Gross domestic product, 1959–93—*Continued*
(billions of dollars, except as noted; quarterly data at seasonally adjusted annual rates)

| Net exports of goods and services | | | Government purchases | | | | | Final sales of domestic product | Gross domestic purchases[1] | Addendum: Gross national product[2] | Percent change from preceding period | |
| | | | | Federal | | | | | | | | |
Net imports	Exports	Imports	Total	Total	National defense	Non-defense	State and local				Gross domestic product	Gross domestic purchases[1]
−1.7	20.6	22.3	99.0	57.1	46.4	10.8	41.8	490.0	495.8	497.0	8.7	9.1
2.4	25.3	22.8	99.8	55.3	45.3	10.0	44.5	510.1	510.9	516.6	3.9	3.0
3.4	26.0	22.7	107.0	58.6	47.9	10.6	48.4	528.9	528.4	535.4	3.6	3.4
2.4	27.4	25.0	116.8	65.4	52.1	13.3	51.4	565.5	569.1	575.8	7.5	7.7
3.3	29.4	26.1	122.3	66.4	51.5	14.9	55.8	597.5	599.8	607.7	5.5	5.4
5.5	33.6	28.1	128.3	67.5	50.4	17.0	60.9	643.0	642.5	653.0	7.4	7.1
3.9	35.4	31.5	136.3	69.5	51.0	18.5	66.8	693.0	698.8	708.1	8.4	8.8
1.9	38.9	37.1	155.9	81.3	62.0	19.3	74.6	756.0	767.9	774.9	9.5	9.9
1.4	41.4	39.9	175.6	92.8	73.4	19.4	82.7	803.8	812.9	819.8	5.8	5.9
−1.3	45.3	46.6	191.5	99.2	79.1	20.0	92.3	880.2	890.6	895.5	9.2	9.6
−1.2	49.3	50.5	201.8	100.5	78.9	21.6	101.3	949.8	960.7	965.6	7.9	7.9
1.2	57.0	55.8	212.7	100.1	76.8	23.3	112.6	1,008.4	1,009.5	1,017.1	5.3	5.1
−3.0	59.3	62.3	224.3	100.0	74.1	25.9	124.3	1,089.2	1,100.2	1,104.9	8.6	9.0
−8.0	66.2	74.2	241.5	106.9	77.4	29.4	134.7	1,197.1	1,215.0	1,215.7	10.0	10.4
.6	91.8	91.2	257.7	108.5	77.5	31.1	149.2	1,331.9	1,349.0	1,362.3	11.8	11.0
−3.1	124.3	127.5	288.3	117.6	82.6	35.0	170.7	1,444.4	1,461.8	1,474.3	8.1	8.4
13.6	136.3	122.7	321.4	129.4	89.6	39.8	192.0	1,591.5	1,572.3	1,599.1	8.7	7.6
−2.3	148.9	151.1	341.3	135.8	93.4	42.4	205.5	1,751.7	1,770.7	1,785.5	11.5	12.6
−23.7	158.8	182.4	368.0	147.9	100.9	47.0	220.1	1,949.4	1,997.8	1,994.6	11.6	12.8
−26.1	186.1	212.3	403.6	162.2	108.9	53.3	241.4	2,204.8	2,258.8	2,254.5	13.1	13.1
−23.8	228.9	252.7	448.5	179.3	121.9	57.5	269.2	2,475.9	2,512.5	2,520.8	11.5	11.2
−14.7	279.2	293.9	507.1	209.1	142.7	66.4	298.0	2,717.5	2,722.8	2,742.1	8.8	8.4
−14.7	303.0	317.7	561.1	240.8	167.5	73.3	320.3	3,005.2	3,045.3	3,063.8	11.9	11.8
−20.6	282.6	303.2	607.6	266.6	193.8	72.7	341.1	3,165.5	3,170.2	3,179.8	3.9	4.1
−51.4	276.7	328.1	652.3	292.0	214.4	77.5	360.3	3,410.6	3,456.5	3,434.4	8.1	9.0
−102.7	302.4	405.1	700.8	310.9	233.1	77.8	389.9	3,706.1	3,879.9	3,801.5	10.9	12.2
−115.6	302.1	417.6	772.3	344.3	258.6	85.7	428.1	4,014.1	4,154.3	4,053.6	6.9	7.1
−132.5	319.2	451.7	833.0	367.8	276.7	91.1	465.3	4,260.0	4,401.2	4,277.7	5.7	5.9
−143.1	364.0	507.1	881.5	384.9	292.1	92.9	496.6	4,513.7	4,683.0	4,544.5	6.4	6.4
−108.0	444.2	552.2	918.7	387.0	295.6	91.4	531.7	4,884.2	5,008.4	4,908.2	7.9	6.9
−79.7	508.0	587.7	975.2	401.6	299.9	101.7	573.6	5,217.5	5,330.5	5,266.8	7.2	6.4
−71.4	557.1	628.5	1,047.4	426.5	314.0	112.5	620.9	5,539.3	5,617.5	5,567.8	5.6	5.4
−19.6	601.5	621.1	1,099.3	445.9	322.5	123.4	653.4	5,731.6	5,742.5	5,737.1	3.2	2.2
−29.6	640.5	670.1	1,131.8	448.8	313.8	135.0	683.0	6,031.2	6,068.2	6,045.8	5.5	5.7
−65.7	660.1	725.8	1,157.1	443.4	303.6	139.8	713.7	6,357.2	6,439.7		5.6	6.1

[1] Domestic product (GDP) less exports and services plus imports of goods and services.

[2] IS net receipts of factor income from rest of the world.

Department of Commerce, Bureau of Economic Analysis.

ECONOMICS

Second Edition

THE IRWIN SERIES IN ECONOMICS

Appleyard and Field
INTERNATIONAL ECONOMICS
second edition

Appleyard and Field
INTERNATIONAL TRADE
second edition

Appleyard and Field
**INTERNATIONAL MONETARY
THEORY**
second edition

Baily and Friedman
**MACROECONOMICS, FINANCIAL
MARKETS, AND THE
INTERNATIONAL SECTOR**
second edition

Barron and Lynch
ECONOMICS
third edition

Baye and Beil
**MANAGERIAL ECONOMICS AND
BUSINESS STRATEGY**

Blair
**URBAN AND REGIONAL
ECONOMICS**

Bornstein
**COMPARATIVE ECONOMIC
SYSTEMS: MODELS AND CASES**
seventh edition

Brown and Moore
**READINGS, ISSUES AND
PROBLEMS IN PUBLIC FINANCE**
fourth edition

Colander
ECONOMICS
second edition

Colander
MICROECONOMICS
second edition

Colander
MACROECONOMICS
second edition

Denzau
**MICROECONOMIC ANALYSIS:
MARKETS & DYNAMICS**

Fisher
**STATE AND LOCAL
PUBLIC FINANCE**

Hadjimichalakis & Hadjimichalakis
**CONTEMPORARY MONEY,
BANKING AND THE
FINANCIAL MARKETS**

Hyman
ECONOMICS
third edition

Hyman
MICROECONOMICS
third edition

Hyman
MACROECONOMICS
third edition

Hyman
**MODERN MICROECONOMICS:
ANALYSIS AND APPLICATIONS**
third edition

Katz and Rosen
MICROECONOMICS
second edition

Lehmann
**REAL WORLD ECONOMIC
APPLICATIONS: THE WALL
STREET JOURNAL WORKBOOK**
third edition

Lindert
INTERNATIONAL ECONOMICS
ninth edition

Maurice and Phillips
**ECONOMIC ANALYSIS: THEORY
AND APPLICATION**
sixth edition

Maurice and Thomas
**MANAGERIAL ECONOMICS:
APPLIED MICROECONOMICS
FOR DECISION MAKING**
fifth edition

Nadler and Hansen
**MICROCOMPUTER
MACROECONOMICS
WITH IBM DISK**

O'Sullivan
URBAN ECONOMICS
second edition

O'Sullivan
**ESSENTIALS OF URBAN
ECONOMICS**

Peterson
**PRINCIPLES OF ECONOMICS:
MICRO**
eighth edition

Peterson
**PRINCIPLES OF ECONOMICS:
MACRO**
eighth edition

Prager
**APPLIED MICROECONOMICS:
AN INTERMEDIATE
APPROACH**

Rima
**DEVELOPMENT OF ECONOMIC
ANALYSIS**
fifth edition

Roger and Daniel
**PRINCIPLES OF ECONOMICS
SOFTWARE SIMULATION**

Rosen
PUBLIC FINANCE
fourth edition

Schwarz and Van Dyken
**MANAGER: MANAGERIAL
ECONOMICS SOFTWARE**

Seo
**MANAGERIAL ECONOMICS:
TEXT, SHORT CASES**
seventh edition

Sharp, Register and Leftwich
ECONOMICS OF SOCIAL ISSUES
eleventh edition

Shepherd
**PUBLIC POLICIES TOWARD
BUSINESS**
eighth edition

Shughart
**THE ORGANIZATION OF
INDUSTRY**

Slavin
ECONOMICS
third edition

Slavin
MICROECONOMICS
third edition

Slavin
MACROECONOMICS
third edition

Streifford
ECONOMIC PERSPECTIVE

Walton and Wykoff
**UNDERSTANDING ECONOMICS
TODAY**
fourth edition

ECONOMICS

Second Edition

DAVID C. COLANDER
Middlebury College

IRWIN

Chicago • Bogota • Boston • Buenos Aires • Caracas
London • Madrid • Mexico City • Sydney • Toronto

Part opener photos
Part 1: Reuters/Bettmann
Part 2: Archive photos
Part 3: © Rafael Macia/Photo Researchers, Inc.

Senior sponsoring editor:	*Gary Nelson*
Developmental editor:	*Jackie Scruggs*
Developmental editor, supplements:	*Amy Winston*
Senior marketing manager:	*Ron Bloecher*
Project editor:	*Denise Santor-Mitzit*
Production supervisor:	*Ann Cassady*
Designer:	*Heidi J. Baughman*
Cover illustrator:	*Richard Tuschman*
Photo research coordinator:	*Michelle Oberhoffer*
Art studio:	*ElectraGraphics, Inc.*
Art manager:	*Kim Meriwether*
Compositor:	*Better Graphics, Inc.*
Typeface:	*10/12 Times Roman*
Printer:	*Von Hoffmann Press, Inc.*

Library of Congress Cataloging-in-Publication Data

Colander, David C.
    Economics / David C. Colander. —2nd ed.
      p.   cm. —(The Irwin series in economics)
    Includes index.
    ISBN 0-256-13799-4
    1. Economics. I. Title. II. Series.
    HB171.5.C788 1995
    330—dc20   94–35112

Printed in the United States of America
2 3 4 5 6 7 8 9 0 VH 1 0 9 8 7 6 5

Dedicated to the memory of Frank Knight and Thorstein Veblen, both of whose economics have significantly influenced the contents of this book.

Preface

One of the first lessons of writing is: Know for whom you are writing. This book is written for students; this preface, however, is written for professors. Why? The answer is simple—the students for whom this book is written don't read prefaces; they don't read anything in a textbook unless it is assigned (and sometimes they don't read that). Their interests lie in the real world, not in texts. The style and structure of the body of this text is made to turn on such students, as much as they can be turned on, to economic ideas. Alas, I recognize that I will fail with many, but I sincerely believe that my success rate of actually getting students to read this textbook will likely be higher than will be the success rate for other economic textbooks written in standard professorial style.

I also recognize that students will never get a chance to read this text unless the professor chooses the book, which is why I write this preface for professors—they read prefaces. (If you're one of those rare students who read textbook prefaces, read on; it will give you a sense of what will be coming in the course.)

I'm pleased to say that the first edition of this book was very well received. As Sally Field would say, ''They like me!'' Since this second edition keeps most of the distinctive components and style of the first edition, the preface I wrote for that first edition remains directly relevant. So let me begin this preface with the key elements of that first edition preface.

Excerpts from Preface to the First Edition

Why write a new introductory economics textbook? Since I am an economist, the answer must be that the expected benefits outweighed the expected costs. But that doesn't mean I had my bank balance in mind when I decided to write this book. Quite honestly, there are easier ways of earning money (my wife's a doctor). There had to be some other benefits out there. For me, those other benefits had to do with a belief about how economics should be taught—what was important and what was not.

Before I started writing this book I had done quite a bit of research on economic education. As part of that research, Arjo Klamer and I had surveyed and interviewed graduate students in a number of top graduate programs. Two of the most disturbing things we discovered were that economic institutions and economic literature were being given short shrift in graduate economics education. For example, in response to the question, ''How important is a knowledge of economic literature to being successful as an economist?'' only 10 percent of the students responded that it was very important, while 43 percent said it was unimportant. In response to the question, ''How important to achieving success as an economist is having a thorough knowledge of the economy?'' only 3 percent said it was very important, while 68 percent said it was unimportant.

I believe that the majority of the profession is concerned with these results. Certainly the students we interviewed were concerned. They said they believed that institutions and literature were very important. Their survey responses simply indicated their perception of how people succeed in the profession, but the current situation was not the way it should be. Almost all economists I know believe that students need to know economic literature and have a thorough knowledge of the institutions. Without the appropriate background knowledge of institutions and literature, all the technical skills in the world aren't going to provide one with the economic sensibility necessary to understand what's going on in the economy or to decide whether or not a model is relevant.

As I thought about these results and considered my own teaching, I realized that the problem was not only in graduate schools; it had filtered down to undergraduate texts. As I looked through the texts, I saw excellent discussions of technical issues and of models, but little discussion of economic sensibility. These books didn't even try to provide the intellectual context within which those models developed or the institutional context to which these models were to be applied. The standard texts had settled into teaching technique for the sake of technique and had shifted away from teaching economic sensibility.

I decided that if I were serious about playing a role in reinstituting economic sensibility and a knowledge of institutions and literature in economic education, I would have to write an introductory textbook that did that. I took it as a challenge. Meeting that challenge was what drove me to write this book; it is what kept me going when all my rational instincts told me it was too much time and too much work.

Teaching Economic Sensibility

The question I faced was: How do you incorporate economic sensibility into a textbook? Economic sensibility is more than a knowledge of modeling techniques; it is a mindset in which one's lens of the world is a latticework of ascending cost/benefit frameworks in which one is deciding on the optimal degree of rationality. Economic sensibility is an enforced reasonableness that provides insight into complicated issues; it is a perspective, not a technique. The argument I heard in favor of teaching technique was that economic sensibility could not be taught. I reject that argument. Economic sensibility may be hard to teach because it does not come naturally for most people, but it can and must be taught. The question is: How do you teach it? The answer I came to: Enthusiastically.

Economics with Passion

I am first and foremost an economics teacher; I am excited by economics. I find economic ideas relevant, challenging, and exciting. In my lectures, I try to convey that excitement, and if the lecture is going right, I can feel the excitement in my students. Then off they go to read the text. All too often when they return to class, the fire in their eyes is gone; the textbook has lulled them into complacency. Those who know me know that I can put up with many things (not quietly, but nonetheless put up with), but one of those things isn't complacency. I want students to think, to argue, to challenge, to get passionate about the ideas. I encourage this reaction from students not just because economists' ideas deserve to be treated passionately, but also because, through a combination of passion and reason, eventually students achieve economic sensibility. I decided what was missing from most textbooks was the passion. I promised myself my book would retain the passion.

Now there's no way I'm going to get passionate about Slutsky equations, phase diagrams, indifference curves, or an AS/AD model. Mathematicians may get passionate about such things, I don't. I do get passionate about the insight economics gives one into the problems we, as individuals and as society, must face: the budget deficit, TANSTAAFL, the environment, and agricultural subsidies. If the techniques help in understanding the ideas, fine, but if they don't, goodbye to the techniques.

Passion without Bias

While not all textbooks are written by passionless people, the conventional wisdom is that authors should hide their passion to make their books more marketable. In some ways this makes sense—often passion and ideological bias go together. Many economists' passions are ideologically linked, and if you remove the ideology, you remove the passion. Good economic sensibility cannot be—and cannot even appear to be—biased; if passion is purged in maintaining neutrality, it is purged for a good cause.

But passion and ideological bias need not go together. I believe it is possible for a passionate textbook to be reasonably objective and unbiased. And I set out to write a book that would be as unbiased as possible (but not more so) and to do so without masking my passion for economic ideas. Various techniques allow me to do this. For example, to keep the students interested in the ideas rather than focusing on technique, I present some ideas in a debate format with two passionate believers on both sides arguing the points. The debate format makes the arguments come alive; they are no longer technical issues that must be memorized; they are passionate ideas, and as the students get caught up in the debate, they think about the ideas much more deeply than they otherwise would.

A Conversational Tone

To transmit that sense of passion to the students, I needed a writing style that allowed it to come through. Quite honestly,

textbookese douses passion faster than a cold shower. So this book is not written in textbookese. It's written in conversational English—I'm talking to the students. When they read the book, they will know me; they may not like me like my mother likes me, but they will know me.

The conversational tone is not a monotone; it ebbs and flows depending on the nature of the material. Sometimes, in the analytic parts, the style approaches textbookese; the important technical aspects of economics require technical writing. When we hit those parts, I tell the students and encourage them to stick with me. But, even here I try to provide intuitive explanations that students can relate to.

The use of conversational style has two effects. First, it eliminates the sense some students have that textbooks provide the ''truth.'' When the textbook author is a real person with peccadilloes and warts, the students won't accept what he or she says unless it makes sense to them. Approaching a textbook with a Missouri ''show me'' attitude stimulates true learning. Second, the conversational style keeps the students awake. If students' heads are nodding as they read a chapter, they're not learning. Now I know this book is not *Catcher in the Rye*; it's a textbook conveying sometimes complex ideas. But the excitement about economic ideas and the real world comes through.

The approach I take allows me to deal simply with complicated ideas. For example, in the book I discuss modern interpretations of Keynesian and Classical economics, real business cycles, strategic pricing, the theory of the second best, rent-seeking, Pareto optimality, and challenges to Pareto optimality. The conversational style conveys the essence of these complex topics to students in a nontechnical fashion without tying the students' brains up in technical tourniquets. The style allows me to relate the ideas to concrete examples rather than mathematical formulas, providing intuitive discussions of the ideas that capture the economic sensibility.

Models in Historical and Institutional Context

Discussing only the minimum of techniques necessary for the students to understand the ideas allows me more leeway to get into, and discuss, institutional and historical issues as they relate to current policy. Models without context are meaningless, and thus you'll find more historical and institutional issues in this book than in other principles books. The book has numerous maps; the discussion conveys the sense that geography, history, and psychology are important, even though it touches on them only tangentially.

One of the ways in which this historical and institutional approach shows up is in the complete coverage of the changing nature of economic systems. Socialism is undergoing enormous changes, and students are interested in what is happening and why it is happening. Their questions cannot be answered with technical models, but they can be discussed informally in a historical context. And that's what this book does.

The Invisible Forces

I've incorporated in the book a pedagogical device I've found useful where I want to include the social and political forces that affect reality. That device is to convey to students a picture of reality being controlled not only by the invisible hand, but also by the invisible foot (politics) and the invisible handshake (social and cultural forces). This *invisible forces* imagery lets me relate economists' abstract models to the real world; it allows me to discuss the real-world interface between economics, politics, and social forces. What makes this device effective is that students can picture these three invisible forces fighting each other to direct real world events; that image allows them to put economic models into perspective.

Some Short Prefatory Comments on the Second Edition

A question the reader might have, and one that I asked myself long and hard, is: "If the first edition was so good, why write a second edition?" One reason I updated the book had to do with money—a reason which isn't discussed in polite prefaces, even those written by economists, so I won't discuss it. A second reason is that it allowed significant improvement in the ancillary package, including two dear to my heart, a classic readings companion text, which lets students go beyond the text, and actually read economists such as Smith, Mill, Marx, Knight, Lerner, and Stigler, and an honors companion text, which presents technical material that would scare away less prepared students. These should help further the critical thought component of the book that is central to my philosophy of how economics should be taught.

A third, and probably the most important, reason for doing a second edition was reviewers' comments. Essentially the reviewers told me, "The first edition was a good first effort, but you can do better." Hearing those comments was initially a real downer; I felt a bit like many of my students feel after I've marked up a first draft of a paper that they hoped would be the final draft—deflated and depressed. But I remembered what I tell my students: "I criticize so that you can learn, so that you can make it better" and resolved to do better—to make the book clearer, more exciting, more dynamic, and more consistent with my overall philosophy than the first edition.

All reviewers agreed that my book was more than a repeat of the standard litany, that it covered the standard introductory material in a more open and accessible way than did other texts. It didn't present economics as a pretentious science, nor did it present economics as a touchy-feely subject. It presented it for what it is—an enormously powerful, but simultaneously potentially confusing and limited, engine of analysis that provides an interesting approach to understanding the problems of society. It was a straightforward presentation of economic ideas—warts and all. But they pointed out that I sometimes strayed from my goals in a number of ways. How did I stray? Let me count the ways.

The first way reviewers said I strayed was that I wasn't always true to my ''math isn't necessary'' view. So in this second edition I eliminated some algebra that scared some students.

Second, they said, "Add more policy discussion." So when doing the second edition I put a sign over my desk: "Policy is where it's at, Stupid—*Policy,*" and, after being reminded by reviewers a few times, I even followed it. Operationally, that meant that the chapter on recent developments in macro theory was eliminated and yet another chapter on macro policy was added. In addition more policy discussion was added throughout the book.

Third, the reviewers said the book needed more questions, so I added them—10 margin questions in each chapter (with answers at the end of the chapter) and at least three additional thought problems at the end of each chapter. The questions remain varied—sometimes serving as a review, sometimes serving to push the student beyond the text.

Fourth, they told me that some reorganization was necessary. So I reorganized. Probably the biggest reorganization concerned the international section. The reviewers told me that if I believe, which I do, that international issues are central to studying economics, there is no justification for an international section separate from micro and macro. So I eliminated it, dividing chapters into macro and micro coverage and placed the relevant chapters directly in the macro and micro sections.

The Usual Revisions: Updates and Improvements

Besides the above substantive changes, there were also the usual revisions. Times and issues change and that change requires modifications; a book quickly becomes out of date. Thus, in the second edition I updated all the discussions and data, and brought the policy discussions up-to-date. For example, I added discussions of health insurance, the macro problems facing the Clinton administration, the problems of the proposed European Currency Union, and the introduction of NAFTA.

The reviewers also told me that, as is inevitably the case, the first edition had pesky little problems. My explanation here wasn't quite clear; my explanation there was too long; I didn't give enough examples here; I got my facts a bit wrong there. It's amazing how many mistakes one can make in 900 pages. This second edition allowed me to clear up all those pesky little problems. (Would you believe, ''eliminate some of them?'') It's also amazing how one can think one is being perfectly clear, when one is actually being very ambiguous. Luckily, reviewers and friends pointed out a number of these places, and because of them the book was improved immensely. Those changes won't be obvious upon glancing at the book, but they will, I believe, be obvious to the students who will have fewer questions upon reading it.

A Change Not Made: My Colloquial Writing Style

One change not made in this second edition, even though it put off some professors, is my colloquial writing style. It's pretty clear that my writing style (and my style in general) isn't professorial. I agree; it isn't. But in my view, students would learn a lot more if professors were a lot less professorial. If students see us as people, they will be encouraged to think through what we have to say, and to challenge us when they think we're wrong. That's the purpose of education—to get students to think. True, it would be nice if students had a love of learning and were thirsting for knowledge. Unfortunately, the reality is that 99% of them don't. It's our job as teachers to make learning fun and exciting for students who don't want to learn, and either get them to learn, or to flunk them out. Being less professorial makes us more real to students and makes learning more fun.

I see the course and the book as an entry point to an enormous store of information, not as the ultimate source. I want to motivate students to learn on their own, to read on their own, to think on their own. These desires have to be taught, and they can only be taught in a language that students can relate to. I believe in going in steps with students, not in leaps. The traditional textbookese is too much a leap for most students to make. It's not a step from the stuff they normally read; it's a leap that most of them aren't willing to make—the same type of leap it is for most of us teachers of economics to read the *Journal of Economic Theory*. There may be some relevant information in those articles, but most of us teachers aren't going to find out because the language the ideas are presented in is incomprehensible to us. So too with a text; it has to talk to students, otherwise they won't read it. I'm pleased to say that students have uniformly related to my style, even if they think my jokes are sometimes corny.

People to Thank

A book this size is not the work of a single person, despite the fact that only one is listed as author. So many people have contributed so much to this book that it is hard to know where to begin thanking them. But I must begin somewhere, so let me begin by thanking the innumerable referees of both the first and second editions who went through the various versions of the text, and kept me on track:

First Edition

Jack Adams
University of Arkansas

Stan Antoniotti
Bridgewater State College

Mahmoud P. Arya
Edison Community College

James Q. Aylsworth
Lakeland Community College

George Bohler
University of North Florida

Bijit K. Bora
Carleton College

Gerald E. Breger
Grand Rapids Junior College

Mario Cantu
Northern Virginia Community College

Tom Carroll
Central Oregon Community College

Carol A. M. Clark
Guilford College

Roy Cohn
Illinois State University

Eleanor Craig
University of Delaware

Jerry L. Crawford
Arkansas State University

Ed Dennis
Franklin Pierce College

Phillip Droke
Highline Community College

Fred Englander
Fairleigh Dickinson University

Valerie Englander
St. John's University

Sharon Erenberg
Eastern Michigan University

Rhona C. Free
Eastern Connecticut State University

Joseph Garwood
Valencia Community College

Bernard Gauci
Hollins College

Robert Gentennar
Hope College

Jack B. Goddard
Northeastern State University

Deniek Gondwee
Gettysburg College

Richard Hansen
Southeast Missouri State University

Raymond N. Harvey
Niagara County Community College

Robert Jantzen
Iona College

Walter Johnson
University of Missouri

Diane E. Kraas
Augustana College

Leonard Lardaro
University of Rhode Island

Randall Lutter
State University of New York at Buffalo

Raymond Mack
Community College of Allegheny County Boyce Campus

Drew Mattson
Anoka-Ramsey Community College

Bruce McCrea
Lansing Community College

H. Neal McKenzie
Dalton College

Debbie A. Meyer
Brookdale Community College

Craig Milnor
Clarke College

William Morgan
University of Wyoming

Mark Morlock
California State University–Chico

H. Richard Moss
Ricks College

Theodore Muzio
St. Vincent College

Hillar Neumann, Jr.
Northern State University

Maureen O'Brien
University of Minnesota–Duluth

Amar Parai
State University of New York College at Fredonia

E. Dale Peterson
Late of Mankato State University

Richard Rosenberg
University of Wisconsin

Linda Schaeffer
California State University–Fresno

Ted Scheinman
Mt. Hood Community College

Timothy Schibik
University of Southern Indiana

Dorothy Siden
Salem State College

R. J. Sidwell
Eastern Illinois University

G. Anthony Spira
University of Tennessee

Mitch Stengel
University of Michigan–Dearborn

Robert Stonebreaker
Indiana University of Pennsylvania

Frank Taylor
McLennan Community College

Wade Thomas
State University of New York College at Oneonta

Joe Turek
Illinois Benedictine College

Alejandro Velez
St. Mary's University

David Weinberg
Xavier University

Kenneth Woodward
Saddleback College

Second Edition

Fatma Antar
Manchester Community College

John Atkins
Pensacola Junior College

Bruce Barnett
Grossmont College

Peter S. Barth
University of Connecticut

William W. Boorman
Palm Beach Community College

Ginny Brannon
Arapahoe Community College

H. L. Brockman
Central Piedmont Community College

Chris Clark
BCIT

Eleanor D. Craig
University of Delaware

Douglas Copeland
Johnson County Community College

Norman V. Cure
Macomb Community College

James W. Eden
Portland Community College

John P. Farrell
Oregon State University

Peter Fortura
Algonquin College

Ann J. Fraedrich
Marquette University

Louis Green
San Diego State University

John B. Hall
Portland State University

Paul A. Heise
Lebanon Valley College

Joseph A. Ilacqua
Bryant College

Susan Kamp
University of Alberta

R. E. Kingery
Hawkeye Community College

Robert Kirk
Indiana University/Purdue University Indianapolis

Evanthis Mavrokordatos
Tarrant County Junior College, N.E.

Diana L. McCoy
Truckee Meadows Community College

Shah M. Mehrabi
Montgomery College

Dennis D. Miller
Baldwin Wallace College

James E. Needham
Cuyahoga Community College

Tim Payne
Shoreline Community College

Harmanna Poen
Houston Community College

Edward R. Raupp
Augsburg College

Donald Reddick
Kwantlen College

Mitchell Redlo
Monroe Community College

Balbir S. Sahni
Concordia University

Dennis Shannon
Belleville Area College

Amrik Singh Dua
Mt. San Antonio College

John D. Snead
Bluefield State College

John Somers
Portland Community College

Annie Spears
University of Prince Edward Island

Delores W. Steinhauser
Brookdale Community College

John Stoudenmire
Methodist College

Deborah L. Thorsen
Palm Beach Community College

Marion Walsh
Lansing Community College

James Watson
Jefferson College

Edgar W. Wood
University of Mississippi

I cannot thank these reviewers enough. They corrected many of my stupid mistakes, they explained to me how a text can contribute to good teaching, and they kept me focused on combining teaching economic sensibility with economic models. They provided me with page upon page of detailed comments and suggestions for improvement. The book strongly reflects their input and is much more usable because of that input.

The formal reviews are only a small portion of the total reviewers. There were many faculty and students who have informally pointed out aspects of the book that they liked, or did not like. There are so many that I can't remember, and don't have room to list, them all, but I hope by listing a few of them I can give you a sense of the importance of these informal reviewers. Some of these individuals (who happen to come to mind at the moment) are:

Roger Adkins, Zahiruddin Alim, John Atkins, Anis Bahreinian, Jim Barbour, Robin Bartlett, Roger Beck, John Bethune, Paula Bracy, Allen Bradley, Jim Bryan, Scott Callan, Kristine Chase, John Conant, John Cornwall, Robert Crofts, Mahmoud Davoudi, Roger Dimick, Rohini Divecha, Jim Esen, Susan Feiner, Ann Fender, Windsor Fields, Richard Fryman, Art Gibb, Derrick Gondwe, Leland Gustafson, John H. Hoag, Janet Harris, Ric Holt, Dave Horlacher, Jim Hubert, Jim Kelsey, Rose Kilburn, Alfred Konuwa, Roger Koppl, Chris Kuehl, Harry Landreth, June Lapidus, Robert Liebman, Peyton Lingle, Lew Marler, Tom Mayer, Susan McGowan, Pat McMahon, Frank Mossadeghi, Joy Newcomb, Michael Paganelli, Tom Porebski, Abdul Qayum, Mary Jean Rivers, James R. Scheib, Sunder Rameswamy, John Ranlett, Nancy Roberts, Sam Rosenberg, Barkley Rosser, Ted Scheinman, Peter Sephton, Scott Sewell, James Smith, Noel Smith, Howard Stein, Keven Stephenson, Terry Stokes, Kit Taylor, Janet Thomas, Roger Traver, Lisa Tuttle, S. V. Char, David Wagenblast, Kristi Weir, Geraldine Welch, Bruce Welz, Peter Wyman. There are many more.

Often their helpful comments were in the form of questions, and in trying to answer them it became clear that the problem was a reflection of my failure of exposition, not in their understanding. I thank all these individuals, (and apologize to the many, many unlisted ones).

I am happy to say that my group of friends throughout the profession is expanding. One of the pleasant aspects of the book is that it led to a large number of invitations to speak throughout the country. At those talks, I met some wonderful economics educators. These talks played a role in the development of an informal group of economics educators who are concerned about the way economics is taught. Together, we've been putting some pressure on the economics establishment to pay more time to teaching and to concern itself more with content teaching issues. The petition we organized (published with all our signatures in the *AER*) of almost 500 undergraduate professors of economics committed to changing the way economics is taught in graduate school made an impact, as did the positive reception given to the first edition of this text. The graduate schools know economists committed to quality undergraduate teaching—which includes conveying a sense of history and institutions—are out there. Eventually, I think we will begin to see some change in the profession—not large change, mind you—institutions don't allow large, sudden changes, but positive, glacial changes in the right direction. My sincere thanks to all who have helped in this effort.

Massaging the Manuscript into a Book

Once the manuscript takes its final form there are still an almost infinite number of jobs to be done on it. Figures must be checked, arguments checked, drafts read, reread, and reread once again. In this second edition, I had immense help in these undertakings from Jenifer Gamber, who is a superbly trained economist and a great organizer. She found last minute data and saw to it that the answers to all the questions were reasonable. Others who helped include Zach Gemignani, who worked as my research assistant in the summer of 1993, and Sandro Wulff, who worked as my research assistant in the summer of 1994. They both did great jobs, and I thank them.

In this entire process many people at Irwin are extremely important and helpful. One is Wendy Hagel, a sales rep at

Irwin, who convinced me that Irwin was the right publisher for me. Two others are Gary Nelson, and his assistant, Tia Schultz. Gary is the economics editor at Irwin. He believed in the project early on and argued for it when others were concerned that I was a bit too blunt for the publishing world. He has seen to it that the project has gone forward and has prospered. The book would not have been what it is without him. And without Tia seeing that things get done, we would have not met any deadlines. A big thanks to both of them.

Then there's Jackie Scruggs, my developmental editor for this second edition. To understand Jackie's role, you have to understand a bit about me. I'm a difficult person to work with. I'm an outlandish perfectionist, a stickler about deadlines, and rather blunt in my assessments. I don't like excuses or bureaucracy. I want things done perfectly, yesterday. Given these characteristics of mine, the fact that I can coexist with publishing houses is unexplainable—except for the existence of people like Jackie within the publishing houses. Jackie is superb. She almost always gets things done perfectly, yesterday, and when she doesn't, she offers no excuses—she simply gets them done today. She operates in a bureaucracy without losing sight of her main duty—to get the job done competently and professionally. She's a gem, and I thank her.

I would also like to thank upper-level management at Irwin—specifically Mike Junior, the publisher, and Jeff Sund, the president. I had less contact with them, but I fully recognize their guiding hands. Their belief in the project and their willingness to make it possible for an anti-bureaucratic author to fit in with a formal publishing institution allowed the first edition to proceed and this second edition to improve. I thank them enormously.

The actual production process of a four-color introductory book is complicated. It requires enormous efforts. Luckily, I had Denise Santor-Mitzit, project editor, directing the manuscript through the process. She did a superb job, as did all the players in the production process: Tom Serb, the copy editor; Heidi Baughman, the designer who made the book look good; Ann Cassady, the production manager, who worked with Better Graphics, Inc., the typesetter, and Von Hoffmann Press, the printer; and Kim Meriwether, art manager, who worked closely with ElectraGraphics, Inc., on the art program.

Of course, as they did their superb job, they created more work for me, reading the galley proofs, the page proofs, and doing all the final checking that must be done in an effort to eliminate those pesky errors that occur out of nowhere. Jenifer Gamber and Helen Reiff went over the manuscript with their fine-tooth combs and discerning eyes, and I went over it with my rake and 20-400 vision, and together we caught things overlooked until then. I thank them enormously for doing what I cannot do, and apologize to them for complaining that they are so picky.

After you have what you believe is a good book, the process still isn't done. You still have to get people to look at it. Ron Bloecher, Bevan O'Callaghan, and John Wood developed a strategy that got the first edition considered, and they have continued that superb work in this second edition. David Littlehale also quickly got a sense of what I was trying to do with the book and captured the essence of it when he explained that I was being "aggressively neutral." I thank him. Mark LaCien and Beth Saviski worked on the advertising and did a great job.

Then, there are the sales reps who are the core of a textbook publishing company. As I traveled around the country giving lectures, I met with many of the Irwin sales reps, discussing the book and learning to see it through their eyes. There are a number I remember very well; they sent me books, comments, and talked with me for hours about publishing and Irwin. Since our talks were often honest, blunt, and off the record, I won't mention them, but I will thank them sincerely. Irwin has one great set of sales representatives out there, and I thank them for getting behind the book.

Creating the Package

These days an introductory economics book is much more than a single book; it is an entire package, and numerous people have worked on the package. Amy Winston was the developmental editor for the ancillaries, and Paul Estenson was the supplements coordinator. I thank them both for their hard work.

The supplements authors were as follows:

Paul Estenson, Supplements Coordinator, *Instructor's Manual, Test Banks, Teaching Transparencies, Economics Issues Videos, Ready Notes, Using Technology to Teach Economics*

Susan Dadres, *Test Banks A & B*

Douglas Copeland, *Student Workbook*

Richard Trieff and Benjamin Shlaes, *Study Guide*

Jenifer Gamber, *Economics Fax Newsletter, Wall Street Journal Applications, Answers to end-of-chapter questions in Instructor's Manual*

Andreas Ortman and Dave Colander, *Experiments in Teaching and Understanding Economics*

Harry Landreth and Dave Colander, *Classic Readings Manual*

David Reese and Larry Wohl, *Essay Test Bank*

Kalash Khandke, Sunder Ramaswamy, and Dave Colander, *Honors Companion*

Craig Roger and Ross Daniel, *Student Workbook for use with Irwin PRESS*

Craig Roger and Ross Daniel, *Instructor's Manual to accompany Irwin PRESS*

Brim Software Group, *Microview/Macroview Software*

There are stories to go with each of these authors—and enormous thanks to be given to them all, but the publisher has told me this preface must be short, so I will simply say thank you to all the supplements authors for making a high-quality and innovative supplements package to the text.

Finally, there's the group of people who helped me at every stage of the process. My colleagues at Middlebury and the Middlebury administration were supportive throughout the project. As usual, my assistant, friend, and conveyer of great insights, Helen Reiff, was my right hand. I appreciate her limiting her law practice to see that justice is done to my books.

Then, there's my wife, Pat, who put her medical practice on hold to give me more time to work on the first two editions of the book, only going back to work once this second edition was in the final stages. Only now that she has gone back to work do I recognize how absolutely necessary to getting this book out her sacrifice was. I strongly believe that, ultimately, family comes first, and as much as I love economics, if it isn't compatible with my family, then it, too, must go. Pat made it possible for me to put enormous effort into economics while still feeling that our family remained a family. Now that she has gone back to work it's my turn to be the primary care giver, and let me tell you, writing an economics textbook is a cinch compared to this job. (Let me add, however, that the world will, in the next edition—if I have time to work on it—hear about medical residency programs that don't provide the type of training a primary care physician needs, but instead seem to be primarily designed to provide cheap labor for hospitals, restrict entry into the medical profession, and give those doctors who have made it through a moral sense that they deserve the outlandish fees they will be charging.)

My love and admiration for Pat remain as unbounded as ever, even if I hardly ever see her these days—since she is working all the time at the hospital.

As you can see, although my name is on the book, many people besides me deserve the credit. I thank them all.

Brief Contents

PART

3

Microeconomics

Contents

PART

2

Macroeconomics

I

Macroeconomic Problems

6 Economic Growth, Business Cycles, Unemployment, and Inflation *133*

7 National Income Accounting *158*

11 Fiscal Policy, and the Debate about Activist Macroeconomic Policy 255

III
Monetary and Financial Institutions

12 Financial Institutions 285

PART

3

Microeconomics

I

Microeconomic Theory: The Basics

22 Individual Choice and Demand   485

23 Supply, Production, and Costs I   515

24 Supply, Production, and Costs II   533

III
Factor Markets

30 Work and the Labor Market   659

31 Nonwage and Asset Income: Rents, Profits, and Interest   684

32 Who Gets What? The Distribution of Income   697

V

International Dimensions of Microeconomics

About the Author

David Colander is the Christian A. Johnson Distinguished Professor of Economics at Middlebury College. He has authored, coauthored, or edited 23 books and over 70 articles on a wide range of economic topics.

He earned his B.A. at Columbia College and his M.Phil and Ph.D. at Columbia University. He also studied at the University of Birmingham in England and at Wilhelmsburg Gymnasium in Germany. Professor Colander has taught at Columbia College, Vassar College, and the University of Miami, as well as having been a consultant to Time-Life Films, a consultant to Congress, a Brookings Policy Fellow, and Visiting Scholar at Nuffield College, Oxford. Recently, he spent two months in Bulgaria, where he worked with former professors of political economy on how to teach Western economics.

He belongs to a variety of professional associations and has served on the Board of Directors and as vice president of the History of Economic Thought Society, the Eastern Economics Association, and is on the Board of Advisors of the *Journal of Economic Perspectives*. He is also on the Editorial Board of *The Journal of Economic Methodology* and *The Eastern Economics Journal*. He is currently the president of the Eastern Economic Association.

He is married to a pediatrician. Patrice, which is fortunate, since they have a family of five boys. In their spare time, the Colanders have designed and built their oak post-and-beam house on a ridge overlooking the Green Mountains to the east and the Adirondacks to the west. The house is located on the site of a former drive-in. (They replaced the speaker poles with fruit trees and used the I-beams from the screen as support for the second story of the carriage house and the garage. Dave's office and library are in the former projection room.)

1
INTRODUCTION

Section I is an introduction, and an introduction to an introduction seems a little funny. But other sections have introductions, so it seemed a little funny not to have an introduction to Section I; and besides, as you will see, I'm a little funny myself (which, in turn, has two interpretations; you will, I'm sure, decide which of the two is appropriate). It will, however, be a very brief introduction, consisting of questions you probably have and some answers to those questions.

SOME QUESTIONS AND ANSWERS

Why study economics?
Because it's neat and interesting and helps provide insight into events that are constantly going on around you.

Why is this book so big?
Because there's lots of important information in it and because the book is designed so your teacher can pick and choose. You'll likely not be required to read all of it, especially if you're on the quarter system. But once you start it, you'll probably read it all anyhow. (Would you believe?)

Why does this book cost so much?
To answer this question you'll have to read the book.

Will this book make me rich?
No.

Will this book make me happy?
It depends.

This book doesn't seem to be written in normal textbook style. Is this book really written by a professor?
Yes, but he is different. He misspent his youth working on cars; he married his high school sweetheart after they met again at their 20th high school reunion. Together they designed and built their own house on the site of a former drive-in theater. (They replaced the speaker poles with a fruit orchard and turned the concession stand into an office and workshop.) At the same time, his wife went back to medical school and got her MD because she was tired of being treated poorly by doctors. Their five kids make sure he doesn't get carried away in the professorial cloud.

Will the entire book be like this?
No, the introduction is just trying to rope you in. Much of the book will be hard going. Learning happens to be a difficult process: no pain, no gain. But the author isn't a sadist; he tries to make learning as pleasantly painful as possible.

What do the author's students think of him?
Weird, definitely weird—and hard. But fair, interesting, and sincerely interested in getting us to learn. (Answer written by my students.)

So there you have it. Answers to the questions that you might never have thought of if they hadn't been put in front of you. I hope they give you a sense of me and the approach I'll use in the book. There are some neat ideas in it. Let's now briefly consider what's in the first five chapters.

A SURVEY OF THE FIRST FIVE CHAPTERS

This first section is really an introduction to the rest of the book. It gives you the background necessary to have the latter chapters make sense. Chapter 1 gives you an overview of the entire field of economics as well as an introduction to my style. Chapter 2 introduces you to supply and demand, and shows you not only the power of those two concepts, but also the limitations.

Chapter 3 tries to put supply and demand in context. It discusses the evolving economic systems and how economic forces interact with political and social forces. In it you'll see how the power of supply and demand analysis is strengthened when it's interpreted with a knowledge of economic institutions. Chapters 4 and 5 then introduce you to some of those economic institutions. Chapter 4 concentrates on domestic institutions; Chapter 5 concentrates on international institutions. Now let's get on with the show.

1

Economics and Economic Reasoning

In my vacations, I visited the poorest quarters of several cities and walked through one street after another, looking at the faces of the poorest people. Next I resolved to make as thorough a study as I could of Political Economy.

~Alfred Marshall

After reading this chapter, you should be able to:

1 State five important things to learn in economics.

2 Explain how to make decisions by comparing marginal costs and marginal benefits.

3 Define opportunity cost, and explain its relationship to economic reasoning.

4 Demonstrate opportunity cost with a production possibility curve.

5 State the principle of increasing marginal opportunity cost.

6 Explain real-world events in terms of three ''invisible forces.''

7 Differentiate between microeconomics and macroeconomics.

8 Distinguish among positive economics, normative economics, and the art of economics.

When an artist looks at the world, he sees color. When a musician looks at the world, she hears music. When an economist looks at the world, she sees a symphony of costs and benefits.[1] The economist's world might not be as colorful or as melodic as the others' worlds, but it's more practical. If you want to understand what's going on in the world that's really out there, you need to know economics.

I hardly have to convince you of this fact if you keep up with the news. Unemployment is up; inflation is down; interest rates are up; businesses are going bankrupt. . . . The list is endless. So let's say you grant me that economics is important. That still doesn't mean that it's worth studying. The real question then is: How much will you learn? Most of what you learn depends on you, but part depends on the teacher and another part depends on the textbook. On both these counts, you're in luck; since your teacher chose this book for your course, you must have a super teacher.[2]

WHAT ECONOMICS IS ABOUT

1 Five important things to learn in economics are:

1. Economic reasoning
2. Economic terminology
3. Economic insights
4. Economic institutions
5. Economic policy options.

Five important things to learn in economics are:

1. *Economic reasoning.*
2. *Economic terminology*.
3. *Economic insights* economists have about issues, and theories that lead to those insights.
4. Information about *economic institutions.*
5. Information about the *economic policy options* facing society today.

By no coincidence this book discusses economic reasoning, economic terminology, economic insights, economic institutions, and economic policy options.

Let's consider each in turn.

Economic Reasoning

Economic reasoning *Making decisions on the basis of costs and benefits.*

The most important thing you'll learn is **economic reasoning**—how to think like an economist. People trained in economics think in a certain way. They analyze everything critically; they compare the costs and the benefits of every issue and make decisions based on those costs and benefits. For example, say you're trying to decide whether protecting baby seals is a good policy or not. Economists are trained to put their emotions aside and ask: What are the costs of protecting baby seals, and what are the benefits? Thus, they are open to the argument that the benefits of allowing baby seals to be killed might exceed the costs. To think like an economist is to address almost all issues using a cost/benefit approach.

Economic reasoning, once learned, is infectious. If you're susceptible, being exposed to it will change your life. It will influence your analysis of everything, including issues normally considered outside the scope of economics. For example, you will likely use economic reasoning to decide the possibility of getting a date for Saturday night, and who will pay for dinner. You will likely use it to decide whether to read this book, whether to attend class, whom to marry, and what kind of work to go into after you graduate. This is not to say that economic reasoning will provide all the

---

[1] Authors are presented with a problem today. Our language has certain ambiguous words that can be interpreted as affording unequal treatment to women. For example, we use the term *man* both to describe all human beings and to describe a specific group of human beings. Similarly, we use the pronoun *he* when we mean all people. One can avoid such usage by writing *he and she* and *men and women* or *human beings,* and in much of this book these terms will be used, although every so often either the masculine or feminine term will appear. This is to see if you notice and to encourage you to think of possible sexist aspects in your own usage.

If you are wondering whether you are sexist, consider the following riddle: A father and son are in a car accident. The father is killed and the boy is injured. When the boy is brought to the hospital, the doctor on emergency room duty says, ''I can't operate on him—he's my son.'' How can this be? If it doesn't seem like a riddle, good; if it does, whenever you see the term *man* think *man and woman,* until the riddle is no longer a riddle.

[2] This book is written by a person, not a machine. That means that I have my quirks, my odd sense of humor, and my biases. All textbook writers do. Most textbooks have the quirks and eccentricities edited out so that all the books read and sound alike—professional but dull. I choose to sound like me—sometimes professional, sometimes playful, and sometimes stubborn. In my view, that makes the book more human and less dull. So forgive me my quirks—don't always take me too seriously—and I'll try to keep you awake when you're reading this book at 3 A.M., the morning of the exam. If you think it's a killer to read a book this long, you ought to try writing one.

answers. As you will see throughout this book, real-world questions are inevitably complicated, and economic reasoning simply provides a framework within which to approach a question.

Second, there's economic terminology, which is tossed around by the general public with increasing frequency. *GDP, corporations,* and *money supply* are just a few of the terms whose meaning any educated person in modern society needs to know. If you go to a party and don't know these terms and want to seem intelligent, you'll have to nod knowingly. It's much better to actually *know* when you nod knowingly.

Economic Terminology

Two terms I want to introduce to you immediately are the *economy* and *economics.* The **economy** is the institutional structure through which individuals in a society coordinate their diverse wants or desires. **Economics** is the study of the economy. That is, economics is the study of how human beings in a society *coordinate* their wants and desires.

Economics   *The study of how human beings coordinate their wants.*

One of society's largest problems is that individuals want more than is available, given the work they're willing to do. If individuals can be encouraged to work more and consume less, that problem can be reduced. Coordination often involves coercion; it involves limiting people's wants and increasing the amount of work individuals are willing to do to fulfill those wants.

Many of society's coordination problems involve scarcity. Therefore, economics is sometimes defined as the study of the allocation of scarce resources to satisfy individuals' wants or desires. I focus the definition on coordination rather than on scarcity to emphasize that the quantity of goods and services available depends on human action: individuals' imagination, innovativeness, and willingness to do what needs to be done.

Many of society's coordination problems involve scarcity.

The reality of our society is that many people would rather play than help solve society's problems. So the basic economic problem involves inspiring people to do things that other people want them to do, and not to do things that other people don't want them to do. Thus, economics is the study of how to get people to do things they're not wild about doing (such as studying) and not to do things they *are* wild about doing (such as eating all the lobster they like), so that the things some people want to do are consistent with the things other people want to do.

Third, you'll learn about some general insights economists have gained into how the economy functions—how an economy seems to proceed or progress without any overall plan or coordinating agency. It's almost as if an invisible hand were directing economic traffic. These insights are often based on **economic theory**—generalizations about the workings of an abstract economy. Theory ties together economists' terminology and knowledge about economic institutions and leads to economic insights.

Economic Insights

Economic theory   *Generalizations about the working of an abstract economy.*

We're so used to the economy's functioning that we may not realize how amazing it is that the economy works as well as it does. Imagine for a moment that you're a visitor from Mars. You see the U.S. economy functioning relatively well. Stores are filled with goods. Most people have jobs. So you ask, "Who's in charge of organizing and coordinating the economic activities of the 260 million people in the United States?" The answer you get is mind boggling: "No one. The invisible hand of the market does it all." Economic theory helps explain such mind-boggling phenomena.

Fourth, you'll learn about economic institutions: how they work, and why they sometimes don't work. An **economic institution** is a physical or mental structure that significantly influences economic decisions. Corporations, governments, and cultural norms are all economic institutions. Many economic institutions have social, political, and religious dimensions. For example, your job often influences your social standing. In addition, many social institutions, such as the family, have economic functions. If any institution significantly affects economic decisions, I include it as an economic institution because you must understand that institution if you are to understand how the economy functions.

Economic Institutions

Economic institutions   *Physical or mental structures that significantly influence economic decisions.*

Since **cultural norms** may be an unfamiliar concept to you, let's consider how such norms affect economies. A cultural norm is a standard people use when they determine whether a particular activity or behavior is acceptable. For example, religious rules once held that Catholics shouldn't eat meat on Friday, so Friday became a day to eat fish. The prohibition ended in the 1960s, but the tendency to eat fish on Friday has endured. In the United States today, more fish is consumed on Fridays than on any other day of the week. This fact can be understood only if you understand the cultural norm that lies behind it. Similarly, in the United States more hams are bought in April and more turkeys are bought in November and December than in other months; more pork is consumed per capita in Sweden than in Israel. Can you explain why?

Economic institutions differ significantly among countries. For example, in Germany banks are allowed to own companies; in the United States they cannot. This causes a difference in the flow of resources into investment. Or alternatively, in Japan, antitrust laws (laws under which companies can combine or coordinate their activities) are loose; in the United States they are restrictive. This causes differences in the nature of competition in the two countries.

Besides helping you understand the economy, knowledge of economic institutions also directly benefits you. How do firms decide whom to hire? How do banks work? How does unemployment insurance work? What determines how much a Japanese car will cost you? How much does the government require your boss to deduct from your paycheck? Knowing the answers to these real-world questions will make your life easier.

Economic Policy Options

Economic policy   Action to influence the course of economic events.

Fifth, you'll learn about economic policy options facing our country. An **economic policy** is an action (or inaction) taken, usually by government, to influence economic events. Examples of economic policy questions are: How should the government deal with the next recession? (Alas, we can be sure that there will be a next recession.) What should the government do about the budget deficit? Will lowering interest rates stimulate the economy? Should government allow two large companies to merge? You won't get specific answers to these questions; instead, you'll simply learn what some of the policy options are, and what advantages and disadvantages each option offers.

A GUIDE TO ECONOMIC REASONING

2 If the benefits of doing something exceed the costs, do it. If the costs of doing something exceed the benefits, don't do it.

Marginal Costs and Marginal Benefits

Marginal costs   Additional costs above what you've already incurred.

Let's now look at each of these five issues more carefully. We'll start with economic reasoning. In the economic way of thinking, every choice has costs and benefits, and decisions are made by comparing the two. The rules are simple:

> *If the benefits of doing something exceed the costs, do it.*
> *If the costs of doing something exceed the benefits, don't do it.*

Economists have found that when one is considering a choice among a variety of alternatives, often it's unnecessary to look at total benefits and total costs. All one need look at are *marginal costs* and *marginal benefits*. These are key concepts in economics, and it pays to learn them early on.

Marginal means additional or incremental. So a **marginal cost** is the additional cost to you over and above the costs you have already incurred. Consider, for

ECONOMIC KNOWLEDGE IN ONE SENTENCE: TANSTAAFL

O nce upon a time, Tanstaafl was made king of all the lands. His first act was to call his economic advisors and tell them to write up all the economic knowledge the society possessed. After years of work, they presented their monumental effort: 25 volumes, each about 400 pages long. But in the interim, King Tanstaafl had become a very busy man, what with running a kingdom of all the lands and everything. Looking at the lengthy volumes, he told his advisors to summarize their findings in one volume.

Despondently, the economists returned to their desks, wondering how they could summarize what they'd been so careful to spell out. After many more years of rewriting, they were finally satisfied with their one-volume effort, and tried to make an appointment to see the king. Unfortunately, affairs of state had become even more pressing than before, and the king couldn't take the time to see them. Instead he sent word to them that he couldn't be bothered with a whole volume, and ordered them, under threat of death (for he had become a tyrant), to reduce the work to one sentence.

The economists returned to their desks, shivering in their sandals and pondering their impossible task. Thinking about their fate if they were not successful, they decided to send out for one last meal. Unfortunately, when they were collecting money to pay for the meal, they discovered they were broke. The disgusted delivery man took the last meal back to the cook, and the economists started down the path to the beheading station. On the way, the delivery man's parting words echoed in their ears. They looked at each other and suddenly they realized the truth. "We're saved!" they screamed. "That's it! That's economic knowledge in one sentence!" They wrote the sentence down and presented it to the king, who thereafter fully understood all economic problems. (He also gave them a good meal.) The sentence?

There Ain't No Such Thing As A Free Lunch—
TANSTAAFL

---

example, attending class. You've already paid your tuition, so the marginal (or additional) cost of going to class does not include tuition.

Similarly, with marginal benefit. The **marginal benefit** of reading this chapter is the *additional* knowledge you get from reading it. If you already knew everything in this chapter before you picked up the book, the marginal benefit of reading it now is zero, except that you now know you are prepared for class, whereas before you might only have suspected you were prepared.

Comparing marginal (additional) costs with marginal (additional) benefits will often tell you how you should adjust your activities to be as well off as possible. If the marginal benefit of engaging in an activity exceeds the marginal cost of doing so, you should do it. But if the marginal benefit is less than the marginal cost, you should do something else.

As an example, let's consider a discussion I might have with a student who tells me that she is too busy to attend my classes. I respond, "Think about the tuition you've spent for this class—it works out to about $30 a lecture." She answers that the book she reads for class is a book that I wrote, and that I wrote it so clearly she fully understands everything. She goes on:

> I've already paid the tuition and whether I go to class or not, I can't get any of the tuition back, so the tuition doesn't enter into my marginal cost decision. The marginal cost to me isn't the tuition; it's what I could be doing with the hour instead of spending it in class. Because I value my time at $75 an hour [people who understand everything value their time highly], and even though I've heard that your lectures are super, I estimate that the marginal benefit of your class is only $50. The marginal cost, $75, exceeds the marginal benefit, $50, so I don't attend class.

I would congratulate her on her diplomacy and her economic reasoning, but tell her that I give a quiz every week, that students who miss a quiz fail the quiz, that those who fail all the quizzes fail the course, and that those who fail the course do not graduate. In short, she is underestimating the marginal benefits of attending my course. Correctly estimated, the marginal benefits of attending my class exceed the marginal costs. So she should attend my class.

There's much more to be said about economic reasoning, but that will come later. For now, all you need remember is that, in economic thinking, *all things have a cost— and a benefit*. Decisions are made on the basis of the **economic decision rule:** If benefits exceed costs, do it. If costs exceed benefits, don't do it.

Marginal benefits   Additional benefits above what you've already derived.

Q–1: Say you bought stock A for $10 and stock B for $20. The price of each is currently $15. Which would you sell if you need $15?

Remember the economic decision rule: If benefits exceed costs, do it. If costs exceed benefits, don't do it.

Economics and Passion

Recognizing that everything has a cost is reasonable, but it's a reasonableness that many people don't like. It takes some of the passion out of life. It leads you to consider possibilities like these:

· Saving some people's lives with liver transplants might not be worth the cost. The money might be better spent on nutritional programs that would save 20 lives for every 2 lives you might save with transplants.

· Maybe we shouldn't try to eliminate all pollution, because the cost of doing so may be too high. To eliminate all pollution would be to forgo too much of some other good activity.

· Buying a stock that went up 20 percent wasn't necessarily the greatest investment if in doing so you had to forgo some other investment that would have paid you a 30 percent return.

· It might make sense for the automobile industry to save $12 per car by not installing a safety device, even though without the safety device some people will be killed.

Q–2: Can you think of a reason why a cost/benefit approach to a problem might be inappropriate? Can you give an example?

You get the idea. This kind of reasonableness is often criticized for being cold-blooded. But, not surprisingly, economists first reason *economically;* the social and moral implications of their conclusions are integrated later.

Economists' reasonableness isn't universally appreciated. Businesses love the result; others aren't so sure, as I discovered some years back when my then-girlfriend told me she was leaving me. "Why?" I asked. "Because," she responded, "you're so, so . . . reasonable." It took me many years after she left to learn what she already knew: There are many types of reasonableness, and not everyone thinks an economist's reasonableness is a virtue. I'll discuss such issues later; for now, let me simply warn you that, for better or worse, studying economics will lead you to view questions in a cost/benefit framework.

Opportunity Cost

3 Opportunity cost is the basis of cost/benefit economic reasoning; it is the benefit forgone, or the cost, of the best alternative to the activity you've chosen. In economic reasoning, that cost is less than the benefit of what you've chosen.

Putting economists' cost/benefit rules into practice isn't easy. To do so, you have to be able to choose and measure the costs and benefits correctly. Economists have devised the concept of opportunity cost to help you do that. The **opportunity cost** of undertaking an activity is the benefit forgone by undertaking that activity. The benefit forgone is the benefit that you might have gained from choosing the next-best alternative. To obtain the benefit of something, you must give up (forgo) something else—namely, the next-best alternative. All activities that have a next-best alternative have an opportunity cost.

Let's consider some examples. The opportunity cost of going out once with Natalia (or Nathaniel), the most beautiful woman (attractive man) in the world, might well be losing your solid steady, Margo (Mike). The opportunity cost of cleaning up the environment might be a reduction in the money available to assist low-income individuals. The opportunity cost of having a child might be two boats, three cars, and a two-week vacation each year for five years.

Examples are endless, but let's consider two that are particularly relevant to you: your choice of courses and your decision about how much to study. Let's say you're a full-time student and at the beginning of the term you had to choose four or five courses to take. Taking one precluded taking some other, and the opportunity cost of taking an economics course may well have been not taking a course on theater. Similarly with studying: you have a limited amount of time to spend studying economics, studying some other subject, sleeping, or partying. The more time you spend on one activity, the less time you have for another. That's opportunity cost.

Notice how neatly the opportunity cost concept takes into account costs and benefits of all other options, and converts these alternative benefits into costs of the decision you're now making. This conversion helps you to compare costs and benefits and to select the activity with the largest difference between benefits and costs.

The relevance of opportunity cost isn't limited to your individual decisions. Opportunity costs are also relevant to government's decisions, which affect everyone in society. A common example is the guns-versus-butter debate. The resources that a

society has are limited; therefore, its decision to use those resources to have more guns (more weapons) means that it must have less butter (fewer consumer goods). Thus, when society decides to spend $50 billion more on an improved health care system, the opportunity cost of that decision is $50 billion not spent on helping the homeless, paying off some of the national debt, or defense.

The opportunity cost concept has endless implications. It can even be turned upon itself. For instance, it takes time to think about alternatives; that means that there's a cost to being reasonable, so it's only reasonable to be somewhat unreasonable. If you followed that argument, you've caught the economic bug. If you didn't, don't worry. Just remember the opportunity cost concept for now; I'll infect you with economic thinking in the rest of the book.

I've just gone over opportunity cost. I'm now going to review the same concept—only this time numerically and graphically. Opportunity cost can be seen numerically with a **production possibility table,** which lists a choice's opportunity cost by summarizing what alternative outputs you can achieve with your inputs. An **output** is simply a result of an activity—your grade in a course is an output. An **input** is what you put in to achieve that output. In this example, study time is an input.

Let's present the study time/grades example numerically. To do so we must be more precise. Say you have exactly 20 hours a week to devote to two courses: economics and history. (So, maybe I'm a bit optimistic.) Grades are given numerically and you know that the following relationships exist: if you study 20 hours in economics, you'll get a grade of 100, 18 hours—94, and so forth.[3]

Let's say that the best you can do in history is a 98 with 20 hours of study a week; 19 hours of study guarantee you a 96, and so on. The production possibility table in Exhibit 1(a) shows the highest combination of grades you can get with various allocations of the 20 hours available for studying the two subjects. One possibility is getting 100 in economics and 58 in history. Another is getting 70 in economics and 78 in history.

Notice that the opportunity cost of studying one subject rather than the other is embodied in the production possibility table. The information in the table comes from experience; we are assuming that you've discovered that if you transfer an hour of study from economics to history, you'll lose 3 points on your grade in economics and gain 2 points in history. Thus, the opportunity cost of a 2-point rise in your history grade is a 3-point decrease in your economics grade.

Q–3: John, your study partner, has just said that the opportunity cost of studying this chapter is about 1/40 the price you paid for this book, since the chapter is about 1/40 of the book. Is he right? Why or why not?

The Production Possibility Table

A production possibility table lists a choice's opportunity costs.

---

[3] Throughout the book I'll be presenting numerical examples to help you understand the concepts. The numbers I choose are often arbitrary. After all, you have to choose something. As an exercise, you might choose different numbers that apply to your own life and work out the argument using those numbers. For those who don't want to make up their own numbers, the study guide has examples with different numbers.

K nowing my students, I can see the red flags rising, the legs tensing up, the fear flooding over many of you. Here it comes—the math and the graphs.

I wish I could change things by saying to you, "Don't worry—mathematics and graphical analysis are easy." But I can't. That doesn't mean math and graphical analysis aren't easy. They are. They're wonderful tools that convey ideas neatly and efficiently. But I've had enough teaching experience to know that somewhere back in elementary school some teacher blew it and put about 40 percent of you off mathematics for life. A tool that scares you to death is not useful; it can be a hindrance, not a help, to learning. I also know that nothing your current teacher or I now can say, write, or do is going to change that for most of those 40 percent. On the other hand, I've had a little bit of luck with about 10 percent of the 40 percent (which makes 4 percent—4 out of 100 students) with the following "conspiracy explanation." So I'll try it on you. Here's what I tell them.

Economics is really simple. Economists know that it is, and they also know that if word got around about how simple economics is, few students would take economics. But economists are smart. They make economics seem more

difficult than it is by couching simple economic ideas in graphs. The graphs convince many students that economics is really hard, allowing economics professors to teach simple ideas that the students think are hard.

About 4 percent of my students become so mad at the thought of being duped that they overcome their math anxiety. The rest just wonder whether this teacher is for real.

If avoiding being duped means something to you, believe the preceding story; if it doesn't, don't. But whatever you do, try to follow the numerical and graphical examples carefully, because they not only cement the knowledge into your minds; they also present the ideas I'm discussing in a rigorous manner.

The ideas conveyed in the numerical and graphical examples will be explained in words—and the graphical analysis (the type of mathematical explanation most used in introductory economics) generally will simply be a more precise presentation of the accompanying discussion in words. In some economics courses, understanding the words may be enough, but in most, the exams pose the questions in graphical terms, so there's no getting around the need to understand the ideas graphically. And it is simple. (Appendix B discusses the basics of graphical analysis.)

The Production Possibility Curve

Production possibility curve *A curve measuring the maximum combination of outputs that can be obtained from a given number of inputs.*

Black

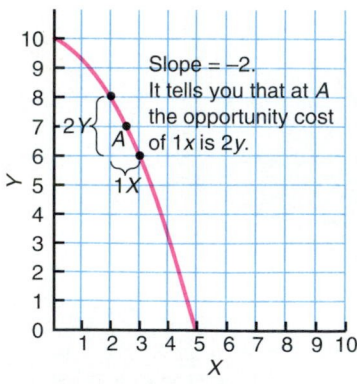

Slope = –2.
It tells you that at *A* the opportunity cost of 1*x* is 2*y*.

2*Y*
A
1*X*

4   Remember this graph:

The slope tells you the opportunity cost of good *X* in terms of good *Y*. You have to give up 2*Y* to get 1*X* when you're around point A.

The information in the production possibility table can also be presented graphically in a diagram. This graphical presentation of the opportunity cost concept is called the **production possibility curve.** This curve indicates the maximum combination of outputs you can obtain from a given number of inputs.

A production possibility curve is created from a production possibility table by mapping the table in a two-dimensional graph. I've taken the information from the table in Exhibit 1(a) and mapped it into Exhibit 1(b). The history grade is mapped, or plotted, on the horizontal axis; the economics grade is on the vertical axis.

As you can see from the bottom row of Exhibit 1(a), if you study economics for all 20 hours and study history for 0 hours, you'll get grades of 100 in economics and 58 in history. Point *A* in Exhibit 1(b) represents that choice. If you study history for all 20 hours and study economics for 0 hours, you'll get a 98 in history and a 40 in economics. Point *E* represents that choice. Points *B, C,* and *D* represent three possible choices between these two extremes.

Notice that the production possibility curve slopes downward from left to right. That means that there is an inverse relationship (a trade-off) between grades in economics and grades in history. The better the grade in economics, the worse the grade in history, and vice versa. That downward slope represents the opportunity cost concept—you get more of one benefit only if you get less of another benefit.

The production possibility curve not only represents the opportunity cost concept; it also measures the opportunity cost. For example, in Exhibit 1(b), say you want to raise your grade in history from a 94 to a 98 (move from point *D* to point *E*). The opportunity cost of that 4-point increase would be a 6-point decrease in your economics grade, from 46 to 40.

To summarize, the production possibility curve demonstrates that:

1. There is a limit to what you can achieve, given the existing institutions, resources, and technology.

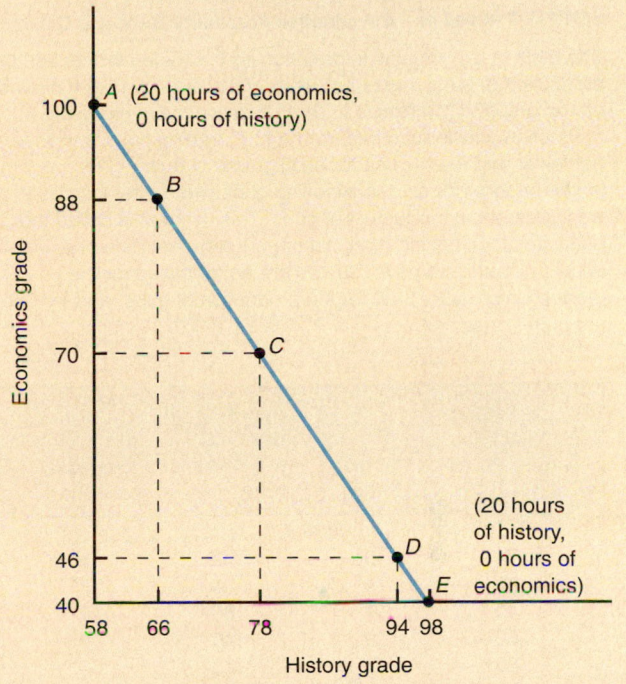

Hours of study in history	Grade in history	Hours of study in economics	Grade in economics
20	98	0	40
19	96	1	43
18	94	2	46
17	92	3	49
16	90	4	52
15	88	5	55
14	86	6	58
13	84	7	61
12	82	8	64
11	80	9	67
10	78	10	70
9	76	11	73
8	74	12	76
7	72	13	79
6	70	14	82
5	68	15	85
4	66	16	88
3	64	17	91
2	62	18	94
1	60	19	97
0	58	20	100

(a) Production possibility table

(b) Production possibility curve

EXHIBIT 1 (a and b)   A Production Possibility Table and Curve for Grades in Economics and History

The production possibility table (a) shows the highest combination of grades you can get with only 20 hours available for studying economics and history.

The information in the production possibility table in (a) can be plotted on a graph, as is done in (b). The grade received in economics is on the vertical axis, and the grade received in history is on the horizontal axis.

2. Every choice you make has an opportunity cost. You can get more of something only by giving up something else.

Increasing Marginal Opportunity Cost   I chose an unchanging trade-off in the study time/grade example because it made the initial presentation of the production possibility curve easier. Since, by assumption, you could always trade two points on your history grade for three points on your economics grade, the production possibility curve was a straight line. But is that the way we'd expect reality to be? Probably not. The production possibility curve is generally bowed outward, as in Exhibit 2(b).

Why? To make the answer more concrete, let's talk specifically about society's choice between defense spending (guns) and spending on domestic needs (butter). The information in Exhibit 2(b) is derived from the table in Exhibit 2(a).

Let's see what the shape of the curve means in terms of numbers. Let's start with society producing only butter (point A). Giving up a little butter (one pound) initially gains us a lot of guns (4), moving us to point B. The next two pounds of butter we give up gains us slightly fewer guns (point C). If we continue to trade butter for guns, we find that at point D we gain almost no guns from giving up a pound of butter. The opportunity cost of choosing guns over butter increases as we increase the production of guns.

The reason the opportunity cost of guns increases as we consume more guns is that some resources are relatively better suited to producing guns, while others are relatively better suited to producing butter. Put in economists' terminology, some resources have a comparative advantage over other resources in the production of butter, while other resources have a comparative advantage in the production of guns. A resource has a **comparative advantage** in the production of a good when, com-

Q–4: If no resource had a comparative advantage in the production of any good, what would the shape of the production possibility curve be? Why?

Comparative advantage   To be better suited to the production of one good than to the production of another good.

EXHIBIT 2 (a and b)   A Production Possibility Table and Curve

The table in (**a**) contains information on the trade-off between the production of guns and butter. This information has been plotted on the graph in (**b**). Notice in (**b**) that as we move along the production possibility curve from *A* to *F*, trading butter for guns, we get fewer and fewer guns for each pound of butter given up. That is, the opportunity cost of choosing guns over butter increases as we increase the production of guns. This concept is called the principle of increasing marginal opportunity cost. The phenomenon occurs because some resources are better suited for the production of butter than for the production of guns, and we use the better ones first.

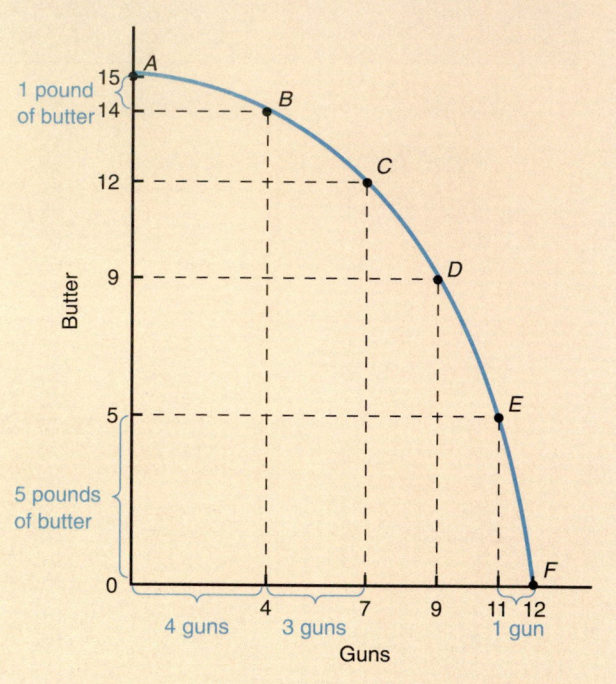

% resources devoted to production of guns	Number of guns	% resources devoted to production of butter	Pounds of butter	Row
0	0	100	15	A
20	4	80	14	B
40	7	60	12	C
60	9	40	9	D
80	11	20	5	E
100	12	0	0	F

(a) Production possibility table

(b) Production possibility curve

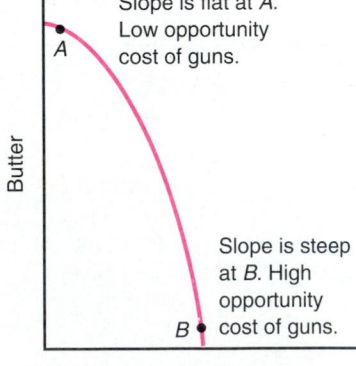

Slope is flat at *A*. Low opportunity cost of guns.

Slope is steep at *B*. High opportunity cost of guns.

Guns

Remember: when the slope is flat, there's a low opportunity cost of guns (a high opportunity cost of butter). When the slope is steep, there's a high opportunity cost of guns (a low opportunity cost of butter).

5   The principle of increasing marginal opportunity cost states that opportunity costs increase the more you concentrate on the activity. In order to get more of something, one must give up ever-increasing quantities of something else.

pared to other resources, it's relatively better suited to producing that good than to producing another good.

When making small amounts of guns and large amounts of butter, in the production of those guns we use the resources whose comparative advantage is in the production of guns. All other resources are devoted to producing butter. Because the resources used in producing guns aren't good at producing butter, we're not giving up much butter to get those guns. As we produce more and more of a good, we must use resources whose comparative advantage is in the production of the other good—in this case, more suitable for producing butter than for producing guns. As we remove resources from the production of butter to get the same additional amount of guns, we must give up increasing amounts of butter. An alternative way of saying this is that the opportunity cost of producing guns becomes greater as the production of guns increases. As we continue to increase the production of guns, the opportunity cost of more guns becomes very high because we're using resources to produce guns that have a strong comparative advantage for producing butter.

Let's consider two more specific examples. Say the United States suddenly decides it needs more wheat. To get additional wheat, we must devote additional land to growing it. This land is less fertile than the land we're already using, so our additional output of wheat per acre of land devoted to wheat will be less. Alternatively, consider the use of relief pitchers in a baseball game. If only one relief pitcher is needed, the manager sends in the best; if he must send in a second one, then a third, and even a fourth, the likelihood of winning the game decreases.

For many of the choices society must make, opportunity costs tend to increase as we choose more and more of an item. The reason is that resources are not easily adaptable from the production of one good to the production of another. Such a phenomenon about choice is so common, in fact, that it has acquired a name: the **principle of increasing marginal opportunity cost.** That principle states:

In order to get more of something, one must give up ever-increasing quantities of something else.

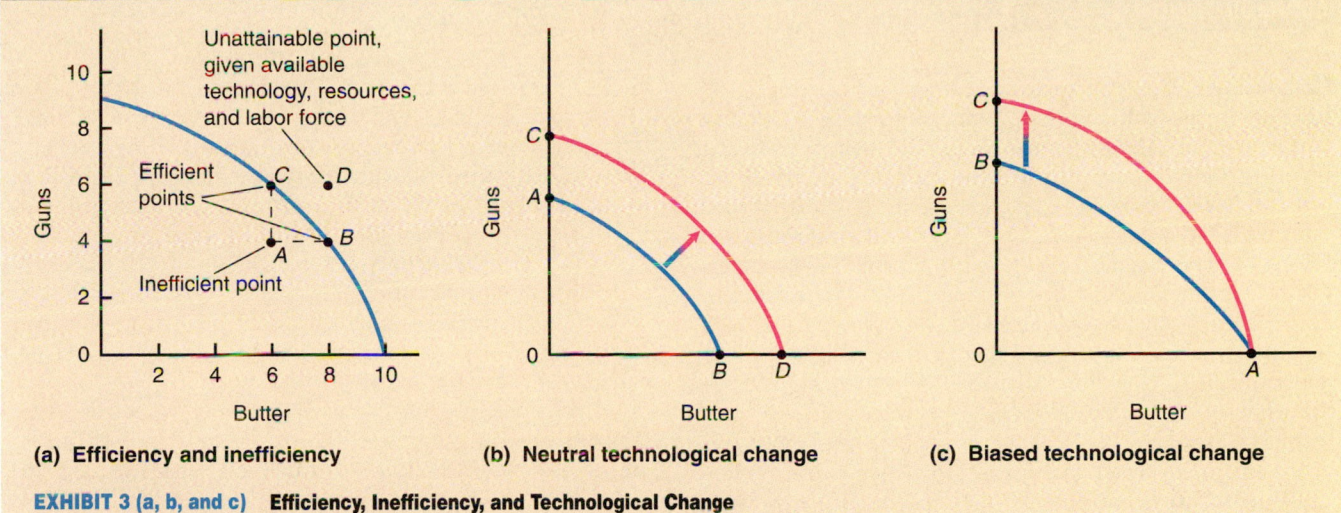

(a) Efficiency and inefficiency   **(b) Neutral technological change**   **(c) Biased technological change**

EXHIBIT 3 (a, b, and c)   Efficiency, Inefficiency, and Technological Change

The production possibility curve helps us see what is meant by efficiency. At point *A*, in **(a)**, all inputs are used to make 6 pounds of butter and 4 guns. This is inefficient since there is a way to obtain more of one without giving up any of the other; that is, to obtain 6 pounds of butter and 6 guns (point *C*) or 4 guns and 8 pounds of butter (point *B*). All points inside the production possibility curve are inefficient. With fixed inputs and given technology, we cannot go beyond the production possibility curve. For example, point *D* is unattainable.

A technological change that improves production techniques will shift the production possibility curve outward, as shown in both **(b)** and **(c)**. How the curve shifts outward depends on how technology improves. For example, if we become more efficient in the production of both guns and butter, the curve will shift out as in **(b)**. If we become more efficient in producing guns, but not in producing butter, then the curve will shift as in **(c)**.

In other words, initially the opportunity costs of an activity are low, but they increase the more we concentrate on that activity. Sometimes this law is called the flowerpot law because, if it didn't hold, all the world's food could be grown in a flowerpot. But it can't be. As we add more seeds to a fixed amount of soil, there won't be enough nutrients or room for the roots, so output per seed decreases.

Efficiency   We like, if possible, to get as much output as possible from a given amount of inputs or resources. That's how **productive efficiency** is defined: achieving as much output as possible from a given amount of inputs or resources. We would like to be efficient. The production possibility curve helps us see what is meant by productive efficiency. Consider point *A* in Exhibit 3(a), which is inside the production possibility curve. If we are producing at point *A*, we are using all our resources to produce 4 guns and 6 pounds of butter. Point *A* represents **inefficiency,** since with the same inputs we could be getting either 4 guns and 8 pounds of butter (point *B*) or 6 pounds of butter and 6 guns (point *C*). Both points *B* and *C* represent efficiency, as long as we prefer more to less. We always want to move our production out to a point on the production possibility curve.

Why not move out farther, say to point *D*? If we could, we would, but by definition the production possibility curve represents the most output we can get from a certain combination of inputs. So point *D* is unattainable, given our resources and technology.

When technology improves, when more resources are discovered, or when the economic institutions get better at fulfilling our wants, we can get more output with the same inputs. What this means is that when technology or an economic institution improves, the entire production possibility curve shifts outward from *AB* to *CD* in Exhibit 3(b). How the production possibility curve shifts outward depends on how the technology improves. For example, say we become more efficient in producing guns, but not more efficient in producing butter. Then the production possibility curve shifts outward to *AC* in Exhibit 3(c).

Productive efficiency   Getting as much output for as few inputs as possible.

Q–5: When a natural disaster hits the midwestern United States, where most of the U.S. butter is produced, what happens to the U.S. production possibility curve for guns and butter?

Production involves transforming *inputs* into *outputs*. For example, seeds, soil, and labor (inputs) combine to produce wheat (output). Many introductory economics texts call inputs *resources* and divide those inputs into three resources: land, labor, and capital. Economists in the 1800s, often called *Classical economists,* discussed production as a means of transforming land, labor, and capital into outputs. Classical economists divided all inputs into those three categories because they were interested in answering the question: How is income divided among landowners, workers, and capitalists? The three divisions helped them focus on that question: landowners' income was rent, workers' income was wages, and capitalists' income was profit.

Modern advanced analysis of production doesn't follow this threefold division. Instead, the modern analysis is more abstract and tells how inputs in general are transformed into outputs in general. Modern economic theory has moved away from the traditional division because the division of income among these three groups isn't central to the questions economists are now asking.

But that leaves open the problem: What division of resources makes the most sense? The answer depends on what question you're asking. For example, in the grade example in this chapter, your time was the input, while in the guns-and-butter example the inputs were machines, natu-

ral resources, and labor. In the most abstract categorization the ultimate resources are space (represented by soil), time (represented by labor), and matter (represented by capital). Thus, in one way of looking at it, the traditional distinction is still relevant. But in another way, it isn't. It directs our focus of analysis away from some important inputs. For example, one of the inputs that economists now focus on is *entrepreneurship,* the ability to organize and get something done. Entrepreneurship is an important input that's distinct from labor. Most listings of general resources today include entrepreneurship.

Here's another important point about resources. The term *resource* is often used with the qualifier *natural,* as in the phrase *natural resources.* Coal, oil, and iron are all called *natural resources.* Be careful about that qualifier *natural.* Whether something is or isn't a natural resource depends on the available technology. And technology is unnatural. For example, at one time a certain black gooey stuff was not a resource—it was something that made land unusable. When people learned that the black gooey stuff could be burned as a fuel, oil became a resource. What's considered a resource depends on technology. If solar technology is ever perfected, oil will go back to being black gooey stuff.

Policies that costlessly shift the production possibility curve outward are the most desirable policies because they don't require us to decrease our consumption of one good to get more of another. Alas, they are the most infrequent. Improving technology and institutions and discovering more resources are not costless; generally there's an opportunity cost of doing so that must be taken into account.

Economics, Institutions, and the Production Possibility Curve   One of the important lessons one learns in economics is that *decisions are made in context:* What makes sense in one context may not make sense in another. For example, say you're answering the question: Would society be better off if students were taught literature or if they were taught agriculture? The answer depends on the institutional context. In a developing country whose goal is large increases in material output, teaching agriculture may make sense. In a developed country, where growth in material output is less important, literature may make sense.

All decisions must be made in context.

Recognizing the contextual nature of decisions is important in interpreting the production possibility curve. Because decisions are contextual, what the production possibility curve looks like depends on the existing institutions, and the analysis can only be applied in institutional context. The production possibility curve is not a purely technical phenomenon. The curve is an *engine of analysis* to make contextual choices, not a definitive tool to decide what one should do in all cases.

Distribution and Productive Efficiency   In discussing the production possibility curve, I avoided questions of distribution: Who gets what? But such questions cannot be ignored in real-world situations. Specifically, if the method of production is tied to a particular income distribution and choosing one method will help some people but hurt others, we can't say that one method of production is efficient and the other inefficient, even if one method produces more total output than the other. The term **efficiency** involves achieving a goal as cheaply as possible. The term has meaning only in regard to a specified goal. Say, for example, that we have a society of ascetics

Efficiency   Achieving a goal as cheaply as possible.

In the 1990s oil has remained an important natural resource. *Bettman Newsphotos.*

who believe that consumption above some minimum is immoral. For such a society, producing more for less (productive efficiency) would not be efficient since consumption is not its goal. Or say that we have a society that cares that what is produced is fairly distributed. An increase in output that goes to only one person and not to anyone else would not necessarily be efficient.

In our society, however, most people prefer more to less, and many policies have relatively small distributional consequences. On the basis of the assumption that more is better than less, economists use their own kind of shorthand for such policies and talk about efficiency as identical to productive efficiency—increasing total output. But it's important to remember the assumption under which that shorthand is used: that the distributional effects that accompany the policy aren't undesirable and that we, as a society, prefer more output.

Q–6: Your firm is establishing a trucking business in Saudi Arabia. The firm has noticed that women are paid much less than men in Saudi Arabia, and the firm suggests that hiring women would be more efficient than hiring men. What should you respond?

The Production Possibility Curve and Tough Choices

The production possibility curve represents the tough choices society must make. Not everyone recognizes these choices. For example, politicians often talk as if the production possibility curve were nonexistent. They promise voters the world, telling them, "If you elect me, you can have more of everything." When they say that, they obscure the hard choices and increase their probability of getting elected.

Economists do the opposite. They promise little except that life is tough, and they continually point out that seemingly free lunches often involve significant hidden costs. Alas, political candidates who exhibit such reasonableness seldom get elected. Economists' reasonableness has earned economics the nickname, *the dismal science.*

Economics and the Invisible Forces

Economic forces are the forces of scarcity.

The opportunity cost concept applies to all aspects of life. It embodies *economic forces.* **Economic forces** are the forces of scarcity; when there isn't enough to go around, goods must be rationed. **Rationing** is a structural mechanism for determining who gets what. For example, dormitory rooms are often rationed by lottery, and permission to register in popular classes is often rationed by a first-come, first-registered rule. The same with food: if food weren't rationed, there wouldn't be enough to go around, so it must be rationed—by charging a price for it. All scarce goods or rights must be rationed in some fashion.

When an economic force operates through the market, it becomes a market force.

Rationing reflects scarcity and economic forces. One of the important choices that a society must make is whether to allow these economic forces to operate freely and openly or to try to rein them in. When society gives an economic force relatively free rein so that an economic force works through the market, it's called a **market force.**

Market forces ration by changing prices. When there's a shortage, the price goes up. When there's a surplus, the price goes down. Much of this book will be devoted to analyzing how the market works like an invisible hand, guiding economic forces to coordinate individual actions and allocate scarce resources. The **invisible hand** is the price mechanism, the rise and fall of prices that guides our actions in a market.

Societies can't choose whether or not to allow economic forces to operate—economic forces are always operating. However, societies may choose whether to allow market forces to predominate. Other forces play a major role in deciding whether to let market forces operate. I'll call these other forces the **invisible handshake** (social and historical forces) and the **invisible foot** (political and legal forces). Economic reality is determined by a contest among these three invisible forces.

6 Economic reality is controlled by three invisible forces:
1. The invisible hand (economic forces);
2. The invisible handshake (social and historical forces); and
3. The invisible foot (political forces).

Let's consider an example in which the invisible handshake prevents an economic force from becoming a market force: the problem of getting a date for Saturday night. If a school (or a society) has significantly more people of one sex than the other (let's say more men than women), some men may well find themselves without a date—that is, men will be in excess supply—and will have to find something else to do, say study or go to a movie by themselves. An ''excess supply'' person could solve the problem by paying someone to go out with him or her, but that would probably change the nature of the date in unacceptable ways. It would be revolting to the person who offered payment and to the person who was offered payment. That unacceptability is an example of the invisible handshake in action—the complex of social and cultural norms that guides and limits our activities. People don't try to buy dates because the invisible handshake prevents them from doing so. The invisible handshake makes the market solution for dating inappropriate.

Q–7: Your study partner Joan states that market forces are always operative. Is she right? Why or why not?

Now let's consider another example in which it's the invisible foot—political and legal influences—that stops economic forces from becoming market forces. Say you decide that you can make some money delivering mail in your neighborhood. You try to establish a small business, but suddenly you experience the invisible foot in action. The U.S. Postal Service has a legal monopoly, so you'll be prohibited from delivering regular mail in competition with the post office. Economic forces—the desire to make money—led you to want to enter the business, but in this case the invisible foot squashes the invisible hand.

Often the invisible foot and invisible handshake work together against the invisible hand. For example, in the United States there aren't enough babies to satisfy all the couples who desire them. Babies born to particular sets of parents are rationed—by luck. Consider a group of parents, all of whom want babies. Those who can, have a baby; those who can't have one, but want one, try to adopt. Adoption agencies ration the available babies. Who gets a baby depends on whom people know at the adoption agency and on the desires of the birth mother, who can often specify the socio-economic background (and many other characteristics) of the family in which she wants her baby to grow up. That's the economic force in action; it gives more power to the supplier of something that's in short supply.

If our society allowed individuals to buy and sell babies, that economic force would be translated into a market force. The invisible hand would see to it that the quantity of babies supplied would equal the quantity of babies demanded at some price. The market, not the adoption agencies, would do the rationing.[4]

Most people, including me, find the idea of selling babies repugnant. But why? It's the strength of the invisible handshake backed up and strengthened by the invisible foot.

---

[4] Even though it's against the law, some babies are nonetheless ''sold'' on a semilegal, or what is called a gray, market. In the early 1990s, the ''market price'' for a healthy baby was about $30,000. If it were legal to sell babies (and if people didn't find having babies in order to sell them morally repugnant), the price would be much lower, since there would be a larger supply of babies.

THE INVISIBLE FORCES

Ideas are encapsulated in metaphors, and Adam Smith's "invisible hand" metaphor has been a central one in economics since 1776. It's a neat metaphor, but it sometimes makes economic forces seem to be the only forces guiding the direction of society. And that just ain't so.

In the 1970s and 1980s, a number of modern-day economists attempted to broaden the dimensions of economic analysis. To explain what they were doing, they introduced metaphors for two other invisible forces. The term *invisible handshake* was coined by Arthur Okun, former chairman of the president's Council of Economic Advisers and an economist at the Brookings Institution, an economic think tank. Okun argued that social and historical forces—the

invisible handshake—often prevented the invisible hand from working.

The term *invisible foot* was coined by Stephen Magee, chairman of the Department of Finance at the University of Texas. Magee summarized the argument of a large number of economists that individuals often use politics to get what they want, expressing this phenomenon with the invisible foot metaphor. Government action to benefit particular pressure groups is the invisible foot. By the late 1980s, these two additional terms were commonly used by the group of economists who were struggling to integrate economic insights with social and political insights.

What is and isn't allowable differs from one society to another. For example, in Russia, until recently, private businesses were against the law, so not many people started their own businesses. In the United States, until the 1970s, it was against the law to hold gold except in jewelry, so most people refrained from holding gold. Ultimately a country's laws and social norms determine whether the invisible hand will be allowed to work.

The invisible foot and invisible handshake are active in all parts of your life. The invisible foot influences many of your everyday actions. You don't practice medicine without a license; you don't sell body parts or certain addictive drugs. These actions are all against the law. But many people do sell alcohol; that's not against the law if you have a permit. The invisible handshake also influences us. You don't make profitable loans to your friends (you don't charge your friends interest); you don't charge your children for their food (parents are supposed to feed their children); many sports and media stars don't sell their autographs (some do, but many consider the practice tacky); you don't lower the wage you'll accept in order to get a job away from someone else (you're no scab). The list is long. You cannot understand economics without understanding the limitations that political and social forces—the invisible foot and the invisible handshake—place on economic actions.

In summary, what happens in a society can be seen as the reaction to, and interaction of, these three forces: the invisible hand (economic forces), the invisible foot (political and legal forces), and the invisible handshake (social and historical forces). Economics has a role to play in sociology, history, and politics, just as sociology, history, and politics have roles to play in economics.

What happens in society can be seen as a reaction to, and interaction of, the invisible hand (economic forces), the invisible foot (political forces), and the invisible handshake (social and historical forces).

Economics is about the real world. Throughout this book I'll use the invisible forces analogy to talk about real-world events and the interrelationships of economics, history, sociology, and politics.

ECONOMIC TERMINOLOGY

Economic terminology needs little discussion. It simply needs learning. As terms come up in discussion, you'll begin to recognize them. Soon you'll begin to understand them, and finally you'll begin to feel comfortable using them. In this book I'm trying to describe how economics works in the real world, so I introduce you to many of the terms that occur in business and in discussions of the economy. Learning economic vocabulary, like learning German or French vocabulary, isn't fun. It's not something that's easily taught in classes. It's something that's learned by study and repetition outside the class. Learning vocabulary takes repetition and memorization, but no one ever said all learning is fun.

Whenever possible I'll integrate the introduction of new terminology into the discussion so that learning it will seem painless. In fact I've already introduced you to a number of economic terms: *opportunity cost, the invisible hand, market forces,*

WINSTON CHURCHILL AND LADY ASTOR

There are many stories about Nancy Astor, the first woman elected to Britain's Parliament. A vivacious, fearless American woman, she married into the English aristocracy and, during the 1930s and 1940s, became a bright light on the English social and political scenes, which were already quite bright.

One story told about Lady Astor is that she and Winston Churchill, the unorthodox genius who had a long and distinguished political career and who was Britain's prime minister during World War II, were sitting in a pub having a theoretical discussion about morality. Churchill suggested that as a thought experiment Lady Astor ponder the question: If a man were to promise her a huge amount of money—say a million pounds—for the privilege, would she sleep with him? Lady Astor did ponder the question for a while and finally answered, yes, she would, if the money were guaranteed. Churchill then asked her if she would sleep with him for five pounds. Her response was sharp: "Of course not. What do you think I am—a prostitute?" This time Churchill won the battle of wits by answering, "We have already established that fact; we are now simply negotiating about price."

One moral that economists might draw from this story is that economic incentives, if high enough, can have a powerful influence on behavior. An equally important moral of the story is that noneconomic incentives can also be very strong. Why do most people feel it's wrong to sell sex for money, even if they would be willing to do so if the price were high enough? Keeping this second moral in mind will significantly increase your economic understanding of real-world events.

economic forces, just to name a few. By the end of the book I'll have introduced you to hundreds more.

ECONOMIC INSIGHTS

Economists have thought about the economy for a long time, so it's not surprising that they've developed some insights into the way it works.

General insights are often embodied in an *economic theory*—a formulation of highly abstract, deductive relationships that capture inherent empirically-observed tendencies of economies. Theories are inevitably too abstract to apply in specific cases and, thus, these theories are often embodied, in turn, in economic models and economic principles that place the generalized insights of the theory in a more specific contextual setting. Then these theories, models, and principles are empirically tested (as best one can) to ensure that they correspond to reality. While these models and principles are less general than theories, they are still usually too general to apply in specific cases. Theories, models, and principles must be combined with a knowledge of real-world economic institutions to arrive at specific policy recommendations.

You've already been introduced to one economic principle, the principle of increasing marginal opportunity cost, which is an insight about the relationship among outputs: In order to get more of one output, you must give up ever increasing quantities of another output. That principle can be applied to a wide variety of examples, so you need to learn only the principle, not each specific example.

To see the importance of principles, think back to grade school when you learned to add. You didn't memorize the sum of 147 and 138; instead you learned a principle of addition. The principle says that when adding 147 and 138, you first add 7 + 8, which you memorized was 15. You write down the 5 and carry the 1, which you add to 4 + 3 to get 8. Then add 1 + 1 = 2. So the answer is 285. When you know that one principle, you know how to add millions of combinations of numbers.

The Invisible Hand Theory

When the quantity supplied is greater than the quantity demanded, price has a tendency to fall.

When the quantity demanded is greater than the quantity supplied, price has a tendency to rise.

In the same way, knowing a theory gives you insight into a wide variety of economic phenomena, even though you don't know the particulars of each phenomenon. For example, much of economic theory deals with the *pricing mechanism* and how the market operates to coordinate *individuals' decisions*. Economists have come to the following insights:

When the quantity supplied is greater than the quantity demanded, price has a tendency to fall.

When the quantity demanded is greater than the quantity supplied, price has a tendency to rise.

Using these generalized insights, economists have developed a theory of markets that leads to the further insight that, under certain conditions, the market will coordinate individuals' decisions, allocating scarce resources *efficiently* so society moves out to its production possibility curve, not inside it. An efficient economy is one that reaps the maximum amount of outputs from the available inputs. Economists call the insight that a market economy will allocate resources efficiently the **invisible hand theory.**

Theories and the models used to represent them are enormously efficient methods of conveying information, but they're also necessarily abstract. They rely upon simplifying assumptions, and *if you don't know the assumptions, you don't know the theory.* The result of forgetting assumptions could be similar to what happens if you forget that you're supposed to add numbers in columns. Forgetting that, yet remembering all the steps, can lead to a wildly incorrect answer. For example,

You've got to know the assumption if you are to know the theory.

$$471$$
$$+\ 327$$
5037 is wrong.

Knowing the assumptions of theories and models allows you to progress beyond gut reaction and better understand the strengths and weaknesses of various economic systems. Let's consider a central economic assumption: the assumption that individuals behave rationally—that what they choose reflects what makes them happiest, given the constraints. If that assumption doesn't hold, the invisible hand theory doesn't hold.

Presenting the invisible hand theory in its full beauty is an important part of any economics course. Presenting the assumptions upon which it is based and the limitations of the invisible hand is likewise an important part of the course. I'll do both throughout the book.

Q–8: John, your study partner, is a free market advocate. He argues that the invisible hand theory tells us that the government should not interfere with the economy. Do you agree? Why or why not?

Economic Theory and Stories

Economic theory, and the models in which that theory is presented, often developed as a shorthand way of telling a story. These stories are important; they make the theory come alive and convey the insights that give economic theory its power. In this book I present plenty of theories and models, but they're accompanied by stories that provide the context that makes them relevant.

At times, because there's much new terminology, discussing models and theories takes up much of the presentation time and becomes a bit oppressive. That's the nature of the beast. As Albert Einstein said, "Theories should be as simple as possible, but not more so." When a theory or a model becomes oppressive, pause and think about the underlying story that the theory is meant to convey. That story should make sense and be concrete. If you can't translate the theory into a story, you don't understand the theory.

Microeconomics and Macroeconomics

Economic theory is divided into two parts: microeconomic theory and macroeconomic theory. Microeconomic theory considers economic reasoning from the viewpoint of individuals and firms and builds up from there to an analysis of the whole economy. I'll define **microeconomics** as *the study of individual choice, and how that choice is influenced by economic forces.* Microeconomics studies such things as the pricing policies of firms, households' decisions on what to buy, and how markets allocate resources among alternative ends. Our discussions of opportunity cost and the production possibility curve were based on microeconomic theory. It is from microeconomics that the invisible hand theory comes.

Microeconomics is the study of how individual choice is influenced by economic forces.

As one builds up from microeconomic analysis to an analysis of the entire society, everything gets rather complicated. Many economists try to uncomplicate matters by taking a different approach—a macroeconomic approach—first looking at the aggregate, or whole, and then breaking it down into components. A micro approach would analyze a person by looking first at each individual cell and then building up. A macro approach would start with the person and then go on to his or her components—arms,

7 Microeconomic theory considers economic reasoning from the viewpoint of individuals and builds up; macroeconomics considers economic reasoning from the aggregate and builds down.

legs, fingernails, feelings, and so on. Put simply, microeconomics analyzes from the parts to the whole; macroeconomics analyzes from the whole to the parts.

Neither approach is independent of the other. In recent years the analysis of macroeconomic issues—inflation, unemployment, business cycles, and growth—has used more and more microeconomic analysis to supplement it. Thus, many economists now define macroeconomics as the study of inflation, unemployment, business cycles, and growth. I'll compromise and define **macroeconomics** as *the study of inflation, unemployment, business cycles, and growth primarily from the whole to the parts—focusing on aggregate relationships and supplementing that analysis with microeconomic insights*.

Macroeconomics is the study of inflation, unemployment, business cycles, and growth; it focuses on aggregate relationships.

To demonstrate the relationship between micro and macro analysis, let's consider again the production possibility curve, which is based on microeconomic principles. If unemployment is high, the economy is operating inside the production possibility curve and hence may be operating inefficiently. In that case, reducing unemployment can be costless. But it might also be that current institutions require such a high level of unemployment in order to prevent other problems like inflation. In that case, reducing unemployment is not costless; it involves significant, and probably costly, institutional changes. Similarly, growth shifts the production possibility curve outward, but that growth may itself be a reflection of inputs. Thus, even though the production possibility curve is derived from microeconomic principles, it can be used to discuss macroeconomic issues.

One must simultaneously develop a micro foundation of macro and a macro foundation of micro.

Neither macro nor micro is prior to the other. Clearly, macro results follow from micro decisions, but micro decisions are formed with a macro context, and can only be understood within that context. For example, say everyone expects low output levels and, given those expectations, everyone produces a low level of output. To make the analysis complete, one must develop simultaneously a microfoundation of macro and a macrofoundations of micro. The macro foundation of micro provides the institutional context within which micro decisions are made, and the micro foundation of macro provides the contextual relation between individual decisions and aggregate outcomes.

ECONOMIC INSTITUTIONS

To know whether you can apply economic theory to reality, you must know about economic institutions. Economic institutions are complicated combinations of historical circumstance and economic, cultural, social, and political pressures. Economic institutions are all around you and affect your everyday life. For example, let's consider three economic institutions: schools, corporations, and cultural norms. Where you go to school plays an important role in the kind of job you'll get. Corporations determine what products are available to buy. Cultural norms determine what you identify as legitimate business activities. Understanding economic institutions requires the wisdom of experience, tempered with common sense—all combined with a desire to understand rather than to accept without question.

Q–9: Canada spends 8 percent of its gross domestic product (GDP) on health care. The United States spends 14 percent. Yet both countries have essentially the same level of healthiness. Based on this information, would you advise the United States to adopt a system like Canada's?

Economic institutions sometimes seem to operate in quite different manners than economic theory says they do. For example, economic theory says that prices are determined by supply and demand. However, a knowledge of economic institutions says that prices are set by rules of thumb—often by what are called cost-plus-markup rules. (That is, you determine what your costs are, multiply by 1.4 or 1.5, and the result is the price you set.) Economic theory says that supply and demand determine who's hired; a knowledge of economic institutions says that hiring is often done on the basis of whom you know, not by economic forces.

These apparent contradictions have two complementary explanations. First, economic theory abstracts from many issues. These issues may account for the differences. Second, there's no contradiction; economic principles often affect decisions from behind the scenes. For instance, supply and demand pressures determine what the price markup over cost will be. In this case, the invisible handshake is guided by the invisible hand. In all cases, however, to apply economic theory to reality—to gain the full value of economic insights—you've got to have a sense of economic institutions.

The final goal of the course is to present the economic policy options facing our society today. For example, should the government restrict mergers between firms? Should it run a budget deficit? Should it do something about the international trade deficit? Should it decrease taxes?

I saved my discussion of this goal for last because there's no sense talking about policy options unless you know some economic terminology, some economic theory, and something about economic institutions. Once you know something about those, you're in a position to consider the policy options available for dealing with the economic problems our society faces.

The first thing to note about policies is that they have many dimensions. Some policies operate within existing institutions without affecting them. Others indirectly change institutions. Still others are designed to change institutions directly. Policies that affect institutions are much more difficult to analyze (because their effects on institutions are generally indirect and nebulous) and to implement (since existing institutions often create benefits for specific individuals who don't want them changed) than are policies that don't affect institutions. For example, consider establishing a government program to promote research. Seems like a good thing—right? But such a policy might undermine the role of existing institutions already promoting research, and the net result of the program might be less, not more, research. When analyzing such policies, we need to take this effect on institutions into account.

On the other hand, policies that directly change institutions, while much more difficult to implement than policies that don't, also offer the largest potential for gain. They shift the production possibility curve, whereas policies that operate within existing institutions simply move society closer to the frontier.

Let's consider an example. In the 1990s, a number of countries decided to abandon socialist institutions and put market economies in place. The result: output in those countries fell enormously as the old institutions fell. Eventually, these countries hope, once the new market institutions are predominant, output will bounce back and further gains will be made. But the temporary hardships these countries are experiencing show the enormous difficulty of implementing policies involving major institutional changes.

I have found it helpful in thinking about institutions to make an analogy to the computer, which has an operating system, software that works within that operating system, and what might be called nested software—software that only works within other software. What's efficient within one software package or operating system may be totally inefficient within another. To use a computer effectively, you must understand the interaction of the different levels of the software. To carry out economic policy effectively, one must understand the interaction and the various levels of institutions.

To carry out economic policy effectively one must understand the interaction of, and the various levels of, institutions.

Let's consider an example: welfare policy and the institution of the two-parent family. In the 1960s, the United States developed a variety of policy initiatives designed to eliminate poverty. These initiatives directed income to single parents with children, and assumed that family structure would be unchanged by these policies. But family structure did not remain unchanged; it changed substantially, and, very likely, these policies to eliminate poverty played a role in the increase in the number of single-parent families. The result was a failure of the programs to eliminate poverty. Now this is not to say that we should not have programs to eliminate poverty, or that two-parent families are preferable to one-parent families; it is only to say that we must build into our policies their effect on institutions.

Objective Policy Analysis

In thinking about policy, we must keep a number of points in mind. The most important is that good economic policy analysis is **objective.** Objective analysis does not say, "This is the way things should be," reflecting a goal established by the

Good policy analysis is as objective as possible.

8 *Positive economics* is the study of what is, and how the economy works.

Normative economics is the study of what the goals of the economy should be.

The *art of economics* is the application of the knowledge learned in positive economics to the achievement of the goals determined in normative economics.

In the art of economics, it is difficult to be objective but it is important to try.

Q–10: State whether the following five statements belong in positive economics, normative economics, or the art of economics.
1. We should support the market because it is efficient.
2. Given certain conditions, the market achieves efficient results.
3. Based on past experience and our understanding of markets, if one wants a reasonably efficient result, markets should probably be relied upon.
4. The distribution of income should be left to markets.
5. Markets allocate income according to contributions of factors.

analyst. That would be **subjective** analysis. Instead it says, ''This is the way the economy works, and if society (or the individual or firm for whom you're doing the analysis) wants to achieve a particular goal, this is how it might go about doing so.'' Objective analysis keeps your subjective views—your value judgments—separate.

To make clear the distinction between objective and subjective analysis, economists have divided economics into three categories: *positive economics, normative economics,* and the *art of economics.* **Positive economics** is the study of what is, and how the economy works. It asks such questions as: How does the market for hog bellies work? How do price restrictions affect market forces? These questions fall under the heading of economic theory. **Normative economics** is the study of what the goals of the economy should be. In discussing such questions, economists must carefully delineate whose goals they are discussing. One cannot simply assume that one's own goals for society are society's goals. Normative economics asks such questions as: What should the distribution of income be? What should tax policy be designed to achieve?

The **art of economics** relates positive economics to normative economics; it is the application of the knowledge learned in positive economics to the achievement of the goals one has determined in normative economics. It looks at such questions as: To achieve a certain distribution of income, how would you go about it, given the way the economy works?[5] Most policy discussions fall under the art of economics.

In each of these three branches of economics, economists separate their own value judgments from their objective analysis as much as possible. The qualifier ''as much as possible'' is important, since some value judgments inevitably sneak in. We are products of our environment, and the questions we ask, the framework we use, and the way we interpret empirical evidence all embody value judgments and reflect our background.

Maintaining objectivity is easiest in positive economics, where one is simply trying to understand how the economy works. In positive economics, one is working with abstract models. Maintaining objectivity is harder in normative economics. It's easy to jump from the way you think the world should be to believing that society agrees with you, and hence not to be objective about whose normative values you are using.

It's hardest to maintain objectivity in the art of economics because it embodies all the problems of both positive and normative economics. It's about how to achieve certain normative ends given the way the economy works, but it also adds more problems. Because noneconomic forces affect policy, to practice the art of economics one must make judgments about how these noneconomic forces work. These judgments are likely to embody one's own value judgments. So one must be exceedingly careful to be as objective as possible in practicing the art of economics.

One of the best ways to find out about feasible economic policy options is to consider how other countries do something and compare their approach to ours. For example, health care is supplied quite differently in various countries. To decide how to improve health care policy in the United States, policy makers study how Canada and Britain do it, and make judgments about whether the approach those countries take will fit our existing institutions. Comparative institutional analysis is an important part of the art of economics.

Policy and the Invisible Forces

When you think about the policy options facing society, you'll quickly discover that the choice of policy options depends on much more than economic theory. One must take into account historical precedent plus social, cultural, and political forces. In an

---

[5] This three-part distinction was made back in 1896 by a famous economist, John Neville Keynes, father of John Maynard Keynes, the economist who developed macroeconomics. This distinction was instilled into modern economics by Milton Friedman and Robert Lipsey in the 1950s. They, however, downplayed the art of economics, which J. N. Keynes had seen as central to understanding the economists' role in policy.

economics course, I don't have time to analyze these forces in as much depth as I'd like. That's one reason there are separate history, political science, sociology, and anthropology courses.

But I don't want to pretend that these forces don't play an important role in policy decisions. They do. That's why I use the invisible force terminology when I cover these other issues. It allows me to integrate the other forces without explaining in depth how they work. I'll use this terminology when discussing policy and applying economic insights to policy questions. In economics, we focus the analysis on the invisible hand, and much of economic theory is devoted to how the economy would operate if the invisible hand were the only force operating. But as soon as we apply theory to reality and policy, we must take into account the other invisible forces.

An example will make my point more concrete. Most economists agree that holding down or eliminating tariffs (taxes on imports) and quotas (numerical limitations on imports) makes good economic sense. They strongly advise governments to follow a policy of free trade. Do governments follow free trade policies? Almost invariably they do not. The invisible foot—politics—leads society in a different direction. If you're advising a policy maker, you need to point out that these other forces must be taken into account, and how other forces should (if they should) and can (if they can) be integrated with your recommendations.

Here's another example. Economic analysis devoid of institutional content would say that the world would be more efficient if we allowed U.S. citizenship to be bought and sold. But to advise policies that would legally allow a market for buying and selling U.S. citizenship would be to recommend a kind of efficiency that goes against historical, cultural, and social norms. The invisible handshake and the invisible foot would prevent the policies from being introduced, and any economist who proposed them would probably be banished to an ivory or other type of tower.

Students find the *Journal of Economic Perspectives* the most relevant of the journals published by the American Economic Association.

CONCLUSION

There's tons more that could be said by way of introducing you to economics, but an introduction must remain an introduction. As it is, this chapter should have:

1. Introduced you to economic reasoning.
2. Surveyed what we're going to cover in this book.
3. Given you an idea of my writing style and approach.

We'll be spending long hours together over the coming term, and before entering into such a commitment it's best to know your partner. While I won't know you, by the end of this book you'll know me. Maybe you won't love me as my mother does, but you'll know me.

This introduction was my opening line. I hope it also conveyed the importance and relevance that belong to economics. If it did, it has served its intended purpose. Economics is tough, but tough can be fun.

CHAPTER SUMMARY

- Learning economics consists of learning: economic reasoning, economic terminology, economic insights, economic institutions, and economic policy options.
- Economic reasoning structures all questions in a cost/benefit frame: If the benefits of doing something exceed the costs, do it. If the costs exceed the benefits, don't.
- Often economic decisions can be made by comparing marginal costs and marginal benefits.
- "There ain't no such thing as a free lunch" (**TAN-STAAFL**) embodies the opportunity cost concept.

- The production possibility curve embodies the opportunity cost concept.
- Economic reality is controlled and directed by three invisible forces: the invisible hand, the invisible foot, and the invisible handshake.
- Economics can be divided into microeconomics and macroeconomics.
- Economics also can be subdivided into positive economics, normative economics, and the art of economics.

KEY TERMS

art of economics *(24)*

comparative advantage *(13)*

cultural norm *(8)*

economic decision rule *(8)*

economic forces *(17)*

economic institution *(7)*

economic policy *(8)*

economic reasoning *(6)*

economic theory *(7)*

economics *(7)*

economy *(7)*

efficiency *(16)*

inefficiency *(15)*

input *(11)*

invisible foot *(18)*

invisible hand *(18)*

invisible hand theory *(21)*

invisible handshake *(18)*

macroeconomics *(22)*

marginal benefit *(8)*

marginal cost *(8)*

market force *(18)*

microeconomics *(21)*

normative economics *(24)*

objective *(23)*

opportunity cost *(10)*

output *(11)*

positive economics *(24)*

principle of increasing marginal opportunity cost *(14)*

production possibility curve *(12)*

production possibility table *(11)*

productive efficiency *(15)*

rationing *(17)*

resources *(7)*

subjective *(24)*

QUESTIONS FOR THOUGHT AND REVIEW

*The number after each question represents the estimated
degree of critical thinking required. (1 = almost none;
10 = deep thought.)*

1. Design a grade production possibility table and curve
   that embody the principle of increasing marginal opportunity cost. *(4)*

2. What would the production possibility curve look like if
   there were decreasing marginal opportunity costs?
   Explain. Think of an example of decreasing marginal
   opportunity costs. *(8)*

3. Show how a production possibility curve would shift if a
   society became more productive in its output of widgets
   but less productive in its output of wadgets. *(5)*

4. List two microeconomic and two macroeconomic
   problems. *(2)*

5. Does economic theory prove that the free market system
   is best? Why? *(4)*

6. Calculate, using the best estimates you can make:
   a. Your opportunity cost of attending college.
   b. Your opportunity cost of taking this course.
   c. Your opportunity cost of attending yesterday's lecture
      in this course. *(6)*

7. List two recent choices you made and explain why you
   made those choices in terms of marginal benefits and
   marginal costs. *(5)*

8. Individuals have two kidneys but most of us need only
   one. People who have lost both kidneys through accident
   or disease must be hooked up to a dialysis machine,
   which cleanses waste from their bodies. Say a person
   who has two good kidneys offers to sell one of them to
   someone whose kidney function has been totally
   destroyed. The seller asks $30,000 for the kidney, and
   the person who has lost both kidneys accepts the offer.
   Who benefits from the deal? Who is hurt? Should a
   society allow such market transactions? Why? *(9)*

9. Is a good economist always objective? Why? *(4)*

10. When all people use economic reasoning, inefficiency is
    impossible, because if the benefit of reducing that ineffi-
    ciency were greater than the cost, the efficiency would
    be eliminated. Thus, if people use economic reasoning,
    it's impossible to be on the interior of a production pos-
    sibility curve. Is this statement true or false? Why? *(8)*

PROBLEMS AND EXERCISES

1. A country has the following production possibility table:

Resources devoted to clothing	Output of clothing	Resources devoted to food	Output of food
100%	20	0%	0
80	16	20	5
60	12	40	9
40	8	60	12
20	4	80	14
0	0	100	15

a. Draw the country's production possibility curve.

b. What's happening to marginal opportunity costs as output of food increases?

c. Say the country gets better at the production of food.
   What will happen to the production possibility curve?

d. Say the country gets equally better at producing food
   and producing clothing. What will happen to the production possibility curve?

2. Go to two stores: a supermarket and a convenience store.

a. Write down the cost of a gallon of milk in each.

b. The prices are most likely different. Using the terminology used in this chapter, explain why that is the

the higher price.

c. Do the same exercise with shirts or dresses in Wal-Mart (or its equivalent) and Saks (or its equivalent).

3. Lawns produce no crops but occupy more land (25 million acres) in the United States than any single crop, such as corn. This means that the United States is operating inefficiently and hence is at a point inside the production possibility curve. Right? If not, what does it mean?

4. Groucho Marx is reported to have said that "The secret of success is honest and fair dealing. If you can fake those, you've got it made." What would likely happen to society's production possibility curve if everyone could fake honesty? Why? (Hint: Remember that society's production possibility curve reflects more than just technical relationships.)

5. Adam Smith, who wrote *The Wealth of Nations* and is seen as the father of modern economics, also wrote *The Theory of Moral Sentiments* in which he argued that society would be better off if people weren't so selfish and were more considerate of others. How does this view fit with the discussion of economic reasoning presented in the chapter?

ANSWERS TO MARGIN QUESTIONS

The numbers in parentheses refer to the page number of the marginal question.

1. Since the price of both stocks is now $15, it doesn't matter which one you sell (assuming no differential capital gains taxation). What price you bought them for doesn't matter. Marginal analysis refers to the future gain, so what you expect to happen to future prices of the stocks—not past prices—should determine which stock you decide to sell. *(9)*

2. Placing a value on a good can be seen as demeaning it. Consider love. Try telling an acquaintance that you'd like to buy his or her spiritual love, and see what response you get. A cost/benefit analysis requires that you put a value on it. *(10)*

3. John is wrong. The opportunity cost of reading the chapter is primarily the time you spend reading it. Reading the book prevents you from doing other things. Assuming that you already paid for the book, the original price is no longer part of the opportunity cost. Bygones are bygones. *(11)*

4. If no resource had a comparative advantage, the production possibility curve would be a straight line connecting the points of maximum production of each product. *(13)*

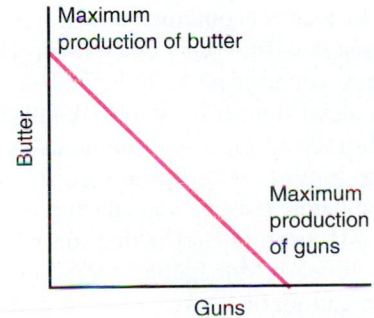

At all points along this "curve," there exists an equal and unchanging trade-off between the production of guns and butter. *(13)*

5. The production possibility curve shifts in along the butter axis. *(15)*

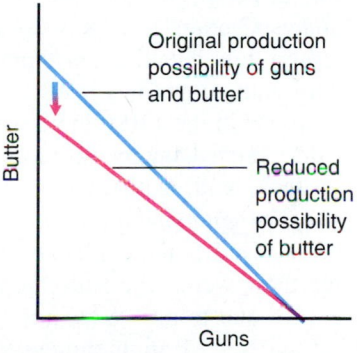

6. I remind them of the cultural forces. Women are not allowed to drive in Saudi Arabia. *(17)*

7. Joan is wrong. Economic forces are always operative; market forces are not. *(18)*

8. He is wrong. The invisible hand theory is a positive theory and does not tell us anything about policy. To do so would be to violate Hume's dictum that a "should" cannot be derived from an "is." This is not to say that government should interfere; whether government should interfere is a very difficult question. *(21)*

9. The answer is not so simple. The adviser must take a careful look at many more issues, such as who has health coverage, who pays for the coverage, how much personal choice is allowed, and how readily available is the most advanced technology. It is a question in the art of economics and such questions never have simple answers. *(22)*

10. (1) Normative; (2) Positive; (3) Art; (4) Normative; (5) Positive. *(24)*

Economics in Perspective

All too often, students study economics out of context. They're presented with sterile analysis and boring facts to memorize, and are never shown how economics fits into the large scheme of things. That's bad; it makes economics seem boring—but economics is not boring. Every so often throughout this book, sometimes in the appendixes and sometimes in boxes, I'll step back and put the analysis in perspective, giving you an idea from whence the analysis sprang and its historical context. In educational jargon, this is called *enrichment.*

I begin here with economics itself.

First, its history: In the 1500s there were few universities. Those that existed taught religion, Latin, Greek, philosophy, history, and mathematics. No economics. Then came the *Enlightenment* (about 1700) in which reasoning replaced God as the explanation of why things were the way they were. Pre-Enlightenment thinkers would answer the question, "Why am I poor?" with, "Because God wills it." Enlightenment scholars looked for a different explanation. "Because of the nature of land ownership" is one answer they found.

Such reasoned explanations required more knowledge of the way things were, and the amount of information expanded so rapidly that it had to be divided or categorized for an individual to have hope of knowing a subject. Soon philosophy was subdivided into science and philosophy. In the 1700s, the sciences were split into natural sciences and social sciences. The amount of knowledge kept increasing, and in the late 1800s and early 1900s social science itself split into subdivisions: economics, political science, history, geography, sociology, anthropology, and psychology. Many of the insights about how the economic system worked were codified in Adam Smith's *The Wealth of Nations,* written in 1776. Notice that this is before economics as a subdiscipline developed, and Adam Smith could also be classified as an anthropologist, a sociologist, a political scientist, and a social philosopher.

Throughout the 18th and 19th centuries, economists such as Adam Smith, Thomas Malthus, John Stuart Mill, David Ricardo, and Karl Marx were more than economists; they were social philosophers who covered all aspects of social science. These writers were subsequently called *Classical economists.* Alfred Marshall continued in that classical tradition, and his book, *Principles of Economics,* published in the late 1800s, was written with the other social sciences much in evidence. But Marshall also changed the questions economists ask; he focused on those questions that could be asked in a graphical supply/demand framework. In doing so he began what is called *neo-classical economics.* Marshall's analysis forms the basis of much of what's currently taught in undergraduate microeconomics courses.

In the 1930s, as economists formalized Marshall's insights, many other social science insights were removed. By the 1950s, these social sciences were cemented into college curricula and organized into college departments. Economists learned economics; sociologists learned sociology.

For a while economics got lost in itself, and economists learned little else. Marshall's analysis was downplayed, and the work of more formal economists of the 1800s (such as Leon Walras, Francis Edgeworth, and Antoine Cournot) was seen as the basis of the science of economics. Economic analysis that focuses only on formal interrelationships is called *Walrasian economics.*

Thus, in the 1990s, there are two branches of neo-classical economics: Marshallian and Walrasian. The Marshallian branch sees economics as a way of thinking and integrates insights from other disciplines. The Walrasian branch sees economics as a logical science and excludes other social sciences. This book falls solidly in the Marshallian tradition. It sees economics as a way of thinking—as an engine of analysis used to understand real-world phenomena, not as a logical exercise in deductive reasoning. My strong belief is that in undergraduate school one should learn Marshallian economics; in graduate school one can learn Walrasian economics.

Marshallian economics is an art, not a science. It sees institutions as well as political and social dimensions of reality as important, and it shows you how economics ties into those dimensions.

Graphish
The Language of Graphs

A picture is worth 1,000 words. Economists, being efficient, like to present ideas in graphs, which are a type of picture. But a graph is worth 1,000 words only if the person looking at the graph knows the graphical language; *Graphish,* we'll call it. (It's a bit like English.) Graphish is usually written on graph paper. If the person doesn't know Graphish, the picture isn't worth any words and Graphish can be babble.

I have enormous sympathy for students who don't understand Graphish. A number of my students get thrown for a loop by graphs. They understand the idea, but Graphish confuses them. This appendix is for them, and for those of you like them. It's a primer in Graphish.

Two Ways to Use Graphs

In this book I use graphs in two ways:

1. To present an economic model or theory visually; to show how two variables interrelate.
2. To present real-world data visually. To do this, I use primarily bar charts, line charts, and pie charts.

Actually, these two ways of using graphs are related. They are both ways of presenting visually the *relationship* between two things.

Graphs are built around a number line, or axis, like the one in Exhibit B1(a). The numbers are generally placed in order, equal distances from one another. That number line allows us to represent a number at an appropriate point on the line. For example, point *A* represents the number 4.

The number line in Exhibit B1(a) is drawn horizontally, but it doesn't have to be; it can also be drawn vertically, as in Exhibit B1(b).

How we divide our axes, or number lines, into intervals, is up to us. In Exhibit B1(a), I called each interval *1;* in Exhibit B1(b), I called each interval *10.* Point *A* appears after 4 intervals of 1 (starting at 0 and reading from left to right), so it represents 4. In Exhibit B1(b), where each interval represents 10, to represent 5, I place point *B* halfway in the interval between 0 and 10.

So far, so good. Graphish developed when a vertical and a horizontal number line were combined, as in Exhibit B1(c). When the number lines are put together

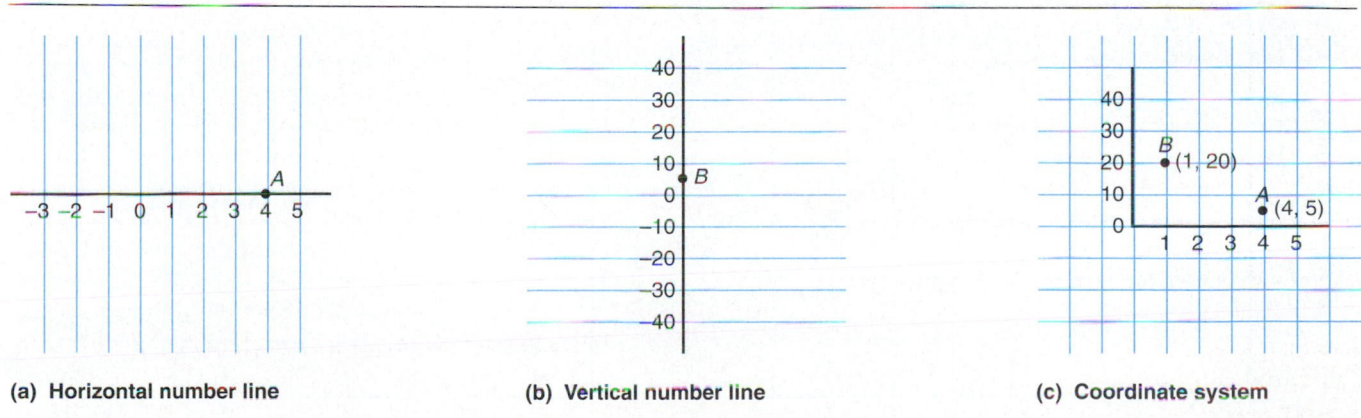

(a) **Horizontal number line**

(b) **Vertical number line**

(c) **Coordinate system**

EXHIBIT B1 (a, b, and c)   Horizontal and Vertical Number Lines and a Coordinate System

they're called *axes*. (Each line is an axis. *Axes* is the plural of *axis*.) I now have a two-dimensional space in which *one point can represent two numbers*. (This two-dimensional space is called a *coordinate space*.) For example, point *A* in Exhibit B1(c) represents the numbers (4, 5)—4 on the horizontal number line and 5 on the vertical number line. Point *B* represents the numbers (1, 20). (By convention, the horizontal numbers are written first.)

Being able to represent two numbers with one point is neat because it allows the relationships between two numbers to be presented visually instead of having to be expressed verbally, which is often cumbersome. For example, say the cost of producing 6 units of something is $4 per unit and the cost of producing 10 units is $3 per unit. By putting both these points on a graph, we can visually see that producing 10 costs less per unit than does producing 6.

Another way to use graphs to present real-world data visually is to use the horizontal line to represent time. Say

that we let each horizontal interval equal a year, and each vertical interval equal $100 in income. By graphing your income each year, you can obtain a visual representation of how your income has changed over time.

Graphs can be used to show any relationship between two variables. (*Variables* are what economists call the units that are measured on the horizontal and vertical axes.) As long as you remember that graphs are simply a way of presenting a relationship visually, you can keep graphs in perspective.

Using Graphs in Economic Modeling   I use graphs throughout the book as I present economic models, or simplifications of reality. A few terms are often used in describing these graphs, and we'll now go over them. Consider Exhibit B2(a), which lists the number of pens bought per day (column 2) at various prices (column 1).

We can present the table's information in a graph by combining the pairs of numbers in the two columns of the

---

EXHIBIT B2 (a, b, c, and d)   A Table and Graphs Showing the Relationships between Price and Quantity

Price of pens (in dollars)	Quantity of pens bought per day	Row
3.00	4	A
2.50	5	B
2.00	6	C
1.50	7	D
1.00	8	E

(a) Price quantity table

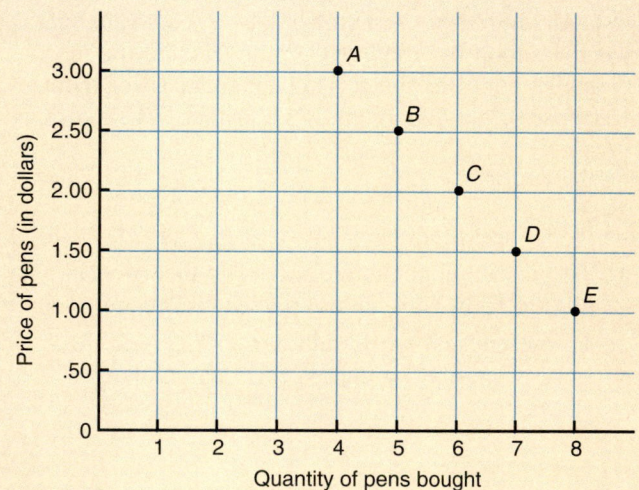

(b) From a table to a graph (1)

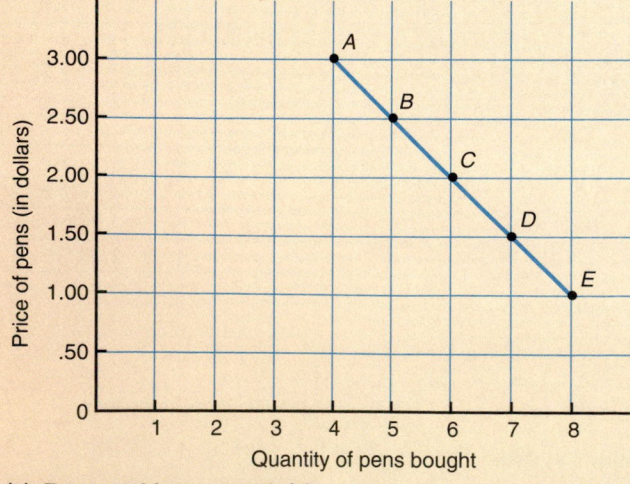

(c) From a table to a graph (2)

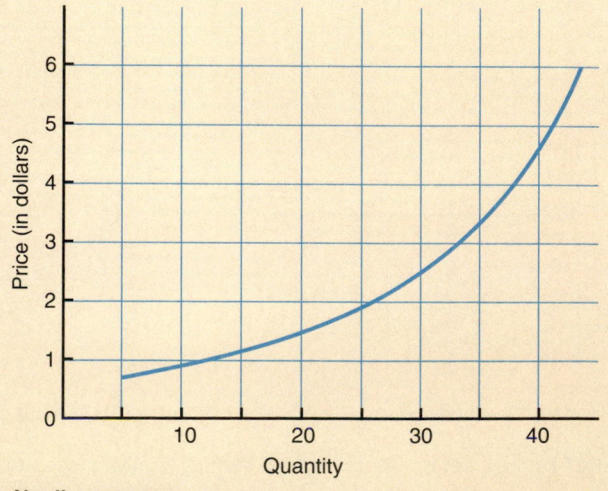

(d) Nonlinear curve

table and representing, or plotting, them on two axes. I do that in Exhibit B2(b).

By convention, when graphing a relationship between price and quantity, economists place price on the vertical axis and quantity on the horizontal axis.

I can now connect the points, producing a line like the one in Exhibit B2(c). With this line, I interpolate the numbers between the points. That is, I make the reasonable assumption (which makes for a nice visual presentation) that the relationship between the variables is the same *between* the points as it is *at* the points. This assumption is called the *interpolation assumption*. It allows us to think of a line as a collection of points and therefore to connect the points into a line.

Even though the line in Exhibit B2(c) is straight, economists call any such line drawn on a graph a *curve*. Because it's straight, the curve in Exhibit B2(c) is called a *linear curve*. Notice that this curve starts high on the left-hand side and goes down to the right. Economists say any curve that looks like that is *downward-sloping*. They also say that a downward-sloping curve represents an *inverse* relationship between the two variables: When one goes up, the other goes down. In this example, the line demonstrates an inverse relationship between price and quantity—that is, when the price of pens goes up, the quantity bought goes down.

Exhibit B2(d) presents a curve that really is curved. It starts low on the left-hand side and goes up to the right. Such curves are called *nonlinear curves*. Economists say any curve that goes up to the right is *upward-sloping*. An upward-sloping curve represents a *direct* relationship between the two variables (what's measured on the horizontal and vertical lines). In a direct relationship, when one variable goes up, the other goes up too. *Downward-sloping* and *upward-sloping* are terms you need to memorize if you want to read, write, and speak Graphish, keeping graphically in your mind the image of the relationships they represent.

Slope   One can, of course, be far more explicit about how much the curve is sloping upward or downward. To be more explicit, mathematicians define the term *slope* as the change in the value on the vertical axis divided by the change in the value on the horizontal axis. Sometimes it's presented as "rise over run":

$$\text{Slope} = \frac{\text{Rise}}{\text{Run}} = \frac{\text{Change in value on vertical axis}}{\text{Change in value on horizontal axis}}$$

Slopes of Linear Curves   In Exhibit B3, I present five linear curves and measure their slope. Let's go through an example to show how we can measure slope. To do so, we must pick two points. Let's use points A (6, 8) and B (7, 4) on curve a. Looking at these points, we see that as we move from 6 to 7 on the horizontal axis, we move from 8 to 4 on the vertical axis. So when the number on the vertical axis falls by 4, the number on the horizontal

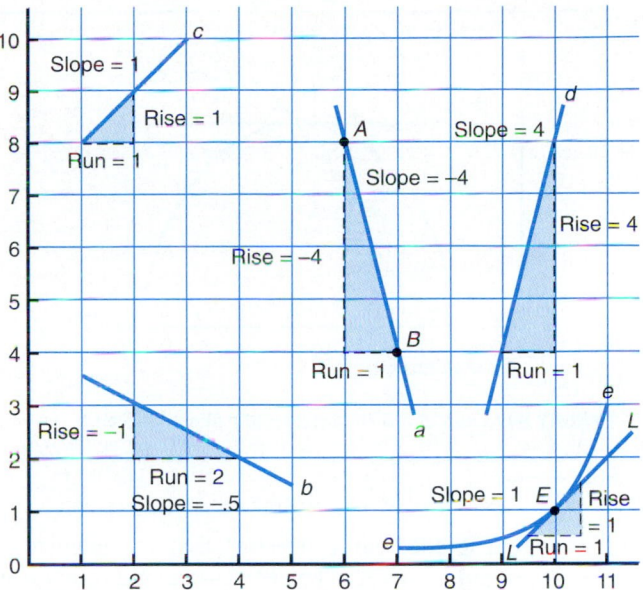

EXHIBIT B3   Slopes of Curves

axis increases by 1. That means the slope is -4 divided by 1, or -4.

Notice that the inverse relationships represented by the two downward-sloping curves, a and b, have negative slopes, and that the direct relationships represented by the two upward-sloping curves, c and d, have positive slopes. Notice also that the flatter the curve, the smaller the numerical value of the slope; and the more vertical, or steeper, the curve, the larger the numerical value of the slope. There are two extreme cases:

1. When the curve is horizontal (flat), the slope is zero.
2. When the curve is vertical (straight up and down), the slope is infinite (larger than large).

Knowing the term *slope* and how it's measured lets us describe verbally the pictures we see visually. For example, if I say a curve has a slope of zero, you should picture in your mind a flat line; if I say "a curve with a slope of minus one," you should picture a falling line that makes a 45° angle with the horizontal and vertical axes. (It's the hypotenuse of an equilateral triangle with the axes as the other two sides.)

Slopes of Nonlinear Curves   The preceding examples were of *linear (straight) curves*. With *nonlinear curves*—the ones that really do curve—the slope of the curve is constantly changing. As a result, we must talk about the slope of the curve at a particular point, rather than the slope of the whole curve. How can a point have a slope? Well, it can't really, but it can almost, and if that's good enough for mathematicians, it's good enough for us.

Defining the slope of a nonlinear curve is a bit more difficult. The slope at a given point on a nonlinear curve is determined by the slope of a linear (or straight) line

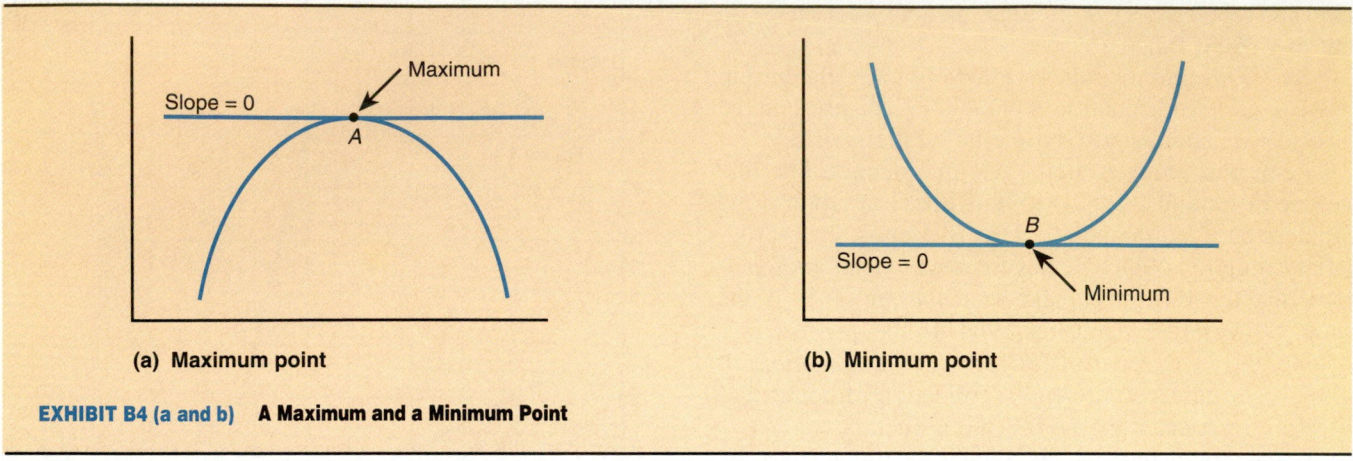

(a) Maximum point

(b) Minimum point

EXHIBIT B4 (a and b)   A Maximum and a Minimum Point

that's tangent to that curve. (A line that's tangent to a curve is a line that just touches the curve, and touches it only at one point in the immediate vicinity of the given point.) In Exhibit B3, the line *LL* is tangent to the curve *ee* at point *E*. The slope of that line, and hence the slope of the curve at the one point where the line touches the curve, is +1.

Maximum and Minimum Points
Two points on a nonlinear curve deserve special mention. These points are the ones for which the slope of the curve is zero. I demonstrate those in Exhibit B4(a) and (b). (At point *A,* we're at the top of the curve so it's at a maximum point; at point *B,* we're at the bottom of the curve so it's at a minimum point.) These maximum and minimum points are often referred to by economists, and it's important to realize that the value of the slope of the curve at each of these points is zero.

There are, of course, many other types of curves, and much more can be said about the curves I've talked about. I won't do so because, for purposes of this course, we won't need to get into those refinements. I've pre-

sented as much Graphish as you need to know for this book.

Presenting Real-World Data in Graphs

The previous discussion treated the Graphish terms that economists use in presenting models which focus on hypothetical relationships. Economists also use graphs in presenting actual economic data. Say, for example, that you want to show how exports have changed over time. Then you would place years on the horizontal axis (by convention) and exports on the vertical axis, as in Exhibit B5(a) and (b). Having done so, you can either connect the data, as in (a), or fill in the areas under the points for that year, as in (b). The first is called a *line graph;* the second is called a *bar graph.*

Another type of graph is a *pie chart,* such as the one presented in Exhibit B5(c). A pie chart is useful in visually presenting how a total amount is divided. The uncut pie is the total amount, and the pie pieces reflect the percentage of the whole pie that the various components make up. Exhibit B5(c) shows the division of grades on a test I gave. Notice that 5 percent of the students got A's.

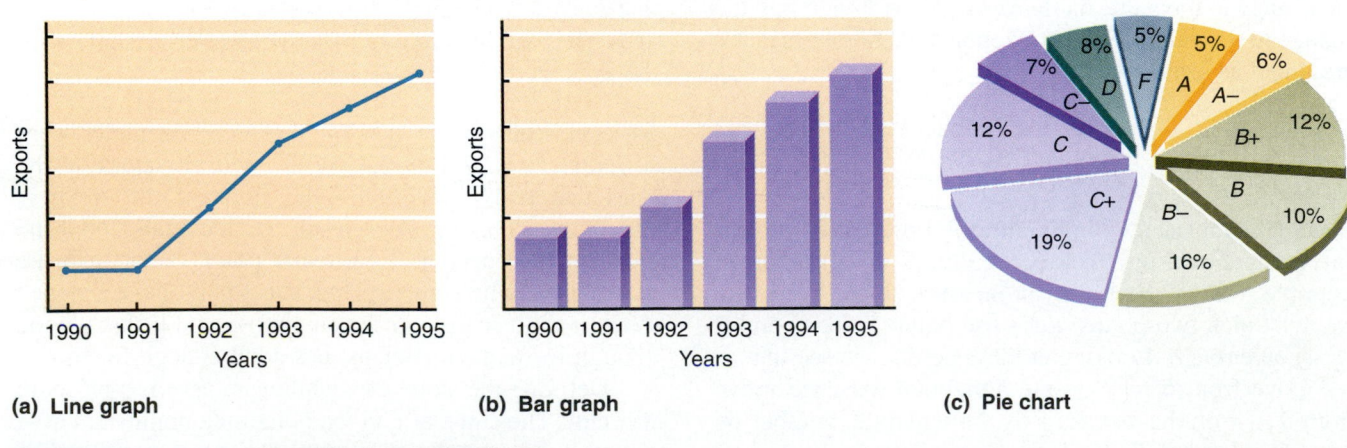

(a) Line graph

(b) Bar graph

(c) Pie chart

EXHIBIT B5 (a, b, and c)   Presenting Information Visually

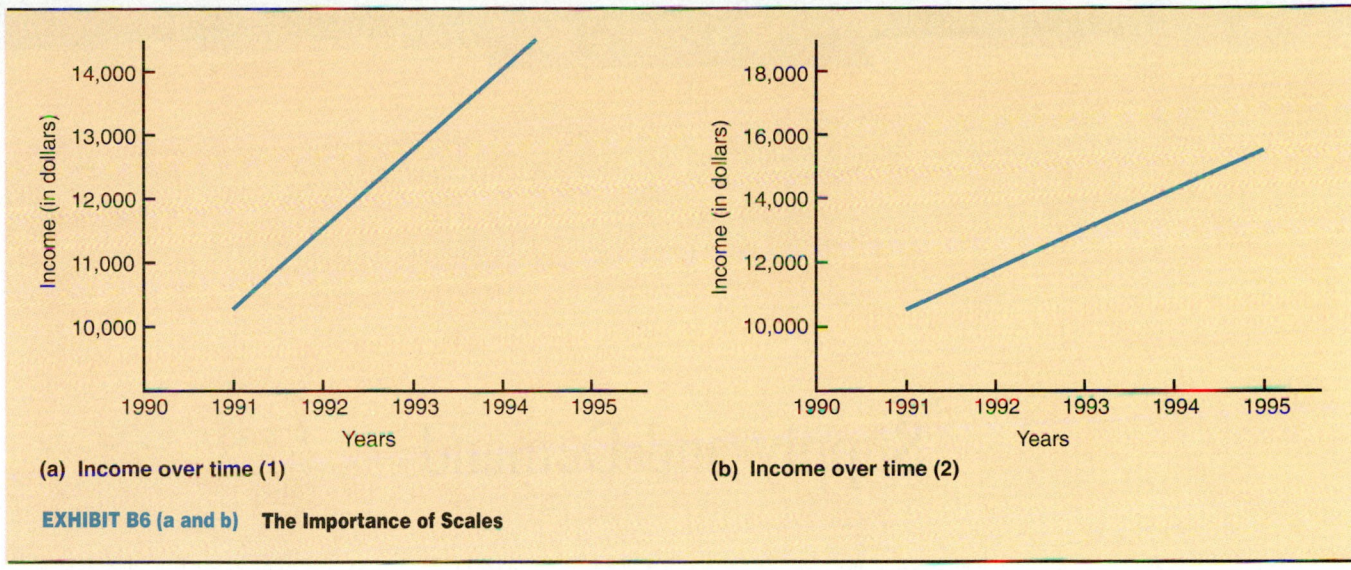

(a) Income over time (1)

(b) Income over time (2)

EXHIBIT B6 (a and b)   The Importance of Scales

There are other types of graphs, but they're all variations on line and bar graphs and pie charts. Once you understand these three basic types of graphs, you shouldn't have any trouble understanding the other types.

Interpreting Graphs about the Real World   Understanding Graphish is important, because if you don't, you can easily misinterpret the meaning of graphs. For example, consider the two graphs in Exhibit B6(a) and (b). Which graph demonstrates the larger rise in income? If you said (a), you're wrong. The intervals in the vertical axes differ, and if you look carefully you'll see that the curves in both graphs represent the same combination of points. So when considering graphs, always make sure you understand the markings on the axes. Only then can you interpret the graph.

Let's now review what we've covered.

· A graph is a picture of points on a coordinate system in which the points denote relationships between numbers.

· A downward-sloping line represents an inverse relationship or a negative slope.
· An upward-sloping line represents a direct relationship or a positive slope.
· Slope is measured by rise over run, or a change of y (the number measured on the vertical axis) over a change in x (the number measured on the horizontal axis).
· The slope of a point on a nonlinear curve is measured by the rise over run of a line tangent to that point.
· At the maximum and minimum points of a nonlinear curve, the value of the slope is zero.
· In reading graphs, one must be careful to understand what's being measured on the vertical and horizontal axes.

2

Supply and Demand

Teach a parrot the terms supply *and* demand *and you've got an economist.*

~Thomas Carlyle

After reading this chapter, you should be able to:

1. State the law of demand.

2. Explain the importance of opportunity cost and substitution to the laws of supply and demand.

3. Draw a demand curve from a demand table.

4. Distinguish a shift in demand from a movement along the demand curve.

5. State the law of supply.

6. Draw a supply curve from a supply table.

7. Distinguish a shift in supply from a movement along the supply curve.

8. State the three dynamic laws of supply and demand.

9. Demonstrate the effect of a price ceiling and a price floor on a market.

Supply and demand. Supply and demand. Roll the phrase around your mouth, savor it like a good wine. *Supply* and *demand* are the most used words in economics. And for good reason. They provide a good off-the-cuff answer for any economic question. Try it.

Why are bacon and oranges so expensive this winter? *Supply and demand.*

Why are interest rates falling? *Supply and demand.*

Why can't I find decent wool socks any more? *Supply and demand.*

The importance of the interplay of supply and demand makes it only natural that early in any economics course, you must learn about supply and demand. Let's start with demand.

DEMAND

Poets and songwriters use literary license. Take the classic song by the Rolling Stones entitled "You Can't Always Get What You Want." Whether the statement is or isn't true depends on how you define *want*. If you define *want* as "being sufficiently desirous of something so that you do what's necessary to buy the good," then in a market in which prices are flexible, you *can* always get what you want. The reason: what you want depends on what the price is. If, however, you define *want* as simply "being desirous of something," then there are many unfulfilled "wants," such as my wanting an expensive sports car. I want to own a Maserati. But, I must admit, I'm not willing to do what's necessary to own one. If I really wanted to own one, I'd mortgage everything I own, increase my income by doubling the number of hours I work, not buy anything else, and get that car. But I don't do any of those things, so there's a question of whether I really want the car. Sure, I'd want one if it cost $10,000, but from my actions it's clear that, at $190,000, I don't really want it. If *want* is defined as "being sufficiently desirous of something that you will do what's necessary to buy the good," you can always get what you want, because your willingness to pay the going price for something is the only way to tell whether you really want it. What you want at a low price differs from what you want at a high price. The quantity you demand varies inversely—in the opposite direction—with the price.

Prices are the tool by which the invisible hand—the market—coordinates individuals' desires and limits how much people are willing to buy—how much they really want. When goods are scarce, the market reduces people's desires for those scarce goods; as their prices go up, people buy fewer of them. As goods become abundant, their prices go down, and people want more of them. The invisible hand sees to it that what people want (do what's necessary to get) matches what's available. In doing so, the invisible hand coordinates individuals' wants. While you can't always get what you want at a low price, you can get it at some price—maybe a super-high price. It isn't surprising that the Stones chose the other definition of *want;* it's unlikely that their song would have become a hit had they put in the appropriate qualifier. You can't dance to "You Can't Always Get What You Want at the Price You Want."

Prices are the tool by which the market coordinates individual desires.

The Law of Demand

What makes the qualifier appropriate is the **law of demand:**

More of a good will be demanded the lower its price, other things constant.

Or alternatively:

Less of a good will be demanded the higher its price, other things constant.

This law is fundamental to the invisible hand's ability to coordinate individuals' desires: as prices change, people change how much of a particular good they're willing to buy.

To be clear about the meaning of the law of demand, economists differentiate the concepts *demand* and *quantity demanded.* **Demand** refers to a schedule of quantities of a good that will be bought per unit of time at various prices. **Quantity demanded** refers to a specific amount that will be demanded per unit of time at a specific price.

In graphical terms, *demand* refers to the entire **demand curve** which tells how much of a good will be bought at various prices. *Quantity demanded* refers to a point

1 The Law of Demand states that the quantity of a good demanded is inversely related to the good's price. When price goes up, quantity demanded goes down.

It is important to distinguish between demand (the entire demand curve) and quantity demanded (a point on the demand curve).

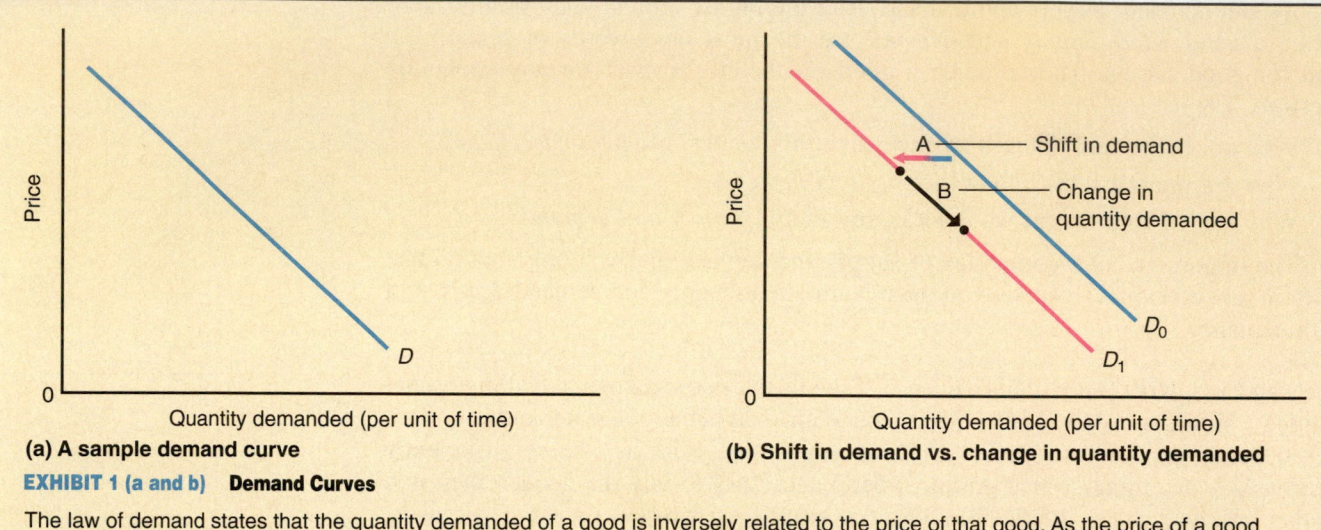

EXHIBIT 1 (a and b)   Demand Curves

The law of demand states that the quantity demanded of a good is inversely related to the price of that good. As the price of a good goes up, the quantity demanded goes down so the demand curve is downward sloping as in Exhibit 1(a). Exhibit 1(b) shows the distinction between a shift in demand (arrow A) brought about by a shift in a nonprice factor, and a change in quantity demanded—a movement along a demand curve—brought about by a change in price (arrow B).

on a demand curve, so when economists talk about movements along a demand curve, they mean changes in quantity demanded.

Exhibit 1(a) shows a demand curve. In graphical terms, the law of demand states that the quantity demanded of a good is inversely related to that good's price, other things constant. As the price goes up, the quantity demanded goes down. As you can see in Exhibit 1(a), price and quantity are inversely related, so the demand curve slopes downward to the right. Exhibit 1(b) distinguishes between a shift in demand—a shift of the entire demand curve as shown by Arrow A—and a change in quantity demanded—a movement along a demand curve as shown by Arrow B.

Just think of something you'd really like but can't afford. If the price is cut in half, you—and other consumers—become more likely to buy it. Quantity demanded goes up as price goes down.

Just to be sure you've got it, let's consider a real-world example: demand for vanity—specifically, vanity license plates. In 1989, the North Carolina state legislature increased the vanity plates' price from $30 to $40. In response, the quantity demanded fell from 60,334 at $30 a year to 31,122 at $40 a year. Assuming other things remained constant, that is the law of demand in action.

Other Things Constant   To understand the law of demand, you must understand the terminology used to discuss that law and the assumptions upon which that law is based. Let's first consider the phrase, "Other things constant."

Notice that in stating the law of demand, I put in a qualification: **other things constant.**[1] That's three extra words, and unless they were important I wouldn't have put them in. But what does "other things constant" mean? Say that over a period of two years, the price of cars rises as the number of cars sold likewise rises. That seems to violate the law of demand, since the number of cars sold should have fallen in response to the rise in price. Looking at the data more closely, however, we see that a third factor has also changed: individuals' income has increased overall. As income increases, people buy more cars, increasing the demand for cars.

The increase in price works as the law of demand states—it decreases the number of cars bought. But in this case, income doesn't remain constant; it increases. That rise in income increases the demand for cars. That increase in demand outweighs the

Q–1:   In the 1980s and 1990s, as animal rights activists made wearing fur coats déclassé, the _____ decreased. Should the missing words be "demand for furs" or "quantity of furs demanded?"

---

[1] *Other things constant* is a translation of the Latin phrase *ceteris paribus.* Sometimes economists just use *ceteris paribus* without translating it.

decrease in quantity demanded that results from a rise in price, so ultimately more cars are sold. If you want to study the effect of price alone—which is what the law of demand refers to—you must make adjustments to hold income constant when you make your study. That's why the qualifying phrase *other things constant* is an important part of the law of demand.

This qualifying phrase, "other things constant," places a limitation on the implications that can be drawn from any analysis based on the law of demand. Alfred Marshall, one of the originators of this law, emphasized these limitations, arguing that it is as much of a mistake to apply supply–demand analysis to areas where these assumptions do not hold as it is not to apply it to those areas where it does apply. To emphasize this point he argued that the law of demand is directly applicable to *partial equilibrium* issues—issues in which other things can reasonably be assumed to remain constant and that supply–demand analysis should be called **partial equilibrium analysis**. He admonished his students to remember that partial equilibrium analysis is incomplete because it assumes other things equal. That it is incomplete does not mean that it cannot be used for other issues, but when applied to issues where other things do not remain constant, it must be used with an educated common sense and one must keep in the back of one's mind what does not remain constant.

How much somebody wants to buy a good depends on many other things besides its price. These include individuals' tastes, prices of other goods, and even the weather. Those other factors must remain constant if you're to make a valid study of the effect of an increase in the price of a good on the quantity demanded of it. In practice it's impossible to keep all other things constant, so you have to be careful when you say that when price goes up, quantity demanded goes down. It's likely to go down, but it's always possible that something besides price has changed.

Economists recognize that many things besides price affect demand. They call them **shift factors of demand.** A shift factor of demand is something, other than the good's price, that affects how much of the good is demanded. Important shift factors of demand include:

1. Society's income.
2. The prices of other goods.
3. Tastes.
4. Expectations.

These aren't the only shift factors. In fact anything—except price changes—that affects demand (and many things do) is a shift factor. While economists agree these shift factors are important, they believe that no shift factor influences how much is demanded as consistently as price of the specific item does. That's what makes economists focus first on price as they try to understand the world. That's why economists make the law of demand central to their analysis.

Relative Price   A second qualification is that the law of demand refers to a good's **relative price.** The relative price of a good is the price of that good compared to the price of another good or combination of goods. For example, if the price of a compact disc is $11 and the price of an apple is 50 cents, the relative price of CDs compared to the price of apples is $11/50¢ = 22. In other words, you can buy 22 apples with one CD or one CD with 22 apples.

The actual price you pay for the goods you buy is called *the money price*. You don't say that a CD has a price of 22 apples; you say that a CD has a price of $11. But don't let that fool you. While the $11 may not look like a relative price, it is. It is the price of the CD compared to a composite price for all other goods. That composite price for all other goods is the price of money. What's the price of money? It's simply how much you'll pay for money. Most people will pay $1 for $1, so the price of $1 is $1. The money price of $11 means that you can trade one CD for 11 one-dollar bills.

Money is not desired for its own sake. You want dollar bills only because you can trade them for something else. You have in the back of your mind a good sense of what else you could do with that $11—what the opportunity cost of spending it on a

Partial equilibrium analysis   In-complete analysis which assumes "other things constant."

Important shift factors of demand include:
1. Society's income.
2. The prices of other goods.
3. Tastes.
4. Expectations.

Relative price   Price of a good compared to the price of some other good.

CD is. You could buy, say, three Big Macs, a double order of fries, and a vanilla shake for $11. The opportunity cost of buying the CD is that big tray of fast food. Thus the money price of an item represents the price of that item relative to the prices of all other goods.

As long as your sense of what that opportunity cost is doesn't change, money price is a good representation of relative price. Over short periods the opportunity cost of $1 doesn't change. Over longer periods, though, because of inflation, money prices are not a good representation of relative prices. Say, for instance, that money prices (including your wage) on average go up 10 percent. (When this happens, economists say the price level has gone up by 10 percent.) Also say the money price of a CD goes up by 2 percent. Has the relative price of CDs gone up or down? Since the *average* money price has gone up 10 percent and the money price of a CD has risen by 2 percent, the relative price of a CD has fallen by 8 percent. The law of demand would say that the quantity of CDs demanded would increase because the relative price has gone down, even though the money price has gone up.

The use of money prices makes life easier for members of society, but it makes life harder for economics students, who must remember that even though they see the money price of an item as an absolute number, it is actually a relative price.

2 The law of demand is based upon individuals' ability to substitute.

I emphasize that the law of demand refers to relative price because the explanation for it involves demanders' ability to *substitute* some other good for that good. If a good's relative price goes up, some people will substitute some other good for it because that substitute's relative price goes down. For example, if the money price of compact discs rises and the money price of music tapes doesn't rise, individuals will substitute music tapes for CDs.

The Demand Table

As I emphasized in Chapter 1, introductory economics depends heavily on graphs and graphical analysis—translating ideas into graphs and back again into words. So let's graph the demand curve.

Exhibit 2(a) describes Alice's demand for renting videocassettes. In this example, the demand is for the temporary use of a videocassette. For example, at a price of $2, Alice will buy the use of six cassettes per week.

There are a number of points about the relationship between the number of videos Alice rents and the price of renting them that are worth mentioning. First, the relationship follows the law of demand: as the rental price rises, quantity demanded decreases. Second, quantity demanded has a specific *time dimension* to it. In this example it is the number of cassette rentals per week that is referred to, not the number of cassettes rented per day, hour, or year. Without the time dimension, the table wouldn't provide us with any useful information. Nine cassette rentals per year is quite a different concept from nine cassette rentals per week. Third, the cassette rentals that Alice buys are interchangeable—the ninth cassette rental doesn't significantly differ from the first, third, or any other cassette rental.

The concept of interchangeable goods causes economists significant problems in discussing real-world demand schedules because the quality of goods often differs in the real world. A pink Volkswagen is quite different from a gray Aston Martin, yet they're both cars. Luckily, in textbooks interchangeable goods cause few problems because we can pick and choose among examples. Textbook authors simply avoid examples that raise significant quality problems. However, it's only fair to point out that in the real world economists spend a great deal of time adjusting their analyses for differences in quality among goods.

Two final points are already familiar to you. Fourth, the price the table refers to is a relative price even though it is expressed as a money price, and fifth, the schedule assumes that everything else is held constant.

From a Demand Table to a Demand Curve

Exhibit 2(b) translates Exhibit 2(a)'s information into a graph. Point A (quantity = 9, price = $.50) is graphed first at the (9, $.50) coordinates. Next we plot points B, C, D, and E in the same manner and connect the resulting dots with a solid line. The result is the demand curve, which graphically conveys the same information that's in the

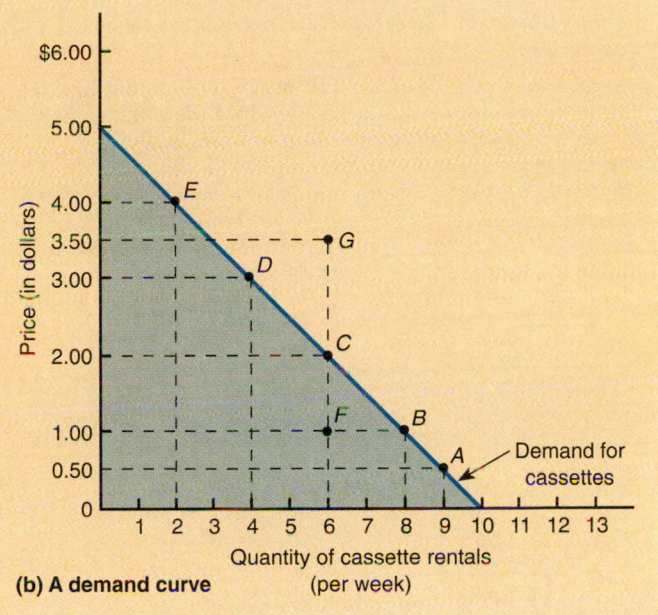

EXHIBIT 2 (a and b)   From a Demand Table to a Demand Curve

The demand table in (a) is translated into a demand curve in (b). Each point on the table corresponds to a point on the curve. For example, point A on the graph represents row A in the table: Alice demands 9 videocassette rentals at a price of 50 cents. A demand curve is constructed by plotting all points from the demand table and connecting the points by a line.

	Price (in dollars)	Cassette rentals demanded per week
A	0.50	9
B	1.00	8
C	2.00	6
D	3.00	4
E	4.00	2

(a) A demand table

(b) A demand curve

demand table. Notice that the demand curve is downward sloping (from left to right), indicating that the law of demand holds in the example. When a curve slopes downward to the right, we say that there is an inverse relationship between the price and the quantity demanded.

The demand curve represents the *maximum price* that an individual will pay for various quantities of a good; the individual will happily pay less. For example, say someone offers Alice six cassette rentals at a price of $1 each (point F of Exhibit 2(b)). Will she accept? Sure; she'll pay any price within the shaded area to the left of the demand curve. But if someone offers her six rentals at $3.50 each (point G), she won't accept. At a rental price of $3.50, she's willing to buy only three cassette rentals.

The demand curve represents the maximum someone would be willing to pay. He or she would happily pay less.

Normally, economists talk about market demand curves rather than individual demand curves. A **market demand curve** is the horizontal sum of all individual demand curves. Market demand curves are what most firms are interested in. Firms don't care whether individual A or individual B buys their good; they care that *someone* buys their good.

It's a good graphical exercise to add the individual demand curves together to create a market demand curve. I do that in Exhibit 3. In it I assume that the market consists of three buyers, Alice, Bruce, and Cathy, whose demand tables are given in Exhibit 3(a). Alice and Bruce have demand tables similar to the demand tables discussed previously. At a price of $3, Alice rents four cassettes; at a price of $2, she rents six. Cathy is an all-or-nothing individual. She rents one cassette as long as the price is equal to or below $1; otherwise she rents nothing. If you plot Cathy's demand curve, it's a vertical line. However, the law of demand still holds: as price increases, quantity demanded decreases.

The quantity demanded by each demander is listed in columns 2, 3, and 4 of Exhibit 3(a). Column 5 gives total market demand; each entry is the sum of the entries in columns 2, 3, and 4. For example, at a price of $3 (row F), Alice demands four cassette rentals, Bruce demands one, and Cathy demands zero, for a total market demand of five cassette rentals.

Exhibit 3(b) shows three demand curves: one each for Alice, Bruce, and Cathy. The market, or total, demand curve is the horizontal sum of the individual demand curves. To see that this is the case, notice that if we take the quantity demanded at $1 by Alice (8), Bruce (5), and Cathy (1) (row B, columns 2, 3, and 4), they sum to 14,

Individual and Market Demand Curves

3   To derive a demand curve from a demand table, you plot each point on the demand table on a graph and connect the points. For example:

Demand table

Q	P
2	5
4	3

EXHIBIT 3 (a and b)   From Individual Demands to a Market Demand Curve

The table (**a**) shows the demand schedules for Alice, Bruce, and Cathy. Together they make up the market for videocassette rentals. Their total quantity demanded (market demand) for videocassette rentals at each price is given in column 5. As you can see in (**b**), Alice's, Bruce's, and Cathy's demand curves can be added together to get the total market demand curve. For example, at a price of $2, Cathy demands 0, Bruce demands 3, and Alice demands 6, for a market demand of 9 (point *D*).

	(1) Price (in dollars)	(2) Alice	(3) Bruce	(4) Cathy	(5) Market demand
A	0.50	9	6	1	16
B	1.00	8	5	1	14
C	1.50	7	4	0	11
D	2.00	6	3	0	9
E	2.50	5	2	0	7
F	3.00	4	1	0	5
G	3.50	3	0	0	3
H	4.00	2	0	0	2

(a) A demand table

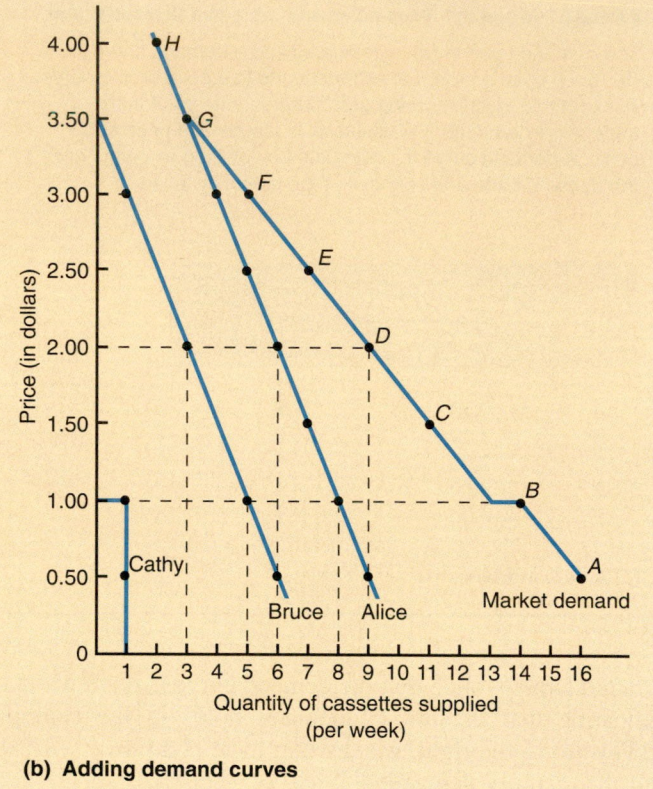

(b) Adding demand curves

Q–2: Derive a market demand curve from the following two individual demand curves:

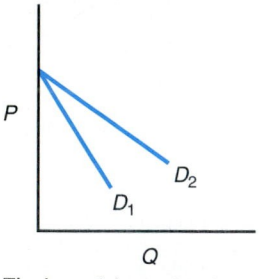

The law of demand is based on two phenomena:
1. *At lower prices, existing demanders buy more.*
2. *At lower prices, new demanders enter the market.*

Shifts in Demand versus Movement along a Given Demand Curve

which is point *B* (14, $1) on the market demand curve. We can do that for each level of price. Alternatively, we can simply add the individual quantities demanded prior to graphing (which we do in column 5 of Exhibit 3(a)) and graph that total in relation to price. Not surprisingly, we get the same total market demand curve.

In practice, of course, firms don't measure individual demand curves, so they don't sum them up in this fashion. Instead, they estimate total demand. Still, summing up individual demand curves is a useful exercise because it shows you how the market demand curve is made up of the sum (the horizontal sum, graphically speaking) of the individual demand curves, and it gives you a good sense of where market demand curves come from. It also shows you that, even if individuals don't respond to small changes in price, the market demand curve can still be smooth and downward sloping. That's because for the market, the law of demand is based on two phenomena:

1. At lower prices, existing demanders buy more.
2. At lower prices, new demanders (some all-or-nothing demanders like Cathy) enter the market.

As I have emphasized already, the demand curves we draw assume other things are held constant. That is, we assume the price of the good, not shift factors, is causing the demand curve to be downward sloping. To distinguish between the effects of price and the effects of shift factors on how much of a good is demanded, we need some terminology.

As I stated above, if how much is demanded is affected by price, we call that effect a change in the quantity demanded. Since a demand curve tells us how much is demanded at different prices, a change in the quantity demanded is represented graphically by a **movement along the demand curve.** If how much is demanded is affected by a shift factor, there is said to be a **shift in demand.** Since a change in a shift factor changes how much would be bought at each different price, a change in demand means that the entire demand curve shifts, to either the right or the left. Thus, a change in a shift factor causes a *shift* in demand; a change in price causes a *movement* along the demand curve. Differentiating between a shift in demand and movement along the demand curve is important but difficult, so it's useful to differentiate the two types of change graphically. I do so for this example in Exhibit 4.

Exhibit 4(a) shows the effect of a change in the price of cassettes from $3.50 to $2. Point A (quantity demanded 3, price $3.50) represents the starting point. Now the price falls to $2 and the quantity demanded rises from 3 to 9, so we move along the demand curve to point B. Notice the demand curve (D_0) has already been drawn to demonstrate the effect that price has on quantity.

Now let's say that price of $3.50 doesn't change but income rises and, as it does, quantity demanded rises to 5. Thus, at a price of $3.50, 5 cassette rentals are demanded rather than only 3. That point is represented by point C in Exhibit 4(b). But if income causes a rise in quantity demanded at a price of $3.50, it will also likely cause an increase in the quantity demanded at all other prices. The demand curve will not remain where it was, but will shift to D_1 to the right of D_0. Because of the change in income, the entire demand curve has shifted. Thus, we say a change in this shift factor has caused a shift in demand.

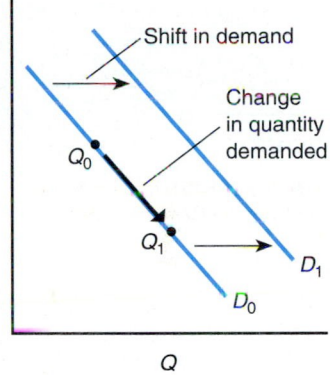

4 Changes in quantity demanded are shown by movements along a demand curve. Shifts in demand are shown by a shift of the entire demand curve.

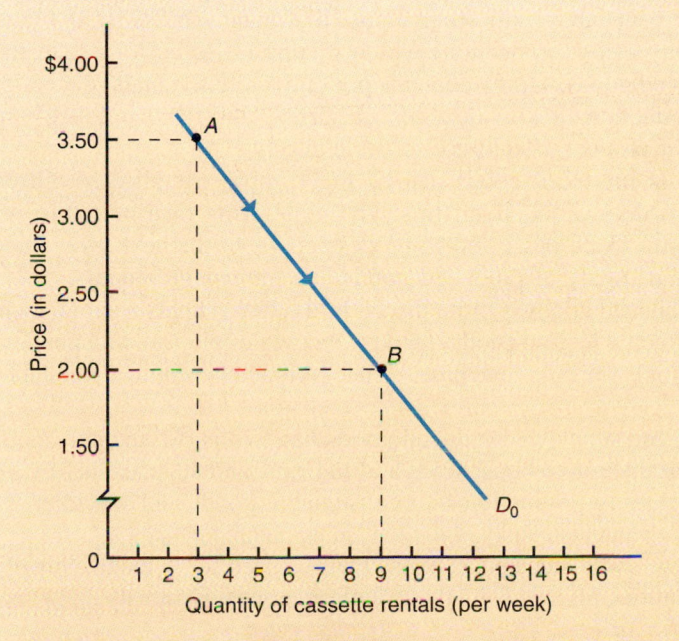

(a) Movement along a demand curve

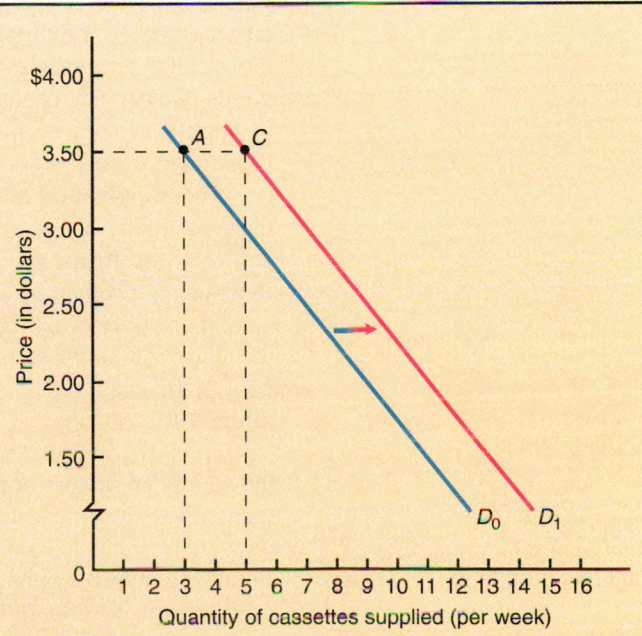

(b) Shift in demand

EXHIBIT 4 (a and b)   Shifts in Demand versus Movement along a Demand Curve

A change in price causes a movement along the demand curve. For example, in **(a)**, if the price of videocassette rentals is $3.50, 3 rentals will be demanded (point A). If the price falls to $2, the quantity of rentals demanded will be 9 (point B). Thus, the fall in price brings about a movement along the demand curve, from point A to point B.

A shift factor change causes a shift in demand. For example, in **(b)**, at the price of $3.50, 3 cassette rentals will be demanded (point A), but if income rises while price remains the same, people are willing to buy 5 cassette rentals for $3.50 (point C) instead of only 3. An increase in income causes the entire demand curve to shift outward from D_0 to D_1.

The difference between shift in demand and movement along a demand curve is that a change in a shift factor causes a shift in the entire demand curve, while a change in the price of a good causes a movement along a demand curve.

To see if you understand, say the local theater decides to let everyone in for free. What will happen to demand for videocassettes? If your answer is there will be a shift in demand—the entire demand curve will shift inward—you've got it. Just to be sure, let's try one last example. Say tastes change: couch potatoes are out, hard bodies are in. What will happen to the demand for cassettes? The entire demand curve shifts in some more.

The difference between shifts in demand and movements along the demand curve deserves emphasis:

· A change in a shift factor causes a shift in demand (a shift of the entire demand curve).

· A change in price of a good causes a change in the quantity demanded (a movement along an existing demand curve).

SUPPLY

Factors of production *Resources, or inputs, necessary to produce goods.*

Firms *Organizations of individuals that transform factors of production into consumer goods.*

In one sense, supply is the mirror image of demand. Individuals control the inputs, or resources, necessary to produce goods. Such resources are often called **factors of production.** Individuals' supply of these factors to the market mirrors other individuals' demand for those factors. For example, say you decide you want to rest rather than weed your garden. You hire someone to do the weeding; you demand labor. Someone else decides she would prefer more income instead of more rest; she supplies labor to you. You trade money for labor; she trades labor for money. Here supply is the mirror image of demand.

For a large number of goods and services, however, the supply process is more complicated than demand. As Exhibit 5 shows, for many goods, there's an intermediate step in supply. Individuals supply factors of production to firms. **Firms** are organizations of individuals that transform factors of production into consumable goods.

Let's consider a simple example. Say you're a taco technician. You supply your labor to the factor market. The taco company demands your labor (hires you). The taco company combines your labor with other inputs like meat, cheese, beans, and tables, and produces many tacos (production) which it supplies to customers in the goods market. For produced goods, supply depends not only on individuals' decisions to supply factors of production; it also depends on firms' ability to produce—to transform those factors of production into consumable goods.

The supply process of produced goods can be much more complicated. Often there are many layers of firms—production firms, wholesale firms, distribution firms, and retailing firms, each of which passes on in-process goods to the next layer firm. Real-world production and supply of produced goods is a multistage process.

The supply of nonproduced goods is more direct. Individuals supply their labor in the form of services directly to the goods market. For example, an independent contractor may repair your washing machine. That contractor supplies his labor directly to you.

Thus, the analysis of the supply of produced goods has two parts: an analysis of the supply of factors of production to households and to firms, and an analysis of why firms transform those factors of production into consumable goods and services.

The Law of Supply

Quantity supplied *Quantity of a good suppliers want to sell, and either have, or are able to produce; it can be represented by a point on a supply curve.*

Positive relationship

Price goes up then quantity supplied goes up.

In talking about supply, the same convention exists that we used for demand. **Supply** refers to the various quantities offered for sale at various prices. **Quantity supplied** refers to a specific quantity offered for sale at a specific price.

There's also a law of supply that corresponds to the law of demand. The **law of supply** states that the quantity supplied of a good is positively related to that good's price, other things constant. Specifically:

Law of supply: More of a good will be supplied the higher its price, other things constant.

Or:

Law of supply: Less of a good will be supplied the lower its price, other things constant.

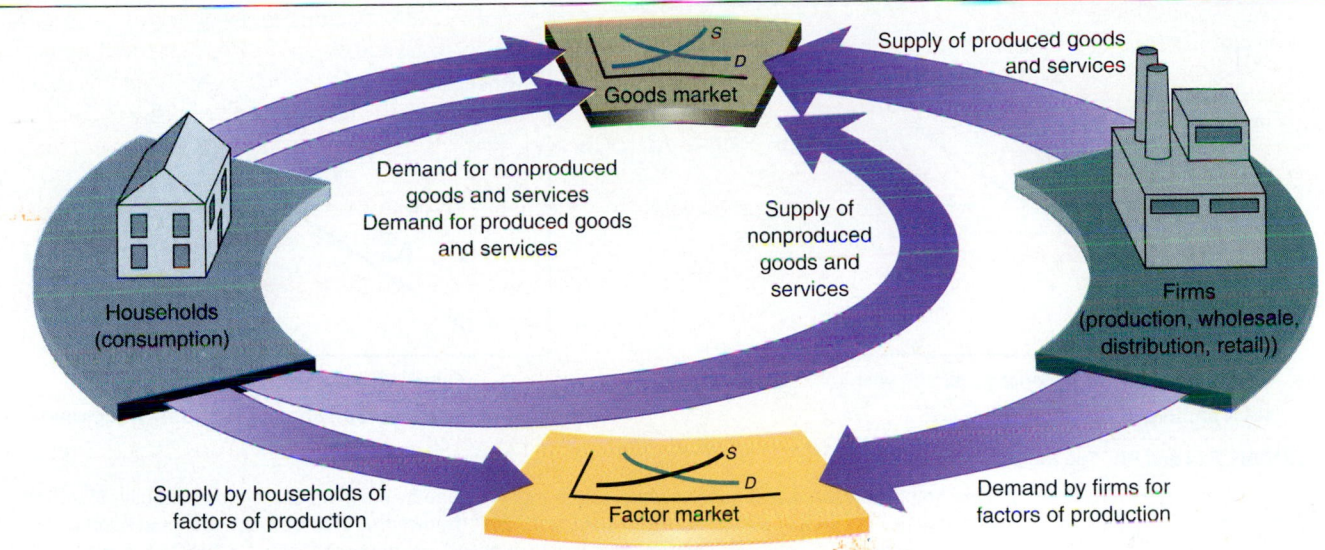

EXHIBIT 5   Transformation of Factors of Production into Consumable Goods and Services

Supply refers to the quantities that will be bought at various prices. When goods are simply traded, supply and demand both come from households. One household supplies the good; another household demands the good. When you mow a neighbor's yard for a fee, you are supplying a nonproduced good.

With produced goods and services, such as a television and insurance, the supply process is more complicated. Households supply factors; firms demand factors and use those factors to produce goods and services. These produced goods are then supplied to households.

Price regulates quantity supplied just as it regulates quantity demanded. Like the law of demand, the law of supply is fundamental to the invisible hand's (the market's) ability to coordinate individuals' actions. Notice how the supply curve in Exhibit 6(a) slopes upward to the right. That upward slope captures the law of supply. It tells us that the quantity supplied varies directly—in the same direction—with the price.

The same graphical distinction holds for the terms *supply* and *quantity supplied* as did for the terms *demand* and *quantity demanded*. In graphical terms, *supply* refers to the entire supply curve because a supply curve tells us how much will be offered for sale at various prices. *Quantity supplied* refers to a point on a supply curve, so if you refer to movements along a supply curve, you're talking about changes in the quantity supplied. The distinction between a shift in supply and a change in quantity supplied is shown in Exhibit 6(b). A shift in supply—a shift of the entire supply curve—is shown by Arrow A. A change in the quantity supplied—a movement along the entire supply curve—is shown by Arrow B.

What accounts for the law of supply? When the price of a good rises, individuals and firms can rearrange their activities in order to supply more of that good to the market, substituting production of that good for production of other goods. Thus, the same psychological tendency of individuals that underlies the law of demand—their determination to want more for less—underlies the law of supply. Individuals and firms want the highest price they can get for the smallest possible quantity they can supply.

With firms, there's a second explanation of the law of supply. Assuming firms' costs are constant, a higher price means higher profits (the difference between a firm's revenues and its costs). The expectation of those higher profits leads it to increase output as price rises, which is what the law of supply states.

Other Things Constant   As with the law of demand, the first qualification of the law of supply is that it assumes other things are held constant. Thus, if the price of wheat rises and quantity supplied falls, you'll look for something else that changed—for example, a drought might have caused the drop in quantity supplied. Your expectations would go as follows: Had there been no drought, the quantity supplied would

5 The law of supply states that the quantity supplied of a good is directly related to the good's price. When prices go up, quantity supplied goes up.

Q–3: In the 1980s and 1990s, as animal activists decreased the demand for fur coats, the prices of furs fell. This caused _____ to decline. Should the missing word(s) be "supply" or "quantity supplied"?

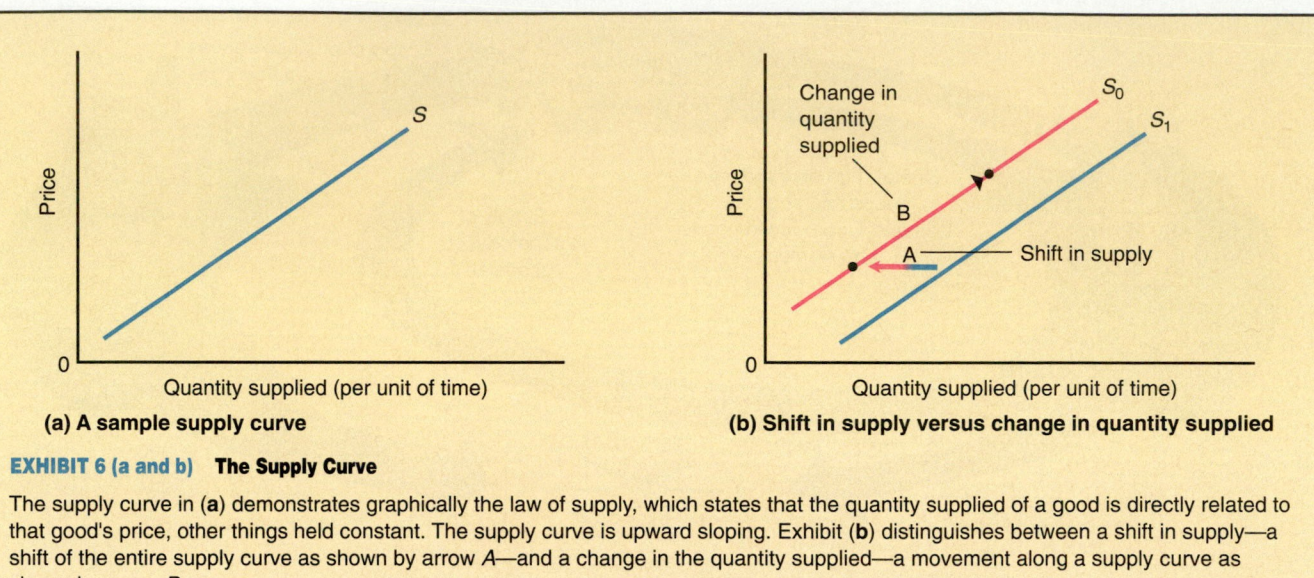

(a) A sample supply curve

(b) Shift in supply versus change in quantity supplied

EXHIBIT 6 (a and b)   The Supply Curve

The supply curve in **(a)** demonstrates graphically the law of supply, which states that the quantity supplied of a good is directly related to that good's price, other things held constant. The supply curve is upward sloping. Exhibit **(b)** distinguishes between a shift in supply—a shift of the entire supply curve as shown by arrow *A*—and a change in the quantity supplied—a movement along a supply curve as shown by arrow *B*.

have increased in response to the rise in price, but because there was a drought, the supply decreased, which caused prices to rise.

As with the law of demand, the law of supply represents economists' off-the-cuff response to the question: What happens to quantity supplied if price rises? If the law seems to be violated, economists search for some other variable that has changed. As was the case with demand, these other variables that might change are called *shift factors*.

This "other things constant" assumption is as important to the law of supply as it is to the law of demand. It limits the direct application of supply–demand analysis to microeconomics. To see why, consider a macroeconomic example (one which affects the entire economy). Say that all firms in an economy cut output—decrease supply— by 10 percent. Is it reasonable to assume that other things remain constant? In answering this question, think about the demand for a firm's product. As all firms cut production, peoples' income will fall and their demand for goods will fall (income is a shift factor). So when considering the aggregate economy, when considering macro issues, changes in aggregate supply and changes in the quantity of aggregate supply will likely be interrelated with changes in aggregate demand. This interaction is one of the primary reasons economists separate the micro analysis presented in this chapter from macro analysis.

Relative Price   A second qualification is that the law of supply refers to *relative price*. The reason is that, like the law of demand, the law of supply is based on individuals' and firms' ability to substitute production of this good for another, or vice versa. If the price of corn rises relative to the price of wheat, farmers will grow less wheat and more corn. If both prices rise by equal percentages, the relative price won't change and it won't be worthwhile to substitute one good for another.

The law of supply, like the law of demand, is based on the individual firm's ability to substitute. Suppliers will substitute toward goods for which they receive higher relative prices.

The Supply Table

6   To derive a supply curve from a supply table, you plot each point on the supply table on a graph and connect the points.

Remember Exhibit 3(a)'s demand table for cassette rentals. In Exhibit 7(a), columns 2 (Ann), 3 (Barry), and 4 (Charlie), we follow the same reasoning to construct a supply table for three hypothetical cassette suppliers. Each supplier follows the law of supply: when price rises, they supply more, or at least as much as they did at a lower price.

EXHIBIT 7 (a and b)   **From a Supply Table to a Supply Curve**

As with market demand, market supply is determined by adding all individual supplies at a given price. Three suppliers—Ann, Barry, and Charlie—make up the market of videocassette suppliers. The total market supply is the sum of their individual supplies at each price (shown in column 5 of (a).

Each of the individual supply curves and the market supply curve have been plotted in (b). Notice how the market supply curve is the horizontal sum of the individual supply curves.

	(1)	(2)	(3)	(4)	(5)
	Price	Ann's	Barry's	Charlie's	Market
Row	(in dollars)	supply	supply	supply	supply
A	0.00	0	0	0	0
B	0.50	1	0	0	1
C	1.00	2	1	0	3
D	1.50	3	2	0	5
E	2.00	4	3	0	7
F	2.50	5	4	0	9
G	3.00	6	5	0	11
H	3.50	7	5	2	14
I	4.00	8	5	2	15

(a) A supply table

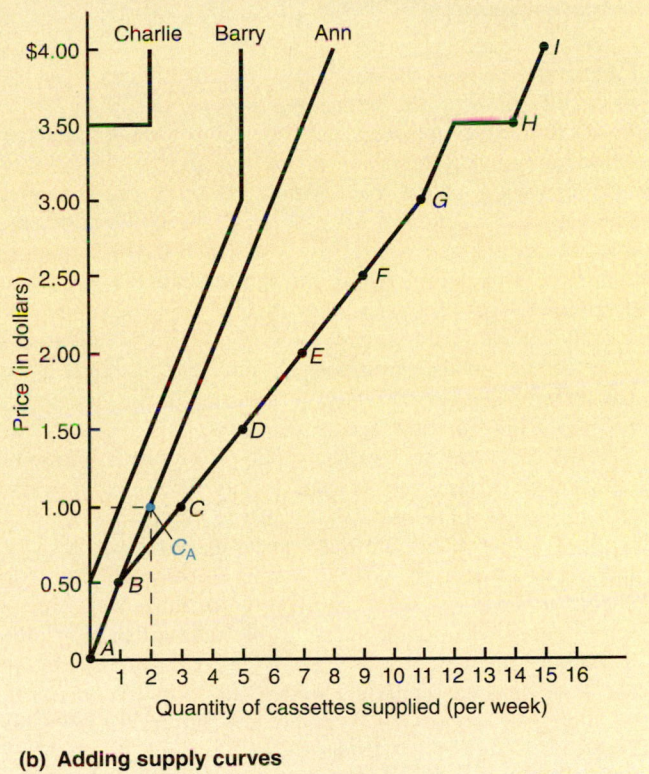

(b) Adding supply curves

Exhibit 7(b) takes the information in Exhibit 7(a)'s supply table and translates it into a graph of Ann's supply curve. For instance, point C_A on Ann's supply curve corresponds to the information in column 2, row C. Point C_A is at a price of $1 and a quantity of 2. Notice that Ann's supply curve is upward sloping, meaning that price is positively related to quantity. Charlie's and Barry's supply curves are similarly derived.

The supply curve represents the set of *minimum prices* an individual seller will accept for various quantities of a good. The market's invisible hand stops suppliers from charging more than the market price. If suppliers could escape the market's invisible hand and charge a higher price, they would gladly do so. Unfortunately for them, and fortunately for consumers, a higher price encourages other suppliers to begin selling cassettes. Competing suppliers' entry into the market places a limit on the price any supplier can charge.

The market supply curve is derived from individual supply curves in precisely the same way that the market demand curve was. To emphasize the symmetry, I've made the three suppliers quite similar to the three demanders. Ann (column 2) will supply 2 at $1; if price goes up to $2 she increases her supply to 4. Barry (column 3) begins supplying at $1, and at $3 supplies 5, the most he'll supply, regardless of how high price rises. Charlie (column 4) has only two units to supply. At a price of $3.50 he'll supply that quantity, but higher prices won't get him to supply any more.

We sum horizontally the individual supply curves to get the market supply curve. In Exhibit 7(a) (column 5), we add together Ann's, Barry's, and Charlie's supply to arrive at the market supply curve, which is graphed in Exhibit 7(b). Notice each point on it corresponds to the information in columns 1 and 5 for a particular row. For example, point H corresponds to a price of $3.50 and a quantity of 14.

From a Supply Table
to a Supply Curve

Q–4: Derive the market supply curve from the following two individual supply curves.

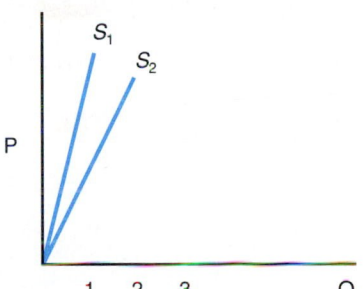

Individual and Market Supply Curves

Many goods must be produced—that is, inputs must be physically transformed before they become desirable goods. Production is complicated and requires a separate analysis before it can be integrated into our analysis.

In what's called *Walrasian economics* (named after famous Swiss economist Leon Walras), the problem of production is assumed away; his is an analysis of a trading economy. This is important to recognize since it's Walrasian economics that provides the logical underpinnings for supply/demand analysis. In Walrasian economics individuals have certain goods they trade; at some prices they sell, at some (lower) prices they buy. It is in this sense that supply is simply the mirror image of demand.

An easy way to see that supply is a mirror image of demand is to think about your supply of hours of work. When we talk of work, we say you're supplying hours of work at $6 per hour. But that same supply of work can be thought of as demand for leisure time. If, at $6 an hour, you choose to work 8 hours a day, you're simultaneously choosing to keep 16 hours for yourself (24 hours a day minus the 8 hours spent working). If we talk in terms of leisure, we speak of demand for leisure; if we talk of work, we speak of supply of labor. One is simply the mirror image of the other.

Another approach to economics is *Marshallian economics* (named after Alfred Marshall, a famous English economist). Marshallian economics does include an analysis of production. It relates costs of production with what firms are willing to sell. The reason production is difficult to integrate with an analysis of supply is that with many production processes, per-unit costs fall as production

increases. For example, in the 1920s Henry Ford produced a lot more Model T cars than either he or any of his competitors had produced before. As he produced more, costs per unit fell and the price of cars fell. Even today many businesses will tell you that if they can increase demand for their good, their per-unit costs and their price will go down. Such examples don't violate the law of supply. Costs per unit fall because of the nature of production. As the nature of production changes, the upward-sloping supply curve shifts outward.

There's another point we should mention about supply. Sometimes students get the impression from textbooks that supply and demand simply exist—that firms can go out, find demand curves, and start supplying. That's not a realistic picture of how the economy works. Demand curves aren't there for students or firms to see. Producing goods and supplying them inevitably involves risk and uncertainty. A company like General Motors may spend $1 billion designing a certain type of car, only to find that consumers don't like its style, or that another company has produced a car consumers like better. In that case, GM suffers a large loss.

To compensate for the potential for losses, suppliers also have the potential to make a profit on goods they sell. When the price of a good is high compared to costs of the resources used in production, expected profits are high, so more producers are encouraged to take the risk. When the price of a good is low compared to the costs, fewer firms take the risk because expected profits are low. Thus, profit is a motivating force of supply in a market economy.

The law of supply is based on two phenomena:
1. At higher prices, existing suppliers supply more.
2. At higher prices, new suppliers enter the market.

The market supply curve's upward slope is determined by two different sources: by existing suppliers supplying more and by new suppliers entering the market. Sometimes existing suppliers may not be willing to increase their quantity supplied in response to an increase in prices, but a rise in price often brings brand new suppliers into the market. For example, a rise in teachers' salaries will have little effect on the amount of teaching current teachers do, but it will increase the number of people choosing to be teachers.

Shifts in Supply versus Movement along a Given Supply Curve

Important shift factors of supply include:
1. The prices of inputs used in the production of a good.
2. Technology.
3. Suppliers' expectations.
4. Taxes and subsidies.

Just as there can be shifts in the demand curve resulting from shift factors, so too can there be shifts in the supply curve caused by shift factors. Important shift factors of supply include:

1. Changes in the prices of inputs used in the production of a good.
2. Changes in technology.
3. Changes in suppliers' expectations.
4. Changes in taxes and subsidies.

These aren't all the shift factors; as was the case with demand, anything that affects supply other than price is a shift factor. Each of these shift factors will cause a **shift in supply,** whereas a change in the price causes a **movement along the supply curve.**

Shift in supply   *A shift of the entire supply curve.*

Movement along a supply curve   *A change in the quantity supplied due to a change in price.*

As with demand, it's useful to graph an example of a shift in supply and to differentiate that from a movement along the supply curve. Exhibit 8 does this for our example. Exhibit 8(a) shows the effect of a change in the price of cassettes from $1.50 to $2.50. Point *A* (5, $1.50) represents the starting point. Now, for some reason, price

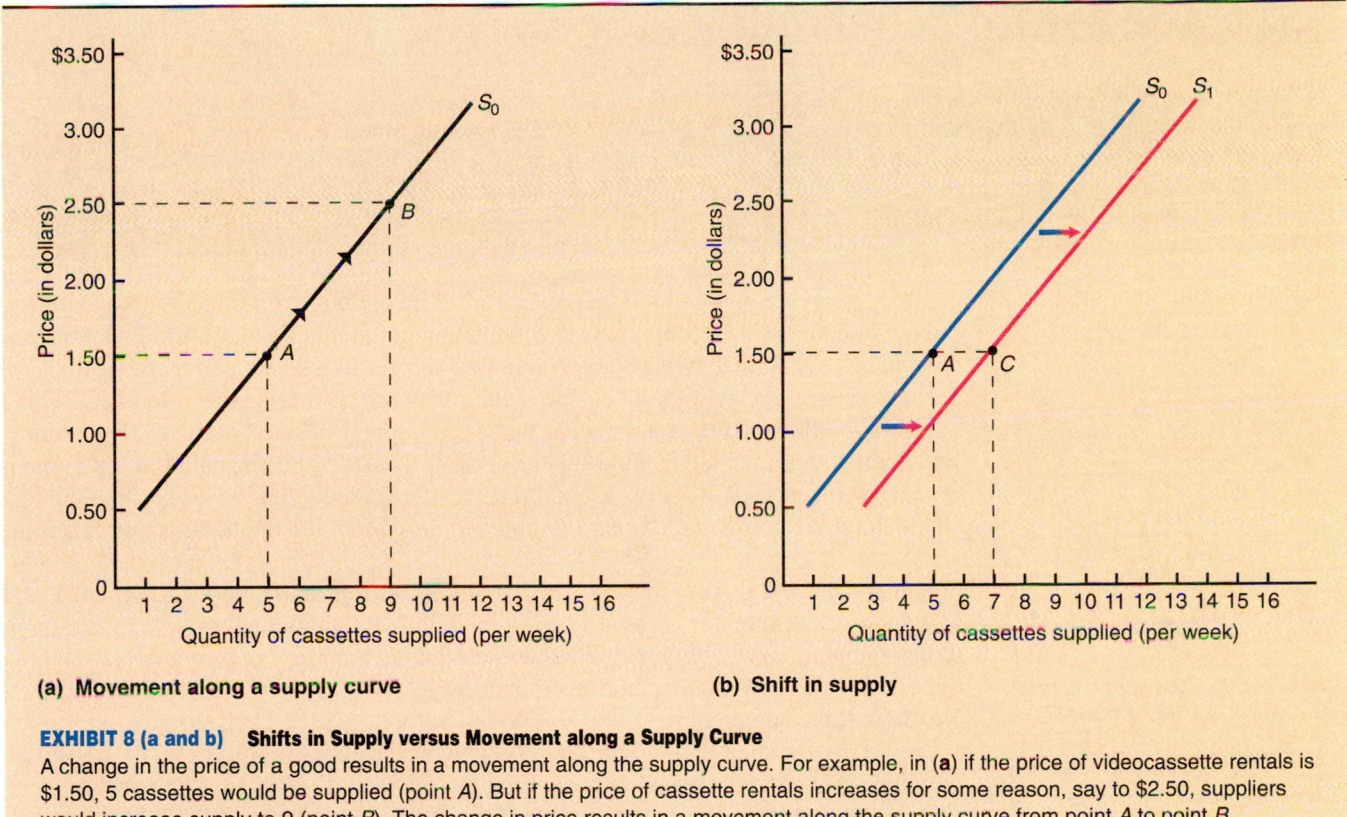

(a) Movement along a supply curve

(b) Shift in supply

EXHIBIT 8 (a and b)   Shifts in Supply versus Movement along a Supply Curve
A change in the price of a good results in a movement along the supply curve. For example, in (**a**) if the price of videocassette rentals is $1.50, 5 cassettes would be supplied (point *A*). But if the price of cassette rentals increases for some reason, say to $2.50, suppliers would increase supply to 9 (point *B*). The change in price results in a movement along the supply curve from point *A* to point *B*.

   Shift factors cause a shift in the supply curve. For example, in (**b**), at the price of $1.50, 5 cassettes would be supplied (point *A*). If some new technology were introduced, lowering the cost of producing the cassette, then suppliers would supply 7 cassettes at the price of $1.50 (point *C*). An improvement in technology results in a shift in the supply curve from S_0 to S_1.

rises to $2.50 and the quantity supplied rises to 9 (point *B*). Because of the price increase, there's a movement along the supply curve.

   Now, however, let's say that there's an improvement in technology: a new type of cassette that's cheaper to make than the existing cassette. Such an advance in technology shifts the supply curve outward to the right. Why? Because it lowers costs for each unit sold, enabling suppliers to offer more for sale at each price. An improvement in technology is shown in Exhibit 8(b). Notice that the entire supply curve shifts from S_0 to S_1, showing that for each price, the quantity supplied will be greater. For example, at price $1.50, 5 cassettes are supplied; but after the technological improvement, at price $1.50, 7 cassettes are supplied. The same reasoning holds for any price.

   Do we see such shifts in the supply curve often? Yes. A good example is computers. For the past 30 years, technological changes have continually shifted computers' supply curve out.

   This should give you an idea of factors that shift supply, and should cement for you the difference between a shift in supply and a movement along a supply curve. But in case it didn't, here it is one more time:

   Shift in supply: A change in a nonprice factor—a shift of the entire supply curve.

   Movement along a supply curve: A change in the quantity supplied due to a change in price—a movement along a supply curve.

Thomas Carlyle, the English historian who dubbed economics ''the dismal science,'' also wrote this chapter's introductory tidbit, ''Teach a parrot the words *supply* and *demand* and you've got an economist.'' In Chapter 1, I hope I convinced you that economics is *not* dismal. In the rest of this chapter I hope to convince you that while

7 Just as with demand, it is important to distinguish between a shift in supply (a shift of the entire supply curve) and a movement along a supply curve (a change in the quantity supplied due to a change in price).

THE MARRIAGE OF SUPPLY AND DEMAND

A REMINDER SIX THINGS TO REMEMBER WHEN CONSIDERING A SUPPLY CURVE

- A supply curve follows the law of supply. When price rises, quantity supplied increases; and vice versa.
- The horizontal axis—quantity—has a time dimension.
- The quantities are of the same quality.
- The vertical axis—price—is a relative price.

- The curve assumes everything else is constant.
- Effects of price changes are shown by movements along the supply curve. Effects of nonprice determinants of supply are shown by shifts of the entire supply curve.

supply and demand are important to economics, parrots don't make good economists. If students think that when they've learned the terms *supply* and *demand* they've learned economics, they're mistaken. Those terms are just labels for the ideas behind supply and demand, and it's the ideas that are important. What's relevant about supply and demand isn't the labels but how the concepts interact. For instance, what happens if quantity supplied doesn't equal quantity demanded? It's in understanding the interaction of supply and demand that economics becomes interesting *and relevant.*

The First Dynamic Law of Supply and Demand

Excess supply *Quantity supplied is greater than quantity demanded.*

Q-5: Explain what a sudden popularity of "Economics Professor" brand casual wear would likely do to prices of that brand.

Excess demand *Quantity demanded is greater than quantity supplied.*

8 The three dynamic laws of supply and demand are:
1. If $Qd > Qs$, P increases; if $Qs > Qd$, P decreases.
2. The larger $Qs - Qd$, the faster P falls; the larger $Qd - Qs$, the faster P rises.
3. If $Qd = Qs$, P does not change.

First dynamic law of supply and demand *When quantity demanded is greater than quantity supplied, prices tend to rise; when quantity supplied is greater than quantity demanded, prices tend to fall.*

When you have a market in which neither suppliers nor demanders can organize and in which prices are free to adjust, economists have a good answer for the question: What happens if quantity supplied doesn't equal quantity demanded? If quantity supplied is greater than quantity demanded (that is, if there is **excess supply**, a surplus), some suppliers won't be able to sell all their goods. Each supplier will think: "Gee, if I offer to sell it for a bit less, I'll be the lucky one who sells my good; someone else will be stuck with not selling their good." But because all suppliers with excess goods will be thinking the same thing, the price in the market will fall. As that happens, demanders will increase their quantity demanded. So the movement toward equilibrium caused by excess supply is on both the supply and demand sides.

The reverse is also true. Say that instead of excess supply, there's **excess demand** (a shortage): quantity demanded is greater than quantity supplied. There are more demanders who want the good than there are suppliers selling the good. Let's consider what's likely to go through demanders' minds. They'll likely call long-lost friends who just happen to be sellers of that good and tell them it's good to talk to them and, by the way, don't they want to sell that . . .? Suppliers will be rather pleased that so many of their old friends have remembered them, but they'll also likely see the connection between excess demand and their friends' thoughtfulness. To stop their phones from ringing all the time, they'll likely raise their price. The reverse is true for excess supply. It's amazing how friendly suppliers become to potential demanders when there's excess supply.

This tendency for prices to rise when demand exceeds supply and for prices to fall when supply exceeds demand is a phenomenon economists call the **first dynamic law of supply and demand:**

When quantity demanded is greater than quantity supplied, prices tend to rise; when quantity supplied is greater than quantity demanded, prices tend to fall.

Exhibit 9 shows the first dynamic law of supply and demand by the arrows labeled *A.* With excess supply the arrows push price down; with excess demand the arrows push price up. It's called a *dynamic law* because *dynamic* refers to change and this law refers to how prices change, not to what prices will be.

The Second Dynamic Law of Supply and Demand

How much pressure will there be for prices to rise or fall? That too will likely depend on differences between quantity supplied and quantity demanded. The greater the difference, the more pressure there is on individuals to raise or lower prices. If you're a seller (supplier) and all your old friends are calling you (there's major excess demand), you'll simply put a message on your answering machine saying, "The price has gone up 200 percent or 300 percent. If you're still interested in talking about old times, stay on the line. Otherwise, it was nice knowing you." If, however, only a

THE DYNAMIC LAWS OF SUPPLY AND DEMAND

1. When quantity demanded is greater than quantity supplied, prices tend to rise; when quantity supplied is greater than quantity demanded, prices tend to fall.
2. The larger the difference between quantity supplied

and quantity demanded, the faster prices will rise (if there is excess demand) or fall (if there is excess supply).
3. When quantity supplied equals quantity demanded, prices have no tendency to change.

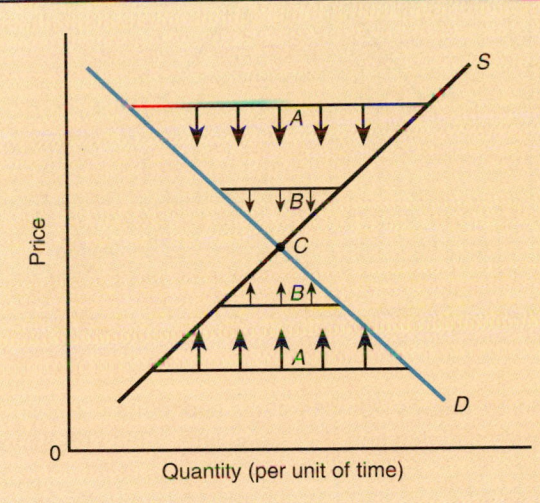

EXHIBIT 9   The Dynamic Laws of Supply and Demand

The dynamic laws of supply and demand tell us what forces will be set in motion when the quantity supplied does not equal the quantity demanded.

couple of old friends call you (there's only minor excess demand), you'll probably raise your price only slightly. Or if you're a buyer (demander) and there's major excess supply, you'll leave the following message: "If you're trying to sell me anything, I'm broke and can only pay less than what you ask."

Thus, the **second dynamic law of supply and demand** is:

In a market, the larger the difference between quantity supplied and quantity demanded, the greater the pressure on prices to rise (if there is excess demand) or fall (if there is excess supply).

The second dynamic law of supply and demand is demonstrated by the smaller *B* arrows in Exhibit 9. Because the difference between quantity supplied and quantity demanded is less than before, the upward and downward pressures aren't as strong.

People's tendencies to change prices exist as long as there's some difference between quantity supplied and quantity demanded. But the change in price brings the laws of supply and demand into play. As price falls, quantity supplied decreases as some suppliers leave the business (the law of supply); and as some people who originally weren't really interested in buying the good think, "Well, at this low price, maybe I do want to buy," quantity demanded increases (the law of demand). Similarly, when price rises, quantity supplied will increase (the law of supply) and quantity demanded will decrease (the law of demand).

Whenever quantity supplied and quantity demanded are unequal, price tends to change. If, however, quantity supplied and quantity demanded are equal, price will stay the same because no one will have an incentive to change it. This observation leads to the **third dynamic law of supply and demand:**

When quantity supplied equals quantity demanded, prices have no tendency to change.

The third dynamic law of supply and demand is represented by point *C* in Exhibit 9. At point *C* there's no upward or downward pressure on price.

Second dynamic law of supply and demand   The larger the difference between quantity supplied and quantity demanded, the greater the pressure for price to rise if there's excess demand or to fall if there's excess supply.

The Third Dynamic Law of Supply and Demand

Third dynamic law of supply and demand   When quantity supplied equals quantity demanded, prices don't tend to change.

EXHIBIT 10   The Marriage of Supply and Demand

Combining supply and demand lets us see the dynamic laws of supply and demand. These laws tell us the pressures on price when there is excess demand (there is upward pressure on price) or excess supply (there is downward pressure on price). Understanding these pressures is essential to understanding how to apply economics to reality.

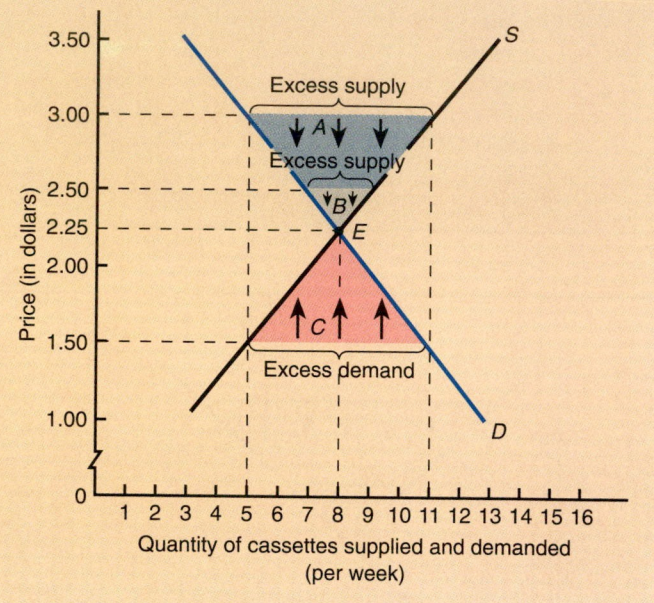

The Graphical Marriage of Demand and Supply

Q–6: In a flood, it is ironic that usable water supplies tend to decline because the pumps and water lines are damaged. What will a flood likely do to the prices of bottled water?

Exhibit 10 shows supply and demand curves for cassettes and demonstrates the operation of the dynamic laws of supply and demand. Let's consider what will happen to the price of cassettes in four cases:

1. When the price is $3;
2. When the price is $2.50;
3. When the price is $1.50; and
4. When the price is $2.25.

1. When price is $3, quantity supplied is 11 and quantity demanded is only 5. Excess supply is 6. At a price of $3, individual demanders can get all they want, but most suppliers can't sell all they wish; they'll be stuck with cassettes that they'd like to sell. Suppliers will tend to offer their goods at a lower price and demanders, who see plenty of suppliers out there, will bargain harder for an even lower price. Both these forces will push the price as indicated by the *A* arrows in Exhibit 10.

2. When price falls from $3 to $2.50, the pressures are the same kind as in (1), only they're weaker, because excess supply is smaller. There aren't as many dissatisfied suppliers searching for ways to sell their cassettes. Generally, the rate at which prices fall depends on the size of the gap between quantity supplied and quantity demanded. This smaller pressure is shown by the *B* arrows in Exhibit 10.

Now let's start from the other side.

3. Say price is $1.50. The situation is now reversed. Quantity supplied is 5 and quantity demanded is 11. Excess demand is 6. Now it's demanders who can't get what they want and suppliers who are in the strong bargaining position. The pressures will be on price to rise in the direction of the *C* arrows in Exhibit 10.

4. At $2.25, price is at its equilibrium: quantity supplied equals quantity demanded. Suppliers offer to sell 8 and demanders want to buy 8, so there's no pressure on price to rise or fall. Price will tend to remain where it is (point *E* in Exhibit 10).

Equilibrium

Equilibrium is a concept in which the dynamic forces cancel each other out.

The concept of equilibrium appears often throughout this text. You need to understand what equilibrium is and what it isn't. The concept itself comes from physics—classical mechanics. To say something is in **equilibrium** is to say that the dynamic forces pushing on it cancel each other out. For example, a book on a desk is in equilibrium because the upward force exerted on the book by the desk equals the downward pressure exerted on the book by gravity. In supply and demand analysis, equilibrium means that the upward pressure on price is exactly offset by the downward pressure on price. **Equilibrium price** is the price toward which the invisible hand drives the market.

So much for what equilibrium is. Now let's consider what it isn't.

First, equilibrium isn't inherently good or bad. It's simply a state in which dynamic pressures offset each other. Some equilibria are awful. Say two countries are engaged in a nuclear war against each other and both sides are blown away. An equilibrium will have been reached, but there's nothing good about it.

Second, equilibrium isn't a state of the world. It's a characteristic of the framework you use to look at the world. A framework for looking at the world is called a **model.** The same situation could be seen as an equilibrium in one framework and as a disequilibrium in another. Say you're describing a car that's speeding along at 100 miles an hour. That car is changing position relative to objects on the ground. Its movement could be, and generally is, described as if it were in disequilibrium. However, if you consider this car relative to another car going 100 miles an hour, the cars could be modeled as being in equilibrium because their positions relative to each other aren't changing.

Understanding that equilibrium is a characteristic of the framework of analysis, not of the real world, is important in applying economic models to reality. For example, in the preceding description I said equilibrium occurs where supply equals demand. In a model where the invisible hand is the only force operating, that's true. In the real world, however, other forces—political and social forces—are operating. These will likely push price away from that supply/demand equilibrium. Were we to consider a model that included all these forces—political, social, and economic— equilibrium would be likely to exist where supply isn't equal to demand. In the real world, the invisible hand, foot, and handshake often work in different directions and vary in strength. For example:

- In agricultural markets, farmers use political pressure (the invisible foot) to obtain higher than supply/demand equilibrium prices. Generally they succeed, so agricultural prices rise above the supply/demand equilibrium price. The laws of supply and demand assume no political pressures on prices.
- In labor markets, social pressures often offset economic pressures and prevent unemployed individuals from accepting work at lower wages than currently employed workers (the invisible handshake). Similarly, when there's a strike, social pressures prevent people who don't have jobs from taking jobs strikers have left. People who do take those jobs are called names like *scab* or *strikebreaker,* and they don't like those names. A pure supply and demand model, though, assumes everyone who wants a job will try to become a scab.
- In product markets, suppliers conspire to limit entry by other suppliers. They work hard to get Congress to establish tariffs and make restrictive regulations (the invisible foot). They also devise pricing strategies that scare off other suppliers and allow them to hold their prices higher than a supply/demand equilibrium. A pure supply and demand model assumes no conspiring at all.
- In the housing rental markets, consumers often organize politically and get local government to enact rent controls (ceilings on rents that can be charged for apartments). Here's an example of government (the invisible foot) putting downward pressure on price.

If social and political forces were included in the analysis, they'd provide a counterpressure to the dynamic forces of supply and demand. The result would be an equilibrium with continual excess supply or excess demand. The invisible hand pushing toward a supply/demand equilibrium would be thwarted by other invisible forces pushing in the other direction.

The Margin is a popular economics magazine written directly for economics students.

Model   Framework for looking at the world.

In the real world, there exist other forces besides pure supply and demand. Political pressure (the invisible foot) and social pressures (the invisible handshake) can be powerful actors in the determination of equilibrium.

Economics is a developing discipline, so the models used in one time period aren't necessarily the models used in another. In their research, economists debate which models are best and how to integrate more insights into their existing models.

Two groups of economists who've recently pushed back the frontiers of economics are the *public choice economists* and the *neo-classical political economists.* Public choice economists, led by Gordon Tullock and James Buchanan, argue that the political dimension must be part of economists' models. To integrate the political dimension, they apply economic analysis to politics and consider how economic forces affect the laws that are enacted and how, in turn, those laws affect economics. Their work was instrumental in leading to the invisible foot metaphor discussed in Chapter 1, and won James Buchanan a Nobel prize in 1986.

Neo-classical political economists share with public choice economists the view that the political dimension must be part of economists' models, and have developed a variety of formal models that significantly modify earlier models' predictions. Many of their models focus on rent seeking (how suppliers can restrict supply and thereby create rents for themselves). *Rent* is defined as an income earned when supply is restricted. For example, say a carpenter's union limits the number of people who can do carpentry. The supply of carpenters will decrease and existing carpenters will earn a higher wage that includes a rent component. Rents can be created either by using politics (the invisible foot) or by special agreements (the invisible handshake). Hence, neo-classical political economists are at the forefront of the movement to broaden economic analysis.

Although the formal analyses of both these groups haven't been adopted by the majority of economists, other economists often use their informal results and insights. Throughout this book I'll discuss these and other groups' views, but I'll focus on the mainstream model that the majority of economists use.

A formal political/social/economic model that included all these forces simultaneously would be complicated, and economists are still working on perfecting one. Meanwhile economists, in their formal analysis, focus on a pure supply and demand model in which only the invisible hand is operating. That model lets you see clearly the economic forces at work. When economists apply the pure supply/demand model to reality, however, they discuss the effects of these other forces.

In this book I'll introduce you to both the formal model (in which only market forces are operating) and the informal model (in which all forces are operating).

Changes in Supply and Demand

Q-7: Demonstrate graphically the effect of a heavy frost in Florida on the quantity and price of oranges.

To ensure that you understand the supply and demand graphs throughout the book and can apply them, let's go through three examples. Exhibit 11(a) deals with an increase in demand; Exhibit 11(b) deals with a decrease in supply.

Let's consider again the supply and demand for cassette rentals. In Exhibit 11(a), the supply is S_0 and initial demand is D_0. They meet at an equilibrium price of \$2.25 and a quantity demanded of 8 (point A). Now say demand for cassette rentals increases from D_0 to D_1. At a price of \$2.25, the quantity of cassette rentals supplied will be 8 and the quantity demanded will be 10; excess demand of 2 exists.

As the first dynamic law of supply and demand dictates, the excess demand pushes prices upward in the direction of the small arrows, decreasing the quantity demanded. As it does so, movement takes place along both the supply curve and the demand curve. The first dynamic law of supply and demand tells us that price will be pushed up.

Q-8: Demonstrate graphically the effect of the discovery of a hormone that increases cows' milk production by 20 percent on the price and quantity of milk sold in a market.

The upward push on price decreases the gap between the quantity supplied and the quantity demanded. As the gap is decreased, the upward pressure decreases, as the second dynamic law requires. But as long as that gap exists at all, price will be pushed upward until the new equilibrium price (\$2.50) and new quantity (9) are reached (point B). At point B the third dynamic law of supply and demand takes hold: quantity supplied equals quantity demanded. So the market is in equilibrium. Notice that the adjustment is twofold: The higher price brings about equilibrium by both increasing the quantity supplied (from 8 to 9) and decreasing the quantity demanded (from 10 to 9).

Exhibit 11(b) begins with the same situation that we started with in Exhibit 11(a); the initial equilibrium quantity and price are 8 and \$2.25 (point A). In this example, however, instead of demand increasing, let's assume supply decreases—say because

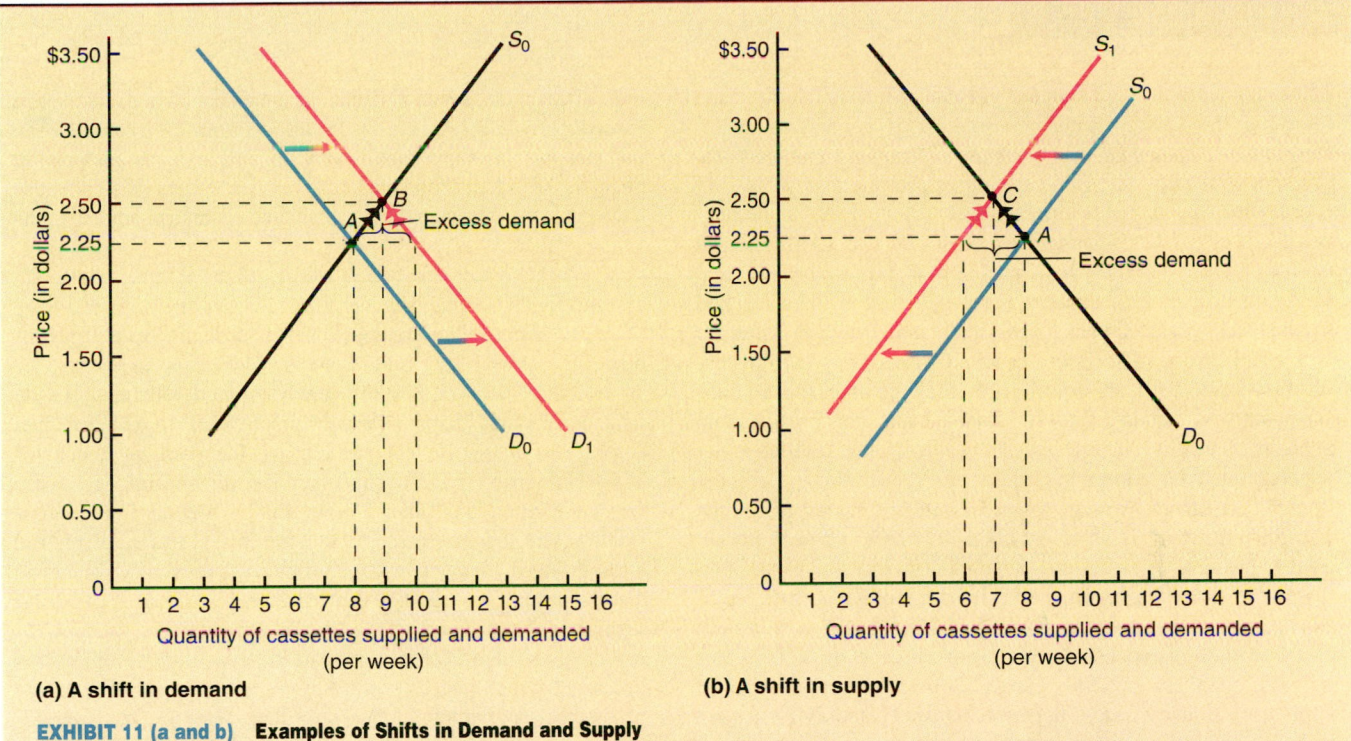

(a) A shift in demand

(b) A shift in supply

EXHIBIT 11 (a and b)   Examples of Shifts in Demand and Supply

When there is an increase in demand (the demand curve shifts outward), there is upward pressure on the price, as shown in (**a**). If there is an increase in demand from D_0 to D_1, the quantity of cassette rentals that was demanded at a price of $2.25, 8, increases to 10, but the quantity supplied remains at 8. This excess demand tends to cause prices to rise. Eventually, a new equilibrium is reached at the price of $2.50, where the quantity supplied and the quantity demanded is 9.

   If supply of cassettes decreases, then the entire supply curve shifts inward to the left, as shown in (**b**), from S_0 to S_1. At the price of $2.25, the quantity supplied has now decreased to 6 cassettes, but the quantity demanded has remained at 8 cassettes. The excess demand tends to force the price upward. Eventually, an equilibrium is reached at the price of $2.50 and quantity 7 (point C).

some suppliers change what they like to do, and decide they will no longer supply this good. That means that the entire supply curve shifts inward to the left (from S_0 to S_1). At the initial equilibrium price of $2.25, the quantity demanded is greater than the quantity supplied. Two more cassettes are demanded than are supplied. (Excess demand = 2.)

   As the dynamic laws of supply and demand require, this excess demand exerts upward pressure on price. Price is pushed in the direction of the small arrows. As the price rises, the upward pressure on price is reduced (in accord with the second dynamic law of supply and demand) but will still exist until the new equilibrium price, $2.50, and new quantity, 7, are reached. At $2.50, the quantity supplied equals the quantity demanded. The adjustment has involved a movement along the demand curve and the new supply curve. As price rises, quantity supplied is adjusted upward and quantity demanded is adjusted downward until quantity supplied equals quantity demanded where the new supply curve intersects the demand curve at point C, an equilibrium of 7 and $2.50.

   I leave a final example as an exercise for you. Demonstrate graphically how the price of computers could have fallen dramatically in the past 10 years, even as demand increased. (Hint: Supply has shifted even more, so even at lower prices, far more computers have been supplied than were being supplied 10 years ago.)

Now that we've discussed the basic analysis and its limitations, we can apply the supply/demand model to a real-world situation.

Q–9: Demonstrate graphically the likely effect of an increase in the price of gas on the quantity and price of compact cars.

SUPPLY AND DEMAND IN ACTION: OIL PRICE FLUCTUATIONS

A model can be interpreted many different ways, and knowing the various interpretations is as central to understanding the lesson of the model as is knowing the technical aspects of the model. For example, most models we use in economics are equilibrium models; they have a definite equilibrium toward which they move. To use such an equilibrium model to analyze a problem is not to believe that the equilibrium of the model is the one that will be reached in the real world. Other forces may, and often do, prevent that equilibrium from being reached. Moreover, the process of moving toward an equilibrium may change the equilibrium one is aiming at. A model only captures certain aspects of reality; in the interpretation of that model, other aspects must be added in.

When the movement toward equilibrium can affect the equilibrium, there is what is called *historeses* or *path dependency* present. When path dependency exists, as it often does, the supply/demand model is incomplete and the equilibrium of the supply/demand model isn't the equilibrium that one would expect. For example, say the price of a pair of Nike sneakers is $200. These $200 sneakers have lots of snob appeal. Now, say, demand declines, and Nike lowers prices. The falling price causes people to think that Nikes are no longer "in," and *because of the fall in price*, tastes change and the demand falls further. In our supply/demand model, such effects are ruled out by our "other things constant" assumption. The real world need not, and generally does not, follow this assumption.

In the analysis of large changes in the economy or small changes in the aggregate economy, the "other things constant" assumption is inevitably broken because movements along a supply curve cause income to change which causes shifts of the demand curve. To capture these interactive effects we need a different analysis, which is where *macroeconomics* comes in. Macroeconomics goes beyond microeconomic supply and demand and tries to include an analysis of interactive effects. (I write "tries to" because macro hasn't done a great job in understanding these interactive effects.)

Another way in which the "other things constant" assumption is violated is demonstrated in the irreversibility of many actions. For example, say you decide to paint your bike pink in a fit of pink-passion. The cost: $2.98 for the spray can. Now you see the newly-painted bike and decide pink isn't your color—you want it back to the original color. You *might* be able to remove the paint at a cost of $75—but probably you can't get the pink paint off. After you've painted the bike, "other things are no longer constant"; you cannot turn back time by pressing a rewind button. Or say you sawed a 10-foot 2×4 to 8' 4". Then, you discover that you really wanted an 8' 5" 2×4. You don't simply run the saw backwards and try again.

The point of these examples is that reality happens in historical time where many actions are irreversible, or are reversible at a much higher cost than was the cost of getting to the situation you'd like to reverse. Supply/demand analysis doesn't capture that dimension of reality, so that dimension must be added back to the analysis in the interpretation.

Economists recognize these problems, but nonetheless they use supply/demand analysis which assumes these problems away to keep the analysis simple. But they keep these limitations in the back of their minds, and add them back, where appropriate, when applying the model to a real-world problem.

Exhibit 12(a) shows the changes in the price of oil from 1973 to 1993. Exhibit 12(b) demonstrates the supply/demand forces associated with those changes in the period 1973–81, during which the price of oil went up substantially. Prior to the 1970s, its price had been relatively stable. In the early 1970s, at a series of meetings of countries who were members of OPEC (the Organization of Petroleum Exporting Countries), some delegates who had studied economics pointed out how OPEC could get more for less. They argued that if they could somehow all decide to limit oil production (to decrease supply), then even though each of them produced less, actually each would make more money. Exhibit 12(b) shows why.

Initially the quantity supplied was 2 billion barrels and the price per barrel was $6. Total OPEC revenue was $12 billion ($6 × 2 billion). Now say OPEC shifts supply back from S_0 to S_1. The quantity of oil supplied falls to 1.5 billion barrels and the price of oil rises to $16 per barrel. Now members' revenue is $24 billion ($16 × 1.5 billion). In cutting production by 25 percent they double their revenues! Even though each producer is selling less oil, each is earning more income. And that's what OPEC did. The member countries restricted supply, and the price of oil started rising drastically worldwide.

The high price provoked a reaction among a large number of non-OPEC oil suppliers (and from OPEC members who could hide their oil sales from other members). They increased their quantity of oil supplied significantly, causing an upward movement along the original supply curve. At the same time oil exploration

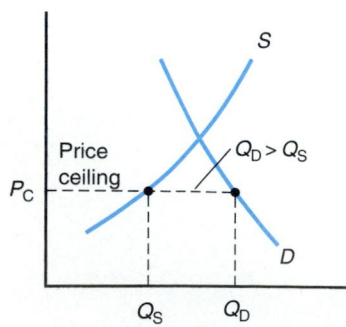

An effective price ceiling will cause $Q_s > Q_d$.

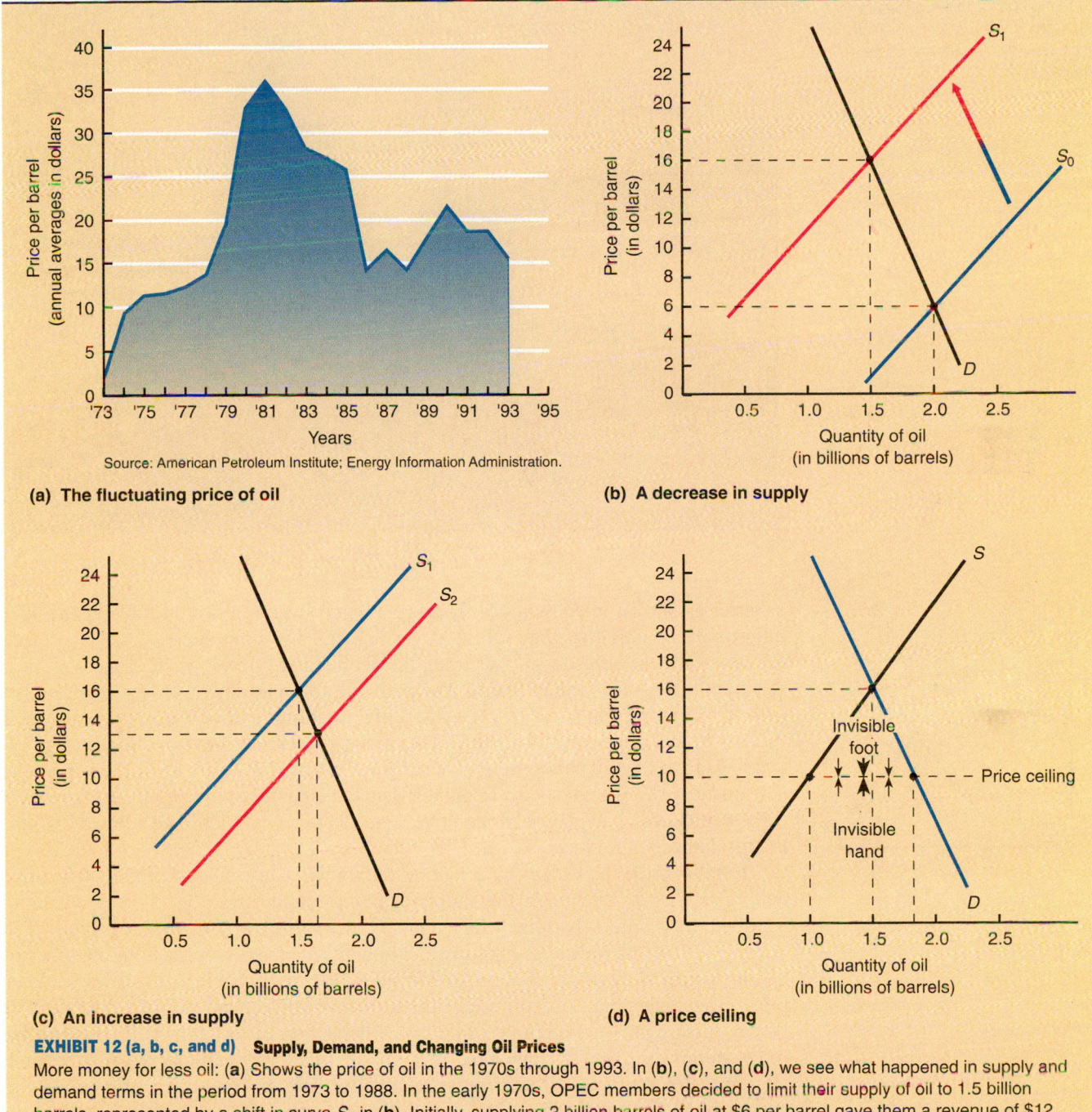

(a) The fluctuating price of oil

Source: American Petroleum Institute; Energy Information Administration.

(b) A decrease in supply

(c) An increase in supply

(d) A price ceiling

EXHIBIT 12 (a, b, c, and d)   Supply, Demand, and Changing Oil Prices

More money for less oil: (a) Shows the price of oil in the 1970s through 1993. In (b), (c), and (d), we see what happened in supply and demand terms in the period from 1973 to 1988. In the early 1970s, OPEC members decided to limit their supply of oil to 1.5 billion barrels, represented by a shift in curve S_1 in (b). Initially, supplying 2 billion barrels of oil at $6 per barrel gave them a revenue of $12 billion, but with restricted supply, the price of oil per barrel rose to $16, giving OPEC members a revenue of $24 billion ($1.5 billion x $16). New exploration shifted the supply curve out, lowering price to $13, as in (c).

Graph (d) shows the response of a market to a price ceiling such as the one imposed in the 1970s in the United States. In (d) the invisible hand is not allowed to operate; quantity demanded exceeds quantity supplied; and the result is shortage. In the 1970s, people lined up to buy limited supplies of gas for their cars.

boomed, shifting the oil supply curve back out to S_2 in Exhibit 12(c). These new discoveries of oil shifted oil's total supply curve outward, even as OPEC countries held their oil back. As supply was responding to higher prices and shortages, so too was quantity demanded. As the price rose, the quantity demanded fell. As people switched to fuel-efficient cars and set their thermostats lower, there was a resulting movement along the demand curve. By the late 1980s, the invisible hand had effectively broken OPEC's limitation on supply, and price fell to between $12 and $15

The long lines and shortages of the 1974 gas crisis are typical results of a price ceiling. © *George Gardner/The Image Works.*

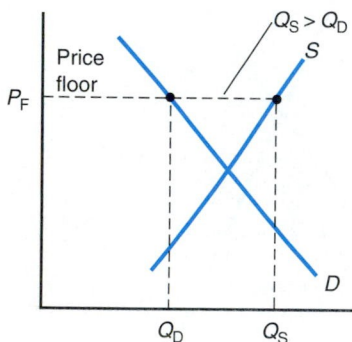

9 An effective price floor will cause $Q_S > Q_d$.

Price ceiling *Government-imposed limit on how high a price may be set.*

Price floor *Government-imposed limit on how low a price may be set.*

Q-10: Draw a supply and demand graph for milk, labeling all axes and curves. Show the effect of a price floor.

a barrel as shown in Exhibit 12(c), approximately where it would have been (after adjustment for inflation) had OPEC never organized to limit supply.

Before these adjustments occurred, the sudden jump in oil price caused political reactions within the United States. The invisible foot put downward pressure on the price of oil in the United States. It led to a **price ceiling** (a government-imposed limit on how high a price can be charged). This political pressure prevented the price of oil from rising to the full new supply/demand equilibrium. The result was an oil shortage. The quantity of oil demanded was greater than the quantity of oil supplied. There were dire predictions that people would freeze to death or wouldn't be allowed to use energy-intensive products.

Exhibit 12(d) shows how such a price ceiling will cause such shortages. The price ceiling is $10, even though the supply/demand equilibrium price is $16. Quantity supplied is 1 billion barrels, while quantity demanded is 1.8 billion barrels. The difference between quantity supplied and quantity demanded reflects the number of people going without oil. When the invisible foot or invisible handshake prevents price from rising to the equilibrium price, the invisible hand doesn't disappear. It places upward pressure on price while the invisible foot places downward pressure on price. In this case the invisible hand won out, and the price ceilings were eliminated, allowing the price of oil to rise substantially. The rise in price eliminated the shortages.

It isn't only price ceilings that have predictable effects. **Price floors** (government-imposed limits on how low a price can be charged) also do. A price floor such as the minimum wage or a government-imposed mandatory price for milk creates a situation of excess supply. The quantity supplied exceeds the quantity demanded, and some way must be found to ration the available quantity demanded among the suppliers. We'll deal with these issues in detail later.

CONCLUSION

Throughout the book I'll be presenting examples of supply and demand. So I'll end this chapter here because its intended purposes have been served. What were those intended purposes? First, the discussion and examples should have exposed you to enough economic terminology and economic thinking to allow you to proceed to my more complicated examples. Second, the discussion should also have set your mind to

THE SUPPLY AND DEMAND FOR CHILDREN

In Chapter 1, I distinguished between an economic force and a market force. Economic forces are operative in all aspects of our lives; market forces are economic forces that are allowed to be expressed through a market. My examples in this chapter are of market forces—of goods sold in a market—but supply and demand can also be used to analyze situations in which economic, but not market, forces operate. An economist who is adept at this is Gary Becker of the University of Chicago. He has applied supply and demand analysis to a wide range of issues, even the supply of and demand for children.

Becker doesn't argue that children should be bought and sold. But he does argue that economic considerations play a large role in people's decisions on how many children to have. In farming communities, children can be productive early in life; by age six or seven, they can work on a farm. In an advanced industrial community, children provide pleasure, but generally don't contribute productively to family income. Even getting them to help around the house can be difficult.

Becker argues that since the price of having children is lower for a farming society than for an industrial society, farming societies will have more children per family. Quantity of children demanded will be larger. And that's what we find. Developing countries that rely primarily on farming often have three, four, or more children per family. Industrial societies average fewer than two children per family.

work putting the events around you into a supply/demand framework. Doing that will give you new insights into the events that shape all our lives. Finally, this chapter should have made you wary of applying supply/demand analysis to the real world without considering the other invisible forces out there battling the invisible hand.

CHAPTER SUMMARY

- The law of demand (supply): More (less) of a good will be demanded (supplied) the lower its price, other things constant.

- A market demand (supply) curve is the sum of all individual demand (supply) curves.

- A shift in quantity demanded (supplied) is a movement along the demand (supply) curve. A shift in demand (supply) is a shift of the entire demand (supply) curve.

- The laws of supply and demand refer to relative prices; they hold true because individuals can substitute.

- When quantity demanded is greater than quantity supplied, prices tend to rise. When quantity supplied is greater than quantity demanded, prices tend to fall.

- When quantity supplied equals quantity demanded, prices have no tendency to change.

- When demand shifts out, the equilibrium price rises. When supply shifts out, the equilibrium price falls.

KEY TERMS

demand *(35)*
demand curve *(35)*
equilibrium *(50)*
equilibrium price *(51)*
excess demand *(48)*
excess supply *(48)*
factors of production *(42)*
firms *(42)*
first dynamic law of supply and
  demand *(48)*
law of demand *(35)*

law of supply *(42)*
market demand curve *(39)*
model *(51)*
movement along the demand
  curve *(40)*
movement along the supply
  curve *(46)*
other things constant *(36)*
partial equilibrium analysis *(37)*
price ceiling *(56)*
price floor *(56)*

quantity demanded *(35)*
quantity supplied *(42)*
relative price *(37)*
second dynamic law of supply and
  demand *(49)*
shift factors of demand *(37)*
shift in demand *(40)*
shift in supply *(46)*
supply *(42)*
third dynamic law of supply and
  demand *(49)*

QUESTIONS FOR THOUGHT AND REVIEW

The number after each question represents the estimated degree of critical thinking required. (1 = almost none; 10 = deep thought.)

1. Draw a demand curve from the following demand table. *(1)*

P	Q
37	20
47	15
57	10
67	5

2. Draw a market demand curve from the following demand table. *(1)*

P	D_1	D_2	D_3	Market Demand
37	20	4	8	32
47	15	2	7	24
57	10	0	6	16
67	5	0	5	10

3. It has just been reported that eating meat is bad for your health. Using supply and demand curves, demonstrate the report's likely effect on the price and quantity of steak sold in the market. *(3)*

4. New York City has had residential rent control for many years. Using supply/demand analysis, explain what effect eliminating those controls would probably have. *(4)*

5. Draw a market supply curve from the following supply table. *(1)*

P	S_1	S_2	S_3	Market Supply
37	0	4	14	18
47	0	8	16	24
57	10	12	18	40
67	10	16	20	46

6. Show, using supply and demand curves, the likely effect of a minimum wage law. If you were a worker, would you support or oppose minimum wage laws? Why? *(6)*

7. Distinguish the effect of a shift factor of demand from the effect of a change in price on the demand curve. *(3)*

8. Say the United States were to legalize the sale of certain currently illegal drugs. Using supply/demand analysis, show what effect legalization would have on the price of those drugs and on the quantity bought. *(7)*

9. Mary has just stated that normally, as price rises, supply will increase. Her teacher grimaces. Why? *(5)*

10. Supply/demand analysis states that equilibrium occurs where quantity supplied equals quantity demanded, but in U.S. agricultural markets quantity supplied almost always exceeds quantity demanded. How can this be? *(5)*

PROBLEMS AND EXERCISES

1. You're given the following individual demand tables for comic books.

Price	John	Liz	Alex
$ 2	4	36	24
4	4	32	20
6	0	28	16
8	0	24	12
10	0	20	8
12	0	16	4
14	0	12	0
16	0	8	0

   a. Determine the market demand table.
   b. Graph the individual and market demand curves.
   c. If the current market price is $4, what's total market demand? What happens to total market demand if price rises to $8?
   d. Say that an advertising campaign increases demand by 50 percent. Illustrate graphically what will happen to the individual and market demand curves.

2. Draw hypothetical supply and demand curves for tea. Show how the equilibrium price and quantity will be affected by each of the following occurrences:
   a. Bad weather wreaks havoc with the tea crop.
   b. A medical report implying tea is bad for your health is published.
   c. A technological innovation lowers the cost of producing tea.
   d. Consumers' income falls.
   e. The government imposes a $5 per pound price ceiling on tea.
   f. The government imposes a $15 per pound price ceiling on tea.
   g. The government imposes a $15 per pound price floor on tea.

3. "Scalping" is the name given to the buying of tickets at a low price and reselling them at a high price. The following information about a Florida State–Notre Dame game in 1993 comes from a newspaper. At the beginning of the season:
   a. Tickets sell for $27 and are sold out in pre-season.
   b. Halfway through the season, both teams have maintained unbeaten records. Resale price of tickets rises to $200.
   c. One week before the game, both teams have remained unbeaten and are ranked 1-2. Ticket price rises to $600.
   d. Three days before the game, price falls to $400.
   Demonstrate, using supply/demand analysis and words, what might have happened to cause these fluctuations in price.

4. In some states and localities ''scalping'' is against the law, although enforcement of these laws is spotty (difficult).
   a. Using supply/demand analysis and words, demonstrate what a weakly-enforced anti-scalping law would likely do to the price of tickets in 3b, 3c, and 3d.
   b. Using supply/demand analysis and words, demonstrate what a strongly-enforced anti-scalping law would likely do to the price of tickets in 3b, 3c, and 3d.
5. This is a question concerning what economists call ''the identification problem.'' Say you go out and find figures on the quantity bought of various products. You will find something like the following:

Product	Year	Quantity	Average Price
VCRs	1990	100,000	$210
	1991	110,000	220
	1992	125,000	225
	1993	140,000	215
	1994	135,000	215
	1995	160,000	220

Plot these figures on a graph.
   a. Have you plotted a supply curve, a demand curve, or what?
   b. If we assume that the market for VCRs is competitive, what information would you have to know to determine whether these are points on a supply curve or on a demand curve?
   c. Say you know that the market is one in which suppliers set the price and allow the quantity to vary. Could you then say anything more about the curves you have plotted?
   d. What information about shift factors would you expect to find to make these points reflect the law of demand?
6. Apartments in New York City are often hard to find. One of the major reasons is that there is rent control.
   a. Demonstrate graphically how rent controls could make apartments hard to find.
   b. Often one can get an apartment if one makes a side-payment to the current tenant. Can you explain why?
   c. What would be the likely effect of eliminating rent controls?
   d. What is the political appeal of rent controls?

7. You're a commodity trader and you've just heard a report that the winter wheat harvest will be 2.09 billion bushels, a 44 percent jump, rather than an expected 35 percent jump to 1.96 billion bushels.
   a. What would you expect would happen to wheat prices?
   b. Demonstrate graphically the effect you suggested in a.
8. Until recently, angora goat wool (mohair) has been designated as a strategic commodity (it used to be utilized in some military clothing). Because of that, in 1992 for every dollar's worth of mohair sold to manufacturers, ranchers received $3.60.
   a. Demonstrate graphically the effect of the elimination of this designation and subsidy.
   b. Explain why the program was likely kept in existence for so long.
   c. Say that a politician has suggested that the government should pass a law that requires all consumers to pay a price for angora goat wool high enough so that the sellers of that wool would receive $3.60 more than the market price. Demonstrate the effect of the law graphically. Would consumers support it? How about suppliers?
9. In the United States, gasoline costs consumers about $1.20 per gallon. In Italy it costs consumers about $4 per gallon. What effect does this price differential likely have on:
   a. The size of cars in the United States and in Italy?
   b. The use of public transportation in the United States and in Italy?
   c. The fuel efficiency of cars in the United States and in Italy?
   What would be the effect of raising the price of gasoline in the United States to $4 per gallon?
10. Mushrooms grow best in carbon-rich soil. The years immediately following a forest fire provide ideal growing conditions for mushrooms. Nowadays wild mushrooms are in demand, which has led to the development of the mushroom-picking profession (individuals travel around to various woods and forests to pick wild mushrooms). Mushroom-pickers often complain that they face a catch-22. Whatever the picking is easy, the prices are low, and whenever the pickings are slim, the prices are high. Can you explain, using supply and demand analysis, why they face this catch-22 situation?

ANSWERS TO MARGIN QUESTIONS

1. *Demand for furs.* The other possibility, *quantity demanded*, is used to refer to movements along (not shifts of) the demand curve. *(36)*

2. When adding two demand curves, you sum them horizontally, as in the diagram below. *(40)*

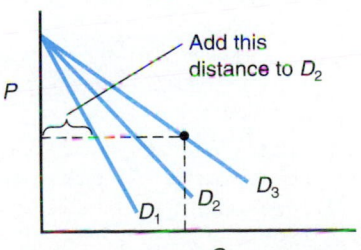

3. The "quantity supplied" declined because there was a movement along the supply curve. The supply curve itself remained unchanged. *(43)*

4. When adding two supply curves, sum the two individual supply curves, as in the diagram below. *(45)*

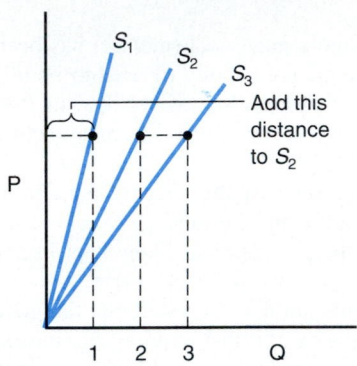

5. Customers will flock to stores demanding that funky "Economics Professor" look, creating excess demand. This excess demand will soon catch the attention of suppliers, and prices will be pushed upward. *(48)*

6. As substitutes—tap water—decrease, demand for bottled water increases enormously, and there will be upward pressure on prices. The other invisible forces will, however, likely work in the opposite direction—against "profiteering" in people's misery. *(50)*

7. A heavy frost in Florida will decrease the supply of oranges, increasing the price, and decreasing the quantity demanded, as in the graph below. *(52)*

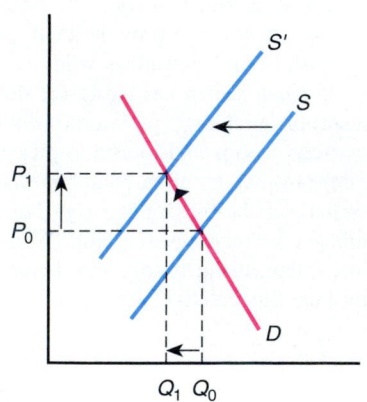

8. A discovery of a hormone that will increase cows' milk production by 20 percent will increase the supply of milk, pushing the price down and increasing the quantity demanded, as in the graph below. *(52)*

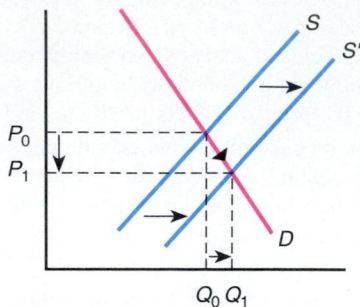

9. An increase in the price of gas will likely increase the demand for compact cars, increasing their price and increasing the quantity supplied, as in the graph below. *(53)*

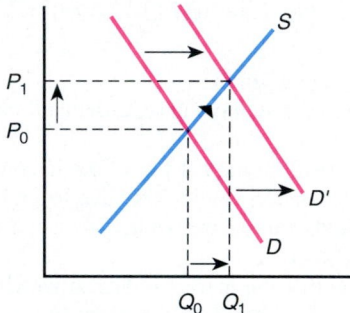

10. A price floor set above the equilibrium price will create excess supply, as in the diagram below. *(56)*

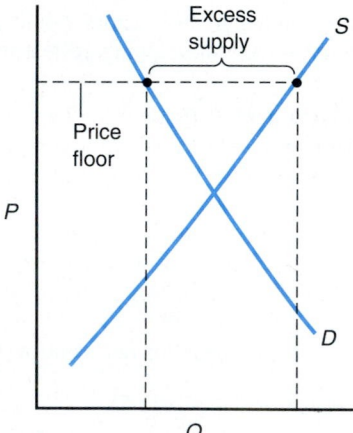

3

The Economic Organization of Society

In capitalism man exploits man;
in socialism it's the other way 'round.

~Abba Lerner

After reading this chapter, you should be able to:

1 List three central questions that every economy must answer.

2 Define capitalism and socialism.

3 Explain how capitalist and socialist economies answer the three central economic questions.

4 Give a brief overview of the history of economic systems: how feudalism begat mercantilism which begat capitalism, and how capitalism and socialism continue to evolve.

5 Explain how markets coordinate economic decisions.

6 Explain what is meant by the phrase "Socialism is the longest path from capitalism to capitalism."

The scene is the People's Court in Bucharest, Romania, December 25, 1989. The newly deposed dictator of Romania, Nicolae Ceausescu, and his wife, Elena, are on trial for crimes against the state.

Judge: *What have you done for society?*

Nicolae Ceausescu: *I built hospitals.*

Judge: *What about the food shortage?*

Nicolae Ceausescu: *The people have 440 pounds of corn a year.*

Judge: *You destroyed the Romanian people and their economy.*

Elena Ceausescu: *I gave my entire life for our people.*

Judge: *We condemn the two of you to death.*

On that same day, Elena and Nicolae Ceausescu were executed by a firing squad for economic crimes against the Romanian people.

The political and economic turmoil in the formerly socialist countries has been much in the news in the 1990s. And with good reason. The Soviet Union is no more; most republics of the former Soviet Union have forsaken socialism and are struggling to introduce a market economy. These events involve some of the most far-reaching changes in the nature of economic systems that the world has seen since the 1930s—changes so major that some social scientists have called the developments ''the end of history.'' Such a sweeping statement is more than a tad too strong, but the developments are certainly important. What's more, they provide me with a good vehicle to introduce some broader issues involving economic systems and the workings of markets.

ECONOMIC SYSTEMS: CAPITALISM AND SOCIALISM

An economic system must coordinate individuals' wants and desires.

In Chapter 1, I discussed how an **economic system** (the set of economic institutions that determine a country's important economic decisions) works via the interaction of three invisible forces: the invisible hand (economic forces), invisible foot (political forces), and invisible handshake (social forces).

An economic system is closely tied to a political system through which people decide what their society desires. In a democracy, voting procedures determine society's will. In an autocracy, a ruling individual or group of individuals decides what society's desires are. Besides determining what a society wants, an economic system must see that individuals' decisions about what they do are coordinated with what society wants, and with what other individuals do. Coordination is necessary so that the whats that the whos want, match the whats that are available.

Before we discuss how the invisible forces operate, we need to consider what people can reasonably expect from an economic system. They can expect it to produce the goods that people want in a reasonably efficient way and to distribute those goods reasonably fairly. Put another way, people can reasonably expect that an economic system will decide:

1 Three central questions that economy must answer:
 1. *What* to produce.
 2. *How* to produce it.
 3. *For whom* to produce it.

1. *What* to produce.
2. *How* to produce it.
3. *For whom* to produce it.

These three decisions that an economic system must make are necessarily vague, because what people expect is vague. But when people feel that an economic system hasn't given them what they want, the result isn't always so vague—as the Ceausescus found out.

Planning, Politics, and Markets

In making their three decisions, societies have a problem. Usually what individuals, on their own, want to do isn't consistent with what ''society'' wants them to do. Society would often like people to consider what's good for society, and to fit what's good for themselves into what society wants them to do. For example, say society has garbage, and society determines that your neighborhood is the best place to set up a garbage dump. Even if you agree a garbage dump is needed, you probably won't want it in your neighborhood. This **NIMBY** (**N**ot **I**n **M**y **B**ack **Y**ard) attitude has become familiar in the 1990s.

Another area in which individual goals and social goals come into conflict is in producing and consuming goods. Individuals generally like to consume much more than they like to produce, so society has the problem of scarcity. It must provide incentives for people to produce more and consume less. It's a sure sign that an economic system isn't working when there are important things that need to be done, but many people are sitting around doing nothing because the system doesn't provide individuals with the incentive to do that work.

How hard is it to make the three decisions I've listed? Imagine for a moment the problem of living in a family: the fights, arguments, and questions that come up. "Do I have to do the dishes?" "Why can't I have piano lessons?" "Bobby got a new sweater. How come I didn't?" "Mom likes you best." Now multiply the size of the family by millions. The same fights, the same arguments, the same questions—only for society the problems are millions of times more complicated than for one family.

How do you solve these complicated coordination problems? Do you create an organization to tell people what to do and when to do it? Or do you let people do what they want, subject to a set of rules? The two main economic systems the world has used in the past 50 years—capitalism and socialism—answer these questions differently.

Capitalism is an economic system based upon private property and the market in which, in principle, individuals decide how, what, and for whom to produce. Under capitalism, individuals are encouraged to follow their own self-interest, while market forces of supply and demand are relied upon to coordinate economic activity. Distribution is to each individual according to his or her ability, effort, and inherited property.

Reliance upon market forces doesn't mean that political, social, and historical forces play no role in coordinating economic decisions, because the other forces influence how the market works. For a market to exist, **private property rights** (in which control over an asset or a right is given to a private individual or firm) must be allocated and defended by government. The concept of private ownership must exist and must be accepted by individuals in society. When you say, "This car is mine," it means that it is unlawful for someone else to take it. If someone takes it without your permission, he or she is subject to punishment through the legal system.

Markets work through a system of rewards and payments. If you do something, you get paid for doing that something; if you get something, you pay for that something. How much you get is determined by how much you give. This relationship seems fair to most people. But there are instances when it doesn't seem fair. Say someone is unable to work. Should that person not get anything? How about Joe down the street who was given $10 million by his parents? Is it fair that he gets lots of toys like Corvettes and skiing trips to Aspen, and doesn't have to work, while the rest of us have to work 40 hours a week and maybe go to school at night?

We'll consider those questions about fairness in a later chapter. For now, all I want to present is the underlying concept of fairness that capitalism embodies: "Them that works, gets; them that don't, starve."[1] In capitalism, individuals are encouraged to follow their own self-interest.

In capitalist economies, individuals are free to do whatever they want as long as it's legal. The market is relied upon to see that what people want to get, and want to

NIMBY *Not In My Back Yard. Phrase used by people who may approve of a project, but don't want it to be near them.*

The coordination problems faced by society are immense.

Capitalism

2a Capitalism is an economic system based on private property and the market. It gives private property rights to individuals, and relies on market forces to coordinate economic activity.

Private property rights give control of an asset or a right to a private individual or firm.

Q–1: John, your study partner, is telling you that the best way to allocate property rights is through the market. How do you respond?

---

[1] How come the professor gets to use rotten grammar but screams when he sees rotten grammar in your papers? Well, that's fairness for you. Actually, I should say a bit more about writing style. All writers are expected to know correct grammar; if they don't, they don't deserve to be called writers. Once one knows grammar, one can individualize his or her writing style, breaking the rules of grammar where the meter and flow of the writing require it. In college you're still proving that you know grammar so, in papers handed in to your teacher, you shouldn't break the rules of grammar until you've proven to the teacher that you know them. Me, I've done lots of books, so my editors give me a bit more leeway than your teachers will give you.

Under capitalism, fluctuations in prices coordinate individuals' wants.

do, is consistent with what's available. If there's not enough of something to go around (if there's excess demand), its price goes up; if more of something needs to get done, the price given to individuals willing to do it goes up. If something isn't wanted or doesn't need to be done (if there's excess supply), its price goes down. Under capitalism, fluctuations in prices coordinate individuals' wants.

Chapters 1 and 2 told how the market works. By almost all accounts, capitalism has been an extraordinarily successful economic system. Since much of this book will be devoted to explaining capitalist economies' success, and since capitalism is probably somewhat familiar to you already, let's discuss socialism first.

Socialism in Theory

In theory, socialism is an economic system based upon individuals' good will toward others, not their own self-interest.

You can best understand the idea behind theoretical socialism by thinking about how decisions are made in a family. In most families, decisions about who gets what are determined by usually benevolent parents. When Sabin gets a new coat and his sister Sally doesn't, it's because Sabin needs a coat while Sally already has two coats that fit her and are in good condition. Victor may be slow as molasses, but from his family he still gets as much as his superefficient brother Jerry. In fact, Victor may get more than Jerry because he needs extra help.

Q–2: Are there any activities in a family that you believe should be allocated by a market? What characteristics do those activities have?

Markets have little role in most families. In my family, when food is placed on the table we don't bid on what we want, with the highest bidder getting the food. In my family, every person can eat all he or she wants, although if one child eats more than a fair share, that child gets a lecture from me on the importance of sharing—of seeing to it that everyone has already had a fair share before you take or even ask for seconds. "Be thoughtful; be considerate. Think of others first," are lessons that many families try to teach.

2b Socialism is an economic system that tries to organize society in the same way as do most families— all people should contribute what they can, and get what they need.

In theory, **socialism** is an economic system that tries to organize society in the same way as these families. Socialism tries to see that individuals get what they need. Socialism tries to get individuals to take other people's needs into account and to adjust their own wants in accordance with what's available. A capitalist economy expects people to be selfish; it relies on markets and competition to direct that selfishness to the general good. In socialist economies, individuals are urged to look out for the other person; if individuals' inherent goodness won't make them consider the general good, government will make them.[2]

Socialism in Practice

In practice, socialism became an economic system based on government ownership of the means of production, with economic activity governed by central planning. Because it is based on a system developed in the former Soviet Union, this is often called Soviet-style socialism.

In the 1980s, a number of countries had Soviet-style socialist economies. In the late 1980s and early 1990s, many of those countries were in turmoil. Total output in the economies had fallen significantly, and their economic and political systems were in chaos. Many of the countries undergoing major changes are shown in Exhibit 1. Why did these countries reject the economic system they had followed for almost 50 years? Some economists argue that Soviet-style socialism self-destructed because socialism did not offer acceptable answers to the questions an economic system must address. They claim socialism didn't provide individuals with incentives to produce enough. Soon, they say, the world will have only one economic system: capitalism. Other economists argue that the Soviet-style socialism was not socialism at all—that, early on, Soviet-style socialism deviated from the socialistic path. True socialism was not rejected, these economists argue, because true socialism was never tried.

Q–3: Which would be more likely to attempt to foster individualism: socialism or capitalism?

---

[2] As you probably surmised, the above distinction is too sharp. Even in capitalist societies, one wants people to be selfless, but not too selfless. Children in capitalist societies are generally taught to be selfless at least in dealing with friends and family. The difficulties parents and societies face is finding a midpoint between the two positions: selfless but not too selfless; selfish but not too selfish.

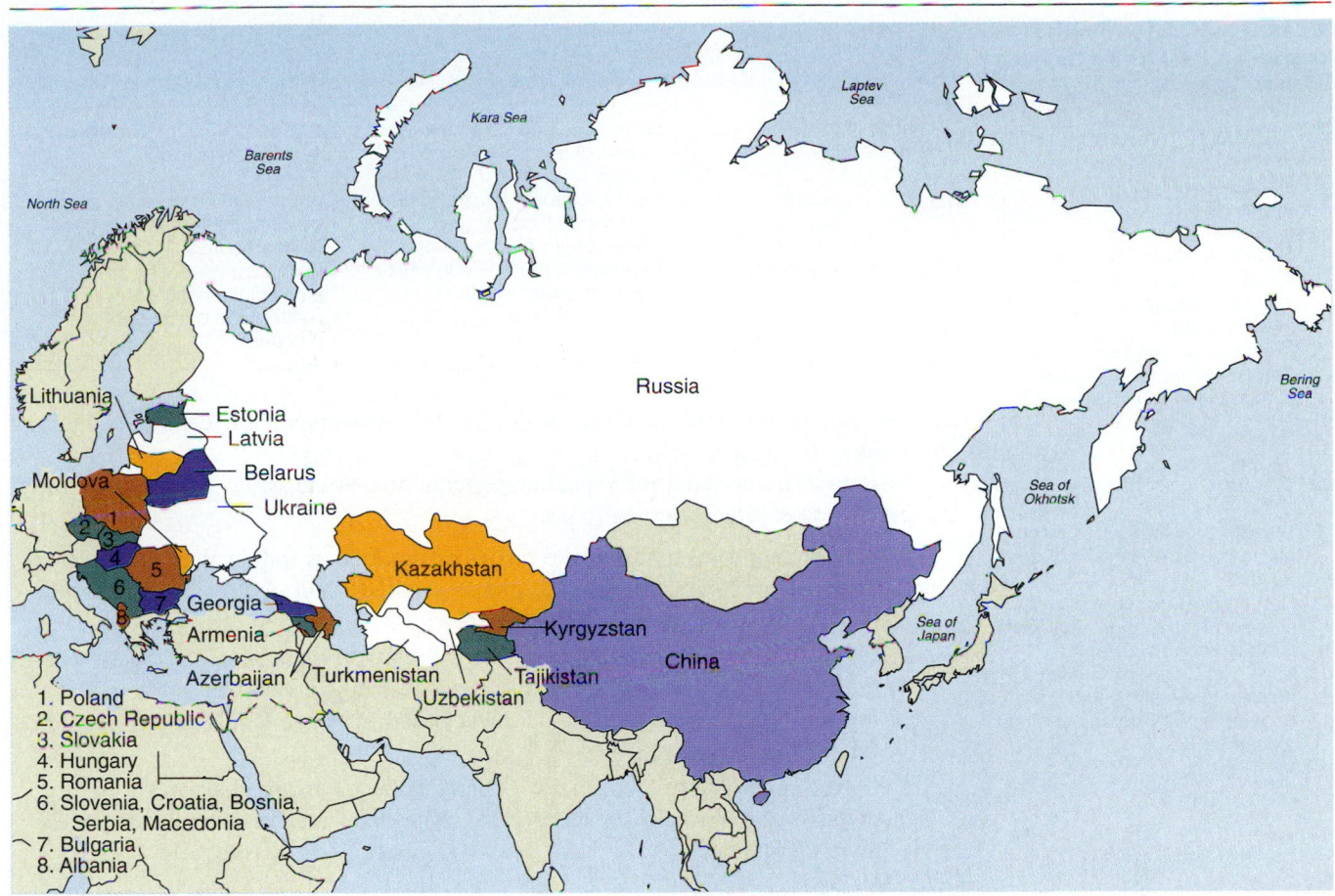

EXHIBIT 1   Socialist Countries in Transition

This map shows the most important formerly traditional socialist economies that are now going through major transitions. China and the former USSR were the largest socialist economies, although there were a number of socialist countries in Eastern Europe, Africa, and Asia.
Source: *CIA World Fact Book.*

Defining Soviet-style socialism precisely is difficult because it embodies both political and economic features. I will concentrate on the economic features. Specifically, **Soviet-style socialism** uses administrative control or central planning to answer the questions *what, how,* and *for whom.* In a Soviet-style socialist economic system, government planning boards set society's goals and then give individuals directives as to how to achieve those goals.

Let's now discuss how a Soviet-style socialist country, if one existed today, and a capitalist country might make different decisions about the what, how, and for whom questions. Let's consider two goods: designer jeans and whole-wheat bread. Compared to their cost in the formerly socialist countries, in most capitalist societies designer jeans are relatively inexpensive while whole-wheat bread is relatively expensive. Why? One reason is that central planners decide that designer jeans are frivolous luxury items, so they produce few or none and charge a high price for what they do produce. Similarly, they decide that whole-wheat bread is good for people, so they produce large quantities and price it exceptionally low. Planners, not supply and demand, determine what, how, and for whom to produce.

To accomplish planners' ends—getting people to do what planners think is best—requires stronger government control than exists in capitalist countries. To maintain that control, government generally owns the means of production, such as factories and machines, and tells people where they will work and how much they will receive. In Soviet-style socialism, individuals' choices are limited and planners'

Soviet-style socialism   An economic system that uses central planning and government ownership of the means of production to answer the questions, what, how, and for whom.

Q–4:   What is the difference between socialism in theory and socialism in practice?

EXHIBIT 2   Capitalism's and Socialism's Answers to the Three Economic Questions

3a Capitalism's answers to the central economic questions:
1. What to produce: what businesses believe people want, and is profitable.
2. How to produce: businesses decide how to produce efficiently, guided by their desire to make a profit.
3. For whom to produce: distribution according to individuals' ability and/or inherited wealth.

Central economic question	Capitalism's answer	Soviet-style socialism's answer
What to produce?	What firms believe people want and will make the firm a profit.	What central planners believe socially beneficial.
How to produce?	Businesspeople decide how to produce efficiently, guided by their desire to make a profit.	Central planners decide, guided by what they believe is good for the country (ideally).
For whom to produce?	Distribution according to ability and inherited wealth.	Distribution according to individual's need (as determined by central planners).

3b Soviet-style socialism's answers to the three questions:
1. What to produce: what central planners believe is socially beneficial.
2. How to produce: central planners decide, based on what they think is good for the country.
3. For whom to produce: central planners distribute goods based on what they determine are individuals' needs.

choices, not individuals' choices, determine the answers to the central economic questions.

In summary, the three principal components of a Soviet-style socialist economy compared to a capitalist economy are:

1. Government ownership of the means of production, rather than private ownership as in capitalism. Central planners, rather than owners of businesses, decide what to produce.
2. Directed labor. Workers are directed by a government planning board where they will work and how much they will be paid, rather than workers making individual choices of employment based on wage levels in different jobs, as in capitalism.
3. Government-determined prices. Usually high prices are charged for luxury goods and low prices for necessities, rather than market-determined prices as in capitalism.

Three principal components of a Soviet-style socialist economy are:
1. Government ownership of the means of production;
2. Directed labor; and
3. Government-determined prices.

There are, of course, markets in Soviet-style socialist economies. Just as in capitalist economies, individuals buy goods by going to the store. The difference between stores in the two kinds of economies is that in a Soviet-style socialist economy, the government tells the storekeeper what goods will be offered, what price to charge, and how much of a good will be delivered to the store, while in a capitalist society, the storeowner can order as much of any good as he or she wants and can charge any price he or she wants—whatever the market will bear.

Differences between Soviety-Style Socialism and Capitalism

Q–5: The difference between capitalism and Soviet-style socialism is that Soviet-style socialism involves planning and capitalism does not. True or false? Why?

The difference between Soviet-style socialist and capitalist economies is not that Soviet-style socialist economies are planned economies and capitalist economies are unplanned. Both economies involve planning. **Planning** simply involves deciding— before the production takes place—what will be produced, how to produce it, and for whom it will be produced. The differences are in who does the planning, what they try to do in planning, and how the plans are coordinated.

In capitalist countries, businesspeople do the planning. Businesspeople decide that they can sell designer jeans, Nintendo games, or economics textbooks. They target their likely customers and decide how much to produce and what price to charge. In Soviet-style socialist countries, government planners decide what people need and should have.

In an idealized capitalist society, businesses design their plans to maximize their profit; the market is relied upon to see that individual self-interest is consistent with society's interest. In an idealized socialist society, the government designs its plans to make society better.

In a capitalist economy, coordination of plans is left to the workings of the market. In a Soviet-style socialist economy, coordination is done by government planners.

Exhibit 2 summarizes how capitalism and Soviet-style socialism answer the three central economic questions: how, what, and for whom.

Soviet people happily tear down a statue of Lenin, which they saw as a symbol of Soviet-style socialism. *Reuters/Bettmann*

Capitalism and socialism have not existed forever. Capitalism came into existence in the mid-1700s; socialism came into existence in the early 1900s.

Both capitalism and socialism have changed over the years, and a look at their evolution will give us a good sense of the struggle among the invisible forces to dominate our lives. In the 1930s, during the Great Depression, capitalist countries integrated a number of what might be called *socialist institutions* with their existing institutions. Distribution was no longer, even in theory, only according to ability; need also played a role. Government's economic role in capitalist societies increased, and some of the how, what, and for whom decisions were transferred from the market to the government. For example, most capitalist nations established a welfare system and a social security system, providing an economic safety net for people whose incomes were inadequate for their needs.

The 1980s saw the reverse process take place, with socialism integrating some capitalist institutions with its existing institutions. Market sectors in socialist countries expanded, government's economic importance decreased, and some how, what, and for whom decisions were transferred from government to the market. Instead of being assigned jobs by the government, workers were often allowed to choose jobs themselves, and some firms were allowed to produce independently of planners' decisions. Even in cases where production decisions weren't transferred, socialist planning boards used market principles more and more in making their decisions.

The result has been a blending of economic systems and a blurring of the distinctions between capitalism and socialism. If the trend toward use of market mechanisms in socialist countries continues, in the 21st century there may be only one general type of economic structure. It won't be pure socialism and it won't be pure capitalism. It will be a blend of the two.

For students of history the recent changes in economic systems are not surprising. Economic systems are in a continual state of evolution. To understand recent movements in socialist countries and to put market institutions in perspective, in the next section I briefly consider the history and nature of economic systems.

Evolving Economic Systems

In the 1930s through the 1960s, capitalist countries became more socialistic; in the 1980s and 1990s, Soviet-style socialistic countries became more capitalistic.

In the 21st century there may well be only one general type of economic structure, which will be a blend of socialist and capitalist institutions.

THE HISTORY OF ECONOMIC SYSTEMS

4A Economic systems evolve because the institutions of the new system offer a better life for at least some—and usually a large majority—of the individuals in a society.

Feudal Society: Rule of the Invisible Handshake

Q–6: In feudalism, how would the *what, how,* and *for whom* questions be answered?

Feudalism Political system divided into small communities in which a few powerful people protect those who are loyal to them.

Q–7: How did the Knights of the Round Table get their food? For example, did they go to the market and buy it?

Remember the distinction between market and economic forces: Economic forces have always existed—they operate in all aspects of our lives; but market forces have not always existed. Markets are social creations societies use to coordinate individuals' actions. Markets developed, sometimes spontaneously, sometimes by design, because they offered a better life for at least some—and usually a large majority of—individuals in a society.

To understand why markets developed, it is helpful to look briefly at the history of the economic systems from which our own system descended.

Let's go back in time to the year 1000 when Europe had no nation-states as we now know them. There was no coordinated central government, no unified system of law, no national patriotism, no national defense, although there was a strong religious institution simply called the Church that fulfilled some of these roles. There were few towns; most individuals lived in walled manors or "estates." These manors "belonged to" the "lord of the manor."[3] I say "belonged to" rather than "were owned by" because most of the empires or federations at that time were not formal nation-states that could organize, administer, and regulate ownership. There were no documents or deeds giving ownership of the land to an individual. Instead there was tradition, and in normal times nobody questioned the lord's right to the land. The land "belonged to" the lord because the land "belonged to" him—that's the way it was.

Because there was no central nation-state, the manor served many functions a nation-state would have served had it existed. The lord provided protection, often within a walled area surrounding the manor house or, if the manor was large enough, a castle. He provided administration and decided disputes. He also decided *what* would be done, *how* it would be done, and *who* would get what, but these decisions were limited. In the same way that the land belonged to the lord because that's the way it always had been, what people did and how they did it were determined by what they always had done. Tradition ruled the manor more than the lord did.

The Life of a Serf   Individuals living on the land were called *serfs.* What serfs did was determined by what their fathers had done. If the father was a farmer, the son was a farmer. A woman followed her husband and helped him do what he did. That was the way it always had been and that's the way it was—tradition again.

Most serfs were farmers, and surrounding the manor were fields of about a half acre each. Serfs were tied by tradition to their assigned plots of land; according to tradition, they could not leave those plots and had to turn over a portion of their harvest to the lord every year. How much they had to turn over varied from manor to manor, but payments of half the total harvest were not unheard of. In return, the lord provided defense and organized the life of the manor—boring as it was. Thus, there was a type of trade between the serf and the lord, but it was nonnegotiable and did not take place through a market.

Problems of a Tradition-Based Society   This system, known as **feudalism,** developed about the 8th and 9th centuries and lasted until about the 15th century, though in isolated countries such as Russia it continued well into the 19th century, and in all European countries its influence lingered for hundreds of years (as late as about 140 years ago in some parts of Germany). Such a long-lived system must have done some things right, and feudalism did: it answered the what, how, and for whom questions in an acceptable way.

But a tradition-based society has problems. In a traditional society, because someone's father was a baker, the son must also be a baker, and because a woman was a homemaker, she wouldn't be allowed to be anything but a homemaker. But what if Joe Blacksmith, Jr., the son of Joe Blacksmith, Sr., is a lousy blacksmith and longs to knead dough, while Joe Baker, Jr., would be a superb blacksmith but hates making

---

[3] Occasionally the "lord" was a lady, but not often.

ADDED DIMENSION

MILESTONES IN
ECONOMICS

6700 B.C.	First known coins (Iran).
3600 B.C.	First system of taxation (Mesopotamia).
2100 B.C.	First welfare system (Egypt).
2000 B.C.	Coins in general use.
2000 B.C.–500 A.D.	International trade flourishes.
100 B.C.	First corporation (Rome).
105 A.D.	Chinese invent paper (a cheap substance to replace parchment).
301 A.D.	First wage and price controls (Emperor Diocletian of Rome).
700–1400	Development of feudal estates.
1275	Development of tariffs in England.
1400–1800	End of feudal estates and development of private property and wage workers.
1600–1800	Mercantilism and state control of economic activity.
1700s	Development of paper money (France).
1750–1900	Industrial Revolution.
1760–1800	Enclosure movement in England, solidifying private property and market economy.
1776	Publication of Adam Smith's *Wealth of Nations*.
1860–1960	Development of social security and unemployment insurance (Germany).
1867	Publication of Karl Marx's *Das Kapital*.
1935–1970	Integration of socialist institutions into capitalism.
1988 onward	Socialist economies in upheaval adopt markets and capitalist institutions.

pastry? Tough. Tradition dictated who did what. In fact, tradition probably arranged things so that we will never know whether Joe Blacksmith, Jr., would have made a superb baker.

As long as a society doesn't change too much, tradition operates reasonably well, although not especially efficiently, in holding the society together. However, when a society must undergo change, tradition does not work. Change means that the things that were done before no longer need to be done, while new things do need to get done. But if no one has traditionally done these new things, then they don't get done. If the change is important but a society can't figure out some way for the new things to get done, the society falls apart. That's what happened to feudal society. It didn't change when change was required.

Some individuals in feudal society just couldn't take life on the manor, and they set off on their own. Because there was no organized police force, they were unlikely to be caught and forced to returned to the manor. Going hungry, being killed, or both, however, were frequent fates of an escaped serf. One place to which serfs could safely escape, though, was a town or city—the remains of what in Roman times had been thriving and active cities. These cities, which had been decimated by plagues, plundering bands, and starvation in the preceding centuries, nevertheless remained an escape hatch for runaway serfs because they relied far less on tradition than did manors. City dwellers had to live by their wits; many became merchants who lived predominantly by trading. They were middlemen; they would buy from one group and sell to another.

Trading in towns was an alternative to the traditional feudal order because trading allowed people to have an income independent of the traditional social structure. Markets broke down tradition. Initially merchants traded using *barter* (exchange of one kind of good for another): silk and spices from the Orient for wheat, flour, and artisan products in Europe. But soon a generalized purchasing power (money) developed as a medium of exchange. Money greatly expanded the possibilities of trading because its use meant that goods no longer needed to be bartered. They could be sold for money, which could then be spent to buy other goods.

In the beginning, land was not one of the goods that could be traded, but soon the feudal lord who just had to have a silk robe but had no money was saying, "Why not?

Douglass North, an economic historian who has emphasized the central role that institutions play in the economy. *Reuters/Bettmann.*

4B Feudalism evolved into mercantilism because markets and the development of money allowed trade to expand, which undermined the traditional base of feudalism. Tradition that can be bought and sold is no longer tradition—it's just another commodity.

In a tradition-based society, the invisible handshake (the social and cultural forces embodied in history) gives a society inertia (a tendency to resist change) which predominates over economic and political forces.

"Why did you do it that way?"

"Because that's the way we've always done it."

Tradition-based societies had markets, but those were peripheral, not central, to economic life. In feudal times what was produced, how it was produced, and for whom it was produced were primarily decided by tradition.

In today's U.S. economy, the market plays the central role in economic decisions. But that doesn't mean that tradition is dead. As I said in Chapter 1, tradition still plays a significant role in today's society, and, in many aspects of society, tradition still overwhelms the invisible hand. Consider the following:

1. The persistent view that women should be home-

makers rather than factory workers, consumers rather than producers.
2. The raised eyebrows when a man is introduced as a nurse, secretary, homemaker, or member of any other profession conventionally identified as *women's work.*
3. Society's unwillingness to permit the sale of individuals or body organs.
4. Parents' willingness to care for their children without financial compensation.

Each of these tendencies reflects tradition's influence in Western society. Some are so deep-rooted that we see them as self-evident. Some of tradition's effects we like; others we don't—but we often take them for granted. Economic forces may work against these traditions, but the fact that they're still around indicates the continued strength of tradition in our market economy.

I'll sell you a small piece of land so I can buy a shipment of silk." Once land became tradeable, the traditional base of the feudal society was undermined. Tradition that can be bought and sold is no longer tradition—it's just another commodity.

From Feudalism to Mercantilism

Toward the end of the Middle Ages, markets went from being a sideshow, a fair that spiced up peoples' lives, to being the main event. Over time, some traders and merchants started to amass fortunes that dwarfed those of the feudal lords. Rich traders settled down; existing towns and cities expanded and new towns were formed. As towns grew and as fortunes shifted from feudal lords to merchants, power in society shifted to the towns. And with that shift came a change in society's political and economic structure.

Q–8: Why did the early traders support the king? What relevance do such actions have to modern-day lobbying?

As these traders became stronger politically and economically, they threw their support behind a king (the strongest lord) in the hope that the king would expand their ability to trade. In doing so, they made the king even stronger. Eventually, the king became so powerful that his will prevailed over the will of the other lords and even over the will of the Church. As the king consolidated his power, nation-states as we know them today evolved. *The invisible foot—government—became an active influence on economic decision making.*

Mercantilism An economic system in which government doles out the rights to undertake economic activities.

As markets grew, feudalism evolved into **mercantilism** (an economic system in which the government determines the what, how, and for whom decisions by doling out the rights to undertake certain economic activities). Political rather than social forces came to control the central economic decisions.

The evolution of feudal systems into mercantilism occurred in somewhat this way: As cities and their markets grew in size and power relative to the feudal manors and the traditional economy, a whole new variety of possible economic activities developed. It was only natural that individuals began to look to a king to establish a new tradition that would determine who would do what. Individuals in particular occupations organized into groups called *guilds,* which were similar to strong labor unions today. These guilds, many of which had financed and supported the king, now expected the king and his government to protect their interests.

As new economic activities, such as trading companies, developed, individuals involved in these activities similarly depended on the king for the right to trade and for help in financing and organizing their activities. For example, in 1492, when Christopher Columbus had the wild idea that by sailing west he could get to the East Indies and trade for their riches, he went to Spain's Queen Isabella and King Ferdinand for financial support.

Since many traders had played and continued to play important roles in financing, establishing, and supporting the king, the king was usually happy to protect their interests. The government doled out the rights to undertake a variety of economic activities. By the late 1400s, Western Europe had evolved from a feudal to a mercantilist economy.

The mercantilist period was marked by the increased role of government, which could be classified in two ways: by the way it encouraged growth, and by the way it limited growth. Government legitimized and financed a variety of activities, thus encouraging growth. But government also limited economic activity in order to protect the monopolies of those it favored, thus limiting growth. So mercantilism allowed the market to operate, but it kept the market under its control. The market was not allowed to respond freely to the laws of supply and demand.

The mercantilist period saw major growth in Western Europe, but mercantilism also unleashed new tensions within society. Like feudalism, mercantilism limited entry into economic activities. It used a different form of limitation—the invisible foot (politics) rather than the invisible handshake (social and cultural tradition)—but individuals who were excluded still felt unfairly treated.

The most significant source of tension was the different roles played by craft guilds and owners of new businesses, who were called **capitalists** or industrialists. Craft guild members were artists in their own crafts: pottery, shoemaking, and the like. New business owners destroyed the art of production by devising machines to replace hand production. Machines produced goods cheaper and faster than craftsmen.[4] The result was an increase in supply and a downward pressure on the price, which was set by government. Craftsmen didn't want to be replaced by machines. They argued that machine-manufactured goods didn't have the same quality as hand-crafted goods, and that the new machines would disrupt the economic and social life of the community.

Industrialists were the outsiders with a vested interest in changing the existing system. They wanted the freedom to conduct business as they saw fit. Because of the enormous cost advantage of manufactured goods over crafted goods, a few industrialists overcame government opposition and succeeded within the mercantilist system. They earned their fortunes and became an independent political power.

Once again the economic power base shifted, and two groups competed with each other for power—this time, the guilds and the industrialists. The government had to decide whether to support the industrialists (who wanted government to loosen its power over the country's economic affairs) or the craftsmen and guilds (who argued for strong government limitations and for maintaining traditional values of workmanship). This struggle raged in the 1700s and 1800s. But during this time, governments themselves were changing. This was the Age of Revolutions, and the kings' powers were being limited by democratic reform movements—revolutions supported and financed in large part by the industrialists.

The Need for Coordination in an Economy   One argument craftsmen put forward was that coordination of the economy was necessary, and the government had to be involved. If government wasn't going to coordinate economic activity, who would? To answer that question, a British moral philosopher named Adam Smith developed, in his famous book *The Wealth of Nations* (1776), the concept of the invisible hand, and used it to explain how markets could coordinate the economy without the active involvement of government. Smith wrote:

Q–9:   In what way did mercantilism foster economic growth, and in what way did it limit economic growth?

From Mercantilism to Capitalism

Capitalists   *Businesspeople who have acquired large amounts of money and use it to invest in businesses.*

4c   Mercantilism evolved into capitalism because the Industrial Revolution undermined the craft-guided mercantilist method of production. Machines produced goods cheaper and faster, making industrialists rich. They used their economic power to change the political support for mercantilism.

Q–10:   Your study partner, Joan, is arguing that mercantilism went down with the king; it was overthrown by the Age of Revolution. How do you respond?

---

[4] Throughout this section I use *men* to emphasize that these societies were strongly male-dominated. There were almost no businesswomen. In fact, a woman had to turn over her property to a man upon her marriage, and the marriage contract was written as if she were owned by her husband!

THE RISE OF MARKETS IN PERSPECTIVE

Back in the Middle Ages, markets developed spontaneously. "You have something I want; I have something you want. Let's trade" is a basic human attitude we see in all aspects of life. Even children quickly get into trading: chocolate ice cream for vanilla, two Zebots for a ride on a motor scooter. Markets institutionalize such trading by providing a place where people know they can go to trade. New markets are continually coming into existence. Today there are markets for baseball cards, pork bellies (which become bacon and pork chops), rare coins, and so on.

Throughout history, societies have tried to prevent some markets from operating because they feel those markets are ethically wrong or have undesirable side effects. Societies have the power to prevent markets. They make some kinds of markets illegal. In parts of the United States, the addictive drug market, the baby market, and the sex market, to name a few, are illegal. In socialist countries, markets in a much wider range of goods (such as clothes, cars, and soft drinks) and activities (such as private business for individual profit) have been illegal.

But, even if a society prevents the market from operating, it cannot escape the dynamic laws of supply and demand. If there's excess supply, there will be downward pressure on prices; if there's excess demand, there will be upward pressure on prices. To maintain an equilibrium in which the quantity supplied does not equal the quantity demanded, a society needs a force to prevent the invisible hand from working. In the Middle Ages, that strong force was religion. The Church told people that if they got too far into the market mentality—if they followed their self-interest—they'd go to Hell.

Until recently in socialist society, the state has provided the preventive force. In their educational system, socialist countries would emphasize a more communal set of values. They taught students that a member of socialist society does not try to take advantage of other human beings but, rather, lives by the philosophy "From each according to his ability; to each according to his need."

For whatever reason—some say because true socialism wasn't really tried; others say because people's self-interest is too strong—the "from each according to his ability; to each according to his need" approach didn't work in socialist countries. They have switched (some say succumbed) to greater reliance on the market.

---

5 Markets coordinate economic activity by turning self-interest into social good. Competition directs individuals pursuing profit to do what society needs to have done.

Man has almost constant occasion for the help of his brethren, and it is in vain for him to expect it from their benevolence only. He will be more likely to prevail, if he can interest their self-love in his favour, and show them that it is for their own advantage to do for him what he requires of them. Whoever offers to another a bargain of any kind proposes to do this. Give me that which I want, and you shall have that which you want, is the meaning of every such offer; and it is in this manner that we obtain from one another the far greater part of those good offices which we stand in need of. It is not from the benevolence of the butcher, the brewer, or the baker, that we expect our dinner, but from their regard to their own interest. We address ourselves, not to their humanity but to their self-love, and never talk to them of our own necessities but of their advantages.

Smith argued that the market's invisible hand would guide suppliers' actions toward the general good. No government coordination was necessary.

With the help of economists such as Adam Smith, the industrialists' view won out. Government pulled back from its role in guiding the economy and adopted a **laissez-faire** policy, leaving coordination of the economy to the invisible hand. (*Laissez faire,* a French term, means "Let events take their course; leave things alone.")

Laissez-faire   *Economic policy of leaving coordination of individuals' wants to be controlled by the market.*

The Industrial Revolution

The invisible hand worked; capitalism thrived. During the **Industrial Revolution,** which began about 1750 and continued through the late 1800s, machine production increased enormously, almost totally replacing hand production. The economy grew faster than ever before. Society was forever transformed. New inventions changed all aspects of life. James Watt's steam engine (1769) made manufacturing and travel easier. Eli Whitney's cotton gin (1793) changed the way cotton was processed. James Kay's flying shuttle (1733),[5] James Hargreaves's

Industrial Revolution   *Period (1750–1900) during which technology and machines rapidly modernized industrial production.*

---

[5] The invention of the flying shuttle frustrated the textile industry because it enabled workers to weave so much cloth that the spinners of thread from which the cloth was woven couldn't keep up. This challenge to the textile industry was met by offering a prize to anyone who could invent something to increase the thread spinners' productivity. The prize was won when the spinning jenny was invented.

THE ROLE OF ECONOMISTS IN ECONOMIC TRANSITIONS

For economics to be relevant, it must have something to say about social policy. Good economists try to be objective and recommend policies that they believe would be good for society in general rather than for any particular group in society.

Deciding what is in society's interest isn't always easy. For economists, it requires interpreting what society wants and comparing different policies, using what economists believe is society's preference. That often means proposing policies that will help some people but hurt others.

Adam Smith's ''invisible hand'' argument for the free working of the market and against government intervention is a good example. Smith favored a laissez–faire policy, meaning the government should not interfere with the operation of the economy. In this argument, Smith and other Classical economists found themselves aligned with the industrialists or manufacturers, who wanted the right to enter into markets as they saw fit, and against the guilds and independent artisans, who wanted government to control who did what.

These two groups each had different reasons for supporting laissez-faire policy, however. Industrialists supported the policy because they believed it benefited them. Sometimes they claimed policies that helped themselves actually benefited society, but they only made this argument because it helped make their case more persuasive. Economists supported the laissez-faire policy because they believed it benefited society.

It's not easy to decide which policies will benefit society when the policies you're looking at will help some people and hurt other people. It's hard to weigh a policy and decide whether the good that it will probably do outweighs the harm that it may cause.

Modern economists have spent a long time struggling with this problem. Some have avoided the problem. They have refused to advocate any policy that might hurt anyone, which pretty much eliminates advocating any policy at all. Good policy-oriented economists make working judgments of what they believe is in society's interest; these working judgments determine which policies they advocate.

In reality, economists' (or anyone's) arguments for the general good of society are unlikely to have much effect on the policies of any government unless their arguments coincide with the interest of one group or another. A policy of less government involvement favored manufacturers over craftspeople. That the policy favored manufacturers or industrialists isn't the reason economists favored it (they argued that less government involvement would be good for society as a whole), but it is the reason industrialists supported laissez-faire, and the industrialists' support of laissez-faire was critical in getting the policy adopted in Britain in the late 1700s.

Once markets were established, the terms of the debate changed. Economists stopped only advocating laissez-faire policies. Good economists recognize the advantages of markets, but they also recognize the problems of markets.

spinning jenny (1765), and Richard Arkwright's power loom (1769), combined with the steam engine, changed the way cloth was processed and the clothes people wore.

The need to mine vast amounts of coal to provide power to run the machines changed the economic and physical landscapes. The repeating rifle changed the nature of warfare. Modern economic institutions replaced guilds. Stock markets, insurance companies, and corporations all became important. Trading was no longer financed by government; it was privately financed (although government policies, such as colonial policies giving certain companies monopoly trading rights with a country's colonies, helped in that trading). The Industrial Revolution, democracy, and capitalism all arose in the middle and late 1700s. By the 1800s, they were part of the institutional landscape of Western society. Capitalism had arrived.

Capitalism was marked by significant economic growth in the Western world. But it was also marked by human abuses—18-hour workdays, low wages, children as young as five years old slaving long hours in dirty, dangerous factories and mines—to produce enormous wealth for an elite few. Such conditions and inequalities led to criticism of the capitalist or market economic system.

From Capitalism to ~~*Socialism*~~ *Welfare Capitalism*

Marx's Analysis   The best-known critic of this system was Karl Marx, a German philosopher, economist, and sociologist who wrote in the 1800s and who developed an analysis of the dynamics of change in economic systems. Marx argued that economic systems are in a constant state of change, and that capitalism would not last. Workers would revolt, and capitalism would be replaced by a socialist economic system.

Marx saw an economy marked by tensions among economic classes. He saw capitalism as an economic system controlled by the capitalist class (businessmen). His class analysis was that capitalist society is divided into capitalist and worker classes.

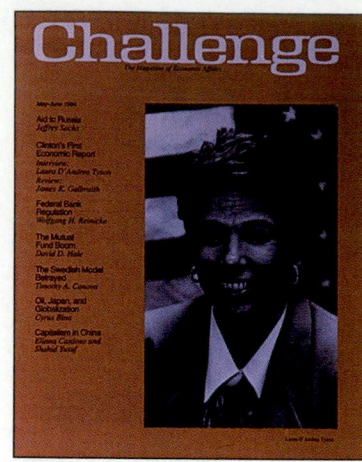

A popular economics magazine written for laypeople.

He said constant tension between these economic classes causes changes in the system. The capitalist class made large profits by exploiting the **proletariat** class (working class) and extracting what he called *surplus value* from workers who, according to Marx's labor theory of value, produced all the value inherent in goods. Surplus value was the profit that, according to Marx's normative views, capitalists added to the price of goods. What economic analysis sees as recognizing a need that society has and fulfilling it, Marx saw as exploitation.

Marx argued that this exploitation would increase as production facilities became larger and larger and as competition among capitalists decreased. At some point, he believed, exploitation would lead to a revolt by the proletariat, who would overthrow their capitalist exploiters.

By the late 1800s, some of what Marx predicted had occurred, although not in the way that he thought it would. Production moved from small to large factories. Corporations developed, and classes became more distinct from one another. Workers were significantly differentiated from owners. Small firms merged and were organized into monopolies and trusts (large combinations of firms). The trusts developed ways to prevent competition among themselves and ways to limit entry of new competitors into the market. Marx was right in his predictions about these developments, but he was wrong in his prediction about society's response to them.

Capitalism did not evolve into socialism because the worst abuses of the market were modified by government.

The Revolution that Did Not Occur   Western society's response to the problems of capitalism was not a revolt by the workers. Whereas Marx said capitalism would fall because of the exploitation of workers by the owners of businesses or capitalists, what actually happened was that the market economy was modified by political forces. Governments stepped in to stop the worst abuses of capitalism. The hard edges of capitalism were softened.

Evolution, not revolution, was capitalism's destiny. The democratic state did not act, as Marx argued it would, as a mere representative of the capitalist class. Competing pressure groups developed; workers gained political power which offset the economic power of businesses.

In the late 1930s and the 1940s, workers dominated the political agenda. During this time, capitalist economies developed an economic safety net which included government-funded programs, such as public welfare and unemployment insurance, and established an extensive set of regulations affecting all aspects of the economy. Today, depressions are met with direct government policy. Antitrust laws, regulatory agencies, and social programs of government softened the hard edges of capitalism. Laws were passed prohibiting child labor, mandating a certain minimum wage, and limiting the hours of work. Capitalism became what is sometimes called **welfare capitalism,** an economic system in which the market is allowed to operate, but in which government plays key roles in determining distribution and making the *what, how,* and *for whom* decisions.

Welfare capitalism Economic system in which the market operates but government regulates markets significantly.

Due to these developments, government spending now accounts for about a third of all spending in the United States, and for more than half in some European countries. Were an economist from the late 1800s to return from the grave, he'd probably say socialism, not capitalism, exists in Western societies. Most modern-day economists wouldn't go that far, but they would agree that our economy today is better described as a welfare capitalist economy than as a capitalist, or even a market, economy. Because of these changes, the U.S. and Western European economies are a far cry from the competitive "capitalist" economy that Karl Marx criticized. Markets operate, but they are constrained by the government.

The concept *capitalism* developed to denote a market system controlled by one group in society, the capitalists. Looking at Western societies today, we see that domination by one group no longer characterizes Western economies. Although in theory capitalists control corporations through their ownership of shares of stock, in practice corporations are controlled in large part by managers. There remains an elite group who control business, but "capitalist" is not a good term to describe them. Managers, not capitalists, exercise primary control over business, and even their control is limited by laws or the fear of laws being passed by governments.

Governments in turn are controlled by a variety of pressure groups. Sometimes one group is in control; at other times, another. Government policies similarly fluctuate. Sometimes they are proworker, sometimes proindustrialist, sometimes pro-government, and sometimes prosociety.

From Feudalism to Socialism

You probably noticed that I crossed out "Socialism" in the previous section's heading and replaced it with "Welfare Capitalism." That's because capitalism did not evolve to socialism as Karl Marx predicted it would. Instead, Marx's socialist ideas took root in Russia, a society that the Industrial Revolution had in large part bypassed. Arriving at a different place and a different time than Marx predicted it would, socialism, you should not be surprised to read, arrived in a different way than Marx predicted. There was no revolution of the proletariat to establish socialism. Instead, there was World War I, which the Russians were losing, and there was Russia's feudal economy and government, which were crippled by the war effort. A small group of socialists overthrew the czar (Russia's king) and took over the government in 1917. They quickly pulled Russia out of the war, and then set out to organize a socialist society and economy.

Russian socialists tried to adhere to Marx's ideas, but they found that Marx had concentrated on how capitalist economies operate, not on how a socialist economy should be run. Thus, Russian socialists faced a huge task with little guidance. Their most immediate problem was how to increase production so that the economy could emerge from feudalism into the modern industrial world. In Marx's analysis, capitalism was a necessary stage in the evolution toward the ideal state for a very practical reason. The capitalists exploit the workers, but in doing so capitalists extract the necessary surplus—an amount of production in excess of what was consumed. That surplus had to be extracted in order to provide the factories and machinery upon which a socialist economic system would be built. But since there had been no capitalism in Russia, a true socialist state could not be established immediately. Instead, the socialists created an economic system that they called **state socialism.** The state would see to it that people worked for the common good until they could be relied on to do so on their own.

State socialism Economic system in which government sees to it that people work for the common good until they could be relied upon to do that on their own.

Socialists saw state socialism as a transition stage to pure socialism. This transition stage still exploited the workers; when Joseph Stalin took power in Russia in the late 1920s, he took the peasants' and small farmers' land and turned it into collective farms. The government then paid farmers low prices for their produce. When farmers balked at the low prices, millions of them were killed.

Simultaneously, Stalin created central planning agencies which directed individuals what to produce and how to produce it, and determined for whom things would be produced. During this period, *socialism* became synonymous with *central economic planning*, and Soviet-style socialism became the model of socialism in practice.

Also during this time, Russia took control of a number of neighboring states and established the Union of Soviet Socialist Republics (USSR), the formal name of the Soviet Union. The Soviet Union also installed Soviet-dominated governments in a number of Eastern European countries. In 1949 most of China, under the rule of Mao Zedong, adopted Soviet-style socialist principles.

Since the late 1980s, the Soviet socialist economic and political structure has fallen apart. The Soviet Union as a political state broke up, and its former republics became autonomous. Eastern European countries were released from Soviet control. Now they faced a new problem: transition from socialism to a market economy. Why did the Soviet socialist economy fall apart? Because workers lacked incentives to work; production was inefficient; consumer goods were either unavailable or of poor

In the late 1980s and early 1990s, the Soviet societies' economic and political structures crumbled.

ADDED DIMENSION   SHAREHOLDERS AND STAKEHOLDERS

orporations (businesses) are technically owned by the owners of capital (shareholders). In theory, at least, they control corporations by electing the officers (the people who make the *what, how,* and *for whom* production decisions). In practice, however, effective control of corporations is generally in the hands of a small group of managing officers.

In the debate about the possible future evolution of capitalism, the question of who controls business decisions is likely to take center stage. Some reformers in the United States argue that the current U.S. system is wrong in both theory and practice. They argue that corporations should reflect the need of stakeholders (all the individuals who have a stake in a corporation's activities). Stakeholders include the corporation's stockholders and officers as well as workers, customers, and the community where the corporation operates. An economy in which all stakeholders, not just shareholders, elect the officers who make the *what, how,* and *for whom* decisions would still use the market. It would still be a market economy, but it would no longer be a capitalist economy.

quality; and high Soviet officials were exploiting their positions, keeping the best jobs for themselves and moving themselves up in the waiting lists for consumer goods. In short, the parents of the socialist family (the Communist party) were no longer acting benevolently; they were taking many of the benefits for themselves.

Recent political and economic upheavals in Eastern Europe and the Soviet Union suggest the kind of socialism these societies tried did not work. However, that failure does not mean that socialist goals are bad; nor does it mean that no type of socialism can ever work. To overthrow socialist-dominated governments it is not necessary to accept capitalism, and many citizens of these countries are looking for an alternative to both systems. Most, however, wanted to establish market economies.

6 Socialism was an attempt to bring out people's social conscience, rather than their self-interest. Many of the countries that attempted to introduce socialism have recently reverted to capitalism.

From Socialism to ?

The upheavals in the former Soviet Union and Eastern Europe have left only China as a major power using a socialist economic system. But even in China there have been changes, and the Chinese economy is socialist in name only. Almost uncontrolled markets exist in numerous sectors of the economy. These changes have led some socialists to modify their view that state socialism is the path from capitalism to true socialism, and instead to joke: "Socialism is the longest path from capitalism to capitalism."

ECONOMIC SYSTEMS OF THE FUTURE

The economic system of tomorrow will mostly likely be quite different from the economic systems of today.

Our economic system will probably be different 30 years from now. If the debate between socialism and capitalism disappears, another debate will rise up to take its place. A new topic for debate may be: Who should be the decision makers in a market economy? In the U.S. economy in the late 1980s, a handful of financiers became celebrities by reaping billions of dollars in profits for themselves. Many people came to wonder whether an economic system that so glorified greed was really desirable, and in the 1990s some of those same financiers found themselves in jail, with the financial institutions they had controlled in ruins. Such widespread reactions may well lead to further evolution of the capitalist system.

Also in the early and mid-1990s, the Asian tigers—a collection of Asian countries such as Singapore, South Korea, and Hong Kong—are the economic stars. As we will discuss in a later chapter, these countries' economies were similar to Japan's economy, which, in turn, has many similarities to mercantilism. In Japan, government and industrialists work closely together, and government plays a key role in the economy. Given the success of the Asian tigers, a push in the United States toward a type of mercantilism similar to theirs exists. And so it's safe to predict that the 1990s will see further evolution of economic systems. The lesson of history seems to be that change remains the one constant in economic systems.

CHAPTER SUMMARY

- Any economic system must answer three central questions:

  What to produce?

  How to produce it?

  For whom to produce it?

- In capitalism, the what, how, and for whom decisions are made by the market.

- In Soviet-style socialism, the what, how, and for whom decisions are made by government planning boards.

- Political, social, and economic forces are active in both capitalism and socialism.

- Economic systems are in a constant state of evolution.

- In feudalism, tradition rules; in mercantilism, the government rules; in capitalism, the market rules.

- In welfare capitalism, the market, the government, and tradition each rule components of the economy.

- Socialism is currently undergoing a major transition; Soviet-style socialism is almost dead, and the future structure of socialist economies is unclear.

KEY TERMS

capitalism *(63)*
capitalists *(71)*
economic system *(62)*
feudalism *(68)*
Industrial Revolution *(72)*

laissez-faire *(72)*
mercantilism *(70)*
NIMBY *(63)*
planning *(66)*
private property rights *(63)*

proletariat *(74)*
socialism *(64)*
Soviet-style socialism *(65)*
state socialism *(75)*
welfare capitalism *(74)*

QUESTIONS FOR THOUGHT AND REVIEW

The number after each question represents the estimated degree of critical thinking required. (1 = almost none; 10 = deep thought.)

1. Is capitalism or socialism the better economic system? Why? *(9)*

2. What three questions must any economic system answer? *(2)*

3. How does Soviet-style socialism answer these three questions? *(3)*

4. How does capitalism answer these three questions? *(3)*

5. What arguments can you give for supporting a socialist organization of a family and a capitalist organization of the economy? *(6)*

6. Why did feudalism evolve into mercantilism? Could feudalism stage a return? Why? *(6)*

7. Why did mercantilism evolve into capitalism? Could mercantilism stage a return? Why? *(6)*

8. Some intellectuals have argued "history has ended" because of recent developments in socialist economies. Respond, basing your answer on Marx's analysis. *(7)*

9. A common joke in socialist countries in the early 1990s was that a person went into a free market store and asked how much a loaf of bread cost. "One dollar," said the clerk. "But that's outrageous. Down the street at the state-run store, it only costs a nickel." "So why don't you buy it there?" said the clerk. "Well," said the customer, "they don't have any." Using supply/demand analysis, show why this situation makes economic sense. *(4)*

10. The Heisenberg principle states that it's impossible to know the true nature of reality because in analyzing that reality, you change it. How might the Heisenberg principle apply to Marx's economic analysis? *(6)*

PROBLEMS AND EXERCISES

1. Suppose a Soviet-style socialist government decided to set all prices at the supply/demand equilibrium price.
   a. Show graphically what price it would set.
   b. How would such an economy differ from a market economy?
   c. Do you think a socialist government could carry out that decision?
   d. Show graphically what would happen if it set the price too high and if it set the price too low.
   e. Which of the preceding two situations best describes what the actual situation was in socialist economies?

2. Poland, Bulgaria, and Hungary (all former socialist countries) were in the process of changing to a market economy in the early 1990s.

a. Go to the library and find the latest information about their transitions.

b. Explain what has happened in those countries, using the invisible hand, invisible handshake, and invisible foot metaphors.

3. Economists Edward Lazear and Robert Michael have calculated that the average family spends two-and-one-half times as much on each adult as they do on each child.

a. Does this mean that children are deprived and that the distribution is unfair?

b. Do you think these percentages change with family income? If so, how?

c. Do you think that the allocation would be different in a family in a Soviet-style socialist country than in a capitalist country? Why?

4. One of the specific problems Soviet-style socialist economies had was keeping up with capitalist countries technologically.

a. Can you think of any reason inherent in a centrally planned economy that would make innovation difficult?

b. Can you think of any reason inherent in a capitalist country that would foster innovation?

c. Joseph Schumpeter, a famous Harvard economist of the 1930s, predicted that as firms in capitalist societies grew in size they would innovate less. Can you suggest what his argument might have been?

d. Schumpeter's prediction did not come true. Modern capitalist economies have had enormous innovations. Can you provide explanations why?

5. In 1993 President Clinton introduced a health care plan that would increase government involvement in the economy.

a. Why might he have done so at precisely the time when government-controlled economies were floundering?

b. Many economists predicted that a government-controlled health care program would have serious problems. What do you think their argument was?

c. What other major areas of the U.S. economy are run by government? Can you give reasons why they are government-run, rather than being privately run?

ANSWERS TO MARGIN QUESTIONS

1. It depends on what he means, but he is probably wrong. Property rights are required for a market to operate. Once property rights are allocated, the market will allocate goods, so the market cannot distribute the property rights that are required for the market to operate. The reason he might be right is that perhaps he was referring what might be called "secondary property rights"—property rights to a newly marketized good. These can be allocated based on existing property rights, as they might be in an auction. Initial property rights, however, must exist before other property rights can be allocated by a market. (63)

2. Most families allocate basic needs through control and command. The parents do (or try to do) the controlling and commanding. Generally they are well-intentioned, trying to meet their perception of their children's needs. However, some family activities which are not basic needs might be allocated through the market. For example, if one child wants a go-cart and is willing to do extra work at home in order to get it, go-carts might be allocated through the market, with the child earning chits that can be used for such nonessentials. (64)

3. Capitalism places much more emphasis on fostering individualism. Socialism tries to develop a system in which the individual's needs are placed second to society's needs. (64)

4. In theory, socialism is an economic system based upon individuals' good will. In practice, socialism follows the Soviet model and involved central planning and government ownership of the primary means of production. (65)

5. False. Both socialism and capitalism involve planning. The difference is in who does the planning. In Soviet-style socialism, central planners do the planning. In capitalism, the managers of firms do the planning, with consumers deciding whether those plans are correct. (66)

6. Feudalism is an economic system based on tradition. The *what, how,* and *for whom* decisions are determined by the past. (68)

7. In the feudal system, knights had the obligation to defend the manor. For fulfilling that duty, they received a certain portion of the produce of the serfs. Thus, tradition determined how the Knights of the Round Table got their food. (68)

8. Early traders supported the king in the hope that he would expand their ability to trade—in other words, improve their economic position. Modern-day lobbying is done for precisely the same reason, and the politicians who will likely bring benefits to a group are supported economically and politically by that group. (70)

9. Mercantilism fostered growth by having government legitimize and finance a variety of activities. It limited economic growth by specific government actions to protect the monopolies of those it favored. (71)

10. I respond that she is generally correct. Mercantilism was a period in which producers, the guilds, and the king were in close alignment. As new technologies developed and industrialists gained economic power, the industrialists supported changing the system in favor of the newly-emerging democratic revolutionary governments. They believed these governments would oppose the guilds and give them, the industrialists, new power. Capitalism, laissez faire, and democracy were all ushered in together. (71)

4

U.S. Economic Institutions

The business of government is to keep the government out of business—that is, unless business needs government aid.

~Will Rogers

After reading this chapter, you should be able to:

1 Provide a bird's-eye view of the U.S. economy.

2 Explain the role of consumer sovereignty in the U.S. economy.

3 Go out and learn more about U.S. economic institutions on your own.

4 Summarize briefly the advantages and disadvantages of various types of business.

5 Explain why, even though households have the ultimate power, much of the economic decision making is done by business and government.

6 List two general roles of government and seven specific roles of government.

You saw in Chapter 2 that supply and demand are the driving forces behind the invisible hand. But the invisible hand doesn't operate in an invisible world; it operates in a very real world—a world of institutions that sometimes fight against, sometimes accept, and sometimes strengthen the invisible hand. Thus, to know how the invisible hand works in practice, we need to have some sense of economic institutions and data about the U.S. economy. Let's first look at some data.

A BIRD'S-EYE VIEW OF THE U.S. ECONOMY

1 For a birds-eye view of the U.S. economy see Exhibit 2.

The powerful U.S. economic machine generates enormous economic activity and provides a high standard of living (compared to most other countries) for almost all its inhabitants. It also provides economic security for its citizens. Starvation is far from most people's minds. Exhibit 1 gives you an idea of what underlies the U.S. economy's strength. For example, in it you can see that the United States is a large country with a temperate climate and a wide range of natural resources. It has excellent transportation facilities and a relatively homogeneous population, most of which speaks the same language, English. Its characteristics are, however, changing. Large-scale immigration is increasing the Hispanic and Asian populations, especially around the southern and western border states.

The Importance of Geographic Economic Information

Such geographic economic information is vitally important. To understand an economy you should know: Where are goods produced? Where are natural resources found? What natural resources does it lack? What are normal transportation routes? To keep their analyses simpler, economists often discuss economic problems without discussing geographic dimensions. But no discussion of an economy should forget that geographic dimensions of economic problems are significant. To determine whether to send my students off to the library to learn this information, I give them a quiz. I present them with two lists like those in the box on page 83. The list on the right gives twenty places in the United States. The list on the left gives a particular economic characteristic, such as an industry, product, activity, or natural condition that has been turned to economic advantage. Students are required to match the numbers with important characteristics of each area.

If you can answer 15 or more of the 20 questions on this quiz correctly, I'm impressed with your knowledge of economic geographic facts. If you answer fewer than 15, I strongly suggest learning more geographic facts. The study guide has a number of other projects, information, and examples. An encyclopedia has even more, and your library has a wealth of information. You could spend the entire semester acquiring facts. I'm not suggesting that, but I *am* suggesting that you follow the economic news carefully and pay attention to *where* various *whats* are produced.

The positive attributes of the U.S. economy don't mean that the United States has no problems. Critics point out that crime is rampant, drugs are omnipresent, economic resources such as oil and minerals are declining, the environment is deteriorating, the distribution of income is skewed toward the rich, and an enormous amount of economic effort goes into economic gamesmanship (real estate deals, stock market deals, deals about deals) which seems simply to reshuffle existing wealth, not to create new wealth. Internationally, the U.S. economic position has deteriorated substantially since the 1950s and 1960s. In some people's eyes, Japan has replaced the United States as the world's economic leader. Rather than lending money to other countries as it had done in the 1950s and 1960s, in the 1980s the United States borrowed enormous amounts from other countries and is now the biggest debtor nation in the world. In short, the U.S. economy of the 1990s is great, but it's far from perfect.

A CIA publication with very up-to-date international and domestic statistics. For example, in it you will find the total railroad mileage in Ghana.

Q–1:   Where would you find the total railroad mileage in Ghana?

Diagram of the U.S. Economy

Exhibit 2 diagrams the U.S. economy. Notice it's divided up into three groups: business, households, and government. Households supply factors of production to business and are paid by business for doing so. The market where this interaction takes place is called a *factor market*. Business produces goods and services and sells them to households and government. The market where this interaction takes place is called the *goods market*.

EXHIBIT 1   CIA Information Survey on United States

GEOGRAPHY

Total area: 9,372,610 km^2

Land area: 9,166,600 km^2; includes only the 50 states and District of Columbia

Comparative area: about half the size of Russia; about three-tenths the size of Africa; about one-half the size of South America (or slightly larger than Brazil); slightly smaller than China; about two and one-half times the size of Western Europe

Land boundaries: total 12,248 km, Canada 8,893 km (including 2,477 km with Alaska), Cuba 29 km (US naval base at Guantanamo), Mexico 3,326 km

Coastline: 19,924 km

Climate: mostly temperate, but tropical in Hawaii and Florida and artic in Alaska, semiarid in the great plains west of the Mississippi River and arid in the Great Basin of the southwest; low winter temperatures in the northwest are ameliorated occasionally in January and February by warm chinook winds from the eastern slopes of the Rocky Mountains

Terrain: vast central plain, mountains in west, hills and low mountains in east; rugged mountains and broad river valleys in Alaska; rugged, volcanic topography in Hawaii

Natural resources: coal, copper, lead, molybdenum, phosphates, uranium, bauxite, gold, iron, mercury, nickel potash, silver, tungsten, zinc, petroleum, natural gas, timber

Land use: arable land: 20%; permanent crops: 0%; meadows and pastures: 26%; forest and woodland: 29%; other: 25%

Irrigated land: 181,020 km^2 (1989 est.)

Environment: pollution control measures improving air and water quality; agricultural fertilizer and pesticide pollution; management of sparse natural water resources in west; desertification; tsunamis, volcanoes, and earthquake activity around Pacific Basin; permafrost in northern Alaska is a major impediment to development

PEOPLE

Population: 235,103,721 (July 1993 est.)

Population growth rate: 1.02% (1993 est.)

Birth rate: 15.48 births/1,000 population (1993 est.)

Death rate: 8.67 deaths/1,000 population (1993 est.)

Net migration rate: 3.41 migrant(s)/1,000 population (1993 est.)

Infant mortality rate: 8.36 deaths/1,000 live births (1993 est.)

Life expectancy at birth: total population: 75.8 years; male: 72.49 years; female: 79.29 years (1993 est.)

Total fertility rate: 2.05 children born/woman (1993 est.)

Ethnic divisions: white 83.4%, black 12.4%, asian 3.3%, native american 0.8% (1992)

Religions: Protestant 56%, Roman Catholic 28%, Jewish 2%, other 4%, none 10% (1989)

Languages: English, Spanish (spoken by a sizable minority)

Literacy: age 15 and over having completed 5 or more years of schooling (1991) total population: 97.9%; male: 97.9%; female: 97.9%

Labor force: 128.548 million (includes armed forces and unemployed; civilian labor force 126.982 million) (1992) *by occupation:* NA

ECONOMY

National product: GDP—purchasing power equivalent—$5.951 trillion (1992)

National product real growth rate: 2.1% (1992)

National product per capita: $23,400 (1992)

Inflation rate (consumer prices): 3% (1992)

Unemployment rate: 7% (April 1993)

Budget: revenues $1,092 billion; expenditures $1,382 billion, including capital expenditures of $NA (FY92)

Exports: $442.3 billion (f.o.b., 1992)
commodities: capital goods, automobiles, industrual supplies and raw materials, consumer goods, agricultural products

partners: Western Europe 27.3%, Canada 22.1%, Japan 12.1% (1989)

Imports: $544.1 billion (c.i.f., 1992)
commodities: crude oil and refined petroleum products, machinery, automobiles, consumer goods, industrial raw materials, food and beverages
partners: Western Europe 21.5%, Japan 19.7%, Canada 18.8% (1989)

External debt: $NA

Industrial production: growth rate 1.5% (1992 est.): accounts for NA% of GDP

Electricity: 780,000,000 kW capacity; 3,230,000 million kWh produced, 12,690 kWh per capita (1992)

Industries: leading industrial power in the world, highly diversified; petroleum, steel, motor vehicles, aerospace, telecommunications, chemicals, electronics, food processing, consumer goods, lumber, mining

Agriculture: accounts for 2% of GDP and 2.8% of labor force; favorable climate and soils support a wide variety of crops and livestock production; world's second largest producer and number one exporter of grain; surplus food producer; fish catch of 4.4 million metric tons (1990)

Illicit drugs: illicit producer of cannabis for domestic consumption with 1987 production estimated at 3,500 metric tons or about 25% of the available marijuana; ongoing eradication program aimed at small plots and greenhouses has not reduced production

Economic aid: donor—commitments, including ODA and OOF, (FY80–89), $115.7 billion

Exchange rates: British pounds: (£) per US$–0.6527 (January 1993), 0.5664 (1992), 0.5652 (1991), 0.5603 (1990), 0.6099 (1989), 0.5614 (1988)

COMMUNICATIONS

Railroads: 240,000 km of mainline routes, all standard 1.435 meter track, no government ownership (1989)

Highways: 7,599,250 km total; 6,230,000 km state-financed roads; 1,369,250 km federally-financed roads (including 71,825 km interstate limited access freeways) (1988)

Inland waterways: 41,009 km of navigable inland channels, exclusive of the Great Lakes (est.)

Pipelines: petroleum 276,000 km (1991), natural gas 331,000 km (1991)

Ports: Anchorage, Baltimore, Beaumont, Boston, Charleston, Chicago, Cleveland, Duluth, Freeport, Galveston, Hampton Roads, Honolulu, Houston, Jacksonville, Long Beach, Los Angeles, Milwaukee, Mobile, New Orleans, New York, Philadelphia, Portland (Oregon), Richmond (California), San Francisco, Savannah, Seattle, Tampa, Wilmington

Merchant marine: 385 ships (1,000 GRT or over) totaling 12,567,000 GRT/19,511,000 DWT; includes 3 passenger-cargo, 36 cargo, 23 bulk, 169 tanker, 13 tanker tug-barge, 13 liquefied gas, 128 intermodal; in addition, there are 219 government-owned vessels

Airports: total: 14,177; usable: 12,417; with permanent-surface runways: 4,820; with runways over 3,659 m: 63; with runways 2,400-3,659 m: 325; with runways 1,200-2,439 m: 2,524

Telecommunications: 126,000,000 telephone access lines; 7,557,000 cellular phone subscribers; broadcast stations—4,987 AM, 4,932 FM, 1,092 TV; about 9,000 TV cable systems; 530,000,000 radio sets and 193,000,000 TV sets in use; 16 satellites and 24 ocean cable systems in use; satellite ground stations—45 Atlantic Ocean INTELSAT and 16 Pacific Ocean INTELSAT (1990)

Source: *CIA World Fact Book,* 1993.

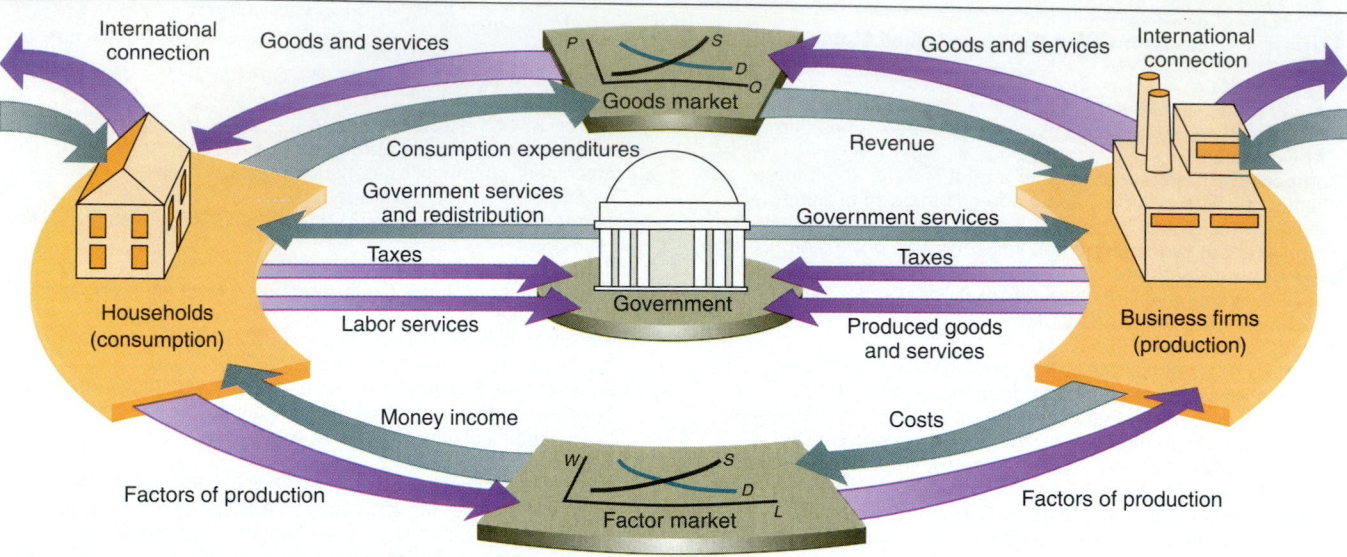

International connection — Goods and services — Goods market — Goods and services — International connection

Consumption expenditures — Revenue

Government services and redistribution — Government services

Taxes — Taxes

Households (consumption) — Government — Business firms (production)

Labor services — Produced goods and services

Money income — Costs

Factors of production — Factor market — Factors of production

EXHIBIT 2   Diagrammatic Representation of the U.S. Economy

Q–2:   What percentage of the economy does agriculture make up?

Notice also the arrows going out and coming in for both business and households. Those arrows represent the international connection, which I'll discuss in Chapter 5.

Finally, consider the arrows connecting government with households and business. Government taxes business and households. It buys goods and services from business and buys labor services from households. Then, with some of its tax revenue, it provides services to both business and households (roads, education) and gives some of its tax revenue directly back to individuals. In doing so, it redistributes income. But government also serves a second function. It oversees the interaction of business and households in the goods and factor markets. Government, of course, is not independent. The United States is a democracy, so households vote to determine who shall govern.

Exhibit 2 gave you an overview of the institutional organization of the U.S. economy. Let's now consider some specifics. First look at business, second at households, and finally at government.

BUSINESS

President Calvin Coolidge once said, "The business of America is business." That's a bit of an overstatement, but business is responsible for over 80 percent of U.S. production. (Government is responsible for the other 20 percent.) In fact, any time a household decides to produce something, it becomes a business. **Business** is simply the name given to private producing units in our society.

Businesses in the United States decide what *to produce,* how *much to produce, and* for whom *to produce it.*

Businesses in the United States decide *what* to produce, *how* much to produce, and *for whom* to produce it. They make these central economic decisions on the basis of their own feelings, which are influenced by market incentives. Anyone who wants to can start a business, provided he or she can come up with the required cash and meet the necessary regulatory requirements. Each year, about 225,000 businesses are started.

Entrepreneurship and Business

Don't think of business as something other than people. Businesses are ultimately made up of a group of people organized together to accomplish some end. In terms of numbers, most businesses are one- or two-person operations. Home-based businesses, at least if they're part-time activities, are easy to start. All you have to do is say you're in business, and you are. If that business becomes complex enough and big enough to have employees (especially if it needs its own building), the difficulties begin. Before the business may expand its operations, a large number of licenses, permits, approvals,

ECONOMIC GEOGRAPHY OF THE UNITED STATES

The Quiz

■n the first column, I list 20 economic characteristics. In the second and third columns, I list 20 states, cities, or areas of the country. Associate the locale with the proper characteristic by printing the letter on the line.

_____ 1. excellent climate for spacecraft launching

_____ 2. major concentration of investment and banking services

_____ 3. film and TV industry

_____ 4. significant fishing and lobstering industries

_____ 5. the maple sugar state

_____ 6. concentration of textile industries

_____ 7. gold is a major product

_____ 8. major oil reserves

_____ 9. iron ore and iron extraction

_____ 10. major automobile production

_____ 11. major port for oil

_____ 12. tourism is a major industry, especially at Mardi Gras

_____ 13. significant irrigation farming

_____ 14. island's seasonal economy driven by summer residents and tourists

_____ 15. nearly all energy needs supplied by hydroelectric power

_____ 16. significant natural gas reserves

_____ 17. staging area for shipment of prime beef

_____ 18. concentration of lead mining

_____ 19. extensive silver mines

_____ 20. major timber production and port for shipping wood products to Japan and the Far East.

a. Colorado
b. Detroit and surrounding area
c. Florida
d. Georgia, South Carolina, and North Carolina
e. Houston
f. Idaho
g. Kansas City
h. Maine
i. Martha's Vineyard (Mass.)
j. New Orleans

k. New York City
l. Northern Minnesota
m. Oklahoma
n. Oregon
o. Pennsylvania and West Virginia
p. Seattle and surrounding area
q. South Dakota
r. Southern California
s. Utah
t. Vermont

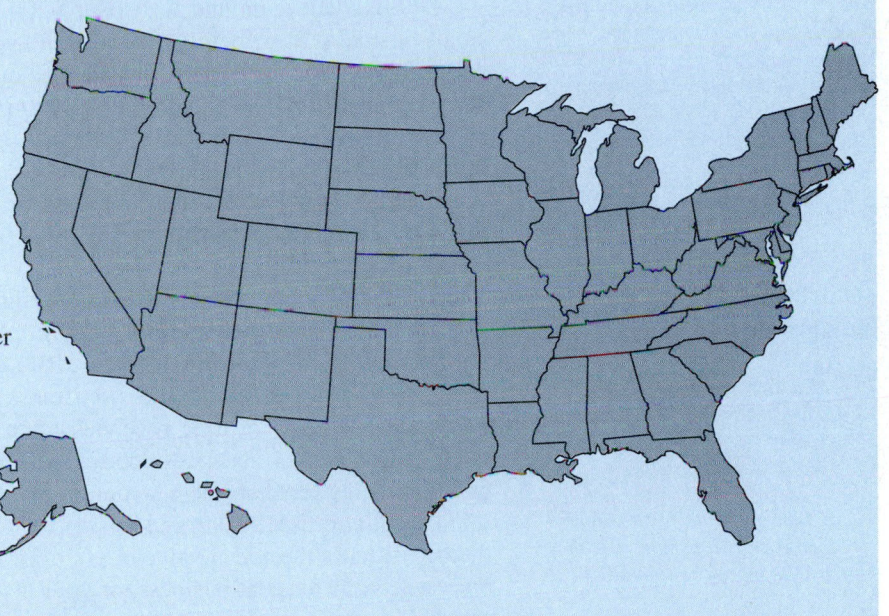

and forms must be obtained from various government agencies. That's why **entrepreneurship** (the ability to organize and get something done) is an important part of business. To give you a sense of what it's like to run a business, let's consider a real-world example.

Entrepreneurship is the ability to organize and get something done; it is an important part of business.

In 1986, Susan and Ralph decided that it would be fun to open a kitchen shop in a prosperous Vermont town. They planned to sell kitchen utensils and light food and drink, including coffee, muffins, cheese, and wine.

They found a building, bought it, and, after getting a building permit, began remodeling. Because it was to be the home of a business, the building had to meet strict fire, electrical, and plumbing codes. Because Susan and Ralph planned to sell wine, they had to apply for a liquor license.

Trials and Tribulations of Starting a Business

Starting your own business is a challenge.

Answers: 1–c, 2–k, 3–r, 4–h, 5–t, 6–d, 7–q, 8–m, 9–l, 10–b, 11–e, 12–j, 13–f, 14–i, 15–n, 16–o, 17–g, 18–a, 19–s, 20–p.

Their plans initially called for an upstairs store area, but state inspectors told Susan and Ralph that, in a building and zone like theirs, an upstairs store was against the law. So much for upstairs.

They had to establish contacts with suppliers, get insurance, and obtain permits from the town to comply with zoning, health, and sanitation codes and regulations surrounding the sale of prepared food.

Then, of course, there are taxes. Any business with employees must withhold taxes from their wages and send those taxes periodically to the various taxing authorities. This includes social security taxes, federal income taxes, and state income taxes. There are also unemployment compensation taxes, property taxes, and sales taxes that the business, not the employees, must pay.

All this costs a lot of money. Susan and Ralph had to open a business checking account with their bank. (They couldn't run all that expense through their personal checking account because sound accounting practice requires people to keep their business checks separate from their personal checks.) They had to have some money to put in the business account. They used some of their savings, but they needed more funds. That meant they had to apply for a loan from the bank. The bank required them to present a formal business plan.

Q-3: Jill has been advised by Jack to start her own business since she is a superb mechanic and can fix a car's engine easily. Unfortunately, she hates forms and bureaucracy. What would you advise?

It took two years and well over $200,000 to start the business. And this was a small business. Somebody without training and background in handling forms, taxes, and bureaucratic regulations usually doesn't do well in business. To such a person, entry into business isn't free; it isn't even possible. Still, many people enter business, and many succeed. Eight years after start-up, 54 percent of new businesses are still in business; 18 percent have failed; and 28 percent will have terminated operations voluntarily. Susan and Ralph were one of the successful ones. They are doing a thriving business in the mid-1990s.

Consumer Sovereignty and Business

2 Although businesses decide what to produce, they are guided by consumer sovereignty.

There's an important if *in people's freedom to start a business: If they can get the money to finance it.*

To say that businesses decide what to produce isn't to say that **consumer sovereignty** (the consumer's wishes) doesn't reign in the United States. Businesses decide what to produce based on what they believe will sell. A key question a person in the United States should ask about starting a business is: Can I make a profit from it? **Profit** is what's left over from total revenues after all the appropriate costs have been subtracted. Businesses that guess correctly what the consumer wants generally make a profit. Businesses that guess wrong generally operate at a loss.

People are free to start businesses for whatever purposes they want. No one asks them: "What's the social value of your term paper assistance business, your Twinkies business, your fur coat business, or your textbook publishing business?" Yet the U.S. economic system is designed to channel individuals' desire to make a profit into the

The Vermont Country Kitchen, a small business like those found across the United States. *Author provided.*

(a) Importance by sales

Agriculture, forest, fishing, mining (4%)
Construction (4%)
Manufacturing (21%)
Trade (wholesale and retail) (18%)
Transportation, communications, utilities (10%)
Services (22%)
Finance, insurance, real estate (21%)

(b) Importance by employment

Agriculture, forest, fishing, mining (4%)
Construction (5%)
Manufacturing (19%)
Trade (wholesale and retail) (27%)
Transportation, communications, utilities (6%)
Services (32%)
Finance, insurance, real estate (7%)

EXHIBIT 3 (a and b)   Importance and Size of Various Types of Business

The general types of business are listed here. (**a**) shows their relative importance by sales. (**b**) shows their relative importance by employment. Notice that less than half the population is involved in what most laypeople consider production—manufacturing, construction, mining, and agriculture.

Source: *Monthly Labor Review* and *Survey of Current Business*, 1994.

general good of society. That's the invisible hand at work. As long as the business doesn't violate a law and conforms to regulations, people in the United States are free to start whatever business they want, if they can get the money to finance it. That's a key difference between the U.S. market economy and a traditional Soviet-style socialist economy where people aren't free to start a business even if they could get the financing.

Exhibit 3(a) shows a selection of various categories of U.S. businesses with their relative amount of receipts (the total income firms take in) for each category. Total receipts aren't necessarily the best indicator of the importance of various types of business to the economy. Exhibit 3(b) ranks businesses by their relative employment.

Businesses in the United States are organized on a variety of levels: manufacturing firms, wholesale firms, and retail firms. For most products, the manufacturer doesn't sell the product to you. Often products are sold five or six times before they reach the consumer. Each of these levels is called a **stage of production.** Thus, most firms *provide a service*—getting you the good when you want it—rather than producing the good. Firms are continually deciding whether to combine these stages of production under one firm, or whether to divide the stages up and allow many firms. Recently, for example, retailing firms such as Wal-Mart have been vertically integrating and combining various stages into their firms. Factory outlets are examples of manufacturing firms undertaking retailing functions.

The Relative Importance of Manufacturing   The percentage of manufacturing output relative to total output has remained constant over the last 40 years; in 1950, it was about 22 percent, and in the early 1990s, it was still about 21 percent. But in terms of jobs, manufacturing has declined significantly, falling from about 34 percent in 1950 to about 19 percent in the mid-1990s. The reason is twofold: first, manufacturing has become more productive, so we get more output per worker; and second, we now import many more components of the products we produce. In the 1990s, parts of manufactured goods are produced throughout the world and service jobs such as retailing have replaced manufacturing jobs.

The growing importance of the service sector to the economy has led some observers to say that we're in a postindustrial society. In their view, the U.S. economy today is primarily a service economy, not a production economy. So classifying the

Categories of Business

Q-4:   Is the category "finance, insurance and real estate" more important when measured by sales or when measured by employment?

Levels of Business

Most firms in the United States provide a service—getting the good to you when you want it—rather than producing the good.

3A   Important industries in the United States include petroleum, steel, motor vehicles, aerospace, telecommunications, electronics, and consumer goods.

ADDED DIMENSION

BALANCE SHEET AND INCOME STATEMENT

Accounting for revenues and expenditures is an important part of business. Elaborate methods of keeping track of those revenues and expenses have developed over the years. A firm's balance sheet (a statement of the firm's net worth at a point in time) is shown in **(a)** below.

COMPANY NAME
Balance Sheet
December 31, 1995

Assets*		Liabilities and stockholders' equity*	
Current assets	$13,859	Current liabilities	$12,675
Property, plant, and equipment	20,362	Long-term liabilities	5,843
		Stockholders' equity	15,703
		Total liabilities and stockholders' equity	
Total assets	$34,221		$34,221

COMPANY NAME
Income Statement*
For the Year Ended December 31, 1995

Sales	$8,710
Cost of goods sold	5,980
Gross profit	2,730
Operating expenses	1,509
Fixed interest payment	165
Income before federal income taxes	1,056
Federal income taxes	509
Net income	$ 547

* Dollars in millions.

(a) Balance sheet

* Dollars in millions.

(b) Income statement

As you can see, the balance sheet is divided into assets on the left side and liabilities and stockholders' equity (also called *net worth*) on the right side. An *asset* is anything of value. An asset need not be a physical item. It might be a right to do something or use something. For example, landing rights are important assets of airline companies. A *liability* is an obligation. When a firm borrows money, it takes on a liability because it has an obligation to pay the money back to the lender. The totals of the two sides must be equal, since *stockholders' equity (net worth)* is defined as the difference between assets and liabilities. That is:

$$\text{Assets} = \text{Liabilities} + \text{Stockholders' equity}$$

or

$$\text{Assets} = \text{Liabilities} + (\text{Assets} - \text{Liabilities})$$

$$\text{Assets} = \text{Assets}.$$

The two sides of the equation are equal by definition. Both assets and liabilities are divided into various subcategories on a balance sheet, but at this stage, all you need to remember is the sheet's general structure.

A firm's income statement is shown in **(b)**. Whereas a balance sheet measures a stock concept (a firm's position at a point in time), an income statement measures a flow concept (the amount of income and expenses passing through a company during a particular period of time). A firm's sales, or total revenue, is given at the top. Then the cost of goods sold is subtracted from total revenue. The resulting number is called *gross profit,* although many income statements don't list gross profits. Next, operating costs and fixed interest payments are subtracted, giving earnings before taxes. Finally, income taxes are subtracted, giving the firm's net income.

economy may or may not be helpful, but you should note how important the provision of services and the distribution of goods are to our economy.

From Manufacturer to You   To give you a sense of the path of a good from manufacturer to ultimate buyer, let's consider a hypothetical example of a window. Clearview Window Corporation bought the glass, wood, and machines needed to make the window from other companies, perhaps spending a total of $20 per window. Those purchases all fell within what is classified as wholesale trade. Clearview Window then assembled the components (cost of assembly: $60), making Clearview's total cost of the window $80.

I needed a window for my house, so I went down to Buildright, a local building supply store, which sells both wholesale to general contractors and retail to plain people who walk in off the street. Wholesale customers get a 20 percent discount from

3B   A useful way to learn about the economy is to trace the path of a product from raw material to final product.

ADDED DIMENSION

IS THE UNITED STATES A POSTINDUSTRIAL SOCIETY?

Producing physical goods is only one of a society's economic tasks. Another task is to provide services (activities done for others). Services do not involve producing a physical good. When you get your hair cut, you buy a service, not a good. Much of the cost of the physical goods we buy actually is not a cost of producing the good, but is a cost of one of the most important services: distribution (getting the good to where the consumer is). After a good is produced, it has to get to the individuals who are going to consume it at the time they need it. If the distribution system gets botched up, it's as if the good had never been produced.

Let's consider a couple of examples. Take Christmas trees. Say you're sitting on 60,000 cut spruce trees in the Vermont mountains, but an ice storm prevents you from shipping them until December 26. Guess what? You're now stuck with 60,000 spruce trees and the problem of somehow getting rid of them. Or take hot dogs. How many of us have been irked that a hot dog that cost 25¢ to fix at home costs $2 at a football game? But a hot dog at home isn't the same as a hot dog at a game. Distribution of the good is as important as production; you're paying the extra $1.75 for distribution.

the retail price, which is deducted at the end of the month from the total bill they've run up. These wholesale customers charge their own customers the full retail price. I'm a plain person, so when I ordered my window, Buildright told me the cost would be $200. However, it didn't have the right size in stock.

Buildright stacked my order with orders from other customers and called up its Clearview distributor (who has a franchise from Clearview Window in the territory where I live) to place one big order for a number of windows, including mine. The Clearview distributor charged Buildright $140 for my window. The Clearview distributor keeps a pile of windows in stock which he replenishes from a shipment of newly made windows that come in once a month from the Clearview plant. For my window, he pays about $100 plus freight.

So it costs Clearview $80 to make my window; Clearview sells it to the distributor for $100 plus freight. The distributor needs to cover his costs for storage, handling, inventory, and billing, and of course he has to make a profit, so he sells the window to Buildright for $140. The owner of Buildright has to cover expenses and make a profit, so he sells me the window for $200 ($160—a 20 percent discount—if he thought I was a wholesale customer).

Producing the good is only a small component of the cost. Distribution—getting the good where it is wanted when it is wanted—makes up 60 percent of the total cost of the window in this example. That large percentage is not unusual. The same story holds true for most goods you buy.

Given the importance of distribution, firms are always looking for new ways to make the distribution process more efficient. Recent approaches include *just-in-time* inventory systems in which computers track a firm's needs; the needed inputs are shipped to the firm just in time, and its outputs are similarly shipped to customers just in time. Another new practice is for retail firms to keep instantaneous tabs on what is selling. That is why, when you buy something, the clerk has to type a whole load of numbers into the computerized cash register (or have the scanner read the bar code with a whole load of numbers). This practice lets the store know what's selling and what isn't so it knows what to order. This makes the distribution process more efficient, and thereby reduces the firm's costs, although it sometimes makes checkouts a pain.

The distribution sector—getting the good where it is wanted when it is wanted—makes up a large portion of the U.S. economy.

Sizes of Business

Another way to classify businesses is by size. Contrary to popular belief, many sectors of the United States contain small (fewer than 500 employees), not large, firms. This is especially true in retail trade and construction industries. The notable exception is manufacturing, which has a group of large producers, such as auto manufacturers.

Exhibit 4 combines activity and size of firms, looking at the largest businesses in various types of activities. Notice the enormous size of some of the businesses, especially in the industrial category. General Motors has sales of well over $100 billion; Sears has sales of well over $50 billion and assets (the physical and financial property that it controls) of almost $100 billion. Compare these figures to the total

EXHIBIT 4 **The Largest Businesses**

Ten largest U.S. corporations*	Sales (in millions)	Assets
General Motors	$138,000	$188,000
Ford Motor	109,000	199,000
Exxon	98,000	84,000
Wal-Mart Stores	67,000	26,000
American Telephone and Telegraph	67,000	61,000
International Business Machines	63,000	81,000
General Electric	61,000	252,000
Mobil	57,000	41,000
Sears Roebuck	55,000	91,000
Philip Morris	51,000	51,000

* Ranking by sales.

Ten largest retailing companies	Sales	Assets
Wal-Mart Stores	$67,000	$ 26,000
Sears Roebuck	55,000	91,000
Kmart	34,000	18,000
Kroger	22,000	4,000
JC Penney	20,000	15,000
Dayton Hudson	19,000	11,000
American Stores	19,000	7,000
Safeway	15,000	5,000
Albertson's	11,000	3,000
May Department Stores	11,000	9,000

Ten largest diversified financial companies	Assets	Revenues
Federal National Mortgage Association	$217,000	$ 16,000
Salomon	185,000	9,000
Merrill Lynch	153,000	166,000
Travelers Insurance	101,000	7,000
American International Group	101,000	20,000
Aetna Life & Casualty	100,000	17,000
Morgan Stanley Group	97,000	9,000
American Express	94,000	20,000
CIGNA	85,000	18,000
Federal Home Loan Mortgage	84,000	5,000

Ten largest commercial banks	Assets	Deposits
Citicorp	$217,000	$145,000
BankAmerica Corp.	187,000	142,000
Nationsbank Corp.	158,000	91,000
Chemical Banking Corp.	150,000	98,000
J.P. Morgan & Co.	134,000	40,000
Chase Manhattan Corp.	102,000	72,000
Bankers Trust New York Corp.	92,000	23,000
Banc One Corp.	80,000	61,000
First Union Corp.	71,000	54,000
PNC Bank Corp.	62,000	33,000

Source:　*Forbes* Magazine, April 25, 1994; *Fortune* Magazine, May 30, 1994.

output of a country like Nepal ($3.5 billion) and you have a sense of the size of some U.S. businesses.

The fact that a business is in the top 10 one year doesn't necessarily mean it will be in the top 10 the next year. Take IBM ("Big Blue")—until the 1990s, it was close to the top of the top 10 of all categories. Then it, like many large companies, went through major restructuring (downsizing) due to its inability to satisfy its customers, and decreased in relative importance.

A sector's relative size does not necessarily capture its importance to the economy.

A sector's relative size does not necessarily capture its importance to the economy. Take agriculture, for example. It's small in terms of both payroll and revenue, but if it stopped doing its job of providing our food, its importance would quickly become apparent. Similarly, the financial sector is relatively small, but modern industry couldn't function without a highly developed financial sector. Just as a missing bolt can bring a car to a sudden halt, so too can problems in one sector of the economy bring about a sudden halt to a much larger part of the economy.

Another way to classify businesses is by their goals. They can be either for-profit businesses or nonprofit businesses. For-profit businesses keep their earnings after they pay expenses (if there are any to keep); **nonprofit businesses** try only to make enough money to cover their expenses with their revenues. If a nonprofit business winds up with a profit, that money goes into "reserves" where it's saved to use in case of later losses.

The goal of a nonprofit business is to serve the community or some segment of the community. Nonprofit businesses include all government-run businesses, some hospitals, pension funds, foundations, many fund-raising organizations such as the American Cancer Society, most universities and colleges, and many museums. Working for a nonprofit organization doesn't mean working for free. Salaries are an expense of a business, and are paid by both for-profit and nonprofit firms. In fact, salaries paid to individuals managing nonprofit organizations can be higher than they are in for-profit organizations, and perks of the job can be fantastic.[1] But perks are classified as "expenses" and aren't included in "profits."

Why discuss the goals of business? Because the goals of business are central to economic theory and economists' insight into how economies function. In a pure capitalist country, all businesses are for-profit businesses. In a pure socialist country, all businesses are nonprofit. As I discussed in Chapter 3, the United States is far from a pure capitalist country, and nonprofit businesses play significant roles in the U.S. economy.

Not only are nonprofit organizations responsible for significant amounts of production in education and medicine, they also often control enormous assets in areas where no production takes place. For example, pension funds (funds held in trust for workers) control over 25 percent of the outstanding stock on the New York Stock Exchange. These nonprofit pension funds make decisions about where to invest money, and they earn very large sums of money. Thus, indirectly, the workers (whose pension funds these are) own a large share of business. In other words, much of the profits of for-profit businesses don't go to capitalists. They go to workers.

The three primary forms of business are sole proprietorships, partnerships, and corporations. Of the 18 million businesses in the United States, approximately 73 percent are sole proprietorships, 8 percent are partnerships, and 19 percent are

Goals of Business

Not all businesses have profit as a motive.

Much of the profits of for-profit businesses don't go to capitalists; they go to workers.

Forms of Business

Q–5: Are most businesses in the United States corporations? If not, what are most businesses?

---

[1] *Perks* is short for *perquisites*. An example of a "fantastic" perk might be the business supplying you with a limousine and driver in New York City or Washington, D.C., an unlimited expense account, trips to Europe and the Far East, and a condo in Honolulu.

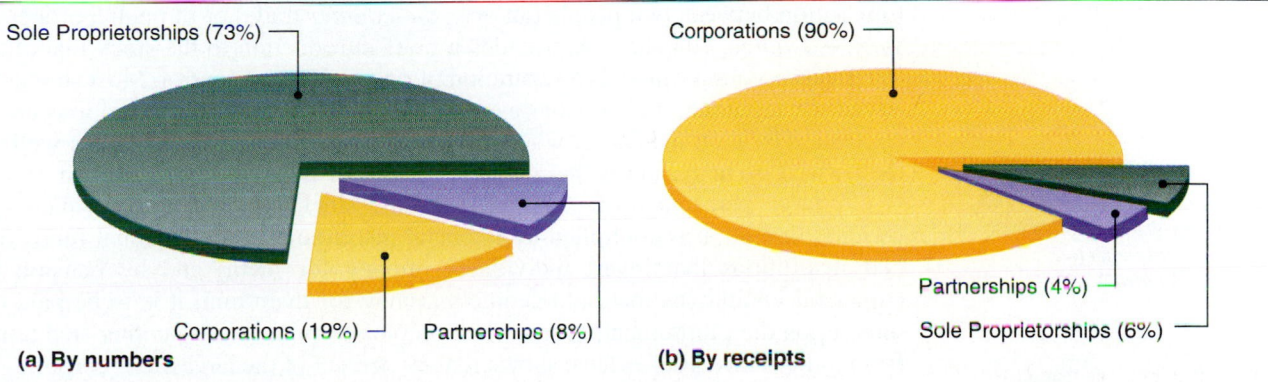

Sole Proprietorships (73%)

Corporations (19%)   Partnerships (8%)

(a) By numbers

Corporations (90%)

Partnerships (4%)

Sole Proprietorships (6%)

(b) By receipts

EXHIBIT 5 (a and b)   Forms of Business

The charts divide firms by the type of ownership. Approximately 74 percent of businesses in the United States are sole proprietorships (**a**). In terms of annual receipts, however, corporations surpass all other forms (**b**).
Source: *Statistical Abstract*, 1993.

The advantages and disadvantages of each are summarized in the following table.

Advantages and Disadvantages of Various Forms of For-Profit Businesses

	Sole Proprietor	Partnership	Corporation
Advantages	1. Minimum bureaucratic hassle 2. Direct control by owner	1. Ability to share work and risks 2. Relatively easy to form	1. No personal liability 2. Increasing ability to get funds 3. Ability to shed personal income and gain added expenses
Disadvantages	1. Limited ability to get funds 2. Unlimited personal liability	1. Unlimited personal liability (even for partner's blunder) 2. Limited ability to get funds	1. Legal hassle to organize 2. Possible double taxation of income 3. Monitoring problems

4 The advantages and disadvantages of the three forms of business are shown in the table.

corporations, as we see in Exhibit 5(a). In terms of total receipts, however, we get a quite different picture, with corporations far surpassing all other business forms, as Exhibit 5(b) shows. In fact, the largest 500 corporations account for 90 percent of the total receipts of all U.S. businesses.

Sole proprietorships are the easiest to start and have the fewest bureaucractic hassles. **Partnerships**—businesses with two or more owners—create possibilities for sharing the burden, but they also create unlimited liability for each of the partners. **Corporations**—businesses that are treated as a person, and are legally owned by their stockholders who are not liable for the actions of the corporate "person"—are the largest form of business when measured in terms of receipts.

When a corporation is formed, it issues **stock** (certificates of ownership in a company) which is sold or given to individuals. Proceeds of the sale of that stock make up what is called the *equity capital* of a company. Ownership of stock entitles you to vote in the election of a corporation's directors.

Limited liability Owner of business is liable only to the extent of his or her own investment.

Corporations were developed as institutions to make it easier for company owners to be separated from company management. A corporation provides **limited liability** for the owners. Whereas with the other two forms of business, owners can lose everything they possess even if they have only a small amount invested in the company, in a corporation the owners can lose only what they have invested in that corporation. If you've invested $100, you can lose only $100. In the other kinds of business, even if you've invested only $100, you could lose everything; the business's losses must be covered by the individual owners.

A corporation's stocks can be distributed among as few as three persons or among millions of stockholders. Stocks can be bought and sold either in an independent transaction between two people (an *over-the-counter* trade) or through a broker and a *stock exchange*. Appendix A provides a brief introduction to the stock market.

In corporations, there is a separation of ownership and control. Most stockholders have little input into the decisions a corporation makes. Instead, corporations are often controlled by their managers, who often run them for their own benefit as well as for the owners'. The reason is that owners' control of management is limited.

Eighty percent of the largest 200 corporations are controlled by managers, with little effective stockholder control.

A large percentage of most corporations' stock is not even controlled by the owners; instead, it is controlled by financial institutions such as mutual funds (financial institutions that invest individuals' money for them) and by pension funds (financial institutions that hold people's money for them until it is to be paid out to them upon their retirement). Thus, ownership of corporations is another step removed from individuals. Studies have shown that 80 percent of the largest 200 corporations in the United States are essentially controlled by managers and have little effective stockholder control.

Q–6: It is obvious that all for-profit businesses in the United States will maximize profit. True or false? Why?

Why is the question of who controls a firm important? Because economic theory assumes business owners' goal is to maximize profits, which would be true of corporations if stockholders made the decisions. Managers don't have the same incentives to maximize profits that owners do. There's pressure on managers to maximize profits, but that pressure can often be weak or ineffective.

HOUSEHOLDS

In the economy, householders vote with their dollars.

The second classification we'll consider in this overview of U.S. economic institutions is households. **Households** (groups of individuals living together and making joint decisions) are the most powerful economic institution. They ultimately control government and business, the other two economic institutions. Households' votes in the political arena determine government policy; their decisions about supplying labor and capital determine what businesses will have available to work with; and their spending decisions or expenditures (the "votes" they cast with their dollars) determine what business will be able to sell.

While the ultimate power does in principle lie with the people and households, we, the people, have assigned much of that power to representatives. As I discussed above, corporations are only partially responsive to owners of their stocks, and much of that ownership is once removed from individuals. Ownership of 1,000 shares in a company with a total of 2 million shares isn't going to get you any influence over the corporation's activities. As a stockholder, you simply accept what the corporation does.

5 Although, in principle, ultimate power resides with the people and households (consumer sovereignty), in practice the representatives of the people—firms and government—are sometimes removed from the people and, in the short run, are only indirectly monitored by the people.

A major decision that corporations make independently of their stockholders concerns what to produce. True, ultimately we, the people, decide whether we will buy what business produces, but business spends a lot of money telling us what services we want, what products make us "with it," what books we want to read, and the like. Most economists believe that consumer sovereignty reigns—that we are not fooled or controlled by advertising. Still, it is an open question in some economists' minds whether we, the people, control business or the business representatives control people. There's similar debate in the political sphere of our lives. U.S. representatives and senators feel only partially responsible to voters. (They feel slightly more responsible around election time.)

Because of this assignment of power to other institutions, in many spheres of the economy households are not active producers of output but merely passive recipients of income. That's why much of the discussion of the household sector focuses on the distribution of household income. Thus, my consideration of households will be short and will focus on their income and their role as suppliers of labor.

Household Types and Income

The U.S. population of about 259 million is composed of about 97 million households. Exhibit 6 looks at three ways income is divided up among households. Notice the relatively low incomes of families where the husband is absent and of black families. Because income determines how many goods and services a person will get, these two groups have fared especially poorly in the *for whom* department.

Q–7: What was the average income of a black family in 1992?

One political concern about income is whether it is fairly (equitably, as opposed to equally) distributed, and whether all households have sufficient income. That's a tough question to answer. For now, let me simply note that the poverty level for a family of four in the United States is defined by the U.S. Department of Commerce as an income below $14,764 per year (1993 figure). By this definition, about 11.7 percent of all households in the United States were below the poverty level in the early 1990s. This percentage is divided unequally between whites and blacks, with 30.9 percent of all black households below the poverty level and 8.9 percent of all white households below it.

Households as Suppliers of Labor

The largest source of household income is wages and salaries (the income households get from labor). Households supply the labor with which businesses produce and government governs. The total U.S. labor force is about 131 million, about 6.0 percent (7.9 million) of whom were unemployed in mid 1994. The average U.S. work week is 42.2 hours for males and 36 hours for females.

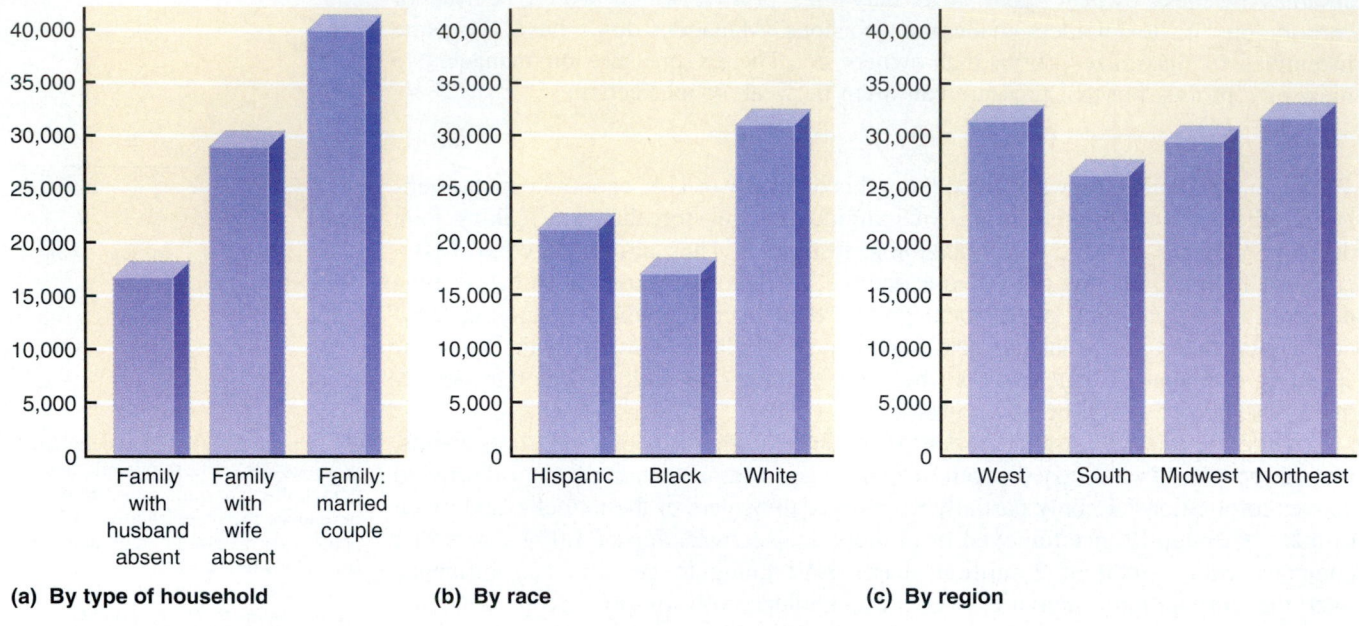

(a) By type of household   **(b) By race**   **(c) By region**

EXHIBIT 6 (a, b, and c)   **Median Household Income by Type of Household, Race, and Region**

These bar charts give you a sense of the distribution of income in the United States in 1992. Notice that the type of household, the race of the household, and the region where the household is located all help to determine household income.
Source: U.S. Bureau of the Census, 1994.

Difference in education and skill level. (handwritten)

Exhibits 7(a) and (b) divide U.S. employment by types of jobs and predicted growth rates of certain jobs. Notice that many of the jobs are service jobs, since the United States has become largely a service economy. Exhibit 7(b) shows that this greater emphasis on services rather than goods is continuing. Many of the fastest-growing jobs are in service industries; many of the fastest-declining are in manufacturing and agriculture.

Other divisions of jobs show even more differences. For example, physicians earn about $150,000 per year; lawyers often earn $100,000 per year, and CEOs of large corporations often make $2,000,000 per year or more. A beginning McDonald's employee generally makes less than $10,000.

In recent times, the power of the unions declined.

One of the biggest changes in the labor markets in recent times has been unions' decline in importance. Labor unions are an economic institution closely associated with households. They were initially created to balance businesses' power. By organizing into unions, workers became an economic institution and gained a larger say in the production process. Unions pushed U.S. wages up relative to wages in other countries, and established in the United States some of the best working conditions in the world. But unions also had a negative effect; part of businesses' response to the high U.S. wages has been to move production facilities to countries where workers receive lower wages. That's one reason the U.S. manufacturing sector has declined relative to the service sector, and union membership and influence have fallen substantially. Service workers have far fewer unions, and their jobs are much more difficult to move to other countries.

People Power

An important way households influence government and business is in their cultural and ideological beliefs. Those beliefs determine what is allowable and what isn't. When those beliefs differ from the existing situation, "people power" has the potential to change the existing institutions significantly. For example, in Eastern Europe by the late 1980s, people's beliefs had become so inconsistent with the existing institutions that people demanded and brought about major economic and political reforms even though there was no formal mechanism, such as free elections, for them to exert their power. People power goes beyond the power people exert in

(a) Job Category	Millions of Females	Millions of Males	Median earnings per week Female	Male
Managerial and professional	11,636	12,454	$580	$791
Technical, sales	16,120	9,774	376	534
Service	4,699	4,680	259	350
Precision products	880	9,609	344	511
Machine operators	3,335	10,685	288	399
Farming, fishing, and forestry	158	1,182	242	274

(b) Fastest-growing jobs*	Fastest-declining jobs*
Home health aides	Electrical and electronic equipment assemblers, precision
Systems analysts and computer scientists	Electrical and electronic assemblers
Personal and home care aides	Child care workers, private household
Medical assistants	Textile draw-out and winding machine operators

*Projection for 1990–2005, based on moderate growth assumptions.
Source: *Monthly Labor Review.*

EXHIBIT 7 (a and b)   Employment and Salaries for Various Full-Time Workers (1993) and Occupation Statistics and Trends

elections. People in an economy have a cultural sensibility, or outlook, which limits actions of both government and business.

Households can exert people power to keep government and business in line. Do people accept the existing situation, or do they feel business or government is wrong? To keep people power on their side, U.S. businesses spend a lot of money on public service and advertisements stating that they, the businesses, are good citizens.

Because of the importance of these cultural and social limitations to business (the invisible handshake), you need some sense of which way the invisible handshake will push. While summarizing the sensibility of a country's people is impossible, it is necessary to make the attempt because it is through those sensibilities—through informal, invisible channels—that households exert much of their power on the economy. Thus, in the next section, I will present my view of the sensibility of the American people.

The Social, Cultural, and Ideological Sensibilities of American People

Ideology   Set of values held so deeply that they are not questioned.

Although, as I've pointed out, the actual U.S. economy is best described as welfare capitalism or a mixed economy due to a number of government programs designed to blunt the sharp edge of the market's forces, the American **ideology** (set of values held so deeply that they are not questioned) is, in word if not in deed, ''let the market do it.'' Like apple pie and motherhood, competition and freedom to undertake economic activities are seen as sacred. Small enterprises and entrepreneurships are especially prized, and many people aspire to starting their own business.

Apple pie and motherhood have changed over the years, and so has competition. In the Great Depression of the 1930s, the U.S. population's unbridled faith in the market was tested. Under President Franklin D. Roosevelt's New Deal in the 1930s, numerous government programs were developed to ease the market's harshness. Laws were passed establishing minimum prices at which goods could be sold. Labor was given the right to organize to achieve its ends; a new farm program limited price fluctuations of agricultural goods; a welfare system, including social security programs and unemployment insurance, was established. These laws and programs are generally viewed as good.

With the advent of World War II (1941–45), defense spending zoomed and government spending as a percentage of total U.S. spending increased from less than 10 percent of total U.S. income in the early 1930s to more than 50 percent of total U.S. income in 1944. After the war, that percentage declined, but the march of government programs to regulate the market continued. In the decade following the war, the government sector's role increased further and the economy grew rapidly. In 1946, the government took responsibility for maintaining high employment. In the 1960s and 1970s, the *safety net* (a set of programs that guaranteed individuals a minimum standard of living) was expanded.

Military-industrial complex Combination of defense industries and U.S. armed forces.

During the postwar period there developed what's called a **military-industrial complex** (a combination of defense industry firms and the U.S. armed forces, which have vested interests in keeping defense spending flowing, regardless of whether that spending is good for society). As outside threats to the United States decreased, the military-industrial complex has been squeezed, and defense spending's percentage of the federal budget has been falling in the early 1990s. In the mid-1990s, defense spending has fluctuated around $290 billion (approximately 20 percent of the federal government budget).

The military-industrial complex is the best known of the vested interests trying to protect themselves, but it's not unique. Other groups' vested interests might also be described as complexes. For example, we could say there's a social-educational complex which protects education interests, while a health industry-welfare complex protects medical benefits. These complexes compete for government expenditures.

These developments may seem to go against the cultural and ideological support the American public gives the market. Support for the market and tolerance of vested interests seem contradictory, but people's ideological views need not be consistent, and they often aren't. A new and larger role for government in the market has been accepted by most people. They believe these programs are proper, so now government programs that restrict the market (for example, the social security system) are seen as fundamentally American as is the market.

Compared to other countries, the United States has a relatively strict standard of economic morals.

Another important aspect of a people's sensibility is their view of morality. Compared to other countries, the United States has a relatively strict standard of economic morals—activities such as direct bribery and payoffs are illegal. (In some countries, these activities aren't illegal. In numerous others, they're illegal but openly tolerated.) The U.S. government bureaucracy, while considered by many to be inefficient, is generally thought to be honest and not corrupt; moreover, by international standards it's actually efficient. Around the fringes of standard morality there's still room for influence peddling, discreet payoffs, and trading favors, but by international standards of corruption they're small potatoes.

There's much more to be said about the cultural sensibilities of the American people, but I'll stop here. Those of you unfamiliar with U.S. cultural and social norms can best find out about them by following the newspapers and by having discussions with friends. My goal in presenting this material isn't to cover the American people's social and cultural sensibilities completely—that would take a whole book by itself—but simply to remind you how important they are: How an economy functions, what types of policies can be instituted, and what people's perceptions of the economic problems are, are all shaped by its people's social, cultural, and ideological sensibilities. The invisible handshake is an important determinant of economic events.

GOVERNMENT

6A Two general roles of government are (1) as a referee and (2) as an actor.

The third major U.S. economic institution I'll consider is government. Government plays two general roles in the economy. It's both a referee (setting the rules that determine relations between businesses and households) and an actor (collecting money in taxes and spending that money on its own projects, such as defense and education). Let's first consider government's role as an actor.

Government as an Actor

The United States has a federal government system, which means we have various levels of government (federal, state, and local), each with its own powers. All levels of government combined consume about 30 percent of the country's total output and employ about 17 million individuals. The various levels of government also have a number of programs that redistribute income through taxation or through a variety of social welfare and assistance programs designed to help specific groups.

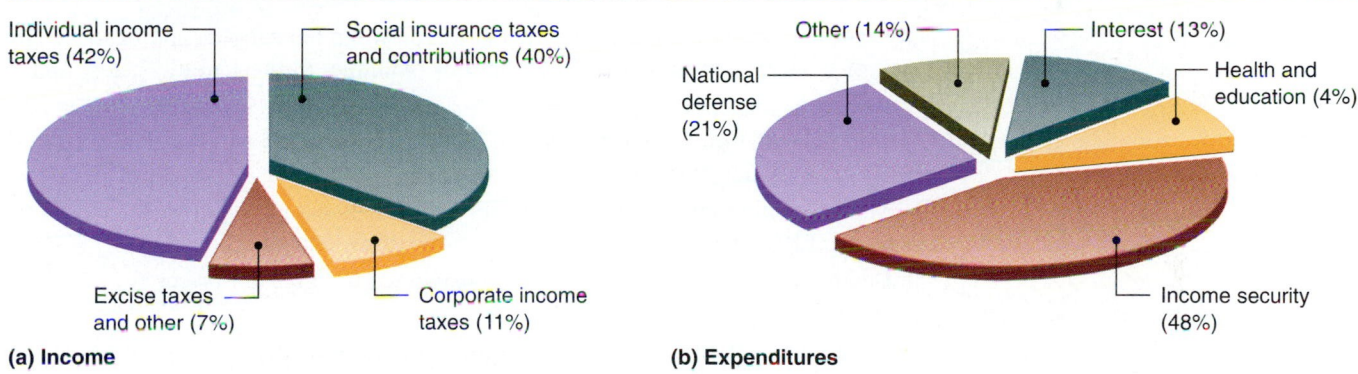

Other (5%)
Insurance trust revenue (8%)
Intergovernmental (21%)
Property tax (21%)
Sales or gross receipts (24%)
Individual and corporation income tax (21%)

(a) Income

Central government administration (6%)
Civilian safety (10%)
Other (13%)
Education (37%)
Highways (8%)
Health and medical (16%)
Public welfare (10%)

(b) Expenditures

EXHIBIT 8 (a and b)   Income and Expenses of State and Local Governments

The charts give you a sense of the importance of state and local government—where they get, **(a)**, and where they spend, **(b)**, their revenues.
Source: *Survey of Current Business,* 1994.

Individual income taxes (42%)
Social insurance taxes and contributions (40%)
Excise taxes and other (7%)
Corporate income taxes (11%)

(a) Income

Other (14%)
Interest (13%)
National defense (21%)
Health and education (4%)
Income security (48%)

(b) Expenditures

EXHIBIT 9 (a and b)   Federal Government Income and Expenditures

The pie diagrams show the sources and uses of federal government revenue.
Source: *Survey of Current Business,* 1994.

State and Local Government   State and local governments employ over 14 million people and spend almost $1 trillion a year. As you can see in Exhibit 8(a), state and local governments get much of their income from taxes: property taxes, sales taxes, and state and local income taxes. They spend their tax revenues on administration, education (education through high school is available free in U.S. public schools), and roads, as Exhibit 8(b) shows. These activities fall within microeconomics, which we'll discuss in the microeconomics sections of this book.

Federal Government   Probably the best way to get an initial feel for the federal government and its size is to look at the various categories of its tax revenues and expenditures in Exhibit 9. Notice income taxes make up about 42 percent of the federal government's revenue, while social security taxes make up about 40 percent. That's more than 80 percent of the federal government's revenues, most of which shows up as a deduction from your paycheck. In Exhibit 9(b), notice the federal government's two largest categories of spending are income maintenance and defense, with expenditures on interest payments close behind.

Interest payments are important because the U.S. government has a large debt. **Debt** is an amount of money that one owes to others. It is a stock concept, which corresponds to the liability portion of a company's balance sheet. The U.S. government has accumulated a large debt, over $4 trillion in the mid-1990s, or over $17,000

Q–8:   The largest percentage of federal expenditure is in what general category?

individual Income tax
Social Security

Debt   *An amount of money one owes to others.*

per U.S. citizen. Interest must be paid on that debt, which explains why the budget's interest component is so high. The national debt has accumulated because the federal government has run almost continual budget deficits since the 1940s. A deficit is a flow concept that corresponds to the net income portion of a company's income statement. A **government budget deficit** occurs when government expenditures exceed government revenues—that is, when tax revenues fall short of budgeted expenditures and the government borrows to make up the difference. A **government budget surplus** occurs when revenues exceed expenditures.

Individuals like government programs that assist them, and they pressure politicians to provide these programs. However, people don't like the taxes they have to pay for those programs, and they put pressure on politicians to lower taxes. These two pressures have resulted in the federal government's significant deficits since the 1940s.

Q–9: A country with a larger debt will also have a larger deficit. True or False? Why?

Government as a Referee

Even if government spending made up only a small proportion of total expenditures, government would still be central to the study of economics. The reason is that, in a market economy, government controls the interaction of business and households. Government sets the rules of interaction and acts as a referee, changing the rules when it sees fit. Government decides whether the invisible hand will be allowed to operate freely.

Government is involved in every interaction between households and business, in the form of laws regulating that interaction. For example, in the United States today:

1. Businesses are not free to hire and fire whomever they want. They must comply with equal opportunity and labor laws. Even closing a plant requires 60 days' notice for many kinds of firms.
2. Many working conditions are subject to government regulation: safety rules, wage rules, overtime rules, hours-of-work rules, and the like.
3. Businesses cannot meet with other businesses to agree on prices they will charge.
4. Workers in a union cannot require all workers in a firm to join the union before they are hired. In many states, they cannot require workers to join the union at all.

Most of these laws evolved over time. Up until the 1930s, household members, in their roles as workers and consumers, had few rights. Businesses were free to hire and fire at will and, if they chose, to deceive and take advantage of consumers.

Over time, laws have changed. New laws to curb business abuses have been passed, and government agencies have been formed to enforce these laws. Now many people think the pendulum has swung too far the other way. They believe businesses are saddled with too many regulatory burdens.

One big question that I'll address throughout this book is: What referee role should the government play in an economy? For example, should government redistribute income from the rich to the poor through taxation? Should it allow a merger between two companies? Should it regulate air traffic? Should it regulate prices?

6B Seven specific roles of government are:
1. Providing a stable structure within which markets can operate.
2. Promoting workable, effective competition.
3. Correcting for external effects of individuals' decisions.
4. Providing public goods that the market doesn't adequately supply.
5. Ensuring economic stability and growth.
6. Providing acceptably fair distribution of society's production among its individuals.
7. Encouraging merit and discouraging demerit goods or activities.

Since considering government's role will be a central element of the entire book, I'll present a few terms and roles now to establish a framework for the later chapters.

Economic Roles of Government   I first consider the economic roles of government. These roles tend to be somewhat less controversial than its political roles.

Providing a Stable Institutional Framework   A basic economic role of government is to provide a stable institutional framework (the set of rules determining what we can and can't do). Before people conduct business, they need to know the rules of the game and have a reasonable belief about what those rules will be in the future. The modern economy requires contractual arrangements to be made among individuals. These arrangements must be enforced if the economy is to operate effectively. Ultimately only the government can create a stable environment and enforce contracts through its legal system. Where governments don't provide a stable environment, as often happens in developing countries, economic growth is difficult; usually such economies are stagnant. Liberia in the early 1990s is an example. As two groups there fought for political control, the Liberian economy stagnated.

Almost all economists believe that providing an institutional framework within which the market can operate is an important function of government. However, they differ significantly as to what the rules for such a system should be. Even if the rules are currently perceived as unfair, an argument can be made for keeping them. Individuals have already made decisions based on the existing rules, so it's unfair to them to change the rules in midstream. Stability of rules is a benefit to society.

Recent economic reforms in the former Soviet Union provide a good example of this point. First, the Soviets modified their rules to encourage profits and entrepreneurship. Within a year they changed the rules again, attacking entrepreneurs as profiteers and confiscating their earnings. Then they began to encourage entrepreneurship again, but the second time few entrepreneurs came forward because of fear that the rules would change once again. Then there was a conservative coup; then a reestablishment of the market. Finally the entire political structure fell apart, and the Soviet Union was no more.

When rules are perceived as unfair and changing them is also perceived as unfair, which often happens, the government finds itself in the difficult position of any referee, trying to strike a balance between the two degrees of unfairness.

Promoting Effective and Workable Competition   One of the most difficult economic functions of government is its role in protecting and promoting competition. As I discussed above, U.S. ideology sees monopoly power as bad. **Monopoly power** is the ability of individuals or firms currently in business to prevent other individuals or firms from entering the same kind of business; thereby monopoly power can raise existing firms' prices. Similarly, U.S. ideology sees **competition** (individuals' or firms' ability to enter freely into business activities) as good. Government's job is to promote competition and prevent monopoly power from limiting competition.

Monopoly power   Ability to prevent others from entering a business field, which enables a firm to raise its price.

Competition   Ability of individuals to freely enter into business activities.

What makes this a difficult function for government is that most individuals and firms believe that competition is far better for the other guy than it is for themselves, that their monopolies are necessary monopolies, and that competition facing them is unfair competition. For example, farmers support competition, but they also support government farm subsidies and import restrictions, which make it harder for foreign individuals to compete in the United States. Likewise, firms support competition, but they also support tariffs which protect them from foreign competition. Professionals, such as architects and engineers, support competition, but they also support professional licensing, which limits the number of competitors who can enter their field.

Correcting for Externalities   When two people freely enter into a trade or agreement, they both believe that they will benefit from that trade. But unless they're required to do so, traders are unlikely to take into account the effect that that agreement or trade may have on others. (An effect of a trade or agreement on a third party that the people who made the trade did not take into account is called an *external effect* or **externality**.) An externality can be positive (in which case society as a whole benefits even more than the two traders) or negative (in which case society as a whole benefits less than the two parties). In either case, externalities provide a potential role for government. If one's goal is to benefit society as much as possible, trades with positive externalities should be encouraged, and trades with negative externalities should be restricted.

Externality   Effect of a trade or agreement on third parties that people did not take into account when they entered the trade or agreement.

An example of a positive externality is education. When someone educates herself or himself, it is not only the person who is helped. All society benefits since better-educated people make better citizens and can often figure out new approaches to solving problems, solutions that benefit everyone.

Q–10:   If there were no externalities, there would be no role for government. True or False? Why?

An example of a negative externality is pollution. For example, when people use air conditioners, they'll probably let loose a small amount of chlorofluorocarbons, which go up into the earth's atmosphere and contribute to the destruction of the ozone layer. The ozone layer protects all living things by filtering some of the sun's ultraviolet light rays, which can contribute to cancer and other harmful or fatal conditions. Neither the firms that produce the air conditioners nor the consumers who buy them pay for the negative effect those chlorofluorocarbons have on society. This means that the destruction of the ozone layer is an externality—the result of an action that is not taken into account by market participants.

When externalities exist, government has a potential role: to step in and change the rules so that the actors must take into account the effect of their actions on society as a whole. I emphasize that the role is a *potential* one, because government often has difficulty dealing with externalities in such a way that society gains. For example, even if the U.S. government totally banned chlorofluorocarbons, the problem wouldn't be solved because ozone layer destruction is an international, rather than a national, problem. I also emphasize *potential* because government isn't simply an institution trying to do good. It's an institution that reflects, and is often guided by, politics and vested interests. It's not clear that, given the political realities, government intervention to correct externalities would improve the situation. In later chapters I'll have a lot more to say about government's role in correcting for externalities.

Public good *Good whose consumption by one individual does not prevent its consumption by other individuals.*

Private good *Good that, when consumed by one individual, cannot be consumed by other individuals.*

Providing for Public Goods   **Public goods** are goods whose consumption by one individual does not prevent their consumption by other individuals. This means that when a supplier supplies a public good to one person, he or she supplies the good to all. In contrast, a **private good** is one that, when consumed by one individual, cannot be consumed by other individuals. An example of a private good is an apple; once I eat that apple, no one else can consume it.

An example of a public good is national defense. National defense must protect all individuals in the country; it cannot protect some people but leave others unprotected. Everyone agrees that national defense is needed. But will everyone, as individuals, supply it, or will everyone rely on someone else doing it? Self-interested people would like to enjoy the benefits of defense, while letting someone else pay for it. Because national defense is a public good, if someone else defends the country you're defended for free; you can be a **free rider.** Everyone has an incentive to be a free rider, but if everyone is a free rider, there won't be any defense. In such cases government can step in to require that everyone pay part of the cost of national defense to make sure that no one is a free rider.

Free rider *Person who participates in something for free because others have paid for it.*

Ensuring Economic Stability and Growth   In addition to providing general stability, government has the potential role of providing economic stability. If it's possible, most people would agree that government should prevent large fluctuations in the level of economic activity; maintain a relatively constant price level; and provide an economic environment conducive to economic growth. These aims, which became U.S. government goals in 1946 when the Employment Act was passed, are generally considered macroeconomic goals. They're justified as appropriate aims for government to pursue because they involve **macroeconomic externalities** (externalities that affect the levels of unemployment, inflation, or growth in the economy as a whole).

Macroeconomic externality *Effect of an individual decision that affects the levels of unemployment, inflation, or growth in an economy as a whole, but is not taken into account by the individual decision maker.*

Here's how a macroexternality could occur. When individuals decide how much to spend, they don't take into account the effects of their decision on others; thus, there may be too much or too little spending. Too little spending often leads to unemployment. But in making their spending decision, people don't take into account the fact that spending less might create unemployment. So their spending decision can involve a macroexternality. Similarly, when people raise their price and don't consider its effect on inflation, they too might be creating a macroexternality.

Political Roles of Government   The other group of possible roles for government, *political roles,* involves more controversial issues.

ADDED DIMENSION

FINDING MORE INFORMATION ABOUT THE ECONOMY

No introductory book is able to provide you with all the information you should have about the economy. You should know about:

- Financial institutions, such as banks, insurance companies, and stock markets.
- The state of the economy: unemployment rates, inflation rates, and growth rates.
- The operations of business, such as advertising and assembly line production.

I'll provide general information on such topics, but you should get up-to-date specifics by following the economic news. Such current information is integral to any economics course. Where should you look? A good beginning is the following:

- Cursory: Business section of your local paper and network news on TV. A slim treatment of the economic issues, but at least it introduces you to the terms.
- One step up from cursory: *Time, Newsweek, U.S. News & World Report;* a national newspaper's business sections (*New York Times, Los Angeles Times, Washington Post*); CNN on TV.
- Reasonably thorough: *Business Week, Forbes, Fortune* magazines; ''Wall Street Week'' and ''The McNeil–Lehrer Report'' on TV.
- Excellent: *The Wall Street Journal, The Economist, The Financial Times.*

Providing for a Fair Distribution of Society's Income   The first, and probably most controversial, of these roles concerns income distribution. Many believe the government should see that the economic system is fair or at least is perceived as fair by the majority of the people in the society.

But determining what's fair is a difficult philosophical question. Let's simply consider two of the many manifestations of the fairness problem. Should the government use a **progressive tax** (a tax whose rates increase as a person's income increases) to redistribute money from the rich to the poor? (A progressive income tax schedule might tax individuals at a rate of 15 percent for income up to $20,000; at 25 percent for income between $20,000 and $40,000; and at 35 percent for every dollar earned over $40,000.) Or should government impose a **regressive tax** (a tax whose rates decrease as income rises) to redistribute money from the poor to the rich? Or should government impose a flat or **proportional tax** (a tax whose rates are constant at all income levels, say 25 percent on every dollar of income, no matter what your total annual income is) and not redistribute money? The United States has chosen a somewhat progressive income tax, while the social security tax is a proportional tax up to a specified earned income.

Another tax question government faces is: Should there be *exemptions* (items of income that aren't taxed at all)? An exemption might be granted for $2,400 of income multiplied by the number of children the taxpayer has. A single mother with five children wouldn't be taxed at all on $12,000 ($2,400 × 5) of her annual income. Or is that a *tax loophole* (a legal but unfair exemption)? Economists can tell government the effects of various types of taxes and forms of taxation, but we can't tell government what's fair. That is for the people, through the government, to decide.

Determining Demerit and Merit Goods or Activities   Another controversial role for government involves deciding what's best for people independently of their desires. The externality justification of government intervention assumes that individuals know what is best for themselves.

But what if people don't know what's best for themselves? What if they do know but don't act on that knowledge? For example, people might know that addictive drugs are bad for them but because of peer pressure, or because they just don't care, they may take addictive drugs anyway. Government action prohibiting such activities through law or high taxes may then be warranted. Goods or activities that are deemed bad for people even though they choose to use the goods or engage in the activities are known as **demerit goods or activities.** The addictive drug is a demerit good; using addictive drugs is a demerit activity.

Demerit goods or activities   Things government believes are bad for you, although you may like them.

Merit goods or activities *Things government believes are good for you, although you may not think so.*

Alternatively, there are some activities that government believes are good for people, even if people may not choose to engage in them. For example, government may believe that going to the opera or contributing to charity is a good activity. But in the United States only a small percentage of the population goes to the opera, and not everyone in the United States contributes to charity. Similarly, government may believe that whole-wheat bread is more nutritious than white bread. But many consumers prefer white bread. Activities and goods that government believes are good for you even though you may not choose to engage in the activities or consume the goods are known as **merit goods or activities,** and government support for them through subsidies or tax benefits may be warranted.

The Limits of Government Action

Economists on all sides of the political spectrum speak in the voice of reason: ''Look at all the costs; look at all the benefits. Then decide whether government should or should not intervene.''

Economic theory doesn't say government should or shouldn't play any particular role in the economy. Those decisions depend on costs and benefits of government action. The public often perceives economic theory and economists as suggesting the best policy is a policy of laissez-faire, or government noninvolvement in the economy. Many economists do suggest a laissez-faire policy, but that suggestion is based on empirical observations of government's role in the past, not on economic theory.

Still, economists as a group generally favor less government involvement than does the general public. I suspect that the reason is that economists are taught to look below the surface at the long-run effect of government actions. They've discovered that the effects of government actions often aren't the intended effects, and that programs frequently have long-run consequences that make the problems worse, not better. Economists, both liberal and conservative, speak in the voice of reason: ''Look at all the costs; look at all the benefits. Then decide whether government should or should not intervene.''

Political pressures often force government to act, regardless of what rational examination suggests. A good example is new air safety regulations after a plane crash. The public generally favors these overwhelmingly. Most economists I know say: ''Wait. Don't act in haste. Consider the benefits and costs that would result.'' After careful consideration, advantages and disadvantages aren't always clear; some economists favor more regulation, some economists favor less regulation—but they all make their assessments on the basis of rational examination, not emotion.

CHAPTER SUMMARY

- The invisible hand doesn't operate in an invisible world. Knowing economics requires knowing real-world information.
- Views about government's appropriate role in the economy have changed over time.
- In the United States, businesses make the *what, how much,* and *for whom* decisions.
- Businesses, households, and government can be categorized in a variety of ways.
- Although businesses decide what to produce, they succeed or fail depending on their ability to meet consumers' desires. That's consumer sovereignty.
- The three main forms of business are corporations, sole proprietorships, and partnerships.
- Income is unequally divided among households. Whether that's bad, and whether anything should be done about it, are debatable.
- Government plays two general roles in the economy: (1) as a referee, and (2) as an actor.

- Government has seven possible economic roles in a capitalist society:

  1. Providing a stable institutional and legal structure within which markets can operate.
  2. Promoting workable and effective competition.
  3. Correcting for external effects of individuals' decisions.
  4. Providing public goods that the market doesn't adequately supply.
  5. Ensuring economic stability and growth.
  6. Providing an acceptably fair distribution of society's products among its individuals.
  7. Encouraging merit and discouraging demerit goods or activities.

- In deciding whether government has a role to play, economists look at the costs and benefits of a given role.

KEY TERMS

business *(82)*
competition *(97)*
consumer sovereignty *(84)*
corporation *(90)*
debt *(95)*
demerit goods or activities *(99)*
entrepreneurship *(83)*
externality *(97)*
free rider *(98)*
government budget deficit *(96)*

government budget surplus *(96)*
households *(91)*
ideology *(93)*
limited liability *(90)*
macroeconomic externality *(98)*
merit goods or activities *(100)*
military-industrial complex *(94)*
monopoly power *(97)*
nonprofit business *(89)*
partnership *(90)*

private good *(98)*
profit *(84)*
progressive tax *(99)*
proportional tax *(99)*
public good *(98)*
regressive tax *(99)*
sole proprietorship *(90)*
stage of production *(85)*
stock *(90)*

QUESTIONS FOR THOUGHT AND REVIEW

The number after each question represents the estimated degree of critical thinking required. (1 = almost none; 10 = deep thought.)

1. A market system is often said to be based on consumer sovereignty—the consumer determines what's to be produced. Yet business decides what's to be produced. Can these two views be reconciled? How? If not, why? *(5)*

2. How many kilometers of highway does the United States have? *(2)*

3. The United States is sometimes classified as a postindustrial society. What's meant by this? And, if it's an accurate classification, is it good or bad to be a postindustrial society? *(7)*

4. A nonprofit company will generally charge lower prices than a for-profit company in the same business because the nonprofit company doesn't factor a profit into its prices. True or false? Why? *(6)*

5. You're starting a software company in which you plan to sell software to your fellow students. What form of business organization would you choose? Why? *(5)*

6. The social security system is inconsistent with pure capitalism, but is almost an untouchable right of Americans. How can this be? *(6)*

7. You've set up the rules for a game and started the game, but now realize that the rules are unfair. Should you change the rules? *(6)*

8. Say the government establishes rights to pollute so that without a pollution permit you aren't allowed to emit pollutants into the air, water, or soil. Firms are allowed to buy and sell these rights. In what way will this correct for an externality? *(9)*

9. What are two general roles of government and seven specific roles? *(3)*

10. According to polls, most U.S. economists classify themselves as liberal, but they generally favor less government involvement in the economy than does the general public. Why? *(6)*

PROBLEMS AND EXERCISES

1. Go to a store in your community.
   a. Ask what limitations the owners faced in starting their business.
   b. Were these limitations necessary?
   c. Should there have been more or fewer limitations?
   d. Under what heading of reasons for government intervention would you put each of the limitations?
   e. Ask what taxes the business pays and what benefits it believes it gets for those taxes.
   f. Is it satisfied with the existing situation? Why? What would it change?

2. You've been appointed to a county counterterrorist squad. Your assignment is to work up a set of plans to stop a group of 10 terrorists the government believes are going to disrupt the economy as much as possible with explosives.
   a. List their five most likely targets in your county, city, or town.

   b. What counterterrorist action would you take?
   c. How would you advise the economy to adjust to a successful attack on each of the targets?

3. The technology is now developing so that road use can be priced by computer. A computer in the surface of the road picks up a signal from your car and automatically charges you for the use of the road.
   a. How could this technological change contribute to ending bottlenecks and rush hour congestion?
   b. What are some of the problems that might develop with such a system?
   c. How would your transportation habits likely change if you had to pay to use roads?

4. Tom Rollins heads a new venture called Teaching Co. He has taped lectures at the top universities, packaged the lectures on audio- and videocassettes, and sells them for $90 and $150 per eight-hour series.

a. Discuss whether such an idea could be expanded to include college courses that one could take at home.

b. What are the technical, social, and economic issues involved?

c. If it is technically possible and cost-effective, will the new venture be a success?

5. In 1938 Congress created a Board of Cosmetology in Washington, D.C., to license beauticians. In 1992 this law was used by the Board to close down a hair-braiding salon specializing in cornrows and braids operated by Mr. Uqdah, even though little is taught in cosmetology schools about braiding and cornrows.

a. What possible reason can you give for why this Board exists?

b. What options might you propose to change the system?

c. What will be the political difficulties of implementing those options?

ANSWERS TO MARGIN QUESTIONS

1. The total railroad mileage in Ghana is 985 kilometers; the information can be found in *The World Fact Book*. *(80)*

2. As a percent of sales, agriculture makes up about 2 percent of the U.S. economy. This information can be found in *The World Fact Book* and also in this book, p. 81. *(82)*

3. Running a successful business in the United States requires a fair amount of paperwork. Businesses are regulated and taxed. I would advise her that she should get a partner or an employee who can deal with such things, be willing to do something she hates, or work for someone else. *(84)*

4. As can be seen in Exhibit 3, the "finance, insurance and real estate" sector is more important when measured by sales. *(85)*

5. As can be seen in Exhibit 5, most businesses in the United States are sole proprietorships, not corporations. Corporations, however, generate the most revenue. *(89)*

6. While profits are important to business, because of internal monitoring problems it is not clear that managers maximize profit. They may waste profit potential in high-priced benefits for themselves and in inefficiency generally. The market, however, provides a limit on inefficiency, and firms that exceed that limit and make losses go out of business. *(90)*

7. As can be seen in Exhibit 6, the average income of an African-American family in 1992 was approximately $18,500. *(92)*

8. The largest percentage of federal expenditure is for income security. *(95)*

9. False. Debt is the accumulated annual deficits, and the current annual deficit has only a slight relationship to the total accumulated debt. A country could be running a current surplus, but have a large debt. *(96)*

10. False. While externalities provide a role for government in many activities, there are other potential roles such as setting up the rules of economic interaction and providing merit goods. *(97)*

Trading in Stocks

Small corporations' stock is usually traded *over-the-counter,* which doesn't mean you go in a store and walk up to the counter. *Over-the-counter* means that the stock is traded in informal markets in which brokers contact other brokers directly. An over-the-counter share has a *bid* price and a higher *ask* price. The bid price is the price someone has offered to pay for shares; the ask price is the price a shareholder has told her brokers she wants to get for her shares. Trades are usually made at some price between the bid and ask figures, with the broker collecting a commission for arranging a trade.

Large corporations' stock is usually traded on a *stock exchange*—a formal market in which stocks are bought and sold. Exhibit A1 shows a typical stock exchange listing. Stocks sold on the New York Stock Exchange have only one price listed. That's because the exchange has a "specialist" market-maker system, in which a particular broker markets a particular group of stocks. This specialist always stands ready to buy or sell shares of a stock at some price. The specialist sets a price and then varies it according to whether he or she is receiving more buy orders or more sell orders.

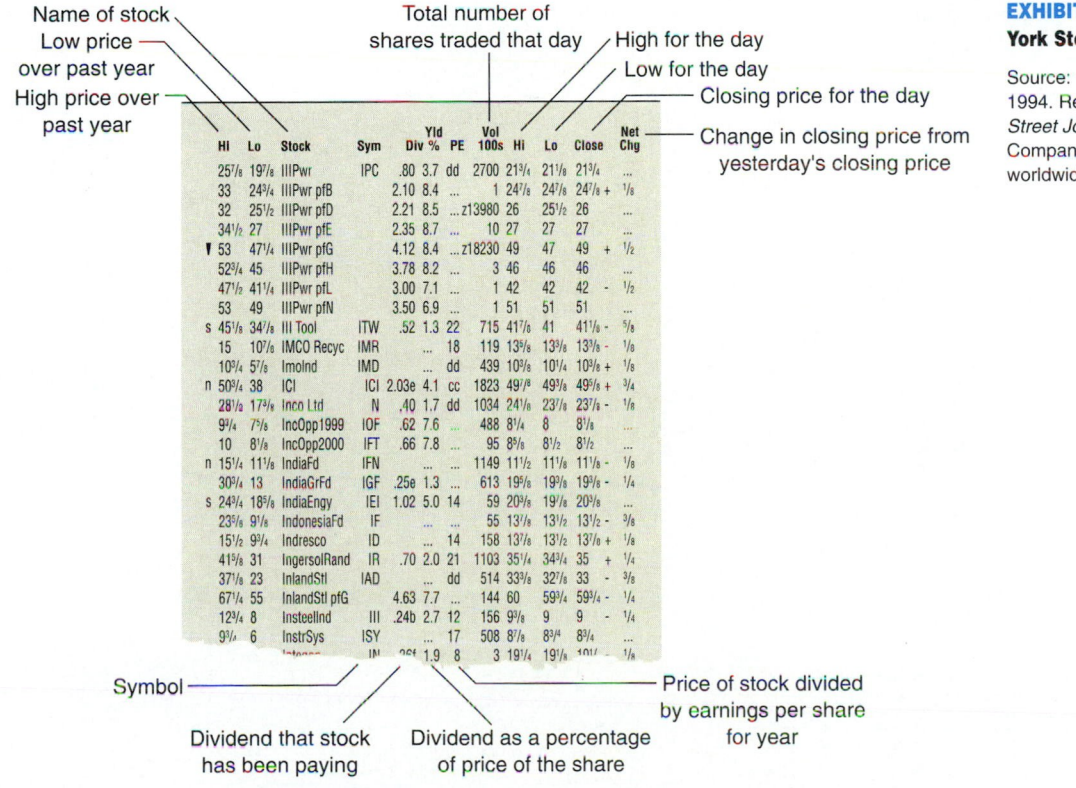

Name of stock
Low price over past year
High price over past year
Total number of shares traded that day
High for the day
Low for the day
Closing price for the day
Change in closing price from yesterday's closing price

Symbol
Dividend that stock has been paying
Dividend as a percentage of price of the share
Price of stock divided by earnings per share for year

EXHIBIT A1 Stock Quotations, New York Stock Exchange

Source: *The Wall Street Journal,* May 6, 1994. Reprinted by permission of *The Wall Street Journal* © 1992 Dow Jones & Company, Inc. All rights reserved worldwide.

In order to buy or sell a New York Stock Exchange stock, you go to a stockbroker and say you want to buy or sell whatever stock you've decided on—say Ford Motor Company. The commission you're charged for having the broker sell you the stock (or sell it for you) varies. Any purchase of fewer than 100 shares of one corporation is called an *odd lot* and you'll be charged a higher commission than if you buy a 100-share lot or more.

There are a number of stock exchanges. The largest and most familiar is the New York Stock Exchange. Somewhere around 50 million individuals own stock they bought on the New York Stock Exchange.

To judge how stocks as a whole are doing, a number of indexes have been developed. These include Standard and Poor's (S&P 500), the Wilshire Index, and the Dow Jones Industrial Average. The Dow Jones is the one you're most likely to hear about in the news.

When a share of a corporation's existing stock is sold on the stock exchange, corporations get no money from that sale. The sale is simply a transfer of ownership from one individual (or organization) to another. The only time a corporation gets money from the sale of stock is when it first issues the shares.

5

An Introduction to the World Economy

As for foreign exchange, it is almost as romantic as young love, and quite as resistant to formulae.

~H. L. Mencken

After reading this chapter, you should be able to:

1 Explain what is meant by *the industrial countries of the world* and *the developing countries of the world.*

2 State where in the world various resources are found and where goods are produced.

3 State two ways international trade differs from domestic trade.

4 Make sense of an exchange rate table in the newspaper.

5 Explain two important causes of a trade deficit.

6 List five important international economic institutions.

7 Give a brief economic history of the European Union and Japan since the 1940s.

International issues must now be taken into account in just about any economic decision a country or a firm faces.

Once there was a time when you could proceed from a discussion of the U.S. economy to a discussion of macroeconomics and microeconomics, the two divisions of economics. No longer. International issues now must also be taken into account in just about every economic decision the United States or a firm in the United States faces. The U.S. economy is now integrated with the world economy, and we cannot reasonably discuss U.S. economic issues without discussing the role that international considerations play in these issues.

Consider the clothes on your back. Most likely they were made abroad. Similarly with the cars you drive. It's likely that half of you drive a car that was made abroad. Of course, it's often difficult to tell. Just because a car has a Japanese or German name doesn't mean that it was produced abroad. Some Japanese and German companies now have manufacturing plants in the United States, and some U.S. firms have manufacturing plants abroad. When goods are produced by **global corporations** (corporations with substantial operations on both the production and sales sides in more than one country are called global, or multinational, corporations), corporate names don't always tell much about where a good is produced. As global corporations' importance has grown, most manufacturing decisions are made in reference to the international market, not the domestic U.S. market.

Global corporation: Corporation with substantial operations on both the production and sales sides in more than one country.

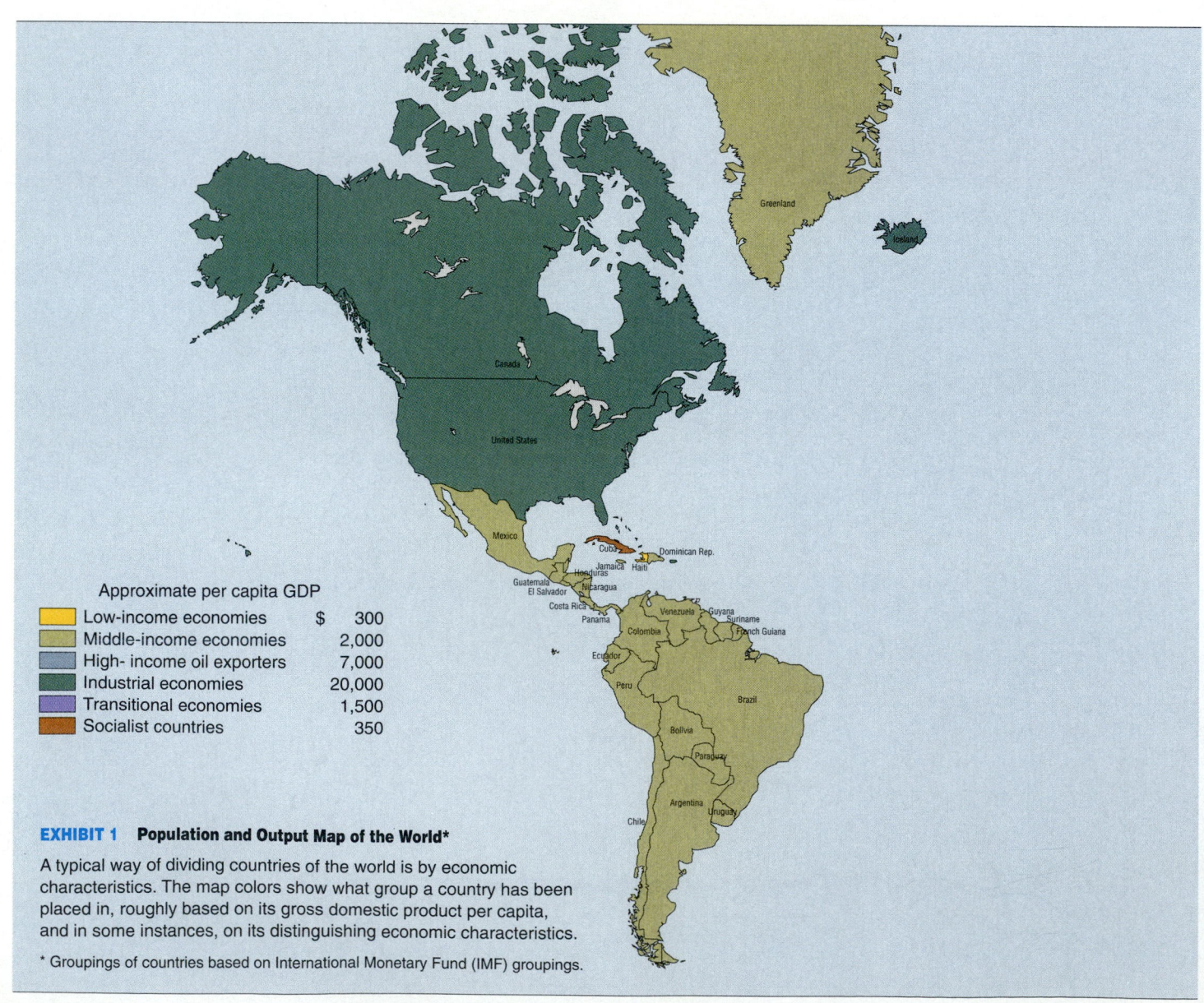

Approximate per capita GDP

🟨 Low-income economies	$	300
🟩 Middle-income economies		2,000
🟦 High- income oil exporters		7,000
🟩 Industrial economies		20,000
🟪 Transitional economies		1,500
🟧 Socialist countries		350

EXHIBIT 1   Population and Output Map of the World*

A typical way of dividing countries of the world is by economic characteristics. The map colors show what group a country has been placed in, roughly based on its gross domestic product per capita, and in some instances, on its distinguishing economic characteristics.

* Groupings of countries based on International Monetary Fund (IMF) groupings.

The economic focus has shifted to the world economy in finance as well as manufacturing. In 1970, the world's 10 largest banks were all headquartered in the United States. Today not even one is in the United States.

The international connection means international economic problems and the policies of other countries—European trade policy, developing countries' debt problems, questions of the United States's competitiveness, transfer of U.S. technology to China, Japanese microeconomic policy, Organization of Petroleum Exporting Countries (OPEC) pricing policies—all have moved to the center of the economic stage. This chapter introduces you to such issues.

In 1993 the ten largest banks in the world were:
1. *Sumitomo*
2. *Dai-Ichi Kangyo*
3. *Sanwa*
4. *Fuji*
5. *Mitsubishi*
6. *Sakura*
7. *Crédit Agricole*
8. *Union Bank of Switzerland*
9. *Industrial Bank of Japan*
10. *HSBC Holdings*

INTERNATIONAL ECONOMIC STATISTICS: AN OVERVIEW

Exhibit 1's map of the world is divided into categories based on per capita output (output per person) and other relevant economic characteristics. *Industrial economies* (such as the United States, Germany, and Britain) have a large industrial production base. A second group of countries, such as Kuwait and Saudi Arabia, have high incomes, but don't have the industrial base. Since their high income is primarily based on oil exports, those countries are known as high-income *oil exporters*. The next two classifications, *middle-income economies* and *low-income economies* (or as they are sometimes called, *developing economies*), make up the majority of countries in the

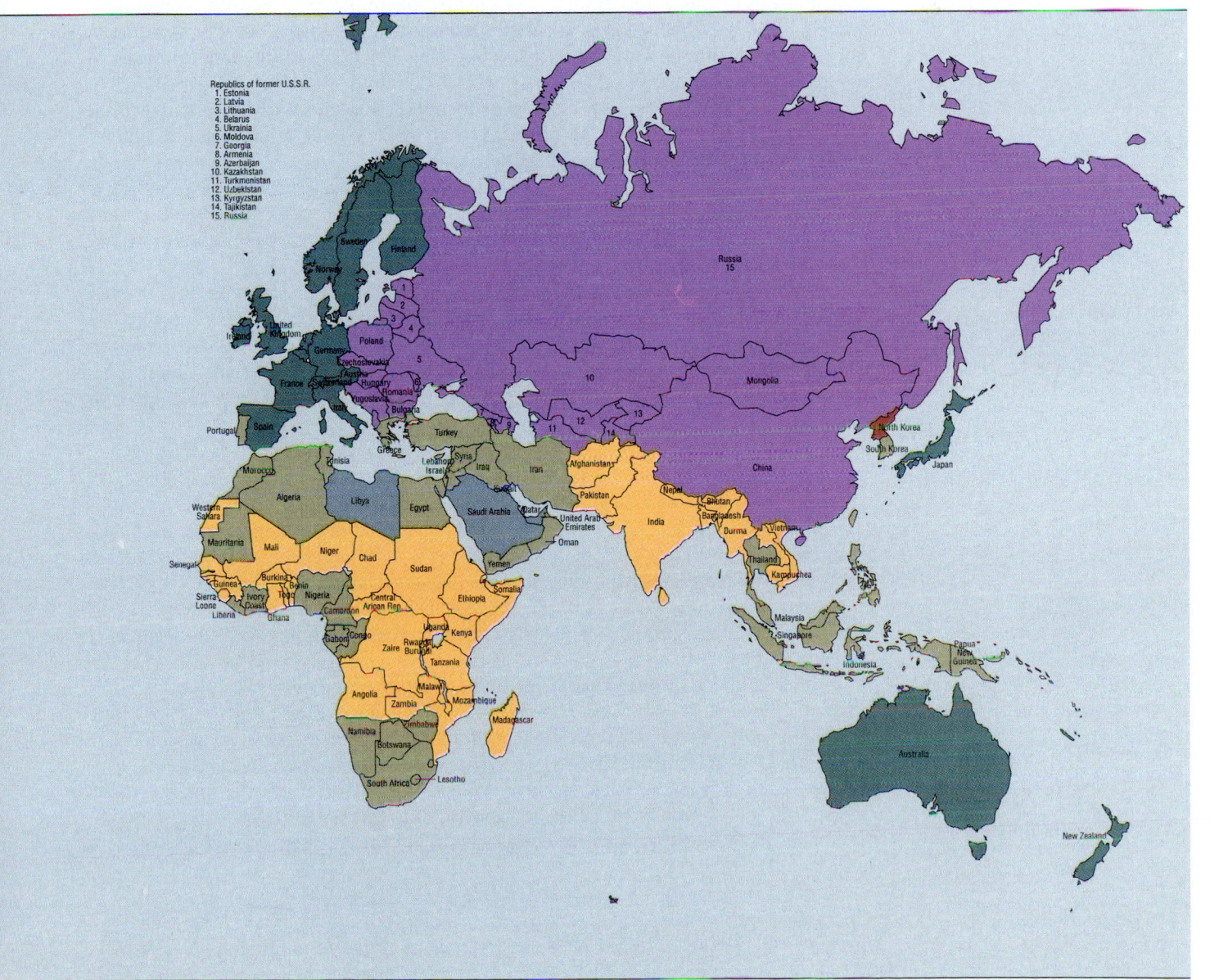

1 The industrial countries of the world have a large industrial base and a per capita income of about $20,000 a year; the developing countries of the world include low- and medium-income economies that have a per capita income of between $300 and $2,000 a year.

world. The *transitional economies* consist of the formerly socialist economies. These economies are in a period of flux and will probably be much in the news in the late 1990s. It is unclear what form of economic organization these transitional economies will take. The final category is *socialist economies;* in the mid-1990s only North Korea and Cuba still fit in this category.

This isn't the only method of classification. An alternative method is by region: Latin American, African, Middle Eastern, Asian, Western European, North American, and Eastern European countries. Since geographically grouped countries often share a cultural heritage, they also often face similar problems.

None of these classifications is airtight. Each country is different from every other, so no grouping works perfectly. Exhibit 1's classification system based largely on output per person is the most commonly used, and should give you a sense of what's meant by such classifications. The next time you hear ''the industrial nations of the world'' or ''the developing countries of the world,'' you should be able to close your eyes and picture the relevant group of economies on a map or, at least, have a general idea of which countries are meant.

Economic Geography

Q–1: On the map in Exhibit 1, Russia looks much larger than Africa. In reality, it isn't. Why does it look larger?

Most classifications are based on a country's total output or production. Production statistics, however, don't necessarily capture a nation's importance or the strategic role it plays in the world economy. Consider Saudi Arabia. Its total output isn't particularly large, but since it's a major supplier of oil to the world, its strategic importance goes far beyond the relative size of its economy. Without its oil, many of the industrial countries of the world would come to a grinding halt. Similarly, Panama's production is minuscule, but its location on a narrow isthmus between the Atlantic and Pacific Oceans and the fact that the Panama Canal runs through its territory make Panama vital to the world economy.

These examples demonstrate why we need, besides a knowledge of countries' productive capacities, a knowledge of economic geography: Where do the world's natural resources lie? Which countries control them? What are the major trade routes? How are goods shipped from one place to another?

Exhibit 2 locates some of the world's major energy resources and trade routes. Note the major flow of energy resources from the Middle East: You can see why it is so important to the world economy (oil and the Suez Canal). Other such resource maps would show why many countries treat South Africa with care (gold, many other alloying metals, and diamonds) and why Chile (with about 27 percent of all copper) is important to the world economy.

2 Some major producing areas for some important raw materials are:
Aluminum—Guinea, Australia
Cobalt—Zaire, Zambia, Russia
Copper—Chile, U.S., Poland
Iron—Russia, Brazil, Australia
Zinc—Canada, Australia, Russia

Differing Economic Problems

The economic problems countries face are determined by a variety of factors such as per capita income levels. High-income countries generally face quite different problems than low-income countries. Even two countries within the same group often face different problems. For example, a significant U.S. problem is its trade deficit. As I'll discuss later in the chapter, the United States **imports** (buys goods produced in foreign countries) much more than it **exports** (sells U.S. goods to foreign countries). A significant Japanese problem is its trade surplus; Japan exports much more than it imports.

Q–2: If you were tracing the flow of copper trade in a map like the one in Exhibit 2, where would you find the information?

Although the identical economic insights apply to all countries, institutions differ substantially among countries. For example, many developing countries have few financial institutions, so when people there want to save, there's no way for them to do so. Similarly with transportation systems. If a firm wants to ship a good from Kansas City to Seattle, it can use trucks, trains, or planes. However, if an African firm wants to ship a good from one city to another in Zaire—say from Kinshasa to Lubumbashi—it must import trucks that can travel on unpaved or even nonexistent roads.

Comparative Advantage and Trade

One reason economies differ is that they produce different goods. Why? That's a question I'll explore in some detail in a later chapter on international trade. For now, I'll simply introduce you to a key term in international trade which plays a major role

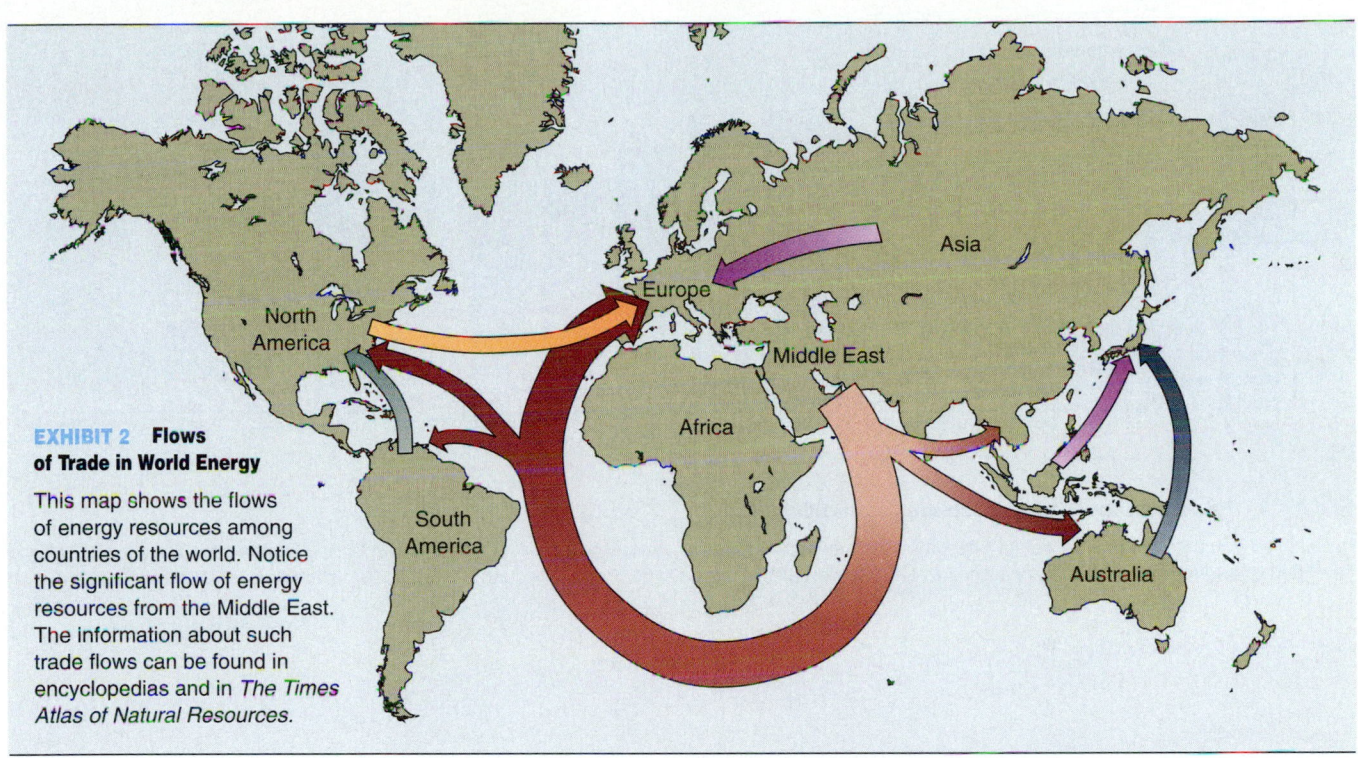

EXHIBIT 2 Flows of Trade in World Energy

This map shows the flows of energy resources among countries of the world. Notice the significant flow of energy resources from the Middle East. The information about such trade flows can be found in encyclopedias and in *The Times Atlas of Natural Resources.*

in what different countries produce. That term is **comparative advantage.** A country has a comparative advantage in producing a good if it can produce that good at a lower opportunity cost (forgone production of another good) than another country can.

For example, say the United States can produce widgets at a cost of $4 apiece and wadgets at $4 apiece, while Korea can produce widgets at a cost of 300 won apiece and wadgets at a cost of 100 won apiece. In the United States, the opportunity cost of one widget is one wadget. (Since each costs $4, the United States must reduce its production of wadgets by one to produce another widget.) In Korea, the opportunity cost of a widget is three wadgets since it costs three times as much to produce a widget as it does to produce a wadget. Because the United States's opportunity cost of producing widgets is lower than Korea's, the United States is said to have a comparative advantage in producing widgets. Similarly, Korea is said to have a comparative advantage in producing wadgets because its opportunity cost of wadgets is one-third of a widget while the United States' opportunity cost of wadgets is one widget.

If one country has a comparative advantage in one good, the other country must necessarily have a comparative advantage in the other good. Notice how comparative advantage hinges on opportunity cost, not total cost. Even if one country can produce all goods cheaper than another country, trade between them is still possible since the opportunity costs of various goods differ.

Countries not only produce different goods, they also consume different goods. Exhibit 3 presents per capita consumption of some goods in selected countries. Notice the differences. The United States ranks high in per capita consumption of beef and veal, but low in consumption of pork. One reason for the differences is that goods' relative prices differ among countries. The United States and Argentina produce lots of beef, so the price of beef is low in these countries and consumption is high. Germany produces lots of pigs, so the price of pork is low and Germans consume lots of pork. Such differences are consistent with economic explanations.

Other differences in consumption (and production) are explained by custom, history, and tradition. For example, Japanese traditionally eat rice with meals; Americans eat bread and potatoes. Drinking alcoholic beverages in Russia is a time-honored tradition; Muslim countries, such as Saudi Arabia, forbid consumption of alcoholic beverages. Understanding international economic issues often requires an in-depth understanding of various countries' histories and cultures.

A country has a comparative advantage in a good if it can produce that good at a lower opportunity cost than another country can. (Remember it is a lower opportunity cost, not necessarily a lower absolute cost.)

Differences in per capita consumption are explained by relative prices, customs, history, and tradition.

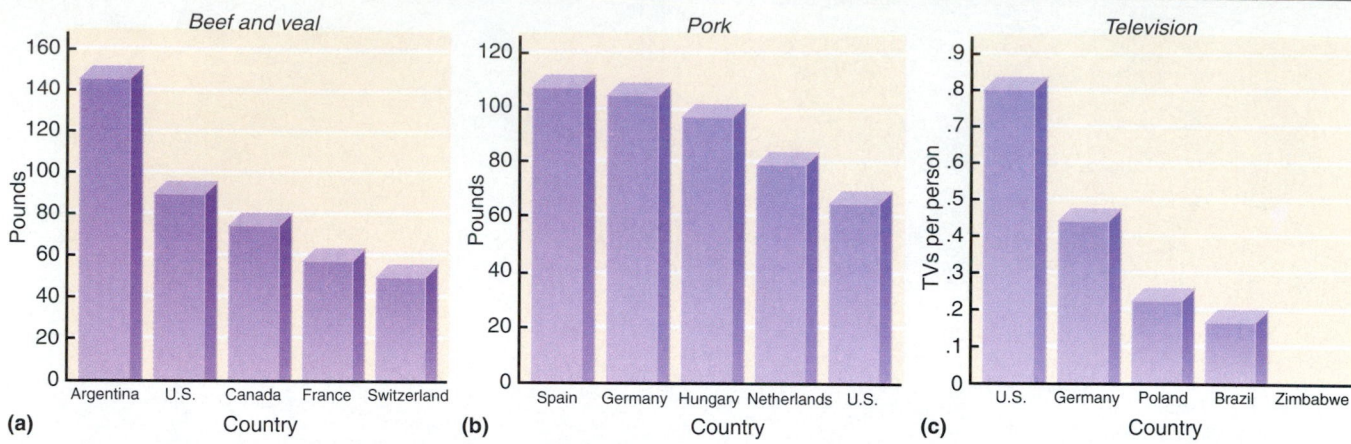

EXHIBIT 3   **Per Capita Consumption of Different Commodities, 1990**

In Exhibit 3 you can see the per capita consumption of selected goods in various countries. Notice that the United States consumes less beef and veal than does Argentina, and its consumption of pork is small compared to all the other countries, but its "consumption" of television is large.

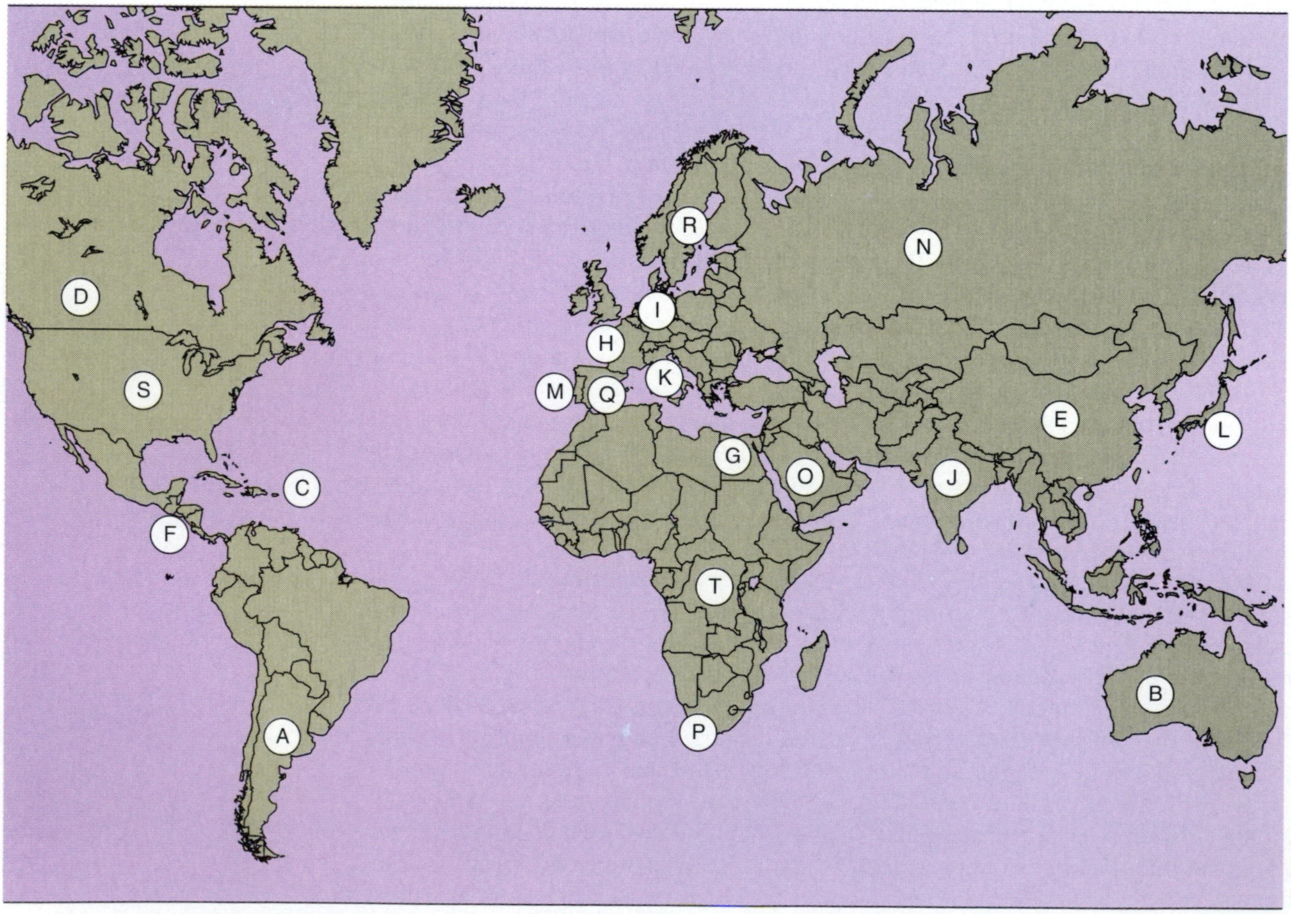

A WORLD ECONOMIC GEOGRAPHY QUIZ

Economic geography isn't much covered in most economics courses because it requires learning enormous numbers of facts, and college courses aren't a good place to learn facts. College is designed to teach you how to interpret and relate facts. Unfortunately, if you don't know facts, much of what you learn in college isn't going to do you much good. You'll be relating and interpreting air. The following quiz presents some facts about the world economy. On the left I list characteristics of countries or regions. On the right I list 20 countries or regions. Associate the characteristics with the country or region.

If you answer 15 or more correctly, you have a reasonably good sense of economic geography. If you don't, I strongly suggest learning more facts. The study guide has other projects, information, and examples. An encyclopedia has even more, and your library has a wealth of information. You could spend the entire semester acquiring facts. I'm not suggesting that; I am suggesting following the economic news carefully, paying attention to where various commodities are produced, and picturing in your mind a map whenever you hear about an economic event.

_____ 1. Former British colony, now small independent island country famous for producing rum.

_____ 2. Large sandy country contains world's largest known oil reserves.

_____ 3. Very large country with few people produces 25 percent of the world's wool.

_____ 4. Temperate country ideal for producing wheat, soybeans, fruits, vegetables, wine, and meat.

_____ 5. Small tropical country produces abundant coffee and bananas.

_____ 6. Has world's largest population and world's largest hydropower potential.

_____ 7. Second–largest country in Europe; famous for wine and romance.

_____ 8. Former Belgian colony has vast copper mines.

_____ 9. European country; exports luxury clothing, footwear, and automobiles.

_____ 10. Large country that has depleted many of its own resources but has enough coal to last its people for hundreds of years.

_____ 11. Long, narrow country of four islands; most thickly populated country in the world; exports majority of the world's electronic products.

_____ 12. Recently politically reunified country; one important product is steel.

_____ 13. Second-largest country in the world; a good neighbor to the United States; leading paper exporter.

_____ 14. European country for centuries politically repressed; now becoming industrialized; chemicals are one of its leading exports.

_____ 15. 96 percent of its people live on 4 percent of the land; much of the world's finest cotton comes from here.

_____ 16. Politically and racially troubled African nation has world's largest concentration of gold.

_____ 17. Huge, heavily populated country eats most of what it raises but is a major tea exporter.

_____ 18. Large country that produces oil and gold; has recently undergone major political and economic changes.

_____ 19. Has only about 50 people per square mile but lots of trees; timber and fish exporter.

_____ 20. Sliver of a country on Europe's Atlantic coast; by far the world's largest exporter of cork.

a. Argentina
b. Australia
c. Barbados
d. Canada
e. China
f. Costa Rica
g. Egypt
h. France
i. Germany
j. India
k. Italy
l. Japan
m. Portugal
n. Russia
o. Saudi Arabia
p. South Africa
q. Spain
r. Sweden
s. United States
t. Zaire

Answers: 1–c, 2–o, 3–b, 4–a, 5–f, 6–e, 7–h, 8–t, 9–k, 10–s, 11–l, 12–i, 13–d, 14–q, 15–g, 16–p, 17–j, 18–n, 19–r, 20–m.

HOW INTERNATIONAL TRADE DIFFERS FROM DOMESTIC TRADE

3 Two ways in which *inter*national trade differs from *intra*national (domestic) trade are:
(1) International trade involves potential barriers to trade; and
(2) International trade involves multiple currencies.

Q–3: What is the difference between a quota and a tariff?

Foreign exchange market Market in which one currency can be exchanged for another.

4 By looking at an exchange rate table, you can determine how much various goods will likely cost in different countries.

Q–4: You are going to Chile and plan to exchange $100. Based on Exhibit 4, how many Chilean pesos will you receive?

*Inter*national trade differs from *intra*national (domestic) trade in two ways. First, international trade involves potential barriers to the flow of inputs and outputs. Before they can be sold in the United States, international goods must be sent through U.S. Customs; that is, when they enter the United States they are inspected by U.S. officials and usually charged fees, known as *customs*. A company in Texas can produce output to sell in any U.S. state without worrying that its right to sell will be limited; a producer outside the U.S. boundary cannot. At any time, a foreign producer's right to sell in the United States can be limited by government-imposed **quotas** (limitations on how much of a good can be shipped into a country), **tariffs** (taxes on imports), and **nontariff barriers** (indirect regulatory restrictions on imports and exports).

The last category, indirect regulatory restrictions on imports and exports, may be unfamiliar to you, so let's consider an example. U.S. building codes require that plywood have fewer than, say, three flaws per sheet. Canadian building codes require that plywood have fewer than, say, five flaws per sheet. The different building codes are a nontariff barrier, making trade in building materials between the United States and Canada difficult.

The second way international trade differs from domestic or intranational trade is countries' use of different currencies. When people in one country sell something to people in another, they must find a way to exchange currencies as well as goods. **Foreign exchange markets** (markets where one currency can be exchanged for another) have developed to provide this service.

How many dollars will an American have to pay to get a given amount of the currency of another country? That depends on the supply of and demand for that currency. To find what you'd have to pay, you look in the newspaper for the exchange rate set out in a foreign exchange table. Exhibit 4 shows such a table.

If you want shekels, you'll have to pay about 33¢ apiece. If you want Punt, one Punt will cost you $1.44. (If you're wondering what shekels and Punt are, look at Exhibit 4.)

Unless you collect currencies, the reason you want the currency of another country is that you want to buy something that country produces or an existing asset of that country. Say you want to buy a Hyundai car that costs 9,684,000 South Korean won. Looking at the table you see that the exchange rate is $1 for 807 won. Dividing 807 into 9,684,000 won tells you that you need $12,000 to buy the car. So before you can buy the Hyundai, somebody must go to a foreign exchange market with $12,000 and exchange those dollars for 9.68 million won. Only then can the car be bought in the United States. Most final buyers don't do this; the importer does it for them. But whenever a foreign good is bought, someone must trade currencies.

THE U.S. INTERNATIONAL TRADE DEFICIT

Balance of trade Difference between the value of the goods and services a country buys from abroad and those it sells abroad.

One reason a U.S. economics course must consider international issues early on is the U.S. **balance of trade** (the difference between the value of the goods a country imports and the value of the goods it exports). When imports exceed exports, a country is running a **trade deficit;** when exports exceed imports, a country is running a **trade surplus.**

Exhibit 5 shows that since the mid-1970s the United States has been running a trade deficit, which increased substantially in the late 1980s. Although it declined a bit in the early 1990s, most economists consider the trade deficit a figure to watch. In 1987, when the trade deficit was at its highest, U.S. imports were about 9 percent of its total output; exports were about 6 percent. The 3 percent difference meant the United States imported about $170 billion worth of goods more than it exported.

Debtor and Creditor Nations

Running a trade deficit isn't necessarily bad. In fact, while you're doing it, it's rather nice. If you were a country, you probably would be running a trade deficit now since, most likely, you're consuming (importing) more than you're producing (exporting). How can you do that? By living off past savings, getting support from your parents or a spouse, or borrowing.

EXCHANGE RATES

Wednesday, March 23, 1994

The New York foreign exchange selling rates below apply to trading among banks in amounts of $1 million and more, as quoted at 3 p.m. Eastern time by Bankers Trust Co., Dow Jones Telerate Inc. and other sources. Retail transactions provide fewer units of foreign currency per dollar.

Country	U.S. $ equil. Wed.	U.S. $ equil. Tues.	Currency per U.S. $ Wed.	Currency per U.S. $ Tues.
Argentina (Peso)	1.01	1.01	.99	.99
Australia (Dollar)	.7120	.7081	1.4045	1.4122
Austria (Schilling)	.08448	.08420	11.84	11.88
Bahrain (Dinar)	2.6525	2.6525	.3770	.3770
Belgium (Franc)	.02882	.02873	34.70	34.80
Brazil (Cruzeiro real)	.0012074	.0012236	828.20	817.25
Britain (Pound)	1.4965	1.4880	.6682	.6720
30-Day Forward	1.4946	1.4862	.6691	.6729
90-Day Forward	1.4917	1.4836	.6704	.6740
180-Day Forward	1.4890	1.4815	.6716	.6750
Canada (Dollar)	.7330	.7313	1.3643	1.3675
30-Day Forward	.7325	.7308	1.3651	1.3684
90-Day Forward	.7314	.7297	1.3672	1.3704
180-Day Forward	.7299	.7276	1.3701	1.3743
Czech. Rep. (Koruna)				
Commercial rate	.0338570	.0338604	29.5360	29.5330
Chile (Peso)	.002395	.002395	417.60	417.60
China (Renminbi)	.114931	.114931	8.7009	8.7009
Colombia (Peso)	.001218	.001218	820.91	820.91
Denmark (Krone)	.1512	.1508	6.6134	6.6296
Ecuador (Sucre)				
Floating rate	.000476	.000476	2099.03	2099.03
Finland (Markka)	.17954	.18034	5.5699	5.5451
France (Franc)	.17393	.17355	5.7495	5.7620
30-Day Forward	.17352	.17314	5.7630	5.7756
90-Day Forward	.17285	.17253	5.7853	5.7960
180-Day Forward	.17219	.17188	5.8075	5.8181
Germany (Mark)	.5944	.5924	1.6825	1.6880
30-Day Forward	.5932	.5913	1.6858	1.6913
90-Day Forward	.5914	.5897	1.6909	1.6959
180-Day Forward	.5897	.5881	1.6958	1.7005
Greece (Drachma)	.004060	.004058	246.30	246.45
Hong Kong (Dollar)	.12945	.12945	7.7250	7.7250
Hungary (Forint)	.0097069	.0097059	103.0200	103.0300
India (Rupee)	.03212	.03212	31.13	31.13
Indonesia (Rupiah)	.0004655	.0004655	2148.04	2148.04
Ireland (Punt)	1.4398	1.4334	.6945	.6976
Israel (Shekel)	.3346	.3346	2.9890	2.9890
Italy (Lira)	.0006010	.0005995	1663.82	1668.17

Country	U.S. $ equil. Wed.	U.S. $ equil. Tues.	Currency per U.S. $ Wed.	Currency per U.S. $ Tues.
Japan (Yen)	.009399	.009436	106.39	105.98
30-Day Forward	.009409	.009445	106.29	105.87
90-Day Forward	.009436	.009473	105.98	105.57
180-Day Forward	.009484	.009522	105.44	105.02
Jordan (Dinar)	1.4556	1.4556	.6870	.6870
Kuwait (Dinar)	3.3538	3.3538	.2982	.2982
Lebanon (Pound)	.000589	.000589	1696.50	1696.50
Malaysia (Ringgit)	3.672	.3670	2.7235	2.7245
Malta (Lira)	2.5641	2.5641	.3900	.3900
Mexico (Peso)				
Floating rate	.3003003	.3014772	3.3300	3.3170
Netherland (Guilder)	.5286	.5269	1.8918	1.8978
New Zealand (Dollar)	.5705	.5685	1.7528	1.7590
Norway (Krone)	.1368	.1363	7.3105	7.3374
Pakistan (Rupee)	.0329	.0329	30.40	30.40
Peru (New Sol)	.4759	.4759	2.10	2.10
Philippines (Peso)	.03690	.03690	27.10	27.10
Poland (Zloty)	.00004535	.00004522	22052.00	22113.00
Portugal (Escudo)	.005769	.005743	173.35	174.12
Saudi Arabia (Riyal)	.26668	.26668	3.7498	3.7498
Singapore (Dollar)	.6305	.6307	1.5860	1.5855
Slovak Rep. (Koruna)	.0305344	.0305530	32.7500	32.7300
South Africa (Rand)				
Commercial rate	.2903	.2903	3.4498	3.4448
Financial rate	.2157	.2170	4.6350	4.6075
South Korea (Won)	.0012384	.0012389	807.50	807.20
Spain (Peseta)	.007254	.007217	137.85	138.57
Sweden (Krona)	.1272	.1271	7.8598	7.8703
Switzerland (Franc)	.7003	.7006	1.4279	1.4273
30-Day Forward	.6999	.7002	1.4288	1.4281
90-Day Forward	.6998	.7002	1.4290	1.4281
180-Day Forward	.7005	.7011	1.4275	1.4263
Taiwan (Dollar)	.037887	.037887	26.39	26.39
Thailand (Baht)	.03949	.03949	25.32	25.32
Turkey (Lira)	.0000461	.0000464	21674.31	21574.40
United Arab (Dirham)	.2723	.2723	3.6725	3.6725
Uruguay (New Peso)				
Financial	.213447	.213447	4.69	4.69
Venezuela (Bolivar)				
Floating rate	.00878	.00878	113.96	113.96
SDR	1.39837	1.40040	.71512	.71408
ECU	1.14530	1.14150	...	...

Special Drawing Rights (SDR) are based on exchange rates for the U.S., German, British, French and Japanese currencies. Source: International Monetary Fund.

European Currency Unit (ECU) is based on a basket of community currencies.

EXHIBIT 4   A Foreign Exchange Rate Table

From the exchange rate table, you learn how much a dollar is worth in other countries. For example, on this day, March 23, 1994, one dollar would buy 5.7495 French francs or 106.39 yen. The table also tells you how many dollars other currencies can buy. For example, one British pound could buy 1.4965 dollars.

Source: Reprinted by permission of *The Wall Street Journal* © 1994 Dow Jones & Company, Inc. All rights reserved worldwide.

EXHIBIT 5   U.S. Trade Balance

The balance of trade is the difference between the value of goods a country imports and the value of goods it sells abroad, or exports. As you can see from the graph, since the early 1980s the United States has imported many more goods than it has exported. Thus, economists say the United States is running a trade deficit. As you can see, the trade deficit declined somewhat in the early 1990s, but it remained large.
Source: U.S. Dept. of Commerce.

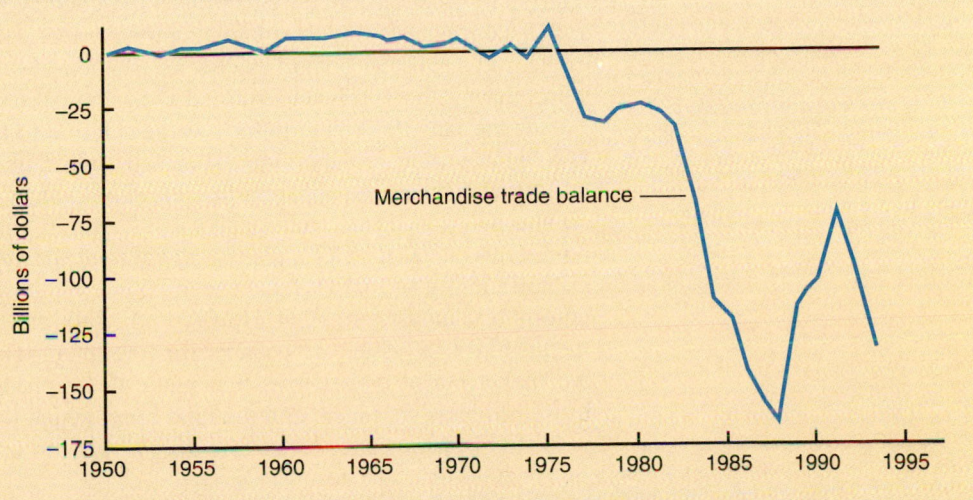

Q–5: Will a debtor nation necessarily be running a trade deficit?

Countries have the same options. They can live off foreign aid, past savings, or loans. For example, the U.S. economy is currently financing its trade deficit by selling off assets—financial assets such as stocks and bonds, or real assets such as real estate and corporations. Since the assets of the United States total many trillions of dollars, it can continue to run trade deficits of similar size for decades to come.

The United States has not always run a trade deficit. Following World War II it ran large trade surpluses with the other countries, so it was an international lender. Thus, it acquired large amounts of foreign assets. Because of the large trade deficits the United States ran in the 1980s, now the United States is a large debtor nation. The United States has borrowed more from abroad than it has lent abroad.

As the United States has gone from being a large creditor nation to being the world's biggest debtor, international considerations have been forced upon us. The cushion of being a creditor—of having a flow of interest income—has been replaced by the trials of being a debtor and having to pay out interest every year without getting anything for it.

Determinants of the Trade Deficit

5 Two important causes of a trade deficit are:
1. A country's competitiveness; and
2. The relative state of a country's economy.

Competitiveness A country's ability to produce goods and services more cheaply than other countries.

In determining the size of the trade deficit, two factors are important:

1. U.S. competitiveness and the value of the dollar.
2. The state of the U.S. economy compared to that of other countries.

Let's look at each factor.

U.S. Competitiveness   Probably the single most important issue in determining whether a country runs a trade deficit or a trade surplus is its **competitiveness** (the ability to produce goods more cheaply than other countries). Competitiveness depends upon productivity—a country's output per worker and its technological innovativeness (its ability to develop new and different products).

In the 1960s and early 1970s, the United States was highly competitive. Even though U.S. workers were paid substantially more than foreign workers, U.S. goods were cheaper, better, and more desired than foreign goods. In the 1950s, the label MADE IN JAPAN was a sign of low-quality, cheap goods. That has changed since the late 1970s. While the United States lost its competitive edge, Japan gained one. Today MADE IN JAPAN is a sign of quality.

Japan's rise from a defeated country after World War II, with few natural resources, little land, and a devastated economy, into an international economic power that outcompetes the United States in many aspects of economics was an important economic story of the 1980s. One reason for Japan's rise was cultural. Another reason was the relative values of the Japanese yen and U.S. dollar. Throughout much of the 1960s, 1970s, and 1980s, the yen's relative value was low. A major determinant of a country's competitiveness is the value of its currency. A currency that is low in value relative to other currencies encourages the country's exports by lowering their prices and discourages its imports by raising their prices. (In 1965, $1 bought about 300 yen; in the mid-1990s, $1 bought as little as 100 yen.) Similarly, the dollar's relatively high value during the 1960s undermined U.S. competitiveness.

In the late 1980s the dollar's value relative to the yen fell substantially, making U.S. goods more competitive. That fall didn't immediately reduce the U.S. trade deficit, and it became apparent that the problems of the United States in international competitiveness have additional causes. But it did eventually help improve U.S. competitiveness. By 1993, the rise in value of the yen had pushed Japanese car prices up sufficiently so that U.S. cars seemed like bargains, causing a recovery of the U.S. automobile industry in 1994. However, the fall in the dollar's value has a downside: It means that U.S. assets are cheaper for foreigners. They can buy not only the products we make, but also the firms that make those products, the buildings within which those products are made, and the land upon which those buildings stand. In the 1990s we'll likely hear much about foreigners "buying up America."

BLACK AND GRAY MARKETS IN CURRENCY

Foreign exchange markets are a good example of supply and demand forces at work. Whenever there's excess supply or demand for something, there's incentive for suppliers and demanders to get together to eliminate the excess.

Let's consider the issue in relation to the former Soviet Union. In 1989, at the official price of 0.64 rubles per dollar, the quantity of dollars demanded far exceeded the quantity of dollars supplied. In the former Soviet Union, adventurous individuals (who weren't worried about the wrath of the invisible foot—that is, about being prosecuted for violating foreign exchange laws) traded in a black market at a higher price, which in 1990 was 30 rubles per dollar.

A black market, which involves trades of a good that can't legally be traded, is a natural result of government price restrictions. Often the government knows that such trading goes on and chooses, for political reasons, not to enforce its own laws strictly. (There are situations like this in the United States. Here the speed limit is 55 miles per hour on many roads, but almost everyone drives at 65 miles per hour, which police tend to accept as a fact of life.)

When a black market is unofficially condoned, trading on it becomes more open and it's often called a *gray market*. Since risk of prosecution is less, upward pressure on price from the invisible foot is less; so gray market prices are usually closer to the supply/demand equilibrium than are black market prices.

The Soviet foreign exchange market became a gray market in late 1989. (The gray market price of a dollar was between 5 and 15 rubles rather than the .64 rubles you'd get at the official rate.) If you went to the former Soviet Union at that time, individuals would come up to you on the street and offer to trade rubles for dollars at something near the gray market price. In 1991 the Soviet Union broke apart and Russia began to let the ruble be freely tradable. Because of political and economic problems, however, the ruble's value fell enormously and it took thousands of rubles to get one dollar.

The State of the U.S. Economy   A second factor in determining the trade balance is the state of the economy. The level of U.S. income affects the trade balance, and the trade balance affects the level of U.S. income. The reason for the first effect is simple. Say the United States is running a trade deficit. When U.S. income rises, the U.S. imports more, so the trade deficit increases.

The second effect—the trade balance's effect on U.S. income—isn't so simple. Say the United States has a trade deficit. When the United States imports more (or exports less), the trade deficit worsens and the rise in imports means U.S. production falls, which means U.S. citizens have less income; they spend less and U.S. income falls even more. So an increase in the trade deficit lowers income. It also works the opposite way: When the United States exports more (imports less), U.S. production rises; as U.S. production rises, U.S. citizens have more income; they spend more and U.S. income rises even more. This effect of exports on domestic income is what economists mean when they say a country has "export-led growth." A country with export-led growth has a trade surplus which stimulates growth in income.

Large trade deficits often inspire politicians to call for trade restrictions prohibiting imports. Most economists, liberal and conservative alike, generally oppose such restrictions. The reason is that even though trade restrictions directly decrease the trade deficit, they also have negative effects on the economy that work in the opposite direction.

One negative effect is that trade restrictions reduce domestic competition. When a group of U.S. producers can't compete with foreign producers—either in price or in quality—that group often pushes for trade restrictions to prevent what they call "unfair" foreign competition. U.S. producers benefit from the trade restrictions, but consumers are hurt. Prices to consumers rise and the quality of the goods they buy falls.

A second negative effect is that trade restrictions bring retaliation. If one country limits imports, the other country responds; the first country responds to that . . . The result is called a *trade war,* and a trade war hurts everyone.

Such a trade war occurred in the 1930s and significantly contributed to the Great Depression of that period. To prevent trade wars, countries have entered into a variety

Economists' View of Trade Restrictions

Q–6: What are two reasons economists generally oppose trade restrictions?

of international agreements. The most important is the **General Agreement on Tariffs and Trade (GATT),** in which countries agree not to impose new tariffs or other trade restrictions except under certain limited conditions.

True to form, the U.S. trade deficit of the 1980s and 1990s has brought about significant political pressure for import restrictions on foreign goods—especially Japanese goods. Supporters of trade restrictions against Japan argue that GATT isn't fair, that Japan has many more barriers to U.S. goods than the United States has barriers to Japanese goods. Japan bashing in the United States, and United States bashing in Japan, have become common, and a trade war between the two countries is a definite possibility.

INTERNATIONAL ECONOMIC POLICY AND INSTITUTIONS

Just as international trade differs from domestic trade, so does international economic policy differ from domestic economic policy. When economists talk about U.S. economic policy, they generally refer to what the U.S. federal government can do to achieve certain goals. In theory, at least, the U.S. federal government has both the power and the legal right of compulsion to make U.S. citizens do what it says. It can tax, it can redistribute income, it can regulate, and it can enforce property rights.

There is no international counterpart to a nation's federal government. Any meeting of a group of countries to discuss trade policies is voluntary. No international government has powers of compulsion. Hence, dealing with international problems must be done through negotiation, consensus, bullying, and concessions.

Governmental International Institutions

6 Five important international economics institutions are:
1. The UN.
2. GATT.
3. The World Bank.
4. The IMF.
5. The EU.

World Bank *A multinational, international financial institution that works with developing countries to secure low-interest loans.*

IMF *A multinational, international financial institution concerned primarily with monetary issues.*

To discourage bullying and to encourage negotiation and consensus, governments have developed a variety of international institutions to promote negotiations and coordinate economic relations among countries. These include the United Nations (UN), General Agreement on Tariffs and Trade (GATT), World Bank, World Court, International Monetary Fund (IMF), and regional organizations such as the Organization of Petroleum Exporting Countries (OPEC), European Union (EU), and North American Free Trade Agreement (NAFTA).

These organizations have a variety of goals. For example, the **World Bank** works closely with developing countries, channeling low-interest loans to them to foster economic growth. The **IMF** is concerned with international financial arrangements. When developing countries encountered financial problems in the 1970s and had large international debts that they could not pay, the IMF helped work on repayment plans.

In addition to these formal institutions, there are informal meetings of various countries. These include **Group of Five** meetings of Japan, Germany, Britain, France, and the United States; and **Group of Seven** meetings with Japan, Germany, Britain, France, Canada, Italy, and the United States.

Since governmental membership in international organizations is voluntary, their power is limited. When the United States doesn't like a World Court ruling, it simply states that it isn't going to follow the ruling. When the United States is unhappy with what the United Nations is doing, it withholds some of its dues. Other countries do the same from time to time. Other member countries complain, but can do little to force compliance. It doesn't work that way domestically. If you decide you don't like U.S. policy and refuse to pay your taxes, you'll wind up in jail.

Q–7: If the United States chooses not to follow a World Court decision, what are the consequences?

What keeps nations somewhat in line when it comes to international rules is a moral tradition: Countries want to (or at least want to look as if they want to) do what's ''right.'' Countries will sometimes follow international rules to keep international opinion favorable to them. But national self-interest often overrides international scruples.

Global Corporations

Q–8: What is a global corporation?

Chapter 4 introduced you to U.S. corporations and listed the largest corporations in the United States. More and more of these and other corporations are transcending national boundaries. They have branches on both the production and sales sides throughout the world. As they do, they become global, or multinational, corporations rather than national corporations.

A REMINDER

INTERNATIONAL ECONOMIC INSTITUTIONS

The *United Nations* was founded in 1945, after World War II, in the hope of providing a place where international problems could be resolved through discussion and negotiation rather than through war.

The *World Bank* is a multilateral, international financial institution established in 1944. One of its main objectives is to provide funding to developing countries.

The *International Monetary Fund* (IMF), another international financial institution founded in 1944, lends money to developing countries in the form of "aid" packages which require recipient countries to try to reach certain economic goals.

The *Organization of Petroleum Exporting Countries* (OPEC) consists of 13 major oil-exporting countries in the Middle East, Far East, Africa, and South America. Formed in 1960, the organization promotes its member countries' joint national interests, such as preventing reductions in oil's price.

The *Organization of Economic Cooperation and Development* (OECD) was set up in 1961 to promote economic cooperation among individual countries. Its 24 members include all major industrial countries and most Western European countries. The OECD is the best source of comparative statistics for Western economies.

Global corporations offer enormous benefits for countries. They create jobs; they bring new ideas and new technologies to a country, and they provide competition for domestic companies, keeping them on their toes. But global corporations also pose a number of problems for governments. One is their implications for domestic and international policy. A domestic corporation exists within a country and can be dealt with using policy measures within that country. A global corporation exists within many countries and there is no global government to regulate or control it. If it doesn't like the policies in one country—say taxes are too high or regulations too tight—it can shift its operations to other countries.

Countries often compete for these global corporations by changing their regulations to encourage companies to use them as their home base. For instance, firms might register their oil tankers in Liberia to avoid paying U.S. wages, and put their funds in Bahamian banks to avoid U.S. financial disclosure laws.

At times it seems that global corporations are governments unto themselves, especially in relation to poorer countries. Consider Exhibit 6(a)'s list of some large global corporations and their sales. Then compare it with Exhibit 6(b)'s list of some small and middle-size economies and their output. In terms of sales, a number of global corporations are larger than the economies of middle-size countries. This comparison is not quite accurate, since sales do not necessarily reflect power; but when a company's decisions can significantly affect what happens in a country's economy, that company has significant economic power.

When global corporations have such power, it is not surprising that they can sometimes dominate a country. The corporation can use its expertise and experience to direct a small country to do its bidding rather than the other way around.

Another problem global corporations present for governments involves multiple jurisdiction. Global corporations can distance themselves from questionable economic activities by setting up *dummy corporations*. A dummy corporation exists only on paper, and is actually controlled by another corporation. Sometimes when a corporation really wants to separate itself from the consequences of certain actions, it creates dummy dummy and dummy dummy dummy corporations, in which one paper corporation controls another paper corporation, which in turn controls another paper corporation. Each corporation is incorporated in a different nation, which makes it difficult, if not impossible, to trace who is actually doing what and who can be held accountable.

Before you condemn globals, remember: Globals don't have it so easy either. Customs and laws differ among countries. Trying to meet the differing laws and ambiguous limits of acceptable action in various countries is often impossible. For example, in many countries bribery is an acceptable part of doing business. If you want to get permission to sell a good, you must pay the appropriate officials *baksheesh* (as it's called in Egypt) or *la mordita* (as it's called in Mexico). In the United States,

The annual report of any company generally is glossy and upbeat about the future.

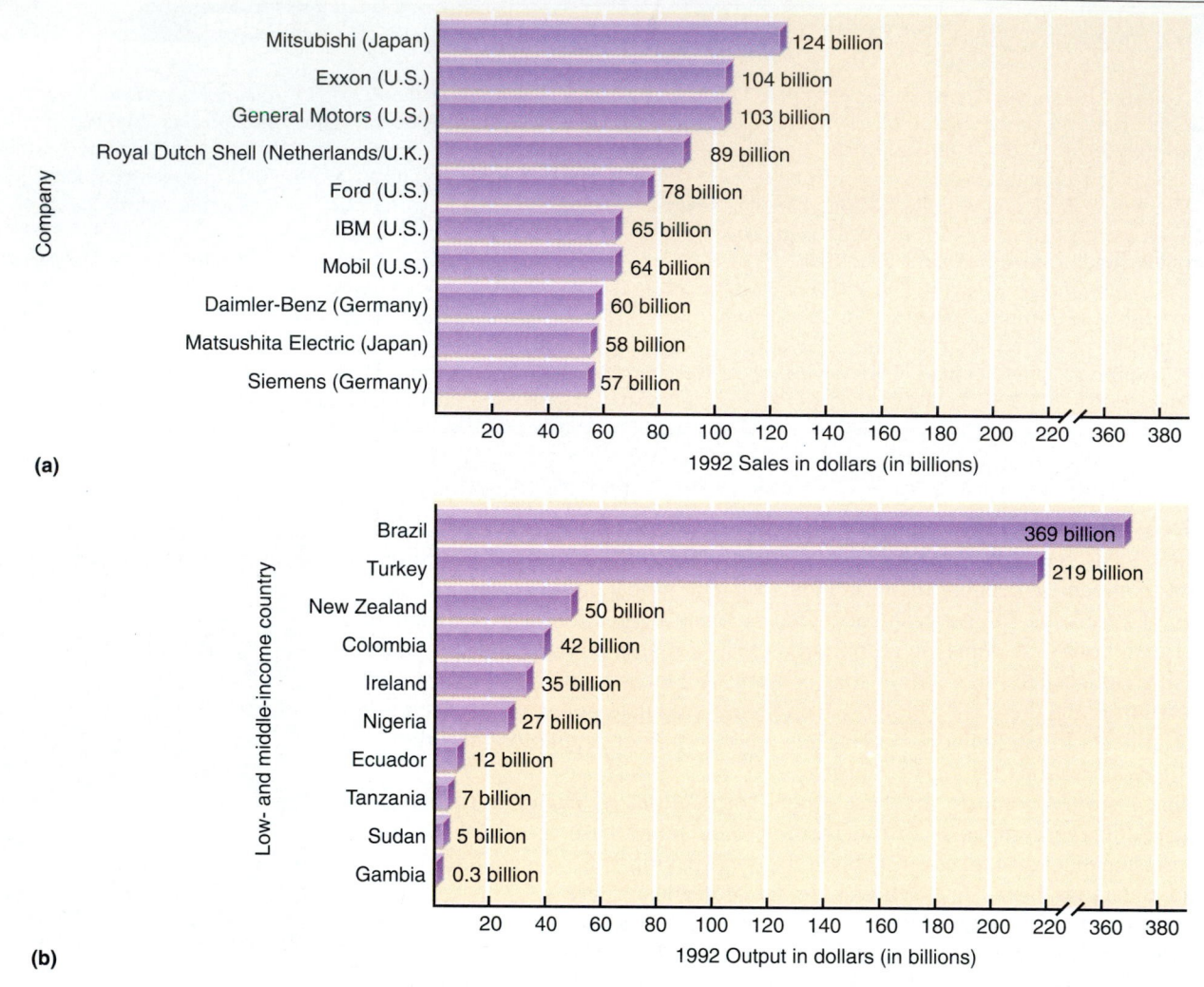

(a)

EXHIBIT 6 (a and b) **Global Corporations**

As you can see in the charts, a number of global corporations are larger than the economies of some countries in terms of sales. This is important to a small country whose economy can be affected by a decision a global corporation might make.
Source: *CIA World Fact Book,* 1993 and *World Almanac,* 1994.

such payments are called bribes and are illegal. Given these differing laws, the only way a U.S. company can do business in some foreign countries is to break U.S. laws.

Moreover, global corporations often work to maintain close ties among countries and to reduce international tension. If part of your company is in an Eastern European country and part in the United States, you want the two countries to be friends. So beware of making judgments about whether global corporations are good or bad. They're both simultaneously.

WHO ARE OUR INTERNATIONAL COMPETITORS?

So far I've given you a brief introduction to the international economic problems the United States faces and to some of the international institutions that exist to coordinate international economic activity. In this section I introduce two of our most important rivals, the European Union and Japan, giving you a brief background of their histories and economic institutions. I also briefly discuss a third competitor—the developing world—and explain why, with the new North American Free Trade Agreement (NAFTA), questions of our economic and political relations with Mexico are likely to be much in the news in the 1990s.

The European Union

In 1957, several governments of Europe formed the European Economic Community. This organization, now called the **European Union (EU)** has undergone many changes since its founding, changes that have strengthened the economic and political

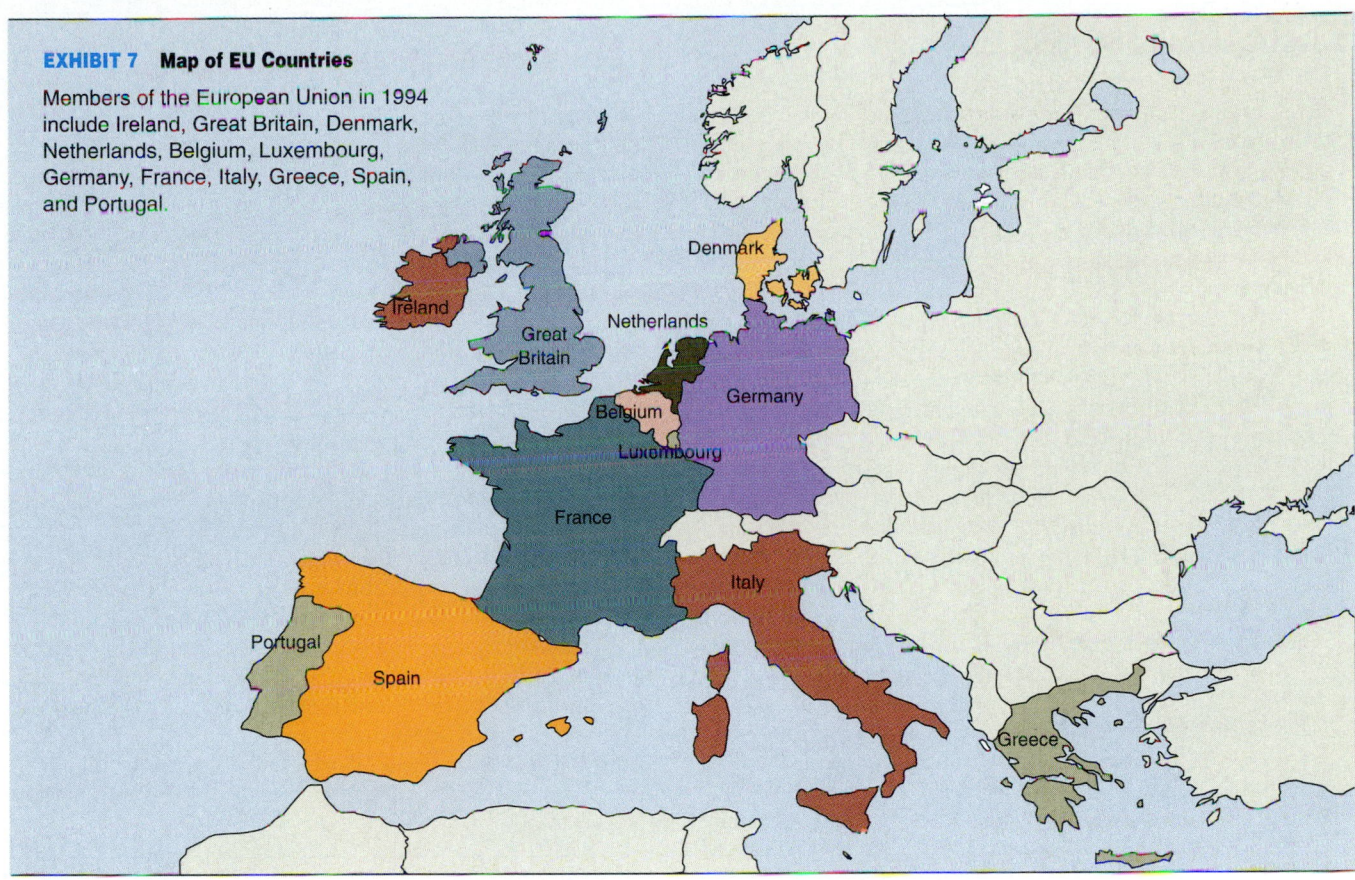

EXHIBIT 7 Map of EU Countries

Members of the European Union in 1994 include Ireland, Great Britain, Denmark, Netherlands, Belgium, Luxembourg, Germany, France, Italy, Greece, Spain, and Portugal.

ties among the countries. The EU is both an economic free trade area and a loose political organization. In the EU, as in any economic union, members allow free trade among themselves to help their economies by providing a larger marketplace and more competition for their own companies. Over time, the EU has expanded from 6 countries to the 12 shown in Exhibit 7's map. In 1995, Austria, Sweden, Norway, and Finland are scheduled to join.

The EU's initial goals were:

1. To remove barriers to trade among member nations;
2. To establish a single commercial policy toward nonmember countries;
3. To better coordinate member countries' economic policies; and
4. To promote competitiveness with other countries.

Meeting those goals hasn't been easy, but the EU has made significant progress.

Why did the countries of the EU combine? Two primary reasons were to establish better markets for European companies and to compete better against U.S. goods. In the 1950s and 1960s, when the United States was highly competitive with other countries and had a trade surplus, it could look beneficently at, and even encourage, such developments. In the 1990s, however, U.S. goods are far less competitive and there's a large trade deficit, so the United States finds it much harder to encourage a potential competitor; the EU's gains likely will come at the expense of the United States.

These U.S. fears have increased as cooperation among EU countries has grown. In 1992, most trade barriers among member nations were removed, and the EU adopted a single commercial policy toward outside nations. The movement toward economic integration has not gone easily, and attempts at further unification have been fraught with political difficulties and confusion. Specifically, the movement toward a common currency—called the ECU (European Currency Unit)—and a single monetary policy broke down in the 1990s and now likely won't take place until the 21st century, if at all.

7A The European Union (EU) is an economic and political union of European countries that allow free trade among member countries. It was created to provide larger marketplaces for member countries.

Q–9: What is the difference between EU and ECU?

he largest European Union economy is Germany. Germany has been on the losing end of two world wars and, nonetheless, has emerged as one of the leading economies of the world. One reason is cultural: German culture reinforces hard work and makes saving a virtue. Also, the country's coal and iron resources helped it establish a strong industrial base as long ago as the early 1900s.

After losing World War II in 1945, Germany was divided into East and West Germany. East Germany, which had a large part of the manufacturing base of prewar Germany, was controlled by a Communist government. West Germany was controlled by the victorious Allied forces, who encouraged it to set up a democratic market economy. The Allies limited West German military spending, while the United States, through the Marshall Plan (an assistance plan for Europe which the United States ran after World War II), pumped in large amounts of money to help the West German economy recover from the war. And recover it did. In the 1960s and 1970s, the West German economy grew so fast that it was called an *economic miracle*.

West Germany's economic story contrasted significantly with East Germany's. East Germany grew more than any of the other Eastern bloc Communist economies, but its growth didn't match West Germany's. To prevent East Germans from emigrating to West Germany, East Germany closed its borders with West Germany in 1961 and built a wall between the two countries. Economic and political changes in East Germany at the end of the 1980s led to the introduction of a market economy in East Germany, an opening of the border, and physical destruction of the wall. In 1990, East and West Germany were reunified.

The problems of economic and political reunification were immense. They placed enormous strains on the German political and economic system. To fund the reunification, the German government borrowed (it ran deficits) and raised taxes. Interest rates rose in Germany, placing significant strains on the European Union. In the 1990s, the German economy remained relatively strong, but it was no longer the economic miracle. It found itself with many of the same difficulties as the United States. In fact, in the early 1990s, Germany had significantly higher unemployment than did the United States, and more serious government budget problems.

The German economy is much more centralized than is the U.S. economy. Banks play a much more important role than do banks in the United States, and often control a variety of German companies. In the United States such control would be illegal. Thus, while Germany, like the United States, is a market economy, it is a different kind of market economy.

The early 1990s saw significant discussions on what the EU's commercial policy will be and whether it will be fair to the United States. Other European countries are also talking about uniting with the EU countries and forming a larger European trading community.

Regardless of what happens with further European economic and political integration, the EU makes a formidable competitor for the United States. Its combined production slightly exceeds U.S. production so it is the larger market. Moreover, the EU has a strong international economic position, since many member countries enjoy trade surpluses while the United States has a trade deficit.

Developments in the EU have been made even more important by recent events in Eastern Europe. Eastern European countries have changed from socialist to more market-oriented economic systems and are attempting to establish closer economic and political ties with the West. East and West Germany are reunified. These developments will open up new markets for which both the United States and the EU will compete. In that competition, the EU has both cultural and geographic advantages over the United States.

In response to the EU's increasing strength, the United States has entered into a free trade agreement with Canada and Mexico called the North American Free Trade Agreement (NAFTA). Once the agreement is in place (it is to be phased in over 15 years), U.S. firms will be able to produce in Mexico—or vice versa—subject to Mexican regulations and at Mexican wage rates, and ship directly into the United States without international legal hurdles. NAFTA raises significant questions about the short-run effects of free trade, such as: Should goods sold in the United States all be subject to the same regulations regardless of where they are produced? Will free trade with Mexico and Canada increase jobs or decrease jobs in the United States? The agreement should be much in the news in the 1990s.

NAFTA will place the United States's economic and political relations with Mexico much in the news in the 1990s.

Besides entering into NAFTA, the United States also argued strongly against high EU protective barriers on imports from foreign countries. Since there are no international organizations specifically designed to coordinate and facilitate international

Japan has become a major player in the world economy.
Reuters/Bettman.

trade among trading areas, a new policy problem of the 1990s may be trade wars among "free trading" areas.

"Japan, Inc."

Japan is a little country with a lot of people—about 125 million, half as many people as the United States—but it fits them into 146,000 square miles, less than 4 percent of the area of the United States. Almost two-thirds of Japan is covered with forest, and much of the rest of the land has poor soil. It has almost no oil; its coal is very low grade; it must import nearly 100 percent of its petroleum and all of its iron ore (used to make steel) and bauxite (used to make aluminum). It has some copper and other minerals such as zinc, but not enough. Even with heavy forestation, it doesn't have enough lumber for domestic use and must make substantial expenditures for imported lumber.

Besides being small, crowded, and poorly endowed, Japan is a chain of islands and has a language that is extremely difficult to learn. These facts have tended, until very recently, to isolate it from the rest of the world. Japan broke its isolation by entering World War II, which it lost, leaving its economy in ruins.

By almost all objective analyses, then, one would expect Japan to be a poor, underdeveloped country. It isn't. Instead, it is one of the most successful and developed economies in the world. In the 1980s its economic strength earned it the nickname *Japan, Inc.* In the 1990s, while still successful, Japan has had its problems. Its stock market crashed in the early 1990s, and the government has spent considerable resources propping up its financial sector. Moreover, with the rise in the value of the yen in the early 1990s and the subsequent rise in price of its exports, Japanese exports declined and the Japanese economy fell into a recession; unemployment rose because exports fell due to limited demand. With these events, Japan has lost its "supereconomy" status, and has joined the ranks of the other industrialized economies. It is successful, but it is not without its problems.

7B Japan is a small, crowded, poorly endowed chain of islands which has been enormously successful economically.

Cultural Reasons for Japan's Success   One reason is cultural. Japan has a social and cultural commitment to hard work. A second cultural trait that has helped Japan's economy is its strong tradition of saving money. These cultural traits are reinforced by social and economic institutions. Japan's educational system is much more demanding than that of the United States. Students go to school longer and are required to work harder than most American students. This imposes on children a discipline and a habit of hard work that persists in later life. Many Japanese enjoy work. Their work is their hobby as well as their job. Only in Japan will you find government-sponsored classes teaching people how not to work so hard.

Some reason's for Japan's economic success include:
(1) Its population's commitment to hard work;
(2) Its high level of savings;
(3) Its institutional commitment to exports; and
(4) Its population's cooperative spirit.

— They live in a co-operative society

The Japanese savings tradition is also encouraged by government policies that keep prices of consumer goods high, make borrowing for consumer goods comparatively expensive, and maintain a skimpy government pension system. One of the reasons the Japanese save a much higher percentage of their incomes than most other people do is that they worry about supporting themselves in their old age.

Japan as a Neomercantilist Country   Another reason that some economists cite for Japanese development is its government's strong role in stimulating export-led growth. These economists argue that Japan's economic growth is not an example of the power of the invisible hand, but of the three invisible forces working together to direct an economy toward growth. In many economists' view, the Japanese economic system is as closely related to mercantilism as it is to capitalism. Some have called it a **neomercantilist** economic system.

Neomercantilism   Market economy guided by government.

The power of Japan's neomercantilist approach is striking. In the 1940s, with few resources and raw materials and devastated by World War II, Japanese firms, under government direction, borrowed in order to finance the purchase of raw materials from abroad. The Japanese government directed firms to allocate a large portion of output for export. They started with small products, paid workers low wages, saved their profits, and learned about international markets. Then they plowed back those savings into more raw materials, more manufacturing, and more exports. They continued this process, each time manufacturing more sophisticated products than before.

Japan put off making improvements in housing, transportation, highways, parks, cultural institutions, and public health while it directed its efforts to rebuilding and developing technology. Government policy encouraged and sheltered business.

MITI   The Japanese agency that guides the Japanese economy.

The Japanese government developed an aggressive trading policy under the control of its Ministry of International Trade and Industry (**MITI**). It encouraged businesses to cooperate with one another, not to compete, in order to be more efficient. The government instituted strong tariffs that are still in force. They prohibit altogether the import of some articles that might compete with Japanese manufacturers. In short, Japan does not follow a laissez-faire policy in either the domestic or the international economy, and it is successful.

Not all economists agree that the government's role in Japanese economic development has been positive. Some economists argue that hard work and high savings led to growth that was partially offset by the government's involvement. They point out that MITI often backed the losing, not the winning, industries. The companies and technologies *it didn't back*, not the ones it did back, were the growth sectors of the Japanese economy. They argue that Japanese growth occurred in spite of, not because of, government involvement.

The Japanese Cooperative Spirit   Japan's labor market is remarkably different from that in the United States. Large companies have what are called *permanent employees.* By tradition, a man, once hired, stays with the same company for his entire working life. Women are unlikely to be permanent employees and are expected to resign their jobs when they get married. The relationship between the company and the worker is close—a worker is a member of the corporate family and his social life revolves around the company. The nature of the Japanese labor market is now changing significantly. Some women can be permanent employees and more and more employees are being laid off and are moving to other companies

Labor unions exist in Japan, but are organized according to industry. In the United States, unions are more likely to be organized by type of skill. Organization by industry allows Japanese workers to do many different jobs within a firm. Until recently, U.S. organized workers would not work outside their specialty.

Japan's pay structure is also different from that in the United States. Japanese workers know that their bonuses, gifts, and special allowances depend on how well their company is doing. Until recently, most U.S. workers received only a wage or salary and no bonus. Another Japanese characteristic contributing to its economic

ECONOMIES THAT DON'T WORK SO WELL

For every economy that works well, there are many more economies that aren't achieving their goals. Considering one of them helps us keep our perspective. Take Pakistan, a country of about 120,000,000 people. Pakistan is poor; the average per capita income is about $400. In the United States the equivalent figure is about $24,000. Pakistan's political structure is, in theory, democratic, but the army plays a major role in determining who will rule. Coups d'état (overthrows of the government) and unexplained deaths of high leaders are common. The resulting political instability keeps out most foreign investments.

Pakistan is an Islamic republic which has had significant fights with India ever since the two nations were created out of the former single British commonwealth country. The British commonwealth ''India'' was divided into ''India'' and ''Pakistan'' in 1947 after World War II. In 1971, Pakistan's internal strife led to half the country declaring its independence and forming a separate country, Bangladesh.

Pakistan's economy is primarily agricultural, although it also manufactures textiles and chemicals. One out of every 60 people has a TV; one out of every 165 has a car. In the United States the equivalent figures are one TV for every 1.3 people, and one car for every 1.8 people. Housing is poor for the majority of the people, and many barely get enough to eat. Income distribution is highly unequal, with a small group being very rich and a great majority being extremely poor.

Most industry has heavy government involvement and is highly inefficient. Without large tariff barriers, it could not compete. Such dependency on the government's prevention of competition breeds corruption. Most Pakistanis have little faith that their government bureaucracy will work for the benefit of society.

---

success is the tradition of cooperation between unions and business; in the United States, labor and management are frequently in conflict.

Another difference is that Japan has few lawyers and is a far less litigious society than the United States. Some cynics have suggested the small number of lawyers is a major reason for Japan's great success. Businesses don't get bogged down by legal maneuvering and litigious behavior. Less cynical people downplay this issue, but they agree Japanese people's cooperative spirit contributes to Japan's success.

Inefficient Japanese Traditions   Not all Japanese institutions promote efficiency. Some Japanese institutions hinder economic progress. Take its agricultural system. Before the war, most farmland in Japan that was not owned by the government was owned by a few individuals who rented it out in small parcels to others. After the war, the big farmland holdings were broken up by the government and sold off to former tenants at low prices. The result was thousands of small farms, averaging an acre in size. Few are larger than three acres. These small farms are highly inefficient, but are kept in business by large government subsidies and tariffs on foreign agricultural products. Because of the structure of Japanese political institutions, these subsidies are almost untouchable, despite U.S. farmers' complaints about trade restrictions.

In the 1990s, a second inefficient Japanese tradition was being seen more and more. That tradition was political corruption in which Japanese politicians received large payoffs from Japanese businesses for government support. In 1993, this corruption brought down the ruling party and led to its replacement by a coalition of reformist parties. Whether this change will improve the system, or whether such corruption is inherent in any neomercantilist system, remains to be seen.

Both the Japanese and U.S. economies are successful, but they differ significantly from each other. There is less competition among firms in Japan than in the United States. Japanese firms work closely with government in planning their industrial strategy. U.S. firms often see government as an opponent, not a partner. Similarly with labor and business: In Japan they generally cooperate; in the United States they generally are opponents.

The Japanese Ministry of International Trade and Industry plays a key role in determining what will be produced and who will produce it. MITI's goal has been to establish strong export-led growth, and that goal has been accomplished, although whether it was because of MITI, or in spite of MITI, is debatable. MITI also has an

Japan, Inc., versus the United States

economic planning board that oversees many parts of the Japanese economy. Japan is no laissez-faire economy.

Don't Overestimate the Differences

The differences between the U.S. and Japanese economies are large but shouldn't be overestimated.

The differences between the U.S. and Japanese economies are large, but shouldn't be overestimated. Both economies rely on markets. In both, profit incentives motivate production.

As global corporations bridge the gap between these two economies, the differences (once very large) are shrinking. U.S. labor unions and firms are cooperating more, while Japanese firms and labor unions are cooperating less. The Japanese system of permanent employment in large firms is breaking down.

With both systems successful, it is difficult to say that one set of institutions is better than the other. They are merely distinct from each other. The differences reflect social, cultural, and geographical conditions in the two countries. Some people have suggested that the United States should adopt a neomercantilist system like Japan's. Maybe it should, but it is not at all clear that Japanese institutions could be transferred to the United States. What works in one country can bomb in another.

The argument that policies that work in one country cannot necessarily be translated into policies that work in another country doesn't mean Japan's experience is of no relevance to the United States. In itself, the fact that a policy works in one country means that that policy deserves consideration by other countries. That's tough for an economist with a strong distrust of government to say, but it must be said. An open mind is a necessary attribute of a good economist.

The Developing Countries of the World as Competitors

Japan and the EU have developed industrial economies similar to the United States's economy. There is, however, a much larger group of countries out there that are at various lower levels of industrial development. Many of them are anxious for industrial development and will likely provide significant competition for the U.S. economy. If Japan and the EU can't out-compete the United States, these other countries often can with low wage rates and governments eager to give global corporations whatever they want. If U.S. firms don't take advantage of this low-cost labor, Japanese and European firms will, and will export the output to the United States.

Of these developing countries, Mexico is of special interest to the United States. The reason is NAFTA, which will allow easy access into the U.S. market for firms producing in Mexico. As NAFTA brings in freer trade, U.S. companies are likely to experience significant Mexican competition. In return, of course, U.S. companies will have a new open market to sell to—Mexico. As inevitably happens with competition, some people will be helped, and some will be hurt.

CONCLUSION

Q–10: If your ancestors emigrated to the United States, state what the annual per capita income in your ancestors' country is today. If your ancestors did not immigrate, what is the annual per capita income of native Americans?

Knowing about other countries' economies helps us keep our own economy in perspective. I don't have the space here (an example of scarcity) to look at other countries' tax structures, public finances, support of education, labor markets . . . the list is endless. But as you wonder about any of the economic policies that are discussed throughout this book, take a few minutes to ask somebody from a foreign country about its economy, and go to the library and look up another country's way of handling its economy (even if you look no further than an encyclopedia). See how that country compares to the United States. Then try to explain what does or doesn't work in that country and whether it would or would not work in the United States. Doing so will make the course more meaningful and your understanding of economics stronger.

CHAPTER SUMMARY

- To understand the U.S. economy, one must understand its role in the world economy.
- Knowledge of the facts about the world economy is necessary to understand the world economy.
- Countries can be classified in many ways, including industrial, middle-income, and low-income economies.
- International trade differs from domestic trade because (1) there are potential barriers to trade and (2) countries use different currencies.
- The relative value of a currency can be found in an exchange rate table.
- The U.S. trade deficit is large. It is financed by selling U.S. assets to foreign owners.
- U.S. competitiveness and the state of the U.S. economy compared to other countries are important in determining the trade deficit's size.
- International policy coordination must be achieved through consensus among nations.
- Global corporations are corporations with significant operations in more than one country.
- Two important international competitors to the United States are the EU and Japan. In Japan and in many EU nations, government plays a larger role in directing the economy than in the United States.

KEY TERMS

balance of trade *(112)*
comparative advantage *(109)*
competitiveness *(114)*
European Union (EU) *(118)*
exports *(108)*
foreign exchange market *(112)*
General Agreement on Tariffs and
  Trade (GATT) *(116)*

global corporations *(106)*
Group of Five *(116)*
Group of Seven *(116)*
IMF *(116)*
imports *(108)*
MITI *(122)*
neomercantilism *(122)*
nontariff barriers *(112)*

quotas *(112)*
tariffs *(112)*
trade deficit *(112)*
trade surplus *(112)*
World Bank *(116)*

QUESTIONS FOR THOUGHT AND REVIEW

The number after each question represents the estimated degree of critical thinking required. (1 = almost none; 10 = deep thought.)

1. A good measure of a country's importance to the world economy is its area and population. True or false? Why? *(5)*

2. The United States exports wheat while Japan exports cars. Why? *(5)*

3. What are the two ways in which international trade differs from domestic trade? *(3)*

4. Find the exchange rate for Swedish krone in Exhibit 4 and also the most current rate from your newspaper. *(3)*

5. If one U.S. dollar will buy .67 Swiss francs, how many U.S. dollars will one Swiss franc buy? *(5)*

6. The U.S. economy is falling apart because the United States is the biggest debtor nation in the world. Discuss. *(7)*

7. What is likely to happen to the U.S. trade deficit if the U.S. economy grows rapidly? Why? *(5)*

8. Why do most economists oppose trade restrictions? *(5)*

9. What effect has the establishment of the EU had on the U.S. economy? Why? *(9)*

10. Japan's successful economy is an example of the power of the invisible hand. True or false? Why? *(6)*

PROBLEMS AND EXERCISES

1. This is a library research question.
   a. What are the primary exports of Brazil, Honduras, Italy, Pakistan, and Nigeria?
   b. Which countries produce most of the world's tin, rubber, potatoes, wheat, marble, and refrigerators?

2. This is an entrepreneurial research question. You'd be amazed about the information that's out there if you use a bit of initiative.
   a. Does the largest company in your relevant geographic area (town, city, whatever) have an export division? Why or why not?
   b. If you were an adviser to the company, would you

suggest expanding or contracting its export division? Why or why not?

   c. Go to a store and look at 10 products at random. How many were made in the United States? Give a probable explanation why they were produced where they were produced.

3. Assume the United States can produce Toyotas at the cost of $8,000 per car and Chevrolets at $6,000 per car. In Japan, Toyotas can be produced at 1,000,000 yen and Chevrolets at 500,000 yen.

   a. In terms of Chevrolets, what is the opportunity cost of producing Toyotas in each country?

   b. Who has the comparative advantage in producing Chevrolets?

   c. Assume Americans purchase 500,000 Chevrolets and 300,000 Toyotas each year. The Japanese purchase far fewer of each. Using productive efficiency as the guide, who should most likely produce Chevrolets and who should produce Toyotas, assuming one is going to be produced in one country and one in the other?

4. From 1990 to 1993, the share of U.S. exports to Western Europe and Japan fell from 41 percent to 35 percent, while the share going to Latin America and Asia rose from 32 percent to 38 percent.

   a. What are likely reasons why this change occurred?

   b. What would you predict would happen to these percentages if the Japanese economy boomed?

   c. Why would President Clinton have urged the Japanese to stimulate their economy?

5. In one of the boxes, a gray market in Russian rubles is discussed.

   a. Draw the supply and demand curves for rubles in terms of dollars and show the Russian government's then-official price of .64 rubles per dollar.

   b. Show the gray market price of dollars mentioned in that box.

   c. Show what the black market price of rubles would have likely been if the Russian government had strictly enforced the exchange laws.

ANSWERS TO MARGIN QUESTIONS

1. While Russia is very large, in terms of square miles of land the continent of Africa is larger. It does not look so on the map because of the nature of the projections used to make the round earth flat. These projections expand the relative size of countries the closer they are to the North or South Pole, and reduce the relative size of countries close to the equator. *(108)*

2. I would find this information in an encyclopedia under "copper" or in *The Times Atlas of Natural Resources.* (The primary producers of copper are Chile, the United States, Poland, and Russia.) *(108)*

3. A quota is a quantitative limitation on trade. A tariff is a type of tax on imports. *(112)*

4. One would receive 41,760 pesos. *(112)*

5. A debtor nation will not necessarily be running a trade deficit. "Debt" refers to accumulated past deficits. If a country had accumulated large deficits in the past, it could run a surplus now but still be a debtor nation. *(114)*

6. Most economists oppose trade restrictions because of their negative effects, such as the reduction of domestic competition and the likelihood that countries upon whom trade restrictions are imposed, in retaliation, will impose trade restrictions of their own, thus beginning a trade war. *(115)*

7. The World Court has no enforcement mechanism. Thus, when a country refuses to follow the Court's decisions, the country cannot be directly punished except through indirect international pressures. *(116)*

8. A global corporation is a corporation with both production and sales facilities in a variety of different countries. *(116)*

9. EU stands for *European Union*. ECU stands for the *European Currency Unit*. The ECU is intended to be to the EU what the dollar is to the United States. *(119)*

10. For foreign countries, I would find this information in *The World Fact Book*. I would look in the *Statistical Abstract of the United States* for data on native Americans. In 1993, native Americans earned a median income of about $11,000. *(124)*

Some Information about The International Economy

Key Provisions of the North American Free Trade Agreement

The NAFTA (North American Free Trade Agreement) is a comprehensive plan to eliminate existing barriers to trade between Canada, the United States and Mexico. NAFTA is open to the inclusion of further participants, but each member country reserves the right to veto against any new applicant.

Some trade restrictions remain in place and some tariffs will only be phased out over a prolonged period of time. Overall, the agreement will remove tariffs on about 10,000 customs goods within 15 years. Some of NAFTA's key provisions are:

Agriculture   Existing tariffs on agricultural produce will gradually be phased out. The NAFTA forsees a complete elimination of all barriers by the end of a fifteen year interim period. The domestic farming sectors may still be subject to government intervention as long as trade in agricultural products will not be distorted by it.

Automobiles   Existing tariffs on automobiles will be phased out over a period of 10 years. Restrictions apply to auto parts imported from outside of the free trade zone. After a transition period of eight years, 62.5% of the value added to each automobile must have originated within North America.

Banking   NAFTA will allow U.S. and Canadian banks to purchase up to 8 percent of Mexican banks immediately. All restrictions on acquiring Mexican banks would be removed by the year 2000.

Disputes   Trade disputes would be subject to arbitration by special appointed judges.

Energy   Access to Mexican oil resources will continue to remain closed to foreign investors. Canadian and U.S. companies will, however, gain access to contracts offered by Mexican oil and electricity monopolies within 10 years.

Immigration   The NAFTA aims to remove restrictions on the free movement of certain special labor groups, chiefly business executives and professionals. Barriers to north-ward immigration of Mexican wage laborers will remain intact.

Patent and Copyright Protection   Mexico pledges to protect the rights to intellectual property. Under the agreement foreign patents on pharmaceuticals would be honored for a period of 20 years.

Textiles   The NAFTA establishes strict guidelines on the free trade of textiles. It foresees the creation of strict rules of origin and manufacture of garments. Tariffs are to be phased out over a 5 year interim period.

Selected International Statistics

Growth rates in real gross domestic product, 1975–93 [percent change]

Area and country	1975–84	1985	1986	1987	1988	1989	1990	1991	1992	1993[1]
World	3.3	3.7	3.6	3.9	4.6	3.4	2.2	0.6	1.7	2.2
Industrial countries	2.5	3.3	2.9	3.2	4.3	3.2	2.3	.5	1.7	1.1
United States	2.5	3.2	2.9	3.1	3.9	2.5	1.2	−.7	2.6	2.7
Canada	3.2	4.8	3.3	4.2	5.0	2.4	−.2	−1.7	.7	2.6
Japan	4.0	5.0	2.6	4.1	6.2	4.7	4.8	4.0	1.3	−.1
European Community	2.0	2.5	2.9	2.9	4.2	3.5	3.0	.8	1.1	−.2
France	2.1	1.9	2.5	2.3	4.5	4.3	2.5	.7	1.4	−1.'
Germany[2]	1.8	1.9	2.2	1.4	3.7	3.6	5.7	1.7	1.9	−1.6
Italy	2.5	2.6	2.9	3.1	4.1	2.9	2.1	1.3	.9	.0
United Kingdom[3]	1.5	3.8	4.3	4.8	5.0	2.2	.4	−2.2	−.5	1.8
Developing countries	4.5	5.2	4.9	5.7	5.3	4.1	3.7	4.5	5.8	6.1
Africa	2.3	3.7	1.9	1.3	3.9	3.6	1.9	1.6	.4	1.6
Asia	6.3	7.3	7.0	8.1	9.0	5.5	5.7	6.1	7.8	8.7
Middle East and Europe	3.6	2.9	2.4	5.9	.7	3.6	4.2	2.4	7.8	3.4
Western Hemisphere	3.2	3.5	4.0	3.2	1.1	1.6	.3	3.3	2.5	3.4
Countries in transition[4]	3.9	2.1	3.6	2.6	4.3	2.3	−3.5	−12.0	−15.4	−10.2
Central Europe	3.3	3.1	3.7	1.9	1.5	.2	−7.1	−12.6	−9.1	−1.8
Former Soviet Union[5]	4.1	1.7	3.6	2.8	5.3	3.0	−2.3	−11.8	−17.8	−13.7

[1] All figures are forecasts except data for United States.
[2] Through 1990 for West Germany only.
[3] Average of expenditure, income, and output estimates of GDP at market prices.
[4] For most countries included in the group, total output is measured by real net material product (NMP) or by NMP-based estimates of GDP.
[5] Data beginning 1990 are weighted averages of separate estimates for the 15 states of the former U.S.S.R.

Civilian Unemployment rate, of Major Industrial Countries, 1967–93
[quarterly data seasonally adjusted]

Year	United States	Canada	Japan	France	Germany[1]	Italy	United Kingdom
				Civilian unemployment rate (percent)[2]			
1967	3.8	3.8	1.3	2.1	1.3	3.4	3.3
1968	3.6	4.5	1.2	2.7	1.1	3.5	3.2
1969	3.5	4.4	1.1	2.3	.6	3.5	3.1
1970	4.9	5.7	1.2	2.5	.5	3.2	3.1
1971	5.9	6.2	1.3	2.8	.6	3.3	3.9
1972	5.6	6.2	1.4	2.9	.7	3.8	4.2
1973	4.9	5.5	1.3	2.8	.7	3.7	3.2
1974	5.6	5.3	1.4	2.9	1.6	3.1	3.1
1975	8.5	6.9	1.9	4.2	3.4	3.4	4.6
1976	7.7	7.1	2.0	4.6	3.4	3.9	5.9
1977	7.1	8.1	2.0	5.2	3.4	4.1	6.4
1978	6.1	8.3	2.3	5.4	3.3	4.1	6.3
1979	5.8	7.4	2.1	6.1	2.9	4.4	5.4
1980	7.1	7.5	2.0	6.5	2.8	4.4	7.0
1981	7.6	7.5	2.2	7.6	4.0	4.9	10.5
1982	9.7	11.0	2.4	8.3	5.6	5.4	11.3
1983	9.6	11.8	2.7	8.6	[3]6.9	5.9	11.8
1984	7.5	11.2	2.8	10.0	7.1	5.9	11.8
1985	7.2	10.5	2.6	10.5	7.2	6.0	11.2
1986	7.0	9.5	2.8	10.6	6.6	[3]7.6	11.2
1987	6.2	8.8	2.9	10.8	6.3	7.9	10.3
1988	5.5	7.8	2.5	10.3	6.3	7.9	8.6
1989	5.3	7.5	2.3	9.6	5.7	7.8	7.3
1990	5.5	8.1	2.1	9.1	p5.0	p7.0	6.9
1991	6.7	10.3	2.1	9.6	p4.4	3p6.9	p8.8
1992	7.4	11.3	2.2	p10.4	p4.7	p7.3	p10.0
1993	6.8	11.2					p10.4

Industrial Production of Major Industrial Countries, 1967–93

Year	United States	Canada	Japan	European Community[5]	France	Germany[6]	Italy	United Kingdom
				Industrial production (1987 = 100)[7]				
1967	57.5	51.1	36.2	59.3	61	57.6	58.5	70.5
1968	60.7	54.3	41.7	63.7	62	62.9	61.9	75.9
1969	63.5	58.1	48.3	69.6	69	70.9	64.2	78.5
1970	61.4	58.8	55.0	73.1	72	75.5	68.3	78.9
1971	62.2	62.0	56.5	74.7	77	77.0	68.0	78.5
1972	68.3	66.7	59.6	78.0	81	79.9	70.8	79.9
1973	73.8	73.8	67.9	83.7	87	85.0	77.7	87.0
1974	72.7	76.1	66.4	84.3	90	84.8	81.2	85.4
1975	66.3	71.6	59.4	78.7	83	79.6	73.7	80.8
1976	72.4	76.0	66.0	84.5	90	86.8	83.9	83.4
1977	78.2	79.3	68.6	86.6	92	88.0	83.8	87.6
1978	82.6	82.1	73.0	95.4	94	90.4	85.4	90.1
1979	85.7	86.1	78.1	93.1	99	94.7	91.1	93.6
1980	84.1	82.8	81.7	92.8	98.9	95.0	96.2	86.9
1981	85.7	84.5	82.6	91.1	98.3	93.2	94.7	84.1
1982	81.9	76.2	82.9	89.9	97.3	90.3	91.7	85.7
1983	84.9	81.2	85.5	90.8	96.5	90.9	88.9	88.9
1984	92.8	91.0	93.4	92.8	97.1	93.5	91.8	89.0
1985	94.4	96.1	96.8	95.8	97.2	97.7	92.9	93.9
1986	95.3	95.4	96.6	98.0	98.0	99.6	96.2	96.2
1987	100.0	100.0	100.0	100.0	100.0	100.0	100.0	100.0
1988	104.4	105.3	109.3	104.2	104.6	103.9	105.9	104.8
1989	106.0	105.2	115.9	108.2	108.9	108.8	109.2	107.0
1990	106.0	101.8	121.4	110.3	111.0	114.1	109.4	106.7
1991	104.1	98.1	123.7	110.2	110.9	117.4	107.1	102.5
1992	106.5	98.5	116.5	108.9	109.8	116.0	106.5	102.0
1993	p 111.0							

Manufacturing Hourly Compensation in U.S. Dollars of Major Industrial Countries (1982 = 100)[4]

Year	United States	Canada	Japan	France	Germany[1]	Italy	United Kingdom
1967		26.1	10.5	17.9	15.2	17.7	16.9
1968		28.2	12.2	20.2	16.3	18.9	15.8
1969		30.4	14.6	20.5	18.1	20.6	17.2
1970		33.9	17.4	21.6	22.9	25.1	19.9
1971		37.7	20.7	24.4	27.0	29.4	23.5
1972		41.3	27.3	29.4	32.5	34.9	27.7
1973		44.3	37.4	38.4	44.2	41.2	31.0
1974		52.2	45.6	42.1	51.6	48.1	35.6
1975		57.3	52.1	58.2	59.7	60.5	44.9
1976		67.7	56.2	59.9	62.9	59.0	42.3
1977	62.8	69.5	68.6	66.1	74.5	65.7	46.2
1978	67.9	69.8	94.0	81.4	92.8	78.8	59.2
1979	74.4	74.8	95.5	97.5	109.1	97.4	77.9
1980	83.3	83.0	98.3	113.3	119.3	111.1	103.7
1981	91.5	93.1	107.6	101.8	102.2	100.9	104.8
1982	100.0	100.0	100.0	100.0	100.0	100.0	100.0
1983	102.7	106.2	107.7	95.3	99.9	104.3	93.2
1984	105.9	105.9	111.0	90.2	93.9	103.5	88.8
1985	111.2	105.6	115.0	95.0	96.0	107.0	94.7
1986	115.8	107.8	171.2	128.4	135.6	142.7	113.7
1987	118.4	116.3	204.2	153.4	171.4	173.3	138.9
1988	123.0	130.9	234.4	160.6	182.1	179.9	158.6
1989	127.9	143.2	231.2	158.1	178.4	188.5	167.3
1990	134.7	155.5	237.5	192.4	222.2	241.0	191.4
1991	141.9	167.8	270.8	193.5	230.6	257.5	210.8
1992	148.1	165.7	300.6	213.5	260.0	271.1	228.4

Consumer Prices of Major Industrial Countries (1982–1984 = 100)

Year	United States	Canada	Japan	European Community[5]	France	Germany[6]	Italy	United Kingdom
1967	33.4	31.3	32.2	23.5	24.6	49.3	16.0	18.5
1968	34.8	32.5	34.0	24.3	25.7	50.1	16.2	19.4
1969	36.7	34.0	35.8	25.3	27.4	51.0	16.6	20.4
1970	38.8	35.1	38.5	26.6	28.7	52.9	16.8	21.8
1971	40.5	36.1	40.9	28.3	30.3	55.6	17.6	23.8
1972	41.8	37.9	42.9	30.1	32.2	58.7	18.7	25.5
1973	44.4	40.7	47.9	32.7	34.5	62.8	20.6	27.9
1974	49.3	45.2	59.0	37.4	39.3	67.2	24.6	32.3
1975	53.8	50.1	65.9	42.8	43.9	71.2	28.8	40.2
1976	56.9	53.8	72.2	47.9	48.1	74.2	33.6	46.8
1977	60.6	58.1	78.1	53.8	52.7	76.9	40.1	54.2
1978	65.2	63.3	81.4	58.7	57.5	79.0	45.1	58.7
1979	72.6	69.1	84.4	65.1	63.6	82.3	52.1	66.6
1980	82.4	76.1	91.0	74.0	72.3	86.8	63.2	78.5
1981	90.9	85.6	95.3	83.2	82.0	92.2	75.4	87.9
1982	96.5	94.9	98.0	92.2	91.6	97.0	87.7	95.4
1983	99.6	100.4	99.8	100.2	100.5	100.3	100.8	99.8
1984	103.9	104.8	102.1	107.4	107.9	102.7	111.5	104.8
1985	107.6	108.9	104.1	114.0	114.2	104.8	121.1	111.1
1986	109.6	113.4	104.8	118.2	117.2	104.7	128.5	114.9
1987	113.6	118.4	104.9	112.2	120.9	104.9	134.4	119.7
1988	118.3	123.2	105.7	126.7	124.2	106.3	141.1	125.6
1989	124.0	129.3	108.0	133.3	128.6	109.2	150.4	135.4
1990	130.7	135.5	111.4	140.8	133.0	112.1	159.6	148.2
1991	136.2	143.1	115.0	147.9	137.2	116.0	169.8	156.9
1992	140.3	145.2	116.9	154.3	140.6	120.6	178.9	162.7
1993	144.5	147.9				125.5	186.4	165.3

[1] Former West Germany.

[2] Civilian unemployment rates, approximating U.S. concepts.

[3] There are breaks in the series for Germany (1983) and Italy (1986, 1991, and 1993). Based on the prior series, the rate for Germany was 7.2 percent in 1983, and the rate for Italy was 6.3 percent in 1986 and 6.6 in 1981. The break in 1993 raised Italy's rate by approximately 1.1 percentage points.

[4] Hourly compensation in manufacturing, U.S. dollar basis. Data relate to all employed persons (wage and salary earners and the self-employed) in the United States and Canada, and to all employees (wage and salary earners) in the other countries. For France and United Kingdom, compensation adjusted to include changes in employment taxes that are not compensation to employees, but are labor costs to employers.

[5] Consists of Belgium-Luxembourg, Denmark, France, Greece, Ireland, Italy, Netherlands, United Kingdom, Germany, Portugal, and Spain. Industrial production prior to July 1981 excludes data for Greece, which joined the Ec in 1981. Data for Portugal and Spain, which became members on January 1, 1986 are excluded to 1982.

[6] Former West Germany

[7] All data exclude construction. Quarterly data are seasonally adjusted.

Source: *Economic Report of the President*, 1994.

2

MACROECONOMICS

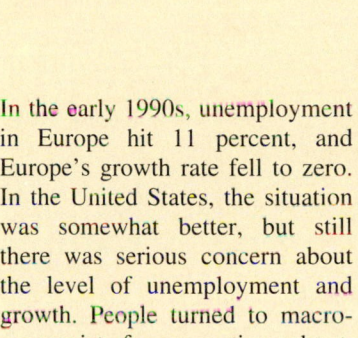

In the early 1990s, unemployment in Europe hit 11 percent, and Europe's growth rate fell to zero. In the United States, the situation was somewhat better, but still there was serious concern about the level of unemployment and growth. People turned to macroeconomists for suggestions about what to do. This section of the book explains the ideas of competing groups of macroeconomists about such issues. It tells you how the ideas developed, and what relevance they have for policy in the 1990s.

The specific focus of macroeconomics is the study of unemployment, business cycles (fluctuations in the economy), growth, and inflation. While the macroeconomic theories studied have changed considerably over the past 60 years, macroeconomics' focus on those problems has remained. Thus, we'll define **macroeconomics** *as the study of the economy in the aggregate with specific focus on unemployment, inflation, business cycles, and growth.*

In the following chapters, I provide you with the background necessary to discuss the modern debate about these issues. Let's begin with a little history.

Macroeconomics emerged as a separate subject within economics in the 1930s when the U.S. economy fell into a Great Depression. Businesses collapsed and unemployment rose until 25 percent of the work force—millions of people— were out of work.

The Depression changed the way economics was taught and the way in which economic problems were conceived. Before the 1930s, economics was microeconomics (the study of partial equilibrium supply and demand). After the 1930s, the study of the core of economic thinking was broken into two discrete areas: microeconomics, as before, and macroeconomics (the study of the economy in the aggregate).

Macroeconomic policy debates have centered on a struggle between two groups: *Keynesian* (pronounced KAIN-sian) economists and Classical economists. Should the government run a budget deficit or a surplus? Should the government increase the money supply when a recession threatens? Should it decrease the money supply when inflation threatens? Can government prevent recessions? Keynesians generally answer one way; Classicals, another.

Each group has many variants. On the Classical side are neo-Classicals, New Classicals, and monetarists. On the Keynesian side are neo-Keynesians, New Keynesians, and post-Keynesians, just to name a few. At the introductory level we

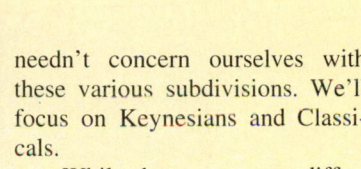

needn't concern ourselves with these various subdivisions. We'll focus on Keynesians and Classicals.

While there are many differences between Keynesians and Classicals, the fundamental policy difference is the following: Classical economists generally oppose government intervention in the economy; they favor a *laissez-faire* policy.[1] Keynesians are more likely to favor government intervention in the economy. They feel a laissez-faire policy can sometimes lead to disaster. Both views represent reasonable economic positions. The differences between them are often subtle and result from their taking slightly different views of what government can do and slightly different perspectives on the economy.

Part I, Macroeconomic Problems (chapters 6 and 7), introduces you to the macroeconomic problems, terminology, and statistics used in tracking the economy's macroeconomic performance.

Part II, Macroeconomics: The Basics (chapters 8–11), provides the background you need to understand macroeconomic theory sufficiently so that you can understand the policy debates that have been going on for the last 60 years and continue unabated. In these chapters the terms of the debate between Keynesians and Classicals will become clear.

Part III, Monetary and Financial Institutions (chapters 12–15), discusses the financial sector and shows you how that sector fits into the macroeconomic landscape. It gives you a sense of the nuts and bolts of macroeconomic policy, the financial institutions in the economy, and how those institutions influence inflation.

Part IV, International Dimensions of Macro Problems (chapters 16 and 17), zero in on the international dimensions of macroeconomic policy. It shows how the additional complications that the international sector brings to macroeconomics can be added to the models and ideas discussed in earlier chapters.

Part V, Macroeconomic Policy Debates (chapters 18–21), discusses the art of macroeconomic policy. It applies the terminology, theory, and knowledge of institutions that you'll have gained from earlier chapters. It includes case studies that bridge the gap between the general discussions in the text and real-life policies.

---

[1] "Laissez-faire" (introduced to you in Chapter 3) is a French expression meaning "Leave things alone; let them go on without interference."

6

Economic Growth, Business Cycles, Unemployment, and Inflation

Remember that there is nothing stable in human affairs; therefore avoid undue elation in prosperity, or undue depression in adversity.

~Socrates

After reading this chapter, you should be able to:

1 Summarize some relevant statistics about growth, business cycles, unemployment, and inflation.

2 Name four ingredients of growth.

3 List four phases of the business cycle.

4 Relate the target rate of unemployment to potential income.

5 Explain how unemployment is measured and state some microeconomic categories of unemployment.

6 Define inflation and distinguish a real concept from a nominal concept.

7 Differentiate between cost-push and demand-pull inflation and expected and unexpected inflation.

8 State two important costs of inflation.

Like people, the economy has moods. Sometimes it's in wonderful shape—it's expansive; at other times, it's depressed. Like people whose moods are often associated with specific problems (headaches, sore back, an itch), the economy's moods are associated with various problems.

Macroeconomics is the study of the aggregate moods of the economy, with specific focus on problems associated with those moods—the problems of growth, business cycles, unemployment, and inflation. These four problems are the central concern of macroeconomics. The macroeconomic theory we'll consider is designed to explain how supply and demand forces in the aggregate interact to create these problems. The macroeconomic policy controversies we'll consider concern these four problems. So it's only appropriate that in this first chapter we consider an overview of these problems, their causes, their consequences, and the debate about what to do about them. It introduces you to some of the terms we'll be using and gives you a sense of the interrelationship of these problems. Just how are business cycles and growth related to inflation and unemployment? The chapter won't answer all your questions (if it did, we wouldn't need the other chapters), but it will provide you with a framework for the remaining chapters.

We'll start with the problems of growth.

GROWTH

1A U.S. economic output has grown at an annual 3 to 3.5 percent rate.

Generally the U.S. economy is growing or expanding. Economic activity—the production of goods and services (output)—is increasing. When people produce and sell their goods, they earn income, so when an economy is growing, both total output and total income are increasing. Such growth gives most people more this year than they had last year. Since most of us prefer more to less, growth is easy to take.

The U.S. Department of Commerce traced U.S. economic growth in output since about 1890 and discovered that, on average, output of goods and services grew about 3.5 percent per year, although in recent years this rate has decreased to slightly under 3 percent. This 3 to 3.5 percent growth rate is sometimes called the *secular trend growth rate*. The rate at which the actual output grows in any one year fluctuates, but on average, the U.S. economy has been growing at that long-term trend. Since population has also been growing, per capita economic growth (growth per person) has been less than 3 to 3.5 percent. This growth trend can be divided into two components, one reflecting growth of population, and one consisting of increased productivity (output per input). When economists talk about economic growth, they generally mean this long-term growth trend of output of 3 to 3.5 percent per year.

The Benefits and Costs of Growth

Economic growth (per capita) allows everyone in society, on average, to have more. Thus, it isn't surprising that most governments are generally searching for policies that will allow them to grow. Indeed, one reason market economies have been so successful is that they have consistently channeled individual efforts toward production and growth. Individuals feel a sense of accomplishment in making things grow and, if sufficient economic incentives and resources exist, individuals' actions can lead to a continually growing economy.

Politically, growth, or predictions of growth, allows governments to avoid hard questions.

Politically, growth, or predictions of growth, allows governments to avoid hard distributional questions of who should get what part of our existing output: With growth there is more to go around for everyone. A growing economy generates jobs, so politicians who want to claim that their policies will create jobs generally predict those policies will create growth. For example, in the early 1990s, Bill Clinton estimated his policies would maintain a 3 percent growth and, because of that growth, create over 8 million jobs.

Of course, there are also costs to material growth—pollution, resource exhaustion, and destruction of natural habitat. These costs lead some people to believe that we would be better off in a non-material-growth society that de-emphasized material growth. (That doesn't mean we shouldn't grow emotionally, spiritually, and intellectually; it simply means we should grow out of our material good fetish). Many people believe these environmental costs are important, and the result is often an environmental–economic growth stalemate.

To reconcile the two goals, some have argued that spending on the environment can create growth and jobs, so the two need not be incompatible. Unfortunately, there's a problem with this argument. It confuses growth and jobs with increased material consumption—what most people are worried about. As more material goods made available by growth are used for anti-pollution equipment, less is available for the growth of an average individual's personal consumption, since the added material goods created by growth have already been used. What society gets, at best, from these expenditures is a better physical environment, not more of everything. Getting more of everything would violate the TANSTAAFL law.

The Causes of Growth

Economists have thought a lot about growth, and have many ideas about it. But they have no magic recipe of policies that can be directly related to growth. They, however, have specified some of the ingredients of that recipe. Four of the most important causes of growth are the following.

1. Institutions with incentives compatible with growth;
2. Technological development;
3. Available resources; and
4. Capital accumulation—investment in productive capacity.

Let's consider each in turn.

> **2** Four important ingredients of growth are:
> 1. Institutions with incentives compatible with growth;
> 2. Technological development;
> 3. Available resources; and
> 4. Capital accumulation— investment in productive capacity.

Institutions with Incentives Compatible with Growth   Throughout this book I have emphasized the importance of economic institutions. Those institutions are vitally necessary for growth. **Growth-compatible institutions**—institutions that foster growth—must have *incentives* built into them that lead people to put out effort—to work hard—and must discourage people from activities that inhibit growth—such as spending a lot of their time in leisure pursuits or in gaining income for themselves by creating impediments for others. Let's consider some examples of each.

When individuals get much of the gains of growth themselves, they have incentives to work harder. That's why private ownership of property plays an important role in growth. It is the institution that *supply-side* economists focus on. In the former Soviet Union, individuals didn't get much of the gain of their own initiative, and hence often spent their time in pursuits other than activities fostering economic growth. Another example of a growth-compatible institution is the corporation, a legal fiction that gives owners limited liability, thereby encouraging large enterprises because people are more willing to invest their savings when they have limited liability than they would be if they did not.

Many developing countries follow a type of mercantilist policy in which government approval is necessary before any economic activity is allowed. Government officials' income often comes from bribes offered to them by individuals who want to be able to undertake economic activity. Such policies inhibit economic growth. Many regulations, even reasonable ones, also tend to inhibit economic growth because they inhibit entrepreneurial activities. But we should mention that to ensure that the growth is of a socially desirable type, some regulation is necessary. The policy problem is in deciding between necessary and unnecessary regulation.

> **Q–1:**   In what way do regulations inhibit growth and in what way are they necessary?

Technological Development   Growth is sometimes thought of as the same things getting bigger, or getting more of the same things. That's an incorrect view of growth. While growth in some ways involves more of the same, a much larger aspect of growth involves changes in technology—*changes* in the goods we buy, and *changes* in the way we make goods. Think of what this generation spends its income on—CDs, cars, computers, fast food—and compare that to what the preceding generation spent money on—LP records, cars that would now be considered obsolete, and tube and transistor radios. (When I was eleven, I saved $30—the equivalent of over $100 now—so I could afford a 6-transistor Motorola radio; computers didn't exist.)

A per capita growth rate of 1 percent per year means on average people will be able to consume 1 percent more per year. Most of you, I suspect, are hoping to do better than that, and most of you will do better, both because you're in college studying economics (so you'll do better than average) and because most individuals in their working years can expect to consume slightly more each year than they did the previous year. Since income also tends to increase with age up to retirement, and ends completely at death, a specific individual's income, and hence his or her consumption, will generally increase by more than the per capita growth in income.

So, if the future is like the past, the average (living) person can look forward to a rate of increase in consumption significantly above average. The average dead person will have a rather significant decrease.

Technological change does more than cause economic growth; it changes the entire social and political dimensions of society.

Contrast this with the goods the next generation might spend its income on: video brain implants (little gadgets in your head to receive sound and full-vision broadcasts—you simply close your eyes and tune in whatever you want, if you've paid your cellular fee for that month), electric cars (gas cars will be considered so quaint, but so polluting), and instant food (little pills that fulfill all your nutritional needs, letting your brain implant gadget supply all the ambiance)—Just imagine! You probably can get the picture even without a video brain implant.

How does society get people to work on these new developments to change the very nature of what we do and how we think? One way is through economic incentives; another is with institutions that foster creativity and bold thinking—like this book; a third is through institutions that foster hard work. There are, of course, trade-offs. Institutions that foster hard work and require discipline—such as the Japanese educational system—don't do as good a job at fostering creativity as the U.S. educational system, and vice versa: the U.S. educational system isn't great at fostering hard work. Thus, many of the new technologies of the 1980s have been thought up in the United States, but have been translated into workable products in Japan.

Available Resources   If an economy is to grow it will need resources. Thus England grew in the late 1700s because it had iron and coal; and the United States grew in the 20th century because it had a major supply of many resources, and it imported people, a resource of which it did not have much.

What is a resource depends on the technology used. A resource in one time period may not be a resource in another.

Of course, you have to be careful in thinking about what is a resource. A resource in one time period may not be a resource in another—what is a resource depends on the technology being used. So creativity can replace resources, and if you develop new technology fast enough, you can overcome any lack of existing resources. Even if a country doesn't have the physical resources it needs, if it can import them, it can grow—as did Japan following World War II.

Investment and Accumulated Capital   At one point, capital accumulation (where capital was thought of as buildings and machines) and investment were seen as forming *the* key element in growth. While buildings and machines are still considered *a* key element in growth, it is now generally recognized that the growth recipe is far more complicated. One of the reasons for this recognition is the empirical evidence; for instance, the former Soviet Union invested a lot and accumulated lots of capital goods, but their economy didn't grow much because that capital was often internationally obsolete. Another reason for this de-emphasis on capital accumulation is a recognition that products change, and useful buildings and machines in one time period may be useless in another. The value of the capital stock depends on the future, and there is no real way of measuring the value of capital independently of its future expectation of earnings. Capital's role in growth is extraordinarily difficult to accurately measure empirically.

Q-2:   The Soviet Union invested a lot but did not grow. What explanation for this can you give?

A third reason for this de-emphasis on capital accumulation is that it became clear that capital was far more than machines. People's knowledge is a type of capital,

INTERPRETING EMPIRICAL EVIDENCE

When I first went to college, I thought that there were facts and there were theories, and that theories were tested by comparing them to the facts. Alas, my college professors delighted in twisting any neat divisions I made, and my neat distinction between fact and theory is one of the things that bit the dust.

The difficulty is that facts are simply empirical observations. What is a fact depends on who is doing the observing. Economic facts (data) must often be collected through more complicated methods than simple observation. Numbers must be collected (presenting first the collector and then the viewer with possible errors). Numbers must be combined, and often subsets of numbers must be chosen (opening up the possibility of more errors). Finally numbers must be interpreted.

Much of the debate in economics is conducted in the statistical trenches: looking at the data and attempting to pull out "facts" from that data. The "fact" that business cycles' peaks and troughs were reduced after World War II was pretty much accepted as a fact until Christina Romer, an economist at Princeton, reanalyzed the data and came up with a different conclusion. She found that no postwar change in business cycles had occurred. Many economists disagreed with her findings, but whether she was right or wrong is not the important point. The important point is that after she presented her new interpretation, the "fact" was in dispute, and no longer a fact. The moral: Beware of "facts."

called **human capital,** and the habitual way of doing things that guides people in how they approach production is **social capital.** For example, the existence of money and a well developed financial market makes many investment projects possible that otherwise wouldn't be possible, and hence such institutions are a type of social capital. In a way, anything that contributes to growth can be called a type of capital, and anything that slows growth can be called a destruction of capital. With the concept of capital including such a wide range of things, it is difficult to say what is *not* capital, which makes the concept of capital less useful.

Turning the Causes of Growth into Growth   The four causes of growth cannot be taken as givens. Even if each of these four ingredients exist, they may not exist in the right proportions. For example, economic growth depends upon people saving and investing rather than consuming their income. Investing now helps create machines that in the future can be used to produce more output with less effort. Growth also depends upon technological change—finding new, better ways to do things. For instance, when Nicolas Appert discovered canning (the ability to cook and store food in a sealed vacuum container so it wouldn't spoil), the economic possibilities of society expanded enormously. But if, when technological changes occur, the savings aren't there to finance the investment, the result will not be growth. It is the *combination* of investing in machines and technological change that plays a central role in the growth of any economy.

There are, of course, many other causes of growth. Nonetheless, this brief introduction should identify some growth issues to keep in the back of your mind as we consider other goals, because policies that sometimes seem to help alleviate other problems, like unemployment or inflation, can have negative effects on growth.

BUSINESS CYCLES

Business cycle   *The upward or downward movement of economic activity that occurs around the growth trend.*

While the secular, or long-term, trend is a 3 to 3.5 percent increase in total output, there are numerous fluctuations around that trend. Sometimes total output is above the trend; at other times total output is below the trend. Such a short-term fluctuation of output around the long-term trend is called a **business cycle.** Thus, a business cycle is the upward or downward movement of economic activity that occurs around the growth trend. Exhibit 1 graphs the fluctuations in the U.S. economy since 1860.

Until the late 1930s, economists took such cycles as facts of life. They had no convincing theory to explain why business cycles occurred, nor did they have policy suggestions to smooth them out. In fact, they felt that any attempt to smooth them through government intervention would make the situation worse.

Since the 1940s, however, many economists have not taken business cycles as facts of life. They have hotly debated the nature and causes of business cycles and of

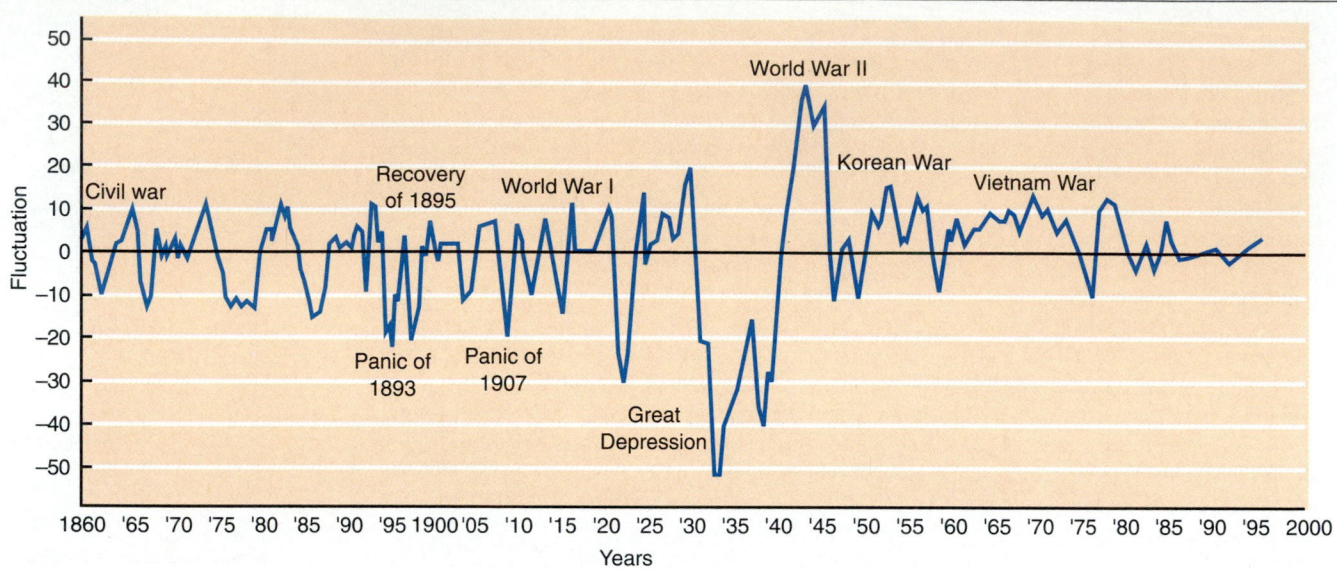

EXHIBIT 1   U.S. Business Cycles

Business cycles have always been a part of the U.S. economic scene.
Source: Courtesy of Ameritrust Co., Cleveland, Ohio, and updated by author.

If prolonged contractions are a type of cold the economy catches, the Great Depression of the 1930s was double pneumonia.

the underlying growth. Classical economists argue that fluctuations are to be expected in a market economy. Indeed, it would be strange if fluctuations did not occur when individuals are free to decide what they want to do. We should simply accept these fluctuations as we do the seasons of the year. If you have no policy to deal with some occurrence, you might as well accept that occurrence. Keynesian economists argue that fluctuations can and should be controlled. They argue that *expansions* (the part of the business cycle above the long-term trend) and *contractions* (the part of the cycle below the long-term trend) are symptoms of underlying problems of the economy, which should be dealt with. Which of these two views is correct is still a matter of debate.

If prolonged contractions (recessions) are a type of cold the economy catches, the Great Depression of the 1930s was double pneumonia. The Great Depression led to changes in the U.S. economy's structure. The new structure included a more active role for government in reducing the severity of cyclical fluctuations. Look at Exhibit 1 and compare the periods before and after World War II. (World War II began in 1941 and ended in 1945.) Notice that the downturns and panics since 1945 have generally been less severe than before.

This change in the nature of business cycles can be better seen in Exhibit 2, which is based on National Bureau of Economic Research data. Notice that since 1945 business cycles' duration has increased, but, more important, the average length of expansions has increased while the average length of contractions has decreased.

How to interpret these statistics is the subject of much controversy. As is the case with much economic evidence, the data are subject to different interpretations. Some economists argue the reduction in fluctuations' severity is an illusion.

If the severity of the fluctuations has been reduced (which most economists believe has happened), one reason is that changes in institutional structure were made as a result of the Great Depression. Both the financial structure and the government taxing and spending structure were changed, giving the government a more important role in stabilizing the economy. Consideration of that stronger government role is a key element of macroeconomics.

The Phases of the Business Cycle

Much research has gone into measuring business cycles and setting official reference dates for the beginnings and ends of contractions and expansions. As a result of this

EXHIBIT 2   Duration of Business Cycles, Pre-World War II and Post-World War II

Cycles	Duration (in months)	
	Pre-World War II (1845–1945)	Post-World War II (1945–1982)
Number	22	9
Average duration (trough to trough)	50	60
Length of longest cycle	99 (1870–79)	117 (1961–70)
Length of shortest cycle	28 (1919–21)	28 (1980–82)
Average length of expansions	29	51
Length of shortest expansion	10 (1919–20)	12 (1980–81)
Length of longest expansion	80 (1938–45)	106 (1961–69)
Average length of recessions	21	11
Length of shortest recession	7 (1918–19)	6 (1980)
Length of longest recession	65 (1873–79)	16 (1981–82)

Source: *Survey of Current Business* and *Economic Report of the President, 1994.*

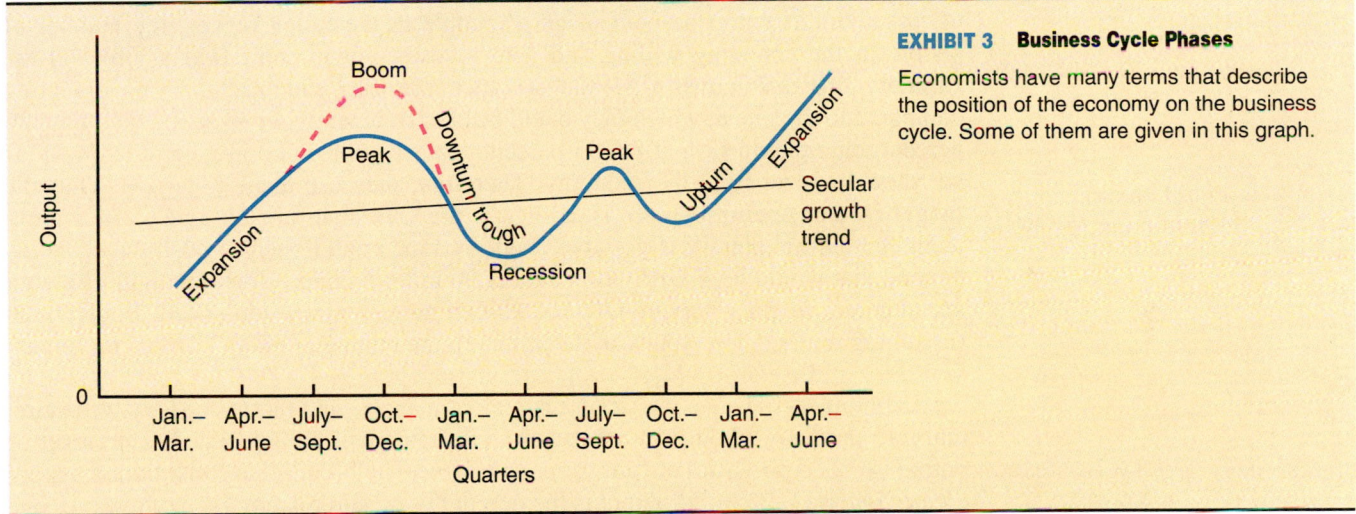

EXHIBIT 3   Business Cycle Phases

Economists have many terms that describe the position of the economy on the business cycle. Some of them are given in this graph.

research, business cycles have been divided into phases, and an explicit terminology has been developed. The National Bureau of Economic Research announces the government's official dates of contractions and expansions. In the postwar era (since mid-1945), the average business expansion has lasted about 51 months. A major expansion occurred from 1982 until mid-1990, when the U.S. economy fell into a recession. In mid-1991 it slowly came out of the recession, but slow growth remained.

Business cycles have varying durations and intensities, but economists have developed a terminology to describe all business cycles and just about any position we might find ourself in on the business cycle. Since this terminology is often used by the press it is helpful to go over it. I do so in reference to Exhibit 3 which gives you a visual picture of a business cycle.

Let's start at the top. The top of a cycle is called the *peak*. A very high peak, representing a big jump in output, is called a **boom.** (That's when the economy is doing great. Most everyone who wants a job has one and everyone is happy.) Eventually an expansion peaks. (At least, in the past, they always have.) When the economy starts to fall from that peak, there's a **downturn** in business activity. If that downturn persists for more than two consecutive quarters of the year, that downturn becomes a **recession.** (In a recession the economy isn't doing so great; many people are unemployed and a number of people are depressed.)

1B Since 1945 the average expansion has lasted about 51 months.

3 The four phases of the business cycle are: the peak, the downturn, the trough, and the upturn.

A large recession is called a **depression.** There is no formal line indicating when a recession becomes a depression. In general, a depression is much longer and more severe than a recession. This ambiguity allows some economists to joke, "When your neighbor is unemployed, it's a recession; when you're unemployed, it's a depression." If pushed for something more specific, I'd say that if unemployment exceeds 12 percent for more than a year, the economy is in a depression.

The bottom of a recession or depression is called the *trough*. When the economy comes out of the trough, economists say it's in an *upturn*. If an upturn lasts two consecutive quarters of the year, it's called an **expansion,** which leads us back up to the peak. And so it goes.

This terminology is important because if you're going to talk about the state of the economy, you need the terminology to do it. Why are businesses so interested in the state of the economy? They want to be able to predict whether it's going into a contraction or an expansion. Making the right prediction can determine whether the business will be profitable or not. That's why a large amount of economists' activity goes into trying to predict the future course of the economy.

Leading, Coincidental, and Lagging Indicators

Unemployment rate   The percentage of people in the labor force who can't find a job.

Capacity utilization rate   Rate at which factories and machines are operating compared to the maximum rate at which they could be used.

Target rate of unemployment   Lowest sustainable rate of unemployment economists believe is possible under existing conditions.

Potential output   Output that would materialize at the target rate of unemployment and the target level of capacity utilization.

4   Potential income is defined as the output that will be achieved at the target rate of unemployment and at the target level of capacity utilization.

Q–3:   List three leading indicators.

Two measures that economists often use when discussing the business cycle are the **unemployment rate** (the percentage of people in the **labor force**—the number of people in the economy willing and able to work—who can't find a job) and the **capacity utilization rate** (the rate at which factories and machines are operating compared to the rate at which they could be used). Generally economists feel that 5–6 percent unemployment and 80–85 percent capacity utilization are about as much as we should expect from the economy. Therefore, they use them as targets. Thus the **target rate of unemployment** is defined as the lowest sustainable rate of unemployment economists believe is possible under existing conditions. To push the economy beyond that would be like driving your car 90 miles an hour. True, the marks on your speedometer might go up to 130, but 90 is a more realistic top speed. Beyond 120 (assuming that's where your car is red-lined), the engine is likely to blow up (unless you have a Maserati).

Economists translate the target unemployment rate and target capacity utilization rate into the level of output with which those rates will be associated. That level of output is called **potential output** (or *potential income,* because, as I mentioned, output creates income). Potential output is the output that would materialize at the target rate of unemployment and the target level of capacity utilization. Potential output grows at the secular (long-term) trend rate of 3 to 3.5 percent per year. When the economy is in a downturn or recession, actual output is below potential output. When the economy is in a boom, actual output is above potential output.

Economists have developed a set of leading and **coincidental indicators** that, as their labels suggest, give us a good idea of when a recession is about to occur and when the economy is in one. **Leading indicators** tell us what's likely to happen 12 to 15 months from now, much as a barometer gives us a clue about tomorrow's weather. They include:

1. Average workweek for production workers in manufacturing.
2. Layoff rate in manufacturing.
3. New orders for consumer goods and materials.
4. Vendor performance, measured as a percentage of companies reporting slower deliveries from suppliers.
5. New business formation.
6. Contracts and orders for plant and equipment.
7. Number of new building permits issued for private housing units.
8. Net change in inventories on hand and on order.
9. Change in sensitive prices (prices that quickly reflect supply and demand pressures).

10. Change in total liquid assets.

11. Changes in the money supply.

Coincidental indicators tell us what phase of the business cycle the economy is currently in, much as a thermometer tells us the current temperature. Coincidental indicators are:

1. Number of employees on nonagricultural payrolls.
2. Personal income minus transfer payments (welfare, social security, war veterans' benefits, and so on).
3. Industrial production.
4. Manufacturing and trade sales volume.

Economists use leading indicators in making forecasts about the economy. Leading indicators are called *indicators,* not *predictors,* because they're only rough approximations of what's likely to happen in the future. For example, before you can build a house, a building permit must be applied for. Usually this occurs six to nine months before the actual start of construction. By looking at the number of building permits that have been issued, you can predict how much building is likely to begin in six months or so. But the prediction might be wrong, since getting a building permit does not require someone to actually build. Business economists spend much of their time and effort delving deeper into these indicators, trying to see what they are really telling us, as opposed to what they seem to be telling us. Business economists joke that the leading indicators have predicted six of the past two recessions.

Sifting through the data to find clues in new statistical series is drudgery detective work, but it's the backbone of business economists' work. Just as TV detectives' antics don't reflect what most detectives do, economists' brief appearances on the TV news don't reflect what economists do.

UNEMPLOYMENT

Business cycles and growth are directly related to unemployment in the U.S. economy. When an economy is growing and is in an expansion, unemployment is usually falling; when an economy is in a downturn, unemployment is usually rising, although often with a lag.

The relationship between the business cycle and unemployment is obvious to most people, but often the seemingly obvious hides important insights. Just why are the business cycle and growth related to unemployment? True, aggregate income must fall in a recession, but, logically, unemployment need not result. A different result could be that everyone's income falls. Looking at the problem historically, we see unemployment has not always been a problem associated with business cycles.

Unemployment became a problem about the time of the Industrial Revolution. In pre-industrial farming societies, unemployment wasn't a problem; there was always work to be done and all had their assigned tasks. The reason is that pre-industrial farmers didn't receive wages—they received net revenue (the income left after all costs had been paid). That means the average amount they netted per hour (the equivalent of a wage) was flexible. In good years they had a high income per hour; in bad years they had a low income per hour.

The flexibility in people's net income per hour meant that when there were fluctuations in economic activity, people's income rose or fell, but they kept on working. Low income was a problem, but, since people didn't become unemployed, **cyclical unemployment** (unemployment resulting from fluctuations in economic activity) was not a problem.

While cyclical unemployment did not exist in pre-industrial society, **structural unemployment** (unemployment resulting from changes in the economy itself) did. For example, say demand for a product falls because of technological change. Some unemployment would likely result; that unemployment would be called *structural unemployment.* But structural unemployment wasn't much of a problem for government, or at least people did not consider it government's problem. The reason is that

Cyclical unemployment *Unemployment resulting from fluctuations in economic activity.*

Structural unemployment *Unemployment resulting from changes in the economy itself.*

ADDED DIMENSION

CAPITALISM, THE FEAR OF HUNGER, AND THE DUTCH DISEASE

sing "the fear of hunger" to see that people work may sound rather mean, but looked at from a societal view it can be "kind." For example, consider the socialist countries that wiped out the fear of unemployment. All people were guaranteed a job. (In fact, all people were required by law to have one.) By law, unemployment was eliminated. But this created other problems. People would show up at work but not really work. After all, they couldn't be fired. The results were shoddy products, shortages, and general dissatisfaction. As one cynical citizen said, "We pretend to work and they pretend to pay us." These negative consequences of eliminating unemployment were a significant reason why people pushed for the elimination or modification of socialism. They said, "If this is the result of eliminating unemployment, bring back unemployment." And the formerly socialist countries have done that with a vengeance in the early 1990s.

I use the term *fear of hunger* rather than *fear of unemployment* to emphasize that if people can expect a good income even if they lose their jobs, the fear of unemployment loses some of its bite. For example, in European countries like the Netherlands people were guaranteed almost as much income if they had no job as they would have earned if they did have a job. The result: the unemployment rate rose and the Dutch economy stagnated. The effect of such high support payments to people who didn't work acquired a name: *the Dutch disease*.

No one argues that unemployment or the fear of hunger is good. But many do argue that going too far in eliminating it has such negative effects on growth that unemployment is the better of two bads.

unemployment of family members was dealt with internally, by the family. If someone in the family had income, that person would share it with unemployed family members.

The Industrial Revolution changed the nature of work and introduced unemployment as a problem for society. This is because the Industrial Revolution was accompanied by a shift to wage labor and to a division of responsibilities. Some individuals (capitalists) took on ownership of the means of production and *hired* others to work for them, paying them a wage per hour. This change in the nature of production marked a significant change in the nature of the unemployment problem.

First, it created the possibility of cyclical unemployment. With wages set at a certain level, when economic activity fell, workers' income per hour did not fall. Instead, when slack periods occurred, factories would lay off or fire some workers. That isn't what happened on the farm; when a slack period occurred on the farm, the income per hour of all workers fell and few were laid off.

Second, the Industrial Revolution was accompanied by a change in how families dealt with unemployment. Whereas in pre-industrial farm economies individuals or families took responsibility for their own slack periods, in a capitalist industrial society factory owners didn't take responsibility for their workers in slack periods. The pink slip (a common name for the notice workers get telling them they are laid off) and the problem of unemployment were born in the Industrial Revolution.

Without wage income, unemployed workers were in a pickle. They couldn't pay their rent, they couldn't eat, they couldn't put clothes on their backs. So what was previously a family problem became a social problem. Not surprisingly, it was at that time—the late 1700s—that economists began paying more attention to the problem of unemployment.

Initially, economists and society still did not view unemployment as a societal problem. It was the individual's problem. If people were unemployed, it was their own fault; hunger, or at least the fear of hunger, and people's desire to maintain their lifestyle would drive them to find other jobs relatively quickly. Thus, early capitalism didn't have an unemployment problem; it had an unemployment solution: the fear of hunger.

As capitalism evolved into welfare capitalism, capitalist societies no longer saw the fear of hunger as an acceptable answer to unemployment.

As capitalism evolved into welfare capitalism, the hunger solution decreased in importance. Capitalist societies no longer saw the fear of hunger as an acceptable answer to unemployment. Social welfare programs such as unemployment insurance and assistance to the poor were developed to help deal with unemployment.

In the Employment Act of 1946, the U.S. government specifically took responsibility for unemployment. The act assigned government the responsibility of creating an economic climate in which just about everyone who wanted a job could have one—a situation that economists defined as **full employment.** It was government's responsibility to offset cyclical fluctuations and thereby prevent cyclical unemployment, and to somehow deal with structural unemployment.

Full employment   Nearly everyone who wants a job has one.

Initially government regarded 2 percent unemployment as a condition of full employment. Two percent became the target rate of unemployment. The 2 percent was made up of **frictional unemployment** (unemployment caused by people quitting a job just long enough to look for and find another one) and of a few "unemployables," such as alcoholics and drug addicts, along with a certain amount of necessary structural unemployment resulting when the structure of the economy changed. Thus, any unemployment higher than 2 percent was considered either unnecessary structural or cyclical unemployment and was now government's responsibility; frictional and necessary structural unemployment were still the individual's problem.

Frictional unemployment   New entrants to the job market and people who have left their jobs to look for and find other jobs.

Macroeconomics developed as a separate field and focused on how to combat cyclical unemployment. As you will see in coming chapters, government believed it could offset cyclical unemployment and achieve full employment by seeing to it that there was sufficient aggregate demand.

By the 1950s, government had given up its view that 2 percent unemployment was consistent with full employment. It raised its target rate of unemployment to 3 percent, then to 4 percent, then to 5 percent. By the 1970s and early 1980s, government raised it further, to 6.5 percent unemployment. In the late 1980s and early 1990s the appropriate target rate of unemployment is a matter of debate, but most economists place it at somewhere between 5 and 7 percent unemployment.

1C In the 1980s and 1990s, the target rate of unemployment has been between 5 and 7 percent.

Why these changing definitions of *full employment?* One reason is that, in the 1970s and early 1980s, a low inflation rate, which also was a government goal, seemed to be incompatible with a low unemployment rate. I'll talk about this incompatibility later when I discuss "stagflation." A second reason is demographics: Different age groups have different unemployment rates, and as the population's age structure changes, so does the target unemployment rate.

Q–4: Why did the definition of full employment change over time?

A third reason is our economy's changing social and institutional structure. These social and institutional changes affected the nature of the unemployment problem. For example, in the post–World War II period, family wealth increased substantially and borrowing became easier than before, giving many unemployed individuals a bit more leeway before they were forced to find a job. For instance, more family wealth meant that upon graduation from high school or college, children who couldn't find the job they wanted could live at home and be supported by their parents for a year or two.

Another example of how changing institutions changed the unemployment problem is women's expanding role in the economy. In the 1950s, the traditional view that "woman's place is in the home" remained strong. Usually only one family member—the man—had a job. If he lost his job, no money came in. In the 1970s to 1990s, more and more women entered the work force so that today over 60 percent of all families are two-earner families. In a two-earner family, if one person loses a job, the family doesn't face immediate starvation. The other person's income carries the family over.

Yet another example involves the changing structure of the economy. In the 1990s the U.S. economy, and much of the European economy, went through major **structural readjustments**—modifications in the types of goods produced and the methods of production. Firms laid off high-wage workers even as they were increasing output. The result was that structural unemployment increased as cyclical unemployment decreased. At times this led to the unemployment rate and the level of output moving in the same direction.

Government institutions also changed. Programs like unemployment insurance and public welfare were created to reduce suffering associated with unemployment. But in doing so, these programs changed the way people responded to unemployment. People in the 1990s are more picky about what jobs they take than they were in the

ADDED DIMENSION   CATEGORIES OF UNEMPLOYMENT

A good sense of the differing types of unemployment and the differing social views that unemployment embodies can be conveyed through three examples of unemployed individuals. As you read the following stories, ask yourself which category of unemployment each individual falls into.

Example 1: Joe is listed as unemployed and collects unemployment insurance. He's had various jobs in the past and was laid off from his last one. He spent a few weeks on household projects, believing he would be called back by his most recent employer—but he wasn't. He's grown to like being on his own schedule. He's living on his unemployment insurance (while it lasts, which usually isn't more than six months), his savings, and money he picks up by being paid cash under the table working a few hours now and then at construction sites.

The Unemployment Compensation office requires him to make at least an attempt to find work, and he's turned up a few prospects. However, some were back-breaking laboring jobs and one would have required him to move to a distant city, so he's avoided accepting regular work. Joe knows the unemployment payments won't last forever. When they're used up, he plans to increase his under-the-table activity. Then, when he gets good and ready, he'll really look for a job.

Example 2: Flo is a middle-aged, small-town housewife. She worked before her marriage, but when she and her husband started their family she quit her job to be a full-time housewife and mother. She never questioned her family values of hard work, independence, belief in free enterprise, and scorn of government handouts. When her youngest child left the nest, she decided to finish the college education she'd only just started when she married.

After getting her degree, she looked for a job, but found the market for middle-aged women with no recent experience was depressed—and depressing. The state employment office where she sought listings recognized her abilities and gave her a temporary job in that very office. Because she was a "temp," however, she was the first to

be laid off when the state legislature cut the local office budget—but she'd worked long enough to be eligible for unemployment insurance.

She hesitated about applying, since handouts were against her principles. On the other hand, while working there she'd seen plenty of people, including her friends, applying for benefits after work histories even slimmer than hers. She decided to take the benefits. While they lasted, she found family finances on almost as sound a footing as when she was working. Although she was bringing in less money, net family income didn't suffer much since she didn't have social security withheld nor did she have the commuting and clothing expenses of going to a daily job.

Example 3: Tom had a good job at a manufacturing plant where he'd worked up to a wage of $450 a week. Occasionally he was laid off, but only a few weeks, and then he'd be called back. In 1989 the plant was bought by an out-of-state corporation which laid off half the work force and put in automated equipment. Tom, an older worker with comparatively high wages, was one of the first to go, and he wasn't called back.

Tom had a wife, three children, a car payment, and a mortgage. He looked for other work but couldn't find anything paying close to what he'd been getting. Tom used up his unemployment insurance and his savings. He sold the house and moved his family into a trailer. Finally he heard that there were a lot of jobs in Massachusetts, 800 miles away. He moved there, found a job, and began sending money home every week. Then the Massachusetts economy faltered. Tom was laid off again, and his unemployment insurance ran out again. Relying on his $100,000 life insurance policy, he figured he was worth more to his family dead than alive, so he killed himself.

As these three examples suggest, unemployment encompasses a wide range of cases. Unemployment is anything but a one-dimensional problem, so it's not surprising that people's views of how to deal with it differ.

1920s and 1930s. People don't just want any job, they want a *fulfilling* job with a decent wage. As people have become choosier about jobs, a debate has raged over the extent of government's responsibility for unemployment.

Whose Responsibility Is Unemployment?

Classical   A macroeconomist who generally favors laissez-faire or non activist policies.

Differing views of individuals' responsibility and society's responsibility affect people's views on whether somebody is actually unemployed. In this book I distinguish two groups of macro economists: **Keynesians** (who generally favor activist government policies) and **Classicals** (who generally favor laissez-faire or non activist policies).

The Classical View of Unemployment

Classical economists take the position that, generally, individuals should be responsible for finding jobs. They emphasize that an individual can always find *some* job at *some* wage rate, even if it's only selling apples on the street for 40¢ apiece. Given this view of individual responsibility, unemployment is impossible. If a person isn't working, that's his or her choice; the person simply isn't looking hard enough for a job. For an economist with this view, almost all unemployment is actually frictional unemployment.

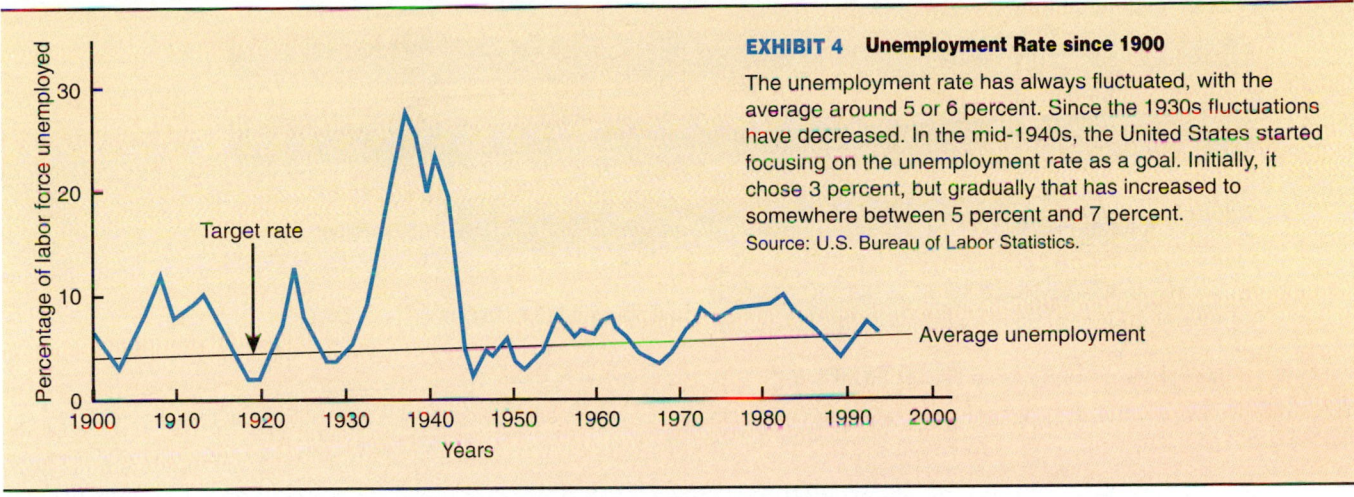

EXHIBIT 4   **Unemployment Rate since 1900**

The unemployment rate has always fluctuated, with the average around 5 or 6 percent. Since the 1930s fluctuations have decreased. In the mid-1940s, the United States started focusing on the unemployment rate as a goal. Initially, it chose 3 percent, but gradually that has increased to somewhere between 5 percent and 7 percent.
Source: U.S. Bureau of Labor Statistics.

The Keynesian View of Unemployment   Keynesian economists tend to say society owes a person a job commensurate with the individual's training or past job experience. They further argue that the job should be close enough to home so a person doesn't have to move. Given this view, frictional unemployment is only a small part of total unemployment. Structural and cyclical unemployment are far more common.

Keynesian   A macroeconomist who generally favors activist policies.

Shifts in the View of Unemployment   Which of these two views—Classical or Keynesian—most people hold depends partly on the general state of the economy. The more people are unemployed, the more tempting it is to see unemployment as a structural or cyclical problem. To see it in either of those ways puts more of the blame on society and less on unemployed individuals. In the Great Depression of the 1930s, with up to 25 percent of the population unemployed, views about unemployment changed. Most people came to see it as society's and not the individual's problem.

Keynesian economics was born in the Great Depression. In the 1950s and 1960s, as Keynesian economics expanded to include a majority of macroeconomists, the Keynesian view of unemployment also became the view of the majority of the population.

But in the 1970s and 1980s that view started to change. In Britain, for example, Prime Minister Margaret Thatcher stated specifically that unemployment was not a societal problem; it was an individual problem. Similar views were expressed in the United States. By 1990 an increasing number of people followed the Classical view and saw unemployment as an individual responsibility. In 1991 the pendulum swung back; as the economy fell into recession, the Keynesian view was once again gaining. When Bill Clinton took office in 1993, he made government creation of jobs a key part of his program.

Q–5:   In what way is the very concept of unemployment dependent upon the value judgments made by the individual?

When there's debate about what the unemployment problem is, it isn't surprising that there's also a debate about how to measure it. When talking about unemployment, economists usually refer to the "unemployment rate" published by the U.S. Department of Labor's Bureau of Labor Statistics (BLS). Fluctuations in the official unemployment rate since 1900 appear in Exhibit 4. In it you can see that during World War II (1941–45), unemployment fell from the high rates of the 1930s depression to an extremely low rate, only 1.2 percent. You can also see that while the rate started back up in the 1950s, reaching 4 or 5 percent, it remained that low up until the 1970s, when the rate began gradually to rise again. After peaking in the early 1980s it began to descend again. In 1990 it was about 5 percent; then in 1991 the economy fell into recession and unemployment rates rose to over 7 percent in 1992. By 1994 the recession had ended, but the unemployment rate remained at about 6.0 percent.

How Is Unemployment Measured?

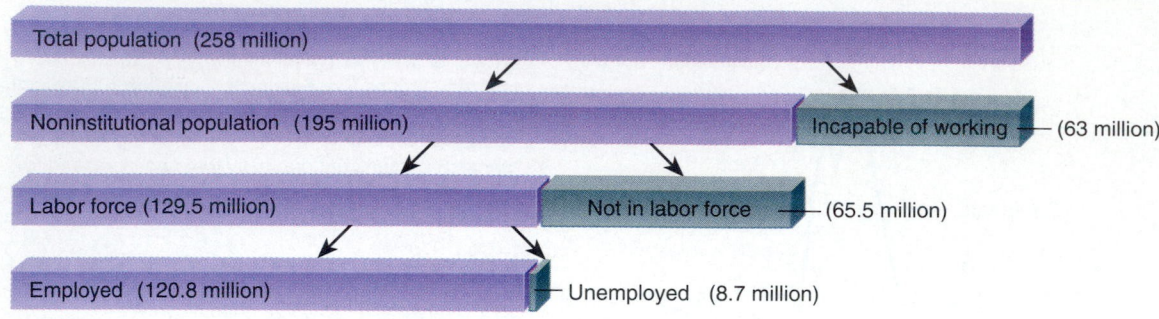

EXHIBIT 5   **Unemployment/Employment Figures (in millions)***

This exhibit shows you how the unemployment rate is calculated and the number in each category for 1993. Notice that the labor force is not the entire population.

* Based on annual 1993 employment/unemployment figures.

Source: *Monthly Labor Review.*

5A The unemployment rate is measured by dividing the number of unemployed individuals by the number of people in the civilian labor force and multiplying by 100.

Calculating the Unemployment Rate   The U.S. unemployment rate is determined by dividing the number of unemployed individuals by the number of people in the civilian labor force and multiplying by 100. For example, if the total unemployed stands at 8 million and the labor force stands at 130 million, the unemployment rate is:

$$\frac{8 \text{ million}}{130 \text{ million}} = .062 \times 100 = 6.2\%$$

To determine the civilian labor force, start with the total population and subtract from that all persons incapable of working, such as inmates of institutions and people under 16 years of age. From that figure another subtraction is made—the number of people not in the labor force, including homemakers, students, retirees, the voluntarily idle, and the disabled. The result is the potential workforce, which is about 50 percent of the total population. We then subtract about 2 million individuals who are in the armed forces, to arrive at a civilian labor force. Today the civilian labor force is about 128 million.

The civilian labor force can be divided into employed and unemployed. The Bureau of Labor Statistics (BLS) defines people as "employed" if they work at a paid job (including part-time jobs) or if they are unpaid workers in an enterprise operated by a family member. The BLS's definition of *employed* includes all those who were temporarily absent from their jobs that week because of illness, bad weather, vacation, labor–management dispute, or personal reasons, whether or not they were paid by their employers for the time off.

The BLS knows the problems with its definitions, and is continually working to improve its estimates. For example, in 1994, it revised the survey system upon which its statistics are based to use a better definition of who is actually a potential worker and whether someone falls into the BLS definition of "unemployed." This change caused the unemployment rate, as measured in January 1994, to rise even though the underlying unemployment rate using the old survey method was little changed. (Such changes cause textbook authors and policy makers difficulty in comparing and presenting statistics.) In mid-1994 the number of unemployed individuals was about 7,900,000. Dividing this number by the labor force (130,800,000) gives us an unemployment rate of 6.0 percent, slightly lower than in 1993.

How Accurate Is the Official Unemployment Rate?   BLS measures unemployment using a number of assumptions that have been the source of debate. For example, people may be staying at home and not looking for a job because they feel they don't have a chance to find one. These workers are called **discouraged workers**. Some Keynesian economists believe these individuals should be considered unemployed. Moreover they question whether part-time workers should be classified as employed.

The *Monthly Labor Review,* a Department of Labor publication, is one of the best sources of labor statistics.

The Keynesian argument is that there is a lack of decent jobs and of affordable transportation to get to the jobs that do exist, resulting in a high degree of discouragement so that many people have simply stopped trying. Because BLS statisticians define these people as voluntarily idle and do not count them as unemployed, Keynesians argue that the BLS undercounts unemployment significantly.

Q–6: Would Keynesians or Classicals be more likely to view the unemployment rate as underestimating the unemployment problems?

The Classical argument about unemployment is that being without a job often is voluntary. People say they are looking for a job, but they're not really looking. Many are working "off the books"; others are simply vacationing. Some Classicals contend that the way the BLS measures unemployment exaggerates the number of those who are truly unemployed. A person is defined as unemployed if he or she is not employed and is actively seeking work.

So is the official unemployment rate too high or too low? The definition of *unemployment* involves value judgments. Both the Keynesian and the Classical arguments are defensible. But both sides agree the unemployment measure is imperfect, missing many people who should be included and including many people who should not be counted. This means that official unemployment figures must be carefully interpreted and modified in the light of other information, such as the number of people employed, part-time employment, and your own perspective on the problem. In short, measuring and interpreting the unemployment rate (like measuring and interpreting most economic statistics) is an art, not a science.

Despite problems, the unemployment rate statistic still gives us useful information about changes in the economy. Except for those times when the BLS changes its procedures, as it did in 1994 when it adjusted part of its unemployment survey (see above), the measurement problems themselves are little changed from year to year, so in comparing one year to another, those problems are not an issue. Keynesian and Classical economists agree that a changing unemployment rate generally tells us something about the economy, especially if interpreted in the light of other statistics. That's why the unemployment rate is used as a measure of the state of the economy.

Despite problems, the unemployment rate statistic still gives us useful information about changes in the economy.

Full Employment and the Target Rate of Unemployment

Right after World War II, economists talked about achieving full employment so that everyone who wanted a job could have one. But, over time, economists increased their perceptions of the level of unemployment consistent with full employment. As this happened, the concept *full employment* no longer seemed an appropriate description of the lowest achievable rate of unemployment. So economists replaced it with other concepts that were more consistent with economic reality. The concept we'll use in this book is the *target rate of unemployment,* which is defined as the lowest sustainable rate of unemployment economists believe possible under existing conditions.

Q–7: What is the "target rate of unemployment," and why is it not zero?

As I've said, the target rate of unemployment changes over time. In the early 1990s, most economists believe that somewhere between 5 and 7 percent is a reasonable target rate. If the economy were to have lower unemployment, they believe the result would be accelerating inflation—too much demand compared to available supply. With more unemployment, economists see the economy going into a downturn or a recession—too much supply compared to available demand. That's why in 1991 and 1992, when the economy had over 7 percent unemployment, most economists believed that the economy was in recession. When the economy is in neither boom nor bust, economists expect between 5 and 7 percent unemployment (the target rate).

Unemployment and Potential Income

The target unemployment rate is used as a reference point for the economy. It establishes potential income (the income in the economy at the target rate of unemployment and target level of capacity utilization). To determine what effect changes in the unemployment rate will have on income, we use **Okun's rule of thumb,** which states that a 1 percent change in the unemployment rate will cause income to change in the opposite direction by 2.5 percent. For example, if unemployment rises from 5 percent to 6 percent, total output of $5 trillion will fall by 2.5 percent, or $125 billion, to $4.875 trillion. In terms of numbers of workers, a 1 percent increase in the unemployment rate means about 1,200,000 additional people are out of work.

Okun's rule of thumb   A 1-percent change in the unemployment rate will cause income in the economy to change in the opposite direction by 2.5 percent.

ADDED DIMENSION

FROM FULL EMPLOYMENT TO THE TARGET RATE OF UNEMPLOYMENT

As I emphasized in Chapter 1, good economists attempt to remain neutral and objective. It isn't always easy, especially when the language we use is often biased. (Think back to the puzzle about the doctor in Chapter 1. Have you solved it yet?)

This problem has proved to be a difficult one for economists in their attempt to find an alternative to the concept *full employment*. An early contender was the *natural rate of unemployment*. Economists have often used the term *natural* to describe economic concepts. For example, they've talked about "natural" rights and a "natural" rate of interest. The problem with this usage is that what's natural to one person isn't necessarily natural to another. The term *natural* often conveys a sense of "that's the way it should be." However, in describing as "natural" the rate of unemployment that an economy can achieve, economists weren't making any value judgments about whether 5.5 percent unemployment is what should, or should not, be. They simply were saying that, given the institutions in the economy, that is what is achievable. So a number of economists objected to the use of the term *natural*.

As an alternative, a number of economists started to use the term *nonaccelerating inflation rate of unemployment (NAIRU)*, but even users of this term agreed it was a horrendous term. And so most avoided its use and shifted to the relatively neutral term, *target rate of unemployment*.

The target rate of unemployment is the rate that one believes is attainable without causing accelerating inflation. It is not determined theoretically; it is determined empirically. Economists look at what seems to be achievable and is historically normal, adjust that for structural and demographic changes they believe are occurring, and come up with the target rate of unemployment.

These figures are rough, but they give you a sense of the implications of a change. For example, say unemployment falls .2 percentage points, from 5.5 to 5.3 percent. That means about 240,000 more people have jobs and that income will be $25 billion higher than otherwise would have occurred if the increase holds for the entire year.

Notice I said "will be $25 billion higher than otherwise would have occurred" rather than simply saying "will increase by $25 billion." As we discussed in the growth section, generally the economy is growing as a result of increases in productivity or increases in the number of people choosing to work. Changes in either of these can cause income and employment to grow, even if there's no change in the unemployment rate. We must point this out because in the 1980s the number of people choosing to work increased substantially, significantly increasing the labor participation rate. Then, in 1993, as many large firms structurally adjusted their production methods to increase their productivity, unemployment sometimes rose, and employment fell, even as output rose. Thus, when the labor participation rate and productivity change, an increase in unemployment doesn't necessarily mean a decrease in employment or a decrease in income.

Microeconomic Categories of Unemployment

In the post–World War II period, unemployment was seen primarily as cyclical unemployment, and the focus of macroeconomic policy was on how to eliminate that unemployment through a specific set of macroeconomic policies—monetary and fiscal policies, which I'll discuss in Part 2.

Understanding monetary and fiscal policies is important, but in the 1990s it's not enough. Unemployment has many dimensions, so different types of unemployment are susceptible to different types of policies. Today's view is that you don't use a sledge hammer to pound in finishing nails, and you don't use macro policies to deal with certain types of unemployment; instead you use micro policies. To determine where microeconomic policies are appropriate as a supplement to macroeconomic policies, economists break unemployment down into a number of categories and analyze each category separately. These categories include how people become unemployed, demographic characteristics, duration of unemployment, and industry. (See Exhibit 6.)

5B   Some microeconomic categories of unemployment are reason for unemployment, demographic unemployment, duration of unemployment, and unemployment by industry.

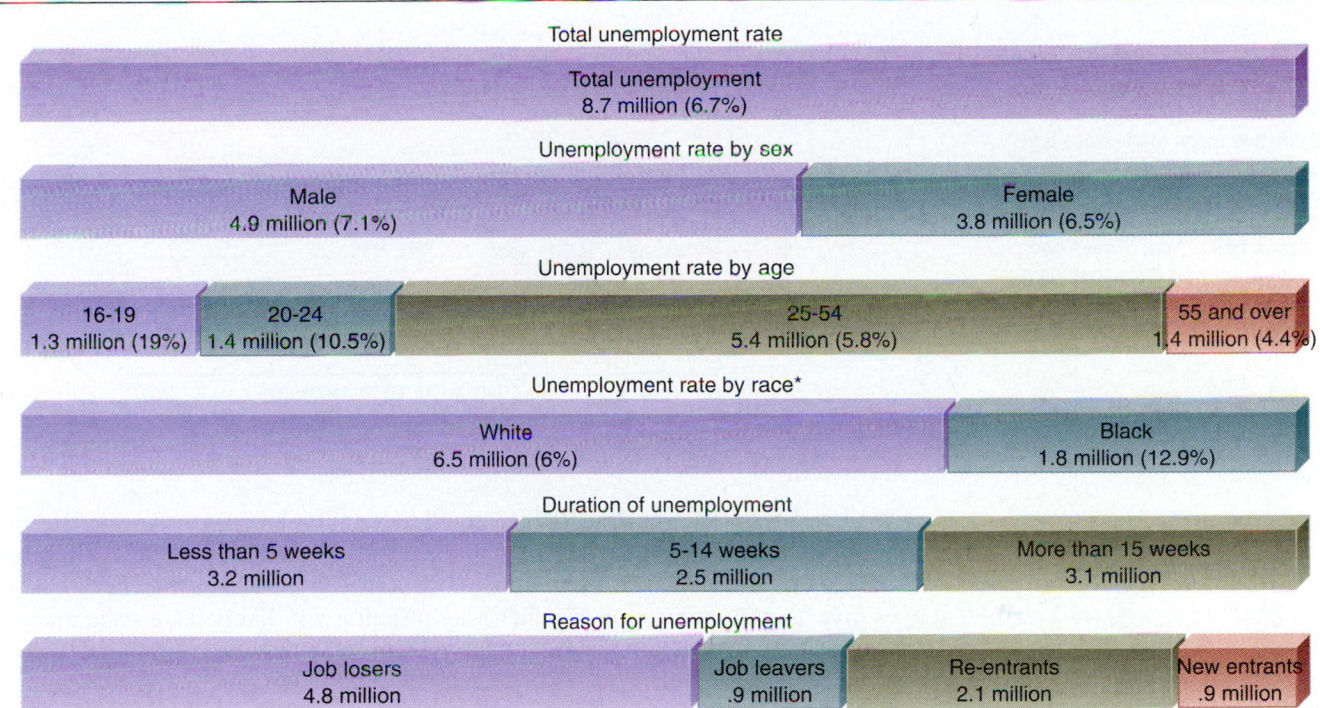

EXHIBIT 6   Unemployment by Microeconomic Subcategories, 1993

Unemployment isn't all the same. This exhibit gives you a sense of some of the subcategories of unemployment.
* Figures adjusted to include estimates of the number of Hispanics.
Source: Dept. of Labor Statistics; *Monthly Labor Review*, 1994.

Inflation is a continual rise in the price level. The price level is an index of all prices in the economy. Even when inflation isn't roaring and inflation itself isn't a problem, the fear of inflation guides macroeconomic policy. Fear of inflation prevents governments from expanding the economy and reducing unemployment. It prevents governments from using macroeconomic policies to lower interest rates. It gets some political parties booted out of office. (Democrat Jimmy Carter lost his bid for a second U.S. presidential term in part because of high inflation at the time.) It gets others elected. (Republican George Bush won the U.S. presidency in 1988 in part because of low inflation in the late 1980s.)

A one-time rise in the price level is not inflation. Unfortunately, it's often hard to tell if a one-time rise in the price level is going to stop, so the distinction blurs in practice, but we must understand the distinction. If the price level goes up 10 percent in a month, but then remains constant, the economy doesn't have an inflation problem. Inflation is an *ongoing rise* in the price level.

From 1800 until World War II the U.S. inflation rate and price level fluctuated; sometimes the price level would rise, and sometimes the price level would fall—there would be deflation. Since World War II the price level has continually risen, which means the inflation rate (the measure of the change in prices over time) has been positive, as can be seen in Exhibit 7. The rate at which the price level rises fluctuates, but the movement has been consistently upward.

Since inflation is a sustained rise in the general price level, one must first determine what the general price level was at a given time and then decide how much it has changed. Because there are a number of different ways of doing this, there are a number of different measures of the price level. The most often used are the Producer Price Index, the GDP deflator, and the Consumer Price Index. Each has certain advantages and disadvantages.

INFLATION

6A Inflation is a continual rise in the price level.

1D Since World War II, the U.S. inflation rate has remained positive and relatively stable.

Measurement of Inflation

EXHIBIT 7   Inflation Since 1990

Until 1940, rises in the price level were followed by falls in the price level, keeping the price level relatively constant. Since the 1940s, inflation has almost always been positive, which means that the price level has been continually rising. Source: U.S. Dept. of Commerce.

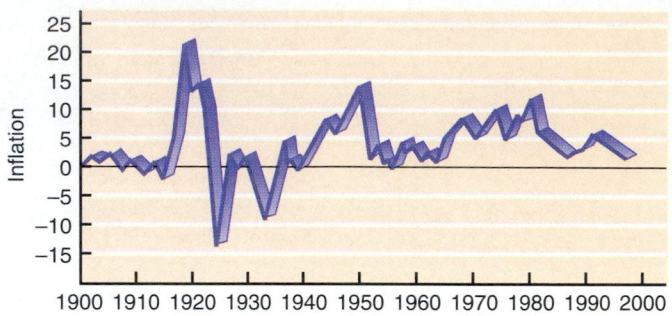

Producer Price Index (PPI)   Composite of prices of certain raw materials.

GDP deflator   Index of the price level of aggregate output or the average price of the components in GDP relative to a base year.

Consumer Price Index (CPI)   Index of inflation measuring prices of a fixed "basket" of consumer goods, weighted according to each component's share of an average consumer's expenditures.

Q–8:   Health care costs make up 15 percent of total expenditures. Say they rise by 10 percent, while the other components of the price index remain constant. By how much does the price index rise?

The **Producer Price Index (PPI)** is an index or ratio of a composite of prices of a number of important raw materials, such as steel, relative to a composite of the prices of those raw materials in a base year. It does not correctly measure actual inflation, but it does give an early indication of which way inflation will likely head since many of the prices that make it up are the prices of raw materials used as inputs in the production of other goods.

The total output deflator, or **GDP deflator** (gross domestic product deflator), is an index of the price level of aggregate output or the average price of the components in total output or GDP relative to a base year.[1] It's the inflation index economists generally favor because it includes the widest number of goods. Unfortunately, since it's difficult to compute, it's published only quarterly and with a fairly substantial lag. (That is, by the time the figures come out, the period the figures measure has been over for quite a while.)

Published monthly, the **Consumer Price Index (CPI)** is the index of inflation most often used in news reports about the economy. As opposed to measuring the prices of all goods, it measures the prices of a fixed "basket" of goods that consumers buy, weighting each component of the basket according to its share of an average consumer's expenditures. Exhibit 8 shows the relative percentages. As you see, housing, transportation, and food make up the largest percentages of the CPI. To give you an idea of what effect the rise in price of a component of the CPI will have on the CPI as a whole, let's say food prices rise 10 percent in a year and all other prices remain constant. Since food is about 20 percent of the total, the CPI will rise 20% × 10% = 2%. The CPI and GDP deflator indices roughly equal each other when averaged over an entire year.

Measuring changes in prices over time is difficult. One of the most vexing price indexing problems is how to include quality changes. For example, say 1995 cars have a new style and, unlike 1994 models, provide airbags as a standard feature. They cost 5 percent more. Has the price of cars really gone up 5 percent, or is the 5 percent simply the cost of improving cars' design and equipment? There are ways to answer these questions, but none are totally satisfactory. With significant changes in goods' quality occurring every year, most economists don't worry about small amounts of inflation (1 or 2 percent), because it's not even certain such small changes actually represent inflation.

Real and Nominal Concepts

Real Output   Aggregate output adjusted for price level changes.

One important way in which inflation indices are used is to separate changes in real output from changes in nominal output. **Real output** is the total amount of goods and services produced, adjusted for price level changes. It is the measure of output that

---

[1] We'll discuss why total output is called GDP in the next chapter.

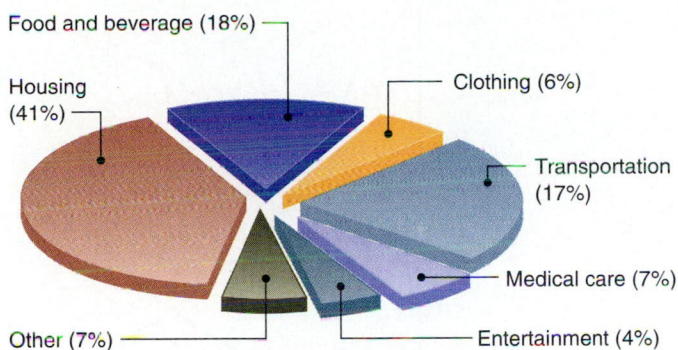

Food and beverage (18%)

Housing (41%)

Clothing (6%)

Transportation (17%)

Medical care (7%)

Other (7%)

Entertainment (4%)

EXHIBIT 8   Composition of CPI

The Consumer Price Index is determined by looking at the prices of the categories listed in this exhibit. These categories represent the rough percentages of people's expenditures. In reality, there are Consumer Price Indexes for two population groups: (1) for all urban consumers (the urban CPI)—about 80 percent of the U.S. population—and (2) for urban wage earners and clerical workers (the wage-earner CPI)—about 32 percent of the U.S. population. The numbers that compose the CPI are collected at 85 separate locations and include prices from over 57,000 housing units and 19,000 business establishments.
Source: Bureau of Labor Statistics, *CPI Detailed Reports*, 1994.

would exist if the price level had remained constant. **Nominal output** is output as measured. For example, say total output rises from $4 trillion to $5 trillion. Nominal output has risen by

$$\frac{\$5 \text{ trillion} - \$4 \text{ trillion}}{\$4 \text{ trillion}} = \frac{\$1 \text{ trillion}}{\$4 \text{ trillion}} = 25\%.$$

Let's say, however, the price level has risen 20 percent, from 100 percent to 120 percent. The inflation index is 120. Because the inflation index has increased, real output (nominal output adjusted for inflation) hasn't risen by 25 percent; it has risen by less than nominal output has increased. To determine how much less, we use our formula to adjust the nominal figures to account for inflation. This is called *deflating* the nominal figures. To deflate we divide the most recent nominal figure, $5 trillion, by the price index of 120 percent (or 1.2):

$$\text{Real Output} = \frac{\text{Nominal Output}}{120} \times 100 = \frac{\$5 \text{ trillion}}{1.2} = \$4.167 \text{ trillion.}$$

That $4.167 trillion is the measure of output that would have existed if the price level had not changed. What output would have been if the price level had remained constant is the definition of real output so $4.167 trillion is the measure of real output. Real output has increased from $4 trillion to $4.167 trillion, or by $167 billion.

When you consider price indices, you mustn't lose sight of the forest for the trees. Keep in mind the general distinction between real and nominal GDP. The concepts *real* and *nominal* and the process of adjusting from nominal to real by dividing the nominal amount by a price index will come up again and again. So whenever you see the word *real*, remember:

The "real" amount is the nominal amount divided by the price index. It is the nominal amount adjusted for inflation.

Inflation results when more people on average raise their nominal prices than lower their nominal prices. Thus, to explain why inflation occurs we must explain why people raise their nominal prices. The logical answer is that they believe that in doing so they can get a larger slice of the total output pie for themselves. But shares of the pie are determined by relative, not nominal, prices. To see the difference, say you raise your nominal price by 10 percent, but everyone else does, too. So the prices of the goods you sell go up by 10 percent and the prices of the goods you buy go up by 10

Q–9:   Nominal output has increased from $5 trillion to $6 trillion. The GDP deflator has risen by 15 percent. By how much has real income risen?

6B   The "real" amount is the nominal amount divided by the price index. It is the nominal amount adjusted for inflation.

Why Does Inflation Occur?

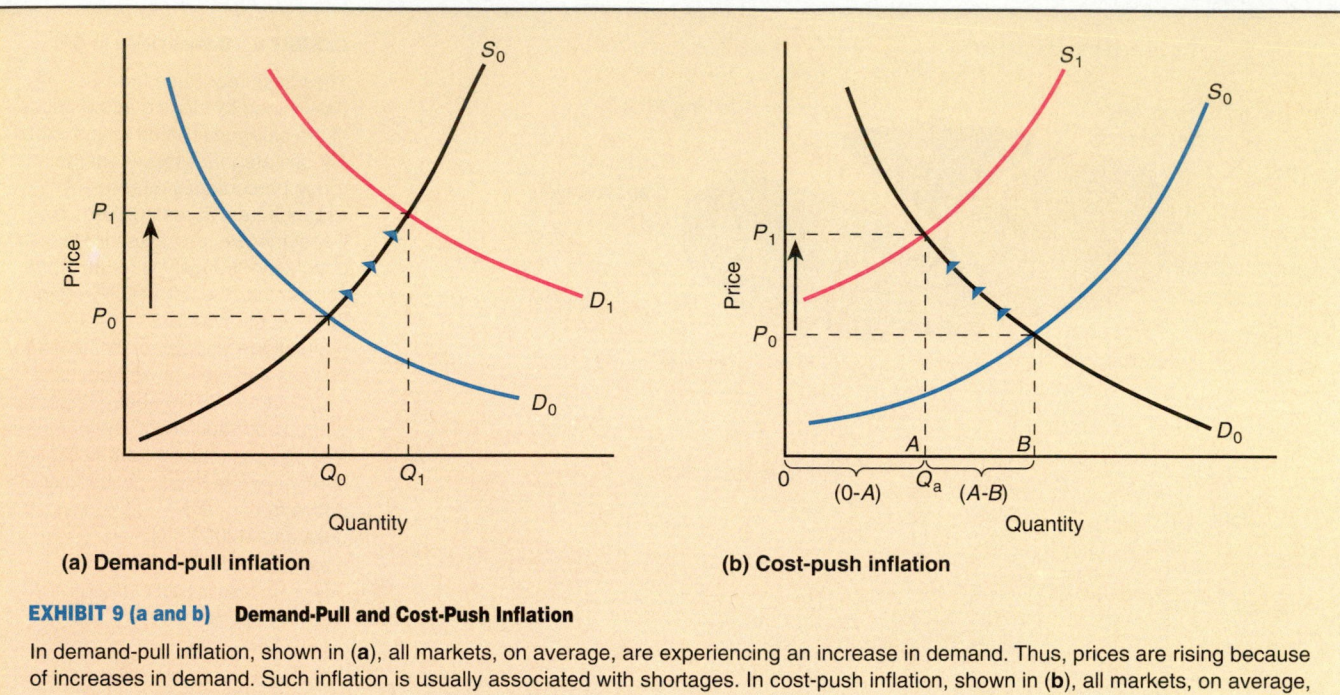

(a) Demand-pull inflation

(b) Cost-push inflation

EXHIBIT 9 (a and b)   **Demand-Pull and Cost-Push Inflation**

In demand-pull inflation, shown in (**a**), all markets, on average, are experiencing an increase in demand. Thus, prices are rising because of increases in demand. Such inflation is usually associated with shortages. In cost-push inflation, shown in (**b**), all markets, on average, do not have excess demand. Instead, prices rise because of increases in nominal supply prices or leftward shifts in supply.

percent. Your nominal price has gone up, but your relative price has not, and you're no better off.

Our economy has nominal wage- and price-setting institutions in which people set their relative prices by setting a nominal price. This means that if we are careful, we can gain insight into inflation by considering a representative market and distinguishing two reasons for individuals wanting to raise their relative price (which, given our price-setting institutions, they do by raising their nominal price).

To see this distinction, think back to Chapter 2's discussion of the dynamic laws of supply and demand. There we saw that a gap between the quantity demanded and the quantity supplied leads to upward pressure on price. Exhibit 9(a) demonstrates this for an individual market. If price is initially P_0 and demand rises from D_0 to D_1, there will be upward pressure on the good's price. When the majority of industries are at close to capacity and they experience increases in demand, we say there's demand-pull pressure, and the inflation that results is called **demand-pull inflation.** Where does this increase in demand come from? It can come from numerous sources, but many economists focus on government's demands and increases in the money supply as important causes of increases in demand in markets on average.

Demand-pull inflation   *Inflation that occurs when the economy is at or above full employment.*

When demand is high, from an individual perspective, a price increase enlarges a person's share. But if overall demand is high, and everyone raises their nominal price, that nominal price increase does not increase a person's share. Overall nominal prices rise, and hence the price level rises, but relative prices are little affected.

Demand-pull inflations are generally characterized by shortages of goods and shortages of workers. Because there's excess demand, firms know that if they raise their prices, they'll still be able to sell their goods, and workers know if they raise their wages, they will still get hired.

Demand-pull pressure can be a catalyst for starting inflation; it is not a cause of continued inflation. If aggregate demand-pull pressure continues unabated even as prices rise, the inflation will quickly blow up into an ever-increasing inflation as expectations of rising price levels cause people to raise their nominal price even more in order to have a desired relative price increase. Remember, Exhibit 9 was a graph of one individual market; it referred to a relative price. If all people are trying to raise their relative prices by raising their nominal prices, everyone will expect the price level to rise, and will raise their price even more. The demand-pull pressure will quickly generate an accelerating expectational inflation. Societies don't want that to happen, so while excess demand may be an explanation of the start of inflation, it is not an explanation of ongoing inflation.

Exhibit 9(b) shows a second possible explanation why people might raise their price in an individual market. Say one group of individuals (0-A) figured out a way to limit the quantity supplied to Q_a. To do so, they must keep suppliers A-B out of the market through some type of legal or social pressure. If they succeed, price rises from P_0 to P_1 as supply shifts to the left. When a significant proportion of markets (or one very important market, such as the labor market or the oil market) experience restrictions on supply, we say that there is cost-push pressure. The resulting inflation is called **cost-push inflation.**

In cost-push inflation, because there is no excess demand (there may actually be excess supply), firms are not sure there will be sufficient demand to sell off their goods and all workers are not sure that after raising their wage they will all be hired, but the ones who actually do the pushing are fairly sure they won't be the ones who can't sell off their goods or the ones fired. A classic cost-push example occurred in the 1970s when OPEC raised its price on oil, triggering cost-push inflation.

The demand-pull/cost-push distinction is helpful as long as one remembers that it must be used with care. The price level is always determined by both demand pressures and cost pressures. In all inflations, both demand-pull and cost-push pressures play a role. As Alfred Marshall (the 19th-century English economist who originated supply and demand analysis) said, it is impossible to separate the roles of supply and demand in influencing price, just as it is impossible to separate which blade of the scissors is cutting a sheet of paper. Both sides always play a role.

To see the difficulty, let's consider the OPEC oil price rise. What would have happened if all prices rose but total quantity demanded did not rise? The result would have been unemployment, a fall in production, and a decrease in the demand for oil. Prices, on average, wouldn't have continued to rise as demand fell. But prices on average *did* continue to rise because total demand did not stay constant—it rose significantly for reasons that we'll discuss in later chapters. So some economists called it demand-pull inflation rather than cost-push inflation. Since inflation is an ongoing rise in prices and, in any ongoing rise, both demand and supply play a role, the cost-push/demand-pull distinction must be used carefully.

A second helpful distinction is between expected and unexpected inflation. **Expected inflation** is inflation people expect to occur. **Unexpected inflation** surprises people.

To see why this expected/unexpected distinction is important, remember when an individual sets a price (for goods or labor) he or she is actually setting a relative price—relative to some price level that they expect to exist out there. The dynamic laws of supply and demand affect relative prices, not nominal prices. Now let's say everyone suddenly expects the price level to rise 10 percent. Let's also say that all individual sellers want a 1/2 percent raise in their relative price. They're not greedy; they just want a little bit more than what they're currently getting.

The reason expectations of inflation are important is the relative price increase people want must be tacked onto the inflation they expect. When people expect a 10 percent inflation, in order to have a one-half of 1 percent rise in their relative price, they have to raise their money price by $10\frac{1}{2}$ percent—10 percent to keep up and 1/2 percent to get ahead. Ten percent of the inflation is caused by expectations of inflation; 1/2 percent of the inflation is caused by cost-push pressures. The cost-push/demand-pull distinction concerns what causes the 1/2 percent pressure. The expected/unexpected distinction refers to the cause of that 10 percent inflation. Thus, whether or not inflation is expected makes a big difference in individuals' behavior. If people expect inflation, they'll raise their prices to get ahead or to keep up. They won't do that for unexpected inflation, because of course they don't know unexpected inflation is coming.

7A Cost-push inflation involves a rise in the price level resulting from restrictions on supply due to some sort of legal or social pressure. When excess demand causes the price level to rise, it is referred to as demand-pull inflation.

Cost-push inflation   *Inflation that occurs when the economy is below full employment with prices rising even though there are no shortages of goods or workers.*

Q–10: Why did some economists see the OPEC oil price rise as a demand-pull, rather than a cost-push, inflation?

Expected and Unexpected Inflation

7B Expected inflation is the amount of inflation that people expect. Unexpected inflation is a surprise to them.

Since prices and wages are often set for periods of two months to three years ahead, whether inflation is expected can play an important role in the inflation process. In the early 1970s people didn't expect the high inflation rates that did occur. When inflation hit, people just tried to keep up with it. By the end of the 1970s, people expected more inflation than actually occurred and raised their prices—and, in doing so, caused the inflation rate to increase.

Expectations of inflation play an important role in any ongoing inflation. They can snowball a small inflationary pressure into an accelerating large inflation. Individuals keep raising their prices because they expect inflation, and inflation keeps on growing because individuals keep raising their prices. That's why expectations of inflation are of central concern to economic policy makers.

Costs of Inflation

8 While inflation may not make the nation poorer, it does cause income to be redistributed, and it can reduce the amount of information that prices are supposed to convey.

Inflation has costs, but not the costs that noneconomists often associate with it. Specifically, inflation doesn't make the nation poorer. True, whenever prices go up somebody (the person paying the higher price) is worse off, but the person to whom the higher price is paid is better off. The two offset each other. So inflation does not make the society on average any poorer. Inflation does, however, redistribute income from people who cannot or do not raise their prices to people who can and do raise their prices. This often creates feelings of injustice about the economic system. Thus, inflation can have significant distributional or equity effects.

A second cost of inflation is its effect on the information content of prices. Consider an individual who laments the high cost of housing, pointing out that it has doubled in 10 years! But if inflation averaged 7 percent a year over the past 10 years, a doubling of housing prices should be expected. In fact, with 7 percent inflation, on average *all* prices double every 10 years. That means the individual's wages have probably also doubled, so he or she is no better off and no worse off than 10 years ago. The price of housing relative to other goods, which is the relevant price for making decisions, hasn't changed. When there's inflation it's hard for people to know what is and what isn't a relative price. People's minds aren't computers, so inflation reduces the amount of information that prices can convey and causes people to make choices that do not reflect relative prices.

Despite these costs, inflation is usually accepted by governments as long as it stays at a low rate. What scares economists is inflationary pressures above and beyond expectations of inflation (for example, if the money supply is increasing at a fast rate). In that case, expectations of higher inflation can cause inflation to build up and compound itself. A 3 percent inflation becomes a 6 percent inflation, which in turn becomes a 12 percent inflation. Once inflation hits 5 percent or 6 percent, it's definitely no longer a little thing. Inflation of 10 percent or more is significant. While there is no precise definition, once inflation hits triple digits—100 percent or more— it is reasonable to say that it has become a **hyperinflation.**

Hyperinflation *Exceptionally high inflation of, say, 100 percent or more per year.*

The United States has been either relatively lucky or wise because it has not experienced hyperinflation since the Civil War (1861–65). Other countries, such as Brazil, Israel, and Argentina, have not been so lucky (or have not followed policies as wise as the United States has). These countries have frequently had hyperinflations. But even with inflations at these levels, economies have continued to operate and, in many cases, continued to do well.

In a hyperinflation people try to spend their money quickly, but they still use the money. Let's say the U.S. price level is increasing 1 percent a day, which is a yearly inflation rate of about 4,000 percent.[2] Is an expected decrease in value of 1 percent per day going to cause you to stop using dollars? Probably not, unless you have a good alternative. You will, however, avoid putting your money into a savings account unless that savings account somehow compensates you for the expected inflation (the expected fall in the value of the dollar), and you will try to ensure your

---

[2] Why about 4,000 percent and not 365 percent? Because of compounding. In the second day the increase is on the initial price level *and* the 1 percent rise in price level that occurred the first day. When you carry out this compounding for all 365 days, you get almost 4,000 percent.

wage *is* adjusted for inflation. In a hyperinflation, wages, the prices firms receive, and individual savings are all in some way adjusted for inflation. Hyperinflations lead to economic institutions with built-in expectations of inflation. For example, usually in a hyperinflation the government issues indexed bonds whose value keeps pace with inflation.

Once these adjustments have been made, substantial inflations will not destroy an economy, but they certainly are not good for it. Such inflations tend to break down confidence in the monetary system, the economy, and the government.

THE INTERRELATIONSHIP OF GROWTH, INFLATION, AND UNEMPLOYMENT

In this chapter, we've talked about growth, inflation, and unemployment. Before we move on, let's briefly address their interrelationship. That interrelationship centers on trade-off between inflation on the one hand and growth and unemployment on the other. If the government could attack inflation without worrying about unemployment or growth, it probably would have solved the problem of inflation by now. Unfortunately, solving inflation often worsens unemployment and slows growth. When the government tries to stop inflation, it often causes a recession—increasing unemployment and slowing growth. Similarly, reducing unemployment by stimulating growth tends to increase inflation. To the degree that inflation and unemployment are opposite sides of the coin, the opportunity cost of reducing unemployment is inflation. The government must make a trade-off between low unemployment and slow growth on the one hand and inflation on the other. Opportunity costs must be faced in macro as well as in micro.

CHAPTER SUMMARY

- The secular trend growth rate of the economy is 3 to 3.5 percent. Fluctuations around the secular trend growth rate are called *business cycles*.
- Two important causes of growth are appropriate economic incentives and people.
- Phases of the business cycle include peak, trough, upturn, and downturn.
- The target rate of unemployment is the lowest sustainable rate of unemployment possible under existing institutions. It's associated with an economy's potential income. The lower the target rate of unemployment, the higher an economy's potential income.
- The microeconomic approach to unemployment subdivides unemployment into categories and looks at those individual components.
- A real concept is a nominal concept adjusted for inflation.
- Inflation is a continual rise in the price level. Both cost-push and demand-pull pressures play a role in any inflation.
- Expectations of inflation can provide pressure for an inflation to continue even when other causes don't exist.
- For inflation to continue, it must be accompanied by an increase in the money supply.
- Two important costs of inflation are an equity cost and an information cost.

KEY TERMS

boom *(139)*
business cycle *(137)*
capacity utilization rate *(140)*
Classical *(144)*
coincidental indicators *(140)*
Consumer Price Index (CPI) *(150)*
cost-push inflation *(153)*
cyclical unemployment *(141)*
demand-pull inflation *(152)*
depression *(140)*
discouraged workers *(146)*
downturn *(139)*
expansion *(140)*

expected inflation *(153)*
frictional unemployment *(143)*
full employment *(143)*
GDP deflator *(150)*
growth-compatible institutions *(135)*
human capital *(137)*
hyperinflation *(154)*
inflation *(149)*
Keynesian *(145)*
labor force *(140)*
leading indicators *(140)*
nominal output *(151)*
Okun's rule of thumb *(147)*

potential output *(140)*
Producer Price Index (PPI) *(150)*
real output *(150)*
recession *(139)*
social capital *(137)*
structural readjustments *(143)*
structural unemployment *(141)*
target rate of unemployment *(140)*
unemployment rate *(140)*
unexpected inflation *(153)*

QUESTIONS FOR THOUGHT AND REVIEW

The number after each question represents the estimated degree of critical thinking required. (1= almost none; 10 = deep thought.)

1. An economist has just made an argument that rules should be followed because they're rules. Which kind of economist is this person: Keynesian or Classical? Why? (*This question uses material from the section introduction.*) *(7)*

2. If unemployment fell to 1.2 percent in World War II, why can't it be reduced to 1.2 percent in the 1990s? *(8)*

3. The index of leading indicators has predicted all past recessions. Nonetheless it's not especially useful for predicting recessions. Explain. *(7)*

4. Distinguish between structural unemployment and cyclical unemployment. *(3)*

5. Does the unemployment rate underestimate or overestimate the unemployment problem? Explain. *(5)*

6. If unemployment rises 2 percent, what will likely happen to income in the United States? *(7)*

7. Why are expectations central to understanding inflation? *(5)*

8. Inflation, on average, makes people neither richer nor poorer. Therefore it has no cost. True or false? Explain. *(7)*

9. Who would be more likely to see a psychiatrist: a Keynesian economist or a Classical economist? Why? (*This question uses material from the section introduction.*) *(8)*

10. Would you expect that inflation would generally be associated with low unemployment? Why? *(7)*

PROBLEMS AND EXERCISES

1. The following questions require library research.
   a. What are the current unemployment rate, capacity utilization rate, and rate of inflation? What do you predict they will be next year?
   b. Find some predictions for each of these figures for next year.
   c. Are these predictions consistent with your predictions? Why?
   d. In what position on the business cycle does the economy currently find itself?

2. The following questions concern statistics and economic institutions.
   a. Go to the local unemployment office and ask to see the form people fill out to collect unemployment insurance. What are the eligibility criteria?
   b. A friend shows you a newspaper article saying unemployment increased but output also increased. He says that this doesn't make sense, it must be a mistake. What do you tell your friend?
   c. Inflation is 5 percent; real output rises 2 percent. What would you expect to happen to nominal output?
   d. Real output rose 3 percent and nominal output rose 7 percent. What happened to inflation?

3. In H. G. Wells's *Time Machine,* a late Victorian time traveler arrives in England in AD 802700 to find a new race of people, the Eloi, in their idleness. Their idleness is, however, supported by another race, the Morlocks, who are underground slaves and who produce the output. If technology were such that the Elois's lifestyle could be sustained by machines, not slaves, is it a lifestyle that would be desirable? What implications does the above discussion have for unemployment?

4. In 1991, Japanese workers' average tenure with a firm was 10.9 years; in 1991 in the United States the average tenure of workers was 6.7 years.
   a. What are two possible explanations for these differences?
   b. Which system is better?
   c. In the mid-1990s Japan has experienced a recession while the United States economy has been growing. What effect will this likely have on these ratios?

5. One quarter prior to the peak in a business cycle, what is most likely happening to the following indicators (up or down)?
   a. Average workweek
   b. Employees on nonagricultural payrolls
   c. Industrial production
   d. Net change in inventories on hand and on order
   e. New business formation
   f. Personal income minus transfer payments

ANSWERS TO MARGIN QUESTIONS

1. Regulations inhibit growth because they discourage and prevent individuals from undertaking entrepreneurial activity. Some regulation is necessary to ensure that growth is of a socially desirable type. *(135)*

2. More capital alone will not lead to growth. Technological change makes older types of capital obsolete, and investment in that older type of capital can be almost a complete waste, as was the case in the former Soviet Union. Its capital didn't embody technological changes. *(136)*

3. Three leading indicators are the average work week, the layoff rate, and changes in the money supply. There are others. *(140)*

4. The definition of full employment changed over time because (1) low inflation was incompatible with what people thought was full employment, and (2) demographics—the age structure of the population—changed, and people of different ages have different rates of unemployment. *(143)*

5. Unemployment is a hypothetical concept, and what "full employment" means is dependent on a value judgment as to what types of possibilities society owes individuals. *(144)*

6. Keynesians emphasize that since to be counted as unemployed by the BLS one must be looking for a job, the unemployment rate does not include discouraged workers. Classicals emphasize that in order to collect unemployment benefits, some people pretend to be unemployed when they are not really unemployed. Thus, Keynesians would be more likely to view the unemployment rate as underestimating the unemployment problem. *(147)*

7. The concept "target rate of unemployment" refers to the lowest sustainable rate of unemployment economists believe possible under existing conditions. It is not zero because existing conditions require some unemployment as individuals change jobs. Also, if unemployment went lower than some level, accelerating inflation would result. *(147)*

8. The price index will rise by $.15 \times .1 = .015 = 1.5\%$. *(150)*

9. Since nominal output has increased by $(6 - 5)/5 = 20\%$, and the price level has increased by 15 percent, real output has increased by 5 percent. *(151)*

10. The oil price rise involved a change in relative prices. If the world money supply and aggregate demand hadn't expanded, that relative price change would have involved a temporary rise in the price level and unemployment. But aggregate demand *did* rise significantly, which leads some economists to call the type of inflation during that time a demand-pull inflation. *(153)*

7

National Income Accounting

The government is very keen on amassing statistics. . . . They collect them, add them, raise them to the nth power, take the cube root and prepare wonderful diagrams. But you must never forget that every one of these figures comes in the first instance from the village watchman, who just puts down what he damn pleases.

~ Sir Josiah Stamp (head of Britain's revenue department in the late 19th century)

After reading this chapter, you should be able to:

1 State why national income accounting is important.

2 Define GDP, GNP, NDP, NI, and NNP.

3 Calculate GDP in a simple example, avoiding double counting.

4 Explain why GDP $= C + I + G + (X - M)$.

5 Distinguish between real and nominal values.

6 State some limitations of national income accounting.

Before you can talk about macroeconomics in depth, you need to be introduced to some terminology used in macroeconomics. That terminology can be divided into two parts. The first part deals with national income accounting, which was specifically developed to handle macroeconomic aggregate concepts (concepts embodying a number of components). Examples include total consumption, total income, and the price level.

The second part distinguishes between real and nominal (or money) concepts. As we discussed in an earlier chapter, **real concepts** are concepts adjusted for inflation; **nominal concepts** are concepts specified in monetary terms with no adjustment for inflation. Real and nominal concepts are used to differentiate and compare goods and services over time.

Real concepts   Economic concepts adjusted for inflation.

Nominal concepts   Economic concepts specified in monetary terms (current dollars) with no adjustment for inflation.

In the 1930s, it was impossible for macroeconomics to exist in the form we know it today because many aggregate concepts of macroeconomics we now take for granted either had not yet been formulated or were so poorly formulated that it was useless to talk rigorously about them. This lack of aggregate terminology was consistent with the Classical economists' lack of interest in the aggregate approach in the 1930s; they preferred to focus on microeconomics.

With the advent of Keynesian macroeconomics in the mid-1930s, development of a terminology to describe macroeconomic aggregates became crucial. Measurement is a necessary step towards rigor. A group of Keynesian economists set out to develop an aggregate terminology and to measure the aggregate concepts they defined, so that people would have concrete terms to use when talking about macroeconomic problems. Their work (for which two of them, Simon Kuznets and Richard Stone, received the Nobel prize) is called **national income accounting** (a set of rules and definitions to use in measuring activity in the aggregate economy—that is, in the economy as a whole). To talk about the aggregate economy without knowing the concepts of national income accounting is equivalent to talking about cricket without knowing what a wicket is, or to talk about rock music without knowing U2.

National income accounting provides a way of measuring total, or aggregate, economic production. In national income accounting aggregate economic production is broken down into subaggregates (such as consumption, investment, and personal income); national income accounting defines the relationship among these subaggregates. In short, national income accounting enables us to measure and analyze how much the nation is producing and consuming.

Learning national income accounting is necessary. Before you play Chopin, you must learn to play scales, and before you fiddle with the aggregate economy, you must learn national income accounting.

NATIONAL INCOME ACCOUNTING

1 National income accounting enables us to measure and analyze how much the nation is producing and consuming.

National income accounting   A set of rules and definitions for measuring economic activity in the aggregate economy.

A firm generally measures how busy it is by how much it produces. To talk about how well the aggregate economy is doing, national income accounting uses a corresponding concept, aggregate output, which goes under the name **gross domestic product (GDP).**

GDP is the total market value of all final goods and services produced in an economy in a one-year period. It's probably the single most-used economic measure. When economists, journalists, and other analysts talk about the economy, they continually discuss GDP: how much it has increased or decreased, and what it's likely to do. In deciding whether a change in GDP means a growth in real output, we must take account of inflation (the rise in prices of goods on average). If we don't, we won't know whether output has really risen.

Up until 1992, the United States (unlike the rest of the world) used gross national product as its primary measure of aggregate output. Economic issues are becoming internationalized and national income accounting has been affected by that internationalization. In 1992, the United States followed the rest of the world and switched to gross domestic product as its primary measure of aggregate output.

Whereas *gross domestic product* measures the economic activity that occurs *within a country*, **gross national product (GNP)** measures the economic activity of

Measuring Total Economic Output of Goods and Services

2A **Gross domestic product (GDP):** Aggregate final output of residents and businesses in an economy in a one-year period.

2B **Gross national product (GNP):** Aggregate final output of citizens and businesses of an economy in a one-year period.

the citizens and businesses *of a country*. So the economic activity of U.S. citizens working abroad is counted in U.S. GNP but isn't counted in U.S. GDP. Similarly for the foreign economic activity of U.S. companies. However, the income of a Mexican or German person or business working in the United States isn't counted in U.S. GNP but is counted in U.S. GDP. Thus, GDP describes the economic output within the physical borders of a country while GNP describes the economic output produced by the citizens of a country. To move from GDP to GNP one must add **net foreign factor income** to GDP. Net foreign factor income is defined as the income from foreign domestic factor sources minus foreign factor incomes earned domestically. Put another way, one must add the foreign income of one's citizens and subtract the income of residents who are not citizens.

GDP is output produced within a country's borders; GNP is output produced by a country's citizens.

Q–1: Which is higher: Kuwait's GDP or its GNP? Why?

For many countries there's a significant difference between GNP and GDP. For example, consider Kuwait. Its citizens have significant foreign income—income that far exceeds the income of the foreigners in Kuwait. This means that Kuwait's GNP (the income of its citizens) far exceeds its GDP (the income of its residents). For the United States, however, foreign output of U.S. businesses and people for the most part offsets the output of foreign businesses and people within the United States. Kuwait's net foreign factor income has been large and positive, while that of the U.S. has been minimal.

Calculating GDP

Aggregate final output (GDP) consists of millions of different services and products: apples, oranges, computers, haircuts, financial advice. . . . To arrive at total output, somehow we've got to add them all together into a composite measure. Say we produced 7 oranges plus 6 apples plus 12 computers. We have not produced 25 comapplorgs. You can't add apples and oranges and computers. You can only add like things (things that are measured in the same units). For example, 2 apples + 4 apples = 6 apples. If we want to add unlike things, we must convert them into like things. We do that by multiplying each good by its *price*. Economists call this *weighting* the importance of each good by its price. For example, if you have 4 pigs and 4 horses and you price pigs at $200 each and horses at $400 each, the horses are weighted as being twice as important as pigs.

Multiplying the quantity of each good by its market price changes the terms in which we discuss each good from a quantity of a specific product to a *value* measure of that good. For example, when we multiply 6 apples by their price, 25¢ each, we get $1.50; $1.50 is a value measure. Once all goods are expressed in that value measure, they can be added together.

Take the example of seven oranges and six apples. (For simplicity let's forget the computers, haircuts, and financial advice.) If the oranges cost 50¢ each, their total value is $3.50; if the apples cost 25¢ each, their total value is $1.50. Their values are expressed in identical measures, so we can add them together. When we do so, we don't get 13 orples; we get $5 worth of apples and oranges.

If we follow that same procedure with all the final goods and services produced in the economy in the entire year, multiplying the quantity produced by the price per unit, we have all the economy's outputs expressed in units of value. If we then add up all these units of value, we have that year's gross domestic product.

There are two important aspects to remember about GDP. First, GDP represents a flow (an amount per year), not a stock (an amount at a particular moment of time). Second, GDP refers to the market value of *final* output. Let's consider these statements separately.

Two important aspects to remember about GDP are:
1. *GDP represents a flow; and*
2. *GDP represents the market value of final output.*

GDP Is a Flow Concept

In economics it's important to distinguish between flows and stock. Say a student just out of college tells you she earns $8,000. You'd probably think, "Wow! She's got a low-paying job!" That's because you implicitly assume she means $8,000 per year. If you later learned that she earns $8,000 per week, you'd quickly change your mind. The confusion occurred because how much you earn is a *flow* concept; it has meaning only when a time period is associated with it: so much per week, per month, per year. A *stock* concept is the amount of something at a given

EXHIBIT 1   U.S. National Wealth Accounts in 1992 (net worth)

	Dollars (in trillions)		Percent of component
Private net worth	$21.8		100%
Tangible wealth		9.5	
Owner–occupied real estate		6.7	31
Consumer durables		2.2	10
Other		0.6	3
Financial wealth		12.2	
Corporate equities		3.7	17
Noncorporate equities		2.3	11
Other (Pension reserves, life insurance, etc.)		6.2	28
Government net financial assets	−3.2		100
Federal		−3.0	94
State and local		−0.2	6
Total net worth	**18.6**		

Source: *Economic Report of the President, 1994.*

point in time. No time interval is associated with it. Your weight is a stock concept. You weigh 150 pounds; you don't weigh 150 pounds per week.

GDP is a flow concept, the amount of total final output a country produces per year. The *per year* is often left unstated, but it is important to keep in your mind that it's essential. GDP is usually reported quarterly or every three months, but it is reported on an *annualized basis,* meaning the U.S. Department of Commerce, which compiles GDP figures, uses quarterly figures to estimate total output for the whole year.

The store of wealth, on the other hand, is a stock concept. The stock equivalent to National Income Accounts is the **Wealth Accounts**—a balance sheet of an economy's stock of assets and liabilities—the stock equivalent to the National Income Accounts. These accounts have recently been developed for the United States, making the U.S. National Income Accounts consistent with the United Nations System of National Accounts, which uses an integrated system of income and wealth accounts. Exhibit 1 shows a summary account of U.S. net worth from the Wealth Accounts for the United States in 1992. These are stock measures; they exist at a moment of time. For example, on December 31, 1992, the accounting date for these accounts, U.S. private net worth was $21.8 trillion.

Q–2: How do Wealth Accounts differ from National Income Accounts?

Sir Richard Stone—Nobel prize, 1984, for work on national accounting. © *The Nobel Foundation.*

GDP Measures Final Output

As a student in my first economics class, I was asked to tell how to calculate GDP. I said, "Add up the value of the goods and services produced by all the companies in the United States to arrive at GDP." I was wrong (which is why I remember it). Many goods produced by one firm are sold to other firms, which use those goods to make something else. GDP doesn't measure total transactions in an economy; it measures *final output.* When one firm sells products to another firm for use in production of yet another good, the first firm's products aren't considered final output. They're **intermediate products** (products used as inputs in the production of some other product). To count intermediate goods as well as final goods as part of GDP would be to double count them. An example of an intermediate good would be wheat sold to a cereal company. If we counted both the wheat (the intermediate good) and the cereal (the final good) made from that wheat, the wheat would be double counted. Double counting would significantly overestimate final output.

If we did not eliminate intermediate goods, a change in organization would look like a change in output. Say one firm that produced steel merged with a firm that produced cars. Both together then produce exactly what each did separately before the merger. Final output hasn't changed, nor has intermediate output. The only difference is that the intermediate output of steel is now internal to the firm. Using only each

Intermediate products Products of one firm used in production of another firm's product.

EXHIBIT 2   Value Added Approach Eliminates Double Counting

Participants	I Cost of materials	II Value of sales	III Value added	Row
Farmer	$ 0	$ 100	$100	1
Cone factory and ice cream maker	100	250	150	2
Middleperson (final sales)	250	400	150	3
Vendor	400	500	100	4
Totals		$1,250	$500	5

firm's sales of goods to final consumers (and not sales to other firms) in one's measure of GDP prevents mere changes in organization from affecting the measure of output.

Two Ways of Eliminating Intermediate Goods   There are two ways to eliminate intermediate goods from the measure of GDP. One is to calculate only final output (goods sold to consumers). To do so, firms would have to separate goods they sold to consumers from intermediate goods used to produce other goods. For example, each firm would report how much of its product it sold to consumers and how much it sold to other producers for use that year in production of other goods; one would eliminate the latter to exclude double counting.

A second way to eliminate double counting is to follow the **value added** approach. Value added is the increase in value that a firm contributes to a product or service. It is calculated by subtracting from the value of its sales the cost of materials that a firm uses to produce a good or service. For instance, if a firm buys $100 worth of thread and $10,000 worth of cloth and uses them in making a thousand pairs of jeans which are sold for $20,000, the firm's value added is not $20,000; it is $9,900 ($20,000 in sales minus the $10,100 in intermediate goods that the firm bought). Exhibit 2 provides another example.

Say we want to measure the contribution to GDP made by a vendor who sells 200 ice cream cones at $2.50 each (they're good cones) for total sales of $500. The vendor bought his cones and ice cream from a middleperson at a cost of $400, who in turn paid the cone factory and ice cream maker a total of $250. The farmer who sold the cream to the factory got $100. Adding up all these transactions, we get $1,250, but that includes intermediate goods. Either by counting only the final value of the vendor's sales, $500, or by adding the value added at each stage of production (column III), we eliminate intermediate sales and arrive at the street vendor's contribution to GDP of $500.

Value added is calculated by subtracting the cost of materials from the value of sales, leaving only the value added at each stage of production. The aggregate value added at each stage of production is, by definition, precisely equal to the value of final sales, since it excludes all intermediate products. In Exhibit 1, the equality of the value added approach and the final-sales approach can be seen by comparing the vendor's final sales of $500 (row 4, column II) with the $500 value added (row 5, column III).

Value added   *The increase in value that a firm contributes to a product or service. It is calculated by subtracting the cost of materials a firm uses to produce a good or service from the value of its sales.*

3   To avoid double counting, you must eliminate intermediate goods, either by calculating only final output (expenditures approach), or by calculating only final income (income approach) by using the value added approach.

Q–3:   If a used car dealer buys a car for $2,000 and re-sells it for $2,500, how much has been added to GDP?

Calculating GDP: Some Examples   To make sure you understand what value added is and what makes up GDP, let's consider some sample transactions and determine what value they add and whether they should be included in GDP. Let's first consider second-hand sales: When you sell your two-year-old car, how much value has been added? The answer is none. The sale involves no current output, so there's no value added. If, however, you sold the car to a used car dealer for $2,000 and he resold it for $2,500, $500 of value has been added—the used-car dealer's efforts transferred the car from someone who didn't want it to someone who did. I point this out to remind you that GDP is not only a measure of the production of goods; it is a measure of the production of goods *and services.*

Now let's consider a financial transaction. Say you sell a bond (with a face value of $1,000) that you bought last year. You sell it for $1,200 and pay $100 commission to the dealer through whom you sell it. What value is added to final output? You might be tempted to say that $200 of value has been added, since the value of the bond has increased by $200. GDP, however, refers only to value that is added as the result of production, not to changes in the values of financial assets. Therefore the price at which you buy or sell the bond is irrelevant to the question at hand. The only value that is added by the sale is the transfer of that bond from someone who doesn't want it to someone who does. Thus, the only value added as a result of economic activity is the dealer's commission, $100. The remaining $1,100 (the $1,200 you got for the bond minus the $100 commission you paid) is a transfer of an asset from one individual to another, but such transfers do not enter into GDP calculations. Only production of goods and services enters into GDP.

Let's consider a different type of financial transaction: The government pays an individual social security benefits. What value is added? Clearly no production has taken place, but money has been transferred. As in the case of the bond, only the cost of transferring it—not the amount that gets transferred—is included in GDP. This is accomplished by including in GDP government expenditures on goods and services, but not the value of government transfers. Thus, social security payments, welfare payments, and veterans' benefits do not enter into calculations of GDP. That's why the government can have a $1.2 trillion budget but only $450 billion ($1.2 trillion minus $750 billion of transfer payments) is included in GDP.

Finally let's consider the work of a house-spouse. How much value does it add to economic activity in a year? Clearly if the house-spouse is any good at what he or she does, a lot of value is added. Taking care of the house and children is hard work. Estimates of the yearly value of a house-spouse's services are often in the $35,000 to $45,000 range. Even though much value is added and hence, in principle, house-spouse services should be part of GDP, by convention a house-spouse contributes nothing to GDP. GDP measures only *market activities;* since house-spouses are not paid, their value added is not included in GDP. This leads to some problems in measurement. For example, suppose a woman divorces her house-spouse and then hires him to continue cleaning her house for $20,000 per year. Then he will be contributing $20,000 value added. That, since it is a market transaction, is included in GDP.

The house-spouse example shows that the GDP measure has some problems. There are other areas in which it also has problems, but since this is an economics text, not an accounting text, I won't go into those problems. What's important for an introductory economics student to remember is that numerous decisions about how to handle various types of transactions had to be made to get a workable measure. Some of those decisions could have gone the other way, but, overall, the terminology of national income accounting is a model of consistency. It focuses on measuring final market output for the entire economy.

GDP can be calculated in two ways: the expenditures method and the income method. This is because of the *national income accounting identity.*

National income accounting is a form of accounting to which you were introduced in Chapter 4. Accounting is a way of keeping track of things. It is based on certain identities; for a firm, its cost plus profit equals revenues because they are identical to revenues. National income accounting is no different. It too is based on an identity. By definition, whenever a good or service (output) is produced, somebody receives an income for producing it. This relationship between output and income, the **national income accounting identity,** can be seen in Exhibit 3, which illustrates the circular flow of income in an economy.[1]

Q–4: How can the government have a $1.5 trillion budget but only have $500 billion of that included in GDP?

TWO METHODS OF CALCULATING GDP

The National Income Accounting Identity

National income accounting identity   The relationship defined between output and income whereby one equals the other.

---

[1] An *identity* is a statement of equality that's "true by definition." In algebra, an identity is sometimes written as a triple equal sign (≡). It is more equal than simply equal. How something can be more equal than equal is beyond me, too, but I'm no mathematician.

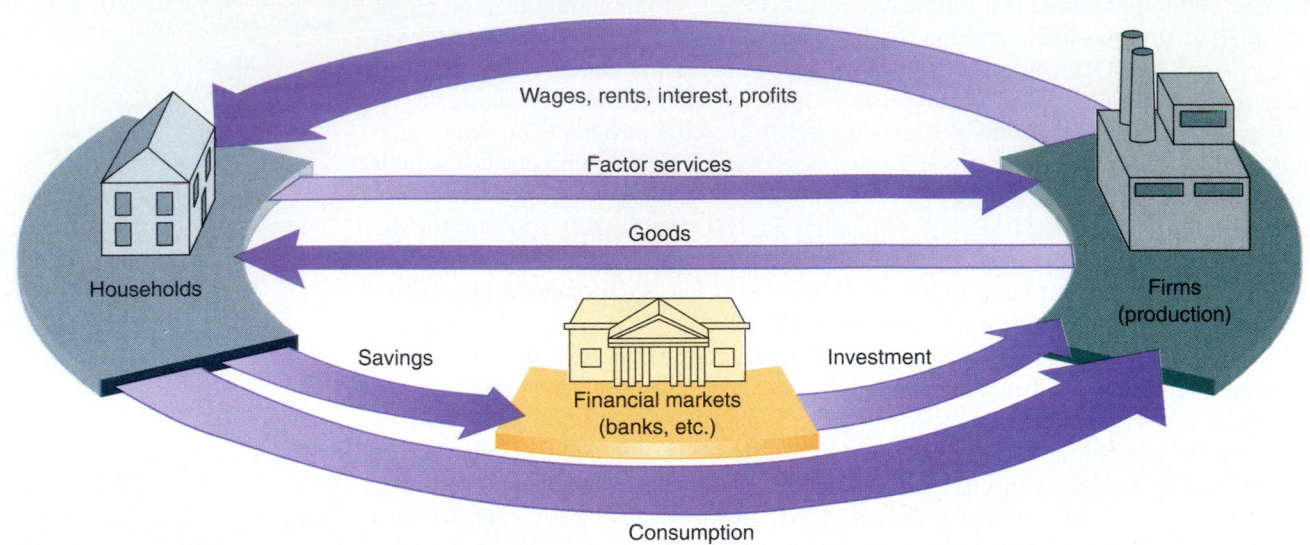

Wages, rents, interest, profits

Factor services

Goods

Households

Savings

Investment

Financial markets
(banks, etc.)

Firms
(production)

Consumption

EXHIBIT 3   The Circular Flow

One of the most important insights about the aggregate economy is that it is a circular flow in which output and input are interrelated.
Households' expenditures (consumption and savings) are firms' income; firms' expenditures (wages, rent, etc.) are households' income.

The *Survey of Current Business*, a
Department of Commerce publication,
is one of the best sources of GDP figures.

In Exhibit 3 we see that as firms produce goods, they create income in the form of wages, rents, interest, and profits (the top flow). Consumers either spend or save their income. Their spending comes back to the firms in the form of consumption (consumers buy firms' output) or, if they save their income, in the form of investment (firms borrow the savings and buy other firms' output), assuming financial markets can translate that savings into investment.

The value of the wages, rents, interest, and profits (the flow along the top in Exhibit 3) equals the value of goods bought (the flow along the bottom). How are these values kept exactly equal? That's the secret of double entry bookkeeping: output must always equal income.

Profit is defined as what remains after all other income (wages, rent, and interest) is paid out. For example, say a firm has a total output of $800 and that it paid $400 in wages, $200 in rent, and $100 in interest. The firm's profit is determined by subtracting that income paid out from the value of total output. Profit equals $800 − $700 = $100. That profit is the income of the owners of the firm. All income (determined by adding profits to wages, rent, and interest) equals $800, which, not surprisingly, equals the value of the output.

The accounting identity even works if a firm incurs a loss. Say that instead of paying $400 in wages, the firm paid $700, along with its other payments of $200 in rent and $100 in interest. Total output is still $800, but total income, excluding profits, is now $1,000. *Profits* are still defined as total output minus income paid out in wages, rent, and interest. Profits in this example are negative: $800 − $1,000 = (−$200). There's a *loss* of $200. Adding that loss to other income ($1,000 + (−$200)) gives total income of $800—which is identical to the firm's total output of $800.

The national income accounting identity (Total output = Total income) allows us to calculate GDP either by adding up all values of final outputs (the *expenditures approach*) or by adding up the values of all earnings or income (the *income approach*).

As with most issues in accounting, there are certain conceptual difficulties in applying seemingly reasonable definitions. In this instance the difficulty is what to do when two economies are interrelated with individuals and businesses of one country producing in another country so that a distinction must be made between GDP and GNP. Although, by definition, expenditures must equal income, there's a question of whose income whose expenditures must equal. If all figures were collected in terms of domestic income and output, there would be no problem, but in the United States, as

NATIONAL INCOME
ACCOUNTING AND DOUBLE
ENTRY BOOKKEEPING

The key to all accounting, including national income accounting, is double entry book-keeping, a system of financial record keeping invented in Italy and attributed to Luigi Pacioli (1494). Double entry bookkeeping is based on redundancy. It requires that accounting terms be defined in such a way that the cost side of the ledger is kept exactly equal to the income side. Since they're exactly equal, in theory one need calculate only one of the two sides, but in practice both sides are calculated, so the accountant can check his or her work. If both sides independently add up to the same figure, it's likely that no mistake was made.

In the national income accounts kept by the U.S. Department of Commerce, the two sides of the ledger are the expenditure accounts and the income accounts. Every entry on one side of the accounts has an offsetting entry on the other side. Whenever production (an increase in output) takes place on the expenditure side, there is a simultaneous increase in income entered on the income side.

As discussed in Chapter 4, in balance sheet accounting (accounting measuring the assets and liabilities of an individual, firm, or country) assets equal liabilities plus net worth. Net worth plays the swing role in balance sheet accounting that profits play in income accounting. *Net worth* is defined as the amount that remains when liabilities are subtracted from assets:

$$\text{Net worth} = \text{Assets} - \text{Liabilities.}$$

Net worth is recorded on the liabilities side of the ledger. Adding liabilities and net worth, we have

$$\text{Assets} = \text{Liabilities} + \text{Net worth.}$$

Substituting in for net worth, we have

$$\text{Assets} = \text{Liabilities} + (\text{Assets} - \text{Liabilities})$$

or

$$\text{Assets} = \text{Assets.}$$

Since by substituting we can get the same term on both sides of the equation, the statement ''Assets = Liabilities + Net worth'' is true by definition.

In national income accounting, profit plays the swing role. Profits are what is left after all other forms of income are accounted for. *Profits* are defined as the difference between total output and other income and are counted as income. So we have

$$\text{Output} = \text{Other income} + \text{Profits}$$

$$\text{Profits} = \text{Output} - \text{Other income.}$$

Substituting in for profits gives

$$\text{Output} = \text{Other income} + \text{Output} - \text{Other income.}$$

Therefore,

$$\text{Output} = \text{Output.}$$

This 17th-century engraving by Rembrandt, "The Money Lender," shows that careful bookkeeping and accounting have been around for a long time. *Bleichroeder Print Collection, Baker Library, Harvard Business School.*

of 1993, the output side is presented as domestic output (the output of firms and residents of the United States) while the input side is still presented as national income (the income of U.S. citizens and firms). These two differ by net foreign factor income. As we've discussed, in the particular case of the United States the difference is minimal, but, conceptually, it's important to keep the distinction in mind so that with either the expenditures approach or the income approach one arrives at the same result.

Let's consider these two approaches in detail.

Exhibit 4 gives the categories of expenditures normally used in the expenditures approach to calculating U.S. GDP: personal consumption expenditures, gross private investment, government purchases, and net exports. All expenditures fall into one or another of these four divisions, so by adding up these four categories, we get total expenditures on U.S. goods and services minus U.S. residents' expenditures on foreign goods. By definition, in national income accounting those expenditures on U.S. goods and services equal the total amount of production of goods and services (GDP).

The Expenditures Approach

EXHIBIT 4   GDP via the Expenditures Approach, 1993

GDP, 1993	Dollars (in billions)		% of GDP
Personal consumption expenditures (*C*)	$4,392		69%
Durable goods		538	
Nondurable goods		1,350	
Services		2,504	
Gross private investment (*I*)	892		14%
Fixed investment		876	
Change in business inventories		16	
Net exports of goods and services (*X − M*)	−64		−1%
Exports		662	
Imports		726	
Government purchases of goods and services (*G*)	1,158		18%
Federal		443	
State and local		715	
	6,378		100%

Source: *Survey of Current Business*, 1994.

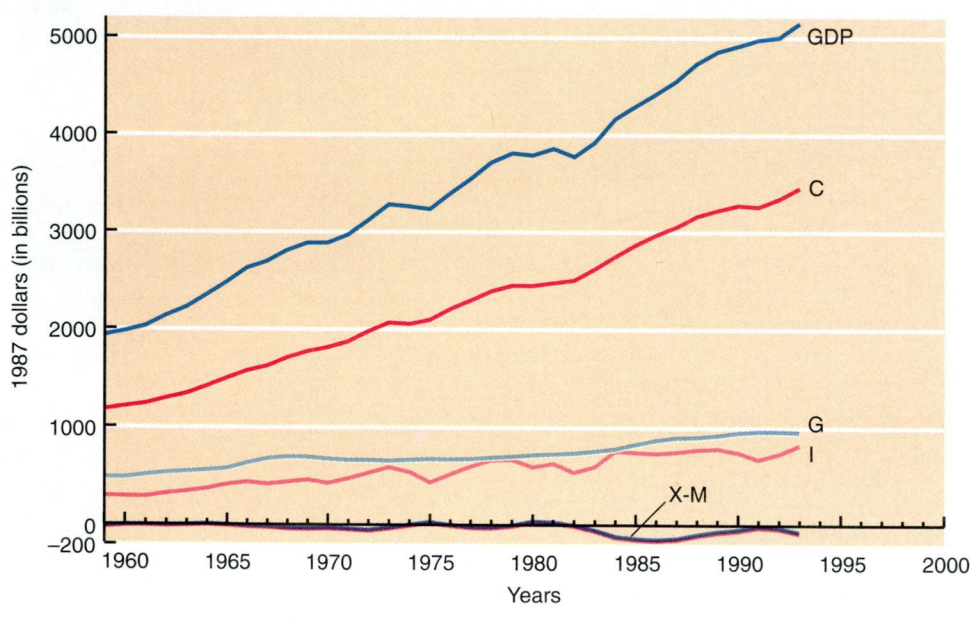

EXHIBIT 5   Movements of U.S. GDP since 1959

This exhibit demonstrates the approximate movement of GDP and its components since 1959. As you can see, gross private investment and net exports fluctuate significantly over the years, and GDP tends to rise overall each year.

Source: *Survey of Current Business*, 1994.

4 GDP = *C* + *I* + *G* + (*X − M*) is an accounting identity because it is defined as true.

Q–5: What are the four components or categories of expenditures in national income?

Gross domestic product is equal to the sum of these four categories of expenditures:

$$GDP = C + I + G + (X - M)$$

where

C = Consumption
I = Investment
G = Government expenditures
$(X - M)$ = Net exports.

Exhibit 5 demonstrates movements in U.S. GDP and its component parts since 1959. As you can see, the individual parts fluctuate in relative importance. Of the components, investment fluctuates most; personal consumption expenditures fluctuate least. Let's consider each component in turn.

Consumption Expenditure (C)   All goods and services bought by households are lumped together under ''consumption.'' This huge category includes such purchases as your visit to the dentist, college tuition, and the new car you buy, as well as all actual and

	Dollars (in billions)		% of Expenditures
Durable goods	$ 538		12%
Motor vehicles and parts		222	
Furniture and household equipment		212	
Other		104	
Nondurable goods	1,350		31
Food		658	
Clothing		237	
Gasoline and oil		104	
Fuel oil		15	
Other nondurable goods		336	
Services	2,504		57
Housing		628	
Household operation		251	
Transportation		170	
Medical care		681	
Other		774	
	4,392		100%

EXHIBIT 6   Breakdown of Consumer Expenditures, 1993

Source: *Survey of Current Business*, 1994.

	Dollars (in billions)		% of Investment
Fixed investment	$876		
Nonresidential		624	70%
Structures		179	
Producers' durable equipment		445	
Residential		252	28
Single-family structures		134	
Multifamily structures		11	
Producers' durable equipment		8	
Other		100	
Change in business inventory	16		2
Subtotal gross investment	892		100%
Depreciation	671		
Net investment	221		

EXHIBIT 7   Gross Private Investment, 1993

Source: *Survey of Current Business*, 1994.

estimated "rents" for existing homes. Consumption is the largest category in GDP, accounting for about 69 percent of the total.

Being so large, consumption is normally broken down into subcategories: durable consumer goods, nondurable consumer goods, and services. **Durable goods** are defined as goods expected to last more than one year. (Why one year? Because one year, although arbitrary, is a reasonable cutoff point.) Durables include cars and household appliances. **Nondurable goods** are goods that last less than one year. The food you eat and the movie tickets you buy fall under this heading. Services are activities done for another person (cutting hair, teaching, and mowing a lawn). They are a form of economic activity, but they do not involve production or sale of goods. Exhibit 6 breaks down these subcategories of consumer expenditures into subsubcategories.

Durable goods   Goods expected to last more than one year.

Nondurable goods   Goods expected to last less than one year.

Gross and Net Private Investment *(I)*   Investment is expenditures by firms or households on goods, often called *capital goods,* that are used over and over to make products or provide services. Housing, tractors, steel mills, and wine barrels are examples. Thus, when economists speak of investment they don't mean the kind of activity taking place when individuals buy stocks or bonds—economists consider that saving, not investing. Gross private investment, the third largest category, makes up about 14 percent of GDP. Exhibit 7 breaks down gross private investment into two subcategories: fixed investment and change in business inventory. Fixed investment is, by far, the larger component. It includes investments in residential and nonresidential buildings and in equipment.

Change in business inventory ("inventory investment" for short) is a different form of investment. It's the increase or decrease in the value of the stocks of inventory that businesses have on hand. Notice I said "increases in the *value* of inventory." Say a car dealership normally keeps 50 cars in stock. Its inventory is 50 cars. In 1995 it increases its stock of cars to 55. Its inventory investment for 1995 is 5 cars times their value. If inventory remains constant from one year to the next, there's no inventory investment. If inventories fall, inventory investment is negative.

Inventory investment is highly volatile. Drawing implications from an increase in inventory investment is difficult, because a change in inventory investment can mean two different things. When firms expect to sell a lot, they usually produce significant amounts for inventory, so an increase in inventory investment may signal expected high sales. But inventory can also increase because goods the firm produces aren't selling. In that case, an increase in inventory investment signals unexpected low sales. Those five extra cars are just sitting on the dealer's lot. Thus, economists keep a close eye on inventory investment as well as on why inventory investment has changed.

Depreciation   Decrease in an asset's value.

Sooner or later, assets such as plants and equipment wear out or become technologically obsolete. Economists call this wearing out process **depreciation** (the decrease in an asset's value). Depreciation is part of the cost of producing a good; it is the amount by which plants and equipment decrease in value as they grow older. Much of each year's private investment involves expenditures to replace assets that have worn out. For example, as you drive your car, it wears out. A car with 80,000 miles on it is worth less than the same type of car with only 1,000 miles on it. The difference in value is attributed to depreciation.

Net private investment   Gross investment minus depreciation.

To differentiate between total or gross investment and the new investment that's above and beyond replacement investment, economists use the term **net private investment** (gross investment minus depreciation). In 1993, gross investment was $892 billion and depreciation was $671 billion, so net investment was $221 billion. Economists pay close attention to net private investment because it gives an estimate of the increase in the country's productive capacity.

Government Purchases (G)

Government purchases are divided into federal expenditures and state and local expenditures. In macroeconomics the main focus is on the federal government because only the federal government is directly concerned with the aggregate economy. This doesn't mean state and local government expenditures don't affect the economy; they do, as do any expenditures. It simply means that state and local governments generally don't take that effect into account since each is relatively small compared to the total economy.

Government uses its tax revenue to build bridges, buy copying machines, print application forms, pay the president, and meet innumerable other expenses. Many of these government goods and services are paid for from general tax revenue and are provided free to consumers of the goods or services. As a result, they have no price at which to value them. By convention, economists value these goods and services at cost. Thus, if the federal government spends $300 billion on defense, government spending on defense is valued at $300 billion.

Total government purchases (the second-largest component) account for about 18 percent of GDP. Exhibit 8 breaks down purchases by various levels of government.

Transfer payments   Payments to individuals by the federal government that aren't payment for a good or service.

Notice that state and local governments make more purchases than does the federal government, and federal government expenditures total $443 billion. Each year the federal government budget (about $1.3 trillion) is much larger than these federal government purchases of $443 billion that enter into GDP. The reason is that the remaining part of the federal government budget involves **transfer payments** (payments made to individuals that *aren't* payment for a good or service). Since they're simply a transfer, not a purchase of a good or service, they don't contribute to GDP. The largest of these transfers is social security payments.

EXHIBIT 8 **Breakdown of Government Expenditures, 1993**

	Dollars (in billions)		% of Total
State and local government expenditures	715		62%
Goods, durable and nonduarble		102	
Services		507	
Structures		106	
Federal government expenditures	443		38%
National defense		303	
Nondefense		140	
Total	1,158		100%

Source: *Survey of Current Business*, 1994.

EXHIBIT 9 **Net U.S. Exports, 1993**

	Dollars (in billions)		% of Total exports or imports
Exports	662		
Merchandise		462	70%
Services		200	30
Imports	726		
Merchandise		592	82
Services		134	18
Net exports	−64		

Source: *Survey of Current Business*, 1994.

Net Exports $(X - M)$ Some goods and services produced in the United States (such as wheat, computers, and U.S. vacations) are bought by people in foreign countries. Other goods and services (such as French champagne and taxi rides in London) are bought from foreign countries by U.S. residents. If these exports and imports are equal, they net out and make no contribution to GDP. If the value of what the United States sells to foreign countries is greater than what it buys from foreign countries, the United States is producing more than it is spending. In this case net exports (exports minus imports) are positive, and the difference between exports and imports must be added to GDP, since the increase represents net foreign expenditure on U.S.-produced goods. It's U.S. production bought by foreigners, but U.S. production nonetheless.

If the United States buys more from foreign countries than it sells to them, imports exceed exports, so net exports are negative. In this case, U.S. spending is more than U.S. production. Since GDP measures production, not spending, the excess of imports over exports must be subtracted from U.S. GDP. If it weren't subtracted, we couldn't measure production by measuring expenditures. To some degree, imports and exports offset each other. However, as I said in Chapter 5, in the United States in the early 1990s imports have significantly exceeded exports.

Exhibit 9 presents U.S. exports and imports. In 1993 exports were $662 billion; imports were $726 billion; so net exports were −$64 billion.

Summing Up the Components Before we move on to the income approach, let's review the expenditure approach. In the expenditure approach you add together consumption, investment, government spending on goods and services, and net exports to arrive at GDP. The division of GDP into the four components differs among countries. Exhibit 10 shows the division for six countries to give you a sense of the differences.

GDP and NDP In the discussion of investment, I differentiated gross investment from net investment. Gross investment minus depreciation equals net investment. Economists have created another aggregate term, **net domestic product (NDP),** to reflect

2c **Net domestic product** GDP adjusted to take account of depreciation.

EXHIBIT 10   Breakdown of GDP for Selected Countries

Country	Nominal GDP, 1992 (U.S. $ in billions)	Personal consumption (% of GDP)	Gross private investment (% of GDP)	Government expenditures (% of GDP)	Exports (% of GDP)	Imports (−% of GDP)
Brazil	$ 369	61%	22%	12%	9%	−5%
Germany	1389	55	19	18	37	−29
Japan	2468	57	24	17	10	−8
Pakistan	48	74	19	12	14	−19
Tunisia	14	79	24	15	26	−44
Tanzania	7	85	19	10	6	−20

the adjustment to investment because of depreciation. NDP is the sum of consumption expenditures, government expenditures, net foreign expenditures, and net investment (gross investment − depreciation). Thus,

$GDP = C + I + G + (X + M)$
$NDP = C$ 2pl (net I) $+ G + (X − M)$

$$GDP = C + I + G + (X − M)$$
$$NDP = C + (net\ I) + G + (X − M).$$

NDP takes depreciation into account, and depreciation is a cost of producing goods; so NDP is actually preferable to GDP as the expression of a country's domestic output. However, measuring true depreciation (the actual decrease in an asset's value) is difficult because asset values fluctuate. In fact, it's so difficult that in the real world accountants don't try to measure true depreciation, but instead use a number of conventional rules of thumb that yield an accepted figure. In recognition of this reality, economists call the adjustment made to GDP to arrive at NDP the *capital consumption allowance* rather than *depreciation*. Since estimating depreciation is difficult, GDP rather than NDP is generally used in discussions.

The Income Approach

Domestic income (DI)   *Total income earned by residents and businesses in a country.*

2D   National income (NI) Total income earned by citizens and businesses of a country.

The alternative way of calculating GDP is the income approach. **Domestic income (DI)** has four components: compensation to employees, rents, interest, and profits. Total domestic income equals NDP, not GDP. Why? Because of depreciation, which is a cost, not an income to anyone. As I stated previously, an economy's domestic income must be separated from an economy's **national income (NI)** (the total income earned by citizens and businesses of a country). Domestic income corresponds to domestic product; national income corresponds to national product. When the United States shifted from GNP to GDP as its primary measure of economic output, it would have been reasonable also to shift to domestic as opposed to national income concepts. Alas, it did not; the primary income statistics reported in the United States are still national income statistics.

To move from domestic income to national income one must add net foreign factor income to domestic income. For the United States in the 1990s, net foreign factor income has been minimal so there's not a lot of difference between the two concepts, but since the primary income figures reported by the U.S. government are national income figures, I discuss the breakdown of national income rather than domestic income, leaving you to make the adjustments to domestic income concepts by subtracting net foreign factor income from national income concepts.

Q–6:   What is the largest component of national income?

Compensation to Employees   Compensation to employees (the largest component of national income) consists of wages and salaries paid to individuals, along with fringe benefits and government taxes for social security and unemployment insurance. As you can see in Exhibit 11, compensation to employees made up about 73 percent of national income.

Rents   Rents are the income from property received by households. Rents received by firms are not included because a firm's rents are simply another source of income to

	Dollars (in billions)		% of national income	
Compensation to employees	$3,772		73%	
Rents	13		0	
Net interest	446		9	
Profits	910		18	
Proprietors' income		443		9
Corporate profits		467		9
National income	5,141		100%	

EXHIBIT 11   Components of National Income, 1993

Source: *Survey of Current Business*, 1994.

the firm and hence are classified as profits. In most years the rent component of GDP is small, since the depreciation owners take on buildings is close to the income they earn from those buildings.

Interest   Interest is the income private businesses pay to households that have lent the businesses money, generally by purchasing bonds issued by the businesses. (Interest received by firms doesn't show up in this category for the same reason that rents received by firms don't show up in the *rent* category.) Interest payments by government and households aren't included in national income since by convention they're assumed not to flow from the production of goods and services. In 1993, net interest was 9 percent of national income.

Profits   Profits are the amount that is left after compensation to employees, rents, and interest have been paid out.[2] Profits are normally divided into two categories: (1) profits of unincorporated businesses and proprietors' income, and (2) profits of incorporated businesses. Both require some discussion.

In an earlier chapter, I pointed out that in most unincorporated businesses, the owner works for the business. The amount that is left over after paying interest, rent, and compensation to employees is both a compensation for the owner's work (valued at his or her opportunity cost of working elsewhere) and the owner's profit. Thus, if a gift shop owner earns $30,000 a year after paying wages, interest, and rent, and she could have earned $20,000 working elsewhere, her compensation is $20,000 and her profits are $10,000. Tabulation of the national income data doesn't show this separation and, by convention, the entire amount ($30,000 in the example) is included as "profit."

As I also discussed in Chapter 4, corporations are fictitious legal entities. For purposes of calculating national income, they can have no income; all income in national income accounting must be attributed to households.

Corporate profits are, in reality, either paid out to stockholders in *dividends* (payments to the holders of a company's stock), in which case they are considered household income; or are not distributed to stockholders but are instead held within the firm as corporate retained earnings. For national income accounting purposes, these retained earnings are undistributed profits, which must be attributed to households. That's what is done. In the national income accounts all undistributed profit is attributed to households. To do so, the U.S. Department of Commerce simply adds all undistributed profits to household income. In 1993 corporate profits were about $467 billion (9% of national income).

---

[2] As we discussed earlier, the national income accounts use accounting profits which must be distinguished from economic profits, which are calculated on the basis of opportunity costs.

National Income and Net National Product: Adjustments for Indirect Business Taxes

Q–7: Why must indirect business taxes be added to national income to make it equal to net national product?

2E   Net national product: GNP adjusted for depreciation.

Other National Income Terms

Personal income (PI)   National income plus net transfer payments from government minus amounts attributed but not received.

Disposable personal income   Personal income minus personal income taxes and payroll taxes.

The sum of compensation to employees, rents, interest, and profits is supposed to equal national income. However, if you added the four components together, you would find national income does not quite equal net national product (NNP). To make the two equal, one must add indirect business taxes to national income. National income *plus* indirect business taxes equals NNP.

Indirect business taxes include sales taxes (a general tax on sales), excise taxes (a sales tax on a particular item or group of items), business property taxes, customs duties, and license fees. These taxes are ultimately paid by households, since according to national income accounting, households ultimately receive all the income. How are they paid for by households? Either the firm raises its prices to include the tax or its earnings fall by the amount of the tax. In either case, households pay. When firms add the cost of taxes to their price, households pay the higher prices. When firms subtract the cost of taxes from their earnings, households pay by receiving lower wages or lower dividends (or both) from those firms. But it is firms, not households, that make the actual payment of these taxes, so to go from national income to **net national product**—GNP adjusted for depreciation—indirect business taxes must be added back to national (or household) income. That means

$$NNP = NI + \text{Indirect business taxes.}$$

Two other often-used concepts deserving mention are personal income and disposable personal income. (These can be either national or domestic concepts. Since the United States still reports them as national concepts, I follow that convention here.)

Personal Income   National income measures the income individuals receive for doing productive work whereas personal income measures all income actually received by individuals. Individuals receive other income that they do not directly earn (for example, social security payments, welfare payments, food stamps, and veterans' benefits). These payments from government to individuals are not part of national income, but they are available to spend.

Similarly in national income accounting, individuals are attributed income that they do not actually receive. This income includes undistributed corporate profits (retained earnings), employers' contributions to the social security system, and corporate income taxes.

If we add to national income the amounts of such payments that households receive, and subtract from national income the amounts attributed to households but not actually received by them, we arrive at **personal income (PI):**

$$PI = NI + \text{Transfer payments from government}$$
$$- \text{ Corporate retained earnings}$$
$$- \text{ Corporate income taxes}$$
$$- \text{ Social security taxes.}$$

Disposable Personal Income   We've accounted for most taxes, but not all. There's still personal income taxes and payroll taxes, which are subtracted from individuals' paychecks or paid directly by self-employed individuals. Personal income taxes and payroll taxes show up on employees' paycheck stubs, but employees don't actually get the money; the government does. Subtracting these personal income taxes from personal income, we arrive at **disposable personal income:**

$$PI - \text{Personal taxes} = \text{Disposable personal income.}$$

Disposable personal income is what people have readily available to spend. Thus, economists follow disposable personal income carefully.

From GDP to Disposable Personal Income   Exhibit 12 reviews the steps involved in moving from GDP to disposable personal income for the United States. Going through these steps should give you a good sense of the relationships among the concepts we've discussed.

W e've covered a lot of definitions quickly, so a review is in order. GDP (the total output of the residents of a society) can be measured in two ways: the expenditures approach and the income approach.

Using the expenditures approach,

$$GDP = C + I + G + (X - M).$$

Much investment is replacement investment—it is made to cover depreciation, and is a cost of production. When one subtracts depreciation from GDP, one arrives at NDP:

$$NDP = GDP - Depreciation.$$

To move from net domestic product to net national product one must add net foreign factor income (foreign earnings of citizens minus domestic earnings of foreigners) to net domestic product:

$$NNP = NDP + Net\ foreign\ factor\ income.$$

To move to national income, one subtracts indirect business taxes from NNP.

$$NI = NNP - Indirect\ business\ taxes.$$

National income can be broken up into four components: compensation to employees, rent, interest, and profits:

$$NI = Compensation\ to\ employees + Rent + Interest + Profits.$$

To move from national income to personal income, one subtracts corporate income taxes, undistributed corporate profits, and social security contributions, and adds transfer payments from the government:

$$PI = NI - Corp.\ income\ taxes - undistrib.\ corp.\ profits - soc.\ sec.\ contrib. + trans.\ pmts.$$

$$Disposable\ personal\ income = Personal\ income - Personal\ taxes.$$

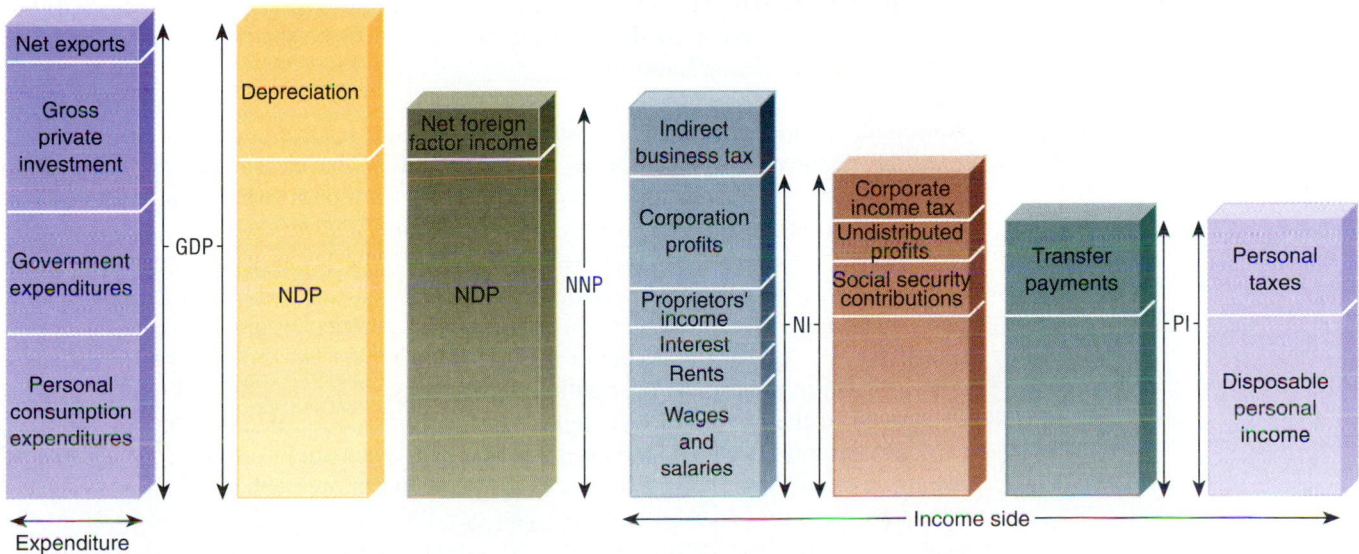

EXHIBIT 12   From GDP to Disposable Personal Income

Here are the steps involved in moving from GDP to disposable personal income.

Now that we've worked our way through two methods of calculating GDP, let's consider what it's used for and what it tells us. The most important way GDP figures are used is to make comparisons of one country's production with another country's and of one year's production with another year's.

USING GDP FIGURES

Comparing GDP among Countries

Q–8: Why are national income statistics not especially good for discussing the income of developing countries?

Most countries use somewhat similar measures to calculate GDP. Thus, we can compare various countries' GDP levels and get a sense of their economic size and power.

Per capita GDP is another measure often used to compare various nations' income. To arrive at per capita GDP, we divide GDP by the country's total population. Doing so gives you a sense of the relative standards of living of the people in various countries.

If you look up some of these measures, some of the comparisons should give you cause to wonder. For example, Bangladesh has per capita GDP of only about $250, compared to U.S. per capita GDP of about $24,000. How do people in Bangladesh live? In answering that question, remember GDP measures market transactions. In poor countries, individuals often grow their own food (subsistence farming), build their own shelter, and make their own clothes. None of those activities are market activities, and while they're sometimes estimated and included in GDP, they often aren't estimated accurately. They certainly aren't estimated at the value of what these activities would cost in the United States. Also, remember GDP is an aggregate measure that values activities at the market price in that society. The relative prices of the products and services a consumer buys often differ substantially among countries. In New York City, $900 a month gets you only a small studio apartment. In Haiti, $900 a month might get you a mansion with four servants. Thus, GDP can be a poor measure of the relative living standards in various countries.

To avoid this problem in comparing per capita GDP, economists often calculate a different concept, *purchasing power parity,* which adjusts for the different relative prices among countries before making comparisons.

Just how much of a difference the two approaches can make can be seen in the case of China. In May 1992, the International Monetary Fund (IMF) changed from calculating China's GDP using the exchange rate approach to calculating it using the purchasing power parity approach. Upon doing so, the IMF calculated that China's GDP grew over 400 percent in one year. Per capita income rose from about $300 to well over $1,000. When methods of calculation can make that much difference, one must use statistics very carefully.

Economic Welfare over Time

Using GDP figures to compare the economy's performance over time is much better than relying merely on our perceptions.

A second way in which the GDP concept is used is to compare one year with another.

Last chapter, when we talked about growth in the economy, we were really talking about growth in total output or GDP. Similarly, when we talked about contractions and expansions, it was in reference to GDP.

Using GDP figures to compare the economy's performance over time is much better than relying merely on our perceptions. Most of us have heard the phrase, *the good old days.* Generally we hear it from our parents or grandparents, who are lamenting the state of the nation or economy. In comparing today to yesterday, they always seem to picture the past with greener grass, an easier life, and happier times. Compared to the good old days, today always comes out a poor second.

Our parents and grandparents may be right when they look back at particular events in their own lives, but if society were to follow such reasoning, it would conclude that all of history has been just one long downhill slide, worsening every year. In actuality, perceptions of the good old days are likely to be biased. It's easy to remember the nice things of yesterday while forgetting its harsh realities. Relying on past perception is not an especially helpful way of making accurate comparisons.

A preferable way is to rely on data that are not changed by emotion or anything else. Looking at GDP over time provides a way of using data to make comparisons over time. For example, say we compare U.S. GDP in 1932 ($58 billion) to GDP in 1993 ($6.4 trillion). Would it be correct to conclude the economy had grown 110 times larger? No. As we discussed in the last chapter, GDP figures aren't affected by emotions, but they are affected by inflation. To make comparisons over time, we can't confine ourselves to a simple look at what has happened to GDP.

In our earlier discussion of supply and demand, I spent quite a bit of space distinguishing between a rise in the price level and a change in relative prices. That's because the distinction is important. A similar important distinction economists make is in comparing output levels over time. Suppose prices of all goods and hence the price level (remember, the price level includes wages) go up 25 percent in one year, but outputs of all goods remain constant. GDP will have risen 25 percent, but will society be any better off? No. To compare GDP over time, you must distinguish between increases in GDP due to inflation and increases in GDP that represent real increases in production and income.

5   A real concept is a nominal concept adjusted for inflation.

Real and Nominal GDP

As I stated in the last chapter, to separate increases in GDP caused by inflation from increases in GDP that represent real increases in production and income, economists distinguish between **nominal GDP** (GDP calculated at existing prices) and **real GDP** (nominal GDP adjusted for inflation). This distinction is sufficiently important to warrant repetition in this chapter. To adjust nominal output for inflation we create a price index (a measure of how much the price level has risen from one year to the next) and divide nominal GDP by that price index.[3]

Nominal GDP   GDP calculated at existing prices.

Real GDP   Nominal GDP adjusted for inflation.

For example, say the price level rises 10 percent (from a price index of 1 to a price index of 1.1) and nominal GDP rises from $4 trillion to $4.6 trillion. Ten percent of that rise in nominal GDP represents the 10 percent rise in the price level. If you divide nominal GDP, $4.6 trillion, by the new price level index, 1.1, you get $4.18 trillion (the amount GDP would have been if the price level had not risen). That $4.18 trillion is called real GDP. To decide whether production has increased or decreased over time, we simply compare the real income. In this example, real income has risen from $4 trillion to $4.18 trillion, so we can conclude that the real economy has grown by 18/400, or 4.5 percent.

Q–9:   If real income has risen from $4 trillion to $4.2 trillion and the price level went up by 10 percent, by how much has nominal income risen?

Real GDP is what is important to a society because it measures what is *really* produced. Considering nominal GDP instead of real GDP can distort what's really happening. Let's say the U.S. price level doubled tomorrow. Nominal GDP would also double, but would the United States be better off? No.

We'll use the distinction between real and nominal continually in this course, so to firm up the concepts in your mind, let's go through another example. Consider Somalia in 1987 and 1988, when nominal GDP rose from 159 billion to 268 billion (measured in their local currency units) while the GDP deflator rose from 100 percent to 173.5 percent. Dividing nominal GDP in 1988 by the GDP deflator, we see *real GDP* fell by over 2 percent. So not only did Somalia's economy not grow; it actually shrank.

The quotation at this chapter's start pointed out that statistics can be misleading. I want to reiterate that here. Before you can work with statistics, you need to know how they are collected and the problems they have. If you don't, the results can be disastrous. Here's a possible scenario:

SOME LIMITATIONS OF NATIONAL INCOME ACCOUNTING

6   Limitations of national income accounting include:
1. Measurement problems;
2. GDP measures national activity, not welfare; and
3. Subcategories are often interdependent.

A student who isn't careful looks at the data and discovers an almost perfect relationship between imports and investment occurring in a Latin American country. Whenever capital goods imports go up, investment of capital goods goes up by an equal proportion. The student develops a thesis based on that insight, only to learn after submitting the thesis that no data on investments are available for that country. Instead of gathering actual data, the foreign country's statisticians estimate investment by assuming it to be a constant percentage of imports. Since many investment goods are imported, this is reasonable, but the estimate is not a reasonable basis for an economic policy. It would be back to the drawing board for the student, whose thesis would be useless because the student didn't know how the country's statistics had been collected.

If you ever work in business as an economist, statistics will be your life's blood. Much of what economists do is based on knowing, interpreting, and drawing infer-

---

[3] Now you know why the total output deflator is called the *GDP deflator*. It is an index of the rise in prices of the goods and services that make up GDP.

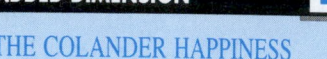

THE COLANDER HAPPINESS INDEX

The only way economists can determine how happy people are is to ask them if they're happy and then develop a happiness index. I've done so in some of my classes by giving students a numerical measure for degrees of happiness:

Ecstatic	5
Very happy	4
Happy	3
Somewhat unhappy	2
Depressed	1

Each student writes down the number that most closely represents his or her average state of happiness for the past year. The average of those calculations forms the "Colander happiness index" for the class—usually between 3 and 3.2. My students are essentially reasonably happy.

In fact, when other economists have taken a type of happiness poll elsewhere, results have been fairly consistent—even in poor countries. Except in times of crisis, people on average are reasonably happy, regardless of their income level, their wealth, or the state of the economy where they live.* I interpret this as meaning there's some level of income below which we'll be unhappy because we're starving, but above that level more output for a society doesn't mean more happiness for a society.

Now this stability of happiness could mean that economics, economic progress, and growth don't matter, that they're irrelevant to happiness. But we economists are naturally loath to give it such an interpretation. Instead, economists slide over such problems and poll people as to how many prefer a higher income to a lower income. I've also conducted these polls and have yet to find an individual who says he or she prefers less income to more income. (If I found one, of course, I'd volunteer to relieve that person of some income, which would make us both happier.)

The fact that everyone, or almost everyone, prefers more output, but that more output or an increase in income doesn't make everyone happier, is not really a contradiction. I know from watching *Star Trek* (and from reading Lord Tennyson) that it's in striving that human beings acquire happiness. Without striving, the human being is but an empty shell. But enough; if this discussion continues, it will, heaven forbid, turn from economics to philosophy.

---

* I've given the test to students in Vermont, New York, and Great Britain, and each time the results have been similar. However, when I gave the test to students in Florida at the University of Miami and to students in Bulgaria, the results were different. In Miami they came up consistently higher for each category. Four students actually checked "ecstatic." I'm not precisely sure what this Florida factor signifies. In Bulgaria, the results were lower (a 2.8 average). Bulgaria was undergoing a wrenching economic change and many incomes had been cut by two-thirds, so this low result was explainable.

---

ences from statistics. Statistics must be treated carefully. They don't always measure what they seem to measure. Though U.S. national income accounting statistics are among the most accurate in the world, they still have serious limitations.

GDP Measures Market Activity, Not Welfare

The first, and most important, limitation to remember is that GDP does not measure happiness nor does it measure economic welfare. GDP measures economic (market) activity. Real GDP could rise and economic welfare could fall. For example, say some Martians came down and let loose a million Martian burglars in the United States just to see what would happen. GDP would be likely to rise as individuals bought guns and locks and spent millions of dollars on protecting their property and replacing stolen items. At the same time, however, welfare would fall.

Welfare is a complicated concept.

Welfare is a complicated concept. The economy's goal should not be to increase output for the sake of increasing output, but to make people better off or at least happier. But a pure happiness measure is impossible. Economists have struggled with the concept of welfare and have decided that the best they can do is to concentrate their analysis on economic activity, leaving others to consider how economic activity relates to happiness. I should warn you, however, that there is no neat correlation

The U.S. government has issued over $320 billion worth of cash. That's about $1,250 for every man, woman, and child. Now ask yourself how much cash you're carrying on you. Add to that the amounts banks and businesses keep, and divide that by the number of people in the United States. The number economists get when they do that calculation is way below the total amount of cash the United States has issued. So what happens to the extra cash?

Let's switch for a minute to a Miami safehouse being raided by drug enforcement officers. They find $50 million in cash. That's what most economists believe happens to much of the extra cash: It goes underground. An underground economy lurks below the real economy.

The underground economy consists of two components: (1) the production and distribution of illegal goods and services; and (2) the nonreporting of legal economic activity.

Illegal activity, such as selling illegal drugs and prostitution, generates huge amounts of cash. (Most people who buy an illegal good or service would prefer not to have the transaction appear on their monthly credit card statements.) This presents a problem for a big-time illegal business. It must explain to the Internal Revenue Service (IRS) where all that money came from. That's where money laundering comes in. Money laundering is simply making illegally gained income look as if it came from a legal business. Any business through which lots of cash moves is a good front for money laundering. Laundromats move lots of cash, which is where the term *money laundering* came from. The mob bought laundromats and claimed a much higher income from the laundromats than it actually received. The mob thus "laundered" the excess money. Today money laundering is much more sophisticated. It involves billions of dollars and international transactions in three or four different countries, but the purpose is the same: making illegally earned money look legal.

The second part of the illegal economy involves deliberately failing to report income in order to escape paying taxes on it. When people work "off the books," when restaurants don't ring up cash sales, when waiters forget to declare tips on their tax returns, they reduce their tax payments and make it look as if they have less income and as if the economy has less production than it actually does.

How important is the underground economy? That's tough to say; it is, after all, underground. A U.S. Department of Commerce economist estimated it at 1.5 percent of the total U.S. economy. The IRS estimates the underground economy at about 10 percent of the total U.S. economy. Some economists estimate it as high as 15 or 20 percent. In other countries, such as Sweden, where the tax rate is higher than in the United States, estimates of the underground economy's size range as high as 30 percent of the above-ground economy.

between increases in GDP and increases in happiness. You can see that in the above box.

Measurement Errors

GDP figures are supposed to measure all economic activity, but they do not. Illegal drug sales, under-the-counter sales of goods to avoid income and sales taxes, work performed and paid for in cash to avoid income tax, nonreported sales, and prostitution are all market activities, yet none of them is included in GDP figures. Estimates of the underground, nonmeasured economy's importance range from 1.5 to 20 percent of GDP in the United States and as high as 40 percent in Italy. That is, if measured U.S. GDP is $6 trillion, inclusion of the underground, nonmeasured activity would raise it to between $6.09 trillion and $7.2 trillion. If we were able to halt underground activity and direct those efforts to the above-ground economy, GDP would rise significantly. For instance, if we legalized prostitution and marijuana sales and quadrupled tax-collection mechanisms, GDP would rise. But that rise in GDP wouldn't necessarily make us better off.

A second type of measurement error occurs in adjusting GDP figures for inflation. Measurement of inflation involves numerous arbitrary decisions about changes in quality of goods. For example, if the price of a Toyota goes up 5 percent from 1995 ($20,000) to 1996 ($21,000), that's certainly a 5 percent rise in price. But what if the

Measurements of inflation can involve significant measurement errors.

1996 Toyota has a "new improved" 16-valve engine? Can you say that the price of cars has risen 5 percent, or should you adjust for the improvement in quality? And if you adjust, how do you adjust? The people who keep track of the price indices used to measure inflation will be the first to tell you there's no one right answer. How that question, and a million other similar questions involved in measuring inflation, is answered can lead to significant differences in estimates of inflation and hence in estimates of real GDP growth.

One recent study for Canada argued inflation could be either 5.4 or 15 percent, depending on how the inflation index was calculated! Which inflation figure one chose would make a big difference in one's estimate of how the economy was doing. Similarly, every five years the United States switches base years (in 1992, it switched from 1982 to 1987), and when it does many of the statistics change.

Misinterpretation of Subcategories

A third limitation of national income accounting concerns possible misinterpretation of the components. In setting up the accounts, a large number of arbitrary decisions had to be made: What to include in "investment"? What to include in "consumption"? How to treat government expenditures? The decisions that were made were, for the most part, reasonable, but they weren't the only ones that could have been made. Once made, however, they influence our interpretations of events. For example, when we see that investment rises, we normally think that our future productive capacity is rising, but remember that investment includes housing investment, which does not increase our future productive capacity. In fact, some types of consumption (say, purchases of personal computers by people who will become computer-literate and use their knowledge and skills to be more productive than they were before they owned computers) increase our productive capacity more than some types of "investment."

Q-10: How can some types of consumption increase our productive capacity by more than some types of investment?

GDP Is Worth Using Despite Its Limitations

Measurement is necessary, and the GDP measurements and categories have made it possible to think and talk about the aggregate economy.

By pointing out these problems, economists are not suggesting that national income accounting statistics should be thrown out. Far from it; measurement is necessary, and the GDP measurements and categories have made it possible to think and talk about the aggregate economy. I wouldn't have devoted an entire chapter of this book to national income accounting if I didn't believe it was important. I am simply arguing that national income accounting concepts should be used with sophistication, with an awareness of their weaknesses as well as their strengths.

Used with that awareness, national income accounting is a powerful tool; one wouldn't want to be an economist without it. For those of you who aren't planning to be economists, it's still a good idea for you to understand the concepts of national income accounting. If you do, the business section of the newspaper will no longer seem like Greek to you. You'll be a more informed citizen and will be better able to make up your own mind about macroeconomic debates.

CHAPTER SUMMARY

- National income accounting is the terminology used to talk about the aggregate economy.
- GDP measures aggregate final output of an economy. It's a flow, not a stock, measure of market activity.
- Intermediate goods can be eliminated from GDP in two ways:
  1. By measuring only final sales.
  2. By measuring only value added.
- National income is directly related to national output. Whenever there's output, there's income.
- GDP is divided up into four types of expenditures:

$$GDP = C + I + G + (X - M).$$

- NDP = GDP − Depreciation.
- NNP = NDP + Net foreign factor income.
- NNP = NI + Indirect business taxes.
- NI = Compensation to employees + Rent + Interest + Profit.
- To compare income over time, we must adjust for price-level changes. After adjusting for inflation, nominal measures are changed to "real" measures. The real amount is the nominal amount divided by the price index.
- National income accounting concepts are powerful tools for understanding macroeconomics, but we must recognize their limitations.

KEY TERMS

depreciation *(168)*
disposable personal income   *(172)*
domestic income (DI)   *(170)*
durable goods   *(167)*
gross domestic product (GDP)   *(159)*
gross national product (GNP)   *(159)*
intermediate products   *(161)*
national income (NI)   *(170)*

national income accounting   *(159)*
national income accounting
  identity   *(163)*
net domestic product (NDP)   *(169)*
net foreign factor income   *(160)*
net national product (NNP)   *(172)*
net private investment   *(168)*
nominal concepts   *(159)*

nominal GDP   *(175)*
nondurable goods   *(167)*
personal income (PI)   *(172)*
real concepts   *(159)*
real GDP   *(175)*
transfer payments   *(168)*
value added   *(162)*
Wealth Accounts   *(161)*

QUESTIONS FOR THOUGHT AND REVIEW

The number after each question represents the estimated degree of critical thinking required. (1 = almost none; 10 = deep thought.)

1. What's the relationship between a stock concept and a flow concept? Give an example that hasn't already been given in this chapter. *(5)*

2. A company sells 1,000 desks for $400 each. Of these, it sells 750 to other companies and 250 to individuals. What is that company's contribution to GDP? *(4)*

3. The United States is considering introducing a value added tax. What tax rate on value added is needed to get the same increase in revenue as is gotten from an income tax with a rate of 15 percent? Why? *(8)*

4. If the United States introduces universal child care, what will likely happen to GDP? What are the welfare implications of that rise? *(5)*

5. You've been given the following data:

Transfer payments	$ 72
Interest paid by consumers	4
Net exports	4
Indirect business taxes	47
Net foreign factor income	2
Corporate income tax	64
Contribution for social insurance	35

Personal tax and nontax payments	91
Undistributed corporate profits	51
Gross private investment	185
Government purchases	195
Personal consumption	500
Depreciation	59

On the basis of these data calculate GDP, GNP, NNP, NDP, NI, personal income, and disposable personal income. *(6)*

6. Rent is $400, investment is $100, interest is $200, savings are $75, profits are −$200, wages are $4,000, and consumption is $3,000. Assuming net foreign factor income and indirect business taxes are zero, what is the level of NDP? *(5)*

7. Economists normally talk about GDP even though they know NDP is a better measure of economic activity. Why? *(3)*

8. How does personal income differ from national income? *(3)*

9. What is the difference between national personal income and domestic personal income? *(4)*

10. If society's goal is to make society happier, and higher GDP isn't closely associated with society being happier, why do economists even talk about GDP? *(9)*

PROBLEMS AND EXERCISES

1. Given the following data about the economy:

Consumption	$700
Investment	500
Corporate income tax	215
Proprietors' income	250
Government expenditure	300
Profits	250
Wages	700
Net exports	275
Rents	25
Depreciation	25
Indirect business taxes	100
Undistributed corporate profits	60
Net foreign factor income	−3
Interest	150
Social security contribution	0
Transfer payments	0
Personal taxes	165

   a. Calculate GDP and GNP with both the expenditures approach and the income approach.
   b. Calculate NDP, NNP, NI, and domestic income.
   c. Calculate PI.
   d. Calculate disposable personal income.

2. There are three firms in an economy: A, B, and C. Firm A buys $250 worth of goods from firm B and $200 worth of goods from firm C, and produces 200 units of output which it sells at $5 per unit. Firm B buys $100 worth of goods from firm A and $150 worth of goods from firm C,

and produces 300 units of output which it sells at $7 per unit. Firm C buys $50 worth of goods from firm A and nothing from firm B. It produces output worth $1,000. All other products are sold to consumers.

a. Calculate GDP.

b. If a value added tax (a tax on the total value added of each firm) of 10 percent is introduced, how much revenue will the government get?

c. How much would government get if it introduced a 10 percent income tax?

d. How much would government get if it introduced a 10 percent sales tax on final output?

3. Below are nominal GDP and GDP deflators for four years.

	Nominal GDP	GDP Deflator	Real GDP
1989	5251	108.5	
1990	5546	113.3	
1991	5723	117.7	
1992	6039	121.1	

a. Calculate real GDP in each year.

b. Did the percent change in nominal GDP exceed the percent change in real GDP in any of the last three years?

c. In which year did society's welfare increase the most?

4. You have been hired as a research assistant and are given the following data.

Compensation	329
Consumption	370
Exports	55
Net foreign factor income	3
Government purchases	43
Gross investment	80
Imports	63
Indirect business taxes	27
Net interest	49
Profits	69
Rental income	1

a. Calculate GNP, GDP, NDP, NNP and NI.

b. What is depreciation in this year?

c. Right after you finish, your boss comes running in to you and tells you that she made a mistake. Imports were really 68 and compensation was 340. She tells you to get her the corrected answers to a. and b. immediately.

5. You've been called in by your boss with some questions.

a. First, she tells you that she has been told that net private investment was negative and gross private investment was positive this year. She says that that is impossible. What do you tell her?

b. Next, she wants you to tell her what national income in the United States was in 1990. She gives you the following data: 1990 GDP was $5546.1 billion, net foreign factor income was $21.7 billion, capital depreciated by $607.7 billion, and indirect business taxes stood at $444.0 billion.

c. Finally, she tells you that GDP fell 32 percent in her country last year, and that she must make a state of the economy speech next week. She wants to know how she can portray this fall in the best possible light. What do you tell her?

ANSWERS TO MARGIN QUESTIONS

1. GNP measures the output of the residents of a country—the output within its geographical borders. GDP measures the output of the citizens and businesses of a country. Kuwait is a very rich country whose residents have a high income, much of it from investments overseas. Thus their GNP will be high. However, Kuwait also has large numbers of foreign workers who are not citizens and whose incomes would be included in GDP but not in GNP. In reality, Kuwait citizens' and businesses' foreign income exceeds foreign workers' and foreign companies' income within Kuwait, so Kuwait's GNP is greater than its GDP. *(160)*

2. Wealth Accounts measure stocks—a country's assets and liabilities at a point in time. Income Accounts measure flows—a country's income and expenditures over a period of time. *(161)*

3. Only the value added by the sale would be added to GDP. In this case the value added is the difference between the purchase price and the sale price, or $500. *(162)*

4. The government budget includes transfer payments, which are not included in GDP. Only those government expenditures that are for goods and services are included in GDP. *(163)*

5. The four components of expenditures in national income are personal consumption, gross private investment, net exports, and government purchases. *(166)*

6. The largest component of national income is compensation to employees. *(170)*

7. By national income accounting convention, all taxes must be paid by households. Since, by definition, households receive all income and produce all output, the taxes paid by businesses must be added back to national income if national income is to equal net product. *(172)*

8. In developing countries, individuals often grow their own food and take part in many activities that are not measured by the GDP statistics. The income figures that one gets from the GDP statistics of developing countries do not include such activities and, thus, can be quite misleading. *(174)*

9. Nominal income must have risen to slightly over $4.6 trillion so that, when it is adjusted for inflation, the real income will have risen to $4.2 trillion. *(175)*

10. Dividing goods into consumption and investment does not always capture the effect of the spending on productive capacity. For example, housing "investment" does little to expand the productive capacity. However, "consumption" of computers or books could expand the productive capacity significantly. *(178)*

8

The Macroeconomic Debate and Aggregate Supply/ Aggregate Demand Analysis*

The Theory of Economics . . . is a method rather than a doctrine, an apparatus of the mind, a technique of thinking which helps its possessor to draw correct conclusions.

~J. M. Keynes

After reading this chapter, you should be able to:

1 State how economists use abstract theory to demonstrate analytic virtuosity.

2 Explain why studying some theory is absolutely necessary to becoming a good policy economist.

3 List two central lessons of macroeconomic theory.

4 State the relevance of the fallacy of composition to macroeconomics.

5 Explain why interrelated supply and demand curves may undermine partial equilibrium supply/demand analysis.

6 Draw an aggregate supply and an aggregate demand curve and explain how they differ from microeconomic supply and demand curves.

7 Distinguish a shift in from a movement along aggregate supply and demand curves.

8 Distinguish a price-level flexibility curve from an aggregate supply curve.

---

* This chapter, which deals with issues of theory, may be skipped in policy-oriented courses. The *AS/AD* curves are briefly explained in Chapter 9, so that policy-oriented courses can proceed immediately to that chapter.

When running for his first term as president, George Bush promised the American public 10 million new jobs if he were elected. He didn't deliver; he was replaced by Bill Clinton. Clinton, in turn, promised prosperity and millions of new jobs in his term of office. Having been elected on these promises, Clinton turned to his economic advisers to tell him how to fulfill them.

The honest answer he would have received from those advisers is that understanding the macro economy is tough and that a simple statement of what he must do to create jobs and prosperity doesn't exist. There are some major policies he could try that would most likely increase jobs, but politically, these major policies would be dangerous; moreover, they would also potentially be highly inflationary. There are also some minor policy initiatives he could try that would push the economy in the right direction; alone, these minor policies couldn't be counted on to achieve the promised result, but at least they would give voters the sense that he was dealing with the problem. The mainstream economic view was that his best political bet, and probably his best economic bet, would be to try these minor macro policy initiatives and hope for some luck. If he was lucky, the economy would pick up on its own, income and jobs would increase, and he could credit his policies.

To argue that you need luck for the economy to achieve macroeconomic prosperity is not to argue that the policies he tried were wrong or irrelevant; it is only to say that any policy strong enough to deliver lots of jobs and sustained prosperity would also probably push the economy perilously close to increasing inflation. In that case, Clinton could find himself "Carterized"—voted out of office because of too much inflation—instead of being "Bushed"—voted out of office because of too much unemployment.

The economists Clinton turned to for answers were generally considered **Keynesian activist economists.** They believed that the government could come up with some policy proposals that could positively impact the economy. Bush's advisers were generally **Classical laissez-faire economists.** They believed that any government policies would probably make things worse, so the best policy was government disinvolvement with the economy—lowering taxes and keeping the government out of the market economy as much as possible.

How do these two groups of economists come to their views about policy? The answer is: through a combination of thorough understanding of past events, deductive reasoning from theory, and gut feelings about the way the economy and politics work. It's difficult to say which of these three methods has most influenced economists' policy views, but the one that is most discussed by economists is deductive reasoning from theory.

Q-1: How does a Keynesian activist economist differ from a Classical laissez-faire economist?

Economists come to their views of policy through a combination of an understanding of past events, deductive reasoning from theory, and gut feelings about the way the economy and politics work.

ECONOMIC THEORIES: THE UNDERPINNINGS OF ACTIVISM AND LAISSEZ-FAIRE ECONOMICS

Most of the work and debate among economists about macroeconomic policy has concerned, and still concerns, theory. Economists love theory. They get as excited about theory as small children get about ice cream. The discussion of theory is so important to economists that anyone who seriously wants to debate any economic policy issue had better know the alternative theories. All serious discussions of economic policy are framed within those theories. A knowledge of theory is an initiation rite through which all policy economists must pass. If you win in the theoretical debate, your policy advice is more likely to be deemed credible.

Is Theory the "Be All and End All" in Economics?

1 In economics, economists often use abstract theory to demonstrate their analytic virtuosity.

Theory is to economics what slam dunks are to basketball.

The role of theory is so pervasive in economics, and so foreign to students, that it needs some explanation. Perhaps the following analogies will put the role of theory in policy discussions in perspective. In competitive sports, success often depends on a competitor's ability to psyche out his or her opponent. Theory is to economics what slam dunks are to basketball or hitting a high C is to a tenor. If you can't slam dunk, you get no respect in basketball. If you can't hit high C, you get no respect at the opera house. So, too, in economics: If you don't deal on the forefront of theory, you get no respect in economics and your policy advice will be dismissed.

The significance economists place on theory can be seen in the economics profession's reaction to President Clinton's choice of Laura Tyson as chairperson of the Council of Economic Advisers. I recount this story to provide insight into the economics profession, and to give you a sense of its heavy theoretical focus.

Tyson's appointment in 1993 created a stir in the economics profession that was initially interpreted as anti-woman by some reporters. (There are few women in the top ranks of the economics profession, so there is definitely reason for such concern.) Upon closer examination, observers generally concluded that gender bias wasn't the direct cause of the rumblings in the profession about her appointment. The direct cause was that she hadn't played the high theory game; she hadn't shown that she could slam dunk. It didn't matter that she was a brilliant policy economist who knew how to use theory and how to push theoretical arguments to their limits. It didn't matter that she knew how to integrate economic issues with political issues. In short, it didn't matter that she was perfect for the job. What mattered to a number of top economists was that she hadn't performed high theory acrobatics, and hence, in those economists' opinion, she was not to be listened to on policy matters.

These economists' rumblings were reported in the popular press, but, relatively quickly, the word went out from some of economics' elder statesmen to the younger theoretical types who were doing the complaining to cool it—they were making themselves look anti-woman to the public—so the issue died. But the point was made, and some males who could both slam dunk and do policy analysis joined the Council. This confirmed the credibility of the group to the profession, and all was well.

The point of the above discussion is that often economists focus too much on theory, especially elaborate theory. The reality is that if a policy economist becomes sufficiently knowledgeable about history and institutions, he or she doesn't have time to become too engrossed in esoteric theory. Nonetheless, the reality also is that theory is, and will continue to be, strongly emphasized by economists. So if you want to understand economists' policy debates, you must understand their theoretical debates.

The above discussion does not mean that theory—even abstract theory—is unimportant. Studying some theory is absolutely necessary to becoming a good policy economist. Just as one can become too engrossed in theory, so too can one become too distanced from it. When I'm with strong ''real-world'' economists, I find myself arguing strongly for economic education that includes a solid grounding in theory and its limits.

There are two reasons why theory is so important. The first is that it defines and highlights definitional truths. TANSTAAFL captures the essence of those definitional truths: There's a cost and benefit to every decision. Theory forces you to recognize the costs and benefits of policies when you take into account the complex interrelationships in the economy. Once you have a solid grounding in theory you build that sense of opposing costs and benefits into your policy considerations, and you think and reason like an economist.

The second reason a solid grounding in theory is necessary is that theory exercises your mind; it gives you practice in understanding interrelationships of economic variables. The reason can be made clear by an analogy again to high school sports. In just about any competitive sport, coaches don't let you compete unless you do calisthenics and exercises in preparation. Generally, the better you do the calisthenics, the better you play the sport. The same is true of economics. Theory and models are economics' calisthenics of the mind.

Students need such calisthenics. Many students' minds are about as flabby as is my body, and I'm a middle-aged male physical mess because I spend all my time exercising my mind and little time exercising my body. Physical exercises would be good for me; I know it, and I keep promising myself that tomorrow I'll do some. But you know how it goes: I find this neat article, or argument, and I'm off to my computer, sitting on my backside. Many students have the same problem with their minds that I have with my body; they know they should exercise their minds, but they put off doing it.

There is no doubt that people can talk about economic policy even though they have no training in theory. It happens all the time. But such talk is the equivalent of

Economists' theoretical focus has led to some good-hearted criticism of the profession.

In Defense of Theory

2 Two reasons theory is important are:
1. Theory defines and highlights definitional truths; and
2. Theory exercises your mind.

Q-2:   State two reasons why economic theory is important.

sandlot baseball or singing in the shower. In a policy discussion with someone trained in economic theory, the untrained are annihilated. The point is, no matter what you are doing, you can't immediately just do it (despite what Nike commercials tell you). Instead, you must prepare yourself to do it right. You do exercises—work with abstract theoretical models.

Having made my pitch for the absolute necessity of theory, I will now say that I'm also a realist; almost none of you are going on to become professional economists, and very few of you will major in economics. For most of you, this is the end of the road in the study of formal economics. But it isn't the end of the road of your consideration of economic policy. All of you, in your role as citizens in our democracy, will be called upon to make decisions about economic policies, and to do that you need some sense of macro theory. So in this book you're going to get the absolute minimal theory necessary to understand the development of economic ideas and make decisions about macroeconomic policies. (A longer introduction to macro theory is included in the appendix of this chapter, for those of you who have teachers who want you to do some more calisthenics of the mind.)

In a policy discussion with someone trained in economic theory, the untrained are often annihilated.

What's the minimum amount of macro theory you've got to know to understand macro policy issues? I've whittled it down to two lessons.

> Lesson 1: You must understand the limits of carrying over the Chapter 2 analysis of supply and demand to the macro economy.
>
> Lesson 2: You must be able to distinguish shifts in aggregate supply and demand curves from movements along aggregate supply and demand curves.

TWO CENTRAL LESSONS OF MACROECONOMIC THEORY

3 Two central lessons of macro-economic theory are:
1. Understanding the limits of supply and demand analysis; and
2. Distinguishing shifts in from movements along aggregate supply and demand curves.

If you can master these two lessons well, you'll have the foundation you need to understand the macro policy debates.

Lesson 1: The Limits of Supply/Demand Analysis

Students often are given a choice of which to study first: macroeconomics or micro-economics. There are advantages and drawbacks to either choice. Those who take micro first will have expanded training in the issues discussed in Chapter 2. That's useful because the student can understand the **microfoundations of macro** better; that is, understand the decisions of individuals that underlie aggregate results. But this can cause problems because it creates in students a tendency to forget the "other things equal" assumptions and think that they can apply the same logic and analysis to macro questions that they apply to micro questions. Doing so is not necessarily correct. The primary reason is the **fallacy of composition** (the false assumption that what is true for a part will also be true for the whole). Let's consider the relevance of the fallacy of composition for macroeconomic reasoning.

Microfoundations of macro   The decisions of individuals that underlie aggregate results.

Fallacy of composition   The false assumption that what is true for a part will also be true for the whole.

Q-3: What is a potential problem of studying micro before macro?

Q-4: Economists assume individuals' decisions are rational, so it is only reasonable that they assume society's decisions are rational. True or false? Why?

4 In macro, small effects can add up and hence cannot be assumed constant.

The Relevance of the Fallacy of Composition   In their microanalysis of an individual's decisions, economists assume individuals are rational—that individuals do what is best for themselves. Can we carry over that reasoning and assume that society is rational—that society does what is best for itself? Not necessarily.

There are many small effects of individuals' actions on others that can influence the aggregate result but that the individual doesn't consider. When you are analyzing one individual's actions (when you are using microanalysis), these small effects can reasonably be assumed constant: the effect of one individual's actions is too small to influence the aggregate significantly, and the feedback effect of those actions' influence on the aggregate can be forgotten. One person's action is as irrelevant to the aggregate as is the size of a grain of sand to the size of a beach. If one grain of sand doubles in size, the beach is unaffected. However, when you are analyzing the whole (when you are using macro analysis), you cannot forget these small effects because, combined, they are no longer necessarily small. If all grains of sand double in size, you've got sand problems. So it isn't at all clear that if individuals are rational, the aggregate result of their combined actions will be collectively rational for society.

To see this, think of one person lowering the price of his or her good. People will substitute that good for other goods, and the quantity demanded of the good will increase. But what if all individuals lower their prices? Since all prices will have gone down, why should demanders switch? The substitution story can't be used in the aggregate. There are many such examples.

One of the important side effects of decisions that must be considered in macro, but not in micro, is the side effect of spending decisions. Your spending decision is someone else's demand, and someone else's spending decision is your demand. In our economy people can spend whatever level of income they want; there is no direct mechanism in the economy that coordinates our spending decisions. Thus the composite of all spending decisions may be too much, or too little, spending. And when there is too little or too much spending, the economy experiences a business cycle.

In macro, one must take into account the side effects of spending decisions.

The **"Other Things Equal" Assumption**   Now that we've gone over the fallacy of composition, let's tie it in with the Chapter 2 discussion about the importance of the "other things equal" assumption and the limits of partial equilibrium analysis. Just in case you forgot, let me review the term *partial equilibrium*. I first used the term in Chapter 2 when I pointed out that supply and demand analysis was a **partial equilibrium** tool. Partial equilibrium means what it says—the analysis is partial or incomplete. It keeps a number of issues at the back of one's mind. To use supply and demand analysis correctly, you've got to remember that the supply and demand curves were designed as an engine of analysis—not as the analysis itself—to be used in combination with reason and educated common sense whenever other things did not remain equal.

Partial equilibrium   The analysis of an issue, holding "all other things constant."

Now let's get specific. The partial equilibrium supply and demand curves focused the analysis on the effect of *a change in the relative price* (the price of a good relative to the composite price level of all other goods) of an individual good in a market in isolation from other markets. If supply and demand decisions of individuals had side effects on other markets which could feed back on the original market, those side effects had to be considered before one applied the results of the analysis to policy. That's why I spent so much time emphasizing that the application of supply and demand analysis depended on the assumption that "other things remain constant."

Obviously, in the real world, other things do not remain constant, and changes in the "other things" must be brought into the analysis through a consideration of shift factors of supply and demand. Considering the effect of such shift factors is the bread and butter of microeconomics.

Independent Shift Factors   Let's review an example in which supply and demand analysis can nicely handle a shift factor: an example of an independent shift factor. Say that consumers' income in a market rises. That's a shift factor, so we will say that the demand for a product will increase (the entire demand curve will shift). The product's relative price will rise from P_0 to P_1, and the quantity produced will increase from Q_0 to Q_1. That case is demonstrated in Exhibit 1(a). You should be able to follow that case with ease.

Interdependent Shift Factors   Now let's consider a case where the supply and demand analysis used above is not enough: the case of an interdependent shift factor. Specifically, let's apply supply and demand analysis to a market in a small town in which the income people earn from supplying a good influences how much they demand of the good. When there is such a relationship, there is an interconnection or interdependence between shift factors of demand and movements along a supply curve. When there is such an interconnection, partial equilibrium supply/demand analysis cannot be used without some modification. The interconnection has violated the "other things constant" assumption necessary to use partial equilibrium analysis.

When there is an interdependence between shift factors of demand and movements along a supply curve, partial equilibrium analysis cannot be used without some modification.

To see the problem such an interconnection creates, let's consider the same example of an increase in demand in Exhibit 1(a), only this time let's assume that the interdependence described above exists—that when suppliers' income increases, their

Q-5: Why is it difficult for supply/demand analysis to deal with interdependent shift factors?

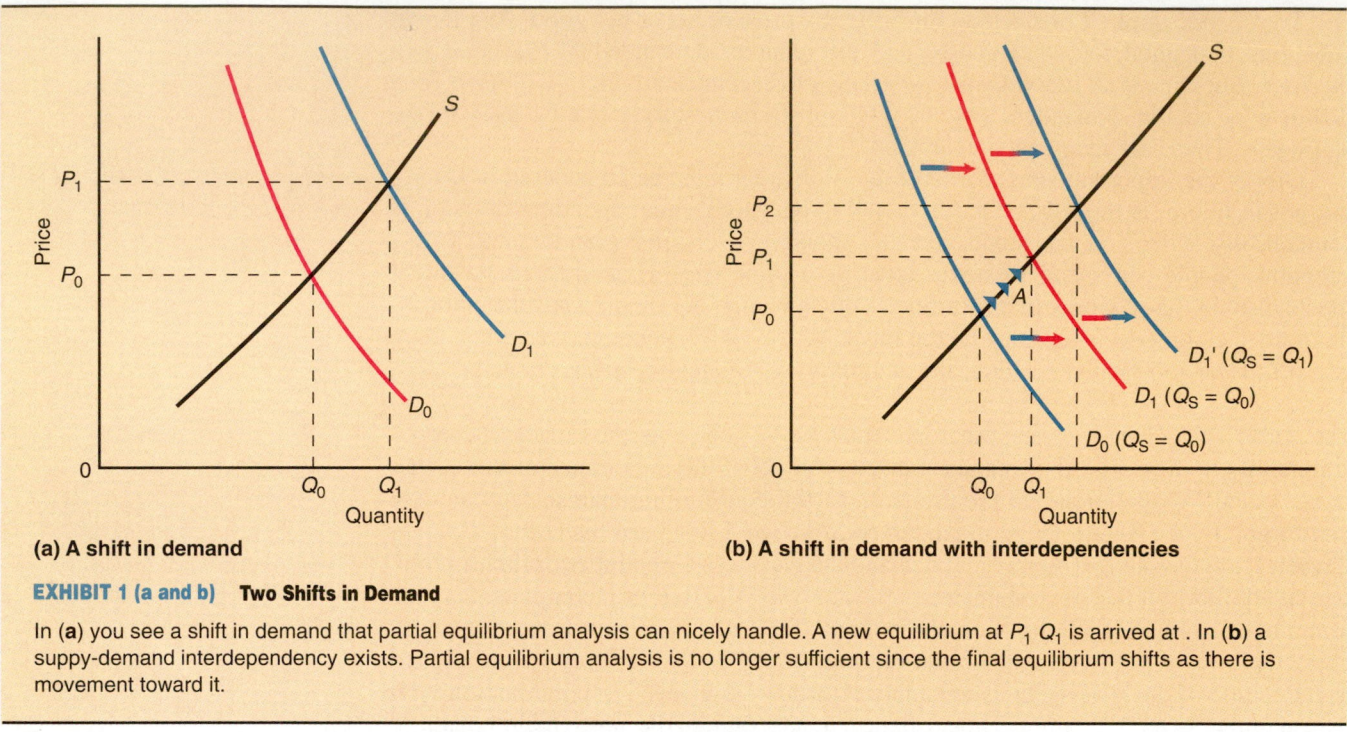

(a) A shift in demand

(b) A shift in demand with interdependencies

EXHIBIT 1 (a and b)   Two Shifts in Demand

In (a) you see a shift in demand that partial equilibrium analysis can nicely handle. A new equilibrium at $P_1 Q_1$ is arrived at . In (b) a suppy-demand interdependency exists. Partial equilibrium analysis is no longer sufficient since the final equilibrium shifts as there is movement toward it.

5 When supply and demand are interrelated, the equilibrium shifts as you move towards it.

demand for the good increases (the demand curve shifts out). Say, for example, that whenever we move along the supply curve—when we change the quantity supplied (move along arrow A in Exhibit 1(b)—that movement in quantity supplied causes people's income to rise and hence causes the demand curve to shift by the same quantity by which supply increased.

I demonstrate this case in Exhibit 1(b). Start the analysis with the market in equilibrium at price P_0. The demand curve shifts out from D_0 to D_1 due to some unspecified shift factor. The excess demand at P_0 causes the quantity supplied to increase, moving us towards price P_1. But because of the assumed interconnection between supply and demand, as that happens, the demand curve, which depends on the quantity supplied, shifts out further than the initial shift. Remember, by assumption, demand shifts whenever quantity supplied increases. Thus, when quantity supplied equals Q_1, the demand curve has shifted out to D_1'. Because of this shift, instead of the market reaching equilibrium at price P_1, excess demand (disequilibrium) will be just as large as it was initially. The situation is like a dog chasing its tail—whenever it tries to catch its tail, the tail moves, and the faster the dog chases, the faster the tail moves. Given the interrelationship between demand and the quantity supplied, there would be no equilibrium in this example—there would simply be an unending chase between the two.

The above example is only one of many possible interrelationships between a shift factor and a movement along a curve. When such interrelationships exist in the real world, they must be added back to the analysis before partial equilibrium supply/demand analysis can be applied to policy analysis. Otherwise you'll fall into the fallacy of composition trap.

The lesson is abstract, but it has direct policy relevance. Say you're predicting the effect of a 10 percent increase in price by your firm on the quantity demanded. If other firms in the industry don't follow suit, there will probably be a large dropoff in the quantity demanded. But if other firms do follow suit and raise their price, other things will not remain constant and there will likely be little effect on demand. So in your analysis you must take into account the interdependent effect of your decisions on your competitors' decisions.

What's all this abstract reasoning about interconnections of supply and demand and the limits of partial equilibrium analysis got to do with macroeconomics? The answer is: everything. Think back to the circular flow diagram presented in Chapter 6. Whenever firms in the aggregate produce (whenever they supply), they create income (demand for their goods). *So in macro, when aggregate supply changes, or when there is movement along an aggregate supply curve, aggregate demand changes.* Aggregate supply and aggregate demand are interdependent. This interdependence is one of the primary reasons we have a separate macroeconomics. In macroeconomics, the "other things constant" assumption central to microeconomic supply/demand analysis cannot hold. In macroeconomics, output creates income and income is spent on output. When the output side increases, so does the income side.

Consider what would happen if in the United States output were to increase by 30 percent in one year. Should you expect that the additional output couldn't be sold? No. As output increases by 30 percent, people's income increases by 30 percent. And as their income rises, it is only reasonable to assume that aggregate demand will also rise, and that an increase in aggregate supply will cause some increase in aggregate demand. It follows that the insights of the partial equilibrium supply and demand model cannot simply be carried over to macroeconomic problems, and that any macro model must take account of the potential interrelationships between aggregate supply and aggregate demand.

One way to bring home these interrelationships to you is by developing aggregate supply and aggregate demand curves that correspond to the partial equilibrium supply and demand curves to which you were introduced in Chapter 2, and to distinguish carefully between shifts in, and movements along, these curves.

The first step in understanding the nature of aggregate supply and aggregate demand is to remember the difference between *price level* and *relative price*. The **price level** is a composite price of all goods. As I discussed in the last chapter, in partial equilibrium supply and demand analysis, **relative price**—the price of the good relative to the price level—goes on the vertical axis, and quantity of the good in the market goes on the horizontal axis. The reason relative price goes on the vertical axis is that the law of supply and the law of demand are based on relative prices: as the relative price of a good rises, demanders buy less of that good—they substitute another good for the higher-priced good. Similarly, suppliers offer more of that good for sale—switching their production towards this good and away from goods whose relative price has declined.

The Framework: The Price Level of Aggregate Output   When we're talking about the aggregate domestic economy, we are not talking about a particular good—we're talking about a composite of all goods, GDP. That means that we're talking about the price level—the price of a composite good. The axes for aggregate supply and aggregate demand are shown in Exhibit 2. Notice that the price level goes on the vertical axis and aggregate output goes on the horizontal axis. This is a fundamentally different framework than the partial equilibrium framework. If we were talking about relative prices, the aggregate supply/demand framework wouldn't make sense. The relative price of all goods—price level—relative to the price of all goods is always one.

There's more to be said about this issue of relative price, but as long as you promise to remember that in macro the *price level* goes on the vertical axis, I won't subject you to those mind exercises here. If you don't promise (or if you're intrigued by the intellectual promise of it all), it's off to the appendix for you.

The Aggregate Demand Curve   Now that we've got the axes down, let's consider the aggregate demand curve. The **aggregate demand curve** is a schedule, graphically

Lesson 2: Distinguish Shifts In from Movements Along Aggregate Supply and Demand Curves

Aggregate supply and aggregate demand are interdependent.

Q-6:   Why can't partial equilibrium analysis be used in macro?

The Tools of Macro Analysis: Aggregate Supply and Aggregate Demand

Price level   *A composite price of all goods.*

Relative prices   *The price of a good relative to the price level.*

In macroeconomics, the price level goes on the vertical axis.

Aggregate demand curve   *A schedule, graphically represented by a curve, that shows how a change in the price level will change the quantity of output demanded, other things (including supply) held constant.*

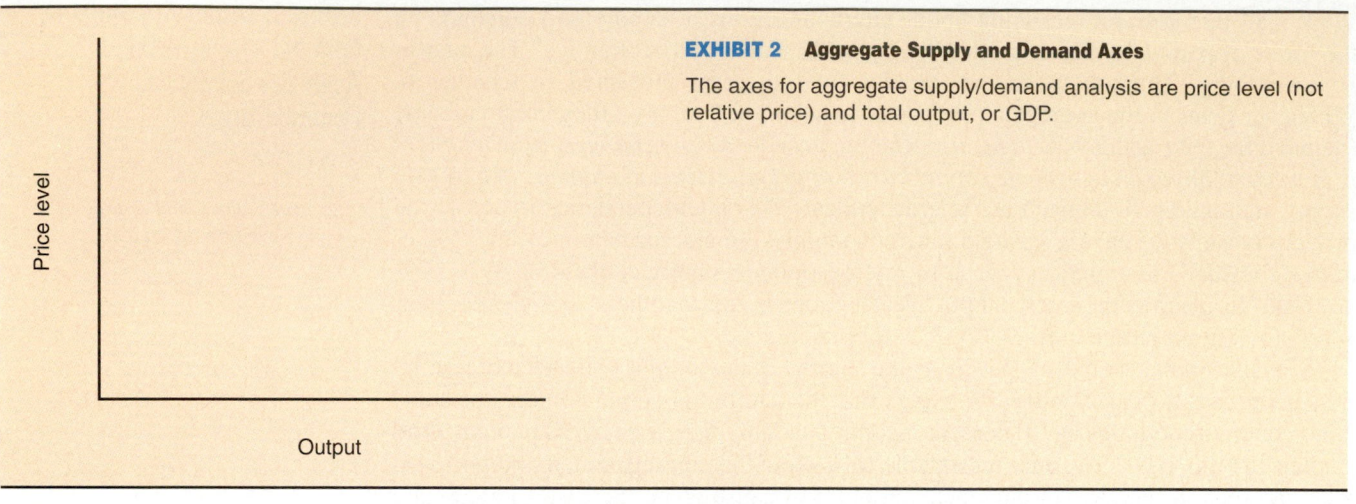

EXHIBIT 2   Aggregate Supply and Demand Axes

The axes for aggregate supply/demand analysis are price level (not relative price) and total output, or GDP.

Price level

Output

represented by a curve, that shows how a change in the price level will change the quantity of output demanded, other things (including supply) held constant.[1]

6A   The *AD* curve is downward sloping.

Generally, economists consider this aggregate demand curve to be downward sloping, as in Exhibit 3(a), which means that a fall in the price level, *other things constant,* will cause the quantity of aggregate demand to increase. This downward-sloping relationship between the price level and the quantity of aggregate demand is called the **law of aggregate demand**—as the price level falls the quantity of aggregate demand will increase, holding everything else constant.

The aggregate demand *(AD)* curve is generally considered to be downward sloping because as the price level falls, certain effects that I discuss in the appendix cause real output to increase. I won't go into these effects here as long as you promise you will remember that the reason that the aggregate demand curve slopes downward is fundamentally different from the reasons a partial equilibrium demand curve (the curve we use in micro) slopes downward. If you don't promise that, it's reading the appendix three times for you.

A change in any factor other than the price level causes a shift in the *AD* curve. For example, say income in the economy rises for *some other reason than a fall in the price level.* That would shift the demand curve out along the *A* arrow in Exhibit 3(b). Similarly, if income fell, that fall would shift the *AD* curve in along the *B* arrow.

A change in any factor other than the price level causes a shift in the AD *curve.*

Since, in national income accounting, income and output are, by definition, equal, it may seem strange to have income a shift factor of aggregate demand for output. The explanation is that national income accounting refers to equilibrium situations, and in *AS/AD* analysis, we are specifically considering the possibility of aggregate disequilibrium and what effect disequilibrium forces will have on the level of income. In disequilibrium, the quantity of output demanded may not equal the quantity of output supplied. The aggregate quantity of output supplied creates income of an equal amount; it does not create quantity demanded of an equal amount. It is the aggregate quantity of output supplied that is being held constant on the aggregate demand curve. It follows that changes in income—changes in aggregate supply—can cause the *AD* curve to shift. The intuition of how this works is clear. If firms increase output by 10 percent, society's income must rise by 10 percent; their spending, however, does

---

[1] (Note to Instructor) This definition of *AD*, while standard in most introductory books, is not the curve (which has sometimes been inappropriately called an *AD* curve) derived from IS/LM analysis or from AE/AP analysis. A curve relating price level and equilibrium output derived from these Keynesian models involves both *hypothesized shifts of, and movements along,* an aggregate demand curve as defined above. Thus such a curve is a locus of points tracing a shifting *AD* curve; it does not distinguish shifts in and movements along the curve. Such a curve is more appropriately called an Aggregate Equilibrium Curve since it maps hypothesized aggregate supply/demand equilibria determined by the interaction of the goods market and the money market against the price level. See Appendix A of this chapter for a full specification of the *AD* curve as defined in this chapter and see Appendix A of Chapter 10 to see how AE/AP analysis and an *AD* curve are related. See the Instructor's Manual for further discussion and references.

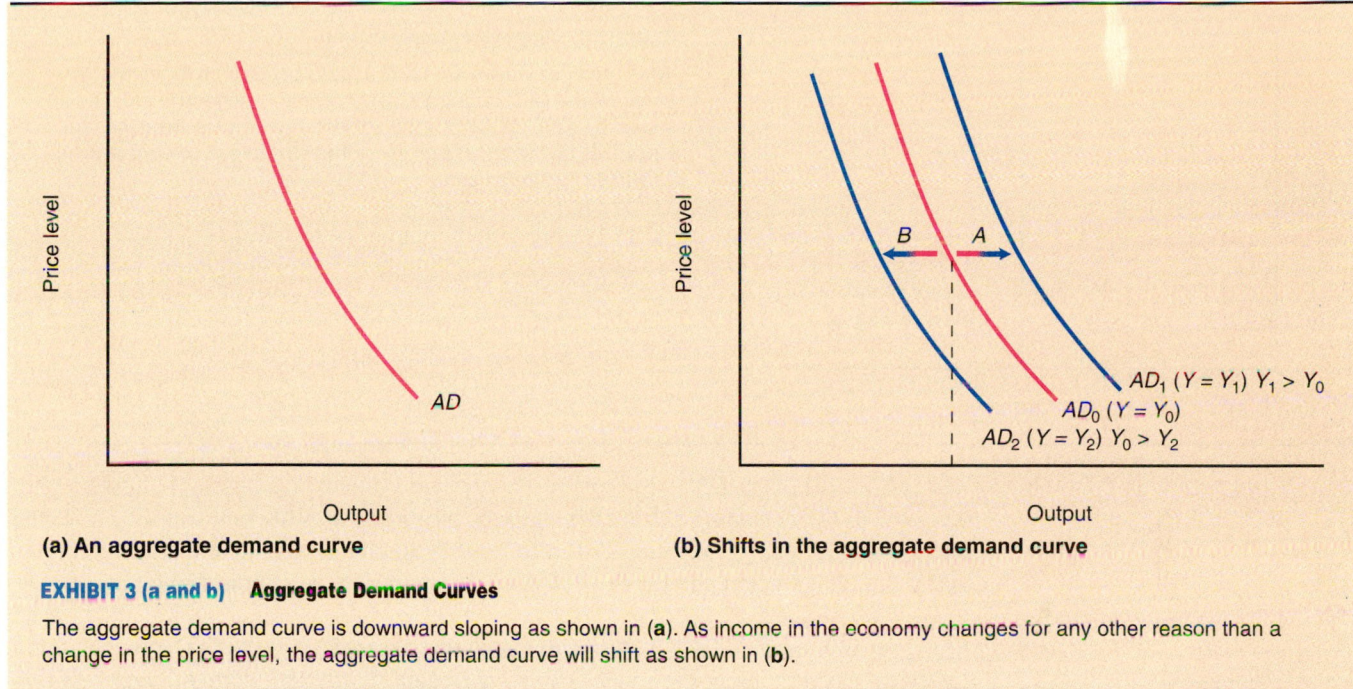

(a) An aggregate demand curve

(b) Shifts in the aggregate demand curve

EXHIBIT 3 (a and b)   Aggregate Demand Curves

The aggregate demand curve is downward sloping as shown in (a). As income in the economy changes for any other reason than a change in the price level, the aggregate demand curve will shift as shown in (b).

not necessarily rise by 10 percent. The only variable that can affect the shape of the *AD* curve is the price level. All other changes must shift the curve; thus, when income changes, the *AD* curve shifts.

The Aggregate Supply Curve   Let's now move on to aggregate supply. The **aggregate supply curve** (*AS*) is a schedule, graphically represented by a curve, which shows how a change in the price level will change the quantity of output supplied, other things (including expectations and aggregate demand) constant.

Economists usually distinguish two *AS* curves—a short-run *AS* curve and a long-run vertical *AS* curve. These two curves are drawn in Exhibit 4. The reasoning for the difference between the shapes of the two curves is that in the short run, input prices, mainly wages, are assumed constant, so as output prices rise relative to input prices, profits increase and firms have an incentive to increase output. This leads to the short-run upward-sloping curve. As long as workers are willing to supply more labor even though their real wage has decreased, this reasoning makes sense.

In the long run, input prices and output prices are assumed to move in tandem. Thus, the reasoning for an upward-sloping *AS* curve does not apply and, in the long run (or in the short run if input prices adjust as fast as output prices), the *AS* curve is perfectly vertical. A vertical *AS* curve means that a change in the price level, other things equal, will not cause the quantity of aggregate supply to change.

The short-run *AS* curve can shift around due to shift factors of supply. One of the most important of these shift factors is expectations of demand. As expectations of demand shift, the short-run aggregate supply curve shifts. If, in the aggregate, businesspeople expect low demand, they decrease their supply—aggregate supply shifts in. Such shifts in short-run aggregate supply correspond to business cycles: a recession corresponds to a shift in of the short-run aggregate supply curve; a boom corresponds to a shift out of the short-run aggregate supply curve. However, outward shifts are limited by the long-run *AS* curve, which corresponds to potential income. Once an economy has reached its potential income, the issue is no longer a business cycle issue; the issue is a growth issue, and a different set of shift factors becomes relevant.

There are lots of neat deductive reasons underlying the shapes of the *AS* curves, but they too will be banished to the appendix—as long as you promise, on your honor, to remember that the reasoning behind the shape of the aggregate supply curve is not

Aggregate supply curve   A schedule, graphically represented by a curve, which shows how a change in the price level will change the quantity of output supplied, other things (including expectations and aggregate demand) constant.

6B   The short-run *AS* curve is upward sloping; the long-run *AS* curve is vertical.

The short-run AS *curve can shift around due to shift factors of supply.*

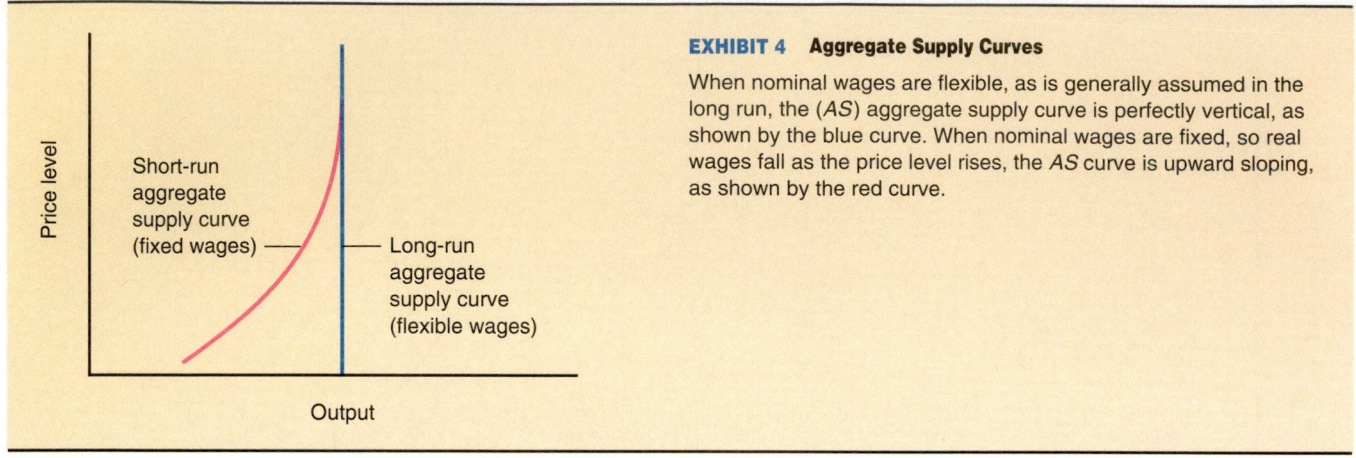

EXHIBIT 4   Aggregate Supply Curves

When nominal wages are flexible, as is generally assumed in the long run, the (AS) aggregate supply curve is perfectly vertical, as shown by the blue curve. When nominal wages are fixed, so real wages fall as the price level rises, the AS curve is upward sloping, as shown by the red curve.

the same as the reasoning behind the shape of the partial equilibrium supply curve (the one we use in micro). My suggestion to your professor is that if any student forgets that point, that student should be sentenced to reading the appendix three more times.

The shapes of the AS *and* AD *curves aren't central to macro analysis.*

Aggregate Adjustment to Shifts in Aggregate Supply and Aggregate Demand   The reason that I can be so cavalier about the shapes of the aggregate supply and demand curves is that these shapes aren't the central part of macro analysis. Just look around you. Do you see the price level fluctuating up and down enormously? No. The price level changes some—generally in an upward direction—but it doesn't change a lot in a short period of time. Moreover, the wage level and the price level tend to move together. Expectations, on the other hand, move around a lot. All you need to do is look at a newspaper and you'll see discussions of how events affect expectations. What this means is that, in our economy, when the quantity of aggregate supply and the quantity of aggregate demand are not equal, firms in the aggregate change their level of production. The result is a shift in the *AS* curve, not a movement along it.

For example, say the economy is in equilibrium and aggregate demand falls unexpectedly. Firms find themselves with products they can't sell and excess capacity. What do they do? They may cut price some, but most firms are very much aware that cutting prices will simply cause their competitors to cut their prices, which means that the decrease in their price will not increase the quantity demanded of their product significantly. Besides, their costs—specifically wages—haven't fallen much, so why cut their price? So, empirically, we just don't see a lot of downward price-level flexibility in the economy in a recession.

The real story of macro concerns the chase between aggregate supply and aggregate demand.

Instead, as firms experience a decrease in demand during a recession, they cut back on output—laying off workers and generally retrenching. As firms in the aggregate cut back, "other things *don't* remain constant." As they cut production, income falls, and as income falls, the aggregate demand curve shifts back and firms cut production some more. There's a chase of aggregate supply and demand in which aggregate equilibrium is brought about by shifting aggregate supply and demand curves, and not simply by movements along aggregate supply and demand curves. An important story of macro concerns that chase. Lesson 2—distinguishing shifts in from movements along aggregate supply and demand curves—is central to your understanding of macro because it focuses you on that chase.

7   Any change in aggregate supply or aggregate demand not caused by a change in the price level is a shift in, not a movement along, the curves.

The Chase in an *AS/AD* Framework—Aggregate Disequilibrium   Let's take a look at the chase in our aggregate supply/demand framework. Consider Exhibit 5(a). In it the aggregate economy is initially in equilibrium at price level P_0 and at output level Q_P—the economy's potential level of output. Now assume that suddenly short-run aggregate demand shifts to the left from AD_0 to AD_1 (arrow A) so that aggregate quantity supplied exceeds aggregate quantity demanded.

Where will the new equilibrium be? Let's consider the two obvious options. The "movement along the curve" option is that we move to the new equilibrium price P_1

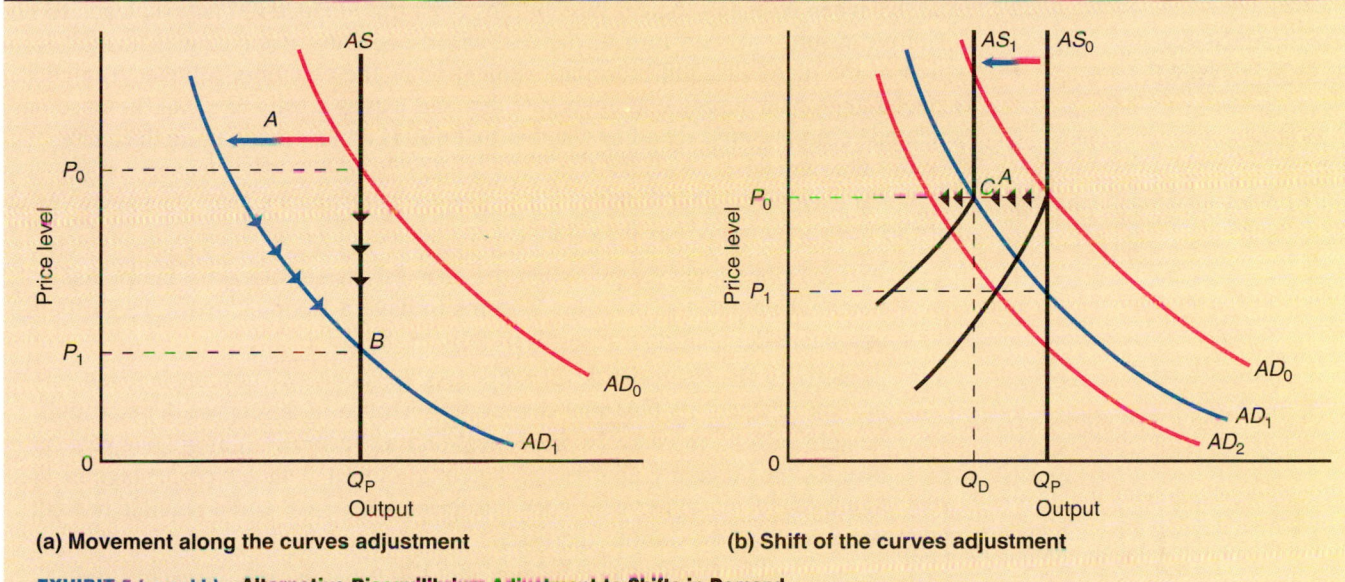

(a) Movement along the curves adjustment

(b) Shift of the curves adjustment

EXHIBIT 5 (a and b)   Alternative Disequilibrium Adjustment to Shifts in Demand

If aggregate supply and demand are independent of each other and nominal wages and the price level are flexible, a decrease in aggregate demand will lead to an adjustment process as shown in (a). Output remains constant and the price level falls. Many other adjustment processes are possible, depending on assumptions. For example, when (1) aggregate supply and demand are interdependent, and (2) a shift in demand causes an equal shift in supply, any shift in supply causes a shift in demand, and (3) when the price level is fixed, the adjustment path will be along arrow A in (b). With interdependent shifts, one must go through an interactive process to determine what the final equilibrium will be.

and equilibrium quantity Q_P (point B), so that the quantity of output demanded in the economy equals the potential output of the economy. For this to happen, the price level would have to adjust sufficiently fast so that chase doesn't occur. That option is shown in Exhibit 5(a).

Unfortunately for the economy, the chase can start more quickly than the price level can adjust, which means that the curves can start shifting quickly, long before you get movements along the curves, i.e., long before the price level falls. For example, faced with excess supply, firms are likely to decrease their expectations of demand, shifting the short-run aggregate supply curve back. If the price level remains constant, short-run aggregate supply could shift back from AS_0 to AS_1 before the price level falls, as in Exhibit 5(b). Thus it might seem to you that the new equilibrium will be at the same price level P_0 and a lower output level Q_D (point C). It won't be there. Why? Because of the interdependency between shifting aggregate supply and shift factors of demand. Specifically, say aggregate supply shifts back to AS_1. As output falls, income falls, and income is a shift factor of demand. So as the AS curve shifts back, that very shift can cause a shift in aggregate demand from AD_1 to AD_2. But it's even more complicated—expected demand is a shift factor of supply, so the mere expectation of the shift in demand can bring about a further shift in supply . . .

The interrelationship between aggregate supply and demand is a fundamentally important insight because it undermines the logical underpinnings of a belief that in the short run a market economy will automatically gravitate toward its potential income. The interdependency between aggregate supply and demand can prevent the economy from arriving at its long-run potential income. I'll stop there, having, I hope, made my point: When you have interdependent shift factors, the analysis of aggregate equilibrium can become very complicated.

At this point in the analysis, I am not interested in determining where the aggregate equilibrium will be. I simply want to impress upon you the complicated nature of aggregate disequilibrium adjustment analysis when all other things are not, as they cannot be in the real world, assumed constant. There are many, many logical possibilities, and the process is mind-boggling. Such mind-boggling processes make theoretical economists' mouths water, and students eyes gloss over. We won't be discussing them here.

Q-7: In *AS/AD* analysis, why is it believed that a shift in an *AD* curve will lead to a further shift in that *AD* curve?

THREE RANGES
IN THE ECONOMY

Q-8: What are the three ranges of the economy?

Luckily, when so many logical possibilities exist that deductive analysis leads to no definitive results, we can turn to the real-world economy itself to gain insight into which of the many disequilibrium-adjustment paths the economy follows. The chase between aggregate supply and aggregate demand leaves a trail. We can then use our educated common sense to tell us whether that trail is a movement along the curves, or shifts in the curves.

When we look at the trail left by the aggregate adjustment process, what we see is that the macro economy has three ranges.

1. A fixed price-level range: When the economy is significantly below its potential output, the price level seems to have a floor—downward shifts in aggregate demand do not result in falls in the price level.

2. A partially flexible price-level range: As the economy approaches, but has not yet reached, its potential output, an increase in aggregate demand will be split into an increase in price level and an increase in aggregate real output. As the economy approaches potential output, a larger percentage of that aggregate demand increase goes into price increases, and a smaller percentage goes into real output increases.

3. An upwardly flexible price-level range: Once the economy reaches its potential output, an excess in aggregate demand will result in price-level changes or in shortages, not in increases, of real output.

Price-level flexibility curve An empirically-observed curve that shows the likely price-level quantity adjustment path of an economy.

These observations mean that in an expansion most economists will see the economy following a price-level/quantity-adjustment path—what we call **price-level flexibility curve**—that looks like the one in Exhibit 6.

At low levels of output relative to potential output (Range *A*), the price level is fixed. This range is also relevant for downward adjustments since the price level seems to have a ratchet; it seldom falls. This means that the historically-determined price level places a floor on the price level, and any adjustment takes place in real output changes, not in price-level changes (probably through interdependent shifts in the supply and demand curves). In intermediate levels of output (Range *B*), the economy's expansion leaves a trail of a rising price level and a rising real output (probably through a combination of shifts in and movements along the curves). At high levels of output relative to potential output (Range *C*), the price level changes quickly in response to changes in aggregate demand. Thus, in Range *C,* we're probably seeing movements along the aggregate supply curve.

The Price-Level Flexibility Curve
Is Not an Aggregate Supply
Curve

8 The price-level flexibility curve is an empirically observed trail of supply/demand equilibria; it is not a deduced curve, and does not hold other things constant.

Q-9: Why is the price-level flexibility curve not an *AS* curve?

Since the price-level flexibility curve in Exhibit 6 is upward sloping and looks a bit like the short-run aggregate supply curve mentioned above, you might be tempted to call it an aggregate supply curve and call everything a movement along an aggregate supply curve. If you do, it's two more readings of the appendix for you. An aggregate supply curve must be derived from deduction: its slope relates to movements along an aggregate supply curve—with no reference to shifts in the curve.

While one can deduce an upward-sloping *AS* curve, it would be difficult, if not impossible, to logically deduce a horizontal aggregate supply curve from first principles. A horizontal aggregate supply curve would imply that a slight change in price level would have a large effect on output, "other things constant." But that just doesn't make sense. No economist argues that small changes in the price level bring about enormous changes in the aggregate quantity supplied. A slight rise in price level and a change in output may be related (that's what it means to say that the price/quantity trail is flat), but the change in the price level does not cause the change in real output; it is simply related to it. Thus, the flat price-level trail in Range *A* is more reasonably seen as the trail of a shifting short-run aggregate supply curve.

Q-10: When aggregate demand falls, what generally happens to the price level?

This observation is further enhanced by the observation of the price-level ratchet. When aggregate demand falls, the price level doesn't fall, whereas when aggregate demand shifts up and the total output is close to potential output, the price level rises. Such an asymmetric response of the price level to shifts in aggregate demand is highly

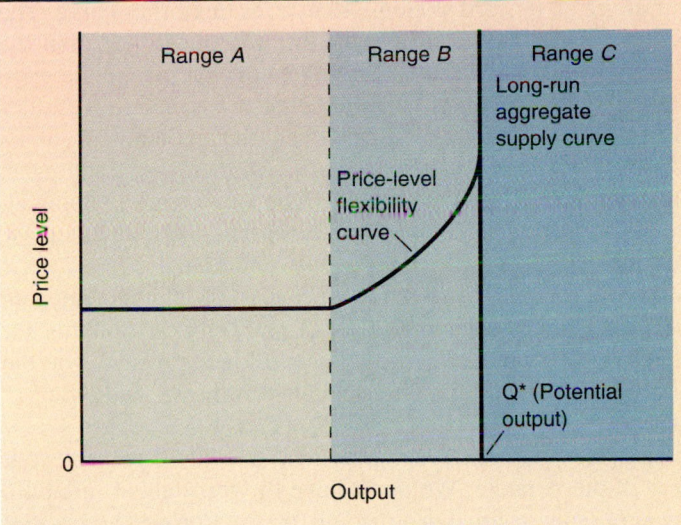

EXHIBIT 6   The Price-Level Flexibility Curve

Most economists agree that the economy has three ranges of price-level flexibility. What they don't know is precisely which range the economy is in.

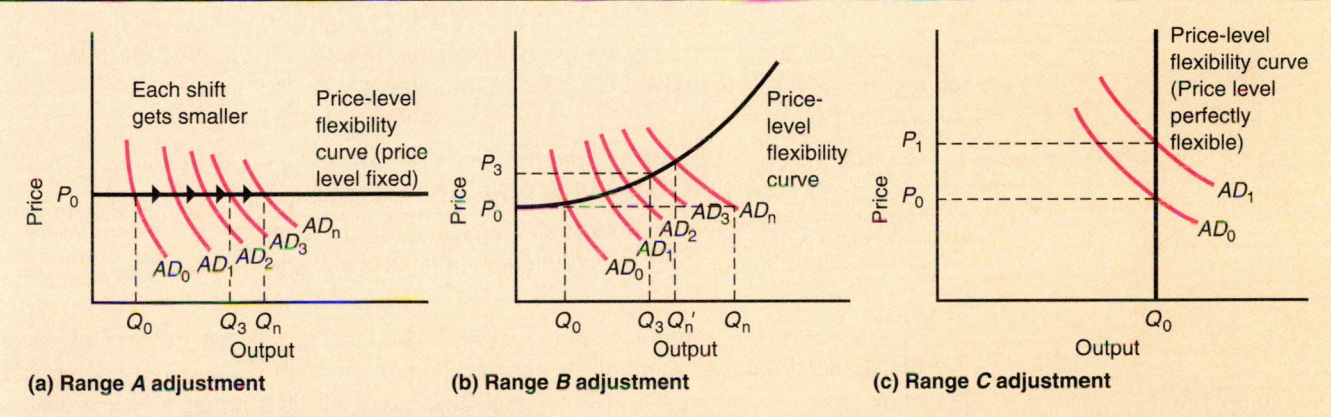

(a) Range *A* adjustment   **(b) Range *B* adjustment**   **(c) Range *C* adjustment**

EXHIBIT 7 (a, b, and c)   Adjustment in the Three Ranges

The adjustment process is divided differently between price and output adjustment in each of the three ranges. In Range *A*, shown in (a), the quantity adjustment is largest. The iterative adjustment ends with output increasing to Q_n. In Range *B*, shown in (b), the output adjustment is smaller at each iteration, and the final adjustment is to Q_n', which is less than Q_n. In Range *C*, shown in (c), no quantity adjustment occurs. Only the price level changes.

unlikely to be derived from first principles. It is far more likely to result from institutional characteristics in an economy that make it easier for nominal wages and prices to rise than to fall. Moreover, when you talk to businesspeople about why they increase or decrease output, they continually tell you that it is in expectation of demand for their product. Such an explanation is consistent with the shifts in aggregate supply occurring due to a shift factor of supply—not due to the effect of a change in the price level on individuals' quantity supplied.

The above discussion leads us to the following basic macro model, presented in Exhibit 7(a, b, and c). In Exhibit 7(a), the economy is in Range *A* where the price level remains relatively constant. The economy is way below potential income. In this range, a policy of increasing aggregate demand from AD_0 to AD_1 will start a chase between supply and demand that will push the aggregate economy along, creating the jobs Bush and Clinton promised. Eventually the chase will end with the demand having shifted all the way out to AD_n.

In Exhibit 7(b), the economy is in Range *B* in which an increase in aggregate demand will cause the price level to rise some, and real output to rise some. The

Aggregate Supply/Demand Analysis and Macro Policy

interdependent shifts occur along an upward sloping price-level flexibility curve. The end result of the shifts is still the AD curve shifting all the way out to AD_n, but the effect on the economy of the shift is not the same as in (a). In (b), the rise in the price level would partially offset the chase; real output would increase less, and the result of the policy would include inflation. In Exhibit 7(c), when the economy is at its potential income, the price-level flexibility curve is vertical. An increase in aggregate demand may still generate an increase in income, but it will be an increase in nominal, not real, income. The increase in aggregate demand will not bring about any increase in real output or additional jobs at all; it will simply cause inflation.

Economists have no way of precisely determining what range the economy is in.

Setting up the policy problem in this way makes the analysis of the aggregate economy look easy. The kicker is that we have no way of precisely determining for sure what range the economy is in, or precisely where potential income is. We do the best we can by basing our judgment on past experience, common sense, and observation, but judgments differ.

Let's consider an example: Europe 1994. Unemployment is over 10 percent, so it would seem the economy is in the A range. We don't have to worry about inflation. But wait—there is major economic restructuring going on in Europe, and social welfare programs significantly reduce people's incentive to work. Thus some economists feel that Europe 1994 is in the high part of range B, or even in range C. What range is Europe 1994 actually in? Economic theory doesn't tell us.

CONCLUSION AND A LOOK AHEAD

I will stop the analysis there. I hope it wasn't too much exercising of the mind, but enough to make the mind a little sore. As a summary of the chapter, I will simply repeat the two lessons.

Lesson 1: You must understand the limits of carrying over the Chapter 2 analysis of supply and demand to the macro economy.

Lesson 2: You must be able to distinguish shifts in aggregate supply and demand curves from movements along aggregate supply and demand curves.

To show you the importance of these two lessons, let's reconsider the policy issue we discussed at the beginning of the chapter: how to get the U.S. economy going and generate jobs. The advice both Clinton and Bush got from their policy advisers was to talk positive and make people believe the economy was going to expand. Bush wasn't good at selling ''positive thinking,'' and the result was that people thought the economy would do poorly—and it did. Clinton was a much better salesperson for ''positive thinking,'' and, with his election, expectations improved—output increased, which caused aggregate demand to increase. This increase improved expectations, and the economy entered an expansionary period. In the last quarter of 1993, real output rose at a 7 percent rate. The debate then turned to inflation and to what range on the price-level flexibility curve the economy was in. We'll return to Bush's and Clinton's dilemma in later chapters.

In the next two chapters, however, we will approach these same theoretical ideas of macro from a historical perspective, showing you the development of the ideas and how they influenced, and were influenced by, real-world events and policies. Then in later chapters we'll use this analysis to discuss the policy problems the U.S. economy is facing today.

CHAPTER SUMMARY

- Economists come to their views about policy through a combination of a study of history, deductive reasoning from theory, and gut feelings about the way the economy and politics work.

- Theory is useful because it (1) defines and highlights definitional truths, and (2) exercises your mind.

- Two central lessons of macroeconomic theory are (1) understanding the limits of supply/demand analysis, and (2) distinguishing shifts in from movements along aggregate supply and demand curves.

- In macroeconomic analysis, one must be careful to avoid the fallacy of composition.

- Aggregate supply and aggregate demand are interdependent, and hence a movement along one curve can cause a shift in the other curve.
- The *AD* curve is downward sloping; the short-run *AS* curve is upward sloping; the long-run *AS* curve is vertical.
- The price-level flexibility curve is not an aggregate supply curve.

- From empirical observation, most economists believe the economy has three ranges—a fixed price-level range, a partially flexible price-level range, and a perfectly upwardly flexible price-level range. The problem of macro policy is deciding what range the economy is in.

KEY TERMS

aggregate demand curve   *(187)*
aggregate supply curve   *(189)*
Classical laissez-faire
   economists   *(182)*
fallacy of composition   *(184)*

Keynesian activist economists   *(182)*
law of aggregate demand   *(188)*
microfoundations of macro   *(184)*
partial equilibrium   *(185)*

price level   *(187)*
price-level flexibility curve   *(192)*
relative price   *(187)*

QUESTIONS FOR THOUGHT AND REVIEW

The number after each question represents the estimated degree of critical thinking required (1 = almost none; 10 = deep thought.)

1. What are three methods economists use to arrive at their view on policy?   *(3)*
2. Why is economic theory like a slam dunk in basketball?   *(4)*
3. What are two central lessons of macroeconomic theory?   *(2)*
4. What is meant by partial equilibrium analysis?   *(2)*
5. What is the difference between a price level and a relative price?   *(2)*

6. What are two reasons why the *AD* curve is downward sloping?   *(8)*
7. What are two reasons why the short-run *AS* curve might be upward sloping?   *(8)*
8. Why must one discuss the shifts in *AS* and *AD* curves as well as the slopes of the curves when discussing the movement to aggregate equilibrium?   *(5)*
9. What range do you think the United States economy is in now?   *(9)*
10. How can ''positive thinking'' cause an economy to expand?   *(4)*

PROBLEMS AND EXERCISES

1. The opening quotation of the chapter refers to Keynes's view of theory.
   a. What do you think he meant by it?
   b. How does it relate to the emphasis on the ''other things constant'' assumption?
   c. Do you think Keynes's interest was mainly in positive economics, the art of economics, or normative economics? Why?
2. State why you believe micro supply/demand analysis, used without additions, is or is not useful in determining the following:
   a. The wage of carpenters.
   b. The average wage rate in the economy.
   c. The price of eggs.
   d. The price level.
   e. The level of income in the economy.
3. In the library:
   a. Find the price level and the level of output (GDP) over the last 10 years. Then:
   b. Graph the data with price level on the vertical axis and the level of GDP on the horizontal axis.

   c. Is the curve you have drawn an *AS* curve, an *AD* curve, or neither? Why?
4. Explain what will likely happen to the shape or position of the *AD* curve in the following circumstances. (The appendix will provide some help in answering this question.)
   a. The exchange rate changes from fixed to flexible.
   b. A fall in the price level doesn't make people feel richer.
   c. A fall in the price level creates expectations of a further fall in the price level.
   d. Income is redistributed from rich to poor people.
   e. Aggregate supply increases.
5. Explain what will happen to the slope or position of the *AS* curve in the following circumstances. (The appendix will provide some help in answering this question.)
   a. Available inputs increase.
   b. A civil war occurs.
   c. The relative price of oil quadruples.
   d. Wages that were fixed become flexible.
   e. The exchange rate changes from fixed to flexible.

ANSWERS TO MARGIN QUESTIONS

1. Keynesian activist economists generally believe that government can come up with some policy that could positively impact the economy. Classical laissez-faire economists generally believe that any government policy would probably make things worse, so the best policy is laissez-faire. *(182)*

2. Two reasons economic theory is important are that (1) it defines and highlights definitional truths, and (2) it exercises your mind. *(183)*

3. A potential problem in studying micro before macro is that it creates in students a tendency to forget the "other things equal" assumption and makes them fall victim of the fallacy of composition. *(184)*

4. False. Individuals' decisions have side effects that individuals do not take into account. These side effects can cause aggregate effects to differ from individuals' desired choices. *(184)*

5. When there are interdependent shift factors, the movement toward equilibrium changes the equilibrium, making the analysis much more complicated. *(185)*

6. Partial equilibrium analysis cannot be used in macro because other things do not remain constant. Aggregate supply and demand are interdependent. *(187)*

7. A shift in the *AD* curve will lead to either a shift in, or a movement along, the *AS* curve. That shift of or movement along the *AS* curve will cause income to change, resulting in a further shift of the *AD* curve. *(191)*

8. The three ranges of the economy are the fixed price-level range, the partially flexible price-level range, and the perfectly-upward flexible price-level range. *(192)*

9. The price-level flexibility curve is an empirically-determined curve of supply/demand equilibrium points which does not separate shifts in from movements along curves. An *AS* curve of that shape cannot be logically deduced from first principles. *(192)*

10. When aggregate demand falls, the price level generally does not fall, but remains constant. Inflation may slow or stop, but deflation—a fall in the price level—does not generally occur. *(192)*

The Foundations of Aggregate Supply and Aggregate Demand

In the chapter I went easy on you, being careful not to pull a muscle in your mind and turn you off to economic theory completely. In this appendix I consider some theoretical issues a bit more carefully. The three issues I will consider are: (1) the way in which the price level can, and cannot, be a relative price; (2) the determinants of the slope of the aggregate demand curve and what makes it shift; and (3) the determinants of the slope of the aggregate supply curve and what makes it shift.

The Price Level as a Relative Price

I stated in the chapter that if we refer to all goods, the price level cannot be a relative price if by relative price we mean the price of one good relative to the price of some other good—there's only one good. I asked you to accept that statement. If you were really thinking about it, you may have thought up some exceptions.

The first exception concerns the time period that we are discussing. If we consider the analysis within a time dimension, the price level in this time period can be high or low compared to some other time period. Thus, the price level can be a price relative to a historically determined past price level and to an expected future price level. For example, if we say the price level went up 10 percent, as we discussed in the last chapter, that means that the composite of all prices has risen 10 percent from what it was the year before.

A second way in which the price level can be a relative price is if we consider the international economy. The price level in one country can be a relative price in relation to the price level in other countries. For example, the price level of U.S. goods can rise or fall relative to the price level of foreign goods.

A third way in which the price level of goods could be a relative price is if we distinguish between the price level of goods and the price level of inputs to produce those goods—then we have separate output price levels and input price levels, and the output price level can be a relative price compared to the input price level. In thinking about the aggregate economy and in applying aggre-

gate supply and demand analysis, it is helpful to keep these possibilities in the back of one's mind, and to be clear about which of these relative price level effects one is talking about.

Incorporating each of these exceptions into the analysis complicates it; one must keep track of the effect of numerous relative price changes, as well as the aggregate shifts. Such complications are best left for intermediate and advanced macro courses. In principles courses, all one need remember is that these issues exist, and that they modify, but do not negate, the central lessons of the macro model.

The Aggregate Demand Curve

In the chapter I defined the aggregate demand curve as a schedule, graphically represented by a curve, that shows how a change in the price level will change the quantity of output demanded, other things (including supply) held constant. I also asserted that it is reasonable to consider it downward sloping. In this appendix I consider the reasons why.

Determinants of the Slope of the Aggregate Demand Curve

There are four effects that have been put forward as explanations of why a fall in the price level will have an effect on the quantity demanded, causing the aggregate demand curve to be downward sloping. These four effects are the *wealth effect*, the *price level interest rate effect*, the *intertemporal price level effect*, and the *international effect*. Each of these effects makes the aggregate demand curve downward sloping and thereby provides a mechanism through which the price level affects the total quantity demanded.

The Wealth Effect The **wealth effect** (sometimes called the Pigou effect, for A. C. Pigou, one of the first economists to point it out) explains the law of aggregate demand as follows: Say the price level falls. That fall will increase the value of money, since each dollar will buy more than it would have at a higher price level. Therefore you could say that the real money supply (the money supply divided by the price level) has increased. As the real money supply rises, the quantity of aggregate goods demanded increases until it has increased enough to equal aggregate supply.

To see how this occurs, let's consider an example. Assume the economy experiences a recession—there is an excess supply of workers and goods. The wage and price levels begin to fall. That fall in the price level increases the value of the dollars in people's pockets, making them richer. Because they're richer, they spend more—the quantity demanded increases. With this adjustment mechanism, the Classicals had an answer to how an aggregate disequilibrium could, in theory, be eliminated through a fall in the price level.

The Price Level Interest Rate Effect   Another explanation of the law of aggregate demand (quantity of aggregate demand increases as price level falls) is called the *price level interest rate effect*. According to the **price level interest rate effect,** a decrease in the price level will increase the real money supply, as in the wealth effect. But the path of the interest rate effect does not depend on making holders of cash balances richer. Instead, the price level interest rate effect focuses on the effect of the increase in real money supply on interest rates: It will lower interest rates, which in turn will increase investment. Why? Because at lower interest rates, businesses will find it cheaper to borrow and hence will undertake more investment projects.[1] Since investment is one component of aggregate demand, the quantity of aggregate demand will increase when the price level falls. Instead of relying on the effect that a lower price level has on cash balances (wealth effect), it concentrates on its effect on interest rates. The price level interest rate effect is another reason why the aggregate demand curve slopes downward to the right.

The Intertemporal Price Level Effect   A third effect is the **intertemporal price level effect.** Say the price level falls and is expected to rise in the next period. People will decide to purchase some goods now that they would have purchased in the future. As they rearrange their intertemporal demand, they will increase their quantity demanded now and decrease their quantity demanded in the future. Thus, as long as the change in the current price level doesn't affect expectations of the future price level, this intertemporal shift in quantity demanded provides another explanation of the law of aggregate demand.

The International Effect   The price level interest rate effect, the wealth effect, and the intertemporal price level effect hold for a closed economy—an economy without international trade. As soon as we allow for international trade, there's another reason why the aggregate demand curve slopes downward: the **international effect,** which works as follows: Given a fixed exchange rate (which most developed countries had in the early 1900s, since they were on the gold standard, which uses fixed exchange rates), when the price level in a country goes down, the price of its exports decreases relative to the price of foreign goods, so a country's exports increase. Similarly for imports: When the price level in a country falls, the relative price of its imports rises, so a country's imports decrease.

For example, say the price level (including wages) in the United States falls by 50 percent. That means that a hamburger that previously cost $2 now will cost $1. Of course, people's incomes also fall, so a person who before had earned $400 per week now earns only $200 per week. However, a fall in the U.S. price level does not affect the price of imports. That means French perfume that previously cost $80 an ounce will still cost $80 an ounce. Since you're now earning only $200 a week, the relative price of French perfume to you will have doubled, and by the law of demand you'll consume less French perfume. You'll substitute American perfume. As the U.S. price level falls, U.S. residents substitute American goods for foreign goods, increasing the quantity of U.S. goods demanded.

The effect is the opposite with exports. Foreigners' income won't have fallen, but the price of U.S. wheat will have declined. So, by the law of demand, foreigners will buy more U.S. wheat than before. As the U.S. price level falls, foreign residents substitute American goods for their own goods, increasing the quantity of U.S. goods demanded. Both of these effects increase aggregate quantity demanded for U.S. goods. Thus, the international effect of a price change is a fourth reason why the aggregate demand curve slopes downward.

The importance of the international effect depends on the importance of international trade to a country. If the country trades very little, the international effect will be small. If the country trades a large amount, the international effect will be large.

If you reflect upon the international effect, you'll see a relationship between it and the reasoning underlying the partial-equilibrium downward-sloping demand curve. Internationally, a country's price level is a relative price. If economists open the analysis to include goods from other countries, a country's overall price level can be equated to the price for a single good—just the opposite of the case of a country's economy examined by itself. In an international context, the aggregate demand curve of a country is the equivalent of a partial-equilibrium demand curve for a single good within a country. So it isn't surprising that the international effect contributes to a downward-sloping aggregate demand curve.

The importance of the international effect depends

---

[1] The price level interest rate effect can't be fully developed here because it depends on issues that themselves won't be fully developed until later chapters. I present it here for completeness, because it is one of the explanations of the downward-sloping aggregate demand curve.

on there being fixed exchange rates. If there are flexible exchange rates, a change in a country's price level will likely be accompanied by an offsetting change in the country's exchange rate. For example, say the price level in a country rises by 10 percent but the country's exchange rate falls by 10 percent. For foreigners, the two effects will be offsetting, and the price they face for U.S. goods will be unchanged. Thus, with flexible exchange rates, the international effect is likely inoperative.

These four effects—the wealth effect, the price level interest rate effect, the intertemporal price level effect, and the international effect—provide an explanation why the *AD* curve is downward sloping.

Shift Factors of Aggregate Demand

Now that we've considered the shape of the *AD* curve, let's consider what makes it shift.

As with micro-demand curves and relative prices, a change in the price level causes a **change in the aggregate quantity demanded**—a movement along the *AD* curve. A change in anything else that affects aggregate demand causes a **change in aggregate demand**—a shift of the entire demand curve. For that reason, these other determinants of aggregate demand are called **shift factors of aggregate demand.** Shift factors of aggregate demand *shift* the demand curve; a change in the price level moves the economy *along* the aggregate demand curve.

Six shift factors of aggregate demand are:

1. Income
2. Expectations
3. Interest rates
4. Distribution of income
5. Exchange rates
6. Wars

I will consider the first four of these shift factors explicitly, and then very briefly consider the final two. In thinking about how these shift factors affect aggregate demand, it is helpful to break aggregate demand into the four component parts discussed in Chapter 7, since shift factors often affect specific components. These four components were consumer spending, investment spending, government spending, and net exports. Let's begin with a discussion of income as a shift factor.

Income   How much aggregate output consumers demand depends first and foremost on their level of income. So consumer spending, the largest component of aggregate demand, is significantly affected by a country's income. A rise in income shifts the *AD* curve out; a fall in income shifts the *AD* curve in.

It is not only a change in domestic income that can cause the *AD* curve to shift; a change in foreign income can also cause the *AD* curve to shift. A rise in foreign income leads to an increase in a country's exports and an outward shift in a country's aggregate demand curve— and a fall in a foreign country's income can lead to a decrease in a country's exports, and an inward shift in a country's aggregate demand curve. An example of this shift occurred in 1993 when Japan's economy fell into a recession. Japanese income fell, and hence Japan's demand for U.S. exports fell; as it did, the U.S. *AD* curve shifted to the left.

Expectations   Another important shift factor of aggregate demand is expectations. Many different types of expectations can affect the *AD* curve. To give you an idea of the role of expectations, let's consider two expectational shift factors.

Expectations about Future Income: When businesspeople expect demand to be high in the future, they will want to increase their output capacity—their investment demand, a component of aggregate demand, will increase. Thus positive expectations about future demand will shift the *AD* curve to the right.

Similarly, when consumers expect the economy to do well, they will be less worried about saving for the future, and they will spend more now—*AD* will shift to the right. Alternatively, if consumers expect the future to be gloomy, they will likely try to save for the future, and will decrease consumption demand. The *AD* curve will shift to the left.

Expectations of Future Prices: Another type of expectation that shifts the *AD* curve concerns expectations of future prices. To see this effect, think back to the intertemporal price level effect. In that case, when the current price level fell relative to the future expected price level, people adjusted their current quantity demanded (movement along the *AD* curve). In this case the price level remains constant, but expectations of future prices rise. If one expects the prices of goods to rise in the future, it pays to buy goods now that you might want in the future—before their price rises. The current price level hasn't changed, but quantity demanded at that price level has increased, indicating an outward shift in the *AD* curve. So an increase in expectations of inflation—an expected rise in the price level—will have a tendency to shift the *AD* curve out.

This effect is seen most clearly in a hyperinflation. In most hyperinflations, people rush out to spend their money quickly—to buy whatever they can to beat the price push. So in hyperinflation, even though prices are rising, aggregate demand stays high because the rise in price creates an expectation of even higher prices—and thus the current high price is seen as a "low price" relative to the future.

I say "have a tendency" rather than "definitely shift the *AD* curve out" because those expectations of inflation are interrelated with a variety of other expectations. For example, an expectation of a rise in the price of goods you buy could be accompanied by an expectation of a fall in income, and that fall in income would work in the opposite direction, decreasing aggregate demand.

This interrelatedness of various types of expectations makes it very difficult to specify precisely what effect certain types of expectation have on the *AD* curve. But it does not negate the importance of expectations as shift factors. It simply means that we often aren't sure what the net effect on aggregate demand of a change in expectations will be.

Interest Rates A third shift factor of aggregate demand is interest rates. That interest rates are a shift factor of aggregate demand may seem strange to you if you remember the price-level interest rate effect explanation of the downward-sloping aggregate demand curve discussed above. It will no longer seem strange if you distinguish changes in interest rates caused by a change in the price level (they cause a movement along the aggregate demand curve) from a change in interest rates not caused by a change in the price level (they are a shift factor of aggregate demand). A rise in interest rates has a tendency to decrease aggregate demand—shift it to the left. A fall in the interest rates has a tendency to shift the *AD* curve to the right. This effect needs some explanation, since interest rates are some people's income, and a fall in interest rates causes that portion of their income to fall, and hence will cause those people to reduce their demand.

The reason a fall in interest rates usually doesn't have that negative effect on aggregate demand is that the negative effect is generally swamped by two stimulative effects. The first stimulative effect is an effect on borrowers. As the interest rate falls, the cost of borrowing falls, which encourages people to borrow more and to spend more. Simultaneously, it causes firms to borrow and spend more. But as people expect firms to borrow and spend more, people expect their income to increase, which causes them to increase their current buying, so through that indirect effect, a decrease in interest rates causes an increase in aggregate production.

The second stimulative effect through which a fall in interest rates affects incomes is through their effect on the value of assets. A fall in interest rates causes bond and stock prices to rise, which raises people's perceived wealth. A rise in interest rates causes bond and stock prices to fall. (This effect of interest rates on stock and bond prices will be considered explicitly in Chapter 12.) As people's perceived wealth increases, so too does their demand for goods.

The importance of these stimulative effects of a fall in interest rates on aggregate demand is why it is generally held that a fall in the interest rate shifts the *AD* curve out to the right. Similarly, a rise in interest rates will have a contractionary effect on aggregate demand, shifting the *AD* curve in to the left.

We can see the effect on the *AD* curve of a rise in the interest rate by reconsidering the hyperinflation case we considered earlier. There, the expectations of rising prices caused the aggregate demand curve to shift out. Now say that the interest rate rises as fast as does the expectation of prices. This rise in interest rates means that people can save and earn as much in interest as they would lose from not buying and having to pay a higher price, which offsets the stimulative effect on current demand of the expected higher price level. For example, if you expect the price of TVs to double in the next year, but you can double your money by putting it in the bank and earning 100 percent interest, you're far less likely to run out and buy TVs.

The movements of expectations of inflation and movements of interest rates are interrelated, which is why economists often talk about **real interest rates**—interest rates adjusted for expected inflation—rather than nominal interest rates. The movement of real interest rates combines the price level interest rate effect and the expectations of the price level effect. Thus a fall in the real interest rate could mean that either the expectations of future price level have fallen and the nominal interest rate has remained constant, or that the nominal interest rate has fallen and expectations of future price level have remained constant. If expectations of future price level rise fast enough, it is possible that a rise in the nominal interest rate can be accompanied by a fall in the real interest rate, making interest rates an important, but complicated, shift factor.

Distribution of Income Some people save more than others and everyone's spending habits differ. Thus, as income distribution shifts, so too will aggregate demand. One of the most important of these distributional effects concerns the distribution of income between wages and profits. Workers receive wage income and are more likely to spend the income they receive; firms' profits are distributed to richer people or are retained, and a higher portion of income received as profits will likely be saved. Thus, as the **real wage**—the ratio of the wage rate to the price level—decreases but total income remains constant, it is likely that aggregate demand will shift back. Similarly, as the real wage increases, it is likely that aggregate demand will shift out.

Effects of Other Shift Factors The above are just four of the many shift factors that can cause the aggregate demand curve to shift. To make sure you are following the analysis, try to reason through the way in which the remaining two shift factors, the exchange rate and war, shift the aggregate demand curve. First consider a fall in the value of the dollar relative to other currencies. Which way will it shift the *AD* curve?

If you answered that it will shift it out because it will increase demand for U.S. goods, you're getting into the analysis.

Second, say there's a war in the Middle East. What will that do to demand for U.S. goods? The most likely answer is that it will increase the demand—it will cause the *AD* curve to shift out as the combatants buy more goods from U.S. firms that produce weapons.

There are many other shift factors, but the above discussion should give you a good sense of both their importance and how they work to shift aggregate demand.

Aggregate Supply

As I stated in the chapter, the aggregate supply curve is a schedule graphically represented by a curve, which shows how a change in the price level will change the quantity of output supplied, other things (including aggregate demand and expectations) held constant.

Determining the Slope of the Aggregate Supply Curve

As was the case with the *AD* curve, specifying precisely what remains constant as we draw this curve is difficult. I will follow the standard practice by ruling out many of the fine points, and focus on constant input prices as the basis for the slope of the short-run *AS* curve. For the long-run *AS* curve, I define the price level in such a way that it includes input prices so that relative input/output price level changes cannot occur.

For both cases, we rule out the international effect on the quantity of aggregate supply either because the exchange rate is flexible, or because the country has no international trade. We also assume that the intertemporal price-level effect on supply is inoperative. (These assumptions can be eliminated, and one could have an upward-sloping aggregate supply curve even without fixed input prices. But since the debate about aggregate supply and demand which we will be discussing at length in this and the next few chapters has focused on the law of aggregate demand, I follow standard practice and assume these additional effects away; doing so does not substantially change the nature of the debate.)

The Slope of the Short-Run Aggregate Supply Curve

The standard argument for an upward-sloping *AS* curve is the following: If input prices are constant, an increase in demand will cause firms' profits to increase, which will lead firms to want to raise output. Thus if output price rises relative to input price, the quantity of aggregate supply can be expected to increase as the price level rises, giving an upward-sloping short-run *AS* curve.

The difficulty with this assumption is in determining where the additional workers are going to come from. If the labor market was initially in equilibrium, then the rise in output price will mean a fall in the real wage—what workers can buy with their pay—which would cause them to work less, not more. So the upward-sloping short-run *AS* curve is based on the assumption that there is excess supply in the labor market. But why should there generally be excess supply in the labor market? Unless one specifies why, the standard argument for an upward-sloping short-run *AS* curve is suspect.

The Slope of the Long-Run *AS* Curve

Questions about the justification for assuming excess supply in the labor market led economists to move away from using the short-run supply curve, and to focus more on the long-run supply curve in which input prices and output prices move together. When input and output prices rise in tandem, the standard explanation of the upward-sloping *AS* curve no longer holds. The assumption of input and output prices rising in tandem, combined with the other above-mentioned assumptions, leads to a vertical long-run *AS* curve.

To see this, ask yourself the following question: What effect on suppliers would there be if the supplier's price went up 100 percent, but all his or her costs also went up 100 percent? The common-sense answer to this question is: There would be no effect on the quantity supplied; it's simply a change in the measuring rod. This common-sense view means that the *AS* curve is vertical—the aggregate quantity people want to supply is unaffected by a change in the price level.

Shift Factors of Aggregate Supply

To say that the quantity of aggregate supply is unaffected by the price level is not to say that aggregate supply cannot change. There are also **shift factors of aggregate supply,** just as there are shift factors of aggregate demand. Shift factors of aggregate supply are factors that shift the aggregate supply curve rather than cause movements along the aggregate supply curve (as does a change in the price level).

In discussing these shift factors of aggregate supply, it is helpful to distinguish between **long-run shift factors** and **short-run shift factors.** Long-run shift factors are shift factors that are unlikely to change substantially in the short run, but in the long run they can change significantly, generally increasing aggregate potential output. Short-run shift factors are shift factors that change significantly in the short run and which can be expected to cause short-run fluctuations in income. The short-run supply curve can shift around within the confines of the long-run supply curve.

Let's consider five of the most important of these potential shift factors of aggregate supply:

1. Available inputs
2. Institutional environment
3. Technology
4. Expectations
5. Wage/price ratio

Long-Run Shift Factors of Aggregate Supply

The first three of the shift factors above—available inputs, institutional environment, and technology—are long-run shift factors; they are unlikely to change substantially in the short run, but in the long run they can change significantly, increasing the output potential of an economy. Combined, they determine an economy's potential output and the level of growth of the aggregate economy.

To incorporate these shift factors into our analysis, economists define a term—**long-run supply.** Long-run supply is the level of supply that is consistent with an economy's potential income; it is the maximum amount of output that can be produced given the institutional structure of the economy. Long-run supply changes only slowly and does not shift much in the short run. The analysis of long-run supply follows the analysis of growth that was presented in Chapter 6, and, if history is a good guide, the shift factors of supply make the long-run supply curve shift out at about 3 percent per year.

Short-Run Shift Factors of Aggregate Supply   The macroeconomic debate about business cycles that we will discuss in the next few chapters is not centered around long-run shift factors of supply. All macroeconomists agree that these long-run shift factors of supply are important causes of growth, although precisely how they each contribute to growth is subject to significant debate. Instead, the macroeconomic debate about business cycles is centered around potential short-run shift factors of supply, especially expectations and the wage/price ratio, which may or may not be a shift factor depending on precisely how the aggregate supply curve is defined.

Once one allows for short-run shift factors, the long-run supply curve—potential output—provides an upper limit beyond which output cannot go. But it can go lower if the short-run shift factors shift the short-run supply curve back—causing a recession. Thus, an understanding of short-run shift factors is essential to understanding recessions, and what policies might pull an economy out of a recession. Let's now consider expectations and the wage/price ratio more carefully.

Expectations: As was the case with aggregate demand, one of the most important shift factors is expectations. Expectations can affect aggregate supply in many ways, but one of the most important, and the one that is the focus of much of the debate in macroeconomics, is *expectations of aggregate demand.*

Say suppliers expect aggregate demand to be low, and hence expect that demand for the product they produce will be low. They will likely decide to reduce supply, shifting the aggregate supply curve back. Alternatively, say expectations of aggregate demand are high, so that suppliers think that demand for their product will be high. Aggregate supply will increase. So, our general conclusion is that *expectations of an increase in aggregate demand will cause the short-run AS curve to shift out, and expectations of a decrease in aggregate demand will cause the short-run AS curve to shift in.* These shifts in expectations play a central role in leading the economy to an aggregate equilibrium.

Just how important expectations of aggregate demand are can be seen by the amount of time and effort firms spend trying to measure what future demand will be. There are large numbers of consumer sentiment surveys, polls, and market research surveys, which firms use

to decide how much to produce—what their supply will be. Recognizing the importance of expectations of demand to supply decisions is easy for businesspeople who are trying to predict demand, and for students trying to understand the economy.

It was somewhat more difficult for Classical economists who were trained to think about the economy as one in which firms had no short-run price-setting role, one in which firms produced and sold whatever they could at whatever price that they could receive. In a perfectly-flexible price world, the quantity demanded would always equal the quantity supplied, so expectations of aggregate demand should not play a role. In any other world—with less than perfectly-flexible prices, such as the world we live in—expectations of aggregate demand are a central shift factor. In the next chapter, we will see that Classical economists failed to consider the role that expectations of demand play, and how that failure led to the Keynesian revolution in macroeconomics in which expectations of demand play a central role in the macroeconomic process.

The Wage/Price Ratio: How much firms decide to produce depends on the expected profit from the sale of a good. When wages are high relative to prices, expected profit is small, or zero, per unit, and firms will have a desire to produce little. When wages are low relative to prices, expected profit per unit is significant, and firms will have a desire to produce a lot. Thus we can expect the *real wage*—the ratio of the wage level to the price level—to be an important factor in their production decision. Whether or not the real wage is an important shift factor depends on which definition of the aggregate supply curve is used. The real wage is an important shift factor if the aggregate supply curve is defined as including wages, so that the wage level and price level move together. This is how the long-run aggregate supply curve is specified. It is also how some economists specify the short-run aggregate supply curve. Such a short-run aggregate supply curve, which allows for instantaneous adjustment of factor prices, will be vertical and any change in the real wage will cause it to shift (in for a rise in the real wage, out for a fall in the real wage).

The real wage is far less important as a shift factor if the short-run aggregate supply curve is defined as it is in the chapter. That definition held the nominal wage constant as the price level changed. This latter definition means that as the price level changes, the real wage will change; these changes in the real wage underlie the slope of the short-run aggregate supply curve specified in this manner. Since this effect of the real wage is already incorporated in the slope of the aggregate supply curve, the real wage is not an important shift factor. If, however, the real wage changes for some other reason—say a change in production technique—that change will be a shift factor.

You should not be surprised that what is a shift factor and what causes a movement along the curve depends on precisely how the aggregate supply curve is defined. Remember the aggregate supply curve is an analytic construct used in modeling; it does not exist independent of its definition. Both the *AS* and *AD* curves are aids in focusing on certain relationships. They are meant to help you hold in the back of your mind other issues that you assume temporarily constant, even though you know they will not remain constant.

When applying the *AS/AD* model to reality it is important to remember that other things are not likely to remain constant, and that shift factors themselves are likely to be interrelated. I mention the "other things constant" proviso because it is unlikely that other things will remain constant. Specifically, think back to the shift factors of aggregate demand. One of the shift factors was the distribution of income and the real wage. A rise in the real wage caused aggregate demand to shift out, and a fall in the real wage caused aggregate demand to shift in. But above, I stated that expectations of demand are a shift factor, and if firms see the real wage falling, they can expect that demand will be low, which will cause the aggregate supply curve to shift in. Similarly, if firms see the real wage rising they can expect that demand will be high, which will cause them to shift their aggregate supply curve out. These shifts are in precisely the opposite direction of the shifts discussed above.

A well-known example of a businessperson trying to take advantage of this real-wage effect on demand for his product occurred with Henry Ford and the production of the Model T automobile. Ford raised the wage of his workers, and encouraged other firms to raise their wages, so that the workers could afford the Model Ts and he could increase output.

The fact that the real wage works through two different, and contradictory, paths means that the net effect of a change in the real wage is unclear when one considers both paths through which a change in the real wage is likely to affect aggregate supply.

Other Shift Factors of Short-Run Supply: There are many other shift factors of short-run supply. For example, bad weather will decrease aggregate supply, and a war in a country can destroy its productive capacity. Alternatively, a major strike by producers could decrease supply so that even if potential output is high, little output is forthcoming as suppliers refuse to work.

Conclusion

I went through the determinants of the slope and the shift factors of aggregate demand and supply so carefully because they have been a source of much confusion in macro theory. Economists who are fastidious about distinguishing these factors in micro often blur over them in macro, much to the detriment of the logic of the argument.

If you went through this appendix carefully, you should have a firm grip on the concepts *aggregate supply* and *aggregate demand,* and be able to distinguish a shift in aggregate supply (and a shift in aggregate demand) from a movement along an aggregate supply curve (and a movement along an aggregate demand curve). Since, as I discussed in the chapter, the empirical observations result from an interaction of aggregate supply and demand, we can't say whether those observations identify a point on a shifting aggregate supply curve or a movement along a supply curve. But businesspeople repeatedly say that they consider expectations of demand—a shift factor of supply—central to their decisions about how much to supply.

KEY TERMS

change in aggregate demand (199)
change in the aggregate quantity
  demanded (199)
international effect (198)
intertemporal price level effect (198)

long-run shift factors (201)
long-run supply (202)
price level interest rate effect (198)
real interest rates (200)
real wage (200)

shift factors of aggregate demand (199)
shift factors of aggregate supply (201)
short-run shift factors (201)
wealth effect (197)

9

The Development of Modern Macroeconomics: The Classical/Keynesian Debate*

The study of economics won't keep you out of the bread line, but at least it will tell you why you are there.

~Al Capp

After reading this chapter, you should be able to:

1 Discuss the reasoning behind Say's Law.

2 Interpret the quantity theory of money.

3 State the essence of Keynes's criticism of the Classical model.

4 Compare the Keynesian and Classical explanations of the effect of a demand shock.

5 Explain why Keynes believed a falling price level would not bring about aggregate equilibrium.

6 Go through the first two steps of a Keynesian income adjustment process.

7 Distinguish a Keynesian economy from a Classical economy.

*This chapter covers much the same ground as does Chapter 8, but it presents the material in historical perspective and with less discussion of technical modelling questions. Policy-oriented courses may proceed immediately from Chapter 7 to this chapter without significant loss of continuity.

The Great Depression of the 1930s marked a significant change in U.S. economic institutions and ideology. In the Depression, not only the deadbeat up the street was unemployed, so were your brother, your mother, your uncle—the hardworking backbone of America. These people wanted to work, and if the market wasn't creating jobs for them, the market system was at fault.

During the Depression, the popular view of government's proper role in the economy changed considerably. Before, the predominant ideology was laissez-faire: keep the government out of the economy. After the Depression, most people believed that government must have a role in regulating the economy.

The Great Depression also led economists to develop theoretical models that allowed for unemployment and left room for government intervention into the market. With these developments, economists started falling into two groups: Economists who generally oppose government intervention fall under the heading **Classical economists.** Those who generally favor government intervention in the aggregate economy are known as **Keynesian economists.** This chapter introduces you to the Classical and Keynesian views on macroeconomic issues by discussing that development.

Classical economists generally oppose government intervention in the economy.

Keynesian economists generally favor government intervention in the aggregate economy.

THE EMERGENCE OF CLASSICAL ECONOMICS

Classical economics began in the late 1700s and early 1800s as economists developed the ideas in Adam Smith's seminal work, *An Inquiry into the Nature and Causes of the Wealth of Nations.* The essence of Classical economics' approach to problems was to use a **laissez-faire** policy (leave the market alone) approach. This policy was based on the view that the market, left to its own devices, was self-adjusting. Wages and prices would adjust to eliminate unemployment. Classicals recognized that in the short run there might be temporary problems, but their analysis focused on the long run.

Classical economists explained unemployment using traditional partial-equilibrium supply and demand curves.

When the Great Depression hit and unemployment became a problem, most Classical economists avoided the issue (as economists, and most people, tend to do when they don't have a good answer). When pushed by curious students to explain how, if the market's invisible hand was so wonderful, the invisible hand could have allowed the Depression and its 25-percent unemployment, Classical economists drew supply-and-demand-for-labor curves like those in Exhibit 1.

They explained, "Unemployment results when the **real wage**—the wage level relative to the price level—is too high. Workers hold their wage above the equilibrium level—that is, they won't take the lower wages offered. Other forces (government policies and economic institutions such as labor unions) can operate to prevent the invisible hand from working its magic." For example, in Exhibit 1, the equilibrium wage is W_e. If the wage is held at W_1 for some reason, quantity of labor supplied is S_1 and quantity of labor demanded is D_1. The difference between the two $(S_1 - D_1)$ is unemployment.

Their laissez-faire policy prescription followed from their analysis: The solution to unemployment was to eliminate labor unions and government policies that held wages too high. If these things happened, the wage rate would fall, and unemployment would be eliminated.

Laymen weren't pleased with this argument. (Remember, economists don't try to present pleasing arguments—only arguments they believe are correct.) But laymen couldn't point to anything wrong with it. It made sense, but it wasn't satisfying. People thought, "Gee, Uncle Joe, who's unemployed, would take a job at half the going wage. But he can't find one—there just aren't enough jobs to go around at any wage."

Most lay people had a different explanation. The popular lay explanation of the Depression was that there was an oversupply of goods which had glutted the market. All that was needed to eliminate unemployment was for government to hire the unemployed, even if it were only to dig ditches and fill them back up. The people who got the new jobs would spend their money, creating even more jobs. Pretty soon, the United States would be out of the Depression.

Classical economists argued against this lay view. They argued that money to hire those people would have to come from somewhere. It would have to be borrowed. Such borrowing would use money that would have financed private economic activity

Adam Smith, a moral philosopher whose book, *The Wealth of Nations,* is seen as the beginning of modern economics. *The Bettmann Archives.*

The popular explanation of the Depression was that an oversupply of goods had glutted the goods market. Classical economists argued against this view.

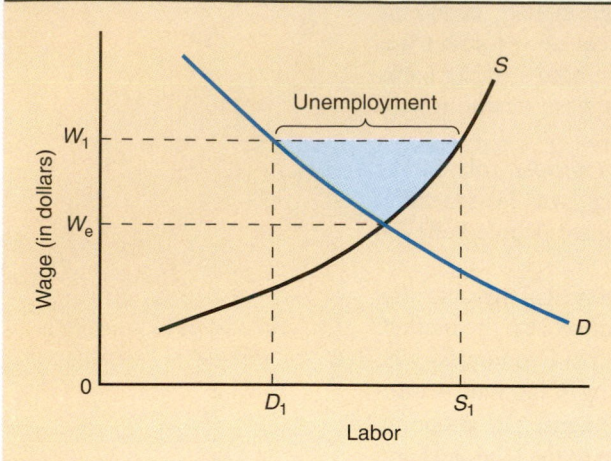

EXHIBIT 1   Unemployment in the Classical Model

If social or political forces hold the wage above the equilibrium wage (at W_1 rather than W_e), the result will be unemployment of $S_1 - D_1$. To eliminate that unemployment, the wage must fall.

and jobs; hence, such borrowing would reduce private economic activity. The net effect would mean no increase in the total number of jobs. In short, the Classicals were saying an oversupply of goods was impossible.

Say's Law

Say's law states that supply creates its own demand.

1   According to Say's Law people work because they want goods; thus supply creates its own demand. Even if people save, supply still creates its own demand because savings leads to investment.

This Classical argument was first made in the 1800s by a French businessman, Jean Baptiste Say, although it was a British stockbroker, David Ricardo, who made it famous. Say's argument went as follows: People work and supply goods to the market because they want other goods. Thus, the very fact that they supply goods means they have income to demand goods of equal value. This idea is normally stated as follows:

Say's law: *Supply creates its own demand.*

Say's law is central to the Classical vision of the economy. It says that there can never be a general glut of goods on the market; aggregate demand will always be sufficient to buy what is supplied.

Not all Classical economists initially accepted Say's law. The most spirited argument against it was put forward by Thomas Malthus, a preacher.[1] Malthus argued that when people saved, part of their income would be lost to the economy and there wouldn't be as much aggregate demand out there as aggregate supply. According to Malthus, Say's law did not necessarily hold true.

Say and Ricardo rejected Malthus's argument. They argued that people's savings were not lost to the economy. When people saved, they did it by lending their savings to other individuals. The people who borrowed the savings would spend what they borrowed on investments. Classical economists argued that the interest rate would fluctuate to equate savings and investment. If people's desire to save increased, the interest rate would fall and the quantity of investment would increase. So any savings seemingly lost to the system would be actually translated into investment, making aggregate demand (total buying power in the economy) equal to aggregate supply (total production), through either a direct route (consumption) or an indirect route (investment by way of savings). Aggregate demand (investment plus consumption) always equaled aggregate supply.

The direct route and indirect route appear in Exhibit 2, the familiar circular flow diagram. Say's law states that total expenditures (consumption plus investment, depicted by flows *b* and *c*), would just equal production or income (depicted by flow *a*). The financial sector would translate all savings into investment to maintain a continual equilibrium between supply and demand.

---

[1] As was pointed out earlier, Thomas Malthus is most famous for the Malthusian doctrine which stated that population grows much faster than food production so the future of mankind is starvation. It was the Malthusian doctrine that earned economics the name of *the dismal science.*

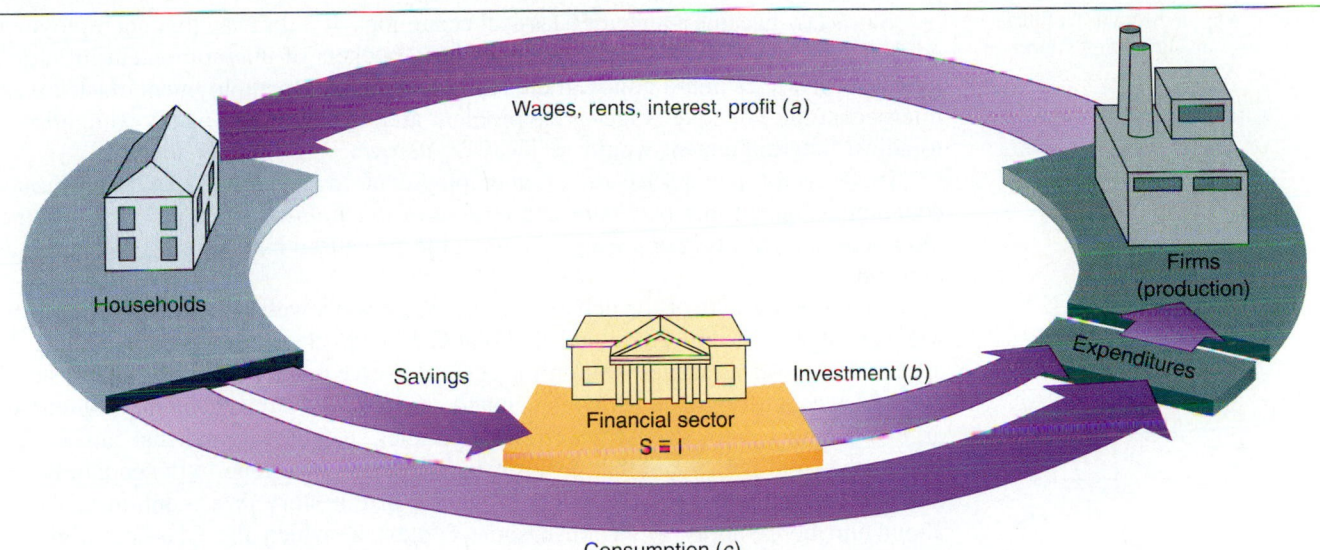

EXHIBIT 2   The Equality of Production (Aggregate Supply) and Expenditures (Aggregate Demand)

According to Say's law, aggregate production always was at the full employment level. Any funds that escaped from the circular flow into the financial sector (savings) would be brought back into the circular flow by the financial sector in the form of investment. Thus, the financial sector was assumed to keep savings always equal to investment.

ADDED DIMENSION

THE TREASURY VIEW, LLOYD GEORGE, AND KEYNES

The Great Depression descended on Britain in the 1920s, before it hit the United States. Therefore many debates about what to do about it occurred first in Britain. British Chancellor of the Exchequer Winston Churchill (a Conservative Party member who later became prime minister) followed the advice of his Treasury Department, which was composed of Classical economists. They advised him that Britain should go back on the gold standard (a monetary system that fixes a currency's price relative to gold and other currencies). All countries that use gold to value their currency have *fixed currency exchange rates*. For example, if 1 British pound = 1 ounce of gold, and 1 U.S. dollar = 1/2 ounce of gold, then 1 British pound = 2 U.S. dollars = 1 ounce of gold.

Churchill followed the Classical economists' advice and returned the pound to the gold standard from which Britain, and all other countries, had departed during World War I. He set a high value on the pound relative to other currencies. As a result, British wages and prices were high relative to those in other countries. Foreign imports were cheap, which was good. British exports were expensive and uncompetitive abroad, which was not good. Unemployment in Britain was high, which was bad. The British Treasury Department's advice on how to eliminate unemployment boiled down to "Keep a stiff upper lip. British wages and prices will eventually fall, or foreign wages and prices will rise."

Regardless of the argument's economic merits, its political merits were dubious. Lloyd George (leader of the opposition Liberal party) advocated a massive government hiring program to eliminate unemployment. Keynes (a prominent advisor to the Liberal party, who had, before Lloyd George's proposals, been seen as a Classical economist) modified his economic analysis in part to justify that shift. That was the beginning of the Keynesian approach to macroeconomics.

Needless to say, many of the Classicals were not very pleased with Keynes's shift, and they saw his economic analysis as opportunism. His shifting position led to a well-known joke about economists: If you ask five economists a question, you will get five different answers; if you ask Keynes a question you will get six different answers.

However, stiff upper lips can carry politicians only so far, and soon thereafter the British Conservative party was also advocating public works programs to help end the depression. Politics often plays a key role in directing economic thinking.

Source: This account is based on Peter Clarke's book, *The Keynesian Revolution in the Making 1924–1936* (Oxford, England: Oxford University Press, 1988).

Q–1: Why doesn't the fact that people save invalidate Say's law?

Say's law became a tenet of Classical economics. It didn't say that unemployment could never exist—there could be lots of little pockets of unemployment in various industries if wages didn't adjust. It did say that whatever unemployment existed was a microeconomic, relative wage–price problem and, if wages and prices were allowed to adjust, unemployment would go away on its own.

In terms of the discussion of unemployment in an earlier chapter, Classical economists agreed that *frictional* and *structural unemployment* could exist, but they did not agree that *cyclical unemployment* could be caused by a shortage of aggregate demand.

That was the state of the debate in the 1930s when a well-known economist, John Maynard Keynes, came along and said that Classical economists were all wrong. He argued that lowering wages wouldn't necessarily solve unemployment and that supply doesn't necessarily create its own demand. Keynes's argument fit the popular lay argument and led to activist government policies. Keynes argued that laissez-faire wasn't the right policy and that government needed to intervene in the economy. But hold it! Talking about Keynes is getting ahead of our story. We mention this much about him here simply to establish some context in which the Classical argument developed.

The Quantity Theory of Money

Money is a medium of exchange that individuals use to buy goods.

The quantity theory of money asserts that the price level varies in response to variations in the money supply.

$MV = PQ$ *is the equation of exchange.*

2 The quantity theory of money holds that increases in money (M) cause increases in the price level, and that real output is independent of the money supply and hence the price level.

Classical economists buttressed their Say's law analysis of the aggregate economy with the quantity theory of money. We will discuss money in much more detail in later chapters. For now all you need have is a general sense of what **money** is: It is a medium of exchange (such as dollar bills) that individuals use to buy goods. Thus, the quantity of money is the amount of the medium of exchange in the economy. In its simplest terms, the **quantity theory of money** says that the price level varies in response to changes in the quantity of money. In other words, changes in the price level are caused by changes in the money supply. If the money supply goes up 20 percent, prices go up 20 percent. If money supply goes down 5 percent, prices go down 5 percent.

The Classical quantity theory of money centers around the **equation of exchange:**

$$MV = PQ$$

where:

M = Quantity of money
V = Velocity
P = Price level
Q = Quantity of real goods sold.

Q is the real output of the economy (real GDP). P is the price level, so PQ is the economy's nominal output (nominal GDP—the quantity of goods valued at whatever price level exists at the time). Remember, real GDP equals nominal GDP divided by (deflated by) the price level; while nominal GDP equals nominal income.

Classical economists strongly favored using gold for money since it placed limits on the quantity of money available. Policy fights about the quantity of money have been around a long time, as can be seen in this hand-colored etching, "The Blessings of Paper Money, or King a Bad Subject." *Bleichroeder Print Collection, Baker Library, Harvard Business School.*

THE BLESSINGS of PAPER MONEY or KING a BAD SUBJECT.

ADDED DIMENSION

CLASSICAL ECONOMISTS AND
THE VEIL OF MONEY

The veil-of-money assumption developed early in Classical economic thought. The predecessors of the Classicals were mercantilists, who had argued that the wealth of nations depended on a nation's store of gold, which was then used as money. (Remember, during this time the international financial system was on a gold standard.)

Countries with balance of payments deficits paid for those deficits with gold, which decreased their money supply. Countries with balance of payments surpluses received gold, which increased their money supply. Mercantilists encouraged countries to protect their gold supplies with tariffs so their gold supplies (their money) wouldn't go into foreign hands.

Adam Smith called his book *The Wealth of Nations* because he argued that the wealth of nations did not depend on the amount of gold or money a country had; it depended on the real output of the country's economy. More money (gold) without more goods would only cause inflation. (This is only simple arithmetic according to the quantity theory of money.) Classical economists argued that a country didn't have to worry about a balance of payments deficit and losing gold. A balance of payments deficit would decrease the money supply and hence the price level. A country's exports would be cheaper, which would tend to eliminate the balance of payments deficit.

Smith, and Classical economists following him, argued that money and the price level were simply veils over the real economy, and the veil of money had to be removed for us to understand the workings of the real economy. The quantity theory of money was a simple way of presenting that insight.

V, the **velocity of money,** is the number of times per year, on average, a dollar goes around to generate a dollar's worth of income. Put another way, velocity is the amount of income per year generated by a dollar of money. *MV* also equals nominal output. Thus, if there's $100 of money in the economy and velocity is 20, GDP is $2,000. We can calculate *V* by dividing nominal GDP by the money supply. In the United States in 1993, GDP was approximately $6.4 trillion, *M* was approximately $1,131 billion, so velocity was GDP/*M* = 5.66, meaning each dollar in the economy circulated enough to support approximately $5.66 in total income.

The equation of exchange is a *tautology,* meaning it's true by definition. What changes it from a tautology to a theory are certain assumptions the Classicals made about the variables in the equation of exchange.

First, Classical economists assumed velocity remains constant. They argued that money is spent only so fast; how fast is determined by the economy's institutional structure, such as how close to stores individuals live, how people are paid (weekly, bi-weekly, or monthly), and what sources of credit are available (can you go to the store and buy something on credit; that is, buy something without handing over cash?). This institutional structure changes slowly, they argued, so velocity won't fluctuate very much. Next year, velocity will be approximately the same as this year.

If velocity remains constant, the quantity theory can be used to predict how much nominal GDP will grow if we know how much the money supply grows. For example, if the money supply goes up 6 percent, using the quantity theory a Classical economist would predict that nominal GDP will go up by 6 percent.

The second Classical assumption concerned *Q*, real output. Classical economists assumed that *Q* was independent of the money supply. That is, the Classicals thought *Q* was **autonomous,** meaning real output was determined by forces outside the quantity theory.

This Classical assumption is sometimes called the **veil-of-money assumption,** which holds that real output is not influenced by changes in the money supply. Classical economists argued that in order to understand what is happening in the real economy, you must lift the veil of money.

This veil-of-money assumption made analyzing the economy a lot easier than it would have been had the financial and real sectors been interrelated and had real economic activity been influenced by financial changes. It allowed Classical economists to separate two puzzles: how the real economy works, and how the price level and financial sector work. Instead of having two different jigsaw puzzles all mixed up,

Velocity of money   The average number of times the same dollar gets spent in a year.

Q-2: What's the difference between the equation of exchange and the quantity theory of money?

Something that is determined by forces outside the model is called autonomous.

The veil-of-money assumption says that real output isn't influenced by changes in money supply.

The veil-of-money assumption allowed Classical economists to separate two puzzles—how the real economy works, and how the financial sector works.

Friedrich von Hayek is a famous Classical economist. He won a Nobel prize, 1974, for work on interdependence of institutional, social, and economic phenomena. © The Nobel Foundation.

each puzzle could be worked separately. They could analyze what happens in the real economy (in the production of real goods and services) separately from what happens to the money supply and price level. Classical economists recognized that there were interconnections between the real and financial sectors, but they argued that most of these interconnections involved short-run considerations. Classical economists were primarily interested in the long run.

In the long run, there is a strong intuitive reason why the real and nominal economies are separate. Say one day you walk into work and your salary has doubled—but all prices also have doubled. What difference will these changes make in your behavior? Since no relative price has changed, it seems fair to say that your behavior won't be affected very much. That's what the Classical economists were saying with the veil-of-money assumption.

With both V (velocity) and Q (quantity or output) unaffected by changes in M (money supply), the only thing that can change is P (price level). Classical economists said that M and P would change by equivalent percentages.

The final assumption of the Classical quantity theory was the *direction of causation*. Classical economists argued that changes in the money supply caused changes in the price level: In the quantity theory of money equation, the direction of causation went from left to right,

$$MV \Rightarrow PQ$$

not the other way around. Thus, when a Classical economist was asked to predict what would happen to inflation, he or she would ask what's happening to the money supply's growth rate. If the money supply were continually increasing at an 8 percent rate, the Classical economist's prediction would be that inflation would be 8 percent.

We've covered a lot of ground in the last few pages, so let's briefly summarize how we went from the equation of exchange to the quantity theory. We start with the equation of exchange:

$$MV = PQ$$

To that we add three assumptions:

1. Velocity is constant.
2. Real output is independent of the money supply.
3. Causation goes from money supply to prices.

The result is the quantity theory of money. It holds that real output is set at levels desired by individuals, and that real output is independent of the wage and price level. An increase in money will not increase real output; it will simply increase the wage and price level.

Classical Economics and *AS/AD* Analysis

Now that I've spelled out the Classical model, let's consider its relationship to *AS/AD* analysis discussed in the last chapter. What the above Classical model says is that the interconnection between aggregate supply and aggregate demand is so great that we don't need any separate aggregate analysis of aggregate demand. Say's law—aggregate supply creates its own demand—makes analysis of aggregate demand unnecessary. To see that it does, let's consider how these Classical assumptions translate into an aggregate supply/aggregate demand framework.

Let's first consider the **Classical long-run aggregate supply curve.** Given these Classical assumptions, what shape will it have, and at what level of output will it be? To answer those questions, think of what the veil-of-money assumption tells us—that real output is independent of the price level: as the price level changes, real output doesn't change. Say that initially the price level is P_1 and real output is Q^* in Exhibit 3(a). Point A represents this combination. Now say the price level rises to P_2. Because the price level does not affect real output, when the price level rises from P_1 to P_2, real output does not change. So point B is also on the aggregate supply curve. By going through this same reasoning you can deduce the vertical long-run aggregate supply curve that I discussed in the last chapter. Exhibit 3(a) shows that vertical Classical aggregate supply curve.

Q–3:   What are the two pillars of the Classical model?

The aggregate supply curve shows the relationship between price level and the total amount of output supplied in an economy.

PILLARS OF THE CLASSICAL MODEL

The two pillars of the Classical model, Say's law (supply creates its own demand) and the quantity theory of money ($MV \Rightarrow PQ$), led to the conclusion that the aggregate economy would always be in equilibrium.

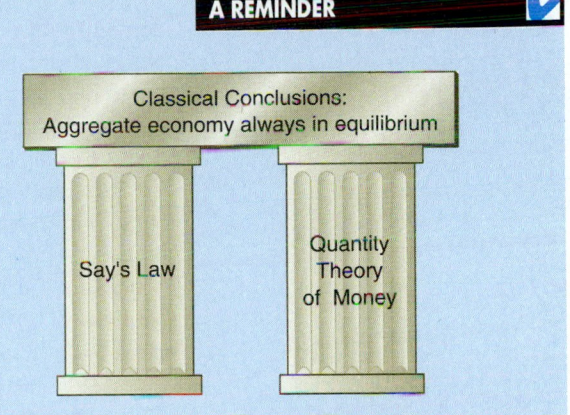

Classical Conclusions: Aggregate economy always in equilibrium

Say's Law

Quantity Theory of Money

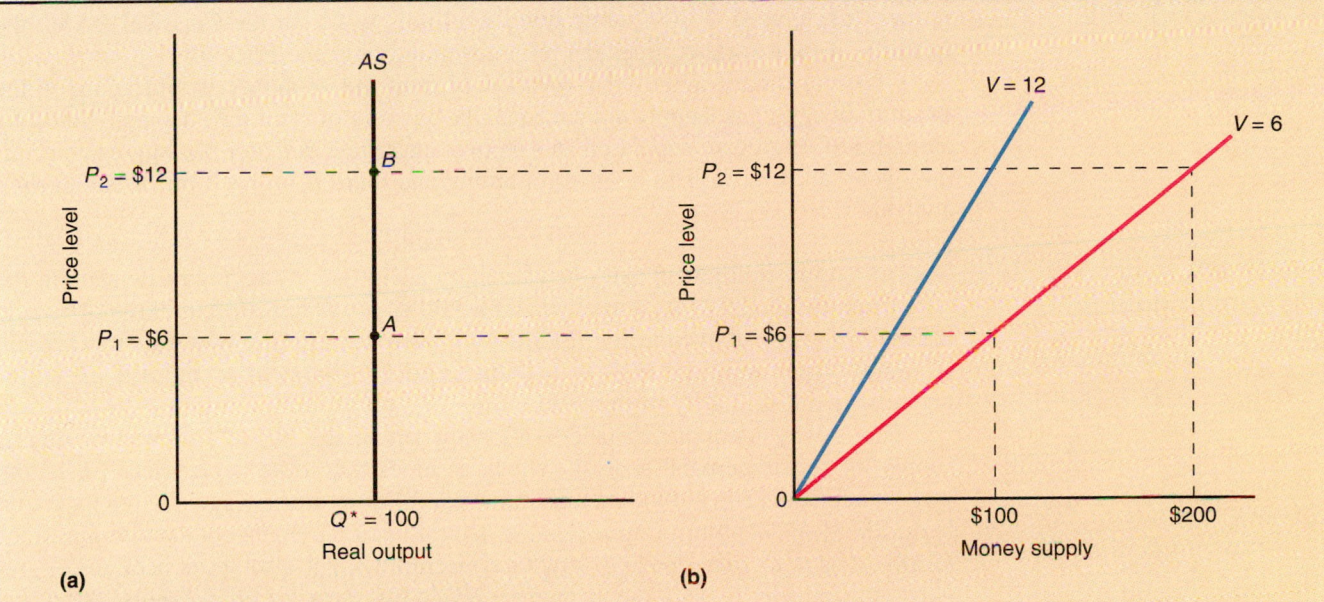

(a)

(b)

EXHIBIT 3 (a and b)   The Long-Run Classical Model

In the Classical model, the aggregate supply curve is perfectly vertical. It determines the level of aggregate demand (Say's law) and output, as in (a). Notice that aggregate demand plays a passive role in the Classical model. It is assumed always to equal aggregate supply (in this example at a real income of 100).

   The quantity of money determines the price level, and only the price level. The velocity is related to the slope of the velocity line in (b). If the velocity were 12 rather than 6, the total nominal income of 1,200 could be supported by a money supply of $100 rather than a nominal income of $600.

Now that we know the shape, let's ask, "At what level of real output will the aggregate supply be?" The answer depends on what people want to supply to the market. Classical economists argued that as long as individuals have free choice about what amount of labor and other resources to supply to the market, and as long as relative wages and prices can fluctuate, whatever level individuals choose to supply must be the *full-employment level*. Remember, the full-employment level is the economy's potential level of income. Thus, assuming flexible wages and prices, Q^* is the full-employment level of output. So the Classical analysis of aggregate supply held that, unless nominal wages were fixed, aggregate supply would be at its long-run potential income and the quantity of aggregate supply would be unaffected by the price level. The Classical aggregate supply curve will be perfectly vertical.

   The next question is "Will there be enough aggregate demand to buy up the aggregate supply?" Say's law answers that question: Supply creates its own demand,

The aggregate demand curve shows the relationship between price level and the total amount of output demanded in an economy.

Q–4: Demonstrate graphically what would happen to the price level if in Exhibit 3 velocity fell to 3.

so *whatever* point we are at on the aggregate supply curve, the quantity of aggregate demand will equal the quantity of aggregate supply! So Say's law tells us we needn't worry about demand. It will be at whatever level is supplied. Thus, Classical economists had no separate analysis of aggregate demand. It was simply assumed to equal aggregate supply via Say's law. If the price level of output rises, people's nominal income (wages, interest, rents, and profits) rises just enough to buy that output.

If supply creates its own demand regardless of what the price level is, aggregate supply and aggregate demand do not determine the price level: Aggregate supply equals aggregate demand at all price levels. And that's exactly what Classical economists argued. They argued that real forces do not determine the price level. Monetary forces determine the price level. According to the Classicals' quantity theory of money, the price level is determined by the money supply.

Exhibit 3(b) graphs the relationship between the money supply and price level that is determined by the quantity theory of money. Say the money supply is $200 and velocity is 6 so total nominal income, PQ, is $1,200. Since we're assuming in part (a) that real output Q^* is 100, the price level must be $12. If the money supply decreases to $100, velocity remains the same and nominal income falls to $600. Real output remains unchanged at 100, while price level falls to $6. In the Classical model, the quantity of money determines the price level and only the price level.

Classical theory avoids the question of how the economy would adjust if the quantity of aggregate supply did not equal the quantity of aggregate demand. Since, by assumption, aggregate supply creates its own aggregate demand, the aggregate economy is assumed always to be in equilibrium, and there is no need for disequilibrium analysis.

Unemployment in the Classical Model

Notice that unemployment can't be caused by a shortage of aggregate demand in the pure Classical model. But unemployment would be possible if structural rigidities held the real wage rate above the equilibrium rate. Such a possibility was shown in Exhibit 1, where wages were too high in relation to prices. Classical economists explained unemployment primarily in this way.

That's why unemployment doesn't show up in the above Classical aggregate supply/aggregate demand analysis, which assumes that all relative prices (including wages) adjust to keep individual markets in equilibrium. If the wage rate remained too high, Classical economists agreed that structural unemployment could exist. But since supply creates its own demand, structural unemployment also shifts back the aggregate demand curve, and the aggregate economy stays in equilibrium. Structural unemployment isn't caused by a shortage of aggregate demand; it's caused by wage rates that are too high.

Classical economists' solution to unemployment followed from their analysis. Since the cause of unemployment is wages that are too high, the solution is to reduce wages. Classical economists recognized that this "reduce the wage rate" solution to unemployment was politically unpopular and was, at best, a long-run solution. But their analysis led to this policy. "Have faith," they said. "Eventually wages will fall and the economy will come out of the depression."

A Problem with the Classical Model

Keynes argued that short-run equilibrium adjutment forces could prevent the aggregate economy from moving to the long-run Classical equilibrium.

As long as the economy was operating smoothly, the above Classical analysis of the aggregate economy met no serious opposition. But the prolonged Depression of the 1930s changed individuals' views about what focus economics should take. The Classical "have faith" solution was no longer acceptable. With a 25-percent unemployment rate, everyone was interested in the short run, not the long run. John Maynard Keynes put that concern most eloquently: "In the long run we're all dead."

Keynes played a major role in the development of macroeconomic thinking in the 1930s. In effect, he said, "Let's forget the long run and focus on the short run." He stopped asking whether the economy would eventually get out of the Depression on its own, and he started asking what short-run forces were causing the Depression and what society could do to escape it. In doing so he argued that a chase between aggregate supply and aggregate demand could prevent the aggregate economy from

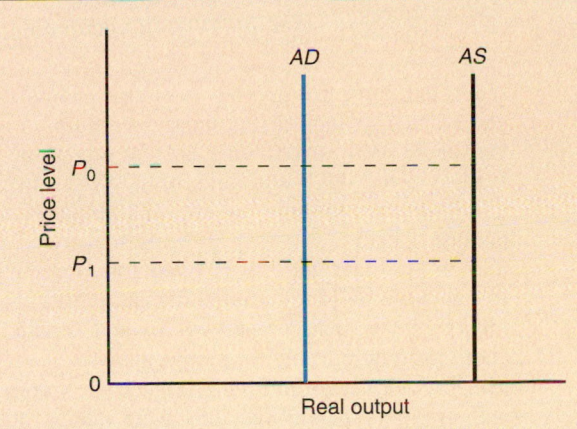

EXHIBIT 4   Keynes's Challenge to the Classical Story

Keynes argued that if the price level were only a veil and did not affect the real economy, there was no way in which a fall in the price level could bring about an aggregate equilibrium. Both the AS and AD curves would be perfectly vertical, and they would never intersect. For example, say that the price level were initially at P_0, at which point the quantity of aggregate supply is greater than the quantity of aggregate demand. The aggregate economy is in disequilibrium.

If the price level falls to P_1, the economy will be no closer to equilibrium. In fact, even if the price level fell without limit (remember, the price level includes the wage level), there would still be no equilibrium.

moving back to the long-run Classical equilibrium, if the economy deviated from that equilibrium. By taking this approach, he created the field of macroeconomics, and at the same time he forced major changes in Classical economics.

In response to Keynes's challenge, Classical economists added an analysis of the short run to their analysis of the long run. They adjusted their long-run Classical model (Exhibit 3) into a more realistic short-run Classical aggregate supply/aggregate demand model (often simply called the *Classical model,* which we'll call it here). This short-run Classical model nicely fits the AS/AD framework developed in the last chapter. Even though, from now on, most of our discussion will be about the short-run model, it's important to remember the short-run model that is now called *the Classical model* developed in response to Keynes's criticism of the "pure" long-run model.

The best way to understand the short-run Classical aggregate supply/aggregate demand model is to briefly consider Keynes's attack on it. Although his attack on the Classical view was multifaceted, its essence can be simply stated: The Classical model worked too neatly since everything was always in equilibrium. He asked, what if, for some reason, everything wasn't in equilibrium? What if there was an aggregate disequilibrium? What if the quantity of aggregate supply exceeded the quantity of aggregate demand, as shown in Exhibit 4?

In that case, Keynes pointed out, if the veil-of-money assumption were true and there were a dichotomy between the real and monetary sectors (as the long-run Classical model assumed), the aggregate demand curve, as well as the aggregate supply curve, would be perfectly vertical because a change in the wage and price level could not affect the real economy. In that case there would be no way a fall in the wage and price level would bring about an equilibrium between the two. By assumption, changes in the price level (which would include changes in the wage level) would have no effect on either the quantity demanded or the quantity supplied, since no relative prices would have changed. Keynes wrote:

> If competition between unemployed workers always led to a very great reduction of the money-wage, there would be a violent instability in the price level. Moreover, there might be no position of stable equilibrium except in conditions consistent with full employment; since the wage-unit might have to fall without limit.

In short, he argued that if the veil-of-money assumption were true and money did not affect the real economy, changes in the price level would only happen if the money supply were changed and would not bring about equilibrium.

Keynes argued that the Classical explanation was confusing the partial equilibrium analysis of supply and demand in micro—in which it is reasonable to assume other things equal—with the analysis of aggregate supply and demand in macro—in which "other things equal" cannot be assumed. In micro the substitution effect, which is based on changes in relative prices, not price levels, can reasonably be assumed to lead to equilibrium. In macro there is no substitution effect for the

3 Keynes argued that the Classical aggregate supply and demand curves had no short-run disequilibrium adjustment mechanism. In response, Classicals created such a mechanism, but Keynes thought it was inadequate. The essence of the Keynesian revolution is that it creates an alternative disequilibrium adjustment mechanism.

ADDED DIMENSION   CLASSICAL ECONOMISTS AND AGGREGATE SUPPLY/AGGREGATE DEMAND ANALYSIS

lassical economists before 1936 wouldn't have put their analysis in an aggregate supply/aggregate demand framework. Their arguments were generally informal arguments with political and social, as well as economic, dimensions. Graphical analysis forced them to specify their arguments in two dimensions, although Classical economists believed the issues had far more than two dimensions.

For example, the aggregate supply/aggregate demand analysis has no time dimension, and most Classical economists of that era were careful to state that their analysis was *long run*, an analysis of where the economy was eventually heading, not where it was at any particular moment. They agreed that in the short run there could be many problems, but they didn't analyze them. They considered short-term problems too complex to deal with.

In the 1930s, the center for Classical economists was England's London School of Economics (LSE). When word got to the LSE students that Keynes, up north in Cambridge, England, was working on a model focusing on demand for output as a whole, they were incredulous. One student at that time recalled:

> We had heard that some very strange things were happening in Cambridge. We couldn't quite make out what it was, something about the elasticity of demand for output as a whole, and we knew that was nonsense, because we were brought up properly on Marshall, and we knew all about elasticity and demand curves.* We knew that if you drew a demand curve you had to assume all the other prices were fixed; otherwise you wouldn't know what the demand curve for this item was. If you were to draw

a demand curve for another item (for example, say you wanted to look at the Consumer Surplus which you could enjoy from being able to buy some item for less than you would have been willing to pay), it was your duty to wipe out the first demand curve because the first one was allowing the price to vary. You had to have the prices fixed for everything else if you were going to draw a demand curve. Knowing this, we knew that demand curves and demand and elasticity referred only to partial analysis; and yet, somehow in Cambridge they must have known that and still, very perversely, they were talking about elasticity of demand for output as a whole. (From an interview with economist Abba Lerner)

The LSE students decided to clear up the confusion; they got in touch with the Cambridge students and agreed to meet once a week at Bishop's Stortford, a town chosen because it's about halfway between London and Cambridge on the railway line. The meetings were to continue until one side or the other won the argument. The result was that many of the LSE students, such as James Meade (who later won a Nobel prize in economics) and Abba Lerner (who's quoted here and who eventually became a key exponent of Keynes's theories) were converted to Keynesian economics. They believed it was both possible and necessary to talk about the demand for output as a whole. In doing so, they gave up Say's law.

---

* *Elasticity* (a term used to describe demand curves) measures the percent change in quantity in response to a percent change in price.

---

domestic economy since the price level, not relative price, goes on the vertical axis and a composite of all goods goes on the horizontal axis. What can be substituted for all goods?

Notice that in his argument Keynes shifted the analysis here from the long run to the short run. He argued that you can't simply assume the long run will arrive without explaining how short-run adjustment forces drive the economy to the long-run equilibrium. Somehow there must be a short-run **disequilibrium adjustment story** to explain how you get to the long run. The original Classical model lacked that story. It was always in equilibrium. That was the essence of Keynes's attack.

The disequilibrium adjustment story provides an explanation of how short-run adjustment forces drive the economy to long-run equilibrium.

To have an adequate disequilibrium adjustment story (a story of how the economy adjusts from disequilibrium to equilibrium), Classical economists needed first to answer two questions: How could an economy get out of equilibrium? And second, how could it get back into equilibrium?

THE CLASSICAL SHORT-RUN DISEQUILIBRIUM ADJUSTMENT STORY

In response to Keynes's arguments, Classicals agreed that the veil-of-money assumption held true only in the long run. They said that in the short run, changes in the price level (which included the wage level) could occur independently of changes in the money supply, and those changes in the price level could affect the aggregate quantity demanded. This argument underlay the downward-sloping aggregate demand curve that we discussed in the last chapter. What that downward-sloping demand curve means is that the quantity of aggregate demand increases whenever the price level falls, and hence the justification for a downward-sloping aggregate demand curve is a justification for how a falling price level would bring about an aggregate equilibrium.

The second part of the Classical disequilibrium story was that if wages were as flexible as prices, *aggregate supply would remain fixed, regardless of what happened*

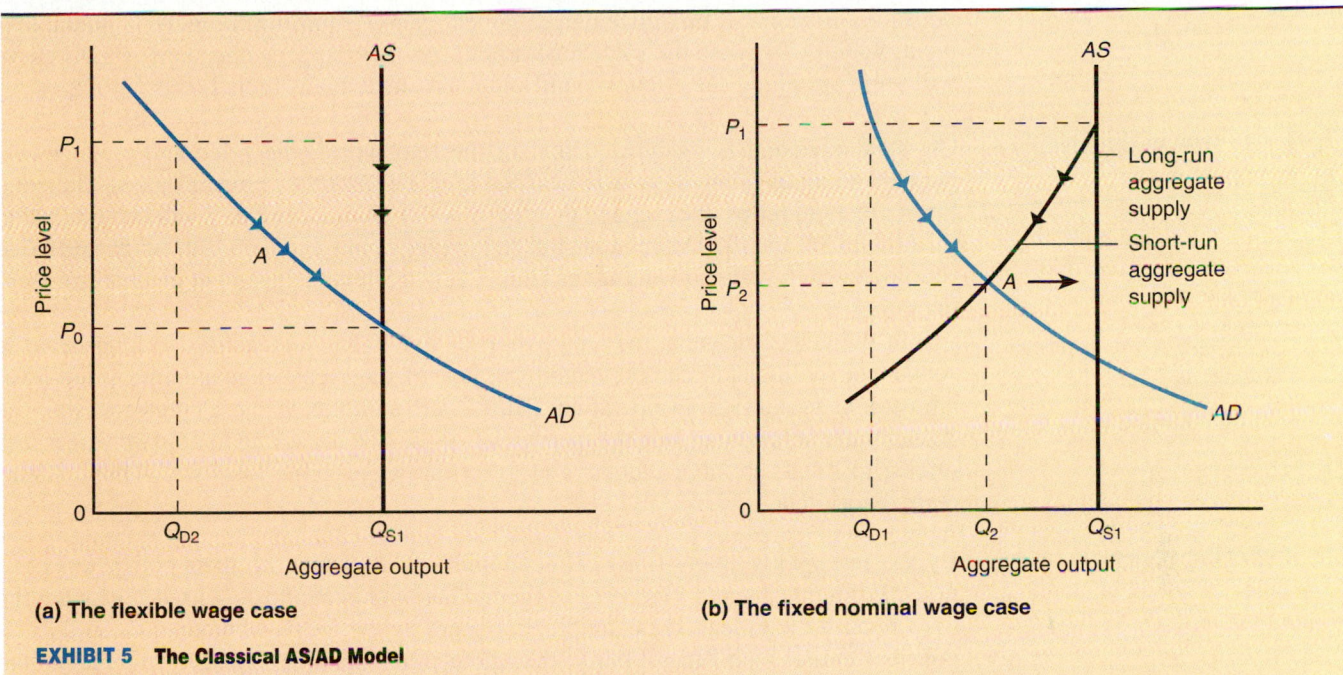

(a) The flexible wage case   **(b) The fixed nominal wage case**

EXHIBIT 5   The Classical AS/AD Model

At price level P_1, the initial quantity of aggregate supply, Q_{S1}, exceeds the quantity of aggregate demand, Q_{D1}, so the price level begins to fall when both wages and prices are flexible. This fall in the wage and price level will cause the quantity of aggregate demand to increase, as shown in (**a**). Eventually an equilibrium is reached at the price level P_0 and aggregate output Q_{S1}. When wages are less flexible than prices, the short run aggregate supply curve is upward sloping, as shown in (**b**). Given fixed wages, the fall in the price level causes unemployment and a fall in output. In the long run, the wage will be flexible, and as the wage falls, the short-run aggregate supply curve shifts out along arrow A to the long-run aggregate supply curve, and equilibrium is achieved at the economy's potential output.

to aggregate demand, and that it would not be affected by changes in the price level, and it would not shift back in response to low expectations of demand. This means that the long-run supply curve will be perfectly vertical and stable. If aggregate demand fell, there would be excess-supply pressure pushing the price level down, thereby increasing the quantity of aggregate demand.

If wages were less flexible than prices, the short-run aggregate supply curve would be upward sloping, and a fall in aggregate demand would bring about a fall in the quantity supplied (a movement down along the upward-sloping short-run *AS* curve). The quantity of aggregate supply of goods could then equal the quantity of aggregate demand at less than the economy's potential income, since there would be unemployment caused by the real wage being too high. That unemployment, however, would bring about a fall in the wage level. As the wage level fell, output would increase as the economy moved back along the upward-sloping short-run aggregate supply curve until, finally, it was once again at its potential income.

To give you a good sense of the Classical theory of aggregate disequilibrium, let's go through the example in Exhibit 5. In Exhibit 5(a), I assume both wages and prices are equally flexible. Assume initially that the price level (P_1) is too high for aggregate supply (AS) and demand (AD) to be in equilibrium. In response, the price level falls. This fall in the price level makes individuals richer, which increases aggregate quantity demanded. That price level fall (shown by the arrows along the *AS* curve) also lowers the relative price of the country's exports and raises the relative price of imports, further increasing aggregate quantity demanded. Thus, in response to the fall in the price level, the aggregate quantity demanded increases along arrow A, until the aggregate economy is once again in equilibrium at P_0 (the law of aggregate demand).

In Exhibit 5(b), I consider the same adjustment, only this time assuming the nominal wage is fixed, which means the short-run *AS* curve is upward sloping. In this case the fall in aggregate demand brings about a fall in the price level until the goods market is in equilibrium at output level Q_2 and price level P_2. But the labor market is

Q–5: What is the shape of the Classical long-run aggregate supply curve?

The Law of Aggregate Demand and the Classical Explanation of Aggregate Disequilibrium Adjustment

4A   In the Classical model, a demand shock leads to a disequilibrium which persists until the price level falls to bring about equilibrium.

not in equilibrium at this price/output goods market equilibrium; there is unemployment, which will cause the wage level to fall. As that happens, the short-run *AS* curve will shift out along the *A* arrow until output is once again at its potential output.

Classicals' View of the Great Depression

In the revised Classical model, wage and price rigidities prevent the Classical aggregate adjustment mechanism from operating, so even Classicals agreed that their solution was not practical.

Classical economists recognized that in the real world, the price and wage levels weren't going to fall to anywhere near the level necessary to bring about equilibrium. So in practical terms, they agreed that their model did not provide a workable solution for how to escape the Depression. But the model pointed to a culprit: wage and price rigidities which were preventing the Classical price-level adjustment mechanism from operating.

In the Classical view, the Depression of the 1930s was lasting so long because social and political forces prevented the law of aggregate demand (the price-level adjustment system) from operating. Thus, their solution to the Depression was the laissez-faire solution: to stop the measures Congress was passing to hold up wages and prices; to break up labor unions; and to let the wage–price level fall. That's where their theory led.

The Rise of Keynesian Economics

By the late 1930s, many Classical economists were giving up their policy prescriptions. Politicians weren't listening to them; Classical economists sensed it was not the time to push their ideas. For example, in Britain by the 1930s all three of the country's political parties (the Liberal party, the Labor party, and the Conservative party) had abandoned support of a laissez-faire policy. Each party was offering a competing government-organized program to fight unemployment.

Many students weren't listening to them, either: Students wanted to discuss policies to end the Depression. They didn't want to hear about the long run. For example, when Canadian exchange student Robert Bryce came back to Harvard after studying at Britain's Cambridge University where Keynes was a professor, his fellow students asked him to organize seminars to discuss the ideas he'd heard Keynes propound. (It was through Bryce's Harvard seminars that Keynes's ideas were transmitted to the United States.) When students organize their own seminars, you know they're interested.

One more reason why Classical economists were giving up their policy prescriptions is that economists are people too. Despite their training, economists are often compassionate people; their gut feelings were the same as the general population's: There must be a better way. Thus, during the Depression some Classical economists advocated a variety of policies that didn't follow from their theory.

While there were many dimensions to Keynes's ideas, their essence was that Say's law (supply creates its own demand) was wrong. Keynes argued that Thomas Malthus was right—general gluts could exist (and certainly did exist in the 1930s).

Keynes (a shrewd investor who was extremely active in the financial sector) argued that the financial sector didn't work the way Say's law assumed it did. It didn't translate savings into investment fast enough to prevent a general glut in output. According to Keynes, the level of savings did not determine the level of investment. Instead, the level of investment would change the level of income and thereby change the level of savings.

Let's consider an example. Say that a large portion of the people in the U.S. economy suddenly decide to save more and consume less. Consumption demand would decrease and savings would increase. If those savings were not immediately transferred into investment (as the Classicals assumed they would be), investment demand would not increase by enough to offset the fall in consumption demand, and aggregate demand would fall. There would be excess supply. Faced with this excess supply, firms would cut back production, which would decrease income. People would be laid off. As people's incomes fell, their desire to consume and their desire to save would decrease. (When you're laid off you don't save.) Eventually income would fall far enough so that once again savings and investment would be in equilibrium, but that equilibrium could be at a lower income level at a point below full employment.

In short, what Keynes argued was that the economy could get stuck in a rut. Once the economy got stuck in a rut with a glut, it had no way out. The government had to

the CATO JOURNAL

AN INTERDISCIPLINARY JOURNAL OF PUBLIC POLICY ANALYSIS

ARTICLES

Justin Yifu Lin   An Economic Theory of Institutional Change: Induced and Imposed Change
Gertrude E. Schroeder   The Implementation and Integration of Innovations in Soviet-Type Economies
Steve Pejovich   Liberty, Property Rights, and Innovation in Eastern Europe
Charlotte Twight   Institutional Underpinnings of Parochialism: The Case of Military Base Closures
Thomas Grennes   The Multifiber Arrangement and the Management of International Textile Trade
Peter Moser   Toward an Open World Order: A Constitutional Economics Approach
William T. Gavin and William G. Dewald   The Effect of Devaluationary Policies on Monetary Velocity
Gregory G. Brunk   The Role of Statistical Heuristics in Public Policy Analysis
Gerald Gunderson   Privatization and the 19th-Century Turnpike
Charles W. Baird   James Buchanan and the Austrians: The Common Ground
Israel M. Kirzner   The Use of Labels in Doctrinal History: Comment on Baird

COMMUNICATIONS

George S. Tavlas   Interpreting Keynes: Reflections on the Leijonhufvud–Yeager Dissension
Edwin G. West   Open Enrollment: A Vehicle for Market Competition in Schooling?

VOLUME 9 NUMBER 1 • PUBLISHED BY THE CATO INSTITUTE • SPRING/SUMMER 1989

Classical economic philosophy still lives in libertarian journals, such as *The Cato Journal.*

do something to pull the economy out of the rut. Keynes and his followers presented a set of models and arguments to explain their views. Those models, which were aggregate models, became the central macroeconomic models.

Keynesian ideas spread like wildfire among the younger economists. By the 1950s, Keynesian economics became accepted by most of the profession. It was taught everywhere in the United States. A terminology developed: national income accounting, which was closely tied to Keynesian concepts. As the terminology became generally used, Keynesian economics became as deeply embedded—and as little thought about—as Say's law had been earlier. That's one of the main reasons why Keynesian economics is not the end of the story and why in this book I emphasize a modern interpretation of the Keynesian model.

Let's now turn to the Keynesian arguments that the students of the 1930s were so interested in—specifically the Keynesian story of how the economy in the 1930s ended up in such a mess. As I stated above, Keynes challenged the Classical view of the macro economy, and the Classicals responded to that challenge with the above formalistic argument of how price level flexibility could, in theory, eventually lead the economy back to its potential income. It was formalistic because it had to be. Almost no one really believed that the price and wage level was going to fall as much as it would have to, or that we'd still have an economy left if the price level fell that much. Keynes said "hogwash" to it. That isn't the way equilibrium comes about.

Keynes's primary argument against that Classical argument did not concern the shape of the *AS* or *AD* curves (although he did argue that the *AD* curve would be almost vertical so that enormous price level flexibility would be needed); it concerned the disequilibrium dynamics. Keynes argued that *all other things could not, and would not, remain equal.* Long before any price level adjustment would take place to the degree needed to bring about significant increases in the quantity of aggregate demand, Keynes argued, an alternative adjustment mechanism—the income adjustment mechanism—would cause the *AS* and *AD* curves to shift, leading the economy to a new short-run equilibrium from which it could not escape on its own.

Keynes believed that the **income adjustment mechanism**—the chase between aggregate supply and demand—is the mechanism by which the aggregate economy arrives at equilibrium through interdependent *shifts* of aggregate supply and aggregate demand, rather than through movements along the aggregate demand curve. Thus for Keynes, equilibrium in the macroeconomy was similar to a dog chasing its tail, and it wasn't clear where the final equilibrium would end up. For Classicals, aggregate equilibrium was set by individuals, and it reflected their desires.

Keynes focused on the income adjustment mechanism, as opposed to the Classical price-level adjustment mechanism, for two reasons. The first is that he felt the price-level adjustment mechanism was, from a practical standpoint, impossible. If it worked at all, it worked too slowly for political and social forces to accept. In response to the Classical argument that the price-level adjustment mechanism would work in the long run, he quipped, "In the long run we're all dead."

Yes, he agreed, there were some theoretical issues raised by the price-level adjustment mechanism, but he argued that those issues weren't especially important during the Depression. Social pressures (the invisible handshake) wouldn't let prices and wages fall fast enough for the Classical price-level adjustment mechanism to work. And even if the social pressures were overcome, political pressures (the invisible foot) would stop the fall in the price level, if it started.

Keynes argued that Classical economists failed to see the importance of the income adjustment mechanism because they were too caught up in Say's law and the quantity theory of money. Classicals assumed velocity constant in the short run without any logical or empirical justification for that assumption. Keynes argued that velocity was not a decision variable of individuals; it was simply a construct that was necessary to relate the quantity of money to the level of income. It could, and did, change considerably. In Keynes's view velocity was flexible in the short run. Hence, the same quantity of money could support different levels of nominal income. Since both Keynes and the Classical economists agreed the price level did not decrease

According to Keynes, once the economy got stuck in a rut with a glut, it had no way out.

Keynes's Alternative Story of Aggregate Equilibrium: The Dog Chasing Its Tail

Keynes's primary argument against the Classicals was that all other things could not, and would not, remain equal.

Income adjustment mechanism *The chase between aggregate supply and aggregate demand.*

Q–6: Why is the dog-chasing-its-tail analogy relevant to the Keynesian adjustment process?

IN THE LONG RUN WE'RE ALL DEAD

W hen Keynes said "In the long run we're all dead," he didn't mean that we can forget the long run. What he meant was that if the long run is sufficiently long so that short-run forces do not let it come about, then for all practical purposes there is no long run. In that case, the short-run problem must be focused on.

Keynes's view of the political and social forces of the time was that voters would not be satisfied waiting for market forces to bring about full employment. Keynes felt that if something were not done in the short run to alleviate unemployment, voters would opt for fascism (as had the Germans) or communism (as had the Russians). He saw both alternatives as undesirable. For him, what would happen in the long run was academic.

Classicals, on the other hand, argued that the short-run problems were not as bad as Keynes made them out to be, so short-run problems should not be focused on to the exclusion of long-run problems. Modern-day Classicals argue that today we are living in Keynes's long run, so that his long-run problems are our short-run problems.

J. M. Keynes   *Bettmann Newsphotos.*

5 Keynes argued that a falling price level would set in motion other dynamic adjustment forces that would more than offset the equilibrating tendencies of the Classical price-level adjustment mechanism.

quickly, flexible velocity meant that aggregate demand for real output could fluctuate around.

The second reason Keynes objected to the Classical disequilibrium dynamics was that he believed that Classical dynamic analysis was theoretically flawed. He believed a falling price level would set in motion other dynamic adjustment forces that would more than offset the equilibrating tendencies of the Classical price-level adjustment mechanism. Specifically, a falling price level would disrupt financial markets and create bearish (negative) expectations in businesspeople, which would cause aggregate supply to decrease. As aggregate supply decreased, aggregate demand would also decrease, and a downward spiral of output would result.

Keynes believed that such alternative dynamic effects of a falling price level would swamp any increase in the quantity of aggregate output caused by a lower price level as the economy moved along the demand curve. To say that theoretically, *other things constant,* an adjustment force exists is one thing; Keynes agreed the price level could be made to fall (if the government wasn't worried about not being re-elected), but if it did, that fall in the price level would cause shifts in the *AS* and *AD* curves. To say a falling price level is strong enough to achieve aggregate equilibrium at an economy's potential output when other things aren't held equal is quite another thing. Keynes said the Classical adjustment mechanism was too weak to bring about an aggregate equilibrium, and that it would, by necessity, violate the "other things equal" assumption.

For much of Keynes's book, *The General Theory of Employment, Interest, and Money,* in which he developed the Keynesian model, he put aside that second, academic reason because the first reason (the real-world reason) was sufficient reason not to consider wage and price-level flexibility. Thus, in the simple Keynesian model that we'll discuss in this chapter and the next, wage and price levels are assumed to be institutionally fixed, leaving the model free to concentrate on what Keynes considered to be the most important dynamic adjustment force: the income adjustment force.

This assumption of fixed wages and prices without a full theoretical explanation of why it is a necessary and justifiable, not an ad hoc (arbitrary), assumption would later come back to haunt Keynesian economists. The reason why is that while wages and prices are slow to adjust downward, they are not so slow to adjust upward when the economy starts approaching its level of potential output. In the 1970s, the wage and price levels rose continuously, and inflation became the economy's biggest

ADDED DIMENSION

WORMHOLES AND THE
CLASSICAL ADJUSTMENT
STORY

Keynes did not spend much time discussing the effect on output of changes in the price level, but later economists have. What they have found is an asymmetry in the effects of price level changes: upward movements in the price level are far less disruptive to the economy than are the equivalent downward movements of the price level. The reason is that the financial system in our economy is built on credit secured by assets. When the price level unexpectedly falls, it undermines the financial system because it transfers wealth away from borrowers, and borrowers are generally the entrepreneurs, the people responsible for supply. When the price level falls significantly, there is a financial panic and chaos. Firms go bankrupt and the institutional foundation of the economy is undermined. This effect might be called the *wormhole effect*.

For those of you who aren't astrophysicists or Trekie IIs, wormholes are disruptions in space. You enter a wormhole and you find yourself in a place somewhere completely different than the one where you started: For example, if you start in a house in Iowa and take just one step, you find yourself on the planet Pluto. That is about what happens when a financial panic is caused by a falling price level. The fall in the price level undermines existing institutions, and both aggregate demand and aggregate supply shift back. The economy finds itself in a depression—because the price level fell!

When the wormhole effect is taken into account the real income equilibrium at which the economy arrives by letting the price level fall may well be at a lower level of output than it began with! Instead of increasing real income, a flexible price which pulls the economy into a wormhole will decrease it. That's why societies seldom let the price level fall significantly.

When the price level rises, the process is different—the wealth transfer is initially in the opposite direction; wealth is transferred from lenders to borrowers. Since these lenders are generally not the entrepreneurs, the same institutional disruption does not occur, at least initially. In fact, as money flows to entrepreneurs the economy often experiences a boom as more and more people try to become entrepreneurs. But to the degree this boom is based on unexpected wealth transfers, the boom is only temporary, and soon the price level increase becomes expected, and inflation becomes built into the economy. The institutional costs of inflation occur over longer periods of time; we'll discuss those costs in the chapter on inflation.

There are a number of complicated institutional issues upon which the above argument depends, such as whether the economy can develop financial institutions that are less fragile in respect to the price level than are our existing financial institutions (i.e., new institutions that avoid the wormhole effect), but that will be as conducive to production as are existing institutions. When, and if, such less-fragile institutions develop, money will be obsolete and we'll all carry our little financial Credit-Debit Wizard with us to pay all our bills. Perhaps, because it's a pain to carry, we will have the Wizard implanted under our skin and directly connected to our brain so that all we have to do is to think "payment" and the Wizard will arrange payment, or think "financing" and the Wizard will arrange financing for us. That is still a few years away, but, hey, it's possible. Don't underestimate those Wizards. (Some economists at the California Institute of Technology are currently designing moneyless computer-payment systems.)

problem. Many Classical economists blamed this inflation on Keynesian policies that were based on a model that assumed the wage and price level fixed. This led to a resurgence of Classical analysis in the 1980s.

In response to that resurgence, Keynesian economists considered the issue of price-level flexibility, and argued that removing that assumption does not change the basic argument as long as the economy is below potential income; it only modifies it slightly. Moreover, they argued that Keynesian economists had never said that the Keynesian model was applicable once the economy has reached its potential output. They refined the interpretation of the Keynesian model so that it *was not* dependent on fixed nominal wages or prices. Rather, it concerned the adjustment dynamics—shifts of the curves, not movements along the curves. It is that refined Keynesian interpretation of the Keynesian model that I present in this chapter. So while the model you see is the traditional Keynesian model, the interpretation is the modern interpretation of 1990s Keynesians.

Q-7: Is the Keynesian argument based on fixed nominal wages or prices?

The Keynesian Aggregate Supply/Aggregate Demand Analysis

In Keynes's view, short-run aggregate supply would shift in response to a shortage in aggregate demand.

Q–8: In Exhibit 6, is the distance Q_1–Q_2 less than the distance Q_0–Q_1? Why and by how much do they differ?

Effective demand The demand that exists after suppliers cut production in response to excess aggregate supply.

Marginal propensity to consume The percentage change in spending that accompanies a percentage change in income.

To see why Keynes thought the Classical model of disequilibrium adjustment was too simple, let's consider his argument against it. As before, let's say that the economy finds itself in aggregate disequilibrium at the existing price level, so the quantity of aggregate supply is greater than the quantity of aggregate demand. This disequilibrium may create a tendency for wages and prices to fall, but that fall will not be instantaneous.

In the meantime a second adjustment force—one of the shift factors discussed in the last chapter—enters the picture.[2] Specifically, firms' expectations cannot be assumed constant. When firms can't sell all their goods, they will cut production—decrease aggregate supply. So unlike the Classical case where aggregate supply was fixed, in Keynes's view short-run aggregate supply would shift in response to a shortage in aggregate demand.

But that shift in supply wasn't the end of the story for Keynes. That shift in short-run aggregate supply would lower income, which is a shift factor of aggregate demand. So the shift back in aggregate supply would cause the aggregate demand curve to shift. But that aggregate demand shift would set in motion a further shift back in aggregate supply.

To understand aggregate equilibrium, Keynes argued, you had to understand the nature of these interdependent shift factors. *The interactions of these shift factors determined the income level at which the economy would equilibrate.*

You can see Keynes's argument in the *AS/AD* framework in Exhibit 6, which has the same starting point as did the discussion of the Classical adjustment process discussed earlier and illustrated in Exhibit 5. Initially, there is disequilibrium of Q_0–Q_1, with the aggregate supply curve AS_0, and the aggregate demand curve AD_0. Keynes argued that the price level was institutionally fixed at P_1. Thus, we can draw a fixed price level line, P_1, which captures the institutional reality of fixed prices.

In the Classical model, if the price level were fixed, the economy would be stuck in a type of permanent disequilibrium. Production—aggregate supply—would remain at the potential output level, but people would not buy the goods. But, as I stated above, Keynes argued that that isn't how the world works. He said that if firms couldn't sell their goods at the existing prices, they would cut output, shifting the aggregate supply curve back from AS_0 to AS_1, in an attempt to eliminate the excess aggregate supply at the existing price level. So in Keynes's model, *aggregate supply depends on expected aggregate demand.* If demand isn't there to buy all that is supplied, the supply will shift back to meet the demand.

But, Keynes argued, that shift back in aggregate supply would not bring about equilibrium. As aggregate supply shifts back, society's income will fall. Therefore the shift back in aggregate supply will cause the aggregate demand curve to shift back from AD_0 to AD_1. What Keynes called effective demand would fall because in Keynes's model not only is aggregate supply dependent on expected aggregate demand, aggregate demand is also dependent on aggregate supply. **Effective demand** is the aggregate demand that exists after suppliers cut production in response to aggregate supply exceeding aggregate demand. Comparing the two shifts in Exhibit 6, we see that the initial difference (Q_0–Q_1) between the AS_0 and AD_0 is more than the difference (Q_1–Q_2) between the AS_1 and AD_1 curves. So as I have drawn it, the AD curve shifts back by less than the AS curve shifts, which means with each shift the two curves move closer together; the shifting is an equilibrating force.

I drew the curves as shifting in this manner because of an assumption Keynes made. He assumed people's **marginal propensity to consume**—the percentage change in spending that accompanies a percentage change in income—is less than one. As income falls, people try to maintain their previous income level by dipping into their savings, so spending decreases by less than does production, which by

---

[2] Keynes did not explore what would happen if nominal prices and wages did not move in tandem. He ruled that possibility out by a wage unit assumption that assumed wages and prices move in tandem. He argued, however, that (1) his conclusions were not based on this assumption, and (2) for the large movement in price level necessary for the Classical price level adjustment mechanism to work, wages and prices would move roughly equally.

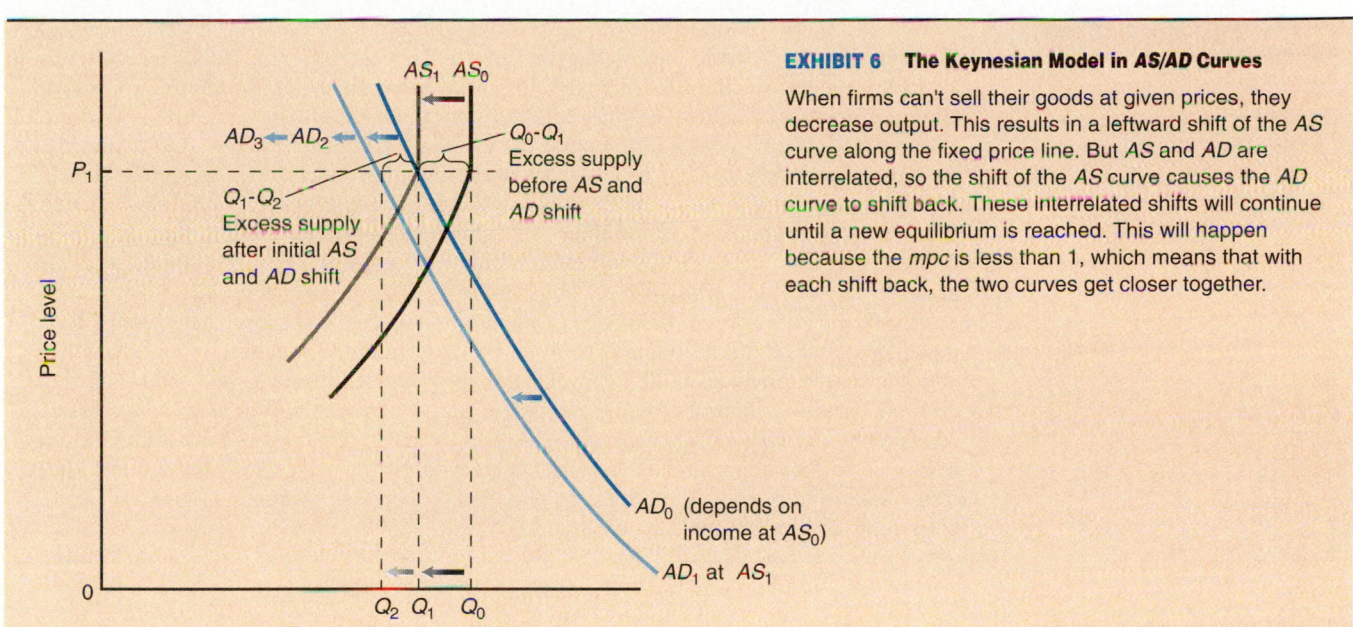

EXHIBIT 6   The Keynesian Model in *AS/AD* Curves

When firms can't sell their goods at given prices, they decrease output. This results in a leftward shift of the *AS* curve along the fixed price line. But *AS* and *AD* are interrelated, so the shift of the *AS* curve causes the *AD* curve to shift back. These interrelated shifts will continue until a new equilibrium is reached. This will happen because the *mpc* is less than 1, which means that with each shift back, the two curves get closer together.

definition equals income. As income decreases, both the *AS* and *AD* curves shift, but the *AS* curve shifts more than does the *AD* curve; so as income falls, the two move closer together.

The fall in production to Q_1 is not the end of the story since after both curves shift there is still excess supply of Q_1–Q_2. Because there is still disequilibrium, the adjustment continues. Both the *AS* and *AD* curves shift further and further to the left, but as they do, the aggregate supply and aggregate demand curves get closer and closer together. AS_2 and AD_2 would be closer together, and AS_3 and AD_3 would be even closer.

Finally, at some level of income they are once again in equilibrium. At that income level Y_e, *AS* = *AD*, at price level P_1. Thus, in response to a negative real shock, the Keynesian model ultimately leads to an aggregate supply/aggregate demand equilibrium at an income level below its potential output. We'll see how that equilibrium is determined in the next chapter.

To bring home the difference between the Keynesian and Classical models, let's review what the effect of an **aggregate demand shock**—a shift in the *AD* curve— will be in each of them. In the Keynesian model, the demand shock will bring about an aggregate supply shift, which would bring about a second round demand shift, which would . . . , and the process would continue, with each iterative shock getting smaller until finally a new equilibrium would be reached. In the Classical model, the demand shock would lead to a disequilibrium, which would put pressure on the price level and wage level to fall. Classicals saw no secondary effect taking place, and no interactive decline, since shift factors in supply did not play a role in their analysis.

The statement that Keynes saw the aggregate short-run supply curve as unstable and the price level as fixed needs an addendum; his analysis focused on an economy experiencing a recessionary shock so that output fell below the output level where it had been. Keynes stated that Classical economics became relevant again once the output level reached its **potential income**—the level it had previously achieved plus a normal growth factor.

Once the economy reaches its potential rate of output, Keynes's analysis of aggregate supply becomes identical to the Classical analysis of aggregate supply: Increases in aggregate demand above potential output will cause the price level to rise,

6 Each step of the Keynesian income adjustment mechanism involves an interdependent shift of the *AD* and *AS* curves, with the *AD* curve shifting by the *mpc* times the shift in the *AS* curve. This interactive process becomes smaller and smaller.

Q–9: If you were going through another iteration of the adjustment process in Exhibit 6, what would the new gap between *AS* and *AD* equal?

A Comparison of the Keynesian and Classical Analyses of a Demand Shock with Fixed Prices

4B In Keynesian analysis, a demand shock causes a supply response which brings about a further demand response which sets in motion an iterative process which continues until a new equilibrium is reached.

The Three Ranges of the Economy

A REMINDER ✓

THE KEY DIFFERENCE IN THE ASSUMPTION ABOUT SHIFT FACTORS OF AGGREGATE SUPPLY AND AGGREGATE DEMAND

To see precisely where the Keynesians and Classicals differed, let's consider once again the modern interpretation of the difference between the Keynesian and Classical views of aggregate supply. Keynes believed that when discussing a decrease in aggregate demand below the level of output the economy had reached, one would find that the aggregate supply curve was unstable—that it was dependent upon expected demand. In this modern interpretation of the Keynesian model, the *AS* curve would shift around, depending on suppliers' expectations of demand. Aggregate equilibrium would be brought about by shifts of the aggregate supply and aggregate demand curves, with the price level remaining constant.

As I discussed above, Classical economists assumed that the aggregate supply curve remained stable at the full-employment income level. Equilibrium was brought about by changes in the price level—by movements along the aggregate supply and aggregate demand curves as opposed to interdependent shifts of these curves. For this Classical adjustment mechanism to work, aggregate supply must remain constant; the *AS* curve cannot shift. According to the Classicals, firms would simply wait for prices to fall, even if the fall in the price level took a long time to operate. Keynes argued that, as a behavioral assumption, that would not do.

Keynes believed that Classical economics became relevant again once the economy reached its potential output.

7 In the Keynesian range of the economy, the price level is constant. In the Classical range, the price level is perfectly flexible.

with no shift in aggregate supply. Keynes's analysis is relevant for recessions—when there is a contractionary shock to the economy or when the economy is significantly below its potential income. Moreover, Keynes recognized an intermediate case where the price level would be partially flexible and hence would rise somewhat in response to expansionary demand shocks.

Thus, using Keynesian analysis, the economy can be divided into the three ranges of the price-level flexibility curve discussed in the last chapter. Those three ranges of the price-level flexibility curve are shown again in Exhibit 7.

In the fixed-price-level Keynesian range, the economy is significantly below its potential income, and the price level can be assumed fixed. In the intermediate range, the price level is partially flexible, and expansionary shocks to the economy bring about a combination of price level adjustment and output adjustment. The closer to potential income the economy is, the more the price level adjustment. Finally, in the Classical range, any expansionary shock to the economy will bring about only a price level adjustment.

Why does how close the economy is to its potential income lead to different responses in terms of price level and output? Because when the output level is significantly below its potential level to expand, the institutional structure to increase production already exists. Increasing output in this case is a lot easier than when the economy is at its potential income. When the economy is at its potential income, the institutional structure must be modified before it is possible for output to increase.

The difference can be made clearer by distinguishing between cyclical and structural unemployment, discussed in an earlier chapter. Cyclical unemployment occurs when output is below potential output. Workers have been laid off, and it is relatively easy to call them back to work and increase production. Structural unemployment occurs when the economy is at its potential output. The problem isn't layoffs; it's appropriate jobs for the existing skills. Structural unemployment is a much more complicated problem than cyclical unemployment.

Q–10: If aggregate demand increases when the economy is at its potential income, what does the Keynesian adjustment process say will happen?

In the 1990s, even though there is significant unemployment, many economists believe that the economy is at, or close to, its potential output.

Unfortunately, when figuring out whether the economy is in a Classical or a Keynesian range, one cannot always simply look to past output level and assume that potential income can reach that level plus a normal growth rate. In some cases, the economy can be undergoing significant **structural readjustment** in which it is trying to change from what it has been doing to something new, not to repeat what it did in the past. If that is true, the economy can find itself in the Classical case at less than the previously-attained output. Unemployment may look like cyclical unemployment, but may actually be structural unemployment.

I mention that possibility because such structural changes have been occurring in many economies in the 1990s. For example, the formerly socialist economies are

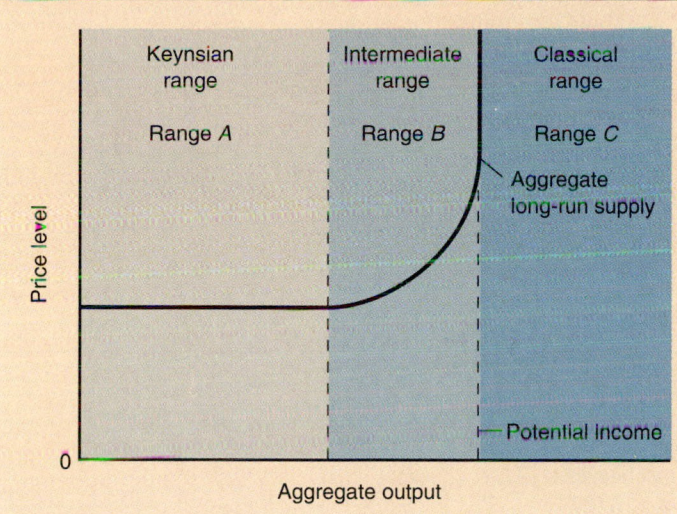

EXHIBIT 7   The Price-Level Flexibility Curve

Most economists believe the economy has three ranges of price-level flexibility. Range *A*, the fixed-price range, is often called the Keynesian range, since in the range, only the income adjustment mechanism is operative. Range *C*, which is reached when the economy reaches its potential income, is often called the Classical range, since only the price-level adjustment mechanism is operative. Range *B* is an intermediate range between the two.

experiencing major structural changes, so even though output has fallen by 40 to 50 percent, they still find themselves in the Classical range—they don't want to produce what, or how, they did before. They are trying to develop whole new institutional structures.

The major industrial countries, the United States included, are also experiencing significant structural changes, which makes Keynesian economics far less relevant than it otherwise would have been. For example, in 1992–1993 the U.S. economy expanded slowly, but that expansion was accompanied by major structural changes. This meant that firms expanded and increased output, but that they often laid off workers simultaneously. Before these workers could be re-employed, they had to structurally change their professions rather than simply being hired back by their former companies. That takes a lot longer—first in realizing that one must redefine one's profession, and then in actually doing it.

Western Europe in the 1990s was experiencing similar structural changes, which is why unemployment could remain at about 10 percent without major attempts to reduce it through policies to increase aggregate demand. In such times of structural change, the economy may well find itself in the Classical case, despite having output significantly below its long-run growth prediction.

You've now been introduced to the central Keynesian and Classical ideas about the adjustment process. You've seen how those ideas relate to the *AS/AD* framework developed in the last chapter. You've also seen how Classical disequilibrium analysis emphasized price level adjustment, and Keynesian adjustment analysis emphasized interdependent shift factors of aggregate supply and aggregate demand.

CONCLUSION

In the next chapter you'll go through Keynes's analysis using a different model—a model that shows how an economy with interdependent supply and demand can reach an aggregate equilibrium, and what that equilibrium will be.

CHAPTER SUMMARY

- In the early 1900s, Classical economics focused on partial-equilibrium microeconomics. It explained unemployment in microeconomic terms: Unemployment was caused by too high a wage level.

- Pure Classical economic analysis of the aggregate economy centered on two propositions: Say's law and the quantity theory of money.

- The quantity theory of money determines the price level, and Say's law sees to it that the aggregate economy is always in equilibrium at full employment.

- In the long-run Classical model, aggregate demand isn't considered. It is simply assumed to exist at a level equal to aggregate supply.

- By the late 1930s, many economists were giving up the Classical view and becoming Keynesian economists who opposed laissez-faire.

- The Keynesian adjustment process is like a dog chasing its tail; each step in the process involves an interdependent shift of the *AS* and *AD* curves.

- Classicals and Keynesians disagreed about the mecha-

nism by which a demand shock affects the economy. Classicals believed it was the price level adjustment mechanism, whereas the Keynesians emphasized the income adjustment mechanism.

- Keynes believed that Classical economics became relevant again once the economy reached its potential output.

KEY TERMS

aggregate demand shock *(221)*
autonomous *(209)*
Classical long-run aggregate supply
  curve *(210)*
Classical economists *(205)*
disequilibrium adjustment story *(214)*
effective demand *(220)*

equation of exchange *(208)*
income adjustment mechanism *(217)*
Keynesian economists *(205)*
laissez-faire *(205)*
marginal propensity to consume *(220)*
money *(208)*
potential income *(221)*

quantity theory of money *(208)*
real wage *(205)*
Say's law *(205)*
structural readjustment *(222)*
veil-of-money assumption *(209)*
velocity of money *(209)*

QUESTIONS FOR THOUGHT AND REVIEW

The number after each question represents the estimated degree of critical thinking required. (1= almost none; 10 = deep thought.)

1. What is the central difference between Keynesian and Classical economists? *(2)*

2. Explain how lowering the wage level will decrease unemployment if the price level doesn't change when the wage is lowered. *(5)*

3. Explain how lowering the wage level will decrease unemployment if the price level is flexible and hence changes when the nominal wage is lowered. *(7)*

4. What three assumptions turn the equation of exchange into the quantity theory of money? *(3)*

5. Assuming the quantity theory of money held true, what would happen if a country on a gold standard ran a balance of payments surplus? *(5)*

6. A popular proposal to end the depression in the 1930s was to create a new money with coupons on it. If the money weren't used within a specific period of time, the coupons would be worthless. Would that proposal help eliminate unemployment, given the Classical analysis? How? *(8)*

7. Why were Classical economists hesitant about using aggregate supply/aggregate demand analysis? *(6)*

8. If a country had a flexible exchange rate rather than a fixed exchange rate, how would the Classical short-run adjustment argument change? *(8)*

9. Classical economists saw the Depression as a political problem, not an economic problem. Why? *(6)*

10. Demonstrate graphically the effect of a demand shock of 20 in the Keynesian model if the *mpc* = .75. *(7)*

PROBLEMS AND EXERCISES

1. Assume the money supply is $500, the velocity of money is 8, and the price level is $2. Using the quantity theory of money:
   a. Determine the level of real output.
   b. Determine the level of nominal output.
   c. Assuming velocity remains constant, what will happen if the money supply rises 20 percent?
   d. If the government established price controls and also raised the money supply 20 percent, what would happen?
   e. How would you judge whether the assumption of fixed velocity is reasonable?

2. The classical analysis of the economy rests on wage and price stability.
   a. Ask a local business what it would do to prices if demand for its product fell 10 percent.
   b. Would its response be the same if the demand for all products fell 10 percent?
   c. Ask a local business how it determines wages. What would it do to wages if unemployment in the community were 8 percent? 10 percent?
   d. Draw an aggregate supply and demand curve. Demonstrate the Classical equilibrium. Now say that demand decreases 10 percent. Using the insights you gained in

parts *a* and *b*, and *AS* and *AD* curves, explain how the economy will likely adjust.

3. The shape of the short-run fixed nominal wage *AS* curve is upward sloping; the slope of the flexible-wage short-run *AS* curve is vertical.
   a. Why?
   b. Assuming the price level is fixed, what effect does that assumption have on the Keynesian adjustment process? Why?
   c. If the price level is somewhat variable, what difference will this make to the Keynesian adjustment process? (Explain in words.)
   d. If the changing price level lowered the quantity of aggregate supply via downward movements along the aggregate supply curve, what effect would that have on the Keynesian adjustment process?

4. Using aggregate supply and demand analysis, demonstrate the effect of the following:
   a. The government runs a large deficit (spends more than it takes in in revenues).
   b. Exports increase.
   c. The value of a country's currency is lowered.

5. The Keynesian adjustment process is an iterative process of interdependent aggregate supply and demand curves.
   a. What role does the *mpc* play in that iterative process?
   b. If the *mpc* is .5 and the initial gap is 10, how much will the two curves shift after five iterations?
   c. How much will they shift after ten iterations?
   d. How would your answers to *b* and *c* change if the *mpc* were .8?

ANSWERS TO MARGIN QUESTIONS

1. When people save, financial markets transfer that savings into investment and as long as financial markets do this, Say's law—that supply creates its own demand—holds true. *(208)*

2. The equation of exchange, $MV = PQ$, is a tautology. What changes it to the quantity theory are assumptions about the variables, specifically that velocity remains constant, that real output is determined separately, and that the causation flows from money to prices. With these assumptions added, the equation of exchange implies that changes in the money supply are reflected in changes in the price level—which is what the quantity theory of money says. *(209)*

3. Two pillars of the Classical model are the quantity theory of money and Say's law. *(210)*

4. If velocity fell to 3, the velocity line in the right-hand graph would shift down, which would cause the price level to fall from $6 to $3, real output remaining constant as in the diagram below. *(211)*

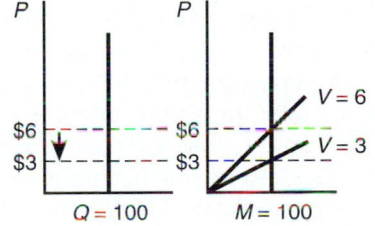

5. The Classical long-run aggregate supply curve is perfectly vertical at full employment. *(215)*

6. The dog-chasing-its-tail analogy is relevant to the Keynesian adjustment process because that adjustment involves shifting interdependent aggregate supply and demand curves. This interconnection causes feedback loops in the adjustment process which start an iterative adjustment process. *(217)*

7. While much of the Keynesian analysis was carried out under the assumption of fixed nominal wages and prices, these are not necessary for the Keynesian adjustment process to take place. Only infinitely fast price-level adjustment (which prevented any disequilibrium) would eliminate it, and if large price-level adjustment caused negative effects on the economy through its effect on contracts and financial markets, even that wouldn't help. *(219)*

8. Yes. The distances differ because of the *mpc*. That *mpc* tells us the amount of feedback spending that occurs in each iteration. Thus $Q_1 - Q_2 = mpc\ (Q_0 - Q_1)$. *(220)*

9. The new gap would equal $mpc\ (Q_1 - Q_2)$, which, in turn, equals $(mpc)^2\ (Q_0 - Q_1)$. *(221)*

10. When the economy is at its potential income, if aggregate demand increases, the aggregate supply curve will not shift out any more. The iterative process will stop and the increase in aggregate demand will only lead to a rise in the price level. *(222)*

The Flexible Price Level and Macrofoundations of Micro

In the chapter I tried to keep the technical discussion to a minimum. In this appendix I discuss two technical issues that should clarify the difference between the Keynesian vision underlying their model and the Classical vision underlying their model. The first concerns the income adjustment mechanism and the price level adjustment mechanism; the second concerns the concept of the economy that underlies their assumptions about the price level and the price-level flexibility curve.

The Income Adjustment Mechanism and a Flexible Price Level

The assumption of a fixed price level is not the distinguishing element of the Keynesian model. Rather, the distinguishing element is the existence of the income adjustment mechanism caused by interdependent aggregate supply and demand. To see that, in the accompanying graph let us start with the same disequilibrium as before.

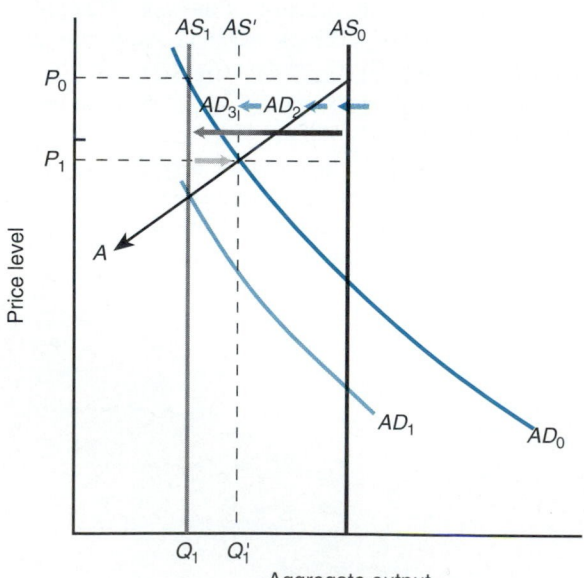

Let's break the adjustment process into periods. In time period 1, the price level falls to P_1. Let's also keep the analysis simple by assuming wages and prices are both equally flexible so the short-run AS curve is perfectly vertical. This fall in the price level to P_1 reduces the shift in the AS curve. It needn't shift all the way over to AS_1 as in the fixed-price case; it only need shift to AS'. This smaller shift in aggregate supply will lead to a smaller shift in aggregate demand, but the interdependent shifts will still be there. The aggregate economy will adjust along the A arrow until, finally, a new equilibrium is reached at a lower output level and a lower price level.

As you can see, the existence of a partially flexible price level modifies the Keynesian analysis but does not change the general result that a below-potential-income level of output is arrived at because of the income adjustment mechanism. The Keynesian analysis is eliminated only if the price-level adjustment occurs instantaneously, so no disequilibrium is possible.

The Macrofoundations of Micro and the Price-Level Flexibility Curve

As I emphasized in the previous chapter, the price-level flexibility curve is not an aggregate supply curve. By definition, an aggregate supply curve represents the quantity suppliers want to supply given a price level, *assuming the price level is free to adjust.* The price-level flexibility curve is, instead, an institutional constraint imposed on the economy by the use of money. Drawing a flat supply curve presupposes that the price level—and hence all individual prices—is free to fluctuate in the short run and that the individuals setting prices would want to eliminate any excess supply or demand by changing prices. That was not the way Keynes pictured the economy. He argued that, in a monetary economy, *the price level was not free to fluctuate in the short run.*

Large fluctuations in the price level would destroy the financial institutions which make our economy so productive. For a monetary economy to operate efficiently, there cannot be perfect price-level flexibility. Thus, the price-level flexibility curve is a curve that reflects a macro-institutional constraint on price-level adjustment; it is not an aggregate supply curve that reflects the aggregate choices of individuals.

Keynes didn't emphasize the point that these real-world institutional constraints on price-level adjustments were not deviations from competitive markets, but were actually necessary institutional constraints imposed by the economy's use of money. That's unfortunate, because his lack of clarity about the role that fixed prices played in his analysis led to an outpouring of discussion about what would happen if there really were price flexibility—discussion that was relevant only to a nonmonetary economy, not a monetary economy like ours.

Most modern macro economists recognize that there are serious problems in using a hypothetical perfectly-competitive economy as a reference point to discuss the macro economics of a monetary economy. That recognition is bringing the previous discussion of the role of fixed wages and prices to an end, and replacing it with discussion of multiple aggregate equilibria and disequilibrium dynamics. The result of that clarification has been that all economists have gained more respect for the role that institutions must play in their analysis.

The modern view is more and more coming to the belief that institutions, such as money, firms, and social conventions, are necessary attributes of an economy and are part of the structural characteristics, or *macrofoundations* of an economy. Those macrofoundations define the economy—but they also impose constraints or limitations on individuals and firms operating within that economy. The existence of these constraints, of which partial price-level rigidity is one, means that it is impossible to analyze the micro economy without a recognition of the constraints imposed by those macrofoundations.

10

The Keynesian Aggregate Production/Aggregate Expenditures Model

Keynes stirred the stale economic frog pond to its depth.
~Gottfried Haberler

After reading this chapter, you should be able to:

1. Explain the difference between induced and autonomous consumption.

2. Show how the level of income is graphically determined in the Keynesian aggregate production/aggregate expenditures model.

3. Use the Keynesian equation to determine equilibrium income.

4. Explain the multiplier process.

5. Relate the Keynesian aggregate production/aggregate expenditures model to the *AS/AD* model.

6. Distinguish between a mechanistic and an interpretative Keynesian model.

Policy fights in economics occur on many levels. Keynes fought on most of them. But it wasn't Keynes who convinced U.S. policy makers to accept his ideas. (Indeed, then-President Roosevelt only met Keynes once and thought he was a pompous academic.) Instead, it was Alvin Hansen, a textbook writer and policy advisor to government who was hired away from the University of Wisconsin by Harvard in the mid-1930s, who played the key role in getting Keynesian economic policies introduced into the United States.

The story of how Hansen converted to Keynes's ideas is somewhat mysterious. At the time, almost all economists were Classicals, and Hansen was no exception. (Otherwise it's doubtful Harvard would have recruited him.) But, somehow, on the train trip from Wisconsin to Massachusetts, Hansen metamorphosized from a Classical to a Keynesian. His graduate seminar at Harvard in the late 1930s and in the 1940s became the U.S. breeding ground for Keynesian economics.

What made Hansen and other economists switch from Classical to Keynesian economics? It was the Depression; the Keynesian story explained it much better than did the Classical real-wage story.

Hansen quickly realized that talking about interdependent shifts of aggregate supply and demand curves didn't work for policy makers and businesspeople. They wanted numbers—specifics—and Keynes's work had no specifics. So Alvin Hansen and his students, especially Paul Samuelson, set about to develop specifics. They developed what is now called the textbook model of Keynesian economics. That textbook model gave the Keynesian ideas a structure embodied in the specific models that policy makers demanded. In the late 1940s, Hansen wrote a book, *A Guide to Keynes*, that was the bible for students studying macro in the 1950s and early 1960s. He also made weekly trips to Washington where he "sold" Keynesian ideas to policy makers.

Hansen's student, Paul Samuelson, wrote a textbook that changed the structure of the economics principles course. Samuelson's text provided an introduction to Keynesian ideas for millions of students throughout the world. At the same time, Dutch and Norwegian economists, including Jan Tinburgen and Ragnar Frisch, developed an empirically-determined macro model that policy makers could use. For their contributions, many in this group won Nobel prizes.

THE TEXTBOOK KEYNESIAN MODEL

In their expositions of Keynesian economics, these policy and textbook economists decided to forget about all the niceties of shapes of the *AS* and *AD* (aggregate supply and aggregate demand) curves. They reasoned: the price level didn't change much in the short run, so why worry about it? Forgetting about the price level let them design a Keynesian model that focused on interdependent shifts in the *AS* and *AD* curves.

The Keynesian model they developed is called the **Aggregate Production/Aggregate Expenditures (AP/AE) Model.** It is called that to separate it from the *AS/AD* model, and to make sure students don't confuse the Keynesian concentration on a shifting aggregate supply and demand (which focuses on total production changes, not on changes in the output caused by price level changes) with the Classical focus on quantity of aggregate supply and demand changes (which result from changes in the price level). In the Keynesian *AP/AE* model, aggregate supply is called "aggregate production." Similarly, economists call the Keynesian concept of aggregate demand "aggregate expenditures" rather than aggregate demand.

The Keynesian *AP/AE* model looks at the relationship between aggregate production and aggregate expenditures. As I will demonstrate below, the *AS/AD* model discussed in the last chapter and the *AP/AE* model are directly related; they both describe the same **income adjustment mechanism** (chase between aggregate supply and demand). That mechanism will be set in motion any time there is aggregate disequilibrium—any time that individuals' planned expenditures differ from firms' planned production. To relate the two models you simply remember that production is another name for supply, that expenditures is another name for demand, and that a shift of a curve in one model is a movement along a curve in the other model.

Q–1: What is the relationship between a change in aggregate production and a change in aggregate supply?

To see Keynes's exposition of the model, we'll start, as Keynes did, by looking separately at production decisions and expenditures decisions.

Aggregate Production in the Keynesian Model

Graphically, aggregate production in the Keynesian model is represented by a 45° line.

Q-2: What is true about the relationship between income and production on the aggregate production curve?

Aggregate production is the total amount of production of all goods and services in every industry in an economy. It is at the center of the Keynesian model. Production creates an equal amount of income, so income and production are always equal; the terms can be used interchangeably.

While aggregate production creates an amount of income equal to that production, it does not necessarily create expenditures equal to that production. Expenditures can be higher or lower than production. Moreover, aggregate production depends on expectations of expenditures. If businesspeople expect high expenditures, they produce a lot; if they expect low expenditures, they produce a little. Keynes's model showed that these expectations of businesspeople can become partially self-fulfilling. Thus, while expectations play no role in production decisions in the Classical model, expectations play a central role in the Keynesian model: Production will be driven by expected expenditures.

Graphically, aggregate production in the Keynesian model is represented by a 45° line on a graph, with real income in dollars measured on the horizontal axis and real production measured in dollars on the vertical axis, as in Exhibit 1. Given the definition of the axes, connecting all the points at which production equals income produces a 45° line through the origin. Since, by definition, production creates an amount of income equal to the amount of production or output, this 45° line is the **aggregate production curve,** or alternatively the aggregate income curve. At all points on the aggregate production curve, income equals production. For example, consider point *A* in Exhibit 1, where income (measured on the horizontal axis) is $4,000 and production (measured on the vertical axis) is also $4,000. That identity between production and income is true only on the 45-degree line. Output and income, however, cannot expand without limit. The model is relevant only when output is below its potential. Once production expands to the capacity constraint of the existing institutional structure—to potential income (line *B*)—no more output expansion is possible. At that point we are no longer in the Keynesian range of the economy.

In Classical analysis, the intersection of the potential income line with the aggregate production line at point *C* would determine expenditures and output. The economy would produce the potential level of output and the income in the economy would be just sufficient to buy the output; in the Classical model, income equals aggregate expenditures. If actual and potential output differed, price flexibility would shift aggregate expenditures until the economy arrived at point *C*.

In the Keynesian model, planned expenditures need not equal production.

Keynes's analysis differs from the Classical analysis because he said that planned aggregate expenditures, while they were related to income, need not be precisely equal to income (production), and if they were not, aggregate supply and demand would start chasing each other; that chase would lead the economy to an undesirable equilibrium. Production brings about equal income, but does not necessarily bring about equal expenditures. Thus, to understand Keynes's argument, one must analyze aggregate expenditures separately from aggregate production.

Aggregate Expenditures in the Keynesian Model

Aggregate expenditures   Total level of expenditures in an economy equals $C + I + G + (X - M)$.

Aggregate expenditures consist of consumption (spending by consumers), investment (spending by business), spending by government, and net foreign spending on U.S. goods (the difference between U.S. exports and U.S. imports). These four components were presented in our earlier discussion of national income accounting, which isn't surprising since the national income accounts were designed around the Keynesian model. We now consider each of those components more carefully.

Consumption   The largest component of expenditures is consumption. While various things affect the level of consumption expenditures, it is most affected by disposable

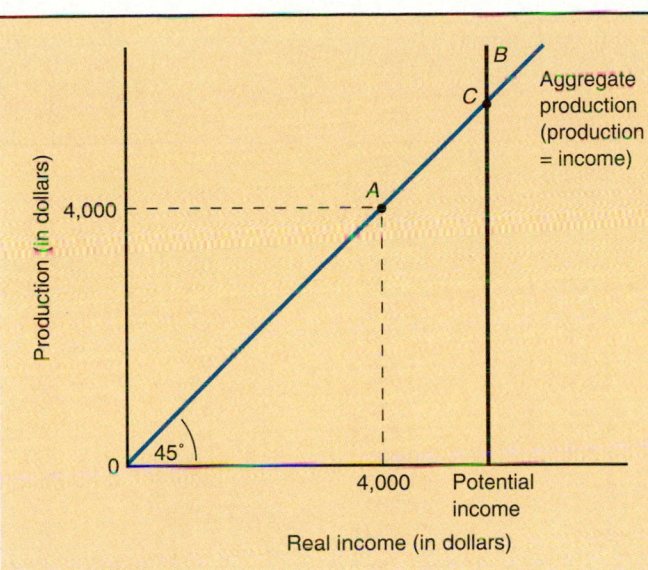

EXHIBIT 1   The Aggregate Production Curve

Since, by definition, output equals income, on each point of the aggregate production curve income must equal production. This equality holds true only on the 45° line.

income. **Disposable income** is that part of income left after paying taxes which, in the simple Keynesian model, are assumed to be constant.

The assumed relationship between consumption and disposable income is reasonable: Most of us look at our disposable income, and then determine how much of it we will spend. Thus in the Keynesian model the central relationship is between consumer spending and disposable income.

Let's consider the consumption decisions of an individual who earned $12,000 and paid $2,000 in taxes last year. That leaves $10,000 in disposable income. Assume $9,000 goes to consumption and $1,000 goes to savings. If next year this person's disposable income rises to $12,000, we would expect consumption also to increase to, say, $10,600. If disposable income fell to $8,000, consumption would fall to $7,400.

Exhibit 2 shows a consumer's entire hypothesized relationship between possible disposable income and consumption levels. Notice that when disposable income is zero, we still assume the person consumes. How? By borrowing or dipping into previous savings. Consumption that would exist at a zero level of disposable income is called **autonomous consumption** (consumption that's unaffected by changes in disposable income). It includes those expenditures a person would make even if he or she were unemployed.

Notice that as disposable income rises, consumption also rises, but not by as much as disposable income. The relationship between changes in disposable income and changes in consumption is shown in columns 2 and 4. The numbers in these columns can be derived from columns 1 and 3. Each entry in column 2 represents the difference between the corresponding entry in column 1 and the entry in the previous row of column 1. Similarly, each entry in column 4 is the difference between the corresponding entry in column 3 and the entry in the previous row of column 3. For example, as disposable income rises from $10,000 to $11,000, the change in disposable income is $1,000. Similarly, as consumption rises from $9,000 to $9,800, the change in consumption is $800.

Since much of Keynes's analysis focuses on changes in expenditures that occur in response to changes in income, it is important to distinguish that portion of consumption that changes in response to changes in income from that portion that does not. As previously stated, that portion of consumption that does not change when income changes is called *autonomous consumption*. **Induced consumption** is consumption that changes as disposable income changes.

The relationship between consumption and disposable income (as in the table in our example) can be expressed more concisely as a **consumption function** (a

Disposable income (Y_d) *Income left over after paying taxes* ($Y_d = Y - T$).

Autonomous consumption (C_0) *Consumption that's unaffected by changes in disposable income.*

1 Autonomous consumption is unrelated to income; induced consumption is directly related to income.

Induced consumption ($mpcY_d$) *Consumption that changes as disposable income changes.*

Consumption function *A functional representation of the relation between consumption and disposable income* ($C = C_0 + mpcY_d$).

EXHIBIT 2   Consumption Related to Disposable Income

(1) Disposable income (Y_d)	(2) Change in disposable income (ΔY_d)	(3) Consumption (C)	(4) Change in consumption (ΔC)	Row
$ 0	—	$ 1,000	—	A
1,000	$1,000	1,800	$800	B
2,000	1,000	2,600	800	C
3,000	1,000	3,400	800	D
4,000	1,000	4,200	800	E
5,000	1,000	5,000	800	F
6,000	1,000	5,800	800	G
7,000	1,000	6,600	800	H
8,000	1,000	7,400	800	I
9,000	1,000	8,200	800	J
10,000	1,000	9,000	800	K
11,000	1,000	9,800	800	L
12,000	1,000	10,600	800	M
13,000	1,000	11,400	800	N
14,000	1,000	12,200	800	O
15,000	1,000	13,000	800	P

THE
GENERAL THEORY
OF
EMPLOYMENT INTEREST
AND MONEY

BY
JOHN MAYNARD KEYNES
FELLOW OF KING'S COLLEGE, CAMBRIDGE

NEW YORK
HARCOURT, BRACE & WORLD, INC.

The General Theory—the book that created macroeconomics as a separate subject.

representation of the relationship between consumption and disposable income as a mathematical function):

$$C = C_0 + mpcY_d$$

where

C = consumption expenditures
C_0 = autonomous consumption
mpc = marginal propensity to consume
Y_d = disposable income

The consumption function corresponding to the table in Exhibit 2 is

$$C = \$1,000 + .8Y_d$$

Notice that if you substitute the data from any row in the table in Exhibit 2, both sides of the consumption function are equal. For example, in row C of Exhibit 2, we see that consumption (C) = $2,600. So $2,600 = $1,000 + .8$Y_d$. Since disposable income (Y_d) = $2,000, we can calculate (.8)($2,000) = $1,600 and add it to $1,000 giving us $2,600. So the two sides are equal.

The Marginal Propensity to Consume   There is one part of the consumption function we haven't talked about yet: the letters mpc (.8 in the numerical example). The letters mpc are the marginal propensity to consume. Keynes was interested in what would happen to consumption spending as disposable income changed. He argued that when disposable income fell by, say $1,000, consumption would fall by somewhat less than that amount ($800 in the example). He defined **marginal propensity to consume (mpc)** as the ratio of a *change* in consumption, ΔC, to a *change* in disposable income, ΔY_d. (The Greek letter Δ, or delta, which corresponds to the letter D in our alphabet, is commonly used to designate *change in.*) The mpc is the fraction consumed from an additional dollar of disposable income.

$$mpc = \frac{\text{Change in consumption}}{\text{Change in disposable income}} = \frac{\Delta C}{\Delta Y_d}$$

Using the data in Exhibit 2, let's determine the level of the mpc by dividing a change in consumption by a corresponding change in disposable income:

$$mpc = \frac{\Delta C}{\Delta Y_d} = \frac{\$800}{\$1,000} = .8$$

Marginal propensity to consume (mpc)   The fraction consumed from an additional dollar of disposable income.

Q–3: If consumption changes by $60 when income changes by $100, what is the mpc?

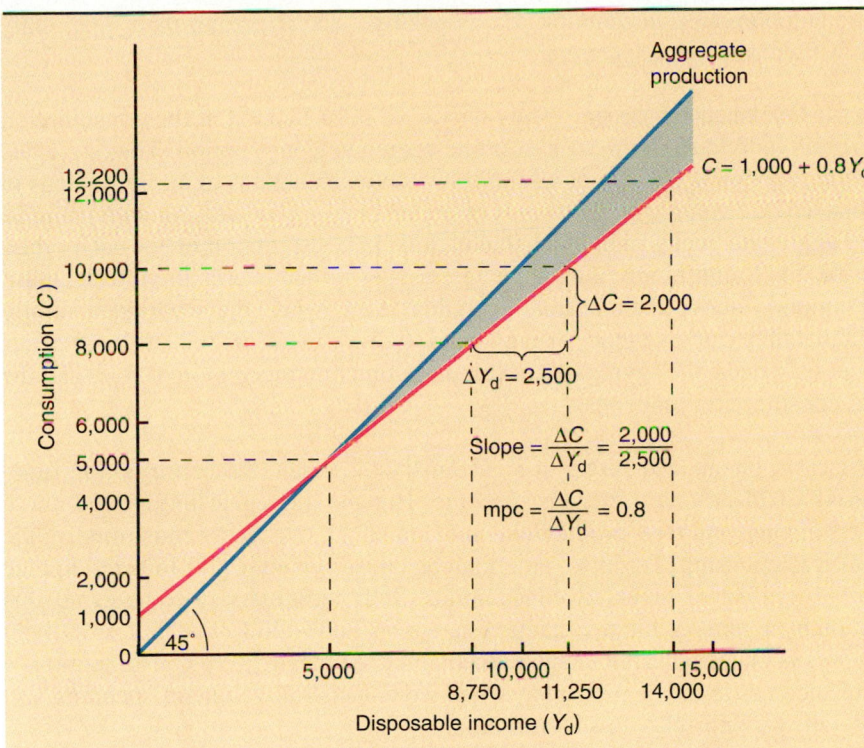

EXHIBIT 3   Graph of Consumption Function

The consumption function graphed here represents the function derived from the information in Exhibit 2. It has a slope of .8, the mpc, and an intercept of 1,000, the level of autonomous consumption. The shaded area is savings, the difference between income and consumption.

Based on figures for consumption and disposable income for Britain at the time, Keynes estimated that the mpc was between .8 and .9. That estimate is not central to his argument, as long as the mpc remains between zero and one.

Graphing the Consumption Function   Now that we're familiar with the components and terminology used with the consumption function, let's see how to graph it. Exhibit 3 graphs the particular consumption function represented by

$$C = \$1,000 + .8Y_d$$

Notice that at zero disposable income, consumption is $1,000. This is the autonomous portion of consumption.

The consumption function's slope tells us how much consumption changes with a particular change in disposable income. In other words, the slope of a consumption function graphically represents the marginal propensity to consume for a total particular consumption function.

The apc and the mpc   Besides the marginal propensity to consume, there's one other term you need to know, both because we'll use it in the future and because it will help cement your understanding of mpc. That term is the **average propensity to consume (apc),** defined as consumption divided by disposable income:

Average propensity to consume (apc)   Consumption divided by disposable income.

$$apc = \frac{\text{Consumption}}{\text{Disposable income}} = \frac{C}{Y_d}$$

For example, if disposable income is 400, and consumption is 370, apc = 370/400 = .925. Alternatively, if disposable income is 500 and consumption is 450, apc = .9.

Notice that the apc changes as income changes. That makes it different from mpc. (By assumption, mpc is constant at all levels of income.) The reason is the constant term, C_0, in the consumption function. (The subscript $_0$ is used throughout the book to indicate what a term such as C will equal when the variable it depends on—in this case, Y_d—is zero.) The relationship between apc and mpc is given by

Q–4:   If the mpc is constant, the apc will also be constant. True or false? Why?

$$apc = \frac{C_0}{Y_d} + mpc$$

As long as autonomous consumption, C_0, is positive, apc is greater than mpc. Only when $C_0 = 0$ are mpc and apc equal.

The Aggregate Consumption Function   Thus far we've been looking at the consumption function for an individual. Now let's examine aggregate consumption. The aggregate consumption function is the sum of all the consumption functions of all individuals in society. Instead of dealing with thousands of dollars, we're now dealing with trillions.

In the aggregate, many individual fluctuations in consumption offset each other. For example, the Smith family may have an emergency that causes them to increase their consumption above their normal spending level, while the Rodriguez family might find that they can save more than planned. Offsetting events such as these occur all the time; they make the aggregate consumption function much more stable than the individual consumption functions.

Disposable Income, Income, and Taxes   It's customary to present the consumption function in terms of disposable (after-tax) income. But the aggregate production curve relates total income and total production, so to make the two fit we must modify the consumption relationship. To do so, autonomous consumption, C_0, is lowered to take account of the effect of taxes on consumption. It is customary, too, to avoid this complication by assuming initially that taxes are zero, and we'll follow this simplification. This means that disposable income and income are identical, so consumption is a function of income. In the next chapter, when we consider government spending and taxes in detail, we will relax this assumption.

Consumption and Savings   Given our assumptions, what people don't consume, they save. Since the aggregate production curve tells us the income that people have, and the consumption function tells us how much they spend, the difference between the two is how much they save. The amount of savings is shown by the shaded area in Exhibit 3. There is no savings at income level $5,000, where expenditures equal income (where the consumption function crosses the aggregate production curve). At lower levels of income, savings is negative; at higher levels of income, savings is positive.

The Keynesian model can be pictured as a combination of injections into and withdrawals from the economy.

Savings, the mps, and the aps   You know from the circular flow diagram that when all individuals spend all their income (which they derive from production), the aggregate economy is in equilibrium. *Injections* into the system will equal *withdrawals* from the system. In this simple Keynesian model, savings represent withdrawals; autonomous expenditures represent injections.

The circular flow diagram expresses the national income identity: aggregate income equals aggregate output. Keynes asked: (1) does aggregate expenditures always equal aggregate production? and (2) if not, what will happen in the economy to bring them into equilibrium? Since individuals save some of their income, expenditures and income need not be equal. The question is: Are the savings translated back into expenditures? If they aren't, injections will not equal withdrawals and income will have to change. Thus, in the hypothesized relationship, and in the economy, savings play an important role. What people don't consume, they save. Specifically,

$$\text{Savings} = \text{Disposable income} - \text{Consumption}$$

If savings is translated back into expenditures, no adjustment is necessary. If savings is not translated back into expenditures, the aggregate economy will not be in equilibrium.

As with consumption, we can use a savings table and savings function to show the relationship between savings and income. Exhibit 4 presents the savings table and graph of the savings function corresponding to the relationships for consumption in Exhibits 2 and 3.

You can see that the amount saved increases as income increases—the higher the level of income, the higher the level of savings. For example, as income goes up from

EXHIBIT 4 (a and b)   Savings Table, Savings Function, and Consumption Function

The information in the table (a) can be translated into a graph. That is done in (b). In the bottom half of (b) you can see the relationship between the savings curve and the difference between the consumption function and the aggregate production curve.

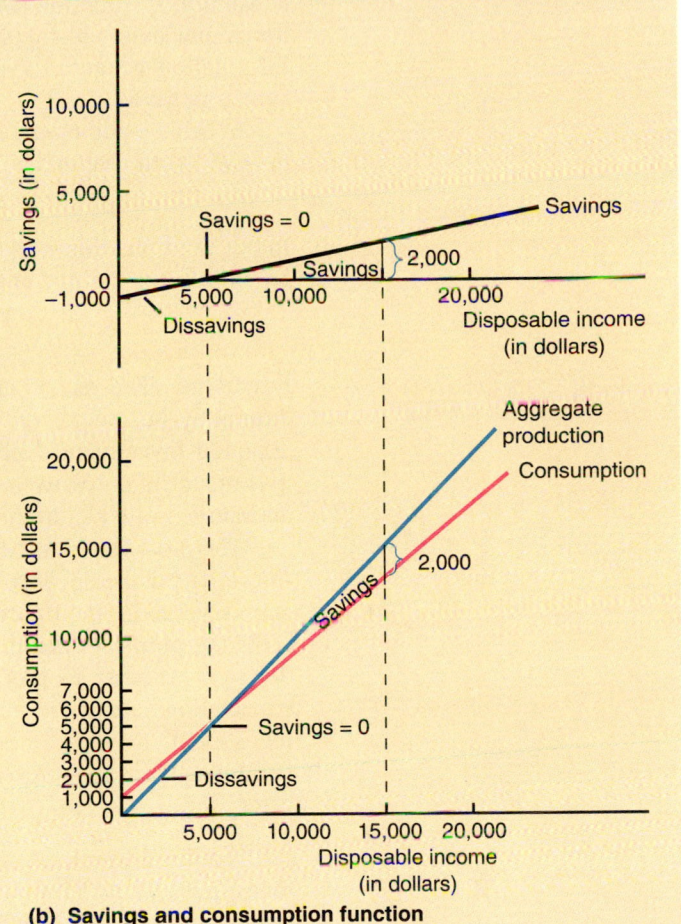

(1) Disposable income (Y_d)	(2) Change in disposable income (ΔY_d)	(3) Savings (S)	(4) Change in savings (ΔS)	Row
0	—	−1,000	—	A
1,000	1,000	−800	200	B
2,000	1,000	−600	200	C
3,000	1,000	−400	200	D
4,000	1,000	−200	200	E
5,000	1,000	0	200	F
6,000	1,000	200	200	G
7,000	1,000	400	200	H
8,000	1,000	600	200	I
9,000	1,000	800	200	J
10,000	1,000	1,000	200	K
11,000	1,000	1,200	200	L
12,000	1,000	1,400	200	M
13,000	1,000	1,600	200	N
14,000	1,000	1,800	200	O
15,000	1,000	2,000	200	P

(a) Savings table

(b) Savings and consumption function

$10,000 to $11,000 (rows *K* and *L* of column 1), savings rises from $1,000 to $1,200 (rows *K* and *L* of column 3).

Column 2 shows the change in disposable income, and column 4 shows the change in savings that occurs as income increases from one row to another. In the example, the change in disposable income was $1,000 and the change in savings was $200.

Just as we defined mpc and apc with the consumption function, so too can we define **marginal propensity to save (mps)** and **average propensity to save (aps).**

The mps is the percentage saved from an additional dollar of disposable income:

$$mps = \frac{\text{Change in savings}}{\text{Change in disposable income}} = \frac{\Delta S}{\Delta Y_d}$$

The aps is savings divided by disposable income:

$$aps = \frac{\text{Savings}}{\text{Disposable income}} = \frac{S}{Y_d}$$

The aps changes with disposable income. If disposable income is $10,000, the aps = 1,000/10,000 = .1. If disposable income is $15,000, savings is $2,000, so aps = 2,000/15,000 = 0.133.

The top half of Exhibit 4(b) graphs the savings function. Notice that it is an upward-sloping function whose slope equals the mps and whose intercept (the point where it crosses the vertical axis) is negative. In this example it is −$1,000.

The consumption function and the savings function are related. The bottom half of Exhibit 4(b) shows the consumption function presented earlier. By extending the income levels between the two graphs you can see that the distance between the

Marginal propensity to save (mps)   The percentage saved from an additional dollar of disposable income.

Average propensity to save (aps)   Savings divided by disposable income.

Both the savings function and the consumption function show the same information.

consumption function and the production curve equals the distance between the horizontal axis and the savings function. Each function provides us with the same information because savings is the mirror image of consumption. What isn't consumed is saved.

When we add up the marginal propensity to consume and the marginal propensity to save, we arrive at 1:

$$mpc + mps = 1$$

Q–5: The *mpc + aps* = 1. True or False? Explain.

In our example, this works. Since *mpc* = .8 and *mps* = .2, the sum equals 1. The same holds true for the *apc* and *aps:*

$$aps + apc = 1$$

Investment   Expenditures by business on plants and equipment.

Investment

The second component of aggregate expenditures is **investment** (expenditures by businesses on plants and equipment). To keep his model simple, Keynes assumed investment depends on the "animal spirits of investors." In other words, investment is *autonomous;* it's independent of the level of disposable income and is determined outside the model.

The most important determinant of autonomous investment is expectations of the future. If businesspeople think the future will be good, they will invest; if they get depressed about the future, they will not invest. For example, this text and ancillaries costs the publisher about $1,000,000 to develop and bring to market. Ultimately the decision whether to proceed or not fell on the CEO's shoulders, and the CEO's expectations about the future played a key role in the decision to go ahead with the investment.

Investment is represented by

$$I = I_0$$

Exhibit 5(a) relates society's income and investment. It represents the amount all firms invest at each level of income. As you can see, the amount of investment doesn't change in response to income changes. Exhibit 5(b) graphs the relationship between investment and income. The relationship is simply the function I = $1,000. Notice that the investment function is a perfectly horizontal line. That means the investment function's slope is zero. When income is $0, investment is $1,000; when income is $5,000, investment is still $1,000. That's because in order to keep the model simple, investment is assumed to be independent of income; that's the meaning of a graphical zero slope.

Just as autonomous consumption can change, so can autonomous investment. Keynes believed investment could shift around a lot, just as he believed the consumption function was capable of shifting. As we'll see shortly, it was precisely those sudden, unexpected shifts in investment spending that Keynes saw as the cause of booms as well as recessions. He also believed investment would be influenced by other variables such as the interest rate, but he didn't include these other influences in the simple model.

Government Expenditures

To keep this first look at the Keynesian model simple, let's also assume government spending is autonomous. That is, it does not change as income changes. Therefore the general equation for government spending on goods and services would be

$$G = G_0$$

which is represented graphically as a horizontal line, just like the investment function. We will assume G_0 = $1,000.

Net exports   A country's exports minus its imports.

Net Exports

When people in the United States spend their income on foreign imports (M), the expenditures are lost to the U.S. economy. However, when foreigners spend their income on U.S. exports (X), that spending adds to U.S. expenditures. The

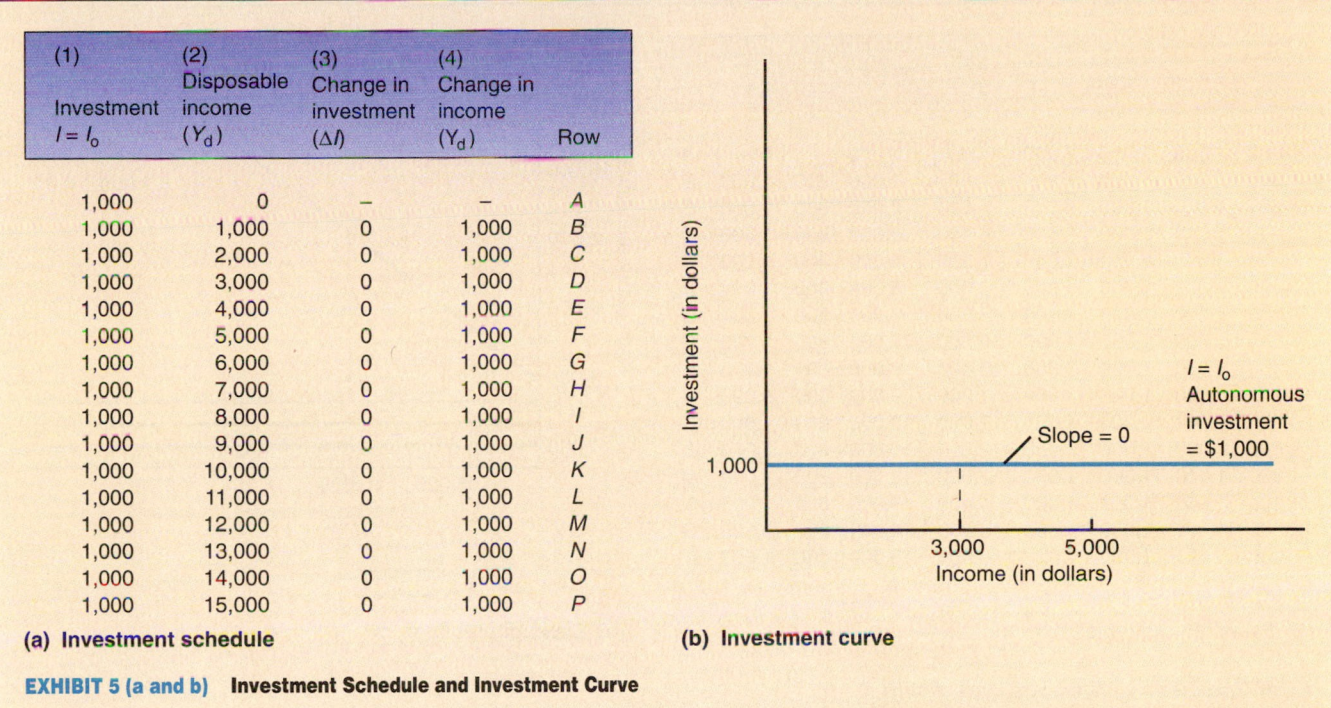

(1) Investment $I = I_0$	(2) Disposable income (Y_d)	(3) Change in investment (ΔI)	(4) Change in income (Y_d)	Row
1,000	0	—	—	A
1,000	1,000	0	1,000	B
1,000	2,000	0	1,000	C
1,000	3,000	0	1,000	D
1,000	4,000	0	1,000	E
1,000	5,000	0	1,000	F
1,000	6,000	0	1,000	G
1,000	7,000	0	1,000	H
1,000	8,000	0	1,000	I
1,000	9,000	0	1,000	J
1,000	10,000	0	1,000	K
1,000	11,000	0	1,000	L
1,000	12,000	0	1,000	M
1,000	13,000	0	1,000	N
1,000	14,000	0	1,000	O
1,000	15,000	0	1,000	P

(a) Investment schedule

(b) Investment curve

EXHIBIT 5 (a and b)   Investment Schedule and Investment Curve

In the table in (a) you can see that the amount of investment does not change with changes in income. It is autonomous—determined outside of the model. That's why there is no change in investment as income changes. Because investment is not affected by changes in income, the investment curve graphed in (b) will have a slope of zero.

common convention is to subtract imports from exports and to talk about **net exports** $(X - M)$. When net exports are positive, exports exceed imports; when net exports are negative, imports exceed exports.

Again, to keep the Keynesian model simple at this point, we assume net exports are autonomous—net exports do not change as income changes. The equation is

$$X - M = X_0 - M_0$$

Since they are autonomous, net exports are graphically represented by a horizontal line, just like the graphs of investment and government spending. To keep the analysis simple, we will assume that net exports are also constant at $1,000.

Aggregate Expenditures *Aggregate expenditures* (AE) is the summation of all four components of expenditures:

$$AE = \text{Aggregate expenditures} = C + I + G + (X - M)$$

$AE = C + I + G + (X - M)$.

Exhibit 6(a) lists the values of each expenditure at a different level of income, or production, as discussed in the preceding several sections. The summation of expenditures, aggregate expenditures, is in column 5. Notice that, by assumption in our example, the only induced expenditure that changes as income changes is consumption.

As you can see in Exhibit 6(b), the aggregate expenditures curve is the graphical sum of all four expenditures curves, and it has the same slope, mpc = 0.8, as the consumption function. Notice that the aggregate expenditures curve crosses the vertical axis at a point that's the sum of all four autonomous expenditures: $C_0 + I_0 + G_0 + (X_0 - M_0) = \$4,000$. A good exercise to help you visualize the relationships involved here is to compare the data in the columns in the table with points on the graph to see how they correspond.

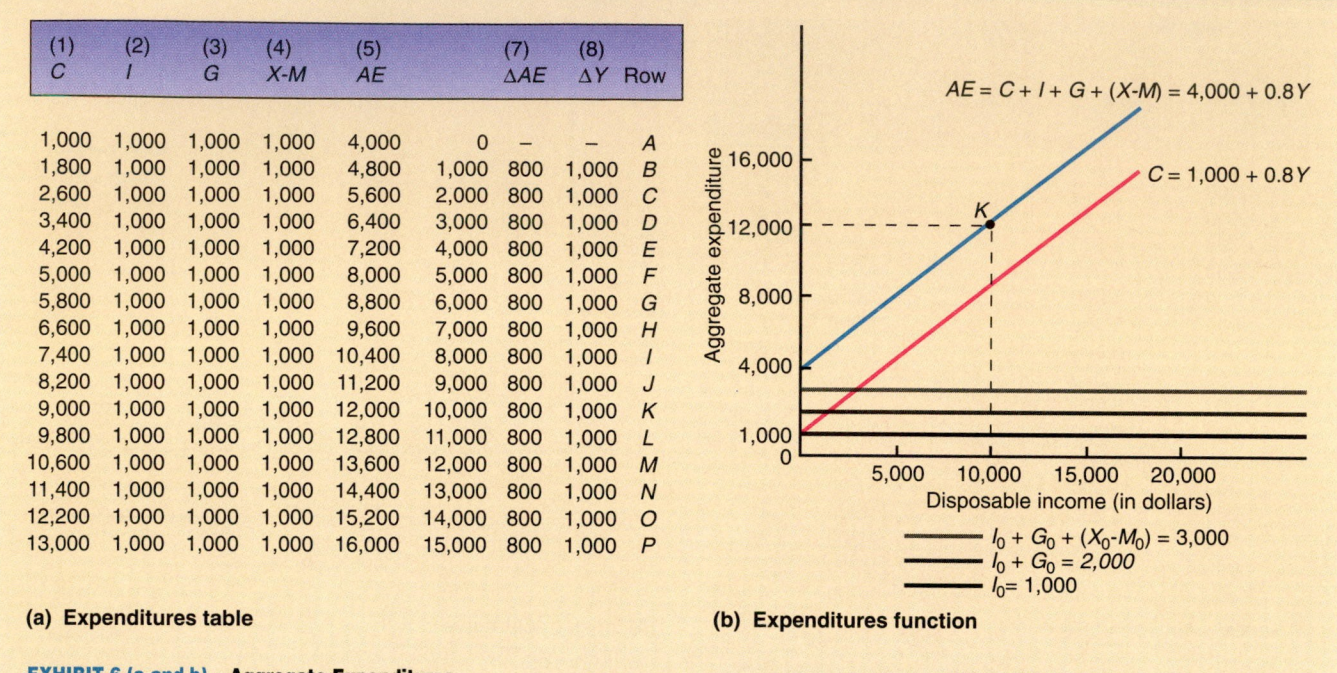

(1) C	(2) I	(3) G	(4) X-M	(5) AE	(7) ΔAE	(8) ΔY	Row
1,000	1,000	1,000	1,000	4,000	0	–	–	A
1,800	1,000	1,000	1,000	4,800	1,000	800	1,000	B
2,600	1,000	1,000	1,000	5,600	2,000	800	1,000	C
3,400	1,000	1,000	1,000	6,400	3,000	800	1,000	D
4,200	1,000	1,000	1,000	7,200	4,000	800	1,000	E
5,000	1,000	1,000	1,000	8,000	5,000	800	1,000	F
5,800	1,000	1,000	1,000	8,800	6,000	800	1,000	G
6,600	1,000	1,000	1,000	9,600	7,000	800	1,000	H
7,400	1,000	1,000	1,000	10,400	8,000	800	1,000	I
8,200	1,000	1,000	1,000	11,200	9,000	800	1,000	J
9,000	1,000	1,000	1,000	12,000	10,000	800	1,000	K
9,800	1,000	1,000	1,000	12,800	11,000	800	1,000	L
10,600	1,000	1,000	1,000	13,600	12,000	800	1,000	M
11,400	1,000	1,000	1,000	14,400	13,000	800	1,000	N
12,200	1,000	1,000	1,000	15,200	14,000	800	1,000	O
13,000	1,000	1,000	1,000	16,000	15,000	800	1,000	P

(a) Expenditures table

(b) Expenditures function

EXHIBIT 6 (a and b) Aggregate Expenditures

Aggregate expenditures are the sum of all the components of expenditures. These can be added numerically in the table, as they are in (a), or graphically, as they are in (b). Notice that the table and the graph correspond. For example, in row K of the table, aggregate expenditures are $12,000, just as they are at point K, which graphs expenditures at income $10,000.

DETERMINING THE LEVEL OF AGGREGATE INCOME

2 To determine income graphically in the Keynesian AP/AE model, you find the income level at which aggregate expenditures equal aggregate production.

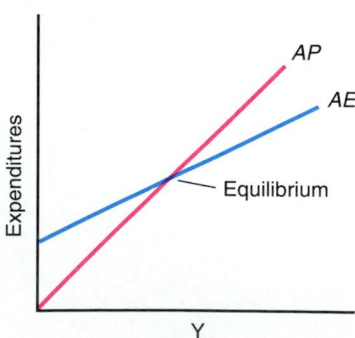

Solving for Equilibrium Graphically

Now that we've developed the graphical framework (the aggregate production/aggregate expenditure, or *AP/AE*, framework), we can put the two together and see how the level of aggregate income is determined in the Keynesian model. We begin by representing a different aggregate expenditures curve and the aggregate production curve on the same graph, as in Exhibit 7.

The aggregate production curve is the 45° line. It tells you the level of aggregate production and also the level of aggregate income since, by definition, income equals production. Expenditures, which do not necessarily equal production or income, are represented by the aggregate expenditures curve. Let's now take a closer look at the relationship between the *AE* and *AP* curves.

Let's first say that income is $12,000. As you can see, at income of $12,000, expenditures are $11,400. Aggregate income exceeds aggregate expenditures. This is true for any income level above $10,000. Similarly, at all income levels below $10,000, aggregate production is less than aggregate expenditures. For example, at a production level of $8,000, aggregate expenditures are $8,600.

The only income level at which aggregate production equals aggregate expenditures is $10,000. Since we know that, in equilibrium, aggregate expenditures must equal aggregate production, $10,000 is the equilibrium level of income in the economy. It is the level of income at which neither producers nor consumers have any reason to change what they are doing. At any other level of income, since there is either a shortage or a surplus of goods, there will be incentive to change. Thus, you can use the aggregate production curve and the aggregate expenditures curve to determine the level of income at which the economy will be in equilibrium.

Let's go through another example. Say the consumption function is

$$C = \$400 + .75Y$$

Government spending is $200. Investment is $100 and net exports are $50. What is the equilibrium level of income in this economy? Exhibit 8 shows the aggregate expendi-

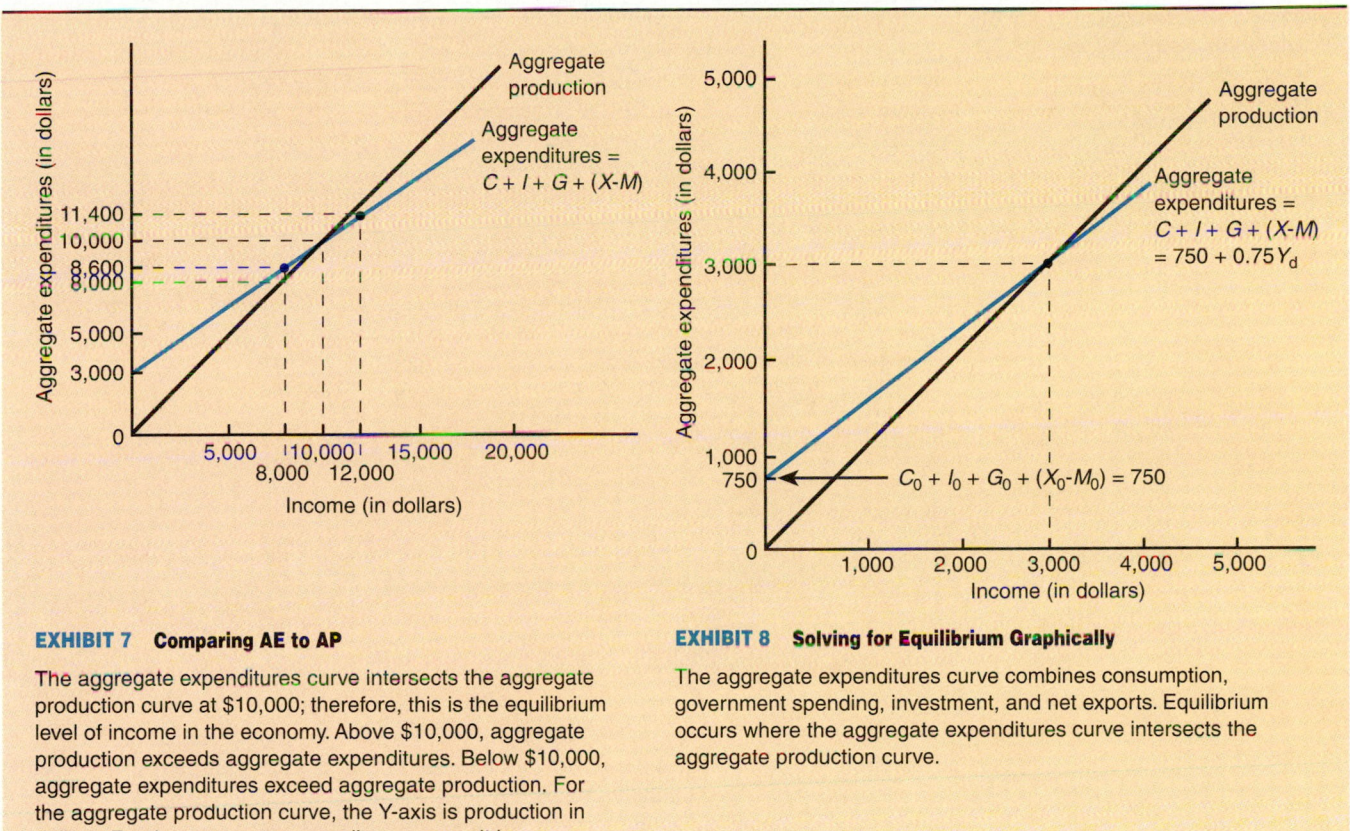

EXHIBIT 7   Comparing AE to AP

The aggregate expenditures curve intersects the aggregate production curve at $10,000; therefore, this is the equilibrium level of income in the economy. Above $10,000, aggregate production exceeds aggregate expenditures. Below $10,000, aggregate expenditures exceed aggregate production. For the aggregate production curve, the Y-axis is production in dollars. For the aggregate expenditures curve, it is expenditures in dollars.

EXHIBIT 8   Solving for Equilibrium Graphically

The aggregate expenditures curve combines consumption, government spending, investment, and net exports. Equilibrium occurs where the aggregate expenditures curve intersects the aggregate production curve.

tures curve and the aggregate production curve that go with these numbers. In it you can see that the equilibrium income is $3,000. This is the only income level where aggregate expenditures equal aggregate production.

Another way to determine the level of income in the Keynesian model (a way that's useful to know) is through the **Keynesian equation,** which tells us that income equals the multiplier times autonomous expenditures.

$$Y = (Multiplier)(Autonomous\ Expenditures)$$

The Keynesian equation does not come out of thin air. It comes from combining the set of equations underlying the graphical presentation of the Keynesian model into the two brackets. The Keynesian equation is derived in the accompanying box.

The multiplier captures the key aspect of the Keynesian model that differentiates it from the Classical model. Specifically, the **multiplier** tells us how much income will change in response to a change in autonomous expenditures.

To calculate the multiplier, you divide 1 by the marginal propensity to save (1 minus the marginal propensity to consume). Thus:

$$Multiplier = 1/mps = 1/(1 - mpc)$$

Once you know the value of the marginal propensity to consume, you can calculate the multiplier by reducing $[1/(1 - mpc)]$ to a simple number. For example, if $mpc = .8$, the multiplier is

$$1/(1 - .8) = 1/.2 = 5$$

The multiplier provided precisely the relationship policy makers needed. It gave them something specific. It gave them an intuitive story of why the Depression

Determining the Level of Aggregate Income with the Keynesian Equation

Keynesian equation   Equation showing the relationship between autonomous expenditures and the equilibrium level of income. Y = (multiplier)(autonomous expenditure).

The Multiplier

Multiplier   A number that tells us how much income will change in response to a change in autonomous expenditures. [1/(1 − mpc)].

Q–6:   If the *mpc* = .5, what is the multiplier?

SOLVING FOR EQUILIBRIUM INCOME ALGEBRAICALLY

For those of you who are mathematically inclined, the Keynesian equation can be derived by combining the equations presented in the text algebraically to arrive at the equation for income. Rewriting the expenditures relationships, and letting $b = $ the *mpc*, we have:

$$C = C_0 + bY$$
$$I = I_0$$
$$G = G_0$$
$$(X - M) = (X_0 - M_0)$$

Aggregate production, by definition, equals aggregate income (Y) and, in equilibrium, aggregate income must equal the four components of aggregate expenditures. Beginning with the national income accounting identity, we have

$$Y = C + I + G + (X - M)$$

Substituting the terms from the first four equations, we have

$$Y = C_0 + bY + I_0 + G_0 + X_0 - M_0$$

Subtracting bY from both sides,

$$Y - bY = C_0 + I_0 + G_0 + X_0 - M_0$$

To arrive at the Keynesian equation we factor out Y:

$$Y(1 - b) = C_0 + I_0 + G_0 + (X_0 - M_0)$$

Now solve for Y by dividing both sides by $(1 - b)$:

$$Y = \underset{multiplier}{[1/(1 - b)]} \ \underset{autonomous \ expenditure}{[C_0 + I_0 + G_0 + (X_0 - M_0)]}$$

This is the Keynesian equation. It embodies all the equations that went into the Keynesian model. When we combine a group of related equations into a single equation, as we did here, that single equation is called a *reduced-form equation.*

---

occurred and, as we will see in the next chapter, it gave them a story of how certain policies can change it. The story went as follows: When the stock market crashed, businesspeople and consumers got scared and cut their investment (remember, investment is spending) and consumption. Aggregate expenditures decreased. That decrease sent the multiplier into action. It induced businesses to further decrease production (shift supply back), which lowered income and induced a further decrease in aggregate expenditures. This cumulative downward spiral of expenditures was the multiplier process. The multiplier story made sense to policy makers and, hence, played a big role in the acceptance of Keynesian economics into policy.

Since the multiplier tells you the relationship between autonomous expenditures and income, once you know the multiplier, calculating the equilibrium level of income is easy. All you do is multiply autonomous expenditures by the multiplier. For example, if autonomous expenditures are $4,000 and the multiplier is 5, equilibrium income in the economy will be $20,000.

3 To determine income using the Keynesian equation, you determine the multiplier and multiply it by the level of autonomous expenditures.

Let's see how the equation works by considering our previous example. In it the *mpc* was .75. Subtracting .75 from 1 gives .25. Dividing 1 by .25 gives 4. (Remember, dividing 1 by 0.25 is asking how many 1/4ths there are in 1.) So our first term is 4. In that example, autonomous consumption (C_0) was $400; investment ($I_0$) was $100; government spending (G_0) was $200; and net exports ($X_0 - M_0$) were $50. Adding these up gives $750. The Keynesian equation tells us to multiply this total autonomous expenditures, $750, by 4. Doing so gives $4 \times \$750 = \$3,000$, the same answer we got graphically.

The Keynesian equation gives you a simple way to determine equilibrium income in the Keynesian model. You determine the multiplier $[1/(1 - mpc)]$ and multiply it by the sum of all autonomous expenditures. Five different marginal propensities to consume and the multiplier associated with each are shown in the table below.

Notice as mpc increases, the multiplier increases. Knowing the multiplier associated with each marginal propensity to consume gives you an easy way to determine equilibrium income in the economy.

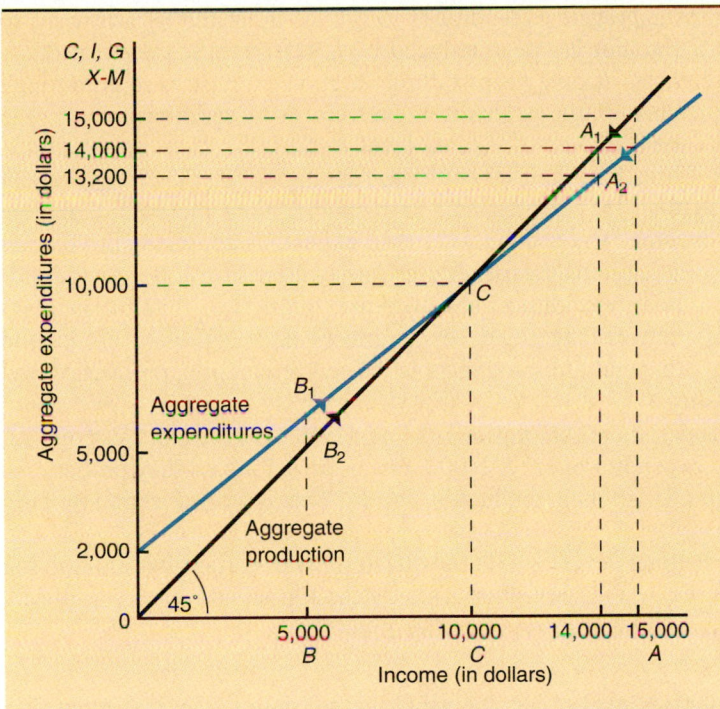

EXHIBIT 9   The Income Adjustment Mechanism

At income levels A and B, the economy is in disequilibrium. Depending on which direction the disequilibrium goes, it generates increases or decreases in production and expenditures until the economy reaches income level C, where aggregate expenditures equal aggregate production.

Marginal Propensities to Consume and Multipliers

mpc	multiplier = $1/(1 - mpc)$
.5	2
.75	4
.8	5
.9	10
.95	20

Let's look at one more example of the multiplier. Say that the *mpc* is .8 but that autonomous expenditures are $4,500 instead of $4,000. What is the level of income? Multiplying the sum of autonomous expenditures, $4,500, by 5 tells us that income is $22,500. With a multiplier of 5, income rises by $2,500 because of the $500 increase in autonomous expenditures.

The preceding discussion provides a technical method of determining equilibrium income in the Keynesian model. But it doesn't help us understand what the model means for the economy and what forces are operating to ensure that the income level we determined is the equilibrium income level. For it to be the equilibrium level of income, there must be adjustment forces that push the economy toward that equilibrium whenever the economy is not in equilibrium. Let's now discuss those forces. Let's ask what happens when the macroeconomy is in disequilibrium—when aggregate production does not equal aggregate expenditures. Exhibit 9 shows us.

Let's first consider the economy at income level A where aggregate production equals $15,000 and aggregate expenditure equals $14,000. Since production exceeds expenditures by $1,000 at income level A, firms can't sell all they produce; inventories pile up. In response, firms make an adjustment. They decrease aggregate production and hence income. As businesses slow production, the economy moves inward along the aggregate production curve as shown by arrow A_1. As income falls, the gap between aggregate production and aggregate expenditures decreases. For example, say businesses decrease aggregate production to $14,000. Aggregate income also falls

Q–7: If autonomous expenditures are $2,000 and the *mpc* = .75, what is the level of income in the economy?

A Closer Look at the Income Adjustment Mechanism

4 The multiplier process works because when expenditures don't equal production, businesspeople change production, which changes income, which changes expenditures, which . . . .

to $14,000, which causes aggregate expenditures to fall, as indicated by arrow A_2, to $13,200. There's still a gap, but it's been reduced by $200, from $1,000 to $800.

Since a gap still remains, income keeps falling. A good exercise is to go through two more steps. With each step, the economy moves closer to equilibrium.

Now let's consider the economy at income level B ($5,000). Here production is less than expenditures. Firms find their inventory is running down. (Their investment in inventory is far less than they'd planned.) In response, they increase aggregate production and hence income. The economy starts to expand as aggregate production moves along arrow B_2 and aggregate expenditures move along arrow B_1. As individuals' income increases, their expenditures also increase, but by less than the increase in income, so the gap between aggregate expenditures and aggregate production decreases. But as long as expenditures and income exceed production, production and hence income keep rising.

Finally, let's consider the economy at income level C, $10,000. At point C, income is $10,000 and expenditures are $10,000. Firms are selling all they produce, so they have no reason to change their production levels. The aggregate economy is in equilibrium.

The equilibrium income level is what we determined earlier by multiplying autonomous expenditures by the multiplier. This discussion should give you insight into what's behind the arithmetic of those earlier models.

SHIFTS IN AUTONOMOUS EXPENDITURES

Determining the equilibrium level of income using the multiplier is an important first step in understanding Keynes's analysis. The second step is to modify that analysis to answer a question that interested Keynes more: How much would a change in autonomous expenditures change the equilibrium level of income? This second step is important since it was precisely those sudden changes in autonomous expenditures Keynes said caused the aggregate disequilibrium, and it was these sudden changes he said the Classical model couldn't handle.

Because Keynes felt autonomous expenditures are subject to sudden shifts, I was careful to point out *autonomous* meant "determined outside the model and not affected by income." Autonomous expenditures can, and do, shift for a variety of other reasons. When they do, the adjustment process is continually being called into play. Let's consider some reasons autonomous expenditures shift.

Shifts in Autonomous Consumption

For example, autonomous consumption can shift because of natural disasters such as the Midwest floods and California earthquake in 1993 (which cause people on average to consume more), but the most important reason it shifts is due to changes in people's expectations about the future. When consumers are confident, the consumption function shifts up. When consumers are scared about the future (as happened in late 1991 and early 1992), the consumption function shifts down. When consumers feel good about the future (as happened in late 1993 and early 1994), the consumption function shifts up. The aggregate expenditures curve shifts up or down accordingly.

Because autonomous consumption shifts around so much, economists measure consumer confidence carefully. These measurements play a large role in economists' estimates of what is likely to happen in the economy.

Shifts in the Investment Function

Another expenditure Keynes believed was continually shifting is the investment function. Reasons the investment function shifts include:

1. Changes in interest rates.
2. Changes in expectations.
3. Technological developments.

Changes in Interest Rates   Keynes believed the interest rate is determined by supply and demand for money, not, as the Classicals believed, by supply and demand for investment. However, Keynes argued the interest rate helps to determine the amount of investment and hence aggregate expenditures. He agreed with the Classicals that as interest rates fall, investment tends to rise. Since the interest rate is the cost of borrowing, when it's cheaper to borrow, you borrow and invest more.

Classical economists believed that interest rate changes would be sufficient to adjust the level of investment so that aggregate expenditures would always equal aggregate production. This belief was based on Say's law. When people saved, financial markets translated that savings into investment, thereby keeping the economy at full employment. Keynes, on the other hand, believed that if for some reason the supply and demand for money caused the interest rate to fall, the lower interest rate would stimulate investments, which in turn would shift up the investment function, the aggregate expenditures function, and equilibrium income. This relationship is the basis of the Keynes effect discussed in the previous chapter.

Notice, however, the difference between the Keynesian view and the Classical view. In the Keynesian view, the monetary sector and real sector are connected; the interest rate is determined in the monetary sector, and that interest rate affects the real sector. In the Classical model, the interest rate is determined in the real sector. It reflects real, not monetary, forces.

In the Keynesian view the real and monetary sectors are connected; in the Classical view they are not.

Changes in Expectations Keynes saw expectations of future sales and profits as the most important determinant of investment demand. When businesspeople expect sales to be good, they invest a lot; when they expect sales to be poor, they cut back on investment.

Keynes believed these expectations could be highly unstable. They were based on rumors, beliefs about future tax policy, and world events. To convey a sense of unpredictability to the expectations, he called them *animal spirits*.

Keynes believed expectations were highly unstable.

For Keynes, unpredictability was not irrationality. Some things in life, he argued, are unpredictable. Future demand for your product was one of these things. Thus, basing your decision on rumors and guesses was the best you could do; it wasn't irrational.

Technological Developments A third major cause of shifts in the investment function is technological developments. When a new technology develops, it makes the old technology obsolete. Firms using that old technology find they can't compete; to keep up they must invest in the new technology. Some economists define periods in economic history by technological development and the investment resulting from that technological development. For example, the 1880s was the railroad period.

A recent major technological advance is the computer revolution beginning in the 1960s. In the 1990s, the biotechnological revolution could dwarf the effects of the computer revolution. These technological advances open up new opportunities and generate large amounts of investment by making past investment obsolete. As investment increases, aggregate expenditures and aggregate income increase.

Shifts in Government Expenditures

In the same way that private expenditures can shift, so too can government expenditures. During a war, government expenditures can increase significantly. In peacetime, government defense expenditures can fall. As we'll see in the next chapter, government's desire to affect the level of income is another reason government expenditures can change.

Shifts in Autonomous Imports and Exports

Even if expenditures within a country are stable, outside expenditures often are not. A war or a shift in political alignments can totally change flows of exports and imports. For example, World Wars I and II brought U.S. trade with Germany to a halt, but significantly increased U.S. exports to other countries. The U.S. economy boomed. The depression in Europe in the middle and late 1920s cut back on European imports from the United States, significantly decreasing U.S. exports and further pushing the U.S. economy into a recession. In the 1990s, the events in the former Soviet Union lowered U.S. exports and lowered Eastern European countries' exports even more. We already know from history that exchange rates and tariff policies impact both imports and exports. All these changes show up as shifts in the autonomous expenditures curve.

Shifts in Autonomous Expenditures and Keynes's Model

To give you a sense of how Keynes saw his model working, let's say that for some reason there is a shock to the economy, decreasing aggregate expenditures so that aggregate production is greater than aggregate expenditures. Suppliers can't sell all they produce. Their reaction, Keynes argued, would be to lay off workers and decrease output. That response would solve the problem if only one firm was in disequilibrium, but wouldn't solve the problem if all firms were in disequilibrium. When *all* producers respond in this fashion, aggregate income, and hence aggregate expenditures, will also fall. The suppliers' cutback will simply start a vicious cycle, which is multiplied. As the laid-off workers cut their expenditures, producers will cut back production, laying off more workers. The economy will enter into a downward spiral with aggregate production and expenditures chasing each other. The result will be an economic depression.

Will the downward spiral ever end? Keynes argued that eventually it would; fired individuals will dip into savings and not cut their expenditures by the full amount of their decrease in income. Because they do, as income falls, aggregate production and aggregate expenditures will get closer and closer together, and at some level of income aggregate production will equal aggregate expenditures. The models we considered in this chapter tell us how much income must fall to bring the economy to aggregate equilibrium.

The Multiplier and Shifts in Autonomous Expenditures   Shifts in autonomous expenditures were important to Keynes. They are what creates *aggregate* disequilibrium. But they are not what distinguishes Keynes from the Classicals. It's the response to that shift that distinguishes the two. The Classicals said that the price level adjustment would bring the economy back into equilibrium. If, as Keynes argued was the case, the price level was institutionally fixed, the Classicals believed that shift would have no secondary effect and that the economy would remain in a disequilibrium until the price level fell.

The essence of the Keynesian revolution was his belief that the Classicals were dead wrong in their belief that the economy would remain in a permanent disequilibrium until the price level fell.

The essence of the Keynesian revolution was his belief that the Classicals were dead wrong in their belief that the economy would remain in a permanent disequilibrium until the price level fell. Keynes argued that a disequilibrium would start the multiplier process in which both production and income would fall. As that happened, the economy would fall into an under–full-employment equilibrium.

Keynes further argued that a fixed price level assumption was not the issue. He argued that the income adjustment process worked very quickly and had a powerful effect, while the price level adjustment process worked slowly and had a weak effect. He agreed that the price level adjustment mechanism might work if a disequilibrium continued into the long run, but he argued it would never have a chance to work because the income adjustment process would have eliminated that disequilibrium. For Keynes, the fixed price assumption was only a simplifying assumption; it was not a necessity, as long as the price level didn't adjust almost instantaneously.

The Income Adjustment Process: An Example   The income adjustment process is directly related to the multiplier. The reason is that any initial shock (a change in autonomous aggregate expenditures) is *multiplied* in the adjustment process. Let's see how this works in Exhibit 10's example, which will also serve as a review of the Keynesian model. In this example, let's say trade negotiations between the United States and other countries have fallen apart and U.S. exports decrease by $20. This is shown in the AE curve's downward shift from AE_0 to AE_1.

Q–8: If exports fall by $30 and the *mpc* = .9, what happens to income?

How far must income fall until equilibrium is reached? To answer that question, we need to know the initial shock, $\Delta X = -\$20$, and the size of the multiplier, $[1/(1 - mpc)]$. In this example, *mpc* = .8, so the multiplier is 5. That means the final decrease in income that brings about equilibrium is $100 (five times as large as the initial shock of $20).

Exhibit 10(b), a blowup of the circled area in Exhibit 10(a), shows the detailed steps of the adjustment process so you can see how it works. Initially, autonomous expenditures fell by $20 (shift *A*), causing firms to decrease production by $20 (shift *B*). But that decrease in income caused expenditures to decrease by another $16 (0.8 ×

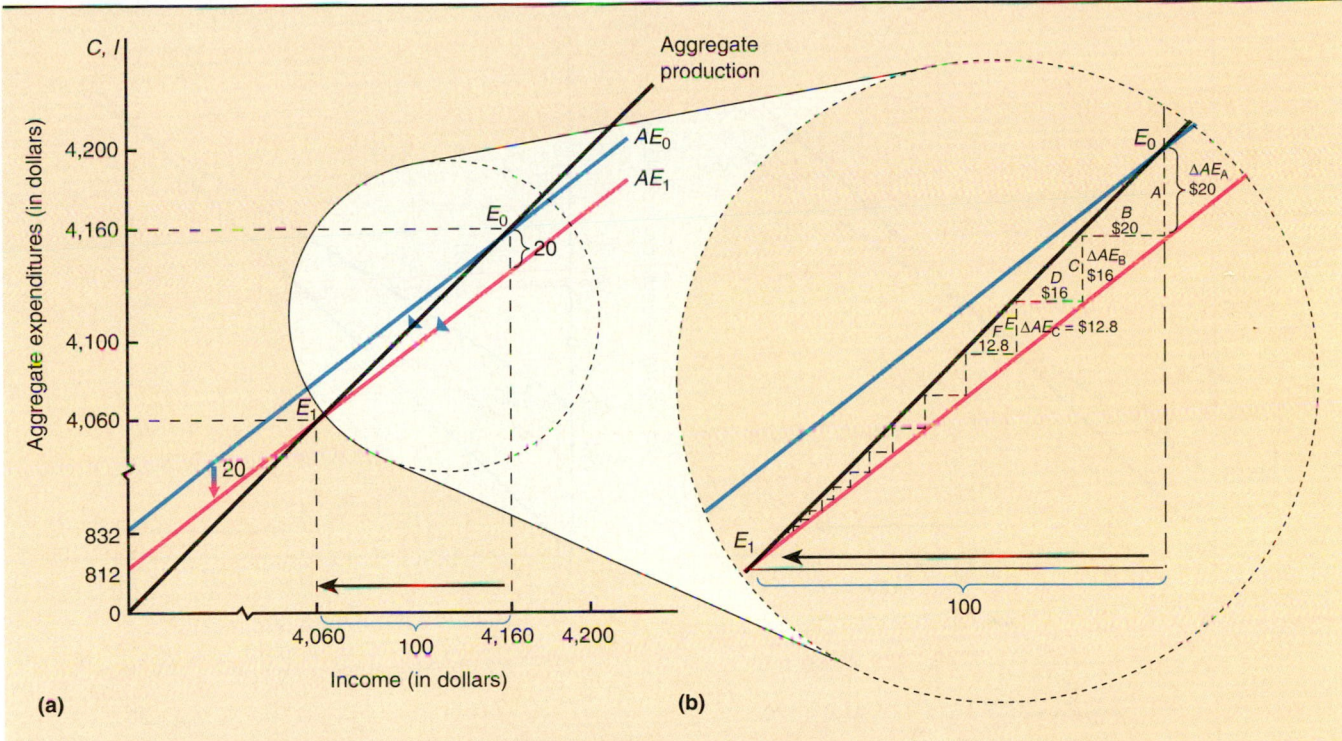

EXHIBIT 10 (a and b)   Shifts in the Aggregate Expenditures Curve

Graph (**a**) shows the effect of a shift of the aggregate expenditures curve. When exports decrease by $20, the aggregate expenditures curve shifts downward from AE_0 to AE_1. In response, income falls by a multiple of the shift, in this case by $100.

Graph (**b**) shows the multiplier process under a microscope. In it the adjustment process is broken into discrete steps. For example, when income falls by 20 (shift B), expenditure falls by (16) (shift C). In response to that fall of expenditures, producers reduce output by 16, which decreases income by 16 (shift D). The lower income causes expenditures to fall further (shift E) and the process continues.

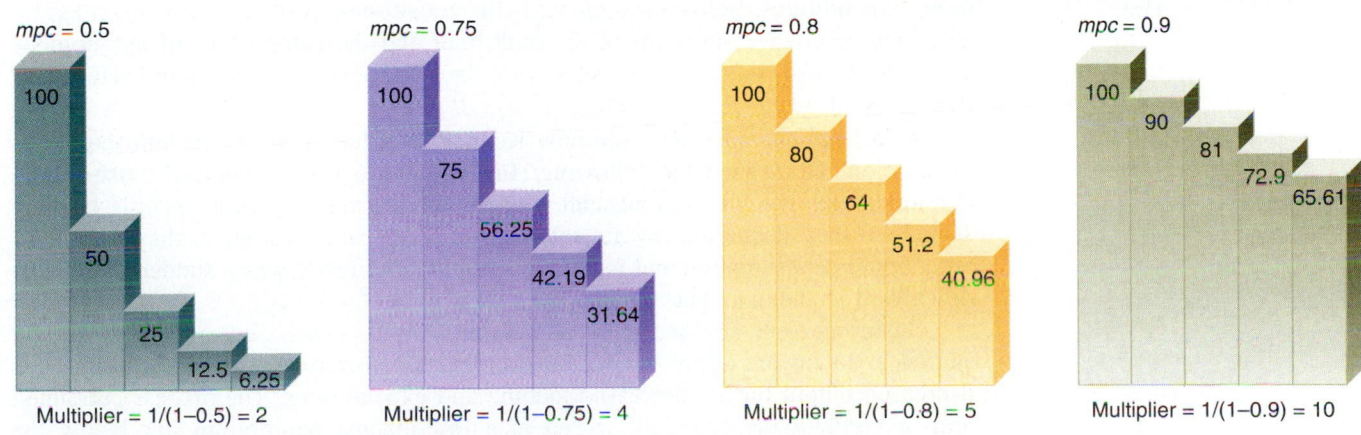

EXHIBIT 11   The First Five Steps of Four Multipliers

The larger the marginal propensity to consume, the more steps are required before the shifts become small.

$20) (shift C). Again firms respond by cutting production, this time by $16 (shift D). Again income falls (shift E) causing production to fall (shift F). The process continues again and again (the remaining steps) until equilibrium income falls by $100, five times the amount of the initial shock. The mpc tells how much closer at each step aggregate expenditures will be to aggregate production. You can see this adjustment process in Exhibit 11, which shows the first steps with multipliers of various sizes.

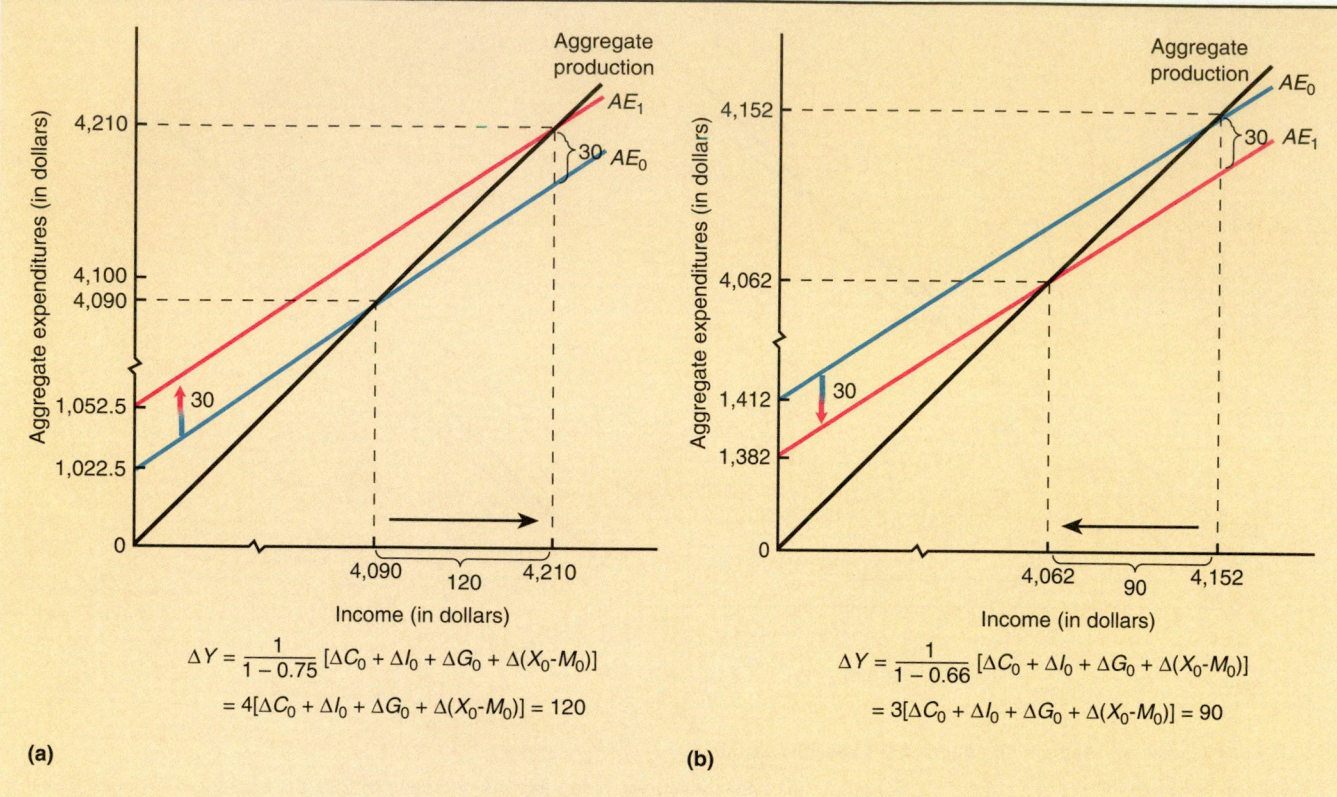

EXHIBIT 12 (a and b)   Two Different Expenditure Functions and Two Different Shifts in Autonomous Expenditures

The steeper the slope of the *AE* curve, the greater the effect on equilibrium income. In (a) the slope of the *AE* curve is .75 and a shift of $30 causes a shift in income of $120. In (b), the slope of the *AE* curve is .66 and a shift of $30 causes a shift in income of $90.

FURTHER EXAMPLES OF THE KEYNESIAN MODEL

Learning to work with the Keynesian model requires practice, so in Exhibit 12(a) and (b) I present two different expenditures functions and two different shifts in autonomous expenditures. Below each model is the equation representing how much aggregate income changes in terms of the multiplier and the components of autonomous expenditures. As you see, this equation calculates the shift, while the graph determines it in a visual way.

As a final example, let's see how Keynes used his model to explain the 1930s Depression. He argued the following: In 1929 there was a financial crash which continued into the 1930s. Financial markets were a mess. Businesspeople became scared, so they decreased investment; consumers became scared, so they decreased autonomous consumption and increased savings. The result was a sudden large shift downward in the aggregate expenditures curve.

Businesspeople responded by decreasing output, which decreased income and started a downward spiral. This downward spiral confirmed business's fears. The decreased output further decreased income and expenditures. The process continued until eventually the economy settled at a low-income equilibrium, far below the potential, or full-employment, level of income.

Paradox of thrift   Individuals attempting to save more cause income to decrease; thereby they end up saving less.

The process that Keynes argued played an important role in bringing about the Depression is sometimes called the **paradox of thrift.** Individuals attempted to save more, but in doing so caused income to decrease, and they ended up saving less.

THE RELATIONSHIP BETWEEN THE *AS/AD* AND THE *AP/AE* MODEL

Let us now consider the relationship between the *AS/AD* and the *AP/AE* models. In Appendix A I discuss the relationship between the *AS/AD* model and the *AP/AE* model in some depth. Here I will briefly consider the relationship.

The relationship between the *AS/AD* model and the *AP/AE* model can be seen in Exhibit 13, which considers a fall in exports of $20 when the multiplier is 2. In Exhibit

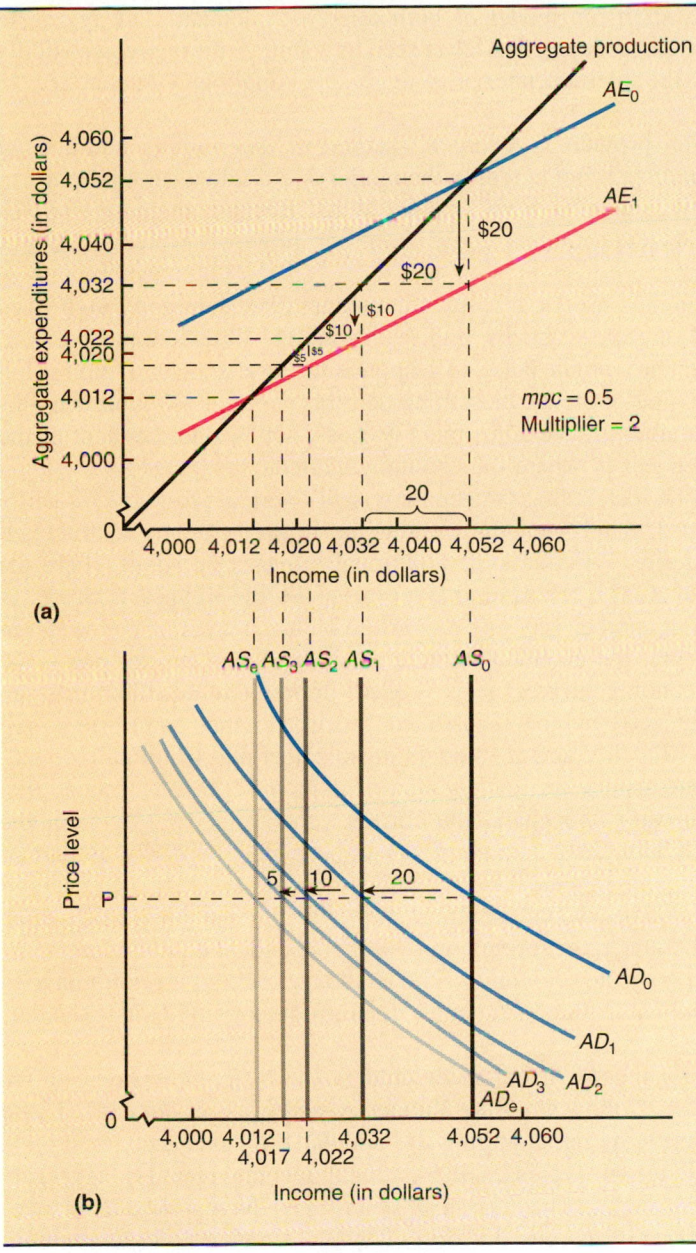

EXHIBIT 13 (a and b)   The Relationship between the AS/AD Model and the AE/AP Model

In these exhibits you can see the equivalency of the AS/AD dynamics and the AP/AE dynamics where there is a fixed price level. Notice that a movement along the AE curve corresponds to a shift of the AD curve, and a movement along the AP curve corresponds to a shift of the AS curve. When AE equals AP, as it does at $4,012, the AS and AD curves will stop shifting. (Since the price level is assumed fixed, the shape of the AS curve doesn't matter. Thus, for simplicity of exposition, I assume wages and prices equally flexible, making the short-run AS curve vertical.) © David Colander.

13(a) you can see that, in the AP/AE model, a fall in exports of $20 will cause income to fall by $40 from $4,052 to $4,012.

Exhibit 13(b) shows that same adjustment in aggregate supply and demand curves. Notice here that the price level remains fixed and the AS and AD curves shift back. Each *shift back* of the AS curve in Exhibit 13(b) is equivalent to a *movement along* the aggregate production curve in Exhibit 13(a). Similarly, each shift back of the AD curve is equivalent to a *movement along* the aggregate expenditures curve. When the AE and AP curves intersect, so do the AS and AD curves.

The key insight into this relationship is to recognize that *shifts in the AS curve are represented by movements along the aggregate production curve* (the 45-degree line). Similarly, *shifts in the AD curve are represented by movements along the aggregate expenditures curve.* In the Keynesian AP/AE model, it is easy to lose sight of aggregate supply because it passively follows aggregate demand, but the supply assumption is there. It is simply dependent on expected demand. Keynes's passive treatment of aggregate supply caused some confusion among macroeconomists and led to some of them mistakenly calling Keynes's model a demand-based model.

5 A shift in the AS curve corresponds to a movement along the AP curve; a movement along the AS curve is represented by a shift in the AP curve. The same process works with the AD curve and the AE curve.

Q–9: If the mpc rises, what happens to the slope of the AD curve?

That's incorrect; it is a short-run model of both aggregate demand and aggregate supply, but the supply response it emphasizes is seen as a shift in the aggregate supply curve brought about by the interdependence of aggregate supply and demand.

The Keynesian Model as an Historical "Model in Time"

At best, what we can estimate are directions and rough sizes of autonomous demand and supply shocks.

The preceding discussion provides a technical method of determining equilibrium income in the Keynesian model. But in reality the model doesn't do what it purports to do—determine equilibrium income from scratch. Why? Because it doesn't tell us where those autonomous expenditures come from, or how we would go about measuring them.

At best, what we can measure, or at least estimate, are directions and rough sizes of autonomous demand or supply shocks, and determine the direction and possible over-adjustment the economy might make in response to those shocks. If you think back to our initial discussion of the Keynesian model, this is how I introduced it—as an explanation of forces affecting the adjustment process, not as a determinant of the final equilibrium independent of where the economy started.

The central Keynesian idea is that the economy will overreact to shocks—shifts in aggregate supply and demand—leading the income in the economy to fluctuate more than individuals desire. Without some additional information about where the economy started from, or what is the desired level of output, the Keynesian theory is not a complete theory. Put another way, *the Keynesian model is a historical model in time.* Each equilibrium that the economy arrives at is dependent on the past—the equilibrium that the economy arrives at is a **path-dependent equilibrium**—an equilibrium that is influenced by the adjustment process to that equilibrium. All history determines current reality and all models must reflect that historical connection. Models that reflect history are called historical models. In any model that involves historeses, you can't understand the current situation separately from the entire past. The future is unfolding in ways that can be understood only as part of historical time.

The Keynesian model is an historical model in time.

There are a number of heavy philosophical points in the last paragraph which have wild mathematical counterpart formulations. Path-dependent equilibria and historeses are all the rage in graduate economics schools today. Luckily, we don't have to get into any of that—the basic ideas are simple for introductory students to understand.

All that introductory students need understand is the different visions of the circular flow of income that follow from the Keynesian and Classical models. Those different visions can be seen by remembering the circular flow analysis.

The circular flow diagram expresses the national income identity: aggregate income equals aggregate output. The Classical school saw forces outside of economics determining the size of the circular flow. It was a circular flow. Keynes did not; he saw the adjustment process to equilibrium changing the size of the income flow and hence changing the equilibrium. Any real shock to the economy would tend to be exaggerated, causing larger than desired fluctuations in income. Thus in a Keynesian model it isn't quite correct to see the aggregate economy as a timeless circular flow; instead it should be seen as a pulsating spiral expanding and contracting in response to unexpected shocks.

In the Keynesian model, the aggregate economy should be pictured as a pulsating spiral, expanding and contracting in response to unexpected shocks.

Understanding the pulsating income (business cycles) could not be accomplished by considering equilibrium separately from disequilibrium adjustment. Keynes's model offered one simple way of considering both simultaneously and arriving at a specific solution. Keynes asked: (1) does aggregate expenditure always equal aggregate production? and (2) if not, what will happen in the economy to bring them into equilibrium?

Mechanistic and Interpretative Keynesians

The "in time" interpretation was not always the interpretation of Keynesian economics that students were taught. In the 1960s, the interpretation of the Keynesian model that was taught was mechanistic. The **mechanistic Keynesian model** pictured the economy as representable by a mechanistic, timeless model with a determinant equilibrium. It involved little or no discussion of the fleetingness of that equilibrium, or of the limitations of that equilibrium with respect to the starting position.

At that time, the Keynesian model was presented as definitive; all economists had to do was to go out and collect the measurements they needed and they could control the level of income in the economy, independent of where the level had been or of what people wanted. Reality proved that interpretation wrong; mechanistic Keynesian economics doesn't work, any more than mechanistic Classical economics does. Modern economists have come to the conclusion that *there is no simple way to understand the aggregate economy.* You can't separate dynamics from the equilibrium analysis; you can't study the economy in a historical vacuum, and any mechanistic interpretation of an aggregate model is doomed to failure.

Mechanistic Keynesianism is not the Keynesian economics presented in this book. The model outlined in this chapter is what I call the **interpretative Keynesian model**—it views the Keynesian model as an aid in understanding complicated disequilibrium dynamics. The specific results of the Keynesian model are a guide to one's common sense, letting one emphasize a particular important dynamic interdependency while keeping others in the back of one's head. With that addendum—that the Keynesian model is not meant to be taken literally, but only as an aid to our intuition—the simple Keynesian model of the 1950s and 1960s is extraordinarily modern and up to date, dealing with the issues with which the highest level macro theorists of the 1990s are struggling.

We've now made it through the Keynesian *AP/AE* model and have related it to the *AS/AD* model. There are a lot of terms and curves there, but I don't want to let those terms and curves get in the way of the ideas. Classical economists said that in a perfectly competitive market economy with a flexible wage and price level, unemployment could not exist. Thus, the existence of unemployment was evidence that the economy was not competitive. The answer to unemployment was to make the economy competitive.

Keynesian economists agreed that if all the Classical assumptions held, the Classical model made sense. But, they argued, all the assumptions could not hold, unless one assumed away the possibility of disequilibrium. A shock to the system could start a multiplier process that magnified the initial shock into a much larger shock. The economy would arrive at a new equilibrium, but it would not be the equilibrium that people wanted. It would not be at the economy's potential level of income.

Keynes said cutting wages (the Classical solution to the depression in a competitive economy) wouldn't help much because, in response to those wage cuts, firms would simply cut prices. Cutting prices might begin the price level adjustment mechanism which would stimulate aggregate demand a bit, but those effects would be overwhelmed by other disequilibrium adjustment processes.

Keynes did not make his argument just for the sake of argument; he was interested in policy—in particular he used his model to demonstrate how specific policies increasing aggregate demand could offset the tendency for the economy to fall below its potential income. We turn to those policies in the next chapter.

Q–10: How does an interpretative Keynesian differ from a mechanistic Keynesian?

6 A mechanistic Keynesian sees the model as a direct guide for policy; it tells you what policy to follow. An interpretative Keynesian sees the model as a guide to one's common sense, highlighting important dynamic interdependencies. Before applying the model, other interdependencies must be considered.

DIFFERENCES BETWEEN THE KEYNESIAN AND CLASSICAL VIEWS

CHAPTER SUMMARY

- The Keynesian model focuses on the chase between aggregate supply and demand.

- Keynes focused on the income adjustment mechanism rather than the price level adjustment mechanism because he felt it was more powerful. He felt the Classical price adjustment mechanism was too weak to bring about an aggregate equilibrium.

- The Keynesian model is made up of the aggregate production and aggregate expenditure curve. In equilibrium, planned aggregate production must equal planned aggregate expenditures.

- Aggregate expenditures (*AE*) is made up of consumption, investment, government spending, and net exports:

$$AE = C + I + G + (X - M)$$

- Consumption depends upon the level of income; the mpc tells us the change in consumption that occurs with a change in income.

- Savings is the mirror image of consumption. When planned aggregate production equals planned aggregate expenditures, planned savings equals planned investment.
- Investment doesn't depend upon the level of income. Shifts in investment or shifts in autonomous consumption can be the initial shock that begins the multiplier process.
- Keynes believed a business cycle is caused by (1) a shock creating a small disequilibrium and (2) the multiplier, which expands that initial shock to a much larger decrease or increase in production and income. The multiplier $(1/(1 - mpc))$ is the income adjustment mechanism.

- The Keynesian equation is

$$Y = \left[\frac{1}{(1 - mpc)}\right]\left[C_0 + I_0 + G_0 + (X_0 - M_0)\right].$$

- The multiplier tells us how much a change in autonomous expenditures will change income.
- Keynesians see aggregate equilibrium occurring in shifts of the aggregate supply and aggregate demand curves. Classicals see aggregate equilibrium occurring by movements along the aggregate supply and aggregate demand curves.
- The Keynesian model cannot be applied mechanistically; it is only a guide to common sense.

KEY TERMS

aggregate expenditures *(230)*
aggregate production curve *(230)*
Aggregate Production/Aggregate Expenditures (*AP/AE*) Model *(229)*
autonomous consumption *(231)*
average propensity to consume (*apc*) *(233)*
average propensity to save (*aps*) *(235)*
consumption function *(231)*

disposable income *(231)*
income adjustment mechanism *(229)*
induced consumption *(231)*
interpretative Keynesian model *(249)*
investment *(236)*
Keynesian equation *(239)*
marginal propensity to consume (*mpc*) *(232)*

marginal propensity to save (*mps*) *(235)*
mechanistic Keynesian model *(248)*
multiplier *(239)*
net exports *(236)*
path-dependent equilibrium *(248)*
paradox of thrift *(246)*

QUESTIONS FOR THOUGHT AND REVIEW

The number after each question represents the estimated degree of critical thinking required. (1 = almost none; 10 = deep thought.)

1. If nominal income, rather than real income, were measured on the vertical axis, what would the *AP* curve look like in each of the three ranges of the economy discussed in the last chapter? *(9)*

2. If savings were instantaneously translated into investment, what would be the multiplier's size? What would be the level of autonomous expenditures? *(7)*

3. Name some forces that might cause shocks to aggregate expenditures. *(2)*

4. Mr. Whammo has just invented a magic pill. Take it and it transports you anywhere. Explain his invention's effects on the economy. *(10)*

5. The marginal propensity to consume is .8. Autonomous expenditures are $4,200. What is the level of income in the economy? Demonstrate graphically. *(3)*

6. The marginal propensity to save is .33 and autonomous expenditures have just fallen by $20. What will likely happen to income? *(5)*

7. The marginal propensity to save is .5 and autonomous expenditures have just risen $200. The economy is at its potential level of income. What will likely happen to income? Why? *(6)*

8. Demonstrate graphically the effect of an increase in autonomous expenditures of $20 in the Keynesian model if the *mpc* = .66. *(3)*

9. Why is the circular flow diagram of the economy an only partially correct conception of Keynesian economics? *(7)*

10. How does a mechanistic Keynesian differ from an interpretative Keynesian? *(3)*

PROBLEMS AND EXERCISES

1. Congratulations. You've been appointed economic advisor to Happyland. Your research assistant says the country's *mpc* is .8 and autonomous investment has just risen by $20.

   a. What will happen to income?
   b. Your research assistant comes in and says he's sorry but the *mpc* wasn't .8; it was .5. How does your answer change?

c. He runs in again and says exports have fallen by $10 and investment has risen by $10. How does your answer change?

d. You now have to present your analysis to the president, who wants to see it all graphically. Naturally you oblige.

2. Congratulations again. You've just been appointed economic advisor to Examland. The *mpc* is .6; investment is $1,000; government spending is $8,000; autonomous consumption is $10,000; and net exports are $1,000.

a. What is the level of income in the country?

b. Net exports increase by $2,000. What will happen to income?

c. What will happen to unemployment? (Remember Okun's rule of thumb.)

d. You've just learned the *mps* changed from .4 to .5. How will this information change your answers in *a, b,* and *c?*

3. In 1992, as President Bush was running (unsuccessfully) for re-election, the economy slowed down; then in late 1993, after President Clinton's election, the economy picked up steam.

a. Demonstrate graphically with the *AP/AE* model a shift in the *AE* curve that would have caused the slowdown. Which component of aggregate expenditures was the likely culprit?

b. Demonstrate graphically with the *AP/AE* model a shift in the *AE* curve that would have caused the improvement. Which component of aggregate expenditures was likely responsible?

c. What policies do you think President Bush could have used to stop the slowdown?

d. What policies do you think President Clinton used to try to speed up the economy?

4. Demonstrate graphically the effect of an increase in autonomous expenditures when the *mpc* = .5 and the price level is fixed:

a. In the *AP/AE* model.

b. In the *AS/AD* model.

c. Do the same thing as in *a* and *b,* only this time assume prices are somewhat flexible. (Appendix B may help in answering this part.)

5. State how the following information changes the slope of the *AD* curve discussed in the previous chapter.

a. The effect of price level changes on autonomous expenditures is reduced.

b. The size of the multiplier increases.

c. Autonomous expenditures increase by $20.

d. Falls in the price level disrupt financial markets which offsets the normally assumed effects of a change in the price level.

ANSWERS TO MARGIN QUESTIONS

1. A shift in aggregate supply is a movement along the aggregate production curve. *(229)*

2. Income equals production on the aggregate production curve. *(230)*

3. The *mpc* is .6. *(232)*

4. False. As long as there is autonomous consumption, the *apc* will change as income changes. *(233)*

5. False. The *mpc* + *mps* = 1. The answer could be "true" only if autonomous consumption = 0. *(236)*

6. The multiplier is 2 when the *mpc* = .5. *(239)*

7. The level of income is $8,000. *(241)*

8. Income falls by $300. *(244)*

9. Nothing. The slope of the *AD* curve is determined by the responsiveness of the quantity of aggregate demand to changes in the price level, not by the size of the multiplier. *(247)*

10. A mechanistic Keynesian sees the economy as a mechanistic timeless model with a determinant equilibrium. He or she would attempt to apply the *AP/AE* model directly. An interpretative Keynesian sees the economy as complicated. He or she sees the *AP/AE* model as an aid to understanding; it cannot be directly applied to the economy. *(249)*

The Relationship Between the *AS/AD* Model and the *AP/AE* Model

In this chapter I briefly considered the relationship between the *AS/AD* model and the *AP/AE* model. In this appendix I discuss that relationship in somewhat more detail.

Deriving the *AD* Curve from the *AP/AE* Model

Let us first derive the aggregate demand curve from the *AP/AE* model. To do so we must remember that the *AD* curve measures the effect of a change in the price level on autonomous expenditures. It includes only the direct responsiveness of aggregate output to changes in the price level (i.e., the initial effect, not the indirect effect caused by the multiplier).

I show this derivation in Exhibit A1. Say that when the price level falls from P_0 to P_1, the direct response will be for expenditures (aggregate quantity demanded) to increase by 10. Similarly when the price level falls from P_1 to P_2, the direct response is for expenditures to increase by 12. This means that we have three different Expenditures Functions—one for each price level. I draw those three expenditures functions in the Exhibit A1(a).

Since this diagram contains the information about the effect of a change in the price level on the quantity of aggregate demand, we can derive an *AD* curve from it. To do so, let's start at equilibrium (point *A*) at price level P_0 and output level Q_0 in Exhibit A2(a). Since at *A*, aggregate demand is Q_0 and the price level is P_0, we can determine one point on the aggregate demand curve. We do so by extending a vertical line down from point *A* in (a) to price level P_0 in (b). Now say that the price level falls from P_0 to P_1. This causes the *AE* curve to shift up by 10, from $AE(P_0)$ to $AE(P_1)$. Initially, expenditures increase from point *A* to point *B*. We can show that increase in expenditures of 10 horizontally by drawing a line over from point *B* to point *C* on the aggregate production line. That increase of 10 is the initial effect of the change in the price level from P_0 to P_1 on aggregate

expenditures. It is the total shift in output that would take place *if there were no multiplier effect.* Extending a vertical line down from point *C* to price level P_1 in (b), we have a second point on the aggregate demand curve (point *C*).

Now say that instead of the price level falling to P_1, it fell to P_2. That would cause the *AE* curve to shift further from $AE(P_0)$ to $AE(P_2)$, for a total increase in expenditures of 22 (from point *A* to point *D*). That increase of 22 can be shown on the horizontal axis by drawing a horizontal line from point *D* to point *E* for a total increase of 22. Extending a vertical line down from point *E* to price level P_2 in (b), we have a third point on the aggregate demand curve (point *E*). If we connect the points *A*, *C*, and *E*, we have part of the aggregate demand curve, and if we continue the thought experiment, we can derive the entire aggregate demand curve.

Notice that when deriving the aggregate demand curve, we specifically did not include the multiplier in determining the slope of the *AD* curve. Those multiplier effects are dependent on interactive shifts in the aggregate supply and demand curve, and including them would have mixed up shifts of the demand curve caused by shift factors, and movements along the demand curve caused by changes in the price level.

Relating the *AS/AD* Model to the *AP/AE* Model

Now, let us consider the relationship between the two models from another perspective. In the text, I considered how the *AD* curve could be related to the *AP/AE* model if the price level were fixed. Here I will consider the relationship between the *AS/AD* model and the *AP/AE* model in the other two ranges of price level flexibility: The partially flexible price level range and the perfectly flexible price level range. Keep in mind that when we talk about changes in aggregate production and aggregate expenditures, we are talking about shifts of the aggregate

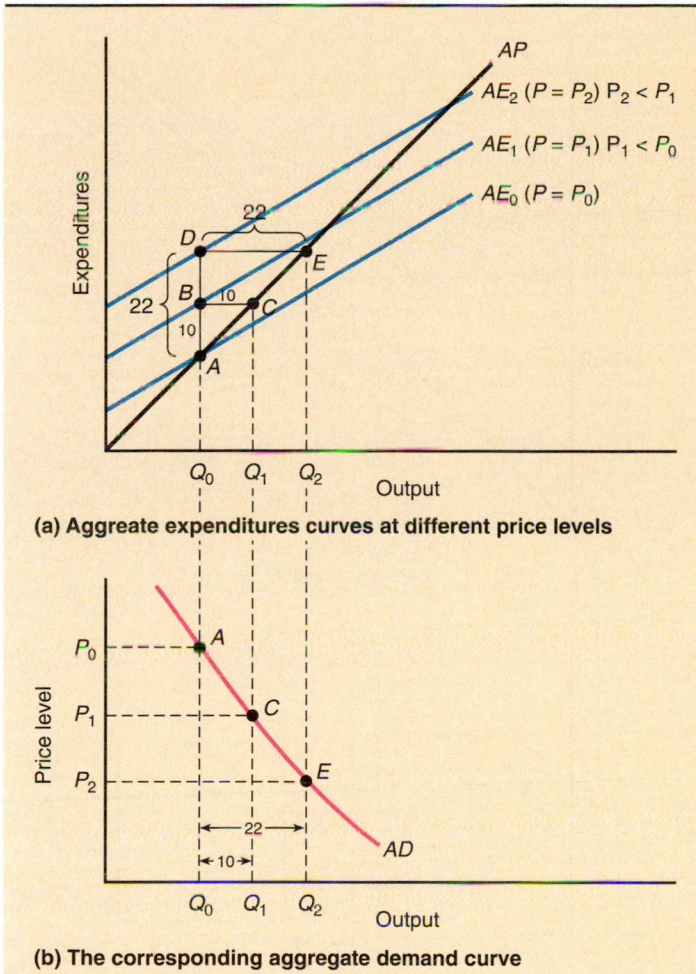

(a) Aggreate expenditures curves at different price levels

(b) The corresponding aggregate demand curve

EXHIBIT A1 (a and b)

The AD curve can be derived from the AP/AE curves by asking what effect a price level change has on aggregate expenditures (other things constant). In (a) three AE curves are drawn, each for a different price level—the lower the price level, the higher the expenditures. Since these three curves give us information about what expenditures will be at different price levels, we can relate these AE curves to an aggregate demand curve. I do that in (b). For example, point A in (a) represents a price level of P_0 and an output level of Q_0. If the price level falls to P_1, the expenditures function shifts up by the 10, which means that the quantity of aggregate demand increases by 10. Tracing over 10 from point B, we arrive at point C. (Notice that I did not move along the AE curve; that includes induced effects—shifts of the demand curve—and they should not be included in the derivation of the slope of the aggregate demand curve). So at the lower price P_1, there is a higher output Q_1. That point can be found by extending a vertical line from C in (a) to price level P_1 (point C) in (b). Doing the same thing for point E, and connecting the three points, gives us the aggregate demand curve.

supply and aggregate demand curves, not movement along these curves. The (a) and (b) parts of Exhibit A2 reproduce the fixed price case discussed in Exhibit 13 of the chapter. It shows how a fall in exports of $20 when the multiplier is 2 is seen in both the AP/AE model and the AS/AD model. As you can see, the net effect of that fall in exports of $20 will cause income to fall $40, from $4,052 to $4,012.

Each shift back of the AS curve in Exhibit A2(b) is equivalent to a movement along the aggregate production curve in (a). Similarly, each shift back of the AD curve is equivalent to a movement along the aggregate expenditures curve. When the AE and AP curves intersect, so do the AS and AD curves.

In Exhibit A2(c) I consider that same shift, only this time I assume the economy is in the intermediate range where the price level is partially flexible. Again for simplicity I assume wages and prices equally flexible, so the AS curve is vertical. As opposed to moving along a fixed price line, we move along a sloping line, shown by

the A arrow in Exhibit A2(d). The multiplier effect is muted by the fall in the price level. As output decreases, the price level falls, and as the price level falls, the AE curve shifts back up from AE_1 to $AE'_1(P_1)$. The new equilibrium is not at income $4,012, but is instead at a slightly higher income level ($4,025), and the new equilibrium price is lower at P_n. The fall in the price level from P_0 to P_n has mitigated, but has not eliminated, the Keynesian multiplier effect. It is possible to go through the same analysis assuming different levels of wage and price level flexibility, and hence with an upward sloping short-run AS curve. Doing so makes it much more complicated, but does not substantially change the analysis.

Finally, to see that you are following the argument, consider that same shift of $20, only this time assume the price level is perfectly flexible. What would the adjustment process look like? That total flexibility of price level means that as soon as the shift from AE_0 to AE_1 occurs, the price level instantaneously falls to P_f (shown in (d)), which shifts the AE curve back to its original

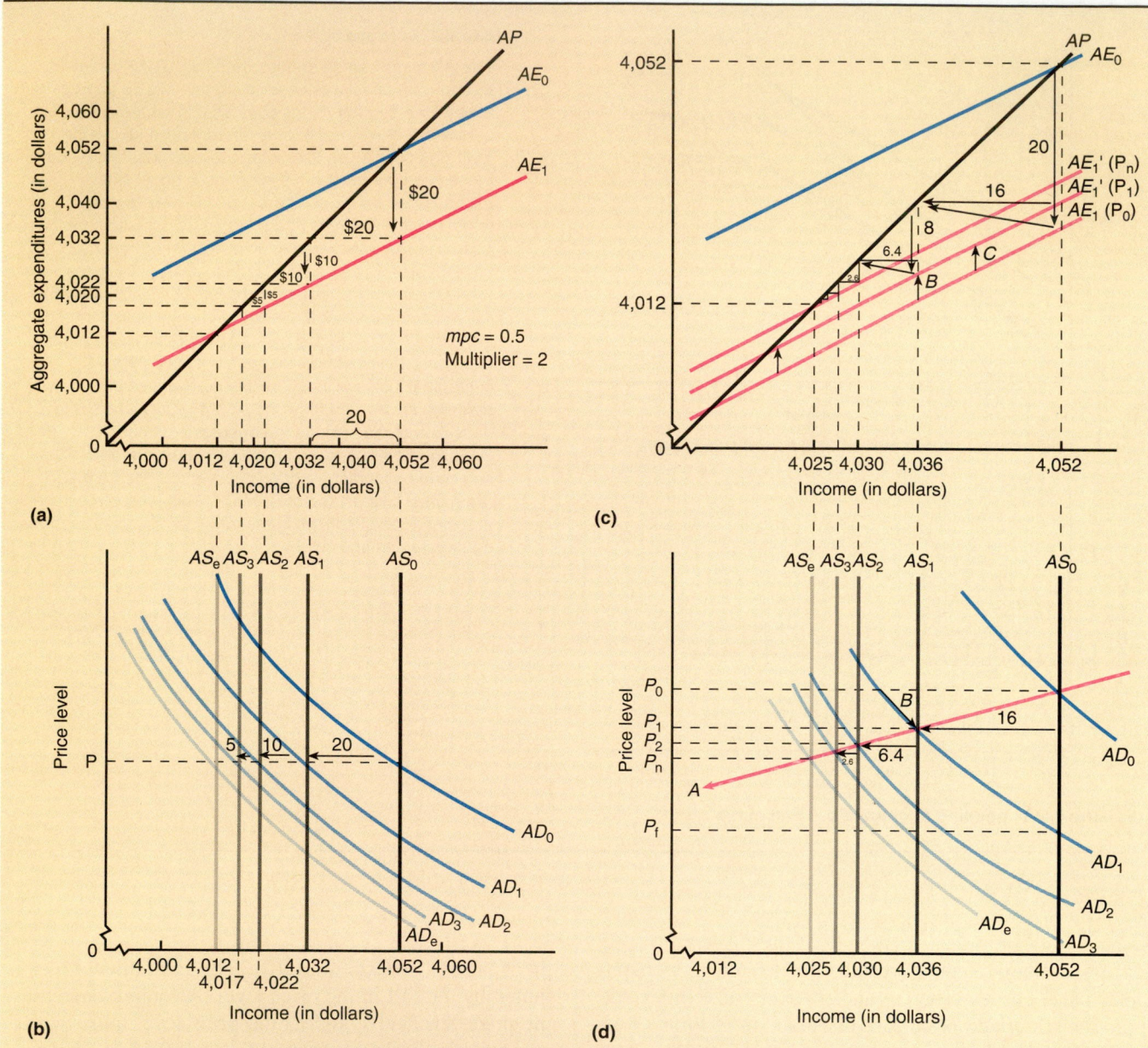

EXHIBIT A2 (a and b)   The Relationship between the *AS/AD* Model and the *AE/AP* Model

In (a) and (b) you can see the equivalency of the *AS/AD* dynamics and the *AP/AE* dynamics where there is a fixed price level. Notice that a movement along the *AE* curve corresponds to a shift of the *AD* curve, and a movement along the *AP* curve corresponds to a shift of the *AS* curve. When *AE* equals *AP*, as it does at $4,012, the *AS* and *AD* curves will stop shifting. In (c) and (d) I consider the equivalency of the two adjustment processes when there is a partially flexible wage and price level. The fall in the wage and price level (shown by arrow *A*) reduces the size of the multiplier at each step. For example, as aggregate demand fell by 20, aggregate supply does not shift by 20, but instead shifts by 16 since the fall in the price level causes the *AE* curve to shift up (arrow *B* in (c)) and movement along the *AD* curve (arrow *B* in (d)). This fall in the price level means that output only falls 16 rather than 20.

A similar type modification occurs for each step of the adjustment process, which makes the final decrease only to $4,025, not to $4,012 as occurred in the fixed price level case. The larger the degree of price level flexibility, the smaller the multiplier. In the limit, with instantaneous price level adjustment, demand shocks are instantaneously offset, the *AE* curve shifts back to its original position, and no output adjustment is required. This, of course, assumes that all other things remain constant and that an equilibrium exists—two highly unlikely assumptions.

position at AE_0. No output change occurs. Thus, instantaneous price level flexibility means there can never be disequilibrium and gives us the Classical position—if that price level flexibility does not cause other things to change. Since, as I discussed in an earlier chapter, price-level flexibility does cause other things to change, even instantaneous price-level flexibility does not necessarily justify the pre-Keynesian Classical position.

11

Fiscal Policy, and the Debate about Activist Macroeconomic Policy

An economist's lag may be a politician's catastrophe.
~George Schultze

After reading this chapter, you should be able to:

1 Explain expansionary and contractionary fiscal policies.

2 Demonstrate fiscal policy using words and graphs.

3 List three alternatives to fiscal policy.

4 Distinguish a structural deficit from a passive deficit.

5 List six problems with fiscal policy and explain how those problems limit its use.

6 Define crowding out and explain how it can undermine the Keynesian view of fiscal policy.

7 Describe how automatic stabilizers work.

The discussion in the previous chapter highlighted the Keynesian story of: (1) how aggregate income is determined, and (2) how small shifts in aggregate expenditure could be multiplied into larger fluctuations in aggregate production and aggregate income. Together these two stories form the Keynesian explanation of why there can be equilibrium at an income level below the full-employment income level and why income in the economy fluctuates.

The Keynesian model was not designed only to understand why fluctuations (booms and busts) occur in the economy; it was also designed to suggest *policies* to deal with the depression, policies that would get the economy out of its under—full-employment equilibrium. Keynes offered an alternative to the Classical laissez-faire policy.

Keynes's initial policy proposals were for public works (for the government to spend more without collecting more taxes to pay for the spending or, in other words, to run a deficit by spending more). Keynesians soon broadened that policy to include: (1) another way to stimulate the economy—by reducing taxes, (2) a way to slow down the economy when it was called for—by decreasing government spending or increasing taxes, (3) policies to change the money supply as a way of controlling the economy, and (4) general policies to influence the four specific components of autonomous expenditures.

We'll see Keynesian policy affecting money in later chapters. In this chapter, we consider government policies that change the level of government spending and taxes as a way of affecting the economy.

FISCAL POLICY AND AGGREGATE DEMAND MANAGEMENT

1 Expansionary fiscal policy involves decreasing taxes or increasing government spending. Contractionary fiscal policy involves increasing taxes or decreasing government spending.

Policy aimed at changing the level of income in the economy by a combination of a change in autonomous expenditures and the multiplied induced expenditures resulting from that change is called **aggregate demand (expenditure) management policy.** One of the most well known of these aggregate demand management policies is **fiscal policy**—the deliberate change in either government spending or taxes to stimulate or slow down the economy. If aggregate income is too low (actual income is below target income), the appropriate fiscal policy is *expansionary fiscal policy:* decrease taxes or increase government spending. If aggregate income is too high (actual income is above target income), the appropriate fiscal policy is *contractionary fiscal policy:* increase taxes or decrease government spending.

Keynesians considered fiscal policy the steering wheel for the aggregate economy. They said Classical economists with their laissez-faire policy were trying to drive an economy without any steering wheel. If that were the case, is it any wonder the economy crashed?

In the 1930s everyone agreed that income was too low and that, if fiscal policy worked, the appropriate fiscal policy was expansionary. Keynesians advocated that governments run deficits. That advocacy made Keynesian economics the center of political debate at the time. Keynesians were accused of being communists, of looking for a way to destroy the U.S. economy, because they advocated running a deficit. In the late 1940s and early 1950s, textbooks that included the Keynesian model were subject to vehement attack; university presidents and trustees were pressured to fire any professor who used a "Keynesian" text. Much has changed since then. By the 1960s and 1970s, fiscal policy was a well-established tool of most governments, and Keynesian economics had become mainstream economics. Such was the influence of the Keynesian model.

The Story of Keynesian Fiscal Policy

Let's start this discussion with the story of fiscal policy for an economy in a depression. What caused that depression? As we saw in the last chapter, when people got scared and cut back their spending, the multiplier took over and expanded that small negative shock into a full-blown depression. In a depression, aggregate production and aggregate expenditures are equal, but at a level of income and production far below the potential level of income—below full employment of all productive resources.

Seeing this low level of income and understanding the Keynesian model of the previous chapter, you should be led to the following insight: If somehow you can

THE ECONOMIC STEERING WHEEL

Our economic system is frequently put to shame in being displayed before an imaginary visitor from a strange planet. It is time to reverse the procedure.

Imagine yourself instead in a Buck Rogers interplanetary adventure, looking at a highway in a City of Tomorrow. The highway is wide and straight, and its edges are turned up so that it is almost impossible for a car to run off the road. What appears to be a runaway car is speeding along the road and veering off to one side. As it approaches the rising edge of the highway, its front wheels are turned so that it gets back onto the road and goes off at an angle, making for the other side, where the wheels are turned again. This happens many times, the car zigzagging but keeping on the highway until it is out of sight. You are wondering how long it will take for it to crash, when another car appears which behaves in the same fashion. When it comes near you it stops with a jerk. A door is opened, and an occupant asks whether you would like a lift. You look into the car and before you can control yourself you cry out, "Why, there's no steering wheel."

"Of course we have no steering wheel," says one of the occupants rather crossly. "Just think how it would cramp the front seat. It's worse than an old-fashioned gearshift lever and it's dangerous. Suppose we have a steering wheel and somebody held on to it when we reached a curb. He would prevent the automatic turning of the wheel, and the car would surely be overturned. And besides, we believe in democracy and cannot give anyone the extreme authority of life and death over all the occupants of the car. That would be dictatorship."

"Down with dictatorship," chorus the other occupants of the car.

"If you are worried about the way the car goes from side to side," continues the first speaker, "forget it. We have wonderful brakes so that collisions are prevented nine times out of ten. On our better roads the curb is so effective that one can travel hundreds of miles without going off the road once. We have a very efficient system of carrying survivors of wrecks to nearby hospitals and for rapidly sweeping the remnants from the road to deposit them on nearby fields as a reminder to man of the inevitability of death."

You look around to see the piles of wrecks and burned-out automobiles as the man in the car continues. "Impressive, isn't it? But things are going to improve. See those men marking and photographing the tracks of the car that preceded us? They are going to take those pictures into their laboratories and pictures of our tracks, too, to analyze the cyclical characteristics of the curves, their degree of regularity, the average distance from turn to turn, the amplitude of the swings, and so on. When they have come to an agreement on their true nature we may know whether something can be done about it. At present they are disputing whether this cyclical movement is due to the type of road surface or to its shape or whether it is due to the length of the car or the kind of rubber in the tires or to the weather. Some of them think that it will be impossible to avoid having cycles unless we go back to the horse and buggy, but we can't do that because we believe in Progress. Well, want a ride?"

The dilemma between saving your skin and humoring the lunatics is resolved by your awakening from the nightmare, and you feel glad that the inhabitants of your own planet are a little more reasonable. But are they as reasonable about other things as they are about the desirability of steering their automobiles? Do they not behave exactly like the men in the nightmare when it comes to operating their economic system? Do they not allow their economic automobile to bounce from depression to inflation in wide and uncontrolled arcs? Through their failure to steer away from unemployment and idle factories, are they not just as guilty of public injury and insecurity as the mad motorists of Mars?

Source: Abba Lerner, "The Economic Steering Wheel," first published in *The University Review* (now *NEW LETTERS*), vol. 7, no. 4 (June 1941), pp. 257–65. Used by permission.

generate a countershock (a jolt in the opposite direction of the shift in autonomous expenditure that started the depression), you can get the multiplier working in reverse, expanding the economy in the same way the initial shock and multiplier had contracted it. You need a countershock to motivate people to spend, and as they increase their spending, society will be better off. But each individual, acting in her own interest, has no incentive to spend more. Each individual would reason: If I spend more, I'll be worse off. Theoretically, my additional spending might help society, but the positive effect would be so diluted that, in terms of my own situation, I don't see how my increased spending is going to benefit me.

For example, if a grocery store clerk increased her shopping expenditures by $100, only about $25 of that expenditure would go into food, so if her store is one of five stores selling various articles in the area where she shops, only $5 would go to her

KEYNES AND KEYNESIAN POLICY

One of the subthemes of this book is that economic thought and policy are more complicated than an introductory book must necessarily make them seem. "Keynesian policy" is a good case in point. In the early 1930s, before Keynes wrote *The General Theory*, he was advocating public works programs and deficits as a way to get the British economy out of the Depression. He came upon what we now call the *Keynesian theory* as he tried to explain to Classical economists why he supported deficits. After arriving at his new theory, however, he spent little time advocating fiscal policy and, in fact, never mentions fiscal policy in *The General Theory*, the book that presents his theory. The book's primary policy recommendation is the need to socialize investments—for the government to take over the investment decisions from private individuals. When one of his followers, Abba Lerner, advocated expansionary fiscal policy at a seminar Keynes attended, Keynes strongly objected, leading Evsey Domar, another Keynesian follower, to whisper to a friend, "Keynes should read *The General Theory*."

What's going on here? There are many interpretations, but the one I find most convincing is the one presented by historian Peter Clarke. He argues that, while working on *The General Theory*, Keynes turned his interest from a policy revolution to a theoretical revolution. He believed he had found a serious flaw in Classical economic theory. The Classicals assumed full employment, but did not show how the economy could move to that equilibrium from a disequilibrium. That's when Keynes's interest changed from a policy to a theoretical revolution.

His followers, such as Lerner, carried out the policy implications of his theory. Why did Keynes sometimes oppose these policy implications? Because he was also a student of politics and he recognized that economic theory can often lead to politically unacceptable policies. In a letter to a friend he later said Lerner was right in his logic, but he hoped the opposition didn't discover what Lerner was saying. Keynes was more than an economist; he was a politician as well.

store. If she were one of 20 employees, her $5 represents only an additional 25¢ spending per employee at the store. If she were about to lose her job, her $100 spending wouldn't save it. However, if *all* individuals, or a large proportion of all individuals, increased their spending by $100 each, spending at her store would rise considerably and her job would likely be saved.

How do you simultaneously get all or most individuals to spend more than they want to? In the 1930s, government found it wasn't easy. President Franklin Roosevelt went on radio to calm people's fears ("We have nothing to fear but fear itself") and to encourage people to spend to create more jobs.

According to the Keynesian model, these admonitions could have worked if they had generated sufficient initial spending; that initial increase would have generated some more spending which, in turn, would have generated even more spending. But these admonitions didn't work. The Keynesian model offered expansionary fiscal policy as an alternative.

With fiscal policy, government could provide the needed increased spending by decreasing taxes, increasing government spending, or both. Fiscal policy would provide the initial expansionary spending, increasing individuals' incomes. As individuals' incomes increased, they would spend more. As they spent more, the multiplier process would take over and expand the effect of the initial spending.

Keynesians argued that fiscal policy—the policy of government changing its spending and taxing to influence production and income levels in the economy—was the missing steering wheel of the economy.

Thus, both cutting taxes and increasing government expenditures are expansionary fiscal policy. The government provides the initial expansionary shock, and then the multiplier takes hold and expands the economy.

2A Expansionary fiscal policy stimulates autonomous expenditures, which increases people's income, which increases people's spending even more.

Keynesians argue that fiscal policy was the missing steering wheel of the economy.

Aggregate Demand Management

Q-1: If spending in the economy is too low, why don't individuals simply increase their spending?

There is nothing special about government's ability to stimulate the economy with additional spending. If a group of individuals wanted to—and had spending power large enough to make a difference—they could do so, but private individuals don't have the incentive to do so. Their spending helps mainly other people and has only a small feedback on themselves. Unless they're altruistic, they don't take into account the effect of their spending on the aggregate spending stream and hence on aggregate income.

The significantly different effects when everyone does something rather than when only one person does it play an important role in economics. This difference has a number of names: the public goods problem, the tragedy of the commons, the fallacy of composition, and the multiperson dilemma.

The problem is neatly seen by reconsidering a football game analogy discussed in an earlier chapter. If everyone is standing, and you sit down, you can't see. Everyone is better off standing. No one has an incentive to sit down. However, if somehow all individuals could be enticed to sit down, all individuals would be even better off. Sitting down is a public good—a good that benefits others—but one that nobody on his or her own will do. Keynes argued that, in times of depression, spending is a public good because it benefits everyone, so government should spend or find ways of inducing private individuals to spend. This difference between individual and economy-wide reactions to spending decisions creates a possibility for government to exercise control over aggregate demand and thereby over aggregate output and income. As I stated above, government's attempt to control the aggregate level of spending in the economy is called aggregate demand management. It involves changing the level of autonomous expenditures through the government's influence of a shift factor of aggregate demand, and then relying on the multiplier effect to multiply that initial effect into a larger effect on income.

The precise size of the multiplier depends on the way in which government changes its spending or its taxes. If it increases spending on goods and services, the full multiplier effect takes place since that initial government spending counts as part of GDP. So the government spending multiplier is $1/(1 - mpc)$. That's the multiplier I discussed in the last chapter. In that chapter, I also mentioned that taxes directly influenced consumption. Taxes shift consumption spending down, making expenditures lower than they would have been had there been no taxes. But, to keep the presentation simple, I didn't explore the issue there. If I had, I would have also mentioned that **transfer payments**—payments by government to individuals that are not in payment for goods or services—work in the opposite direction than taxes; transfer payments shift the consumption function up, making expenditures higher than they would have been.

Unfortunately, when discussing fiscal policy that specifically involves changing taxes and government expenditures, I cannot avoid discussing these issues in a bit more detail. The reason is that the way in which the expenditures enter the income stream make a difference to the size of the multiplier. Specifically, if the government decreases taxes or increases transfer payments, the multiplier is smaller since that initial injection is not counted in GDP. Thus the multiplier starts not with the initial injection, but with the resulting increase in individuals' spending. Say government decreases taxes by x. Expenditures will rise by a fraction of x—specifically $mpc \cdot x$. The multiplier then operates on that increased spending. So, since people spend only a portion of their additional income—the mpc times the added income—the tax and transfer multiplier is $mpc \cdot x \cdot [1/(1 - mpc)] = mpc/(1 - mpc)$.

Let's consider an example: say the marginal propensity to consume is 0.67. The spending multiplier is $1/(1 - 0.67) = 3$ so if government increases spending by $100, income will rise by $300. Now, say that government cuts taxes by $100, or raises transfer payments by $100. Because this fiscal policy is being implemented by a tax cut or a transfer payment, only a fraction of the $100 tax cut translates into increased spending ($0.67 \times \$100$). This increase [$0.67 \times \$100$] is then multiplied by the spending multiplier [$1/(1 - 0.67)$] to arrive at increased income of $200. In this case the tax/transfer multiplier is [$.67/(1 - .67)$] = 2, less than the spending multiplier of 3.

You should try a couple other examples to be sure you've got it. Here's one: government spending on goods rises by $30 and transfer payments are lowered by $20. The $mpc = .5$. How much will income change? Your answer should be: Income goes up by $40. If that wasn't your answer, work through a couple more examples.

The Tax/Transfer Multiplier and the Government Spending Multiplier

The tax/transfer multiplier is $mpc/1 - mpc)$.

Q-2: If the marginal propensity to consume is .75 and government cuts taxes by $100, what will happen to income?

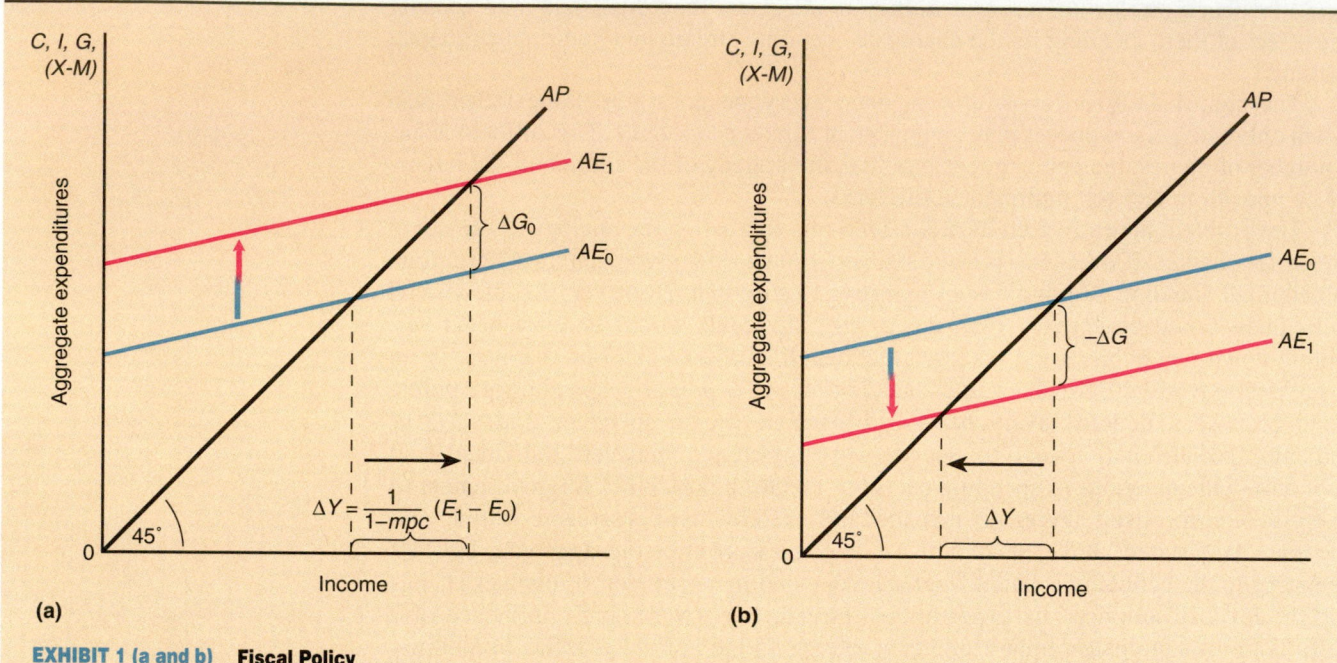

EXHIBIT 1 (a and b)   Fiscal Policy

The government can use fiscal policy as a tool to shift the *AE* curve. An increase in government spending (or a decrease in taxes) **(a)** shifts the *AE* curve upward by ΔG_0 (−mpc T_0). A decrease in government spending (or an increase in taxes) **(b)** shifts the *AE* curve down by −ΔG_0 (mpc T_0). Income changes by a multiple of the change in taxes or spending.

In practice, the difference between the tax/transfer multiplier and the spending multiplier is not very important. As I emphasized throughout the last chapter, the Keynesian model is about tendencies only—it is about dynamic processes that might push the economy off course, not about final equilibria. The Keynesian theory simply tells us that fiscal policy can modify the direction of income movement of the economy, not that it can precisely control the level of income. The Keynesian *AP/AE* model gives us a concrete example of how the control of income might work, but it does not directly describe reality, which is far more complicated than this model allows.

As I will discuss below, the actual practice of fiscal policy is a very rough practice indeed; no Keynesian I know of now believes that we can fine tune the equilibrium income of the economy with fiscal policy, and an increasing number of Keynesians wonder whether, given the politics of today, we can even significantly affect it. Still, as an exercise in logical thinking and modeling, it is helpful to make the distinction between the differential effects of a tax cut and a spending cut on income. As long as you remember not to take the actual solution of the Keynesian model too literally, it is a useful calisthenic for the mind.

Fiscal Policy in Graphs

2B Expansionary fiscal policy shifts up the aggregate expenditure curve and increases income by a multiple of that shift.

Exhibit 1 shows the way fiscal policy works in graphs. An increase in government expenditures (or a decrease in taxes) shifts the aggregate expenditures curve up as in Exhibit 1(a); a decrease in government expenditures (or an increase in taxes) shifts the aggregate expenditures curve down as in Exhibit 1(b). In both cases, notice that income changes by a multiple of the change in government expenditure. That's the multiplier in action.

Controlling the Level of Income with Fiscal Policy   Having determined how an increase in government spending can shift the aggregate expenditures curve, let's now consider how, in this model, government can control the level of aggregate income in the economy with fiscal policy.

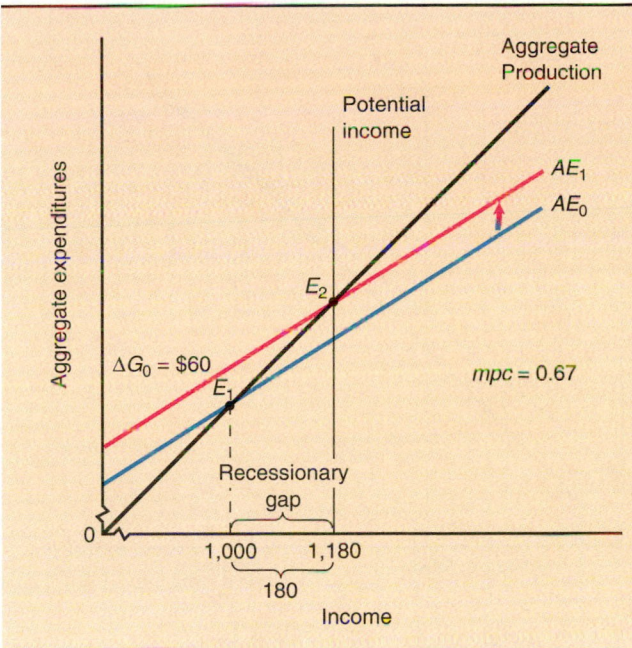

EXHIBIT 2   Fighting a Recession

If the economy is below its potential income level, the government can increase its expenditures to stimulate the economy. The multiplier process takes over and expands the initial shock of the additional spending until actual income equals potential income.

Fighting Recession: Expansionary Fiscal Policy   Let's first consider the case where the economy is in a recession (Exhibit 2). Initially the economy is at equilibrium at income level $1,000, which is below potential income ($1,180). When equilibrium income is below potential income, this difference is called a **recessionary gap.** If everything goes as it should in the Keynesian story, this is what happens: The government recognizes this recessionary gap in aggregate income of, say, $180, and responds by increasing government expenditures by $60. This shifts the AE curve from AE_0 upward to AE_1, increasing aggregate income to the full-potential aggregate income level. Such government action is called *expansionary fiscal policy.*

Recessionary gap   The difference between equilibrium income and potential income when potential income exceeds equilibrium income.

Businesses that receive government contracts hire the workers who have been laid off by other firms and open new plants; income increases by $60. But the process doesn't stop there. At this point, the multiplier process sets in. As the newly employed workers spend more, other businesses find that their demand increases. They hire more workers, who spend an additional $40 (since their *mpc* = .67). This increases income further. The same process occurs again and again. By the time the process has ended, income has risen by $180 and is back at $1,180, the potential level of income.

How did the government economists know to increase spending by $60? They knew by backward induction. They empirically estimated that the *mpc*—the slope of the aggregate expenditures curve—was .67, which meant that the multiplier was $1/(1 - .67) = 1/.33 = 3$. They divided the multiplier, 3, into the recessionary gap, $180, and determined that if they increased spending by $60, income would increase by $180.

Fighting Inflation: Contractionary Fiscal Policy   Keynes devised and developed his model around a depression. However, in principle there's no reason why fiscal policy can't work in reverse (decreasing expenditures that are too high), given the assumptions of the model. You might think that it's impossible for income to be too high, and that, instead, at higher incomes everyone is better off. This is not always the case. Expenditures are "too high" when the economy is in the vertical range of the price level flexibility curve. In this range, instead of causing real income to increase, additional expenditures cause inflationary pressure. If there's inflationary pressure, people on average want to raise their prices, which either causes shortages if wages and prices are fixed (can't be raised) or inflation if wages and prices are not fixed. When this is the case, the aggregate supply curve cannot shift out any further so there is excess demand and demand-pull inflation, as Exhibit 3(a) shows.

Q–3:   Demonstrate graphically the effect of contractionary fiscal policy.

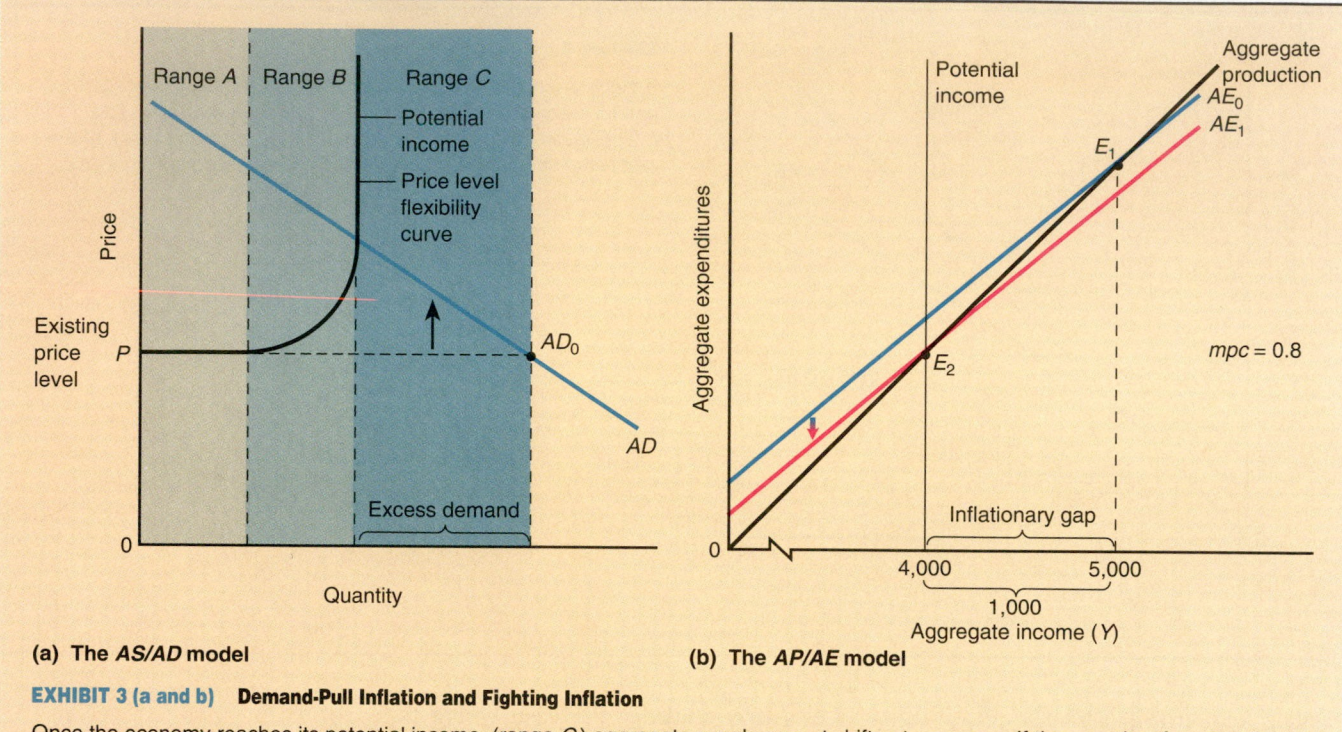

(a) The *AS/AD* model

(b) The *AP/AE* model

EXHIBIT 3 (a and b)   Demand-Pull Inflation and Fighting Inflation

Once the economy reaches its potential income, (range *C*) aggregate supply cannot shift out any more. If the quantity of aggregate demand (*AD₀*) exceeds the quantity of aggregate supply (*AS₀*) at that fixed price level, there will be excess demand *and pressures for demand-pull inflation*. This case is shown in (**a**). When equilibrium income exceeds potential income, the economy has an inflationary gap. There will be either shortages, or inflation, or both. In (**b**), the same situation is shown in the *AP/AE* model. In this case, contractionary fiscal policy, shifting the *AE* curve downward, is called for.

Inflationary gap   The difference between equilibrium income and potential income when equilibrium income exceeds potential income.

Remember from the previous chapter, the Keynesian *AP/AE* model is a *fixed price* model that tells a story about a chase between aggregate supply and demand when the economy is in Range *A*. For that chase to occur, aggregate supply must be below potential output. Once the quantity of aggregate demand shifts up beyond potential output, the fixed price assumption is no longer relevant and inflation occurs. Whenever equilibrium income exceeds potential income, there's said to be an **inflationary gap.** When there's an inflationary gap, expenditures are too high. To prevent inflation, Keynesians believe that the government should exercise contractionary fiscal policy (cutting government spending or raising taxes).

Exhibit 3(b) shows a numerical example of contractionary fiscal policy at work. Potential income is $4,000, *mpc* = .8, but the equilibrium level of income is $5,000. Thus, there is an inflationary gap of $1,000, which causes upward pressure on wages and prices with no additional output resulting.

An inflationary gap calls for contractionary fiscal policy. The government increases taxes by $250, shifting the *AE* curve from *AE₀* to *AE₁*, which decreases the equilibrium level of income by $1,000, back to $4,000, the potential level of income. The government has offset the expansionary shock with contractionary fiscal policy.

How did the government know to increase taxes by $250? Again, by backward induction. The spending multiplier, $[1/(1 - mpc)]$, is 5, but the government knows that not all the tax increase will decrease expenditures since people will reduce their savings in order to hold their expenditures up. Expenditures will initially fall by the *mpc* multiplied by the increased taxes, or $(.8 \times \$250) = \$200$ rather than $250. The tax/transfer multiplier $mpc/(1 - mpc) = .8/.2 = 4$ takes that into account so they use the tax multiplier of 4 rather than the spending multiplier of 5. So the total decrease in income is $4 \times \$250 = \$1,000$. As you can see, once the government knows the multiplier and the inflationary or recessionary gap, it can determine what fiscal policy it should use to achieve the potential level of income.

There are two ways to think about the effectiveness of fiscal policy—in the model, and in reality.

Effectiveness of Fiscal Policy in the Model   How effective fiscal policy is in the model depends on the size of the multiplier which, as we saw in the last chapter, depends on the size of the marginal propensity to consume. That model was a highly simplified model that focused on induced consumption spending—spending dependent on income. That is why the multiplier depended on the size of the marginal propensity to consume.

In reality, consumption is not the only component of income with an induced component. Other expenditures also have induced elements and hence provide leakages from the circular flow. We can include the induced component of these other expenditures by discussing the **marginal propensity to expend** (mpe)—the additional spending that will be translated into the income stream when all induced expenditures are included. The marginal propensity to expend is the generalized equivalent of the marginal propensity to consume. As with the mpc a high marginal propensity to expend means a large multiplier; a low marginal propensity to expend means a low multiplier. Thus, in a generalized model, the multiplier is:

$$\text{generalized expenditures multiplier} = 1/(1 - mpe).$$

The size of the marginal propensity to expend depends in turn on the size of the induced expenditures and leakages from the circular flow, the three most important of which are the marginal propensity of individuals to save, the marginal propensity to import, and the marginal tax rate. The larger these three are, the smaller is the multiplier. Why? Because each of these draws income from the circular flow and reduces the degree to which expenditure is connected to income. (In Appendix A, I go through explicitly what the relationship between these three variables and the multiplier is.)

When one includes all induced expenditures for the United States, one comes up with a marginal propensity to expend of about .5 or .6, which means that 40 to 50 percent of all spending escapes the circular flow and does not induce new spending. Thus, for the United States, a realistic multiplier is about $1/(1 - .5)$ or $1/(1 - .6)$, or between 2 and 2.5.

Expanding the model to include all induced expenditures gives us a way of thinking about relative sizes of multipliers for various countries. For example, would you say that small countries will likely have higher or lower multipliers than the United States? They probably will have smaller multipliers than the United States since they will have high marginal propensities to import. This means that expansionary policy in small countries is in large part exported abroad.

Effectiveness of Fiscal Policy in Reality   Models are great, and simple models, like the one I've presented in this book, that you can understand intuitively are even greater. You put in the numbers, and out comes the answer. Questions based on such models make great exam questions. But don't think that policies that work in a model will work in the real world.

The effectiveness of fiscal policy in reality depends on the government's ability to perceive a problem, and to react appropriately to it. The essence of fiscal policy is government changing its taxes and its spending to offset any deviation that would occur in other autonomous expenditures, thereby keeping the economy at its potential at level of income. If the model is a correct description of the economy, and if the government can act fast enough and change its taxes and spending in a *countercyclical* way, depressions can be prevented. A fiscal policy in which the government offsets any shock that would create a business cycle is called **countercyclical fiscal policy.** Such countercyclical policy designed to keep the economy always at its target at potential level of income is called **fine tuning.**

As I will discuss below, almost all economists, whether Keynesian or Classical, agree the government is not up to fine tuning the economy. The debate in the 1990s is whether it is up to any tuning of the economy at all.

Q-4:   The marginal propensity to expend is .33 and there is an inflationary gap of $100. What fiscal policy would you recommend?

A high marginal propensity to expend means a large multiplier; a low marginal propensity to expend means a low multiplier.

Q-5:   If the marginal propensity to import rises, what happens to the size of the multiplier? Why?

A countercyclical fiscal policy designed to keep the economy always at its target or potential level of income is called fine tuning.

Almost all economists, whether Keynesian or Classical, agree the government is not up to fine tuning the economy.

At one time, some Keynesians thought the economy followed a simple adjustment process such as described by this model, and that it could be modeled simply, and controlled. No more. Why? Because this, or any, simple model captures only one aspect of the dynamic adjustment process.

All economists now recognize that the dynamic adjustment in the economy is extraordinarily complicated, and that once you take into account reasonable expectations of future policy, the formal model becomes hopelessly complex. Graduate students in economics get PhDs for worrying about such hopeless complexities. At the introductory level, all we require is that you (1) know this simple Keynesian model, and (2) remember that, in the real world, it cannot be used in a mechanistic manner; it must be used with judgment.

ALTERNATIVES TO FISCAL POLICY

As questions about the effectiveness of fiscal policy have developed, policy discussions have moved toward alternatives to fiscal policy. To understand how these alternatives work, you must simply remember that any change in autonomous expenditures, ΔE, not just changes in the government deficit, will affect the level of income. You can see the alternatives to fiscal policy by thinking of the Keynesian equation:

$$\Delta Y = \text{multiplier} \times \begin{pmatrix} \Delta \text{ autonomous consumption} \\ + \\ \Delta \text{ autonomous investment} \\ + \\ \Delta \text{ autonomous government spending} \\ + \\ \Delta \text{ autonomous net exports} \end{pmatrix}$$

3 Three alternatives to fiscal policy are directed investment policies, trade policies, and autonomous consumption policies.

Any policy that affects any of these four components of autonomous expenditures—autonomous consumption, autonomous investment, autonomous government spending, and autonomous net exports—can achieve the same results as fiscal policy. So three alternatives to fiscal policy are directed investment policies, trade policies, and autonomous consumption policies. The above requires one addendum: any policy that can influence *autonomous* expenditures *without having offsetting effects on other expenditures* can be used to influence the direction and movement of the aggregate income. That addendum in italics is important because, in the Classical view, no expenditure is autonomous. If you push on one type of expenditure, you simply pull on another, and the net effect is a wash. But in the Keynesian view there is an autonomous component of each of those expenditures that in principle can be affected by policy. We have already considered government spending policy when we talked about fiscal policy. Let us briefly consider some of the other policies that could be used to influence income. I discuss investment first, then net exports, and, finally, consumption.

Directed Investment Policies: Policy Affecting Expectations

Let's first consider investment. Remember our discussion in the last chapter in which I explained that Keynes thought that the Depression was caused by some type of collective psychological fear on the part of investors who, because they predicted that the economy was going into a recession, decided not to invest. As a result, the economy went into a recession, and then eventually a depression, as the fear built upon itself. If somehow government could have supported investment, it could have avoided the Depression.

A Numerical Example To give you some practice with the model, let's consider a numerical example. Say that income is $400 less than desired and that the marginal propensity to expend is .5. How much will government policy have to increase autonomous investment in order to achieve the desired level of income? Working backwards, we see that the multiplier is 2, so autonomous investment must be increased by $200.

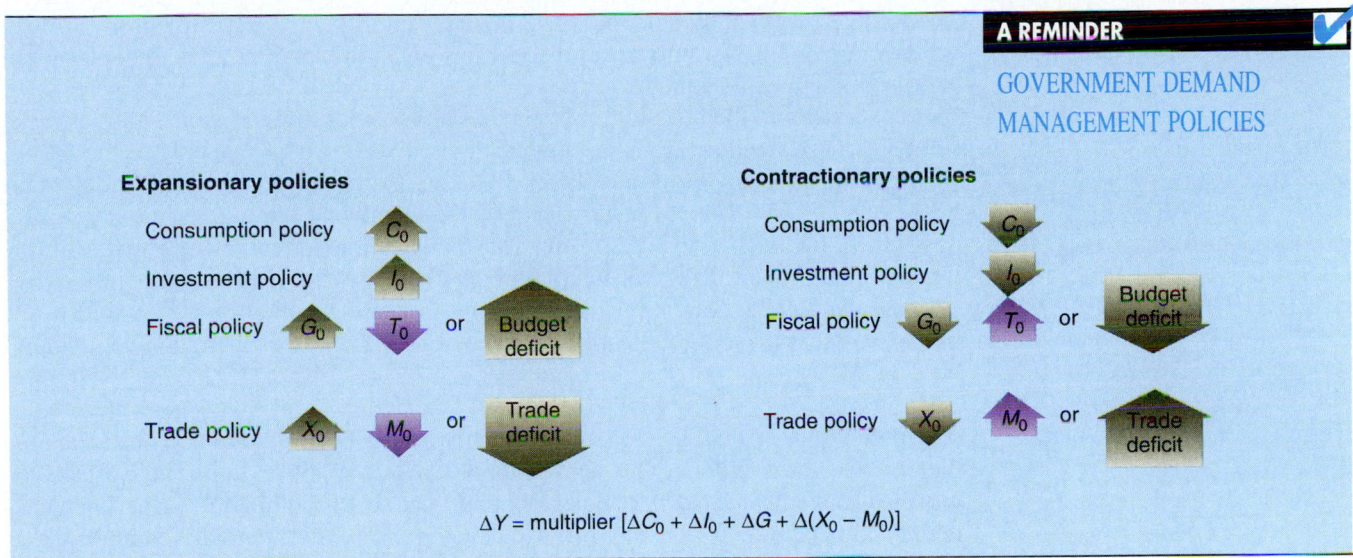

Q–6: How is it possible to "talk" the economy into a boom?

Rosy Scenario: Talking the Economy Well   Numerical examples like the one above are a bit far-fetched since it is difficult to relate a specific policy to a specific numerical result or investment. But the relationship is there, and you can see examples of government trying to exploit it every day. For example, listen to government officials on the radio or television. Almost inevitably you will hear rosy scenarios from them— the **Rosy Scenario policy.** You almost never hear a policy-level government economist telling the newspapers how bad the economy is going to be. Why? Because a gloomy prediction could affect expectations and decrease investment and consumption spending. If you're a high-level government policy economist and you have a gloomy forecast, you're told to keep quiet or quit. In the Great Depression, President Roosevelt, in a famous radio address, told the nation not to fear—that the only thing it had to fear was fear itself. George Bush's and Bill Clinton's upbeat talk about the economy is another example: if they can get people to think the economy in the 1990s will be in good shape, it will be in good shape because people expect it to be.

Another way to influence investment is to protect the financial system by government guarantees or promises of guarantees. Nothing can decrease business confidence quite like a large number of bank and financial institution failures. Precisely that type of financial institution failure changed a recession in the 1930s to the Great Depression. As we will see in later chapters, to prevent such failures in the future the government instituted a number of guarantee-type policies after the Depression.

Let's consider how such investment-expectations policies work in practice. Say the economy is in a slight recession, and because of that, banks are in financial trouble. The government recognizes that if the public decides that banks are in trouble, they will try to get their money out of the banks, in which case banks will have to close. As banks close, loans will dry up, investment will decrease, and the economy will fall into a deep recession. To prevent that, the government comes along and tells everyone that it will bail out the banks so that people's money is safe. If the government is believed, everything stays fine and the recession doesn't happen (and, hopefully, the banks get themselves out of their financial trouble).

Japan used such a "save the financial institutions" policy in the 1990s. When the Japanese stock and real estate markets collapsed in the early 1990s, the Japanese government loosened bank accounting rules in order to prevent banks from failing. Similarly, in the early 1990s, when the U.S. banking system was seriously in trouble due to loan losses, the U.S. government modified institutional rules to increase banking profitability. It worked, and by the mid-1990s the U.S. banking system had recovered.

Another way in which the government can influence investment is through influencing the interest rate. I will discuss this policy in detail in a later chapter when we discuss monetary policy.

The answer to the question, "When do such policies affecting expectations make sense?" doesn't follow from the models; it is a matter of judgment. In the 1930s, Keynes didn't see any of these policies affecting investment as being sufficient; in his book, *The General Theory,* he advocated the government taking over the investment decisions—nationalizing investment. That policy didn't receive high marks in the United States.[1] Instead, Keynesian policy quickly came to mean fiscal policy. Why? Because politically, Keynesians quickly saw that fiscal policy could be sold to the public, whereas the more radical Keynesian nationalizing investment policies couldn't be.

Trade Policy and Export-Led Growth

Any policy that increases autonomous exports or decreases autonomous imports (and thereby increases autonomous expenditures) will also have multiplied effects on income. Examples of such policies abound. The U.S. Commerce Department has entire sub-departments assisting firms to develop their export markets. Similarly, U.S. trade delegations frequent other nations, pushing to get the other nations' trade restrictions on U.S. goods lowered. The idea is to stimulate U.S. exports and increase aggregate expenditures on U.S. goods, and hence to have a multiplied effect on U.S. income. Such policies are part of a set of policies that generally go under the name **export-led growth policies.**

Export-led growth policies Policies designed to stimulate exports and hence have a multiplied effect on U.S. income.

Notice that it is the trade balance (exports minus imports) that affects aggregate expenditures, so any policy that will reduce imports, such as tariffs, will have the same expansionary effect on income. That's why you hear so much about trade restrictions from Washington. They're a way of protecting U.S. jobs and of stimulating the U.S. economy.

A Numerical Example   Let's start with a numerical example of a small country with a large percentage of imports. Say one country's income is $300 million too low and its marginal propensity to expend is .33. How must it affect net exports to achieve its desired income? Since the *mpe* is low, the multiplier is small (1.5), which means that net exports must be increased by approximately $200 million (either by decreasing imports or increasing exports by that amount).

Interdependencies in the Global Economy   I'll discuss these trade policies in much more detail in later chapters, but for now, let me remind you that one country's exports are another country's imports, so that every time the United States is out pushing its exports in an attempt to follow an export-led growth policy, it is the equivalent to getting another country to follow an *import-led decline* for its economy. Similarly, every trade restriction on foreign goods has an offsetting effect on another country's economy, an effect that will often lead to retaliation. So a policy of trying to restrict imports can often end up simultaneously restricting exports as other countries retaliate. Expectations of such retaliation is one of the reasons many economists support free trade agreements, such as the North American Free Trade Association (NAFTA), in which member countries agree not to engage in restrictive trade policies on imports.

A final way in which the trade balance can be affected is through **exchange rate policy,** deliberately affecting a country's exchange rate in order to affect its trade balance. In the long run, a low value of a country's currency relative to currencies of other countries encourages exports and discourages imports; a high value of a country's currency relative to other countries discourages exports and encourages imports.

The effect of such exchange rates can be seen in the automobile industry. In the 1970s and 1980s, Japanese exports of cars were increasing enormously. An important

Q-7: In the 1990s, the value of the U.S. dollar has fallen. What effect would you expect that to have on income in the United States?

---

[1] In some ways, enormous defense expenditure made by the government after the 1940s was a version of such a policy, and it led to many complaints that the U.S. economy was a war-based economy.

reason for that was the relative value of the Japanese yen (somewhere around 300 to the dollar). In the 1990s, the value of the dollar fell relative to the yen, so that in 1994 it was about one-third the value (100 to the dollar) of what it was in the 1970s. With this change, Japanese cars no longer seemed the good buy that they were before, and the U.S. automobile industry made a comeback. Again, we'll discuss such policies in more detail in a later chapter.

The third alternative to fiscal policy are consumption policies. Any policy designed to encourage autonomous consumption can hold autonomous expenditures up and have the same effect as fiscal policy. Increasing consumer credit availability to individuals by making the institutional environment conducive to credit is one way of achieving this.

Autonomous Consumption Policy

The growth of the U.S. economy from the 1950s through the 1980s was marked by significant institutional changes that made credit available to a larger and larger group of people. This increased consumer credit allowed significant expansion in income of the U.S. economy. In the 1990s, there was some cutback by consumers as they tried to consolidate their financial obligations, and that has played a major role in the slow growth of the U.S. economy in the early 1990s. Similarly, the resolution of those problems played a major role in the rise in growth in the mid-1990s.

As a final review, to be sure you have the model down pat, calculate how much autonomous expenditures should change to decrease income by $60 if the *mpe* = ⅔.[2]

The above discussion of autonomous expenditure policy made it look as if there were a one-way flow from autonomous expenditure to income. Thus one could talk about fiscal policy, and the size of the deficit, or trade policy, and the size of the trade balance, as policies to control the level of income. But when one is thinking about such policies, it is important to remember that not all of these expenditures are autonomous. Most consumption is induced, and separating out an autonomous component is difficult. Imports are also partially dependent on income, so some portion of them are induced. When income in a country goes up, the country's imports go up.

Structural versus Passive Government Budget and Trade Deficits

Similarly with taxes: when income goes up, so do taxes, so taxes have an induced effect as well. Each of these induced elements affects the marginal propensity to expend, and thereby affects the size of the multiplier. (How these effects are mathematically related to the size of the multiplier is shown in Appendix A.) Higher tax rates and higher marginal propensities to import decrease the size of the multiplier; lower tax rates and lower marginal propensities to import increase the size of the multiplier.

Higher tax rates and higher marginal propensities to import decrease the size of the multiplier.

The induced elements of taxes and imports mean that when we are discussing export-led growth policies or fiscal policy, we must remember that while *the budget deficit and the trade balance will affect aggregate income, simultaneously aggregate income will affect the budget deficit and trade balance.* So if we're using the deficit or the trade balance as policy tools, they themselves will change as income changes, and the ending trade balance and ending budget deficit might be quite different than the initial trade balance or initial budget deficit.

The budget deficit and the trade balance will affect aggregate income, but they will also be affected by it.

For example, say the multiplier is two and the government is running expansionary policy. It increases government spending by $100, which causes income to rise by $200. If the tax rate is 20 percent, tax revenues will increase by $40 and the final deficit will be $60, not $100. Alternatively, consider a successful export-led growth policy. Say the multiplier is again 2, the marginal propensity to import is .3, and the government wants to eliminate a $40 billion trade deficit. The government introduces policies that expand exports by $40 billion and income by $80 billion. That $80 billion increase in income causes imports to increase by $24 billion, so the $40 billion trade deficit will not be eliminated. It will instead be reduced by $16 billion.

---

[2] If you came up with any answer but "Decrease C_0 by 20," a review is in order.

REGIONAL MULTIPLIERS

The macro policies discussed in the book are national policies. A parallel policy discussion goes on in just about every community when regional planning units consider the effect of the pullout of a military base, or the relocation of a new company into a community. All such policies to affect such decisions are based on the assumption that regional multipliers exist—that the impact of an expenditure will have a multiplied effect on the income of the community.

We can fit such policies into our Keynesian model by thinking of a community as having imports and exports. While there are no measured exports and imports, there are unmeasured imports and exports. For example, colleges are an export of a regional area (why?), and the maintenance of a college in an area can be seen as a regional export-led growth policy. Building expensive stadiums for professional sports teams is usually similarly justified by such multiplier-effect reasoning.

Looking in your local paper, you will most likely see evidence of such policies; most regional areas give tax benefits and other concessions to firms that locate there. (Ironically, many of these initiatives are supported by businesspeople who, on a national level, reject Keynesian policies.)

When thinking about these regional policies, it is important to remember that all the same problems that exist with Keynesian policy on the national level also exist on the local level: retaliation, inability to decide what to affect, and inability to decide what is the "appropriate" target level of income. In the Classical view, in the aggregate, all these regional policies are simply offsetting each other, and the net effect of such policies on the aggregate economy is more waste in government. But even if one is persuaded by this Classical argument, one might still support regional policies based on multiplier analysis. The reason is that unless such regional incentives are prohibited for all communities, once one area introduces them, the others must follow or lose out.

---

4 A structural deficit is a deficit that would exist at potential income. A passive deficit is the deficit that exists because income is below potential income.

To differentiate between a budget deficit being used as a policy instrument to affect the economy, and a budget deficit that is the result of income being below its potential, economists use a reference income level at which to judge fiscal policy. That reference income level is their estimate of the economy's potential level of income. They then ask: Would the economy have a budget deficit if it were at its potential level of income? The portion of the budget deficit that would exist even if the economy were at its potential level of income is called a **structural deficit.** If an economy is operating below its potential, the actual deficit will be larger than the structural deficit. The portion of the deficit that exists because the economy is operating below its potential level of output is called a **passive deficit.** Economists believe that an economy can eliminate a passive budget deficit through growth in income, whereas it can't grow out of a structural deficit. Because the economy can't grow out of structural budget deficits, they are of more concern to policy makers than are passive budget deficits.

Q-8: An economy's actual income is $1 trillion; its potential income is also $1 trillion. Its actual deficit is $100 billion. What is its passive deficit?

Let me give an example. Say potential income is $7 trillion and actual income is $6.8 trillion, a shortfall of $200 billion. The actual deficit is $250 billion and the marginal tax rate is 25 percent. If the economy were at its potential income, tax revenue would be $50 billion higher and the deficit would be $200 billion. That $200 billion is the structural deficit. The $50 billion (25 percent multiplied by the $200 million shortfall) is the passive portion of the deficit.

In reality there is significant debate about what an economy's potential income level is, and hence there is disagreement about what percentage of a deficit is structural and what part is passive. Nonetheless, the distinction is often used and is important to remember.

Some Real-World Examples

So much for our discussion of the theoretical issues surrounding Keynesian economics and policies. Let's now turn to how they work in practice. To give you an idea of how fiscal and other expenditures policies work in the real world, we'll look at a couple of examples. Let's first consider what happened in World War II.

Until the 1980s, most Keynesian economists were primarily interested in policy, and theoretical revolution in Keynes's work was not expanded upon. A truce was arrived at between Keynesians and Classicals. The truce stated that (1) Classical theory was theoretically correct, but the assumptions it made were inapplicable to many real-world situations, and (2) Keynesian theory was, theoretically, a special case of Classical theory, but it was a special case that just happened to be relevant to the real world. This gave Keynesians the policy applicability they were interested in, and Classicals the theoretical laurels.

In the 1980s, Keynesian policy came under fire and the truce broke down on the real-world policy side. More and more economists came to believe that Keynesian policy wasn't so relevant after all. As that happened, modern Keynesians returned to Keynes's work and argued against the other part of the truce that gave the theoretical laurels to the Classicals. These modern Keynesians argued that Keynes's theory was the more general theory since it allowed for the aggregate economy to have multiple equilibria, which modern theoretical work concluded it would likely have unless one assumed them away with ad hoc assumptions.

Thus in the 1990s, a new truce is developing. While modern macro theorists agree that the mechanistic multiplier models of Keynesian economics are far too simple, they are more and more accepting that, in its general approach, Keynesian economics (the interpretive, not the mechanistic brand) is the more general theory because it includes the effects of dynamic disequilibrium feedback on the equilibrium—what in mathematics is called path dependency. Almost all modern theoretical work—both Keynesian and Classical—is being directed at such dynamic issues, making the Keynesian/Classical distinction almost irrelevant when talking about theoretical work. What this development means is that in theory, what in this book I call Keynesian economics has been accepted as more general than what in this book I call Classical economics (although many modern Classical economists would argue that it is they, not the Keynesians, who led the modern theoretical charge into path dependency).

In the real world, however, many Keynesian economists now also agree that the dynamic interactions are so complicated that, in most circumstances—except for serious recession—Classical economics, with its focus on establishing a system of rules within an institutional environment, is the most relevant. So the new truce is precisely the reverse of the old truce. In the new truce, Keynesians have the theoretical laurels and Classicals have the policy relevance.

Fiscal Policy in World War II   The Depression in the United States continued through the 1930s. However, by the beginning of the 1940s it was no longer the focus of U.S. policy as the war in Europe (which had started in 1939) and in the Pacific (where it had started somewhat earlier) became more and more the central issue, especially after December 7, 1941, when Japan attacked the United States by bombing Pearl Harbor in Hawaii. At that point the United States entered the war against Japan and soon thereafter entered the war against Germany.

Fighting a war costs money, so economists' attention turned to how to raise that money. Taxes went up enormously, but government expenditures rose far more. The result can be seen in Exhibit 4(a), which tabulates GNP, the deficit, and unemployment data for 1937–46. As you can see, the deficit increased greatly and income rose by more than the deficit. Exhibit 4(b) shows the Keynesian multiplier model which describes those effects. As predicted, the U.S. economy expanded enormously in response to the expansionary fiscal policy that accompanied the war. (The wartime expansion was accompanied by wage and price controls and a large increase in the money supply, so we must be careful about drawing too strong an inference from this expansion.)

It might seem from the example of World War II, when the U.S. economy expanded sharply, that wars are good for the economy. They certainly do bring about expansionary policy, increase GDP, and decrease unemployment. But remember, GDP is *not* welfare and a decrease in unemployment is not necessarily good. In World

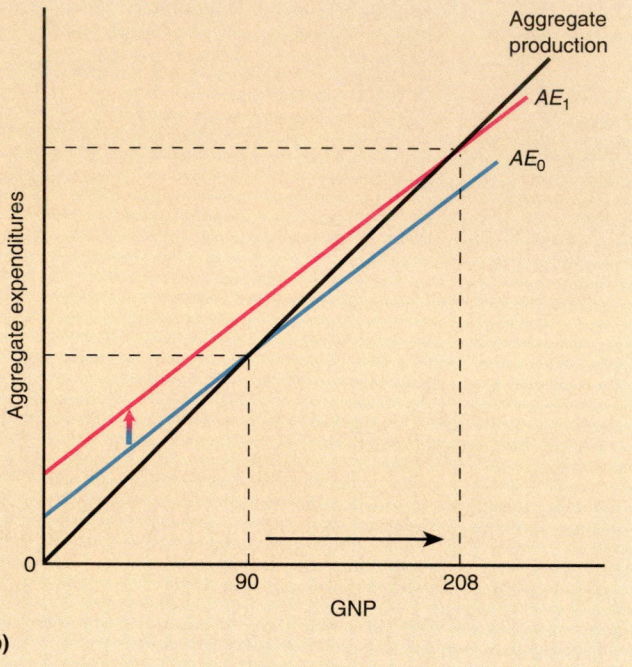

EXHIBIT 4 (a and b)   War Finance: Expansionary Fiscal Policy

During wars, government budget deficits have risen significantly. As they have, unemployment has fallen and GNP has risen enormously. You can see the effect in the table in (a), which presents the U.S. government budget deficit and unemployment rate during World War II. The graph in (b) shows that this is what would be predicted by the Keynesian model.

Year	GNP (billions of dollars)	Deficit (billions of dollars)	Unemployment rate
1937	90	−2.8	14.3
1938	84	−1.0	19.0
1939	90	−2.9	17.2
1940	99	−2.7	14.6
1941	124	−4.8	9.9
1942	157	−19.4	4.7
1943	191	−53.8	1.9
1944	210	−46.1	1.2
1945	211	−45.0	1.9
1946	208	−18.2	3.9

(a)

(b)

War II people went without many goods; production of guns and bombs increased but production of butter decreased. Many people were killed or permanently disabled, which decreases unemployment but can hardly be called a good way to expand the economy and lower unemployment.

Fiscal Policy in the 1990s   As a second example of how economists think about fiscal policy, let's look into the future to the late 1990s when the revenue that the U.S. government gets from social security taxes is predicted to be much higher than expenditures on social security benefits paid out to people. Economists have pointed out that, in the absence of any change in policy, U.S. fiscal policy will likely turn highly contractionary. Using the simple Keynesian model, they have predicted that that surplus will slow down the economy and push it into a period of slow growth and possibly recession.

Now let's talk about a more recent example: 1993 and President Bill Clinton's policy proposal to get the economy going—to increase income. Clinton is a Democrat, and has generally Keynesian advisers. So what kind of policy do you think he advocated? If you said, ''Increase the budget deficit to stimulate the economy,'' you've learned the model we discussed above, but you haven't been reading the paper. Instead, from reading the newspaper you should know that he proposed a policy of *decreasing the deficit* to stimulate the economy! (The path by which a decrease in the deficit was to stimulate the economy was through the deficit's effect on the long-term interest rate and investment. A smaller deficit means less government borrowing which, as we will discuss later, means lower interest rates, which means higher investment.)

Actually, his policy was more complicated than that; he did propose to initially increase the budget deficit slightly to stimulate the economy, but Congress didn't go along. Moreover, like much in politics, a lot of his deficit reduction was political rhetoric. But the lesson of this 1993 case is clear: applying the simple Keynesian model discussed above is not going to give you an understanding of policy discussions today.

But that does not mean you don't have to know the above models. It means you must know them better than did earlier students. As I've emphasized continually—to

Applying the simple Keynesian model discussed above is not going to give you an understanding of policy discussions today.

During World War II unemployment fell enormously, and the government issued many posters to get women to work. After the war, the government issued many posters to get women to give up their jobs for "their men." *Shaffer Archives.*

understand a model you must understand the limitations of the model and the assumptions that make it work, and determine whether those assumptions fit the reality. It's clear that in the 1990s, the assumptions of the simple model discussed above don't fit the facts of the 1990s. In the following pages I consider some reasons why.

Keynesian fiscal policy, and activist government policy in general, sounds so easy— and in the model it is. If there's a contraction in the economy, the government runs an expansionary fiscal policy; if there's inflation, the government runs a contractionary fiscal policy, keeping the economy at the desired level of income.

   In reality, that's not the way it is. A number of important problems arise, which makes the actual practice of fiscal policy difficult. These problems don't mean that the model is wrong; they simply mean that for fiscal policy to work, the policy conclusions drawn from the model must be modified to reflect the real-world problems. Let's consider how the reality might not fit the model. The model assumes:

PROBLEMS WITH FISCAL AND OTHER ACTIVIST KEYNESIAN POLICY

1. Financing the deficit doesn't have any offsetting effect. In reality, it often does.

2. The government knows what the situation is (for instance, the size of the *mpc*, and other exogenous variables). In reality, the government must estimate them.

3. The government knows the economy's potential income level (the highest level of income that doesn't cause inflation). In reality, the government may not know what this level is.

4. The government has flexibility in changing spending and taxes. In reality, government cannot change them quickly.

5. The size of the government debt doesn't matter. In reality, the size of the government debt often does matter.

6. Fiscal policy doesn't negatively affect other government goals. In reality, it often does.

Let's consider each a bit further.

5 Six assumptions of the model that could lead to problems with fiscal policy are:
   1. Financing the deficit doesn't have any offsetting effects.
   2. The government knows what the situation is.
   3. The government knows the economy's potential income.
   4. The government has flexibility in terms of spending and taxes.
   5. The size of the government debt doesn't matter.
   6. Fiscal policy doesn't negatively affect other government goals.

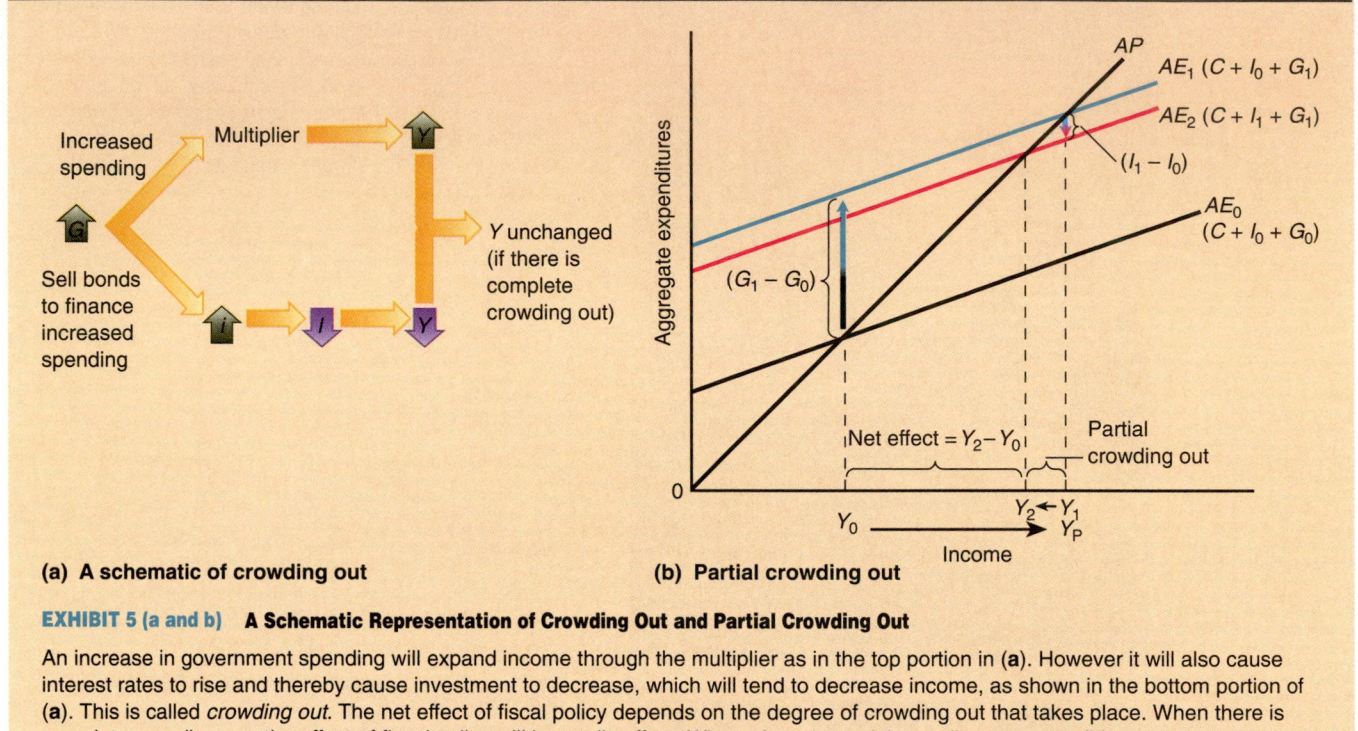

(a) A schematic of crowding out   **(b) Partial crowding out**

EXHIBIT 5 (a and b)   A Schematic Representation of Crowding Out and Partial Crowding Out

An increase in government spending will expand income through the multiplier as in the top portion in **(a)**. However it will also cause interest rates to rise and thereby cause investment to decrease, which will tend to decrease income, as shown in the bottom portion of **(a)**. This is called *crowding out*. The net effect of fiscal policy depends on the degree of crowding out that takes place. When there is complete crowding out, the effect of fiscal policy will be totally offset. Where there is partial crowding out, as in **(b)**, an increase in government spending will still have an expansionary effect, but the effect will be smaller than it otherwise would have been.

Financing the Deficit Doesn't Have Offsetting Effects

One of the most important limitations of the Keynesian model is that it assumes that financing the deficit has no offsetting effects on income. Classicals argue that that is not the case—that fiscal policy will have significant offsetting effects, and that the government financing of a deficit will offset the deficit's expansionary effect.

Classical economists say that the Keynesian model assumes savings and investment are unequal, and that the government can increase its expenditures without at the same time causing a decrease in private expenditures. Classical economists object to that assumption. They believe the interest rate equilibrates savings and investment. They argue that when the government sells bonds to finance the deficit, that sale of bonds will crowd out private investment.

Crowding out occurs as follows: When the government runs a deficit, it must sell bonds to finance that deficit. To get people to buy and hold the bonds, the government must make them attractive. That means the interest rate the bonds pay must be higher than it otherwise would have been. This tends to push up the interest rate, which makes it more expensive for private businesses to borrow, so they reduce their borrowing and their investment. That private investment is crowded out by expansionary fiscal policy. Hence the name "crowding out." Increased government spending crowds out private spending.

Exhibit 5(a) shows the interconnection. The top arrows represent the direct effect of increased spending. The bottom arrows represent the effects of financing that increased spending. Each set of arrows works in the opposite direction from the other set. Crowding out is shown graphically in the Keynesian model in Exhibit 5(b). Income in the economy is Y_0 and government has decided to expand that income to Y_1 by increasing its spending by ΔG.

If financing were not an issue, expansionary fiscal policy would shift up aggregate expenditures from AE_0 to AE_1, increasing income from Y_0 to Y_1. Financing the deficit, however, increases interest rates and decreases investment by ΔI, which shifts the AE curve back to AE_2. Income falls back to Y_2. Because of crowding out, the net expansionary effect of fiscal policy is much smaller than it otherwise would have been. Some Classicals argue that crowding out could totally offset the expansionary effect of fiscal policy, so the net effect is zero, or even negative, since they consider private spending more productive than government spending.

The crowding out effect also works in reverse on contractionary fiscal policy. Say the government runs a surplus. That surplus will slow the economy via the multiplier effect. But it also means the Treasury can buy back some of its outstanding bonds, which will have a tendency to push bond prices up and interest rates down. Lower interest rates will stimulate investment which, in turn, will have an offsetting expansionary effect on the economy. So when we include financing the deficit in our consideration of fiscal policy, the net multiplier effect is reduced.

How large this financing offset to fiscal policy will be is a matter of debate. Classicals see the crowding out effect as relatively large, in many cases almost completely negating the effect of expansionary fiscal policy. Keynesians see it as relatively small, as long as the economy is in a recession or operating below its potential income level. Some Keynesians even argue that often the crowding out will be offset by **crowding in**—positive effects of government spending on other components of spending. Where there is crowding in, the increased government spending will cause investment to increase as businesses prepare to meet the government's demand for goods.

The empirical evidence is mixed and has not resolved the debate. Both sides see some crowding out occurring as the debt is financed by selling bonds. The closer to the potential income level the economy is, the more crowding out is likely to occur.

6 Crowding out is the offsetting effect on private expenditures caused by the government's sale of bonds to finance expansionary fiscal policy.

Q–9: Demonstrate graphically what would happen if government expenditures policy stimulated private investment.

Knowing What the Situation Is

All our examples used numbers that were chosen arbitrarily. In reality, the numbers used in the model must be estimated since data upon which estimates can be made aren't always available. Most economic data are published quarterly, and it usually takes six to nine months of data to indicate, with any degree of confidence, the state of the economy and which way it is heading. Thus, we could be halfway into a recession before we even knew it was happening. (Data are already three months old when published; then we need two or three quarters of such data before they compose a useful body of information to work with.)

In an attempt to deal with this problem, the government relies on large macroeconomic models and leading indicators to predict what the economy will be like six months or a year from now. As part of the input to these complex models, the government must predict economic factors that determine the size of the multiplier. These predictions are imprecise so the forecasts are imprecise. Economic forecasting is still an art, not a science.

Economists' data problems limit the use of fiscal policy for fine tuning. There's little sense in recommending expansionary or contractionary policy until you know what policy is called for.

Knowing the Level of Potential Income

This problem of not knowing the level of potential income is related to the problem we just discussed. The target level of employment and the potential level of income are not easy concepts to define. At one time it was thought 3 percent unemployment meant full employment. Some time later it was generally thought 6 percent unemployment meant full employment. About that time economists stopped calling the potential level of income the *full-employment* level of income.

Any variation in potential income can make an enormous difference in the policy prescription that could be recommended. To see how big a difference, let's translate a 1 percent change in unemployment into a change in income. According to **Okun's law,** the general rule of thumb economists use to translate changes in the unemployment rate into changes in income is that a 1 percent fall in the unemployment rate equals a 2.5 percent increase in income. Thus, in 1994 with income at about $7 trillion, a 1 percent fall in the unemployment rate would have increased income $175 billion.

Now let's say one economist believes 6 percent is the long-run achievable target unemployment level, while another believes it's 4.5 percent. That's a 1.5 percent

Okun's law   A general rule of thumb economists use to translate the unemployment rate into changes in income. A 1 percent fall in the unemployment rate equals a 2.5 percent increase in income.

The CBO Report—*The Economic and Budget Outlook* is one of the many government publications that discusses macroeconomic policy options.

Differences in estimates of potential income often lead to different policy recommendations.

In most cases the U.S. economy is in an ambiguous state where some economists are calling for expansionary policy and others are calling for contractionary policy.

difference. Since a 1 percent decrease in the unemployment rate means an increase of about $175 billion in national income, their views of the income level we should target differ by over $263 billion (1.5 × $175 = $263). Yet both views are reasonable. Looking at the same economy (the same data), one economist may call for expansionary fiscal policy while the other may call for contractionary fiscal policy.

In practice, differences in estimates of potential income often lead to different policy recommendations. Empirical estimates suggest that the size of the multiplier is between 2 and 2.5. Let's say it's 2.5. That means autonomous expenditures must be predicted to shift either up or down by more than $105 billion before an economist who believes the target unemployment rate is 4.5 percent would agree in policy recommendation with an economist who believes the rate is 6 percent. Since almost all fluctuations in autonomous investment and autonomous consumption are less than this amount, there's no generally agreed upon policy prescription for most fluctuations. Some economists will call for expansionary policy; some will call for contractionary policy; and the government decision makers won't have any clear-cut policy to follow.

You might wonder why the range of potential income estimates is so large. Why not simply see whether the economy has inflation at the existing unemployment and income levels? Would that it were so easy. Inflation is a complicated process. Seeds of inflation are often sown years before inflation results. The main problem is that establishing a close link between the level of economic activity and inflation is a complicated statistical challenge to economists, one that has not yet been satisfactorily met. That leads to enormous debate as to what the causes are.

Economists believe that outside some range (perhaps 3.5 percent unemployment on the low side and 10 percent on the high side), too much spending causes inflation and too little spending causes a recession. That 3.5 to 10 percent range is so large that in most cases the U.S. economy is in an ambiguous state where some economists are calling for expansionary policy and others are calling for contractionary policy.

Once the economy reaches the edge of the range or falls outside it, the economists' policy prescription becomes clearer. For example, in the Depression, when this Keynesian model was developed, unemployment was 25 percent—well outside the range. Should the economy ever go into such a depression again, economists' policy prescriptions will be clear. The call will be for expansionary fiscal policy. Most times the economy is within the ambiguous range so there are disagreements among economists.

Expenditures on war-related products have been a major source of government expenditures in the past 60 years. With the end of the Cold War in the early 1990s these expenditures are proving hard to cut.
UPI/Bettmann.

For argument's sake, let's say economists agree that contractionary policy is needed and that's what they advise the government. Will the government implement it? And, if so, will it implement contractionary fiscal policy at the right time? The answer to both questions is: probably not. There are also problems with implementing economists' calls for expansionary fiscal policy. Even if economists are unanimous in calling for expansionary fiscal policy, putting fiscal policy in place takes time and has serious implementation problems.

Numerous political and institutional realities in the United States today make the task of implementing fiscal policy difficult. Government spending and taxes cannot be changed instantaneously. New taxes and new spending must be legislated. It takes time for the government to pass a bill. Politicians face intense political pressures; their other goals may conflict with the goals of fiscal policy. For example, few members of Congress who hope to be reelected would vote to raise taxes in an election year. Similarly few members would vote to slash defense spending when military contractors are a major source of employment in their districts, even when there's little to defend against. Squabbles between Congress and the president may delay initiating appropriate fiscal policy for months, even years. By the time the fiscal policy is implemented, what may have once been the right fiscal policy may have ceased to be right, and some other policy may have become right.

Imagine trying to steer a car at 60 miles an hour when there's a five-second delay between the time you turn the steering wheel and the time the car's wheels turn. Imagining that situation will give you a good sense of how fiscal policy works in the real world.

There is no inherent reason why the adoption of Keynesian policies should have caused the government to run deficits year after year and hence to incur ever-increasing debt. Keynesian policy is consistent with running deficits some years and surpluses other years. In practice, the introduction of Keynesian policy has been accompanied by many deficits and few surpluses, and by a large increase in government debt. If that increase in government debt hurts the economy, one can oppose Keynesian policy, even if one believes that policy might otherwise be beneficial.

There are two reasons why Keynesian policy has led to an increase in government debt. First, early Keynesian economists favored large increases in government spending as well as favoring the government's using fiscal policy. These early Keynesians employed the Keynesian economic model to justify increasing spending without increasing taxes. A second reason is political. Politically it's much easier for government to increase spending and decrease taxes than to decrease spending and increase taxes. Due to political pressure, expansionary fiscal policy has predominated over contractionary fiscal policy.

Whether debt is a problem is an important and complicated issue as we'll see in a later chapter devoted entirely to the question. For now, all you need remember is that if one believes that the debt is harmful, then there might be a reason not to conduct expansionary fiscal policy, even when the model calls for it.

An economy has many goals; achieving potential income is only one of those goals. So it's not surprising that those goals often conflict. In an earlier example in this chapter, we saw those conflicts. When the government ran expansionary fiscal policy, the balance of trade deficit grew. As the economy expands and income rises, exports remain constant but imports rise. If a nation's international considerations do not allow a balance of trade deficit to become larger, as is true in many countries, those governments cannot run expansionary fiscal policies—unless they can somehow prevent this balance of trade deficit from becoming larger.

So where do these six problems leave fiscal policy? While they don't eliminate it, they restrict its usefulness. Fiscal policy is a sledgehammer, not an instrument for fine tuning. When the economy goes into a depression, the appropriate fiscal policy is clear. Similarly when the economy has a hyperinflation, the appropriate policy is

The Government's Flexibility in Changing Taxes and Spending

Size of the Government Debt Doesn't Matter

Fiscal Policy Doesn't Negatively Affect Other Government Goals

Fiscal Policy in Practice: Summary of the Problems

Fiscal policy is a sledgehammer, not an instrument for fine tuning.

ADDED DIMENSION

FIGHTING THE VIETNAM INFLATION

One time economists were united in their views on appropriate fiscal policy was during the Vietnam War, from the early 1960s until 1975, when the economy was pushed to its limits. About 1965, President Lyndon B. Johnson's economic advisers started to argue strongly that a tax increase was needed to slow the economy and decrease inflationary pressures. President Johnson wouldn't hear of it. He felt a tax increase would be political suicide. Finally in mid-1968, after Johnson had decided not to run for reelection, a temporary income tax increase was passed. By then, however, many economists felt that the seeds of the 1970s inflation had already been sown.

clear. But in less extreme cases, there will be debate on what the appropriate fiscal policy is—a debate economic theory can't answer conclusively.

Building Keynesian Policies into Institutions

7 An automatic stabilizer is any government program or policy that will counteract the business cycle without any new government action.

Economists quickly recognized the political problems with instituting direct counter-cyclical fiscal policy. To avoid these problems they suggested policies that built fiscal policy into U.S. institutions so that it would be put into effect without any political decisions being necessary. They called a built-in fiscal policy an **automatic stabilizer,** which is any government program or policy that will counteract the business cycle without any new government action. Automatic stabilizers include welfare payments, unemployment insurance, and the income tax system.

To see how automatic stabilizers work, consider the unemployment insurance system. When the economy is slowing down or is in a recession, the unemployment rate will rise. When people lose their jobs, they will reduce their consumption, starting the multiplier process, which decreases income. Unemployment insurance immediately helps offset the decrease in individuals' incomes as the government pays benefits to the unemployed. Thus, the budget deficit increases, and part of the fall in income is stopped without any explicit act by the government. Automatic stabilizers also work in reverse. When income increases, they decrease the size of the deficit.

Another automatic stabilizer is our income tax system. Earlier in this chapter we said that tax revenue fluctuates as income fluctuates and that this makes the deficit hard to predict. When the economy expands unexpectedly, the budget deficit is lower than originally expected; when the economy contracts unexpectedly, the budget deficit is higher than expected. Let's go through the reasoning why. When the economy is strong, people have more income and thus pay higher taxes. This increase in tax revenue reduces expenditures from what they would have been, and moderates the economy's growth. When the economy goes into a recession, the opposite occurs.

Q–10 What effect do automatic stabilizers have on the size of the multiplier?

Automatic stabilizers may seem like the solution to the economic woes we have discussed, but they, too, have their shortcomings. One problem is that when the economy is first starting to climb out of a recession, automatic stabilizers will slow the process, rather than help it along, for the same reason they slow the contractionary process. As income increases, automatic stabilizers increase government taxes and decrease government spending, and as they do, the discretionary policy's expansionary effects are decreased.

Despite these problems, most Keynesians believe automatic stabilizers have played an important role in reducing fluctuations in our economy. They point to the kind of data we see in Exhibit 6, which they say show a significant decrease in fluctuations in the economy. Other economists aren't so sure; they argue the apparent decrease in fluctuations is an optical illusion. As usual, economic data are sufficiently ambiguous to give both sides strong arguments. The verdict is still out.

Fiscal Policy in Perspective

By now you should be able to think in terms of the Keynesian model and see how disequilibria between aggregate production and aggregate expenditures can be resolved by adjustments in aggregate income. But beware. The Keynesian model is only a model. It's a tool, a crutch, to help you see certain relationships. It does so by obscuring others, including interest rate adjustment, price level adjustment, and supply incentive effects.

EXHIBIT 6   Decrease in Fluctuations in the Economy

One of the arguments in favor of Keynesian economics is that since it was introduced into the U.S. economy, fluctuations in the economy have decreased. Source: Federal Reserve Historical Charts and Economic Report of the President.

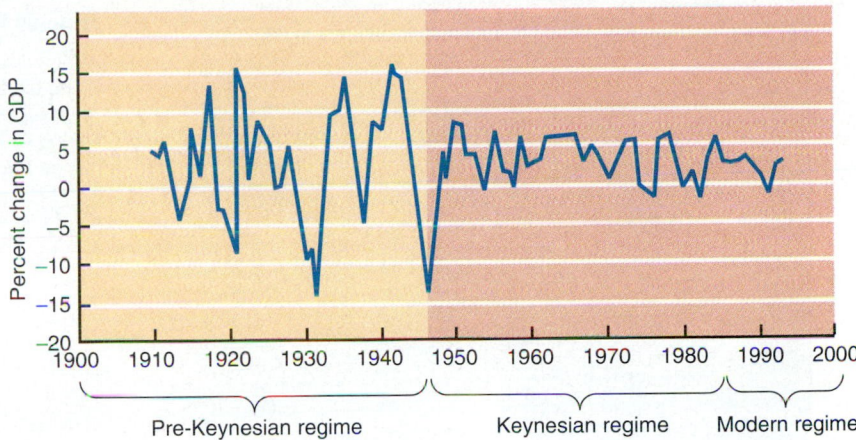

Consideration of these aspects led to significant changes in macroeconomic thinking over the years. In the 1970s Classical economics rose like a phoenix from the ashes and re-emerged. Modern Classical economists challenged the way Keynesian economists thought about expansionary effects of fiscal policy. They won many converts and modified the presentation of Keynesian economics so that it focuses on dynamic adjustment and is no longer presented mechanistically.

The modern Classical economists argue that expectations of policy can change the dynamic adjustment process, and that any simple dynamic adjustment models are unlikely to describe the aggregate economy. But while they are working on alternative aggregate dynamic adjustment models, they haven't come up with any that have been accepted as a way of describing the adjustment process of the aggregate economy. In the absence of an alternative model, the Keynesian model is the model used by most macro policy economists. Therefore, it is useful to know this model, as long as you keep in mind that it is only a first approximation to analyzing what happens in the economy.

The Keynesian model is the model used by most macro policy economists.

I went through the Keynesian model so carefully in this chapter for two reasons. (1) It describes tendencies that affect economies and highlights important dynamic inter-relationships among aggregates. The equilibrium it describes doesn't matter much; it is never reached, but the tendencies the model highlights for the economy to move in certain directions do matter. (2) It is the model that is in the back of most macro policy economists' minds when they discuss macro policy. This means that to understand how most policy economists talk about the macro economy, you must understand the tendencies given in the Keynesian model.

Not only did I carefully go through the model, I also carefully went through limitations of the model. The reason I did so is that the United States has gotten about as much as it can out of Keynesian demand management policy. To see this it is helpful to think back to the discussion of the three ranges of the economy presented in earlier chapters—the Keynesian range, the Classical range, and the Intermediate range shown in Exhibit 7.

Demand management policies are useful in keeping the economy out of range *A* and range *C*. And they are used that way. But that means that the economy is almost always in the Intermediate range—where there is significant debate about whether an expansionary demand management policy is going to be inflationary, or will lead to higher output.

The dilemma of macro policy is that we have no way of specifying precisely where these ranges are. There is no signpost on the economy saying, "This is the economy's potential income, and this is the appropriate target unemployment." Thus at the 1994 American Economic Association meeting you could have two former presidents of the American Economic Association, William Vickrey and Robert

THE KEYNESIAN MODEL AND THE PRACTICE OF FISCAL POLICY IN THE 1990S

The economy is generally in an ambiguous range; in this range macro policy is an art, not a science.

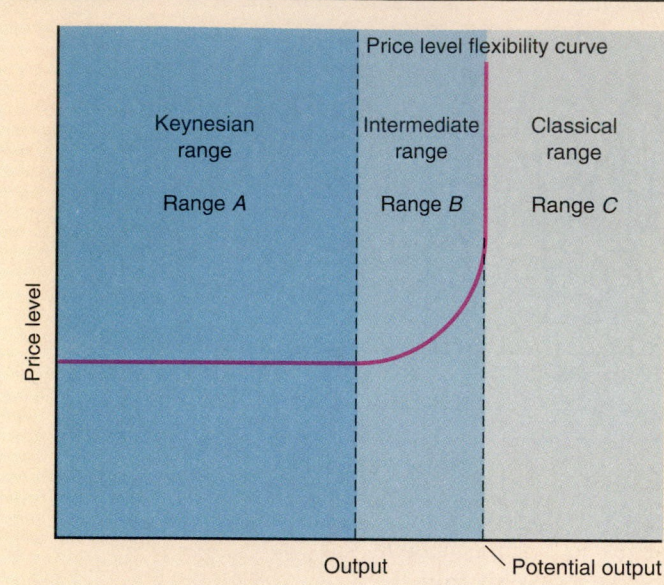

EXHIBIT 7   The Three Ranges of Output

When discussing macro policy, it is important to keep in mind the three ranges of output. Demand management policies are useful in keeping the economy out of ranges A and C, which means the economy is generally in range B where the appropriate policy is debatable.

Eisner, arguing that we are still in the Keynesian range and our target should be 3.5 percent unemployment—that's the old-time Keynesian position. Looking at the same reality, you could have some modern Classical economists, such as Robert Barro, arguing that even if the unemployment rate is 10 percent, we are still at the economy's potential income—that we are in Range C. The majority of the profession, however, see the economy in the mid-1990s as being in the Intermediate range (Range B). In this Intermediate range the science of economics does not present a policy guide, and we enter the art of economics which involves choosing between conflicting goals when one is not sure of the results. We'll discuss the art of macroeconomics in later chapters.

CHAPTER SUMMARY

• Aggregate demand management policy attempts to influence the level of output in the economy by influencing aggregate demand and relying on the multiplier to expand any policy-induced change in aggregate demand.

• Fiscal policy—the change in government spending or taxes—works by providing a deliberate countershock to offset unexpected shocks to the economy.

• Expansionary fiscal policy is represented graphically as an upward shift of the aggregate expenditures curve.

• Contractionary fiscal policy is represented graphically as a downward shift of the aggregate expenditures curve.

• The effect of fiscal policy can be determined by using the Keynesian model.

• The size of the deficit or surplus influences the level of income in the economy, but is also influenced by it.

• The size of the trade balance (net exports) influences the

level of income in the economy but is also influenced by it.

• Fiscal policy is affected by the following problems, among others:

 1. Lack of knowledge of what policy is called for.
 2. Government's inability to respond quickly enough.
 3. Government debt.
 4. Crowding out.

• Keynesian fiscal policy is now built into U.S. economic institutions through automatic stabilizers.

• Aggregate demand management policies are most effective in the Keynesian range of the economy—when the economy is significantly below its potential income.

KEY TERMS

aggregate demand management
  policy   *(256)*
automatic stabilizer   *(276)*
countercyclical fiscal policy   *(263)*
crowding in   *(273)*
crowding out   *(272)*
exchange rate policy   *(266)*

export-led growth policies   *(266)*
fine tuning   *(263)*
fiscal policy   *(256)*
inflationary gap   *(262)*
marginal propensity to expend   *(263)*
Okun's law   *(273)*

passive deficit   *(268)*
recessionary gap   *(261)*
Rosy Scenario policy   *(265)*
structural deficit   *(268)*
transfer payments   *(259)*

QUESTIONS FOR THOUGHT AND REVIEW

*The number after each question represents the estimated
degree of critical thinking required. (1 = almost none;
10 = deep thought.)*

1. Explain how Franklin D. Roosevelt's statement, "We
   have nothing to fear but fear itself," pertains to macroeconomic policy.   *(4)*

2. Congratulations! You've just been appointed chairman of
   the Council of Economic Advisers in Textland. The *mpc*
   is .8; all nonconsumption expenditures and taxes are
   exogenous. There is a recessionary gap of $400, which
   the government wants to eliminate by changing taxes.
   What policy would you suggest?   *(4)*

3. Your research assistant comes running in and tells you
   that instead of changing taxes, the government wants to
   achieve the same result by increasing expenditures. What
   policy would you recommend now?   *(4)*

4. Your research assistant has a worried look on her face.
   "What's the problem?" you ask. "I goofed," she confesses. "I thought taxes were exogenous when actually
   there's a marginal tax rate of .1." Before she can utter
   another word, you say, "No problem. I'll simply recalculate my answers to Questions 2 and 3 and change
   them before I send them in." What are your corrected
   answers? (Requires reading Appendix A.)   *(5)*

5. She still has a pained expression. "What's wrong?" you
   ask. "You didn't let me finish," she says. "Not only
   was there a marginal tax rate of .1; there's also a marginal propensity to import of .2." Again you interrupt to
   make sure she doesn't feel guilty. Again you say, "No
   problem," and recalculate your answers to Questions 2
   and 3 to account for the new information. What are your
   new answers? (Requires reading Appendix A.)   *(5)*

6. That pained look is still there, but this time you don't
   interrupt. You let her finish. She says, "And they want
   to see the answers graphically." You do the right
   thing.   *(4)*

7. Two economists are debating whether the normal rate of
   unemployment is 4 or 6 percent. Mr. A believes it's 4
   percent; Ms. B believes it's 6 percent. One says the
   structural deficit is $40 billion; the other says it is $20
   billion. Which one says which? Why?   *(5)*

8. What is the current state of U.S. fiscal policy? Would
   you advise the United States to change its fiscal policy?
   Why?   *(7)*

9. If interest rates have no effect on investment, what percentage of crowding out will there be?   *(5)*

10. A country has a balance of trade deficit and a recession-
    ary gap. Advise it how to eliminate both.   *(9)*

PROBLEMS AND EXERCISES

1. Congratulations. You've just been appointed economic
   adviser to Easyland. You go to your first board meeting
   and are asked the following questions. What are the
   answers you would give?
   a. Why does cutting taxes by $100 have a smaller effect
      on GDP than increasing expenditures by $100?
   b. If they cut taxes and want a neutral fiscal policy, what
      should they do with their trade policy?
   c. Why does the trade deficit generally increase as the
      economy improves?
   d. How does your answer to c change if all world econ-
      omies are moving together?

2. Congratulations. You've just been appointed economic
   advisor to Dreamland. The president wants your advice
   on how to reduce unemployment from 8 to 6 percent.
   Income is $40,000, and the *mpe* is .4.
   a. Advise her.

   b. She wants to know what would happen to her formerly
      balanced budget if she follows your advice. You natu-
      rally tell her.
   c. Now she wants to know what will happen to her for-
      merly zero trade deficit. You tell her.
   d. Hearing your answers, she tells you that your policy is
      unacceptable. She wants to reduce unemployment and
      keep both the trade and the government budget in bal-
      ance. How do you respond?

3. Condolences. You've been fired from your job in Dreamland, but you found another job in neighboring
   Fantasyland. Its economy is almost the same as Dreamland's but you must rely on your research assistant for the
   specific numbers. He says income is $50,000, *mpe* is .75,
   and the president wants to lower unemployment from 8 to
   6 percent.
   a. Advise him.

b. Your research assistant comes in and says "Sorry, I meant that the *mpe* is .66." You redo your calculations.

c. You're just about to see the president when your research assistant comes running, saying "Sorry, sorry, I meant that the *mpe* is .5." Redo your calculations.

4. President Clinton's policy in 1993 was designed to reduce the deficit but increase employment.

a. Why would such a policy not fit well in the Keynesian model presented in this chapter?

b. Explain in words how such a policy might achieve the desired effect.

c. Graphically demonstrate your answer in *b*.

d. What data would you look at to see if your explanations in *b* and *c* are appropriate?

5. Explain the following observations in terms of the Keynesian model.

a. In the early 1990s, the United States was pushing Japan to increase its budget deficit.

b. In the early 1990s, the United States was pushing Japan to decrease its trade surplus.

c. In the early 1990s, unemployment in Europe exceeded 10 percent but few economists were pushing for an increase in European governments' budget deficits.

d. When running for re-election most presidents increase government spending programs.

e. A maxim in politics is that if you are going to increase taxes, the time to do it is right after your election, when re-election is far off.

ANSWERS TO MARGIN QUESTIONS

1. Each individual's spending primarily affects others' income, not their own. The feedback effects on their own income are so small that they do not take them into account. Only coordinated effort, in which many people increase their spending simultaneously, will have a strong enough effect to create a significant multiplier effect. Thus people's spending decision is a type of externality. *(258)*

2. Income will increase by 3 × $100, or $300. *(259)*

3. As you can see, contractionary fiscal policy shifts aggregate expenditure down and shifts income down by a multiple of that amount. *(261)*

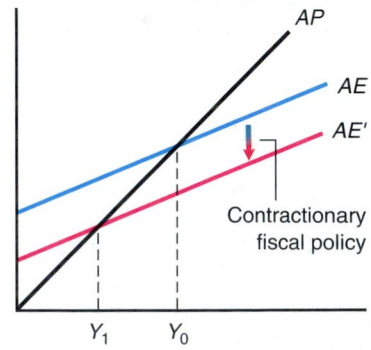

4. Since there is an inflationary gap, I would recommend contractionary fiscal policy. Since the multiplier is 1.5 (given the marginal propensity to expend of .33), I would recommend decreasing government spending by $66. *(263)*

5. If the marginal propensity to import rises, the multiplier becomes smaller since the marginal propensity to import is a leakage from the circular flow. *(263)*

6. Expectations play a central role in both spending and production decisions. If positive talk about the economy

can influence expectations, it may be possible to "talk" an economy into a boom. *(265)*

7. According to the Keynesian model, a fall in the value of the dollar should increase exports, which would have a multiplied positive effect on income. *(266)*

8. Since the economy is at its potential income, its passive deficit is zero. All of its budget deficit is a structural deficit. *(268)*

9. If government spending stimulated private spending, the phenomenon of what might be called "crowding in" might occur. The increase in government spending would shift the *AE* curve up from AE_0 to AE_1 as in the diagram below. The resulting shift in income would

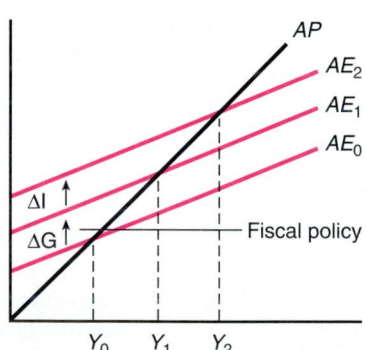

cause a further shift up in investment, shifting the aggregate expenditure curve up further to AE_2. Income would increase from Y_0 to Y_2—by more than what the simple Keynesian model would predict. *(273)*

10. Automatic stabilizers tend to decrease the size of the multiplier, decreasing the fluctuations in the economy. *(276)*

The Algebraic Keynesian Model

In this chapter I used a multiplier based on the marginal propensity to consume and briefly introduced the marginal propensity to expend. This kept the math to a minimum, but obscured some of the ways in which the components of expenditures affected income, and in turn how those components of income are affected by income. In this appendix I briefly outline a fuller presentation and show the relationship between the marginal propensity to expend (mpe), specified as e in the equations, and the marginal propensities to consume (mpc), specified as b in the equations, and the marginal propensity to import (mpm), specified as m in the equations, and the marginal tax rate, specified as t in the equations.

The basic Keynesian model consists of the following equations:

(1) $C = C_0 + bY_d$

(2) $Y_d = Y - T + R$

(3) $I = I_0$

(4) $G = G_0$

(5) $R = R_0$

(6) $T = T_0 + tY$

(7) $X = X_0$

(8) $M = M_0 + mY$

(9) $C + I + G + (X - M) = Y$

Equation (1) is the consumption function. C_0 is autonomous consumption; bY_d is the *mpc* multiplied by disposable income.

Equation (2) defines disposable income as a function of real income minus taxes plus government transfers.

Equation (3) is the investment function. I_0 is autonomous investment.

Equation (4) is the government expenditures function. G_0 is autonomous spending.

Equation (5) is the government transfer function. R_0 is autonomous transfer payments.

Equation (6) is the tax function. Taxes are composed of two parts. The autonomous component, T_0, is unaffected by income. The induced portion of taxes is tY. The tax rate is represented by t.

Equation (7) is the exogenous export function.

Equation (8) is the import function. Imports are composed of two parts. M_0 is the autonomous portion. The induced portion is mY. The marginal propensity to import is represented by m.

Equation (9) is the national income accounting identity: Total expenditures = income.

To use this model meaningfully, we must combine all these equations into a single equation, called a *reduced-form equation,* which will neatly show the effect of various shifts on the equilibrium level of income. To do so we first substitute Equation (2) into Equation (1) giving us:

(1a) $C = C_0 + b(Y - T + R_0)$

We then substitute (1a), (3), (4), (5), (6), (7), and (8) into Equation (9), giving:

$$C_0 + b[Y - (T_0 + tY) + R_0] + I_0 + G_0 + (X_0 - (M_0 + mY)) = Y$$

Removing the parentheses:

$$C_0 + bY - bT_0 - btY + bR_0 + I_0 + G_0 + X_0 - M_0 - mY = Y$$

Moving all of the Y terms to the right side:

$$C_0 - bT_0 + bR_0 + I_0 + G_0 + X_0 - M_0 = Y - bY + btY + mY$$

Factoring out Y on the right side:

$$C_0 - bT_0 + bR_0 + I_0 + G_0 + X_0 - M_0 = Y(1 - b + bt + m)$$

Dividing by $(1 - b + bt + m)$ gives:

$$(C_0 - bT_0 + bR_0 + I_0 + G_0 + X_0 - M_0)[1/(1 - b + bt + m)] = Y$$

$1/(1 - b + bt + m)$ is the multiplier for a simple Keynesian model with endogenous taxes and endogenous imports.

The marginal propensity to expend, *mpe,* discussed in the text would equal $b - bt - m$. The additional terms adjust b, the *mpc,* for the other induced expenditures that the simple model did not consider. Notice that they both make the multiplier smaller. For example, if the *mpc* is .8, $t = .25$, and $m = .1$, the multiplier using only the *mpc* would be $1/(1 - .8) = 5$. Taking into account other induced expenditures we can calculate the *mpe*. It equals $.8 - .8(.25) - .1 = .5$. Substituting .5 into our generalized multiplier formula, $1/(1 - .5)$ we see that the multiplier becomes $(1/(.5)) = 2$.

Thus, the general structure of the reduced form equation is:

$$Y = (\text{multiplier})(\text{autonomous expenditures})$$

When we discuss changes in autonomous expenditures, the general form is:

$$\Delta Y = (\text{multiplier})(\Delta \text{ autonomous expenditures})$$

To see whether you follow the argument, let's try another numerical example. Say you want to increase income (Y) by 100. Assume $b = .8$, $t = .2$, and $m = .04$. Substituting in these numbers your find that $mpe = .8 - .8(.2) - .04 = .6$. Thus, in this example we get a multiplier of 2.5. (The approximate multiplier for the United States is usually considered to be somewhere between 2 and 2.5; the additional terms play an important role in making it this small.)

Having calculated the multiplier we can now determine how much to change autonomous expenditure to affect income. For example, to increase income by 100, we must increase autonomous expenditures by $(100/2.5) = 40$.

The Circular Spiral, Real Business Cycles, and Dynamic Externalities

It is important, when thinking about Keynesian policies, that you remember that *it is only autonomous expenditures that have no offsetting effects on other expenditures that cause a multiplied effect on income.* When the expenditures we make aren't autonomous, the expansion won't necessarily take place. For example, when we increase consumption, we might be decreasing saving which might lead to decreased investment, and hence to a direct offsetting effect. That's precisely what Classicals contend happens in general—when the government pushes on one of these supposedly autonomous expenditures. it simply pulls down on another and the net effect is a wash. *Classicals see everything as induced—dependent on everything else—so forget activist government policy and rely on a laissez-faire policy.*

The Keynesian Spiral

When you think of the circular flow diagram, the Classical conception of a flow in which everything depends on everything else seems to make sense in the aggregate: Something can't come out of nothing. Thus a reasonable question for you to ask is: "Where do Keynesians see this autonomous expenditure coming from; isn't any expenditure going to have to come from somewhere?"

For Keynesians the answer to this question is: Not necessarily. They don't see financial markets as operating smoothly in translating savings into investment. More generally, they don't see the economy operating efficiently in translating all leakages from the circular flow into injections into the circular flow. What that means is that, for Keynesians, the circular flow is not a flow at all, but is, instead, a spiral that shrinks or expands in response to the dynamic disequilibrium adjustment forces in the economy. If people save too much, the spiral will shrink and aggregate income will fall, causing people to save less; people will end up sitting around doing nothing— unemployed, not saving, and not earning income. If people save too little, the spiral will expand beyond what the

current institutions can handle and an accelerating inflation will result.

Keynesians see policies directed at autonomous expenditures as preventing that from happening, or at least preventing the income from shrinking or expanding too much. Expansionary autonomous policies generate income, and as they do, they generate saving, which prevents the offsetting effect on other autonomous investment. Contractionary policies decrease income and as they do, they decrease spending.

Real Business Cycles, Keynesian Business Cycles, and Macro Policy

Recent developments in modern Classical economics have also accepted a version of this circular spiral notion of the economy. It is called the *real business cycle* theory. It says that business cycles occur because of technological and other "natural" shocks.

The difference between the Classical real business cycle theory and the Keynesian business cycle theory is that, in the Classical view, the spiraling nature of income in the economy simply reflects individuals' desires, while in the Keynesian view, the initial fluctuations may begin from individuals' desires, or from some other cause, but those fluctuations are multiplied into larger-than-desired fluctuations. In that sense, the Keynesian economic theory of business cycles presented in this book can be interpreted as a modification of the Classical real business cycle theory—one that allows for deviations from the desired dynamic equilibrium path. It follows that in their policies Keynesians should not be trying to prevent all the fluctuations in income—only larger-than-individually-desired fluctuations.

Another way of expressing this dynamic interpretation of Keynesian economics is to say that Keynesians see the aggregate income level as fluctuating more than individuals' desires due to **dynamic externalities**— effects of adjustment decisions that are not taken into account by the decision maker. Keynesians' policies are designed to offset these dynamic externalities. Some Classicals see the aggregate income reflecting the desires of individuals, and hence see the Keynesian policies designed to affect aggregate income as inappropriate. Other Classicals agree that, in principle, dynamic externalities can exist; they argue, however, that generally the dynamic interrelationships are so complicated that the government is not going to be able to react to them in a reasonable manner. So even though they accept the Keynesian intuitive model of the aggregate economy, they still reject the use of Keynesian policies and come to Classical policy conclusions.

12

Financial Institutions

*Finance is a means of assuring the flow of capital. Historically it
has also been a means for guiding that flow. In the first case, it is
a mechanism in aid of the industrial system as we know it. In the
second, it is a power controlling it.*

~Adolf A. Berle, Jr.

After reading this chapter, you should be able to:

1 Explain how financial assets can be created by an agreement between two people.

2 List four types of financial institutions.

3 Distinguish a primary financial market from a secondary financial market.

4 List three money market assets and two capital market assets.

5 Explain why, when interest rates fall, bond prices rise—and vice versa.

6 Roughly determine the present value of an amount of money at a future date.

7 Differentiate the Classical and Keynesian views of the financial sector.

Markets make specialization and trade possible and thereby make the economy far more efficient than it otherwise would be. But the efficient use of markets requires a financial sector that facilitates and lubricates those trades.

In thinking about the economy, students often focus on the *real* economy: producing real goods or services such as shoes, operas, automobiles, and textbooks. That's an incomplete view of the economy. The financial sector plays a central role in organizing and coordinating our economy; it makes modern economic society possible. A car won't run without oil; a modern economy won't operate without a financial sector.

In thinking about the financial sector's role, remember the following insight. *For every real transaction there is a financial transaction that mirrors it.* For example, when you buy an apple, the person selling the apple is buying 35¢ from you by spending his apple. The financial transaction is the transfer of 35¢; the real transaction is the transfer of the apple.

For larger items, the financial transaction behind the real transaction can be somewhat complicated. When you buy a house, you'll probably pay for part of that house with a mortgage, which requires that you borrow money from a bank. The bank, in turn, borrows from individuals the money it lends to you. There's a similar financial transaction when you buy a car, or even a book, on credit.

There's a financial transaction reflecting every real transaction. The financial sector is important for the real sector. If the financial sector doesn't work, the real sector doesn't work. All trade involves both the real sector and the financial sector. Thus in this book I don't have a separate section on the steel sector or even the computer sector of the economy, but I do have a separate section on the financial sector of the economy.

For every real transaction there is a financial transaction that mirrors it.

FINANCIAL ASSETS AND FINANCIAL LIABILITIES

1 A financial asset—or financial liability—is simply a promise of someone to pay something to someone in the future. Such a promise simultaneously creates an asset for the holder of the promise and a liability for the maker of the promise.

To understand the financial sector and its relation to the real sector, you must understand: (1) what financial assets are, (2) how financial institutions work, (3) what financial markets are, and (4) how financial markets work.

An *asset* is something that provides its owner with expected future benefits. There are two types of assets: real assets and financial assets. Real assets are assets such as houses or machinery whose services provide direct benefits to their owners, either now or in the future. A house is a real asset—you can live in it. A machine is a real asset—you can produce goods with it.

Financial assets are assets, such as stocks or bonds, whose benefit to the owner depends on the issuer of the asset meeting certain obligations. These obligations are called **financial liabilities.** *Every financial asset has a corresponding financial liability;* it's that financial liability that gives the financial asset its value. In the case of bonds, for example, a company's agreement to pay interest and repay the principal gives bonds their value. If the company goes bankrupt and reneges on its liability to pay interest and repay the principal, the asset becomes worthless. The corresponding liability gives the financial asset its value.

The financial liability created by a financial asset can be either an *equity liability* or a *debt liability.* An example of an equity liability is a share of stock that a firm issues. It is a liability of the firm; it gives the holder ownership rights which are spelled out in the financial asset. An equity liability, such as a stock, usually conveys a general right to dividends, but only if the company's board of directors decides to pay them.

A debt liability conveys no ownership right. It's a type of loan. An example of a debt liability is a bond that a firm issues. The bond is a liability of the firm but an asset of the individual who holds the bond. A debt liability, such as a bond, usually conveys legal rights to interest payments and repayment of principal.

Real assets are created by real economic activity. For example, a house or a machine must be built. Financial assets are created whenever somebody takes on a financial liability. For example, say I promise to pay you $1,000,000,000 in the future. You now have a financial asset and I have a financial liability. Understanding that financial assets can be created by a simple agreement of two people is fundamentally important to understanding how the financial sector works.

Q–1: If the government prints new $1,000 bills and gives them to all introductory students who are using the Colander text, who incurs a financial liability and who gains a financial asset?

A **financial institution** is a business whose primary activity is buying, selling, or holding financial assets. For example, some financial institutions (depository institutions and investment intermediaries) sell promises to pay in the future. These promises can be their own promises or someone else's promises. When you open a savings account at a bank, the bank is selling you its own promise that you can withdraw your money, plus interest, at some unspecified time in the future. Such financial institutions are called **depository institutions.** When you buy a government bond or security from a securities firm, it's also selling you a promise to pay in the future. But in this case, it's a third party's promise. So a securities firm is a financial institution that sells third parties' promises to pay. It's a type of investment intermediary.

As financial institutions sell financial assets, they channel savings from savers (individuals who give other people money now in return for promises to pay it back with interest later) to borrowers (investors or consumers who get the money now in return for their promise to pay it and the interest later).

As economists use the term, *to save* is to buy a financial asset. *To invest* (in economic terminology) is to buy real, not financial, assets that you hope will yield a return in the future.[1] How do you get funds to invest if you don't already have them? You borrow them. That means you create a financial asset that you sell to someone else who saves.

Some financial institutions also hold and store individuals' financial assets. Such financial institutions are called **contractual intermediaries** because they intermediate (serve as a go-between) between savers and investors. For example, a pension fund is a financial institution that holds individuals' savings and pays back those savings plus interest after the individuals retire. It uses individuals' savings to buy financial assets from people and firms who want to borrow. Similarly, a commercial bank is a financial institution that holds an individual's cash in the form of checking deposits; it distributes that cash to others when that individual tells it to. A checking deposit is a financial asset of an individual and a financial liability of the bank.

Exhibit 1 lists four types of financial institutions and shows the percentage of total U.S. financial assets each holds, along with the sources and uses of funds for each. These percentages give you an idea of the institution's importance, but institutions' importance can come in other ways. For example, although financial brokers hold no financial assets, they're important because they facilitate buying and selling such assets. Let's consider each grouping separately.

Depository institutions, the first category listed, are financial institutions whose primary financial liability is deposits in checking accounts. They hold approximately 35 percent of all the financial assets in the United States. This category includes commercial banks, savings banks, savings and loan associations (S&Ls), and credit unions. The primary financial liability of each is deposits. For example, the amount in your checking account or savings account is a financial asset for you and a financial liability for the bank holding your deposit.

Banks make money by lending your deposits (primarily in the form of business and commercial loans), charging the borrower a higher interest rate than they pay the depositor. Those loans from banks to borrowers are financial assets of the bank and financial liabilities of the borrower.

Laws governing financial institutions changed significantly in the 1980s and early 1990s. In the 1970s, each financial institution was restricted to specific types of financial transactions. Savings banks and S&Ls handled savings accounts and mortgages; they were not allowed to issue checking accounts. Commercial banks were not allowed to hold or sell stock; they did, however, issue checking accounts. These restrictions allowed us to make sharp, clear distinctions among financial institutions. Changes in the laws have eliminated many of these restrictions, blurring the distinction between the various types of financial institutions. Now all depository institutions can issue checking accounts. In the late 1990s, many more changes are likely.

FINANCIAL INSTITUTIONS

Financial institution   A business whose primary activity is buying, selling, or holding financial assets.

Depository institution   Financial institution whose primary financial liability is deposits in checking or savings accounts.

Q–2:   Joe, your study partner, has just said that, in economic terminology, when he buys a bond he is investing. Is he correct? Why?

Contractual intermediary   A financial institution that holds and stores individuals' financial assets.

2   Four types of financial institutions are: (1) depository institutions; (2) contractual intermediaries; (3) investment institutions; and (4) financial brokers.

Depository Institutions

In the 1990s financial institutions are changing, and the distinctions among them are becoming blurred.

Q–3:   Joan, your study partner, has just made the following statement: "A loan is a loan and therefore cannot be an asset." Is she correct? Why or why not?

---

[1] This terminology isn't the terminology most lay people use. When a person buys a stock, in economic terms that person is *saving*, though most lay people call that *investing*.

EXHIBIT 1   1993 Holdings of Financial Institutions

Financial Institutions	% of Total Financial Assets	Primary Assets (Uses of Funds)	Primary Liabilities (Sources of Funds)
Depository institutions:			
Commercial banks	26%	Business and consumer loans, mortgages, U.S. government securities, and municipal bonds	Checkable deposits and savings deposits
Savings and loan associations and mutual savings banks	7	Mortgages	Savings deposits (and checkable deposits)
Credit unions	2	Consumer loans	Savings deposits (and checkable deposits)
Contractual intermediaries:			
Pension funds	30	Corporate bonds and stock	Employer and employee contributions
Life insurance companies	12	Corporate bonds and mortgages	Policy premiums
Fire and casualty insurance companies	4	Municipal bonds, corporate bonds and stock, and U.S. government securities	Policy premiums
Investment intermediaries:			
Money market mutual funds	4	Money market instruments	Shares
Mutual funds	10	Stocks and bonds	Shares
Finance companies	5	Consumer and business loans	Commercial paper, stocks, and bonds
Financial brokers:			
Investment banks	0	None	None
Brokerage houses	0	None	None

Source: Federal Reserve System.

Some differences remain that reflect their history. Commercial banks' primary assets are loans, and their loans include business loans, mortgages, and consumer loans. Savings banks' and S&Ls' primary assets are the same kind as those of commercial banks, but their loans are primarily mortgage loans.

Contractual Intermediaries

The most important contractual intermediaries are insurance companies and pension funds. These institutions promise, for a fee, to pay an individual a certain amount of money in the future, either when some event happens (a fire or death) or, in the case of pension funds and some kinds of life insurance, when the individual reaches a certain age or dies. Insurance policies and pensions are a form of individual savings. Contractual intermediaries manage those savings. As the average age of the U.S. population increases, as it will throughout the 1990s, the share of assets held by these contractual intermediaries will increase.

Investment Intermediaries

Investment intermediaries provide a mechanism through which small savers pool funds to invest in a variety of financial assets rather than in just one or two. An example of how pooling works can be seen by considering a mutual fund company, which is one type of investment intermediary.

A mutual fund enables a small saver to diversify (spread out) his or her savings (for a fee, of course). Savers buy shares in the mutual fund which, in turn, holds stocks or bonds of many different companies. When a fund holds many different companies' shares or bonds, it spreads the risk so a saver won't lose everything if one company goes broke. Such spreading of risks by holding many different types of financial assets is called **diversification.**

A finance company is another type of investment intermediary. Finance companies make loans to individuals and businesses, as do banks, but instead of holding deposits, as banks do, finance companies borrow the money they lend. They borrow from individuals by selling them bonds and commercial paper. **Bonds** are promissory notes specifying that a certain amount of money plus interest will be paid back in the future. **Commercial paper** is a short-term promissory note that a certain amount of money plus interest will be paid back on demand.

Diversification   *Spreading, and therefore lowering, risk by holding stocks or bonds of many different companies.*

Bonds   *Promissory notes that a certain amount of money plus interest will be paid back in the future.*

Commercial paper   *Short-term promissory note that a certain amount of money plus interest will be paid back on demand.*

DO FINANCIAL ASSETS MAKE SOCIETY RICHER?

Financial assets are neat. You can call them into existence simply by getting someone to accept your IOU. *Remember, every financial asset has a corresponding financial liability equal to it.* So when you say a country has $1 trillion of financial assets, you're also saying that the country has $1 trillion of financial liabilities. An optimist would say a country is rich. A pessimist would say it's poor. An economist would say that financial assets and financial liabilities are simply opposite sides of the ledger and don't indicate whether a country is rich or poor.

To find out whether a country is rich or poor, you must look at its *real assets*. If financial assets increase the economy's efficiency and thereby increase the amount of real assets, they make society better off. This is most economists' view of financial assets. If, however, they decrease the efficiency of the economy (as some economists have suggested some financial assets do because they focus productive effort on financial gamesmanship), financial assets make society worse off.

The same correspondence between a financial asset and its liability exists when a financial asset's value changes. Say stock prices fall significantly. Is society poorer? Clearly the people who own the stock are poorer, but the people who might want to buy stock in the future are richer since the price of assets has fallen. So in a pure accounting sense, society is neither richer nor poorer when the prices of stocks rise or fall.

But there are ways in which changes in the value of financial assets might signify that society is richer or poorer. For example, the changes in the values of financial assets might *reflect* (rather than cause) real changes. If suddenly a company finds a cure for cancer, its stock price will rise and society will be richer. But the rise in the price of the stock doesn't cause society to be richer. It reflects the discovery that made society richer. Society would be richer because of the discovery even if the stock's price didn't rise.

There's significant debate about how well the stock market reflects real changes in the economy. Classical economists believe it closely reflects real changes; Keynesian economists believe it doesn't. But both sides agree that that the changes in the real economy, not the changes in the price of financial assets, underlie what makes an economy richer or poorer.

Finance companies charge borrowers higher interest than banks do, in part because their cost of funds (the interest rate they pay to depositors) is higher than banks' cost of funds. (The interest rate banks pay on savings and checking accounts is the cost of their funds.) As was the case with depository institutions, a finance company's profit reflects the difference between the interest rate it charges on its loans and the interest rate it pays for the funds it borrows.

Why do people go to finance companies if finance companies charge higher interest than banks? Because of convenience and because finance companies' loan qualifications are easier to meet than banks'.

Financial Brokers

Q-4: What is the difference between an investment bank and a commercial bank?

Securities firms are of two main types: investment banks and brokerage houses. Investment banks assist companies in selling financial assets such as stocks and bonds. They provide advice, expertise, and the sales force to sell the stocks or bonds. They handle such things as *mergers* and *takeovers* of companies. A merger is when two or more companies join to form one new company. A takeover occurs when one company buys out another company. Investment banks do not hold individuals' deposits and do not make loans to consumers. That's why in Exhibit 1 they have zero assets and hence zero liabilities. They are nonetheless financial institutions because they assist others in buying and selling financial assets.

Brokerage houses assist individuals in selling previously issued financial assets. Brokerage houses create a secondary market in financial assets, as we'll see shortly. A **secondary financial market** is a market in which previously issued financial assets can be bought and sold.

FINANCIAL MARKETS

A financial market is a market where financial assets and financial liabilities are bought and sold. The stock market, the bond market, and bank activities are all examples of financial markets.

Financial institutions buy and sell financial assets in financial markets. Sometimes these markets are actual places, like the New York Stock Exchange, but generally a market simply exists in the form of a broker's Rolodex files, computer networks, telephone lines, and lists of people who sometimes want to buy and sell. When individuals want to sell, they call their broker and their broker calls potential buyers; when individuals want to buy, the broker calls potential sellers. A market is an institution that brings buyers and sellers together; a **financial market** is an institution (the Rolodex cards and the telephone) that brings buyers and sellers of financial assets together.

Financial market   *Institution that brings buyers and sellers of financial assets together.*

The market for financial instruments is sometimes rather hectic, as suggested by this famous painting. © *New York Historical Society.*

Primary and Secondary Financial Markets

3   A primary financial market is one in which *newly issued* financial assets are sold; a secondary financial market is one in which *previously issued* financial assets are sold.

The Wall Street Journal is must reading material for businesspeople; only the editorial page is highly conservative.

Q–5:   The difference between primary and secondary financial markets is that primary markets are more important. True or false? Why or why not?

There are various types of financial markets. A **primary financial market** is a market in which newly issued financial assets are sold. These markets transfer savings to borrowers who want to invest (buy real assets). Sellers in this market include *venture capital firms* (which sell part ownerships in new companies) and *investment banks* (which sell new stock and new bonds for existing companies). Whereas investment banks only assist firms in selling their stock, venture capital firms often are partnerships that invest their own money in return for part ownership of a new firm.

Many new businesses will turn to venture capital firms for financing because only established firms can sell stock through an investment bank. Risks are enormous for venture capital firms since most new businesses fail. But potential gains are huge. A company that's already established will most likely use an investment bank to get additional funds. Investment banks know people and institutions who buy stocks; with a new stock offering they use those contacts. They telephone these leads to try to *place* (sell) the new issue.

Generally new offerings are too large for one investment bank to sell. So it contracts with other investment banks and brokerage houses to sell portions of the new stock or bond issue. Exhibit 2(a) shows an advertisement announcing a stock offering. In this advertisement, a group of investment banks announces it's selling 3,000,000 shares of stock for Petco at $15.50 per share. The lead bankers listed in the first line have subcontracted with all the other investment banks and brokerage houses listed to assist in the sale. Exhibit 2(b) shows a tombstone ad announcing the successful completion of a sale.

There are many different types of buyers for newly issued financial assets. They include rich individuals and financial institutions, such as life insurance companies, pension funds, and mutual funds.

A secondary financial market transfers existing financial assets from one saver to another. (Remember, in economics, when an individual buys a financial asset such as a stock or bond, he or she is a saver. In economics, investment occurs only when savings are used to buy items such as machines or a factory.) A transfer on a secondary market does not represent any new savings; it is savings for one person and dissavings for another. One cancels out the other. The New York Stock Exchange is

(a) Announcement of sale

(b) Tombstone ad

EXHIBIT 2 (a and b)   Stock Offering Announcements

An advertisement (**a**) annoucing the availability of a new stock issue notes that it is *not* "a solicitation of an offer to buy," but that a formal prospectus containing all the details is available from the listed investment banks. When the shares have been sold, a second advertisement (**b**) announces completion of the stock or bond offering. The second, self-congratulatory ad is called a *tombstone advertisement*.

probably the best-known secondary financial market. It transfers stocks from one stockholder to another.

The secondary market does, however, have an important role to play in new savings. The existence of a secondary market lets the individual buyer of a financial asset know that she can resell it, transferring the asset back into cash at whatever price the secondary market sets. This ability to turn an asset into cash quickly is called **liquidity.** Secondary markets provide liquidity for financial asset holders and thereby encourage them to hold financial assets. If no secondary market existed, most people would hesitate to buy a stock or a 30-year bond. What if they needed their money in, say, 10 years? Or 10 weeks?

Besides the organized secondary financial markets we often hear about—the New York Stock Exchange, AMEX (American Stock Exchange), and Chicago Mercantile Exchange—there are informal *over-the-counter* markets. Over-the-counter markets work like the primary financial markets: Brokers know of other individuals interested in buying what's for sale. Buying and selling takes place over the phone, with the broker acting as an intermediary.

Liquidity   Ability to turn an asset into cash quickly.

The floor of the New York Stock Exchange is often a hectic place.   *UPI/Bettmann.*

Money Markets and Capital Markets

Money markets *Markets in which financial assets with maturity of less than one year are bought and sold.*

Capital markets *Markets in which financial assets with maturity of more than one year are bought and sold.*

Financial markets can also be divided into two other categories: **money markets** (in which financial assets having a maturity of less than one year are bought and sold) and **capital markets** (in which financial assets having a maturity of more than one year are bought and sold). (*Maturity* refers to the date the issuer must pay back the money that was borrowed plus any remaining interest, as agreed when the asset was issued.) For example, say the U.S. government issues an IOU (sometimes called a *Treasury bill*) that comes due in three months. This will be sold in the money market because its maturity is less than a year. Or say the government or a corporation issues an IOU that comes due in 20 years. This IOU, which is called a *bond,* will be sold in a capital market.

TYPES OF FINANCIAL ASSETS

Now that you've been introduced to financial institutions and markets, we can consider some specific financial assets. Financial assets are generally divided into money market assets and capital market assets.

Money Market Assets

Money market assets are financial assets that mature in less than one year. They usually pay lower interest rates than do longer-term capital assets because they offer the buyer more liquidity. A general rule of thumb is: The more liquid the asset, the lower the return. As in the over-the-counter market, money market and capital market transactions are made over the phone lines using computers. Newly issued money market assets are sold through an investment bank or a securities dealer. Exhibit 3 gives you a visual sense of some of the most important money market assets and their growth over time. Notice how the relative importance of various assets changes over time.

Some of the most important money market assets are negotiable CDs, commercial paper, and U.S. Treasury bills.

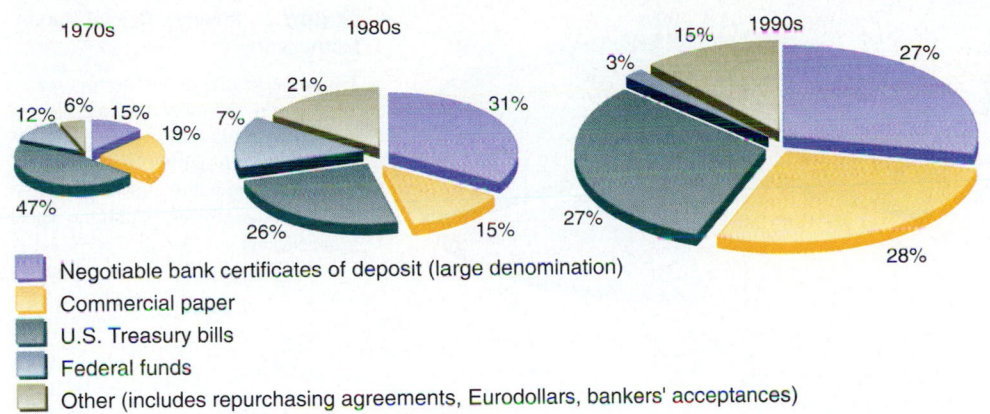

1970s   1980s   1990s

12% 6% 15%
19%
47%

21% 7%
31%
26% 15%

15% 3%
27%
27% 28%

EXHIBIT 3 **Principal Money Market Instruments**

These pie charts show the growth and relative importance of money market instruments over time. The increasing size of the pies reflects the increasing value over time.
Source: Federal Reserve Bank and author extrapolations

■ Negotiable bank certificates of deposit (large denomination)
■ Commercial paper
■ U.S. Treasury bills
■ Federal funds
■ Other (includes repurchasing agreements, Eurodollars, bankers' acceptances)

Negotiable CDs   CD is short for *certificate of deposit*. Think of it as a large amount of savings you agree to hold in an account at the bank for a specified period of time. But what if you need cash before the time is up? That's where the "negotiable" comes in. (Not all CDs are negotiable.) You can sell a negotiable CD in a secondary market and get cash for it if you need cash. The new owner can either sell it again on the secondary market or simply withdraw the money from the bank that issued it, including interest, when the required time is up (when the CD matures).

CD (certificate of deposit)   A piece of paper certifying that you have a sum of money in a savings account in the bank for a specified period of time.

Commercial Paper   Why borrow from a bank if you can borrow directly from the public? Why not cut out the middleman? Large corporations often do precisely that. The borrowings are called *commercial paper*. Commercial paper is a short-term IOU of a large corporation. Commercial paper pays a higher interest rate than U.S. Treasury bills, but a lower interest rate than banks would charge the corporation. The same reasoning holds for a person who buys commercial paper. Commercial paper generally pays a higher interest rate than a CD, which is why people are willing to lend directly to the firm. Since the bank is an intermediary between the lender of funds and the borrower, the process of lending directly and not going through a financial intermediary is called **disintermediation.**

Disintermediation   Borrowing directly from an individual without going through an intermediary bank.

U.S. Treasury Bills   These are U.S. government IOUs that mature in less than a year. Since it's unlikely the U.S. government will go broke, IOUs of the U.S. government are very secure, so U.S. Treasury bills need pay a relatively low rate of interest.

Where do these government IOUs come from? Think back to the discussion of fiscal policy in which the government spent more than it took in in revenues. That deficit must be financed by borrowing. Selling U.S. Treasury bills is one way the U.S. government borrows money.

Differences among Money Market Assets   Money market assets differ slightly from each other. For example, Treasury bills are safer than commercial paper and pay slightly lower interest. For the most part, however, they are interchangeable, and the interest rates paid on them tend to increase or decrease together.

Capital market assets have a maturity of over one year. Exhibit 4 gives you a visual sense of the principal capital market instruments and their relative importance over time. As you can see, the most important are stocks, bonds, and mortgages. Since mortgages are discussed later in this chapter, we'll focus here on stocks and bonds.

Stocks   A **stock** is a partial ownership right to a company. The stock owner has the right to vote on company policy, although generally, for smaller shareholders, this right doesn't convey much power. A stockholder can, however, attend the firm's stockholder meeting and ask questions of the firm's officers. Exhibit 5 shows a stock certificate certifying that the holder (who's named on the certificate's face) owns a

Capital Market Assets

4 Three important money market assets are CDs, commercial paper, and U.S. Treasury bills. Two capital market assets are corporate stocks and corporate bonds.

Stock   Ownership right to a company.

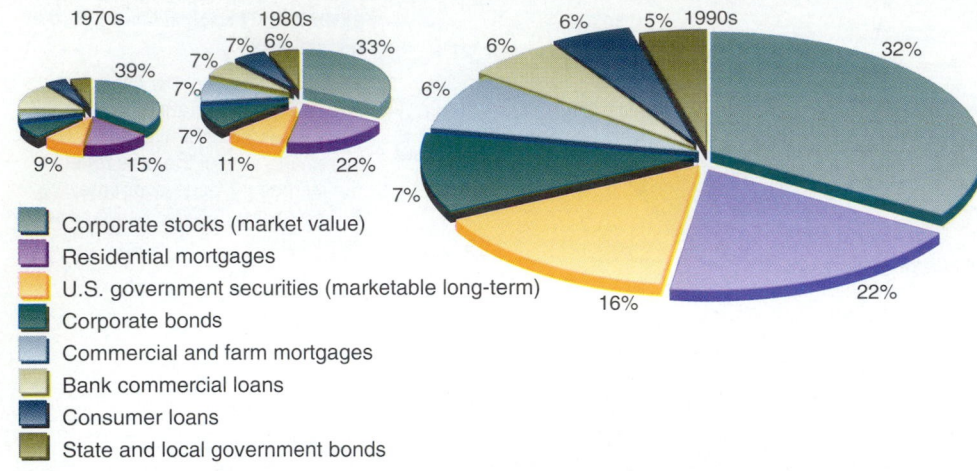

EXHIBIT 4   Principal Capital Market Instruments

These pie charts show the relative importance of capital market instruments since the 1970s. The increasing size of the pies reflects the increasing value over time.
Source: Federal Reserve Bank and author extrapolations

- Corporate stocks (market value)
- Residential mortgages
- U.S. government securities (marketable long-term)
- Corporate bonds
- Commercial and farm mortgages
- Bank commercial loans
- Consumer loans
- State and local government bonds

EXHIBIT 5   A Stock Certificate

Stock certificates generally look impressive to make holders think they have something valuable. Recently there has been a move to replace certificates with computer entries, but somehow a computer entry doesn't give one a feeling of real value. Most people care about such things; large companies, that hold much of the stock on the exchange, don't. They prefer computer entries.

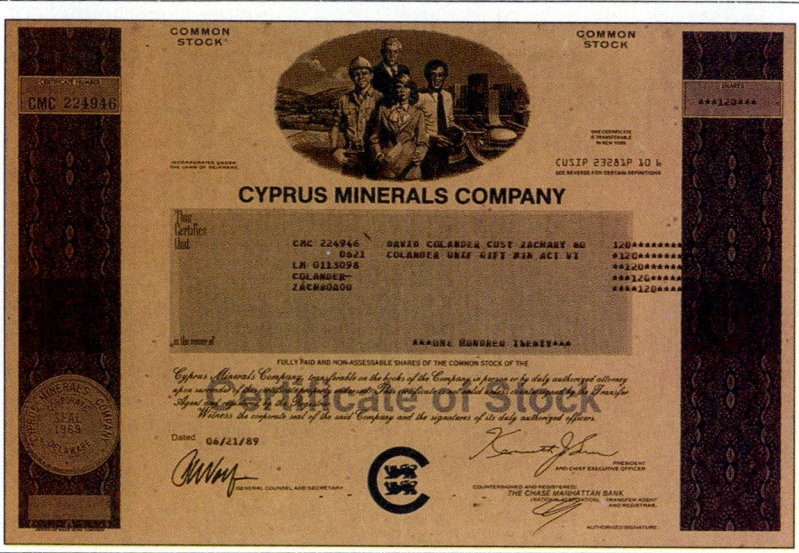

Stocks have no maturity date.

specified number of shares in the firm—in this case, 120 shares of Cyprus Minerals. This is a valuable certificate, printed on special paper, which will last indefinitely without turning yellow or crumbling away. If the stock certificate is lost or stolen, the owner's investment will still be safe because no one can sell a stock certificate unless the owner has endorsed it on the back (somewhat like a check), which she should not do until the moment she's ready to sell it or confer it as a gift. If a stock certificate is lost or destroyed, the owner can get another one from the company because the company keeps a list of its owners (the people who own stock) and their addresses, but the owner must pay a fee.

The owner of a stock can sell it at any time she pleases, provided someone wants to buy it. She will get whatever the going price is at the moment her sale is closed, minus a commission to the broker. Or she can keep it, hoping that its price will go up and it will be worth more. If the company is paying dividends (periodic payments to owners of its stock), every three months she gets a check for those dividends. She doesn't have to do anything to get these checks—the company mails them automatically to "the shareholder of record."

Stocks have no maturity date. The money you paid for them never has to be paid back to you. Stocks require no periodic payments to you every year. So it's possible to buy a stock and get nothing for it. So why would anyone buy a stock? Because with it

THE DOW

Of all the current economic institutions, perhaps the one you hear most about is Wall Street. Wall Street is a real street in New York City, but the term *Wall Street* is often used to refer to the entire financial sector. Probably the most important institution on Wall Street is the New York Stock Exchange, where ownership rights in corporations are traded. These ownership rights are called *stocks*. Stocks are also called *shares,* because they represent the share of a business the stockholder owns. While individuals who own stocks are chiefly interested in the price of shares they own, they also want to know the general movement of prices in the market as a whole.

A measure indicating this is the *Dow Jones Industrial Average,* commonly called *the Dow.* The Dow Jones average was created in 1884 when newsman Charles Dow (founder of *The Wall Street Journal*) chose a group of what he felt were representative stocks and began reporting their prices as typical of general movements in the market. Initially he chose 12 stocks, added up their prices, divided the total by 12, and arrived at an average price per share.

Unfortunately for the statistician, the financial people who manage the firms represented by the stocks do funny things with stocks, such as splitting stocks or issuing stock dividends. A *stock split* occurs when the company decides to give each owner extra shares—say two shares for each one the owner already has. A stock dividend means that instead of using money to pay you the earnings on your shares, the company gives you one or more additional shares of stock. Stock splits and stock dividends, both of which increase the number of shares in the market, lower the price of all the company's shares but do not make the owners worse off, because the people own more shares. Often, in fact, owners are made better off, because the price of the shares soon starts to rise again.

But after stock splits and stock dividends of any of the stocks comprising the Dow average, dividing by 12 no longer gives us a representative measure of what happened to the average price. Statisticians did some fancy adjusting, and now, even though the number of stocks included in the Dow has risen from 12 to 30, the divisor used is less than .5. So to compute the Dow Jones Industrial Average, you simply add the prices of the following 30 big, well-known companies, and divide by a number slightly less than .5.

Dow Jones Industrial Stocks

Alcoa	Goodyear Tire and Rubber
Allied Signal	IBM
American Express	International Paper
AT&T	McDonald's
Bethlehem Steel	Merck
Boeing Co.	Minnesota M&M
Caterpillar, Inc.	J. P. Morgan
Chevron	Philip Morris
Coca-Cola	Procter & Gamble
Disney	Sears, Roebuck
Du Pont	Texaco
Eastman Kodak	Union Carbide
Exxon	United Technologies
General Electric	Westinghouse
General Motors	Woolworth

There are many other measures of the market, such as the NASDAQ 500 and Wilshire 5000. But the Dow Jones average is most used. Most TV news programs include a few spoken words or message flashed on the screen: "The Dow Jones Average is down 5.63 for the day," or "Dow— + 26.9."

comes ownership rights—all the company's income that isn't paid out to factors of production belongs to the stockholders. For example, say you own one share of the million shares Cyprus Minerals has issued, and after paying all costs and debts due, Cyprus Minerals has $6 million in after-tax profits. Your percentage of that $6 million is $6. This $6 can be paid out to stockholders in dividends. Or the company can retain the $6 (which would then be called *retained earnings*), in which case the stock's value will likely increase because the firm can invest the retained earnings and earn more profit. (An increase in the value of a stock is called a *capital gain.*) The company's board of directors decides which option the company will follow.

Notice that a share of stock gives you the right to a percentage of the company's profits this year and all future years. Because it does, the price of a stock depends upon investors' opinions of a company's prospects. A company with excellent prospects sells for a high price; a company whose prospects are dim sells for a low price. What's high? What's low? That depends. A rough rule of thumb is to take a multiple of the company's earnings (its *earnings per share*) to determine the price a person would be willing to pay for a share. For instance, "15 times earnings" means a share is selling for 15 times the company's annual earnings divided by the number of shares outstanding. If Cyprus Minerals in our previous example was expected to continue earning $6 a share, and stock buyers applied the 15-times-earnings rule of thumb, the stock would sell for $90 a share.

DEBTOR AND CREDITOR.

Published by M. Shushan, Boston, Mass.

The divergent interests of debtors and creditors are nicely captured in this late 19th-century drawing by W. W. Chenery. *Bleichroeder Print Collection, Baker Library, Harvard Business School.*

Q–6: A company's stock is selling for three times earnings. How is the market valuing the prospects of that company?

A bond is a promise of the bond-issuers to pay interest of a certain amount at specified intervals to the bondholder and to pay the bond's face value when the bond matures.

Q–7: If the interest rate in the economy goes down, what will likely happen to the price of a previously issued bond?

An average company stock sells for somewhere around 15 times earnings. (This average price/earnings ratio fluctuates somewhat over time.) A company with excellent future prospects might sell for 30 or 40 times earnings. A company with poor prospects might sell for merely 2 or 3 times earnings. The price/earnings ratio for a company is reported in the newspaper stock tables.

Bonds   A bond is a promise of the bond-issuer to pay interest of a certain amount at specified intervals (usually semi-annually) to the bondholder and to pay the bond's face value when the bond matures. Bonds are different from stocks. They generally have a maturity date when borrowers pay back the money. Exhibit 6(a) shows an unregistered bond.

A bond's value depends on a bond's face value and its coupon rate (the interest rate stated on the bond). Exhibit 6(a)'s bond has a face value of $5,000 and a coupon rate of 12.75 percent per year. That means that the bondholder receives $637.50 each year in interest payments. When the bond matures, the bond holder receives $5,000.

Printed on the bond is the *maturity date*, October 1, 2002. There's no sense hanging onto that bond after October 1, 2002, because after that its interest is all used up.

If you need the money from the bond before the maturity date, you'll enter into the secondary bond market. Call your bond broker and ask what your bond is selling for. What price you will get depends in large part on the interest rate.

Generally when bonds are issued, their coupon rate is close to the market interest rate prevailing in the economy for bonds of similar risk. These bonds sell *at par* (at their face value). If market interest rates rise, the future stream of income becomes worth less and the bond sells at a discount (at less than its face value). If the market interest rate falls, the future stream of income becomes worth more and the bond sells at a premium (at more than its face value).

Exhibit 6(b) shows a bond table. Let's see what it tells us. Alpine bonds, the first bond issue on the list, pay a coupon rate of $13\frac{1}{2}$ percent annual interest and come due in 1996. They sell for $66 for every $100 of their par value (the value stated on the bond), which means that their yield (the net interest rate you get if you buy the bond at the closing price) is $20\frac{1}{2}$ percent. Each year you get $13.50 from the bond that cost you $66. Dividing $13.50 by $66 gives $20\frac{1}{2}$ percent.

At the time this bond table appeared, $20\frac{1}{2}$ percent was higher than the interest rate on most bonds in the United States. That suggests there were fears Alpine might

CAPITAL GAINS AND LOSSES

c apital gains and losses aren't limited to stock. They can occur with any asset—financial or real. A capital gain or loss is simply the change in the value of an asset.

Noneconomists often call capital gains and losses *paper gains and losses* because no money transfers hands as the gain or loss occurs. Often you'll hear, "Oh, it's only a paper loss," as if somehow a capital loss wasn't quite as bad as a loss that has to be paid for in money. It's the same for a "paper gain," which they feel isn't as good as a gain that puts money in your pocket.

Economists don't use the "paper" terminology. They emphasize the opportunity cost concept. When you have a capital gain, you have the option of realizing that gain by selling the asset for the increased price. The opportunity cost of not selling that asset is the price of that asset including the capital gain. Say the price of a share of Cyprus Minerals goes from $21 to $30. If you sell the share, you get $9 (minus transaction costs) in your pocket. If you don't sell the share, the cost of not selling the share is $30. If you didn't sell the share at $21, the cost of not selling it was only $21. Thus, using the opportunity cost framework, a capital gain or loss is as real as any other gain or loss.

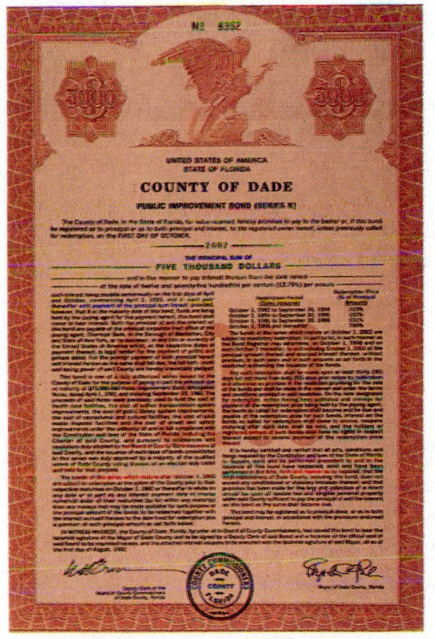

(a) A bond

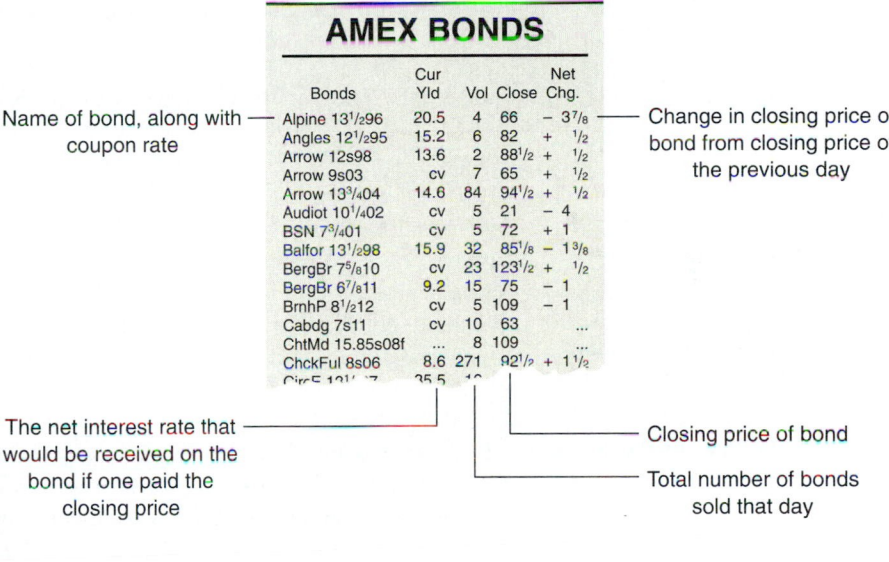

Name of bond, along with coupon rate —

The net interest rate that would be received on the bond if one paid the closing price

Change in closing price of bond from closing price of the previous day

Closing price of bond

Total number of bonds sold that day

(b) A bond table

EXHIBIT 6 (a and b)   A Bond and a Bond Table

Bonds used to be impressive pieces of paper like the one in (**a**). Some still are, but most are now simply computer entries. To determine the market price of a bond, you look at a bond table. (**b**) shows such a table and gives you the meaning of each of the entries ("cv" means a bond that is convertible into a stock; therefore its value depends on the price of the stock as well as the interest rate).

default on the bonds. Notice some other bonds in the table are selling at premiums. They were issued with a face value of $100, but their current prices are over $100. If you sell a "BrnhP" bond for $109 but paid only $100 for it, you make a gain of $9 on the sale price, but the new owner's yield or net annual interest per dollar is lower than the $8\frac{1}{2}$ percent stated for these bonds. That's because $8\frac{1}{2}$ percent of $100 is $8.50, but $8.50 as a percentage of $109 is only 7.8 percent. This 7.8 percent is the bond's yield.

THE VALUE OF A FINANCIAL ASSET

To understand financial assets, you must understand how financial asset prices are determined. Why does an average share of stock sell for about 15 times earnings? How come bond prices rise as market interest rates fall, and fall as market interest rates rise? In answering such questions, the first point to recognize is that $1 today is

WHAT WILL A BOND SELL FOR?

To determine what a bond will sell for, first remember a bond is a flow of payments over time. Its selling price depends on how much those payments are worth. If it's unlikely those payments will continue (for example, if the company issuing the bond is close to bankruptcy), the bond isn't worth much. This *risk* plays an important role in determining the bond's price.

A second factor in determining a bond's price is the current interest rate in the economy. If the interest rate today (for bonds of similar riskiness) is higher than the bond's coupon rate (which generally represents the interest rate that existed when the bond was originally issued), a bond will sell for less than its face value on the secondary market. Why? Because if it sold at its face value, it would make more sense for people to buy newly issued bonds paying higher interest rates. When a bond sells for less than its face value, its yield (the rate of return you receive per dollar of purchase price per year from a bond) increases. For example, say there's a one-year 5 percent coupon bond with $100 face value, and this bond is selling for $50. For $50 you'll get a $5 payment (5 percent of $100). That comes out to a 10 percent yield.

If the interest rate is lower than the coupon rate, bonds will sell for more than their face value. Why? Because at its face value, the bond is much more desirable than newly issued bonds. The market value of the bond will rise until the yield on the bond equals the interest rate on similar newly issued bonds. Only then will the buyer be indifferent between the old and new bonds.

Because of this relationship between interest rates and bond prices, generally whenever market interest rates rise, bond prices fall; whenever market interest rates fall, bond prices rise. Thus, the interest rate in the economy plays an important role in determining a bond's price on the secondary market.

---

5 The value of a financial asset is determined by the present value of the future flow of income it represents. As the interest rate goes up, the value of income in the future goes down and hence so does the value (price) of a fixed-interest financial asset.

Present Value and Interest Rate

Present value   *Value now of income payments in the future.*

Q–8: How much is $50 to be received 50 years from now worth if the interest rate is 5 percent? (Use Exhibit 7.)

not equal to $1 next year. Why? Because if I have $1 today I can invest it and earn interest (say 10 percent per year), and next year I will have $1.10, not $1. So if the annual interest rate is 10 percent, $1.10 next year is worth $1 today or, alternatively, $1 next year is worth roughly 91 cents today. A dollar two years in the future is worth even less today, and dollars 30 years in the future are worth very little today.

How much less $1 in the future is worth today depends on the interest rate. If the interest rate is close to zero, $1 is worth only a little bit less; if the interest rate is 5 percent, $1 is worth quite a bit less. The higher the interest rate, the less a dollar is worth in the future. How do I know? Because I pulled out my handy business calculator and pressed in the numbers to calculate the **present value** (the value now of income payments in the future).

Exhibit 7 graphically displays, for three different annual interest rates, how much a given amount of money at various lengths of time in the future is worth now. Notice that: (1) the higher the interest rate, the less a given amount of money in the future is worth now; and (2) how quickly the present value falls at higher annual interest rates. At 15 percent interest, $100 to be received 30 years from now is currently worth $1.50, as shown in Exhibit 7(c).

The present value reasoning also works in reverse. You can determine the future value of a given amount of money today. Say you have $100 now. If you earn 8 percent annual interest on it, it will be $215.89 in 10 years and $466.10 in 20 years. The higher the interest rate and the longer the time frame, the greater the future value will be.

Most of you, I suspect, don't have business calculators. For people who don't, there are bond tables to tell you present values of future dollars. A table or a calculator is extremely helpful in determining the price a bond should sell for. That's because a bond consists of a stream of income payments over a number of years *and* the repayment of the face value of the bond. Each year's interest payment and the eventual repayment of the face value must be calculated separately and then the results added together.

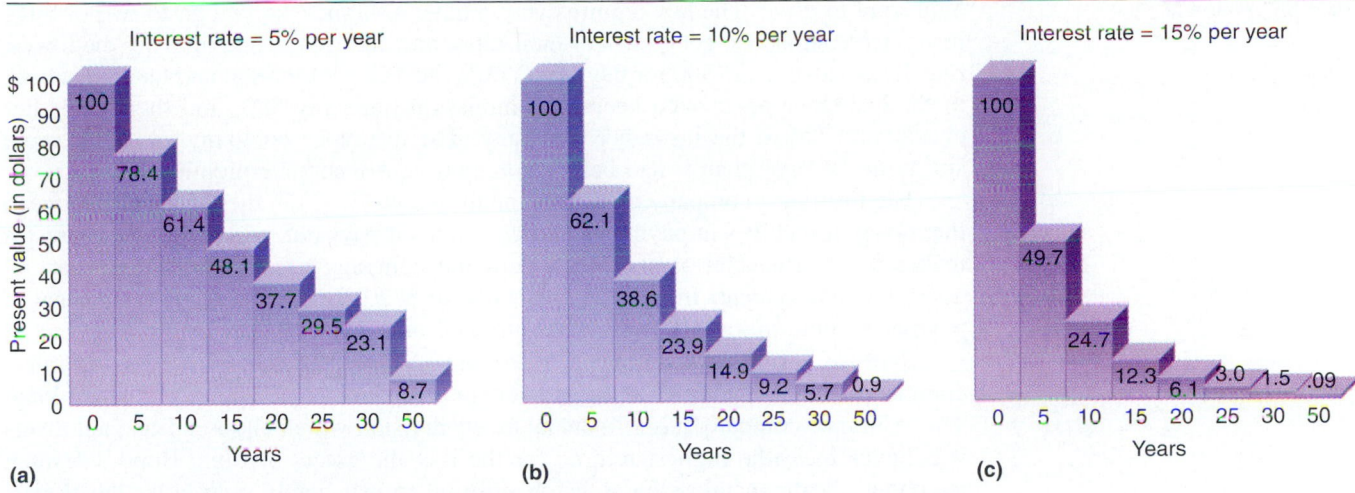

EXHIBIT 7 (a, b, and c)   Present Value of $100 to be Received a Certain Number of Years in the Future

The present value of money in the future declines as the interest rate increases. Notice how once the interest rate hits 10% or more, (**b**), (**c**), the present value of money to be received 50 years in the future is close to worthless.

All financial assets can be broken down into promises to pay certain amounts at certain times in the future, or, if the financial asset is a share of stock, not a promise but an expectation of such payment. So all financial assets (stocks or bonds) can be valued. You simply calculate the present value of all expected future payments. For example, say a share of stock is earning $1 per share and is expected to do so long into the future. If the interest rate is 6½ percent, the present value of that future stream of expected earnings is about $15. With this knowledge, let's return to our question, "Why do stocks generally sell for 15 times earnings?" We now have an answer. It's because that's roughly what the present value formula says they should sell for.

There is, however, a proviso to the preceding reasoning. If promises to pay aren't trustworthy, you don't put the amount that's promised into your calculation; you put in the amount you expect. That's why when a company or a country looks as if it's going to default on loans or stop paying dividends, the value of its bonds and stock will fall considerably. For example, in the late 1980s many people thought Brazil would default on its bonds. That expectation caused the price of Brazilian bonds to fall to about 30¢ on the dollar. Then in the 1990s, when people believed total default was less likely, the value rose.

This chapter isn't meant to cover the intricacies of valuation over time. That's done in a finance course. The point of this chapter is to help you understand the relationship between interest rates and asset prices. Increases in interest rates (because they make future flows of income coming from an asset worth less now) make financial asset prices fall. Decreases in interest rates (because they make the future flow of income coming from an asset worth more now) make financial asset prices rise.

Since a slight change in interest rates can lead to a large change in asset prices, many individuals speculate on what's going to happen to interest rates and switch their investments from one type of financial asset to another, causing potential problems for the macroeconomy. So understanding how assets are valued is fundamental to understanding the macroeconomic debate.

We've covered a lot of material quickly, so the institutions discussed may be a bit of a blur in your mind. To get a better idea of how these financial markets work, let's follow two transactions you'll likely make in your lifetime and see how they work their way through the financial system.

6 To determine the present value of a future amount of money, you use a calculator or a computer, or a present value chart like the one in Exhibit 7.

Q–9: How much is $50 to be received 50 years from now worth if the interest rate is 10 percent? (Use Exhibit 7.)

Asset Prices, Interest Rates, and the Economy

LEADING YOU THROUGH TWO FINANCIAL TRANSACTIONS

Insuring Your Car

You want to drive. The law requires you to have insurance, so you go to two or three insurance companies, get quotes of their rates, and choose the one offering the lowest rate. Say it costs you $800 for the year. You write a check for $800 and hand the check to the insurance agent who keeps a commission (let's say $80) and then sends her check for $720 to the insurance company. The insurance company has $720 more sitting in the bank than it had before you paid your insurance premium.

The insurance company earns income in two ways: (1) in the difference between the money it receives in payments and the claims it pays out, and (2) in the interest it makes on its financial assets. What does the company use to buy these financial assets? It has payments from its customers (your $720, for example) available because payments come in long before claims are paid out.

Because earnings on financial assets are an important source of an insurance company's income, your $720 doesn't stay in the insurance company's bank for long. The insurance company has a financial assets division which chooses financial assets it believes have the highest returns for the risk the assets involve. Bond salesmen telephone the financial assets division offering to sell bonds. Similarly, developers who want to build shopping malls or ski resorts go to the financial assets division, offering an opportunity to participate (really asking to borrow money).

The financial assets division might decide to lend your $720 (along with $10 million more) to a mall developer who builds in suburban locations. The division transfers the $720 to the mall developer and receives a four-year, 12 percent promissory note (a promise to pay the $720 back in four years along with $86.40 per year in interest payments). The promissory note is a financial asset of the insurance company and a financial liability of the developer. When the developer spends the money, the $720 leaves the financial sector and re-enters the spending stream in the real economy. At that point it becomes investment in the economic sense.

Buying a House

Mortgage   A special name for a secured loan on real estate.

Most people, when they buy a house, don't go out and pay the thousands of dollars it costs in cash. Instead they go to a bank or similar financial institution and borrow a large portion of the sales price, taking out a mortgage on the house. A **mortgage** is simply a special name for a secured loan on real estate. By mortgaging her house, a person is creating a financial liability for herself and a financial asset for someone else. This financial asset is secured by the house. If the person defaults on the loan, the mortgage holder (who, as you will see, may or may not be the bank) can foreclose on the mortgage and take title to the house.

The funds available in banks come primarily from depositors who keep their savings in the bank in the form of savings accounts or checking accounts. Balances in these accounts are often small, but with lots of depositors they add up and provide banks with money to lend out. If you're planning to buy a house, you'll most likely go to a bank.

The bank's loan officer will have you fill in a lengthy form, and the bank will send an appraiser out to the house to assess its value. The appraiser asks questions about the house: Does it meet the electrical code? What kind of pipes does it have? What kind of windows does it have? All this information about you and the house is transferred onto a master form that the loan officer uses to decide whether to make the loan. (Contrary to what many lay people believe, in normal times a loan officer wants to make the loan. Remember, a bank's profits are the difference between what it pays in interest and what it receives in interest; it needs to make loans to make profits. So he or she often looks at hazy answers on the form and puts an interpretation on them that's favorable to making the loan.)

In a month or so, depending on how busy the bank is, you hear back that the loan is approved for, say, $80,000 at 9 percent interest and two points. A point is 1 percent of the loan; it is a charge the bank makes for the loan. So two points means the bank is charging you $1,600 for making you a loan of $80,000 at 9 percent interest. (And you wondered why the bank was anxious to make you a loan!) The bank credits your account with $78,400, which allows you to write a check to the seller of the house at a meeting called the *closing*.

The bank gets a lot of money in deposits, but generally it doesn't have anywhere near enough deposits to cover all the mortgages it would like to make. So the process doesn't stop there. Instead the bank generally sells your mortgage on the secondary market to Fannie Mae (the Federal National Mortgage Association) or Ginnie Mae (the Government National Mortgage Association), which pay, say, $80,400 for the $80,000 mortgage. They're buying your mortgage (which you paid $1,600 in points to be allowed to get) for $400 more than its amount. The bank makes money both ways: when it makes the loan and when it sells the loan.

Fannie Mae and Ginnie Mae are nonprofit companies organized by the government to encourage home ownership. They do this by easing the flow of savings into mortgages. They take your mortgage and a number of similar ones from different areas and make them into a bond package: a $100,000,000 bond fund secured by a group of mortgages. (Remember the long forms and the questions the appraiser asked? Those forms and answers allow Fannie Mae and Ginnie Mae to classify the mortgage and put it in a group with similar mortgages.) They then sell shares in that bond fund to some other institution that gives Fannie Mae and Ginnie Mae money in return. The Maes use that money to buy more mortgages, thereby channeling more savings into financing home ownership.

Who buys Fannie Mae and Ginnie Mae bonds? Let's go back and consider our insurance company. If the insurance company hadn't made the loan to the developer, the company might have decided the Ginnie Mae bonds were the best investment it could make. So who knows? Your insurance company may hold the mortgage to your house.

You, of course, don't know any of this. You simply keep making your mortgage payments to the bank which, for a fee, forwards it to Ginnie Mae, which uses it to pay the interest on the bond it sold to the insurance company.

We could go through other transactions, but these two should give you a sense of how real-world financial transactions work their way through financial institutions. Financial institutions make money by the fees and commissions they charge for buying and selling loans, and on the difference between the interest they pay to get the money and the interest they receive when they lend the money out.

Summary

Now that you have a sense of the financial sector, let's briefly consider how it fits into the macroeconomic models and debates discussed in earlier chapters. The debate was between Classicals who believed government should follow a laissez-faire policy and Keynesians who believed government should take an activist role in controlling the aggregate economy with policies such as fiscal policy.

WHY FINANCIAL INSTITUTIONS ARE IMPORTANT FOR MACROECONOMICS

The Classical View of the Financial Sector

Classical economists see the financial sector operating relatively smoothly. It is like a mirror that reflects the real sector, and as long as government doesn't disturb that mirror the financial sector won't be a problem. That's why Classical economists said that savings will be translated into investment relatively smoothly and that the Keynesian problem of insufficient demand wouldn't arise. Say's law is based on a smoothly working financial sector.

Q–10: Which would be more likely to believe the financial sector operates smoothly, a Keynesian or a Classical?

Exhibit 8(a) shows the Classical view of the financial market. The supply of savings is upward sloping, and the demand for investment is downward sloping. The interest rate adjusts to maintain savings equal to investment at the full-employment level of income.

Because Classicals see the financial sector working smoothly, they generally oppose any meddling with the financial system (last-ditch loans to companies about to go out of business, credit controls, limitation on interest rates, and other government involvement in financial markets).

The Keynesian View of the Financial Sector

Keynesian economists see the financial sector differently. While they also see the financial sector as a mirror, often it's more like a reflecting pond with waves. These waves in the financial sector can have serious repercussions in the real sector.

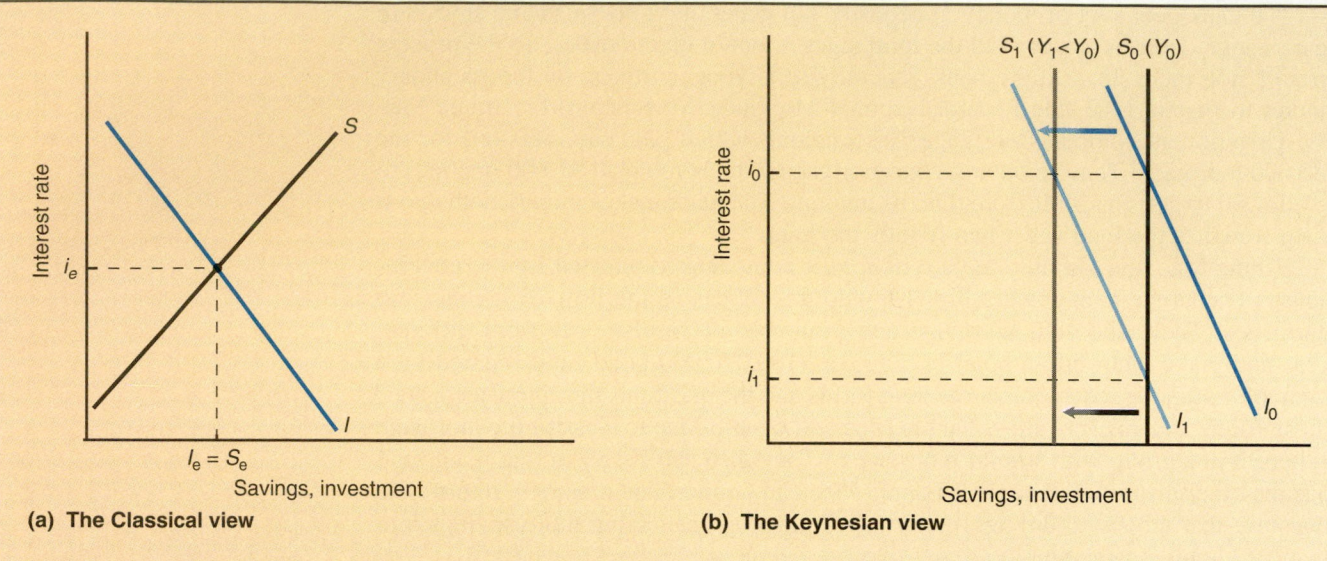

(a) The Classical view

(b) The Keynesian view

EXHIBIT 8 (a and b)   The Classical View of the Financial Sector and the Keynesian View of the Financial Sector

Classical economists see the financial market working smoothly so that savings and investment would always be equal. If they weren't, the interest rate would change so they were equal. Since savings always equal investment, there can be no Keynesian-type multiplier process.

Keynesians see financial markets working in fits and starts and often staying in disequilibrium for long periods of time. If the interest rate adjusts, it does so slowly. Before the interest rate adjusts to bring savings and investment into equilibrium, the multiplier process would be set in motion, causing income to shift and the savings curve to shift. Shifts in the savings curve, not changes in the interest rate, bring about equilibrium in the Keynesian model.

7 Classicals see interest rates equilibrating financial markets; Keynesians see fluctuations in income causing shifts in supply and demand curves before interest rates equilibrate the financial markets.

Specifically, Keynesians do not believe that the financial market efficiently translates savings into investment. Sometimes, because the financial sector isn't working correctly, there's too much savings; sometimes there's too little savings. When the financial sector fails to translate savings back into investment, the quantity of aggregate supply differs from the quantity of aggregate demand. When this occurs, the multiplier process starts, causing unwanted business cycles. Put simply, Keynesians believe the financial sector can get messed up, and when it gets messed up it messes up the real economy too.

The Keynesian view of financial markets can best be seen in Exhibit 8(b). In it you can see that the supply of savings is relatively vertical—the interest rate doesn't have much effect on it. Similarly with the demand for investment. Keynes argued that investment was not a simple decision based on interest rates but was a difficult decision based on expectations of the future and gut feelings. Why are the shapes of these curves important? Because those shapes tell us how much the interest rate must change to bring the financial market back into equilibrium. If the curves are relatively vertical (as Keynesians believe) and there's a shift in demand for investment from I_0 to I_1, the interest rate must change enormously (from i_0 to i_1) to bring the economy back into equilibrium. Such large interest rate fluctuations would cause serious problems in the financial sector.

If a change in the interest rate doesn't bring about equilibrium in the savings/investment market, what does? Changes in income. Since saving often doesn't equal investment, the result is income fluctuations in the real economy. Those fluctuations change income and hence savings. Equilibrium between savings and investment is brought about by the savings curve shifting (shown in Exhibit 8(b) as the shift from S_0 to S_1) as income falls from Y_0 to Y_1.

If the interest rate isn't determined in the savings/investment market in the Keynesian model, where is it determined? Keynesians believe it's determined in the money market, by people's demand for highly liquid assets and the supply of those liquid assets, specifically money. This means that a change in the money supply could affect interest rates and could play a role in equilibrating savings and investment.

We'll discuss these questions more in later chapters. Before we do, we'll take a much closer look at how one particular financial institution—banks—and one particular financial asset—money—fit into the macroeconomic landscape.

CHAPTER SUMMARY

- Every financial asset has a corresponding financial liability.
- Financial institutions buy, sell, or hold financial assets.
- Primary financial markets sell newly issued financial assets. Secondary financial markets transfer existing financial assets from one individual to another.
- Financial assets with a maturity of less than one year (such as Treasury bills and commercial paper) are sold in money markets. Financial assets with a maturity of over one year (such as bonds and mortgages) are sold on capital markets. They usually pay a higher rate of return than money market assets because they are less liquid.

- Bonds pay a fixed interest on an investment each year until maturity, at which point the face value is paid.
- Stocks have no maturity date, pay no interest, and do not return your original investment, but they give you ownership rights to a company and, thus, its profits.
- Present value is the current value of a future amount of money. As the interest rate rises, the present value of a future amount of money falls.
- Classicals believe the financial market works efficiently; Keynesians believe it often gets messed up.

KEY TERMS

bonds *(288)*
CD (certificate of deposit) *(293)*
capital market *(292)*
commercial paper *(288)*
contractual intermediary *(287)*
depository institution *(287)*

disintermediation *(293)*
diversification *(288)*
financial asset *(286)*
financial institution *(287)*
financial liability *(286)*
financial market *(290)*

liquidity *(291)*
money market *(292)*
mortgage *(300)*
present value *(298)*
primary financial market *(290)*
secondary financial market *(289)*
stock *(293)*

QUESTIONS FOR THOUGHT AND REVIEW

The number after each question represents the estimated degree of critical thinking required. (1 = almost none; 10 = deep thought.)

1. Is the cash in your pocketbook or wallet a real or a financial asset? Why? *(3)*

2. If financial institutions don't produce any tangible real assets, why are they considered a vital part of the U.S. economy? *(4)*

3. Which market, the primary or secondary, contributes more to the production of tangible real assets? Explain why. *(6)*

4. Why do money market assets generally yield lower interest payments than capital assets? *(3)*

5. Suppose that in 1995 you bought a newly issued bond with a $10,000 face value, a coupon rate of 9 percent, and a maturity date of 2020. How much interest would it pay each year? If the interest rate in the economy is 8

percent, would the bond be likely to sell for more or less than $10,000? *(4)*

6. Consider a company whose stock sells for $24 a share, has about $2 million in annual earnings, and has a million shares outstanding. What's that firm's price/earnings ratio? *(3)*

7. If a bond with a $5,000 face value and a 7.5 percent coupon rate is selling on the secondary bond market for $4,000, what can you say about the interest rate in the economy? *(3)*

8. A presidential candidate favors little government intervention in the economy. Would Classicals or Keynesians be more likely to support his candidacy? Why? *(3)*

9. How might a Keynesian economist explain a stock market crash? *(5)*

10. How might a Classical economist explain a stock market crash? *(9)*

PROBLEMS AND EXERCISES

1. A bond has a face value of $10,000 and a coupon rate of 10 percent. It is issued in 1995 and matures in 2005.
   a. How much does the bond pay annually?
   b. If the bond is currently selling for $9,000, what is its yield?
   c. If the interest rate in the economy rises, what will happen to the bond's price? Why?

2. Go to a local bank.
   a. Ask for a loan application. Inquire if you will be eligible for a loan.
   b. Ask why or why not.
   c. Find out how many different types of accounts they have and how these accounts differ.
   d. Ask if they will cash a $1,000 out-of-state check. If so, how long will it take for them to do so?

3. For the following financial instruments, state for whom it is a liability and for whom it is an asset. Also state, if appropriate, whether the transaction occurred on the capital or money markets.
   a. Lamar purchases a $100 CD at his credit union.
   b. First Bank grants a mortgage to Sandra. The bank then sells the mortgage to FNMA, who packages the mortgage in a fund and sells shares of that fund to Pension USA.
   c. Sean purchases a $100 jacket using his credit card with First Bank.

   d. City of Providence issues $1 billion in municipal bonds to build a community center, most of which were purchased by Providence residents.
   e. Investment broker sells 100 shares of existing stock to Lanier.
   f. Investment broker sells 1,000 shares of new-issue stock to Lanier.

4. Your employer offers you a choice of two bonus packages: $1,400 today or $2,000 five years from now. Assuming 5 percent rate of interest, which is the better value? Assuming an interest rate of 10 percent, which is the better value?

5. State whether you agree or disagree with the following statements:
   a. If stock market prices go up, the economy is richer.
   b. A real asset worth $1,000,000 is more valuable to an individual than a financial asset worth $1,000,000.
   c. Financial assets have no value to society since each has a corresponding liability.
   d. The United States has much more land than does Japan. Therefore, the value of all U.S. land should significantly exceed the value of land in Japan.
   e. U.S. GDP exceeds Japan's GDP; therefore, the stock market valuation of United States–based companies should exceed that of Japan-based companies.

ANSWERS TO MARGIN QUESTIONS

1. If the government prints a new $1,000 bill and gives it to an introductory student who is using the Colander text, the government incurs a $1,000 financial liability, and the student gains a financial asset, which is the $1,000 bill. *(286)*

2. No, he is not correct. In economic terminology, the buying of the bonds is actually saving. Investing is the spending of money on capital goods. This may be confusing because in business terminology the purchase of bonds is referred to as *investing*. In economic terminology, remembering the distinction between saving and investment is vital. *(287)*

3. No, she is not correct. A loan is definitely a loan, but it is an asset to the person who made the loan and a liability to the person who has incurred the debt. *(287)*

4. An investment bank is a bank that assists firms in their financing activities. A commercial bank is a bank that takes in deposits and makes loans. Because of recent regulatory changes, this distinction is blurring. *(289)*

5. False. The difference between primary and secondary financial markets lies in whether first issues are being sold, as they are in primary markets, or bonds and stock

are being re-sold, as they are in secondary markets. *(290)*

6. For a company's stock to sell for only three times earnings is far below normal. Therefore, the market must be valuing the prospects of that company at a very low level. *(296)*

7. The interest rate varies inversely with the current price of a previously-issued bond. Thus, if the interest rate in the economy goes down, the price of the bond should go up. *(296)*

8. If the interest rate is 5 percent, $50 to be received 50 years from now is worth approximately $4.35 currently, as can be seen in Exhibit 7(a). *(298)*

9. If the interest rate is 10 percent, $50 to be received fifty years from now is worth approximately $0.45 currently, as can be seen from Exhibit 7(b). *(299)*

10. Keynesians see the financial markets as having problems. Therefore, an economist who believes the financial sector operates smoothly is likely to be a Classical. *(301)*

13

Money and Banking

The process by which banks create money is so simple that the mind is repelled.

~John Kenneth Galbraith

After reading this chapter, you should be able to:

1 Explain what money is.

2 Enumerate the three functions of money.

3 State the alternative definitions of money and their primary components.

4 Explain how banks create money.

5 Calculate both the simple and the approximate real-world money multiplier.

6 Explain how a financial panic can occur and the potential problem with government guarantees to prevent such panics.

The financial institutions and assets discussed in the previous chapter are many and complicated. Each has its own peculiarities and interrelationships with the economy. Absorbing as my overview of them was, I suspect you've had enough, and if I tried to present in its entirety, the debate between Keynesians and Classicals about the financial sector that was introduced at the end of the last chapter, I would soon send you into a mental institution or at least into art history or sociology.

So instead, to simplify, I will follow the usual practice and focus on one of a group of the most important financial assets, which collectively are called *money,* and on a single financial institution, banks, which directly affect money.

THE DEFINITION AND FUNCTIONS OF MONEY

1 Money is a financial asset that makes the real economy function smoothly by serving as a medium of exchange, a unit of account, and a store of wealth.

At this point you're probably saying, "I know what money is; it's cash—the dollar bills I carry around." In one sense you're right; cash is money. But in another sense you're wrong. Money is much more than cash. In fact a number of short-term financial assets are included as money. To see why, let's consider the definition and uses of money and then see which financial assets meet that definition.

The definition is as follows: **Money** is a highly liquid financial asset that's generally accepted in exchange for other goods and is used as a reference in valuing other goods. Consider the dollar bill that you know is money. Look at it; it states on it that it is a *Federal Reserve Note,* which means that it is an IOU (a liability) of the **Federal Reserve Bank** (the **Fed**), which is the U.S. central bank. (We'll discuss the Fed in depth in the next chapter, but at this point all you need know is that the Fed's liabilities serve as cash in the United States.)

Functions of Money

2 The three functions of money are:
1. Medium of exchange;
2. Unit of account; and
3. Store of wealth.

From the previous chapter we know what a liquid financial asset is. It's an asset that can be quickly exchanged for another good. But the definition of money also requires that these financial assets are generally accepted in exchange for other goods and are used as a reference in valuing other goods. This definition says money serves three functions:

1. It serves as a medium of exchange.
2. It serves as a unit of account.
3. It serves as a store of wealth.

To get a better understanding of what money is, let's consider each in turn.

Money as a Medium of Exchange

The easiest way to understand money's medium-of-exchange use is to imagine what an economy would be like without money. Say you want something to eat at a restaurant. Without money you'd have to barter with the restaurant owner for your meal. *Barter* is a direct exchange of goods and/or services. You might suggest bartering one of your papers or the shirt in the sack that you'd be forced to carry with you to trade for things you want. Not liking to carry big sacks around, you'd probably decide to fix your own meal and forgo eating out. Bartering is simply too difficult.

Money being processed at a bank. *Federal Reserve Bank of Boston.*

The use of money as a medium of exchange makes it possible to trade real goods and services without bartering. It facilitates exchange by reducing the cost of trading. Instead of carrying around a sack full of goods, all you need to carry around is a billfold full of money. You go into the restaurant and pay for your meal with money; the restaurant owner can spend (trade) that money for anything she wants.

Money doesn't have to have any inherent value to function as a medium of exchange. All that's necessary is that everyone believes that other people will accept it in exchange for their goods. This neat social convention makes the economy more efficient.

Money doesn't have to have any inherent value to function as a medium of exchange.

That social convention depends on there not being too much or too little money. If there's too much money compared to the goods and services offered at existing prices, the goods and services will sell out, and money won't buy you anything. The social convention will break down, or prices will rise. If there's too little money compared to the goods and services offered at the existing prices, there will be a shortage of money and people will have to resort to barter, or prices will fall.

In order to maintain money's usefulness and to prevent large fluctuations in the price level, the money issuer, which in the United States is the Federal Reserve Bank, or Fed, must issue neither too much nor too little money. (As I stated previously, the Fed is the central bank of the United States; its liabilities serve as money for the U.S. economy.) People accept money in payment and agree to hold money because they believe the Fed will issue neither too little nor too much money. This explains why the Fed doesn't freely issue large amounts of money. To issue money without restraint would destroy the social convention that gives money its value.

Q–1: Since the cost of printing money is low compared to its value, why doesn't the Fed print up lots of money?

Money as a Unit of Account   A second use of money is as a unit of account. Throughout the book we've emphasized that money prices are actually relative prices. A nominal price, say 25¢, for a pencil conveys the information of a relative price: 1 pencil = $\frac{1}{4}$ of 1 dollar or $\frac{1}{6}$ of a hamburger because money is both our unit of account and our medium of exchange. When you think of 25¢, you think of $\frac{1}{4}$ of a dollar and of what a dollar will buy. The 25¢ a pencil costs only has meaning relative to the information you've stored in your mind about what it can buy. If a hamburger costs $1.50, you can compare hamburgers and pencils (1 pencil = $\frac{1}{6}$ of a hamburger) without making the relative price calculations explicitly.

Having a unit of account makes life much easier. For example, say we had no unit of account and you had to remember the relative prices of all goods. For instance, with three goods you'd have to memorize that an airplane ticket to Miami costs 6 lobster dinners in Boston or 4 pairs of running shoes, which makes a pair of shoes worth $1\frac{1}{2}$ lobster dinners.

Memorizing even a few relationships is hard enough, so it isn't surprising that societies began using a single unit of account. If you don't have a single unit of account, to know the relative prices of all combinations of just 20 goods you need to remember over a million relative prices. If you have a single unit of account, you need know only 20 prices. A single unit of account saves our limited memories and helps us make reasonable decisions based on relative costs.

Money is a useful unit of account only as long as its value relative to other prices doesn't change too quickly. That's because it's not only used as a unit of account at a point in time, it's also a unit of account *over time*. Money is a standard of deferred payment. The value of payments that will be made in the future (such as the college loan payments many of you will be making in the future) are determined by the future value of money. A hyperinflation would significantly reduce the value of what you have to pay back. So a hyperinflation would help you, right? Actually, probably not— because a hyperinflation would also rapidly destroy money's usefulness as a unit of account and thereby destroy the U.S. economy.

Money is a useful unit of account only as long as its value relative to other prices doesn't change too quickly.

In a hyperinflation, all prices rise so much that our frame of reference is lost. Is 25¢ for a pencil high or low? If the price level changed 33,000 percent (as it did in 1988 in Nicaragua) or over 100,000 percent (as it did in 1993 in Serbia), 25¢ for a pencil would definitely be low, but would $100 be low? Without a lot of calculations

In a hyperinflation, all prices rise so much that our frame of reference is lost.

CHARACTERISTICS OF A GOOD MONEY

The characteristics of a good money are that its supply be relatively constant, that it be limited in supply (sand wouldn't make good money), that it be difficult to counterfeit, that it be divisible (have you ever tried to spend half a horse?), that it be durable (raspberries wouldn't make good money), and that it be relatively small and light compared to its value (watermelon wouldn't make good money either). All these characteristics were reasonably (but not perfectly) embodied in gold. Many other goods have served as units of account (shells, wampum, rocks, cattle, horses, silver), but gold historically became the most important money, and in the 17th and 18th centuries gold was synonymous with money.

But gold has flaws as money. It's relatively heavy, easy to counterfeit with coins made only partly of gold, and, when new gold fields are discovered, subject to fluctuations in supply. These flaws led to gold's replacement by paper currency backed only by trust that the government would keep its commitment to limit its supply.

Paper money can be a good money if somehow people can trust the government to limit its supply and guarantee that its supply will be limited in the future. That trust has not always been well placed.

we can't answer that question. A relatively stable unit of account makes it easy to answer.

The unit-of-account usefulness of a money also requires that prices don't change too quickly. If the government printed money to pay all its expenses, money's relative price would fall quickly (an increase in supply lowers price), which is another way of saying that the price level would explode and the unit-of-account function of money would be seriously undermined. Maintaining the unit-of-account usefulness of money is a second reason government doesn't pay all its bills by printing money.

Given the advantages to society of having a unit of account, it's not surprising that a monetary unit of account develops even in societies with no government. For example, in a prisoner of war camp during World War II, prisoners had no money, so they used cigarettes as their unit of account. Everything traded was given a price in cigarettes. The exchange rates on December 1, 1944, were:

> 1 bar of soap: 2 cigarettes
> 1 candy bar: 4 cigarettes
> 1 razor blade: 6 cigarettes
> 1 can of fruit: 8 cigarettes
> 1 can of cookies: 20 cigarettes

As you can see, all prices were in cigarettes. If candy bars rose to 6 cigarettes and the normal price was 4 cigarettes, you'd know the price of candy bars was high.

Money as a Store of Wealth

In an earlier chapter, we saw that financial assets serve as a store of wealth. Whenever you save, you forgo consumption now so that you can consume in the future. To bridge the gap between now and the future, you must acquire a financial asset. This is true even if you squirrel away cash under the mattress. In that case, the financial asset you've acquired is simply the cash itself. Money is a financial asset. (It's simply a bond that pays no interest.) So a third use of money is as a store of wealth. As long as money is serving as a medium of exchange, it automatically also serves as a store of wealth. The restaurant owner can accept your money and hold it for as long as she wants before she spends it. (But had you paid her in fish, she'd be wise not to hold it more than a few hours.)

As long as money is serving as a medium of exchange, it automatically also serves as a store of wealth.

Q–2: Why do people hold money rather than bonds when bonds pay higher interest than money?

Money's usefulness as a store of wealth also depends upon how well it maintains its value. If prices are going up 100,000 percent per year, the value of a stated amount of money is shrinking fast. People want to spend their money as quickly as possible before prices rise any more. Thus, once again, money's usefulness as a social convention depends upon the government not issuing too much money.

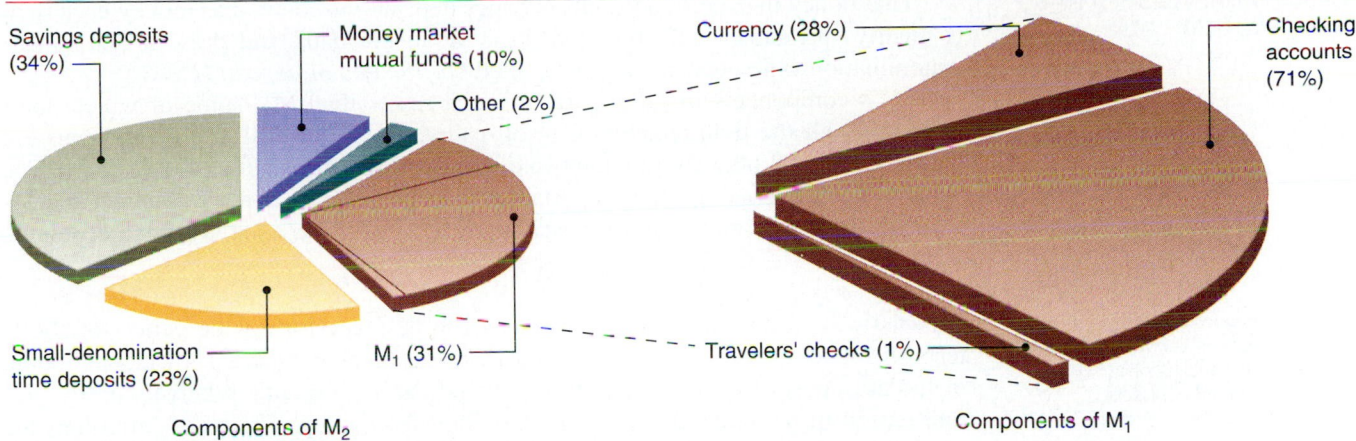

EXHIBIT 1   Components of M₂ and M₁

The two most-used definitions of the money supply are M₁ and M₂. The primary components of M₁ are cash and checking accounts. M₂ includes all of M₁, plus savings accounts and time deposits.
Source: *Federal Reserve Bulletin*, 1994.

Even if prices aren't rising, you might wonder why people would hold money which pays no interest, rather than holding a government bond which does pay interest. The reason is that money is more easily translated into other goods than are bonds. Since money is also the medium of exchange, it can be spent instantaneously (as long as there's a shop open nearby). Our ability to spend money for goods makes money worthwhile to hold even if it doesn't pay interest.

According to the definition of *money,* what people believe is money is a determining factor in deciding whether a financial asset is money. What is money depends on what people will accept as money; consequently it's difficult to define *money* unambiguously. A number of different financial assets serve some of the functions of money and thus have claims to being called *money.* To handle this ambiguity, economists have defined different concepts of money and have called them M₁, M₂, and L. Each is a reasonable concept of money. Let's consider their components.

Alternative Definitions of Money

M₁   **M₁** consists of cash in the hands of the public and checking account balances. Clearly, cash in the hands of the public (the dollar bills and coins you carry around with you) are money, but how about your checking account deposits? The reason they're included in this definition of money is that just about anything you can do with cash, you can do with a check. You can store your wealth in your checking account; you can use a check as a medium of exchange (indeed, for some transactions you have no choice but to use a check), and your checking account balance is denominated in the same unit of account (dollars) as is cash. If it looks like money, acts like money, and functions as money, it's a good bet it's money. Indeed, checking account deposits are included in all definitions of money.

The same arguments can be made about traveler's checks. (Some advertisements even claim that traveler's checks are better than money because you can get them replaced.) Currency, checking account deposits, and traveler's checks make up the components of M₁, the narrowest definition of money. Exhibit 1 presents the relative sizes of M₁'s components.

3 M₁ is the component of the money supply that consists of cash in the hands of the public plus checking accounts and travelers' checks.

M₂   **M₂** is made up of M₁ plus savings deposits, small-denomination time deposits, and money market mutual fund shares, along with some esoteric financial instruments that won't concern us here. The relative sizes of the components of M₂ are given in Exhibit 1. (The esoteric instruments are classified as ''Other.'')

3 M₂ is the component of the money supply that consists of M₁ plus other relatively liquid assets.

Q–3:   Which would be a larger number, M_1 or M_2? Why?

The money in savings accounts (savings deposits) is counted as money because it is readily spendable—all you need do is go to the bank and draw it out. Small-denomination time deposits are also called *certificates of deposit (CDs)*.

M_2's components include more financial assets than M_1, some of which don't quite meet all the requirements of being called money. But all the components are highly liquid and play an important role in providing reserves for commercial banks. What makes the M_2 definition important is that economic research has shown that M_2 is the definition of money most closely correlated with the price level and economic activity.

3   The broadest definition of the money supply is L (which stands for liquidity). It consists of almost all short-term financial assets.

Beyond M_2: L   The same type of argument can be made for a wide variety of short-term financial assets (assets whose maturity is less than one year). They all have some of the attributes of money. They're liquid and can be "spent" relatively easily. For that reason they're included in some definitions of money. There are definitions for M_3, M_4, and beyond. Most economists concern themselves only with the first two definitions (M_1 and M_2) and the broadest definition, which is called L (for *liquidity*). The **L** definition of money includes almost all short-term assets.

Credit card balances cannot be money since they are assets of a bank. In a sense, they are the opposite of money.

Distinguishing between Money and Credit   You might have thought that credit cards would be included in one of the definitions of *money*. But we didn't include them. In fact, credit cards are nowhere to be seen in a list of financial assets. Credit cards aren't a financial liability of the bank that issues them. Instead credit cards create a liability for their holders (money owed to the company or bank that issued the card) and the banks have a financial asset as a result.

Let's consider how a credit card works. You go into a store and buy something with your credit card. You have a real asset—the item you bought. The store has a financial asset—an account receivable. The store sells that financial asset to the bank (for a fee, of course) and gets cash in return. Either the bank collects cash when you pay off your financial liability or, if you don't pay it off, the bank earns interest on its financial asset (usually at a high rate, about 18 percent per year).

This distinction between credit and money should be kept in mind. Money is a financial asset of individuals and a financial liability of banks. Credit is savings made available to be borrowed. Credit is not an asset.

Credit cards and credit impact the amount of money people hold. When credit is instantly available (as it is with a credit card) there's less need to hold money. (If you didn't have a credit card, you'd carry a lot more cash.) Liquidity is less valuable to people. So credit and credit cards do make a difference in how much money people hold, but because they are not financial assets, they are not money.

Now that we've considered what money is, both in theory and in practice, let's consider the banking system's role in creating money.

BANKS AND THE CREATION OF MONEY

Banks are financial institutions that borrow from people (take in deposits) and use the money they borrow to make loans to other individuals. Banks make a profit by charging a higher interest on the money they lend out than they pay for the money they borrow.

Banking is generally analyzed from the perspective of **asset management** (how a bank handles its loans and other assets) and **liability management** (how a bank attracts deposits and what it pays for them). When banks offer people "free checking" and special money market accounts paying 4 percent, they do so after carefully considering the costs of those liabilities to them.

It is important to think of banks as both borrowers and lenders.

To think of banks as borrowers as well as lenders may seem a bit unusual, but borrowing is what they do. When you keep money in a savings account or a checking account, the bank is borrowing from you, paying you a zero (or low) interest rate and lending your money to other people at a high interest rate. Much of banks' borrowing is short-term borrowing, meaning banks must pay the money back to the lender either on demand (as in the case of checking accounts or savings accounts) or within a specific period of time (as in the case of certificates of deposit).

ADDED DIMENSION

NOW ACCOUNTS AND MONEY
MARKET ACCOUNTS

At one time the only checking accounts were those of commercial banks. You put your money in a commercial bank and wrote a check. Then savings banks (banks allowed only to have savings accounts) started allowing individuals to write *negotiable orders of withdrawals* on their savings accounts (NOW accounts). So if you held $10,000 in a savings account you could write an IOU to someone and the savings bank promised to pay it. That IOU looked like a check, and for all practical purposes it was a check. But unlike a checking account, NOW accounts paid interest on depositors' balances. Many people started shifting from checking accounts to NOW accounts, and soon commercial banks complained of unfair competition by savings banks. These complaints led to commercial banks being allowed to pay interest on their checking accounts.

Mutual funds saw how nicely NOW accounts worked and decided to imitate them. Individuals who kept their money stored with a mutual fund were allowed to write IOUs based on their deposits (up to three IOUs per month, each for a minimum of, say, $500). The mutual fund invested depositors' money in the money market (short-term bills, commercial paper, and CDs). Hence, accounts with mutual funds are called *money market accounts*. These accounts pay slightly higher interest than savings banks' accounts, and, like the NOW account, are close to a checking account.

So today people have a choice of depository institutions, which is nice for people, but tough for textbook writers and students who have to learn more divisions.

In the United States, banks operate in a regulated environment. They have limits on what kinds of loans they can make and what types of borrowing they're allowed to do. The primary regulator of the money supply in the United States is the Federal Reserve Bank (the Fed), which we'll consider in detail in the next chapter.

How Banks Create Money

How do banks create money? As John Kenneth Galbraith's epigram at the start of this chapter suggested, the process is simple—so simple it seems almost mystical to many.

4 Banks ''create'' money because a bank's liabilities are defined as money. So when a bank incurs liabilities it creates money.

The key to understanding how banks create money is to remember the nature of financial assets: Financial assets can be created from nothing as long as an offsetting financial liability is simultaneously created. Since money is any financial asset that serves the function of money, money can be created rather easily. Seeing how dollar bills are created is the easiest way to begin examining the process. Dollar bills are IOUs of the Fed that serve the three functions of money. So whenever the Fed issues an IOU, it creates money.[1] Similarly, other banks create money by creating financial assets that serve the functions of money. As we saw when we considered the definition of *money*, bank checking accounts serve those functions, so they are money, just as cash is. When a bank places the proceeds of a loan it makes to you in your checking account, it is creating money. You have a financial asset that did not previously exist.

The First Step in the Creation of Money   To see how banks create money, let's consider what would happen if you were given a freshly printed $100 bill. Remember, the Fed created that $100 bill simply by printing it. The $100 bill is a $100 financial asset of yours and a financial liability of the Fed, which issued it.

If the process of creating money stopped there, it wouldn't be particularly mysterious. But it doesn't stop there. Let's consider what happens next as you use that money.

The Second Step in the Creation of Money   Say you decide to put the $100 bill in your checking account. To make the analysis easier, let's assume that your bank is a branch of the country's only bank, Big Bank. All money deposited in branch banks goes into Big Bank. After you make your deposit, Big Bank is holding $100 cash for you, and you have $100 more in your checking account. You can spend it whenever you want

---

[1] As we'll see in the next chapter, dollar bills aren't the Fed's only IOUs.

Gold coins once served as our economy's medium of exchange. These have been almost totally replaced by paper money. *David Pollack/The Stock Market.*

simply by writing a check. So Big Bank is performing a service for you (holding your money and keeping track of your expenditures) for free. Neat, huh? Big Bank must be run by a bunch of nice people.

But wait. You and I know that bankers, while they may be nice, aren't as nice as all that. There's no such thing as a free lunch. Let's see why the bank is being so nice.

Banking and Goldsmiths   To see why banks are so nice, let's go way back in history to when banks first developed.[2] At that time, gold was used for money and people carried around gold to make their payments. But gold is rather heavy, so if they had to make a big purchase, it was difficult to pay for the purchase. Moreover, carrying around a lot of gold left them vulnerable to being robbed by the likes of Robin Hood. So they looked for a place to store their gold until they needed some of it.

From Gold to Gold Receipts   The natural place to store gold was the goldsmith shop, which already had a vault. For a small fee, the goldsmith shop would hold your gold, giving you a receipt for it. Whenever you needed your gold, you'd go to the goldsmith and exchange the receipt for gold.

Pretty soon most people kept their gold at the goldsmith's, and they began to wonder: Why go through the bother of getting my gold out to buy something when all that happens is that the seller takes the gold I pay and puts it right back into the goldsmith's vault? That's two extra trips.

Consequently, people began using the receipts the goldsmith gave them to certify that they had deposited $100 worth (or whatever) of gold in his vault. At that point gold was no longer the only money—gold receipts were also money. However, as long as the total amount in the gold receipts directly represented the total amount of gold, it was still reasonable to say, since the receipts were 100 percent backed by gold, that gold was the money supply.

Q-4:   Most banks prefer to have many depositors rather than one big depositor. Why?

Gold Receipts Become Money   Once this process of using the receipts rather than the gold became generally accepted, the goldsmith found that he had substantial amounts of gold in his vault. All that gold, just sitting there! On a normal day only 1 percent of the gold was claimed by ''depositors'' and had to be given out. Usually on the same

---

[2] The banking history reported here is, according to historians, apocryphal (more myth than reality). But it so nicely makes the point that I repeat it anyhow.

day an amount at least equal to that 1 percent came in from other depositors. What a waste! Gold sitting around doing nothing! So when a good friend came in, needing a loan, the goldsmith said, "Sure, I'll lend you some gold receipts as long as you pay me some interest." When the goldsmith made this loan, he created more gold receipts than he had covered in gold in his vault. He created money.

Pretty soon the goldsmith realized he could earn more from the interest he received on loans than he could earn from goldsmithing. So he stopped goldsmithing and went full-time into making loans of gold receipts. At that point the number of gold receipts outstanding significantly exceeded the amount of gold in the goldsmith's vaults. But not to worry; since everyone was willing to accept gold receipts rather than gold, the goldsmith had plenty of gold for those few who wanted actual gold.

It was, however, no longer accurate to say that gold was the country's money or currency. Gold receipts were the money. They met the definition of *money*. These gold receipts were backed partially by gold and partially by people's trust that the goldsmiths would pay off their deposits on demand. The goldsmith shops had become banks.

Money is whatever meets the definition of money.

Banking Is Profitable   The banking business was very profitable for goldsmiths. Soon other people started competing with them, offering to hold gold for free. After all, if they could store gold, they could make a profit on the loans to other people (with the first people's money). Some even offered to pay people to store their gold.

The goldsmith story is directly relevant to banks. People store their cash in banks and the banks issue receipts—checking accounts—which become a second form of money. When people place their cash in banks and use their receipts from the bank as money, those receipts also become money because they meet the definition of *money:* They serve as a medium of exchange, a unit of account, and a store of wealth. So money includes both cash that people hold and their deposits in the bank.

Which brings us back to why banks hold your cash for free. They do it, not because they're nice, but because when you deposit cash in the bank, your deposit allows banks to make profitable loans they otherwise couldn't make.

The Money Multiplier

With that background, let's go back to your $100, which the bank is now holding for you. You have a checking account balance of $100 and the bank has $100 cash. As long as other people are willing to accept your check in payment for $100 worth of goods, your check is as good as money. In fact it *is* money in the same way gold receipts were money. But when you deposit $100, no money has been created yet. The form of the money has simply been changed from cash to a checking account or demand deposit.

Now let's say Big Bank lends out 90 percent of the cash you deposit, keeping only 10 percent as **reserves** on hand—that is, enough money to manage the normal cash inflows and outflows. This 10 percent is the **reserve ratio** (the ratio of cash or deposits the bank holds at the central bank to deposits a bank keeps as a reserve against withdrawals of cash). This reserve ratio is determined by the percentage of deposits that banks are required to hold (required reserve ratio) and the percentage that banks may choose to hold in excess of that required reserve ratio. Thus it is at least as large as the required reserve ratio, but it can be larger.

Reserve ratio   The ratio of cash (or deposits at the central bank) to deposits a bank keeps as a reserve against cash withdrawals. The reserve ratio consists of required and excess reserves.

So, like the goldsmith, Big Bank lends out $90 to someone who needs a loan. That person the bank loaned the money to now has $90 cash and you have $100 in a demand deposit, so now there's $190 of money, rather than just $100 of money. The $10 in cash the bank holds in reserve isn't counted as money since the bank must keep it as reserves and may not use it as long as it's backing loans. Only cash held by the public is counted as money. By making the loan, the bank has created $90 in money.

Of course, no one borrows money just to hold it. The borrower spends the money, say on a new sweater, and the sweater store owner now has the $90 in cash. The store owner doesn't want to hold it either. She'll deposit it back into the bank. Since there's only one bank, Big Bank discovers that the $90 it has loaned out is once again in its coffers. The money operates like a boomerang: Big Bank loans $90 out and gets the $90 back again.

The same process occurs again. The bank doesn't make any money holding $90, so it lends out $81, keeping $9 (10 percent of $90) in reserve. The story repeats and repeats itself, with a slightly smaller amount coming back to the bank each time. At each step in the process, money (in the form of checking account deposits) is being created.

Determining How Many Demand Deposits Will Be Created   What's the total amount of demand deposits that will ultimately be created from your $100? To answer that question, we continue the process over and over: 100 + 90 + 81 + 72.9 + 65.6 + 59 + 53.1 + 47.8 + 43.0 + 38.7 + 34.9. Adding up these numbers gives us $686. Adding up $686 plus the numbers from the next 20 rounds gives us $961.08.

As you can see, that's a lot of adding. Luckily there's an easier way. Mathematicians have shown that you can determine the amount of money that will eventually be created by such a process by multiplying the initial $100 in money that was found and deposited by $1/r$, where r is the reserve ratio (the percentage banks keep out of each round). In this case the reserve ratio is 10 percent.
Dividing,

$$1/r = 1/.10 = 10$$

so the amount of demand deposits that will ultimately exist at the end of the process is

$$(10 \times \$100) = \$1,000.$$

The $1,000 is in the form of checking account deposits (demand deposits). The entire $100 in cash that you were given, and which started the whole process, is in the bank as reserves, which means that $900 ($1,000 − $100) of money has been created by the process.

5 The money multiplier is the measure of the amount of money ultimately created per dollar deposited by the banking system. When people hold no cash it equals $1/r$. When people hold cash the approximate money multiplier is $1/(r + c)$.

Calculating the Money Multiplier   The ratio $1/r$ is called the **simple money multiplier.** It tells us how much money will ultimately be created by the banking system from an initial inflow of money. In our example, $1/.10 = 10$. Had the bank kept out 20 percent each time, the money multiplier would have been $1/.20 = 5$. If the reserve ratio were 5 percent, the money multiplier would have been $1/.05 = 20$. The higher the reserve ratio, the smaller the money multiplier, and the less money will be created.

Banks are not the only holders of cash. Firms and individuals hold cash too, so in each round we must also make an adjustment in the multiplier for what people and firms hold. The math you need to formally calculate the money multiplier gets a bit complicated when firms and people hold cash. Since for our purposes a rough calculation is all we need, we will use an approximate money multiplier in which individuals' cash holdings are treated the same as reserves of banks. Thus the **approximate real-world money multiplier** in the economy is:

$$1/(r + c)$$

Approximate real-world money multiplier $1/(r + c)$.

Q-5:   If banks hold 20 percent of their deposits as reserves, and the ratio of money people hold as cash to deposits is 20 percent, what is the approximate money multiplier?

Q-6:   If people suddenly decide to hold more cash, what happens to the size of the approximate money multiplier?

where r = the percentage of deposits banks hold in reserve and c is the ratio of money people hold in cash to the money they hold as deposits.[3] Let's consider an example. Say the banks keep 10 percent in reserve and the ratio of individuals' cash holdings to their deposits is 25 percent. This means the approximate real-world money multiplier will be

$$1/(.1 + .25) = 1/.35 = 2.9.$$

Faith as the Backing of Our Money Supply

The creation of money and the money multiplier are easy to understand if you remember that money (the financial asset created) is offset by an equal amount of financial liabilities of the bank. The bank owes its depositors the amount in their

---

[3] In the Appendix I discuss the precise calculation of the money multiplier when individuals hold cash.

Life keeps getting tougher. In the old days economics students only had to learn the simple money multiplier. Recent reforms in the U.S. banking system have made that impossible. The Depository Institutions Deregulation Act of 1980 extended the reserve requirement to a wide variety of financial institutions besides banks, but it also lowered the reserve requirement for most deposits. In the 1990s, the average reserve requirement for all types of bank deposits is about 2 percent and banks hold very few excess reserves. (The U.S. reserve requirement on checking accounts is between 3 and 12 percent. In Great Britain, there are no reserve requirements.)

If you insert that low average ratio into the simple money multiplier, you get a multiplier of 50! The real-world money multiplier is much lower than that because of people's holding of cash; the ratio of money people hold as cash, c, is over .4. (For each person in the United States there's about $1,000 in cash. Don't ask me where that cash is, but according to the data it's out there.) Thus, despite the fact that it makes calculating the approximate real-world money multiplier a bit more difficult, these holdings must be included in the story. Otherwise you won't have a sense of how the real-world system works.

checking accounts. Its financial liabilities to depositors, in turn, are secured by the loans (the bank's financial assets) and by the financial liabilities of people to whom the loans were made. Promises to pay underlie any modern financial system.

The initial money in the story about the goldsmiths was gold, but it quickly became apparent that it was far more reasonable to use gold certificates as money. Therefore gold certificates backed by gold soon replaced gold itself as the money supply. Then, as goldsmiths made more loans than they had gold, the gold certificates were no longer backed by gold. They were backed by promises to get gold if the person wanted gold in exchange for the gold certificate. Eventually the percentage of gold supposedly backing the money became so small that it was clear to everyone that the promises, not the gold, underlay the money supply.

The same holds true with banks. Initially cash (Federal Reserve IOUs) was backed by gold, and banks' demand deposits were in turn backed by Federal Reserve IOUs. But by the 1930s the percentage of gold backing money grew so small that even the illusion of the money being backed by anything but promises was removed. All that backs the modern money supply are banks' promises to pay.

All that backs the modern money supply are banks' promises to pay.

You've already been introduced to the basis of financial accounting: the T-account presentation of balance sheets. The balance sheet is made up of assets on one side and liabilities and net worth on the other. By definition the two sides are equal; they balance (just as the T-account must).

To cement the money creation process in your mind, let's discuss how banks create money using transactions that affect the balance sheet. To keep the analysis simple, we limit the example to the case where only banks create money. (In the appendix we do the more complicated example in which people also hold cash.)

Exhibit 2 shows the initial balance sheet of an imaginary Textland Bank, which we assume is the only bank in the country. As you can see, Textland has $500,000 in assets: $30,000 in cash, $300,000 in loans, and $170,000 in property. On the liabilities side, it has $150,000 in demand deposits and $350,000 in net worth. The two sides of the balance sheet are equal.

Creation of Money Using T-Accounts

EXHIBIT 2   Textland Bank Balance Sheet   Beginning Balance

Assets		Liabilities and Net Worth	
Cash	$ 30,000	Demand deposits	$150,000
Loans	300,000	Net worth	350,000
Property	170,000		
Total assets	$500,000	Total liabilities and net worth	$500,000

The first thing to notice about this balance sheet is that if all holders of checking accounts (demand deposits) wanted their cash, the bank couldn't give it to them. The cash it holds is only a portion—20 percent—of the total deposits:

$$\$30,000/\$150,000 = .20.$$

Banks rely upon statistical averages and assume that not all people will want their money at the same time. Let's assume Textland Bank has decided 20 percent is an appropriate reserve ratio.

Now let's say that John Finder finds $10,000 in cash. He deposits that $10,000 into Textland Bank. After he does so, what will happen to the money supply? The first step is seen in Transaction 1, which shows the effect of John Finder's deposit on the bank's account. The bank gains $10,000 in cash, but its liabilities also increase by $10,000, so, as you can see, the two sides of the balance sheet are still equal. At this point no additional money has been created; $10,000 cash has simply been changed to a $10,000 demand deposit.

EXHIBIT 2   (continued) Transaction 1

Assets		Liabilities and Net Worth	
Cash (beginning balance)	$30,000	Demand deposits (beginning balance) . . . $150,000	
Cash from John	10,000	John's deposit	10,000
Total cash	$ 40,000	Total demand deposits	$160,000
Loans	300,000	Net worth	350,000
Property	170,000		
Total assets	$510,000	Total liabilities and net worth	$510,000

Now let's assume the bank uses a reserve ratio of 20 percent, meaning it can lend out 80 percent of the cash it receives in new deposits. Say it lends out 80% × $10,000 = $8,000 to Fred Baker, keeping 20 percent × $10,000 = $2,000 in reserve. The change in the bank's balance sheet is seen in Transaction 2. This step creates $8,000 in money. Why? Because John Finder still has $10,000 in his checking account, while Fred Baker has $8,000 cash, so, combining John's checking account balance with Fred's cash, the public has $8,000 in money. As you can see, loans have increased by $8,000 and cash in Textland Bank has decreased by $8,000.

EXHIBIT 2   (continued) Transaction 2

Assets		Liabilities and Net Worth	
Cash (after Trans. 1)	$ 40,000	Demand deposits (after Trans. 1)	$160,000
Cash given to Fred	8,000	Net worth	350,000
Total cash	$ 32,000		
Loans (beginning balance)	300,000		
Loan to Fred	8,000		
Total loans	308,000		
Property	170,000		
Total assets	$510,000	Total liabilities and net worth	$510,000

Fred Baker didn't borrow the money to hold onto it. He spends it buying a new oven from Mary Builder, who, in turn, deposits the $8,000 into Textland Bank (the only bank according to our assumptions). Textland's balance sheet now looks like Transaction 3.

EXHIBIT 2   (continued)   Transaction 3

Assets			Liabilities and Net Worth		
Cash (after Trans. 2)	$32,000		Demand deposits	$160,000	
Cash from Mary	8,000		Mary's deposit	8,000	
Total cash		$ 40,000	Total demand deposits		$168,000
Loans		308,000	Net worth		350,000
Property		170,000			
Total assets		$518,000	Total liabilities and net worth		$518,000

EXHIBIT 3   The Money-Creating Process

Bank Gets	Bank Keeps (Reserve Ratio: 20%)	Bank Loans (80%) = Person Borrows
$10,000	$2,000	$8,000
8,000	1,600	6,400
6,400	1,280	5,120
5,120	1,024	4,096
4,096	819	3,277
3,277	656	2,621
2,621	524	2,097
2,097	419	1,678
1,678	336	1,342
1,342	268	1,074
$44,631 (total deposits)	$8,946	+	$35,705

Total money existing (after 10 rounds) = $44,631

Mary Builder has a demand deposit of $8,000, and John Finder has a demand deposit of $10,000. But Textland Bank has excess reserves of $6,400, since it must keep only $1,600 of Mary's $8,000 deposit as reserves:

$$80\% \times \$8,000 = \$6,400$$

So the bank is looking to make a loan.

Now the process occurs again. Exhibit 3 shows the effects of the process for 10 rounds, starting with the initial $10,000. Each time it lends the money out, the money returns like a boomerang and serves as reserves for more loans. After 10 rounds we

Q–7: How would the answer to the total amount of money created in this example have differed if, in addition to the 20 percent reserve the banks hold, individuals' ratio of cash to deposits were 30 percent?

reach a point where total demand deposits are $44,631, and the bank has $8,946 in reserves. This is approaching the $50,000 we'd arrive at using the money multiplier:

$$1/r(\$10,000) = [1/.2](\$10,000) = 5(\$10,000) = \$50,000.$$

If we carried it out for more rounds, we'd actually reach what the formula predicted.

Note that the process ends only when the bank holds all the cash, and the only money held by the public is in the form of demand deposits. Notice also that the total amount of money created depends on the amount banks hold in reserve.

To see that you understand the process, say that banks suddenly get concerned about the safety of their loans, and they decide to keep **excess reserves**—reserves in excess of what they are required to hold. What will happen to the money multiplier? If you answered that it will decrease, you've got it. Excess reserves decrease the money multiplier as much as do required reserves. I mention this example because this is precisely what happened to the banking system in the early 1990s. Banks became concerned about the safety of their loans; they held large excess reserves, and the money multiplier decreased.

In summary, the process of money creation isn't difficult to understand as long as you remember that money is simply a bank's financial liability held by the public. Whenever banks create financial liabilities for themselves, they create financial assets for individuals, and those financial assets are money.

REGULATION OF BANKS AND THE FINANCIAL SECTOR

You just saw how easy it is to create money. The banking system and money make the economy operate more efficiently, but they also present potential problems. For example, say that for some reason suddenly there's an increase in money (that is, in promises to pay) without any corresponding increase in real goods and services. As the money supply increases without an increase in real goods to buy with that money, more money is chasing the same number of goods. Aggregate demand exceeds aggregate supply. The result will be a fall in the value of money (inflation), meaning real trade will be more complicated. Alternatively, if there's an increase in real goods but not a corresponding increase in money, there will be a shortage of money, which will hamper the economy. Either the price level will fall (deflation) or there will be a recession.

Societies have continually experienced these problems, and the financial history of the world is filled with stories of financial upheavals and monetary problems. For example, there are numerous instances of private financial firms who have promised the world, but their promises have been nothing but hot air. One instance occurred in the 1800s in the United States, when banks were allowed to issue their own notes (their own promises to pay). These notes served as part of the U.S. money supply. Sharp financial operators soon got into the process and created banks out in the boonies called *wildcat banks* because they were situated in places where only a wildcat would go. These wildcat banks issued notes even though they had no deposits, hoping that no one would cash the notes in. Many such banks defaulted on their promises, leaving holders of the notes with only worthless pieces of paper. Merchants quickly caught on, and soon they began checking in a "book of notes" which listed whether the notes the buyer was offering were probably good or not.

Anatomy of a Financial Panic

6 Financial systems are based on trust that expectations will be fulfilled. Banks borrow short and lend long, which means that if people lose faith in banks, the banks cannot keep their promises.

Another problem that can develop in the banking system is a financial panic. Banking and financial systems are based on promises and trust. People put their cash into other financial assets (such as demand deposits) and believe that these demand deposits are as good as cash. In normal times, demand deposits really are as good as cash. When times get bad, people become concerned about the financial firms' ability to keep those promises and they call upon the firms to redeem the promises. But banks have only their reserves (a small percentage of their total deposits) to give depositors. Most of the depositors' money is loaned out and cannot be gotten back quickly, even though the banks have promised depositors that their deposits will be given back "on demand." Put another way, banks borrow short and lend long.

When a lot of depositors lose faith in a bank and, all at one time, call on the bank to keep its promises, the bank cannot do so. The result is that the bank fails when depositors lose faith, even though the bank might be financially sound for the long run. Fear underlies financial panics and can undermine financial institutions.

To prevent such panics, the U.S. government has guaranteed the obligations of various financial institutions. Guaranteeing programs include the Federal Deposit Insurance Corporation (FDIC), Federal Savings and Loan Insurance Corporation (FSLIC), and a variety of government-guaranteed bonds. These guarantees work as follows: The financial institutions pay a small premium for each dollar of deposit to the government-organized insurance company. That company puts the premium into a fund used to bail out banks experiencing a run on deposits. These guarantees have two effects:

1. They prevent the unwarranted fear that causes financial crises. Depositors know that the government will see that they can get their cash back even if the bank fails. This knowledge stops them from responding to a rumor and trying to get their money out of a suspect financial institution before anyone else does.

2. They prevent warranted fears. Why should people worry about whether or not a financial institution is making reasonable loans on the basis of their deposits if the government guarantees the financial institutions' promises to pay regardless of what kind of loans the institutions make?

Guarantees prevent unwarranted fears. The illusion upon which banks depend (that people can get their money in the short run, even though it's only in the long run that they can *all* get it) can be met by temporary loans from the government. Guarantees can prevent unwarranted fears from becoming financial panics. The guarantee makes the illusion a reality. If people can indeed get their money in the long run, seeing to it that this illusion *is* reality isn't expensive to the government. As long as the bank has sufficient long-term assets to cover its deposits, the government will be repaid its temporary loan.

Unfortunately, covering the unwarranted fear can also mean preventing the warranted fear from putting an effective restraint or discipline on banks' lending policies. If deposits are guaranteed, why should depositors worry whether banks have adequate loans to cover their deposits in the long run? Thus, when there's a bigger illusion than the short-run/long-run illusion, and depositors can't get their money in the long run (that is, their fears were warranted), guaranteeing deposits can be expensive indeed. The U.S. government found this out in the late 1980s in connection with its guarantees of federal savings and loan institutions' deposits.

The Savings and Loan Fiasco of the Late 1980s and Early 1990s   As we said, the United States has guaranteed the deposits of a variety of financial institutions, including savings and loan institutions (S&Ls). S&Ls had developed as institutions to hold savings and invest those savings back into the community. Up until 1980, S&Ls were heavily regulated by the government and weren't allowed to invest in anything except private residential mortgages, which generally are relatively safe investments. The only place S&Ls were allowed to get their funds from was their depositors' savings accounts. During the period when S&Ls were heavily regulated, the U.S. government began to guarantee S&L deposits.

In 1982 financial institutions were deregulated, and S&Ls were allowed to invest in anything they wished and to compete for funds with commercial banks by issuing interest-bearing checking accounts (called *NOW accounts*) and negotiable CDs. They did so. They paid high interest on their deposits and, to justify that high interest, they invested in high-interest financial assets such as high-risk junk (low-grade) bonds and commercial real estate. Unfortunately S&Ls didn't have the management capability to assess the risks, and they made billions of dollars worth of bad loans which would

Q–8: Why does borrowing short and lending long present a potential problem for banks?

Government Policy to Prevent Panic

Q–9: What are two effects that a government guarantee of financial institutions can have?

The Benefits and Problems of Guarantees

The fact that deposits are guaranteed doesn't serve to inspire banks to make certain deposits are covered by loans in the long run.

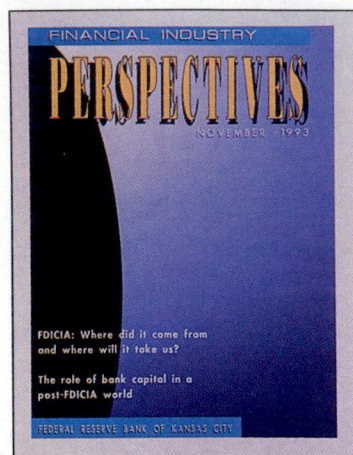

Each reserve bank has its own journal, and these are excellent sources of information and readable articles about financial issues.

Spread *The difference between a bank's costs of funds and the interest it receives on lending out those funds.*

never be paid back. During the 1980s the U.S. economy also changed. Banking policies that had made sense in the late 1970s and early 1980s no longer made sense in the mid-1980s. The result was the savings and loan fiasco of the late 1980s and early 1990s. Many S&Ls failed and didn't have enough money to pay back depositors. The U.S. government, which had guaranteed those deposits, had to bail out the S&Ls by paying the depositors.

Because of the complexity and vast number of deals so many S&Ls made, it will probably be years before the government actually knows the final cost, but it will be in the hundreds of billions of dollars.

How Could the Savings and Loan Fiasco Happen?

How, you ask, can banks make so many bad loans that they don't have enough money to pay back depositors? Part of the answer is fraud—banks made loans to friends that they knew were more like gifts than like loans. Part of the answer is that it doesn't take many bad loans to pull a bank under. Remember, banks take deposits in and lend those deposits out, hoping to make a profit from the **spread** (the difference between their costs and the interest they pay out, and the interest they take in minus bad loans). If, on average, more loans go bad than expected and the banks' costs are higher than expected, banks' profit can evaporate, leaving a loss. When that happens, deposits must be covered by the banks' net worth, which is small—about 1 percent of total deposits—so there isn't much room for many bad loans. As was just pointed out, the S&Ls paid high interest rates and made many risky loans.

Another part of the answer is that it isn't hard to make a bad loan. Making loans is inherently risky. A person walks in with a grand idea for a mall—all she needs is a $10,000,000 loan. The mall is needed by the community and will be worth $30,000,000 once it's built. She has investors willing to put up $2,000,000 of their own money and she's willing to pay 12 percent interest and give the mall as collateral. She's built successful malls before. So the bank makes the loan.

The building starts, only to have the builder discover there's a stone ledge beneath the site. Blasting is required—costs go up 12 percent. A builders' strike delays construction—costs go up 4 percent. When things are ready to proceed once the strike

This 18th-century etching by Robert Goez, "The Speculator," captures a popular view of financial activities. It shows a man reduced to rags by bad speculation. *Bleichroeder Print Collection, Baker Library, Harvard Business School.*

is settled, it rains daily, slowing construction—costs go up another 8 percent. The economy goes into a recession and one store that had promised to rent space in the mall pulls out. Let's say the store that pulled out was an ''anchor'' store (that is, the mall relied on that store's presence to attract large numbers of shoppers, who would then wander around and shop in the mall's smaller stores). Now the major industry in town shuts down. The mall's finished value falls 40 percent. You get the picture.

Making loans requires taking chances and, when you take chances, once in a while you lose. S&Ls bet that there would be no recession. When a recession started, they lost their bet, and a number of their loans went bad.

The last part of the answer is the government guarantee. Had the government not guaranteed the S&L's deposits, depositors (not the government) would have incurred the loss. They likely would have become alarmed as they saw troubles coming to their S&Ls and would have withdrawn their money before the situation became a disaster. But they didn't watch carefully and had no reason to be alarmed, because they knew the government had guaranteed their deposits (at least, up to $100,000).

Should the government have guaranteed S&L deposits? That's an open question. The guarantees did serve their purpose; they prevented unwarranted runs on S&Ls. (That is, depositors didn't all run to the bank at the same time and ask to withdraw their money in cash.) But the guarantee program had serious flaws. If the government was going to guarantee deposits, it should have charged banks much higher fees. Government then would have had enough money to cover the losses resulting from bad loans. Or government should have maintained a strong regulatory presence, limiting the risks the S&Ls undertook.

The S&L crisis didn't answer the debate between the two goals: avoiding unwarranted fears while not limiting warranted fears. Keynesians blame the crisis on the bank deregulation that let S&Ls make risky loans and investments. They claimed the S&Ls' crisis showed the need for regulation. Classicals blame government guarantees that stopped the market forces from operating. As usual, both Keynesians and Classicals have reasonable arguments.

Q–10: What is a benefit and what is the cost of government guarantees of deposits?

CHAPTER SUMMARY

- Money is a useful financial instrument.
- Money serves as a unit of account, a medium of exchange, and a store of wealth.
- There are various definitions of money: M_1, M_2, and L.
- Since money is what people believe money to be, creating money out of thin air is easy. How banks create money out of thin air is easily understood if you remember that money is simply a financial liability of a bank.
- The simple money multiplier is $1/r$.
- The approximate real world multiplier is $1/(r + c)$.
- Financial panics are based on fear. They can be prevented by government, but only at a cost.

KEY TERMS

approximate real-world money multiplier *(314)*
asset management *(310)*
excess reserves *(318)*
Federal Reserve Bank (Fed) *(306)*

L *(310)*
liability management *(310)*
M_1 *(309)*
M_2 *(309)*
money *(306)*

reserve ratio *(313)*
reserves *(313)*
simple money multiplier *(314)*
spread *(320)*

QUESTIONS FOR THOUGHT AND REVIEW

The number after each question represents the estimated degree of critical thinking required. (1= almost none; 10 = deep thought.)

1. Money is to the economy as oil is to an engine. Explain. *(4)*

2. List the three functions of money. *(1)*

3. Why doesn't the government pay for all its goods simply by printing money? *(4)*

4. What are two components of M_2 that are not components of M_1? *(1)*

5. Assuming individuals hold no cash, calculate the simple money multiplier for each of the following reserve requirements: 5%, 10%, 20%, 25%, 50%, 75%, 100%.   *(3)*

6. Assuming individuals hold 20% of their money in the form of cash, recalculate the approximate real-world money multipliers from Question 5.   *(5)*

7. If dollar bills (Federal Reserve notes) are backed by nothing but promises and are in real terms worthless, why do people accept them?   *(4)*

8. If the U.S. government were to raise the reserve requirement to 100 percent, what would likely happen to the interest rate banks pay? Why?   *(6)*

9. What was the cause of the S&L crisis? What role did government guarantees play in that crisis?   *(6)*

10. Is the current U.S. banking system susceptible to panic? If so, how might a panic occur?   *(5)*

PROBLEMS AND EXERCISES

1. While Jon is walking to school one morning, a helicopter flying overhead drops a $100 bill. Not knowing how to return it, Jon keeps the money and deposits it in his bank. (No one in this economy holds cash.) If the bank keeps 5 percent of its money in reserves:
   a. How much money can the bank now lend out?
   b. After this initial transaction, by how much is the money in the economy changed?
   c. What's the money multiplier?
   d. How much money will eventually be created by the banking system from Jon's $100?

2. Assume that there's only one bank in the country, that the reserve requirement is 10 percent, and that the ratio of individuals' cash holdings to their bank deposits is 20 percent. The bank begins with $20,000 cash, $225,000 in loans, $105,000 in physical assets, $200,000 in demand deposits, and $150,000 in net worth.
   a. An immigrant comes into the country and deposits $10,000 in a bank. Show this deposit's effect on the bank's balance sheet.
   b. The bank keeps enough of this money to satisfy its reserve requirement and loans out the rest to Ms. Entrepreneur. Show the effect on the bank's balance sheet.
   c. Ms. Entrepreneur uses the money to pay Mr. Carpenter, who deposits 84 percent of what he gets in the bank. Show the effect on the bank's balance sheet.
   d. Show the bank's balance sheet after the money multiplier is all through multiplying (based on the Appendix).

3. Assume there is one bank in the country whose reserve requirement is 20 percent. It has $10,000 in cash; $100,000 in loans; $50,000 in physical assets; $50,000 in demand deposits; and $110,000 net worth. Mr. Aged withdraws $1,000 from the bank and dies on the way

home without spending a penny. He is buried with the cash still in his pocket.
   a. Show this withdrawal's effect on the bank's balance sheet.
   b. What happened to the bank's reserve ratio and what must the bank do to meet reserve requirements?
   c. What is the money multiplier? (Assume no cash holdings.)
   d. What will happen to total money supply because of this event after the money multiplier is through multiplying?

4. Assume reserve requirements are 15 percent. Textland Bank's balance sheet looks like this:

Assets		Liabilities	
Cash	30,000	Deposits	150,000
Loans	320,000	Net Worth	550,000
Property	350,000		
Total	700,000		700,000

   a. How much is the bank holding in excess reserves?
   b. If the bank eliminates excess reserves by making new loans, how much new money would be created (assuming no cash holdings)?
   c. Assuming cash holdings are 20 percent of deposits, approximately how much new money would be created?

5. Categorize the following as components of M_1, M_2, both, or neither.
   a. State and local government bonds.
   b. Checking accounts.
   c. Money market mutual funds.
   d. Cash.
   e. Stocks.
   f. Corporate bonds.
   g. Travelers' checks.

ANSWERS TO MARGIN QUESTIONS

1. For money to have value, it must be in limited supply. People will use paper money as a medium of exchange, unit of account, and store of value only as long as it *is* limited in supply, which means that the Fed cannot print up lots of money and maintain its use as money.   *(307)*

2. Money provides liquidity and ease of payment. People hold money rather than bonds to get this liquidity and hold down transactions costs.   *(308)*

3. M_2 would be the larger number, since it includes all of the components of M_1 plus additional components.   *(310)*

4. Banks operate on the law of large numbers—the law that, on average, many fluctuations will affect each other, and hence their effect will be much smaller than the sum of all fluctuations—so that they will have some money flowing in and some money flowing out at all

times. This allows them to make loans on the "float," the average amount that they are holding. If there is one big depositor at a bank, the law of large numbers does not necessarily hold, and the bank must hold larger reserves in case that big depositor withdraws that money. *(312)*

5. The approximate money multiplier is $1/(r + c)$, which is equal to $1/.4 = 2.5$. *(314)*

6. The approximate real-world money multiplier would decrease since it makes the denominator of the money multiplier larger. *(314)*

7. Since the approximate real-world money multiplier is $1/(r + c)$, when $r = .2$ and when individuals hold cash to deposits at a ratio of 30 percent, the money multiplier is reduced from 5 to 2 and the total amount of money created would be $20,000. *(318)*

8. When banks borrow short and lend long, they are susceptible to a financial panic. Unless they have a place where they can borrow, they may not have the liquidity to pay off depositors immediately. *(319)*

9. Government guarantees of financial institutions can prevent unwarranted fears that cause financial crisis, but they can also prevent warranted fears and thereby undermine financial institutions. *(319)*

10. Government guarantees of deposits tend to eliminate unwarranted fears, but they also eliminate warranted fears and hence eliminate a market control of bank loans. *(321)*

Precise Calculation of the Money Multiplier when People Hold Cash

In the text we used the approximate money multiplier to determine what the effect of people holding cash will be. In this appendix we go through a similar example using precise formula, first in an example, then in T-accounts.

Mathematicians have found a simple formula to determine the money multiplier when people hold cash. It's $(1 + c)/(r + c)$. The formula $(1 + c)/(r + c)$ is the actual money multiplier when individuals hold cash.

Before we substitute in, it's important to call your attention to the definition of c. It's not the ratio of the money people keep to the total money they receive. It's the ratio of money people hold as cash to the money people hold as demand deposits. The two ratios are, however, related. If people deposit in the bank 80 percent of the money they receive, they're keeping 25 percent of the money they deposit. For example, if they receive $100 and keep $20, they're depositing $80.

The ratio of cash to money they receive is

$$20/100 = 20\%$$

Measuring c (the ratio of cash to money they deposit), we get

$$c = 20/80 = 25\%.$$

So in our example, $c = .25$.

With this formula we can calculate precisely how much the money multiplier would be when people hold cash. Say banks hold 10 percent of their deposits in reserve ($r = .10$) and individuals hold cash equal to 25 percent of the amount they deposit ($c = .25$). Substituting the numbers into the formula gives

$$(1 + .25)/(.1 + .25) = 3.57.$$

This tells us that when people hold 20 percent of their money as cash and 80 percent as checking account deposits, and banks hold 10 percent of their deposits as reserves, the complex money multiplier is 3.57. So in our example in the text, from that initial $100, $357 in money would be created. Thus our approximate multiplier calculated in the text, 2.9, was too small. Why was it too small? Because it didn't take into account the fact that when people hold money as cash, the money they hold must also be included in the money supply; when banks hold money, it need not be included.

To cement the money creation process in your mind, let's go through the same example we did in the chapter, only this time allowing for individuals to hold cash.

Exhibit A1 shows the effects of the money multiplier process for 10 rounds, starting with the initial $10,000, with a reserve requirement of .2 and a ratio of money people hold in cash to the money they hold as deposits of .3. Each time it lends the money out, 77 percent of what it lends comes back to the bank like a boomerang and serves as the basis for more loans. After 10 rounds we reach a point where the public holds $5,961 in cash and total demand deposits are up to $19,949. Adding these two gives us a total money supply of $25,910. This is approaching the $26,000 we'd arrived at using the precise calculations of the money multiplier:

$$[(1 + c)/(r + c)](\$10,000) =$$
$$[(1 + .3)/(.2 + .3)]\,(\$10,000)$$
$$= 2.6(\$10,000) = \$26,000.$$

If we carried it out for a few more rounds, we'd actually reach what the formula predicted.

Note the $10,000 in currency notes is held jointly by the bank and the public. After 10 rounds the bank holds $3,979 in cash and the public holds $5,961 in cash. Thus, a total of $9,940 (approaching $10,000) is held in cash. However, the money supply, which includes both cash and checking account deposits, has been increased to almost $26,000. The additional money is in the form of checking account deposits.

Bank Gets	Bank Keeps (Reserve Ratio: 20%)	Bank Loans (80%) = Person Borrows	Demand Deposits (77% of What Person Gets)	Person Keeps (23% of What Person Gets)
			$ 7,700	$2,300
$7,700	$1,540	$6,160	4,743	1,417
4,743	949	3,794	2,921	873
2,921	584	2,337	1,799	538
1,799	360	1,439	1,108	331
1,108	222	886	682	204
682	136	546	420	126
420	84	336	259	77
259	52	207	159	48
159	32	127	98	29
98	20	78	60	18
	$3,979		$19,949 +	$5,961

EXHIBIT A1   The Money-Creating Process

14

Central Banks, the Fed, and Monetary Policy

There have been three great inventions since the beginning of time: fire, the wheel and central banking.

~Will Rogers

After reading this chapter, you should be able to:

1 Recount a brief history of the Fed.

2 State what monetary policy is.

3 List the three tools of monetary policy and explain how they work.

4 Go through the effect of an open market operation on a bank, using T-accounts.

5 Explain how monetary policy works in the Keynesian model.

6 Explain how monetary policy works in the Classical model.

7 List five problems often encountered in conducting monetary policy.

The preceding chapter ended with a discussion of financial panics which can occur when people lose faith in one financial asset and want to shift to another. Financial panics are no stranger to banking. In the 1800s the United States suffered a financial panic every 20 years or so. Initially, a few people would suddenly fear they wouldn't be able to get their money out of their bank. They'd run down to the bank to get it. Others would see them getting their money and would do likewise. This was referred to as *a run on the bank*. As a result, their bank would have to close. If a bank closed, people would worry about other banks closing, and they'd run to *their* banks. That process could spread uncontrollably; banks would close and there would be a general financial panic. These panics led to considerable debate about what government should do to regulate and control the banking system.

Much of the initial debate about the U.S. banking industry concerned whether there should be a central bank (a bank that could make loans to other banks in times of crisis and could limit those banks' expansionary loans at other times). Supporters of a central bank argued that a central bank would create financial stability. Opponents argued that it would cause recessions and favor industrial interests over farming interests, and increase centralized power in the economy.

HISTORY AND STRUCTURE OF THE FEDERAL RESERVE SYSTEM

Initially central bank supporters predominated, and it wasn't long before the Bank of the United States, the first central U.S. bank chartered by the U.S. government, was established. Debates about the bank were rancorous and in 1811 its charter was not renewed. It went out of existence.

Five years later, in 1816, the political forces changed and the Second Bank of the United States was chartered. Its attempt to stop the inflationary spiral of 1817 and 1818 caused a depression. The bank was blamed. Political forces once again changed, and in 1832 the Second Bank was dismantled.

The next hundred years were marked by periodic financial crises and recessions—every 10 or 20 years. These crises led to arguments that the country needed a central bank to help prevent future crises, but when a particular crisis ended, the argument would fade away. In 1907, however, there was a major financial panic. In response the government established the Federal Reserve Bank (the Fed) in 1913.

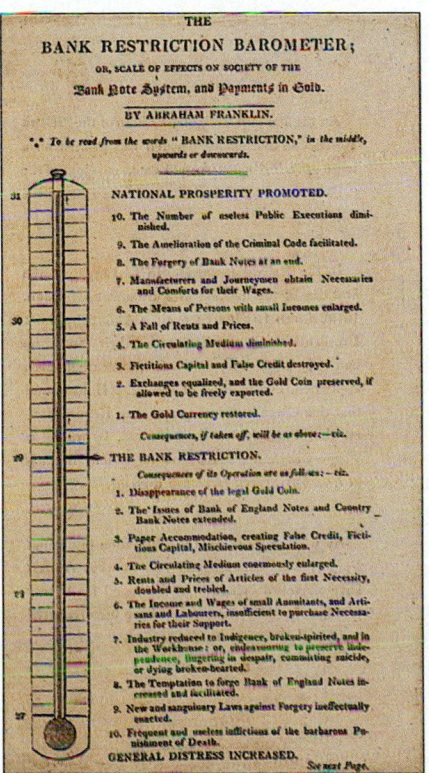

The issue of regulating banks has been at the forefront of economic policy discussions for centuries as can be seen in this 18th- or 19th-century English print of unknown origin, "The Bank Restriction Barometer." *Bleichroeder Print Collection, Baker Library, Harvard Business School.*

CENTRAL BANKS IN OTHER COUNTRIES

In the United States, the Central Bank is the Fed, and much of this chapter is about its structure. But the Fed is only one of many Central Banks. Let's briefly introduce you to some of the others.

Bundesbank In Germany, the Central Bank is called the *Bundesbank*. It has a reputation as a fierce inflation fighter, in large part because of the historical legacy of the German hyperinflation of the late 1920s and early 1930s. In the mid-1990s, to fight inflation it maintained high interest rates relative to the rest of the world, causing international monetary disruption, which will be discussed in a later chapter. It has a much higher reserve requirement than does the Fed.

The Bank of England The Bank of England is sometimes called the Old Lady of Threadneedle Street (because it's located on that street, and the British like such quaint characterizations). It does not use a required reserve mechanism. Instead, individual banks determine their own needed reserves, so any reserves they have would, in a sense, be excess reserves. Needless to say, bank reserves are much lower in England than they are in Germany.

How does the Old Lady control the money supply? With the equivalent of open market operations and with what might be called "tea control." Since there are only a few large banks in England, the Old Lady simply passes on the word at tea as to which direction she thinks the money supply should be going. Alas for sentimentalists, "tea control" is fading in England, as are many of the quaint English ways.

The Bank of Japan Of the three banks I discuss here, the Bank of Japan is most similar to the Fed. It uses primarily open market operations to control the money supply. Reserve requirements are similar to the Fed's, but because it allows banks a longer period in which to do their averaging, and Japan does not have the many small banks that the United States does—banks which often hold excess reserves—excess reserves are much lower in Japan than in the United States. Until the 1990s the Bank of Japan held the Japanese interest rate far below the world rate, which caused an international outflow of savings and a corresponding trade surplus. In the 1990s the Japanese interest rate has been increased substantially, in part due to the actions of the Bank of Japan.

Clearly, there's more to be said about each of these central banks, but this brief introduction should give you a sense of both the similarities and the diversities among the central banks of the world.

The Federal Reserve Bank has remained in existence ever since and is now the United States central bank.

The Fed Is a Central Bank

1 The Fed was created in 1913 in response to a financial crisis that had begun in 1907.

Central bank A banker's bank; it conducts monetary policy and supervises the financial system.

2 Monetary policy is a policy that influences the economy through changes in the money supply and available credit.

A **central bank** is a type of bankers' bank. If banks need to borrow money, they go to the central bank, just as when you need to borrow money, you go to a neighborhood bank. If there's a financial panic and a run on banks, the central bank is there to make loans to the banks until the panic goes away. Since its IOUs are cash, simply by issuing an IOU it can create money. A central bank's duties also include assisting government with its financial affairs. A central bank serves as a financial advisor to government. As is often the case with financial advisors, the government sometimes doesn't like the advice and doesn't follow it.

Besides being a bankers' bank and a financial advisor, the Fed also conducts monetary policy for the government. **Monetary policy** is a policy of influencing the economy through changes in the money supply and credit availability in the economy. Monetary policy is one of the two main macroeconomic tools (the other is fiscal policy) by which government attempts to control the aggregate economy. Unlike fiscal policy, which is controlled by the government directly, monetary policy is controlled by the Fed.

Historical Influences in the Federal Reserve Bank's Structure

In many countries, such as Germany, Great Britain, and France, the central bank is a part of their government, just as this country's Department of the Treasury and the Department of Commerce are part of the U.S. government. In the United States the central bank is not part of the government in the same way as in some European countries.

Because of political infighting about how much autonomy the central bank should have in controlling the economy, the Federal Reserve Bank was created as a semi-autonomous organization. The bank is privately owned by the member banks. However, member banks have few privileges of ownership. For example, the Board of Governors of the Federal Reserve is appointed by the U.S. president, not by the owners. Also, almost all the profits of the Fed go to the government, not to the owners. In short, the Fed is owned by the member banks in form only. In practice the Fed is an agency of the U.S. federal government.

The Fed is a semi-autonomous organization.

Although it is an agency of the federal government, the Fed has much more independence than most agencies. One reason is that creating money is profitable, and while it returns its income after expenses to Congress, it is not dependent on Congress for appropriations. A second reason is that once appointed for a term of 14 years, Fed governors cannot be removed from office, nor can they be reappointed. Because they cannot be removed and because they have little incentive to try to get reappointed, they feel little political pressure. If the president doesn't like what they do, tough luck, until their appointments expire or one of them decides to resign or retire.

There are seven officers of the Federal Reserve Bank; they are called the Governors of the Federal Reserve. In practice, since pay at the Federal Reserve is much lower than at private banks and consulting firms, many appointees stay less than 14 years. When your job resumé includes "Governor of the Federal Reserve," private organizations are eager to hire you and pay you five or six times as much as you earned at the Fed. This means that none of the Federal Reserve Governors are hard up for a job. So while they are at the Federal Reserve, they can pretty much follow the policies they believe are best without being concerned about political retaliation, even if their terms aren't for life.

The president appoints one of the seven members to be chairman of the Board of Governors for a four-year term. The chairman has enormous influence and power, and is often called the second-most-powerful person in the United States. This is a bit of an exaggeration, but the chairman's statements are more widely reported in the financial press than any other government official's.

Q–1: Who appoints the chairman of the Board of Governors of the Federal Reserve System?

The Fed's general structure reflects its political history. Exhibit 1 demonstrates that structure. Notice in Exhibit 1(a) most component banks are in the East and Midwest. The South and West have only three banks: Atlanta, Dallas, and San Francisco. The reason is that in 1913, when the Fed was established, the West and South were smaller and less important economically than the rest of the country, so fewer banks were established there.

As these regions grew, the original structure remained because no one wanted to go through the political wrangling restructuring would bring about. Instead, the southern and western regional Feds established a number of branches to handle their banking needs.

In legislation establishing the Fed, Congress gave it six explicit functions:

1. Conducting monetary policy (influencing the supply of money and credit in the economy).
2. Supervising and regulating financial institutions.
3. Serving as a lender of last resort to financial institutions.
4. Providing banking services to the U.S. government.
5. Issuing coin and currency.
6. Providing financial services to commercial banks, savings and loan associations, savings banks, and credit unions.

Of these, the most important policy is monetary policy.

In this chapter I emphasize the monetary policy function of the Fed because, in macroeconomics, that is the most important of the Fed's normal functions. But the Fed has other duties which include important microeconomic functions. Let's consider one

The Fed's Other Functions

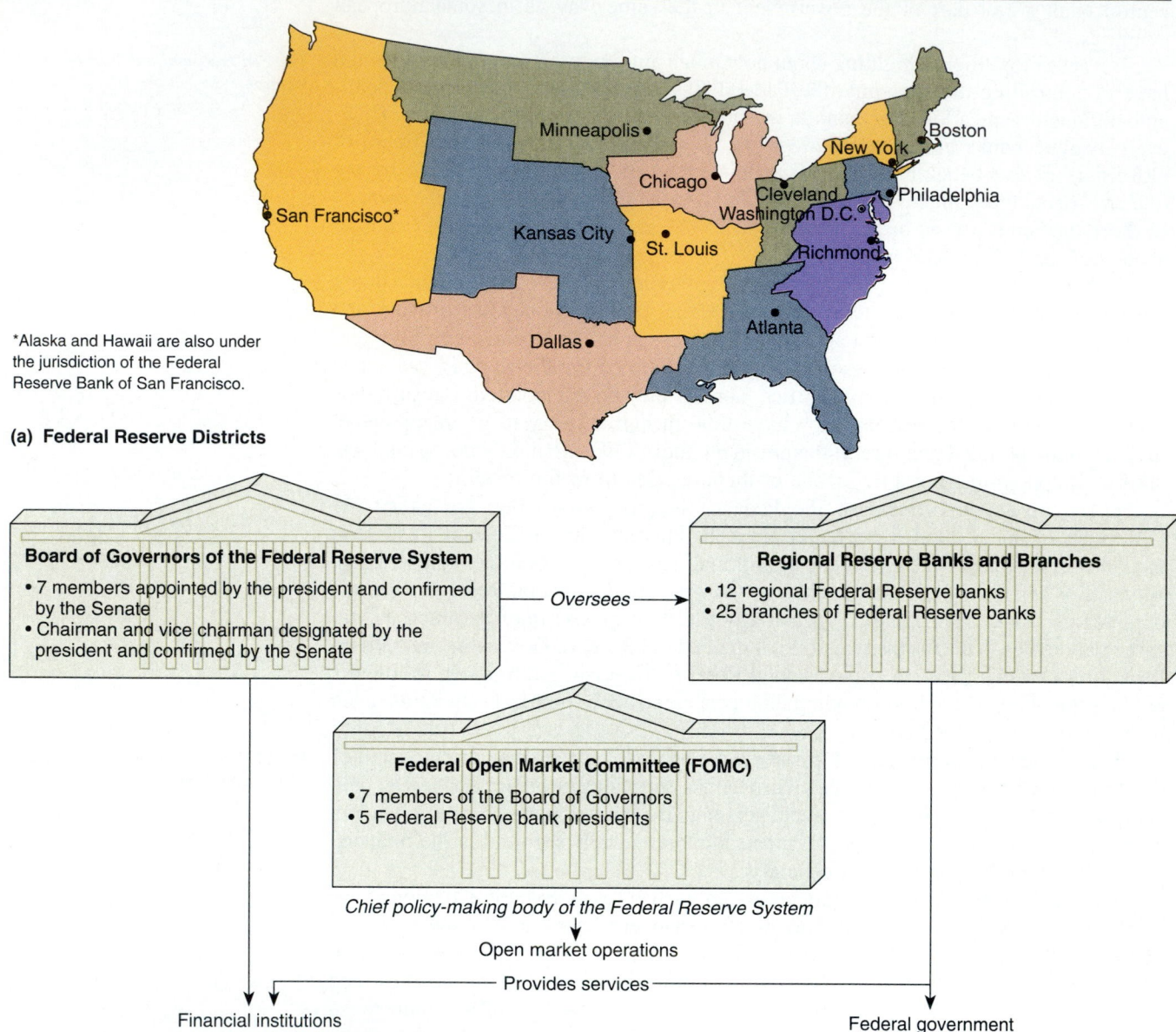

*Alaska and Hawaii are also under the jurisdiction of the Federal Reserve Bank of San Francisco.

(a) Federal Reserve Districts

Board of Governors of the Federal Reserve System
• 7 members appointed by the president and confirmed by the Senate
• Chairman and vice chairman designated by the president and confirmed by the Senate

Oversees →

Regional Reserve Banks and Branches
• 12 regional Federal Reserve banks
• 25 branches of Federal Reserve banks

Federal Open Market Committee (FOMC)
• 7 members of the Board of Governors
• 5 Federal Reserve bank presidents

Chief policy-making body of the Federal Reserve System

Open market operations

Provides services

Financial institutions

Federal government

(b) Federal Reserve Structure

EXHIBIT 1 (a and b)   The Federal Reserve System

The Federal Reserve System is composed of 12 regional banks. It is run by the Board of Governors. The Federal Open Market Committee (FOMC) is the most important policy-making body.
Source: The Federal Reserve System.

that will likely be much in the news in the 1990s: the function of regulating financial institutions.

This function will be in the news because of bank's inherent tendencies to make loans to people who don't need them and to judge a borrower's eligibility for a loan by the geographic area in which the borrower is located. What this means is that certain geographic areas—poor areas, inner cities, minority areas—have traditionally either explicitly or implicitly been red-lined (circled in red on the bank's map of the area), and few, or no, loans have been made there. When an area cannot get loans it almost inevitably fulfills a bank's negative expectations that it isn't worthy of getting loans. As a consequence, the area goes downhill, since no loans are available to keep it up.

Such actions by banks may, and in some instances definitely do, violate federal anti-discrimination laws and, in its role as regulator, the Fed will be looking for ways to end such practices.

Monetary policy is probably the most used policy in macroeconomics. The Fed conducts and controls it, whereas fiscal policy is conducted directly by the government. Both policies are directed toward the same end: influencing the level of aggregate economic activity, hopefully in a beneficial manner. (In many other countries institutional arrangements are different; the central bank is a part of government, so both monetary and fiscal policy are directly conducted by the government, albeit by different branches of government.)

Actual decisions about monetary policy are made by the Federal Open Market Committee (FOMC), the Fed's chief policy-making body. All seven members of the Board of Governors, together with the president of the New York Fed and a rotating group of four of the presidents of the other regional banks, sit on the FOMC. The financial press and business community follow their discussions closely. There are even Fed watchers whose sole occupation is to follow what the Fed is doing and to tell people what it will likely do.

The three tools of monetary policy are:

1. Changing the reserve requirement.
2. Changing the discount rate.
3. Executing open market operations (buying and selling bonds).

Let's discuss each in turn.

Changing the Reserve Requirement   Earlier you saw how the total amount of money created from a given amount of cash depends on the percentage of deposits that a bank keeps in reserves (the bank's reserve ratio). These reserves are IOUs of the Fed—either vault cash or deposits at the Fed. By law, the Fed controls the percentage of deposits banks keep in reserve by controlling the reserve requirement of all U.S. banks. The percentage the Federal Reserve System sets as the minimum amount of reserves a bank must have is called the **reserve requirement.**

Required Reserves and Excess Reserves   The amount banks keep in reserves depends partly on Federal Reserve requirements and partly on how much banks feel they need for safety (the cash they need to keep on hand at any time to give to depositors who claim some of their deposits in the form of cash). The amount most banks need for safety is much smaller than what the Fed requires. For them, it's the Fed's reserve requirement that determines the amount they hold as reserves.

Banks hold as little in reserves as possible. Why? Because reserves earn no interest for a bank. And we all know that banks are in business to earn profits. How much is as little as possible? That depends on the type of liabilities the bank has. In the early 1990s, required reserves for large banks for their checking accounts (also called *demand deposits*) were about 10 percent. The reserve requirement for savings accounts and time deposits that mature in less than one-half year was 3 percent. The reserve ratio for many other of the banking system's liabilities was even lower, making the reserve requirement for total liabilities about 2 percent.

In the early 1990s, total reserves were about $60 billion and required reserves were about $59 billion. This means excess reserves (reserves in excess of requirements) were about $1 billion. Thus, the reserve requirement generally plays a central role in how much money banks have to lend out. However, excess reserves can increase substantially for short periods, as they did in the spring of 1992. Banks had reserves available, but did not lend them out.

The Reserve Requirement and the Money Supply   By changing the reserve requirements, the Fed can increase or decrease the money supply. If the Fed increases the reserve requirement, it contracts the money supply; banks have to keep more reserves so they have less money to lend out; the decreased money multiplier (the multiple contraction of deposits occurring in response to a change in reserves) further contracts the money supply. If the Fed decreases the reserve requirement, it expands the money supply; banks have more money to lend out; the money multiplier further expands the money

MONETARY POLICY

Q–2:   What is the difference between monetary policy and fiscal policy?

Tools of Monetary Policy

3   The three tools of monetary policy are:
1. Changing the reserve requirement;
2. Changing the discount rate; and
3. Executing open market operations.

Reserve requirement   *Minimum ratio of reserves to deposits that a bank must have.*

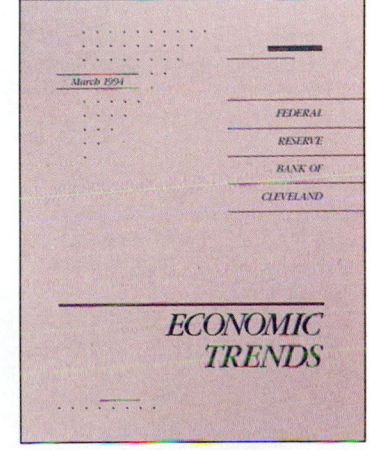

Economic Trends, a publication of the Federal Reserve Bank of Cleveland, is an excellent source for graphs and current information about monetary and fiscal policy.

The approximate real-world money multiplier is $1/(r + c)$.

supply. The Fed has seldom used changes in the reserve requirement to control the money supply, but in April 1992 it lowered the reserve requirement on large banks from 12 to 10 percent for demand deposits in an attempt to expand the money supply.

The total effect on the money supply of changing the reserve requirement can be determined by thinking back to the approximate real-world money multiplier, which, as you saw in the last chapter, should equal $1/(r + c)$ [1 divided by the sum of r (the percentage of each dollar that banks hold in reserves) plus c (the ratio of people's cash to deposits)]. When banks hold no excess reserves and face a reserve requirement of 15 percent, and people's cash-to-deposit ratio is 25 percent, the approximate money multiplier will be $1/.4 = 2.5$, so $1,000,000 in cash will support a total $2,500,000 money supply. In reality the cash-to-deposit ratio is about 0.4 ($c = .4$), the average reserve requirement for demand deposits is about .1 ($r = .1$), and banks hold little in the way of excess reserves. So the realistic approximate money multiplier for demand deposits (M_1) is

$$(1)/(0.1 + 0.4) = 1/0.5 = 2$$

A $100 increase of reserves will support a $200 increase in demand deposits.[1] For other deposits the reserve requirement is much lower, so the money multiplier is larger for those.

Q–3: What would happen to the approximate money multiplier if the cash-to-deposit ratio were .2 rather than .4?

Q–4: Why would a bank hold Treasury bills as secondary reserves when it could simply hold primary reserves—cash?

What do you do if you're a bank and you come up short of reserves? The Fed funds option is one solution, as the accompanying box says. The bank can borrow from another bank that has excess reserves. But if the entire banking system is short of reserves, that option won't work since there's no one to borrow from. Another option is to stop making new loans and to keep as reserves the proceeds of loans that are paid off. Still another option is to sell Treasury bonds to get the needed reserves. (Banks often hold some of their assets in Treasury bonds so that they can get additional reserves relatively easily if they need them.) These Treasury bonds are sometimes called *secondary reserves*. They do not count as bank reserves—only IOUs of the Fed count as reserves. But Treasury bonds can be easily sold and transferred into cash which does count as reserves. Banks use all these options.

Changing the Discount Rate   A second tool of monetary policy concerns another alternative banks have if they are short of reserves. A bank can also go to its bank (the Federal Reserve, the banker's bank) and take out a loan.

Discount rate   Rate of interest the Fed charges on loans it makes to banks.

The **discount rate** is the rate of interest the Fed charges for those loans. An increase in the discount rate makes it more expensive for banks to borrow from the Fed. A discount rate decrease makes it less expensive for banks to borrow. Therefore changing the discount rate is a second way the Fed can expand or contract the money supply.

---

[1] As c, the cash-to-deposit ratio, increases, the approximation becomes less exact. The actual multiplier is $(1 + c)/(r + c) = 1.4/.5 = 2.8$. Since the marginal amount held varies rather substantially, and various measures of money are used, this difference between our approximation and the actual cash multiplier is not of operational significance. In estimating the effect of policy on the different measures of the money supply, banks use only very rough estimates of the money supply.

Although banks find it difficult to be both fully loaned out and to stay within the reserve requirement (which is determined by biweekly averages), they've developed ways to manage.

Say your bank didn't make as many loans as it expected to so that it has a surplus of reserves (excess reserves). Say also that another bank has made a few loans it didn't expect to make so it has a shortage of reserves. The bank with surplus reserves can lend money to the bank with a shortage—and it can lend it overnight. At the end of a day, a bank will look at its balances and see whether it has a shortage or surplus of reserves. If it has a surplus, it will call a federal funds ("Fed funds") dealer to learn the interest rate for Fed funds. Say the rate is 6 percent. The bank will then agree to lend its excess reserves overnight to the other bank for the daily equivalent of 6 percent per year. It's all simply done electronically, so there's no need actually to transfer funds. In the morning the money (plus overnight interest) is returned. The one-day interest rate is low, but when you're dealing with millions or billions, it adds up.

The market in which banks lend and borrow reserves (the *federal funds market*) is highly efficient. When money is tight (most banks have shortages of reserves), the Fed funds rate is high; when money is loose (most banks have excess reserves), the rate is low. Generally, large city banks are borrowers of Fed funds; small country banks are lenders of Fed funds.

Economists keep a close eye on the Fed funds rate in determining the state of monetary policy.

On the surface, the reasoning seems straightforward. A discount rate decrease lowers the bank's cost and allows it to borrow more from the Fed. More reserves (IOUs of the Fed) are in the system so the money supply increases and the interest rates banks charge customers fall. An increase in the discount rate works in the opposite way.

In practice, however, the way the discount rate works is more complicated. The discount rate that the Fed charges is usually much lower than competing interest rates, such as the Fed funds rate that the banks would pay if they didn't borrow from the Fed. Thus, based on pure economic costs, banks should borrow lots of money from the Fed. But the invisible handshake is at work here, and the Fed discourages banks from using this option. It's a bit like having your parents lend you money. They'll lend you money, probably at a zero interest rate, but they may frown upon it and lecture you if you borrow from them. As a result, you use them only as a last resort. Similarly most banks borrow from the Fed only as a last resort.

Banks generally are very responsive to the Fed's desires. They know that the Fed controls the auditors of the banks, and if a bank borrows too often, the Fed may well suggest the auditors make a special visit to the bank to see why it needs to borrow. With such "moral suasion," the actual discount rate is not the determinant; the Fed's reproach is.

Nonetheless, the changes in the discount rate affect the money supply as we'd expect them to. The reason is that the Fed uses the discount rate as a signal to banks and to the general public: An increase in the discount rate signals that the Fed wants money tightened; a decrease signals that the Fed wants the money supply expanded. Banks usually respond appropriately.

The Fed's use of this signal could be seen in 1993 when it cut the discount rate substantially (from 3.5% to 3%) as a signal that it believed more aggressive bank lending policy was warranted, or in mid-1994 when it raised it back to 3.5%.

Open Market Operations   Changes in discount rate and reserve requirement are not used in day-to-day Fed operations. They're used mainly for major changes. For day-to-day operations, the Fed uses a third tool: **open market operations**—the Fed's buying and selling of government securities (the only type of asset the Fed is allowed by law to hold in any appreciable quantity). These open market operations are the primary tool of monetary policy.

When the Fed buys a Treasury bill or bond, it pays for it with its IOU. This IOU doesn't have to be a written piece of paper. It may be simply a computer entry credited to the bank's account, say $1 billion. As you saw in Chapter 13, an IOU of the Fed is money.

Q–5: The discount rate works primarily through market channels. True or false? Why?

Open market operations   The Fed's buying and selling of government securities is the most important tool of monetary policy.

Q–6: Besides open market operations, what are two tools of monetary policy?

The Federal Reserve banks process millions of checks every day through automated machines, such as this one. *Federal Reserve Bank of Boston.*

Because the IOU the Fed uses to buy a government security serves as reserves to the banking system, with the simple act of buying a Treasury bond and paying for it with its IOU the Fed can increase the money supply (since this creates reserves for the bank). To increase the money supply, the Fed goes to the bond market, buys a bond, and pays for it with its IOU. The individual or firm who sold the bond now has an IOU of the Fed. When the individual or firm deposits the IOU in a bank, presto! The reserves of the banking system are increased. If the Fed buys $1,000,000 worth of bonds, it increases reserves by $1,000,000 and the total money supply by $1,000,000 times the money multiplier.

When the Fed sells Treasury bonds, it collects back some of its IOUs, reducing banking system reserves and decreasing the money supply. Thus,

To expand the money supply, the Fed buys bonds. To contract the money supply, the Fed sells bonds.

> *To expand the money supply, the Fed buys bonds.*
> *To contract the money supply, the Fed sells bonds.*

Open market operations are the Fed's most-used tool in controlling the money supply. Periodically the Open Market Committee looks at trading in the financial markets and decides what its open market operations will be and whether it wants to expand or contract the money supply.

4 An open market operation changes reserves, which leads the banks to increase or decrease loans, which affects the income and price levels in the economy.

Let's go through an example using T-accounts. Say there's only one bank, Textland Bank, with branches all over the country. Textland is fully loaned out at a 10 percent reserve requirement. For simplicity, assume people hold no cash. Textland's beginning balance sheet is presented below.

EXHIBIT 2   **Textland Bank Balance Sheet**   Beginning Balance

Assets		Liabilities and net worth	
Cash (reserves)	$ 300,000	Demand deposits	$3,000,000
Loans	2,000,000	Net worth	1,000,000
Treasury bonds	400,000		
Property	1,300,000		
Total assets	$4,000,000	Total liabilities and net worth	$4,000,000

Now say the Fed sells $10,000 worth of Treasury bonds to individuals. The person who buys them pays with a check to the Fed for $10,000. The Fed, in turn, presents that check to the bank, getting $10,000 in cash from the bank. This step is shown in Transaction 1.

EXHIBIT 2   **(continued)**   Transaction 1

Assets		Liabilities and net worth	
Cash (reserves)................... $ 300,000		Demand deposits.................. $3,000,000	
Payment to Fed (person's Treasury		Deposit for cash (person's check) .... (10,000)	
purchase) .... (10,000)		Total deposits.......................	$2,990,000
Total cash	$ 290,000	Net worth	1,000,000
Loans	2,000,000		
Treasury bonds.....................	400,000		
Property	1,300,000		
Total assets........................	$3,990,000	Total liabilities and net worth...........	$3,990,000

As you can see, bank reserves are now $290,000, which is too low to meet requirements on demand deposits of $2,990,000. With a 10 percent reserve requirement, $2,990,000 in deposits would require $(1/10) \times \$2,990,000 = \$299,000$, so the bank is $9,000 short of reserves. It must figure out a way to meet its reserve requirement. Let's say that it calls in $9,000 of its loans. After doing so it has assets of $299,000 in cash and $2,990,000 in demand deposits, so it looks as if the bank has met its reserve requirement.

If the bank could meet its reserve requirement that way, its balance sheet would be as shown in Transaction 2. Loans would decrease by $9,000 and cash would increase by the $9,000 necessary to meet the reserve requirement.

EXHIBIT 2   **(continued)**   Transaction 2

Assets		Liabilities and net worth	
Cash (reserves)................... $ 290,000		Demand deposits....................	$2,990,000
Loans (repaid) 9,000		Net worth..........................	1,000,000
Total cash	$ 299,000		
Loans........................... 2,000,000			
Loans called in.................... (9,000)			
Total loans	1,991,000		
Treasury bonds	400,000		
Property...........................	1,300,000		
Total assets	$3,990,000	Total liabilities and net worth	$3,990,000

Unfortunately for the bank, meeting its reserve requirement isn't that easy. That $9,000 in cash had to come from somewhere. Most likely, the person who paid off the loans in cash did it partly by running down her checking account, borrowing all the cash she could from others, and using whatever other options she had. Since by assumption in this example, people don't hold cash, the banking system was initially fully loaned out, and Textland Bank was the only bank, the only cash in the economy was in Textland Bank's vaults! So that $9,000 in cash had to come from its vaults. Calling in the loans cannot directly solve its reserve problem. It still has reserves of only $290,000.

But calling in its loans did *indirectly* help solve the problem. Calling in loans decreased investment which, because it decreased aggregate demand, decreased the income in the economy. (If you're not sure why this is the case, think back to the Keynesian model.) That decrease in income decreases the amount of demand deposits people want to hold. As demand deposits decrease, the bank's need for reserves decreases.

Calling in loans doesn't directly solve the banking system's reserve problem, but it does indirectly do so.

Contraction of the money supply in this example works in the opposite way to an expansion of the money supply discussed in the last chapter. Banks keep trying to meet their reserve requirement by getting cash, only to find that for the banking system as a whole the total cash is limited. Thus, the banking system as a whole must continue to call in loans until that decline in loans causes income to fall sufficiently to

Q–7: If the Fed wants to increase the money supply, should it buy bonds or sell bonds?

cause demand deposits to fall to a level that can be supported by the smaller reserves. In this example, with a money multiplier of 10, when demand deposits have fallen by $100,000 to $2,900,000, total reserves available to the system ($290,000) will be sufficient to meet the reserve requirement.

Think back to the discussion of the Fed's structure. Recall the FOMC is the Fed's chief policy-making body. Now you know why. It decides on open market operations, and open market operations are the Fed's chief tool for controlling the economy.

How Monetary Policy Works

Both Keynesians and Classicals agree that monetary policy is important, but they differ in how they see monetary policy affecting the economy, and in their recommendations to the Fed about how to conduct monetary policy. These differences will become more apparent when we discuss macro policy in later chapters, but to provide a good foundation for those later discussions, let's now briefly consider these differences.

Monetary Policy in the Keynesian Model
In Keynesian terms, monetary policy can be seen as an alternative method of shifting the aggregate expenditures curve up or down, thereby controlling the level of income in the economy. Let's see how.

In Exhibit 3(a) we see that when the Fed decreases the money supply (uses contractionary monetary policy), it increases the interest rate. Exhibit 3(b) shows the effect of that increased interest rate on investment. As you can see, because the demand for investment is downward sloping, as discussed in an earlier chapter, the rise in interest rate decreases the quantity of investment.

5 In the Keynesian model, monetary policy works as follows:

$$M \downarrow \rightarrow i \uparrow \rightarrow I \downarrow \rightarrow Y \downarrow$$
$$M \uparrow \rightarrow i \downarrow \rightarrow I \uparrow \rightarrow Y \uparrow$$

A decrease in investment starts the income multiplier process and decreases income by a multiple of the amount that investment decreased. Exhibit 3(c) shows the effect of a fall in investment on income. Thus, *contractionary* monetary policy tends to *decrease* the money supply, *increase* the interest rate, *decrease* investment, and *decrease* income and output:

contractionary monetary policy

$$M \downarrow \rightarrow i \uparrow \rightarrow I \downarrow \rightarrow Y \downarrow$$

Expansionary monetary policy works in the opposite manner, as Exhibit 3(d) shows. *Expansionary* monetary policy tends to *increase* the money supply, *decrease* the interest rate, *increase* investment, and *increase* income and output:

expansionary monetary policy

$$M \uparrow \rightarrow i \downarrow \rightarrow I \uparrow \rightarrow Y \uparrow$$

The preceding discussion of how monetary policy works in theory is helpful, but it probably isn't very intuitive. Let's go through the reasoning again, only this time focusing on trying to provide an intuitive feel for what is happening. Say the Fed uses open market operations. As the Fed either injects or pulls out reserves, it influences the amount of money banks have to lend and the interest rate at which they can lend it. When banks have more reserves than required, they want to lend. (That's how they make their profit.) To get people to borrow more from them, banks will decrease the interest rate they charge on loans. So expansionary monetary policy tends to decrease the interest rate banks charge their customers; contractionary policy tends to increase the interest rate banks charge customers. Expansionary monetary policy increases the amount of money banks have to lend, which tends to increase investment. Contractionary monetary policy decreases the amount of money banks have to lend, which tends to decrease investment.

One of the best known economists who developed the Keynesian analysis of monetary policy is James Tobin. He won a Nobel Prize in 1981 for his contribution.

Keynesian Monetary Policy in the Circular Flow
Exhibit 4's familiar circular flow diagram shows how monetary policy works in the Keynesian model. In the Keynesian view monetary policy works inside the financial sector to help equate the flow of savings with investment. When the economy is operating at too low a level of income and when savings exceeds investment, in the absence of monetary policy, income will

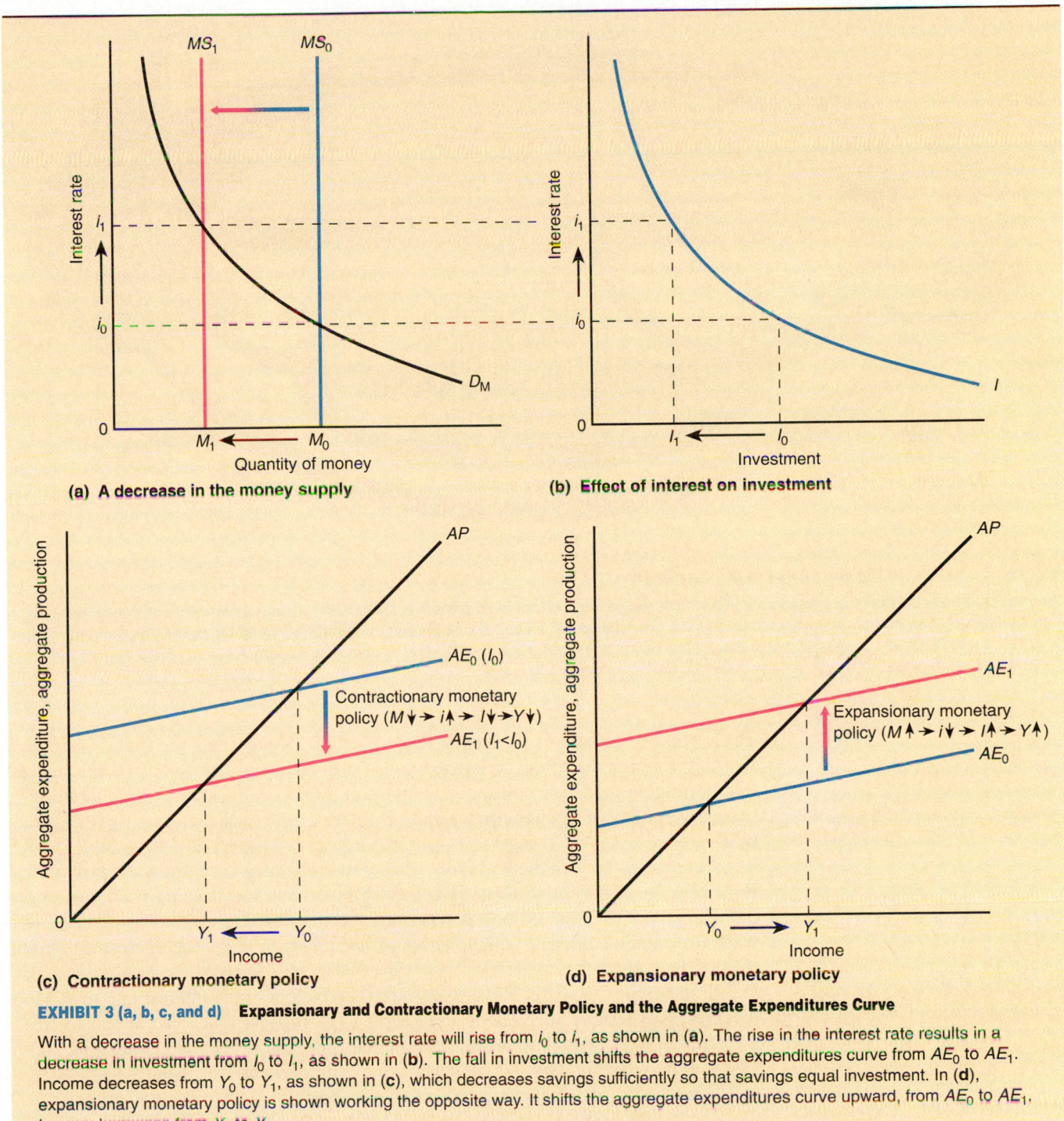

(a) **A decrease in the money supply**

(b) **Effect of interest on investment**

(c) **Contractionary monetary policy**

(d) **Expansionary monetary policy**

EXHIBIT 3 (a, b, c, and d)   Expansionary and Contractionary Monetary Policy and the Aggregate Expenditures Curve

With a decrease in the money supply, the interest rate will rise from i_0 to i_1, as shown in (a). The rise in the interest rate results in a decrease in investment from I_0 to I_1, as shown in (b). The fall in investment shifts the aggregate expenditures curve from AE_0 to AE_1. Income decreases from Y_0 to Y_1, as shown in (c), which decreases savings sufficiently so that savings equal investment. In (d), expansionary monetary policy is shown working the opposite way. It shifts the aggregate expenditures curve upward, from AE_0 to AE_1. Income increases from Y_0 to Y_1.

fall. Expansionary monetary policy tries to channel more savings into investment so the fall in income is stopped. It does so by increasing the available credit, lowering the interest rate, and increasing investment and hence income.

Contractionary monetary policy is called for when savings is smaller than investment and the economy is operating at too high a level of income, causing inflationary pressures. In this case, monetary policy tries to restrict the flow of savings into investment. Thus, to control the economy, Keynesians tend to favor an activist monetary policy, with the Fed taking an active role in controlling the interest rate.

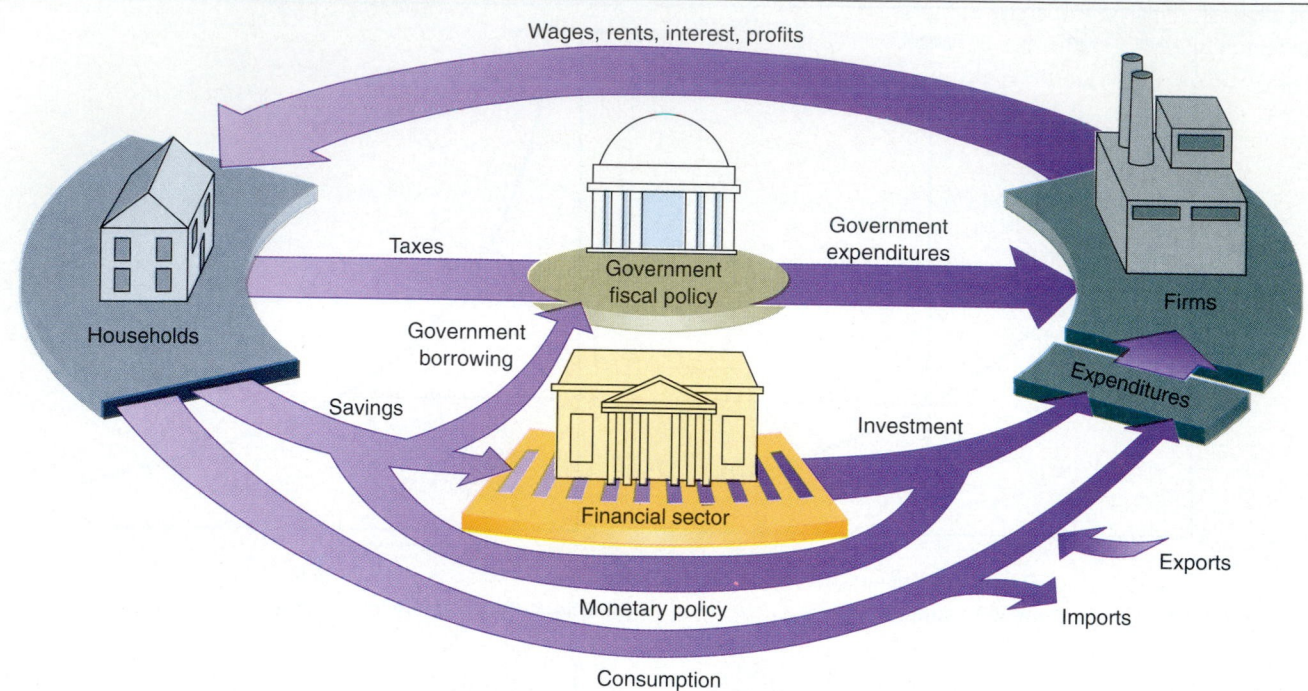

EXHIBIT 4　**Keynesian Monetary Policy in the Circular Flow**

If monetary and fiscal policy are needed, it is because the financial sector is, in some ways, clogged and is not correctly translating savings into investment. Monetary policy works to unclog the financial sector. Fiscal policy provides an alternative route for savings around the financial sector. A government deficit absorbs excess savings and translates it back into the spending stream. A surplus supplements the shortage of savings and reduces the flow back into the spending stream.

The Keynesian Emphasis on the Interest Rate　　Because Keynesians see monetary policy working through the effect of interest rates on investment, they focus on the interest rate in judging monetary policy. They interpret a rising interest rate as a tightening of monetary policy. They interpret a falling interest rate as a loosening of monetary policy.

Keynesians believe the Fed should target interest rates in setting monetary policy. For example, if the interest rate is currently 6 percent and the Fed wants to loosen monetary policy, it should buy bonds until the interest rate falls to $5\frac{1}{2}$ percent. If it wants to tighten monetary policy, it should sell bonds to make the interest rate go up to, say, $6\frac{1}{2}$ percent.

Keynesians focus on interest rates as an indicator of monetary policy.

In the 1950s, the early Keynesians advocated keeping the interest rate low. More recently, Keynesians have advocated keeping the interest rate low enough to foster growth, but high enough to prevent inflationary pressures. As you can imagine, it's a fine line between the two, so whatever policy the Fed chooses usually has critics.

Discussions of whether interest rates are too high or too low and the effect of monetary policy on interest rates fill our newspapers' financial pages. These articles reflect the Keynesian focus on monetary policy.

6　In the Classical model, monetary policy works through the quantity theory:

$$MV = PQ$$

It has short-run effects on real output, Q, but in the long run it affects only the price level, P.

Monetary Policy in the Classical Model　　In the Classical model, monetary policy is best seen in the quantity theory of money. Expansionary monetary policy increases M (the money supply) and in the long run simply increases P (price level):

$$MV = PQ$$

Thus, in the long run monetary policy has no effect on real economic variables such as income or employment. This view is consistent with the Classical proposition that there is a dichotomy between the real and nominal sectors. The Classical position on monetary policy is best seen in this theory.

The Classical Emphasis on Money Supply   The quantity theory of money framework and the long-run relationship between money and prices that Classicals emphasize lead them to focus on the money supply as the key variable in judging whether monetary policy is tight or loose. A large increase in the money supply indicates expansionary monetary policy; a large decrease in the money supply indicates contractionary monetary policy.

Q–8:   An economist emphasizes the interest rate in her discussion of monetary policy. Is she more likely to be a Keynesian or a Classical?

"Steady-as-You-Go" Policy   Because of the Classicals' focus on the long run, they favor a "steady-as-you-go" monetary policy, increasing the money supply just enough each year to allow for the normal real growth in the economy. That increase is to be maintained regardless of the state of the economy. Following that rule, Classicals claim, is most likely to provide the stable financial setting necessary for a market economy to operate. Thus, Classicals oppose the Keynesian policy of an activist monetary policy.

The reason for their steady-as-you-go policy proposal is that, in the short run, Classical economists are much less certain about the workings of monetary policy. They argue that in the short run it operates in numerous ways that are too hard to analyze because they're constantly changing. How long monetary policy takes to work, by what channels it influences the real economy, and how, in the short run, it will influence prices versus real income—all this is unknowable. But what is knowable is that expansionary monetary policy will have some unknown strong effect in the short run and will raise the price level in the long run.

Classicals don't believe that monetary policy can ease or hinder the link between savings and investment because they believe the financial markets are already coordinating the flow from savings into investment as well as possible. True, sometimes savings and investment might get screwed up a bit, but monetary policy, with its uncertain effect, will likely screw it up even more. Moreover, Classicals believe that since politicians focus on short-run effects, political pressures will generally be toward increasing the money supply. In the long run these increases in the money supply will lead to an increase in the price level, so a Keynesian activist monetary policy that does not follow a predetermined rule will have an undesirable effect on inflation.

Real and Nominal Interest Rates   In support of their argument that the money supply rather than the interest rate should be considered in judging the looseness or tightness of monetary policy, Classicals point out the distinction between real and nominal interest rates. **Nominal interest rates** are the rates you actually see and pay. When a bank pays 7 percent interest, that 7 percent is a nominal interest rate. **Real interest rates** are rates adjusted for expected inflation.

Nominal interest rate   Interest rates you actually see and pay.

Real interest rates   Nominal interest rates adjusted for expected inflation.

For example, say you get 7 percent interest from the bank, but the price level goes up 7 percent. At the end of the year you have $107 instead of $100, but you're no better off than before, because the price level has risen—on average, things cost 7 percent more. What you would have paid $100 for last year now costs $107. (That's the definition of *inflation*.) Had the price level remained constant, and had you received 0 percent interest, you'd be in the equivalent position to receiving 7 percent interest on your $100 when the price level rises by 7 percent. That 0 percent is the *real interest rate*. It is the interest rate you would expect to receive if the price level remains constant.

The real interest rate cannot be observed because it depends on expected inflation, which cannot be directly observed. To calculate the real interest rate, you must subtract what you believe to be the expected rate of inflation from the nominal interest rate. For example, if the nominal interest rate is 7 percent and expected inflation is 4 percent, the real interest rate is 3 percent. The relationship between real and nominal interest rates is important both for your study of economics and for your own personal finances.

Nominal interest rate = Real interest rate + Expected inflation rate.

Nominal interest rate = Real interest rate + Expected inflation rate.

Real and Nominal Interest Rates and Monetary Policy What does this distinction between nominal and real interest rates mean for monetary policy? It supports the Classical argument against using monetary policy to control the economy because it adds yet another uncertainty to the effect of monetary policy. Keynesians say that expansionary monetary policy lowers the interest rate and contractionary monetary policy increases the interest rate. However, if the expansionary monetary policy leads to expectation of increased inflation, Classicals point out that expansionary monetary policy can increase nominal interest rates (the ones you see). Why? Because of expectations of increasing inflation.

The distinction between nominal and real interest rates strengthens the Classical case that the best monetary policy is an unchanging policy. In the short run, the effects of monetary policy's effects are too uncertain; in the long run, they simply lead to changes in the price level.

Given the ambiguity of the short-run effect and the negative effect of the long run, monetary policy should not be used to influence the economy. Instead, according to Classical economists, the economy should be governed by a specific rule that sets the money supply at a predetermined level and either holds it there or increases it at a constant rate.

Q–9: Does Fed policy generally reflect Classical theory or Keynesian theory?

Monetary Policy in the Fed Model of the 1990s

While it is important to know both the Keynesian and Classical models, it is also important to know that the Fed is eclectic, sometimes using a Keynesian model, sometimes a Classical model, but generally an *eclectic* model that combines both Keynesian and Classical models with a "feel of the markets." Thus, the Fed will use both interest rates and money supply measures, deciding on which to place more emphasis by using common sense and knowledge of institutional factors. The Fed is in constant communication with players in financial markets, and it has many economists whose job it is to fit the theories into the institutions. This results in swings in focus. In the mid-1990s, the swing was toward emphasizing interest rates and away from emphasizing money supply measures, but if the past is any indication, this swing won't be permanent.

Problems in the Conduct of Monetary Policy

Earlier, after discussing fiscal policy's structure and mechanics, I presented the problems with using fiscal policy. Now that you've been through the structure and mechanics of monetary policy, let's consider the problems with using it too.

Knowing What Policy to Use

To use monetary policy effectively, you must know the potential level of income. Otherwise you won't know whether to use expansionary or contractionary monetary policy. Let's consider an example: mid-1991. The economy seemed to be coming out of a recession. The Fed had to figure out whether to use expansionary monetary policy to speed up and guarantee the recovery, or use contractionary monetary policy and make sure inflation didn't start up again. Initially the Fed tried to fight inflation, only to discover that the economy wasn't coming out of the recession. In early 1992, the Fed switched from contractionary to expansionary monetary policy. It continued that policy through 1994 when fears of inflation caused it to start tightening the money supply slightly.

7 Five problems of monetary policy:
1. Knowing what policy to use.
2. Understanding what policy you're using.
3. Lags in monetary policy.
4. Political pressure.
5. Conflicting international goals.

Understanding the Policy You're Using

To use monetary policy effectively, you must know whether the monetary policy you're using is expansionary or contractionary. You might think that's rather easy, but it isn't. In our consideration of monetary policy tools, you saw that the Fed doesn't directly control the money supply. It indirectly controls it, generally through open market operations. It controls what's called the **monetary base** (the vault cash and reserves banks have at the Fed). Then the money multiplier determines the amounts of M_1, M_2, and other monetary measures in the economy.

Monetary base Vault cash plus reserves banks have on deposit at the Fed.

That money multiplier is influenced by the amount of cash that people hold as well as the lending process at the bank. Neither of those is the stable number that we used in calculating the money multipliers. They change from day to day and week to week, so even if you control the monetary base, you can never be sure exactly what will happen to M_1 and M_2 in the short run. Moreover, the effects on M_1 and M_2 are sometimes different; one measure is telling you that you're expanding the money supply and the other measure is telling you you're contracting it.

And then, of course, there are changes in the interest rate—the measure of monetary policy that Keynesians focus on. If interest rates rise, is it because of expected inflation (which is adding an inflation premium to the nominal interest rate) or is it the real interest rate that is going up? There is frequent debate over which it is. Combined, these measurement problems make the Fed often wonder not only about what policy it should follow, but what policy it is following.

Lags in Monetary Policy   Monetary policy, like fiscal policy, takes time to work its way through the economic system. The Fed can change the money supply or interest rates; people don't have to borrow, however. An increased money supply may simply lead to excess reserves and have no influence on income. This problem can be especially difficult in a recession.

For example, in the 1930s the Fed increased banks' reserves, but the money supply fell by about 25 percent. This led early Keynesians to focus on fiscal policy rather than monetary policy as a way of expanding the economy. They likened expansionary monetary policy to pushing on a string. The same problem exists with using contractionary monetary policy. Banks have been very good at figuring out ways to circumvent cuts in the money supply, making the intended results of contractionary monetary policy difficult to achieve.

Political Pressure   While the Fed is partially insulated from political pressure by its structure, it's not totally insulated. Presidents place enormous pressure on the Fed to use expansionary monetary policy (especially during an election year) and blame the Fed for any recession. When interest rates rise, the Fed takes the pressure, and if any members of the Board of Governors are politically aligned with the president, they find it difficult to persist in contractionary policy when the economy is in a recession.

Conflicting International Goals   Monetary policy is not conducted in a vacuum. It is conducted in an international arena and must be coordinated with other governments' monetary policy. Similarly, as we'll see a little later, monetary policy affects the exchange rate and trade balance. Often the desired monetary policy for its international effects is the opposite of the desired monetary policy for its domestic effects.

Q-10: What are five problems in the conduct of monetary policy?

CONCLUSION AND A LOOK AHEAD

I could continue with a discussion of the problems of using monetary policy, but the above should give you a good sense that conducting monetary policy is not a piece of cake. It takes not only a sense of the theory; it also takes a feel for the economy. In short, the conduct of monetary policy is not a science. It does not allow the Fed to steer the economy as it might steer a car. It does work well enough to allow the Fed to *influence* the economy—much as an expert rodeo rider rides a bronco bull.

This chapter is not the end of our discussion of monetary policy. We'll see more of monetary policy when we discuss how to conduct macroeconomic policy in the next section. There you'll learn how monetary policy works in practice, the central role it plays in understanding inflation, and how it is integrated with fiscal policy. Before we turn to those issues, however, it is helpful to specifically consider the issue of inflation, and the role it plays in the policy debates about macroeconomic policy. That is what we do in the next chapter.

CHAPTER SUMMARY

- The Fed is a central bank; it conducts monetary policy for the United States and regulates financial institutions.
- Monetary policy influences the economy through changes in the money supply and credit availability.
- The three tools of monetary policy are:
    1. Changing the reserve requirement.
    2. Changing the discount rate.
    3. Open market operations.
- A change in reserves changes the money supply by the change in reserves times the money multiplier.
- Open market operations is the Fed's most important tool:

    To expand the money supply, the Fed buys bonds.

    To contract the money supply, the Fed sells bonds.

- In the Keynesian model, contractionary monetary policy works as follows:

$$M \downarrow \rightarrow i \uparrow \rightarrow I \downarrow \rightarrow Y \downarrow$$

Expansionary monetary policy works as follows:

$$M \uparrow \rightarrow i \downarrow \rightarrow I \uparrow \rightarrow Y \uparrow$$

- As an indicator of monetary policy, Keynesians focus on interest rates; Classicals focus on money supply.
- Classical economists see the short-run effects of monetary policy as ambiguous. They favor a long-run monetary rule.
- The Fed uses an eclectic model that combines both Keynesian and Classical insights.
- Problems of monetary policy include knowing what policy to use, knowing what policy you are using, lags, political pressure, and conflicting international goals.

KEY TERMS

central bank *(328)*
discount rate *(332)*
monetary base *(340)*
monetary policy *(328)*

nominal interest rates *(339)*
open market
  operations *(333)*

real interest rates *(339)*
reserve requirement *(331)*

QUESTIONS FOR THOUGHT AND REVIEW

The number after each question represents the estimated degree of critical thinking required. (1 = almost none; 10 = deep thought.)

1. Is the Fed a private or a public agency? *(5)*
2. Why are there few regional Fed banks in the western part of the United States? *(2)*
3. The Fed wants to change the reserve requirement in order to increase the money supply (which is currently 4,000) by 200. The money multiplier is 3. What's the current reserve requirement and how should the Fed change it? *(6)*
4. The Fed wants to increase the money supply (which is currently 4,000) by 200. Assume that for each 1 percent the discount rate falls, banks borrow an additional 20. If instead of changing the reserve requirement, the Fed decides to change the discount rate, how much should the Fed change the rate to increase the money supply by 200? *(6)*
5. The Fed wants to increase the money supply (which is currently 4,000) by 200 as in (4). Only now, it decides

to use open market operations. What should it do to achieve the desired change? *(6)*

6. You can lead a horse to water, but you can't make it drink. How might this adage be relevant to expansionary (as opposed to contractionary) monetary policy? *(7)*
7. The interest rate has just fallen. How might Classical and Keynesian economists draw different implications from that event? *(7)*
8. Investment increases by 20 for each interest rate drop of 1 percent. The income multiplier is 3. If the money multiplier is 4, and each change of 5 in the money supply changes the interest rate by 1 percent, what open market policy would you recommend to increase income by 240? *(6)*
9. If the nominal interest rate is 6 percent and inflation is 5 percent, what's the real interest rate? *(3)*
10. "The effects of open market operations are somewhat like a stone cast in a pond." After the splash, discuss the first three ripples. *(4)*

PROBLEMS AND EXERCISES

1. Suppose the Fed decides it needs to pursue an expansionary policy. Assume people hold no cash, the reserve requirement is 20 percent, and there are no excess reserves.
   a. Show how the Fed would increase the money supply by $2 million by changing the reserve requirement.
   b. Show how the Fed would increase the money supply by $2 million through open market operations.

2. Suppose the Fed decides that it needs to pursue a contractionary policy. It wants to decrease the money supply by $2 million. Assume people hold 20 percent of their money in the form of cash balances, the reserve requirement is 20 percent, and there are no excess reserves.
   a. Show how the Fed would decrease the money supply by $2 million by changing the reserve requirement.
   b. Show how the Fed would decrease the money supply by $2 million through open market operations.
   c. Go to your local bank and find out how much excess reserves they hold. Recalculate (a) and (b) assuming all banks held that percentage in excess reserves.

3. Some individuals have suggested raising the required reserve ratio for banks to 100 percent.
   a. What would the money multiplier be if this change were made?

b. What effect would such a change have on the money supply?
   c. How could that effect be offset?
   d. Would banks likely favor or oppose this proposal? Why?

4. Using T-accounts, show the effect of an increase in the reserve requirement from 0.1 to 0.15 given the following initial position (Textland, again, is the only bank in town and there no one holds cash).

Assets		Liabilities	
Reserves	10,000	Demand deposits	100,000
T-bill holdings	5,000	Net worth	85,000
Property	70,000		
Loans	100,000		

5. One of the proposals to reform monetary policy has been to have the central bank pay interest on reserves held at the bank.
   a. What effect would that proposal have on excess reserves?
   b. Would banks generally favor or oppose this proposal? Why?
   c. Would central banks generally favor or oppose this proposal? Why?
   d. What effect would this proposal probably have on interest rates paid by banks?

ANSWERS TO MARGIN QUESTIONS

1. The President of the United States appoints the Chairman of the Board of Governors of the Federal Reserve System. *(329)*

2. Monetary policy is conducted by the Fed and involves changing the money supply or interest rates. Fiscal policy is conducted by the U.S. Treasury, or government, and involves running a surplus or deficit. *(331)*

3. If the cash to deposit ratio were .2, the approximate money market multiplier would be $1/(.1 + .2) = 3.33$ rather than 2. *(332)*

4. Banks receive no interest on their primary reserves (cash), and hence prefer to hold Treasury bills because they pay interest. *(332)*

5. False. The Fed limits access to the discount window. Banks do not make decisions about borrowing from the Fed based on the fact that they can get a low interest rate at the discount window, but see it, instead, as a last resort. *(333)*

6. The other tools of monetary policy are changing the discount rate and changing the reserve requirement. *(333)*

7. When the Fed buys bonds, it pays for those bonds with

its IOUs—money—so to increase the money supply the Fed should buy bonds. *(336)*

8. Keynesians are more likely to emphasize the interest rate in discussions of monetary policy. Classical economists are more likely to emphasize measures of the money supply. *(339)*

9. It depends. The Fed is generally eclectic, sometimes using a Keynesian model and sometimes a Classical model, combining the use of both of those models with a feel for the market. In other words, the Fed does what it wants. In 1993, the Fed leaned toward emphasizing interest rates and away from money supply measures, but, if the past is any indication, the swing won't be permanent. *(340)*

10. Five problems of monetary policy are:
   1. Knowing what policy to use:
   2. Understanding what policy you're using;
   3. The lags in monetary policy;
   4. Political pressure; and
   5. Conflicting international goals. *(341)*

Keynesian and Classical Theories of Interest and Their Implications for Monetary Policy

To understand the theoretical differences between Keynesian and Classical economists' theories of monetary policy, we must understand their alternative theories of interest. Unfortunately, these theories are complicated, confusing, and quite possibly confused—all at the same time.

The way these theories try to treat money is as simply another good—a good that has a supply and demand curve that can be analyzed separately from the other supply and demands. Having specified the analysis of the money market, both Keynesian and Classical theories then try to integrate it back into the aggregate analysis. There have been many articles written trying to do this on both the Keynesian and Classical sides, but the formal attempts to do so lead to one of two conclusions: (1) that money doesn't matter; or (2) that money matters but only as a third- or fourth-order effect on the economy.

If one believes money matters in a more substantive way, one is forced to make some ad hoc assumptions that money *does* matter (it is desired for its own sake). That approach doesn't come close to making money matter as much as it seems to in the real world. Only Robert Clower, and Peter Howitt, in their recent work on the role of money, have, in my view, provided a reasonable discussion of how it might be integrated.

In the Clower view, money matters so much to the economy that its deep theoretical analysis must go beyond supply and demand analysis. Money is part of the institutional structure of our economy, and its effects are so substantial and interrelated with that institutional structure that it doesn't make a lot of sense to separate out the analysis of money independent of that institutional structure. Money is part of the macrofoundation of the economy. What this means is that output is not a function of money, i.e., $Q = F(M)$, but that the production function, F, is dependent on money and that production function cannot be specified independently of the existence of money. At the introductory level, we needn't worry about such high-level theoretical issues. We simply need to recognize that money does matter, and it matters a lot.

An analogy that Classical economists used might make this argument clear. They compared money's role in the economy to the role of oil in a gas engine. As inputs into running an engine go, oil plays a supplemental role. Gas, together with electrical sparks, would be seen as the primary input. Oil would likely be seen as a tangential input. Moreover, any formal analysis of how oil reduces friction and heat would be extraordinarily complicated. But try running an engine without oil, and you will see oil's importance, just as you will also see the importance of money if you try to run an economy without money.

That said, let me now review very briefly the Keynesian and the Classical theories of money. Keynesians believe the interest rate is primarily a monetary phenomenon, so they have a monetary theory of the rate of interest. For Keynesians, the interest rate is determined by the supply and demand for money. Classicals believe the interest rate is a real phenomenon, so they have a real theory of the rate of interest. In an earlier chapter you were introduced to the Keynesian and Classical theories of the interest rate. This appendix further develops their theories and discusses their implications for conducting monetary policy.

The Keynesian Supply and Demand for Money Theory of the Interest Rate

As we saw in the last chapter, money is a financial asset people want to hold. But how much do they want to hold? It shouldn't surprise you that economists' answer is that it depends upon the supply and demand for money.

The Supply of Money   The Fed determines the money supply by setting the amount of reserves in the system. Then the total amount of money in the economy is determined by the reserve requirement and the money multiplier.

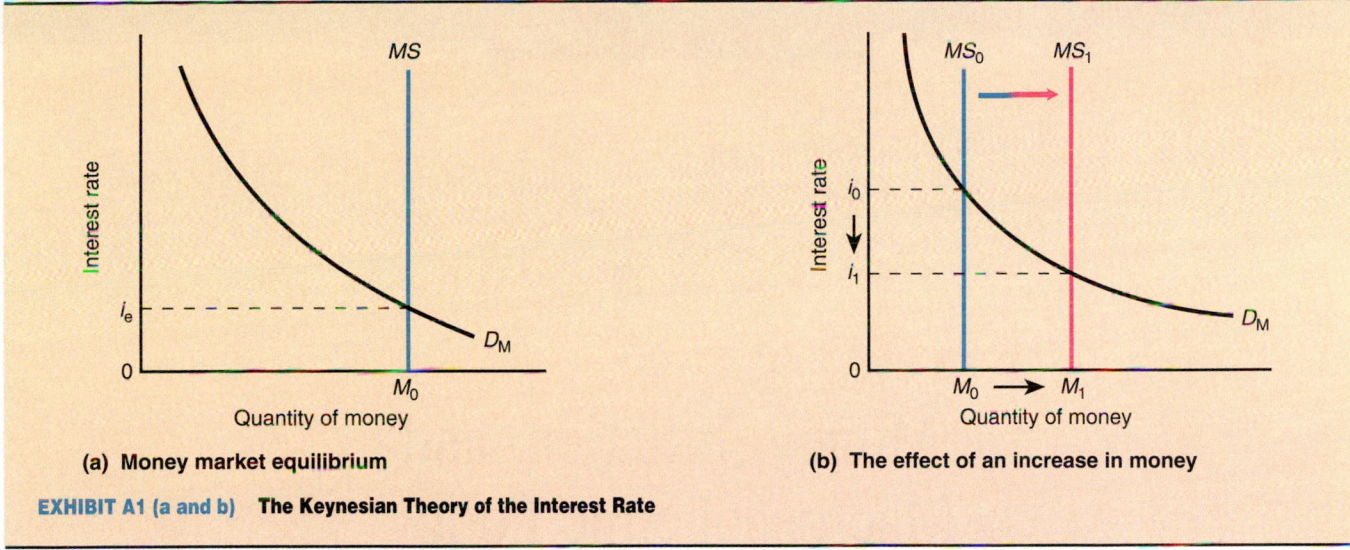

(a) Money market equilibrium   **(b) The effect of an increase in money**

EXHIBIT A1 (a and b)   The Keynesian Theory of the Interest Rate

Here we'll assume that the Fed can perfectly determine the amount of money supplied to the economy and that that amount of money supplied isn't influenced by the interest rate. That makes the supply of money perfectly vertical, as in Exhibit A1.

The Demand for Money   As we saw in the last chapter, people want to hold money because it's useful to them as a medium of exchange and as a store of wealth. But holding money isn't costless. *Money pays lower interest than other financial assets.* So how much money people want to hold depends on the interest rate on those other financial assets. The higher the interest rate on other financial assets, the greater the opportunity cost of holding money and the lower the quantity of money demanded. At lower interest rates, quantity of money demanded is larger because the opportunity cost of holding money is lower. Demand for money as a function of the interest rate is shown by the curve D_M in Exhibit A1.

The Keynesian theory of interest comes from combining the supply of money with the demand for money as in Exhibit A1. The interest rate is determined where the quantity of money supplied equals the quantity of money demanded (i_e). If the supply of money increases, say from M_0 to M_1 as in Exhibit A1(b), the interest rate will fall from i_0. If the demand for money increases, interest rate will rise. Keynes argued that, in the short run, the money market determines the interest rate.

The Classical Savings Investment Theory of the Interest Rate

The supply and demand for money isn't the only market that plays a role in determining the interest rate. The Classical view is that the interest rate is determined by the supply of savings and the demand for those savings for investment purposes. Money doesn't affect the interest rate, so it doesn't affect the real economy. It only affects the price level. So the best monetary policy is a policy that provides stability of the price level. It's a long-run policy that emphasizes a constant predetermined growth rate of the money supply.

Implications of Keynesian and Classical Theories for Monetary Policy

In the Classical model, interest rate fluctuations keep savings equal to investment at the full-employment level of income. Changes in the interest rate equilibrate the savings/investment market.

That's not the way it works in Keynes's model. Income fluctuations, not interest rate fluctuations, bring the savings/investment market into equilibrium. As discussed in the text, this happens in the following way: Income fluctuates, which causes savings to fluctuate. That fluctuation in savings brings the savings/investment market into equilibrium.

So in Keynes's model, the real economy is affected by money. In the Classical model, money only affects the price level.

The implication of the Keynesian theory of interest for monetary policy is it's necessary to maintain an *active* discretionary monetary policy to keep the interest rate at a level that will maintain a savings/investment equilibrium at the target level of income. Classicals believe in a monetary rule.

15

Money, Inflation, and Macroeconomic Policy

The first few months or year of inflation, like the first few drinks, seem just fine. Everyone has more money to spend and prices aren't rising quite as fast as the money that's available. The hangover comes when prices start to catch up.

~Milton Friedman

After reading this chapter, you should be able to:

1 Explain why sustained high inflation is inevitably accompanied by a roughly equal increase in the money supply and expectations of inflation.

2 Differentiate between long-run and short-run Phillips curves.

3 Outline the Classical theory of inflation.

4 Explain why Classical economists favor a monetary rule.

5 Outline the Keynesian theory of inflation.

6 Distinguish the Keynesian and Classical views of the Phillips curve trade-off.

7 Explain why a Keynesian would be more likely to support an incomes policy than a Classical economist would.

Inflation and its relationship to unemployment were introduced earlier. Now that we've worked our way through macroeconomic theory and financial institutions, we're ready to consider these issues again and discuss the problems societies have had in trying to cope with inflation.

Inflation is a continuous rise in the price level. All economists agree on that. They also agree (1) that high inflation rates are inevitably accompanied by a roughly proportional increase in the money supply, and (2) that high inflation rates are associated with expectations of inflation of approximately that rate. Thus, most economists accept that when inflation is really high, say 40 percent, the money supply will be increasing by about 40 percent, and people will be expecting approximately 40 percent inflation.[1] Why do these rough equalities hold? Let's consider the money supply and inflation first.

Say, for example, that the U.S. money supply growth rate is 40 percent. What will likely happen? From the equation of exchange ($MV = PY$), you can deduce that something else must also change. Assuming velocity, V, isn't decreasing enormously and real output, Y, isn't increasing enormously, that 40 percent increase in the money supply, M, must be accompanied by a rise in the price level, P, of about 40 percent. Otherwise there will be a shortage of goods. Alternatively, say prices are rising at a 40 percent rate but the money supply isn't growing at all. Unless velocity is increasing by 40 percent a year, firms will be unable to sell their goods at the higher prices because the amount of money people are spending won't buy the goods that firms are offering to sell at those higher prices. Given the shortage of aggregate demand, firms will be forced to stop increasing their prices.

Notice that so far we've said nothing about what's causing what to increase, which clearly is something policymakers would like to know. Determining the cause of inflation is important in determining how to fight it.

To distinguish cases in which price increases cause the money supply increases from cases in which money supply increases cause the price increases, inflation is divided into **cost-push inflation** (price increases cause money supply increases) and **demand-pull inflation** (money supply increases cause price increases).

In an ongoing inflation, it's often impossible to distinguish whether it's cost-push or demand-pull. The reason is expectations of inflation. Say money supply is expected to increase. Firms will expect demand for their goods to increase and will raise prices on the basis of that expectation. Then, even though price increases may come before money supply increases, it's the expected increase in the money supply that causes prices to rise. However, regardless of whether prices are being pulled by the money supply or are pushing the money supply, all economists agree that, for substantial inflation to continue, the money supply must rise.

The second relationship that most economists agree exists is between inflation and expectations of inflation. The relationship is based on common sense. For example, if inflation is currently 20 percent, assuming no major change in policy, it is reasonable to expect that it will remain about 20 percent. So people's natural tendency is to base their expectations on what is or has recently been. Expectations based on what has been in the past are called **adaptive expectations.**

Adaptive expectations aren't the only reasonable type. People likely will also base their expectations of inflation on their understanding of the economy, economists' predictions of inflation, and their own past experience. For example, if the money supply is increasing substantially, many economists will predict high inflation. To the degree that people believe economists, people will expect high inflation, even though it's not yet high. So the relationship between current inflation and expectations of future inflation is not perfect.

INFLATION

Inflation   A continuous rise in the price level.

The Money Supply and Inflation

1 High inflation rates are inevitably accompanied by high money growth and high inflationary expectations. The reason is that the velocity of money generally cannot increase enormously and people's expectations of the future are determined in large part by what is occurring now.

Cost-push inflation   Inflation where price increases cause money supply increases.

Demand-pull inflation   Inflation where money supply increases cause price increases.

Regardless of whether prices are being pulled by the money supply or are pushing the money supply, all economists agree that, for substantial inflation to continue, the money supply must rise.

Inflation and Expectations of Inflation

Adaptive expectations   Expectations of the future based on what has been in the past.

Q-1: If inflation exists when there are fairly large amounts of unemployment, is it more likely to be a cost-push inflation or a demand-pull inflation?

---

[1] Where economists disagree is on what causes what to increase. Is inflation causing the money supply to increase, or are increases in the money supply causing inflation? We'll address these issues shortly.

EXAMPLES OF COST-PUSH AND DEMAND-PULL INFLATION

There have been periods when it wasn't difficult to distinguish between cost-push and demand-pull inflations. For example, during the post–World War II period, which began in late 1945, there was large pent-up demand. Because of shortages of goods during the war, people had saved up buying power. After the war, most economists were expecting strong inflationary pressures from demand-pull forces. And that's what happened. There was general agreement that the period's inflation was demand-pull inflation.

But in the early 1970s, that stored-up buying power didn't exist. Then there was a significant supply shock—oil prices rose substantially, placing cost-push pressure on prices. That's why most economists call the inflation of the early 1970s cost-push inflation.

But, on average, most economists agree that expectations of inflation approximately equal the amount of inflation in the economy.

Inflation and Unemployment: The Phillips Curve Trade-Off

Perhaps the most vexing dilemma policy makers face in dealing with inflation is the inflation/unemployment policy dilemma: Whenever they try to fight inflation, unemployment seems to increase, and whenever they try to fight unemployment, inflation seems to increase. It is captured graphically in a curve, shown in Exhibit 1(b), called the short-run Phillips curve. In it, unemployment is measured on the horizontal axis; inflation is on the vertical axis. The Phillips curve tells us what combinations of inflation and unemployment are possible. It tells us that when unemployment is low, say 4 percent, inflation tends to be high, say 4 percent (point *A* on the short-run Phillips curve). It also tells us that if we want to lower inflation, say to 1 percent, we must be willing to accept high unemployment, say 7 percent (point *B* in Exhibit 1(b)).

The **Phillips curve** was initially a representation of historical inflation and unemployment data. As economists looked at unemployment and inflation data over time, they noticed that there seemed to be a trade-off between inflation and unemployment. When unemployment was high, inflation was low; when unemployment was low, inflation was high. That empirical relationship seemed rather stable in the 1950s and 1960s. Exhibit 1(a) shows this empirical relationship for the United States for the years 1954–68, when it became built into the way economists looked at the economy.

Because it seemed to represent a relatively stable trade-off, in the 1960s the Phillips curve played a central role in discussions of macroeconomic policy. Republicans (often advised by Classical economists) generally favored contractionary monetary and fiscal policy, which maintained high unemployment and low inflation (a point like *B* in Exhibit 1(b)). Democrats (often advised by Keynesian economists) generally favored expansionary monetary and fiscal policies which brought about low unemployment but high inflation (a point like *A* in Exhibit 1(b)).

Phillips curve   A representation of the relation between inflation and unemployment.

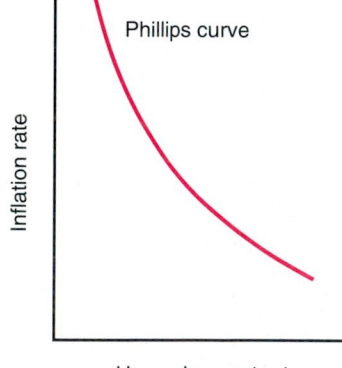

The Breakdown of the Short-Run Phillips Curve   In the early 1970s, the empirical short-run Phillips curve relationship seemed to break down. When one looked at the data, there no longer seemed to be a trade-off between unemployment and inflation. Instead, when unemployment was high, inflation was also high. Exhibit 1(c) shows the empirical relationship between inflation and unemployment from 1969 to 1981. Notice that the relatively stable relationship up until 1969 breaks down in the 1970s. In the 1970s, there doesn't seem to be any trade-off between inflation and unemployment at all. Something clearly changed in the 1970s. In the 1980s, inflation fell substantially, and beginning in 1986, a Phillips curve–type relationship began to reappear, as can be seen in Exhibit 1(d).

To discover what changed in the 1970s, economists devoted much thought to explaining the theory underlying the Phillips curve. What caused inflation? How would inflation interact with unemployment if people acted in certain reasonable ways? As economists thought about these problems, they developed and refined their theories and models of both inflation and unemployment.

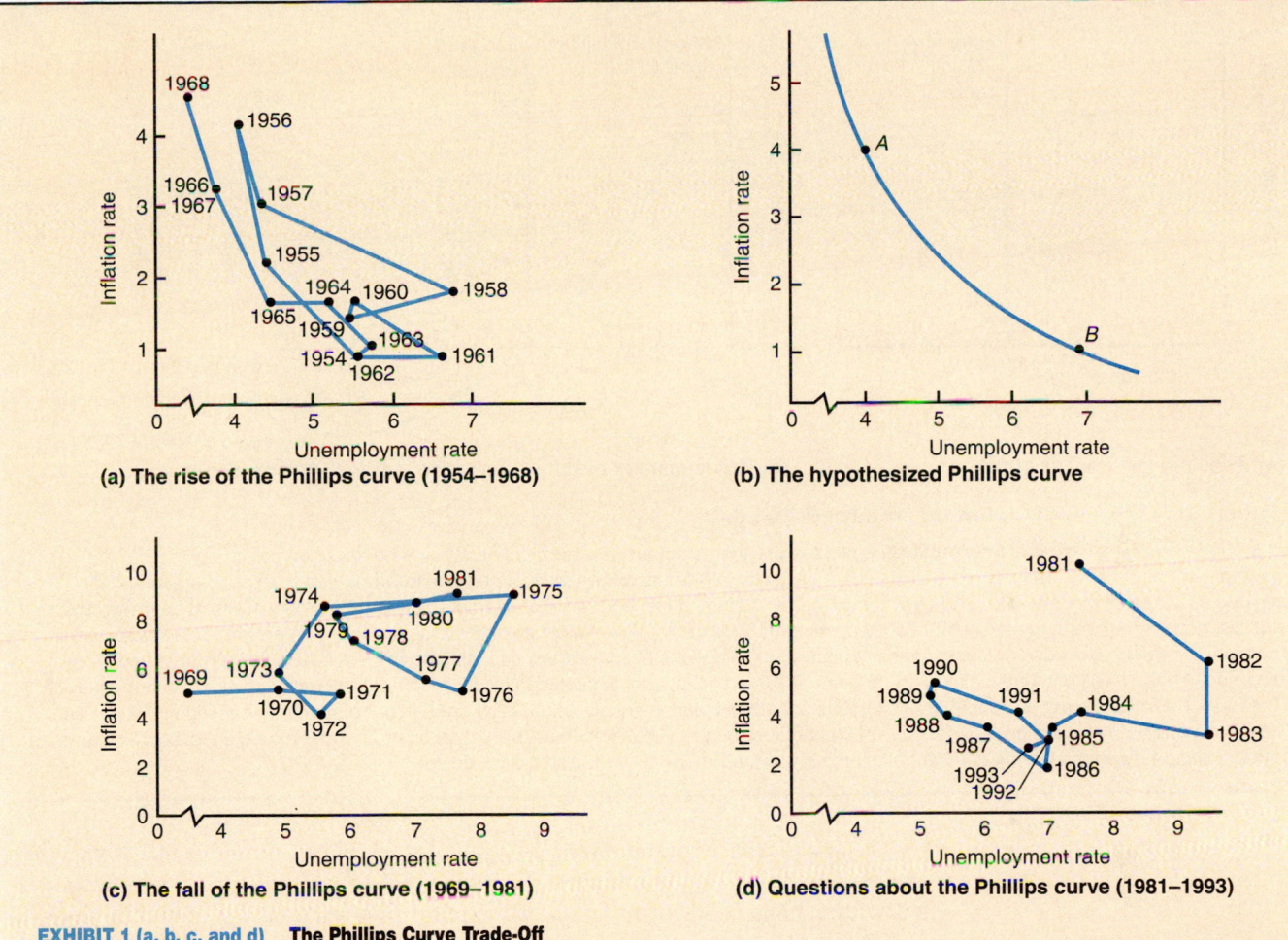

EXHIBIT 1 (a, b, c, and d)   The Phillips Curve Trade-Off

Analyzing the empirical relationship between unemployment and inflation from 1954 to 1968—shown in (**a**)—led economists to believe there was the relatively stable Phillips curve which, for policy choices, could be represented by the smooth Phillips curve in (**b**). In the 1970s the empirical Phillips curve relationship between inflation and unemployment broke down, leading many economists to question the existence of any Phillips curve relationship that allowed policy makers to choose between inflation and unemployment. In (**c**) you can see how in the 1970s, no stable Phillips curve existed, while in (**d**) you can see how in the 1980s and 1990s, the evidence is mixed. Specifically, from 1985 to 1993, a Phillips curve relationship seemed to exist. This allows some economists to say a Phillips curve–type relationship exists and others to say it doesn't.
Source: Economic Report of the President.

The Distinction between the Short-Run and Long-Run Phillips Curves   As views of the Phillips curve changed, economists began distinguishing between a short-run Phillips curve and a long-run Phillips curve. The key element of that distinction is based on **expectations of inflation** (the rise in the price level that the average person expects). On each point on the **short-run Phillips curve,** expectations of inflation are constant and hence will not, generally, equal actual inflation. At each point on the **long-run Phillips curve,** expectations of inflation change so that they equal actual inflation. Economists used this distinction to explain why the short-run Phillips curve relationship broke down in the 1970s.

The reason expectations are so central to the Phillips curve is seen by considering an individual's decision about what wage or price to set. Say you expect 0 percent inflation and you want a 2 percent wage or price increase. You'll raise your wage or price by 2 percent. Now say you expect 20 percent inflation and you want a 2 percent real wage increase. To get it, you must increase your wage by 22 percent. If everyone expects 20 percent inflation, everyone will raise their wage or price by 20 percent just to keep up.

Expectations of inflation   *The rise in the price level that the average person expects.*

Short-run Phillips curve   *A curve showing the trade-off between inflation and unemployment when expectations of inflation are constant.*

Long-run Phillips curve   *A curve showing the trade-off (or complete lack thereof) when expectations of inflation equal actual inflation.*

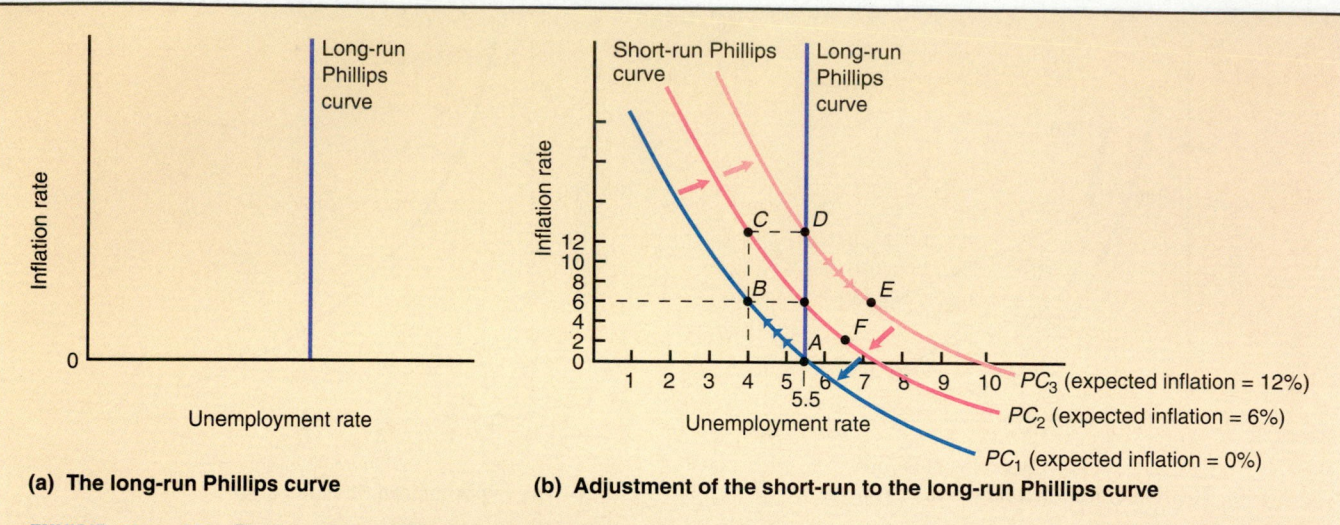

(a) The long-run Phillips curve   **(b) Adjustment of the short-run to the long-run Phillips curve**

EXHIBIT 2 (a and b)   The Long-Run and Short-Run Phillips Curve

In the long run, when expectations of rates of inflation are met, changes in rates of inflation have no effect on the level of unemployment, making the long-run Phillips curve perfectly vertical as shown in (**a**). If the government tries to expand the economy beyond its potential income, it can do so in the short run but not in the long run. For example, say the economy starts at point A in (**b**) and the government runs expansionary policy pushing the economy to point B. At point B, actual inflation, 6 percent, exceeds expected inflation, 0 percent. Because actual exceeds expected, expectations of inflation will rise, shifting the short-run Phillips curve up in the direction of PC_2. It will continue shifting up (to point C, for example) until expected inflation once again equals actual inflation (point D). The long-run Phillips curve is such that at all points expected inflation equals actual inflation. Once the economy has high inflation, one way to eliminate it is for the government to run contractionary policy, pushing the economy to point E where expected inflation exceeds actual inflation. As expectations of inflation fall, the short-run Phillips curve will shift back down to PC_2 and PC_1.

This means that expectations of inflation play a significant role in inflation. When expectations of inflation are higher, the same level of unemployment will be associated with a higher rate of inflation. To capture this relationship, it makes sense to assume that the short-run Phillips curve moves up or down as expectations of inflation change.

Q–2: Draw the long-run Phillips curve. Why does it have that shape?

The Shape of the Long-Run Phillips Curve   To determine what the long-run Phillips curve would look like, economists asked themselves: What difference should expectations of inflation make to the target level of unemployment? Their answer was none. If people expect 20 percent inflation and are raising their wages and prices 20 percent on average, the situation is just the same as if they expect 4 percent inflation and are raising their wages and prices 4 percent on average. Since their real incomes will be the same in both situations, their real decisions—how much labor to supply and demand—will be the same, so employment will not change. People aren't fooled by expected inflation. Thus, economists theorized that the long-run Phillips curve would be a vertical line, as in Exhibit 2(a). As you can see, in the long run, when expectations of inflation are fully built into people's wage- and price-setting decisions, there's no trade-off between inflation and unemployment.

This vertical long-run Phillips curve fits the empirical data for the 1970s and provides an explanation for why the short-run trade-off broke down. To see this, let's consider the years 1964 and 1970. Unemployment in both years was approximately 5 percent, but inflation in 1970 was over 5 percent while inflation in 1964 was less than 2 percent. Why the difference? Consider what happened in the interim: Inflation was consistently rising, so it's reasonable to assume that expectations of inflation were higher in 1970 than in 1964. Expectations of inflation explain the difference. When expectations are higher, actual inflation at each level of unemployment will be higher.

Q–3: If people's expectations of inflation didn't change, would the economy move from a short-run to a long-run Phillips curve?

Moving from a Short-Run to a Long-Run Phillips Curve   We can see how an economy moves from a short-run to a long-run Phillips curve by examining Exhibit 2(b). Say, for example, that initially the economy is at point *A*. Expected inflation is zero, unemployment is 5.5 percent, a level consistent with potential income. Since expected inflation is zero, the relative short-run Phillips curve is PC_1, which assumes zero expected inflation. (Each short-run Phillips curve is consistent with one level of expected inflation.)

Now, say that the government expands aggregate demand with expansionary monetary policy. Initially, expectations of inflation remain constant, so the economy moves along the initial short-run Phillips curve, PC_1. Unemployment falls from 5.5 percent to 4 percent and inflation rises from 0 percent to 6 percent (point *B*).

If the rise of inflation to 6 percent caused no change in individuals' expectations, the economy could remain at point *B*. But generally people change their expectations to match the actual inflation. As they do, the short-run Phillips curve shifts, since each short-run Phillips curve represents the trade-off for a given level of inflationary expectation. In this case the short-run Phillips curve shifts to PC_2. This means that people who wanted a 2 percent raise are now asking for a 2 + 6, or 8, percent raise. If the government wanted to maintain the 4 percent unemployment rate, it would have to use far more expansionary policies and accept 12 percent inflation (point *C*). But if the government did so, the short-run Phillips curve would shift up to PC_3, and the same expectation adjustment would occur. The short-run Phillips curve will continue to shift up as long as actual inflation exceeds expected inflation.

Now, the economy is on PC_3 where inflationary expectations are 12 percent. The only way for the government to stop this upward spiral is to back off on its unemployment goal, and to accept the level of unemployment consistent with potential income—5.5 percent unemployment. If it does so, the economy will arrive at point *D*—with expected inflation of 12 percent equaling actual inflation of 12 percent and the unemployment rate at 5.5 percent. If you connect points *A* and *D* you will see that they are both points on a vertical line—the long-run Phillips curve—in which expectations of inflation equal actual inflation.

Notice that the economy has arrived at a new equilibrium, but it is an equilibrium with 12 percent inflation. The attempt to achieve the lower level of unemployment has left a legacy of 12 percent expected inflation. A good exercise is to ask yourself how the government can rid itself of that inflation. The answer is an **induced recession**—a deliberate attempt by government to rid the economy of inflationary expectations. The government would decrease the money supply growth to, say, 6 percent, which would cause unemployment to rise above 5.5 percent but inflationary expectations to fall, shifting the short-run Phillips curve down. The economy would follow a path from point *D* to *E* to *F* to *A* as shown in Exhibit 2(b). The adjustment would stop when expectations of inflation equaled actual inflation again (point *A*).

In summary, policies that decrease unemployment below the level of unemployment consistent with an economy's potential income will lead to increasing inflation, expectations of inflation, and hence to accelerating inflation. To rid the economy of those expectations of inflation, the government must be prepared to accept an unemployment rate above that consistent with potential income—it must induce a recession. The most well-known induced recession in the United States occurred in the early 1980s, when inflation had reached 12 percent. In response, the Fed cut the money supply growth, causing a recession and high unemployment. This recession brought down inflation and inflationary expectations.

By the 1980s, most economists accepted the view that there was a short-run trade-off but no long-run trade-off. Once again, however, economists' beliefs were challenged by empirical observation. As unemployment decreased from 7 percent in 1986 to about 5 percent in 1989, inflation increased, but there were no signs of accelerating inflation, even though expectations had had time to adjust. Then in 1990 and 1991 as unemployment rose, inflation fell and it remained low in the first part of the 1990s. This led some economists to argue that a long-run trade-off between inflation and unemployment was returning. Because of these new observations, the inflation/unemployment trade-off is likely to be much in debate in the 1990s.

2 The long-run Phillips curve is vertical; it takes into account the feedback of inflation on expectations of inflation. The short-run Phillips curve does not take this feedback into account.

THEORIES OF INFLATION AND THE PHILLIPS CURVE TRADE-OFF

Keynesians blur the relationship between inflation and money in order to focus on the institutional process of setting prices and on cost-push pressures as the underlying causes of the inflationary process.

Q–4: If an inflation theory focuses on the money supply and competitive markets, is it more likely to be a Keynesian theory or a Classical theory?

Classicals blur the price-setting process and the cost-push pressures in order to focus on demand-pull pressure and the relationship between increases in the money supply and inflation.

The Classical Theory of Inflation

3 The Classical theory of inflation is summarized by the sentence: Inflation is everywhere and always a monetary phenomenon.

Q–5: What is another name for Classical macroeconomists?

Most economists accept the existence of a short-run Phillips curve and the rough equality between expectations of inflation, increases in the money supply, and the actual rate of inflation. In a theory, however, one must blur out a number of aspects of reality to focus on those aspects one believes are most important. That's what Keynesians and Classicals do with their theories of inflation.

Keynesians blur the relationship between inflation and money in order to focus on the institutional process of setting prices and on cost-push pressures as the underlying causes of the inflationary process. According to Keynesians, the money supply increases with inflation, but these increases aren't the cause of inflation; the money supply increases occur because government tries to see that inflation (the rise in the price level) doesn't lead to unemployment and cost-push pressures. When government increases aggregate demand to see that the price increases don't lead to unemployment, it ratifies the inflation. According to Keynesians, money supply increases are a necessary, but not a causal, link in the inflation process.

Classicals blur the price-setting process and the cost-push pressures in order to focus on demand-pull pressure and the relationship between increases in the money supply and inflation. When Classicals see inflation they see the government increasing the money supply. Both theories shed light on inflation. Let's now consider them a bit more carefully.

The Classical theory of inflation can be summed up in one sentence: *Inflation is everywhere and always a monetary phenomenon.* If the money supply doesn't rise, the price level won't rise. Forget all the other stuff. It obscures the connection between money and inflation. (As I stated above, this focus on money is why Classicals were called *monetarists* in the 1960s and 1970s.)

The Quantity Theory of Money and Inflation   That connection between money and inflation is relatively simple and can be seen in the quantity theory: When the money supply rises, prices go up; if the money supply doesn't continue to rise, inflation won't continue. Consider the quantity theory of money:

$$MV = PQ$$

Classicals assume velocity, *V*, and real output, *Q*, are relatively constant. They also consider the price level, *P*, relatively flexible. According to Classical theory, any

The Classical view that printing money causes inflation is seen in the 18th-century satirical drawing by James Gilray showing William Pitt spewing paper money out of his mouth while gold coins are locked up in his stomach. *Bleichroeder Print Collection, Baker Library, Harvard Business School.*

inflation is caused by demand-pull pressures—which are generated by increases in the money supply. Therefore,

$$\Delta M \rightarrow \Delta P$$

Lawrence Davidson, a Classical economist at the St. Louis Federal Reserve Bank, summarizes that view:

> Monetarists (another name for Classical economists) also believe that there are numerous sources of price change, yet only changes in money growth can permanently alter the rate of inflation. Therefore, we expect that non-monetary factors will sometimes affect short-term measured inflation rates. If these non-monetary sources of measured inflation arise unexpectedly over time, and if they only temporarily affect the inflation rate, then the only lasting, predictable, and controllable source of inflation would be monetary growth. ("Inflation Misinformation and Monetary Policy," *St. Louis Federal Reserve Bank Review,* 1982, p. 21.)

Classical Modifications of the Quantity Theory   The quantity theory of money embodies the central element of the Classical theory of inflation. There are many modifications which explain why the connection between money and inflation in the short run isn't perfectly tight. One important modification is that Classicals believe that people are often fooled into thinking an increase in nominal demand caused by an increase in the money supply is actually an increase in real demand. The result will be a short-run expansionary effect on the real economy, as suggested in this chapter's opening quotation from Milton Friedman.

Examples of Money's Role in Inflation   Let's consider an example. In 1971 the Fed increased the money supply significantly; as a result, income rose and unemployment fell. In response, in 1972 inflation fell slightly, as did unemployment. However, in 1974 and 1975 both inflation and unemployment rose substantially. Here's an example of expansionary monetary policy increasing real output as prices are slow to respond to increases in aggregate demand. But in the long run the expansionary monetary policy caused inflation. Classical economists also believe that people can be fooled in the opposite direction—thinking that a decrease in nominal demand is actually a decrease in real demand. This makes it difficult to stop an ongoing inflation because the initial short-run effect is on real output. The effect on inflation occurs in the long run.

Let's consider another example, again from the 1970s, when significant inflation—10 percent—had become built into the economy. In late 1979 and the early 1980s, the Fed decreased the money supply growth significantly. This led to a leap in unemployment from 7 to 10 percent, but initially no decrease in inflation. By 1984, however, inflation had fallen to about 4 percent, and it remained low throughout the 1980s and early 1990s.

Now let's consider a couple of more recent examples. In the early 1990s, the German central bank felt Germany's inflation rate was too high. It cut the money supply growth considerably. Initially, the impact was on output, and the tight money pushed the German economy into a recession. It remained in recession through early 1994, but the forecasts for 1995 were for growth, albeit slow.

Another example is Russia in the early 1990s. The Russian government was short of revenue and was forced to print money to finance its debt. As a result, inflation blew up into hyperinflation, and the Russian ruble became almost worthless.

Despite these and many other examples, the simple view connecting inflation with money supply growth lost favor in the late 1980s and early 1990s as formerly stable relationships between certain measurements of money and inflation broke down. Part of the reason for this was the enormous changes in financial institutions that were occurring because of technological changes and changing regulations. Another part was the increased global interdependence of financial markets, which increased the flow of money among countries. In the 1990s it seemed that, for low inflation, the random elements (called *noise*) in the relationship between money and inflation

Economic Review, published by the Federal Reserve Bank of Kansas City, is an excellent source of articles concerning financial issues.

The core of the Classical theory is that inflation is everywhere and always a monetary phenomenon.

Q–6: What one sentence best summarizes the Classical theory of inflation?

ADDED DIMENSION

THE KEEPER OF THE
CLASSICAL FAITH:
MILTON FRIEDMAN

B y most accounts, Milton Friedman was a headstrong student. He didn't simply accept the truths his teachers laid out. If he didn't agree, he argued strongly for his own belief. He was very bright and his ideas were generally logical and convincing. He needed to be both persistent and intelligent to maintain and promote his views in spite of strong opposition.

Throughout the Keynesian years of the 1950s and 1960s, Friedman stood up and argued the Classical viewpoint of economics. He kept Classical economics alive. He was such a strong advocate of the quantity theory of money that, during this period, Classical economics was called monetarism. Friedman was the leader of the monetarists.

Friedman argued that fiscal policy simply didn't work. It led to expansions in government's size. He also opposed an activist monetary policy. The effects of monetary policy, he said, were too variable for it to be useful in guiding the economy. He called for a steady growth in the money supply, and argued consistently for a laissez-faire policy by government.

He has made his mark in both microeconomics and macroeconomics. In the 1970s, his ideas caught hold and helped spawn a renewal of the Classical school of economics. He was awarded the Nobel prize in economics in 1976.

Milton Friedman—Nobel prize, 1976, for work on monetary theory. Friedman is the macroeconomist who most strongly argued the monetarist view. © *The Nobel Foundation.*

Monetary rule *A prescribed monetary policy to be followed regardless of what is happening in the economy.*

Natural rate of unemployment
Classical term for the unemployment rate in long-run equilibrium when expectations of inflation equal the actual level of inflation.

4 Classical economists favor a monetary rule because they believe the short-run effects of monetary policy are unpredictable and the long-run effects of monetary policy are on the price level, not on real output.

overwhelmed the connection. For large inflation of the type experienced by many developing and transitional economies, the connection was still evident.

Classical Policy to Fight Inflation In terms of policy, monetary policy is powerful, but unpredictable in the short run. Because of this unpredictability monetary policy cannot, and should not, be used to control the level of output in the economy. Thus, paradoxically, monetarists favor a *laissez-faire* monetary policy.

Classicals, or monetarists as they are sometimes called because of their focus on money, believe that in the long run money affects only the price level. Since the short-run effects are unpredictable and in the long run only the price level is affected, Classicals say that monetary policy should follow a **monetary rule** (a prescribed monetary policy that's to be followed regardless of what's happening in the economy). They argue that:

1. The money supply should be increased by a determined percentage, say 3 percent per year, to allow for changes in productivity and real growth.
2. Monetary policy should not be used in the short run to try to steer the economy.

Classicals believe that monetary policy should be used only to achieve long-run objectives, the most important of which is price stability.

There are many alternative ways in which short-run Classical theory of inflation makes adjustments for changes in velocity, real output, and inflationary expectations, but the core of their theory is inevitably that *inflation is everywhere and always a monetary phenomenon.* That core connection between money and inflation is pleasant for students because it makes it possible to present succinctly the Classical view.

The Classical View of the Phillips Curve Trade-Off The Classical view of the trade-off centers around the **natural rate of unemployment** (the rate of unemployment to which the economy naturally gravitates).[2] This natural rate of unemployment is independent of the inflation rate and expectations of inflation. It is the unemployment rate that will exist in long-run equilibrium when expectations of inflation equal the actual level of inflation. The long-run Phillips curve is vertical at this natural rate of unemployment.

Unemployment rates below the natural unemployment rate would lead to actual inflation higher than expected inflation, which would bring about a future increase in

---

[2] The natural rate concept is the Classical equivalent of what this book calls the *target rate of unemployment.* The Keynesian equivalent for the target rate is the *nonaccelerating inflation rate of unemployment* (NAIRU).

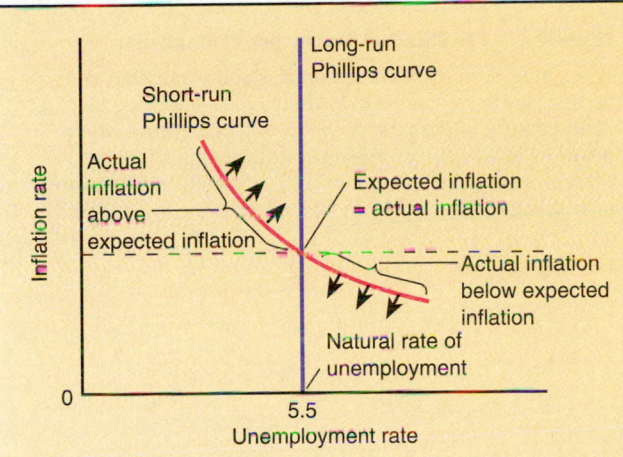

EXHIBIT 3   The Classical View of the Phillips Curve Trade-Off

In the Classical view, the long-run Phillips curve is vertical at the natural rate of unemployment. Because expectations of inflation lag behind actual inflation, there exists a temporary trade-off between inflation and unemployment. But the trade-off is an illusion, and as soon as expectations catch up with actual inflation, the economy will return to the natural rate of unemployment.

expectations of inflation, and an upward shift of the short-run Phillips curve. This Classical view is shown in Exhibit 3.

At unemployment rates to the left of the long-run Phillips curve (unemployment rates below the natural rate), actual inflation is above expectations of inflation so the short-run Phillips curve will shift upward (shown by the upward arrows in Exhibit 3). To the right of the long-run Phillips curve (at unemployment rates higher than the natural rate), actual inflation is below expectations of inflation and the short-run Phillips curve will shift downward (shown by the downward arrows in the exhibit).

Maintaining an unemployment rate below the natural rate would cause an ever-increasing acceleration of inflation. Such an accelerating inflation is unsustainable because it destroys the benefits of money. It would cause hyperinflation and a breakdown of the economy. Eventually the government must give up its attempt to lower the unemployment rate below the natural rate. But even after giving up its attempt to achieve an unemployment rate below the natural rate, the government will have left a legacy of high inflation. The combination of high and accelerating inflation and high unemployment is known as **stagflation.**

Exhibit 4 graphs the Classical explanation of how stagflation occurs. Say the economy starts at an equilibrium of zero actual inflation, zero expected inflation, and 5.5 percent unemployment, which, let's suppose, happens to be the natural rate of unemployment. Now government comes along and expands the economy with expansionary monetary or fiscal policy to point *A* on the short-run Phillips curve so that there will be 3 percent inflation and 4 percent unemployment. The 3 percent actual inflation exceeds 0 percent expected inflation, which causes a shift up in expectations of inflation. This increase in expectations causes the short-run Phillips curve to shift up from PC_1 to PC_2.

After expectations of inflation have shifted up fully, instead of being able to achieve 4 percent unemployment with a 3 percent inflation rate, it would take a 6 percent inflation rate to maintain unemployment at 4 percent (point *B*). Let's say the government is willing to accept 6 percent inflation and uses expansionary monetary or fiscal policy to try to maintain unemployment at 4 percent, which is 1.5 percent below the natural rate. Expectations of inflation would shift up to 6 percent and the short-run Phillips curve would shift up to PC_3. Now the government finds that to keep the economy at 4 percent unemployment would require an even more expansionary policy and an inflation rate of 9 percent (point *C*). And even that 9 percent is only temporary; as long as the unemployment rate is less than the natural rate, actual inflation will be above expected inflation, the short-run Phillips curve will be shifting up, and inflation will be accelerating.

That's what Classicals said happened in the 1970s. Government, following Keynesians' advice, expanded the economy and reduced unemployment below the natural rate, causing expectations of inflation to rise and the short-run Phillips curve to

6   The Classical view of the Phillips curve trade-off centers around the natural rate of unemployment. Any attempt to maintain unemployment at a rate below the natural rate is unsustainable because doing so would cause accelerating inflation.

Stagflation   Combination of high inflation and high unemployment.

Q–7: If the economy is at point *A* on the Phillips curve below, what prediction would you make for unemployment and inflation?

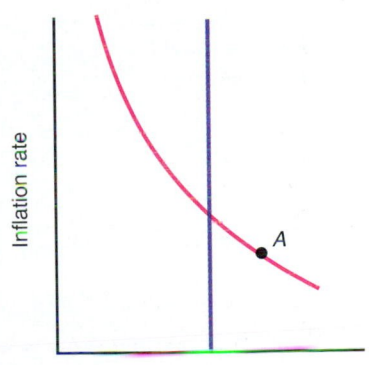

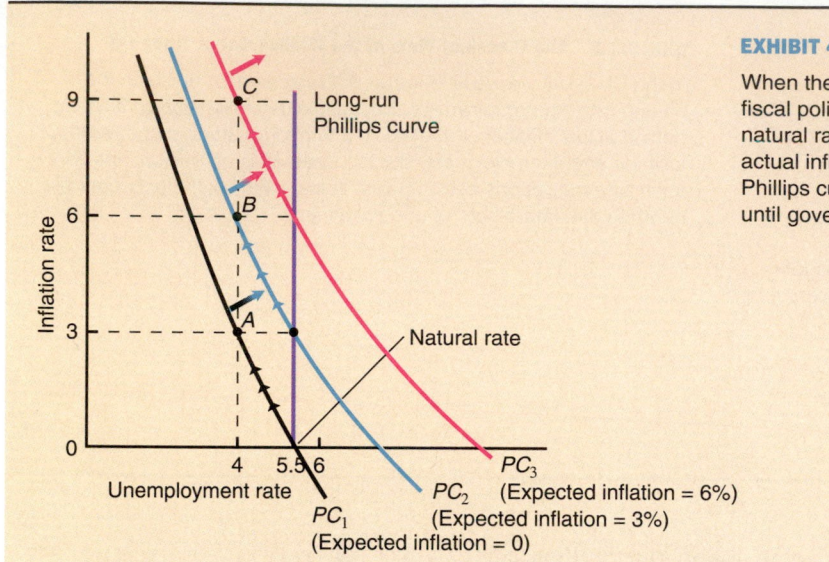

EXHIBIT 4   The Classical Explanation of Stagflation

When the government utilizes expansionary monetary or fiscal policy in an attempt to lower unemployment below the natural rate, it pushes the economy to a point like *A* where actual inflation exceeds expected inflation; the short-run Phillips curve shifts upward. Inflation continually increases until government gives up its attempt to do the impossible.

shift up. Inflation stopped rising only when the government accepted the natural rate of unemployment as inevitable. In the Classical view, government expansionary policy caused stagflation.

The Keynesian Theory of Inflation

5 The Keynesian theory of inflation holds that institutional and structural aspects of inflation, as well as increases in the money supply, are important causes of inflation.

Keynesian theories of inflation emphasize institutional and social causes of inflation.

Keynesians would agree with much of what the Classicals have to say but believe that they aren't focusing on the important institutional and structural aspects of inflation. Keynesians argue that when firms and individuals set prices, they do not take into account the effect of their pricing decisions on the price level. Since generally firms, rather than consumers, set prices, those prices quickly adjust upward in response to an increase in demand, but are much slower to adjust downward in response to a decrease in demand.

The revenue that firms receive is divided among profits, wages, and rent. All this income is ultimately paid to individual owners of the factors of production. Firms are simply intermediaries between individuals as owners of the factors of production and individuals as consumers. Keynesians argue that, given the institutional structure of our economy, it's often easier for firms to increase wages, profits, and rents to keep the peace with their employees and other factors of production than it is to try to hold those costs down. Firms then pay for that increase by raising the prices they charge consumers. That works as long as, in response to the rising price level, the government increases the money supply so that the demand is there to buy the goods at the higher prices.

Let's consider an example: A zuka firm is happy with its competitive position in the zuka market. It expects 0 percent inflation. Productivity (output of zukas per unit input) is increasing 2 percent, the same as the increase in productivity in the economy as a whole, so the firm can hold its nominal price of zukas constant even if it increases wages by 2 percent. Since the price level isn't expected to change, holding the price of zukas constant should maintain the firm's share of the zuka market. The firm offers workers a 2 percent increase.

The firm meets its workers to discuss the 2 percent offer. At that meeting it becomes clear to the firm that its workers will push for a 4 percent pay increase. What should the firm do? In a highly competitive market in which supply and demand forces alone determine wages and prices, there's no question what it would do; it would increase wages only 2 percent and hold its price constant. Real-world firms, however, often meet workers' demands under the expectation that other firms will do so too. Meeting these demands helps maintain morale and prevents turnover of key workers. This occurs whether or not there are unions. The result is an upward push on nominal wages and prices.

THE DISTRIBUTIONAL EFFECTS OF INFLATION

■f inflation is a distributional fight, who wins and who loses? The winners are people who can raise their wages or prices and still keep their jobs and sell their labor or goods. The losers are people who can't.

The composition of these groups changes over time. For example, at one time people on social security and pensions lost out during inflations since social security and pensions were, on the whole, set at fixed rates. Inflation lowered recipients' real income. But social security payments and many pensions are now indexed (automatically adjusted to compensate for inflation), so their recipients are no longer losers. Their real income became independent of inflation.

Similarly, it's sometimes said that bond holders are hurt by inflation, since the value of the money with which the bonds are redeemed falls during inflation. That's true, but whether bond holders lose depends on how the interest rate on bonds adjusts to the expected inflation rate. In recent years, the nominal interest rate has adjusted quickly to expectations of inflation. When that happens, it is unclear how much bond holders have lost. If nominal interest rates adjust quickly to expectations of inflation, the real interest rate may remain as high as it otherwise would have been.

For example, in the 1950s bond holders received 2 percent interest; inflation was low, so 2 percent interest was close to a 2 percent real interest rate. In the early 1970s, interest rates on bonds were 8 percent, in large part because people expected 6 percent inflation. Six percent compensated bond holders for inflation, leaving them the same 2 percent real return they had received in the 1950s. So we must be careful in generalizing about distributional effects of inflation.

What we can say about the distributional consequences of inflation is that people who don't expect inflation and who are tied in to fixed contracts denominated in unindexed monetary values will likely lose in an inflation. However, these people are rational and probably won't let it happen again. They'll be prepared for a subsequent inflation.

This upward push on nominal wages and prices can exist only if the labor and product markets are not highly competitive. In a highly competitive market, even small amounts of unemployment and excess supply would cause wages and prices to fall. Keynesians believe that most real-world markets are not highly competitive in this fashion. While they agree that some competition exists, they argue that in most sectors of the economy, competition works slowly. The invisible handshake, as well as the invisible hand, influences wages and prices. The result is that even when there is substantial unemployment and considerable excess supply of goods, existing workers can still put an upward push on nominal wages, and existing firms can put an upward push on nominal prices.

The Insider/Outsider Model and Inflation   To get a better picture of how existing workers can push up wages despite substantial unemployment, let's consider a Keynesian model which divides the economy into insiders and outsiders. Insiders are workers who have good jobs with excellent long-run prospects, and current business owners. Both receive above-equilibrium wages, profits, and rents. If the world were competitive, their wages, profits, and rents would be pushed down to the equilibrium level. To prevent this from happening, Keynesians argue, insiders develop sociological and institutional barriers that prevent outsiders from competing away those above-equilibrium wages, profits, and rents. Because of those barriers, outsiders (often minorities) must take dead-end, low-paying jobs or attempt to undertake marginal businesses that pay little return for many hours worked. Even when outsiders do find better jobs or business opportunities, they are first to be fired and their businesses are the first to suffer in a recession. Thus, outsiders have much higher unemployment rates than insiders. For example, in the United States blacks tend to be outsiders; black unemployment rates are generally twice as high as white unemployment rates for the same age groups.

In short, Keynesians see an economic system that's only partially competitive. In their view, the invisible hand is often thwarted by other invisible forces. Such partially competitive economies are often characterized by insiders' monopolies. Insiders get the jobs and are paid monopoly wage levels. Outsiders are unemployed at those higher wages. Imperfect competition allows workers (and firms) to raise nominal wages (and prices) even as unemployment (and excess supply of goods) exists. Then, as other insiders do likewise, the price level rises. This increase in the price level lowers

Q–8:   How would a Classical economist likely respond to an insider-outsider model of inflation?

workers' real wage. In response, workers further raise their nominal wages to protect their real wages. The result is an ongoing chase in which the insiders protect their real wage, while outsiders (the unemployed) suffer. (If the ideas of *nominal* and *real* are unclear to you, a review of earlier chapters may be in order.)

Within this imperfectly competitive system, both wages and prices develop their own inertia that causes inflation to take on a life of its own. Keynesians believe that to understand inflation you must understand the psychology of the individuals with wage- and price-setting power, including both firms and organizations of workers.

Thus, Keynesians see the nominal wage- and price-setting process as generating inflation. As one group pushes up its nominal wage or price, another group responds by doing the same. More groups follow until finally the first group finds its relative wage or price hasn't increased. Then the entire process starts again. Once the nominal wage and price levels have risen, government has two options: It can either ratify the increase by increasing the money supply, thereby accepting the inflation; or it can refuse to ratify it, causing unemployment.

The Role of Unemployment in Keynesian Theories of Inflation

Keynesians believe that, under current conditions, the costs of unemployment are borne heavily by minorities and other outsiders.

What role does unemployment play in the inflation process for Keynesians? They see the fear of unemployment as a way of "disciplining" workers to accept lower pay. The reality that there are a number of unemployed people out there waiting to take the jobs of employed workers who ask for too high a wage increase helps prevent existing workers from raising their wage. Thus, unemployment helps fight inflation. But unemployment is not a complete retardant of inflation because many workers and firms have insulated themselves from unemployment through implicit or explicit contracts providing them with job and market security regardless of the level of unemployment. This means that the unemployment costs of fighting inflation are borne heavily by minorities and other outsiders. Insiders are more protected and have less to fear from unemployment. The resulting unemployment is not "natural" in the sense that it reflects people's choices; it is simply the amount of unemployment that is necessary to create competitive pressure on insiders and thereby limit their attempts at further monopolization.

Another difference between Keynesians and Classicals is that Keynesians are far less likely to see a specific level of unemployment as the "natural rate" of unemployment. Because they believe that aggregate supply and demand are interrelated, they are far more cautious about specifying a single rate of unemployment toward which the aggregate economy gravitates. For them the target rate of unemployment can shift around; it is to be empirically determined, not theoretically deduced.

The Keynesian View of the Phillips Curve Trade-Off

6 Keynesians believe that institutional factors play a major role in determining inflation, and that expected inflation need not precisely equal actual inflation. Within a range of output levels, a trade-off is possible.

As I've stated, Keynesians see an economy of imperfectly competitive markets. Keynesians believe that, in the short run, social forces (the invisible handshake, which creates a type of implicit contract between buyers and sellers) and explicit contracts play a large role in price determination. Because of these social forces, there is no reason that, in the short run, expected inflation must precisely equal actual inflation. Keynesians argue that if the economy is kept close to the existing level of inflation (say within 2 or 3 percent), these social forces can hold inflationary expectations in check at their existing level and prevent them from being built into higher inflationary demands, and thereby shifting up the short-run Phillips curve. Thus, within a limited range of inflation rates around the actual inflation rate, many Keynesians believe that the short-run Phillips curve can be relatively stable, and not shift up even though actual inflation exceeds expected inflation. They argue that the trade-off existing up to 1969 was not an illusion and that that relationship did exist in the late 1980s. There can be a long-run trade-off between inflation and unemployment, as there was up until 1969. In a sense, Keynesians are saying that the long run never comes.

The reason many Keynesians believe there can be a long-run trade-off between inflation and unemployment is not that they believe people are irrational; it is that they believe people are reasonable. Keynesians argue that, given the cost of rationality, it would be unreasonable for most people to make explicit calculations about inflation's

The debate on what to do about inflation has an analogy to dieting. Fasting will cause you to lose about a pound a day. Want to lose 30 pounds? A Classical dietitian would say, "Fast. Thirty pounds equals 105,000 calories. When you've managed to complete a period in which you've eaten 105,000 fewer calories than are necessary to maintain your present weight, you'll have lost 30 pounds." A Keynesian dietitian would offer a variety of diets or would explore your soul to discover why you want to overeat, and would perhaps suggest a liquid protein plan. The Keynesian diet would also involve your taking in 105,000 fewer calories than if you'd continued to overeat. But, Keynesians argue, you can't stick with a diet unless you've discovered what makes you want to overeat.

effect on their incomes. People have a general feeling, but that is all they have. Consequently people's calculations about their relative wage and prices based on the price level are inexact. Three or four percent inflation per year is about .008 percent per day, meaning that $1,000 will lose about 8¢ in value each day. That 8¢ is hardly noticeable. Price indices are more inexact than that. Therefore, say many Keynesians, low inflation levels (2 or 3 percent) will be accepted by individuals without leading them to immediate increases in their nominal wages or prices.

Keynesians argue that people will rationally respond quite differently to a 2 percent decrease in their real wage caused by a 2 percent decrease in their nominal wage than they would to a 2 percent decrease in their real wage caused by a 2 percent increase in the price level. This argument accounts for the Keynesian explanation of the reasonably stable trade-off that existed before 1969.

How then do these Keynesians explain the 1970s? The answer is that the economy experienced a combination of unfortunate events, including oil price shocks and overly expansionary government policies. These events caused inflation to exceed what psychologists called the *just-noticeable difference.*

The **just-noticeable difference** is the threshold where our senses realize that something has changed. For example, say it gets 3°F warmer; most people won't notice. But if it gets 10°F warmer, most people will notice. Thus, the just-noticeable difference is a change of somewhere between 3°F and 10°F. Keynesians argue that, in the 1970s, inflation exceeded that threshold. As it did, inflation became built into people's expectations and everyone who previously had wanted a 4 percent wage hike now asked for a 9 percent hike, while firms that wanted a 3 percent price increase raised their prices by 8 percent to account for the expected higher price level due to inflation. The entire short-run Phillips curve shifted up, as suggested by the Classicals. But that happened only because the economy was pushed too far; it doesn't negate the existence of a continuing trade-off between inflation and unemployment within certain limits.

Thus, there is a central difference between the Keynesian and Classical views of the Phillips curve. The Keynesian view allows that, within a limited range, there is a long-run trade-off between inflation and unemployment. That's why Keynesians generally support a more expansionary policy than do Classical economists, and also why they support more activist monetary and fiscal policies. In the Keynesian view, government macroeconomic policy can do good; in the Classical view, it cannot.

The preceding discussion highlighted differences between Keynesian and Classical theories of inflation. Keynesians see inflation as an institutional phenomenon; Classicals see it as a monetary phenomenon.

Classicals and Keynesians on Supply Shocks   The distinction between the Keynesian and Classical theories of inflation comes out most clearly when we consider the effects of a supply-price shock, such as a sudden increase in the price of oil. Keynesians see such a supply-price shock as a cost-push pressure, likely to lead to significant inflationary pressures as people try to maintain their relative income at their previous level.

Just-noticeable difference   A threshold below which our senses don't recognize that something has changed.

Q–9:   How do Keynesians explain a relatively stable trade-off between inflation and unemployment that persists year after year?

Similarities and Differences between Keynesian and Classical Theories

Q–10:   A price supply shock has just hit the economy. Who is likely to predict higher inflation, a Keynesian or a Classical? Why?

EXHIBIT 5   Inflation, Money Supply
Growth, and Unemployment

Year	Inflation (measured by Implicit Price Deflator of GDP)	Rate of Money Supply Growth			Civilian Unemployment
		M_1	M_2	M_3	
1990	4.4	4.1	3.5	1.4	5.5
1991	3.9	8.7	3.0	1.3	6.7
1992	2.9	14.2	1.4	0.1	7.4
1993	2.6	10.2	1.6	1.1	6.8

Classical economists see a supply-price shock as simply a relative price change. They argue that as long as the government does not increase the money supply, other relative prices will fall and there will be little inflationary pressure from a supply-price shock. So they advocate maintaining a monetary rule and not increasing the money supply to accommodate higher prices.

Classicals and Keynesians on Recent Inflation   To see these differences, let's compare how Classicals and Keynesians explain the inflation that's been occurring in the early 1990s.

First, the facts, which I present in Exhibit 5. As you can see, in the early 1990s, inflation remained low, while unemployment fluctuated. Different measures of the money supply were changing at different rates. There were no major price shocks during this time, but there were significant changes in financial institutions. The monetarists argued that, once one accounted for financial institutional changes, the core relationship between changes in the money supply and inflation could be seen.

Thus, the period, while not perfectly consistent with the Classical view, was not a refutation of it. Classicals claimed that if the Fed held constant an appropriate measure of the money supply, inflation could be totally stopped.

Keynesians would say that the inflation was relatively low because the unemployment rate was being kept higher than the economy could handle, and that the remaining inflation was a combination of supply shock inflation and inflation caused by existing institutions. They would claim that holding down the appropriate measure of the money supply was impossible (since one couldn't decide what the appropriate measure was), but that even if one could hold it down, holding it down further would only cause more unemployment since the inflation was inherent in the institutions.

Similarities in the Keynesian and Classical Views   These differences between the theories shouldn't obscure the similarities. Once the economy reaches its potential output, both Keynesians and Classicals see inflation as an excess demand phenomenon: too much money chasing too few goods. The differences in views occur when the economy is not at its potential output. Keynesians believe inflation is still possible; Classicals believe it is not.

KEYNESIAN AND CLASSICAL POLICIES TO FIGHT STAGFLATION

The two different theories of inflation lead to two different sets of policies to fight inflation and the unemployment/inflation dilemma.

Classicals say to stop inflation one must reduce the rate of growth of the money supply. Control the money supply and you will control inflation.

Keynesians agree that controlling the money supply will ultimately control inflation, but they argue that it will do so in an inefficient and unfair manner. They argue that tight monetary policy usually causes unemployment among those least able to handle it. Keynesians ask, ''Why should this group bear the cost of fighting inflation?'' Their argument is that putting a brick wall in front of a speeding car will stop the car, but that doesn't mean that's how you should stop a car. Instead,

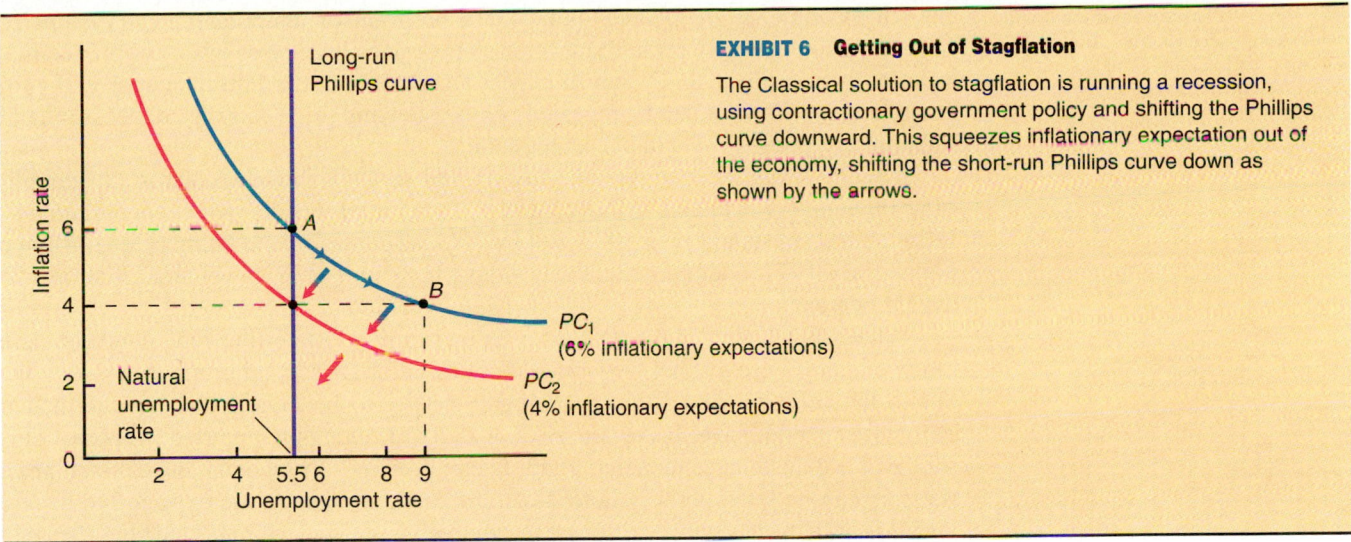

EXHIBIT 6   Getting Out of Stagflation

The Classical solution to stagflation is running a recession, using contractionary government policy and shifting the Phillips curve downward. This squeezes inflationary expectation out of the economy, shifting the short-run Phillips curve down as shown by the arrows.

Keynesians are more likely to favor the use of supplemental policies in conjunction with contractionary monetary policy. Let's consider both views more carefully.

The Classical Approach to Fighting Stagflation

One way to escape a stagflation is embodied in the Classical analysis of the natural rate of unemployment. If you got into the problem by actual inflation exceeding expected inflation because you tried to hold unemployment below the natural rate, you can get out of inflation by having actual inflation below expected inflation. To do that you must maintain the unemployment rate higher than the natural rate. In essence, you cause a recession. Exhibit 6 graphs this method of getting out of stagflation.

7 Classicals see monetary growth and competitive markets determining the level of inflation and unemployment. No role for an incomes policy remains.

Say that initially the economy was in equilibrium at 6 percent inflation and 5.5 percent unemployment, and that the natural rate of unemployment was 5.5 percent (point A). Say that the government runs contractionary aggregate policy so that the unemployment rate increases to 9 percent and inflation falls to 4 percent (point B). As expectations of inflation fall, the short-run Phillips curve shifts down from PC_1 (6 percent inflationary expectation) to PC_2 (4 percent inflationary expectation).

As long as the actual unemployment rate remains above the natural rate of unemployment, the Phillips curve trade-off will keep falling as expectations of inflation keep falling in response to lower-than-expected inflation. If government policies hold unemployment above the natural rate, eventually expectations of inflation will fall to zero. At that point, the government can stop squeezing inflation out of the economy and it can be allowed to return to the natural rate of unemployment. This is the Classical solution to stagflation: contractionary monetary and fiscal policies squeezing the inflationary expectation out of the economy. True, it involves suffering, but the economy must atone for the expansionary sins of the Keynesians.

Classicals tend to favor a strict monetary rule; Keynesians favor more discretion.

For Classicals, however, since people's expectations are rational and the rate of increase in the money supply determines the rate of inflation, the suffering need not be that great if the government is firm. If a strict monetary rule can be adopted and people can know that, no matter what, the government won't exceed the monetary growth rate specified in the rule, expectations of inflation will fall quickly.

The Keynesian Approach to Fighting Stagflation

Inducing a recession to rid the economy of expected inflation isn't a pleasant policy, so it isn't surprising that a Keynesian alternative has often been tried. The Keynesian alternative is to use a supplemental policy that directly holds down inflation. Such a policy is often called an *incomes policy*. An **incomes policy** is a policy that places direct pressure on individuals to hold down their nominal wages and prices. Because it holds down inflation, an incomes policy can help to eliminate expectations of inflation, thereby reducing the cost in unemployment necessary to fight inflation.

Incomes policy A policy placing direct pressure on individuals to hold down their nominal wages and prices.

7 Keynesians see institutional and social forces determining the level of inflation and unemployment, and hence see a role for an incomes policy.

An example of an incomes policy is a program of temporary *wage and price controls,* which directly prohibit inflation. Keynesians argue that when people see that inflation is at a lower level, they'll expect less inflation, the Phillips curve will shift down, and the controls can be repealed. With wage and price controls, expectations of inflation are eliminated without a recession.

It seems a highly desirable alternative, and in 1971 President Nixon, a Republican, instituted wage and price controls. The initial results were encouraging— inflation fell substantially in 1972. But in 1973, as controls were being lifted, inflation jumped. By 1974, unemployment was almost back to its 1972 level and inflation was over 8 percent.

What went wrong? One problem was bad timing. About the time controls were removed, an oil price shock generated more inflation. A second problem was that the fall in the inflation rate allowed aggregate policy to be more expansionary than it otherwise would have been. In 1972 and 1973, unemployment decreased. This suggests expansionary monetary and fiscal policies. Temporary wage and price controls can only temporarily hold down inflation. If controls are expected to have a long-run effect, they must be long-run controls—but no one expected the 1971–74 wage and price controls to be long run. Thus, temporary controls change nothing in the underlying reality. Using controls often tempts government to be too expansionary.

It's unclear what the inflation rate in the absence of these controls would have been. Supporters of temporary wage and price controls argue that the controls stopped a bad situation from getting worse. Opponents of temporary price controls as a way to reduce expectations of inflation argue that, inevitably, such price controls will be used to camouflage expansionary policy and thus should be avoided.

CONCLUSION

The Classical and Keynesian views of inflation and the Phillips curve trade-off reflect two consistent worldviews. Keynesians see a world in which sociological and institutional factors interact with market forces, keeping the economy in a perpetual disequilibrium when considered in an economic framework. Classicals see a world in which market forces predominate. They consider institutional and sociological factors insignificant, and view the overall economy as one in continual equilibrium. These two worldviews carry over to their analyses of the central policy issue facing most governments as they decide on their monetary and fiscal policies: the trade-off between inflation and unemployment.

These different worldviews are why there are major disagreements about policy. Classicals believe the best policy is laissez-faire; Keynesians believe an activist policy is needed. Given their contrasting worldviews, the debate will likely continue for a long time.

CHAPTER SUMMARY

- High inflation is inevitably accompanied by roughly proportional increases in the money supply and expectations of inflation.
- The short-run Phillips curve differs from the long-run Phillips curve because on the long-run Phillips curve expected inflation must equal actual inflation.
- The Classical theory of inflation blurs out the institutional process of setting prices and focuses on the relation between money and inflation.
- Classical economists favor a monetary rule that is to be followed regardless of economic conditions.
- The Keynesian theory of inflation blurs out the relation-

ship between inflation and money and focuses on the institutional process of setting prices.
- In the Classical theory of inflation, the only equilibrium is on the long-run Phillips curve.
- In the Keynesian theory of inflation, a short-run Phillips curve trade-off can persist into the long run as long as inflation doesn't exceed a certain range.
- Classicals argue that the only way to stop inflation is to stop increasing the money supply. Keynesians argue that supplemental policies (such as an incomes policy) are needed.

KEY TERMS

adaptive expectations   *(347)*
cost-push inflation   *(347)*
demand-pull inflation   *(347)*
expectations of inflation   *(349)*
incomes policy   *(361)*

induced recession   *(351)*
inflation   *(347)*
just-noticeable difference   *(359)*
long-run Phillips curve   *(349)*
monetary rule   *(354)*

natural rate of unemployment   *(354)*
Phillips curve   *(348)*
short-run Phillips curve   *(349)*
stagflation   *(355)*

QUESTIONS FOR THOUGHT AND REVIEW

The number after each question represents the estimated degree of critical thinking required. (1 = almost none; 10 = deep thought.)

1. Distinguish cost-push from demand-pull inflation.   *(2)*

2. Draw a short-run and a long-run Phillips curve.   *(2)*

3. How would a Keynesian explain the relatively stable inflation/unemployment trade-off existing before 1969?   *(5)*

4. How would a Classical economist explain the relatively stable inflation/unemployment trade-off existing before 1969?   *(9)*

5. What policy implications would a Classical draw from the quotation at the beginning of the chapter?   *(4)*

6. What policy implications would a Keynesian draw from the quotation at the beginning of the chapter?   *(6)*

7. What implication does the insider/outsider view of the economy have for macroeconomic policy?   *(6)*

8. What arguments would a Classical economist give in opposing an incomes policy?   *(3)*

9. Demonstrate graphically how an induced recession will eliminate stagflation.   *(4)*

10. The Phillips curve is nothing but a figment of economists' imagination. True or false?   *(9)*

PROBLEMS AND EXERCISES

1. People's perception of inflation often differs from actual inflation.
   a. List five goods that you buy relatively frequently.
   b. Looking in old newspapers (found in the library on microfiche), locate sale prices for these goods since 1950, finding one price every five years or so. Determine the average price rise of each of these five goods from 1950 until today.
   c. Compare that price rise with the rise in the Consumer Price Index.

2. Congratulations. You've just been appointed finance minister of Inflationland. Inflation has been ongoing for the past five years at 5 percent. The target rate of unemployment, 5 percent, is also the actual rate.
   a. Demonstrate the economy's likely position on both short-run and long-run Phillips curves.
   b. The president tells you she wants to be reelected. Devise a monetary policy strategy for her that might help her accomplish her goal.
   c. Demonstrate that strategy graphically, including the likely long-run consequences.

3. In the early 1990s, Argentina stopped increasing the money supply and fixed the exchange rate of the Argentine austral at 10,000 to the dollar. It then renamed the Argentine currency the "peso" and cut off four zeros so that one peso equaled one dollar. Inflation slowed substantially. After this was done, the following observations were made. Explain why these observations did not surprise economists.

   a. The golf courses were far less crowded.
   b. The price of goods in dollar-equivalent pesos in Buenos Aires, the capital of the country, was significantly above that in New York City.
   c. Consumer prices—primarily of services—rose relatively to other goods.
   d. Luxury auto dealers were shutting down.

4. Grade inflation is widespread. In 1990, 81 percent of the students who took the SATs had an A or B average, but 40 percent of them scored less than 390 on the verbal SAT. Students' grades are increasing but what they are learning is decreasing. Some economists argue that grade inflation should be dealt with in the same way that price inflation should be dealt with—by creating a fixed standard and requiring all grades to be specified relative to that standard. One way to accomplish this is to index the grades professors give: specify on the grade report both the student's grade and the class average, and deflate (or inflate) the professor's grade to some common standard.
   a. Discuss the advantages and disadvantages of such a proposal.
   b. What relationship does it have to economists' proposals for fixed exchange rates?

5. In 1990 Japan's money supply growth rate fell from 11–12 percent to 3–4 percent. What effect would you expect this decline to have on:
   a. Japanese real output?
   b. Japanese unemployment?
   c. Japanese inflation?

ANSWERS TO MARGIN QUESTIONS

1. The more unemployment there is, the more inflation is likely to be cost-push, since unemployment relates to excess supply. One should keep in mind, however, that the cost-push/demand-pull distinction is more useful for describing the *initial causes* of inflation than they are for describing an ongoing inflation. *(347)*

2. As you can see in the graph, the long-run Phillips curve is perfectly vertical. Its shape is dependent on the assumption that people's expectation of inflation completely adjusts to inflation in the long run, and that that adjustment is not institutionally constrained. *(350)*

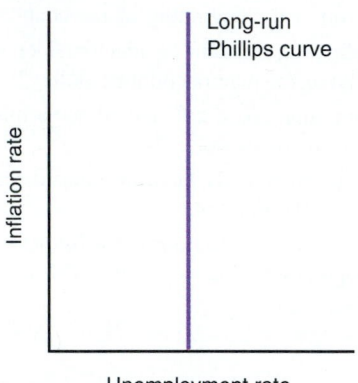

3. If people's expectations of inflation didn't change, the economy would stay on a short-run Phillips curve rather than move to the long-run Phillips curve. *(350)*

4. Classical theories of inflation are more likely to focus on money supply and competitive markets. Keynesian theories of inflation focus on institutional and structural problems in the market. *(352)*

5. Another name for Classical macroeconomists is "monetarists." *(352)*

6. "Inflation is everywhere and always a monetary phenomenon" is the sentence that best summarizes the Classical theory of inflation. *(353)*

7. If the economy is at point *A* on the Phillips curve below, inflation is below expected inflation and unemployment is higher than the target rate of unemployment. If this were the only information I had about the economy, I would expect both unemployment and inflation to fall. *(355)*

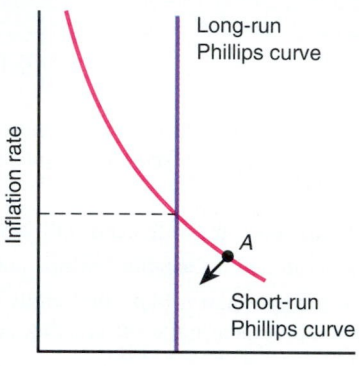

8. A Classical economist would likely say that the insider-outsider model of inflation tended to obscure the central cause of inflation: increases in the money supply. *(357)*

9. Keynesians would use the "just noticeable difference" concept to explain a relatively stable trade-off between inflation and employment that persists year after year. They see small changes in inflation as being too costly for people to adjust to, so they accept such changes without making adjustments. Most Keynesians see some flexibility between nominal and real rates. *(359)*

10. A Keynesian would be most likely to predict higher inflation. Classicals, who focus on the money supply, would say the price shock would be temporary and would essentially be a relative price change. *(359)*

16

International Dimensions of Monetary and Fiscal Policies

The actual rate of exchange is largely governed by the expected behavior of the country's monetary authority.

~Dennis Robertson

After reading this chapter, you should be able to:

1 Explain why there is significant debate about what U.S. international goals should be.

2 State why domestic goals generally dominate international goals.

3 Explain the paths through which monetary policy affects exchange rates and the trade balance.

4 Explain the paths through which fiscal policy affects exchange rates and the trade balance.

5 Summarize the reasons why governments try to coordinate their monetary and fiscal policies.

6 State the potential problem of internationalizing a country's debt.

In the 1990s, it's impossible to talk about macroeconomic policy without talking about international issues. That's what we do in this chapter: We discuss the effect that monetary and fiscal policies have on international macroeconomic goals, plus the effect that certain international phenomena have on domestic macroeconomic goals of low inflation, low unemployment, and high growth.

The discussion in this chapter is not totally new to you. Earlier chapters have introduced you to many international concepts and touched upon the international dimensions of fiscal and monetary policies. But now it's time to put those discussions together and consider the issues more carefully. This discussion will provide you with the necessary international base for understanding the macroeconomic policy you'll be reading about in the newspapers. In the next chapter we'll consider international finance in more depth.

THE AMBIGUOUS INTERNATIONAL GOALS OF MACROECONOMIC POLICY

Macroeconomics' international goals are less straightforward than its domestic goals. There is general agreement about the domestic goals of macroeconomic policy: We want low inflation, low unemployment, and high growth. There's far less agreement on what a country's international goals should be.

Most economists agree that the international goal of U.S. macroeconomic policy is to maintain the U.S. position in the world economy. But there's enormous debate about what achieving that goal means. Do we want a high or a low exchange rate? Do we want a balance of trade surplus? Or would it be better to have a balance of trade deficit? Or should we not even pay attention to the balance of trade? Let's consider the exchange rate goal first.

The Exchange Rate Goal

An **exchange rate** is the rate at which one country's currency can be traded for another country's currency. We discuss exchange rates at length in the next chapter; for now, let's briefly consider the three types of exchange rates that exist.

Exchange rate The rate at which one country's currency can be traded for another country's currency.

Fixed and Flexible Exchange Rates Countries can have fixed exchange rates, flexible exchange rates, or a partially flexible exchange rate. With a **fixed exchange rate,** the exchange rates are set and governments are committed to buying and selling currencies at a fixed rate. With a **flexible exchange rate,** the exchange rate is set by market forces (supply and demand for a country's currency). With a **partially flexible exchange rate,** the government sometimes buys and sells currencies to influence the price directly, and at other times the government simply accepts the exchange rate determined by supply and demand forces. In the 1990s, the United States uses a partially flexible exchange rate.

Q–1: If a country has flexible exchange rates, how can it influence those exchange rates?

In this chapter, to keep the analysis at a manageable level, I assume that the country in question has a flexible exchange rate. Thus, it accepts that its exchange rate will be determined by the forces of supply and demand. But that doesn't mean that the country can't indirectly influence the exchange rate through monetary and fiscal policies' effects on the economy and on the supply and demand for dollars. It is that indirect effect that we focus on in this chapter. In the following chapter on international finance, I extend the analysis to include a country's ability to affect exchange rates directly.

Do Countries Want a High or a Low Exchange Rate? There is a debate over whether a country should have a high or a low exchange rate. A high exchange rate for the dollar makes foreign currencies cheaper, lowering the price of imports. Lowering import prices places competitive pressure on U.S. firms and helps to hold down inflation. All of this benefits U.S. residents' living standard. But a high exchange rate encourages imports and discourages exports. In doing so, it can cause a balance of trade deficit which can exert a contractionary effect on the economy by decreasing aggregate demand for U.S. output. So a high exchange rate also has a cost to U.S. residents.

Q–2: What effect does a low exchange rate have on a country's exports and imports?

A low exchange rate has the opposite effect. It makes imports more expensive and exports cheaper, and it can contribute to inflationary pressure. But, by encouraging exports and discouraging imports, it can cause a balance of trade surplus and exert an expansionary effect on the economy.

Thus, depending on the state of the economy, there are arguments for both high and low exchange rates. Hence there's often a divergence of views about what the exchange rate goal should be. Because of that divergence of views, many economists argue that a country should have no exchange rate policy because exchange rates are market-determined prices that are best left to the market. These economists question whether the government should even worry about the effect of monetary policy and fiscal policy on exchange rates. According to them, government should simply accept whatever exchange rate exists and not consider it in its conduct of monetary and fiscal policies.

1 Exchange rates have conflicting effects and, depending on the state of the economy, there are arguments for both high and low exchange rates.

The Trade Balance Goal

A deficit in the **trade balance** (the difference between imports and exports) means that, as a country, we're consuming more than we're producing. Imports exceed exports, so we're consuming more than we could if we didn't run a deficit. A surplus in the trade balance means that exports exceed imports—we're producing more than we're consuming. Since consuming more than we otherwise could is kind of nice, it might seem that a trade deficit is preferred to a trade surplus.

Trade balance *The difference between a country's exports and its imports.*

But wait. A trade deficit isn't without costs, and a trade surplus isn't without benefits. We pay for a trade deficit by selling off U.S. assets to foreigners—by selling U.S. companies, factories, land, and buildings to foreigners, or selling them financial assets such as U.S. dollars, stocks, and bonds. All the future interest and profits on these assets will go to foreigners, not U.S. citizens. That means eventually, some time in the future, we will have to produce more than we consume so we can pay them *their* profit and interest on *their* assets. Thus, while in the short run a trade deficit allows more current consumption, in the long run it presents problems.

As long as a country can borrow, or sell assets, a country can have a trade deficit. But if a country runs a trade deficit year after year, eventually the long run will arrive and the country will run out of assets to sell and run out of other countries from whom to borrow. When that happens, the trade deficit problem must be faced.

World Economic Outlook—This IMF publication provides useful economic surveys of problems facing the world economy.

The debate about whether a trade deficit should be of concern to policy makers involves whether these long-run effects should be anticipated and faced before they happen.

Opinions differ greatly. Some say not to worry. We should accept what's happening and not concern ourselves about a trade deficit. These "not-to-worry" economists argue that the trade deficit will end when U.S. citizens don't want to borrow from foreigners any more and foreigners don't want to buy any more of our assets. They argue that the inflow of financial capital (money coming into the United States to buy our assets) from foreigners is financing new investment which will make the U.S. economy strong enough in the long run to reverse the trade deficit without serious disruption to the U.S. economy. So why deal with the trade deficit now when it will take care of itself in the future?

1 Running a trade deficit is good in the short run but presents problems in the long run; thus there is debate about whether we should worry about a trade deficit or not.

Others argue that, yes, the trade deficit will eventually take care of itself, but the economic distress accompanying the trade deficit taking care of itself will be great. By dealing with the problem now, the United States can avoid a highly unpleasant solution in the future.

Q–3: Why do some people argue that we should not worry about a trade deficit?

Both views are reasonable, which is why there's no consensus on what a country's trade balance goal should be.

International versus Domestic Goals

In the real world, when there's debate about a goal, that goal generally gets far less weight than goals about which there's general agreement. Since there's general agreement about our country's domestic goals (low inflation, low unemployment, and high growth), domestic goals generally dominate the U.S. political agenda.

2 Domestic goals generally dominate international goals because (1) international goals are ambiguous, and (2) international goals affect a country's population indirectly and, in politics, indirect effects take a back seat

Even if there weren't uncertainty about a country's international goals, domestic goals would likely dominate the political agenda. The reason is that inflation, unemployment, and growth affect a country's citizens directly. Trade deficits and exchange rates affect them indirectly—and in politics, indirect effects take a back seat.

Often a country responds to an international goal only when the international community forces it to do so. For example, when in the 1980s Brazil couldn't borrow any more money from other countries, it reluctantly made resolving its trade deficit a key goal. Similarly, when other countries threatened to limit Japanese imports, Japan took steps to increase the value of the yen and decrease its trade surplus. When a country is forced to face certain economic facts, international goals can become its primary goals. As countries become more economically integrated, these pressures from other countries become more important.

THE EFFECTS OF MONETARY AND FISCAL POLICIES ON INTERNATIONAL GOALS

To say that achieving international goals is not the determining factor in the choice of macroeconomic policies isn't to say that economists don't consider the effects of monetary and fiscal policies on international goals. They watch these carefully.

For example, the United States ran trade deficits through much of the 1980s and early 1990s. By the late 1980s other countries were placing heavy pressure on the United States to do something. You can understand U.S. macroeconomic policy during that period only if you understand that international pressure. To follow the debates about macroeconomic policy, you must be familiar with how monetary and fiscal policies affect the exchange rate and the trade balance. Those effects often can significantly influence the choice of policies. We begin by considering the effect of monetary policy.

Monetary Policy's Effect on Exchange Rates

Monetary policy affects exchange rates in three ways: (1) through its effect on the interest rate, (2) through its effect on income, and (3) through its effect on price levels and inflation.

Q-4: What effect does the lowering of a country's interest rates have on exchange rates?

The Effect on Exchange Rates via Interest Rates   Expansionary monetary policy pushes down the U.S. interest rate, which decreases the financial capital inflow into the United States, decreasing the demand for dollars, pushing down the value of the dollar, and decreasing the U.S. exchange rate via the interest rate path. Contractionary monetary policy does the opposite. It raises the U.S. interest rate, which tends to bring in financial capital flows from abroad, increasing the demand for dollars, increasing the value of the dollar, and increasing the U.S. exchange rate.

To see why these effects take place, consider a person in Japan in the late 1980s, when the Japanese interest rate was about 2 or 3 percent. He or she reasoned, "Why should I earn only 2 or 3 percent return in Japan? I'll save (buy some financial assets) in the United States where I'll earn 8 percent." If the U.S. interest rate goes up due to contraction in the money supply, other things equal, the advantage of holding one's financial assets in the United States will become even greater and more people will want to save here. People in Japan hold yen, not dollars, so in order to save in the United States they must buy dollars. Thus, a rise in U.S. interest rates increases demand for dollars and, in terms of yen, pushes the U.S. exchange rate up.

It's important to recognize that it's the relative interest rates that govern the flow of financial capital. In the early 1990s, Japan tightened its money supply, raising interest rates there to 6 percent. This relative increase in the Japanese interest rate decreased demand for dollars and thus lowered the U.S. exchange rate.

Another example of how important relative international interest rates are involves Germany and the European Union (EU). In 1992, the EU was heading toward a monetary union in which all member countries would use a common currency. As a stepping stone, the EU countries had exchange rates set within a narrow band. Because of fiscal problems caused by German reunification, The German central bank, the Bundesbank, felt it had to raise its interest rates. That rise put upward pressure on the mark, and destroyed the fixed exchange rate system and the upcoming monetary union. Many economists are willing to say that relative interest rates, because of their importance in the short run, are *the primary* short-run determinant of exchange rates.

The Effect on Exchange Rates via Income   Monetary policy also affects income in a country. As money supply rises, income expands; when money supply falls, income

For international trade to take place, currencies must be convertible into other currencies. Here we see a Japanese currency trader taking bids on buying and selling currencies. *Fujifotos/The Image Works.*

contracts.[1] This effect on income provides another way the money supply affects the exchange rate. As we saw earlier, when income rises, imports rise while exports are unaffected. To buy foreign products, U.S. citizens need foreign currency which they must buy with dollars. So when U.S. imports rise, the supply of dollars to the foreign exchange market increases as U.S. citizens sell dollars to buy foreign currencies to pay for those imports. This decreases the dollar exchange rate. This effect through income and imports provides a second path through which monetary policy affects the exchange rate: Expansionary monetary policy causes U.S. income to rise, imports to rise, and the U.S. exchange rate to fall via the income path. Contractionary monetary policy causes U.S. income to fall, imports to fall, and the U.S. exchange rate to rise via the income path.

The Effect on Exchange Rates via Price Levels   A third way in which monetary policy can affect exchange rates is through its effect on prices in a country. Expansionary monetary policy pushes the U.S. price level up. As the U.S. price level rises relative to foreign prices, U.S. exports become more expensive, and goods the United States imports become cheaper, decreasing U.S. competitiveness. This increases demand for foreign currencies and decreases demand for dollars. Thus, via the price path, expansionary monetary policy pushes down the dollar's value for the same reason that an expansion in income pushes it down.

Contractionary monetary policy puts downward pressure on the U.S. price level and slows down any existing inflation. This tends to decrease the U.S. price level relative to foreign prices, making U.S. exports more competitive and the goods the United States imports more expensive. Thus, contractionary policy pushes the value of the dollar up via the price path.

The Net Effect of Monetary Policy on Exchange Rates   Notice that all these effects of monetary policy on exchange rates are in the same direction. Expansionary monetary policy pushes a country's exchange rate down; contractionary monetary policy pushes

Q–5: What effect would contractionary monetary money policy have on a country's exchange rates via the income and price routes?

---

[1] When there's inflation, it's the rate of money supply growth relative to the rate of inflation that's important. If inflation is 10 percent and money supply growth is 10 percent, the rate of increase in the real money supply is zero. If money supply growth falls to, say, 5 percent while inflation stays at 10 percent, there will be a contractionary effect on the real economy.

a country's exchange rate up. Summarizing these effects, we have the following relationships for expansionary and contractionary monetary policy:

3 Monetary policy affects exchange rates through the interest rate path, the income path, and the price level path, as shown in the accompanying diagram.

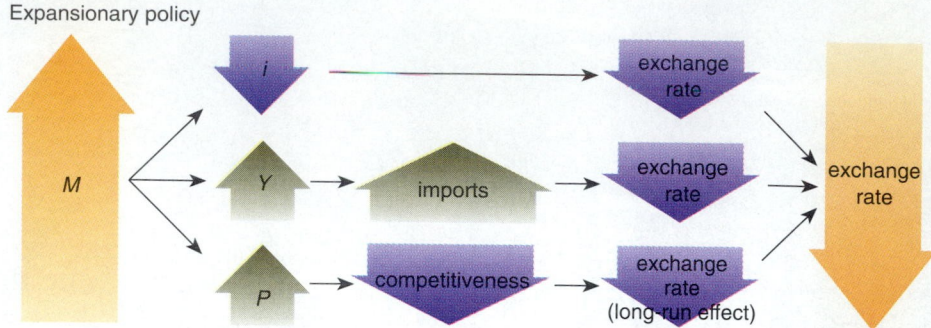

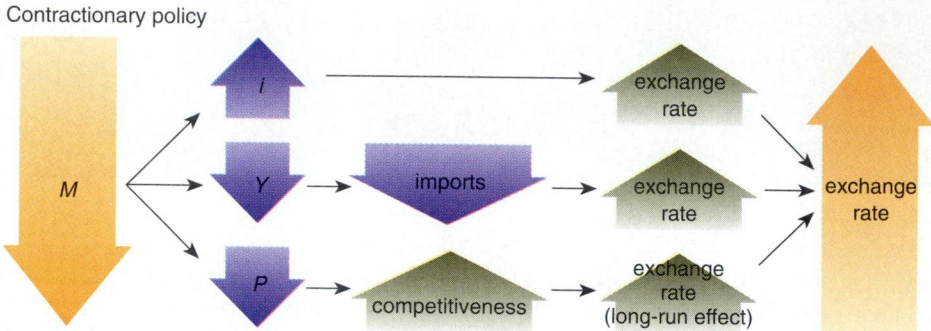

There are, of course, many provisos to the relationship between monetary policy and the exchange rate. For example, as the price of imports goes up, there is some inflationary pressure from that rise in price and hence some pressure for the price level to rise as well as fall. Monetary policy affects exchange rates in subtle ways, but if an economist had to give a quick answer to what effect monetary policy would have on exchange rates it would be:

Expansionary monetary policy lowers exchange rates. It decreases the relative value of a country's currency.

Contractionary monetary policy increases exchange rates. It increases the relative value of a country's currency.

Expansionary monetary policy lowers exchange rates. It decreases the relative value of a country's currency.

Contractionary monetary policy increases exchange rates. It increases the relative value of a country's currency.

Monetary Policy's Effect on the Trade Balance

When a country's international trade balance is negative (in deficit), the country is importing more than it is exporting. When a country's international trade balance is positive, the country is exporting more than it is importing.

Monetary policy affects the trade balance in three ways: through income, through the price level, and through the exchange rate.

The Effect on the Trade Balance via Income
Expansionary monetary policy increases income. When income rises, imports rise, while exports are unaffected. As imports rise, the trade balance shifts in the direction of deficit. So, via the income path, expansionary monetary policy shifts the trade balance toward a deficit.

Contractionary policy works in the opposite direction. It decreases income. When income falls, imports fall, while exports are unaffected, so the trade balance shifts in the direction of surplus. Thus, via the income path, expansionary monetary policy increases the trade deficit; contractionary monetary policy decreases the trade deficit.

The Effect on the Trade Balance via Price Levels
A second way monetary policy affects the trade balance is through its effect on a country's price level. Expansionary monetary policy pushes a country's price level up. This decreases its competitiveness and increases a trade deficit. So, via the price path, expansionary monetary policy increases a trade deficit.

Contractionary monetary policy works in the opposite direction. It tends to push a country's price level down; this fall makes exports more competitive and imports less competitive. Both these effects tend to decrease a trade deficit. So, via the price path, contractionary monetary policy decreases a trade deficit.

Monetary policy's effect on the price level is a long-run, not a short-run, effect. It often takes a year for changes in the money supply to affect prices, and another year or two for changes in prices to affect imports and exports. Thus, the price path is a long-run effect. Price level changes don't significantly affect the trade balance in the short run.

The Effect on the Trade Balance via Exchange Rates   A third path through which expansionary monetary policy influences the trade balance is the exchange rate. Expansionary U.S. monetary policy decreases the interest rate which tends to push the dollar exchange rate down, increasing U.S. competitiveness. This decreases a trade deficit and hence works in a direction opposite to the effects of income changes and price level changes on the trade balance. Like the price level effect, the effect of the exchange rate on the trade balance is a long-run effect. This path doesn't have a significant effect in the short run.

Contractionary monetary policy works in the opposite direction. It raises the exchange rate, increasing the relative price of U.S. exports and lowering the relative price of imports into the United States. Both effects tend to increase a trade deficit.

Q–6: What effect will contractionary monetary policy have on the trade balance through the price level and income paths?

The Net Effect of Monetary Policy on the Trade Balance   Since the effects are not all in the same direction, talking about the net effect of monetary policy on the trade balance is a bit more ambiguous than talking about its net effect on a country's exchange rate. However, only one of these paths—the income path—is a short-run effect. Thus, in the short run the net effect of monetary policy is relatively clear: Expansionary monetary policy tends to increase a trade deficit; contractionary monetary policy tends to decrease it. Since, in the long run, the price path effect and the exchange rate effect tend to offset each other, the short-run effects of monetary policy through the income path often carry over to the long-run effect.

Q–7: What will be the net effect of contractionary monetary policy on the trade balance?

Summarizing these three relationships, we have the following relationships for expansionary and contractionary monetary policy:

3 Monetary policy affects the trade deficit through the income path, the price level path, and the exchange rate path, as shown in the accompanying diagram.

Expansionary monetary policy makes a trade deficit larger.

Contractionary monetary policy makes a trade deficit smaller.

While many complications can enter the trade balance picture, most economists would summarize monetary policy's short-run effect on the trade balance as follows:

Expansionary monetary policy makes a trade deficit larger.
Contractionary monetary policy makes a trade deficit smaller.

Fiscal Policy's Effect on Exchange Rates

Now we'll consider fiscal policy's effect on exchange rates. Fiscal policy, like monetary policy, affects exchange rates via three paths: via income, via price, and via interest rates. Let's begin with its effect through income.

The Effect on Exchange Rates via Income   Expansionary fiscal policy expands income and therefore increases imports, increasing the trade deficit and lowering the exchange rate. Contractionary fiscal policy contracts income, thereby decreasing imports and increasing the exchange rate. These effects of expansionary and contractionary fiscal policies via the income path are similar to the effects of monetary policy, so if it's not intuitively clear to you why the effect is what it is, it may be worthwhile to review the slightly more complete discussion of monetary policy's effect presented previously.

The Effect on Exchange Rates via Price Levels   Let's turn to the effect of fiscal policy on exchange rates through prices. Expansionary fiscal policy increases aggregate demand and increases prices of a country's exports; hence it decreases the competitiveness of a country's exports, which pushes down the exchange rate. Contractionary fiscal policy works in the opposite direction. These are the same effects that monetary policy had. And, as was the case with monetary policy, the price path is a long-run effect.

The Effect on Exchange Rates via Interest Rates   Fiscal policy's effect on the exchange rate via the interest rate path is different from monetary policy's effect. Let's first consider the effect of expansionary fiscal policy. Whereas expansionary monetary policy lowers the interest rate, expansionary fiscal policy raises interest rates because the government sells bonds to finance that deficit. The higher U.S. interest rate causes foreign capital to flow into the United States, which pushes up the U.S. exchange rate. Therefore expansionary fiscal policy's effect on exchange rates via the interest rate effect is to push up a country's exchange rate.

Contractionary fiscal policy decreases interest rates since it reduces the bond financing of that deficit. Lower U.S. interest rates cause capital to flow out of the United States, which pushes down the U.S. exchange rate.

Q–8: What is the net effect of expansionary fiscal policy on the exchange rate?

The Net Effect of Fiscal Policy on Exchange Rates   Of these three effects, the interest rate effect and the income effect are both short-run effects. These two work in opposite directions to each other, so the net effect of fiscal policy on the exchange rate is ambiguous. Let's summarize these three effects.

4   Fiscal policy affects exchange rates through the income path, the interest rate path, and the exchange rate path, as shown in the accompanying diagram.

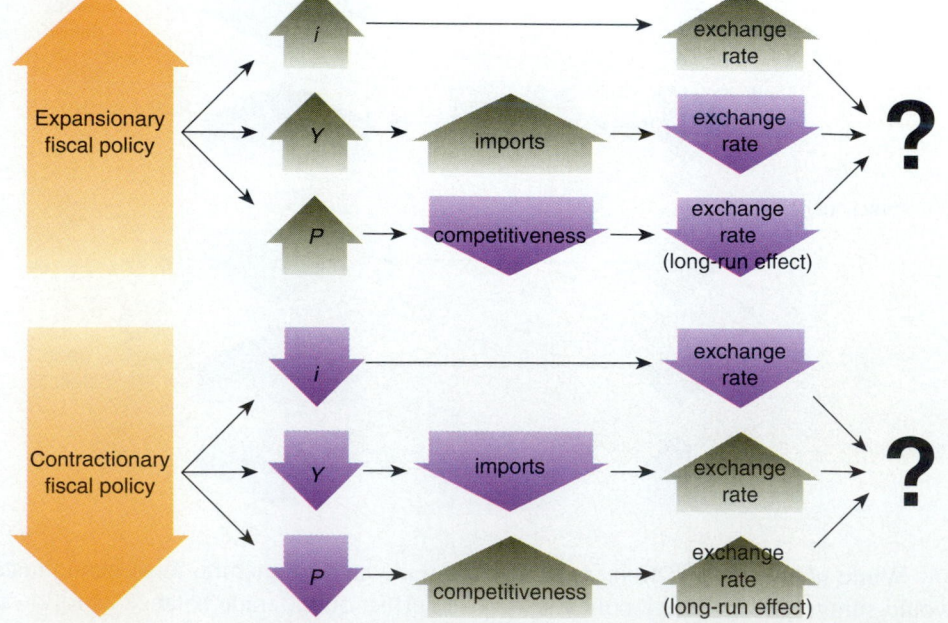

Thus, it's unclear what the effect of expansionary or contractionary fiscal policy will be on exchange rates.

Fiscal policy works on the trade deficit primarily through its effects on income and prices. (Since fiscal policy's effect on the exchange rate is unclear, there is no need to consider its effect through exchange rates.)

Fiscal Policy's Effect on the Trade Deficit

The Effect on the Trade Deficit via Income   Let's begin by looking at the income path. As with expansionary monetary policy, expansionary fiscal policy increases income. This higher income increases imports, which increases the size of the trade deficit.

Contractionary fiscal policy decreases income and decreases imports. Hence it decreases the size of a trade deficit. These are the same effects as those of monetary policy.

The Effect on the Trade Deficit via Prices   The effect via the price level route is also similar to the effects of monetary policy. Expansionary fiscal policy pushes up the price level, increasing the price of a country's exports and decreasing its competitiveness. Hence it increases the trade deficit.

Contractionary fiscal policy pushes down the price level, decreasing the price of a country's exports, increasing its competitiveness, and decreasing the trade deficit. This effect via price is a long-run effect, as it is with monetary policy.

The Net Effect of Fiscal Policy on the Trade Deficit   Since these two effects work in the same direction, fiscal policy's net effect on the trade balance is clear:

   Expansionary fiscal policy increases a trade deficit.

   Contractionary fiscal policy decreases a trade deficit.

   Summarizing these two effects schematically, we have:

Expansionary fiscal policy increases a trade deficit.

Contractionary fiscal policy decreases a trade deficit.

4 Fiscal policy affects the trade balance through the income path and the price level path, as shown in the accompanying diagram.

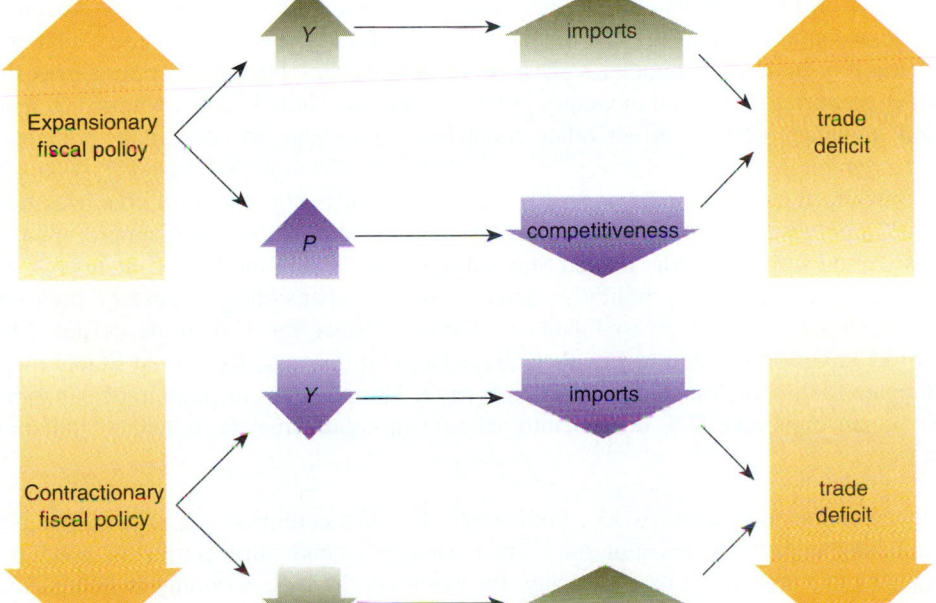

Exhibit 1 summarizes the primary net short-run effects of both expansionary monetary and fiscal policies on international goals. (The effects of contractionary policy work in the opposite direction.)

Q–9: What is the net effect of expansionary fiscal policy on the trade deficit?

So far, we've focused on the effect of monetary and fiscal policies on international goals. But often the effect is the other way around: International phenomena change and have significant influences on the domestic economy and on the ability to achieve domestic goals.

INTERNATIONAL PHENOMENA AND DOMESTIC GOALS

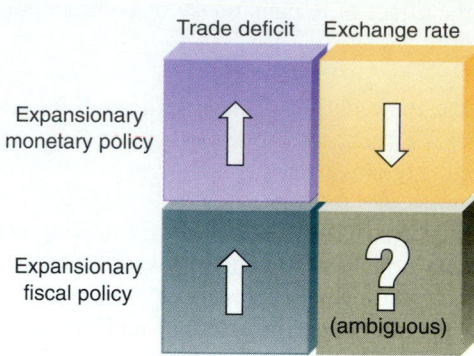

EXHIBIT 1   **The Effect of Expansionary Monetary and Fiscal Policy on International Goals**

In the short run, expansionary monetary policy tends to increase a trade deficit and decrease the exchange rate. Expansionary fiscal policy tends to increase the trade deficit. Its effect on the exchange rate is ambiguous.

For example, say that Japan ran contractionary monetary policy. That would increase the Japanese exchange rate and increase Japan's trade surplus, which means it would decrease the U.S. exchange rate and increase the U.S. trade deficit, both of which would affect U.S. domestic goals. So the monetary and fiscal policies of other countries can have significant effects on the U.S. domestic economy. This has led to significant pressure for countries to coordinate their economic policies.

International Monetary and Fiscal Coordination

5 Governments try to coordinate their monetary and fiscal policies because their economies are interdependent.

Unless forced to do so because of international pressures, most countries don't let international goals guide their macroeconomic policy. But for every effect that monetary and fiscal policies have on a country's exchange rates and trade balance, there's an equal and opposite effect on the combination of other countries' exchange rates and trade balances. When one country's exchange rate goes up, by definition another country's exchange rate must go down. Similarly, when one country's balance of trade is in surplus, another's must be in deficit. This interconnection means that other countries' fiscal and monetary policies affect the United States, while U.S. fiscal and monetary policies affect other countries, so pressure to coordinate policies is considerable.

Because of this interdependence, many economists argue that all countries must work together to coordinate their monetary and fiscal policies. For example, if Japan has a trade surplus and the United States has a trade deficit, the United States can run contractionary monetary policy or Japan can use expansionary monetary policy to help expand U.S. exports to Japan and thereby reduce the U.S. trade deficit. Why would Japan do something like that? Because, if it doesn't, the United States might threaten to directly limit Japanese exports to the United States through trade sanctions. So Japan must take U.S. desires into account in conducting its monetary and fiscal policies.

Coordination Is a Two-Way Street

Q-10: If domestic problems call for expansionary monetary policy and international problems call for contractionary monetary policy, what policy will a country likely adopt?

Coordination, of course, works both ways. If other countries are to take the U.S. economy's needs into account, the United States must take other countries' needs into account in determining its goals. Say, for example, the U.S. economy is going into a recession. This domestic problem calls for expansionary monetary policy. But expansionary monetary policy will increase U.S. income and U.S. imports and lower the value of the dollar. Say that, internationally, the United States has agreed that it must work toward eliminating the U.S. trade deficit in the short run. Does it forsake its domestic goals? Or does it forsake its international commitment?

There's no one right answer to those questions. It depends on political judgments (how long until the next election?), judgments about what foreign countries can do if the United States doesn't meet its international commitments, and similar judgments by foreign countries about the United States. The result is lots of international

The world has become much more interdependent in recent years. In this picture you see cars made in Germany being unloaded for sale in the United States. © *David Wells/The Image Works.*

economic parleys (generally in rather pleasant surroundings) to discuss these issues. Nicely worded communiques are issued which say, in effect, that each country will do what's best for the world economy as long as it's also best for itself.

Each country will likely do what's best for the world economy as long as it's also best for itself.

Crowding Out and International Considerations

As a final topic in this chapter, let's reconsider the issue of *crowding out* that we considered in an earlier chapter, only this time we'll take into account international considerations. Say a government is running a budget deficit, and that the central bank has decided it won't accommodate the deficit. This happened in the 1980s with the Fed and the U.S. government. What will be the result?

The basic idea of crowding out is that the budget deficit will cause the interest rate to go up. But wait. There's another way to avoid the crowding out that results from financing the deficit: Foreigners could buy the debt at the existing interest rate. This is called *internationalizing the debt,* and is what happened to the U.S. economy in the late 1980s.

In the 1980s, there were massive inflows of financial capital from abroad. These inflows held down the U.S. interest rate even as the federal government ran large budget deficits. Thus, those large deficits didn't push up interest rates because foreigners, not U.S. citizens, were buying U.S. debt.

But, as we discussed, internationalization of the U.S. debt is not costless. While it helps in the short run, it presents problems in the long run. Foreign ownership of U.S. debt means that the United States must pay foreigners interest each year on that debt. To do so, the United States must export more than it imports, which means that the United States must consume less than it produces at some time in the future to pay for the trade deficits it's running now.

As you can see, the issues become complicated quickly.

Despite the complications, the above discussion gives you an understanding of many of the events that may have previously seemed incomprehensible. To show you the relevance of what I have said above about crowding out and international considerations, let's look at two situations that occurred in the early 1990s.

The first concerned Germany and the EU (discussed above). For political reasons, Germany was running loose fiscal policy. Fearing inflation from this loose fiscal policy, the Bundesbank ran tight monetary policy, forcing both the German interest rate and the German exchange rate up. This disrupted the movement toward a European Monetary System and a common European currency—the ECU—as other European countries refused to go along. Here we see domestic goals superseding international goals.

6 While internationalizing a country's debt may help in the short run, in the long run it presents potential problems, since foreign ownership of a country's debts means the country must pay interest to those foreign countries and that debt may come due.

The second concerns Japan in 1993 and early 1994. Japan was experiencing a recession, in part because its tight monetary policy had pushed up interest rates and hence pushed up the exchange rate for the year. Other countries, especially the United States and European countries, put enormous pressure on Japan to run expansionary fiscal policy which would keep the relative value of the yen high, but simultaneously increase Japanese income, and hence Japanese demand for imports.

There are many more examples, but these two should give you a good sense of the relevance of the issues.

CONCLUSION: SELECTING POLICIES TO ACHIEVE GOALS

Throughout this chapter I have organized the discussion around the effects of policies. Another way to organize the discussion would have been around goals, and to show how alternative policies will achieve those international goals.

The following table does this, and will serve as a useful review of the chapter. It shows alternative policies that will achieve specified goals.

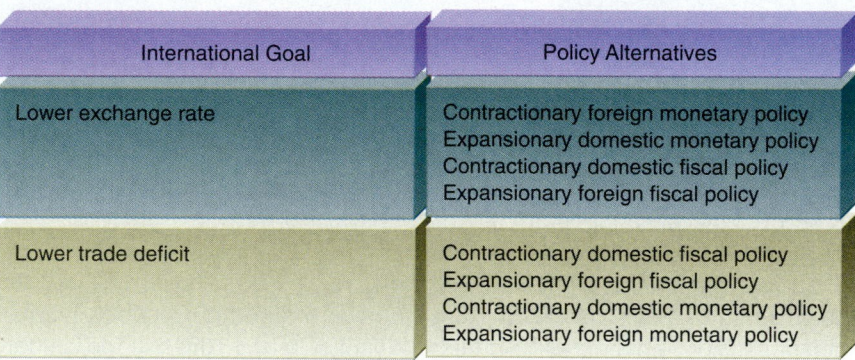

International Goal	Policy Alternatives
Lower exchange rate	Contractionary foreign monetary policy Expansionary domestic monetary policy Contractionary domestic fiscal policy Expansionary foreign fiscal policy
Lower trade deficit	Contractionary domestic fiscal policy Expansionary foreign fiscal policy Contractionary domestic monetary policy Expansionary foreign monetary policy

EXHIBIT 2 **Selecting Policies to Achieve Goals**

You can see in the table why coordination of monetary and fiscal policies is much in the news, since a foreign country's policy can eliminate or reduce the need for domestic policy.

This brief chapter in no way exhausted the international topics. Countries use many policies to effect their international goals. But this chapter has, I hope, made you very aware of the international dimensions of our economic goals, and of how monetary and fiscal policies affect those goals. That awareness is necessary to discuss the real-world macroeconomic policies that we turn to in the next chapter.

CHAPTER SUMMARY

- The international goals of a country are often in dispute.
- Domestic goals generally dominate international goals; countries often respond to an international goal when forced to do so by other countries.
- Expansionary monetary policy tends to lower a country's exchange rate and increase its trade deficit.
- Contractionary fiscal policy has an ambiguous effect on a country's exchange rate but tends to decrease its trade deficit.

- For every effect that monetary and fiscal policies have on a country's exchange rate and trade balance, there is an equal and opposite effect on the combination of foreign countries' exchange rates and trade balances.
- International capital inflows can reduce crowding out.
- Internationalizing a country's debt means that at some time in the future the country must consume less than it produces.

KEY TERMS

exchange rate *(366)*   partially flexible exchange rate *(366)*   trade balance *(367)*
fixed exchange rate *(366)*
flexible exchange rate *(366)*

QUESTIONS FOR THOUGHT AND REVIEW

The number after each question represents the estimated degree of critical thinking required. (1 = almost none; 10 = deep thought.)

1. Look up the current U.S. exchange rate relative to the yen. Would you suggest raising it or lowering it? Why? *(7)*

2. Look up the current U.S. trade balance. Would you suggest raising it or lowering it? Why? *(7)*

3. What effect on the U.S. trade deficit and exchange rate would result if Japan ran an expansionary monetary policy? *(4)*

4. What would be the effect on the U.S. trade deficit and the U.S. exchange rate if Japan ran a contractionary fiscal policy? *(4)*

5. If modern Classicals are correct and expansionary monetary policy immediately increases inflationary expectations and the price level, how might the effect of monetary policy on the exchange rate be different than that presented in this chapter? *(9)*

6. What effect will a combination of expansionary fiscal policy and contractionary monetary policy have on the exchange rate? *(5)*

7. How would a Classical economist differ from a Keynesian economist in their policies for dealing with an oil price shock? Why? *(8)*

8. Is the United States justified in complaining of Japan's use of an export-led growth policy? Why? *(8)*

9. What effect would you expect a fall in the price of oil to have on the U.S. economy? Why? *(6)*

10. How is the Bundesbank's running a tight monetary policy in the early 1990s an example of domestic goals superseding international goals? *(2)*

PROBLEMS AND EXERCISES

1. Draw the schematics to show the effect of contractionary fiscal policy on exchange rates.

2. Draw the schematics to show the effect of expansionary monetary policy on the trade deficit.

3. You observe that over the past decade a country's competitiveness has been continually eroded and its trade deficit has risen.
   a. What monetary or fiscal policies might have led to such results? Why?
   b. You also observe that interest rates have steadily risen along with a rise in the exchange rate. What policies would lead to this result?
   c. What policy might you suggest to improve the country's competitiveness? Explain how that policy might work.

4. Congratulations! You have been appointed an adviser to the IMF. A country that has run trade deficits for many years now has difficulty servicing the accumulated international debt and wants to borrow from the IMF to meet its obligations. The IMF requires that the country set a target trade surplus.

   a. What monetary and fiscal policies would you suggest the IMF require of that country?
   b. What would be the likely effect of that plan on domestic inflation and growth?
   c. How do you think the country's government will respond to your proposals? Why?

5. Congratulations! You've been hired as an economic advisor to Textland, a country that has perfectly flexible exchange rates. State what monetary and fiscal policy you might suggest in each of the following situations, and explain why you would suggest those policies.
   a. You want to lower the interest rate, decrease inflationary pressures, and lower the trade deficit.
   b. You want to lower the interest rate, decrease inflationary pressures, and lower a trade surplus.
   c. You want to lower the interest rate, decrease unemployment, and lower the trade deficit.
   d. You want to raise the interest rate, decrease unemployment, and lower the trade deficit.

ANSWERS TO MARGIN QUESTIONS

1. A country can influence its exchange rates indirectly through its monetary and fiscal policies. Contractionary monetary policy pushes up the exchange rate; contractionary fiscal policy pushes down the exchange rate. *(366)*

2. A low exchange rate of a country's currency will tend to stimulate exports and curtail imports. *(366)*

3. A trade deficit means a country is consuming more than it is producing. Consuming more than you produce is pleasant. It also means that capital is flowing into the

country, which can be used for investment. So why worry? *(367)*

4. A fall in a country's interest rate will push down its exchange rate. *(368)*

5. Contractionary monetary policy pushes up the interest rate, decreases income and hence imports, and has a tendency to decrease inflation. Therefore, through these paths, contractionary monetary policy will tend to increase the exchange rate. *(369)*

6. Contractionary monetary policy will tend to decrease income and the price levels, decreasing imports and increasing competitiveness. Since the income and price level paths work in the same direction, contractionary monetary policy is likely to decrease the trade deficit. The exchange rate path can, however, work in the opposite direction. *(371)*

7. In the short run, the net effect of contractionary monetary policy on the trade balance is to decrease the trade deficit, or increase the trade surplus. *(372)*

8. The net effect of expansionary fiscal policy on exchange rates is uncertain. Through the interest rate effect it pushes up the exchange rate, but through the income and price level effects it pushes down the exchange rate. *(372)*

9. The net effect of expansionary fiscal policy on the trade deficit is to increase the trade deficit. *(373)*

10. Generally, when domestic policies and international policies conflict, a country will choose to deal with its domestic problems. Thus, it will likely use expansionary monetary policy if domestic problems call for that. *(374)*

17

International Finance

A foreign exchange dealer's office during a busy spell is the nearest thing to Bedlam I have struck.

~Harold Wincott

After reading this chapter, you should be able to:

1 Describe the balance of payments and the balance of trade.

2 Explain why a country might have simultaneously a balance of trade surplus and a balance of payments deficit.

3 Discuss how real-world exchange rates are set.

4 Explain why many developing countries have nonconvertible currencies.

5 Differentiate fixed, floating, partially floating, and nonconvertible exchange rates, and discuss the advantages and disadvantages of each.

6 Give a brief history of the gold standard.

As I have emphasized throughout the book, in the 1990s economic questions must be considered in an international setting. Earlier chapters introduced international financial issues such as exchange rates and the balance of payments. This chapter expands on those discussions and presents the central issues of international finance.

Let's first review two conclusions of the last chapter. In the short run:

Expansionary monetary policy pushes down the exchange rate and increases the trade deficit; contractionary monetary policy does the opposite.

Expansionary fiscal policy has an ambiguous effect on the exchange rate, but, like expansionary monetary policy, it increases the trade deficit; contractionary fiscal policy does the opposite.

You should be able to work through the reasons expansionary monetary and fiscal policies have those effects. If not, you will benefit from a review of earlier chapters.

THE BALANCE OF PAYMENTS

1A The balance of payments is a country's record of all transactions between its residents and the residents of all foreign countries.

The best door into an in-depth discussion of international financial issues is a discussion of **balance of payments** (a country's record of all transactions between its residents and the residents of all foreign nations).[1] These include buying and selling of goods and services (imports and exports), interest and profit payments from previous investments, together with all the capital inflows and outflows. Exhibit 1 presents the 1987 and 1993 balance of payments accounts for the United States. It records all payments made by foreigners to U.S. citizens and all payments made by U.S. citizens to foreigners in those years.

In the balance of payments accounts, flows of payments into the United States have a plus sign. Goods the U.S. exports must be paid for in dollars; they involve a flow of payments into the United States, so they have a plus sign. Similarly, U.S. imports must be paid for in foreign currency; they involve a flow of dollars out of the United States and, thus, they have a minus sign. Notice that the bottom line of the balance of payments is $0. By definition, the bottom line (which includes *all* supplies and demands for currencies, including those of the government) must add up to zero.

Current account *The part of the balance of payments account that lists all short-term flows of payments.*

Capital account *The part of the balance of payments account that lists all long-term flows of payments.*

Official transactions account *The part of the balance of payments account that records the amount of a currency or other international reserves a nation buys.*

As you can see in Exhibit 1, the balance of payments account is broken down into the *current account,* the *capital account,* and the *official transactions account.* The **current account** (lines 1–13) is the part of the balance of payments account in which all short-term flows of payments are listed. It includes exports and imports, which are what one normally means when one talks about the trade balance. The **capital account** (lines 14–17) is the part of the balance of payments account in which all long-term flows of payments are listed. If one buys a German stock, or if a Japanese company buys a U.S. company, the transaction shows up on the capital account.

The government can influence the exchange rate by buying and selling currencies, or by buying and selling other international reserves, such as gold. Such buying and selling is recorded in the **official transactions account,** line 20 of Exhibit 1. To get a better idea of what's included in the three accounts, let's consider each of them more carefully.

The Current Account

At the top of Exhibit 1, the current account is composed of the merchandise (or goods) account (lines 2–5), the services account (lines 6–9), the net investment income account (line 10), and the net transfers account (lines 11 and 12).

Starting with the merchandise account, notice that in 1987 the United States imported $410 billion worth of goods and exported $250 billion worth of goods. The difference between the two is sometimes called the **balance of trade.** Looking at line 5, you can see that the United States had a balance of trade deficit of $160 billion in 1987 and $132 billion in 1993.

1B The balance of trade is the difference between the value of goods a nation exports and the value of goods it imports.

The trade balance is often discussed in the press as a summary of how the United States is doing in the international markets. It's not a good summary. Trade in services is just as important as trade in merchandise, so economists pay more attention to the

---

[1] These records are not very good. Because of measurement difficulties, many transactions go unrecorded and many numbers must be estimated, leaving a potential for large errors.

EXHIBIT 1   The Balance of Payments Account, 1987 and 1993

	1987		1993	
1. Current account				
2. Merchandise				
3. Exports	+250		+457	
4. Imports	−410		−589	
5. Balance of trade		−160		−132
6. Services				
7. Exports	+ 98		+187	
8. Imports	− 90		−131	
9. Balance on services		+ 8		+ 56
10. Net investment income	+ 8		+ 1	
11. Net transfers	− 23		− 33	
12. Invest. trans. balance		− 15		− 32
13. Balance on current account		−167		−108
14. Capital account				
15. Capital inflows	+230		+226	
16. Capital outflows	− 71		−144	
17. Balance on capital account		**+159**		**+ 82**
18. Current and capital balance		− 8		− 26
19. Statistical discrepancy		− 1		+ 27
20. Official transactions account		+ 9		− 1
21. Totals		0		0

Source: Survey of Current Business 1994.

combined balance on goods and services. Notice that in both 1987 and 1993 most of the U.S. trade deficit resulted from an imbalance in the merchandise account. The service account worked in the opposite direction. It was slightly positive in 1987; in 1993 the services account reduced the trade deficit by $56 billion. Such services include tourist expenditures and insurance payments by foreigners to U.S. firms. For instance, when you travel in Japan, you spend yen, which you must buy with dollars; this is an outflow of payments or a negative contribution to the services account.

There is no reason that the goods and services sent into a country must equal the goods and services sent out in a particular year, even if the current account is in equilibrium, because the current account also includes payments from past investments and net transfers. When you invest, you expect to make a return on that investment. The payments to foreign owners of U.S. capital assets is a negative contribution to the U.S. balance of payments. The payment to U.S. owners of foreign capital assets is a positive contribution to the U.S. balance of payments. These payments on investment income are a type of holdover from past trade and services imbalances. So even though they relate to investments, they show up on the current account.

The final component of the current account is net transfers, which include foreign aid, gifts, and other payments to individuals not exchanged for goods or services. If you send $100 to your aunt in Mexico, it shows up with a minus sign here.

Adding up the pluses and minuses on the current account, we arrive at line 13, the current account balance. Notice that in 1987 the United States ran a $167 billion deficit on the current account, and in 1993 the United States had a deficit of $108 billion (line 13). That means that, in the current account, the supply of dollars greatly exceeded the demand for dollars. If the current account represented the total supply of and demand for dollars, the value of the dollar would have fallen. But it doesn't. There are also the capital account, statistical discrepancies, and the official transactions account.

The capital account measures the flow of payments between countries for assets such as stocks, bonds, and real estate. As you can see in Exhibit 1, in 1987 there was a

Q–1: If you, a U.S. citizen, are traveling abroad, where will your expenditures show up in the balance of payments accounts?

The Capital Account

significant inflow of capital into the United States in excess of outflows of capital from the United States. Capital inflows (payments by foreigners for U.S. real and financial assets) were $159 billion more than capital outflows (payments by U.S. citizens for foreign assets). In 1993, there was an inflow of $226 billion (line 17), but there was also a much larger outflow of $144 billion, so the net balance on the capital account was only $82 billion as compared to $159 billion in 1987.

To buy these U.S. assets foreigners needed dollars, so these net capital inflows represent a demand for dollars. In both these years the demand for dollars to buy capital goods went a long way toward balancing the excess supply of dollars on the current account. In 1987 they were $8 billion short, and in 1993 they were $26 billion short.

In thinking about what determines a currency's value, it's important to remember both the demand for dollars to buy goods and services and the demand for dollars to buy assets.

Thus it would seem that the government would have to buy dollars. That wasn't the case, however. The reason is statistical discrepancies, as we see in line 19. In 1987 there was a −$1 billion discrepancy, and in 1993 there was +$27 billion discrepancy. These discrepancies arise because many international transactions, especially on the capital account, go unrecorded and hence must be estimated. With these discrepancies taken into account, in the absence of government policy there would have been downward pressure on the value of the dollar in 1987 and slight upward pressure on the dollar in 1993. Because of the importance of capital flows, when you think about what's likely to happen to a currency's value, it's important to remember both the demand for dollars to buy goods and services and the demand for dollars to buy assets.

2 Since the balance of payments consists of both the capital account and the trade account, if the capital account is in surplus and the trade account is in deficit, there can still be a balance of payments surplus.

There is, of course, a difference between demand for dollars to buy currently produced goods and services and demand for dollars to buy assets. Assets earn profits or interest, so when foreigners buy U.S. assets, they earn income from those assets just for owning those assets. The net investment income from foreigners' previous asset purchases shows up on line 10 of the current account. It's the difference between the income U.S. citizens receive from their foreign assets and the income foreigners receive from their U.S. assets. If assets earned equal returns, one would expect that when foreigners own more U.S. capital assets than U.S. citizens own foreign capital assets, net investment income should be negative. And when U.S. citizens own more foreign capital assets than foreigners own U.S. capital assets, net investment income should be positive. Why is this? Because net investment income is simply the difference between the returns on U.S. citizens' assets held abroad and foreign citizens' assets held in the United States.

Q–2: How can net investment income be positive if a country is a net debtor nation?

In the 1980s, the inflow of capital into the United States greatly exceeded the outflow of capital from the United States, and this trend has continued into the early 1990s. As a result, the United States became a net debtor nation; the amount foreigners own in the United States now exceeds the amount U.S. citizens own abroad by well over $500 billion. So one would expect that U.S. investment income would be negative. But looking at Exhibit 1 we see that was not the case. The reason? Foreigners' returns have been low, and much of the U.S. investment abroad is undervalued. For example, the Japanese bought a lot of real estate at very high prices and have been losing money on those investments. But one cannot expect this trend to continue. In the 1990s, net investment income will likely become negative.

The Official Transactions Account

The current account and the capital account measure the private and non-U.S. government supply of and demand for dollars. The net amount of these two accounts is called the *balance of payments surplus* (if demand for a currency exceeds supply), or *deficit* (if supply of a currency exceeds demand). In 1987 the private supply of dollars exceeded the private demand by $9 billion and in 1993 the private demand for dollars exceeded the private supply of dollars by $1 billion. In 1987 the United States had a balance of payments deficit; in 1993, the United States had a small balance of payments surplus.

A balance of payments deficit will put downward pressure on the value of a country's currency.

A balance of payments deficit will put downward pressure on the value of a country's currency. If a country wants to prevent that from happening, it can buy its own currency. The third component of the balance of payments account, the official transactions account, records the amount of dollars that the United States bought. As you can see on line 20 of Exhibit 1, in 1987 the government entered into the foreign exchange market and bought $9 billion worth of U.S. dollars, using $9 billion of foreign reserves that it had. In 1993, it sold $1 billion. When a government buys its own currency to hold up the currency's price, we say that the government has supported its currency. It's holding the exchange rate higher than it otherwise would have been. If it sells its currency, it's attempting to depress the value of the currency.[2]

Now let's return to the point made at the beginning of the chapter: As long as a currency is freely exchangeable for another currency, the three accounts (current, capital, and official transactions) must sum to zero. Why is this? Because that's what it means to be freely exchangeable. Whenever anybody wants, they can take their currency and trade it for another. The supply must equal the demand.

The concepts *balance of payments* and *surplus* or *deficit* refer to the balance of payments not counting a country's official reserve transactions. Thus, if a currency is freely exchangeable, any deficit in the balance of payments must be offset by an equal surplus in the official reserve transactions, and any surplus must be offset by an equal deficit. This means that the supply of and demand for a freely exchangeable currency must sum to zero by definition.

EXCHANGE RATES

The balance of payments has two sides: the flow of goods or assets, and the flow of money to pay for those goods. International finance is more complicated than domestic finance because international finance always involves two financial transactions: the exchange of a real good or asset for money, and the exchange of money of one country for the money of another country. For international trade to take place, one must be able to exchange currencies. If either of these financial transactions is difficult or costly, trade is impeded.

As I will discuss later, a number of countries' currencies cannot be freely exchanged today. These countries have what are called **nonconvertible currencies.** International trade is greatly impeded by that lack of free exchange. The former Soviet Union is an example of a country whose currency did not trade freely. In the 1980s, as the Soviet Union attempted to expand its international trade, it looked for ways to make its currency (the ruble) convertible (exchangeable) into other currencies.

Nonconvertible currency   A currency that cannot be freely exchanged with currencies of other countries.

Thinking about the problem of trade with nonconvertible currencies gives one a deeper appreciation of the role of money in an economy. Money makes an economy operate efficiently—but only if everyone agrees to the monetary convention. You accept dollars because you know that someone else will accept dollars who in turn knows that someone else will accept dollars. Dollars have no inherent value, but they acquire value because our government declares that dollars are legal tender and that it will accept only dollars in payments of taxes, and because people believe that dollars have value. Hence dollars do have value.

Money makes an economy operate efficiently—but only if everyone agrees to the monetary convention.

In the international sphere there is no legally mandated monetary convention, so a foreign exchange market in which one currency can be exchanged for another must be set up. That foreign exchange market is a system of formal or informal international monetary markets governed by a set of internationally agreed upon conventions. These conventions provide the framework within which international financial affairs are conducted.

Supply, Demand, and Fundamental Analysis of Exchange Rates

Supply and demand are the two central forces of economics, and so it shouldn't be surprising that our initial discussion of the determination of exchange rates uses supply and demand curves.

At first glance, the analysis of foreign exchange rates seems simple: You have an upward-sloping supply curve and a downward-sloping demand curve. But what goes

---

[2] Support for the dollar can also come from foreign central banks. In 1987, foreign central banks bought $45 billion, and in 1993 bought $71 billion, worth of dollar-denominated assets, thereby playing a big role in holding the value of the dollar higher than it otherwise would have been.

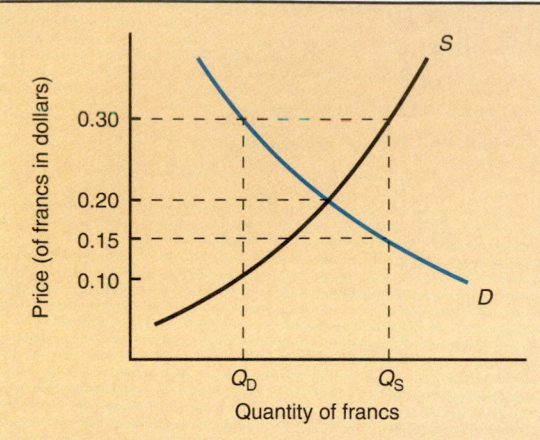

EXHIBIT 2   The Supply and Demand for Francs

As long as one keeps "quantities and prices of what" straight, the standard, or fundamental, analysis of the determination of exchange rates is easy. Exchange rates are determined by the supply and demand for a country's currency. Just remember that if you're talking about the supply and demand for francs, the price will be measured in dollars and the quantity will be in francs, as in this exhibit. If you're talking about the supply of and demand for dollars, the quantity will be in dollars, but the price of dollars will be measured in another currency. Otherwise the price of a dollar would be a dollar.

Q–3: Show graphically the effect of an increase in demand for francs on the exchange rate for francs.

on the axes? Obviously price and quantity, but what price? And what quantity? Because you're talking about the relative prices of currencies—that's basically what exchange rates are—you have to specify which currencies you're using.

In Exhibit 2, I present the supply and demand for French francs in terms of dollar prices. Notice that the quantity of francs goes on the horizontal axis and the dollar price of francs goes on the vertical axis.

The first point to recognize is that when you are comparing the currencies of only two countries, the supply of one currency is equal to the demand for the other currency. To demand one currency, you must supply the other. In Exhibit 2 we are assuming that there are only two countries: the United States and France. This means that the supply of francs is the equivalent of a demand for dollars. The demand for dollars comes from the French who want to buy U.S. goods or assets. To do so, they supply francs to buy dollars. Let's consider an example showing why. Say a French person wants to buy an IBM computer made in the United States. She has francs, but IBM wants dollars. So, in order to buy the computer, she or IBM must somehow exchange francs for dollars. She is *supplying* francs and *demanding* dollars.

The supply curve of francs is upward sloping because the more dollars French citizens get for their francs, the cheaper U.S. goods and assets are for them. Say, for example, that the dollar price of one franc rises from 15¢ to 20¢. That means that the price of a dollar to a French person has fallen from 6.67 francs to 5 francs. For a French person, a good that cost $100 now falls in price from 667 francs to 500 francs. U.S. goods are cheaper, so the French buy more U.S. goods and more dollars, which means they supply more francs.

The demand for francs comes from Americans who want to buy French goods or assets. The demand curve is downward sloping because the lower the dollar price of francs, the more francs U.S. citizens want to buy, for the same reasons I just described.

Equilibrium is where the quantity supplied equals the quantity demanded. In my example, equilibrium occurs at a dollar price of 20¢ for one franc. If the price of francs is above or below 20¢, quantity supplied won't equal the quantity demanded and there will be pressure for the exchange rate to move to equilibrium. Say, for example, that the price is 30¢. The quantity of francs supplied will be greater than the quantity demanded. People who want to sell francs won't be able to sell them. To find buyers, they will offer to sell their francs for less. As they do, the price of francs falls.

The supply/demand framework directly relates to the balance of payments. When quantity supplied equals quantity demanded, the balance of payments is in equilibrium. If the exchange rate is too high, there will be a deficit in the balance of payments; if the exchange rate is too low, there will be a surplus in the balance of payments. Thus, in Exhibit 2 when the price of francs is 30¢, quantity of francs supplied exceeds the quantity demanded so France is running a balance of payments deficit. When the price of francs is 15¢, the quantity of francs demanded exceeds the quantity supplied, so France is running a balance of payments surplus.

ADDED DIMENSION

DETERMINING THE CAUSES OF FLUCTUATIONS IN THE DOLLAR'S VALUE

A s you can see on the graph, the dollar's value has fluctuated considerably since 1973. A good exercise to see if you understand movements in the value of the dollar is to try to choose which factors caused the fluctuation.

Let's start with fluctuations in 1973 and 1974. These probably reflected expectational bubbles—in which speculators were more concerned with short-run than long-run fundamentals—while the dollar's low value in 1979 and 1980 reflected high inflation, relatively low real interest rates, and the booming U.S. economy during this period.

The rise of the dollar in the early 1980s reflected higher interest rates and the falling U.S. inflation rate, although the rise was much more than expected and probably reflected speculation, as did the sudden fall in the dollar's value in 1985. Similarly, the fluctuations in the late 1980s and early 1990s reflected both changing interest rates in the United States and changing foreign interest rates, as well as changing relative inflation rates.

As you can see, after the fact we economists are pretty good at explaining the movements in the exchange rates.

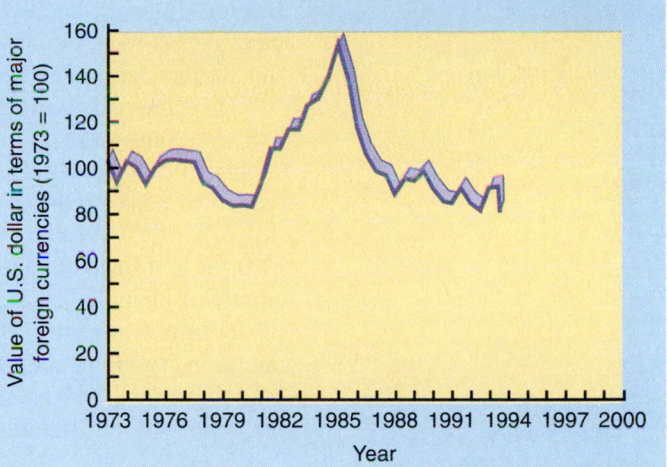

Alas, before the fact we aren't so good because often speculative activities make the timing of the movements unpredictable.

Supply/Demand, Traders, and Exchange Rates   It would appear from Exhibit 2 that the determination of exchange rates is a relatively simple process: All one need do is determine the supply and demand curves and decide where equilibrium occurs. And in some ways, it is relatively easy. But in other ways it isn't; if it were as simple as determining supply and demand curves and equilibrium, the quotation at the head of this chapter about the bedlam in a foreign exchange dealer's office wouldn't have been appropriate, and governments would not agonize over exchange rates as they do. There's more to the story of exchange rates than is told in those two curves.

The reason is that the curves in Exhibit 2 reflect long-run considerations; they reflect the effect of normal market forces on the supply and demand for currency. It was normal market forces that we used to justify the shapes of the curves. An analysis of curves based on normal market forces like that in the discussion of Exhibit 2 is often called **fundamental analysis** because the forces described there are the forces one arrives at by applying normal or fundamental economic analysis to the exchange rates. The normal market forces are the forces that will determine exchange rates in the long run—say in two, three, or four years.

Most movements in exchange rates that are discussed in the newspapers are influenced by these normal market forces, but are not determined by them. Thus, the short-run analysis of exchange rates (what will happen to the exchange rate in the next week, month, or year) is not directly based on fundamental analysis but upon a variety of effects that influence traders' decisions whether to buy, sell, or hold a currency. Those decisions depend much more on a variety of forces that cause *shifts in* the supply and demand curves for a country's currency than on forces governing the shapes of the supply and demand curves.

In the real world, shifts in the supply of and demand for currencies are extremely important, and the exchange rate fluctuations necessary to keep the balance of payments in equilibrium in the short run are large. As we will see, such large shifts in exchange rates cause problems and lead to attempts to reduce exchange rate fluctuations. But before we consider this problem, let's consider the forces that cause supply of and demand for currencies to shift.

Forces that Cause Shifts in the Supply of and Demand for Currencies   The major forces that can cause shifts include changes in a country's income, changes in a country's prices, changes in interest rates, and changes in expectations. Let's consider each in turn.

Q–4: Show graphically the effect of an increase in the demand for dollars by French people on the price of francs.

Fundamental analysis   Analysis of curves describing fundamental forces that will be operating in the long run.

3 In the long run, fundamental analysis only influences the value of a currency. Expectations of traders are far more important in determining short-run exchange rates than are fundamentals.

Four shift factors for supply and demand for currencies are:
1. *changes in a country's income;*
2. *changes in a country's prices;*
3. *changes in interest rates; and*
4. *changes in expectations.*

Changes in a Country's Income

The demand for imports depends on the income in a country. When a country's income falls, demand for imports falls. Hence demand for foreign currency to buy those imports falls, which means that the supply of the country's currency to buy the foreign currency falls. That's why, in our presentation of the Keynesian model, we said that imports depend on income.

How important is this relationship? Very important. For example, in late 1990 the U.S. economy went into recession and, as it did, the trade deficit was reduced and the supply of dollars was also reduced significantly. This decrease in the supply of dollars tended to push up the price of U.S. dollars relative to foreign currencies.

Changes in a Country's Prices

The United States's demand for imports and foreign countries' demand for U.S. exports depend on prices of U.S. goods compared to prices of foreign competing goods. If the United States has more inflation than other countries, foreign goods will become cheaper, U.S. demand for foreign currencies will tend to increase, and foreign demand for dollars will tend to decrease. This rise in U.S. inflation will shift the dollar supply outward and the dollar demand inward.

Changes in Interest Rates

People like to invest their savings in assets that will yield the highest return. A rise in U.S. interest rates relative to those abroad will increase demand for U.S. assets as long as that rise is a rise in the real interest rate—that is, as long as the rise isn't accompanied by a rise in inflation. As a result of a rise in the U.S. interest rate, demand for dollars will increase, while simultaneously the supply of dollars will decrease as fewer Americans sell their dollars to buy foreign assets. A fall in the U.S. interest rate or a rise in foreign interest rates will have the opposite effect.

Changes in Expectations

If the value of a currency falls, the holders of that currency and of assets denominated in that currency lose; if the value of a currency rises, the holders of that currency and of assets denominated in that currency gain. So everyone tries to hold currencies whose value will rise and get rid of currencies whose value will fall. Thus, expectations of whether a currency will rise or fall can cause large shifts in the supply and demand. Expectations can even be self-fulfilling. For example, the expectation of a rise in the dollar's value will increase the demand for dollars and decrease the supply, which will cause a rise in the value of the dollar. The dollar rises because it is expected to rise.

Stability and Instability in Foreign Exchange Markets

Given that these large shifts in the supply and demand for currencies are constantly occurring, one might expect that there would be enormous shifts in exchange rates. But that doesn't often happen. Usually exchange rates are rather stable for two reasons. First, government enters into exchange markets to maintain stability. When people buy, the government sells; when people sell, the government buys. Government action counters the shifts.

A second reason is that foreign exchange traders and speculators stabilize the rates. Traders know that eventually market forces will be strong and will lead to fundamental forces that will control the exchange rates, and they base their expectations on those fundamentals. Which of these two reasons is more important is debatable. Since that debate centers on whether private traders or government are better at stabilizing exchange rates, we need to look behind the supply and demand curves for currencies—at the traders who make the markets work.

Exchange Rate Markets, Traders, and the Spread

International currency traders are interested in making money. They buy and sell currencies. If they buy low and sell high, they make a profit. If they buy high and sell low, they lose money. The currency trader is constantly on the phone offering to buy a currency at one rate and to sell it at another rate.

The **spread** is the difference between the price at which they buy a currency and the price at which they sell it. To see how the spread works, let's consider a trader of francs and dollars. She might post the following rates:

Spread *The difference between the price at which traders buy and sell a currency.*

Today's Rates

Sell: $1 . . . . 4.5 francs
Buy: $1 . . . . 4.4 francs

Sell: 1 franc . . . . 23¢
Buy: 1 franc . . . . 22¢

The spread is 1¢ for every franc traded, and 10 centimes (100 centimes equals one franc) for every dollar traded. The greater the spread, the greater the profit per transaction but the smaller the number of transactions that are likely to go through that trader. Traders become known as aggressive or nonaggressive. Aggressive traders have the smallest spread. They buy high and sell cheap, relying on volume for their profit.

How does an international currency trader choose what rates she will set? The answer is that she must choose a rate that brings her about the same amount of dollars that other people want to buy. That is, she must choose a rate for which the quantity of dollars supplied roughly equals the quantity of dollars demanded.

Thus, after a trader sets her rates, she will see how many dollars her advertised rates are bringing in, and how many dollars are going out. If fewer dollars are coming in than going out, she'll raise the price of dollars in terms of French francs. Instead of 4.5 francs to the dollar, she'll make it 4.6 francs to the dollar. Dollars become more expensive in terms of francs; francs become cheaper in terms of dollars. International traders hope that if everything goes right, that change will bring the two currencies into equilibrium. Traders set exchange rates to equate supply and demand for dollars.

The Short-Run Determination of Exchange Rates   Most currency traders will have taken an introductory economics course, so they'll look at the factors that cause shifts in supply and demand and think about the general long-run direction of exchange rates. As stated before, they call the analysis of the long-run determinants of exchange rates *fundamental analysis.* But traders recognize that in the very short run the quantities of currencies supplied and demanded aren't significantly influenced by exchange rates, but are significantly influenced by expectations. They expect that supply and demand for currencies will shift enormously, which means the equilibrium price will fluctuate widely. Traders' time horizon is the very short run (minutes, hours, or days). Thus, you'll seldom hear currency traders talking about fundamentals of exchange rate determination. They're far more concerned with the short-run factors that shift demand, especially expectations.

Currency traders are active in markets for most of the major currencies. The spreads are extremely narrow. The traders are constantly buying or selling—listening for trade figures, rumors on the street, and interest rate policy changes by governments. They don't limit themselves to buying and selling for customers. They can buy for their own accounts, speculating on whether a currency is about to go up or down. Often a trader has millions of dollars riding on whether a currency will go up or down a single percentage point.

Traders see only a small part of a currency's supply and demand—the part that flows through their offices as they buy and sell. Given their very limited observations, they have to guess what's going on. They're making judgments not about shifts in demand, but about their belief about other traders' beliefs about . . . . Rumors can, and do, drive international currency markets wild.

Predicting how much of a foreign currency all the people in a country will want in the short run is a complicated task. If a currency trader predicts wrong, she gets stuck with some currencies that nobody wants. When the spread is wide, she can afford a few losses, but when the bid/ask spread is narrow, she must predict very carefully and must try to make sure that she chooses a rate for which the supply of and demand for various currencies flowing through her office are equal.

Q–5: Will a trader with a larger, or a smaller, spread make a larger profit?

Rumors can, and do, drive international currency markets wild.

International currency traders often deal in a variety of currencies, and when they do they must be continually on the lookout for discrepancies among the exchange rates for various countries. For example, let's say a trader opens an office with several windows and sets up the following exchange rates:

Window 1: $1 = 4.5 francs or 1 franc = 22.5¢
Window 2: $1 = 707.9 won or 1 won = 0.14¢
Window 3: 1 won = 0.005 francs or 1 franc = 200 won.

Enter Mr. Arbitrage, who's always keeping his eye on international currency traders. Mr. Arbitrage goes up to window 1 and says, "I'll buy $1,000 worth of French francs." He receives 4,500 francs. He then goes to window 3 and says, "I'd like to buy Korean won for these 4,500 French francs, please." Handing over 4,500 francs, he receives 900,000 won. He then goes to window 2 and says, "I'd like to exchange these 900,000 won for dollars, please." He hands over 900,000 won, for which he receives $1,260. Next he takes the $1,260 back to window 1 and says, "I'd like to buy French francs, please." At this point the currency trader should know that she's goofed: In setting the exchange rates she has forgotten the principle of arbitrage.

Arbitrage is the buying of a good in one market at a low price and selling that good in another market at a higher price. It limits the exchange rates a currency trader can set in various markets and still make a profit. Specifically, the roundabout exchange rates must be identical to the direct exchange rates. Recognizing this, she changes the exchange rate between won and francs so that 1 won = 0.0063 francs and no arbitrage profits are to be made.

Our little story and example make it look as if arbitrage is simple. But remember, there are hundreds of currencies, and with even as few as 50 currencies there are many thousands of possible roundabout exchange rates. The table shows some of them.

Key Currency Cross Rates Late New York Trading Mar. 23, 1994

	Dollar	Pound	SFranc	Guilder	Peso	Yen	Lira	D-Mark	FFranc	CdnDlr
Canada	1.3636	2.0432	.95591	.72133	.40949	.01283	.00082	.81157	.23746	....
France	5.7425	8.605	4.0256	3.0377	1.72447	.05405	.00345	3.4177	....	4.2113
Germany	1.6802	2.5176	1.1778	.88881	.50456	.01581	.00101	....	.29259	1.2322
Italy	1662.3	2490.8	1165.32	879.35	499.20	15.645	....	989.36	289.48	1219.1
Japan	106.25	159.21	74.483	56.205	31.907	....	.06392	63.237	18.502	77.92
Mexico	3.3300	4.9897	2.3344	1.7615	....	.03134	.00200	1.9819	.5799	2.4421
Netherlands	1.8904	2.8326	1.3252	....	.56769	.01779	.00114	1.1251	.32919	1.3863
Switzerland	1.4265	2.1375	....	.75460	.42838	.01343	.00086	.84901	.24841	1.0461
U.K.	.66738	....	.46784	.35304	.20041	.00628	.00040	.39720	.11622	.48942
U.S.	....	1.4984	.70102	.52899	.30030	.00941	.00060	.59517	.17414	.73335

Real-world arbitragers have computers that constantly monitor these exchange rates. If they find a difference, they buy and sell quickly, keeping the people who set exchange rates on their toes to set all exchange rates so that arbitragers can't make money by arbitraging markets.

Foreign exchange markets have become sophisticated and the spread is small. Computers, programmed to spot any potential for arbitrage, monitor exchange rates and keep exchange rates among currencies in line so that roundabout trading does not bring about long-term profits for arbitragers. Arbitragers, like others in a competitive market, cover their costs (which include normal profits) but don't make so much profit that they attract others into the business.

Government's Role in Determining Exchange Rates

So far I haven't discussed government's role in exchange rate determination. Where does government policy come in?

Every country has goals for its international exchange rate and trade balance, and uses monetary and fiscal policies to achieve those goals. Through these policies governments can influence income and, hence, the current account and interest rates

Foreign exchange traders often have millions of dollars riding on small movements in exchange rates.
© *David H. Wells/The Image Works.*

and, hence, the capital account. This means that, through monetary and fiscal policies, government can indirectly affect a country's balance of payments and, hence, exchange rates.

In addition to monetary and fiscal policies, countries can use other economic policies to influence the exchange rate. A government might simply pass a law flatly specifying what the exchange rate will be. Alternatively, a government can directly affect its currency's exchange rate by means of capital control policies and exchange rate policies. Still another possibility is for it to use trade policies, such as quotas and tariffs, to influence the trade balance. Let us look more specifically at setting exchange rates by legal mandate, exchange rate policies, and capital control policies.

Exchange Rates Set by Law: Nonconvertible Currency and Capital Controls A government can simply pass a law outlawing international currency trading and prohibiting the buying and selling of foreign currencies except at a rate determined by the government. Many developing countries set their exchange rates in this manner. When governments do so, they make international trade difficult, because their currencies can't be freely exchanged with other currencies—that is, their currencies are *nonconvertible.*

Nonconvertible currencies' exchange rates don't fluctuate in response to shifts in supply and demand. Often the only legal way to deal in such currency is to buy it from the government and sell to the government. It is illegal to trade nonconvertible currencies privately or even to carry large amounts of nonconvertible currency out of the country. Such prohibitions against currency flowing freely into and out of a country are called **capital controls.** If one country's currency can't be exchanged for another's at anything reflecting a market price, it's very difficult to buy each other's goods.

If nonconvertible currencies make trade so difficult, why do countries use them? The answer is: to avoid making the economic adjustments that international considerations would otherwise force upon them. Say that a country is running a large balance of payments deficit and the value of its currency is falling. This fall is pushing up the price of imports, causing inflation, and making its assets cheaper for foreigners. Foreigners can come in and buy up the country's assets at low prices.

The country can avoid this political problem simply by passing a law that fixes the exchange rate at a certain level. This action indirectly limits imports, since most foreign firms won't sell their goods at the official exchange rate. They don't want the country's currency at the official exchange rate. It also limits exports since the price of

Capital controls   A government's prohibitions on its currency freely flowing into and out of the country.

4 Developing countries often have nonconvertible currencies to avoid making economic adjustments that international considerations would otherwise force upon them.

When many U.S. banks first got seriously involved in international currency markets in the 1970s, traders had relatively loose limits on the speculative positions they could take. A *speculative position* is the net amount of a currency a trader holds from buying or selling currency for his or her own account in the hope that its value will rise or fall.

Speculative positions can be either long or short. Holding a currency in the hope that its price will rise is a *long position;* selling a currency you don't have but will buy when you must supply it, in the hope that its price will have fallen, is a *short position.*

Some traders lost millions of dollars for their banks in a short time. In the famous case of Franklin National Bank, the losses in trading currencies brought the bank under— that is, it went bankrupt and had to be bailed out by the Federal Deposit Insurance Corporation.

In response to such problems, most banks instituted stringent controls over the positions that traders could take. Most traders weren't allowed to have unauthorized positions at the end of each trading day.

Who are these foreign exchange traders? Usually they're not Ph.D. economists or even MBAs; such people often don't have the guts or personality to be traders. Instead traders are often people who are directly out of high school or college, people who have been discovered to have an ability to make split-second correct decisions (to buy or sell); who have few regrets ("If only I'd . . ."); and who want to earn about $60,000 a year to start. They're a bungee-type group. (Bungee is a sport in which you tie one end of an elastic rope to a rock or a tree and the other end to your feet and dive off a cliff, hoping the rope will stop you right before you hit the ground. If you're successful, you yo-yo up and down for two or three minutes.) Bungee is a trader's hobby. I prefer gardening.

a country's exports is held high. The government can and often does give favored firms special dispensation to import or export. Thus, having a nonconvertible currency enables the government to control what can and can't be imported and exported. Generally when there's a nonconvertible currency, there is a large incentive for people to trade currencies illegally in a black market.

Exchange Rate Policy and Government Intervention in the Currency Market

Even if a government doesn't establish a nonconvertible currency, it can still directly affect the exchange rate. The government can buy and sell currencies, just like an individual trader. If it buys or sells enough of a particular currency, it can affect that currency's relative price (its exchange rate). So an **exchange rate policy** is a policy in which the government buys and sells a currency in order to affect its price.

Exchange rate policy Government policy of buying and selling a currency to affect its price.

Say the Federal Reserve wants to raise the value of the U.S. dollar. If it buys lots of dollars (paying for them with other currencies), it will increase the demand for dollars, which will push the price of dollars up. If it wants to lower the price of dollars (in terms of other currencies), it can sell dollars and buy other currencies.

Think back to the U.S. balance of payments as summarized in Exhibit 1. When the United States bought $9 billion worth of dollars in 1987, paying for them from its reserves, it was using exchange rate policy to support the value of the dollar.

In the autumn of 1993, there was a typical example of United States intervention. The value of the dollar had been falling relative to the Japanese yen, and in August that fall accelerated, bringing the value to about 100 yen per dollar. While some fall was seen as desirable since the United States had a significant trade deficit, in mid-August the Fed felt that the fall was too fast. It feared the market was being disorderly. The Fed entered into the exchange markets, buying dollars and maintaining an "orderly market." The amount it bought compared to the total yen/dollar transactions was small, but the mere presence of the Fed in the market changed expectations and brought pressure on the dollar to rise.

The actual intervention is generally too small to move the market, but the expectations that the intervention generates are often large enough. It's like a rolling snowball that grows as it collects snow from the snowy ground. This autumn 1993 intervention was typical: The Fed will let the dollar fall, but if it can stop the fall, it won't let the dollar fall "too fast."

Q–6: In general, would it be easier for the United States to push the value of the dollar down, or up? Why?

Since the United States can create all the dollars it wants, it's easier for the United States to push the value of its currency down by selling dollars than to hold it up. In contrast, it's easier for another country (say, Japan) to push the value of the dollar up

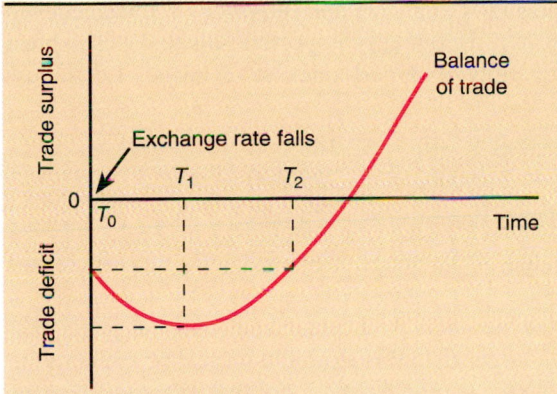

EXHIBIT 3   The J-Curve

Generally, a depreciation of the currency does not initially improve the balance of trade deficit; it makes it worse. Eventually it starts to get better, and eventually, eventually, a depreciation will eliminate a trade deficit. Tracing out the time path of the balance of trade gives one a curve that looks like a J.

(by pushing the value of the yen down). Thus, if the two countries can decide which way they want their exchange rates to move, they have a large incentive to cooperate. Of course, cooperation requires an agreement on the goals. One role of the various international economic organizations discussed in Chapter 5 is to provide a forum for reaching agreement on exchange rate goals and a vehicle through which cooperation can take place.

The Effect of Exchange Rates on the Balance of Goods and Services and Balance of Payments   A government's exchange rate goal can be an end in itself, or it can be a means to an end. A decrease in a country's exchange rate—that is, a decline in its currency's value relative to that of another country's currency—pushes the price of imports up and the price of exports down. Thus, it tends to decrease the *quantity* of imports coming into a country and to increase the *quantity* of exports going out of a country. It also makes a country's assets cheaper to foreigners. These changes in quantity *eventually* improve the balance of trade and hence the balance of payments.

I emphasize the words *eventually* and *quantity* to highlight a paradox that often occurs when exchange rates change. Often initially a fall in the exchange rate doesn't decrease the balance of trade deficit and the balance of payments deficit; it increases them. This phenomenon has occurred so often that it has acquired a name, the **J-curve.** I'll explain why it's called that in a moment.

Why do trade deficit increases initially occur when a country's exchange rate falls? To answer that question, remember that a country's imports and exports are determined by two variables: price multiplied by quantity. When a country's exchange rate falls, the *quantity* of imports tends to decrease and the *quantity* of exports tends to rise, but the *price* of imports tends to rise and the *price* of exports tends to fall. In the short run these price effects tend to predominate over the quantity effects, so the balance of payments and balance of trade deficits become larger. Eventually, however, the quantity effects tend to predominate over the price effects, so the balance of trade and balance of payments deficits get smaller.

If one were graphing what happens to the balance of trade and balance of payments after an exchange rate falls, the graph would look something like Exhibit 3. The fall in the exchange rate occurs at time T_0, and initially the balance of trade and hence the balance of payments worsen. The balance of trade keeps worsening until time T_1, whereupon it starts to improve. At time T_2, it's back where it was at the start, and thereafter it substantially improves. The curve looks like a ''J''—hence the name *the J-curve.*

Let's go through a numerical example to place the J-curve concept into your deep memory. Say that at an exchange rate of 2.5/1 (2.5 German marks to $1.00), the United States is importing 40 Mercedes at $50,000 (125,000 German marks) each, and is exporting to Germany 200,000 videos at $9 (22.5 German marks) each. Imports are $2,000,000 (40 × $50,000) and exports are $1,800,000 (9 × $200,000). The United States thus has a $200,000 trade deficit with Germany.

J-curve   Curve describing the rise and fall in the balance of trade deficit following a fall in the exchange rate.

Now say that the value of the dollar falls to 2.27/1 and the price of a Mercedes to U.S. citizens goes to $55,000. In response, the quantity imported falls to 39. The price of videos falls to $8.20, and the quantity exported rises to 210,000. Let's now calculate the trade balance:

$$\text{Imports } (\$55,000 \times 39) = \$2,145,000$$
$$\text{Exports } (\$8.20 \times 210,000) = \underline{\$1,722,000}$$
$$\text{Trade deficit} \quad \$\ \ 423,000$$

In response to a *fall* in the relative value of the dollar, the trade deficit has increased from $200,000 to $423,000.

This result was dependent on the numbers I chose. Experience suggests that eventually, the quantity effect is much larger than this example indicates, and a fall in the value of a currency improves a country's trade balance, but that *eventually* can be as long as five to seven years. This possibility presents policymakers with a serious long-run/short-run dilemma in using exchange rate policy to achieve government's balance of trade and payments goals. Escaping that dilemma is one reason that many developing countries use nonconvertible currencies. Politically, often they can't afford to make their balance of payments deficit larger in the short run in order to achieve a long-run improvement.

The J-curve phenomenon—which suggests that normal market forces don't operate to keep the exchange rate in short-run equilibrium—is the reason that in our earlier discussion we separated the short-run determination of the exchange rate from the long-run determination of exchange rates. Fundamental analysis only works in the long run. In the short run, normal market forces don't determine exchange rates.

Understanding the limited, and possibly even perverse, short-run effect of normal market forces on achieving equilibrium is important to understanding why most governments don't leave determination of the exchange rate to the market, but instead play varying roles in its determination. We now turn to a consideration of three alternative exchange rate regimes and how they affect short-run determination of exchange rates.

Fundamental analysis only works in the long run. In the short run, normal market forces don't determine exchange rates.

Q–7: Why don't most governments leave determination of the exchange rate to the market?

FLEXIBLE, PARTIALLY FLEXIBLE, AND FIXED EXCHANGE RATES

5 Three exchange rate regimes are:

Flexible exchange rate   Determination of exchange rates is left totally up to the market.

Partially flexible exchange rate The government sometimes affects the exchange rate and sometimes leaves it to the market.

Fixed exchange rate   The government chooses an exchange rate and offers to buy and sell currencies at that rate.

When governments do not enter into foreign exchange markets at all, but leave the determination of exchange rates totally up to currency traders, the country is said to have a **flexible exchange rate.** The price of its currency is allowed to rise and fall as market forces dictate.

When governments sometimes buy or sell currencies to influence the exchange rate, while at other times they let private market forces operate, the country is said to have a **partially flexible exchange rate.** A partially flexible exchange rate is sometimes called a *dirty float* because it isn't purely market determined or government determined.

If the government chooses a particular exchange rate and offers to buy and sell currencies at that price, it is imposing a **fixed exchange rate.** For example, suppose the U.S. government says it will buy francs at 20¢ and sell dollars at 5 francs. In that case, we say that the country has a fixed exchange rate of 5 francs to the dollar.

Notice that, in principle, any trader could establish a fixed exchange rate by guaranteeing to buy or sell a currency at a given rate. Any "fix," however, is only as good as the guarantee, and to fix an exchange rate the trader would require many more resources than she has; only governments have sufficient resources to fix an exchange rate, and often even governments run out of resources. To maintain a fix they must borrow other currencies to prevent the price of their currency from falling.

History of Exchange Rate Systems

6 The gold standard is the system by which the value of a country's currency is fixed in relation to the price of gold. Its heyday was from 1867 until about 1933.

A good way to give you an idea of how the various systems work is to present a brief history of international exchange rate systems.

The Gold Standard: A Fixed Exchange Rate System   Governments played a major role in determining exchange rates until the 1930s. Beginning with the Paris Conference of 1867 and lasting until 1933 (except for the period around World War I), most of the world economies had a system of relatively fixed exchange rates under what was called a **gold standard.**

Under a gold standard, the amount of money a country issued had to be directly tied to gold, either because gold coin served as the currency in a country (as it did in the United States before 1914) or because countries were required by law to have a certain percentage of gold backing their currencies. Gold served as currency or backed all currencies. Each country participating in a gold standard agreed to fix the price of its currency relative to gold. That meant a country would agree to pay a specified amount of gold upon demand to anyone who wanted to exchange that country's currency for gold. To do so, each country had to maintain a stockpile of gold. When a country fixed the price of its currency relative to gold, it fixed its currency's price in relation to other currencies as a result of the process of arbitrage.

Under the gold standard, a country made up a difference between the quantity supplied and the quantity demanded of its currency by buying or selling gold to hold the price of its currency fixed in terms of gold. How much a country would need to buy and sell depended upon its balance of payments deficit or surplus. If the country ran a surplus in the balance of payments, it was required to sell its currency—that is, buy gold—to stop the value of its currency from rising. If a country ran a deficit in the balance of payments, it was required to buy its currency—that is, sell gold—to stop the value of its currency from falling.

The gold standard enabled governments to prevent short-run instability of the exchange rate. If there was a speculative run on its currency, the government would buy its currency with gold, thereby preventing the exchange rate from falling.

But for the gold standard to work, there had to be a method of long-run adjustment; otherwise countries would run out of gold and would no longer be able to fulfill their obligations under the gold standard. That long-run adjustment mechanism was called the **gold specie flow mechanism.** Here's how it worked: Since gold served as reserves to a country's currency, a balance of payments *deficit* (and hence a downward pressure on the exchange rate) would result in a flow of gold out of the country and hence a decrease in the country's money supply. That decrease in the money supply would contract the economy, decreasing imports, lowering the country's price level, and increasing the interest rate, all of which would work toward eliminating the balance of payments deficit.

Similarly a country with a balance of payments *surplus* would experience an inflow of gold. That flow would increase the country's money supply, increasing income (and hence imports), the price level (making imports cheaper and exports more expensive), and lowering the interest rate (increasing capital outflows). These would work toward eliminating the balance of payments surplus.

Thus, the gold standard determined a country's monetary policy and forced it to adjust any international balance of payments disequilibrium. Adjustments to a balance of payments deficit were often politically unpopular; they led to recessions, which, because the money supply was directly tied to gold, the government couldn't try to offset with expansionary monetary policy.

The gold adjustment mechanism was called into play in the United States when the Federal Reserve in late 1931, in response to a shrinking U.S. gold supply, decreased the amount of money in the U.S. economy, deepening the depression that had begun in 1929. The government's domestic goals and responsibilities conflicted with its international goals and responsibilities.

That conflict led to partial abandonment of the gold standard in 1933. At that time the United States made it illegal for individual U.S. citizens to own gold. Except for gold used for ornamental and certain medical and industrial purposes, all privately owned gold had to be sold to the government. Dollar bills were no longer backed by gold in the sense that U.S. citizens could exchange dollars for a prespecified amount of gold. Instead dollar bills were backed by silver, which meant that any U.S. citizen could change dollars for a prespecified amount of silver. In the late 1960s that changed also. Since that time, for U.S. residents, dollars have been backed only by trust in the soundness of the U.S. economy.

Gold specie flow mechanism *Long-run adjustment mechanism under the gold standard in which gold flows and price level changes bring about equilibrium.*

Q–8: Explain how a country can move from a balance of payments surplus to a balance of payments equilibrium, using the gold specie flow mechanism.

Gold continued to serve, at least partially, as international backing for U.S. currency. That is, other countries could still exchange dollars for gold. However in 1971, in response to another conflict between international and domestic goals, the United States totally cut off the relationship between dollars and gold. After that a dollar could be redeemed only for another dollar, whether it was a U.S. citizen or a foreign government who wanted to redeem the dollar.

The Bretton Woods System: A Fixed Exchange Rate System

As World War II was coming to an end, the United States and its allies met to establish a new international economic order. After much wrangling they agreed upon a system called the **Bretton Woods system,** named after the resort in New Hampshire where the meeting was held.

Bretton Woods system   An agreement that governed international financial relationships from the period after World War II until 1971.

The Bretton Woods system established the International Monetary Fund (IMF) to oversee the international economic order. The IMF was empowered to arrange short-term loans between countries. The Bretton Woods system also established the World Bank, which was empowered to make longer-term loans to developing countries. Today the World Bank and IMF continue their central roles in international financial affairs.

The Bretton Woods system was based upon mutual agreements about what countries would do when experiencing balance of payments surpluses or deficits. It was essentially a fixed exchange rate system. For example, under the Bretton Woods system, the exchange rate of the dollar for the British pound was set at slightly over $4 to the pound.

The Bretton Woods system was not based on a gold standard. When countries experienced a balance of payments surplus or deficit, they did not necessarily buy or sell gold to stabilize the price of their currency. Instead they bought and sold other currencies. To ensure that participating countries would have sufficient reserves, they established a stabilization fund from which a country could obtain a short-term loan. It was hoped that this stabilization fund would be sufficient to handle all short-run adjustments that did not reflect fundamental imbalances.

In those cases where a misalignment of exchange rates was determined to be fundamental, the countries involved agreed that they would adjust their exchange rates. The IMF was empowered to oversee an orderly adjustment. It could authorize a country to make a one-time adjustment of up to 10 percent without obtaining formal approval from the IMF Board of Directors. After a country had used its one-time adjustment, formal approval was necessary for any change greater than 1 percent.

The Bretton Woods system reflected the underlying political and economic realities of the post-World War II period in which it was established.

The Bretton Woods system reflected the underlying political and economic realities of the post–World War II period in which it was set up. European economies were devastated; the U.S. economy was strong. To rebuild, Europe was going to have to import U.S. equipment and borrow large amounts from the United States. There was serious concern over how high the value of the dollar would rise and how low the value of European currencies would fall in a free market exchange. The establishment of fixed exchange rates set limits on currencies' relative movements; the exchange rates that were chosen helped provide for the rebuilding of Europe.

In addition, the Bretton Woods system provided mechanisms for long-term loans from the United States to Europe that could help sustain those fixed exchange rates. The loans also eliminated the possibility of competitive depreciation of currencies, in which each country tries to stimulate its exports by lowering the relative value of its currency.

Special Drawing Rights (SDRs)   IOUs of the IMF.

Reserve currency   A currency in which countries hold reserves.

One difficulty with the Bretton Woods system was a shortage of reserves and international liquidity. To offset that shortage, the IMF was empowered to create a type of international money called **Special Drawing Rights (SDRs).** But SDRs never became established as an international currency and the U.S. dollar soon began serving as a **reserve currency** (a currency in which countries hold their liquid financial assets) for individuals and countries. To get the dollars to foreigners, the United States had to run a deficit in the current account. Since countries could exchange the dollar for gold at a fixed price, the use of dollars as a reserve currency meant that, under the Bretton Woods system, the world was on a gold standard once removed.

The number of dollars held by foreigners grew enormously in the 1960s. By the early 1970s, those dollars far exceeded in value the amount of gold the United States had. Most countries accepted this situation; even though they could legally demand gold for their dollars, they did not. But Charles de Gaulle, the nationalistic president of France, wasn't pleased with the U.S. domination of international affairs at that time. He believed France deserved a much more prominent position. He demanded gold for the dollars held by the French central bank, knowing that the United States didn't have enough gold to meet his demand. As a result of his demands, on August 15, 1971, the United States ended its policy of exchanging gold for dollars at $35 per ounce. With that change, the Bretton Woods system was dead.

The Present System: A Partially Flexible Exchange Rate System   International monetary affairs were much in the news in the early 1970s as countries groped for a new exchange rate system. The makeshift system finally agreed upon involved partially flexible exchange rates. Most Western countries' exchange rates are allowed to fluctuate, although at various times governments buy or sell their own currencies to affect the exchange rate.

Under the present partially flexible exchange rate system, countries must continually decide when a balance of payments surplus or deficit is a temporary phenomenon and when it is a signal of a fundamental imbalance. If they believe the situation is temporary, they enter into the foreign exchange market to hold their exchange rate at what they believe is an appropriate level. If however they believe that the balance of payments imbalance is a fundamental one, they let the exchange rate rise or fall.

While most Western countries' exchange rates are partially flexible, certain countries have agreed to fixed exchange rates of their currencies in relation to rates of a group of certain other currencies. For example, European Union countries maintained almost fixed exchange rates among their currencies until 1993, although this group of EU currencies could float relative to other currencies. Other currencies are fixed relative to the dollar.

Deciding what is, and what is not, a fundamental imbalance is complicated, and such decisions are considered at numerous international conferences held under the auspices of the IMF or governments. A number of organizations such as G-5 (Group of Five) and G-7 (Group of Seven), which were introduced in Chapter 5, focus much of their discussion on this issue. Often the various countries meet and agree, formally or informally, on acceptable ranges of exchange rates. Thus, while the present system is one of partially flexible exchange rates, the range of flexibility is limited.

Now that I've summarized the history of exchange rate systems, let's consider the advantages and disadvantages of each of the three exchange rate systems.

Fixed Exchange Rates   The advantages of a fixed exchange rate system are:

1. Fixed exchange rates provide international monetary stability.
2. Fixed exchange rates force governments to make adjustments to meet their international problems.

The disadvantages of a fixed exchange rate system are:

1. Fixed exchange rates can become unfixed. When they're expected to become unfixed, they create enormous monetary instability.
2. Fixed exchange rates force governments to make adjustments to meet their international problems. (Yes, this is a disadvantage as well as an advantage.)

Let's consider each in turn.

Fixed Exchange Rates and Monetary Stability   To maintain fixed exchange rates, the government must choose an exchange rate and have sufficient reserves to support that rate. If the rate it chooses is too high, its exports lag and the country continually loses reserves. If the rate it chooses is too low, it is paying more for its imports than it needs

Advantages and Disadvantages of Alternative Exchange Rate Systems

Q–9: Would someone who believes price stability is the main goal of central bank policy be more likely to prefer fixed or flexible exchange rates?

A country that is continually gaining or losing reserves must eventually change its fixed exchange rate.

ADDED DIMENSION

TURMOIL WITHIN THE EUROPEAN EXCHANGE RATE MECHANISM

In the 1980s, it all looked so easy. After economic union in 1992 would come monetary union. A single European central bank would take over for individual banks, and a single currency—the ECU (European Currency Unit)—would replace the domestic currencies of Europe and would challenge the dollar as the reserve currency of the world economy.

But, as often happens with grand plans, there's a big jump between the plan and the reality. Let's consider the history of that case, and the case itself, again, now that we've discussed exchange rates.

The problems began when Germany, the dominant EU economy, changed its focus from EU unity to German reunification and the financing of that reunification. To bring about the reunification, the German government ran large deficits, which forced the German interest rate up as the Bundesbank refused to monetize the deficit. The high relative interest rate increased demand for the deutsche mark, putting pressure on other EU countries to keep their exchange rates within the agreed-upon band. After using all their reserves to defend their currencies, the only remaining tool available to them to keep within the range was contractionary monetary policy. (They had already agreed that goods could flow freely among member countries, and that no capital controls were allowed.)

But many of these countries were in a recession; contractionary monetary policy would worsen the recession. Sensing a contradiction, speculators entered the market, increasing the upward pressure on the mark. The result was inevitable. First Britain, Spain, and Italy, and finally France, broke their EU commitment to a fixed exchange rate, and let their currencies float to a lower level relative to the mark. Speculators made billions, and the idea of the EU having a single monetary policy and a single currency ended, at least for the near future.

Eventually, in the autumn of 1993, the countries agreed to a wide 15 percent band within which EU countries would confine their currencies, but, given the experience of the early 1990s when domestic concerns overwhelmed EU concerns, this band was seen as a fixed exchange rate limit that would probably be broken as it imposed constraints on countries' domestic monetary policies.

to and is building up reserves, which means that some other country is losing reserves. A country that is continually gaining or losing reserves must eventually change its fixed exchange rate.

The difficulty is that as soon as the country gets close to its reserves limit, foreign exchange traders begin to expect a drop in the value of the currency, and they try to get out of that currency because anyone holding that currency when it falls will lose money. False rumors of an expected depreciation or decrease in a country's fixed exchange rate can become true by causing a "run on a currency," as all traders sell that currency. Thus, at times fixed exchange rates can become highly unstable because expectation of a change in the exchange rate can force the change to occur. As opposed to small movements in currency values, under a fixed rate regime these movements occur in large, sudden jumps.

Fixed Exchange Rates and Policy Independence   Maintaining a fixed exchange rate places limitations on a central bank's actions. In a country with fixed exchange rates, the central bank must ensure that the international supply of and demand for its currency are equal at the existing exchange rate.

Say, for example, that the United States and the Bahamas have fixed exchange rates: \$1 B = \$1 U.S. The Bahamian central bank decides to run an expansionary monetary policy, lowering the interest rate and stimulating the Bahamian economy. The lower interest rates will cause financial capital to flow out of the country, and the higher income will increase imports. Demand for Bahamian dollars will fall. To prop up their dollar and to maintain the fixed exchange rate, the Bahamas will have to buy their own currency. They can do so only as long as they have sufficient reserves of other countries' currencies.

Because most countries' international reserves are limited, a country with fixed exchange rates is limited in its ability to conduct expansionary monetary and fiscal

This British newspaper is one of the best sources for up-to-date news on international finance.

ADDED DIMENSION

INTERNATIONAL TRADE
PROBLEMS FROM SHIFTING
VALUES OF CURRENCIES

Major fluctuations in exchange rates can cause problems for international trade. Say, for instance, that a firm decides to build a plant in the United States because costs in the United States are low. But say the value of the dollar then rises significantly; the firm's costs rise significantly too, making it uncompetitive.

Or let's take a recent real-world example: Korean companies decided to make a major drive to sell Korean VCRs in the United States. They decided on a low-price strategy, which was justified by their cost advantage. Their export drive was a success, but the value of the Korean won relative to the dollar rose significantly. The result was that in 1989 Korean VCR companies were losing money on each VCR they sold in the United States. They kept the price low, hoping that the won would fall in value. (In other words, their average variable costs were less than the price; their average total costs were greater than the price.)

policies. It loses its freedom to stimulate the economy in response to a recession. That's why, when a serious recession hits, many countries are forced to abandon fixed exchange rates. They run out of international reserves, and choose expansionary monetary policy to achieve their domestic goals over contractionary monetary policy to achieve their international goals.

Flexible Exchange Rates   The advantages and disadvantages of flexible exchange rates are the reverse of those of fixed exchange rates.

The advantages are:

1. Flexible exchange rates provide for orderly incremental adjustment of exchange rates, rather than large, sudden jumps.
2. Flexible exchange rates allow government to be flexible in conducting domestic monetary and fiscal policies.

The disadvantages are:

1. Flexible exchange rates allow speculation to cause large jumps in exchange rates that do not reflect market fundamentals.
2. Flexible exchange rates allow government to be flexible in conducting domestic monetary and fiscal policies. (This too is a disadvantage as well as an advantage.)

Let's consider each in turn.

Flexible Exchange Rates and Monetary Stability   Advocates of flexible exchange rates argue as follows: Why not treat currency markets like any other market and let private market forces determine a currency's value? There is no fixed price for TVs; why should there be a fixed price for currencies? The opponents' answer is based on the central role that international financial considerations play in an economy and the strange shapes and large shifts that occur in the short-run supply and demand curves for currencies.

As you saw in the discussion of the J-curve, short-run changes in the exchange rate do not necessarily improve the balance of payments. This suggests that the short-run supply of and demand for currencies may be a little bit strange. As opposed to sloping up and sloping down nicely (as normal supply and demand curves do), short-run supply and demand curves for currencies often slope in a way that makes the invisible hand push the wrong way: Supply curves are likely to bend backward, and demand curves are likely to fall backward.

With supply and demand curves that slope the wrong way and shift around all the time, there's no guarantee that a fall in the exchange rate will help achieve equilibrium. As you saw with the J-curve, it can take the economy further from equilibrium. If equilibrium is to be achieved, it must be achieved because speculators enter in and buy an undervalued currency in expectation of its future rise. Thus, two arguments against flexible exchange rates are that they don't necessarily help achieve equilib-

With supply and demand curves that slope the wrong way and shift around all the time, there's no guarantee that a fall in the exchange rate will help achieve equilibrium.

rium in the short run, and that they allow far too much fluctuation in exchange rates, making trade difficult.

Flexible Exchange Rates and Policy Independence   The policy independence arguments for and against flexible exchange rates are the reverse of those given for fixed exchange rates. Individuals who believe that national governments should not have flexibility in setting monetary policy argue that flexible exchange rates don't impose the discipline on policy that fixed exchange rates do. Say, for example, that a country's goods are uncompetitive. Under a fixed exchange rate system, the country would have to contract its money supply and deal with the underlying uncompetitiveness of its goods. Under a flexible exchange rate system, the country can maintain an expansionary monetary policy, allowing inflation simply by allowing the value of its currency to fall.

Advocates of policy flexibility argue that it's stupid for a country to go through a recession when it doesn't have to; flexible exchange rates allow countries more flexibility in dealing with their problems. True, policy flexibility may lead to inflation, but inflation is better than a recession.

Partially Flexible Exchange Rates   Faced with the dilemma of choosing between these two unpleasant policies, most countries have opted for a policy in between the two: partially flexible exchange rates. With such a policy they try to get the advantages of both a fixed and a flexible exchange rate.

When policymakers believe there is a fundamental misalignment in a country's exchange rate, they will allow private forces to determine it—they allow the exchange rate to be flexible. When they believe that the currency's value is falling because of speculation, or that too large an adjustment in the currency is taking place, and that that adjustment won't achieve their balance of payment goals, they step in and fix the exchange rate, either supporting or pushing down their currency's value.

Q-10:   If currency traders expect the government to devalue a currency, what will they likely do?

If policymakers are correct, this system of partial flexibility would work smoothly and would have the advantages of both fixed and flexible exchange rates. If policymakers are incorrect, however, a partially flexible system has the disadvantages of both fixed and flexible systems.

Which view is correct is much in debate. Most foreign exchange traders that I know tell me that the possibility of government intervention increases the amount of private speculation in the system. In private investors' view, their own assessments of what exchange rates should be are better than those of policymakers. If private investors knew the government would not enter in, private speculators would focus on fundamentals and would stabilize short-run exchange rates. When private speculators know government might enter into the market, they don't focus on fundamentals; instead they continually try to outguess government policymakers. When that happens, private speculation doesn't stabilize; it destabilizes exchange rates as private traders try to guess what the government thinks.

Many of my economics colleagues who work for the Fed aren't convinced by private investors' arguments. They maintain that some government intervention helps stabilize currency markets. I don't know which group is right.

CONCLUSION

Even though you've stayed with me through the chapter's in-depth introduction to international finance, you still won't be able to predict exchange rates. Nobody can do that. But at least I hope you know why you can't. The most honest prediction that one can make is that exchange rates are likely to be highly volatile—unpredictable in the short run and even unpredictable in the long run as new short-run phenomena develop. To make even a reasonable guess about what will happen in such markets, you will likely need a psychologist (who can tell you what other people are thinking, what other people think you're thinking, what other people think you think you're thinking, and so on), and perhaps also a psychiatrist to handle the mental marshmallow you might become if you get into international currency markets.

Being an international currency trader isn't for most people; when my students suggest that they'd like to become international currency traders, I suggest they go into a more pleasant, less stressful field—like, say, air traffic control.

Our story has a moral, however. The moral is that in many so-called economic phenomena, noneconomic criteria play a significant role in what happens; in the short run they swamp the long-run economic forces. Economists can predict which types of markets will have these fluctuations (foreign exchange markets are definitely one type), but they can't predict exactly how prices will fluctuate in these markets.

Being an international currency trader isn't for most people. I suggest most people would prefer a more pleasant and less stressful field like, say, air traffic control.

CHAPTER SUMMARY

- The balance of payments is made up of the current account, the capital account, and the official transactions account.

- In 1988 the United States became a net debtor nation. In the early 1990s it is the largest debtor nation in the world.

- Exchange rates in a perfectly flexible exchange rate system are determined by the supply of and demand for a currency.

- When a country sets an exchange rate by law, it has a nonconvertible currency.

- It is easier technically for a country to bring the value of its currency down than it is to support its currency.

- In many so-called economic phenomena, noneconomic criteria play a significant role in what happens.

- Often, in the short run, a fall in a country's exchange rate can increase a balance of payments deficit and balance of trade deficit. In the long run, a fall tends to improve those balances.

- Flexible, partially flexible, and fixed exchange rates have advantages and disadvantages.

KEY TERMS

balance of payments *(380)*
balance of trade *(380)*
Bretton Woods system *(394)*
capital account *(380)*
capital controls *(389)*
current account *(380)*
exchange rate policy *(390)*

fixed exchange rate *(392)*
flexible exchange rate *(392)*
fundamental analysis *(385)*
gold specie flow
  mechanism *(393)*
gold standard *(393)*
J-curve *(391)*

nonconvertible currency *(383)*
official transactions account *(380)*
partially flexible exchange rate *(392)*
reserve currency *(394)*
Special Drawing Rights (SDR's) *(394)*
spread *(386)*

QUESTIONS FOR THOUGHT AND REVIEW

The number after each question represents the estimated degree of critical thinking required. (1 = almost none; 10 = deep thought.)

1. If a country is running a balance of trade deficit, will its current account be in deficit? Why? *(3)*

2. When someone sends 100 British pounds to a friend in the United States, will this transaction show up on the capital or current account? Why? *(3)*

3. Support the statement: "It is best to offset a capital account surplus with a current account deficit." *(7)*

4. Support the statement: "It is best to offset a capital account deficit with a current account surplus." *(5)*

5. Which is likely to have the larger spread: South Korean won or U.S. dollars? Why? *(7)*

6. What are the advantages and disadvantages of a nonconvertible currency? *(5)*

7. What is the J-curve and why might its existence provide an argument for a country having a nonconvertible currency? *(6)*

8. Explain how an international financial adjustment would occur under a gold standard. *(6)*

9. Which is preferable: a fixed or a flexible exchange rate? Why? *(7)*

10. Explain how high interest rates in Germany placed downward pressure on other EU countries' currencies and ended the European fixed exchange rate system. *(5)*

PROBLEMS AND EXERCISES

1. Draw the fundamental analysis of the supply and demand for British pound sterling in terms of dollars. Show what will happen to the exchange rate with those curves in response to each of the following events:
   a. The U.K. price level rises.
   b. The U.S. price level rises.
   c. The U.K. economy experiences a boom.
   d. The U.K. interest rates rise.

2. At an exchange rate of Rs20 to \$1 (Rs is the sign for rupees), Pakistan is exporting 100,000 bales of cotton to the United States at \$5 (or Rs100) each. It's importing 60 cars from the United States at \$10,000 (Rs200,000) each. Now say that the value of the rupee falls to Rs22 to \$1. Pakistan's exports rise to 103,000 bales of cotton while car imports fall to 58.
   a. What has happened to the trade balance?
   b. What will likely happen in the long run?
   c. What would happen if Pakistani exporters raised their price for cotton so that they were getting the same revenue as before the rupee's fall in value?
   d. How would that response affect what would happen in the long run?

3. Will the following be suppliers or demanders of U.S. dollars in foreign exchange markets?
   a. A U.S. tourist in Latin America.
   b. A German foreign exchange trader who believes that the dollar exchange rate will fall.
   c. A U.S. foreign exchange trader who believes that the dollar exchange rate will fall.
   d. A Costa Rican tourist in the U.S.
   e. A Russian capitalist who wants to protect his wealth from expropriation.
   f. A British investor in the United States.

4. You've been hired as an economic advisor to Yamaichi Foreign Exchange Traders. What buy or sell recommendations for U.S. dollars would you make in response to the following news?
   a. Faster economic growth in the EU.
   b. Expectations of higher interest rates in the United States.
   c. U.S. interest rate rises, but rises less than expected.
   d. Expected loosening of U.S. monetary policy.
   e. Higher inflationary predictions for the United States.

5. State whether the following will show up on the current account or the capital account:
   a. IBM's exports of computers to Japan.
   b. IBM's hiring of a British merchant bank as a consultant.
   c. A foreign national living in the U.S. repatriates money.
   d. Ford Motor Company's profit in Hungary.
   e. Ford Motor Company uses that Hungarian profit to build a new plant in Hungary.

ANSWERS TO MARGIN QUESTIONS

1. The expenditures of a U.S. citizen traveling abroad will show up as a debit on the services account. As tourism or traveling, it is a service. *(381)*

2. Net investment income is the return a country gets on its foreign investment minus the return foreigners get on their investment within a country. A country is a net debtor nation if the value of foreign investment within a country exceeds the value of its investment abroad. A country can be a net debtor nation and still have its net investment income positive if its foreign investment is undervalued at market values (valuation is generally done at book value), or if its foreign investment earns a higher rate of return than foreigners' investment within that country. *(382)*

3. As in the diagram below, an increase in the demand for francs pushes up the exchange rate of francs in terms of dollars. *(384)*

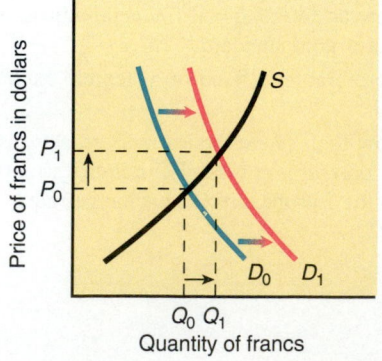

4. An increase in the demand for dollars is the equivalent of an increase in the supply of francs, so an increase in the demand for dollars pushes down the price of francs in terms of dollars, as in the diagram below. *(385)*

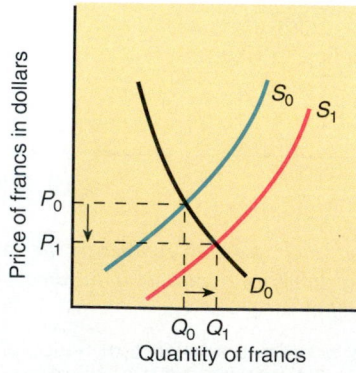

5. It depends. The spread is the difference between the bid and ask price. The smaller the spread, the more volume but the lower profit per unit volume. *(387)*

6. In general, it would be easier for the United States to push the value of the dollar down because doing so involves the United States buying up foreign currencies, which it can pay for simply by printing more dollars. To push the dollar up requires foreign reserves. *(390)*

7. In the short run, normal market forces have a limited, and possibly even perverse, effect on exchange rates, which is why most governments don't leave determination of exchange rates to the market. *(392)*

8. According to the gold specie flow mechanism, a country experiencing a surplus will have an inflow of gold, which will push prices up and will decrease exports and increase imports, moving a balance of payments surplus into a balance of payments equilibrium. *(393)*

9. Someone who believes price stability is the main goal of central bank policy is more likely to prefer fixed exchange rates, because these rates place an international anchor on domestic monetary policy and prevent governments from running as expansionary a monetary policy as they otherwise might like. *(395)*

10. Currency traders expecting devaluation will likely sell a currency, forcing the devaluation even if it might otherwise not have had to take place. *(398)*

18

Deficits and Debt

Any government, like any family, can for a year spend a little more than it earns. But you and I know that a continuance of that habit means the poorhouse.

~Franklin D. Roosevelt

After reading this chapter, you should be able to:

1 Define the terms *deficit* and *debt*.

2 State why economists focus on financial health rather than on deficits.

3 Explain why, in an expanding economy, a government can run a limited, but continual, deficit without serious concern about the consequences.

4 Differentiate between a real deficit and a nominal deficit.

5 Explain why, even though the real budget deficit of the United States is much lower than the nominal deficit, there is still reason for concern about the deficit.

6 Explain why there are alternative reasonable views about the deficit.

In our discussion of macroeconomic policies and problems, two concepts come up continually: deficits and debt. Is the U.S. budget deficit something we have to worry about? Is the $4.5 trillion U.S. government debt going to be an unbearable burden on our grandchildren? These and similar questions are sufficiently important to warrant a separate chapter that explores the government budget deficit and debt.

> **1** A deficit is a shortfall of incoming revenue under outgoing payments. A debt is accumulated deficits minus accumulated surpluses.

Before we begin the exploration, let's briefly consider the definitions. A **deficit** is a shortfall of revenues under payments; it is a flow concept. If your income (revenues) is $20,000 per year and your expenditures (payments) are $30,000 per year, you are running a deficit. If revenues exceed payments, you are running a surplus. This means that a *government budget deficit* occurs when government expenditures exceed government revenues.

Debt is accumulated deficits minus accumulated surpluses; it is a stock concept. For example, say you've spent $30,000 a year for 10 years and have had annual income of $20,000 for 10 years. So you've had a deficit of $10,000 per year. At the end of 10 years, you will have accumulated a debt of $100,000:

$$10 \times \$10,000 = \$100,000.$$

(Spending more than you have in income means that you need to borrow the extra $10,000 per year from someone, so in later years much of your expenditure will be on interest on your previous debt.)

Let's begin with a consideration of the historical record of deficits in the United States. Exhibit 1(a) graphs the U.S. budget deficits since 1945. As you can see, for many years the U.S. budget has been significantly in deficit. But that hasn't always been the case. Before the 1940s, the U.S. government ran a budget surplus sometimes (mainly in peacetime) and a budget deficit at other times (mainly during wartime). After World War II—that is, after 1945—that changed, and since that time the United States has run consistent deficits.

U.S. GOVERNMENT DEFICITS AND DEBT: THE HISTORICAL RECORD

Because debt is accumulated deficits, and the United States has a deficit almost every year, you would expect United States debt to have increased substantially since World War II. Exhibit 1(b) shows that is indeed the case.

Why was there a change after World War II? A reason many economists suggest is the change in macroeconomic **policy regimes**—the general set of rules that governs the monetary and fiscal policies that a country follows—that occurred after World War II.

Policy Regimes, the Deficit, and the Debt

Policy regime   The general set of rules, whether explicit or implicit, governing the monetary and fiscal policies a country follows.

The big difference in policy regimes before and after World War II was the introduction of Keynesian economics and its use of discretionary fiscal policy. Before World War II, Classical economics dictated that government budget deficits were bad and that, except in wartime, they should be avoided. And that was the policy the U.S. government followed. That was changed by Keynesian economics which prescribed deficits to stimulate the economy and achieve a higher level of output. According to Keynesian economics, deficits were not necessarily bad. You had to look at the state of the economy to decide whether a deficit was good or bad.

Because Keynesian economics removed the stigma connected with deficits, some economists argue that government budget deficits are the result of Keynesian policies. Others argue that view is too simplistic. They point out that Keynesian economics never said that all deficits are good—it only said that deficits aren't necessarily bad, and when the economy is in a recession deficits might actually be good.

The argument that Keynesian economics accounts for the deficit is weakened by the fact that, in the 1980s, when there was a second change in policy regimes—Keynesian economics was discarded and replaced with a modern Classical supply-side economic policy regime—the deficit did not disappear. In fact, the deficit grew. The modern Classical supply-side policy regime has led to an even larger deficit than existed in the Keynesian policy regime.

> **Q-1:** In the 1980s, when the United States changed to a modern Classical supply-side policy regime, what happened to the size of the deficit?

The modern Classical supply-side regime focuses on the need for tax cuts whenever they can possibly be implemented. This supply-side Classical focus on tax cuts as the key to economic prosperity with little concern about the deficit is why you

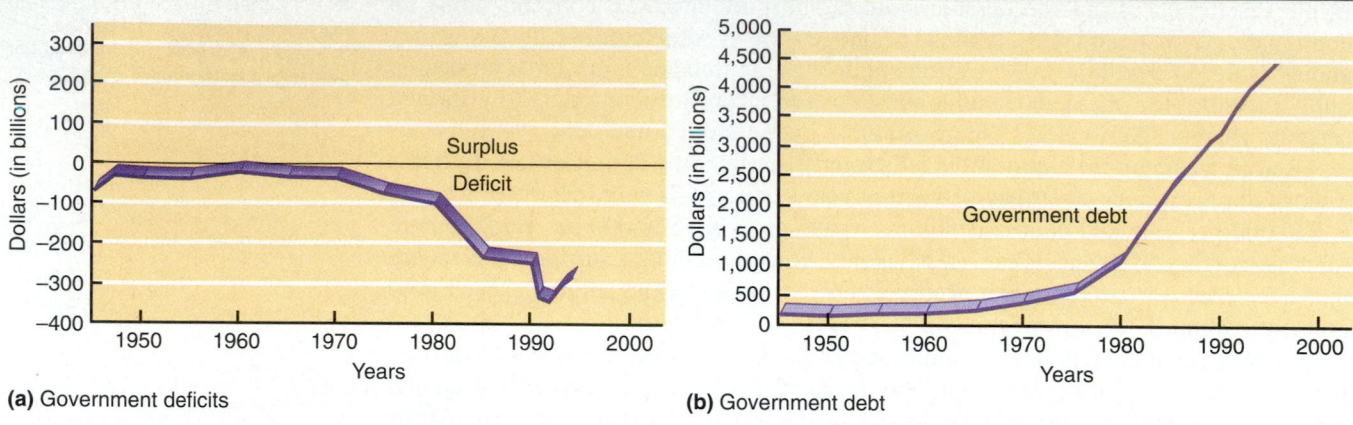

(a) Government deficits

(b) Government debt

EXHIBIT 1 (a and b)   U.S. Budget Deficits and Debt

Since the end of World War II, the U.S. government has run almost consistent deficits. These deficits increased substantially in the 1980s and early 1990s. They fell some in the mid-1990s, but they remained high and were expected to rise in the late 1990s. The result has been a large rise in government debt held by the public. (This exhibit excludes debt held by public agencies.)
Source: *Economic Report of the President.*

are now likely to see role reversals—Keynesians arguing against a deficit and Classicals arguing in favor of government running a deficit!

Politics and the Deficit

Gramm-Rudman-Hollings Act   *A law establishing mandatory deficit targets for the United States. (Large deficits continued despite the law.)*

Budget Enforcement Act of 1990   *A law establishing a pay-as-you-go test for new spending and tax cuts, along with additional spending limits for government.*

Differing groups of economists' changing views of deficits have had little impact on the lay public's view about deficits and debt. The lay public doesn't like either. In response, politicians say that they too don't like deficits and debt and that they're greatly concerned about the deficit problems.

In the 1980s political concern about the deficit grew so large that Congress passed the **Gramm-Rudman-Hollings Act** in 1985, establishing mandatory deficit targets for the United States. This act was designed to eliminate deficits by 1991. When it became clear that it would not achieve its goals, it was supplemented by the **Budget Enforcement Act of 1990.** This law put caps on certain aspects of federal spending, and established a ''pay-as-you-go'' test for new spending or tax cuts so that, up until

This lithograph, entitled "Legislative assault (on the budget)," appeared in a French newspaper in 1835.
Bleichroeder Print Collection, Baker Library, Harvard Business School.

1996, any new legislation, except for emergencies, must be accompanied by offsetting tax increases or spending cuts.

In 1993, as deficits continued high, the Clinton administration pushed through a deficit reduction law, the Omnibus Budget Reconciliation Act of 1993, that consisted of a combination of tax measures, spending cuts, and some new spending programs. Even with these laws, most observers projected continued high deficits throughout the 1990s, as government spending increased due to already-passed health and income maintenance entitlement programs.

For some politicians, these laws were not strong enough. They suggested a balanced budget amendment to the U.S. Constitution that would make it unconstitutional for the government to run a deficit. Support for such an amendment grew in the early 1990s as budget deficits reached $300 billion. Even economists who support that balanced budget amendment agree that the reason for not running a budget deficit is not the immediate economic consequences of a deficit. The reason is political. They believe that a balanced budget requirement would work like a lock on the refrigerator and that the political structure of the United States lacks self-control in spending and hence needs that lock. If you unlock a refrigerator, people without self-control will grow fat. Similarly, without the discipline of a mandatory balanced budget, government and politicians without self-control won't make the hard choices. Instead they'll say, "We can have both guns and butter. We'll pay for them by running a deficit."

Judging by events since the 1940s, there's substance to the political argument that most democracies lack self-control in spending and taxing decisions. Most political observers agree that democracy tends to put off difficult decisions. People want lots of goods and services from government, but nobody wants to pay for them with taxes. Running a deficit (buy now, pay later) allows democracies to buy current goods and services but delay paying for them, and hence to avoid the hard choices for the present.[1]

Where do economists come out in the debate about the deficit? On most sides of the issue. But the reasons for their differences are quite unlike the reasons lay people and politicians differ. Why? Because there are a number of technical aspects behind the deficits and debt that most economists understand, and most lay people (and politicians) don't. Thus, to understand economists' views on deficits and debt, you've got to understand these technical aspects behind applying those definitions. We'll now examine these technical aspects and see how understanding them changes our ideas about problems deficits and debt pose for society.

The definitions of *deficits* and *debt* are simple, but their simplicity hides important aspects that will help you understand current debates about deficits and debt. Thus, it's necessary to look carefully at some ambiguities in the definitions. Let's start with deficits.

Deficits are a shortfall of revenues compared to expenditures. So whether you have a deficit depends on what you include as a revenue and what you include as an expenditure. How you make these decisions can make an enormous difference in whether you have a deficit.

For example, consider the problem of a firm with revenues of $8,000 but no expenses except a $10,000 machine expected to last five years. Should the firm charge the $10,000 to this year's expenditures? Should it split the $10,000 evenly among the five years? Or should the firm use some other approach? Which method the firm chooses makes a big difference in whether its current budget will be in surplus or deficit.

This accounting issue is central to the debate about whether we should be concerned about the U.S. budget deficit. Say, for example, that government promises

Each year the federal government publishes its budget, which details its spending programs.

Most political observers agree that democracy tends to put off difficult decisions.

ECONOMISTS' WAY OF LOOKING AT DEFICITS AND DEBT

Arbitrariness in Defining Deficits

Q-2: Distinguish between deficit and debt.

---

[1] The fact that democracy has problems doesn't mean that some other form of government is preferable to democracy. As Winston Churchill said, democracy is the worst form of government, except for all the other forms.

to pay an individual $1,000 ten years from now. How should government treat that promise? Since the obligation is incurred now, should government count as an expense now an amount that, if saved, would allow government to pay that $1,000 later? Or should government not count it as an expenditure until it actually pays out the money?

The same ambiguity surrounds revenues. For example, say you're holding government bonds valued at $100,000, which pay $10,000 interest per year, while you're spending $10,000 per year. You might think your budget is balanced. But what if the market value of the bonds (the amount you can sell them for) rises from $100,000 to $120,000? Should you count that $20,000 rise in value of the bonds as a revenue? Using an opportunity cost approach which economists use, a person holding bonds should count the rise in the bond's market value as revenue, which means that your income for the year is $30,000, not $10,000. Similarly the government that issued the bond should count the rise in the market value of the bond it issued as an expenditure and count any fall in the market value of a bond it issued as income.[2]

Many such questions must be answered before we can determine whether a budget is in deficit or surplus. Some questions have no right or wrong answer. For others there are right or wrong answers that vary with the question being asked. For still others, an economist's "right way" is an accountant's "wrong way." In short, there are many ways to measure expenditures and receipts so there are many ways to measure deficits.

To say that there are many ways to measure deficits is not to say that all ways are correct. Pretending to have income that you don't have is wrong by all standards. Similarly, inconsistent accounting practices—sometimes to measure an income flow one way and sometimes another—are wrong. Standard accounting practices rule out a number of "creative," but improper, approaches to measuring deficits. But even eliminating these, there remain numerous reasonable ways of defining deficits, which accounts for much of the debate.

There are many ways to measure expenditures and receipts, so there are many ways to measure deficits.

Deficits as a Summary Measure

2 The deficit is simply a summary measure of the financial health of the economy. To understand that summary you must understand the methods that were used to calculate it.

The point of the previous discussion is that deficits are simply a summary measure of a budget. As a summary, a deficit figure reduces a complicated set of accounting relationships down to one figure. To understand whether that one summary measure is something to worry about, you've got to understand the accounting procedures used to calculate it. Only then can you make an informed judgment about whether a deficit is something to worry about.

The Need to Judge Debt Relative to Assets

Debt is accumulated deficits. If you spend $1,000 more than you earn for each of three years, you'll end up with a $3,000 debt. (To make things simple, we assume that spending includes paying interest on the debt.)

Debt is also a summary measure of a country's financial situation. As a summary measure, debt has even more problems than deficit. Unlike a deficit (which is the difference between outflows and inflows and hence provides at least a full summary measure), debt by itself is only half of a picture. The other half of the debt picture is assets. For a country, assets include its skilled work force, its natural resources, its factories, its housing stock, and its holdings of foreign assets. For a government, assets include the buildings and land it owns but, more importantly, it includes a portion of the assets of the people in the country, since government gets a portion of all earnings of those assets in tax revenue.

To get an idea why the addition of assets is necessary to complete the debt picture, consider two governments: one has debt of $3 trillion and assets of $500 trillion; the other has $1 trillion in debt but only $1 trillion in assets. Which is in a better position? The government with more debt is, because its debt is significantly exceeded by its

Q–3: Why is debt only half the picture of a country's financial situation?

To judge a country's debt, you must view its debt in relation to its assets.

---

[2] Since a fixed rate bond's price varies inversely with the interest rate in the economy, a rise in the interest rate creates an income for bond issuers and an expense for bond holders. Reviewing the reasons why in relation to the present value formula is a good exercise.

assets. The example's point is simple: To judge a country's debt, you must view its debt in relation to its assets.

Like income and revenues, assets and debt are subject to varying definitions. Say, for example, that an 18-year-old is due to inherit $1 million at age 21. Should that expected future asset be counted as an asset now? Or say that the government buys an aircraft for $1 billion and discovers that it doesn't fly. What value should the government place on that aircraft? Or say that a country owes $1 billion, due to be paid 10 years from now, but inflation is ongoing at 100 percent per year. The inflation will reduce the value of the debt when it comes due by so much that its current real value will be $1 million—the approximate present value of $1 billion in 10 years with 100 percent inflation. It will be like paying $1 million today. Should the country list the debt as a $1 billion debt or a $1 million debt?

Arbitrariness in Defining Debt

As was the case with income, revenues, and deficits, there's no unique answer to how assets and debts should be valued. So even after you take assets into account, you still have to be careful when deciding whether or not to be concerned about debt.

Another important fact about debt is that all debt is not the same. In particular, government debt is different than an individual's debt. There are three reasons for this.

Difference between Individual and Government Debt

First, government is ongoing. There's no real need for government ever to pay back its debt. An individual's lifespan is limited; when a person dies, there's inevitably an accounting of assets and debt to determine whether anything is left to go to heirs. Before any part of a person's estate is passed on, all debts must be paid. The government, however, doesn't ever have to settle its accounts.

Second, government has an option for paying off a debt that individuals don't have. Specifically, it can pay off a debt by creating money. As long as people will accept a country's currency, a country can always exchange its interest-bearing debt for money (non–interest-bearing debt). By doing so, it pays off its debt.

Third, much of a government debt is **internal government debt** (government debt owed to its own citizens). Paying interest on the debt involves a redistribution among citizens of the country, but it does not involve a net reduction in income of the average citizen. For example, say that a country has a $3 trillion debt, all of which is internal debt. Say also that the government pays $300 billion interest on its debt each year. That means the government must collect $300 billion in taxes so people are $300 billion poorer; but it pays out $300 billion in interest to them, so on average, people in the country are neither richer nor poorer because of the debt.[3]

Internal government debt *Government debt owed to its own citizens.*

External government debt (government debt owed to individuals in foreign countries) is different, being more like an individual's debt. Paying interest on it involves a net reduction in domestic income. U.S. taxpayers will be poorer; foreign holders of U.S. bonds will be richer.

External government debt *Government debt owed to individuals in foreign countries.*

These three differences between government debt and individual debt must be continually kept in mind when considering governments' debt problems.

Let's now apply some of these insights. In Exhibits 1(a) and (b), we saw that U.S. government debt and deficits have been increasing since World War II. Let's now consider the question from a slightly different perspective, taking into account government's ability to handle debt and deficits. That different perspective is to look at deficits and debt relative to GDP, as in Exhibits 2(a) and (b). As you can see, relative to GDP recent deficits look much smaller. As a percentage of GDP, deficits haven't shown the same alarming trend as when they're considered in absolute terms. And it's the same with debt. Relative to GDP, debt has not been continually increasing. Instead, from after World War II to the 1970s and in the period from 1988 to 1990, the debt/GDP ratio actually decreased. In the mid 1990s it stabilized at somewhat under 70% of GDP.

Deficits, Debt, and Debt Service Relative to GDP

---

[3] There are, of course, distributional effects. The people who pay the taxes are not necessarily the same people who receive the interest.

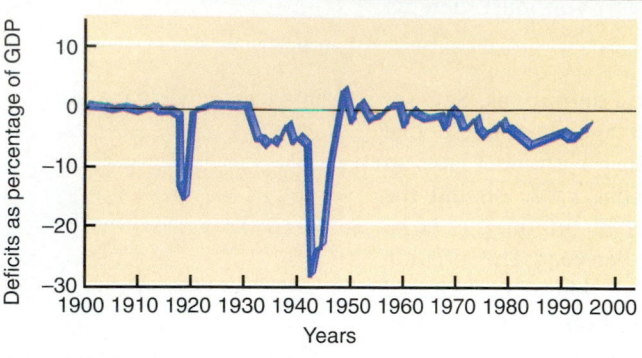

(a) Deficits as percentage of GDP

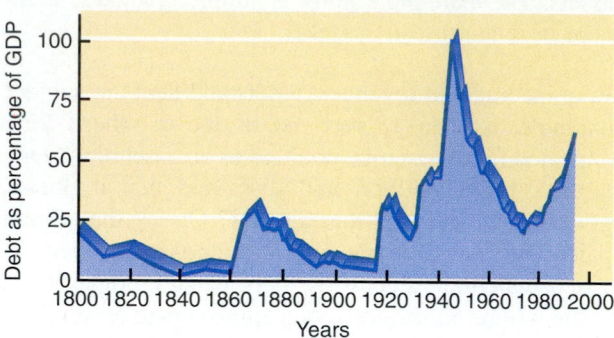

(b) Debt as percentage of GDP

EXHIBIT 2 (a and b)   **U.S. Deficits and Debt Relative to GDP**

The size of the deficits and the size of the debt look somewhat different when considered relative to the GDP. Notice specifically how the total debt to GDP declined substantially from the 1950s to the 1980s and how it has increased in the 1980s and 1990s.
Source: *Economic Report of the President* and *Historical Statistics.*

Q–4: Why is it reasonable to measure debt relative to GDP?

Debt service   *The interest rate on debt times the total debt.*

Structural deficit   *The deficit that would remain when the cyclical elements have been netted out.*

Why measure deficits and debt relative to GDP? Because the ability to pay off a deficit depends upon a nation's productive capacity. Government's ability to bring in revenue depends upon GDP. So GDP serves the same function for government as income does for an individual. It provides a measure of how much debt, and how large a deficit, government can handle.

Considering deficits and debt relative to GDP should ease our concern about the large U.S. deficit and growing U.S. debt. Although the absolute size of the deficits is much larger today than earlier, their relative importance compared to GDP is not. Similarly for debt. Though the debt has been increasing continuously, the problem it presents hasn't necessarily increased.

Considering debt relative to GDP is still not quite sufficient. Economists are also concerned about the interest rate paid on the debt. How much of a burden a given amount of debt imposes depends on the interest rate that must be paid on that debt. The interest rate on debt times the total debt is the **debt service** a country must pay each year. Money spent on debt service cannot be spent on buying new goods and services.

Over the past 50 years, the interest rate has fluctuated considerably; when it has risen, the debt service has increased; when it has fallen, debt service has decreased. Exhibit 3 shows the federal interest rate payments relative to GDP. This ratio increased substantially in World War II and then again in the 1970s and early 1980s. In the early 1990s, it rose but in the mid 1990s it has fallen to slightly over 3% of GDP. Thus, this measure of the debt problem suggests that the debt is more of a problem than the debt/GDP measure, but less of a problem than when we simply looked at debt.

Let's now turn to a consideration of how growth in GDP reduces problems posed by deficits and debt service.

Two Ways GDP Growth Reduces Problems Posed by Deficits

GDP can grow either because there's *real* growth or because there's *inflationary* growth. Both types of growth play major roles in economists' assessment of deficits. So we must consider how both types of GDP growth affect deficits and debt.

Structural Deficits, Cycles, and Growth In my earlier discussion of fiscal policy, I pointed out that the level of income in the economy affected the deficit. As income increases, tax revenue increases and the deficit declines. This meant that in a cyclical downturn, the deficit increases, and in a cyclical upturn, the deficit decreases. In talking about the problem of total debt, economists generally focus on the **structural deficit**—the deficit that would remain when the cyclical elements have been netted out (when the economy is at its potential income). In theory, determining the structural

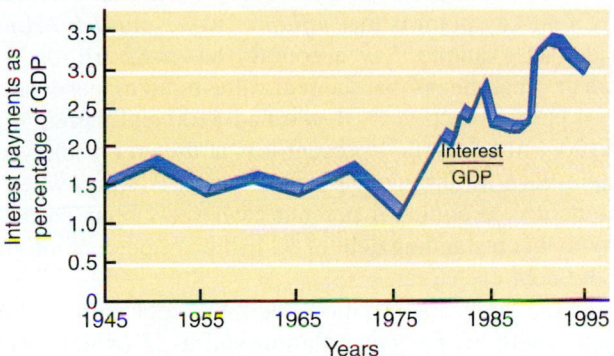

EXHIBIT 3   Federal Interest Payments Relative to GDP

Interest payments as a percentage of GDP remained relatively constant until the 1970s, after which they rose significantly due to high interest rates and large increases in debt. In the late 1980s, they fell as GDP increased, but with the recession in the early 1990s they rose substantially again, even as interest rates fell.
Source: *Economic Report of the President.*

deficit is easy to do; in practice, it is difficult since there is significant debate about where potential income is and how much it is increasing from one year to the next. Despite this, in discussing the deficit problem, economists focus on the structural deficit; the cyclical component of the deficit will solve itself.

Real Growth and the Deficit   When a society experiences real growth, it becomes richer, and, being richer, it can handle more debt. Real growth in the United States has averaged about 2.5 percent per year, which means that U.S. debt can grow at a rate of 2.5 percent without increasing the debt/GDP ratio. But for debt to grow, government must run a deficit, so a constant debt/GDP ratio in a growing economy is consistent with a continual deficit.

When a society experiences real growth, it becomes richer, and, being richer, it can handle more debt.

How much of a deficit are we talking about? U.S. federal government debt is about $4.6 trillion and GDP is about $6.4 trillion, so the government debt/GDP ratio is about 70 percent. A real growth rate of 2.5 percent means that real GDP is growing at about $160 billion per year. That means that government can run a deficit of $112 billion a year without increasing the debt/GDP ratio:

3   Since in a growing economy a continual deficit is consistent with a constant ratio of debt to GDP, and GDP serves as a measure of the government's ability to pay off the debt, a country can run a continual deficit.

$$70\% \times \$160 \text{ billion} = \$112 \text{ billion}.$$

Of course, for those who believe that total U.S. government debt is already too large relative to GDP, this argument (that the debt/GDP ratio is remaining constant) is unsatisfying. They'd prefer the debt/GDP ratio to fall.

Is the current U.S. debt/GDP ratio too high? That's a difficult question. The United States can afford its current debt, in the sense that it can afford to pay the interest on that debt. In fact, it could afford a much higher debt/GDP ratio since U.S. government bonds are still considered one of the safest assets in the world. No one is worried about the U.S. government defaulting. So technically the current debt can be handled, and can probably be increased by trillions of dollars without problem.

But, of course, that debt requires interest to be paid on it. In 1994, the U.S. government paid out approximately $200 billion in interest. A larger debt would require even higher interest payments. The $200 billion in interest payment is government revenue that can't be spent on defense or welfare; it's a payment for past expenditures. Ultimately the interest payments are the burden of the debt. That's what people mean when they say a deficit is burdening future generations. That burden is the interest payments future generations will have to make to the holders of U.S. debt.[4]

Summarizing: Real growth makes it possible for a country to run a deficit without increasing the debt/GDP ratio. Since that ratio is a key ratio for judging economists' concern about debt, real growth lessens concern about the deficit.

We now turn to inflation's effect on deficits and debt.

---

[4] This statement about the burden of the debt doesn't contradict my earlier statement that government's internal debt doesn't directly decrease income in a country. With internal debt, those interest payments are paid to someone in the country. Thus, the burden of the debt isn't the loss of income to society. The burden is the prior commitment of government revenue to paying interest on government bonds. If collecting those tax revenues necessary to pay off bond holders has negative incentive effects and reduces income, then the debt indirectly lowers income in the economy.

Q-5: Explain how inflation can wipe out debt.

Inflation, Debt, and the Real Deficit Inflation's subtle effect on deficits and debt requires careful consideration. The first key point is that *inflation wipes out debt*. How much does it wipe out? Consider an example. Say a country has a $2 trillion debt and inflation is 4 percent per year. That means that the real value of all assets denominated in dollars is declining by 4 percent each year. If you had $100 and there's 4 percent inflation in a year, that $100 will be worth 4 percent less at the end of the year—the equivalent of $96 had there been no inflation. By the same reasoning, when there's inflation the value of the debt is declining 4 percent each year. Four percent of $2 trillion is $80 billion, so with an outstanding debt of $2 trillion, 4 percent inflation will eliminate $80 billion of the debt each year.

The larger the debt and the larger the inflation, the more debt will be eliminated with inflation. For example, with 10 percent inflation and a $2 trillion debt, $200 billion of the debt will be eliminated by inflation each year. With 4 percent inflation and a $4 trillion debt, $160 billion of the debt will be eliminated.

If inflation is wiping out debt, and the deficit is equal to the increases in debt from one year to the next, inflation also affects the deficit. Economists take this into account by defining two types of deficits: a nominal deficit and a real deficit.

A **nominal deficit** is the deficit determined by looking at the difference between expenditures and receipts. It's what most people think of when they think of the budget deficit; it is the value that is generally reported.

A **real deficit** is the nominal deficit adjusted for inflation's effect on the debt. It is the nominal deficit *minus* the decrease in the value of the government's total outstanding debts due to inflation. Thus, to calculate the *real* deficit one must know the nominal deficit, the rate of inflation, and the total outstanding government debt. Let's consider some examples.

In our first example, assume:

> Nominal deficit = $100 billion
> Inflation = 4%
> Total debt = $2 trillion.

The definition of *real deficit* states:

Real deficit = Nominal deficit − (Inflation × Total debt).

Substituting in the numbers gives us:

$$\text{Real deficit} = \$100 \text{ billion} - (4\% \times \$2 \text{ trillion})$$
$$= \$100 \text{ billion} - \$80 \text{ billion}$$
$$= \$20 \text{ billion}$$

Though the nominal deficit is $100 billion, the real deficit is only $20 billion.

In our second example, assume:

> Nominal deficit = $100 billion
> Inflation = 10%
> Total debt = $2 trillion.

The only change from the first example is the inflation rate. But look what happens to the real deficit.

$$\text{Real deficit} = \$100 \text{ billion} - (10\% \times \$2 \text{ trillion})$$
$$= \$100 \text{ billion} - \$200 \text{ billion}$$
$$= -\$100 \text{ billion}$$

In this case, the country is not running a real deficit. After adjusting for inflation, the $100 billion nominal deficit becomes a −$100 billion deficit (a $100 billion real surplus)!

In our third example, assume:

> Nominal deficit = $100 billion
> Inflation = 4%
> Total debt = $4 trillion.

Nominal deficit *The deficit determined by looking at the difference between expenditures and receipts.*

Real deficit *The nominal deficit adjusted for inflation's effect on the debt.*

4 Real deficit = Nominal deficit − (Inflation × Total debt).

Q-6: The nominal deficit = $40 billion; inflation = 2 percent, and the total debt = $4 trillion. What is the real deficit?

In this example we've changed both the inflation rate and the amount of total debt. Now see what happens:

$$\text{Real deficit} = \$100 \text{ billion} - (4\% \times \$4 \text{ trillion}) = -\$60 \text{ billion}.$$

The $100 billion deficit becomes a $60 billion surplus. As you can see, the real deficit can differ significantly from the nominal deficit.

Inflation, Debt, and Nominal Deficits   This distinction between the nominal deficit and the real deficit is not an illusion. Inflation wipes out debt, and that fact must be considered when evaluating the effect of a deficit. Inflation is an important reason why the U.S. debt/GDP ratio declined in the postwar period. When inflation increases, the debt/GDP ratio can decrease even when the nominal deficit is large.

Inflation wipes out debt, and that fact must be considered when evaluating the effect of a deficit.

You may be somewhat hesitant to accept the preceding argument about how inflation eliminates debt and can change a nominal deficit into a real surplus. The first time I was presented with the argument, I was dubious. Somehow, inflation as a way of reducing debt's burden sounds too good to be true. If you are hesitant, it's with good reason. While the argument that inflation wipes out debt is correct, your fears are not groundless. Inflation is not a costless answer to eliminating debt.

To see that it isn't, let's carefully consider how inflation eliminates the debt. Say you bought U.S. bonds having a 4 percent annual interest rate with the expectation that the price level would remain constant. That's not a bad return; in each year you expect $4 for each $100 you loaned the government, and as each bond matures you expect to get $100 back. Now let's say that inflation is 6 percent per year. For each year of the loan the dollars with which the government pays you back are worth 6 percent less than the dollars you loaned the government, so instead of getting 4 percent more, you're losing 2 percent—the 4 percent interest you get minus the 6 percent inflation.

For you (the holder of debt), inflation isn't a costless way to eliminate a debt. It's very costly to creditors, who lose what the government gains. The government's gain from an inflation is the bond holder's loss from inflation. So the effect of inflation on debt is no illusion; it is simply a transfer of money from bond holders to the government.

Nominal and Real Interest Rates and Deficits   Such transfers of income do not make bond holders (creditors) very happy. Yes, the government's real debt is being reduced by inflation, but it's being reduced by bond holders' losses. And bond holders aren't helpless people. What can they do about it? For the fixed interest rate bonds they already hold, they can do nothing. When they bought the bonds, the contract was set. But they can do something about future bonds. The next time a bond salesman suggests buying government bonds, purchasers will likely take any expected inflation into account. Instead of buying a bond with a 4 percent interest rate, they will require an additional 6 percent to compensate them for the 6 percent expected inflation, for a total of 10 percent.

Expectations of inflation push up the nominal interest rate and cause bond holders to demand an inflation premium on their bonds. Expected future inflation causes the real interest rate to be different from the nominal interest rate. Thus, in the absence of inflation the nominal interest rate might be 4 percent. With 6 percent inflation, the nominal interest rate might be 10 percent: 4 percent real interest rate plus 6 percent expected inflation.

If the nominal interest rate is 6 percent higher than the real interest rate, bond holders have fully adjusted their 6 percent expectations of inflation into their bond purchases. In this case they won't lose if there's 6 percent inflation. Bond holders do not lose when they correctly expect inflation and build that expectation into their financial dealings. But if bond holders don't lose when they make a full adjustment for expected inflation, government can't win.

To see that, with full interest rate adjustment for inflation, creditors don't lose, it is helpful to divide the government's deficit into two components: a spending-on-current-needs component and a debt service component.

With Full Adjustment in Expectations, Creditors Don't Lose

Let's say the government has a total debt of $2 trillion, total expenditures of $500 billion, and a nominal deficit of $100 billion. Let's also assume that initially there's no expected inflation. Because there's no expected inflation, the 4 percent nominal interest rate will also be the real interest rate, and the nominal deficit will equal the real deficit. This means that the government is paying $80 billion a year in interest ($2 trillion debt × 4 percent interest). The debt service component of the deficit is $80 billion, leaving $420 billion to finance spending on current needs.

Q–7:   Explain why, when there is full adjustment for expectations, creditors don't lose in an inflation.

Now assume that there's a 6 percent inflation but the interest rate remains 4 percent. That 6 percent inflation decreases real debt by $120 billion (6 percent × $2 trillion). Using the real deficit formula, you can calculate that the government is actually running a real surplus of $20 billion:

$$\text{Real deficit} = \$100 \text{ billion} - (6\% \times \$2 \text{ trillion})$$

$$= \$100 \text{ billion} - \$120 \text{ billion}$$

$$= -\$20 \text{ billion}$$

But what happens if the 6 percent inflation were fully expected? In that case, the nominal interest rate on the debt, assuming it's all short term, will rise from 4 to 10 percent to account for the expected inflation. Debt service will be $200 billion (10 percent × $2 trillion), $120 billion more than government would have had to pay had there been no inflation adjustment to the interest rate. That $120 billion increase in the debt service expenditures just equals the $120 billion that the inflation wiped out.

This $120 billion increase in the debt service component of the deficit decreases the $420 billion current-spending component of the budget to $300 billion. So when nominal interest rates go up, simply in order to maintain the nominal deficit at its current level government must either reduce spending on current needs or it must raise taxes and collect more in revenues. It's paying extra interest to bond holders to compensate them for their loss due to inflation.

This distinction between nominal and real is necessary to make a judgment about a given nominal deficit. When there's high expected inflation and a large debt, much of the nominal deficit is a debt service component which is simply offsetting the decrease in the debt due to inflation.

This insight into debt is directly relevant to the budget situation in the United States. For example, back in 1990 the nominal U.S. deficit was about $280 billion, while the real deficit was about half of that—$140 billion. But that low real deficit was not costless to the government. When inflationary expectations were much lower, as they were in the 1950s, government paid 3 or 4 percent on its bonds. In 1990 it paid 8 or 9 percent, which is about 5 percent more than it paid in the 1950s. With its $2.75 trillion debt, the United States was paying about $140 billion more in interest than it would have had to pay if no inflation had been expected and the nominal interest rate had been 3 rather than 8 percent. That reduced the amount it could spend on current services by $140 billion. This means that much of the 1990 nominal U.S. deficit existed because of the rise in debt service necessary to compensate bond holders for the expected inflation.

As inflationary expectations and nominal interest rates fell in the 1990s, the difference between the real and nominal deficit decreased. Still, a 2 percent gap between nominal and real interest rates and a $5 trillion debt would mean that $100 billion of any deficit is due to the inflation premium raising the nominal interest rate.

Summary to This Point

Deficits are a summary measure of the state of the economy.

It is the financial health of the economy, not the deficit, that we should be concerned with.

We've covered a lot of material, so before we move on let's review four important points:

1. Deficits are summary measures of the state of the economy. They are dependent on the accounting procedures used.
2. It is the financial health of the economy, not the deficit, with which we should be concerned.
3. Deficits and debt should be viewed relative to GDP to determine their importance.

INFLATION AND INDEXED BONDS

ere's a proposal that some economists have suggested could significantly reduce the nominal U.S. deficit. Currently most bonds are fixed-interest bonds. They pay back a stated number of dollars in a given period. For example, at 10 percent interest a $1,000 five-year bond pays $100 interest each year for five years, and pays back another $1,000 at the end of five years.

Some economists have proposed the following: make the amount that is to be paid back, the $1,000, indexed to inflation. Thus, if price level rises 40 percent, the amount paid back would be $1,400 rather than $1,000. Bonds that pay back an amount dependent on inflation are called *indexed bonds*.

Let's now ask: What would happen if the United States were to issue indexed bonds? Since bond holders are compensated for inflation, the interest on bonds would fall. If 5 percent inflation were the expected rate and the nominal interest rate were 7 percent, the real interest rate would be 2 percent—so the interest rate on bonds would be 2 instead of 7 percent, U.S. debt service would fall from about $200 billion to between $50 billion and $60 billion, and the measured U.S. deficit would decrease significantly.

Most economists oppose having the government issue indexed bonds. Yes, they agree, it would lower the measured deficit, but it would not change real U.S. debt. At the same time, indexing would introduce new complexities of government finance as the inflation index came under even more scrutiny because so much money would be riding on it.

Whether or not you favor the proposal, it is a superb proposal from an academic perspective. It helps us recognize the difference between real and nominal deficits.

4. The real deficit is the nominal deficit adjusted for the inflation reduction in the real debt:

$$\text{Real deficit} = \text{Nominal deficit} - (\text{Inflation} \times \text{Debt})$$

Considering real deficits rather than nominal deficits and viewing the deficit and debt relative to GDP should have lessened your concern about the size of the U.S. deficit. Given inflation, the real deficit is lower than the nominal deficit, and given real growth we can stand an increase in total debt without the burden becoming intolerable.

But, as with most issues in economics, we must think about "on the other hand." The most important "on the other hand" concerns how future commitments are calculated in the U.S. budget, and the accounting gimmicks used to make the nominal deficit seem low. To see how these work, let's consider the accounting system used by the U.S. government budget.

Some Reasons for Concern about the U.S. Government Budget Deficit

The U.S. Budget Does Not Include Many Government Obligations

The U.S. government uses a **cash flow accounting system.** When it spends or collects money, these outflows or inflows show up on the budget. When the government doesn't have a cash inflow or outflow, nothing shows up on the budget. This cash flow accounting system leads to a number of important aspects of the budget and the deficit.

Cash flow accounting system   An accounting system entering expenses and revenues only when cash is received or paid out.

First, a number of obligations government incurs do not show up as part of the deficit. One such obligation is federal loan guarantees, such as guarantees on student loans, pensions, and deposits in banks. Since no cash is spent when these guarantees are made, they don't show up as an expenditure.

Just how important these can be became apparent in 1989 when numerous savings and loan associations went bankrupt and the Federal Savings and Loan Insurance Corporation (FSLIC), the organization that guarantees S&L deposits, was called upon to meet its obligation. The cost to government was over $200 billion—all from off-budget obligations that never showed up in the government budget when they were incurred! So here we have a case of government incurring a huge obligation that never showed up as an expense at the time it was incurred.

The FSLIC doesn't have the United States's only outstanding obligation that doesn't appear in the budget. There are also obligations of the FDIC (Federal Deposit Insurance Corporation), a government organization that guarantees bank deposits, Penny Benny (Pension Benefit Guarantee Corporation), a government organization that guarantees pension payments by firms through pension benefits insurance, and others. Through these programs, the U.S. government has guaranteed trillions of

Q–8: How can a government that isn't running a deficit still get itself into financial trouble?

dollars of obligations out there, meaning that even if it had a real deficit of zero, its overall financial health might still be questionable.

The Government Uses Accounting Tricks to Make the Deficit Look Smaller Of even more concern is the way in which the U.S. government met its obligation to bail out the savings and loan corporations. What it did not do is admit to the obligation and enter it into the books as an expense. Entering the S&L bailout on the books would have increased the nominal deficit and made it look as if the government weren't reducing the deficit—but the government was committed to reducing the deficit.

Instead, the government increased insurance fees on savings and loans institutions slightly and counted those fees as additional current revenue. These fees were no way near enough to cover the cost of the S&L bailout. To cover most of the costs, the government sold special bonds. But these expenditures were *not* counted as expenditures so they didn't increase the deficit in 1989 or 1990. Instead, they were called **off-budget expenditures** (expenditures of money that are not to be counted as expenditures in the budget).

So here's what happened with the S&L bailout. The fees increased current revenues; the expenditures weren't entered on the books. As it worked out, incurring a multibillion dollar obligation in 1989 *lowered* the measured budget deficit for 1989!

Were this FSLIC action an isolated incident, it could be shaken off. It's much like failing a quiz: It might be no problem if the reason you failed the quiz was that your child or your father was sick that day: not to worry, because it was an isolated incident. But if you failed a quiz because you did no studying, failing is much more important. It suggests that, unless you start studying, you will likely fail all your other quizzes. The FSLIC fiasco was the government equivalent to not studying.

The U.S. government has often dealt with its budgetary problems with gimmicks to make the deficit look smaller than it is. Thus, many economists argue that the government has serious financial health problems that are hidden by the accounting procedures it uses. And it has those problems even if its real deficit is zero or in surplus.

The Social Security Retirement System

Let's consider the old-age retirement portion of the social security system as another example of how the government's financial health may be questionable even when its budget is not in deficit. According to some observers, that system has a built-in financial problem that will likely explode some time about the year 2020.

Funded and Unfunded Retirement Systems Pension systems can be either funded or unfunded. A **funded pension system** is one in which money is collected and invested in a special fund from which pension payments are made. An **unfunded pension system** is one in which pensions are paid from current revenues.

The social security system, which provides pensions for a large majority of the U.S. population, is largely an *unfunded* pension system. Until recently, most of the social security taxes that the government collected as part of that pension system were not invested in a special fund to be used to pay out benefits when the person retires or otherwise becomes eligible to receive benefits. Instead, to a large degree, the government paid social security benefits from current tax revenue.

An unfunded pension system is not necessarily unsound. In an ongoing system, there will always be revenue coming in and payments going out. There are always current workers to support a system that pays the aged. The benefit of the unfunded system is that it allows initial payments to individuals to exceed what they paid in. The problem with an unfunded system is that there's no trust fund of assets earning interest to cover future payments.

A Potential Problem with Unfunded Systems As long as the population's age distribution, the annual death rate, and the number of people working do not change much, an unfunded system presents no problem. But an unfunded system does present a potential problem if the amount paid in and the amount paid out differ.

Off-budget expenditure An expenditure that is not counted in the budget as an expenditure.

5 Even though the real deficit is lower than the nominal deficit, there is still cause for concern because the U.S. budget fails to include many obligations and the government uses many accounting tricks.

Funded pension system One in which money is collected and invested in a special fund from which payments are made.

Unfunded pension system One in which pensions are paid from current revenues.

COMPARISONS OF GOVERNMENT DEBT TO GDP

One way to get a handle on whether the U.S. government debt is "too high" is to compare it to the debt of some other countries, as is done in the bar chart. Since debt is defined slightly differently in different countries, and since fluctuation in GDP can change ratios, these percentages should be interpreted as measures of magnitude only.

In the chart you can see that the United States comes out in the middle of these eight countries. Of course, there is no economic law stating that the other countries are right, or that the economic situation might not change, making these current ratios unsustainable. Still, it's nice to know that the United States is not alone in its deficit and debt problems.

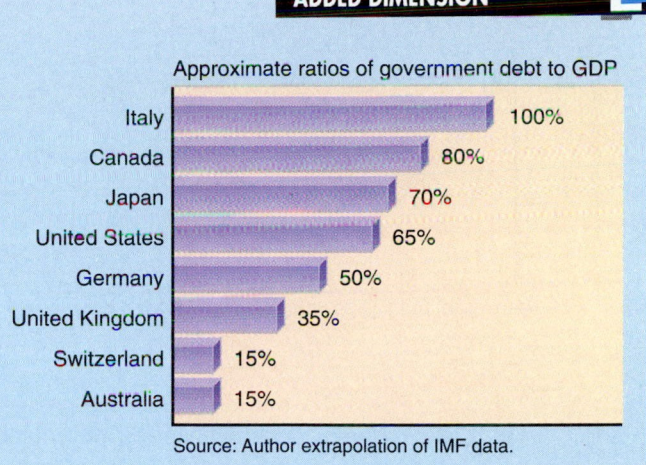

Approximate ratios of government debt to GDP

Italy	100%
Canada	80%
Japan	70%
United States	65%
Germany	50%
United Kingdom	35%
Switzerland	15%
Australia	15%

Source: Author extrapolation of IMF data.

To see this, say we have only three groups of people: workers, the retired elderly, and the very young (who aren't yet working). Now suddenly we start a pension program. We use the money that we collect from the workers to pay pensions to the elderly retired people. These elderly people have paid nothing in, because they retired before the system started up. In short, this group gets benefits without having paid anything into the system. In the next generation, the elderly die, the workers become elderly, and the young become workers. The new group of elderly get paid by the new workers. As long as the three groups remain at equivalent relative sizes, the process works neatly—each generation will get paid when its time comes.

But let's consider what happens when there's a "baby boom" and one group suddenly has a large number of children in a short period of time. In this case, the sizes of the generations are no longer equal. Initially things work out well. The baby boom young become workers, and there are lots of them relative to the elderly. There's plenty of money coming in and comparatively little going out. This allows for an increase in payments to the elderly, or a decrease in the taxes paid by the working group, or both.

But what happens in the next generation when the baby boom workers become elderly? Then, assuming the baby boomers have a "normal" number of children, rather than the larger numbers of children their own parents had, the number of people collecting benefits becomes larger but the number of workers contributing to the system becomes smaller. In this case, payments per person must decrease, contributions coming in per worker must increase, or some combination of the two must occur. None of these alternatives is particularly pleasant.

This example doesn't come out of nowhere. It represents the current situation in the U.S. social security system. From 1946 through the late 1960s there was a baby boom, and these baby boomers are currently in the labor force. They'll start retiring in large numbers in the early 2000s and, when they do, the number of workers per retiree will decrease dramatically, so that in 2020 there will be about 2.5 workers per retiree instead of more than 15 workers per retiree as in the 1950s and 1960s. Exhibit 4 shows these unpleasant projections.

There are a number of ways to avoid these unpleasant alternatives. One way is to partially fund the system. With a partially funded pension system, some of the money paid in by the baby boom generation is put in a trust fund (when the proportion of workers to elderly is high). That trust fund and the interest it earns is used to pay part of the benefits of the elderly when the proportion of workers to elderly is low.

A second way is to vary the retirement age so that a large group of workers retires later and a small group of workers retires earlier. After age 65, people in each age group die off faster than people in younger age groups. This means that if the retirement age were raised, there would be fewer people to collect benefits than there

Q–9: How can a baby boom cause problems for an unfunded pension system?

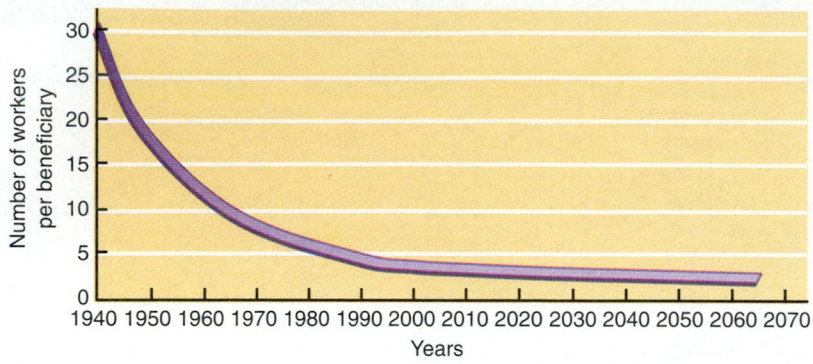

EXHIBIT 4 **Projection of Workers Compared with Social Security Retirees**

The number of workers per retiree declined considerably from 1940 to 1994, and it will continue to decline until about 2010.This will be the "crunch" period for social security. Source: Social Security Administration.

are when the retirement age is 65. This higher retirement age would help keep the ratio of workers to elderly roughly equal, again eliminating the mismatch of revenue coming in with payments going out.

Social Security and the Budget Deficit In the 1970s and 1980s, economists pointed out that this problem would be occurring. In response, the government made a number of changes. The retirement age was moved up slightly and, most important, there was a large increase in the rate of social security or FICA (Federal Insurance Contribution Act) contributions. This tax increase was to create a large trust fund that would provide significant budget surpluses in the 1980s and 1990s. These surpluses could be used to make the payments coming due in the 2000s without requiring huge tax increases or massive borrowing at that future time. Thus, in 1994, about $70 billion more in social security taxes was collected than was paid out. Therefore it seems as if the supplemental trust fund solution is the one the government is following.

Unfortunately, that tax increase is not resulting in government surpluses. Instead, the government is running large current deficits, so it is financing the trust fund with government bonds (promises to pay). (The only asset the trust fund is allowed to hold is government bonds.) But the social security system has already promised to pay anyway. So the only difference the trust fund makes is that, with the "trust fund," the government has issued pieces of paper (bonds) as backing for that promise.

Q–10: How could raising the retirement age at which people become eligible to receive social security payments help the economy without affecting the deficit?

An Alternative Let's look at another possible solution to the social security problem. Say that the retirement age at which people become eligible to receive social security payments were raised in increments so that, in 2010, the retirement age at which they could get full benefits would be 70. (It's now about 65.)[5] Then say that the current social security tax rates were lowered 10 percent. This combination of policies would increase the current budget deficit, but would significantly improve the U.S. financial picture because future commitments would have been so significantly lowered that there would be no need to collect as much current social security tax revenue. So here's a case in which the deficit would increase, but the United States would be in better financial shape.

THE DEFICIT DEBATE: WOLVES, PUSSYCATS, OR TERMITES

6 Because the deficit has many dimensions and each is widely debated, there are many alternative reasonable views about the deficit.

The accounting used in the social security system is only one of the U.S. government's many problem accounting areas. That's why economists emphasize that it's the financial health of the economy that's important, not the deficit. But economists also recognize that the measured deficit will be at the center of the debate about govern-

---

[5] Government pension systems were started by the 19th-century German leader Otto von Bismarck. He reportedly chose 65 as the retirement age because his advisors told him that vital statistics for the country showed most people died before age 65.

ment spending and taxes, so they take positions on the deficit and its meaning to the economy.

Charles Schultze, chairman of the Council of Economic Advisers in the Carter administration and currently an economist at the Brookings Institution, has divided economists' views about the deficit and its relationship to the economy's financial health into three groups:

1. The wolf-at-the-door group, who believe the deficit will bring about imminent doom.
2. The domesticated-pussycat group, who believe the deficit doesn't matter.
3. The termites-in-the-basement group, who believe the deficit will cause serious problems in the long run.

Few economists belong to the wolf-at-the-door group. A small but vocal group of economists comprise the domesticated pussycats. They include both liberal Keynesian economists who feel the economy needs more expansion and conservative Classical economists who believe deficits don't influence behavior and hence make no difference to the real economy. The largest group of economists belong to the termites-in-the-basement group.

Charles Schultze—Chairman of the Council of Economic Advisers under President Carter. *UPI/Bettmann.*

Three alternative views about the deficit are demonstrated in an exchange between William Proxmire, Robert Eisner, Robert Solow, and Franco Modigliani. Proxmire is a retired politician. Eisner, Solow, and Modigliani are well-known economists.

Three Alternative Views of the Deficit

'WIZARDS' SAY FORGET THE DEFICIT—DON'T LISTEN

William Proxmire
U.S. Senator
Washington, D.C.

Now some eminent economists are telling Congress and the administration to forget the deficit and the $2.6 trillion national debt. These objects of our deepest concern don't matter, they say. When people of the stature of Robert Eisner, a former president of the American Economic Association, whisper these seductive words, it's going to be hard for members of Congress to resist. And when the view is echoed by such Wall Street wizards as John Gutfreund and Peter Bernstein, it's like a teenager being told by her revered family doctor that smoking doesn't really threaten her health—it might even relax her and ease tensions.

After more than 30 years in the Senate, I cannot think of a more alluring or dangerous philosophy for a member of Congress than the economic gospel according to Mr. Eisner. How

irresistible it would be if a congressman could justify voting for increased spending and cutting taxes because it's good, hard economic sense.

The two most painful actions a member of Congress can take are first, a vote to cut popular spending programs and, second—and even more painful—a vote to increase taxes. But if these economic and Wall Street gurus are right, every day of a congressman's service in this debt-ridden government can be Christmas. A few years ago the so-called supply-side economists promised that a cut in taxes, even without a corresponding reduction in spending, would permit the country to grow its way out of deficits and debt. A trillion and a half dollars of additional national debt has made the supply siders a laugh.

Now we're told by Mr. Eisner that the $155 billion deficit for 1988 is a mirage. In the Eisner view, expenditures on roads, aircraft carriers and fighter planes are not really spending. They're investments. Mr. Eisner claims that when we include state and local surpluses, and then allow for inflation,

the government at all levels is running an Eisner surplus. Mr. Eisner computes that surplus at $42 billion for 1988. Right now, in his view, Congress isn't spending enough—it's taxing too much. According to him, this surplus is a serious drag on the economy. So come on Congress, spend more. Tax less. The deficit is not big enough. It's not even a deficit.

What's wrong with this Eisner analysis? Plenty. First, buying a highway or a warship is indeed an investment. It's also something else. It's a cost. When this kind of investment is made with borrowed money, it can be an exacting and painful cost.

Here's "an investment" that rarely pays a tangible cash return to the government. Take the federal government's biggest spender, the military: 85% of its expenditure is for military personnel, including retired pay, operations and maintenance, and procurement. None of these expenditures yield a penny of return to the government. In fact, military procurement, far from being an investment representing a source of future income, creates an "asset"—an aircraft carrier, for example, that will, once constructed, cost tens of billions of dollars to operate throughout its useful life in addition to its original cost. Some investment.

Overwhelmingly, government "investment" is of the same "wasting-asset" kind. Yes indeed, government expenditures may constitute useful services, often services to be consumed for years to come. During those years the government that borrows to "buy" the investment—the building or highway—must pay interest on its borrowing. It must maintain and operate its public asset.

As time goes on, the government must rehabilitate or replace the public asset or terminate the service it provides. Certainly the present government accounting system of counting all expenditures as outlay without offsetting credit for their future value is crude. But it is also roughly accurate and fair. This follows because every year Americans live off past government "investments" as well as buy "investments" that provide government services for the future. One could argue that, by failing to maintain the pace of highway building and other capital construction, recent congresses have been accumulating bigger deficits than reported. On this basis, I could as easily contend that the true federal deficit is $300 billion for 1988 as Mr. Eisner can argue that it is not a deficit at all, but a surplus.

The simplest, most obvious evidence that the federal government is living beyond its means is the colossal new burden of an immensely expanded national debt that now commands $155 billion a year in interest. That interest is both the fastest growing cost of government and the one cost that must be paid on time, in full. Interest and interest alone can not be cut, stretched out or reduced. It is a grim, unavoidable reminder of debt that all the sophistries of the brightest on Wall Street and academia cannot diminish.

The Eisner argument should be very appealing to your 19-year-old son who wants you to buy him a $30,000 Porsche. His pitch to you goes like this: "We're not really and truly going into debt when we spring for this Porsche. This isn't debt. This is an investment. Look, we can finance it over five years. You'll pay only about $45,000 total. I know you think I'm nuts, Dad, but this is the way the former president of the American Economic Association and the brightest guys on Wall Street see it. So how about it, Daddio? Let's get with it."

The Wall Street Journal, September 7, 1989.

DEFICIT ISN'T TOO TAXING

Robert Eisner
Professor of Economics
Northwestern University
Evanston, Ill.

Re William Proxmire's Feb. 3 editorial-page article " 'Wizards' Say Forget the Deficit—Don't Listen'': Despite his alarm, deficits—at least as they are conventionally measured—may not be bad for the economy. Mr. Proxmire taxes me—forgive the expression—for pointing out that by meaningful measure the official 1988 budget deficit of $155 billion was actually a real surplus of $42 billion. The calculations, though, are simple and illuminating.

- Apply standard business accounting practices to the federal budget and include as expenses or costs only the depreciation of capital, not capital expenditures. Substituting a reasonable estimate of depreciation for the more than $200 billion of federal investment spending (Office of Management and Budget estimate) would knock some $70 billion off the deficit, reducing it to $85 billion.

- Recognize that deficits are significant because they add to debt but what matters then is the real debt, adjusted for inflation. With inflation running at 3.6%, there was an "inflation tax" of some $72 billion on the $2 trillion of Treasury debt held by the public. Counting this inflation tax reduces the deficit to $13 billion.

- In terms of impact on the economy, we are interested in all of government, not just Washington. State and local governments over the past fiscal year ran a surplus of some $55 billion—not unrelated to $108 billion of federal grants in aid that amounted to more than two-thirds of the official federal deficit. If we add the plus $55 billion to the minus $13 billion we reach that real government budget surplus of $42 billion.

The critical issue—however we measure the budget—is what it does to the economy. Republicans since the days of Franklin D. Roosevelt have been denouncing Democratic budget deficits. Democrats have tried to have a field day denouncing the Reagan deficits that began in 1982. (They are in fact now much less, running some 3% of gross national product while they were more than 6% of GNP a few years ago.) Few politicians have been inspired to face the facts.

Despite recent record deficits, the sky has not fallen. Rather, the economy moved from deep recession and 10.7% unemployment to more than six years of sustained recovery. Unemployment fell by half. Corporate profits and the stock market soared. Business investment grew smartly.

All this indeed occurred not in spite of the budget deficits but in large part because of them. Government spending in excess of what it took from the public in taxes fueled aggregate demand, private and public, so that we were able to purchase more and more of what our productive economy could offer.

This is not to argue, contrary to Mr. Proxmire's charge, that there should be no limit to deficits. They can be too large if they bring us to the point where we are trying to buy more than can possibly be produced, a point that, despite our relative prosperity, we have hardly yet reached. And this is not to argue for wasteful government spending—or any other kind of wasteful spending. It makes a difference whether a person borrows to finance a gambling binge in Las Vegas or to buy a house or pay for his child's education. It makes a difference whether a firm borrows to finance productive capital expenditures or frivolous extravagance.

It is vitally important that in addition to maintaining current prosperity—it hardly makes sense to slow down the economy now because it might slow down later—we invest adequately in the future. I see no reason to second-guess household and business decisions on how much to save and invest as long as the economy is prosperous. But by far the greatest portion of investment in the future is by its nature public. Private productivity and our future well-being depend critically on public investment in human capital—in education, training and health, in basic research, in our vast tangible infrastructure of roads, bridges and airports, and in the protection of natural resources of land, water and air.

This is where Mr. Proxmire's counsel and all the near-hysteria about our mismeasured budget deficits, can lead us seriously astray. Our 13-year-olds score last in international comparisons on tests of math and science ability. Much of a generation grows up semiliterate or illiterate and crazed by drugs. Workers spend hours on choked highways and business travelers spend hours waiting for clearance to land at or fly to our congested airports.

Yet our "education president" is told that there is little or no more money to be invested in education, that the war to end the scourge of drugs will have to be fought on a shoestring, that there is virtually no room for new expenditures of any kind because "the deficit" must be brought down to some arbitrary target.

I am not telling "Daddio" to borrow to buy his 19-year-old son a $30,000 Porsche—although something that will give service for five years is properly considered an investment. But worthwhile public investment does have a payoff to the economy in higher productivity and national income. And indeed out of this higher income flows increased government revenues, even if Mr. Bush keeps that famous pledge to lip readers.

The Wall Street Journal, March 3, 1988. Reprinted by permission of THE WALL STREET JOURNAL © 1988 Dow Jones & Company, Inc. All rights reserved worldwide.

Who's Right?

The Proxmire letter is typical of many intelligent lay people's view of the deficit. Proxmire attacks the adjustments that almost all economists believe should be made to the deficit. He represents the wolf-at-the-door view, which few economists endorse.

Eisner's response represents the domesticated-pussycat view held primarily by liberal Keynesian economists (of whom Eisner is one) and conservative supply-side and Classical economists, although their reasons for holding that view are quite different from those of liberal Keynesians. Liberal Keynesians believe that it is important to stimulate the economy by running a deficit. As long as the economy needs stimulation, deficits don't matter. Supply-side economists and Classical economists who fall into this group of domesticated pussycats believe that deficits don't influence the economy, period: Since people are rational and fully discount expected future tax payments that the deficit would entail, deficits make no difference to the economy.

The termites-in-the-basement view in the Solow/Modigliani letter on the next page represents the ideas of the majority of economists. They see the deficit gnawing away at the structure of the economy. They agree that the deficit per se doesn't matter, but they believe that the economy's underlying health isn't good and that it needs to be treated. Superficial cover-up work that makes the deficit look smaller, but doesn't deal with the underlying health problems, won't treat the disease.

William Proxmire—Former senator from Wisconsin who chaired the Senate Budget Committee.
UPI/Bettmann.

CUTTING DEFICIT IS OUR ONLY ACCEPTABLE COURSE

Franco Modigliani
Robert Solow
Professors of Economics
M.I.T., Cambridge, Mass.

To the Editor:
It is unfortunate that Prof. Robert Eisner, whose contributions have made him a leading member of the economics profession, has now chosen to devote much of his attention to a contrary campaign in favor of more government expenditure and bigger deficits. Does he have a point?

Many of the arguments in ''Let's Stop Worrying About the Budget Deficit'' (letter, Feb. 19) are perfectly acceptable; for example, his assertion that any expenditure that primarily benefits future generations might be paid out of deficits without damaging them. The same goes for his assertion that the deficit, as measured in the budget, has numerous shortcomings. He calls attention to some that go in the direction of exaggerating the deficit (though one could argue with his specific corrections).

But he fails to mention others going in the opposite direction. Of these the most conspicuous is the treatment of Social Security; as a pension system it should not be included in the budget. It is running a surplus of some $50 billion (which should be devoted to capital formation to meet the coming bulge in the population of old relative to young). Hence, if Social Security were properly taken out of the budget, the deficit would be $50 billion larger.

But his argument is faulty on other grounds. The first is his concern that reducing the deficit at this time is likely ''to slow the economy and hence bring less investment.'' This preoccupation must be regarded as entirely misplaced under conditions of high demand pressure and high interest rates.

Even more serious is Mr. Eisner's failure to come to grips with the fact that, since the beginning of the huge fiscal deficits in 1982, national savings (inclusive of durable goods accumulation) have plummeted from a comparatively low level of around 10 percent in the 1960's and 70's to a distressingly low one of around 5 percent in recent years. Though net national saving may

not be exactly measured, there is no ground to doubt the trend. Only the large increase in capital imports (the trade deficit) has made it possible nearly to maintain the level of investment.

Professor Eisner seems to agree about some proper concern over our presumed growing debt to the rest of the world. But what he fails to realize is that none of his proposed solutions will reduce the trade deficit, unless we free resources to be used for more net exports. This requires that we either cut the deficit or cut investment. Failure to do so under conditions of full, if not overfull, employment would threaten to overload the economy, courting the risk of serious inflation.

Most thoughtful people agree that cutting investment is the last thing we should consider, and no one in his right mind thinks we should push output at the risk of inflation. This leaves cutting the deficit as the only acceptable option.

Reprinted by courtesy of Franco Modigliani and Robert Solow from a letter in the *New York Times* of March 12, 1989.

CHAPTER SUMMARY

- A deficit is a shortfall of incoming revenues over outgoing payments; debt is accumulated deficits.

- A budget deficit should be judged in light of economic and political conditions.

- The deficit is a summary measure of a budget. Whether a deficit is a problem depends on the budgeting procedures that measure it.

- A country's debt must be judged in relation to its assets.

- To judge the importance of deficits and debt, economists look at them relative to GDP.

- A real deficit is nominal deficit adjusted for the effect of inflation.

- When expectations of inflation have fully adjusted, inflation involves no transfer from creditors to debtors.

- The U.S. government often deals with its deficit problem with gimmicks.

- There are various reasonable views about the U.S. budget deficit.

KEY TERMS

Budget Enforcement Act of 1990   *(404)*
cash flow accounting system   *(413)*
debt   *(403)*
debt service   *(408)*
deficit   *(403)*

external government debt   *(407)*
funded pension system   *(414)*
Gramm-Rudman-Hollings Act   *(404)*
internal government debt   *(407)*
nominal deficit   *(410)*

off-budget expenditure   *(414)*
policy regime   *(403)*
real deficit   *(410)*
structural deficit   *(408)*
unfunded pension system   *(414)*

QUESTIONS FOR THOUGHT AND REVIEW

The number after each question represents the estimated degree of critical thinking required. (1 = almost none; 10 = deep thought.)

1. Your income is $40,000 per year; your expenditures are $45,000. $10,000 of your $45,000 expenditure is for tuition. Is your budget in deficit or surplus? Why? *(6)*

2. "The deficit should be of concern." What additional information do you need to undertake a reasonable discussion of that statement? *(5)*

3. "The debt should be of concern." What additional information do you need to undertake a reasonable discussion of that statement? *(5)*

4. Inflation is 20 percent. Debt is $2 trillion. The nominal deficit is $300 billion. What is the real deficit? *(2)*

5. How would your answer to Question 4 differ if you knew that expected inflation was 15 percent? *(5)*

6. If the government were to issue inflation-adjusted bonds, the deficit would fall. Would you suggest such a policy? Why? *(6)*

7. State the arguments of the pussycat view of the deficit. *(6)*

8. State the arguments of the wolf-at-the-door view of the deficit. *(6)*

9. State the arguments of the termites-in-the-basement view of the deficit. *(6)*

10. In what sense is the social security trust fund an accounting gimmick? *(7)*

PROBLEMS AND EXERCISES

1. Calculate the real deficit in the following cases.
   a. Inflation is 10 percent. Debt is $3 trillion. Nominal deficit is $220 billion.
   b. Inflation is 2 percent. Debt is $1 trillion. Nominal deficit is $50 billion.
   c. Inflation is −4 percent. (Price level is falling.) Debt is $500 billion. Nominal deficit is $30 billion.

2. Using the latest figures available from your library, calculate the real budget deficits for the United States, Britain, France, Brazil, and Nigeria.

3. Assume a country's nominal GDP is $600 billion, government expenditures less debt service are $145 billion, and revenue is $160 billion. The nominal debt is $360 billion. Inflation is 3 percent while real interest rates are 3 percent. Expected inflation is fully adjusted.
   a. Calculate debt service payments.
   b. Calculate the nominal deficit.
   c. Calculate the real deficit.

   d. What would you expect to happen if expectations of inflation fall? Why?

4. Assume a country's real growth is 2 percent per year, while its real deficit is rising by 5 percent per year. Can a country continue to afford such deficits ad infinitum? What problems might this country face in the future?

5. You've been hired by Creative Accountants, consultants to Textland. Your assignment is to make suggestions about how to structure its accounts so that the current deficit looks as small as possible. Specifically, they want to know how to treat the following:
   a. Government pensions.
   b. Sale of land.
   c. Social security taxes.
   d. Proceeds of a program to allow people to prepay taxes for a 10 percent discount.
   e. Expenditures on F-52 bombers.

ANSWERS TO MARGIN QUESTIONS

1. When the United States changed to a modern Classical supply-side policy regime, the size of the deficit increased, suggesting that it was politics as much as Keynesian economics that led to deficits. *(403)*

2. The deficit is a flow concept, the difference between income and expenditures. A debt—accumulated deficits—is a stock concept. *(405)*

3. To get a full picture of a country's financial situation, you have to look at assets as well as debt, since a large debt for a country with large assets poses no problem. *(406)*

4. GDP provides a measure of an economy's ability to service the debt and hence it is reasonable to measure the debt relative to GDP. *(408)*

5. Inflation reduces the value of the dollars with which the

debt will be repaid and hence, in real terms, wipes out debt. *(410)*

6. The real deficit equals the nominal deficit minus inflation times the total debt. Inflation times the total debt in this case equals $80 billion (.02 × $4 trillion). Since the nominal deficit is $40 billion, the real deficit is actually a surplus of $40 billion. ($40 billion − $80 billion = −$40 billion). *(410)*

7. When there is full adjustment for expectations, nominal interest rates rise to fully compensate creditors for any loss due to inflation. *(412)*

8. Deficits are simply a summary measure of an economy's health. By undertaking obligations in the future that don't show up as a deficit, a country can still get itself into financial trouble. *(413)*

9. An unfunded pension system is a pay-as-you-go system. It collects taxes from current workers and uses the proceeds to pay out benefits to current retirees. A baby boom changes the ratio between workers and retirees. Initially, it increases the number of workers to retirees, lowering the tax rate that must be paid to meet a given per-person retirement goal. However, when the baby boomers retire, it increases the necessary tax rate because there are so many more retirees for whom a per-person retirement goal must be met, and there are fewer working taxpayers from whom the necessary amount of taxes must be collected. *(415)*

10. Raising the social security retirement age does not reduce the deficit, but it does significantly reduce the future obligations of the country and hence can help the country's fiscal health. *(416)*

19

The Art of Macro Policy

*The worst episodes of recent monetary history—the great
inflations—have been marked by the subjection of central bankers
to overriding political pressures.*

~R. S. Sayers

After reading this chapter, you should be able to:

1 Summarize the conflicting goals of macro policy.

2 Explain why macroeconomic policy is an art, not a science.

3 Distinguish a policy model from a theoretical model.

4 Explain why modern macro policy focuses on credibility.

5 State the main points of agreement between Keynesians and Classicals.

6 Explain why the macroeconomic debate in the early 1990s was based on supply-side macro policies.

7 Summarize macroeconomic policy since the 1940s.

8 Take a hypothetical situation and develop a reasonable macroeconomic strategy for dealing with that situation.

In earlier chapters I introduced you to the terminology, the institutions, and the theory of the macroeconomy. It's now time to put it all together.

· What should government do if the economy seems to be falling into a recession?
· What should government do if inflation seems to be increasing?
· What should government do if the economy seems to be falling into a recession but, simultaneously, inflation seems to be increasing?
· What should government do if there's a large trade deficit at the same time that it's worried about a recession?
· What should government do if its currency's value is falling and there's concern about inflation?

Policymakers face these and similar questions every day. In this chapter, using the terminology, knowledge of institutions, theory, and insights we developed in previous chapters, we'll try to come to grips with these difficult real-world issues.

The first two sections provide some context for discussing these questions by considering the conflicting goals of macroeconomic policy. These two sections summarize and review similarities and differences between Keynesians and Classicals described in earlier chapters. The first section updates some recent theoretical developments relevant for policy and discusses the interaction between theory and policy. The second section considers the similarities and differences between Keynesians and Classicals on macro policy.

The third section of the chapter reviews important episodes in the recent history of macroeconomic policy, showing you how things worked out in real-world cases. The final section presents you with a hypothetical case and shows how the understanding you've gained in earlier chapters can let you function as an economic advisor to a government.

THE LIMITS OF MACROECONOMIC THEORY AND POLICY

1 Too contractionary a policy will cause unemployment and recession. Too expansionary a policy will accelerate inflation and expand trade deficits.

One reason why macroeconomic policy is so complicated is that it involves conflicting goals. As we saw in the chapter on inflation, the low inflation goal often conflicts with the low unemployment/high growth goal. And as we saw in a previous chapter, international trade balance and exchange rate goals often conflict with one another and with domestic goals. Thus, the government finds itself and the economy on a tightrope. Too expansionary a policy will accelerate inflation and expand trade deficits. But the government also knows that if it's too contractionary, it will cause a recession.

To maintain the economy on this tightrope, governments use monetary and fiscal policies as a balance bar. If the economy seems to be falling into inflation, governments can use contractionary monetary and fiscal policies; if it seems to be falling into recession, they can use expansionary monetary and fiscal policies. If they face both problems simultaneously, they must choose between the two and hope for the best.

The Limits of Macroeconomic Policy

In thinking about these goals, we must recognize that there are limits to what can be achieved with macroeconomic policy. Economists often tell governments that they're asking for too much. These governments are like a patient who asks his doctor for a health program that will enable him to forget about a training program, eat anything he wants, and run a four-minute mile. Some things just can't be done, and it's important for governments to recognize the inevitable limitations and trade-offs, at least with the monetary and fiscal policy tools currently available. Good economists are continually pointing out those limits.

Q-1: The President comes to you and says she wants very low unemployment, zero inflation, and very high growth. How do you respond?

But, like the patient who doesn't like to hear there are limits, governments often go to other advisors who offer more upbeat advice. Economists are often put in the position of the stick in the mud who sees only problems, not potentials.

This stick-in-the-mud image isn't appropriate. We economists are often dynamic, innovative, positive sorts of people (would you believe?) who've just been cast in a difficult role of pointing out that there are no free lunches.

	Option	Advantages	Disadvantages
Monetary policy	Expansionary	1. Interest rates may fall. 2. Economy may grow. 3. Decreases unemployment.	1. Inflation may worsen. 2. Exchange rate may fall. 3. Capital outflow. 4. Trade deficit may increase.
	Contractionary	1. Exchange rate may rise. 2. Helps fight inflation. 3. Trade deficit may decrease. 4. Capital inflow.	1. Risks recession. 2. Increases unemployment 3. Slows growth. 4. May help cause short-run political problems. 5. Interest rates may rise.
Fiscal policy	Expansionary (borrow and spend)	1. Maybe growth will continue. 2. May help solve short-run political problems. 3. Decreases unemployment.	1. Budget deficit worsens. 2. Hurts country's ability to borrow in the future. 3. Trade deficit may increase. 4. Upward pressure on interest rate.
	Contractionary (reduce deficit)	1. May help fight inflation. 2. May allow a better monetary/fiscal mix. 3. Trade deficit may decrease. 4. Interest rates may fall.	1. Risks recession. 2. Increases unemployment. 3. Slows growth. 4. May help cause short-run political problems.

EXHIBIT 1   Macroeconomic Policy Dilemmas

What makes economists' stick-in-the-mud role so difficult is that the trade-offs are often uncertain, meaning that once in a while the "promise-them-everything" advisors turn out to be right. Here's an example:

In 1984 and 1985, most economists were convinced that there was serious concern about inflationary pressures. Based on this concern, they warned against too expansionary monetary and fiscal policies. They kept predicting higher inflation. But due in part to some unexpected falls in the prices of oil and raw materials, that inflation didn't occur, even though government listened instead to a set of "full-speed-ahead" advisors. Because the inflation didn't occur, the advisors who said "Full speed ahead" could point to this period and correctly say that they were right.

With policy effects so uncertain, most economists are hesitant to make unambiguous predictions about policy. But they do have a sense of the effects of certain policies and the trade-offs each involves. Exhibit 1 summarizes those trade-offs.

When advising governments about real-world macro policy, economists are very aware that economic relationships aren't certain, and that conducting macroeconomic policy is an art, not a science. In practicing the **art of macro policy,** Keynesians and Classicals have different styles, and before we talk about some real-world episodes, it's helpful to contrast those styles. We begin by reviewing some recent policy-relevant theoretical developments in macroeconomics.

With policy effects so uncertain, most economists are hesitant to make unambiguous predictions about policy.

2 Economic relationships are not certain, which makes macroeconomic policy an art rather than a science.

The Difference between Theoretical Models and Policy Models

Q–2:   What are rational expectations?

In the 1980s and 1990s, there have been a lot of theoretical developments in thinking about macroeconomic problems, but most of those developments have had only tangential effects on macro policy makers. The reason is that those new developments lead to the conclusion that the aggregate economy is enormously complicated. Once one takes full account of that complexity, it's unclear, theoretically, what policies, if any, should be followed.

Recent theoretical work that often goes under the name **rational expectations** has focused on building dynamic feedback effects into macro models. Rational expectations are expectations about the future based on the best current information. Such expectations are important because if people expect a policy, and make adjustments in anticipation of it, the policy will have a different effect than if they didn't expect it. Affecting the expectations becomes the channel through which policy actions affect the economy.

The influence of the rational expectations work is woven into much of the discussion in this book. It is why, for example, when I discuss monetary policy, I talk about Fed posturing—*seeming to be* absolutely resolute about fighting inflation—in addition to *being* resolute. If people believe the Fed will do nothing but fight inflation, people will react differently than if they do not believe that. One Fed economist nicely summarized this distinction when he differentiated ''bark policy'' from ''bite policy.'' If the Fed barks loudly and convincingly enough, it doesn't have to bite.

In this book Keynesian economics is interpreted as a theory where, because of interdependencies of individuals' expectations, what is individually rational is not necessarily collectively rational. This interpretation is influenced by the work on rational expectations. It is a modern interpretation of Keynesian economics that makes it theoretically sound, even if all individuals have rational expectations. In modern macroeconomic theory, the key Keynesian insight is that the aggregate economy involves enormous interdependencies.

Q–3:   What is the problem with mechanistic Keynesianism?

What is undermined by rational expectations is what has sometimes been called **mechanistic Keynesianism**—the belief that the simple multiplier models (or even complex variations) actually describe the aggregate adjustment process, and lead to a deterministic solution that policy makers can exploit in a mechanistic way.

Modern macroeconomists do not believe the economy works this way, and even the most complicated models leave out most interdependencies to make those models tractable. When one adds back these interdependencies, the solutions to the models are indeterminate. Once one takes into account these many interdependencies, one recognizes that Keynesian models, at best, describe tendencies toward an exaggeration of external real shocks to the economy. This more limited interpretation of Keynes' insight is the modern interpretation of Keynesian theory.

The last three paragraphs summarize about 5,000 articles and lots of fancy math that have been done over the past 10 years. This chapter is policy-oriented, so I can summarize that work briefly because, while recent theoretical developments have been influential in the interpretation given to macro models, they have not had a significant effect on macro policy. These developments have simply brought home the fact that if you build dynamic feedback effects into an aggregate model, you can come up with just about any result. Slightly different assumptions in models lead to substantially different results and policy recommendations. These models describing that complexity are grist for tenure for academic economists but are of little use to policy makers. Policy makers don't want complexity. They want models that come to definite conclusions, because policy makers don't have the luxury of waffling on issues.

Policy makers don't want complexity. They want models that come to definite conclusions.

The Interface between Theoretical and Policy Models

Most theoretical work of macroeconomists involves abstract models that omit institutional context to try to capture those aspects of economic behavior that transcend institutions. However, most actions by individuals do not transcend institutions. So it should not be surprising that those theoretical models don't come to policy conclusions until the institutional context is added back. And adding back institutional context involves judgment—judgment about which reasonable people may differ.

This differing institutional judgment explains why no conclusion can be reached regarding whether the Keynesian model or the Classical model is the best guide for policy. Once one adds the institutional context back, both Classical and Keynesian macro models become reasonable guides, depending on the situation, and that's how policy makers use them—as guides, not as directives.

The introductory Keynesian and Classical models presented in the text are the ones in the back of policy makers' minds. They use them not as mechanical guides, but, with judgment, as working models—as descriptions of empirical regularities that they assume will be maintained—unless something else comes up. Policy makers do not care whether these models can be deductively derived from micro principles, or even whether they involve logical inconsistencies; what they care about is that these models fit with their intuition, describe observed reality, and predict reasonably well.

Let me give an example. Some farmers use the following rule of thumb: When the cows lie down, it is going to rain. The larger the percentage of their cows that lie down, the higher the probability of rain. If this rule of thumb usually works, it is a good rule of thumb. People who use this rule to predict don't care about the cows' decision-making process. They care about observable empirical regularity that they can base policy decisions on (such as whether to harvest the hay immediately, or wait a day).

Academic cowonomists would have a different focus. They would look into the cows' decision-making process and would try to explain the cow's lying-down decision in cost/benefit terms consistent with a cow's utility function.

What I am saying is that there are two fundamentally different types of models used in economics: policy models and theoretical models. A policy model is a working tool that captures empirical regularities that may be caused by features of the current institutional framework or by inherent economic tendencies; for short-run policy, policy makers don't care which, as long as the model leads to the best prediction.

An academic theoretical model has a different purpose. Academic economists care passionately about whether an empirical regularity reflects inherent economic tendencies or the current institutional framework. Which of these is the cause of an empirical regularity has significant long-run policy relevance, and that is an academic economist's focus. By separating out institutionally-determined effects from institution-transcendent economic tendencies, their models can be used to predict whether a policy can be used indefinitely, or whether it only works temporarily—until institutions change. The recent Classical and Keynesian theoretical work on micro-foundations is an attempt to make that separation for macroeconomics.

When teaching this subject, the instructor must discuss both types of models. That presents a problem, because on the one hand, the theoretical models are highly abstract and mathematically too complicated to present to anyone but specialists. On the other hand, the policy-oriented observational models are not really models at all. They are simply empirical generalizations, and they often fail to bring out the differences between those empirical regularities based on institutional constraints that will likely change and those that transcend existing institutions.

Let's now briefly consider the influence of some of this modern theoretical work on macro policy and some of the ideas underlying it.

As I stated before, modern Classical economics is centered around rational expectations. The essence of the modern Classical policy argument based on rational expectations is the following: Say the government uses an activist monetary and fiscal policy. People aren't stupid; they'll soon come to expect that activist monetary and fiscal policy will be used and, in anticipation, will change their behavior. But if they change their behavior, the government's estimates of what is going to be the effect of policy, based on past experience, will be wrong.

Let's consider an example. Say everyone knows government will run expansionary fiscal policy if the economy is in a recession. In the absence of any expected policy response by government, people would have lowered their prices when they saw a recession coming. Expecting government expansionary policy, however, they

The introductory Keynesian and Classical models presented in the text are the ones in the back of policy makers' minds. They are used not as mechanical guides, but, with judgment, as working models.

3 Theoretical models are abstract; they try to capture certain aspects of economic behavior that transcend institutions. Policy models combine individuals' actions that transcend institutions and individual actions that depend on institutions; they try to capture empirical regularities.

People Aren't Stupid

Modern Classical economics is centered around rational expectations.

Q-4: How does the fact that people aren't stupid tend to undermine activist policy?

won't lower their prices. Thus, an activist policy creates its own problems, which can be avoided by establishing a set of rules that limit government's policy responses. Modern Classical economics has formalized that insight.

As we can see from this discussion, the key element of modern Classical ideas about policy is that you must consider the effects of policy on people's behavior, and that those effects place limits on policy options. Specifically, the fact that the economy is falling into a recession is not a sufficient reason for the government to run expansionary monetary and fiscal policies. Some modern Classicals go further than that, arguing that if all people have rational expectations and the economy is competitive, there's no room for any activist monetary policy.

Modern Keynesians generally agree with this modern Classical argument about expectations. But they argue that it doesn't rule out activist monetary and fiscal policies in all instances. As I discussed above, they argue that many fluctuations in the economy are due to a collective irrationality, which leaves room for government to correct that irrationality.

Credibility and Macro Policy

A good way to see how modern Classical and Keynesian ideas have affected macroeconomic policy, or at least the thinking about that policy, is the discussion in the 1990 *Economic Report of the President.* There's little or no mention of an activist fiscal policy and sizes of multipliers. Instead, the central theme is, "Fiscal policy should move toward *credible, systematic* policies that would promote strong noninflationary growth" (p. 77). By **credible systematic policies,** they mean policies that people believe will be implemented regardless of the consequences.

Similarly with the report's discussion of monetary policy. A key statement of principle for monetary policy is:

> Monetary policy needs to maintain credibility, because credibility helps ensure that the goals of policy will be attained during a period of dynamic economic and financial developments. Policy credibility is enhanced by building a record of achievement of the stated goals of policy and by consistently following stated policy principles.

I suspect the redundancy in those descriptions is by design. The economists who wrote the report wanted to emphasize that one cannot think of macroeconomic policy without thinking about what effect expectations of macroeconomic policy will have. The policy must be credible, systematic, and consistent. All these statements emphasize that you cannot think of policy choices in one time period as not affecting individuals' behavior in another time period.

An analogy to raising a child might make the point clear. Say that your child is crying in a restaurant. Do you hand out a piece of candy to stop the crying or do you maintain your "no candy" rule? Looking only at the one situation, it might make sense to give the candy, but doing so will undermine your credibility and consistency, and therefore has an additional cost. This emphasis on credibility is the primary effect modern theoretical work has had on macroeconomic policy. In conducting macro policy, one must consider the effect that expectations of that policy will have on the economy generally, and not only in a particular case.

Emphasis on credibility is the primary effect modern theoretical work has had on macroeconomic policy.

Classicals and Keynesians also agree that, in practice, credibility is hard to achieve. The 1990 *Economic Report of the President* summarizes the problem nicely:

> Policy credibility is clearly useful to have, but achieving it may not be easy. Simply announcing a change in policy does not make it believable. Credibility depends in part on the plausibility and consistency of the announced policy in the context of the overall economic environment and other policies. Credibility probably depends most importantly on a track record of following the stated principles of policy.

4 Modern economists focus on credibility because they see macro policy operating through expectations as much as through the real channels emphasized in the traditional models.

Most economists can agree with this statement. Keynesians' and Classicals' disagreement concerns what policy is plausible and hence what policy can be credible.

THE KEYNESIAN/CLASSICAL POLICY DEBATE

Debates about economic theory often mask debates about economic policy. Economists use theories to guide their reasoning, but before they can translate the results of a theory into a policy prescription, they must add a sense of institutions and history,

The Classical view of government as a tool that individuals use to enrich themselves has been around for a long time, as can be seen in this 19th-century lithograph.

adjusting the model to fit reality. Keynesians and Classicals differ not only in the theoretical models they prefer, but also, and probably more importantly, in their sense of institutions and history.

The Classical View of Government Policy

As you saw in earlier chapters, Classicals have a profound distrust of government and the political process. They tend to believe that, even if theoretically the government might be able to help solve a recession, there's a serious question whether, given the political process, it will do so. Politics will often guide government to do something quite different than "further the general good." In the Classical view, real-world government intervention is more likely to do harm than good.

Classicals have a profound distrust of government and the political process.

Classicals see democratic government as being significantly controlled by special interest groups. While, in theory, government might be an expression of the will of the people, in practice it's not. Thus, government is not a legitimate method of correcting problems in the economy. True, government sometimes does good, but this is the exception. Overall the costs of government action outweigh the benefits.

In the Classical view, politicians often are guided by politics, not by society's best interest. Therefore any policy that increases the government's role is highly suspect and should be avoided. Modern Classical models reflect this view and focus on a model that highlights a laissez-faire policy for government.

In the Classical view, politicians often are guided by politics, not by society's best interest.

The Keynesian View of Government Policy

Keynesians tend to have more faith in government not only being able to recognize what's wrong, but also in being willing to work to correct it. Thus, for a Keynesian it's worthwhile to talk about a model that highlights an activist role for government.

Q–5: Distinguish between Keynesian and Classical views of government policy.

Keynesians tend to see government as an expression of the will of the people. Thus, they see it as a legitimate method of correcting problems in the economy. True, government is sometimes misled by interest groups who direct government to do their own bidding rather than follow the general interest, but this is simply a cost of government. In the Keynesian view, the benefits of government generally outweigh the costs.

Keynesians tend to see government as an expression of the will of the people.

Who's Right on Policy?

Notice that these differences between Keynesians and Classicals are based on judgment calls requiring a knowledge of the workings of the market and the social institutions that tie our country together. They're judgments upon which reasonable individuals may differ; between the two extremes are innumerable shades of

Keynesians and Classicals. There's no objective way of deciding which group is right or wrong.

Flip-Flopping Views of the Deficit

Now that we've considered the complex interaction between policy and theoretical models, let's consider how that interaction can lead to confusion about policy positions. Specifically, let's consider the recent flip-flopping of Keynesian and Classical views on the deficit.

Historically, as we saw in earlier chapters, Classical economists opposed budget deficits whereas Keynesian economists supported them. Both positions were simplifications—but reasonable simplifications. In the 1980s, however, many modern Classicals put forward a view of the deficit quite outside the Classical tradition. Modern Classicals said that deficits didn't matter. This switch occurred about the time that many Keynesians were arguing that the government budget deficit was too large and should be reduced. Thus, the 1980s saw Classicals and Keynesians flip-flop their positions on the budget deficit.

Why Modern Classicals Flipped   One reason for the modern Classical switch in position was the rediscovery of a theoretical argument for ignoring the effects of deficits. That argument was called the *Ricardian equivalence theorem,* named for David Ricardo, an early Classical economist who first developed the argument. The **Ricardian equivalence theorem** states that it makes no difference whether government spending is financed by taxes or by a deficit. The effect of an increase in government spending is the same in either case: a transfer of resources from the private sector to the government with *no* net effect on the aggregate economy.

Ricardian equivalence theorem Proposition that it makes no difference whether government spending is financed by taxes now or by a deficit (taxes later).

The reasoning for the Ricardian equivalence theorem is based on rational expectations. If the government runs a deficit, at some time in the future that deficit must be paid off—meaning that, eventually, taxes will be higher than if there were no deficit. Rational individuals will take those future taxes into account in their decisions and will spend less now, just as they would have spent less on themselves now if current taxes had been raised. So individuals with rational expectations will save more now to pay for future taxes, and therefore will be unaffected by a government deficit.

Earlier Classical economists didn't emphasize the Ricardian equivalence theorem because they saw it as primarily a *theoretical* argument of little practical relevance. They opposed deficits because of their concern that government would waste the money. Modern Classicals focused more on formal theory, so they gave this argument more weight.

A second reason for the flip-flop was a change in the political realities. Even for those modern Classicals who didn't believe that tax cut incentives would stimulate the economy, or didn't believe in the Ricardian equivalence theorem, there was a major reason to support tax cuts. Tax cuts would limit new government programs. It was as if you had a spendthrift spouse who spent money faster than you could earn it. You've tried many strategies to get the spouse to stop spending, but nothing has worked. So you adopt the final strategy: earn less money and spend it immediately yourself so the bills pile up higher and higher so that your spouse won't have anything to spend.

Thus, some modern Classicals supported supply-side tax cuts because of the limitation they placed on government social programs. And it worked. In the 1980s, large cuts occurred in many social programs—cuts that many had believed were impossible. The modern Classical support for tax cuts also helped to put in office presidential candidates who opposed government activism (primarily Republicans) and helped to keep out of office presidential candidates in favor of government activism (primarily Democrats).

Why the Keynesians Flipped   The argument that one didn't have to worry about deficits was at the center of the Keynesian policy revolution. Indeed, because he made that argument, Alvin Hansen, a Harvard economist who was instrumental in introducing Keynesian economics to the United States in the late 1930s, had been called a radical communist. Most 1930s Classical economists opposed Keynesianism precisely because it led to deficits. A balanced budget placed a constraint on government that was consistent with Classicals' judgment about governments.

Part of the early Keynesians' support of the federal deficit was based upon the political position that allowing budget deficits would allow an expansion of government programs. By the 1980s, government programs had expanded about as much as was politically feasible, so that reason to favor deficits ended.

Many Keynesians also felt that the large deficit was forcing government to hold down the economy with its other tool, monetary policy. Heavy reliance on monetary policy to slow the U.S. economy in the 1980s and 1990s, while government ran large deficits, is one reason Keynesians have argued for a more contractionary fiscal policy. They believed that a more contractionary fiscal policy would allow the Fed to run a more expansionary monetary policy, lowering interest rates, increasing investment, and increasing growth. In short, crowding out would be reduced. Thus, even though Keynesians supported a more expansionary aggregate policy than Classicals, they criticized the monetary/fiscal mix: They supported a somewhat less expansionary fiscal policy but a much more expansionary monetary policy. They believed that if the deficit were reduced, monetary policy could provide a stronger stimulus to the economy without generating inflation.

Not all Keynesians flip-flopped, but enough of them did so that it was no longer an acceptable simplification to say that Keynesians generally supported deficits and expansionary fiscal policy. So, in the 1990s, we find both Classicals and Keynesians divided in their views of the deficit.

With that update on modern theoretical developments and their relevance for policy, let's consider the three central problems of macroeconomics—inflation, unemployment, and growth—and see where Keynesians and Classicals tend to come out in their judgments about what to do about each of these. Exhibit 2 provides a summary comparison.

As you can see in Exhibit 2, there are some differences, but those differences reflect differences in emphasis, interpretation, and judgment, as much as they reflect differences in theory.

Similarities and Differences between Keynesians and Classicals on Macro Policy

Similarities and Differences between Keynesians and Classicals on Fiscal Policy   Classicals tend to worry slightly more about inflation than do Keynesians. Thus, Classicals tend to be willing to believe that a higher unemployment rate is consistent with potential income than is a Keynesian. Moreover, Classicals see expansionary monetary and fiscal policy as having far less effect on real income and unemployment. All Classicals see expansionary monetary policy as inflationary. However, they are divided on their view of expansionary fiscal policy's effect on inflation. The monetarist school of Classical thought says the deficit isn't important for inflation; some modern Classicals say that the deficit doesn't make any difference, since people with rational expectations offset any effect of the deficit. But the majority Classical position is that expansionary fiscal policy can contribute to inflationary pressures because it increases aggregate demand, while aggregate supply doesn't change. The result is inflation.

These theoretical differences between Keynesians and Classicals and among different subgroups of Classical economists on the expansionary effect of fiscal policy aren't too important in practice, since, in the real world, fiscal policy is a difficult tool to use. The reason these theoretical differences are not too important in practice is political reality. A country's fiscal policy generally reflects political considerations as much as or more than economic stabilization considerations. Due to these political considerations, economists of all persuasions tend to believe that governments usually lean toward expansionary fiscal policy, regardless of economists' advice.

The theoretical differences between Keynesians and Classicals and among different subgroups of Classical economists on the expansionary effect of fiscal policy aren't too important in practice.

If expansionary aggregate policy (a deficit) is needed, fiscal policy generally turns expansionary. Tax cuts or spending increases are politically popular, and if the need for them is recognized in time, usually we can count on expansionary fiscal policy.

Turning the other way—contractionary fiscal policy—isn't so easy. When the U.S. president says, "Read my lips: No new taxes," and the U.S. Congress says, "No

EXHIBIT 2   A Comparison of Classical and Keynesian Policies

Problem	Keynesian Policy	Classical Policy
Inflation	• *Cause: Inflation is a combination institutional and monetary problem* • Use contractionary monetary and fiscal policy • Supplement above policy with policies to change wage–and price–setting institutions— possibly consider a temporary income policy • Some small amount of inflation may be good for economy, and it is not worth trying to push inflation to zero if it involves significant unemployment	• *Cause: Inflation is a monetary problem* • Avoid inflation by relying on strict monetary rule—use contractionary monetary policy • Be careful about expanding output too high and causing inflation • Push inflation to zero by following strict monetary rule
Slow Growth	• *Cause: Slow growth is a combination institutional and aggregate demand problem* • Use expansionary monetary and fiscal policy • Supplement above policy with policies to establish incentives for growth	• *Cause: Growth rate reflects people's desires; probable cause of slow growth is too much regulation, too high tax rates, and too few incentives for growth* • Remove government impediments to growth; go back to laissez-faire policy
Recessionary Unemployment	• *Cause: Recessionary unemployment is a combination institutional and aggregate demand problem* • Use expansionary monetary and fiscal policy	• *Cause: Recessionary unemployment was probably caused by earlier government policies which were too expansionary, causing inflation* • If unemployment is very high, use expansionary monetary and fiscal policy. Generally, however, government policies should focus on the long run.

cuts in government programs,'' it's rather difficult to have contractionary fiscal policy. The fiscal policy steering wheel is consistently being pulled toward being inflationary.

Both Keynesians and Classicals agree about the political difficulties of using fiscal policy to slow inflation. Thus, much of the debate about what types of macroeconomic policy to use generally focuses on monetary policy.

Q–6: Do Keynesians and Classicals agree or disagree more about the long-run or the short-run effects of monetary policy on inflation?

Similarities and Differences between Keynesians and Classicals on Monetary Policy   The majority Keynesian and Classical views on monetary policy agree that expansionary monetary policy can stimulate the economy in the short run (although some modern Classicals argue that people with rational expectations will immediately push up prices, so expansionary monetary policy can only cause inflation, even in the short run). But Keynesians and Classicals disagree about the long run, and hence they disagree on the effectiveness of expansionary policy. Classicals tend to see the long-run effect of monetary policy as exclusively on inflation; Keynesians believe that the inflationary effect of monetary policy is dependent on how close the economy is to its potential income. Because of this difference, Keynesians tend to advocate more activist policies, while Classicals tend to advocate more laissez-faire policies.

Theoretically these differences show up in their views on the aggregate supply curve. Keynesians see the aggregate supply curve as dependent upon expected demand. Thus, an increase in nominal demand can increase real output. Classicals see aggregate supply as independent of expected aggregate demand. Unless expansionary monetary policy fools suppliers into thinking there's been an increase in real demand, it can only cause inflation.

Most Keynesians and Classicals agree that in the short run, expansionary monetary policy can stimulate growth and keep the economy out of a recession. But it can do so only at the cost of creating inflationary pressure. That inflationary pressure leads to increased rates of inflation in the long run, as it breaks down institutional constraints on firms raising wages and prices and as it becomes built into expectations. Therefore, the initial inflationary side effects of expansionary monetary policy are often hidden. This hiding of costs creates enormous political pressure for expansionary monetary policy. With politicians' short-run time horizon, a push for expansionary monetary policy is almost inevitable, especially around election time. Given the Fed's quasi-independence, there is debate about whether the Fed responds to that pressure as well.

The debate about whether or not to use expansionary monetary policy arises because of disagreement about whether moderate expansionary pressures will always lead to inflation in the long run. This difference in views means that there's a range of inflation and unemployment where it's not clear whether expansionary or contractionary monetary policy should be used. The economy is often in this range. On the one hand, to use expansionary policy in that range is to take a chance that inflationary expectations will get built into expectations and institutions. On the other hand, to use contractionary policy can lead to a slow-growth, high-unemployment economy.

Amid these debates between Keynesians and Classicals we shouldn't lose sight of the convergence of views. There's more agreement about policy than disagreement. Both Keynesians and Classicals generally agree that:

1. *Expansionary monetary and fiscal policies have short-run stimulative effects on income.*
2. *Expansionary monetary and fiscal policies have potential long-run inflation effects.*
3. *Monetary policy is politically easier to use than fiscal policy.*
4. *Expansionary monetary and fiscal policies tend to increase a trade deficit.*
5. *Expansionary monetary policy places downward pressure on the exchange rate.*
6. *Expansionary fiscal policy has an ambiguous effect on the exchange rate.*

In the actual conduct of policy, these agreements often mean that various economists' advice is similar, whether they're Keynesian or Classical.

Another way to see the consistency of policy advice is to consider macro policy in terms of the three ranges of price level flexibility that I presented in earlier chapters. I reproduce those ranges in Exhibit 3. In range *A,* where unemployment is very high and the economy is a long way from potential output, both Classicals and Keynesians agree that expansionary macro policy is called for. In range *C,* where aggregate demand exceeds potential income, both Keynesians and Classicals agree that contractionary macro policy is called for. The debate concerns range *B,* where unemployment may be too high but, simultaneously, there are inflationary pressures that could lead to an accelerating inflation. Because there is agreement about policy action in ranges *A* and *C,* the economy is generally pushed into range *B.*

Let's now turn to macroeconomic policy over the past 50 years. We begin with a discussion of recent events, and then look back in history. As you read it, try to determine which periods reflect Keynesian advice, which reflect Classical advice, and which reflect consensus advice.

The period 1983–1990 set the stage for the recent history of macro policy. This was a period of substantial growth in the economy. Ronald Reagan was president during

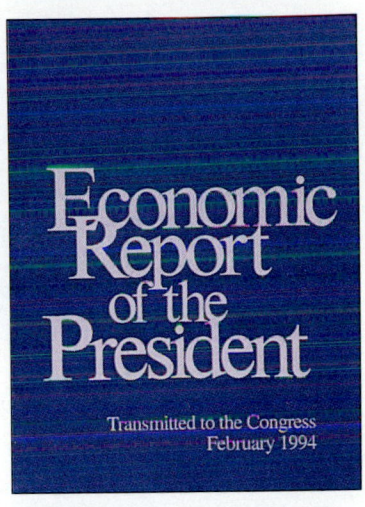

The *Economic Report of the President* provides a summary of the past year's economic events as well as a variety of data such as that found on the endpapers.

Agreement about Macroeconomic Policy

5 Both Keynesians and Classicals generally agree that:
1. Expansionary monetary and fiscal policies have short-run stimulative effects on income.
2. Expansionary monetary and fiscal policies have potential long-run inflation effects.
3. Monetary policy is politically easier to implement than fiscal policy.
4. Expansionary monetary and fiscal policies tend to increase a trade deficit.
5. Expansionary monetary policy places downward pressure on the exchange rate.
6. Expansionary fiscal policy has an ambiguous effect on the exchange rate.

A HISTORY OF POST–WORLD WAR II MACROECONOMIC POLICY

Recent History of Macroeconomic Policy

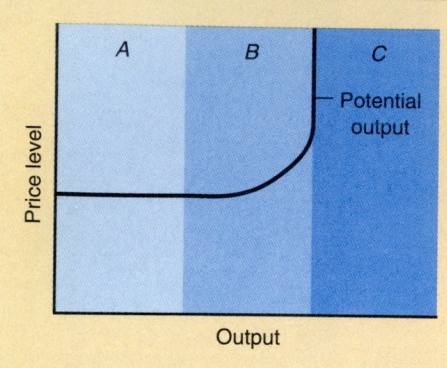

EXHIBIT 3   The Three Ranges of Price Level Flexibility

Most economists see the economy as having three ranges of price level flexibility. In range *A*, when the economy is significantly below potential income, most economists agree that expansionary policy is useful. In range *C*, when the economy is above its potential income, most economist favor contractionary policy. In range *B*, the intermediate range, there is debate about policy. The economy is generally thought to be in range *B* so there is generally debate about what is the appropriate policy.

most of this time. His successor, George Bush, was elected in 1988 on an economic platform similar to Reagan's: keep tax rates low, rely on growth and cutting government expenditures to cut the deficit, and enjoy the prosperity.

In the first half of Bush's term the economy kept on its path of growth, but in the fall of 1990 the string of good luck ended. Due to a Middle East military conflict, oil prices rose substantially, leading many to fear that inflationary pressures would result in an inflationary spurt like that of the mid- and late 1970s. Those fears of policy makers and businesspeople led to contractionary monetary policy and a fall in investment, and that led to the 1990 recession.

The 1990 Recession   Going into the 1990s, the consensus view was that fiscal policy was expansionary, not for macroeconomic reasons, but for political reasons. This was unlikely to change significantly, so if inflationary pressures were going to be nipped in the bud, monetary policy had to provide the contractionary effect.

In 1990, regardless of how one measured monetary policy—by interest rates or by money supply—the Fed policy was contractionary, and there was significant debate about whether it should have loosened up policy to avoid a recession. The tight monetary policy had stronger-than-desired effects as banks limited loans to meet regulatory requirements, which had been tightened in response to the Savings and Loan problem of the 1980s. The arguments for loosening were countered by the fear that, if the Fed did loosen up, or even showed weakness in its resolve to fight inflation, inflation would take off. Whether that would have happened is unclear; what is clear is that there were problems with the anti-inflationary policy the Fed followed.

The Fed's resolve to fight inflation was strengthened by international pressures. In September 1990, as concern about the Middle East political situation grew, the G-7 countries met and decided to coordinate their monetary policies. All would maintain relatively contractionary policies, so that the 1974 and 1979 experiences, in which an oil price rise led to serious world-wide inflation, wouldn't be repeated—they would come down on the side of fighting inflation. Many economists felt that this would be the path to a serious recession, which would lead the Fed and other countries' central banks to change their policies from contractionary to expansionary, as they had in the past.

The United States had an even stronger reason to maintain contractionary policy. The country already had a significant trade balance deficit which was expected to worsen due to rising prices of oil imports.

The policy most economists advocated for the United States was to reduce the deficit by tightening up somewhat on fiscal policy, but not too much—for fear of furthering recessionary pressures. This contractionary fiscal policy was meant to be counteracted by expansionary monetary policy. The combination of policies would lower the interest rate some, decreasing the value of the dollar, which, in the long run, would stimulate U.S. exports.

The Fed worked behind the scenes to achieve these goals, arguing that the economy could go a lot more smoothly if fiscal policy would become slightly more contractionary. It offered to loosen up on monetary policy, but only if Congress and the president made some movements toward tightening up the deficit—to make fiscal policies more contractionary.

By the end of summer 1990, the president and Congress hadn't made any progress in eliminating the government deficit, which had actually increased because the government was taking in less than the expected amount of revenue, thanks to a slowdown in the U.S. economy.

In October the deficit was reduced somewhat. In response, the Fed eased monetary policy slightly but, for fear of inflation, didn't ease up significantly. Once again the Fed and other central banks had to decide whether to accommodate and possibly trigger accelerating inflation, or to hold the line and possibly cause a recession. They tried to find a middle road: running expansionary, but not too expansionary, policy. It didn't work. In fall 1990 the economy went into recession. Unemployment increased from 5.1 to 7 percent and real GDP fell. The Fed's response was to fight the recession, although initially that response was muted because the Fed didn't want to rekindle inflation.

The recession lingered on through all of 1991 despite signs that it was ending. When it was clear that the recovery was slow in coming and that inflation was remaining low, the Fed forgot about inflation and its desire for tighter fiscal policy before it would institute a looser monetary policy. Despite the government's increasing budget deficit, the Fed loosened monetary policy significantly. Interest rates fell to their lowest level in 30 years. Their fall pushed down the U.S. exchange rate and that decrease, combined with the recession, temporarily lowered the U.S. foreign trade deficit. Simultaneously, recessions in the EU and Japan refocused international concern away from inflation.

The Sort-of Recovery, 1992—and the Debate about Supply-Side Macro Policies

The pickup in the economy did not occur fast enough for George Bush. Entering the presidential election of 1992 with the economy in the doldrums, he lost the election to the Democratic nominee, Bill Clinton, who ran on a platform of getting the economy going again.

Precisely how Clinton planned to do this was unclear, not because he lacked an understanding of the economic problems facing the country, but because the situation the economy was in made traditional policies contradictory. The goals he set were beyond the normal macroeconomic tools of monetary and fiscal policy. His problems were compounded by recession in Europe and Japan that reduced U.S. exports and caused the U.S. trade deficit to expand.

Pointing out the limitations of normal macro policies would not have gotten him elected, so instead, he promised to do everything. After he was elected, he had to figure out how to achieve those contradictory goals, or at least how to appear to be doing so.

The dilemma Clinton faced provides a good statement of the modern confusion about macroeconomic policy. The difficulty was the following: To expand the economy and create jobs, both Keynesian and Classical economics tell us to run deficits and increase the money supply (although Classical economics says this will only work temporarily). But the political imperatives of the 1990s were to *decrease the size of the deficit* and to prevent inflation by not increasing the money supply.

Within this new situation, the difference between the Classical and Keynesian theories becomes of minor importance, since both theories say that to stimulate the economy you must do what is politically infeasible. It is at this point that supply-side policies enter in.

Supply-side policies expand potential output by creating supply-side incentives by lowering tax rates or by modifying the composition of government spending and taxes to stimulate supply. Because they expand potential output, they allow the economy to grow; that growth decreases the budget deficit and creates jobs. Thus, supply-side policies offer the hope of having it all—growth, prosperity, and low

Q-7: Why could President Clinton use neither Keynesian nor Classical traditional macro policy?

The Allure of Supply-Side Policies

6 Traditional macro policies offer trade-offs. To expand the economy, one must run deficits and increase the money supply. Doing so causes inflation. Supply-side policies offered hope of expanding potential output and hence having it all—growth, prosperity, and low unemployment—without deficits.

unemployment. It isn't surprising that both Democratic and Republican politicians have been attracted to such policies.

Classical Supply-Side Economics

Classical supply-side economics focuses on incentive effects of taxes. It argues that low tax rates are central to an economy's success. Classical supply-side economics developed not in the economics profession, but in the popular press, in Jude Wanniski's book *The Way the World Works.* Wanniski, a former newspaper reporter, prides himself on never having taken an economics course. He bases his arguments on some ideas of economist Arthur Laffer, who argued that the U.S. economy's problem was that tax rates were too high and that if rates were cut, the economy would expand.

Classical supply-side rhetoric worked well for Reagan, but not so well for Bush. The deficits kept mounting up as the supply-side incentives didn't create the needed increase in the growth of potential output and didn't end the political push for more and more government spending. But that did not undermine its political appeal because supply-side policies were the only set of policies in town that promised everything.

Differences between Classical Supply-Side and Keynesian Explanations of How a Tax Cut Stimulates the Economy

At first glance, Wanniski's supply-side argument may look very much like a Keynesian argument for fiscal policy in which cutting taxes stimulates the economy via the multiplier effect. But there's an important difference between the Keynesian and supply-side views. The supply-side explanation of how the tax cut would stimulate the economy is by microeconomic incentives. It focuses on tax rates, not tax revenues.

The supply-side explanation of how a tax cut would stimulate the economy is by microeconomic incentives.

The supply-side argument goes as follows: If the government cuts tax rates, people will have greater incentive to work, to save, and to invest. As they do all these things, output will increase, not because of expectations of increased demand, but because of the incentive effects of lower tax rates on supply. (The aggregate supply curve, and hence potential income, will shift out.) Since supply creates its own demand, aggregate demand will also increase. The economy will expand because of greater incentives to work. Exhibit 4(a) shows the supply-side view. A decrease in taxes directly shifts the *AS* curve out and, since supply creates its own demand, also shifts the demand curve out. In the supply-side view, aggregate supply is the best estimate of potential income, which means the tax rate cut increases potential income too.

Q–8: What's the difference between a Classical supply-side and a Keynesian explanation of the effect of a tax rate cut?

The Keynesian explanation of the effect of a cut in taxes, shown in Exhibit 4(b) differs. The Keynesian theoretical explanation holds that a tax cut increases income and expected aggregate demand. If the level of potential income is greater than the actual level of income, producers will increase output because of that increased expected demand, which further increases aggregate demand. If, however, the economy is initially at potential income, the tax cut shifts aggregate demand, but not aggregate supply, because aggregate supply can't increase beyond potential income. The result will be either shortages or inflation.

In the Keynesian explanation of the effect of a tax cut, demand leads supply and potential income is unaffected. In the supply-side explanations, supply leads demand and potential income is increased.

The Keynesian explanation of a tax cut's effect is the multiplier process: In it, *demand* leads *supply* and potential income is unaffected. In the supply-side explanation, *supply* leads *demand* and potential income is increased. The differences are important because the supply-side explanation has specific policy implications. The supply-side explanation says that a deficit financed by a tax cut will not be inflationary. Politically, this was a desirable argument: society can have its free lunch.

Economists and Classical Supply-Side Economics

Most economists were not convinced by the supply-side arguments. While all agreed that there are supply-side effects on incentives to save, on labor supply and effort, the majority see the time dimension needed for these supply-side policies to take effect—two to four years—as longer than the focus of short-run macro policy. Therefore, most economists saw the supply-side arguments as involving significant political rhetoric without much substance for

Few economists were convinced by the supply-side arguments.

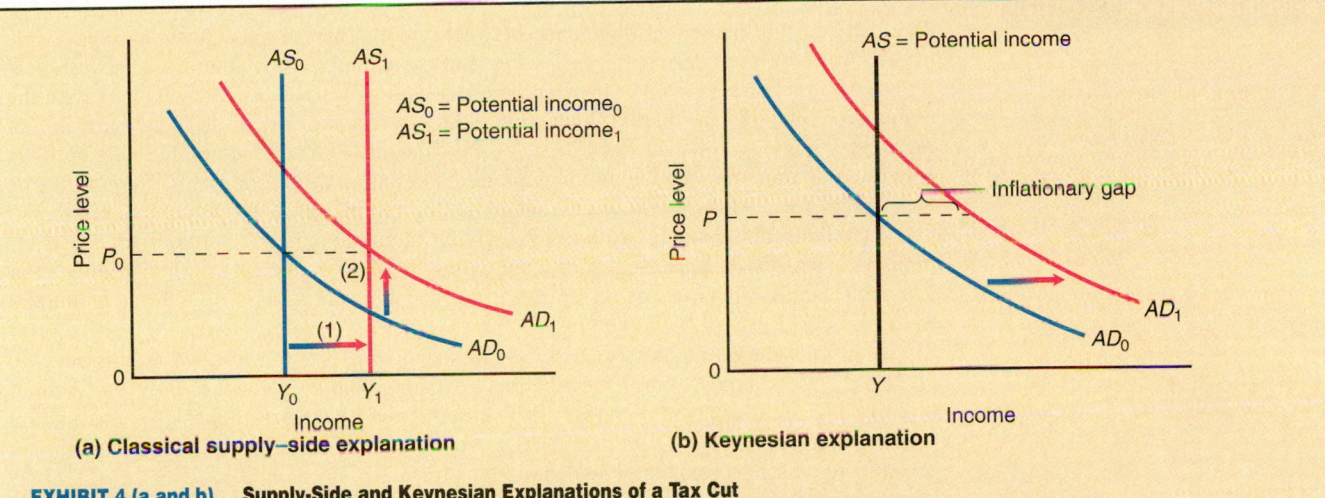

EXHIBIT 4 (a and b)   Supply-Side and Keynesian Explanations of a Tax Cut

The Classical supply-side explanation of how a tax cut stimulates an economy already at its potential income is shown in (**a**), where (1), an outward shift of the AS curve, leads to (2), an increase in aggregate demand. Supply leads demand and the tax rate cut shifts potential income out. The Keynesian explanation, shown in (**b**), has demand leading supply—the AD curve shifts outward from AD_0 to AD_1, resulting in an inflationary gap if the economy is at its potential income.

short-run aggregate policy.[1] Setting tax rates could stimulate the economy in the short-run through expectations. If the economy were below its potential income (and remember, it's unclear where potential income is) and if the tax cuts positively affected expectations, they could lead to a boom because people believed they would work. Some economists supported supply-side policies on these grounds.

Other economists supported supply-side policies for a different reason. They argued that since much of government spending was a waste, some way had to be found to reduce it. Cutting taxes thereby created a large deficit, making it impossible for the government (like the spendthrift spouse) to spend more, while at the same time introducing positive long-run incentive effects. Compared with the alternatives, many economists believed that the supply-side policies offered the best hope for the economy, even if they might not achieve the short-run benefits claimed in the political rhetoric through the path that supply-siders claimed.

Keynesian Supply-Siders   Clinton's supply-side policy was based on a variation of the Classical supply-side policy, but it had definite Keynesian overtones, so I call it **Keynesian supply-side policy.** A Keynesian supply-side policy goes beyond the traditional Keynesian demand-side analysis that has been so far discussed. The Keynesian version of supply-side economics focuses on the composition of government spending and taxes. It says that that composition can be modified to expand supply and potential output, decreasing the deficit at the same time that it expands the economy. Thus, the policy does not look at the level of total taxes and spending; instead it focuses on the composition of total taxes and spending.

Here's how it is supposed to work: You design a policy that combines tax cuts with tax increases; you call the tax cuts "investments in productivity," and you don't discuss the tax increases. Similarly, you combine spending cuts with spending increases; you call the spending increases "supply-enhancing" spending, and you call the spending cuts "supply-enhancing" cuts.

If you're a good orator, and lucky, you can make the policy sound attractive and, perhaps, even pull it off, if you are lucky with inflation remaining low, expectations

---

[1] On the state level, where substitution effects from one state to another are likely, supply-side arguments have many more supporters among economists.

ADDED DIMENSION

DISTINGUISHING THE KEYNESIAN AND CLASSICAL SUPPLY-SIDE ARGUMENTS

■ e can see the theoretical difference between the Keynesian and Classical supply-side explanations by considering the following thought experiment: Assume the government replaced the income tax (a tax in which the total amount a person pays changes with the amount of income she earns) with a poll tax (a tax in which the total amount an individual pays is constant regardless of his income). Also assume that the poll tax generated as much revenue as the income tax, and that marginal propensities to consume were equal for all income groups. What would be the effect on the aggregate economy?

Classical supply-siders would say that the aggregate output would increase enormously since the reward for additional work would be increased significantly. For Classical supply-siders, a cut in tax rates, not a cut in tax revenues, is what stimulates the economy.

A Keynesian would say that a shift from an income tax to a poll tax would have no effect on the economy. Why? Because tax revenues wouldn't change; only the method of assessing the taxes would change. In the traditional Keynesian model, it is the amount of tax collected, not the tax rate, that affects the economy. A change in the tax rates, tax revenue remaining constant, would have no effect.

In reality, tax revenues are almost invariably changed by changing tax rates, so the effect of a tax cut is difficult to discover, which is why there is so much debate about which side is right.

holding up private demand, and monetary policy holding the interest rate down. How? By affecting expectations, and thereby stimulating private investment and consumption. As I discussed earlier, there is a self-fulfilling nature to the economy. If you can convince people the economy is going to be great, and get them to act on that conviction, the economy *will* be great. The policy works through expectations and beliefs, and then through economic channels—not directly through economic channels.

In late 1993 and early 1994, this policy worked for Clinton. The economy picked up and started to expand considerably, creating the usual debates about how close to potential income the U.S. economy was and how much inflation would be generated. In early 1994, the Fed started tightening monetary policy slightly to ward off inflation. Economists were divided on whether this was the right policy or not.

The above may sound like an unsympathetic discussion of Clinton's policy, but it should be kept in mind that he had almost no other options. Both Keynesian and Classical theory said what the political demands for him to accomplish—cut the deficit, hold inflation down, expand growth, and increase jobs—could not be achieved through traditional policies.

The problem some economists have with this Keynesian supply-side policy is three-fold:

> **Q–9:** What concerns do many economists (even Keynesian economists) have with Keynesian supply-side policies?

1. The government is deciding which activities are, and are not, supply-enhancing. Past experience is not heartening about the government's ability to make those decisions.

2. Politically, getting the tax and spending changes to follow the structure that has actually been decided upon is difficult. Politics, not economics, usually guides those decisions.

3. Supply-side effects of compositional changes in taxes and spending are second-order, long-term effects. In the short run, the aggregate effects of the budget deficit will predominate.

These three reasons leave a number of economists, even those who generally support the goals Clinton advocated, wary of the long-run success of his Keynesian supply-side policies. While such policies sound good politically and reconcile the otherwise irreconcilable goals, it is unclear how long the high expectations could support the economy. Like the Classical supply-side proposals, the Keynesian supply-side proposals were seen by the majority of economists as political rhetoric without much substance for short-run aggregate policy, except through the expectational path.

Like the Classical supply-side proposals, the Keynesian supply-side proposals were seen by the majority of economists as political rhetoric without much substance for short-run aggregate policy.

Now that we've gone through the recent history, let's take a brief look back at the earlier history of macroeconomic policy to see how we got to where we are. That earlier history has been a history of the eclectic use of monetary and fiscal policy to attempt to stay within the boundary between too-high inflation and too-high unemployment.

The New Deal and the Rise of Keynesian Economics

Keynesian economics developed in the 1930s during the Depression. This early work in the United States was primarily theoretical, and Keynesian economists didn't have significant input into policy. President Franklin Roosevelt opposed deficits (and hence the use of expansionary fiscal policy). Moreover, he didn't like Keynes, whom he met during one of Keynes's visits to the United States. The Fed had a number of Keynesian advisors but, at the time, monetary policy wasn't the focus of Keynesian economics.

Nonetheless the U.S. government was running deficits and starting public works programs as part of Roosevelt's **New Deal.** These programs, however, reflected the practical "do something" approach to policy rather than the influence of Keynesian (or Classical) economics.

The first half of the 1940s brought World War II. U.S. government spending increased enormously; U.S. taxes increased significantly (income tax rates of over 90 percent on high incomes). But the increase in spending was so large that the U.S. government started running wartime deficits significantly larger than anything it had run in the Depression. The Fed agreed to hold interest rates on government bonds constant to help the government finance wartime spending. This agreement meant the Fed could not conduct an independent monetary policy, but was forced to accommodate a highly expansionary fiscal policy. In response, the U.S. economy boomed. Economic activity expanded enormously. Much of the production, however, was used for the war effort; consumer goods were in short supply. To keep the resulting inflationary pressures in check, wage and price controls were instituted.

During the war, the combination of price controls and high government expenditures led to low unemployment and low inflation. The U.S. economy came out of World War II operating at capacity output. The major economic questions of the immediate postwar period were: (1) how to convert the economy from wartime to peacetime production without falling back into a depression, and (2) how to eliminate price controls without generating a large inflation. Both questions were successfully answered.

Soon after the war ended, price controls were lifted. The results were positive: While inflation picked up, it remained low, even as aggregate demand remained high.

The economy also avoided a recession or depression, at least initially, due in part to pent-up demand. Despite high tax rates, aggregate demand remained high as people spent some of their forced wartime savings. Their increased consumption offset much of the decrease in government spending. In spring 1948, the high wartime income tax rates were cut, giving the economy an additional expansionary push. But that push didn't offset the contractionary effect of the further decline in government spending, and the economy started to fall into a recession by the end of 1949.

That recession was short-lived because, in 1950, the Korean War started, the United States got involved, and government spending jumped due to rearmament. The economy quickly came out of the recession. Thus, in this first postwar recession we see fiscal policy working. But the fiscal policy (changes in government spending) was not implemented for stabilization purposes. Instead it reflected wartime and political needs.

The economy continued strong through the Korean War. Monetary policy during this period was still limited by the earlier agreement between the Fed and the Treasury that required the Fed to hold the interest rate on government bonds constant. In 1951, the Fed and the Treasury met to adjust this earlier agreement, and in the **Treasury Accord** it was agreed that the Fed no longer was bound by the earlier agreement.

Earlier History of Macroeconomic Policy

7 The history of macroeconomic policy since the 1940s has been one of the eclectic use of monetary and fiscal policy to attempt to stay within the boundary between too-high inflation and too-high unemployment.

New Deal   President Franklin Roosevelt's name for his practical "do-something" approach to economic policy.

The 1949 Recession

Treasury Accord   An agreement between the Fed and U.S. Department of the Treasury in which the Fed was freed from holding the interest rate on government bonds constant.

The 1953–1954 Recession

In the summer of 1953, the Korean War ended and government expenditures decreased. Consumer confidence fell. To try to prevent a recession, the Fed loosened monetary policy. The expansionary monetary policy didn't work (or at least it wasn't enough), and industrial production fell almost 10 percent from July 1953 to May 1954. No specific expansionary fiscal policy was implemented, but automatic stabilizers, such as unemployment insurance, helped slow output's fall. By the end of 1954, consumer confidence was picking up and sales were increasing. By mid-1955, the economy was moving into a boom, and the concern turned from recession to inflation.

The 1955–1956 Inflation

To fight this inflation, the Fed tightened the money supply, increasing the reserve requirement and raising the discount rate. It hoped that the tightened money supply would stop the inflation, but not stop real output from growing nor cause unemployment to increase. These hopes weren't met. The contractionary monetary policy did slow inflation, but it also decreased real output. By 1957, that decrease had become significant, and the concern changed back from inflation to unemployment and recession.

The 1957–1958 Recession

The tight monetary policy of 1956 hit the capital goods industry especially hard; business investment dropped 16 percent, and consumers' expenditures for durable items fell almost as much. This decline was worsened by the end of a Middle East Crisis (such crises have been almost continual since World War II), which caused U.S. exports to decrease. (During the crisis, U.S. exports had boomed as foreign countries bought food and goods from the United States to stockpile for a potential war.) During this period, the Fed was still concerned about inflation. This was the time when the inflation/unemployment Phillips curve trade-off became part of economists' lexicon.

Faced with this dual problem, the Fed had to choose which problem to fight. Initially it chose to fight inflation; it didn't loosen monetary policy significantly. But in late 1958 and early 1959, the Fed reversed itself and moved toward a more expansionary monetary policy, causing interest rates to fall. Combined with a large increase in mortgages guaranteed by the Federal Housing Administration and the Veterans' Administration, this expansionary monetary policy worked. By mid-1959, the economy was in a boom. Once again the policy concern changed, and inflation, not unemployment, became the focus of policymakers' concern.

The 1960 Inflation and Recession   To fight the inflation, the Fed used contractionary monetary policy and decreased the money supply. Again, the results were the same. Contractionary monetary policy slowed the inflation, but it also brought the economy into recession.

Industrial production fell during the second half of 1960 and into the first part of 1961. Unemployment increased substantially. This was one of the few times that the economy had fallen into a recession during a presidential election. Many observers believe that the recession played a significant role in Richard Nixon's defeat by John F. Kennedy.

The Sustained Expansion of the 1960s   Partly because of the 1950s experience in fighting inflation and partly because of a change in policy advisors (from Classical economists advising Republicans to Keynesian economists advising Democrats), the focus of monetary and fiscal policies changed in the 1960s from fighting inflation to avoiding a recession. (John F. Kennedy's administration marked the first time that strong Keynesians were in key positions on the Council of Economic Advisers.[2]) The result was that generally, up until 1969, monetary policy was expansionary. The economy remained in a sustained expansion through much of the 1960s.

During the early 1960s, fiscal policy was also somewhat expansionary. Then, in 1966–67, it became highly expansionary as the government attempted to fight a large

---

[2] Actually, during Harry S Truman's presidency (1945–1953), economists sympathetic to Keynes were on the council, but they were primarily Roosevelt New Dealers rather than Keynesian economists.

war in Vietnam while simultaneously maintaining domestic programs such as President Lyndon Johnson's War on Poverty. By 1966 most economists, Keynesian as well as Classical, had concluded that significant inflationary pressures were developing, and that both monetary and fiscal policies needed tightening. Politically, the government didn't want to hear such advice. It's true that monetary policy was tightened for about six months in 1966, but then it was loosened again until 1969, by which time inflation had picked up significantly. Fiscal policy was even less responsive to economists' advice, and, for political reasons, fiscal policy remained highly stimulative until 1968, when the government instituted a 10 percent income tax surcharge.

This 1968 tax increase and 1969 tight monetary policy both worked to slow down the economy. But about that same time, government war spending decreased. The result was a more contractionary fiscal policy than desired. Combined with a highly contractionary monetary policy, this policy led to a sudden braking of the economy which caused interest rates to rise to their highest levels in decades, leading to the 1969–70 recession. With this recession, the sustained expansion of the 1960s ended, as did economists' hopes of eliminating the business cycle with fine-tuning of monetary and fiscal policies.

The 1969 Recession and the 1970–1973 Boom   Faced with a substantial economic downturn in 1969, the Fed acted relatively fast to reverse its policy to fight the recession. Since inflation hadn't yet responded to the tight monetary policy of 1969, fighting the recession required forgetting about using monetary policy to meet its inflation goals (which weren't being met anyway). Instead, the government instituted partial **wage and price controls** (legal limits on prices and wages).

Wage and price controls   Legal limitations on the prices and wages that can be set.

Wage and price controls began in August 1971. The combination of price controls and expansionary monetary policy worked. In 1972, economic output increased significantly, and inflation stayed low. This significant monetary expansion right before a presidential election led some people to believe that Nixon and his economic advisors had learned a lesson from their 1960 election loss when, as mentioned before, the economy went into a recession right before the election. You never use contractionary monetary or fiscal policies right before a presidential election if you want to be reelected. In November 1972, President Nixon was reelected by a large majority.

Soon after the 1972 election, wage and price controls were loosened. Finally, in 1973, they were dismantled. The result was a significant increase in inflation which, by 1973, had reached 9 percent.

How much of this inflation was due to the removal of price controls and the expansionary monetary policy, and how much was due to exogenous supply price shocks, is a matter of debate between Keynesians and Classicals. Classicals argue that the inflation was primarily caused by the removal of price controls and the expansionary monetary policy. Keynesians disagree, pointing out that three **supply price shocks** hit the economy during this period.

Supply price shock   A shock that causes a rise in nominal wages and prices.

The first supply price shock concerned import prices. In 1972 and 1973, the U.S. economy had a fixed exchange rate with other major currencies, which meant that the U.S. government was committed to buying and selling currencies to maintain that fixed exchange rate whenever the quantity of dollars demanded didn't equal the quantity of dollars supplied. In 1971 the dollar was valued at a high relative exchange rate, imports significantly exceeded exports, and the United States had a significant balance of trade deficit. In response to that deficit, the United States and other countries agreed that the dollar would be devalued by 12 percent in December 1971. This raised import prices by 12 percent, causing a supply price shock.

The second supply price shock—the poor grain harvest of 1972—pushed up food prices. The third supply price shock—the Arab oil embargo—limited oil shipments to the United States and tripled the price of oil. Combined, these three supply price shocks caused significant inflationary pressure. They presented the Fed with a dilemma: either (1) expand the money supply, ratify the supply shock inflation, and allow other prices to rise in response, thereby avoiding a recession but building inflation into the economy, or (2) don't expand the money supply, trying to prevent

ADDED DIMENSION POLITICS AND ECONOMICS

The discussion of economic policy history touched only briefly on the politics of the decisions, but as you read through it I hope you were thinking of who was in office. If you didn't, it might be helpful to reconsider that history, taking into account the following information about the presidents and their parties, the chairmen of the Council of Economic Advisers and their political classifications, and the chairmen of the Fed and their political affiliations.

Thinking about this information should convince you that while, in theory, the differences between Classicals and Keynesians are substantial, in practice they are often blurred by politics.

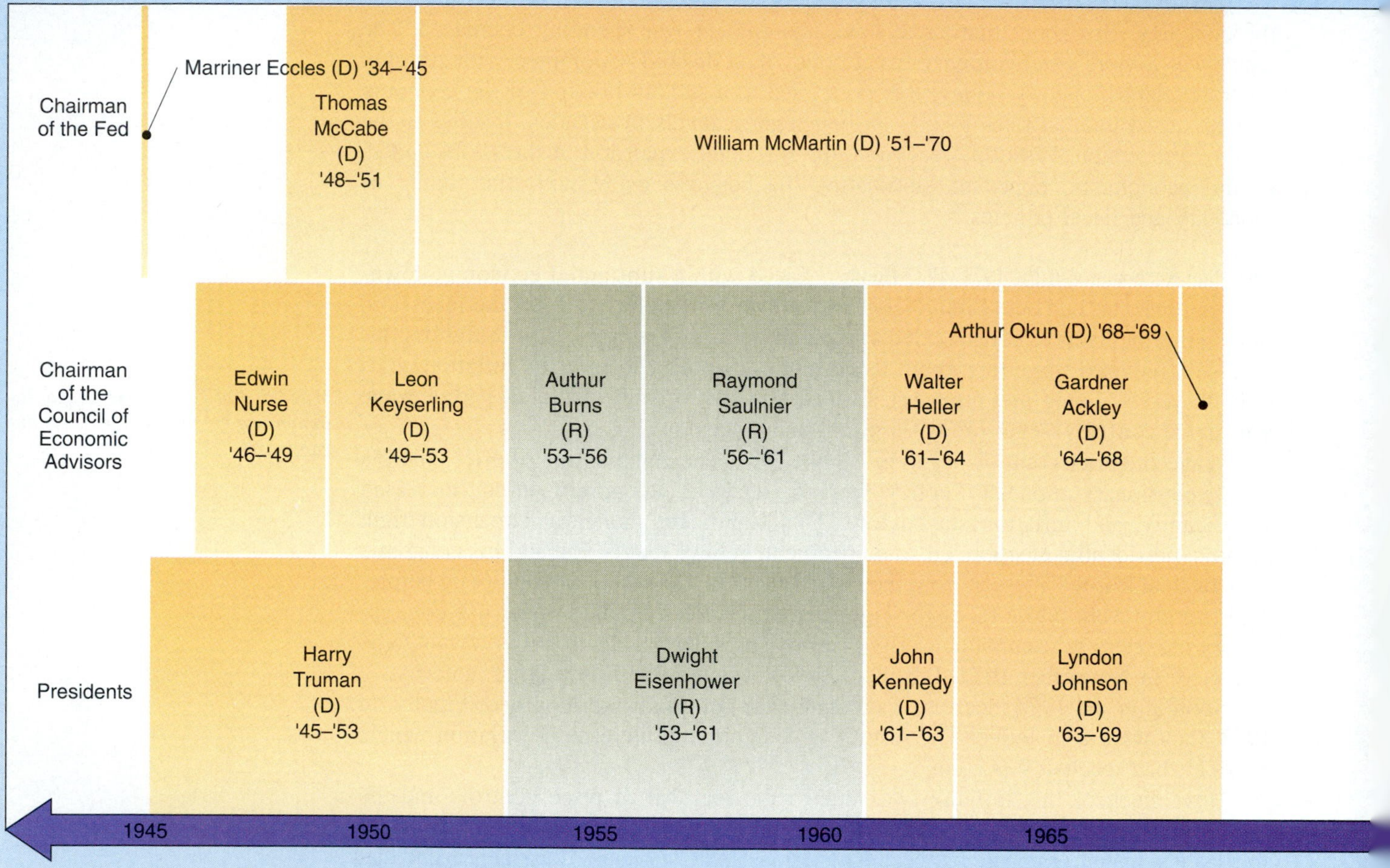

Chairman of the Fed	Marriner Eccles (D) '34–'45	Thomas McCabe (D) '48–'51	William McMartin (D) '51–'70			
Chairman of the Council of Economic Advisors	Edwin Nurse (D) '46–'49	Leon Keyserling (D) '49–'53	Authur Burns (R) '53–'56	Raymond Saulnier (R) '56–'61	Walter Heller (D) '61–'64	Gardner Ackley (D) '64–'68 — Arthur Okun (D) '68–'69
Presidents	Harry Truman (D) '45–'53		Dwight Eisenhower (R) '53–'61		John Kennedy (D) '61–'63	Lyndon Johnson (D) '63–'69

1945   1950   1955   1960   1965

the supply price shocks from being built into expectations of inflation, and risk recession.

Initially, the Fed expanded the money supply, but in 1973 it decided that it must do something about the inflation. It significantly tightened the money supply. The economy responded predictably and went into a recession.

The 1973–1975 Recession   The result of the tight monetary policy in 1973 was a severe recession, not only in the United States but in all major industrialized countries, as decreased U.S. imports had contractionary effects on foreign countries' exports. Inflation was reduced, but it remained high by historical standards. This recession lasted well into 1975, when the focus of policy once again shifted from concern about inflation to concern about the recession.

That concern led to an expansionary fiscal policy (a large 1975 tax cut) and expansionary monetary policy. Combined, these policies helped pull the economy out of the recession. Inflation, however, which had remained very high during the recession, grew even higher, causing the Fed serious concern over which problem it

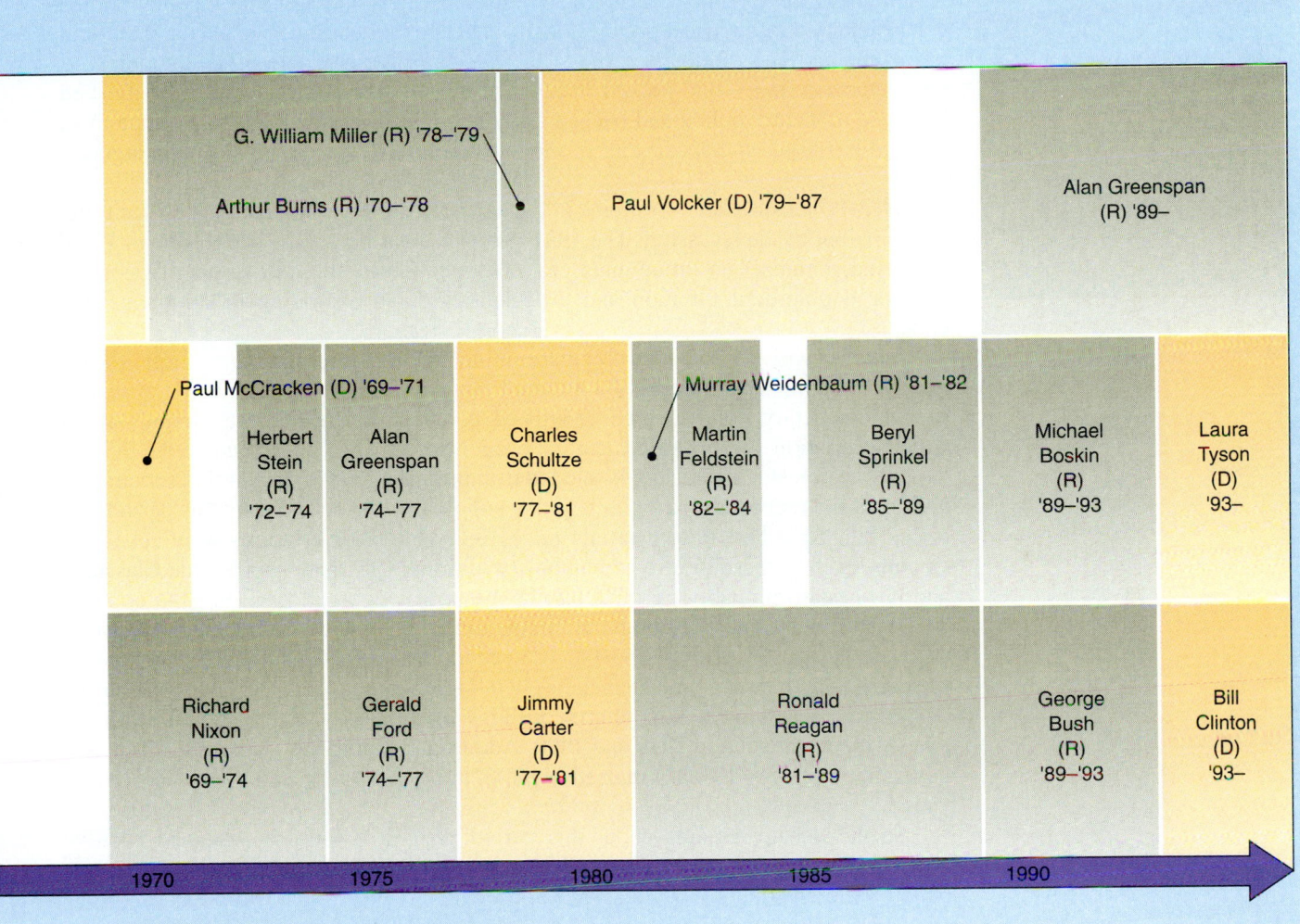

G. William Miller (R) '78–'79

Arthur Burns (R) '70–'78

Paul Volcker (D) '79–'87

Alan Greenspan
(R) '89–

Paul McCracken (D) '69–'71

| Herbert Stein (R) '72–'74 | Alan Greenspan (R) '74–'77 | Charles Schultze (D) '77–'81 | Murray Weidenbaum (R) '81–'82
Martin Feldstein (R) '82–'84 | Beryl Sprinkel (R) '85–'89 | Michael Boskin (R) '89–'93 | Laura Tyson (D) '93– |

| Richard Nixon (R) '69–'74 | Gerald Ford (R) '74–'77 | Jimmy Carter (D) '77–'81 | Ronald Reagan (R) '81–'89 | George Bush (R) '89–'93 | Bill Clinton (D) '93– |

1970   1975   1980   1985   1990

should be fighting. Despite this concern, through the late 1970s the Fed maintained an expansionary monetary policy.

The 1980–1982 Recession–Expansion–Recession   In October 1979, however, the Fed abruptly changed its focus from recession to inflation. At that point it also stopped focusing on interest rate targets as a measure of monetary policy, and announced that, henceforth, it would focus instead on the money supply.

The result was an enormous increase in short-term interest rates, which rose to more than 20 percent, and a sudden decrease in the money supply. In the short run, these policies had few effects upon inflation which, partly due to a second oil-price shock, had reached double digits in late 1979 and early 1980. But they significantly affected real output. In response to these measures the U.S. economy went into a large contraction. Industrial production fell by well over 10 percent.

In May 1980, the Fed moderated and backed off on its highly contractionary policy. In response, business activity picked up; by November 1980 the economy was in a major expansion. The expansion didn't take place soon enough for President

Q–10:   What well-known policy change did the Fed implement in October 1979?

Stagflation *Simultaneous high infla-tion and high unemployment.*

Jimmy Carter. He was voted out of office partly because the public blamed him for the period's **stagflation** (simultaneous high inflation and high unemployment).

After the election, the concern changed from recession to inflation; the Fed tightened the money supply significantly. Again the interest rate rose to almost 20 percent, causing large decreases in spending on housing and consumer durables. By June 1981 the economy was deep into a recession. By November 1982, 12 million people were unemployed. The term *stagflation* was used with increasing frequency.

In response to this recession, both fiscal policy and monetary policy turned expansionary. On the fiscal policy side, in 1981 the United States enacted a major cut in income tax rates, although some of the effects of the cut were offset by increased social security taxes that kicked in about this same time. Simultaneously, the Fed loosened monetary policy and backed away from its strict monetary rule. Since then, the Fed has used an eclectic mix of money supply targets and interest rate targets.

The 1983–1990 Expansion Combined, these expansionary policies helped pull the economy out of the recession. The 1981–82 recession, unlike the earlier one in 1980, had a major impact on inflationary expectations, and by the mid-1980s it was clear that the double-digit inflation and expectations of an exploding inflation rate had ended.

Exactly why this sudden decrease in inflation and inflationary expectations occurred is a matter of debate. Traditional Classical economists attributed it primarily to tight monetary policy which convinced people that the Fed was serious about fighting inflation. Supply-side Classical economists attributed it to cuts in the income tax rates which stimulated supply and led to significant growth. Keynesian economists attributed the reduced inflation to negative supply price shocks during this period: Oil prices fell, food and raw materials prices fell, and labor relations were relatively smooth. Each of these three explanations (traditional Classical, supply-side Classical, and Keynesian) probably captures part of the truth.

Whatever the cause, throughout this period employment was increasing substantially, inflation stayed low, and the U.S. economy seemed strong. But there were problems. The banking and financial system significantly overextended itself during this period, resulting in hundreds of billions of dollars of government-guaranteed loans which came due in 1989 and 1990. Additionally, both the U.S. trade deficit and government budget deficit remained high, creating serious potential long-term problems.

So the debate remains about this period: Was it a time of sustained positive growth, or was it merely a time in which a group of yuppies and rich people became richer while creating serious long-term problems for the United States?

Assessment of Policy

The history of macroeconomic policy since the 1930s should have given you a sense of the changing focus, the political difficulties of using the fiscal policy tool, and the shifting back and forth over concern about inflation and recession. A natural reaction to that history is that, in hindsight, the handling of monetary and fiscal policy leaves much to be desired.

Fiscal policy has often had the wrong effects at the right time, or the right effects at the wrong time, but it has seldom had the right effect at the right time. There wasn't much discussion of fiscal policy in this history because it hasn't been used much to try to direct the economy. That's why much of this history concerned monetary policy.

In its conduct of monetary policy, the Fed has seemed to switch goals from one moment to the next and to continually go too far in both directions. The result has been a stop-go set of policies, causing the economy to alternate between inflationary booms and recessions. This leads modern Classical economists to argue that the Fed's policies have lacked credibility. Keynesians emphasize, however, that such an assessment can only be made with hindsight. Given the knowledge available to policymakers and the political and institutional constraints under which they operate, many

Keynesians believe that the past 50 years, while not pretty, are representative of about as good a macroeconomic policy as can be expected. In short, macroeconomics is an art, and art isn't always pretty or neat.

Now that we've been through the history of macroeconomic policy, let's switch gears and consider a hypothetical example that raises some of the same issues. Only this time you don't have hindsight to assist you.

In this example, you've been appointed head of the Xanadu central bank. You have the following information about the economy:

· The current interest rate is 10 percent.
· The unemployment rate is 8 percent.
· The government is running a budget deficit of 1 billion xanadi (the Xanadu currency), which is 2 percent of its GDP.
· The country has a trade deficit of 2 billion xanadi.
· Inflation is 6 percent.
· Your central bank has almost no international reserves so you can do little to affect the exchange rate in the market.

Prime Minister Xorcist, who appointed you, is running for reelection. He tells you that, to win, he must lower the unemployment rate and reduce the interest rate. He also remembers, from the introductory economics course he took with you when you were teaching at Xanadu U., that increasing the money supply will accomplish these goals.

How do you respond? You tell him that yes, in the short run, expansionary monetary policy will accomplish his goals, but that it will have some side effects. Specifically it will likely increase the trade deficit, push down Xanadu's exchange rate, and boost inflation.

"Why?" he asks. First, you tell him that imports depend upon income, so when income increases, imports will increase so the trade deficit will worsen. Then you explain that lower interest rates will mean fewer people will want to hold their money in xanadi (Xanadu's currency). That will lower demand for xanadi, while higher income and higher imports will increase demand for foreign currencies. The result will be a fall in Xanadu's exchange rate. This fall will cause import prices to rise, while the increased money supply will contribute directly to inflation.

The prime minister will likely respond that he wants you to expand the money supply while avoiding the side effects. How can you do that? You'll have to do something to stop imports from increasing as income increases. You'll have to introduce an **import control law** that prevents people from importing. Similarly, you'll need a **capital control law** that prevents people from investing abroad, and a **foreign exchange control law** that prevents people from buying foreign currency. And of course you'll have to do something to prevent inflation, which means price controls. In short, with import controls, price controls, capital controls, and exchange controls, you can for a short time prevent the effects. The prime minister tells you, "But those policies will be unpopular!" You answer, "Yes, but don't you remember the other lesson we learned in economics at Xanadu U.? There's no such thing as a free lunch." At that point the prime minister fires you, and you go into exile.

Dealing with such difficult trade-offs is what real-world macro policy is all about.

As you can see, real-world monetary and fiscal policies are not cut and dried. Working with these policies is an art, not a science, and involves politics and psychology as well as economics. But the messiness of real-world policy doesn't mean that one can forget the simplified theories and relationships of economic models. Far from it. Real-world policy problems require a much deeper understanding of the models so that one can see through the messiness and design a policy consistent with the general principles embodied in those models.

CONGRATULATIONS! YOU ARE NOW A POLICY ADVISOR

8 By remembering the relationships among economic variables, one can conduct a reasonable analysis for dealing with any economic situation, but it may not be politically desirable.

Import control law   *A law preventing people from importing.*

Capital control law   *A law preventing people from investing abroad.*

Foreign exchange control law   *A law preventing people from buying foreign currency.*

Dealing with such difficult trade-offs is what real-world macro policy is all about.

CONCLUSION

CHAPTER SUMMARY

• The goals of macro policy often conflict with one another.

• A policy model has a different focus than a theoretical model.

• Modern macroeconomists emphasize the need for policy to be credible.

• Modern Classicals and Keynesians have flip-flopped in their views of a deficit.

• Keynesians tend to favor activist policy; Classicals tend to favor laissez-faire policy.

• Keynesian and Classical economists agree about many aspects of macroeconomic policy.

• Monetary policy has been used far more often than fiscal policy over the past 50 years.

• Macro policy is chosen through a combination of economic and political considerations.

• Supply-side policies are policies that expand potential output by creating incentives for individuals to increase output, either by lowering tax rates or changing the composition of spending and taxes.

• Monetary policy has been characterized by stop-go measures as the Fed's concern has shifted from inflation to recession.

• Often short-run solutions to problems create even worse long-run problems.

• Macroeconomic policy is an art, not a science.

KEY TERMS

art of macro policy *(425)*
capital control law *(445)*
Classical supply-side economics *(436)*
credible systematic policies *(428)*
foreign exchange control law *(445)*
import control law *(445)*

Keynesian supply-side policy *(437)*
mechanistic Keynesianism *(426)*
New Deal *(439)*
rational expectations *(426)*
Ricardian equivalence theorem *(430)*

stagflation *(444)*
supply price shock *(441)*
supply-side policies *(435)*
Treasury Accord *(439)*
wage and price controls *(441)*

QUESTIONS FOR THOUGHT AND REVIEW

The number after each question represents the estimated degree of critical thinking required. (1 = almost none; 10 = deep thought.)

1. What is the difference between a mechanistic Keynesian view and a modern Keynesian view? *(3)*

2. How do policy models and theoretical models differ? *(3)*

3. What is the relationship between rational expectations and the modern macro emphasis on credibility? *(4)*

4. Keynesians and Classicals are in direct opposition on macroeconomic policy. True or false? Why? *(5)*

5. Why did Keynesians and Classicals flip-flop in their view of the deficit? *(5)*

6. Distinguish between Keynesian supply-side policy and Classical supply-side policy. *(5)*

7. The experience with price controls during World War II demonstrates that price controls work. True or false? Why? *(7)*

8. The experience of the New Deal suggests that economists' theoretical debates have little effect on government's real-world policies. True or false? Why? *(7)*

9. Give three possible explanations for the increase in inflation in the 1970s. *(3)*

10. Give three possible explanations for the 1983–90 decrease in inflation. *(6)*

11. How might the policy advice given to Prime Minister Xorcist have changed if he hadn't needed to run for reelection for three more years? *(6)*

PROBLEMS AND EXERCISES

1. In the library, research one of the Fed's responses to a recession discussed in this chapter.
   a. Would you have done anything differently?
   b. If you did something differently, what would be the possible negative effects of your actions?
   c. Who was president, Fed chairman, and chairman of the Council of Economic Advisers during the recession you looked at? Give their political affiliations.
   d. If individuals from the opposite party were in office during that recession, how might the responses have been different?

2. Find the current unemployment, inflation, and growth rates.
   a. What fiscal policy is government using to deal with the problems?
   b. What monetary policy is government using?
   c. Who is currently president, Fed chairman, and chairman of the Council of Economic Advisers? What are their political affiliations?
   d. How might the policies be different if individuals from another party were in power?

3. In a recent article, two economists proposed that the United States implement a plan of mandatory forced savings of 4 percent of a person's income per year.
   a. Explain the likely effect of this plan on interest rates and savings.
   b. Discuss the macroeconomic implications of the plan.
   c. Discuss the administrative problems of the plan.

4. As Europe's unemployment rates rose to over 10 percent in the early 1990s, a number of proposals were put forward for work-sharing, in which individuals work one day less per week and have their pay reduced by from 10 to 20 percent. Do you think such proposals could play a significant role in reducing unemployment in Europe? Why or why not?

5. The U.S. unemployment insurance system spends about $26 billion a year. President Clinton's Labor Secretary Robert Reich proposed that:
   a. Cash rewards be given to workers who find jobs quickly;
   b. Individuals be allowed to take their total unemployment benefits out in a lump sum, rather than over the normal 26-week period, if they are starting a small business;
   c. Individuals who want to retool their skills be given the benefits as "training subsidies."

Discuss the advantages and disadvantages of each of these three proposals.

ANSWERS TO MARGIN QUESTIONS

1. I would respond that it is important for governments to recognize the inevitable limitations and trade-offs of goals, at least with the monetary and fiscal tools currently available. *(424)*

2. Rational expectations are expectations about the future based on the best information currently available. *(426)*

3. The simple multiplier model (or even complex variations of that model) does not include sufficient dynamic interdependencies. At best, the modern Keynesian model describes tendencies toward an exaggeration of autonomous real shocks to the economy. *(426)*

4. The fact that people aren't stupid tends to undermine activist monetary and fiscal policy because, in the expectation of policies, people will change their behavior. *(427)*

5. Classicals see democratic government as being significantly controlled by special interests, and believe that the costs of government action tend to outweigh the benefits. Keynesians tend to have more faith in government. *(429)*

6. Keynesians and Classicals disagree more about the long-run effects of monetary policy on inflation. Both agree that monetary policy can have short-run real effects. Classicals tend to believe, however, that in the long run, the real effects will disappear, and only the inflationary effects will remain. Keynesians believe monetary policy can have long-run real effects. *(432)*

7. President Clinton could use neither Keynesian nor Classical policy because both policies told him that to create jobs he had to run deficits and increase the money supply, but, in the early 1990s, the political imperatives were to decrease the size of the deficit and prevent inflation by refraining from increasing the money supply. *(435)*

8. In the Keynesian view, a tax rate cut works by affecting demand which in turn affects supply if the economy is below potential income. In the Classical supply-side view, a tax rate cut works by affecting supply-side incentives, increasing potential income and demand simultaneously. Thus a tax rate cut will not be inflationary even if the economy is at its potential income. *(436)*

9. The problems some economists have with Keynesian supply-side policies are that the government is not very likely to make the right decisions about what are supply-enhancing policies and what aren't, and that the effects are too small and long-run to achieve the desired short-run benefits. *(438)*

10. In October 1979, the Fed stopped focusing on interest rate targets and started focusing on money supply targets. The immediate result was an enormous increase in short-term interest rates and a recession. The long-term result was an end to the inflationary expectations that had existed in the late 1970s. *(443)*

20

Growth and the Macroeconomics of Developing and Transitional Economies

Rise up, study the economic forces which oppress you. . . . They have emerged from the hand of man just as the gods emerged from his brain. You can control them.

~Paul LaFargue

After reading this chapter, you should be able to:

1 Distinguish between growth and development.

2 Explain why there might be a difference in normative goals between developing and developed countries.

3 Explain why economies at different stages in development have different institutional needs.

4 Explain what is meant by ''the dual economy.''

5 Distinguish between a régime change and a policy change.

6 Explain why the statement that inflation is a problem of the central bank issuing too much money is not sufficient for developing and transitional countries.

7 Distinguish between convertibility on the current account and full convertibility.

8 Explain the ''borrowing circle'' concept and why it was successful.

Throughout this book I have emphasized that macro policy is an art in which one takes the abstract principles learned in *positive economics*—the abstract analysis and models that tell us how economic forces direct the economy—and examines how those principles work out in a particular institutional structure to achieve goals determined in *normative economics*—the branch of economics that considers what goals we should be aiming for. In this chapter we see another aspect of that art.

Most of this book has emphasized the macroeconomics of Western industrialized economies, the United States in particular. That means I have focused on their goals and their institutions. In this chapter I shift focus and discuss the macroeconomic problems of *developing economies* and *transitional economies*. As discussed in Chapter 5, a **developing economy** is an economy that has a low level of GDP per capita and a relatively undeveloped market structure, and has never had an alternative, developed economic system. As discussed in Chapter 3, a **transitional economy** is an economy that has had an alternative, developed, socialist economic system, but is in the process of changing from that system to a market system.

Economists use the terms developing and transitional, rather than growing, to emphasize that the goals of these countries involve more than simply an increase in output; these countries are changing their underlying institutions. Put another way, these economies are changing their production function; they are not increasing inputs given a production function. Thus *development* refers to an increase in productive capacity and output brought about by a change in the underlying institutions, and *growth* refers to an increase in output brought about by an increase in inputs.

The distinction can be overdone. Institutions, and hence production functions, in developed as well as in developing countries are continually changing, and output changes are essentially a combination of both changes in production functions and increases in inputs. For example, in the 1990s the major Western economies have been **restructuring** their economies—changing the underlying economic institutions—as they work to compete better in the world economy. As they restructure, they change their methods of production, their laws, and their social support programs. Thus, in some ways, they are doing precisely what developing and transitional countries are doing—developing rather than just growing. Despite the ambiguity, the distinction between growth and development can be a useful one if you remember that the two blend into each other.

The reason economists separate out developing and transitional economies is that these economies have (1) different institutional structures and (2) a different weighting of goals than do Western developed economies. These two differences—in institutional structure, and in goals—change the way in which the lessons of abstract theory are applied and discussed.

The chapter begins with a consideration of how the goals of developing countries differ from the goals of developed countries. Then I turn my attention to how the institutions differ. In the process of that discussion, I consider the general conduct of macro policy in developing countries, and some case studies that bring to life important aspects of the macroeconomic problems they face.

When discussing macro policy within Western developed economies, I did not dwell on questions of normative goals of macroeconomics. Instead, I used generally accepted goals in the United States as the goals of macro policy—achieving low inflation, low unemployment, and an acceptable growth rate—with a few caveats. You may have noticed that the discussion focused more on what might be called stability goals—achieving low unemployment and low inflation—than it did on the acceptable growth rate goal. I chose that focus because growth in Western developed countries is desired because it holds unemployment down, and because it avoids difficult distributional questions, as much as it is desired for its own sake. Our economy has sufficient productive capacity to provide its citizens, on average, with a relatively high standard of living. The problem facing Western societies is as much seeing that all members of those societies share in that high standard of living as it is raising the standard.

1 Growth occurs because of an increase in inputs, given a production function; development occurs through a change in the production function.

Q–1: Why does restructuring in developed countries suggest that the distinction between growth and development can be overdone?

While the lessons of abstract theory do not change when we shift our attention to developing and transitional economies, the institutions and goals change enormously.

DIFFERING GOALS OF DEVELOPED AND DEVELOPING COUNTRIES

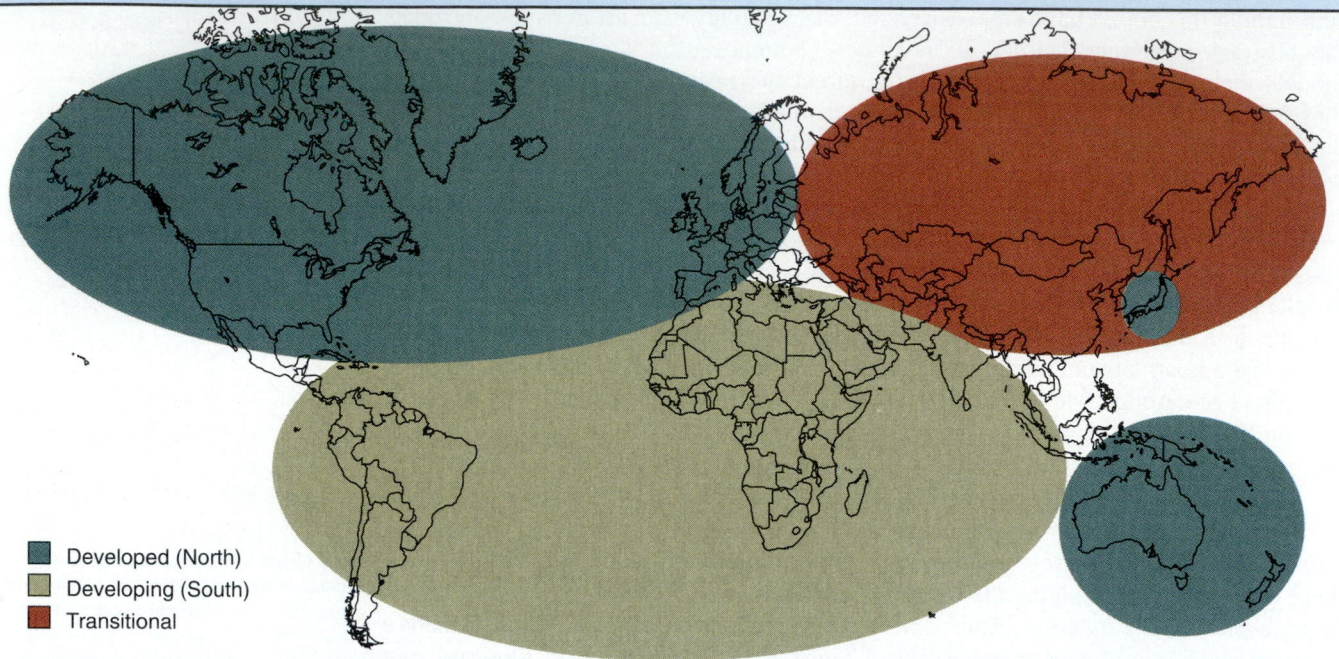

Developed (North)
Developing (South)
Transitional

Consider the map of the world and you will see that most of the developed nations are in the Northern hemisphere and most of the developing nations are in the Southern hemisphere. This has led to a characterization of the normative questions about growth as the "North/South conflict." Roughly, "North" refers to North America and Western Europe (together with Japan and Australia). "South" refers to Latin America and Africa.

The South's Position

In this conflict, the "South" takes the following position:

Economic growth uses natural resources or, more precisely, modifies the forms certain resources take. Much of the modification of resources that occurs due to current Northern production processes is, in the South's view, undesirable. For example, in many production processes we start with beautiful raw materials—forests, mountains, and pristine rivers—and we end up with trash heaps—dumps and polluted cesspools. In short, current production processes create too many of what society considers waste products in order to create goods that people don't really need, but which, instead, reflect needs created for them by society. The South asks: "Do Northern industrialized economies really need closets filled with this year's fashions—to be thrown out and replaced with next year's fashions? Or would something simpler—less resource-intensive—suffice?" Alternatively, think of automobiles. Do Western consumers really need air-conditioned automobiles at the cost of the depletion of the ozone layer?

The normative value judgments that must be made to answer these questions posed by the South are enormous, and I do not intend to deal with them here. But that does not mean that such judgments are not important. It is, in my view, legitimate to question whether further growth along the lines that Western economies are currently following is a goal to which the majority of people in Western society would subscribe, if they thought seriously about the issue.

The South points out that even if Northern societies have chosen the growth path, that path may still be suspect when one considers the normative issue of growth from an international perspective. Western economic growth imposes costs on the rest of the world. The world has a population of about 5.5 billion. The population of the industrialized countries is less than 1 billion, or 17 percent of the world's population, yet they use 60 percent of the world's resources and create many of the waste products which influence the entire atmosphere of the world. The South argues that, if we had a worldwide democratic government and a vote were taken on whether the majority of all people felt that physical growth in Western economies was a worthwhile goal, that growth would not be supported.

The North's Response

The Northern response to this philosophical question is varied. One response is to feel somewhat guilty about the North's success and use of the world's resources, and to establish aid programs to try to assuage that guilt. A number of international development programs have been started to try to offset the costs, but these programs are not large.

A second response is that the world isn't a democracy, and so in reality the question is moot. It doesn't matter what is right in some abstract philosophical sense. What matters simply is "what is."

A third response is that the South has the argument backwards. True, the North uses resources, but it is also creating new technologies. Technological changes are occurring faster than resource depletion, and with modern technological improvements in waste disposal, wastes are decreasing, not increasing. These pro-economic-growth economists argue that economic growth of Northern industrial countries is good not only for people in Northern countries; it is good for the entire world.

CLASSICAL ECONOMISTS AND LONG-RUN GROWTH

ADDED DIMENSION

How did Classical economists advise countries to grow? They advised: (1) keep the government out of the economy; (2) channel income to entrepreneurs and capitalists who consume little and who have a fetish for investing; (3) channel income away from landowners, who use it on servants and good living, not on growth-creating activities; and (4) channel income away from government that spends it on who-knows-what (but certainly not on growth-creating activities).

They also generally opposed programs to raise wages of workers because (1) workers would use the raises to have more children (the Malthusian doctrine), and (2) high wages would make the economy internationally uncompetitive in a fixed exchange rate system as then existed.

Early Classical economics—Adam Smith, Thomas Malthus, and David Ricardo—were strongest in their support of these propositions. Later Classical economists—John Stewart Mill and Alfred Marshall—were less adamant in their

support and often advocated contrary policies. Likely reasons for the change include changing institutions and increased wealth in the economy.

Democracy entered into society together with capitalism, and as the democratic nature of government became part of the institutional structure, the Classical arguments against government intervention were modified. Similarly, as industrialists lost their investment fetish and started to enjoy life (i.e., as they (or their children) started to consume some of their profits, not invest), it made less sense to channel income to industrialists to bring about investment and growth. Also, with the development of financial markets, savings from others, such as landowners or workers, could be channeled into investment and hence into growth. And finally, as society got richer, other goals besides growth became more important. In short, as Western institutions changed and Western wealth grew, so, too, did Classical economists' proposed policies.

In the developing countries, the weighting of goals is different. Growth—an increase in the economies' output—and development—a transition of the economies' institutions so that the economies can achieve higher levels of output—are primary goals. When people are starving and the economy isn't fulfilling people's **basic needs**—adequate food, clothing, and shelter—a main focus of macro policy will be on how to increase the economy's growth rate through development so that the economy can fulfill those basic needs.

When Classical economics developed, its focus was almost totally on economic growth. Early developers of that Classical economics—Adam Smith, Thomas Malthus, and David Ricardo—took growth as economics' central area of concern. As Western market economies grew, the focus of macroeconomics changed from issues of long-run growth to issues of short-run stability. The macroeconomic models developed in this book reflect that change in focus. Keynesian economics, specifically, has a short-run focus, and has little relevance to long-term growth. That part of Classical economics that we concentrated on in earlier chapters was a response to Keynes, which means that the Classical economics I presented earlier concerned more short-run than long-run issues. I left out a discussion of Classical long-run economics, which did focus on growth. (See the accompanying box for a brief discussion of Classical long-run economics.)

In summary, the goals of developed and developing countries differ; for developing countries, growth in economic output is a more generally agreed-upon goal than it is for developed countries. The central policy question facing these developing countries is: What set of macro policies will lead to growth?

Developing and transitional countries differ from developed countries not only in their goals, but also in their macroeconomic institutions. These macroeconomic institutions are qualitatively different from institutions in developed countries. Their governments are different; their financial institutions—the institutions that translate savings into investment—are different; their fiscal institutions—the institutions through which government collects taxes and spends its money—are different; and their social and cultural institutions are different. Because of these differences, the way in which one discusses macroeconomic policy is different.

One of the differences concerns very basic market institutions—such as Western-style property rights and contract law. In certain groups of developing countries, most

Growth and Basic Needs

2 There are differences in normative goals between developing and developed countries because their wealth differs. Developing countries face true economic needs whereas developed countries' economic needs are considered by most people normatively less pressing.

Economic Growth as an Appropriate Goal for Developing Countries

---

INSTITUTIONAL DIFFERENCES

Q–2: What are two ways in which developed countries differ from developing countries?

3 Economies at different stages of development have different institutional needs because the problems they face are different. Institutions that can be assumed in developed countries cannot necessarily be assumed to exist in developing countries.

notably sub-Saharan Africa, these basic market institutions don't exist; instead, communal property rights and tradition structure economic relationships. In the transitional economies, where the government previously owned large portions of the economy, ownership is often unclear. Decades ago, before the government owned large portions of the economy, there was private ownership, and claims based on those old conditions are surfacing, often placing clouds on current "ownership" and control. How can one talk about market forces in such economies?[1] On a more mundane level, consider the issue of monetary policy. Talking about monetary policy via open market operations (the buying and selling of bonds by the central bank) is not all that helpful when there are no open market operations, as there are not in many developing countries.

Let's now consider some specific institutional differences more carefully.

Political Differences and Laissez Faire

In many developing countries, institutional checks and balances on government leaders often do not exist.

Views of how activist macroeconomic policy should be are necessarily contingent on the political system an economy has. One of the scarcest commodities in developing countries is socially-minded leaders. Not that developed countries have any overabundance of them, but at least in most developed countries there is a tradition of politicians seeming to be fair and open-minded, and a set of institutionalized checks and balances that limits leaders using government for their personal benefit. In many developing countries, those institutionalized checks and balances on governmental leaders often do not exist.

Let's consider a few examples. First, consider Saudi Arabia, which, while economically rich, maintains many of the institutions of a developing country. It is an absolute monarchy in which the royal family is the ultimate power. Say a member of that family comes to the bank and wants a loan that, on economic grounds, doesn't make sense. What do you think the bank loan officer will do? Grant the loan, if the banker is smart. Thus, despite the wealth of the country, it isn't surprising that many economists believe the Saudi banking system reflects that political structure, and may find itself in serious trouble in the 1990s.

In 1994, Rwanda provides another example of the enormous political problems facing the developing countries of Africa.

Another example is Lebanon, which has so many competing political factions fighting for power that even to talk about macro policy proposals that assume a central government, let alone a government out to do good, is misplaced. The government in Lebanon is mainly concerned with continued existence; a primary institutionalized check on government leaders is a bullet.

A third example is the new transitional countries of the former Soviet Union. They face enormous political instability problems, and in the early 1990s the largest growth industry there was the private protection agency business. In such an institutional setting, government policy often has little to do with economics or what's good for the economy, and any proposed macroeconomic policy must take that into account.

A final example is Nigeria, which had enormous possibilities for economic growth in the 1980s because of its oil riches. It didn't develop. Instead, politicians fought over the spoils, and bribes became a major source of their income. Corruption was rampant, and the Nigerian economy went nowhere. I will stop there, but, unfortunately, there are many other examples.

Q–3: Why might an economist favor activist policies in developed countries and laissez-faire policies in developing countries?

Because of the structure of government in many developing countries, many economists who, in Western developed economies, favor activist government policies may well favor Classical laissez-faire policies for the same reasons that early Classical economists did—because they have a profound distrust of the governments. That distrust, however, must have limits. As I discussed in Chapter 4, even a laissez-faire policy requires some government role in setting the rules. So there is no escaping the need for socially-minded leaders.

---

[1] One can, of course, talk about economic forces. But, as discussed in Chapter 1, economic forces only become market forces in a market institutional setting.

A second institutional difference between developed and developing countries is the dual nature of developing countries' economies. Whereas it often makes sense to talk about Western economies as a single economy, it does not for most developing countries. Their economies are generally characterized by a duality—a traditional sector and an internationally-oriented modern market sector.[2]

The Dual Economy

4 "The dual economy" refers to the existence of the two sectors in most developing countries: a traditional sector and an internationally-oriented modern market sector.

Often, the largest percentage of the population participate in the traditional economy. It is a local currency, or no currency, sector in which traditional ways of doing things take precedence. The second sector—the internationally-oriented modern market sector—is often indistinguishable from Western economies. Activities in the modern sector are often conducted in foreign currencies, rather than domestic currencies, and contracts are often governed by international law. This **dual economy** aspect of developing countries creates a number of policy dilemmas for them and affects the way they think about macroeconomic problems.

Q–4: What is meant by the term "dual economy"?

For example, take the problem of unemployment. Many developing countries have a large, subsistence farming economy. Subsistence farmers aren't technically unemployed, but often there are so many people on the land that, in economic terms, their marginal product is minimal or even negative, so for policy purposes one can consider the quantity of labor that will be supplied at the going wage unlimited. But to call these people unemployed is problematic. These subsistence farmers are simply outside the market economy. In such cases one would hardly want, or be able, to talk of an unemployment problem in the same way we talk in the United States.

A third institutional difference concerns developing and transitional countries' fiscal systems. To undertake discretionary fiscal policy—running a deficit or surplus to affect the aggregate economy—the government must be able to determine expenditures and tax rates, with a particular eye toward the difference between the two. As discussed above, discretionary fiscal policy is difficult for Western developed countries to undertake; it is almost impossible for developing and transitional economies. Often, the governments in these economies don't have the institutional structures with which to collect taxes (or, when they have the institutional structure, it is undermined by fraud and evasion), so their taxing options are limited; that's why they often use tariffs as a primary source of revenue.

Fiscal Structure of Developing and Transitional Economies

Often developing countries do not have the institutional structures with which to collect taxes.

In the traditional sector of many developing and transitional countries, barter or cash transactions predominate, and such transactions are especially difficult to tax. For example, consider Bulgaria, which at the beginning of the 1990s was attempting to transform from a centrally-planned economy to a market economy. Initially it had no agency for tax collection since all previous economic activity was under the control of the state. Under its old institutional structure, revenues automatically flowed into the state. As the country shifted to a market economy, that changed dramatically. With no experience in tax collection, and with no tradition of paying taxes, initially all the fiscal policy discussion concerned how to collect enough to finance the basic core of government in order to keep it functioning.

Similar problems exist with government expenditures. Many expenditures of developing countries are mandated by political considerations—if the government doesn't make them, it will likely be voted out of office. Within such a setting, to talk about Keynesian fiscal policy—choosing a deficit for its macroeconomic implications—even if it might otherwise be relevant, is not much help since the budget deficit is not a choice variable, but instead is a result of other political decisions.

Many government expenditures in developing countries are mandated by political considerations.

The political constraints facing developing and transitional countries can, of course, be overstated. The reality is that developing countries do institute new fiscal régimes. Take, for example, Mexico. In the early 1980s, Mexico's fiscal problems seemed impossible to solve, but in the late 1980s and early 1990s, Carlos de Salinas, a U.S.-trained economist, introduced a fiscal austerity program and an economic

---

[2] I discuss these two economies as if they were separate, but in reality, they are interrelated. Portions of the economy devoted to the tourist trade span both sectors, as do some manufacturing industries. Still, there is sufficient independence of the two economies that it is reasonable to treat them as separate.

5 A régime change is a change in the entire atmosphere within which the government and the economy interrelate; a policy change is a change in one aspect of government's actions.

Financial Institutions of Developing and Transitional Economies

The primary difference between financial institutions in developing countries and developed countries arises from the dual nature of developing countries' economies.

An Example of the Different Roles of Financial Institutions in Transitional Economies

Soft budget constraint   Loose financial constraints on firm's decisions in centrally-planned economies.

liberalization program that lowered Mexico's deficit and significantly reduced its inflation. But such changes are better called a **régime change**—a change in the entire atmosphere within which the government and the economy interrelate—rather than a **policy change**—a change in one aspect of government's actions, such as monetary policy or fiscal policy.

I spent three chapters discussing the complex financial systems of developed countries because you had to understand those financial systems in order to understand macro policy. While some parts of that discussion carry over to developing countries, other parts don't, since financial systems in developing countries are often quite different than those in developed countries.

The primary difference arises from the dual nature of developing countries' economies. In the traditional part of developing economies, the financial sector is embryonic; trades are made by barter, or with direct payment of money; trades requiring more sophisticated financial markets, such as mortgages to finance houses, just don't exist.

In the modern international part that isn't the case. Developing countries' international financial sectors are sometimes as sophisticated as Western financial institutions. When one walks into a currency trading room in Bulgaria or Nigeria, one will see a room similar to a room that one would see in New York, London, or Frankfurt. That modern financial sector is integrated into the international economy (with pay rates that often approach or match those of the West). This dual nature of developing countries' financial sectors imposes constraints on the practice of monetary policy and changes the regulatory and control functions of central banks.

Let's consider an example of a transitional economy—Bulgaria, where I spent some time trying to understand the banking system and teaching Bulgarian professors about Western banking. Before going over there, I had expected to teach about money and banking the same way I had done in the West, explaining how the quantity of high-powered money serves as a basis for loans, and how the money multiplier works. Then, I had expected to explain how the banks made decisions on long-term loans, and how those decisions were related to central bank policy.

I soon discovered that much of this was not directly relevant for Bulgaria. While Bulgarian private banks had many long-term loans on the books, when I was there they were making almost no new long-term loans, and those that already existed were, in large part, worthless. The reason was that the Bulgarian private banks had been created out of the former Bulgarian National Bank. In the transition, that single bank was broken up into the Central Bank and a number of private banks, with the private banks carrying on their books some portion of the loans of the central bank from which they were created. These loans had little value; as part of the planned economy, the bank had systematically extended whatever credit was needed to the companies it served. These firms simultaneously extended **inter-firm credit** (loans from one firm to another) to other firms so that monetary payment for whatever they wanted was easy to obtain. This is what Harvard economist James Kornai called the **soft budget constraint.** By this term he meant that, since firms could get loans without difficulty, financial constraints—the need to pay for inputs—placed little constraint on firms' decisions in centrally-planned economies. With the end of the central planning and an attempt to switch their economies from centrally-planned to market economies, the soft budget constraint came to a hard end.

The private banks that evolved from the government bank inherited the loans of their predecessor banks, and it was these long-term loans that they carried on their books. The loans were uncollectable. Even if the firms to whom the loans were made were still viable, those viable firms had so many trade credits extended to other, unviable firms that the viable firms couldn't pay off the loans. Most firms couldn't even afford to pay the interest, and the only reason they didn't default was that the banks kept lending them the money to pay the interest. Luckily or unluckily, depending on where you stood, the real interest rate was negative, and inflation was wiping out many of these loans. (For whom was this unlucky? Remember: inflation makes the society neither richer nor poorer, so someone was losing. Who? Holders of cash whose wealth was being wiped out.)

New long-term loans weren't being made for three reasons. The first was that the central bank was attempting to restrict credit in order to restrain the inflationary pressures. Thus, private banks had a hard time getting loans from the central bank. An important reason why the central bank was concerned about making too much credit available was, in turn, a second reason why new long-term loans weren't being made. Since the private banks had never made loans based on sound lending principles (remember the soft budget constraint), they had no loan officers or procedures to determine who should get loans.

Third, even if they had had such a system, there was little demand for what I'd call sound long-term loans. These were two reasons for their low demand. First, the Bulgarian economy was in a serious downward spiral. With expectations of a downward economic spiral, sound long-term investment doesn't make much sense. Second, the interest rate charged by the Bulgarian banks was about 50 percent. Such high nominal interest rates have a tendency to discourage loans. But, you must remember, the inflation was around 60 percent, making the real interest rate minus 10 percent. A negative real interest rate should, according to simple economic theory, encourage firms to take out loans. That wasn't taking place. Why? It seems that once inflation and nominal interest rates get that high, they are accompanied by enormous uncertainty about future inflation and, in particular, about relative prices of products. To make a business plan work with a 60 percent rate of inflation and a 50 percent nominal interest rate, you must build a 50 or 60 percent price rise into your business plan, making your profitability analysis on the basis of an expected rise in prices.

When I asked businesspeople why they didn't do that, I discovered that the business texts that they were using to guide them didn't include such an inflation adjustment—their texts did break-even analysis (an analysis of whether an investment makes sense or not) at fixed prices. (Remember, these were people new to business, and they were looking to the Western textbooks to guide them). Even those who understood that the break-even analysis could be adjusted for expected inflation didn't want their success or failure to be dependent on an inflation rate over which they had no control. Entrepreneurial types generally like control, and the inflation made them feel controlled rather than in control. In short, they felt the financial situation was too uncertain to take a chance, and so they didn't want to invest.

To say that there was no demand for solid productive investment loans is not to say there was no demand for loans. There was a large demand for long-term loans, but most of that demand was connected to high-risk investments in which the borrower received most of the return in the unlikely event that the project turned out to be successful and the bank bore all the loss in the likely event the project was unsuccessful. The end result was that the banks were making almost no long-term loans.

Despite the fact that the banking system was not making any long-term loans, it provided significant short-term loans (one to two weeks) called trade credits to facilitate inter-firm trade. In Western economies this necessary function for a working economy is provided primarily by firms. When a firm orders a product from another firm, the bill is sent payable in about 30 days—weeks after the product is sent. Accounts payable and accounts receivable representing short-term loans from one firm to another, are parts of every Western firm's balance sheet. The Bulgarian firms were unwilling to extend such trade credits to other Bulgarian firms; they wanted payment guaranties before they would sell to another firm. (In the United States, firms want such guaranties when the firms they are dealing with are close to bankruptcy.) The Bulgarian banking system was providing this guarantee function. It extended large amounts of **trade credits** making inter-firm trade possible.

This trade credit role of banking is hardly mentioned in modern Western money and banking books, and is not even discussed in the financial and monetary institutions chapters of this book. It is, however, an absolutely necessary function for an economy to work. In developed countries, one takes the fulfillment of that function for

Trade credits *Short-term loans to facilitate inter-firm trade.*

Q–5: Why is the trade credit function of banks barely mentioned in financial and monetary chapters of this book?

granted; in Bulgaria one couldn't. (This function of banking was not always taken for granted in the United States; academic discussion of banking in the early 1800s often included discussion of this vital role and how to maintain sufficient "elasticity" in the money supply to meet the trade credit needs. Western institutions simply became so good at fulfilling this function that we don't discuss it.)

It is important to have specific knowledge of a country's institutions before one can understand its economy and meaningfully talk about policy.

The above is one of many institutional examples of differences that exist and that change the nature of the macro problem. What's important is not so much the specifics of the example but, rather, the general point it brings home. Economies at different stages of development have different institutional, and policy, needs. Institutions with the same names in different countries can have quite different roles. Such institutions can differ in subtle ways, making it important to have specific knowledge of a country's institutions before one can understand its economy and meaningfully talk about policy for them.

Monetary Policy in Developing and Transitional Countries

Now that I've discussed some of the ways in which financial institutions differ in developing and transitional countries, let's consider some issues of central banking and monetary policy for those economies.

The first thing to note about central banking in developing and transitional countries is that its primary goal is often different than a central bank's primary goal in developed countries. The reason is that, while all central banks have a number of goals, at the top of them all is the goal of keeping the economy running. In the 1990s, Western central banks have the luxury of assuming away the problem of keeping the economy running—inertia, institutions, and history hold Western industrial economies together, and keep them running. Central banks in developing and transitional countries can't make that assumption.

Central banks in developing and transitional countries have far less independence than do central banks in developed countries.

What this means in practice is that central banks in developing and transitional countries have far less independence than do central banks in developed countries. With a political and fiscal system that generates large deficits and cannot exist without those deficits, the thought of an independent monetary policy goes out the window.

A second difference concerns the institutional implementation of monetary policy. In a developing or a transitional country, a domestic government bond market seldom exists. So if the government runs a deficit and is financing it domestically, the central bank usually must buy the bonds, which means that it must increase the money supply.

Monetary Policy and Inflation   The above institutional background gives us some insight into the significant inflation problem many developing and transitional countries face. The extent of that inflation can be seen in Exhibit 1.

It shows recent inflation rates for various countries. Notice that for a number of developing countries, the U.S. inflation rate wouldn't be seen as inflation at all, but only as background noise in the price level. For example in the 1990s inflation in Brazil has averaged over 1,000% per year. Thus, talking about inflation as a macroeconomic problem of developing countries would seem to make sense. But it cannot be talked about as a simple economic problem; it must be talked about as a macro-political problem.

Q-6: If everyone knows that the cause of inflation in developing countries is the creation of too much money, why don't these countries stop inflation?

Let me explain. In the United States, there's significant debate about the cause and nature of inflation. The cause and nature of developing and transitional countries' inflation is clear. Economists of all persuasions agree that large inflations can continue only if the central bank issues large amounts of money. So the cause of developing countries' inflation is that the central bank is issuing too much money. But, as discussed above, the central bank knows that. The real policy debate is not about the economic cause but is about the political cause—does the central bank have a choice about issuing so much money. That debate concerns issues related to the political consequences of not issuing too much money.

6 Central banks recognize that printing too much money causes inflation, but often feel compelled to do so for political reasons. Debate about inflation in developing and transitional countries generally concerns those political reasons, not the relationship between money and inflation.

As I discussed above, often, in developing countries, the government's sources of tax revenue are limited, and the low level of income in the economy makes the tax base small. A government, attempting to collect significantly more taxes might risk

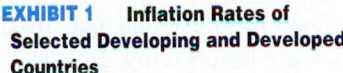

EXHIBIT 1   Inflation Rates of Selected Developing and Developed Countries

Inflation is a problem of many developing countries, especially in Latin and South America. Notice the generally lower rates of inflation in the developed as compared to the developing countries.
Source: *U.N. Statistical Yearbook*, various years.

— Bangladesh
— Brazil
— Gambia
— Germany
— Hungary
— Italy
— Korea
— U.S.

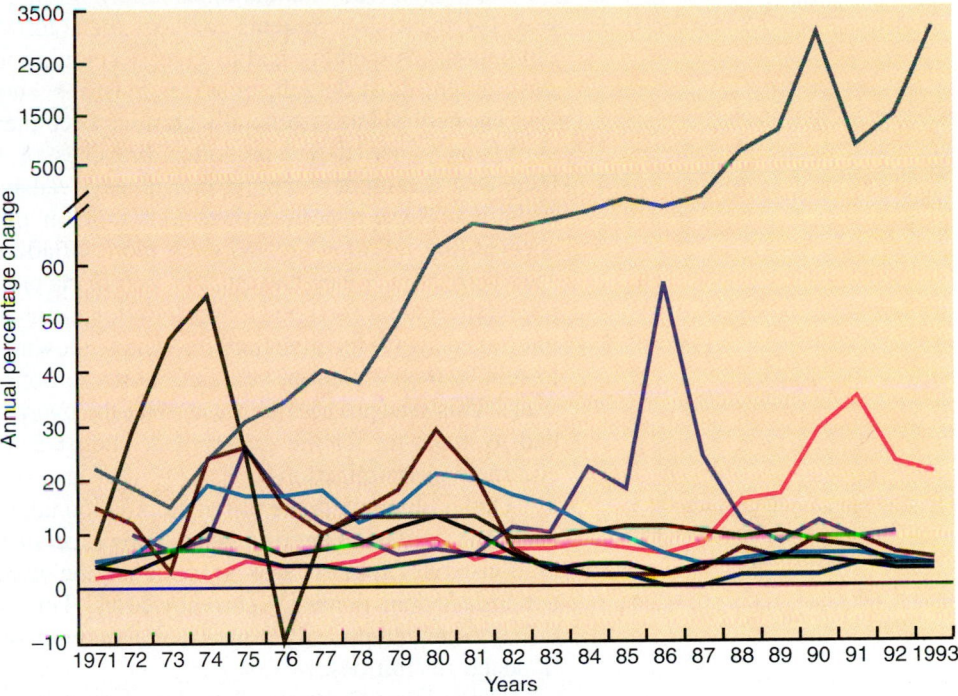

being overthrown. Similarly its ability to cut expenditures is limited. If it cuts expenditures, it will be overthrown. With new tax sources unavailable and with no ability to cut expenditures, the government uses its only other option to meet its obligations—it issues debt. And, if the central bank agrees with the conclusion that the government is correct in its assessment that it has no choice, then if the central bank doesn't want the government to be overthrown, it has no choice but to monetize that debt. Sometimes the central bank's choices are even more limited; dictatorships simply tell the central bank to provide the needed money, or be eliminated.

The problem for transitional economies is slightly different. As socialist countries, they had their taxes built into their pricing structure. Their government received the difference between the revenue received for the goods they sold and the cost to them to produce those goods. Their "tax" was that difference. As they moved toward a market economy, this source of revenue was eliminated and they had no taxing institutions—such as the U.S. Internal Revenue Service—in place to implement new taxes and supply that revenue. Moreover, people had no tradition of paying taxes and, hence, avoided and evaded taxes whenever they could. With the legal system in transition, the government could do little to force individuals to pay taxes.

The Inflation Tax   Issuing money to finance budget deficits may be a short-term solution but it is not a long-term solution. It is an accounting identity that real resources consumed by the economy must equal the real resources produced or imported. If the government deficit doesn't increase output, the real resources the government is getting because the central bank is monetizing its debt must come from somewhere. Where do those real resources come from? From the **inflation tax:** an implicit tax on the holders of cash and the holders of any obligations specified in nominal terms. Inflation works as a type of tax on these individuals.

Let's consider that inflation tax in relation to the transitional economies. With the end of central planning, there was an enormous monetary overhang—large stores of currency in excess of real goods in the economy at market prices. This monetary overhang existed because most individuals had stored their financial wealth in the currency of their country. This currency represented the enormous past obligations of the former socialist governments—obligations that far exceeded the governments', or the economies', ability to meet them.

Inflation works as a tax on holders of obligations specified in nominal terms.

As they moved to a market economy without an acceptable tax base there was no way for these governments to meet their current obligations, let alone their past obligations. Something had to give; accounting identities are unforgiving. Either the government must default, or prices must rise enormously.

The central banks generally chose to keep the governments operating (which isn't surprising, since they were often branches of the government). To do that they increased the money supply enormously, causing hyperinflation in many of these countries. These hyperinflations soon took on a life of their own. The expectation of accelerating inflation created even more inflationary pressure as individuals tried to spend any money they had quickly, before the prices went up. This increased velocity, nominal demand for goods, and inflationary pressures. These hyperinflations wiped out (taxed away) the monetary overhang, allowing most of those transitional countries to rein in their inflation, getting it down to double digits (less than 100 percent per year). This was possible because, with the overhang wiped out, the inflation tax only had to make up for the government budget deficit; it no longer had to be used to eliminate past obligations.

Q–7: In an inflation, who else, besides government, gets revenue from an inflation tax?

One problem with the use of an inflation tax is that in an inflation, the government is not the only recipient of revenue; any issuer of fixed-interest-rate debt denominated in domestic currency also gains. And the holder of any fixed-interest-rate debt denominated in domestic currency loses. This income redistribution caused by an inflation can temporarily stimulate real output, but it can also undermine the country's financial institutions.

The point of the above discussion is that the central banks know that issuing large quantities of money will cause inflation. What they don't know, and what the policy discussions are about, is which is worse: the inflation or the unpleasant alternatives. Should the central bank bail out the government? There are legitimate questions about whether countries' budget deficits are absolutely necessary or not. It is those assessments in which the debate about developing countries' inflation exists; the debate is not about whether the inflation is caused by the issuance of too much money.

The fact that inflation is only a temporary solution doesn't stop developing and transitional countries' leaders from using it.

Opponents of any type of bailout point out that any "inflation solution" is only a temporary solution that, if used, will require ever-increasing amounts of inflation to remain effective. Proponents of bailouts agree with this argument, but argue that inflation buys a bit more time, and the alternative is the breakdown of the government and the economy. Because of the unpleasant alternative, the fact that inflation is only a temporary solution doesn't stop developing and transitional countries' leaders from using it. They don't have time for the luxury of long-run solutions, and are often simply looking for policies that will hold their governments together for a month at a time.

Focus on the International Sector and the Exchange Rate Constraint

Another difference between the monetary policies of developed and developing countries concerns the policy options they consider for dealing with foreign exchange markets. Developed countries are generally committed to full exchange rate convertibility on both the current and capital accounts. With full exchange rate convertibility, individuals can exchange their currency for any other country's currency without significant government restrictions.

Transitional and developing countries often do not have fully convertible currencies. Individuals and firms in these countries face restrictions on their ability to exchange currencies—sometimes general restrictions and sometimes restrictions depending on the purpose for which they wish to use the foreign exchange.

Various Types of Convertibility

Q–8: Distinguish between convertibility on the current account and full convertibility.

Since convertibility plays such a central role in developing countries' macro policies, let's review the various types of convertibility. The United States has **full convertibility.** That means that U.S. law does not prevent individuals from changing dollars into any currency they want for whatever legal purpose they want. (There are, however, reporting laws about movements of currency.) Most Western developed countries have full convertibility.

A second type of convertibility is **convertibility on the current account.** This system allows people to exchange currencies freely to buy goods and services, but not to buy assets in other countries.

The third type of convertibility is **limited capital account convertibility.** This system allows full current account convertibility and partial capital account convertibility. There are various levels of restrictions on what types of assets one can exchange, so there are many types of limited capital account convertibility.

Almost no developing country allows full convertibility. Why? One reason is that they want to force their residents to keep their savings, and to do their investing, in their home country, not abroad. Why don't their citizens want to do that? Because when there is a chance of a change in governments—and government seizure of assets—as there often is in developing countries, rich individuals generally prefer to have a significant portion of their assets abroad, away from the hands of their government.

These limits on exchange rate convertibility explain a general phenomenon found in most developing countries—the fact that much of the international part of the dual economy in developing countries is "dollarized"—contracts are framed in, and accounting is handled in, dollars, not in the home country's currency. Dollarization exists almost completely in the international sectors of countries that have nonconvertible currencies, and largely in the international sectors of countries where the currency is convertible on the current account, but not on the capital account. This dollarization exists because of non-convertibility, or the fear of nonconvertibility. Thus, ironically, nonconvertibility increases the focus on dollarized contracts in the international sector, and puts that sector beyond effective control by the central bank.

Nonconvertibility does not halt international trade—it merely complicates it, since it adds another layer of uncertainty and bureaucracy to the trading process. Each firm that is conducting international trade must see that it will have sufficient foreign exchange to carry on its business. Developing and transitional governments will often want to encourage this international trade, while preventing outflows of their currencies for other purposes.

When developing countries have partially convertible exchange rates, **exchange rate policy**—buying and selling foreign currencies in order to help stabilize the exchange rate—often is an important central bank function. This is such an important function because trade in most of these countries' currencies is *thin*—there is not a large number of traders or trades. When trading is thin, large fluctuations in exchange rates are possible in response to a change in a few traders' needs. Even the uncertainties of the weather can affect traders. Say an expected oil tanker is kept from landing in port because of bad weather. The financial exchange—paying for that oil—that would have taken place upon landing does not take place, and the supply/demand conditions for a country's currency could change substantially. In response, the value of the country's currency could rise or fall dramatically unless it were stabilized. The central bank often helps provide exchange rate stabilization.

Conditionality and the Balance of Payments Constraint

In designing their policies, transitional and developing countries often rely on advice from the International Monetary Fund (IMF). One reason is that the IMF has economists who have much experience with these issues. A second reason is that, for these countries, the IMF is a major source of temporary loans that they need to stabilize their currencies.

These loans usually come with conditions that the country meet certain domestic monetary and fiscal stabilization goals. Specifically, these goals are that government deficits be lowered and money supply growth be limited. Because of these requirements, IMF's loan policy is often called **conditionality**—the making of loans that are subject to specific conditions.

Even a partially flexible exchange rate régime presents the country with the **balance of payments constraint**—limitations on expansionary domestic macroeconomic policy due to a shortage of international reserves. Attempts to expand the

7 Full convertibility means one can exchange one's currency for whatever legal purpose one wants. Convertibility on the current account limits those exchanges to buying goods and services.

Almost no developing country has full convertibility.

Nonconvertibility does not halt international trade; it merely makes it more difficult.

The basis for most IMF loans is conditionality.

Balance of payments constraint
Limitation on expansionary domestic macro policy due to a shortage of international reserves.

domestic economy with expansionary monetary policy continually push the economy to its balance of payments constraint. To meet both its domestic goals and international balance of payments constraints, many developing countries turn to loans from the IMF, not only for the exchange rate stabilization reasons discussed above, but also for a more expansionary macro policy than otherwise possible. Because of the IMF's control of these loans, macro policy in developing countries is often conducted with one eye toward the IMF, and sometimes with a complete bow.

MACRO INSTITUTIONAL POLICY IN DEVELOPING COUNTRIES

Macro institutional policies
Policies to change the underlying macro institutions and thereby increase output.

The above discussion may have made it seem as if conducting domestic macro policy in developing countries is almost hopelessly dominated by domestic political concerns and international constraints. If, by macro policy, one means using traditional monetary and fiscal policy tools as they are used in standard ways, that's true. But macro policy, interpreted broadly, is much more than using those tools. It is the development of new institutions that expand the possibilities for growth. It is creating a new production function, not operating within an existing one. Macro policy, writ large to include the development of new institutions, can have enormous effects. To undertake such policies requires an understanding of the role of institutions, the specific nature of the problem in one's country, and creativity.

Let's consider a recent World Bank report on the developmental success of ''The Asian Tigers'' to see how economists view what might be called **macro institutional policies**—policies to change the underlying macro institutions and thereby increase output. The report asked what were the causes of these countries' high growth rates, and whether their success provides lessons for other developing countries.

The report concluded that the most important reason for these countries' success was that they ''got the economic fundamentals right, with low inflation, sound fiscal policies, high levels of domestic savings, heavy investment in education; and they kept their economies more open to foreign technology than most other developing countries.'' In a sense, what the World Bank concluded was that these high growth rates were not a miracle at all, but simply the result of sound economic policies.

Macro policy in developing countries involves getting the infrastructure right—creating a climate within which individual initiative is directed toward production.

While economists will disagree with particulars of many of these fundamentals, almost all would agree with the general argument: macro policy in developing countries involves getting the infrastructure right—creating a climate within which individual initiative is directed toward production.

Generating Saving and Investment and the Lingering Shadow of the Debt Crisis

Growth depends on investment, and investment depends on savings.

Let's now consider some of these fundamentals more carefully.

Growth depends on investment, and investment depends on saving. This saving can come from domestic sources, or it can come from international sources, either in the form of foreign private investment or foreign aid.

Because it is difficult to generate domestic savings, developing countries often look abroad for savings to finance investment. But many of the firms in these countries are unable to borrow abroad because they lack creditworthiness. This leads the governments of many of these developing countries to guarantee loans by private firms, thereby creating large government debt overhangs, all denominated in dollars, leaving the monetary policy with a serious external debt problem.

Had the loans that led to this debt gone for productive investments that paid a return greater than the principal and interest on the loans, these investments would have been helpful. But in reality, as a result of political corruption and economic mismanagement, the investments were often unproductive. Returns on the investments didn't even cover the interest payments, let alone the principal. The situation was worsened by tight U.S. monetary policy that simultaneously raised interest rates, increasing the interest burden of these floating rate loans, and raised the value of the dollar, increasing the developing countries' indebtedness far beyond their expectations. In short, the governments that had guaranteed the loans found themselves responsible for repaying the loans without the wherewithal to do so. They found themselves in a debt crisis.

In the early 1990s, the total debt of Latin American countries was about $400 billion, much of it owned by U.S. banks, while all the developing countries combined had about $1.4 trillion in outstanding debt. That meant that they had to have a large annual trade surplus simply to pay the interest of about $100 billion a year on their debt. Some countries' annual interest was more than they could afford to pay from their export earnings. But if they paid only the interest on the debt and did not make payments on the principal, the debt would remain as large as ever. And as long as that debt remained unpaid, there would be no new incoming foreign investment to devote to development. The developing countries found themselves trapped by debt, and that trap became known as the debt crisis.

In the late 1980s, when the debt situation looked hopeless, some economists urged the developing countries simply to repudiate their debt—to say it was guaranteed by corrupt former officials, that fraud was involved, and that it was time to start over. This would have allowed the countries to make a new start, declaring that they owe nothing. For obvious reasons this strategy was extraordinarily tempting, and in the late 1980s a number of Latin American countries threatened to repudiate their debt, and some partially did so.

The Debt Repudiation Strategy

Apart from the moral argument that a debt should be repaid, the major argument against repudiation is that it will destroy the country's ability to get loans in the future. The counter-argument is that the country already has so much debt that it won't be able to get new credit anyway, so why worry about obtaining future loans? If they repudiate their debt, they won't need much in the way of loans since they can use the interest they were paying on the debt to finance internal development. Moreover, if all the developing countries were to collectively repudiate their debts, forming a debtors' cartel, the banks would be unable to single out one or two countries that had repudiated and, according to many observers, would start making loans to them again in a year or two.

Q–9:   What is the disadvantage of the debt repudiation strategy?

Whether or not that strategy made sense, the threat of it made lots of sense, and worry about total repudiation increased banks' willingness to give developing countries leeway in repaying loans. This worry also made those existing loans to developing countries, which can be sold on the secondary market just like bonds, sell for far less than par—some for only about 15 to 30¢ on the dollar. (Each dollar of the loan amount is sold at anywhere between 15 and 30¢.) Thus countries could buy their debt back at only a portion of what they had borrowed.

In the 1990s, the fall in the value of the dollar and the fall in international market rates of interest assisted developing countries so that by 1993 the debt, while still a problem, was no longer considered a crisis. The value of developing country debt rose substantially, making significant profits for those who had bought it at 15¢ to 30¢ on the dollar.

The IMF and the World Bank are superb sources of international data and articles about development issues.

Unfortunately there were new debt problems in the making, and many economists saw the debt incurred by Russia and other former republics of the Soviet Union as being un-repayable, and hence a new international debt crisis of the late 1990s is a potential problem.

How the Debt Crisis Was Managed   There's a saying in banking, "If you owe the bank a million, you're in trouble; if you owe the bank a billion, your trouble is the bank's trouble." When a lender will go broke if a borrower defaults, the lender will try as hard as it can to work something out. Accordingly, the 1980s were years of intense negotiation designed to prevent developing countries from defaulting on their loans. The U.S. government, other Western governments, and the International Monetary Fund were active in these negotiations.

If you owe a bank a million, you are in trouble; if you owe a bank a billion, your trouble is the bank's trouble.

In the late 1980s, default was prevented by (1) restructuring the debt, (2) lending developing countries even more money to pay the interest on the debts, (3) writing off some of the old loans (essentially forgiving them), and (4) lowering the interest rate on the remaining loans.

The Debt Restructuring Strategy   Since the process by which these debts were reduced shows the role of the IMF in developing countries' economies, let's consider portions of it a bit more carefully.

The fall in the value of developing countries' debt led to an alternative strategy— the debt restructuring strategy—which achieved the same goals as debt repudiation would have—a decrease in the debt—but without a bankruptcy or repudiation of the debt. The basic plan followed, called The Brady Plan, involved banks accepting a reduction in indebtedness of the developing country (at, say 40¢ on the dollar) in trade for either a U.S. government or IMF guarantee of the "restructured" debt. These restructuring plans were instituted in the early 1990s and, by the mid-1990s, the developing countries were once again in a reasonably strong debt position and banks were making new, unguaranteed loans to them.

Generating Domestic Savings

Because of the problems of international debt, generating domestic saving is, in many ways, preferable to borrowing from abroad. But it is a difficult strategy—poor people don't have much discretionary income, and hence can't save much, and rich people are concerned about confiscation of their wealth, and hence save abroad, either legally or illegally. Moreover, for the small middle class that does exist, there are few financial instruments that effectively channel savings into investment. Macro monetary policy in such countries involves setting up such institutions. Let's now consider two case studies that give some insight into these issues.

A Real Names Policy   Macro policies in developing countries often deal with setting up laws and institutional structures to handle attempts to circumvent policies that restrict freedom of movement, rather than conducting macro policy given an unchanging institutional structure. Thus, our first case study involves an attempt by the South Korean government to control the way its citizens save money. It was called a "real names" policy.

The Wall Street Journal reported the South Korean real names policy as follows: "President Kim Young Sam staged a surprise raid on [South] Korea's underground economy, introducing a real-names financial transaction system." (*The Wall Street Journal,* Aug. 13, 1993, A4.)

The background that led to the policy is as follows: As in most developing countries, businesspeople are concerned about holding too much of their wealth in South Korea because of taxes and fear of government confiscation. Having wealth means they may have to explain how they got it, and the ways they got it may not always have been legal. Moreover, many politicians had significant wealth, and it is unclear how they came to have that wealth.

Q–10:   Why did South Korea institute a "real names" policy?

They could have simply put their money outside South Korea, and many of them did. But South Korea, like most developing countries, limits the flow of domestic capital abroad. Moreover, South Korea's economy is one of the success stories of development, and the rates of return on South Korean investments were high. This led many South Koreans to want to invest in South Korea, but they didn't want it to be known that it was their money. They managed to solve these conflicting goals by investing their money in South Korea using fictional names to hide their holdings. The "real names" policy made that fictional name strategy illegal.

Making that strategy illegal sounds like a good policy, but it has a problem. Consider the economic effect of the law. It will drive South Koreans to hold more of their money abroad rather than at home, and will tend to depress investment, and hence income, in the South Korean economy. Soon after the introduction of the policy, the South Korean government lowered economic growth estimates by 25 percent.

If the policy depresses the economy, why did Kim Young Sam institute it? One of the reasons was political pressure from the middle class to control the excesses of the rich. During his election campaign, Kim Young Sam had promised to institute this popularly favored policy if he won the presidency. After he was elected he backed off, but the expectation that he might actually implement the policy led to a withdrawal of funds from South Korea and into other countries.

Those expectations that he would institute the law were destabilizing. To stop the destabilizing effects of those expectations, he had to really institute the policy. That said, it should also be said that the law very likely won't be all that effective. The

[M]aking productive loans in developing countries involves more than simply lending money. It involves changing cultural norms and creating a market economy. Thus, when the Grameen Bank makes a loan, it has the borrower promise to abide by the following 16 decisions, in an effort to change the culture and ways of life of the borrower.

The 16 Decisions

1. The four principles of Grameen Bank—discipline, unity, courage, and hard work—we shall follow and advance in all walks of our lives.

2. We shall bring prosperity to our families.

3. We shall not live in dilapidated houses. We shall repair our houses and work towards constructing new houses as soon as possible.

4. We shall grow vegetables all the year round. We shall eat plenty of them and sell the surplus.

5. During the planting seasons, we shall plant as many seedlings as possible.

6. We shall plan to keep our families small. We shall minimize our expenditures. We shall look after our health.

7. We shall educate our children and ensure that they can earn enough to pay for their education.

8. We shall always keep our children and the environment clean.

9. We shall build and use pit latrines.

10. We shall drink tube-well water. If it is not available, we shall boil water or use alum.

11. We shall not take any dowry in our sons' weddings, neither shall we give any dowry in our daughters' weddings. We shall keep the center free from the curse of dowry. We shall not practice child marriage.

12. We shall not inflict any injustice on anyone, neither shall we allow anyone to do so.

13. For higher income we shall collectively undertake bigger investments.

14. We shall always be ready to help each other. If anyone is in difficulty, we shall all help.

15. If we come to know of any breach of discipline in any center, we shall all go there and help restore discipline.

16. We shall introduce physical exercise in our centers. We shall take part in all social activities collectively.

---

reason is that there is a high threshold level specified by the law. It only applies to accounts of more than 50 million won (about $62,000). This lessens the impact on a number of small businesspeople using the fictitious name accounts, letting the President seem as if he is a reformist while still assuring South Korean businesspeople that he will support them. Still, more than a thousand high-ranking government officials reported wealth of $1.3 million or more, and a Chief Justice of the South Korean Supreme Court resigned after it was revealed that he had $3.5 million. Such are the ironies of macro policies in developing countries.

The Borrowing Circle   Our next case study considers the development of an institution in one of the poorest countries of the world—Bangladesh. There, Mohammed Yunus, a U.S.-trained economist, created a bank—the Grameen Bank—that made market-rate-interest loans to poor village women. According to reports, the loans had a 97 percent payback rate, and Yunus made a profit.

How did he do it? As I discussed above, most banks in developing countries are internationally oriented. They use the same structure that Western banks use. This leaves the traditional part of many developing countries' economies without an effective way to translate savings into investment, leaving many entrepreneurial individuals without ways to develop their ideas.

Yunus recognized that Western financial institutional structures were not well suited to the traditional sectors of developing countries. He further recognized that the purpose of financial institutions is to direct resources to those with good ideas who can back up their promises to pay back their loans in the future with increased output.

What Yunus did was to reconsider the fundamental role of banking in an economy—to make it possible for people with ''good'' ideas to develop those ideas by providing them with funds to develop their ideas—and to devise a structure that allowed such lending to take place.

He saw that Western banking institutions did not provide the answer for Bangladesh. By basing their lending decisions on the amount of collateral a borrower had, they essentially made it impossible for most people in Bangladesh to get loans. But Yunus also recognized that the collateral function served a useful purpose: it forced people to make the hard decision about whether they really needed the loans, and to work hard to see that they could pay it back, even if the going got tough. If you eliminate the role of collateral, something else must replace it.

The ingenious solution he came up with was the **borrowing circle** concept. Recognizing that the invisible handshake was extremely strong in Bangladesh, he made use of that handshake in his bank's lending practices. He offered to make loans to any woman who could find four friends who would agree that they would, if necessary, help her pay the loan back. If the borrower defaulted, the others could not borrow until the loan was repaid. The invisible handshake replaced the traditional collateral.

Notice a couple of things about the concept:

- It used economic insights creatively, and it recognized the essence of the problem, not the superficial aspects.
- It relied on an individual rather than governmental initiative. Yunus made a profit, and the individuals getting the loans made profits. Thus it encouraged development without a government plan.
- It created a new institution that fit the social structure, rather than importing outside institutions.
- It was directed at the traditional economy, rather than the international economy, and the successful loans improved the lot of millions.

This simple concept worked. In ten years it developed into a large bank that has made more than 1,600,000 loans. The loans have been taken out to buy such things as a cow or material to make a fishing net—not large items, but items to use in precisely the types of activity that generate bottom-up development.

Mr. Yunus' work has received enormous accolades (President Clinton said he should get a Nobel Prize), and even developed countries are looking into the borrowing circle concept as a way of getting credit to the poor. While the concept was extraordinarily simple, his borrowing circle concept made use of economic insights but simultaneously reflected an understanding of and concern about the cultural and social dimensions of the economy. It is the type of macro policy most needed in developing countries.

The above two case studies are quite different from each other, but they both involved attempts to change institutions to make them more efficient at translating saving into investment. Such attempts at changing institutions are characteristic of macro policy in developing and transitional countries.

CONCLUSION

Examples of macro policy in developing countries like the above exist, but not as often as I would like to report. They are most likely to be found in Asian countries, although in the early 1990s there were some bright spots in Latin America. These cases show that creative macro institutional policies play an important role in development, and that the future of developing countries can be brighter than the present.

Whether their futures will be brighter depends on the imagination, drive, and creativity of their policy makers. It doesn't surprise me that the originator of this

---

8 The ''borrowing circle'' concept replaced traditional collateral with guarantees by friends of the borrower. It was successful because the invisible handshake in Bangladesh, where the borrowing circle originated, was very strong.

To undertake beneficial macro institutional policy requires an understanding of the role of institutions, the specific nature of the problems in one's country, and creativity.

Bangladeshi plan (whom, in case you haven't guessed, I greatly admire) studied economics, because economic thinking directs one to solutions that combine economic insight with existing institutions. It doesn't promise easy answers, but it does allow one to see the type of institutions that are sustainable. The economic way of thinking can lead to institutional change and economic takeoff.

CHAPTER SUMMARY

- Economists separate out developing and transitional economies because these economies have different institutional structures and different weighting of goals than do Western economies.
- Many developing economies have serious political problems which make it impossible for government to take an active, positive role in the economy.
- Many developing countries have dual economies—one a traditional, non-market economy, and the other an internationalized market economy.
- Inflation in developing countries is usually related to the printing of too much money; the debate is about the political reasons why this occurs, and the viability of the alternatives.

- Most monetary policies in developing countries focus on the international sector and are continually dealing with the balance of payments constraint.
- Most developing countries have some type of limited convertibility.
- Macro policies in developing and transitional countries are more concerned with institutional policies and régime changes than are macro policies in developed countries.
- The debt crisis of the 1980s was resolved by a combination of write-downs and restructuring.
- The borrowing circle is an example of an innovative macro institutional policy designed to better translate savings into investment.

KEY TERMS

balance of payments constraint *(459)*
basic needs *(451)*
borrowing circle *(464)*
conditionality *(459)*
convertibility on the current account *(459)*
developing economy *(449)*

dual economy *(453)*
exchange rate policy *(459)*
full convertibility *(458)*
inflation tax *(457)*
inter-firm credit *(454)*
limited capital account convertibility *(459)*

macro institutional policies *(460)*
policy change *(454)*
régime change *(454)*
restructuring *(449)*
soft budget constraint *(454)*
trade credits *(455)*
transitional economy *(449)*

QUESTIONS FOR THOUGHT AND REVIEW

The number after the questions represents the estimated degree of critical thinking required. (1 = almost none; 10 = deep thought)

1. Do different economic theories apply to developing countries than to developed countries? *(2)*
2. What is the difference between development and growth? *(2)*
3. What are three ways in which the institutions of developing countries differ from those in developed countries? *(2)*
4. Why do governments in developing countries often seem more arbitrary and oppressive than governments in developed countries? *(3)*

5. What is meant by "the dual economy"? *(2)*
6. How does a régime change differ from a policy change? *(2)*
7. What was the soft budget constraint? *(2)*
8. What is the inflation tax? *(2)*
9. Why doesn't the fact that the "inflation solution" is only a temporary solution stop many developing countries from using it? *(4)*
10. What is conditionality, and how does it relate to the balance of payments constraint? *(4)*

PROBLEMS AND EXERCISES

1. Could the borrowing circle concept be adopted for use in the United States?
   a. Why or why not?
   b. What modifications would you suggest if it were to be adopted?
   c. Minorities in the United States often do not use banks. In what ways are U.S. minorities' problems similar to those of people in developing countries?

2. Choose any developing country and answer the following questions about it:
   a. What is its level of per capita income?
   b. What is its growth potential?
   c. What is the exchange rate of its currency in relation to the U.S. dollar?
   d. What policy suggestions might you make to the country?

3. Bulgarian private banks rarely made long-term loans, but made substantial short-term loans in the early 1990s.

   a. List three reasons why long-term loans were not made and two reasons why short-term loans were extended.
   b. Contrast this with banking practices in the United States.

4. It has been argued that development economics has no general theory; it is instead the application of common sense to real-world problems.
   a. Do you agree or disagree with that statement? Why?
   b. Why do you think this argument about that lack of generality of theories is made for developing countries more than it is made for developed countries?

5. In 1993 and 1994 President Fujimori of Peru instituted a set of policies that turned the Peruvian economy around. Research the following questions:
   a. How did he engineer this turnaround?
   b. Why has the U.S. government limited aid to Peru?
   c. What monetary and fiscal policy did he use?
   d. How would you judge his policies?

ANSWERS TO MARGIN QUESTIONS

1. Restructuring in developed countries suggests that the distinction between growth and development can be overdone since it is an example of developed countries' growth occurring through changing institutions—development—rather than through increasing inputs—growth. *(449)*

2. Two ways in which a developed country differs from a developing country are: (1) their institutions are qualitatively different; and (2) their goals are different. *(451)*

3. An economist might favor activist policies in developed countries and laissez-faire policies in developing countries because the policies one favors depend upon the desire and ability of government to work for and achieve the goals of its policies. Different views of government can lead to different views of policy. Since many economists have a serious concern about the political structure in developing counties, but less such concern about it in developed countries, they can favor one set of policies for developing countries and another set for developed countries. *(452)*

4. The "dual economy" refers to developing countries' tendency to have two economies that have little interaction—one a traditional non-market economy, and one an internationally-oriented modern market economy. *(453)*

5. The trade credit function of banks in Western market economies is barely mentioned because the institutional structure almost eliminates it as a function. *(455)*

6. While everyone agrees that inflation in developing countries is caused by the central bank issuing too much money, the real policy question concerns what the political consequences of not issuing too much money may be. Sometimes the cure for inflation can be worse than the problem. *(456)*

7. In an inflation, any issuers of fixed-interest-rate debt denominated in the domestic currency gain from the holders of these debts. *(458)*

8. Full convertibility includes convertibility on the capital account as well as on the current account. It means that people are allowed to buy foreign financial assets—to save abroad. Convertibility on the current account means that people are allowed to buy foreign currencies in order to buy foreign goods, but not necessarily in order to buy foreign financial assets. *(458)*

9. The disadvantage of the debt repudiation strategy is that it will lessen the country's ability to get loans in the future. *(461)*

10. Rich individuals in developing countries often like to hide their wealth, or get it out of the country to avoid possible confiscation. In South Korea, they had an incentive to keep it in South Korea because of the high rates of return they earned there, but they hid its ownership under fictitious names. This was politically unpopular, which led to political pressure to make holding wealth under fictitious names illegal. *(462)*

21

Macroeconomics, Social Policy, and Economic Reasoning

Economists are not solely that but also human beings, and their own values undoubtedly affect their economics.

~Milton Friedman

After reading this chapter, you should be able to:

1 Summarize four nonmainstream economic approaches.

2 Explain why nonmainstream economists often use a less formal analysis than mainstream economists.

3 Read economic articles with a more discerning eye.

4 Predict what will happen in the economy as well as some economists predict.

5 Be on the lookout for positive and negative spin in economic writing.

6 Analyze an economic article on your own.

By now you should have a good sense of Keynesian and Classical macroeconomic theory, policy, and institutions. The differing Keynesian and Classical approaches capture the diversity within mainstream economics, but leave untouched the broader range of diversity among macroeconomists who disagree with the mainstream. In the first part of this chapter, I supplement the mainstream focus of the previous discussion and briefly review some of the nonmainstream approaches to macroeconomics.

Then, in the second part, I put the theory and knowledge you have learned in previous chapters to work. This part of the chapter follows some real-life events and discusses three real-world articles—the type you see every day in newspapers and magazines. By considering these, not only will you get a deserved break from me, you will also get some practice in translating the economic knowledge you've gained in the classroom into the real world.

The readings were chosen to reflect the type of reading you'll likely be doing (if I've infected you with the economic bug) once you're out of the course. After presenting the first two selections, I consider their arguments and reasoning, showing my view of how they apply macroeconomic reasoning and how seriously they should be taken. Views about applying macroeconomic reasoning differ, even among experts, so my discussion should be seen as a jumping-off point for you or your professor to consider these or similar articles. Interpretation is an art, not a science. The third article I leave to you as an exercise to interpret.

NONMAINSTREAM APPROACHES TO MACRO

Heterodox economist *An economist who does not accept that the mainstream economic model is the appropriate way to analyze the economy.*

Mainstream economist *An economist who analyzes the world in a manner similar to that presented in this book.*

Austrians

1 Four nonmainstream macroeconomic approaches are the Austrian, the Post-Keynesian, the Institutionalist, and the Radical approaches.

Austrian economists believe in liberty of individuals first and in other social goals second.

The Keynesian and Classical views presented in earlier chapters differed in policy emphasis, but the policy implications of the differences were limited to slight variations. Keynesians favored somewhat more activist policies; Classicals favored somewhat less activist policies—but both operated within the current institutional structure.

A characteristic of nonmainstream, or heterodox, economists is that they are far more open to discuss major institutional changes than are mainstream economists. More specifically, a **heterodox economist,** or nonmainstream economist, is one who doesn't accept the basic underlying model used by a majority of economists as the most useful model for analyzing the economy. Economists who do accept that model are called **mainstream economists.**

In this section I will briefly introduce four heterodox macroeconomists' approaches to give you a sense of how their analysis differs from the mainstream analysis presented in this book. The four heterodox approaches are Austrian, Post-Keynesian, Institutionalist, and Radical.

Austrian economists are not all economists from Austria; rather, they are economists from anywhere who follow the ideas of Ludwig von Mises and Friedrich von Hayek, two economists who were from Austria. Austrian economists are sometimes classified as conservative, but they are more appropriately classified as **libertarians,** by which they mean that they believe in liberty of individuals first and in other social goals second. They view much of government—collective action—as violating individual liberty, and therefore they strongly oppose any state intrusion into private property and private activities. Consistent with their views, they are often willing to support what are sometimes considered radical ideas, such as legalizing addictive drugs or eliminating our current monetary system—ideas that conservative economists would oppose.

In macroeconomics, Austrian economists emphasize the uncertainty in the economy, and the inability of a government controlled by self-interested politicians to undertake socially beneficial policy. Well-known Austrian macroeconomists include Murray Rothbard, Peter Boethke, and Mario Rizzo.

One proposal of Austrian economists will give you a flavor of their approach. That proposal is to eliminate the Federal Reserve System and to establish a **free market in money**—a policy that would leave people free to use any money they want, and would significantly reduce banking regulation. In a sense, their proposal carries the Classical argument in favor of laissez faire to its logical conclusions. Why should the government have a monopoly of the money supply? Why shouldn't people be free to use whatever money they desire, denominated in whatever unit they want?

Why don't we rely upon competition to prevent inflation? Why don't we have a free market in money?

A sub-group of Austrian economists is *public choice* economists. They use the mainstream supply and demand approach, but apply it much more broadly than do mainstream economists. Specifically, they see government decisions as reflecting economic forces rather than attempts by government to do good. Well-known public choice economists include Gordon Tullock, James Buchanan, and Robert Tollison.

Post-Keynesian macroeconomists are economists who follow Keynes's approach more so than do mainstream macroeconomists. They agree with Austrians about the importance of uncertainty in understanding the macro economy, but their policy response to that uncertainty is not to have government get out of the macro economy; it is for the government to take a larger role in guiding the economy.

One of their policy proposals that gives you a flavor of their approach is **tax-based incomes policies**—policies in which the government tries to directly affect the nominal wage- and price-setting institutions. Under a tax-based incomes policy, any firm raising its wage or price would be subject to a tax, and any firm lowering its wage or price would get a subsidy. Such a plan, they argue, would reduce the upward pressure on the nominal price level, and reduce the rate of unemployment necessary to hold down inflation. Well-known Post-Keynesian economists include Paul Davidson, Hy Minsky, and John Cornwall.

Institutionalist economists are economists who argue that any economic analysis must involve specific considerations of institutions. Institutionalists have a long history in economics; their lineage goes back to the early 1930s and the writings of Thorstein Veblen, J. M. Clarke, and John R. Commons. Institutionalists were early supporters of welfare capitalism, and they helped set up many of the institutions of welfare capitalism, such as Social Security, which we now take for granted. Institutionalists are very close to Post-Keynesians in their approach to macroeconomics, but they give stronger emphasis to the role of institutions, and to the role of government in establishing new institutions, than do Post-Keynesians.

You can get a sense of their policy approach from one of the policies many Institutionalists support: **indicative planning**—a macroeconomic policy in which the government sets up an overall plan for various industries and selectively directs credit to certain industries. Thus for Institutionalists the invisible foot directs the invisible hand. Well-known Institutionalists include Marc Tool, Warren Samuels, and John Adams.

Radical economists are economists who believe substantial equality-preferring institutional changes should be implemented to our economic system. Radical economists evolved out of Marxian economics. Compared to mainstream economists, Radicals are far more willing to consider major institutional changes in our macro economy. They focus on the lack of equity in our current economic system, and their political discussions focus on institutional changes that might bring about a more equitable system. Specifically, they see the current economic system as one in which a few people—capitalists and high-level managers—benefit enormously, while others—minority groups such as African-Americans and Hispanics—are left out, without a job. To incorporate such issues, Radical economists often use a class-oriented analysis and are much more willing to talk about social conflict and tensions in our society than are mainstream economists.

Compared to mainstream economists, Radical economists' analysis focuses much more on distributional fights between capitalists and workers and their different savings propensities. According to one important branch of radical theory, when profits are high, because capitalists save a large portion of their income, aggregate demand will be too low, and the economy goes into a recession; then government must run a deficit to bail out the economy. Mainstream economists agree that such distributional effects exist, but they consider them too small to worry about. Main-

Post-Keynesians

Post-Keynesian economists believe that uncertainty is a central issue in macroeconomics.

Institutionalists

Institutionalist economists believe that the important macroeconomic policy decisions involve institutional design.

Radical economists focus their analysis on major institutional changes whose purpose is to alleviate inequities in our current system.

Radical economists use a more class-oriented analysis because it better focuses on conflict than does mainstream analysis.

Radicals

Dollars & Sense—An economic magazine that interprets current economic events from a socialist perspective.

stream economists focus on fluctuations in business investment and consumers' spending decisions, not on differences in people's marginal propensity to consume.

Policy proposals some Radicals favor and that give you a sense of their approach are policies to establish worker cooperatives to replace the corporation. Radicals argue that such worker cooperatives would see that the income of the firm was more equitably allocated. Well-known radical economists include Samuel Bowles, Herbert Gintis, and Howard Sherman.

Consistency of the Various Approaches

2 Nonmainstream economists tend to use a less formal model because they can include more variables and make the models more realistic.

Q–1: Why are nonmainstream approaches to macroeconomics often less formal than mainstream approaches?

There's nothing necessarily inconsistent between mainstream and heterodox economists' approaches.

A characteristic of almost all heterodox economists of all types is that their analyses tend to be less formal than mainstream analysis. *Less formal* doesn't mean better or worse. There are advantages and disadvantages to formality, but *less formal* does mean that there's more potential for ambiguity in interpretation. It's easy to say whether the logic in a formal model is right or wrong. It's much harder to say whether the logic in an informal model is right or wrong because it's often hard to see precisely what the logic is. The advantage of an informal model is that it can include many more variables and can be made more realistic, so you can discuss real-world problems more easily with that model. Nonmainstream economists often want to talk about the real world, which is why they use informal models.

Often, after I discuss the mainstream and nonmainstream approaches, some student asks which is right. I respond with a story told by a former colleague of mine, Abba Lerner; the story goes as follows:

> "But look," the rabbi's wife remonstrated, "when one party to the dispute presented their case to you, you said, 'You are quite right,' and then when the other party presented their case you again said, 'You are quite right.' Surely they cannot both be right?" To which the Rabbi answered, "My dear, you are quite right!"

The moral of the story is that there's nothing necessarily inconsistent among mainstream and heterodox economists' approaches.[1] They are simply different ways of looking at the same event. Which approach is most useful depends on what issues and events one is analyzing. The class analysis used by radicals is often more appropriate to developing countries than it is to the United States, and in analyzing developing countries many mainstream economists also include class fights in their approach. Similarly, Austrian analysis provides more insight into the role of the entrepreneur and individual in the economy than does mainstream analysis, while Post-Keynesian and Institutionalist analysis is useful when considering major institutional changes.

The distinctions between nonmainstream and mainstream economists can be overdone. One economist may well fall into two or three different groupings and use a combination of various analyses.

Let's now move on to some case studies that give you a sense of how to apply macroeconomic reasoning.

CASE STUDY 1

3 Reading articles with a more discerning eye comes with lots of practice.

In one Sherlock Holmes story the clue is the dog that did not bark. The economy is often as much a mystery as one of Sherlock Holmes's cases; the clues about what is to come are often as obscure as the hound's silence. Case Study 1 is a report of such silence and economists' attempt to interpret it. The article was written by a reporter, not an economist. As you read it, ask yourself, "What is the reporter's incentive in writing this article? What about the economists she interviews? What do they base their information on? Is the conclusion the article comes to sound? Are the differences among economists discernible?"

---

[1] Many economists, both mainstream and heterodox, will likely object to this statement. They, like the rabbi's wife, believe that someone must be right and someone wrong. I, like the rabbi, agree with them.

CASE STUDY 1

LEADING INDEX OF ECONOMY CLIMBS 0.3%

By Hilary Stout

WASHINGTON—The economy's slow, methodical growth is likely to continue into next year, the government's chief economic forecasting gauge suggests, although pockets of weakness still worry some economists.

The index of leading indicators, a composite of 11 statistics designed to foretell economic activity six to nine months hence, made its best showing since April, climbing 0.3% in August, the Commerce Department reported.

The increase—the second in as many months—suggests the economy is on "a pattern of slow but stable growth," said Gordon Richards, an economist at the National Association of Manufacturers.

In July, the index rose a revised 0.1%, originally estimated at a 0.2% increase. All the figures are adjusted for seasonal changes.

Five of the indicators pushed the index up; they included stock prices, building permits and factory orders for consumer goods, which were driven by a surge in automobile demand.

But some economists believe the economy is exhibiting enough weakness to keep alive the threat of recession. Among the leading indicators, an index of consumer expectations dropped significantly. Plant and equipment orders also fell. And the average work week shrank.

"Basically we don't see any strong sector of the economy, and we see several that are weak," said David Levy, a partner in Levy Economic Forecasts, Chappaqua, N.Y. "We believe the economy is going to have a very close brush with recession this year or early next, and the critical factor deciding whether it will drop (into a recession) or manage to avoid it is going to be Federal Reserve policy."

The Fed policy-making committee is due to meet this week to set monetary policy for the next several weeks. After pushing up interest rates from March 1988 to March 1989 to head off inflation, the Fed let rates slip a few

times this summer. But lately it has held them steady, waiting to see just where the economy is headed. Many analysts believe the central bank won't make any further changes in policy for now, amid signs that inflation is tapering while growth continues.

"I have to think the Fed is quite pleased with themselves at this point," said Daniel Van Dyke, head of the economic forecasting group at Bank of America in San Francisco.

The index showed that the weakest area of the economy is clearly manufacturing. For example, the prices of raw materials declined, making a negative contribution to the index. "That's good news for inflation but indicates there is slack in the industrial commodity area," noted Richard Peterson, senior vice president at Continental Bank in Chicago. Economists also said they expected August's boost in the factory orders component to drop back after orders for cars—brought on by sales incentives and new models—subside.

Many economists don't take the leading indicators index seriously as a forecasting gauge, reading it as an indication of current activity. Nevertheless, the numerous monthly declines in the index this year had triggered fears that the economy was edging toward a recession.

After the latest report, however, Lawrence Hunter, deputy chief economist for the U.S. Chamber of Commerce, contended that the leading indicators "show that the economic slowdown should come to an end in the fourth quarter," and "the real gross national product should rise throughout 1990."

Statistics Released in the Week Ended Sept. 29

	Total	Change (from prior period)
Money supply		
M1 Week ended		
Sept. 18 (in billions)	$ 790.8	−$1.8
M2 Week ended		
Sept. 18 (in billions)	$3,158.2	+$3.9
M3 Week ended		
Sept. 18 (in billions)	$4,017.8	−$0.5
Durable goods orders		
August (in billions)	$ 126.74	+3.8%
Leading indicators		
August, index	144.4%	+0.3%

Auto sales		
Sept. 11–20		
vs. year ago	211,966	−10.2%
Farm prices		
August index	143%	−0.7%
New jobless claims		
Week ended Sept. 16	319,000	+2.6%

Statistics to Be Released This Week

Purchasing management survey (Mon.)
September
Construction spending (Mon.)
August
New-home sales (Tues.)
August
Factory orders (Tues.)
August
New-car sales (Wed.)
September
Chain store sales (Thurs.)
September
Money supply (Thurs.)
September 25
Unemployment rate (Fri.)
September
Consumer installment credit (Fri.)
August

LEADING INDICATORS

Here are the net contributions of the components of the Commerce Department's index of leading indicators. After various adjustments, they produced a 0.3% rise in the index for August and a 0.1% rise in July.

	August 1989	July 1989
Workweek	−.07	.00
Unemployment claims	.19	−.08
Orders for consumer goods	.58	−.26
Slower deliveries	−.08	−.03
Plant and equipment orders	−.16	.09
Building permits	.10	−.06
Durable order backlog	−.19	.02
Materials prices	−.20	−.30
Stock prices	.24	.14
Money supply	.20	.24
Consumer expectations	−.39	.26

The seasonally adjusted index numbers (1982 = 100) for August, and the change from July, are:

Index of leading indicators	144.4	0.3
Index of coincident indicators	133.9	0.4
Index of lagging indicators	122.3	0.9

The ratio of coincident to lagging indicators was 1.09, down from 1.10 in July.
The Wall Street Journal, October 2, 1989. Reprinted by permission of THE WALL STREET JOURNAL © 1989 Dow Jones & Company, Inc. All rights reserved worldwide.

Interpretation and Discussion

Detectives spend most of their time watching and waiting; so do business economists who forecast the future direction of the economy. Most economic theories involve relationships among variables that take one to five years to work their way through the economy. Economists know that in shorter time spans there are too many random blips—too much uncertainty—for economists, or anyone, to say much that is specific. In the very short run, many economic relationships that will occur even in the short run are overwhelmed by other, often random, events. But that doesn't mean that a knowledge of economics isn't relevant. Economics includes an understanding of economic institutions and how they operate. That knowledge can be useful in interpreting data and events. When people ask, ''What's going to happen to the economy?'' they generally don't want to know what's going to happen in one or two years; they want to know what's going to happen tomorrow, next week, or next month. Thus, when answering reporters' questions, economists are generally relying on their knowledge of economic institutions as much as, or more than, they're relying on their knowledge of economic theory.

When answering reporters' questions, economists are generally relying on their knowledge of economic institutions as much as, or more than, they're relying on their knowledge of economic theory.

Perspective

Q–2: Why don't reporters write articles explaining that economists don't have a lot to say about what's happening in the economy in the short run?

Most economic reporters aren't trained economists; often they've had a course or two in economics, but economic training isn't required. They report; they don't interpret.

A reporter's job is to report about the news that people want to know about and to write articles that people want to read. Reporters are assigned a beat, and their job is to report the events that happen on that beat. Even when little is happening, economic reporters must write something. An article stating simply, ''Nothing significant happened this week,'' is unlikely to sell many newspapers or endear its writer to the editor. Instead, economic reporters resort to what one of my teachers called ''barking at straws.''

Such barking at straws fills up much of even the best newspapers' articles about the economy. Some articles sound as if they say something significant, but they don't say much at all. Like clockwork, you can expect to see an article about the economy following the release of each new economic statistic, even though movements in these short-run statistics are as likely to be caused by some extraneous event as they are to reflect something significant.

This article is, I suspect, a reporter's attempt to write an interesting article about nothing happening. It appeared in *The Wall Street Journal* in a space that, once a week, looks at the forecasts for the economy.[2]

The article is an example of the best economic reporting. I chose an example of the best to emphasize that it is not the fault of the reporter that the many articles about economics in the newspapers say little or nothing. It's that there's little or nothing to say.

Content

Q–3: If you're predicting the economy in the very short run, how much economic theory do you have to know?

Economists follow economic events and statistics carefully. They also recognize that there are many different interpretations to the clues those events and statistics provide. Generally a new statistic adds more questions about where the economy is heading than it answers.

So what should an economist reply when a reporter asks about some short-run trend? Most economists answer the best they can. But they almost all admit that their very short-run predictions are based more on a knowledge of economic data, and how one set of data often leads (precedes in time) another set, rather than on the theories discussed in this book. For example, an increase in building permits and factory orders usually leads to an increase in income, so economists look at increases in those statistics and forecast that income will go up.

Now that isn't very heavy theory; it doesn't take a Ph.D. in economics to figure out that increases in building permits and factory orders will likely lead to increases in

---

[2] *The Wall Street Journal* has a reputation as a conservative, almost reactionary, newspaper. On the editorial pages, that reputation is earned. The rest of the newspaper is, however, quite different. It portrays a wide diversity of views and is committed to objective reporting.

income, and that is why I don't spend more time in this book discussing short-term relationships of leading indicators and economic activity.

While an in-depth discussion is left for classes on economic forecasting, a few comments are appropriate here. Forecasting is a serious study in its own right. Finding and interpreting clues isn't easy. Analyzing these clues and their relationship to the economy often becomes highly sophisticated. There's much discussion among business economists about what group of indicators should be in the index of leading indicators.

The difficulty of predicting the economy is increased by three complications. Notice that:

1. The report of leading indicators is significantly revised months after it is first issued. This often happens and makes forecasting more tricky. The clues might not be what they at first are presented to be.

2. Economists know that what will happen in the economy depends on what policy the government follows. Thus, all predictions must be hedged with qualifying statements about what policy will be. When predictions depend on unknown policy responses, those predictions can never be certain.

3. Finally, there's the operation of a type of **Heisenberg principle** (a principle of quantum physics stating that observation changes what is observed and therefore knowledge is necessarily limited). Economists' predictions affect what people expect and what people expect affects what happens. Thus, economists are not simply observers. What they say (their predictions) affects what happens in the economy. Their predictions can become self-fulfilling prophecies, and they can never know what the economy would be like independent of their predictions.

Heisenberg principle   The act of looking at something changes its nature.

Combined, these three complications create a situation in which even the most informed predictions about the economy are often wrong.

Moving away from forecasting, let's consider what the article tells us about macroeconomic policy. Notice that there's much discussion of how the data will affect Fed policy, but not a single mention of fiscal policy. That's telling. Political realities have made discretionary fiscal policy an unusable tool in the short run. Fiscal policy has an effect, but fiscal policy is generally determined by political goals, not macroeconomic goals.

Q–4:   Why is monetary policy much more discussed in the newspapers than fiscal policy?

That's not the case with monetary policy. Notice the continual mention of Federal Reserve policy and economists' discussion about how the Fed will react. In order to predict what will happen in the economy, simply looking at how events will affect the economy isn't enough. Instead you must predict how an event will affect Fed policy and how that policy will affect the economy. This indirect path of influence often makes for some seemingly paradoxical predictions. Say, for instance, that the indicators had been stronger—definitely pointing to a growing economy. That might cause some economists to predict that the economy will experience a slowdown. Why? Because a growing economy could lead the Fed to institute contractionary monetary policy in order to offset possible inflationary pressures. The contractionary monetary policy would cause interest rates to rise, which would slow down the economy.

Alternatively, say statistics reported a fall in the money supply. Remember that a fall in the money supply is associated with an increase in interest rates. So you might expect that if the money supply falls, interest rates will rise. But reality is more complicated; the Fed doesn't control the money supply directly. The Fed discovers how its open market operations (its policy of buying or selling bonds) has affected the money supply at the same time as others do. It might well react to that fall in the money supply by increasing the money supply more than it would have otherwise, so interest rates would be expected to fall, not rise. As you can see, to apply economic theory to reality you must have a good understanding of the institutional and political realities.

In summary, predicting the economy in the short run is almost impossible. Most academic economists avoid making short-run predictions, or if they do make predictions, they couch them in uncertainty, leaving themselves an out. Economists who

Predicting the economy in the short run is almost impossible.

4 The best way to predict the future is to say that what will happen is what will happen, unless, of course, it doesn't happen.

CASE STUDY 2

have mastered the art of predicting have generally mastered the art of saying, ''What will happen is what will happen, unless, of course, it doesn't happen.'' When you're predicting what is almost impossible to predict, that's not a bad way to go.

The period 1981–88 (the Reagan years) was important in shaping modern macroeconomics. In response to a highly restrictive monetary policy exercised in 1981 and 1982, inflation came down substantially in 1983, but the short-run cost of that decrease in inflation was high unemployment. In 1982, the economy fell into the worst recession since the Great Depression of the 1930s.

The following selection from the *1986 Economic Report of the President* concerns the Reagan policies for that year. The *Economic Report of the President* is a political, not an academic, document issued yearly by the president's Council of Economic Advisers. This 1986 report discussed events in 1985 and the last part of 1984, plus proposed policies for 1986.

CASE STUDY 2

INFLATION, DISINFLATION, AND THE STATE OF THE MACROECONOMY

The American economy is now in the fourth year of a robust expansion that has increased employment by more than 9 million, sustained the greatest advance in business fixed investment of any comparable period in the postwar era, while inflation has remained at less than a third of the rate prevailing when the Administration took office. Interest rates are at the lowest levels of this decade. Long-term interest rates, in particular, have declined 5 percentage points from their peaks in 1981, and home mortgage rates are down by 7 percentage points. Worldwide confidence in the vitality of the U.S. economy has been restored, as is reflected in the unprecedented inflow of foreign investment and the substantial appreciation of the dollar since 1980. The outlook is favorable for continuation of a healthy expansion. After slowing in the second half of 1984, economic activity is again accelerating. The recent moderate decline in the dollar bodes well for an eventual improvement in the trade balance. A modest and temporary acceleration of inflation is possible in 1986. But with appropriate economic policies, lower inflation, and ultimately price stability are achievable goals for an economy that continues to grow and to generate opportunities for all Americans.

Despite the impressive progress of the U.S. economy, important problems remain. Although the 3.8 percentage point decline in the unemployment rate

since November 1982 far exceeds the average decline for a comparable period in earlier postwar expansions, the total unemployment rate remains high by postwar standards. Federal spending consumes an unprecedentedly large share of gross national product (GNP) for a peacetime period, diverting resources that could be more productively employed in the private sector. Determined efforts and politically difficult decisions will be required to bring Federal spending into line with revenues and thereby reduce the fiscal deficit. Inflation, now in abeyance, could be reignited by excessive monetary growth. Alternatively, a sudden move to sharply lower money growth could push the economy once again into recession.

Two central themes dominate this Report and, not coincidentally, the Administration's approach to economic policy. First, the private enterprise, free market system is generally the best mechanism to organize efficient and full employment of the economy's resources and to generate genuine opportunity and rising living standards for all. To assist the private sector, the government should limit itself to providing essential public services and should avoid blunting or distorting economic incentives by high or uneven tax rates and by unnecessary or inappropriate regulation.

Second, economic performance is seriously injured by the macroeconomic instability inevitably associated with cycles of inflation and disinflation. Such injury was reflected in the relatively sluggish economic growth of the 1970s. It was most acute and most apparent when rising inflation

confronted efforts to reduce inflation by lowering monetary growth: in 1969–70, in 1974–75, briefly in late 1979 and early 1980, and finally on a more persistent basis in 1981–82. In each confrontation, the outcome was a recession; in two cases, a severe and prolonged recession.

Even now, the consequences of earlier inflation and disinflation are still felt in the problems afflicting the American economy. The present level of unemployment is partly the heritage of past inflation and necessary actions to control it. Problems in agriculture, in industry, and in international trade are related to fluctuations in commodity prices, asset values, and the value of the dollar that, in turn, are linked to the process of inflation and disinflation and to the economic policies that underlie that process. Problems of the credit system—of borrowers, lenders, and government insurance agencies—derive partly from sharp, unexpected movements in interest rates, asset values, and income levels that accompany the inflation–disinflation process.

The healthy overall performance of the U.S. economy may be small comfort to those affected by its remaining problems. But with time and with appropriate policies, these remaining problems can be corrected. The cure, however, does not lie in policies that would reignite inflation and once again inflict its debilitating effects on the American economy. Rather, the cure lies with policies that will enhance private incentives for growth, while maintaining a stable macroeconomic environment.

Economic Report of the President, 1986.

This selection presents President Reagan's economic advisors' view of the 1984–85 expansion out of the 1982–83 recession. Unlike our first selection (in which objectivity was the writer's goal), the *Economic Report of the President* is a political document designed to cast events and the policies of the Reagan economic advisors in a favorable light. This doesn't mean that what the passage has to say isn't true; it only means that the chosen viewpoint will likely highlight certain aspects of reality while obscuring other less favorable interpretations. In 1984–85 the economy was coming out of the 1983 recession, as seen in Exhibit 1, so President Reagan's advisors had much to be positive about.

Let's look for some examples where favorable light is placed on the events. First, notice that the report emphasizes what happened to employment (it increased substantially) rather than what happened to unemployment. From 1980 to 1986, labor force participation increased as the number of women in the labor force rose dramatically. When labor force participation increases, both unemployment and employment can increase at the same time. In the period the report addresses, unemployment was falling, but was still high by historical standards. Employment, however, was rising substantially. Focusing on employment rather than unemployment gives a positive spin to the data; it directs the reader away from the still-high unemployment. (In the 1990s, *spin control* has become a popular term to describe attempts to interpret events to the interpreter's greatest advantage.)

Another passage that casts events in a good light is the discussion of interest rates. When the council was writing the report, nominal interest rates were declining but were still high. Real interest rates were very high by historical standards—a fact the council doesn't mention. It discusses only the change in nominal interest rates rather than real interest rates.

A third example of positive spin is seen in what is not discussed. As Exhibit 1 suggests, the economy in 1984 was emerging from a severe recession. The budget deficit had increased significantly as automatic stabilizers kicked in. These automatic stabilizers had kept expenditures high and reduced tax revenue. The deficit was made even higher when taxes were cut by the Economic Recovery Tax Act of 1981. That deficit played a key role in the macroeconomic events of the time and in the political and economic discussions. Keynesian economists claimed it was the deficit that pulled the economy out of the recession. Yet the article's only mention of the deficit is a statement that the deficit will need to be brought into line by holding down spending. The possibility of increasing taxes is not discussed because that was not part of President Reagan's political agenda.

A fourth example of putting events in a positive light is the statement, "Worldwide confidence in the vitality of the U.S. economy . . . is reflected in the unprecedented inflow of foreign investment." That foreign investment was the mirror image of the large U.S. trade deficit beginning at that time. An alternative interpretation of that flow of foreign investment into the United States is that *in this time period the U.S. is selling off its assets to finance its trade deficit*. That inflow of foreign

Interpretation and Discussion

Perspective

5 Generally, there are a number of ways to make a point, and good economic writers try to put positive spin on the points they are making.

	GNP (in billions of $)	Net exports (in billions of $)	Inflation rate	Labor force (in millions)	Unemployment rate
1980	$2,732	+$32.1	13.5%	107	7.1%
1981	3,052	+33.9	10.3	109	7.6
1982	3,166	+26.3	6.2	110	9.7
1983	3,405	−6.1	3.2	112	9.6
1984	3,772	−58.9	4.3	114	7.5
1985	4,014	−78.0	3.6	116	7.2
1986	4,240	−104.4	1.9	118	7.2
1987	4,526	−123.0	3.6	120	6.2
1988	4,861	−93.2	4.1	122	5.5

EXHIBIT 1   Facts on the U.S. Economy, 1980–1988

Source: Council of Economic Advisers.

It is important when reading political documents to adjust for spin.

investment was caused in large part by the high real interest rates resulting from the large U.S. budget deficit combined with the tight monetary policy of the time. But to say that would have given negative spin to the interpretation. It is important, when reading political documents, to find a zero spin position between different interpretations of the same issue.

Content

The preceding discussion of spin control shouldn't obscure the fact that the Reagan administration's economic policies were a success in the following sense: During the Reagan years, the economy experienced one of the longest peacetime expansions since World War II. When the economy is doing well, not much spin control is needed to convince people that your policies are shrewd.

In economics, it's almost impossible to prove that certain policies caused certain outcomes. Too many other things invariably change. Thus, there was significant debate about what the Reagan policy was, whether some other policies would have been even more successful, and whether the policies would have long-run negative effects. To consider these issues, let's look at what those policies were.

The 1981 tax cut was directed at high-income individuals. Designed to lower marginal tax rates to encourage supply incentive effects, it was an application of the supply-side economics discussed in an earlier chapter. Keynesians claimed that the supply incentive effects were minimal; they argued that the deficit resulting from the tax incentive, together with looser monetary policy, fueled the recovery. Thus, according to Keynesians, Reagan's policy succeeded because it was a Keynesian policy.

Supply-side Classical economists whose position is reflected in this report disagreed; they argued that the lower tax rates worked through the supply side, fueling the recovery by giving people incentives to produce more. This debate between Keynesians and Classicals was not settled when this report was written in 1985, and is still not settled in the 1990s. The empirical evidence is ambiguous.

Q–5: If economists emphasize free enterprise and laissez faire, what type of economists are they likely to be?

You can tell that the report's authors are Classical economists by their emphasis on free enterprise and laissez-faire. They blame economic instability on previous government policies. They don't see economic instability inherent in the private economy. Thus, they blame existing unemployment on ''past inflation and necessary actions to control it.''

This report has very little discussion of what type of fiscal policy to use. In part that is because Classical economists are doing the writing, but it is also due to the acceptance that politics, not economic goals, will govern the size of the government budget deficit. That's why more and more of the responsibility for controlling the economy has shifted to the Fed and monetary policy.

Despite the report's Classical political overtones, it contains much with which a Keynesian economist could agree. For example, the council argues that ''excessive'' monetary growth could ignite inflation and that sharply lower money growth could push the economy into recession. Keynesians would be in general agreement with those views.

Similarly, most Keynesians would agree that economic performance is seriously injured by macroeconomic instability. Where Keynesians and Classicals would disagree is in what is ''excessive monetary growth'' and what causes macroeconomic instability. Keynesians argue that the aggregate economy is inherently unstable and that discretionary monetary policy reduces that instability. Most Classicals argue that discretionary policy decreases the stability, and that a monetary rule is needed.

In assessing this report, we have the benefit of hindsight, and in that assessment the report comes out reasonably well. Specifically, the economic expansion that began in 1983 continued through 1989 without generating significant inflation. Many Keynesian economists had expected a downturn in economic activity or an increase in inflation in the late 1980s. They were wrong. Neither that downturn nor a rise in inflation occurred in the 1980s. Thus, in one sense the economic report was vindicated. However, throughout the period the federal budget deficit and U.S. trade deficit remained high, allowing Keynesians to claim that it was the government deficit that fueled the expansion, and that Reagan had simply bought economic expansion for the present by mortgaging the future. They claimed that the recession of the early 1990s was the long-run consequence of the policies of the 1980s.

One area where the report was probably mistaken is in the problem with the credit system, which the council attributed to ''sharp unexpected movements in interest rates.'' If this were true, one would have expected that ending the sharp unexpected changes in interest rates would alleviate the problem. But even though those sharp unexpected movements didn't occur in the late 1980s, the private credit system and government insurance agencies that guarantee that system were severely battered as numerous S&Ls and other financial institutions defaulted, costing the government hundreds of billions of dollars. So the debate goes on.

I present as a final case study an article on President Clinton's economic program. I present it without interpretation of content or perspective. To get you started I do, however, provide questions at the end of the article (with answers at the end of the chapter), and hope that you analyze the case study in class or in discussions with friends.

CASE STUDY 3

CASE STUDY 3

CLINTON'S BUDGET— WHAT'S THE THEORY?

Herbert Stein

''On what thee-o-ry?'' Henry Kissinger cried out, when the referee called a penalty against the Redskins at RFK Stadium. I am tempted to make the same cry when I see in the papers that the administration is preparing a campaign to sell its budget package to the American people. The administration believes that its budget package has been misreported and misunderstood. So its spokespeople are going to get on the trail and on the airwaves to persuade people that the program will really reduce the budget deficit, really impose taxes almost entirely on the rich and really cut spending.

I am willing to concede all these claims. But for me, at least, they ''don't get anywhere near where the trouble is,'' to quote Adelaide in ''Guys and Dolls.'' The trouble is a failure to explain what good this deficit cut, this ''progressive'' tax increase, and these expenditure cuts will do for the American people, and especially how they will produce the promised ''jobs, jobs, jobs.'' In short, there is no theory.

Undoubtedly, there could be a theory. Economists are good at that. Probably there are five young economists on the staff of the Council of Economic Advisers who, if given the assignment, could produce a theory to explain how the budget package not only will create jobs but will create eight million jobs. They also could adduce statistical evidence in support of the theory. Perhaps the paper doing all that now lies on someone's desk on the third floor of the Old Executive Office Building next to the White House. But they have not revealed the theory or the evidence to the public.

Textbook Theory

You see, the argument that raising taxes and cutting spending will create jobs is counter-the-textbook, and by now, almost 60 years after Keynes, counterintuitive. We teach our sophomores that reducing government expenditures cuts demand for goods and services, and that raising taxes cuts private after-tax income and so cuts private demand for goods and services. The cut in demand reduces employment.

We teach our juniors who take macroeconomics courses that, while cutting the budget deficit will probably reduce employment, it might not do so. Reduction of the budget deficit will lower interest rates, which will stimulate investment demand and so offset, in part, the declines in demand resulting from increased taxes and lower government spending. This offset is unlikely to be complete, because a decline in interest rates will increase the desire to hold money; unless the Federal Reserve supplies more money, the shortage of money will keep interest rates from falling enough to offset the direct contractionary effects of tax increases and expenditure cuts.

In its limited efforts to explain its budget package so far, the administration has relied upon the plan's effect in reducing interest rates and so stimulating investment demand. But that is, of course only one side of the story, and we have been offered no reason for thinking that the positive effect of reducing interest rates will be sufficient to offset the negative effects of higher taxes and lower expenditures.

As I have said, theories are imaginable that would explain how the budget package will create jobs, and I can think of a few:

The administration's plan includes some ''targeted'' incentives for investment—in small business, for example—that will increase the demand for output. If sufficiently powerful, the effect of this could offset the combined effects of the expenditure cuts, the reduction of after-tax incomes by the tax increases, and the negative incentives for investment generated by the boosts in corporate and individual income-tax rates.

This seems implausible to me, but econometricians might be able to test it.

Recovery has been slow so far because long-term interest rates have not fallen enough to boost investment very much. Interest rates have not

A former chairman of the president's Council of Economic Advisers, Herbert Stein is currently an American Enterprise Institute fellow. *UPI/Bettmann.*

fallen more because there is an expectation that when the economy recovers, the deficit will still be very large and interest rates will then rise. People are reluctant to buy long-term assets now if they think that a rise of interest rates, and fall of asset prices, is coming. Enactment of a credible deficit reduction package will allay the fear of future interest-rate increases and permit a decline of interest rates now, which will stimulate investment now.

This leaves open the question of whether the prospect of higher taxes and lower government expenditures in the future will dim the outlook for recovery and thereby depress investment now.

• The prospect of deficit reduction will warm the cold heart of the Federal Reserve and encourage it to expand the money supply more rapidly, thus stimulating demand and boosting employment.

This assumes that we know something about the heartbeat of the Federal Reserve.

• The level of employment will depend on the relation between and the real productivity of labor and the real wages that workers require to get them to accept employment. The budget package will increase the rate of growth of productivity. Reducing the budget deficit will increase the supply of savings available for private investment at any level of national output. In that way it will increase the productivity of labor, raise the wages that employers can offer, and induce more workers to accept employment.

This, it seems to me, would be a peculiar argument for the Clinton administration to make but there is probably something in it, although how much and how fast is unclear. There may be other and better theories to explain how the Clinton budget package would create jobs. But I am sure that they would be as complex and uncertain as those I have suggested.

Republicans cannot take much comfort from what I believe to be the difficulty of explaining how the administration's program would increase jobs. The Republicans, or at least most of them most of the time, claim to be as devoted to reducing the budget deficit as Mr. Clinton is. Indeed, they usually say that the Clinton plan would not actually reduce the deficit while theirs would. So they cannot make the argument that deficit-reduction is per se depressing. Also, this is a Keynesian argument, and even though Richard Nixon declared himself a Keynesian as long ago as 1971, Republicans generally still regard "Keynesianism" as a kind of perversion. As for the argument that the preferred GOP way of reducing the deficit is more stimulative than the Democratic way, it would take some pretty fancy footwork to demonstrate that.

Probably both the Democrats and the Republicans are wise to avoid theory and stick to reiteration of words like "tax and spend," "jobs" and "change." The number of people who would like to hear some rational debate is small. But we are at a moment when all kinds of "special interests" are being served, and someone ought to say a word for the "special interest" in theory and evidence.

Just Do It

Despite what I have said, I am in favor of the budget package. I feel about substantial deficit reduction the way I felt about sending a man to the moon. I didn't see any great gain from doing it, but once it became an agreed-upon national objective, I thought its success was important. It is good for the country—for its morale and feeling of competence—to be able to accomplish some big difficult task it has set for itself, as long as the task is not too foolish. The country—Democrats, Republicans and Perotistas—seems to have agreed that substantial deficit reduction is a very high priority. We should just do it. And since the country has elected a Democratic president, a Democratic House and a Democratic Senate, the only way to do it is the Democratic way.

The Wall Street Journal, July 26, 1993. Reprinted by permission. The Wall Street Journal, © 1993 Dow Jones & Company, Inc. All rights reserved worldwide.

6 The following questions may help you analyze an article on your own.

Q–6: Herbert Stein is a Republican who was President Richard Nixon's Chairman of the Council of Economic Advisers. Is he being objective in this article?

Q–7: If the present Council of Economic Advisers produced a theory underlying President Clinton's policy, do you think Stein would be convinced by it?

Q–8: Why can't President Clinton rely on either Keynesian or Classical theory to provide support for his policies?

Q–9: Why will "cutting the budget deficit probably reduce employment," and why "might it not do so"?

Q–10: In the time that has passed since this article was written in 1993, what has happened to the economy, and should what has happened be attributed to Clinton's policies?

As you can see, as soon as we start getting into real-world situations, the neat models you learned in earlier chapters don't fit so well, but that doesn't mean they're useless. Far from it. Keeping those models in the back of your mind gives logic and structure to a set of economic events and views that would otherwise be gobbledygook to you. You simply must apply them with insight and a knowledge of political and social economic institutions.

I hope that by going through these three selections in some detail, I prepared you for using the macroeconomics you've learned to interpret the everyday economic events that influence your life. It's in applying macroeconomics to those real-world events that economics changes from a course you must complete to a hobby and avocation which can give you pleasure and understanding for the rest of your life.

CONCLUSION

CHAPTER SUMMARY

- Four heterodox approaches to macroeconomics are the Austrian (focuses on liberty), the Post-Keynesian (emphasizes uncertainty), the Institutionalist (sees institutions as central), and the Radical (focuses on inequities and class tensions).

- The different approaches used by various macroeconomic groups differ in emphasis; they are not necessarily inconsistent with one another.

- The approach one takes to understanding macroeconomic problems depends on the issues being addressed and one's normative goals for the analysis.

- Interpreting economics articles is an art, not a science.

- When interpreting an article one must consider its source.

- Short-run movements in the macroeconomy are often random. They can be explained but not predicted.

- In the short run, economic interrelationships are complicated and can move contrary to economic theories' predictions.

- The same economic set of events can be given two reasonable, contradictory interpretations.

- Two different types of economic writing are the informative and the persuasive.

- It's important to distinguish a writer's goal when you're interpreting an article.

- President Clinton had to rely on luck and non-standard theory to explain how cutting the deficit would create jobs.

KEY TERMS

Austrian *(468)*
free market in money *(468)*
Heisenberg principle *(473)*
heterodox economist *(468)*

indicative planning *(469)*
Institutionalist *(469)*
libertarians *(468)*
mainstream economists *(468)*

Post-Keynesian *(469)*
Radical *(469)*
tax-based incomes policies *(469)*

QUESTIONS FOR THOUGHT AND REVIEW

The number after each question represents the estimated degree of critical thinking required. (1 = almost none; 10 = deep thought.)

1. An economist has suggested that the stock market crash of October 1987 is a prime example of the inherent instability of the equities market. Outside certain daily trading ranges, prices are very volatile. She prescribes government regulation of trading practices. With what

schools of nonmainstream thought is this consistent? *(4)*

2. Which nonmainstream school of thought would be most likely to agree with the insider/outsider theory discussed in a previous chapter? Why? *(6)*

3. Which of the four types of nonmainstream economists do you think would be most likely to support President Clinton's health care reform proposals? Why? *(6)*

4. When interpreting an economics article, why is it important to determine the writer's goals? *(4)*

5. Most newspaper articles about the future direction of the economy are the equivalent of astrology columns. True or false? Why? *(6)*

6. Telephone your local newspaper and ask to speak to its economics and business reporter. Interview the reporter about his or her training in economics and classify that reporter as to what type of economist he or she would most likely find most compatible with his or her own approach. *(8)*

7. Give two alternative explanations for why foreign investment in the United States rose in the late 1980s. *(5)*

8. You've just read that the interest rate has fallen. Does this suggest expansionary monetary policy? Why? *(5)*

9. As what kind of economist would you classify your professor? Analyze one of your professor's lectures in terms of content and perspective. *(9)*

10. As what kind of economist would you classify yourself? Analyze one of your views in terms of content and perspective. *(10)*

PROBLEMS AND EXERCISES

1. Read the introduction of the most recent *Economic Report of the President* and analyze its content and perspective.

2. Find a recent newspaper report on the state of the economy and analyze its content and perspective.

3. You are at a party and you overhear the following:
   a. Mr. A: What this country needs is major institutional change.
   b. Ms. B: There's too much government monopoly.
   c. Ms. C: What this country needs is a tax-based incomes policy.
   d. Mr. D: Indicative planning would have kept the economy out of its current predicament.
   For each statement, give the type of nonmainstream economist who most likely was talking.

4. Find out what has happened to leading indicators this month, and based on those indicators, predict GDP growth, inflation, and unemployment for the next three-month period. Explain your reasoning.

5. Find an economic article in a recent magazine or economic newspaper. Analyze that article for both content and perspective. Specifically state whether the presentation has some spin, what the author's purpose in writing the article was, and whether he or she achieved his or her objectives. What additional sources would you turn to before you made a judgment on the issue being discussed?

ANSWERS TO MARGIN QUESTIONS

1. Nonmainstream analysis is often less formal than mainstream analysis because nonmainstream economists want to include a broader set of issues (such as sociological and cultural issues) that are less susceptible to formal analysis. *(470)*

2. Reporters' job is to fill up their columns. If they were to say that economists didn't have a lot to say about what's happening in the economy in the short run, individuals might wonder why they are reading the column. *(472)*

3. If you are predicting the economy in the very short run, economic theory plays very little role. Instead, common sense and a knowledge of institutions and statistics are far more important. *(472)*

4. Monetary policy is discussed more than fiscal policy because monetary policy is essentially the only game in town. Political problems generally prevent discretionary fiscal policy from being used. *(473)*

5. Economists who emphasize free enterprise and laissez-faire are likely to be Classical economists. *(476)*

6. Although Herbert Stein is a Republican, in this article he is not taking a partisan position; he is being reasonably objective in his analysis of the issues. *(478)*

7. It is highly unlikely that any theory the Council of Economic Advisers came up with would be convincing to Herbert Stein, since he understands both the Classicals' and Keynesians' views and has explained how the policy doesn't fit either one. *(478)*

8. The difficulty for Clinton—and for anybody else trying to reduce the deficit, increase jobs, and expand the economy all at the same time—is that the two main theories, Keynesian and Classical, both say that, at least in the short run, achieving those goals simultaneously is almost impossible—unless you get very lucky. *(478)*

9. Using the standard Classical and Keynesian approaches, Clinton's two goals are inconsistent. Cutting the budget deficit means running contractionary fiscal policy. Contractionary fiscal policy will reduce, not increase, employment, using standard macro analysis. The two goals might not be contradictory if cutting the budget—contractionary fiscal policy—reduces the interest rate so much, and positively affects expectations by such a large degree, that autonomous private expenditures increase by more than the government deficit falls. That, at least, is what Clinton had to hope would happen. *(478)*

10. In 1993 and early 1994 the economy expanded, at least initially. While this expansion could be attributed, in part, to Clinton's policy, most economists attributed it to a combination of luck, positive expectations, expansionary monetary policy (partially made possible by Clinton's budget policy), and a fall in oil prices that kept inflation pressure down. Attributing short-run movements to any specific macro policy is inevitably a debatable activity. *(478)*

3

MICROECONOMICS

In my vacations, I visited the poorest quarters of several cities and walked through one street after another, looking at the faces of the poorest people. Next I resolved to make as thorough a study as I could of Political Economy.

real life. (5) Burn the mathematics. (6) If you can't succeed in (4), burn (3). This last I did often. (From a letter from Marshall to A. L. Bowley, reprinted in A. C. Pigou, *Memorials of Alfred Marshall*, p. 427.)

You may remember having already seen this quotation from Alfred Marshall. It began the first chapter. I chose this beginning for two reasons. First, it gives what I believe to be the best reason to study economics. Second, the quotation is from a hero of mine, one of the economic giants of all times. His *Principles of Economics* was economists' bible in the late 1800s and early 1900s. How important was Marshall? It was Marshall who first used the supply and demand curves as an engine of analysis.

I repeat this quotation here in the introduction to the microeconomics section because for Marshall economics was microeconomics, and it is his vision of economics that underlies this book's approach to microeconomics. For Marshall, economics was an art that was meant to be applied—used to explain why things were the way they were, and what we could do about them. He had little use for esoteric theory that didn't lead to a direct application to a real-world problem. Reflecting on the state of economics in 1906, Marshall wrote to a friend:

I had a growing feeling in the later years of my work at the subject that a good mathematical theorem dealing with economic hypotheses was very unlikely to be good economics: and I went more and more on the rules—(1) Use mathematics as a shorthand language, rather than as an engine of inquiry. (2) Keep to them until you have done. (3) Translate into English. (4) Then illustrate by examples that are important in

Marshall didn't feel this way about mathematical economics because he couldn't do mathematics. He was trained as a formal mathematician, and he was a good one. But, for him, mathematics wasn't economics, and the real world was too messy to have applied to it much of the fancy mathematical economic work that some of his fellow economists were doing. Marshall recognized the influence of all three invisible forces and believed that all three had to be taken into account in applying economic reasoning to reality.

Since 1906 when Marshall wrote this letter, the economics profession has moved away from its Marshallian roots. The profession has found other heroes who have created a mathematical foundation for economics that's both impressive and stultifying. Mathematical economics that has only the slightest connection to the real world has overwhelmed much of the real-world economics that Marshall followed. That's sad.

Not to worry. You won't see such highfalutin mathematical economics in these microeconomic chapters. The chapters follow the Marshallian methodology and present the minimum of formal theory necessary to apply the concepts of economics to the real world, and then they do just that; they start talking about real-world issues.

Part I (chapters 22–24), presents that minimum of theory necessary to understand the economic way of thinking. It introduces you to the foundations of economic reasoning. Part II (chapters 25–29) introduces you to various market structures, providing you with a way of approaching real world markets. But even in these theoretical chapters the focus is on intuition and putting the economic approach to problems into perspective rather than on presenting technique for the sake of technique.

Part III (chapters 30–32) looks at a particular set of markets—factor markets. These markets play a central role in determining the distribution of income. These chapters won't tell you how to get rich (you'll have to wait for the sequel for that), but it will give you new insights into perplexing problems. Part IV (chapters 33–36) integrates economic reasoning with real-world institutions and normative issues to give insight into what's happening. It will explain why economists differ, and how they come up with policy proposals.

Finally, in Part V (chapters 37–39) I consider international issues. While international issues were considered in earlier chapters, given their importance in modern day economies this specific consideration seems warranted.

22

Individual Choice and Demand

The theory of economics must begin with a correct theory of consumption.

~ Stanley Jevons

After reading this chapter, you should be able to:

1. Discuss the principle of diminishing marginal utility.

2. Summarize economists' analysis of rational choice.

3. Explain how marginal utility accounts for the law of demand.

4. Distinguish a complementary good from a substitute good.

5. Explain why economists can believe there are many explanations of individual choice, but nonetheless focus on self-interest.

6. Define the concept *price elasticity of demand* and explain what it tells us about total revenue.

7. Explain the importance of substitution in determining the elasticity of demand.

No analysis is more important to economics than the analysis of individual choice. It is the foundation of economic reasoning and it gives economics much of its power.

We touched on the analysis of individual choice in Chapters 1 and 2. Chapter 1 introduced you to examples of economic reasoning using individual choice. In Chapter 2 you were introduced to the law of demand: The quantity demanded increases as the price decreases. In this chapter we extend that analysis and explore the formal reasoning that underlies individual choice theory and the law of demand.

This formal economic analysis of choice centers on self-interest: People do what they do because doing so is in their interest. The first part of this chapter shows you that foundation and leads you through some exercises to make sure you understand the reasoning. The second part of the chapter relates that analysis to the real world, giving you a sense of when the model is useful and when it's not. Finally the third part of the chapter introduces you to elasticity, a term economists use to describe demand curves.

As you go through this chapter, think back to Chapter 1, which set out the goals for this book. One goal was to get you to think like an economist. This chapter, which formally develops the reasoning process behind economists' cost/benefit approach to problems, examines the underpinnings of how to think like an economist.

INDIVIDUAL CHOICE, SELF-INTEREST, AND ECONOMIC REASONING

Why do people do what they do? There are many explanations. Freudian psychology tells us we do what we do because of an internal fight between the id, ego, and superego plus some hangups people have about their bodies. Other psychologists tell us it's a search for approval by our peers; we want to be OK. Economists agree that these are important reasons, but argue that if we want an analysis that's simple enough to apply to problems, these heavy psychological explanations are likely to get us all mixed up. At least to start with, we need an easier underlying psychological foundation. And economists have one—self-interest. People do what they do because it's in their self-interest.

Economists' analysis of individual choice doesn't deny that most of us have our quirks. Each individual is unique and often strange. That's obvious in what we buy. On certain items we're penny-pinchers; on others we're big spenders. For example, how many of you or your parents clip coupons to save 40¢ on cereal but then spend $20 on a haircut? How many save 50¢ a pound by buying a low grade of meat but then spend $10 on a bottle of wine, $40 on dinner at a restaurant, or $30 for a concert ticket?

Economists' analysis of individual choice doesn't deny that most of us have our quirks.

But through it all comes a certain rationality. Much of what people do reflects their rational self-interest. Thus, a good beginning in understanding individual choice is to focus on the rational part of people's behavior. That's why economists start their analysis of individual choice with a relatively simple, but powerful, underlying psychological foundation.

Jeremy Bentham, the 19th-century economist and philosopher who strongly advocated utilitarianism. *The Bettmann Archive.*

Using that simple theory, two things determine what people do: the pleasure people get from doing or consuming something, and the price of doing or consuming that something. Price is the market's tool to bring the quantity supplied equal to the quantity demanded. Changes in price provide incentives for people to change what they're doing. Through those incentives the invisible hand guides us all. Thus, to understand economics you must understand how price affects our choices. That's why we focus on the effect of price on the quantity demanded. We want to understand the way in which a change in price will affect what we do.

In summary, economists' theory of rational choice is a simple, but powerful, theory that shows how these two things—pleasure and price—are related.

UTILITARIAN FOUNDATIONS OF INDIVIDUAL CHOICE

Let's start with an analysis of what we buy. Why do we buy what we buy? Economists' analysis of individual choice starts with the proposition that individuals try to get as much pleasure as possible out of life. To analyze the choice formally we must measure pleasure.

Measuring Pleasure

How does one measure pleasure? I don't know the answer to that, but back in the 1800s economists such as Jeremy Bentham thought that eventually they would be able to measure pleasure by measuring brain waves. In the expectation of this discovery they even developed a measure of pleasure which they called a *util*. They predicted that someday a machine that could measure utils would be developed. Not surprisingly they called this machine a *utilometer*. This utilometer was to be connected to people's heads and an economist would read it as people went through their daily activities. Eating broccoli might give 10 utils; eating a hot fudge sundae might give 10,000 utils. (OK, so I'm a chocoholic.)

Eventually these 19th-century economists gave up hope of developing a utilometer, but economists use the term **utility** as a quaint, shorthand term for the pleasure or satisfaction that one expects to get from consuming a good or service. (And you thought that economists didn't have a sense of humor.) Utility serves as the basis of economists' analysis of individual choice.

In discussing utility, economists initially used what are called *cardinal measures*. (An example of a cardinal measure is anything that can be measured by an actual number.) But no economist today believes that these actual numbers given to utility have meaning. Economists have gone to great lengths to show that only ordinal measures are necessary. To have an ordinal measure all you need is a ranking of goods that people reveal when they choose one good over another. (That means you can say "John is cuter than Bob," but you don't need to say how much cuter.)

It's important to keep in the back of your mind that economists don't need to measure utils, especially if you're going on in economics, but it's not important to keep it in the front of your mind. In introductory economics there's nothing quite as useful as a good old util. It gives one real numbers to work with, rather than all kinds of fancy measure theories. So here's the deal: I'll use real numbers in discussing utility and you promise that you'll remember they're not really needed. (If you don't accept this deal, see Appendix A where I go through the same analysis without using cardinal measures.)

In thinking about utility, it's important to distinguish between *total utility* and *marginal utility*. **Total utility** refers to the total satisfaction one gets from one's consumption of a product. **Marginal utility** refers to the satisfaction one gets from the consumption of an incremental or additional product above and beyond what one has consumed up to that point. For example, eating a whole pound of Beluga caviar might give you 4,700 utils (units of utility).[1] Consuming the first 15 ounces may have given you 4,697 utils. Consuming the last ounce of caviar might give you an additional 3 utils. The 4,700 is total utility; the 3 is the marginal utility of eating that last ounce of caviar.

An example of the relationship between total utility and marginal utility is given in Exhibit 1. Let's say that the marginal utility of the first slice of pizza is 14, and since you've eaten only one slice, the total utility is also 14. Let's also say that the marginal utility of the second slice of pizza is 12, which means that the total utility of two slices of pizza is 26 (14 + 12). Similarly for the third, fourth, and fifth slices of pizza, whose marginal utilities are 10, 8, and 6, respectively. If we add the marginal utilities you get from eating each of these five slices, we arrive at the total utility of your eating those five pieces of pizza. We do so in row E, column 2, of Exhibit 1(a).

Notice that marginal utility shows up between the lines. It is the utility of changing consumption levels. Thus, the marginal utility of changing from one to two slices of pizza is 12. The relationship between total and marginal utility can also be seen graphically. In Exhibit 1(b) we graph total utility (column 2 of Exhibit 1(a)) on the vertical axis, and number of slices of pizza (column 1 of Exhibit 1(a)) on the horizontal axis. As you can see, total utility increases up to seven slices of pizza; after eight slices it starts decreasing—after eight pieces of pizza you're so stuffed that you can't stand to look at another slice.

Cardinal and Ordinal Utility

Q–1: One of the assumptions of economists' theory of choice is that one can measure utility. True or false? Why?

The Relationship between Total Utility and Marginal Utility

Total utility   *The satisfaction one gets from one's entire consumption of a product.*

Marginal utility   *The satisfaction one gets from the consumption of an incremental or additional product above and beyond what one has consumed up until that point.*

Utility   A measure of the pleasure or satisfaction one gets from consuming a good or service.

---

[1] I choose specific numbers to make the examples more understandable and to make the points I want to make. A useful exercise is for you to choose different numbers and reason your way through the same analysis.

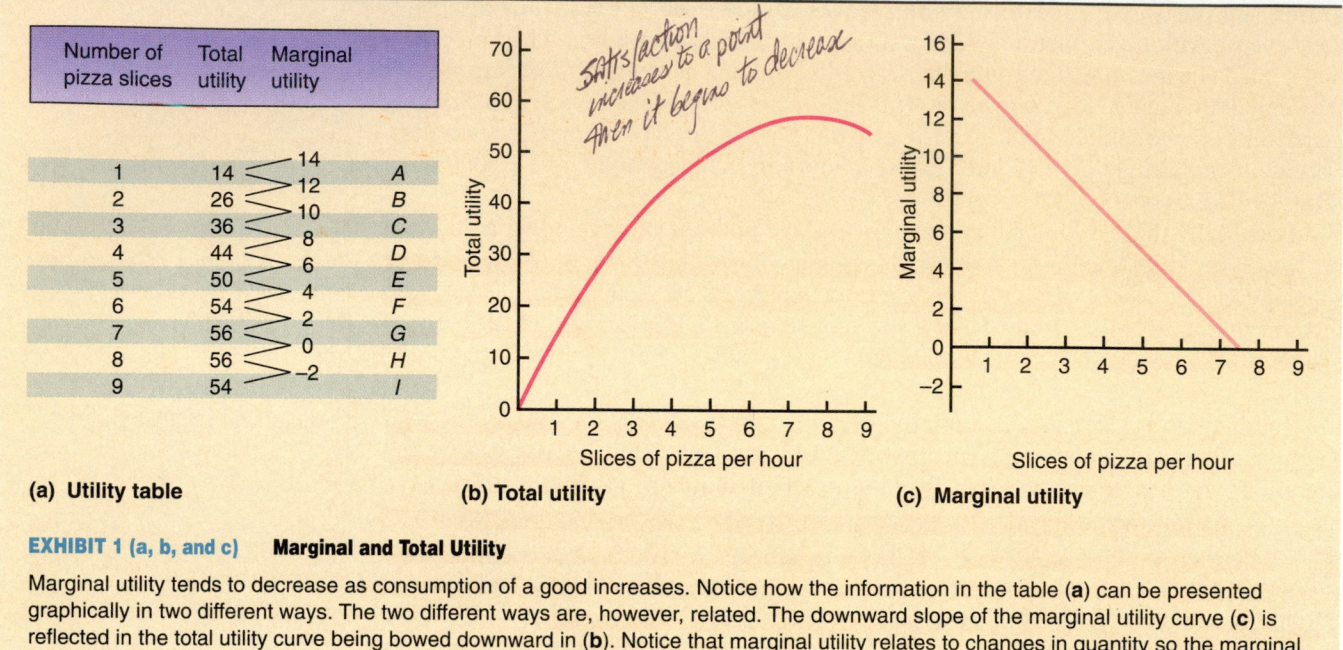

EXHIBIT 1 (a, b, and c)   Marginal and Total Utility

Marginal utility tends to decrease as consumption of a good increases. Notice how the information in the table (**a**) can be presented graphically in two different ways. The two different ways are, however, related. The downward slope of the marginal utility curve (**c**) is reflected in the total utility curve being bowed downward in (**b**). Notice that marginal utility relates to changes in quantity so the marginal utility line is graphed at the halfway point. For example, in (**c**), between 7 and 8, marginal utility becomes zero.

Q–2: If the total utility curve were a straight line—that is, did not exhibit diminishing marginal utility—what would the marginal utility curve look like?

Diminishing Marginal Utility

1 The principle of diminishing marginal utility states that, after some point, the marginal utility received from each additional unit of a good decreases with each unit consumed.

As you consume more of an item, X, beyond some point the additional units of consumption will yield fewer utils than the previous units. In general:
$X \uparrow \rightarrow MU_x \downarrow (X \downarrow \rightarrow MU_x \uparrow)$.

In Exhibit 1(c) we graph marginal utility (column 3 of Exhibit 1(a)) on the vertical axis and slices of pizza (column 1) on the horizontal axis. Notice how marginal utility decreases while total utility increases. When total utility stops increasing (between 7 and 8 slices), marginal utility is zero. Beyond this point total utility would decrease and marginal utility would be negative. An additional slice of pizza will actually make you worse off.

Now let's consider the shapes of these curves a bit more carefully: What are they telling us about people's choices? As we've drawn the curves, the marginal utility that a person gets from each additional slice of pizza decreases with each slice of pizza eaten. Economists believe that the shapes of these curves accurately describe the pattern of people's enjoyment. They have given this principle a name: **diminishing marginal utility.** As individuals increase their consumption of a good, at some point consuming another unit of the product will simply not yield as much additional pleasure as did consuming the preceding unit.

Consider, for example, that late-night craving for a double cheese and pepperoni pizza. You order one and bite into it. Ah, pleasure! But if you've ordered a large pizza and you're eating it all by yourself, your additional pleasure is going to decrease with each additional slice that you consume. In other words you get fewer utils from each additional slice of pizza that you consume. That's the principle of diminishing marginal utility:

As you consume more of an item, x, beyond some point the additional units of consumption will yield fewer utils than the previous units. In general:
$$X \uparrow \rightarrow MU_x \downarrow \text{ and conversely, } (X \downarrow \rightarrow MU_x \uparrow).$$

Notice that the principle of diminishing marginal utility does not say that you don't enjoy consuming more of a good; it simply states that as you consume more of the good, you enjoy the additional units less than you did the initial units. A fourth slice of pizza still tastes good, but it doesn't match the taste of the third slice. At some point, however, marginal utility can become negative. Say you had two large pizzas and only two hours in which to eat them. Eating the last slice could be pure torture. But in most situations you have the option *not* to consume any more of a good. When consuming a good becomes torture (meaning its utility is negative), you simply don't consume any more of it. If you eat a slice of pizza (or consume an additional unit of any other good), that's a good indication that its marginal utility is still positive.

Q–3:   Increasing consumption of a good generally increases its marginal utility. True or false? Why?

The analysis of rational choice is the analysis of how individuals choose goods in order to maximize total utility, and how maximizing total utility can be accomplished by considering marginal utility. That analysis begins with the premise that rational individuals want as much satisfaction as they can get from their available income. How do they achieve that?

Rational Choice and Marginal Utility

Let's start by considering a number of choices. (Answer each choice as you read it.)

Choice 1:   Between a $1 slice of pizza giving you 41 utils and a $1 hero sandwich that gives you 30 utils.

Choice 2:   Between a Maserati at $170,000 that gives you 120,000 utils and a Yugo at $5,000 that gives you 20,000 utils.

Choice 3:   Between reading an additional chapter in this book that gives you an additional 200 utils at a cost of one hour of your time, and reading a chapter in psychology that gives you an additional 100 utils at a cost of 40 minutes of your time, or 150 utils for a chapter and a half at a cost of one hour. (Psychology is easier but less fulfilling than economics.)

Choice 4:   Between having a date with that awesome guy Jerry, which gives you 2,000 utils and costs you $70, and taking out plain Jeff, which gives you 200 utils and costs you $10.

The correct choices, in terms of marginal utility, are: (1) the pizza, (2) the Yugo, (3) a chapter of this book, and (4) Jerry.

If you answered all four correctly, either you're lucky or you have a good understanding of the principle of rational choice. Now let's explore the principle of rational choice more thoroughly by considering each of the four examples.

Choice 1   Since the slice of pizza and the hero both cost $1, and the pizza gives you more utils than the hero, the pizza is the rational choice. If you spend $1 on the hero rather than the pizza, you're losing 11 utils and not making yourself as happy as you could be. You're being irrational. Any choice (for the same amount of money) that doesn't give you as many utils as possible is an irrational choice.

But now let's say that the price of heroes falls to 50¢ so that you can buy two heroes for the same price you previously had to pay for only one. Let's also say that two heroes would give you 56 utils (not $2 \times 30 = 60$—remember the principle of diminishing marginal utility). Which would now be the more rational choice? The two heroes, because their 56 utils are 15 more than you would get from that dollar spent on one slice of pizza.

Another way of thinking about your choice is to recognize that essentially what you're doing in your choices is buying utils. Obviously you want to get the most for your money, so you make those choices that have the highest util per unit of cost. Let's see how this way of thinking about it works by considering our second choice.

The *Critical Review* is a provocative journal analyzing economic issues from an Austrian perspective.

Choice 2   The Maserati costs $170,000 and we get 120,000 utils from it. Per dollar spent we get:

$$\frac{120,000 \text{ utils}}{\$170,000} = .71 \text{ utils.}$$

With the Yugo, for each dollar spent we get

$$\frac{20,000 \text{ utils}}{\$5,000} = 4 \text{ utils.}$$

You get more utils per dollar for the Yugo than for the Maserati, so we choose the Yugo. To say something has the highest util per unit of cost is to say that it has the highest marginal utility per dollar. Alternatively, you can decide to choose the cheapest, lowest cost per util, item. The Maserati gives you 0.71 utils per dollar, so one util costs about $1.43 ($1 divided by 0.71). The Yugo gives you 4 utils per dollar, so a util costs 25¢. The util from a Yugo is cheaper. Since the cost per util is determined by dividing a $1 by the marginal utility per dollar, having the lowest cost per util is equivalent to having the highest marginal utility.

Choice 3   Here the two alternatives have a cost in time, not money. The analysis, however, is the same. You calculate the marginal utility (number of utils) of the choice facing you, and divide that by the cost of the activity; that gives you the marginal utility per unit of cost. Then choose the activity that has the highest MU per unit of cost or lowest cost per util. When you do that, you see that this chapter gives you $3\frac{1}{3}$ utils per minute ($200/60 = 3\frac{1}{3}$), while the psychology chapter gives you $2\frac{1}{2}$ utils per minute. So you choose to read another chapter in this book.[2]

Choice 4   Taking out Jerry gives you $28\frac{1}{2}$ utils per dollar ($2,000/$70$), while taking out Jeff gives you 20 utils per dollar ($200/$10$). So you choose to take out Jerry.

The basic **principle of rational choice** is as follows: *Spend your money on those goods that give you the most marginal utility (MU) per dollar.* The principle of rational choice is important enough for us to emphasize.[3]

$$If \ \frac{MU_x}{P_x} > \frac{MU_y}{P_y}, \ choose \ to \ consume \ an \ additional \ unit \ of \ good \ x.$$

$$If \ \frac{MU_x}{P_x} < \frac{MU_y}{P_y}, \ choose \ to \ consume \ an \ additional \ unit \ of \ good \ y.$$

$$If \ \frac{MU_x}{P_x} = \frac{MU_y}{P_y}, \ you're \ maximizing \ utility; \ you \ cannot \ increase \ your \ utility \ by \ adjusting \ your \ choices.$$

By substituting the marginal utilities and prices of goods into these formulas, you can always decide which good it makes more sense to consume. Consume the one with the highest marginal utility per dollar.

Let's apply these formulas by substituting in the numbers from one of our previous examples: the choice between the Maserati and the Yugo. The marginal utility of the Maserati was 120,000; the price was $170,000. The marginal utility of the Yugo was 20,000; the price was $5,000. Substituting,

$$\frac{20,000}{\$5,000} = 4 \ utils \ per \ \$ > \frac{120,000}{\$170,000} = .7 \ utils \ per \ \$.$$

So choose the Yugo.

In each of the previous four examples, there was a clear winner. If in the examples you had been maximizing utility and hence were in equilibrium, there couldn't have been a clear winner. Why? As you make choices, it's important to remember the principle of diminishing marginal utility: As we consume more of an item, the marginal utility we get from the last unit consumed decreases. Conversely as we consume *less* of an item, the marginal utility we get from the last unit consumed *increases*. (The principle of diminishing marginal utility operates in reverse.)

The principle of rational choice tells you to keep adjusting your spending if the marginal utility per dollar (*MU/P*) of two goods differs. The only time you don't adjust your spending is when there is no clear winner. When you've maximized utility, the ratios of the marginal utility to price of the two goods are equal. This insight accounts for the third formula in the principle of rational choice:

$$If \ \frac{MU_x}{P_x} = \frac{MU_y}{P_y}, \ you're \ maximizing \ utility; \ you're \ in \ equilibrium.$$

---

2   Principle of rational choice: spend your money on those goods that give you the most marginal utility per dollar.

If $\frac{MU_x}{P_x} > \frac{MU_y}{P_y}$, choose to consume an additional unit of good x.

If $\frac{MU_x}{P_x} < \frac{MU_y}{P_y}$, choose to consume an additional unit of good y.

If $\frac{MU_x}{P_x} = \frac{MU_y}{P_y}$, you're maximizing utility; you cannot increase your utility by adjusting your choices.

Rational Choice and Maximizing Utility

Q-4:   If goods A and B both give the same marginal utility but good B costs twice as much as good A, how should you change your purchases?

---

[2] As I've pointed out before, I choose the numbers to make the points I want to make. A good exercise for you is to choose different numbers that reflect your estimate of the marginal utility you get from choice, and see what your rational choices are. And remember our deal.

[3] The symbol > means "greater than." The symbol < means "less than."

EXHIBIT 2   Maximizing Utility

Big Macs (P = $2)				Ice Cream (P = $1)			
Q	TU	MU	MU/P	Q	TU	MU	MU/P
0	0			0	0		
		20	10			29	29
1	20			1	29		
		14	7			17	17
2	34			2	46		
		10	5			7	7
3	44			3	53		
		3	1.5			2	2
4	47			4	55		
		0	0			1	1
5	47			5	56		
		−5	−2.5			0	0
6	42			6	56		
		−10	−5			−4	−4
7	32			7	52		

So far in discussing our examples, we've considered each of the four choices separately. But in real life, choices aren't so neatly separated. Say you were presented with all four choices simultaneously. If you make all four of the decisions given in the examples, are you being rational? The answer is no. Why? The pizza gives you 46 utils per dollar; taking out Jerry gives you 28 utils per dollar; and the Yugo gives you only 4 utils per dollar. You aren't being rational; you aren't maximizing your utility. It would clearly make sense to dump the Yugo and take out Jerry on pizza binges instead (assuming, of course, that he'll go out with you without your Yugo).

But what about the fourth choice: studying psychology or economics? We can't compare the costs of studying to the costs of the other goods because, as I noted earlier, the costs of both studying alternatives are expressed in terms of time, not money. If we can assign a money value to the time, however, we can make the comparison. Let's say you can earn $6 per hour, so the value of your time is 10¢ per minute. This allows us to think about both alternatives in terms of dollars and cents. Since a chapter in economics takes an hour to read, the cost in money of reading a chapter is 60 minutes × 10¢ = $6. Similarly the cost of the 40 minutes you'd take to read the psychology chapter is $4.

With these values we can compare our studying decisions with our other decisions. The value in utils per dollar of reading a chapter of this book is:

$$\frac{200}{\$6} = 33\frac{1}{3} \text{ utils per dollar}$$

So forget about dating Jerry with its value of 28 utils per dollar. Your rational choice is to study this chapter while stuffing yourself with pizza.

But wait. Remember that, according to the principle of diminishing marginal utility, as you consume more of something, the marginal utility you get from it falls. So as you consume more pizza and spend more time reading this book, the marginal utilities of these activities will fall. Thus, as you vary your consumption, the marginal utilities you get from the goods are changing.

When do you stop varying your consumption? When you maximize utility—when the marginal utility per dollar spent on each choice is equal. Achieving equilibrium by maximizing utility (juggling one's choices, adding a bit more of one and choosing a bit less of another) requires more information than I've so far presented. We need to know the marginal utility of alternative amounts of consumption for each choice and how much income we have to spend on all those items. With that information we can choose among alternatives.

An Example of Rational Choice   In Exhibit 2 we consider an example in which we have the necessary information to make simultaneous decisions. In this example, we have $7 to spend on ice cream cones and Big Macs. The choice is between ice cream at $1 a

Rational Choice and Simultaneous Decisions

Q–5:   What are the three formulas for the principle of rational choice?

cone and Big Macs at $2 apiece. In the exhibit you can see the principle of diminishing marginal utility in action. The marginal utility (*MU*) we get from either good decreases as we consume more of it. Marginal utility (*MU*) becomes negative after five Big Macs or six ice cream cones.

The key columns for your decision are the *MU/P* columns. They tell you the *MU* per dollar spent on each of the items. By following the rule that we choose the good with the higher marginal utility per dollar, we can quickly determine the optimal choice.

Let's start by considering what we'd do with our first $2. Clearly we'd only eat ice cream. Doing so would give us 29 + 17 = 46 utils, compared to 20 utils if we spent the $2 on a Big Mac. How about our next $2? Again the choice is clear; the 10 utils per dollar from the Big Mac are plainly better than the 7 utils per dollar we can get from ice cream cones. So we buy one Big Mac and two ice cream cones with our first $4.

Now let's consider our fifth and sixth dollars. The *MU/P* for a second Big Mac is 7. The MU/P for a third ice cream cone is also 7, so we could spend the fifth dollar on either—if McDonald's will sell us half a Big Mac. We ask them if they will, and they tell us no, so we must make a choice between either two additional ice cream cones or another Big Mac for our fifth and sixth dollar. Since the marginal utility per dollar of the fourth ice cream cone is only 2, it makes sense to spend our fifth and sixth dollar on another Big Mac. So now we're up to two Big Macs and two ice cream cones and we have one more dollar to spend.

Now how about our last dollar? If we spend it on a third ice cream cone we get 7 additional utils. If McDonald's maintains its position and only sells whole Big Macs, this is our sole choice since we only have a dollar and Big Macs sell for $2. But let's say that McDonald's wants the sale and this time offers to sell us half a Big Mac for $1. Would we take it? The answer is no. The next Big Mac gives us only 5 utils per dollar whereas the third ice cream cone gives us 7 utils per dollar. So we spend the seventh dollar on a third ice cream cone.

With these choices we've arrived at equilibrium—we're maximizing total utility. Our total utility is 34 from two Big Macs and 53 utils from the three ice cream cones, making a total of 87 utils.

Why do these two choices make sense? Because they give us the most utility per dollar and hence the highest total utility. These choices make the marginal utility per dollar equal as between the last Big Mac and the last ice cream cone. The marginal utility per dollar we get from our last Big Mac is:

$$\frac{MU}{P} = \frac{14}{\$2} = 7$$

The marginal utility per dollar we get from our last ice cream cone is:

$$\frac{MU}{P} = \frac{7}{\$1} = 7$$

The marginal utility per dollar of each choice is equal, so we know we can't do any better. For any other choice we would get less total utility, so we could increase our total utility by switching to one of these two choices.

The General Principle of Rational Choice

The General Principle of Rational Choice

$\dfrac{MU_x}{P_x} > \dfrac{MU_z}{P_z}$, consume more of good *x*.

$\dfrac{MU_y}{P_y} < \dfrac{MU_z}{P_z}$, consume more of good *y*.

Our example involved only two goods, but the reasoning can be extended to the choice among many goods. Our analysis of rational choice has shown us that the principle of rational choice among many goods is simply an extension of the basic principle of rational choice applied to two goods. That general principle for maximizing utility is to equate, as closely as possible, the marginal utility per dollar of the activities or goods being considered.

When $\dfrac{MU_x}{P_x} > \dfrac{MU_z}{P_z}$, *consume more of good* x.

When $\dfrac{MU_y}{P_y} > \dfrac{MU_z}{P_z}$, *consume more of good* y.

Stop adjusting your consumption when the marginal utilities per dollar are equal.

So the general principle of rational choice is this:

Choose goods and activities so that the marginal utilities per dollar of the goods consumed are equal:

$$\frac{MU_x}{P_x} = \frac{MU_y}{P_y} = \frac{MU_z}{P_z}$$

When this principle is met, the consumer is in equilibrium; the marginal cost per util is equal for all goods and the consumer is as well off as it is possible to be.

Notice that the rule does not say that the rational consumer should consume a good until its marginal utility reaches zero. The reason is that the consumer doesn't have enough money to buy all she wants. She faces an income constraint and does the best she can under that constraint—that is, she maximizes utility. To buy more goods she has to work more, so she should work until the marginal value of another dollar earned just equals the marginal value of another dollar spent. According to economists' analysis of rational choice, a person's choice of how much to work is made simultaneously with the person's decision of how much to consume. So when you say you want a Porsche but can't afford one, economists ask whether you're working two jobs and saving all your money to buy a Porsche. If you aren't, you're demonstrating that you don't really want a Porsche, given what you would have to do to get it.

Now that you know the basic rule for maximizing utility, let's bring in the law of demand and see how it relates to marginal utility. The law of demand says that the quantity demanded of a good depends inversely on the relative price of that good. Accordingly when the price of a good goes up, the quantity we consume of it goes down.

Now let's consider the law of demand in relation to our marginal utility rule. When the price of a good goes up, the marginal utility *per dollar* we get from that good goes down. So when the price of a good goes up, if we were initially in equilibrium, we no longer are. Therefore we lower our consumption of that good. The principle of rational choice shows us formally that following the law of demand is the rational thing to do.

Let's see how. If:

$$\frac{MU_x}{P_x} = \frac{MU_y}{P_y}$$

and the price of good *y* goes up, then:

$$\frac{MU_x}{P_x} > \frac{MU_y}{P_y}$$

Our condition for maximizing utility is no longer satisfied. Consider the preceding example, in which we were in equilibrium with 87 utils (34 from two Big Macs and 53 from three ice cream cones) with the principle of rational choice fulfilled:

Big Mac   ice cream

$$\frac{14 \text{ marginal utils}}{\$2} = \frac{7 \text{ marginal utils}}{\$1} = 7$$

If the price of an ice cream cone rises from $1 to $2, the marginal utility per dollar for one Big Mac (whose price hasn't changed) exceeds the marginal utility per dollar of ice cream cones:

Big Mac   ice cream

$$\frac{14}{\$2} > \frac{7}{\$2}$$

To satisfy our condition for maximizing utility so that our choice will be rational, we must somehow raise the marginal utility we get from the good whose relative price has risen and lower the *MU* we get from a good whose relative price has fallen. Following

Choose goods and activities so that the marginal utilities per dollar of the goods consumed are equal:

$$\frac{MU_x}{P_x} = \frac{MU_y}{P_y}$$

Marginal Utility
and the Law of Demand

3 According to the principle of rational choice, if there is diminishing marginal utility and the price of a good goes up, we consume less of that good. Hence, the principle of rational choice leads to the law of demand.

the principle of diminishing marginal utility, we can increase marginal utility only by *decreasing* our consumption of the good whose price has risen. As we consume fewer ice cream cones and more Big Macs, the marginal utility of ice cream rises and the marginal utility of a Big Mac falls.

This example can be extended to a general rule: If the price of a good rises, you'll increase your total utility by consuming less of it. When the price of a good goes up, consumption of that good must go down. Our marginal utility rule underlies the law of demand:

> *Law of demand: The quantity demanded of a good will rise the lower its price, other things constant.*

Or alternatively:

> *The quantity demanded of a good will fall the higher its price, other things constant.*

This discussion of marginal utility and rational choice shows the relationship between marginal utility and the price we're willing to pay. When total utility is low but *MU* is high, as it is with diamonds, the price we're willing to pay is high. When total utility is high but *MU* is low, as it is with water, the price we're willing to pay is low. Since our demand for a good is an expression of our willingness to pay for it, quantity demanded is related to marginal utility.

Complements, Substitutes, and Shift Factors of Demand

In Chapter 2, I spent a lot of time distinguishing between movements along a demand curve—a change in the quantity demanded—and shifts in demand caused by a change in a shift factor. Now that we've studied the foundations of choice theory, it is useful to reconsider those distinctions. A shift factor changes the marginal utility one gets from a good and hence changes how much of a good is desired at all prices. Say, for example, that it rains. That raises the *MU* of umbrellas and puts people off their rational choice equilibrium. They adjust—buy more umbrellas—and that adjustment shifts the demand for umbrellas out.

Similarly, a change in the price of a good puts people off their rational choice equilibrium and causes them to modify their consumption of that good, and of other goods. They continue to do so until the ratio of marginal utilities is in line with the new price ratios. For example, say the price of pencils goes up; one reduces one's consumption of pencils, raising the marginal utility of pencils.

In the adjusting process, a price change of one good indirectly affects the marginal utility of, and hence the demand for, another good. For example, when the price of a Big Mac goes up, one consumes fewer Big Macs, raising the marginal utility of consuming Big Macs. One then also consumes more of other goods—say, pizza—lowering the marginal utility one gets from pizzas. So, a change in the price of Big Macs will affect the demand for pizzas. That's why price of related goods is a shift factor of demand for a good.

There are actually two ways in which a price change of a related good can affect the demand for a good. The Big Mac/pizza example is an example in which goods were **substitutes**—goods that can be used in place of one another. When goods X and Y are substitutes, the rise in price of good Y will decrease the marginal utility one gets from good Y, and hence will increase the demand for good X. For example, say the price of hot dogs goes up. The demand for hamburgers will increase—hot dogs and hamburgers are substitutes for each other. This is the most common way the price-of-a-related good effect works.

It is possible, however, for the price-of-a-related good effect to work in another manner. For example, if the goods are **complements**—goods that are used in conjunction with other goods—a fall in the price of good Y will directly increase the marginal utility of good X, and hence will *increase* the demand for good X. For example, say the price of hot dogs goes up and that people use lots of mustard on hot dogs (but not on hamburgers; on hamburgers they use ketchup). The increase in price and the related decrease in the consumption of hot dogs will directly lower the *MU* one gets

---

Law of demand   *The quantity demanded of a good will rise the lower its price, other things constant.*
or
Law of demand   *The quantity demanded of a good will fall the higher its price, other things constant.*

When there is a cost of decision making, it is rational to be "irrational."

4   A good is a substitute for another good if its consumption goes up when the price of the other good goes up. A good is a complement for another if its consumption goes down when the price of the other good goes up.

ADDED DIMENSION

INCOME AND SUBSTITUTION EFFECTS

■n the discussion of the law of demand I didn't say precisely how much the quantity demanded would decrease with a price rise. I didn't because of a certain ambiguity that arises when one talks about changes in nominal prices. To understand the cause of this ambiguity, notice that with $7 we can no longer consume two big Macs and three ice cream cones. We've got to cut back for two reasons: First, we're poorer due to the rise in price. This is called the *income effect.* Second is the change in the *relative* prices. The price of ice cream has risen relative to the price of Big Macs. This is called a *substitution effect.* Technically the law of demand is based only upon the substitution effect.

To separate the two effects, let's assume that somebody compensates us for the rise in price of ice cream cones. Since it would cost $10 [(2 × $2 = $4) + (3 × $2 = $6)] to buy what $7 bought previously, we'll assume that someone gives us an extra $3 to compensate us for the rise in price. This eliminates the income effect. We now have $10 so we can buy two Big Macs and the three ice cream cones as we did before. If we do so, our total utility is once again 87 (34 utils from two Big Macs and 53 utils from three ice cream cones). But will we do so?

We see that Big Macs give us more *MU* per dollar. What happens if we exchange an ice cream cone for an additional Big Mac, so instead of buying three ice cream cones and two Big Macs, we buy three Big Macs and two ice cream cones? The *MU* per dollar of Big Macs falls from 7 to 5 and the *MU* per dollar of the ice cream cone (whose price is now $2) rises from 3.5 to 8.5. Our total utility rises to 44 from three Big Macs and 46 from two ice cream cones, for a total of 90 utils rather than the previous 87. We've increased our total utility by shifting our consumption out of ice cream, the good whose price has risen. The price of ice cream went up and, even though we were given more money so we could buy the same amount as before, we did not; we bought fewer ice cream cones. That's the substitution effect in action: It tells us that when the relative price of a good goes up, the quantity purchased of that good decreases, *even if you're given money to compensate you for the rise.*

from mustard, and hence will decrease the demand for mustard. The same is true for all complementary goods.

Other shift factors also affect marginal utility, and hence affect demand. An increase in income, for example, increases the total utility one gets from one's income, and thereby increases one's consumption of almost all goods, although the increase may be greater for some goods than for others. Goods whose consumption increases with an increase in income are called **normal goods.** It is, however, possible that an increase in income can affect relative preferences so much that an increase in income can cause a decrease in the consumption of a particular good. Goods whose consumption decreases when income increases are called **inferior goods.** In some instances, potatoes are an example of an inferior good. As income goes up, people might so significantly shift their consumption toward meat and away from potatoes that their total consumption of potatoes decreases.

Understanding a theory involves more than understanding how a theory works; it also involves understanding the limits the assumptions underlying the theory place on the use of the theory. So let us consider some of the assumptions upon which economists' analysis of choice is based. The first assumption we'll consider is the implicit assumption that decisions can be made costlessly.

Applying Economists' Theory of Choice to the Real World

The Cost of Decision Making and Bounded Rationality   The theory of rational choice makes reasonably good intuitive sense when we limit our examples to two or three choices, as I did in this chapter. But in reality, there are hundreds of thousands of choices that we must make simultaneously. It simply doesn't make intuitive sense that we're going to apply rational choice to all those choices simultaneously—that would exceed our decision-making abilities. This cost of decision making means that it is only rational to be somewhat irrational—to do things without applying the rational choice model. Thinking about decisions is one of the things we all economize on.

How real-world people decide in real-world situations is an open question that modern economists are spending a lot of time researching. Following the work of Nobel Prize winner Herbert Simon, a number of economists have come to believe that, to make real-world decisions, most people use **bounded rationality**—rationality based on *rules of thumb*—rather than using the rational choice model. They argue that many of our decisions are made with our minds on automatic pilot. This view of

Herbert Simon was awarded the Nobel Prize in 1978 for work on the importance of institutions and process to economic theory. © *The Nobel Foundation.*

Advertising is designed to mine rules of thumb.

rationality has significant implications for interpreting and predicting economic events. For example, one rule of thumb is that "you get what you pay for," which means that if something has a high price we tend to think it is better than something that has a low price. Put technically, we rely on price to convey information about reality. This reliance on price for information changes the inferences one can draw from the analysis, and can lead to upward-sloping demand curves.

A second rule of thumb that people sometimes use is "follow the leader." When one doesn't know what to do, one does what one thinks smart people are doing. Consider the clothes you're wearing. I suspect many of your choices of what to wear reflect these rules of thumb. Suppliers of these goods certainly think so and spend enormous amounts of money to exploit these rules of thumb. They try to steer your automatic pilot toward their goods. The suppliers emphasize these two rules ("you get what you pay for" and "follow the leader") to convince people their product is the "in" thing to buy. If they succeed, they've got a gold mine; if they fail, they've got a flop. Advertising is designed to mine these rules of thumb.

In technical terms, the "follow the leader" rule leads to **focal point equilibria** in which a set of goods is consumed, not because the goods are objectively preferred to all other goods, but simply because through luck, or advertising, they have become focal points to which people have gravitated. Once some people started consuming a good, others followed.

Given Tastes   A second assumption implicit in economists' theory of rational choice is that utility functions are given, and are not shaped by society. In reality our preferences are determined not only by nature, but also by our experiences—by nurture. Let's consider an example: Forty percent of major league baseball players chew tobacco, but close to zero percent of college professors chew tobacco. Why? Are major league baseball players somehow born with a tobacco-chewing gene while college professors are not? I doubt it. Tastes often are significantly influenced by society.

Tastes and Individual Choice   One way in which economists integrate the above insights into economics is by emphasizing that the analysis is conducted on the assumption of "given tastes." As discussed above, in reality, economists agree that often forces besides price and marginal utility play a role in determining what people demand. They fully recognize that there is a whole other analysis necessary to supplement theirs—an analysis of what determines taste.

Ask yourself what you ate today. Was it health food? Pizza? Foie gras? Whatever it was, it was probably not the most efficient way to satisfy your nutritional needs. The most efficient way to do that would be to eat only soybean mush and vitamin supplements at a cost of about $300 per year. That's less than one-tenth of what the average individual today spends on food per year. Most of us turn up our noses at soybean mush. Why? Because tastes are important.

I emphasize this point about the importance of tastes because some economists have been guilty of forgetting their simplifying assumption. An example of this is that some economists in the 1800s thought that society's economic needs eventually would be fully satisfied and that we would enter a golden age of affluence where all our material wants would be satisfied. They thought there would be surpluses of everything. Clearly that hasn't happened. Somehow it seems that whenever a need is satisfied, it's replaced by yet another want, which soon becomes another need.

There are, of course, examples of wants being temporarily satisfied, as a U.S. company on a small island in the Caribbean is reported to have discovered. Employees weren't showing up for work. The company sent in a team of efficiency experts who discovered the cause of their problem: The firm had recently raised wages, and workers had decided they could get all they wanted (warm weather, a gorgeous beach, plenty of food, and a little bit of spending money) by showing up for work once, maybe twice, a week. Such a situation was clearly not good for business, but the firm found a solution. It sent in thousands of Sears catalogs, and suddenly the workers were

MAKING STUPID DECISIONS

It is hard to make good decisions. You need lots of training—in math, in economics, in logic. Think of kids—do five-year-olds make rational decisions? Some dyed-in-the-wool utilitarians might argue that whatever decision one makes must, by definition, be rational, but such usage makes the concept tautological—true by definition.

When applying the theory of rational choice, most economists agree that some decisions people make can be irrational. For example, they will concede that five-year-olds make a lot of what most parents would call "stupid (or irrational) decisions." By a stupid decision they mean a decision that has expected consequences which, if the child had logically thought about them, would have caused the child not to make that particular decision. But five-year-olds often haven't learned how to think logically about expected consequences, so economists don't assume decisions made by five-year-olds reflect the rational choice model.

In the real world, parents and teachers spend enormous effort to teach children what is rational, reasonable, and "appropriate." Children's decision-making process reflects that teaching. But parents and teachers teach more than a decision-making process; they also teach children a moral code that often includes the value of honor and the value of selflessness. These teachings shape their children's decision-making process (although not always in the way that parents or teachers think or hope) and modify their preferences. So our decision-making process and our preferences are, to some degree, taught to us.

Recognizing that preferences and decision-making processes are, to some degree, taught, not inherent, eliminates the fixed point by which to judge people's decisions: Are they making decisions that reflect their true needs, or are they simply reflecting what they have been taught? Eliminating that fixed point makes it difficult to draw unambiguous policy implications from economists' model of rational choice.

no longer satisfied with what they already had. They wanted more and went back to work to get it. When they were presented with new possibilities, their wants increased. Companies know that tastes aren't constant, and they spend significant amounts of money in advertising to make consumers have a taste for their goods. It works, too.

Tastes are also important in explaining differences in consumption between countries. For example, in Japan one wouldn't consider having a meal without rice. Rice has a ceremonial, almost mystical value there. In many parts of the United States supper means meat and potatoes. In Germany, carp (a large goldfish) is a delicacy; in the United States many people consider carp inedible. In the United States corn is a desirable vegetable; in parts of Europe, until recently, it was considered pig food.

To say we don't analyze tastes in the core of economic theory doesn't mean that we don't take them into account. Think back to Chapter 2 when we distinguished shifts in demand (the entire demand schedule shifts) from movements along the demand curve. Those movements along the demand curve were the effect of price. Tastes were one of the shift factors of demand. So economists can include tastes in their analysis; a change in tastes makes the demand curve shift.

Economists take account of changes in tastes as shift factors of demand.

We began this chapter with a discussion of the simplifying nature of the economists' analysis of rational choice. Now that you've been through it, you may be wondering if it's all that simple. In any case, I'm sure most of you would agree that it's complicated enough. When we're talking about formal analysis, I'm in total agreement.

But if you're talking about informal analysis and applying the analysis to the real world, most economists would also agree that this theory of choice is in no way acceptable. Economists believe that there's more to life than maximizing utility. We believe in love, anger, and doing crazy things just for the sake of doing crazy things. We're real people.

But, we argue, simplicity has its virtue, and often people hide their selfish motivations. Few people like to go around and say, "I did this because I'm a selfish, calculating person who cares primarily about myself." Instead they usually emphasize other motives. "Society conditioned me to do it"; "I'm doing this to achieve fairness"; "It's my upbringing." And they're probably partially right, but often they hide and obscure their selfish motives in their psychological explanations. The beauty of economists' simple psychological assumption is that it cuts through many obfuscation (that's an obfuscating word meaning smokescreens) and, in doing so, it often captures a part of reality that others miss. Let's consider a couple of examples.

Individual Choice
Theory in Context

5 Economists use their simple self-interest theory of choice because it cuts through many obfuscations, and in doing so often captures a part of reality that others miss.

Why does government have restrictions on who's allowed to practice law? The typical layperson's answer is that these restrictions exist to protect the public. The economists' answer is that many of the restrictions do little to protect the public. Instead their primary function is to restrict the number of lawyers and thereby increase the marginal utility of existing lawyers and the price they can charge.

Why do people pollute? The layperson's answer is that people haven't been educated about the importance of the environment. The economists' answer is that people aren't paying enough for their polluting activities.

Why do museum directors almost always want to increase the size of their collections? The layperson's (and museum directors') answer is that they're out to preserve our artistic heritage. The economists' answer is that it often has more to do with maximizing the utility of the museum staff. (Economist William Grampp recently made this argument in a book about the economics of art. He buttressed his argument by pointing out that more than half of museums' art is in storage and not accessible to the public. Acquiring more art will simply lead to more going into storage.)

Now in no way am I claiming that the economic answer based on pure self-interest is always the correct one. But I am arguing that approaching problems by asking the question, "What's in it for the people making the decisions?" is a useful approach that will give you more insight into what's going on than many other approaches. It gets people to ask tough, rather than easy, questions. After you've asked the tough questions, then you can see how to modify the conclusions by looking deeply into the real-world institutions.

All too often students think of economics and economic reasoning as establishment reasoning. That's not true. Economic reasoning can be extremely subversive to existing establishments. But whatever it is, it is not subversive in order to be subversive, or proestablishment to be proestablishment. It's simply a logical application of a simple idea—individual choice theory—to a variety of problems.

Approaching problems by asking the question "What's in it for the people making the decision?" is a useful approach that will give you more insight than many other approaches.

Q-6: In what way can economic reasoning be subversive to existing establishments?

ELASTICITY OF DEMAND

6a Price elasticity of demand is defined as a measure of the percent change in the quantity demanded divided by the percent change in the price.

Now that we've examined the foundations of the law of demand, it's time to talk about a term economists use to describe the responsiveness of quantity demanded to changes in price: **price elasticity of demand** (or often just *elasticity of demand*). It's a measure of the percent change in quantity of a good demanded divided by the percent change in the price of that good. Price elasticity of demand is an important concept, so let's write it down formally:

$$E_d = \frac{\text{Percent change in quantity}}{\text{Percent change in price}}$$

Let's consider an example. Say the price of a good goes up by 10 percent and, in response, the quantity demanded falls by 20 percent. The price elasticity of demand would be −2. Alternatively, say the price goes down by 5 percent and the quantity rises by 2 percent. In that case the price elasticity of demand would be −.4.

Elasticity uses percentages, not absolute amounts, and by convention ignores the minus sign.

Two things to remember in thinking about elasticity are:

1. By convention, we ignore the minus sign.
2. It uses percentages, not absolute amounts.

Let's briefly consider each.

Ignoring the Minus Sign

The first point to notice about the discussion of elasticity is that when I said what the price elasticity of demand was, I said −2. This follows because whenever price goes up, quantity demanded falls. This inverse relationship is deeply ingrained in every economist's mind. But negative numbers are a pain, especially when you're comparing two negative numbers, say −2 and −4. Which is larger? (The answer is −2.) To avoid this confusion, generally economists talk about elasticity as a positive number and remember that it's actually negative. (Those of you who remember some math can think of the definition of elasticity as being an absolute value, rather than a simple number.) We'll follow that convention in this book, which means that you've got to remember that the elasticity of demand is actually negative even though we talk about it as positive.

The second point to notice is that elasticity uses percentages, not absolute amounts. In describing demanders' responsiveness, we use percentages rather than absolute amounts for two reasons. The first is that percentage changes are unaffected by our choice of units. For example, say the price rises from $1.00 to $1.20 per quart and quantity demanded falls from 400 to 380 quarts. Is that highly responsive or not? If we use cents, the change seems relatively responsive, with a change of price of 20 cents bringing about a change in quantity demanded of 20 quarts. But if we use dollars, it seems far more responsive—with the change of one-fifth of a dollar bringing about a change in quantity demanded of 20 quarts. So there seems to be a difference in responsiveness, depending on the units we're using. Using percentages eliminates this difference caused by the unit we measure in. Measuring in cents or dollars, the percentage change in our price is 20/100 or .20/1.00, both of which are 20 percent. A 20 percent change in price brings about a 5 percent change in quantity demanded.

The second reason for using percentages is that it makes comparisons of responsiveness of different goods easier since the percentage change gives us insight into what will happen to total revenue. Say a $1.00 increase in the price of a $2,000 computer decreases the quantity demanded by one, from 10 to 9. Say also that a $1.00 increase in the price of a pen, from $1.00 to $2.00, decreases quantity demanded by one—from 10,000 to 9,999. Using absolute numbers, the $1.00 price increase had the same effect on the quantities.

But such a comparison of absolute numbers is not very helpful. To see that, ask yourself which good you'd rather be selling. As a percentage of price, the computer price increase of 1/2,000 of the original price is relatively small, and the decrease in quantity demanded of 1/10 of original sales is large, so total revenue would decrease. As a percentage, the price increase in pens was relatively large—100 percent—and the percentage quantity decrease is small. So, if you raised the price of pens there will be an increase in total revenues. Clearly, if you're raising your price in these examples you'd rather be selling pens than computers. By using percentages, this is made clear: a .05 percent increase in price decreases quantity demanded by 10 percent, so the elasticity is 200. With pens, a 100 percent increase in prices decreases quantity demanded by .01 percent, an elasticity of .0001. So the elasticities measure tells us the two situations are substantially different.

The usefulness for sellers of comparing responsiveness to price changes derives from elasticity's relationship with total revenues. (E_d represents price elasticity of demand.)

- If E_d is greater than 1, a rise in price lowers total revenue. (Price and total revenue move in opposite directions.) The demand in that price range is described as **elastic.** When demand is elastic, the percent change in quantity is greater than the percent change in price.

- If E_d is equal to 1, a rise in price leaves total revenue unchanged. The demand is described as having **unitary elasticity.** When demand is unit elastic, the percent change in quantity equals the percent change in price.

- If E_d is less than 1, a rise in price increases total revenue. (Price and total revenue move in the same direction.) The demand in that price range is described as **inelastic.** When demand is inelastic, the percent change in quantity is less than the percent change in price.

Elastic Percent change in quantity is greater than percent change in price. $E_d > 1$.

Unitary elasticity Percent change in quantity equals percent change in price. $E_d = 1$.

Inelastic Percent change in quantity is less than percent change in price. $E_d < 1$.

Now let's try some real-world examples. The first is a university president thinking of raising tuition. Say that raising tuition by 10 percent will decrease the number of students by only 1 percent. What's the elasticity? The percent change in quantity is 1 percent; the percent change in price is 10 percent. Dividing the percent change in quantity by the percent change in price, we have an elasticity of .1. That's an inelastic demand ($E_d < 1$), so raising tuition will increase the college's total revenue.

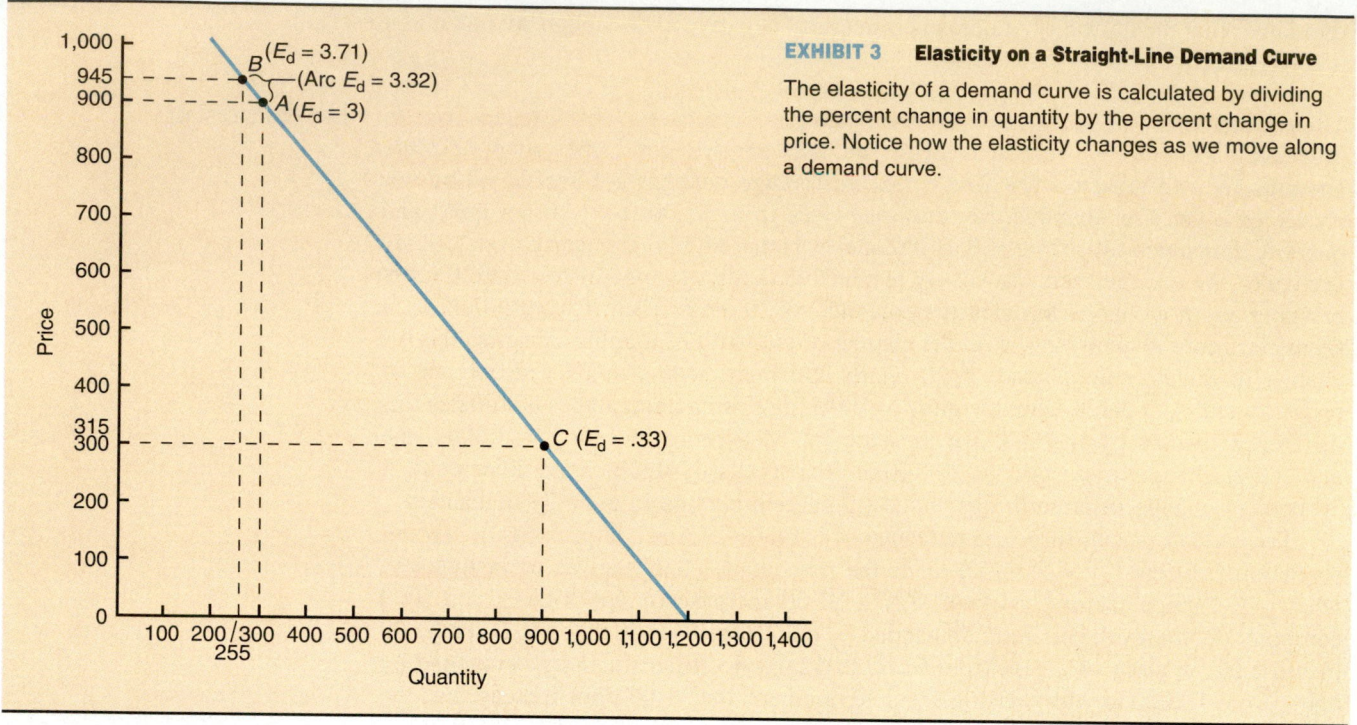

EXHIBIT 3   Elasticity on a Straight-Line Demand Curve

The elasticity of a demand curve is calculated by dividing the percent change in quantity by the percent change in price. Notice how the elasticity changes as we move along a demand curve.

Q–7: If price goes up by 20 percent and quantity decreases by 20 percent, what is the elasticity of demand?

6b If demand is inelastic, a rise in price increases total revenue. If demand is elastic, a rise in price lowers total revenue. If demand is unitary elastic, a rise in price has no effect on revenue.

But if a 10 percent rise in tuition will decrease the enrollment by 25 percent, the elasticity will be large (2.5). In response to an increase in tuition, the college's total revenue will significantly decrease. When you have an elastic demand you should hesitate to increase price. (To make sure you're following the argument, explain the likely effect an elastic demand will have on lowering tuition.)

As another example, recall the vanity license plates that we used to illustrate the law of demand in Chapter 2. A rise in the price of vanity plates of 33 percent, from $30 to $40, decreased the quantity demanded about 50 percent, from 60,334 to 31,122, so the elasticity was about 50%/33% = 1.5. The percent decrease in quantity exceeded the percent increase in price, so total revenue fell from

$$\$30 \times 60{,}334 = \$1{,}810{,}020$$

to

$$\$40 \times 31{,}122 = \$1{,}244{,}880$$

Elasticity and the Demand Curve

Let's now see how to calculate the elasticity in the area around a point on a demand curve. In Exhibit 3 we do so for a hypothetical demand curve facing a college.

Say it's thinking of raising tuition from $900 to $945, an increase of 5 percent (45/900). Doing so will cause it to move along the demand curve from point *A* to point *B*. Extending lines down to the quantity axis we can see that this will cause enrollment to fall from 300 to 255, a decrease of 15 percent (45/300). Remembering that elasticity is defined as the percent change in quantity divided by the percent change in price, we can now calculate the elasticity of the demand curve at point *A*. It's 15%/5% = 3.

The elasticity at the initial price and initial quantity (point *A*) is 3. But after the price change, we will be at point *B*—the new price of $945 and the new quantity of 255. The elasticity at point *B* is (45/255)/(45/945) which equals 3.71. That's as exact a measure as we can give of elasticity over a range of points on a demand curve. It's somewhere between 3 and 3.71.

Q–8: As you move down along a straight line demand curve, what happens to the elasticity of that demand curve?

These calculations point out an important fact: elasticity changes at different points on a straight line demand curve. To see this more clearly, let's consider a point further away from points *A* and *B*—point *C*—and, again, a 5 percent tuition increase. What is the elasticity of demand at this point? Extending our lines down to the quantity axis, we can see that quantity will decrease from 900 to 885, a decrease of $15/900 = 1.67\%$. So the elasticity of point C is approximately $(15/900)/(15/300) = .33$. It's fallen substantially.

Now let's think a bit more about the question of what elasticity was facing the university president who was thinking of raising price from $900 (point A) to $945 (point B). The elasticity at the initial point was 3 and at the point she would move to it was 3.7. So what do you tell her the elasticity facing her is?

Economists, quite reasonably, use an average of the two when describing the elasticity of a section of a demand curve. The average can be calculated using the *arc elasticity method*. **Arc elasticity** is the average elasticity of a range of points on a demand curve. It's calculated in the following manner: Instead of dividing the changes in price and quantity by one end point or the other, you add both end points and divide them by 2. Doing so using the facts in our previous example gives:

Arc elasticity   The average elasticity of a range of points on a demand curve.

$$\text{Arc } E_d = \frac{\dfrac{45}{(255 + 300)/2}}{\dfrac{45}{(900 + 945)/2}} = 3.32$$

In the real world, elasticities are calculated with statistical techniques, with a great amount of effort devoted to distinguishing between movement along a demand curve and shifts of a demand curve. Because of difficulties in distinguishing these two, our estimates of elasticities are rough and ready and can easily vary by, say, 20 or even 40 percent up or down. Thus, while economists give specific elasticities for demand curves, we interpret those numbers loosely.

Elasticity Is Not a Slope   In thinking about elasticity in relation to a demand curve, students make the common mistake of saying *elasticity* but thinking *slope*. Remember that elasticity isn't the same as slope. Slope tells us what will happen to quantity demanded when price changes. In Exhibit 3 the slope of the demand curve is -1. And since it's a straight line, its slope is -1 at every point on that demand curve. That isn't the case for elasticity. Elasticity changes at each point on a straight-line demand curve.

As a review of elasticity, let's consider more carefully the relationship between elasticity and total revenue and see how it can be demonstrated graphically.

The relationship between elasticity and total revenue is no mystery. There's a very logical reason why they are related, which can most neatly be seen by recognizing that total revenue $(P \times Q)$ is represented by the area under the demand curve at that price and quantity. For example, at point A on demand curve D_1 in Exhibit 4(a), the total revenue at price $4 and quantity 6 is the area designated by the A and B rectangles, $24.

If we increase price to $5, quantity demanded decreases to 5, so total revenue is now $25. Total revenue has increased slightly, so the demand curve at point A is slightly inelastic, but close to unit elasticity. The new total revenue is represented by the A and C rectangles. The difference between the old total revenue (A and B) and the new total revenue (A and C) is the difference between the rectangles B and C. Comparing these rectangles provides us with a visual method of estimating elasticities. Comparing the size of these two rectangles, let's see what happens to total revenue.

In Exhibit 4(b) we consider an inelastic point; in Exhibit 4(c) we consider a highly elastic point. While in Exhibit 4(b) the slope of the demand curve is the same as in Exhibit 4(a), we're at a different point on the demand curve (point B). If we raise our price from $1 to $2, quantity demanded falls from 9 to 8. The gained area (rectangle C) is much greater than the lost area (rectangle B). In other words, total revenue increases significantly, so the demand curve at point B is highly inelastic.

In Exhibit 4(c) the demand curve is again the same, but we're at still another point, C. If we raise our price from $8 to $9, quantity demanded falls from 2 to 1. The gained area (rectangle C) is much smaller than the lost area (rectangle B). In other

Elasticity and Total Revenue: A Closer Look

Q–9: If you are a seller, would you be more likely to raise your price with an inelastic or an elastic demand curve? Why?

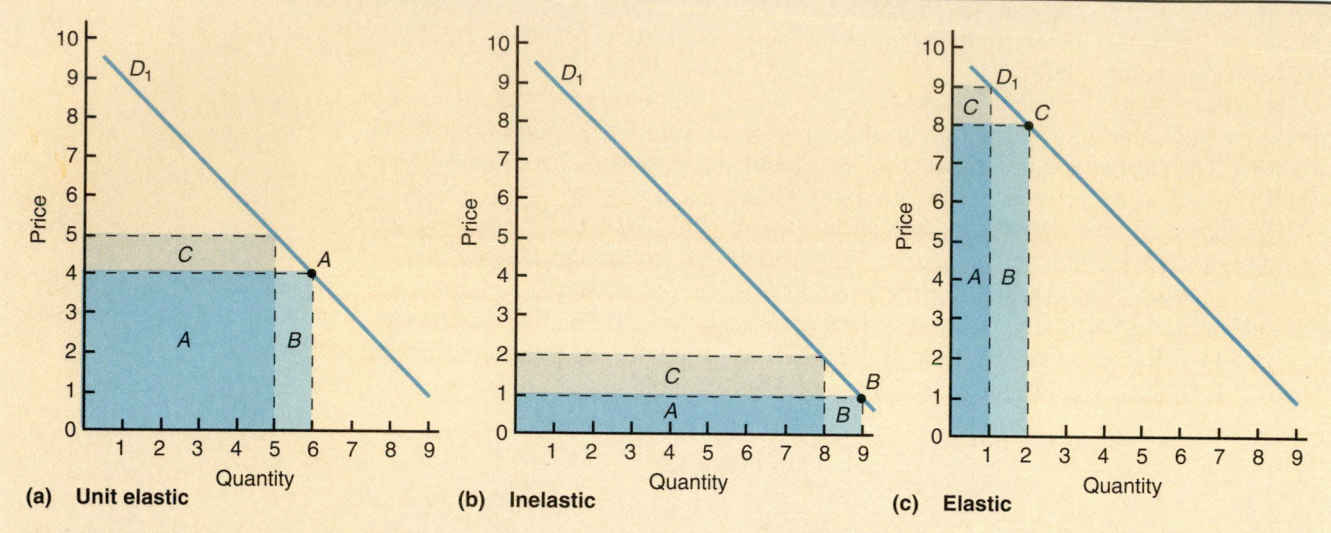

EXHIBIT 4 (a, b, and c)   **Elasticity and Total Revenue**

Total revenue is measured by the rectangle one gets by extending lines from the demand curve to the price and quantity axes. The change in total revenue resulting from a change in price can be estimated by comparing the size of the before and after rectangles. If price is being raised, total revenue increases by rectangle *C* and decreases by rectangle *B*. As you can see, the effect of a $1 price rise on total revenue differs significantly at different points on a demand curve. **(a)** shows an almost unitary elastic point, **(b)** shows an inelastic point, and **(c)** shows an elastic point.

words, total revenue decreases significantly, so the demand curve at point *C* is highly elastic.

Notice that the elasticity of a straight-line demand curve changes as you move along that demand curve. The way in which elasticity changes and its relationship to total revenue can be seen in Exhibit 5.

When output is zero, total revenue is zero; similarly when price is zero, total revenue is zero. That accounts for the two end points of the total revenue curve in Exhibit 5(b). Let's say we start at a price of zero, where demand is very inelastic. As we increase price (decrease quantity demanded), total revenue increases significantly. As we continue to do so, the increases in total revenue become smaller until finally, after output of Q_0, total revenue actually starts decreasing. It continues decreasing at a faster and faster rate until finally, at zero output, total revenue is zero. These relationships are summarized in Exhibit 5(c).

Perfectly Elastic and Inelastic Demand Curves   Economists have developed terminology other than *elastic* and *inelastic* to describe two special cases; the case in which the demand curve is perfectly horizontal (slope = 0) and the case in which the demand curve is perfectly vertical (slope = infinity). When the demand curve is perfectly horizontal, the elasticity is infinite. Economists describe such a curve as **perfectly elastic.**

When the demand curve is perfectly vertical, the elasticity is zero. Economists describe such a demand curve as **perfectly inelastic.** If one raises price with a perfectly elastic demand curve, total revenue falls to zero; and if one raises price with a perfectly inelastic demand curve, total revenue increases proportionately. A perfectly elastic (D_2) and a perfectly inelastic (D_1) demand curve are demonstrated in Exhibit 5(d).

Perfectly elastic   *Horizontal demand curve. E_d = infinity.*

Perfectly inelastic   *Vertical demand curve. E_d = 0.*

The Influence of Substitution on the Elasticity of Demand

Now that you know how to measure elasticity of demand, let's consider some of the factors that are likely to make demand more or less elastic. The influence of these factors can be summed up in one word: *substitution.* As a general rule, *the more substitutes a good has, the more elastic is its demand.*

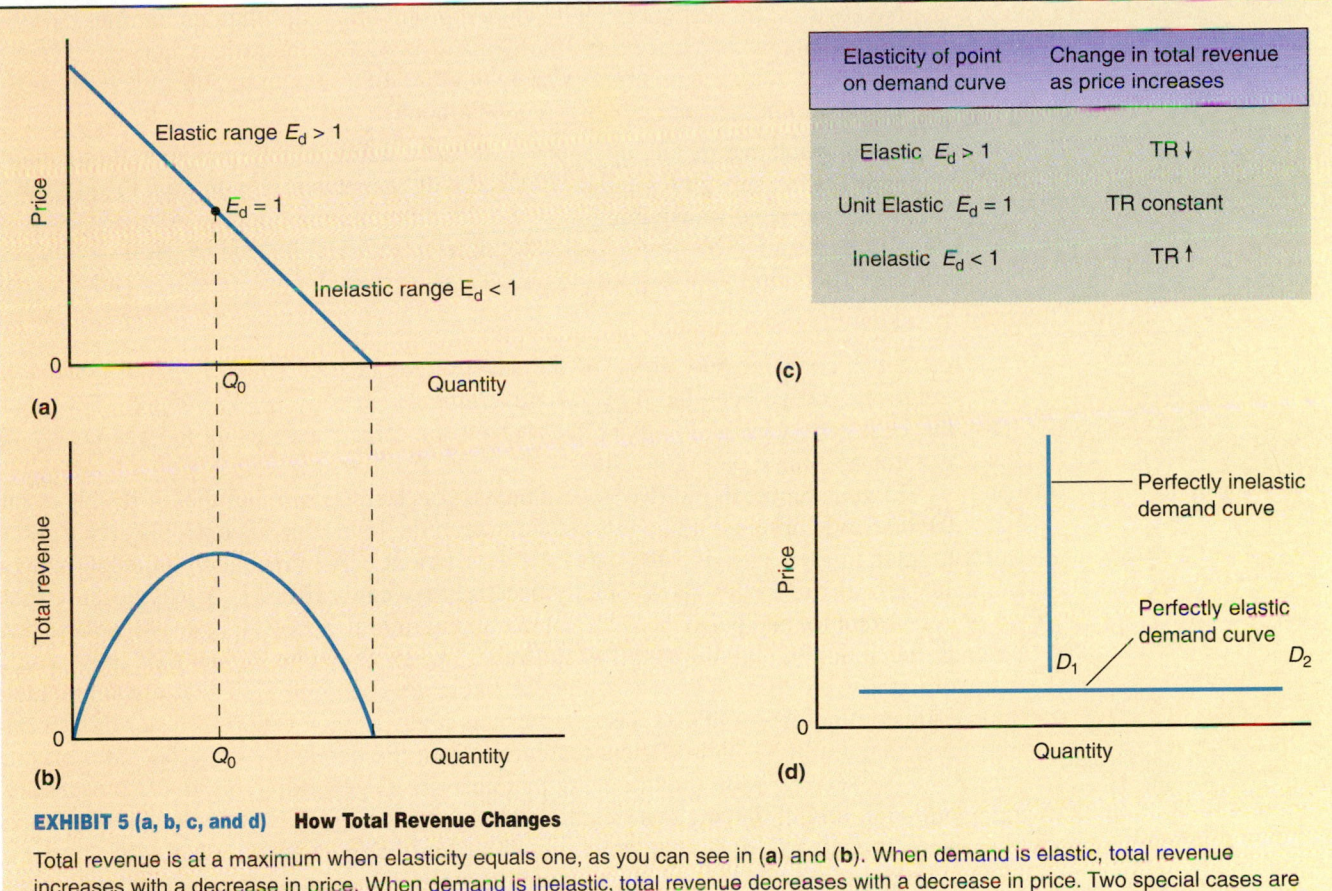

Elasticity of point on demand curve	Change in total revenue as price increases
Elastic $E_d > 1$	TR ↓
Unit Elastic $E_d = 1$	TR constant
Inelastic $E_d < 1$	TR ↑

EXHIBIT 5 (a, b, c, and d)   How Total Revenue Changes

Total revenue is at a maximum when elasticity equals one, as you can see in (a) and (b). When demand is elastic, total revenue increases with a decrease in price. When demand is inelastic, total revenue decreases with a decrease in price. Two special cases are shown in (d). A perfectly inelastic curve is vertical; total revenue will increase substantially with any rise in price. A perfectly elastic curve is horizontal; total revenue will fall to zero with any rise in price.

The reasoning is as follows: If a good has substitutes, a price rise for that good will cause the demander to shift consumption to those substitute goods. When a satisfactory substitute for a good is available, a rise in that good's price will have a large effect on the quantity demanded, and the demand curve will tend to be elastic. For example, I think a Whopper is a satisfactory substitute for a Big Mac; if most people agree with me, the demand for Big Macs is very elastic.

The number of substitutes a good has is affected by several factors:

1. The larger the time interval considered, or the longer the run, the more elastic is the demand curve for the goods.

2. The less a good is a necessity, the more elastic is its demand curve.

3. The more specifically a good is defined, the more elastic is its demand curve.

7 As a general rule, the more substitutes a good has, the more elastic is its demand.

These three reasons are derivatives of the substitution factor. Let's consider each to see why.

1. There are more substitutes in the long run than in the short run. That's because the long run provides more options for change. For example, let's consider the World War II period when the price of rubber went up considerably. In the short run, there were few substitutes; the demand for rubber was inelastic. In the long run, however, the rise in the price of rubber stimulated research for alternatives. Many alternatives were found. Today automobile tires, which were all made of rubber at the time World War II broke out, are almost entirely made from synthetic materials. In the long run, the demand curve was very elastic.

2. Necessities, by definition, tend to have fewer substitutes than do luxuries. Insulin for a diabetic is a necessity; the demand is highly inelastic. Chocolate ecstasy cake, however, is a luxury. A variety of other luxuries can be substituted for it (for example, cheesecake, a ball game, or a book).

3. If the good we're talking about is broadly defined (say, transportation), there aren't many substitutes and the demand will be inelastic. If you want to get from *A* to *B*, you need transportation. If the definition of the good is narrowed (say, to "transportation by bus"), there are more substitutes. Instead of taking a bus you can walk, ride your bicycle, or drive your car. In that case the demand curve is more elastic.

Let's consider how some of the substitution factors affect a specific decision. Let's say you've been hired by two governments (the city of Washington, D.C., and the U.S. government) to advise them about the effect that raising the gas tax by 10 percent will have on tax revenues.

In your report to the two governments, you would point out that in the short run the demand curve would be less elastic than in the long run, since people aren't going to trade in their gas-guzzling cars for fuel-efficient cars immediately in response to a 10 percent rise in gas taxes—partly because they can't afford to, partly because they don't want to, and partly because not that many fuel-efficient cars are available to buy at the moment. In the long run, however, when the time comes that they would ordinarily purchase a new car, they're likely to switch to cars that are more fuel-efficient than their old cars, and to switch as much as they can to forms of transportation that are more fuel-efficient than cars. Then the demand will be far more elastic.

The second point you'd note is that gasoline is generally considered a necessity, although not all driving is necessary. However, since gasoline is only a small part of what it costs to drive a car, the demand will probably tend to be inelastic.

Q–10: Why is price elasticity generally larger in the long run than in the short run?

As for the third factor (how broadly defined the good we're talking about is) you have to be careful. It makes your recommendations for the government of the city of Washington, D.C., and the U.S. government quite different from each other. For the U.S. government, which is interested in the demand for gasoline in the entire United States, gasoline has a relatively inelastic demand. The general rule of thumb is that a 1¢ rise in tax will raise tax revenues by $1 billion. That inelasticity can't be carried over to the demand for gasoline in a city such as Washington, D.C. Because of the city's size, people in Washington have a choice. A large proportion of the people who buy gas in Washington could as easily buy gas in Maryland or Virginia. Gasoline in Washington is a narrowly defined good and therefore has a quite *elastic* demand. A rise in price will mean a large fall in the quantity of gas demanded.

I mention this point because in August 1980 someone forgot about it when the city of Washington raised the tax on a gallon of gasoline by 8¢, a rise at that time of about 5 percent. In response, monthly gasoline sales in Washington fell from 16 million gallons to 11 million gallons, a 40 percent decrease! The demand for gas in Washington was not inelastic, as it was for the United States as a whole; it was very elastic ($E_d = 8$). Washingtonians went elsewhere to buy gas. Within four months the city had repealed the tax increase.

The fact that smaller geographic areas have more elastic demands limits how highly state and local governments can tax goods relative to their neighboring localities or states. Where there are differences, new stores open all along the border and existing stores expand to entice people to come over that border and save on taxes. For example, the liquor tax is higher in Vermont than in New Hampshire, so it isn't surprising that right across the border from Vermont, New Hampshire has a large number of liquor stores. Here's one final example: If you look at license plates in Janzen Beach, Oregon (right across the Washington state border), you'll see mostly Washington license plates. Why? If you answered that it likely has something to do with differential sales taxes in Washington and Oregon, you've got the idea.

W hile price elasticity is the elasticity that economists most often talk about, elasticity is a general concept that relates percent changes in something with percent changes in something else.

One frequently used elasticity is *cross price elasticity of demand* (the percent change in quantity of one good divided by the percent change in price of another good). An example of where cross price elasticity might be important is a hot dog and ketchup. The price of hot dogs can influence the demand for ketchup. (Notice we used "demand," not "quantity demanded," to emphasize that in response to a change in anything but the price of that good, the entire demand curve shifts; there's no movement along the demand curve.)

Another commonly used elasticity term is *income elasticity of demand,* the percent change in demand that will result from a percent change in income.

$$E_I = \frac{\text{Percent change in demand}}{\text{Percent change in income}}$$

As an example, say your income goes up by 100 percent and your demand for Big Macs goes up by 50 percent. Your income elasticity for Big Macs would be:

$$\frac{50\%}{100\%} = \frac{1}{2}$$

The following table presents income elasticities measured for some groups of goods.

Commodity	Income Elasticity Short run	Income Elasticity Long run
Motion pictures	.81	3.41
Foreign travel	.24	3.09
Household electricity	.14	1.94
Intercity bus transportation	.17	1.89
Tobacco products	.21	0.86
Radio and TV repairs	.64	5.20
Food produced and consumed on farms	−.61	—
Furniture	2.60	0.53
Jewelry and watches	1.00	1.64

Source: Hendrik S. Houthakker and Lester D. Taylor, *Consumer Demand in the United States: Analyses and Projections,* 2nd ed. (Cambridge, Mass.: Harvard University Press, 1970).

In the short run, people often save increases in income, so most goods, other than impulse-bought goods, have low income elasticities. To avoid this problem, economists generally focus on long-run income elasticities. Notice that some goods have long-run income elasticities less than 1, which means that their consumption doesn't keep pace with rises in income. These tend to be relative necessities (goods that are necessities compared to other goods). Other goods have long-run elasticities greater than 1; their consumption more than keeps pace with rises in income. They tend to be relative luxuries.

Finally, notice the one good—food produced and consumed on farms—with a negative income elasticity. As mentioned earlier in the text, such goods are called *inferior goods.* As income rises, people not only decrease the proportionate amount they spend on such goods; they decrease the absolute amount they spend.

Exhibit 6 presents empirical estimates of elasticity of demand. Notice that, as expected, different estimates are provided for the short- and long-run elasticities of each good. Also notice that the estimates are for the entire United States; if one were doing estimates for a specific region in the United States, the estimates could be expected to show more elasticity.

Taking an example from Exhibit 6, notice that the long-run demand for movies is elastic. If movie theaters raise their prices, it's relatively easy for individuals simply to

EXHIBIT 6   Short-Run and Long-
Run Elasticities of Demand

Product	Price Elasticity	
	Short run	Long run
Radio and television repair	0.47	3.84
Tobacco products	0.46	1.89
Electricity (for household consumption)	0.13	1.89
Stationery	0.47	0.56
Medical care and hospitalization insurance	0.31	0.92
Intercity bus trips	0.20	2.17
Toys (nondurable)	0.30	1.02
Movies/motion pictures	0.87	3.67
Foreign travel by U.S. residents	0.14	1.77

Source: Hendrik S. Houthakker and Lester D. Taylor, *Consumer Demand in the United States: Analyses and Projections,* 2nd ed. (Cambridge, Mass.: Harvard University Press, 1970).

stay home and watch television. Thus, intuitively we consider movies to have close substitutes, so we would expect the demand to be relatively elastic.

As a second example, in the short run the demand for electricity is highly inelastic. People either have electrical appliances or they don't. In the long run, however, it becomes elastic since people can shift to gas for cooking and oil for heating, and can buy more energy-efficient appliances.

As an exercise, you might see if you can explain why each of the other goods listed in the table has the elasticity of demand reported.

Individual and Market Demand Elasticity

In thinking about demand elasticity, keep in mind the point made in Chapter 2: The market demand curve is the horizontal summation of individual demand curves, and some individuals have highly inelastic demands and others have highly elastic demands. A slight rise in the price of a good will cause some people to stop buying the good; the slight increase won't affect other people's demand for the good at all. Demand elasticity is influenced both by how many people drop out totally and by how much an existing consumer marginally changes his or her quantity demanded.

If a firm can somehow separate the people with less elastic demand from those with more elastic demand, it can charge more to the individuals with inelastic demands and less to individuals with elastic demands. We see examples of firms trying to do just that throughout the economy. Let's consider three:

1. Airlines' Saturday stay-over specials. If you stay over a Saturday night, usually you can get a much lower airline fare than if you don't. The reason is that businesspeople have inelastic demands and don't like to stay over Saturday nights, while pleasure travelers have more elastic demands. By requiring individuals to stay over Saturday night, airlines can separate out businesspeople and charge them more.

2. The phenomenon of selling new cars. Most new cars don't sell at the listed price. They sell at a discount. Salespeople are trained to separate out comparison shoppers (who have more elastic demands) from impulse buyers (who have inelastic demands). By not listing the selling price of cars so that the discount can be worked out in individual negotiations, salespeople can charge more to customers who have inelastic demands.

3. The almost-continual-sale phenomenon. Some items, such as washing machines, go on sale rather often. Why don't suppliers sell them at a low price all the time? Because some buyers whose washing machines break down have inelastic demand. They can't wait, so they'll pay the "unreduced" price. Others have

Stores conduct short-run sales in order to price discriminate.   © *Susan McCartney/Photo Researchers, Inc.*

elastic demands; they can wait for the sale. By running sales (even though they're frequent sales), sellers can separate demanders with inelastic demand curves from demanders with elastic demand curves.

CONCLUSION

That's the end of our introduction to individual choice theory. There was a lot to learn, but I hope that the facts and applications that were combined with it made it more palatable. Whether it was or was not palatable, it's a necessary chapter. Economists are continually thinking about, empirically measuring, and applying the analysis and terminology in this chapter. Their conversations are dotted with *elastic, inelastic,* and applications of the principle of rational choice.

An economist friend, Arjo Klamer, and I did a survey in which we asked economics graduate students whether they often applied the principle of rational choice in their daily lives. They overwhelmingly answered yes. A few students wrote, "Doesn't everyone?" Even those graduate economics students who didn't like the principle of rational choice and the selfishness it implied about human nature still applied the principle of rational choice in analyzing real-world events. Their comments included, "Yes, I am brainwashed," and "Very often in spite of myself."

One of the goals of the book set forth in Chapter 1 is to get you to think like an economist. If I were to choose one principle that's central to thinking like an economist, the principle of rational choice would be it. Look at the world around you and apply the principle: Look for some phenomenon that doesn't seem as if it could have been a rational choice and then think harder because, from some perspective, it will have an explanation that accords with the principle of rational choice.

The fact that the principle of rational choice can explain everything doesn't mean that it's the best explanation imaginable. It's important to look at as many different explanations as possible, empirically testing when possible to choose among alternative explanations and, when it's impossible to test, keeping in the back of your mind various alternative explanations. Some economists believe that the principle of rational choice provides the best explanation of almost all events. Other economists believe that social and political factors must be built into the explanations of almost all events. But all economists in some way use the principle of rational choice in approaching problems. That's why this chapter is so important.

The fact that the principle of rational choice can explain everything doesn't mean that it's the best explanation imaginable.

CHAPTER SUMMARY

- The principle of diminishing marginal utility states that as you consume more of an item, the additional units of consumption will yield fewer utils than the first units.
- The principle of rational choice is:

If $\dfrac{MU_x}{P_x} > \dfrac{MU_y}{P_y}$, choose to consume more of good x.

If $\dfrac{MU_x}{P_x} < \dfrac{MU_y}{P_y}$, choose to consume more of good y.

If $\dfrac{MU_x}{P_x} = \dfrac{MU_y}{P_y}$, you're maximizing utility; you're indifferent between good x and good y.

- The law of demand can be derived from the principle of rational choice.
- To apply economists' analysis of choice to the real world, one must carefully consider, and adjust for, the underlying assumptions, such as costlessness of decision making and given tastes.
- A good is a substitute for another good if its consumption goes up when the price of the other good goes up; a good is a complement for another good if its consumption goes down when the price of the other good goes up.
- Economists describe demand curves by their elasticity.
- If one raises price and has: an elastic demand curve, total revenue falls; an inelastic demand curve, total revenue rises; a unitary elastic demand curve, total revenue is unchanged.
- The more substitutes a good has, the more elastic its demand curve.

KEY TERMS

arc elasticity *(501)*
bounded rationality *(495)*
complements *(494)*
diminishing marginal utility *(488)*
elastic *(499)*
focal point equilibrium *(496)*

inelastic *(499)*
inferior goods *(495)*
marginal utility *(487)*
normal goods *(495)*
perfectly elastic *(502)*
perfectly inelastic *(502)*

price elasticity of demand *(498)*
principle of rational choice *(490)*
substitutes *(494)*
total utility *(487)*
unitary elasticity *(499)*
utility *(487)*

QUESTIONS FOR THOUGHT AND REVIEW

The number after each question represents the estimated degree of critical thinking required. (1 = almost none; 10 = deep thought.)

1. How would the world be different than it is if the principle of diminishing marginal utility seldom held true? *(8)*

2. It is sometimes said that an economist is a person who knows the price of everything but the value of nothing. Is this statement true or false? Why? *(9)*

3. Assign a measure of utility to the study you are putting into your various courses. Do your study habits follow the principle of rational choice? *(6)*

4. The marginal utility of your consumption of widgets is 40; it changes by 2 with each change in widgets consumed. The marginal utility of your consumption of wadgets is also 40 but changes by 3 with each change in widgets consumed. The price of widgets is $2 and the price of wadgets is $3. How many widgets and wadgets should you consume? *(4)*

5. What key psychological assumptions do economists make in their theory of individual choice? *(7)*

6. Explain your motivation for four personal decisions you have made in the past year, using economists' model of individual choice. *(7)*

7. Determine the elasticity of demand if, in response to an increase in price of 10 percent, quantity decreased by 20 percent. Would it be elastic or inelastic? *(3)*

8. A firm has just increased its price by 5 percent over last year's price, and it found that quantity sold remained the same. The firm comes to you and wants to know its elasticity of demand. How would you calculate it? What additional information would you search for before you did your calculation? *(7)*

9. Why would an economist be more hesitant about making an elasticity estimate of the effect of an increase in price of 1 percent rather than an increase in price of 50 percent? *(6)*

10. Demand for "prestige" college education is generally considered to be highly inelastic. What does this suggest about tuition increases at prestige schools in the future? Why don't colleges raise tuition by amounts even greater than they already do? *(9)*

PROBLEMS AND EXERCISES

1. *a.* The following table gives the price and total utils of three goods: A, B, and C.

		Total utility							
Good	Price	1	2	3	4	5	6	7	8
A	$10	200	380	530	630	680	700	630	430
B	2	20	34	46	56	64	72	78	82
C	6	50	60	70	80	90	100	90	80

As closely as possible, determine how much of the three goods you would buy with $20. Explain why you chose what you did.

b. The following table gives the marginal utility of John's consumption of three goods: A, B, and C.

Units of consumption	MU of A	MU of B	MU of C
1	20	25	45
2	18	20	30
3	16	15	24
4	14	10	18
5	12	8	15
6	10	6	12

(1) Good A costs $2 per unit, good B costs $1, and good C costs $3. How many units of each should a consumer with $12 buy to maximize his or her utility?

(2) How will the answer change if the price of B rises to $2?

(3) How about if the price of C is 50¢ but the other prices are as in part (1)?

2. As your annual income increases from $50,000 to $55,000, your quantity of meat demanded increases from 300 to 350 pounds.
   a. Calculate your income elasticity of demand for meat.
   b. What additional information would you want to have to ensure that your answer is correct?
   c. If your income falls to $25,000, what would you predict would happen to your quantity of meat demanded?

3. In the "Added Dimension" box on income elasticities, the short-run elasticity for furniture was higher than the long-run elasticity. What is a likely explanation for that?

4. Early Classical economists found the following "diamond/ water" paradox perplexing: "Why is water, which is so useful and necessary, so cheap, when diamonds, which are

so useless and unnecessary, so expensive?" Using the utility concept explain why it is not really a paradox.

5. The president of a liberal arts college in Pennsylvania asked economist Paul Heise about the effect of a particular proposal on net income, enrollment, and student GPA. The proposal was the following: "For the incoming class: (a) cut tuition for students in the top 10 percent of their high school class by 50 percent; (b) cut tuition for students in the 10th to 20th percent of their high school class by 33 percent; (c) cut tuition for students in the 20th to 30th percent of their high school class by 25 percent; (d) leave tuition the same for all others." He believed the demand was highly elastic.
   a. What was Professor Heise's response?
   b. What would his response have been if the demand had been highly inelastic?

6. Nobel Prize-winning economist, George Stigler, explains how the famous British economist, Phillip Wicksteed, decided where to live. His two loves were fresh farm eggs, which were more easily obtained the farther from London he was, and visits from friends, which decreased the further he moved away from London. Given these two loves, describe the decision rule that you would have expected Wicksteed to follow.

7. You are buying your spouse, significant other, or close friend a ring. You decide to show your reasonableness, and buy a cubic zirconium ring that sells at 1/50 the cost of a mined diamond and that any normal person could not tell from a mined diamond just by looking at it. In fact, the zirconium will have more brilliance and fewer occlusions (imperfections) than a mined diamond.
   a. How will your spouse (significant other, close friend) likely react?
   b. Why?
   c. Is this reaction justified?

8. Economists William Hunter and Mary Rosenbaum wrote an article in which they estimated the demand elasticity for motor fuel as between .4 and .85.
   a. If the price rises 10 percent and the initial quantity sold is 10 million gallons, what is the range of estimates of the new quantity demanded?
   b. In carrying out their estimates they came up with different elasticity estimates for rises in prices than for falls in prices, with an increase in price having a larger elasticity than a decrease in price. What hypothesis might you propose for their findings?

ANSWERS TO MARGIN QUESTIONS

1. False. Economists' theory of choice does not require them to measure utility. It only requires that the marginal utility of one good be compared to the marginal utility of another. *(487)*

2. If the total utility curve were a straight line, the marginal utility curve would be flat with a slope of zero since

marginal utility would not change with additional units. *(488)*

3. False. The principle of diminishing marginal utility is that as one increases consumption of a good, the good's marginal utility decreases. *(489)*

4. Because both give the same marginal utility but good B

costs twice as much, we should decrease our consumption of good B and increase our consumption of good A. This will increase the marginal utility of good B and decrease the marginal utility of good A. We should continue changing until the ratio of marginal utility to prices of the goods are equal. *(490)*

5. The three formulas for the principle of rational choice are: *(490)*

If $\dfrac{MU_x}{P_x} > \dfrac{MU_y}{P_y}$, choose to consume an additional unit of good x.

If $\dfrac{MU_x}{P_x} < \dfrac{MU_y}{P_y}$, choose to consume an additional unit of good y.

If $\dfrac{MU_x}{P_x} = \dfrac{MU_y}{P_y}$, you're maximizing utility; you cannot increase your utility by adjusting your choices.

6. Economic reasoning is the logical application of a simple idea, individual choice theory, to a variety of problems. It leads people to ask about institutions: ''What's in it for the people making the decisions?'' This question can often be subversive to existing establishments. *(498)*

7. The elasticity of demand is defined as the percentage change in quantity divided by the percentage change in price. In this case, it would be 1. *(500)*

8. As you move down along a straight line demand curve, the elasticity of demand decreases until, at the quantity axis, it equals zero. *(500)*

9. As a seller, I would be more likely to raise my price with an inelastic demand, since then a rise in price would increase my total revenue. *(501)*

10. There tend to be more substitutes in the long run than in the short run, which is why the price elasticity is generally larger in the long run. *(504)*

Indifference Curve Analysis

As I stated in the chapter, analyzing individual choice using cardinal utility (giving utility actual numbers) is unnecessary. In the chapter, I asked you to make a deal with me: You'd remember that cardinal utility is unnecessary and I'd use cardinal numbers. This appendix is for those who didn't accept my deal (and for those whose professors want them to get some practice in graphish). It presents an example of a more formal analysis of individual choice.

Sophie's Choice

Sophie is a junk food devotee. She lives on two goods: chocolate bars, which cost $1 each, and cans of soda, which sell for 50¢ apiece. Sophie is trying to get as much pleasure as possible, given her income. Alternatively expressed, Sophie is trying to maximize her utility, given an income constraint.

By translating this statement of Sophie's choice into graphs, I can demonstrate the principle of individual choice without ever mentioning any specific amount of utility.

The graph we'll use will have chocolate bars on the vertical axis and cans of soda on the horizontal axis, as in Exhibit A1.

Graphing the Income Constraint

Let's begin by asking: How can we translate her income constraint (the $10 maximum she has to spend) into graphish? The easiest way to do that is to ask what would happen if she spent her $10 all on chocolate bars or all on cans of soda. Since a chocolate bar costs $1, if she spends it all on chocolate bars she can get 10 bars (point A in Exhibit A1). If she spends it all on cans of soda, she can get 20 cans of soda (point B). This gives us two points.

But what if she wants some combination of soda and chocolate bars? If we draw a line between points A and B, we'll have a graphical picture of her income constraint and can answer that question because that line shows us

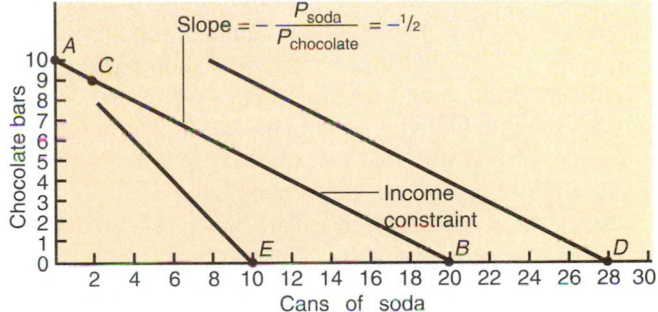

EXHIBIT A1   **Graphing the Income Constraint**

the various combinations she can buy. The line is her income constraint in graphish.

To see that it is, say Sophie is spending all her money on chocolate bars. She then decides to buy one fewer chocolate bar. That gives her $1 to spend on soda, which, since those cans cost 50¢ each, allows her to buy 2 cans. Point C (9 chocolate bars and 2 cans of soda) represents that decision. Notice how point C is on the income constraint. Repeat this exercise from various starting points until you're comfortable with the fact that the line does indeed represent the various combinations of soda and chocolate bars Sophie can buy with the $10. It's a line with a slope of −1/2 and intersects the chocolate bar axis at 10 and the cans-of-soda axis at 20.

To be sure that you've got it, ask yourself what would happen to the income constraint if Sophie got another $4 to spend on the two goods. Going through the same reasoning should lead you to the conclusion that the income constraint will shift to the right so that it will intersect the cans-of-soda axis at 28 (point D), but its slope won't change. (I started the new line for you.) Make sure you can explain why.

Now how about if the price of a can of soda goes up to $1? What happens to the income line? (This is a question many people miss.) If you said the income line becomes steeper, shifting in along the cans-of-soda axis to point *E* while remaining anchored along the chocolate bar axis until the slope equals −1, you've got it. If you didn't say that, go through the same reasoning we went through at first (if Sophie buys only cans of soda . . .) and then draw the new line. You'll see it becomes steeper. Put another way, the absolute value of the slope of the curve is the ratio of the price of cans of soda to the price of chocolate bars; the absolute value of the slope becomes greater with a rise in the price of cans of soda.

Graphing the Indifference Curve

Now let's consider the second part of Sophie's choice: the pleasure part. Sophie is trying to get as much pleasure as she can from her $10. How do we deal with this in graphish?

To see, let's go through a thought experiment. Say Sophie had 14 chocolate bars and 4 cans of soda (point *A* in Exhibit A2). Let's ask her, ''Say you didn't know the price of either good and we took away 4 of those chocolate bars (so you had 10). How many cans of soda would we have to give you so that you would be just as happy as before we took away the 4 chocolate bars?''

Since she's got lots of chocolate bars and few cans of soda, her answer is probably ''Not too many; say, 1 can of soda.'' This means that she would be just as happy to have 10 chocolate bars and 5 cans of soda (point *B*) as she would to have 14 chocolate bars and 4 cans of soda (point *A*). Connect those points and you have the beginning of a ''just-as-happy'' curve. But that doesn't sound impressive enough, so, following economists' terminology, we'll call it an *indifference curve*. She's indifferent between points *A* and *B*.

If you continue our thought experiment, you'll get a set of combinations of chocolate bars and cans of soda like that shown in the table in Exhibit A2.

If you plot each of these combinations of points on the graph in Exhibit A2 and connect all these points, you have one of Sophie's indifference curves: a curve representing combinations of cans of soda and chocolate bars among which Sophie is indifferent.

Let's consider the shape of this curve. First, it's downward sloping. That's reasonable; it simply says that if you take something away from Sophie, you've got to give her something in return if you want to keep her indifferent between what she had before and what she has now.

Second, it's bowed inward. That's because as Sophie gets more and more of one good, it takes fewer and fewer of another good to compensate for the loss of the good she incurred in order to get more of the other good. The underlying reasoning is similar to that in our discussion of the law of diminishing marginal utility, but notice we haven't even mentioned utility. Technically the reasoning for the indifference curve being bowed inward is called *the law of diminishing marginal rate of substitution*. It tells us that as you get more and more of a good, if some

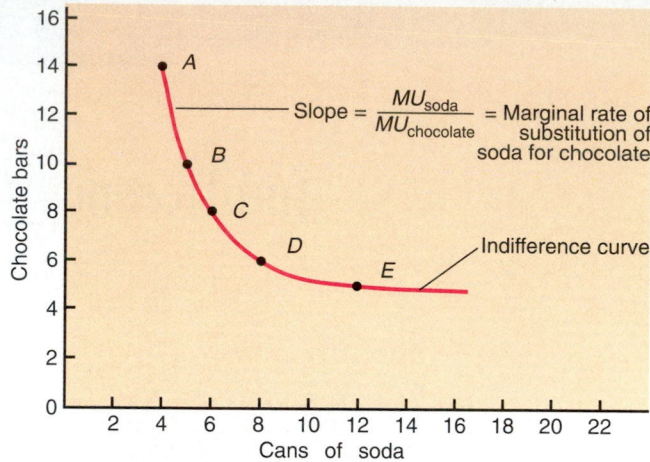

Chocolate bars	Cans of soda	
14	4	*A*
10	5	*B*
8	6	*C*
6	8	*D*
5	12	*E*

EXHIBIT A2   **Sophie's Indifference Curve**

of that good is taken away, then the marginal addition of another good you need to keep you on your indifference curve gets less and less.

Even more technically one can say that the absolute value of the slope of the indifference curve equals the ratio of the marginal utility of cans of soda to the marginal utility of chocolate bars:

$$\text{Slope} = \left| \frac{MU_{\text{soda}}}{MU_{\text{chocolate}}} \right| = \begin{array}{l}\text{Marginal rate} \\ \text{of substitution}\end{array}$$

That ratio equals the marginal rate of substitution of cans of soda for chocolate bars. Let's consider an example. Say that in Exhibit A2 Sophie is at point *A* and that the marginal utility she gets from an increase from 4 to 5 cans of soda is 10. Since we know that she was willing to give up 4 chocolate bars to get that 1 can of soda (and thereby move from point *A* to point *B*), that 10 must equal the loss of utility she gets from the loss of 4 chocolate bars out of the 14 she originally had. So the marginal rate of substitution of cans of soda for chocolate bars between points *A* and *B* must be 4. That's the absolute value of the slope of that curve. Therefore her *MU* of a chocolate bar must be about 2.5 (10 for 4 chocolate bars).

One can continue this same reasoning, starting with various combinations of goods. If you do so, you can get a whole group of indifference curves like that in Exhibit A3. Each curve represents a different level of happiness. Assuming she prefers more to less, Sophie is better off if she's on Curve II than if she's on Curve I, and even better

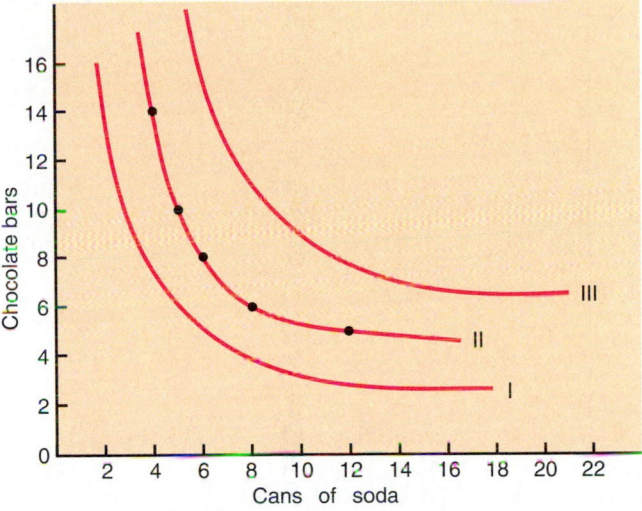

A Group of Indifference Curves

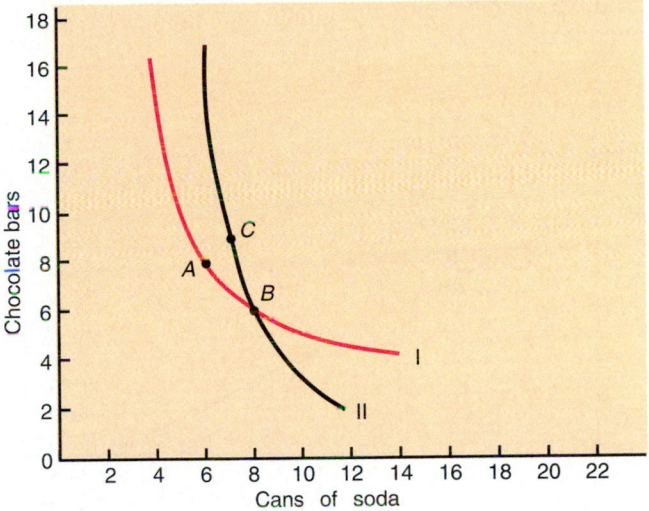

Why Indifference Curves Cannot Cross

off if she's on Curve III. Her goal in life is to get out to the furthest indifference curve she can.

To see whether you've followed the reasoning, ask yourself the following question: "Assuming Sophie prefers more of a good to less (which seems reasonable), can any two of Sophie's indifference curves cross each other as the ones in Exhibit A4 do?"

The answer is no, no, no! Why? Because they're indifference curves. If the curves were to cross, the "prefer-more-to-less" principle would be violated. Say we start at point A: Sophie has 8 chocolate bars and 6 cans of soda. We know that since A (8 chocolate bars and 6 sodas) and B (6 chocolate bars and 8 cans of soda) are on the same indifference curve, Sophie is indifferent between A and B. Similarly with points B and C: Sophie would just as soon have 9 chocolate bars and 7 cans of soda as she would 6 chocolate bars and 8 cans of soda.

It follows by logical deduction that point A must be indifferent to C. But consider points A and C carefully. At point C, Sophie has 7 cans of soda and 9 chocolate bars. At point A she has 6 cans of soda and 8 chocolate bars. At point C she has more of both goods than she has at point A, so to say she's indifferent between these two points violates the "prefer-more-to-less" criterion. Ergo (that's Latin, meaning "therefore") two indifference curves cannot intersect. That's why we drew the group of indifference curves in Exhibit A3 such that they did not intersect.

Combining Indifference Curves and Income Constraint

Now let's put the income constraint and the indifference curves together and ask how many chocolate bars and cans of soda Sophie will buy if she has $10, given the psychological makeup described by the indifference curves in Exhibit A3.

To answer that question, we must put the income line

of Exhibit A1 and the indifference curves of Exhibit A3 together, as we do in Exhibit A5.

As we discussed, Sophie's problem is to get to as high an indifference curve as possible, given her income constraint. Let's first ask if she should move to point A (8 chocolate bars and 10 cans of soda). That looks like a good point. But you should quickly recognize that she can't get to point A; her income line won't let her. (She doesn't have enough money.) Well then, how about point B (7 chocolate bars and 6 cans of soda)? She can afford that combination; it's on her income constraint. The problem with point B is the following: She'd rather be at point C since point C has more chocolate bars and the same amount of soda (8 chocolate bars and 6 cans of soda). But, you say, she can't reach point C. Yes, that's true, but she can reach point D. And, by the definition of indifference curve, she's indifferent between point C and point D, so point D (6 chocolate bars and 8 cans of soda), which she can reach given her income constraint, is preferred to point B.

The same reasoning holds for all other points. The reason is that the combination of chocolate bars and cans of soda represented by point D is the best she can do. It is the point where the indifference curve and the income line are tangent—the point at which the slope of the income line ($-P_s/P_c$) equals the slope of the indifference curve ($-MU_s/MU_c$). Equating those slopes gives $P_s/P_c = MU_s/MU_c$ or:

$$MU_c/P_c = MU_s/P_s$$

This equation, you may remember from the chapter, is the equilibrium condition of our principle of rational choice. So by our graphish analysis we arrived at the same conclusion we arrived at in the chapter, only this time we did it without mentioning cardinal utility. This means that even without a utilometer, economists' principle of rational choice is internally logical.

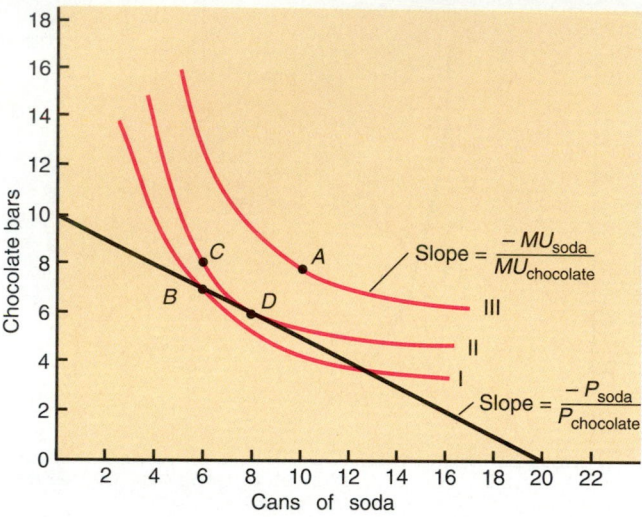

EXHIBIT A5 **Combining Indifference Curves and Income Constraint**

Deriving a Demand Curve from the Indifference Curve

Not only can one derive the principle of rational choice with indifference curve/income line analysis, one can also derive a demand curve. To do so, ask yourself what a demand curve is. It's the quantity of a good that a person will buy at various prices. Since the income line gives us the relative price of a good, and the point of tangency of the indifference curve gives us the quantity that a person would buy at that price, we can derive a demand curve from the indifference curves and income lines. To derive a demand curve we go through a set of thought experiments asking how many cans of soda Sophie would buy at various prices. We'll go through one of those experiments.

We start with the analysis we used before when Sophie started with $10 and chose to buy 8 cans of soda when the price of a can of soda was 50¢ (point A in Exhibit A6(a). That analysis provides us with one point on the demand curve. I represent that by point A in Exhibit A6(b). At a price of 50¢, Sophie buys 8 cans of soda.

Now say the price of a can of soda rises to $1. That rotates the income line in, from income line 1 to income line 2 as in Exhibit A6(a). She can't buy as much as she could before. But we can determine how much she'll buy by the same reasoning we used previously. She'll choose a point at which her lower indifference curve is tangent to her new income line. As you can see, she'll choose point B, which means that she buys 6 cans of soda when the price of a can of soda is $1. Graphing that point (6 cans of soda at $1 each) on our price/quantity axis in Exhibit

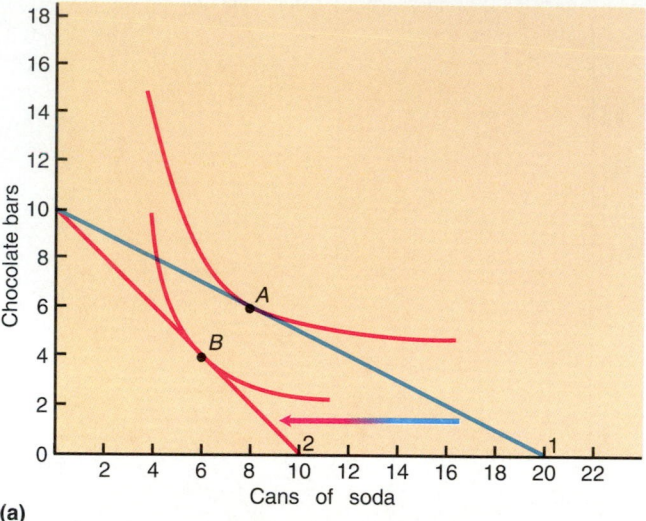

(a)

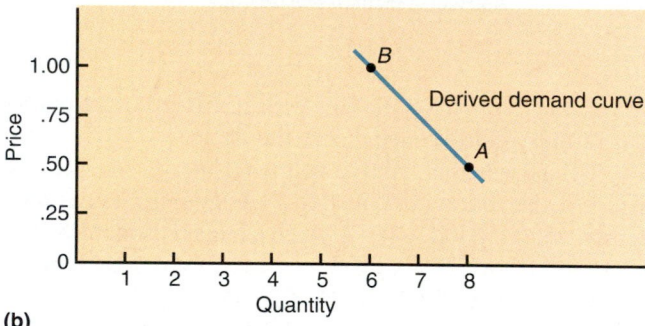

(b)

EXHIBIT A6 (a and b) **From Indifference Curves to Demand Curves**

A6(b), we have another point on our demand curve, point B. Connect these two together and you can see we're getting a downward-sloping demand curve, just as the law of demand said we would. To make sure you understand, continue the analysis for a couple of additional changes. You'll see that the demand curve you derive will be downward-sloping.

There's much more one can do with indifference curves. One can distinguish income effects and substitution effects. (Remember, when the price of a can of soda rose, Sophie was worse off. So to be as well off as before, as is required by the substitution effect, she'd have to be compensated for that rise in price by an offsetting fall in the price of chocolate bars.) But let's make a deal. You tentatively believe me when I say that all kinds of stuff can be done with indifference curves and income constraints, and I'll leave the further demonstration and the proofs for you to experience in the intermediate microeconomics courses.

23

Supply, Production, and Costs

I

*Production is not the application of tools to materials,
but logic to work.*

~Peter Drucker

After reading this chapter, you should be able to:

1 Explain why opportunity costs underlie the law of supply.

2 Define and use the elasticity of supply concept.

3 Distinguish between the long run and the short run.

4 State the law of diminishing marginal productivity and explain its role in determining the shape of short-run cost curves.

5 Distinguish the various kinds of cost curves and describe the relationships among them.

6 Explain why the marginal cost curve always goes through the minimum point of an average cost curve.

The ability of Western market economies to supply material goods and services to members of their societies makes them the envy of many other societies and is one of the strongest arguments for using the market as a means of organizing society. Somehow markets are able to channel individuals' imagination, creativity, and drive into the production of material goods and services that other people want. They do this by giving people incentives to supply goods and services to the market.

Ultimately all supply comes from individuals. Individuals control the factors of production such as land, labor, and capital. Why do individuals supply these factors to the market? Because they want something in return. This means that industry's ability to supply goods is dependent on individuals' willingness to supply the factors of production they control. This connection became obvious in the formerly socialist countries in the late 1980s and early 1990s when consumer goods were unavailable. People in those countries stopped working (supplying their labor). They reasoned: Why supply our labor if there's nothing to get in return?

The analysis of supply is more complicated than the analysis of demand because it involves the production of goods as well as the supply of factors to produce those goods.

The analysis of supply is more complicated than the analysis of demand. In the supply process, people first offer the factors of production they control to the market. Then the factors are transformed by firms, such as GM or IBM, into goods that consumers want.

Complications are a pain for textbook writers; we want to make the analysis simple for you. (Really we do.) So what we do is to separate out the analysis of the supply of factors of production (considered in detail in later chapters) from the supply of produced goods. This allows us to assume that the prices of factors of production are constant in our analysis of the supply of produced goods, which simplifies the analysis enormously. There's no problem with doing this as long as you remember that behind any produced goods are individuals' factor supplies. Ultimately people, not firms, are responsible for supply.

Even with the analysis so simplified, there's still a lot to cover—so much, in fact, that we devote two chapters (this chapter and the next) to considering production, costs, and supply. In this chapter I introduce you to the production process and short-run cost analysis. Then, in the next chapter, I focus on long-run costs and how cost analysis is used in the real world.

SUPPLY, OPPORTUNITY COST, AND REAL PEOPLE

To emphasize the reality that people, not firms, are responsible for supply, let's talk briefly about individuals' decisions to supply factors of production. How do you decide how much labor, capital, or land to supply? The answer lies in the opportunity cost to you of keeping the factor for yourself. Let's use the most relevant example for most of you—your labor.

Opportunity Costs and the Law of Supply

Opportunity cost *The forgone benefit of the next-best alternative.*

1 When you supply a factor, you are forgoing its benefits for yourself. The opportunity cost of that forgone pleasure tends to increase the more you supply, which is why opportunity costs underlie the law of supply.

How much labor will you supply to the market? Think about it using the economic reasoning that is becoming second nature to you (I hope). The answer I'm sure you've arrived at is that it depends on how much you value your leisure, because leisure is what you're forgoing when you work. An hour of leisure is the **opportunity cost** (the forgone pleasure of the next-best alternative) of an hour of work. The same holds true for anything else you supply. Supply ultimately depends on the opportunity cost of the supplier.

Let's consider another example: housing. I worked on this chapter in Bulgaria where there are few hotels. If there are no hotels, where does one stay, you ask? In people's houses. A number of Bulgarians have determined that, given the right price, they're willing to provide visitors with rooms in their houses. The higher the price, the more rooms that are supplied. (The same holds true around college campuses and in places that have special events.) As the price rises, the quantity of a factor supplied to a market expands. Still another example involves truck drivers in the United States. Their hourly pay has fallen in the last ten years as the trucking industry has become more competitive. As this has happened, the quantity of individuals wanting to be truck drivers has decreased.

Some ''goods'' are actually ''bads'' because of the costs associated with holding them (for example, garbage, old tires, and broken cars). The opportunity cost of having them is negative. In that case more people want to get rid of the good than want to hold the good, so the good has a negative price.

Whether something has a positive or negative price depends on supply and demand. If it were discovered that garbage made an excellent fuel, people would pay for garbage. If everyone wanted to be a doctor, instead of paying doctors to treat them, people would pay to be allowed to doctor someone. If you could convince people that work is fun, they would pay you to allow them to work for you. Supply and demand determine the price of goods, but underlying supply and demand are social mores, technology, people's tastes, and the availability and usefulness of resources.

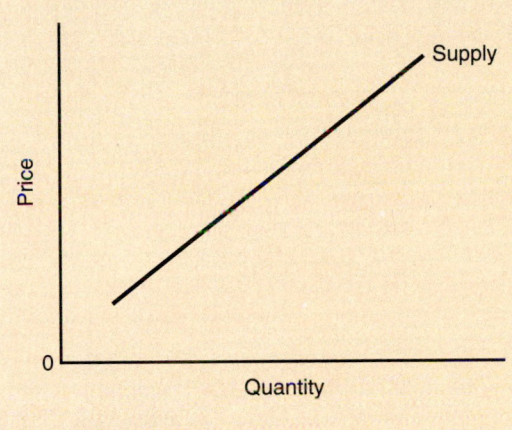

(a) A supply curve

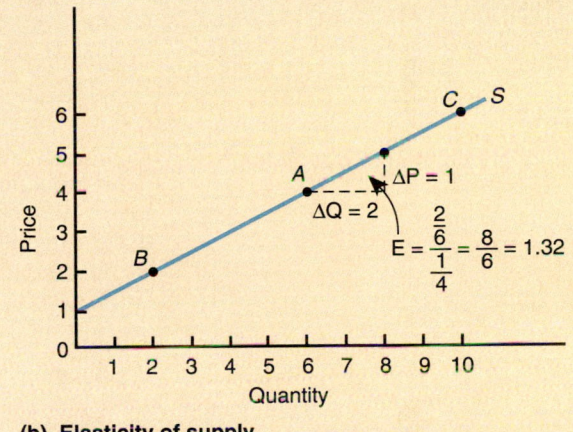

(b) Elasticity of supply

EXHIBIT 1 (a and b)   Supply of Factors of Production

The supply curve of a factor of production is upward sloping as in **(a)**. This follows from the law of supply: When the price of a good increases, the quantity of that good supplied will increase. In **(b)** you can see how elasticity can be calculated. You divide percent change in quantity by percent change in price, and the result is the elasticity at that point.

What this means is that ultimately there's a law of supply, just as there's a law of demand. The law of supply is:

> *When the price of a good increases, the quantity of that good supplied will increase.*

It tells us that the supply curve will be upward sloping as in Exhibit 1.

Like the shape of demand curves, supply curves' shape is described by the concept of elasticity. **Price elasticity of supply** is the percent change in quantity supplied divided by the percent change in price. In common sense terms, it measures the relative responsiveness of quantity supplied evoked by a change in price. Because the supply curve slopes upward, the elasticity of supply is positive so you don't need to use the convention of remembering, but not using, the minus sign, as you had to with the elasticity of demand:

$$E_s = \frac{\text{Percent change in quantity}}{\text{Percent change in price}}$$

Let's consider an example. Say that the quantity of housing supplied to the rental market in an area increases 20 percent when the price goes up 10 percent. The elasticity of supply would be 2.

When the price of a good increases, the quantity of that good supplied will increase.

Elasticity of Supply

Price elasticity of supply   The percent change in quantity supplied divided by the percent change in price.

2 $E_s = \dfrac{\text{Percent change in quantity}}{\text{Percent change in price}}$

Q–1: What is the elasticity of point C in Exhibit 1(b)?

A GEOMETRIC TRICK FOR
ESTIMATING THE ELASTICITY
OF SUPPLY

There's an easy way to estimate the elasticity of any straight-line supply curve. You simply extend it (or a line tangent to it, if it's curved) to one of the axes, as in the accompanying graph. The point at which this extension intersects the axes indicates the elasticity of the supply curve:

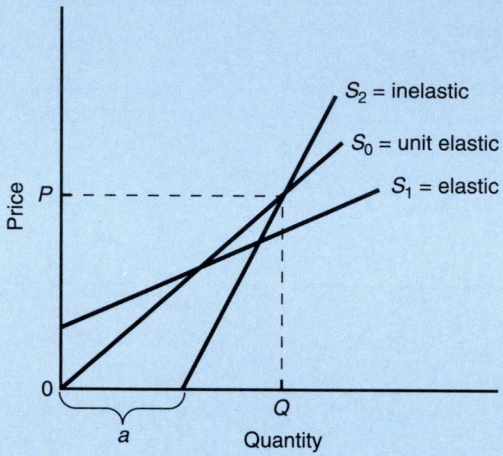

- If the extension intersects the vertical (price) axis, as does S_1, the supply curve has an elasticity greater than 1; the supply curve is elastic.
- If the extension intersects the horizontal (quantity) axis, as does S_2, all points on the supply curve have an elasticity less than 1; the supply curve is inelastic.
- If the extension intersects the two axes at the origin, the supply curve has an elasticity of 1; the supply curve has unit elasticity.

If you combine this trick with a knowledge that a perfectly elastic supply curve is horizontal and a perfectly inelastic supply curve is vertical, you can even remember which is which. If a straight line supply curve crosses the horizontal axis, all points on it are inelastic; if it crosses the vertical axis, all points on it are elastic.

In Exhibit 1(b) you can see how elasticity at a point on the supply curve can be calculated graphically. The point we are considering is point *A,* where $P = \$4.00$ and $Q = 6$. We want to find how much quantity will change when price changes from $4 to $5. As you can see, when price rises from $4 to $5, the quantity rises by 2. So the percent change in quantity is $2/6 = 33$ percent, and the percent change in price is $1/4 = 25$ percent. Then we substitute in our formula (percent change in quantity/percent change in price), which gives us $(2/6)/(2/8)$, or $33\%/25\%$, and arrive at our answer: $33\%/25\% = 1.32$. To see if you've got it, try calculating the elasticity at point B. You should come up with an answer of approximately 2.

Terminology Used to Describe Elasticity of Supply   The same terminology is used to describe elasticity of supply as is used to describe elasticity of demand:

- If the percent change in quantity supplied is less than the percent change in price, the elasticity of supply is less than 1 and the supply is said to be *inelastic.*
- A supply curve that is perfectly vertical (i.e., for which quantity supplied does not change in response to a change in price) is called *perfectly inelastic.*
- If the percent change in the quantity supplied equals the percent change in the price, the elasticity of supply is equal to 1 and the supply has *unit elasticity.*
- If the percent change in the quantity supplied exceeds the percent change in price, the elasticity of supply is greater than 1 and the supply is *elastic.*
- A supply curve that's perfectly horizontal (i.e., for which there's an infinite, or larger than imaginable, quantity response to a change in price) is called *perfectly elastic.*

VALUE ADDED AND THE CALCULATION OF TOTAL PRODUCTION

This book (like all economics textbooks) treats production as if it were a one-stage process—as if a single firm transformed a factor of production into a consumer good. Economists write like that to keep the analysis manageable. (Believe me, it's complicated enough.) But you should keep in mind that reality is more complicated. Most goods go through a variety of stages of production.

For example, consider the production of desks. One firm transforms raw materials into usable raw materials (iron ore into steel); another firm transforms usable raw materials into more usable inputs (steel into steel rods, bolts, and nuts); another firm transforms those inputs into desks, which it sells wholesale to a general distributor, which then sells them to a retailer, which sells them to consumers. Many goods go through five or six stages of production and distribution. As a result, if you added up all the sales of all the firms you would overstate how much total production was taking place.

To figure out how much total production is actually taking place, economists use the concept *value added.* **Value added** is the contribution that each stage of production makes to the final value of a good. A firm's value added is determined by subtracting from the firm's total output the cost of the inputs bought from other firms. For example, if a desk assembly firm spends $4,000 of its revenue on component parts and sells its output for $6,000, its value added is $2,000, or $33\frac{1}{3}$ percent of its revenue.

When you add up all the stages of production, the value added of all the firms involved must equal 100 percent, and no more, of the total output. When I discuss "a firm's" production of a good in this book, to relate that discussion to reality, you should think of that firm as a composite firm consisting of all the firms contributing to the production and distribution of that product.

Why is it important to remember that there are these various stages of production? Because it brings home to you how complicated producing a good is. If any one of those stages gets messed up, the good doesn't get to the consumer. Producing a better mousetrap isn't enough. The firm must also be able to get it out to consumers and let them know that it's a better mousetrap. The standard economic model doesn't bring home this point. But if you're ever planning to go into business for yourself, you'd better remember it. Many people's dreams of supplying a better product to the market have been squashed by this reality.

The Influence of Substitution on the Elasticity of Supply   Just as was the case with elasticity of demand, the most important determinant of elasticity of supply is the number of substitutes for the good. If substitution is easy, supply will be elastic; if substitution is difficult, the supply will be inelastic.

Since most of the issues concerning elasticity of supply are parallel to those of elasticity of demand which I discussed at length last chapter, I'll be brief. As was the case with demand, the ease of substitution depends on the time dimension considered. The shorter the time period, the fewer possibilities of substitution, and the less elastic the supply. Some economists distinguish three time periods. (1) In the instantaneous period, quantity supplied is fixed so the elasticity of supply is perfectly inelastic. This supply is sometimes called the *momentary supply.* (2) In the short run, some substitution is possible, so the *short-run supply* curve is somewhat elastic. (3) In the *long run,* significant substitution is possible—including totally different technologies. The supply curve becomes very elastic and may even become downward sloping.

In determining the elasticity of supply, one must remember that many supplied goods are produced, so we must take into account how easy it is to substitute for existing goods by producing more of that good. And before we can do that we need to talk about the production process in detail.

To make sure you have the general idea, however, let's go through a couple of examples to check whether you can intuitively determine elasticity of supply. Let's first consider land. There's a fixed amount of it; you can't make more of it (at least not easily), so land is very inelastic in supply. (The supply curve is close to vertical.) Now how about ballpoint pens? It's relatively easy to make another pen, so it seems reasonable that the supply of pens will be quite elastic (close to horizontal). As a third example, think about the supply of your labor. How many more hours would you supply if your wage went up by various percentages? Based on that information, determine what your elasticity of labor supply is. (For doing economics, mine is very inelastic.)

Ronald Coase won the Nobel Prize in 1991 for work on the theory of firms and markets. He argued that firms come into existence when the cost of organizing via markets exceeds the cost of organizing via command and control. © *The Nobel Foundation.*

THE PRODUCTION PROCESS

With examples like housing and labor, the law of supply is rather intuitive. These goods already exist and their supply to the market depends on people's opportunity costs of keeping them for themselves and for supplying them to the market. But many of the things we buy (such as VCRs, cars, and jackets) don't automatically exist; they must be produced. The supply of such goods depends upon production. So let's now consider production and see how production relates to supply.

The Role of the Firm in Production

Firm   Economic institution that transforms factors of production into consumer goods.

Transactions costs   Costs of undertaking trades through the market.

A key concept in production is the firm. A **firm** is an economic institution that transforms factors of production into consumer goods. A firm (a) organizes factors of production, (b) produces goods, and/or (c) sells produced goods to individuals.

The firm operates within a market, but, simultaneously, it is a negation of the market in the sense that it replaces the market with command and control. How an economy operates—which activities are organized through markets, and which activities are organized through firms—depends upon **transactions costs**—costs of undertaking trades through the market—and the rent or command over resources that organizers can appropriate to themselves by organizing production in a certain way. Ronald Coase won a Nobel Prize in 1991 for pathbreaking work on the nature of the firm and transactions costs.

In Chapter 4 we talked about the myriad firms that exist in real life. They include sole proprietorships, partnerships, corporations, for-profit firms, nonprofit firms, and cooperatives. These various firms are the production organizations that translate factors of production into consumer goods.

The Long Run and the Short Run

Long-run decision   A decision in which the firm can choose among all possible production techniques.

Short-run decision   Firm is constrained in regard to what production decisions it can make.

The production process is generally broken down into a *long-run* planning decision, in which a firm chooses the least expensive method of producing from among all possible methods, and a *short-run* adjustment decision, in which a firm adjusts its long-run planning decision to reflect new information.

In a **long-run decision** a firm chooses among all possible production techniques. This means that it can choose the size of the plant it wants, the type of machines it wants, and the location it wants. In a **short-run decision** the firm has fewer options; it is constrained in regard to what production decisions it can make.

The terms *long run* and *short run* do not necessarily refer to specific periods of time independent of the nature of the production process. They refer to the degree of flexibility the firm has in changing the level of output. In the long run, by definition, the firm can vary the inputs as much as it wants. In the long run all inputs are variable. In the short run some of the flexibility that existed in the long run no longer exists. In the short run some inputs are so costly to adjust that they are treated as fixed. *So in the long run all inputs are variable; in the short run some inputs are fixed.*

Production Tables and Production Functions

Production table   A table showing the output that will result from various combinations of factors of production or inputs.

How a firm combines factors of production to produce consumer goods can be presented in a **production table** (a table showing the output resulting from various combinations of factors of production or inputs).

Real-world production tables are complicated. They often involve hundreds of inputs, hundreds of outputs, and millions of possible combinations of inputs and outputs. Studying these various combinations and determining which is best requires expertise and experience. Business schools devote entire courses to it (operations research and production analysis); engineering schools devote entire specialties to it (managerial engineering).

Studying the problems and answering the questions that surround the production relationship make up much of what a firm does: What combination of outputs should it produce? What characteristics should those outputs have? What combination of inputs should it use? What combination of techniques should it use? What new techniques should it explore? To answer these questions, the managers of a firm look at a production table.

Production tables are so complicated that in introductory economics we concentrate on short-run production analysis in which one of the factors is fixed. Doing so allows us to capture some important technical relationships of production without

Modern production often involves quite different technology than production formerly did. In this picture we see the status display board in the network operations center of the Ameritech Company.
© *Cameramann/The Image Works.*

getting too tied up in numbers. The relevant part of a production table of widgets appears in Exhibit 2(c).[1] In it the number of the assumed fixed inputs (machines) has already been determined. Columns 1 and 2 of the table tell us how output varies as the variable input (the number of workers) changes. For example, you can see that with 3 workers the firm can produce 17 units of output. Column 3 tells us workers' **marginal product** (the additional output that will be forthcoming from an additional worker, other inputs constant). Column 4 tells us workers' **average product** (output per worker).

It is important to distinguish marginal product from average product. Workers' average product is the total output divided by the number of workers. For example, let's consider the case of five workers. Total output is 28, so average product is 5.6 (28 divided by 5). To find the marginal product we must ask how much additional output will be forthcoming if we change the number of workers. For example, if we change from 4 to 5 workers, the additional worker's marginal product will be 5; if we change from 5 to 6, the additional worker's marginal product will be 3. That's why the marginal products are written between the lines.

The information in a production table is often summarized in a production function. A **production function** is a curve that describes the relationship between the inputs (factors of production) and outputs. Specifically, the production function tells the maximum amount of output that can be derived from a given number of inputs. Exhibit 2(a) is the production function that displays the information in the production table in Exhibit 2(c). The number of workers is on the horizontal axis and the output of widgets is on the vertical axis.

Exhibit 2(b) graphs the workers' average and marginal productivities from the production function in Exhibit 2(a). (Alternatively you can determine those graphs by plotting columns 3 and 4 from the table in Exhibit 2(c).) Notice that both marginal and average productivities are initially increasing, but that eventually they both decrease. Between seven and eight workers, the marginal productivity of workers actually becomes negative.

Marginal product *Additional output forthcoming from an additional input, other inputs constant.*

Average product *Total output divided by the quantity of the input.*

Production function *Equation that describes the relationships between inputs and outputs, telling the maximum amount of output that can be derived from a given number of inputs.*

The Law of Diminishing Marginal Productivity

---

[1] What's a widget? It's a wonderful little gadget that's the opposite of a wadget. (No one knows what they look like or what they are used for.) Why discuss widgets? For the same reason that scientists discuss fruit flies—their production process is simple, unlike most real-world production processes.

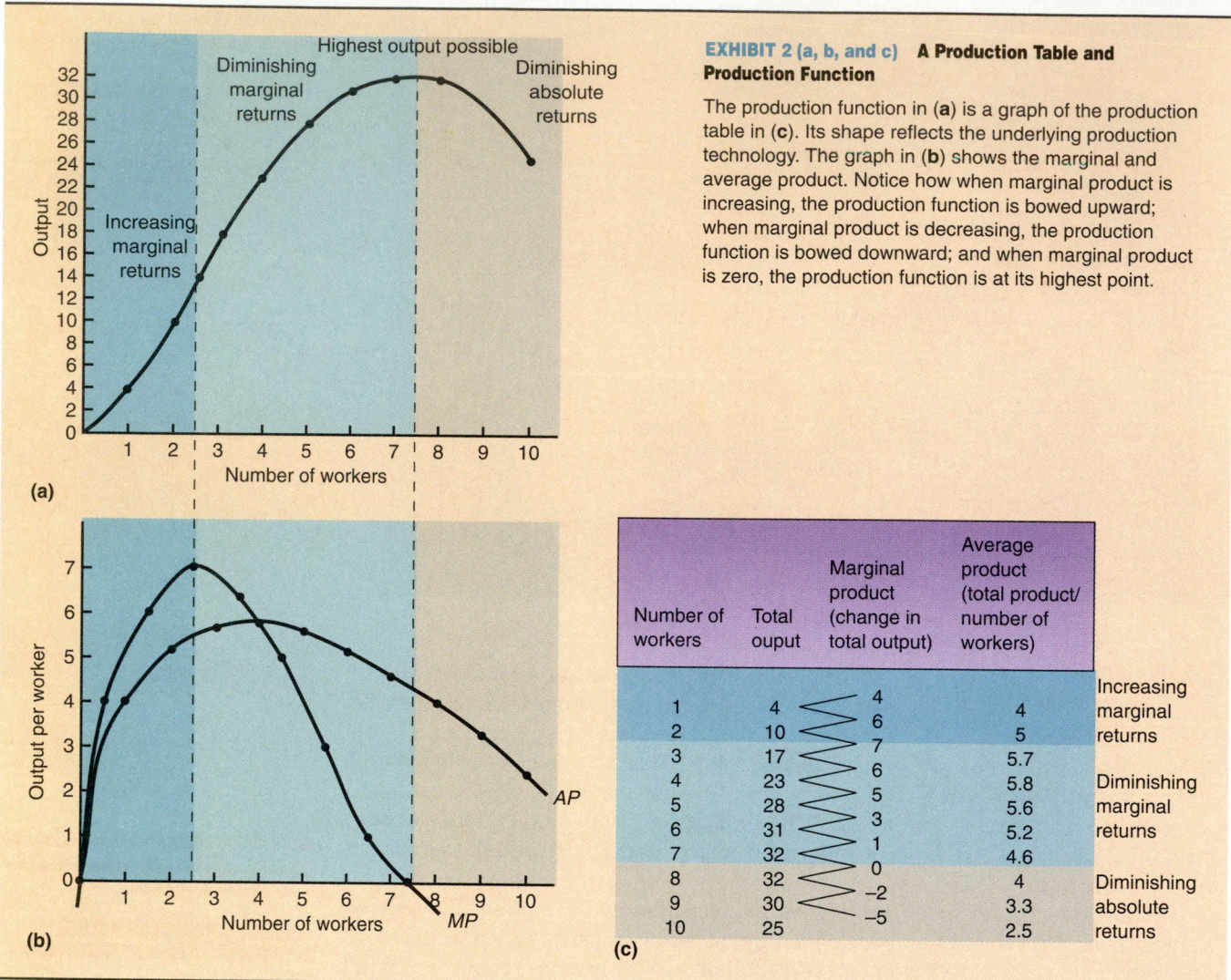

(a)

Highest output possible

Diminishing marginal returns

Diminishing absolute returns

Increasing marginal returns

Output

Number of workers

(b)

Output per worker

Number of workers

AP

MP

EXHIBIT 2 (a, b, and c)   A Production Table and Production Function

The production function in (a) is a graph of the production table in (c). Its shape reflects the underlying production technology. The graph in (b) shows the marginal and average product. Notice how when marginal product is increasing, the production function is bowed upward; when marginal product is decreasing, the production function is bowed downward; and when marginal product is zero, the production function is at its highest point.

Number of workers	Total ouput	Marginal product (change in total output)	Average product (total product/ number of workers)	
1	4	4	4	Increasing marginal returns
2	10	6	5	
3	17	7	5.7	
4	23	6	5.8	Diminishing marginal returns
5	28	5	5.6	
6	31	3	5.2	
7	32	1	4.6	
8	32	0	4	Diminishing absolute returns
9	30	−2	3.3	
10	25	−5	2.5	

(c)

Q–2:   What are the normal shapes of a marginal productivity and an average productivity curve?

This means that initially this production function exhibits increasing marginal productivity and then it exhibits *diminishing marginal productivity*. Eventually it exhibits negative marginal productivity.

The same information can be gathered from Exhibit 2(a), but it's a bit harder to interpret.[2] Notice that initially the production function is bowed upward. Where it's bowed upward there is increasing marginal productivity, as you can see if you extend a line down to Exhibit 2(b). Then, between 2.5 and 7.5 workers, the production function is bowed downward but is still rising. In this range there's diminishing marginal productivity, as you can see by extending a line down to Exhibit 2(b). Finally there's negative marginal productivity.

The most important area of these relationships is the area of diminishing marginal productivity. Why? Because that's the most likely area for a firm to operate in. For example, if it's in the first range and marginal productivity is increasing, a firm can increase its existing workers' output by hiring more workers; it will have a strong incentive to do so and get out of that range. Similarly if hiring an additional worker actually cuts total output (as it does when marginal productivity is negative), the firm would be crazy to hire that worker. So it stays out of that range. This means that the most relevant part of the production function is that part exhibiting diminishing marginal productivity.

---

[2] Technically the marginal productivity curve is a graph of the slope of the total product curve.

THE HISTORY OF THE LAW OF DIMINISHING MARGINAL PRODUCTIVITY

When economists were first formulating their analysis of production, farming was the most important economic activity and most individuals worked on the land. Economists devised their analysis of production to help them structure their ideas about what would happen to total production as the population grew and hence the number of workers increased. In thinking about this issue, they came up with the law of diminishing marginal productivity, which describes what will happen if more and more of a flexible input (labor) is added to a fixed input (land).

The law of diminishing marginal productivity states that eventually, when more and more of a variable input is added to a fixed input, the additional output that results from that additional input decreases.

Initially the law of diminishing marginal productivity was the basis of some gloom-and-doom predictions, which prompted writer Thomas Carlyle to call economics *the dismal science*. The gloom-and-doom predictions were that since the amount of land is fixed, as the population grows, with more workers working the fixed amount of land, eventually the point of diminishing marginal productivity will be reached and the amount of food available per person will decline. Starvation will result, decreasing the population to the subsistence level of output per person. If given any more wages, workers will have more kids and reduce the output per person again to subsistence. This was known as the *iron law of wages:*

Diminishing marginal productivity combined with human beings' uncontrolled sexual drive will result in increases in the supply of labor so that average output and wages will decrease to the subsistence level.

For most Western economies the gloom-and-doom predictions have not come true. Even the originator of the predictions, Thomas Malthus, eliminated them from later editions of *An Essay on Population,* the book in which he first propounded them. Similarly the iron law of wages was soon dropped.

It was not because the law of diminishing marginal productivity doesn't hold true that the gloom-and-doom predictions were dropped. Rather they were dropped because technological changes overwhelmed the law of diminishing marginal productivity. Over time, fewer and fewer individuals have been able to grow more and more output on a smaller amount of land.

While in the United States gloom-and-doom predictions have been overtaken by events, in many developing countries the law of diminishing marginal productivity is very much in effect. In those countries output per individual is decreasing, often to the subsistence level or even below it. Economists in some developing countries believe that not only has the point of diminishing marginal productivity set in, but the point of input saturation has been reached: Output, rather than merely not increasing with additional inputs, actually decreases, and the marginal productivity of additional workers is negative.

This range of the relationship between fixed and variable inputs is so important that economists have formulated a law that describes what happens in production processes when they reach this range—when more and more of one input is added to a fixed amount of another input. It's called the **law of diminishing marginal productivity,** which states that as more and more of a variable input is added to an existing fixed input, eventually the additional output one gets from that additional input is going to fall.

Let's consider the underlying reasoning for this law a bit more carefully. Within the range of diminishing marginal productivity, as you add more workers, they must share the existing machines, so the marginal product of the machines increases and the marginal product of the workers decreases.

As I stated in the introductory chapter, the law of diminishing marginal productivity is sometimes called *the flower pot law* because if it didn't hold true, the world's entire food supply could be grown in one flower pot. In the absence of diminishing marginal productivity, one could take a flower pot and keep adding seeds to it, getting more and more food per seed until one had enough to feed the world. In reality, however, a given flower pot is capable of producing only so much food no matter how many seeds you add to it. At some point, as you add more and more seeds, each additional seed will produce less food than did the seed before it. Eventually the pot reaches a stage of diminishing absolute productivity in which the total output, not simply the output per unit of input, decreases as inputs are increased.

Probably in a firm, far more discussion is about costs than about anything else. Invariably costs are too high and the firm is trying to figure out ways to lower costs. But the concept *costs* is ambiguous; there are many different types of costs and it's

4A The law of diminishing marginal productivity states that as more and more of a variable input is added to an existing fixed input, after some point the additional output one gets from the additional input will fall.

THE COSTS OF PRODUCTION

EXHIBIT 3   **The Cost of Producing Earrings**

1 Output	2 Fixed costs (FC)	3 Variable costs (VC)	4 Total costs (TC) (FC + VC)	5 Marginal costs (MC) (change in total costs)	6 Average fixed costs (AFC) FC/Output	7 Average variable costs (AVC) VC/Output	8 Average total costs (ATC) AFC + AVC
4	$50	$ 50	$100		$12.50	$12.50	$25.00
				$10			
5	50	60	110		10.00	12.00	22.00
10	50	100	150		5.00	10.00	15.00
				6			
11	50	106	156		4.54	9.64	14.18
17	50	150	200		2.94	8.82	11.76
				7			
18	50	157	207		2.78	8.72	11.50
21	50	182	232		2.38	8.67	11.05
23	50	200	250		2.17	8.70	10.87
				10			
24	50	210	260		2.08	8.75	10.83
28	50	250	300		1.79	8.93	10.72
				15			
29	50	265	315		1.72	9.14	10.86
32	50	350	400		1.56	10.94	12.50

important to know these different types. Let's consider some of the most important categories of costs in reference to Exhibit 3, which gives a table of costs associated with making between 4 and 32 pairs of earrings.

Fixed Costs, Variable Costs, and Total Costs

Fixed costs Costs that are spent and cannot be changed in the period of time under consideration.

Fixed costs are costs that are spent and cannot be changed in the period of time under consideration. There are no fixed costs in the long run since all inputs are variable and hence their costs are variable. In the short run, however, a number of costs will be fixed. For example, say you make earrings. You buy a machine for working with silver, but suddenly there's no demand for silver earrings. Assuming that machine can't be modified and used for other purposes, the money you spent on it is a fixed cost.

Fixed costs are shown in column 2 of Exhibit 3. Notice that fixed costs remain the same ($50) regardless of the level of production. As you can see, it doesn't matter whether output is 15 or 20; fixed costs are always $50.

Variable costs The costs of variable inputs; they change as output changes.

Besides buying the machine, the silversmith must also hire workers. These workers are the earring maker's **variable costs.** Variable costs are costs that change as output changes. The earring maker's variable costs are shown in column 3. Notice that as output increases, variable costs increase. For example, when she produces 11 pairs of earrings, variable costs are $106; when she produces 17, variable costs rise to $150.

Total cost Sum of the fixed and variable costs.

All costs are either fixed or variable in the standard model so the sum of her fixed and variable costs equals her **total cost.**

$$TC = FC + VC$$

The earring maker's total costs are presented in column 4. Each entry in column 4 is the sum of the entries in columns 2 and 3 in the same row. For example, to produce 17 pairs of earrings, fixed costs are $50 and variable costs are $150 so total cost is $200.

Average Total Cost, Average Fixed Cost, and Average Variable Cost

Total cost, fixed cost, and variable cost are important, but much of firms' discussion is of average cost. So next distinction we want to make is between total cost and average cost. To arrive at the earring maker's average cost, we simply divide the total amount of whatever cost we're talking about by the quantity produced. Each of the three costs we've discussed has a corresponding average cost.

For example, **average total cost** (often called average cost) equals total cost divided by the quantity produced. Thus:

$$ATC = TC/Q$$

Average fixed cost equals fixed cost divided by quantity produced:

$$AFC = FC/Q$$

Average variable cost equals variable cost divided by quantity produced:

$$AVC = VC/Q$$

Average fixed cost and average variable cost are shown in columns 6 and 7 of Exhibit 3. The most important average cost concept, average total cost, is shown in column 8. Average total cost can also be thought of as the sum of average fixed cost and average variable cost:

$$ATC = AFC + AVC$$

As you can see, the average total cost of producing 17 pairs of earrings is $11.76. It can be calculated by dividing total cost ($200) by output (17).

All these costs are important to our earring maker, but they are not the most important cost she considers in her decision as to how many pairs of earrings to produce. That distinction goes to marginal cost, which appears in column 5.[3] **Marginal cost** is the increased (decreased) total cost of increasing (or decreasing) the level of output by one unit. Let's find marginal cost by considering what happens if our earring maker increases production by one unit—from 10 to 11. Looking again at Exhibit 3, we see that the total cost rises from $150 to $156. In this case the marginal cost of producing the eleventh unit is $6.

The marginal cost concept is extremely important to economic reasoning. But before we get into that, it is important to see how these cost concepts can be presented graphically. It's important for two reasons: First, graphs reinforce your understanding of the cost concepts; and, second, one of the most efficient ways of testing whether you understand the cost concepts is with graphs. So let's say that our earring maker is a visually oriented person who asks you (an economics consultant) to show her what all those numbers in the table in Exhibit 3 mean.

To do so, you first draw a graph, putting quantity on the horizontal axis and a dollar measure of various costs on the vertical axis. In this graphical presentation we will focus on average cost curves because that's what economists generally do. But, for completeness, we will also briefly discuss total cost curves, which, since they are directly related to average cost curves, provide the same information.

Total Cost Curves   Exhibit 4 graphs the total cost, total fixed cost, and total variable cost of all the levels of output given in Exhibit 3.[4] Thus, the total cost curve is determined by plotting the entries in column 1 and the corresponding entries in column 4. For example, point *L* corresponds to a quantity of 10 and a total cost of $150. Notice that the curve is upward sloping: Increasing output increases total cost.

The total fixed cost curve is determined by plotting column 1 and column 2 on the graph. The total variable cost curve is determined by plotting column 1 and column 3.

As you can see, the total variable cost curve has the same shape as the total cost curve: Increasing output increases variable cost. This isn't surprising, since the total cost curve is the vertical summation of total fixed cost and total variable cost. For

---

Average total cost (often called average cost)   Total cost divided by the quantity produced.

Average fixed cost   Fixed cost divided by quantity produced.

Average variable cost   Variable cost divided by quantity produced.

$$ATC = AFC + AVC$$

Marginal Cost

Marginal cost   The cost of changing the level of output by one unit.

Q–3: What is the normal shape of a marginal cost curve?

Graphing Cost Curves

---

[3] Since only selected output levels are shown, not all entries have marginal costs. For a marginal cost to exist, there must be a marginal change, a change by only one unit.

[4] To keep the presentation simple, we focus only on the most important part of the total cost curve, that part that follows the simplest rules. Other areas of the total cost curve can be bowed downward rather than bowed upward.

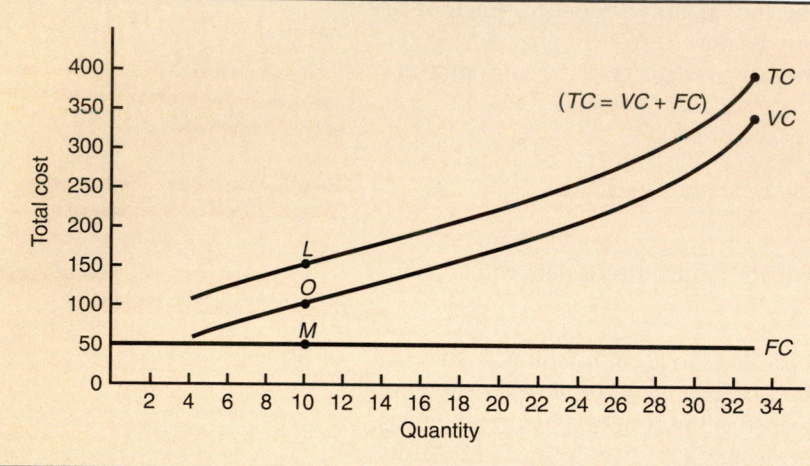

EXHIBIT 4 Total Cost Curves

Total fixed costs are always constant; they don't change with output. All other total costs increase with output. As output gets high the rate of increase has a tendency to increase.

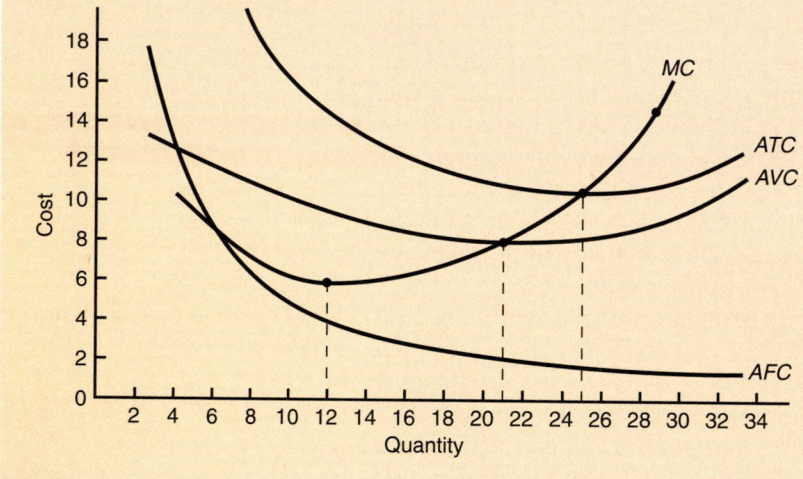

EXHIBIT 5 Per Unit Output Cost Curves

The average fixed cost curve is downward sloping; the average variable cost curve and average total cost curve are U-shaped. The U-shaped *MC* curve goes through the minimum points of the *AVC* and *ATC* curves..

5 As can be seen in Exhibit 5, the marginal cost curve goes through the minimum point of the average total cost curve and average variable cost curve; each of these curves is U-shaped. The average fixed costs curve slopes down continuously.

Q–4: Draw a graph of both the marginal cost curve and the average cost curve.

Q–5: What determines the distance between the average total cost and the average variable cost?

example, at output 10, total fixed cost equals $50 (point *M*); total variable cost equals $100 (point *O*); and total cost equals $150 (point *L*).

Average and Marginal Cost Curves   In Exhibit 5, I present the average fixed cost curve, average total cost curve (or average cost curve, as it's generally called), average variable cost curve, and marginal cost curve associated with the cost figures in Exhibit 3. Each point on the four curves represents a combination of two corresponding entries in Exhibit 3. Points on the average variable cost curve are determined by plotting the entries in column 1 and the corresponding entries in column 7. Points on the average fixed cost curve are determined by entries in column 1 and the corresponding entries in column 6. Points on the average total cost curve are determined by entries in column 1 and the corresponding entries in column 8. Finally, the marginal cost curve is determined by plotting the entries in column 1 and the corresponding entries in column 5. As was the case with the total cost curves, all our earring maker need do is look at this graph to find the various costs associated with different levels of output.

One reason the graphical visualization of cost curves is important is that the graphs of the curves give us a good sense of what happens to costs as we change output.

Downward Sloping Shape of the Average Fixed Cost Curve   Let's start our consideration with average fixed cost. Average fixed cost is decreasing throughout. The average fixed cost curve looks like a child's slide: It starts out with a steep decline; then it

THE $5,000 FLASHLIGHT

■ I've used simple examples in this chapter to keep the terminology clear. Now, let's briefly discuss a more relevant example: LEDs (light-emitting diodes). These diodes are the little electronic gadgets that light up digital watches, calculator displays, and the like. A small number of companies produce these.

As part of the development process, all major producers continually try to find new uses for these LEDs. One company recently made a technological breakthrough that allowed it to produce a much more powerful version, which lights up brightly enough to illuminate large signs and uses far less electricity than the alternatives. To demonstrate the power of these new LEDs, the company had somewhere around 200 flashlights built, like the one pictured here.

Because the developmental costs of these LEDs were enormous, the division of the company that worked on them was assigned a large overhead cost, all of which was fixed in relation to output. But only a small number of flashlights were made. If one were to calculate the average costs of these flashlights, that average total cost would be about $5,000 apiece. The company gave them away. Was the

John Thoeming.

company simply being nice? No. These flashlights helped create demand and show the power of the company's technological breakthrough, increasing the demand for LEDs and thereby spreading the fixed costs to a greater number of units, significantly lowering the average cost per unit.

---

becomes flatter and flatter. What this tells us about production is straightforward: As output increases, the same fixed cost can be spread over a wider range of output, so average fixed cost falls. Average fixed cost initially falls quickly but then falls more and more slowly. As the denominator gets bigger while the numerator stays the same, the increase has a smaller and smaller effect.

The Law of Diminishing Marginal Productivity and the U-Shape of the Average and Marginal Cost Curves

Let's now move on to the average and marginal cost curves. Why do they have the shapes they do? Or expressed another way, how does our analysis of production relate to our analysis of costs? You may have already gotten an idea of how production and costs relate if you remembered Exhibit 2 and recognized the output numbers that we presented there were the same output numbers that we used in the cost analysis. The reason they were the same is that the cost analysis is of that earlier production analysis. The laws governing costs are the same laws governing productivity that we just saw in our consideration of production.

When output is increased in the short run, it can only be done by increasing the variable input. But as more and more of a variable input is added to a fixed input, the law of diminishing marginal productivity enters in. Marginal and average productivities fall. The key insight here is that when marginal productivity falls, marginal cost must rise, and when average productivity of the variable input falls, average variable cost must rise. So to say that productivity falls is the equivalent to saying that cost rises.

It follows that if eventually the law of diminishing marginal productivity holds true, then eventually both the marginal cost curve and the average cost curve must be upward sloping. And, indeed, in our examples they are. It's also generally held that at low levels of production, marginal and average productivities are increasing. This means that marginal cost and average variable cost are initially falling. If they're falling initially and rising eventually, at some point they must be neither rising nor falling. This means that both the marginal cost curve and the average variable cost curve are U-shaped.

The average total cost curve is the vertical summation of the average fixed cost curve and the average variable cost curve, so it's always higher than both of them. As you can see in Exhibit 5, the average total cost curve has the same general U-shape as

4B As more and more of a variable input is added to a fixed input, the law of diminishing marginal productivity causes marginal and average productivities to fall. As these fall, marginal and average costs rise.

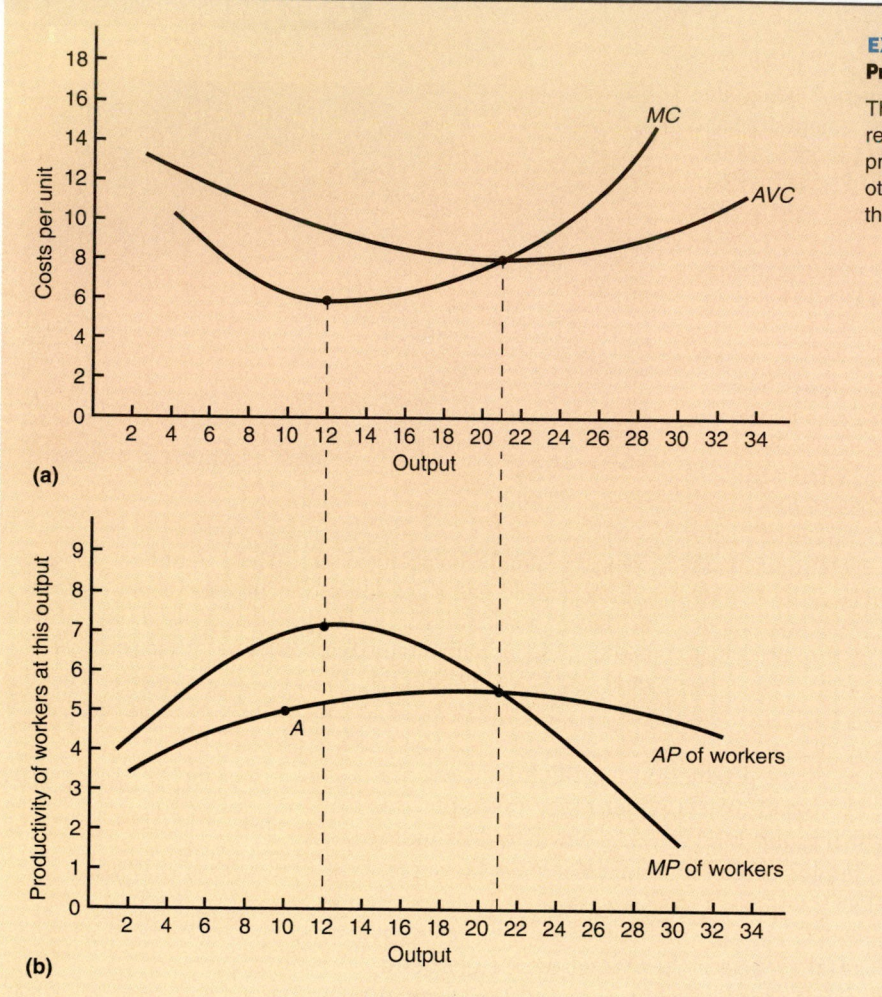

EXHIBIT 6 (a and b) The Relationship between Productivity and Costs

The shapes of the cost curves are mirror-image reflections of the shapes of the corresponding productivity curves. When one is increasing, the other is decreasing; when one is at a minimum, the other is at a maximum.

the average variable cost curve, but its low point is to the right of the low point for the average variable cost curve. We'll discuss why after we cover the shape of the average variable cost curve.

Average total cost initially falls faster and then rises more slowly than average variable cost. If one increased output enormously, the average variable cost curve and the average total cost curve would almost meet. Average total cost is of key importance to our earring maker. She wants to keep it low.

Q–6: If you increase output enormously, what two cost curves would almost meet?

The Relationship between the Marginal Productivity and Marginal Cost Curves
In Exhibit 6(a), I redraw the marginal cost curve and average variable cost curve presented in Exhibit 5. Notice their U-shape. Initially costs are falling. Then there's some minimum point. After that, costs are rising.

In Exhibit 6(b), I graph the average and marginal productivity curves that we first developed in Exhibit 2(b), although this time I relate average and marginal productivities to output, rather than to the number of workers. Thus, we know that the average product of two workers is 5, and that two workers can produce an output of 10, so when output is 10, the worker's average productivity is 5. Point A corresponds to an output of 10 and average productivity of 5.

Now let's compare the graphs in (a) and in (b). If you look at the two graphs carefully, you'll see that one is simply the mirror image of the other. The minimum point of the average variable cost curve (output = 21) is at the same level of output as the maximum point of the average productivity curve; the minimum point of the marginal cost curve (output = 12) is at the same level of output as the maximum point on the marginal productivity curve. When the productivity curves are falling, the

Q–7: When the marginal cost equals the minimum point of the average variable cost, what is true about the average productivity and marginal productivity of workers?

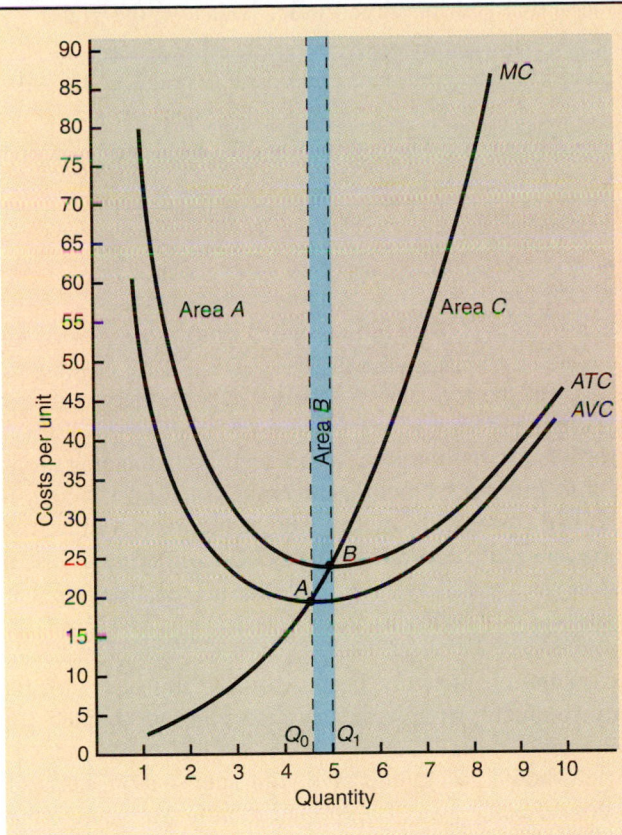

EXHIBIT 7 **Relationship of Marginal Cost Curve to Average Variable Cost and Average Total Cost Curves**

EXHIBIT 7 **Relationship of Marginal Cost Curve to Average Variable Cost and Average Total Cost Curves**

The marginal cost curve goes through the minimum point of both the average variable cost curve and the average total cost curve. Thus there is a small range where average total costs are falling and average variable costs are rising.

corresponding cost curves are rising. Why is that the case? Because as productivity falls, costs per unit increase; and as productivity increases, costs per unit decrease.

When the productivity curves are falling, the corresponding cost curves are rising.

The Relationship between the Marginal Cost and Average Cost Curves Now that we've considered the shapes of each cost curve, let's consider some of the important relationships among them—specifically the relationships between the marginal cost curve on the one hand and the average variable cost and average total cost curves on the other. These relationships are shown graphically for a different production process in Exhibit 7.

Let's first look at the relationship between marginal cost and average total cost. In areas *A* and *B* at output below 5, even though marginal cost is rising, average total cost is falling. Why? Because in areas *A* and *B* the marginal cost curve is below the average total cost curve. At point *B,* where average total cost is at its lowest, the marginal cost curve intersects the average total cost curve. In area *C,* above output 5, where average total cost is rising, the marginal cost curve is above the *ATC* curve.

The positioning of the marginal cost curve is not happenstance. The position of marginal cost relative to average total cost tells us whether average total cost is rising or falling.

6 When marginal cost exceeds average cost, average cost must be rising. When marginal cost is less than average cost, average cost must be falling. This relationship explains why marginal cost curves always intersect the average cost curve at the minimum of the average cost curve.

If MC > ATC, then ATC is rising.
If MC = ATC, then ATC is at its low point.
If MC < ATC, then ATC is falling.

If $MC > ATC$, then ATC is rising.
If $MC = ATC$, then ATC is at its low point.
If $MC < ATC$, then ATC is falling.

To understand why this is, think of it in terms of your grade point average. If you have a B average and you get a C on the next test (that is, your marginal grade is a C), your grade point average will fall below a B. Your marginal grade is below your average grade, so your average grade is falling. If you get a C+ on the next exam (that is, your marginal grade is a C+), *even though your marginal grade has risen from a C to a C+,* your grade point average will fall. Why? Because your marginal grade is still below your average grade. To make sure you understand the concept, explain the next two cases:

Q-8: If marginal costs are increasing, what is happening to average total costs?

Q–9: If marginal costs are decreasing, what is happening to average variable costs?

If $MC > AVC$, then AVC is rising.
If $MC = AVC$, then AVC is at its low point.
If $MC < AVC$, then AVC is falling.

Q–10: Why does the marginal cost curve intersect the average total cost curve at the minimum point?

1. If your marginal grade is above your average grade, your average grade will rise.
2. If your marginal grade and average grade are equal, the average grade will remain unchanged.

Marginal and average reflect a general relationship that also holds for marginal cost and average variable cost.

If $MC > AVC$, then AVC is rising.
If $MC = AVC$, then AVC is at its low point.
If $MC < AVC$, then AVC is falling.

This relationship is best seen in area B of Exhibit 7 when output is between Q_0 and Q_1. In this area the marginal cost curve is above the average variable cost curve, so average variable cost is rising; but the MC curve is below the average total cost curve, so average total cost is falling.

The intuitive explanation for what is represented in this area is that average total cost includes average variable cost, but it also includes average fixed cost, which is falling. As long as short-run marginal cost is only slightly above average variable cost, the average total cost will continue to fall. Put another way: Once marginal cost is above average variable cost, as long as average variable cost doesn't rise by more than average fixed cost falls, average total cost will still fall.

At this point I'm going to cut off the chapter, not because we're finished with the subject, but because there's only so much that anyone can absorb in one chapter. It's time for a break.

Those of you who are married should go out and give your spouse a big kiss; tell him or her that the opportunity cost of being away for another minute was so high that you couldn't control yourself. Those of you with kids, go out and read them a Dr. Seuss book. (My favorite is about Horton.) Let's face it—Seuss is a better writer than I, and if you've been conscientious about this course, you may not have paid your kids enough attention. Those of you with significant others, go out and do something significant. Those of you with parents bearing the cost of this education, give them a call and tell them that you appreciate their expenditure on your education. Think of the opportunity cost of that education to them; it's not peanuts. We'll return to the grind in the next chapter.

INTERMISSION

Dr. Seuss books are often more interesting than economics books.

CHAPTER SUMMARY

• No one is going to supply a good to the market unless the price he will get for that good exceeds the opportunity cost of that good.

• Price elasticity of supply is the percent change in quantity divided by the percent change in price.

• In the long run a firm can choose among all possible production techniques; in the short run it is constrained in its choices.

• The law of diminishing marginal productivity states that as more and more of a variable input is added to a fixed

input, the additional output the firm gets will eventually be decreasing.

• Costs are generally divided into fixed costs, variable costs, and total costs.

• The average variable cost curve and marginal cost curve are mirror images of the average product curve and the marginal product curve, respectively.

• If $MC > ATC$, then ATC is rising.
If $MC = ATC$, then ATC is constant.
If $MC < ATC$, then ATC is falling.

KEY TERMS

average fixed cost *(525)*
average product *(521)*
average total cost *(525)*
average variable cost *(525)*
firm *(520)*
fixed costs *(524)*
law of diminishing marginal
  productivity *(523)*

long-run decision *(520)*
marginal cost *(525)*
marginal product *(521)*
opportunity cost *(516)*
price elasticity of supply *(517)*
production function *(521)*
production table *(520)*
short-run decision *(520)*

total cost *(524)*
transactions costs *(520)*
value added *(519)*
variable costs *(524)*

QUESTIONS FOR THOUGHT AND REVIEW

The number after each question represents the estimated degree of critical thinking required. (1 = almost none; 10 = deep thought.)

1. State the law of supply and explain how it relates to opportunity cost. *(5)*

2. If the supply curve is perfectly inelastic, what is the opportunity cost of the supplier? *(6)*

3. "There is no long run; there are only short and shorter runs." Evaluate that statement. *(8)*

4. What is the difference between marginal product and average product? *(3)*

5. If average product is falling, what is happening to short-run average variable cost? *(3)*

6. If marginal cost is increasing, what do we know about average cost? *(4)*

7. If average productivity falls, will marginal cost necessarily rise? How about average cost? *(4)*

8. Say that neither labor nor machines are fixed but that there is a 50 percent quick order premium paid to both workers and machines for delivery of them in the short run. Once you buy them, they cannot be returned, however. What do your short-run marginal cost and short-run average total cost curves look like? *(9)*

9. If machines were variable and labor fixed, how would the general shapes of the short-run average cost curve and marginal cost curve change? *(6)*

10. If you increase production to an infinitely large level, the average variable cost and the average total cost will merge. Why? *(4)*

PROBLEMS AND EXERCISES

1. Find and graph the *TC, AFC, AVC, AC,* and *MC* from the following table.

Units	FC	VC
0	$100	$ 0
1	100	40
2	100	60
3	100	70
4	100	85
5	100	130

2. An economic consultant is presented with the following table on average productivity and asked to derive a table for average variable costs. The price of labor is $15 per hour.

Labor	TP
1	5
2	15
3	30
4	36
5	40

   a. Help him do so.
   b. Show that the graph of the average productivity curve

and average variable cost curve are mirror images of each other.

   c. Show the marginal productivity curve for outputs between 1 and 5.
   d. Show that the marginal productivity curve and marginal cost curve are mirror images of each other.

3. In one of the "Added Dimension" boxes in this chapter, there are three statements about the elasticities of straight-line supply curves. One of those statements is that supply curves intersecting the quantity axis are inelastic. Can you prove that that is true by algebraic manipulation of the elasticity formula?

4. A firm has fixed costs of 100 and variable costs of the following:

Output	1	2	3	4	5	6	7	8	9
Variable costs	35	75	110	140	175	215	260	315	390

   a. Graph the AFC, ATC, AVC, and MC curves.
   b. Explain the relationship between the MC curve and the two average cost curves.
   c. Say fixed costs dropped to 50. Graph the new AFC, ATC, AVC, and MC curves.
   d. Which curves shifted in *c?* Why?

5. Say that a firm has fixed costs of 200 and constant variable costs of 25.
    a. Graph the AFC, ATC, AVC, and MC curves.
    b. Explain why the curves have the shapes they do.
    c. What law is not operative for this firm?
    d. Say that instead of increasing by a constant 25, variable costs increase by 5 for each unit, so that

the cost of 1 is 25, the cost of 2 is 30, the cost of 3 is 35, and so on. Graph the AFC, ATC, AVC, and MC curves associated with these costs.
    e. Explain how costs would have to increase in *d* in order for the curves to have the "normal" shapes of the curves presented in the text.

ANSWERS TO MARGIN QUESTIONS

1. The elasticity of point C is 1.2. *(517)*

2. Normally the marginal productivity curve and average productivity curve are both inverted U-shaped. *(522)*

3. The normal shape of a marginal cost curve is U-shape. *(525)*

4. As you can see in the graph below, both these curves are U-shaped and the marginal cost curve goes through the average cost curve at the minimum point of the average cost curve. *(526)*

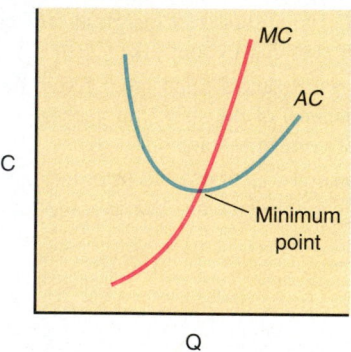

5. The distance between the average total cost and the average variable cost is determined by the average fixed

cost at that quantity. If quantity increases, the average fixed cost decreases, so the two curves get closer and closer together. *(526)*

6. As output increases, the average total costs and average variable costs come closer and closer together. *(528)*

7. Since the average productivity and marginal productivity of workers are the mirror images of average costs and marginal costs, and when the marginal costs and average costs intersect the two are equal, it follows that the average productivity and marginal productivity of workers must be equal at that point. *(528)*

8. It is impossible to say what is happening to average total costs on the basis of what is happening to marginal costs. It is the position of marginal costs relative to average total costs that is important. *(529)*

9. It is impossible to say because it is the position of marginal cost relative to average variable cost that determines what is happening to average variable cost. *(530)*

10. The marginal cost curve intersects the average total cost curve at the minimum point because once the marginal cost exceeds average total costs, the average total costs must necessarily begin to rise, and vice versa. *(530)*

24

Supply, Production, and Costs

II

Economic efficiency consists of making things that are worth more than they cost.

~J. M. Clark

After reading this chapter, you should be able to:

1 Distinguish technical efficiency from economic efficiency.

2 Explain how economies of scale influence the shape of long-run cost curves.

3 Differentiate diminishing marginal productivity from diseconomies of scale.

4 State the envelope relationship between short-run cost curves and long-run cost curves.

5 Explain the central role of opportunity costs in all supply decisions.

6 Discuss some of the problems of using cost analysis in the real world.

7 Apply the marginal cost concept to decisions facing you.

Welcome back. I hope you've reestablished your relationship with the real world and are ready to return, with renewed vigor, to the world of economics. When we took our intermission last chapter we had worked our way through the various short-run costs. That short run is a time period in which some inputs are fixed. A key determinant of the shape of the short-run cost curve is marginal productivity. If those last two sentences don't ring some bells and create images of cost curves dancing in your head, you may have been intermissioning before intermission, so a review of the last chapter is in order. If those bells are ringing, then we can continue and consider firms' long-run decisions and the determinants of the long-run cost curves. We'll do that in the first part of this chapter. Then in the second part we'll talk about applying cost analysis to the real world.

MAKING LONG-RUN PRODUCTION DECISIONS

In the long run, firms have many more options than they do in the short run. They can change any input they want. Plant size is not given; neither is the technology available given.

To make their long-run decisions, firms look at the costs of the various inputs and the technologies available for combining those inputs, and then decide which combination offers the lowest cost.

Say you're opening a hamburger stand. One decision you'll have to make is what type of stove to buy. You'll quickly discover that many different types are available. Some use more gas than others but cost less to buy; some are electric; some are self-cleaning and hence use less labor; some are big; some are little; some use microwaves; some use convection. Some have long-term guarantees; some have no guarantees. Each has a colorful brochure telling you how wonderful it is. After studying the various detailed specifications and aspects of the production technology, you choose the stove that has the combination of characteristics that you believe best fits your needs.

Next you decide on workers. Do you want bilingual workers, college-educated workers, part-time workers, experienced workers . . . ? You get the idea: Even simple production decisions involve complicated questions. These decisions are made on the basis of the expected costs, and expected usefulness, of inputs.

Technical Efficiency and Economic Efficiency

Technical efficiency *A situation in which as few inputs as possible are used to produce a given output.*

1 Technical efficiency is efficiency that does not consider cost of inputs. The least-cost technically efficient process is the economically efficient process.

One important distinction to keep in mind in considering firms' long-run production decisions is the distinction between technical efficiency and economic efficiency. The production process transforms inputs into outputs. Any firm will want to choose a technically efficient production process. **Technical efficiency** in production means that as few inputs as possible are used to produce a given output.

Many different production processes can be technically efficient. For example, say you know that to produce 100 tons of wheat you can use 10 workers and 1 acre or use 1 worker and 100 acres. Which of these two production techniques is more efficient? Both can be technically efficient since neither involves the use of more of both inputs than the other technique. But that doesn't mean that both are equally efficient. That question can't be answered unless you know the relative costs of the two inputs. If an acre of land rents for $1,000,000 and each worker costs $10 a day, our answer likely will be different than if land rents for $40 an acre and each worker costs $100 a day. This is no longer a technical question; this is an economic question whose answer depends upon the costs of production. Which of the variety of technically efficient methods of production is *economically efficient?* The **economically efficient** method of production is that method that produces a given level of output at the lowest possible cost.

In long-run production decisions, firms will look at all available production technologies and choose the technology that, given the available inputs and their prices, is the economically efficient way to produce. These choices will reflect the prices of the various factors of production. Those prices, in turn, will reflect the factors' relative scarcities.

Economically efficient *Using the method of production that produces a given level of output at the lowest possible cost.*

Consider the use of land by firms in the United States and in Japan. The United States has large amounts of land (10 acres) per person, so the price of land is lower than in Japan, which has only .78 acre per person. An acre of rural land in the United States might cost about $700; in Japan it costs about $15,000. Because of this difference in price of inputs, production techniques use land much more intensively in Japan than in the United States. Similarly with China: Labor is more abundant so production techniques are more labor-intensive than in the United States. Whereas China would utilize hundreds of people to build a road, primarily using human labor, the United States would use three or four people along with three machines. Both countries are being economically efficient, but because costs of inputs differ, the economically efficient method of production differs. Thus, the economically efficient method of production is that technically efficient method of production that has the lowest cost.

Q–1:   Why does China use more labor-intensive techniques than does the United States?

✓**Determinants of the Shape of the Long-Run Cost Curve**   In the last chapter we saw that the law of diminishing marginal productivity accounted for the shape of the short-run cost curve. That followed since we kept adding more of a variable input to a fixed input. The law of diminishing marginal productivity doesn't apply to the long run since in the long run all inputs are variable. The most important determinants of what is economically efficient in the long run are economies and diseconomies of scale. Let's consider each of these in turn and see what effect they will have on the shape of the long-run average cost curve.

The shape of the long-run cost curve is due to the existence of economies and diseconomies of scale.

Economies of Scale   When the per-unit output cost of all inputs decreases as output increases, we say that there are **economies of scale** in production. For example, if producing 40,000 VCRs costs the firm $16,000,000 ($400 each), but producing 200,000 VCRs costs the firm $40,000,000 ($200 each), there are significant economies of scale associated with choosing to produce 200,000 rather than 40,000.

Economies of scale   A decrease in per-unit cost as a result of an increase in output.

In real-world production processes, at low levels of production economies of scale are extremely important. The reason is that many production techniques are indivisible—they must be used at a certain minimum level before they begin to become useful. For example, say you want to produce a pound of steel. You can't just build a mini blast furnace, stick in some coke and iron ore, and come out with your single pound of steel. Technology requires that technically efficient blast furnaces be of a minimum size with a production capacity that is measured in tons per hour, not pounds per year. The cost of the blast furnace is said to be an **indivisible setup cost** (the cost of an indivisible input for which a certain minimum amount of production must be undertaken before the input becomes economically feasible to use).

Indivisible setup cost   The cost of an indivisible input for which a certain minimum amount of production must be undertaken before the input becomes economically feasible to use.

Indivisible setup costs are important because they create many real-world economies of scale: As output increases, the costs per unit of output decrease. As an example, consider this book. Setting the type for it is an indivisible setup cost; it is a cost that must be incurred if any production is to take place, but it is not a cost that increases with the number of books produced. That means that the more copies of the book that are produced, the lower the typesetting cost per book. That's why it costs more per book to produce a textbook for an upper-level, low-enrollment course than it does for a lower-level, high-enrollment course. The same amount of work goes into both (both need to be written, edited, and set into type), and the printing costs differ only slightly.

The actual print run costs of printing a book are only about $1 to $8 per book. The other costs are indivisible setup costs. Because of these indivisible setup costs, large economies of scale are possible in printing books. Prices of produced goods, including books, reflect their costs of production. As you move to upper-level academic courses, you'll likely discover that the books are smaller and less colorful but cost as much as, or more than, this introductory text.

Q–2:   Why are larger production runs often cheaper per unit than smaller production runs?

In the long-run planning decisions about the cost of producing this book, the expected number of copies to be sold was an important element. That figure influenced the number of books produced, which in turn affected the expected cost per unit. This will be the case any time there are economies of scale. With economies of

PRODUCING THE
MAZDA MIATA

The normal production run of a U.S. automobile is 200,000 units per year. Why is it so high? Because of indivisible setup costs. In order to reduce those indivisible setup costs to an acceptable level, the production level per year must equal at least 200,000 or the car is considered an economic failure. The Pontiac Fiero, a sporty two-seater, was dropped in 1988 because it didn't sell well enough to sustain that production level.

But what is an indivisible setup cost depends on the structure of production. Japanese companies structure production differently from U.S. companies and have a much lower level of indivisible setup costs. For example, at just about the same time as Pontiac dropped the Fiero, a Japanese company, Mazda, entered the market with the Miata, another sporty two-seater. Because Mazda's assembly line is designed to handle different sizes and shapes of vehicles (which permits economies of scope discussed later in the text), its minimum profitable production level for the Miata is about 30,000, not 200,000. This alternative structure of production made it possible for the Miata to do well in a market that buys a total of about 40,000 two-seater sports coupes annually.

Quantity	Total costs of labor	Total costs of machines	Total costs $= TC_L + TC_M$	Average total costs $= TC/Q$
11	381	254	635	58
12	390	260	650	54
13	402	268	670	52
14	420	280	700	50
15	450	300	750	50
16	480	320	800	50
17	510	340	850	50
18	549	366	915	51
19	600	400	1,000	53
20	666	444	1,110	56

(a)

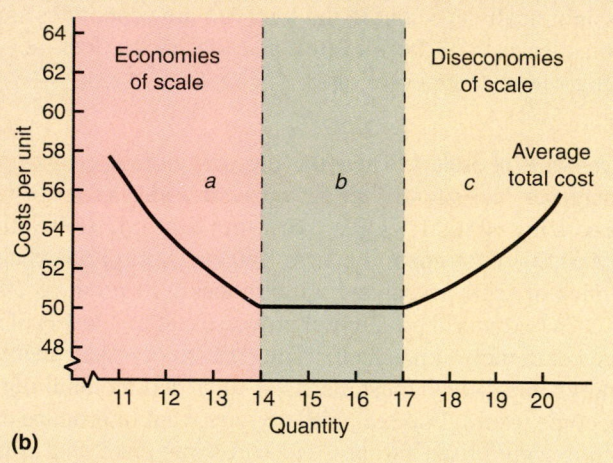

(b)

EXHIBIT 1 (a and b)   A Typical Long-Run Average Total Cost Table and Curve

In the long run, average costs initially fall because of economies of scale; then they are constant for a while, and finally they tend to rise due to diseconomies of scale.

2 In the longer run all inputs are variable, so only economies of scale can influence the shape of the long-run curve.

Minimum efficient level of production *The amount of production run that spreads out setup costs sufficiently for a firm to undertake production profitably.*

3 Diminishing marginal productivity refers to the decline in productivity caused by increasing units of a variable input being added to a fixed input. Diseconomies of scale refer to the decreases in productivity which are brought about because of increases of all inputs equally.

Diseconomies of scale *An increase in per-unit cost as a result of an increase in output.*

scale, cost per unit of a small production run is higher than cost per unit of a large production run.

Exhibit 1(a) demonstrates a normal long-run production table; Exhibit 1(b) shows the related typical shape of a long-run average cost curve. (Notice that there are no fixed costs. That's because we're in the long run so all costs are variable.) Economies of scale account for the downward-sloping part. Cost per unit of output is decreasing.

Because of the importance of economies of scale, businesspeople often talk of a minimum efficient level of production. What they mean by **minimum efficient level of production** is that, given the price at which they expect to be able to sell a good, the indivisible setup costs are so high that production runs of less than a certain size don't make economic sense. Thus, the minimum level of production is the amount of production that spreads setup costs out sufficiently for a firm to undertake production profitably.

Diseconomies of Scale   Notice that on the right side of the graph the long-run average cost curve is upward sloping. Average cost is increasing. When the per-unit cost of all inputs increases as a result of an increase in output, we say that there are **diseconomies of scale** in production. For example, if producing 200,000 VCRs costs the firm $40,000,000 ($200 each) and producing 400,000 VCRs costs the firm

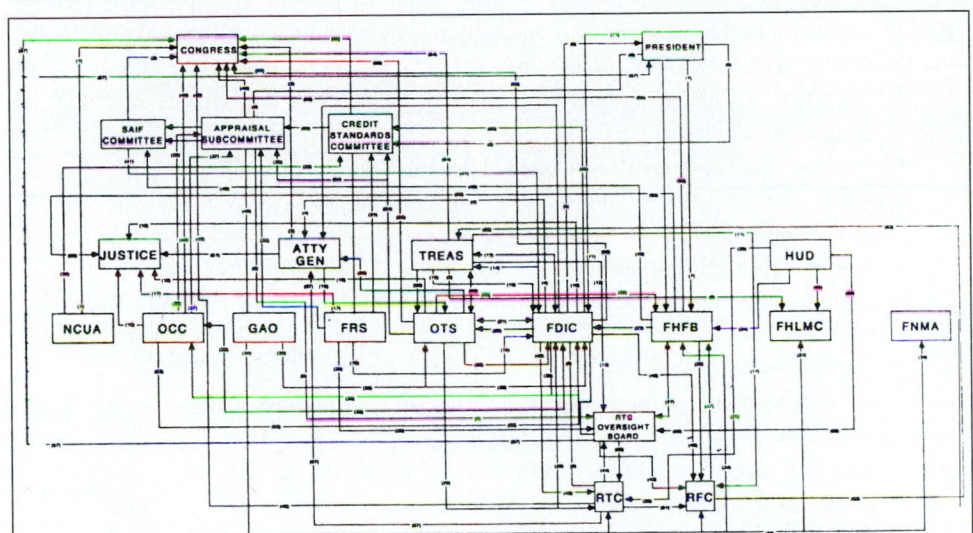

EXHIBIT 2   The S&L Maze

Decision making within large organizations is complicated. It often results in significant economies of scale. In this exhibit, we see the organizational maze of controls on the Resolution Trust Corporation. Internal structures of large corporations are similarly complex.

$100,000,000 ($250 each), there are diseconomies of scale associated with choosing to produce 400,000 rather than 200,000. Diseconomies of scale usually, but not always, start occurring as firms get large.

Diseconomies of scale could not occur if production relationships were only technical relationships. If that were the case, the same technical process could be used over and over again at the same cost. In reality, however, production relationships have social dimensions, which introduce the potential for important diseconomies of scale into the production process in two ways:

1. As the size of the firm increases, monitoring costs generally increase.
2. As the size of the firm increases, team spirit or morale generally decreases.

Monitoring costs are the costs incurred by the organizer of production in seeing to it that the employees do what they're supposed to do. If you're producing something yourself, the job gets done the way you want it done; monitoring costs are zero. However, as the scale of production increases, you have to hire people to help you produce. This means that if the job is to be done the way you want it done, you have to monitor (supervise) your employees' performance. The cost of monitoring can increase significantly as output increases; it's a major contributor to diseconomies of scale. Most big firms have several layers of bureaucracy devoted simply to monitoring others. The job of middle managers is, to a large extent, monitoring.

The other social dimension that can contribute to diseconomies of scale is the loss of **team spirit** (the feelings of friendship and being part of a team that bring out people's best efforts). Most types of production are highly dependent on team spirit. When that team spirit or morale is lost, production slows considerably. A good example is the former Soviet Union in its earlier transition from capitalism to socialism and its ongoing transition from socialism to capitalism. During both transitions, people lost faith in the system; whatever team spirit had existed fell apart, and production decreased by 25 percent or more.

An important reason diseconomies of scale can come about is that the bigger things get, the more checks and balances are needed to ensure that the right hand and the left hand are coordinated. The larger the organization, the more checks and balances and the more paperwork.

Probably the largest diseconomies of scale exist in government, where checks and balances are required on many levels. Exhibit 2, a flow chart of the controls over the the Resolution Trust Corporation, gives you a visual sense of why diseconomies of scale exist. Each line implies a connection, a need for meetings, and paperwork.

Some large firms manage to solve these problems and thus avoid diseconomies of scale. But as a firm's size increases, it's much harder to maintain that team spirit

Q–3: If production had no social dimension, what would be true about the long-run average cost curve?

Monitoring costs   Costs incurred by the organizer of production in seeing to it that employees do what they are supposed to do.

Team spirit   The feelings of friendship and being part of a team that bring out people's best effort.

A REMINDER ✔

REVIEW OF COSTS

W e've covered a lot of costs and cost curves quickly so a review is in order. First, let's list the cost concepts and their definitions.

1. Marginal cost: the additional cost resulting from a one-unit change in output.
2. Total cost: all costs.
3. Average total cost: total cost divided by total output (TC/Q).
4. Fixed cost: cost that is already spent and cannot be recovered. (It exists only in the short run.)
5. Average fixed cost: fixed cost divided by total output (FC/Q).
6. Variable cost: cost of variable inputs. Variable cost does not include fixed cost.
7. Average variable cost: variable cost divided by total output (VC/Q).

Each of these costs can be represented by a curve. A number of these curves have specific relationships to the other cost curves.

1. *MC: MC* intersects *AVC* and *ATC* at their minimum points.
2. If $MC > AVC$, then *AVC* is rising. If $MC < AVC$, then *AVC* is falling.
3. If $MC > ATC$, then *ATC* is rising. If $MC < ATC$, then *ATC* is falling.
4. *ATC:* a U-shaped curve.
5. *AVC:* a U-shaped curve lower than the *ATC,* with the minimum point slightly to the left.
6. *AFC:* a downward-sloping curve that starts high, initially decreases rapidly, and then decreases slowly.
7. The long-run *ATC* curve is a U-shaped curve which forms an envelope around the various short-run *ATC* curves.

---

effectively and to monitor employees. So, often these problems of monitoring and loss of team spirit limit the size of firms. They underlie diseconomies of scale in which relatively less output is produced for a given increase in inputs, so that per-unit costs of output increase.

Economies and diseconomies of scale play important roles in real-world long-run production decisions.

The Importance of Economies and Diseconomies of Scale   Economies and diseconomies of scale play important roles in real-world long-run production decisions. Economies of scale underlie firms' attempts to expand their markets either at home or abroad. If they can make and sell more at lower per-unit costs, they will make more profits. Diseconomies of scale prevent a firm from expanding and can lead corporate raiders to buy the firm and break it up in the hope that the smaller production units will be more efficient, thus eliminating some of the diseconomies of scale.

The long-run and the short-run average cost curves have the same U-shape. But it's important to remember that the reasons why they have this U-shape are quite different. The assumption of initially increasing and then eventually diminishing marginal productivity (as a variable input is added to a fixed input) accounts for the shape of the short-run average cost curve. Economies and diseconomies of scale account for the shape of the long-run average total cost curve.

Q-4: Why is the short-run average cost curve a U-shaped curve?

Q-5: Why is the long-run average total cost curve generally considered to be a U-shaped curve?

The Relationship between Short-Run Average Total Cost and Long-Run Average Total Cost

4 The envelope relationship is the relationship explaining that, at the planned output level, short-run average total cost equals long-run average total cost, but at all other levels of output, short-run average total cost is higher than long-run average total cost.

Since in the long run all inputs are flexible, while in the short run some inputs are not flexible, long-run cost will always be less than or equal to short-run cost. To see this, let's consider a firm that had planned to produce 100 but now adjusts its plan to produce more than 100. We know that in the long run the firm chooses the lowest-cost method of production. In the short run it faces an additional constraint: All expansion must be done using only the variable input. That constraint must increase average cost (or at least not decrease it) compared to what average cost would have been had the firm planned to produce that level to begin with. If it didn't, the firm would have chosen that new combination of inputs in the long run. Additional constraints increase cost. This relationship between long-run and short-run average total costs is known as the **envelope relationship,** shown in Exhibit 3.

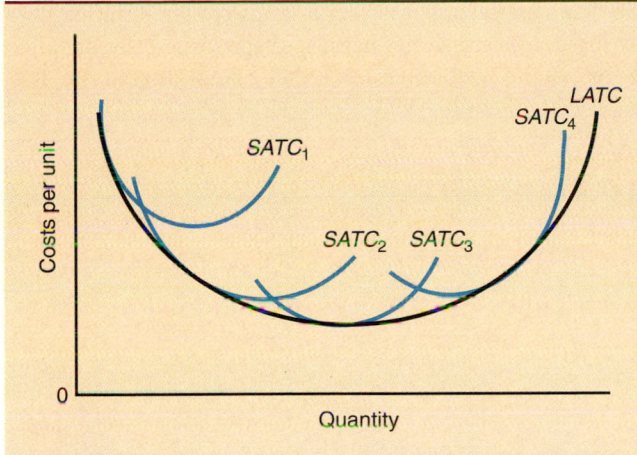

EXHIBIT 3   Envelope of Short-Run Average Total Cost Curves

The long-run average total cost curve is an envelope of the short-run average total cost curves. Each short-run average total cost curve touches the long-run average total cost curve at only one point.

Why it's called an *envelope relationship* should be clear from the exhibit. Each short-run average total cost curve touches the long-run average total cost curve at one, and only one, output level; at all other output levels, short-run average cost exceeds long-run average cost. The long-run average total cost curve is an envelope of short-run average total cost curves.

In this chapter and the last we have discussed the technical nature of costs and production. In the next chapter we will formally relate costs of production to the supply of goods. As a bridge between the two chapters, let's conclude this chapter with a consideration of the entrepreneur, who establishes the relationship between costs and the supply decision, and of some of the problems of using cost analysis in the real world.

In thinking about the connection between cost and supply, one fundamental insight is that the revenue received for a good must be greater than the planned cost of producing it. Otherwise why would anyone supply it? The difference between the expected price of a good and the expected average total cost of producing it (the good's opportunity cost) is the supplier's expected economic profit per unit. It's profit that underlies the dynamics of production in a market economy.

An **entrepreneur** is an individual who sees an opportunity to sell an item at a price higher than the average cost of producing it. The entrepreneur is the organizer of production and the one who visualizes the demand and convinces the individuals who own the factors of production that they want to produce that good. Similarly, the entrepreneur also must convince demanders that what the entrepreneur is producing is what the demanders want. Cost enters into these decisions as a cutoff. Entrepreneurs who don't cover their cost generally don't stay in business.

Cost curves do not become supply curves through some magic process. To move from cost to supply, entrepreneurial initiative is needed. The entrepreneur analyzes costs and supplies output. An entrepreneur must organize people to do something that he or she wants them to do. He or she must be a psychologist, a cheerleader, a boss, a confessor, and an engineer, to name just a few of the skills an entrepreneur needs. It's these dynamic, driven individuals who underlie supply and who instigate production. They're people who get other people off their behinds.

By allowing entrepreneurs to earn profit, market economies encourage people to channel their drive into supplying material goods. Entrepreneurs create production and hence supply. Without entrepreneurs there would be little supply because there would be no one to recognize and act on demand potential.

The greater the difference between price and average total cost, the greater the entrepreneur's incentive to tackle the organizational problems and supply the good. That insight underlies the dynamic laws of supply discussed in Chapter 2.

COSTS, ENTREPRENEURIAL ACTIVITY, AND THE SUPPLY DECISION

Price Must Be Expected to Exceed Cost for a Good to Be Supplied

5 The difference between the expected price of a good and the expected average total cost of producing it—the good's opportunity cost—is the supplier's expected economic profit per unit. The opportunity cost must be below price for a good to be supplied.

Entrepreneur Visionary individual who makes production happen; she visualizes demand and makes things happen.

The Entrepreneur and Supply

Cost curves do not become supply curves through some magic process. To move from cost to supply, entrepreneurial initiative is needed.

Q–6: Why is the role of the entrepreneur central to the production process in the economy?

USING COST ANALYSIS IN THE REAL WORLD

6   Some of the problems of using cost analysis in the real world include:
1. Economies of scope;
2. Learning by doing and technological change;
3. Many dimensions;
4. Unmeasured costs;
5. Joint costs;
6. Indivisible costs;
7. Uncertainty;
8. Asymmetries; and
9. Multiple planning and adjustment periods with many different short runs.

All too often students walk away from an introductory economics course thinking that cost analysis is a relatively easy topic. Memorize the names, shapes, and relationships of the curves, and you're home free. In the textbook model, that's right. In real life, it's not, because actual production processes are marked by:

1. Economies of scope;
2. Learning by doing and technological change;
3. Many dimensions;
4. Unmeasured costs;
5. Joint costs;
6. Indivisible costs;
7. Uncertainty;
8. Asymmetries; and
9. Multiple planning and adjustment periods with many different short runs.

The general model provides a nice framework with which to approach production, but before the model can be really applied it must be expanded to incorporate these complications. Alas, in introductory economics we don't have time to discuss these complications in detail, but we do have time to give you a sense of their importance. We'll do so by briefly considering four qualifications.

Economies of Scope

Economies of scope   *The costs of producing products are interdependent so that producing one good lowers the cost of producing another.*

The cost of production of one product often depends on what other products a firm is producing. When the costs of producing products are interdependent, so that it's less costly for a firm to produce one good when it's already producing another, economists say that there are **economies of scope** in the production of the two goods. For example, once a firm has set up a large marketing department to sell cereal, the department might be able to use its expertise in marketing a different product—say, dog food. A firm that sells gasoline can simultaneously use its gas station attendants to sell soda, milk, and incidentals. The minimarts so common along our highways and neighborhood streets developed because gasoline companies became aware of economies of scope.

✓Q–7:   What is the difference between an economy of scope and an economy of scale?

Economies of scope play an important role in firms' decisions of what combination of goods to produce. They look for both economies of scope and economies of scale. When you read about firms' mergers, think about whether the combination of their products will generate economies of scope. Many otherwise unexplainable mergers between seemingly incompatible firms can be explained by economies of scope.

Learning by Doing and Technological Change

The production terminology that we've been discussing is central to the standard economic models. In the real world, however, other terms and concepts are also important. The production techniques available to real-world firms are constantly changing because of *learning by doing* and *technological change*. These changes occur over time and cannot be accurately predicted.

Unlike events in the standard economic model, all events in the real world are influenced by the past. That's why learning by doing is important in the real world, but isn't a part of the standard economic model. **Learning by doing** simply means that as we do something, we learn what works and what doesn't, and over time we become more proficient at it. Practice may not make perfect, but it certainly makes better and more efficient. Many firms estimate that output per unit input will increase by 1 or 2 percent a year, even if no changes in inputs or technologies occur, as employees learn by doing.

✓*Learning by doing*   *Becoming more proficient at doing something by actually doing it; in the process, learning what works and what doesn't.*

Q–8:   Does learning by doing cause the cost curve to be downward sloping?

The concept of learning by doing emphasizes the importance of the past in trying to predict performance. Let's say a firm is deciding between two applicants for the job of managing its restaurant. One was a highly successful student but has never run a restaurant; the other was an OK student who has run a restaurant that failed. Which one does the firm hire? The answer is unclear. The first applicant may be brighter, but the lack of experience will likely mean that the person won't be hired. Businesses give

PROFILES OF TWO ENTREPRENEURS

William Lear

William Lear was an inventor extraordinaire. After completing eighth grade he quit school to go to work as a mechanic. In the early 1920s he invented the automobile radio. He failed to get financial backing for his invention, however, and sold it to Motorola.

In 1934 he developed a frequency amplifier that could be used in any radio set and which lowered the cost of radios significantly. Selling that invention to RCA made him a millionaire. During World War II he developed an automatic pilot device which made it possible for planes to take off, fly, and land even when visibility was zero. Similar systems are still in use today.

In 1962 he wanted to develop a small, low-price jet aircraft. His company, Lear, Inc. (which by then was being run by corporate managers), wouldn't go along with his idea, so he left the company and started again. In 1965 the Lear Jet was born, the fastest and cheapest small jet that then existed. Next he turned his ingenuity to audiotape and developed the first eight-track tape system.

Lear lived for inventing. He made things work, not only inventing them but also bringing them into production. After production of his inventions got underway, he often found himself at odds with the organization he'd created.

He died in 1978 while working on a turboprop plane which was meant once again to revolutionize small plane transportation.

Steven Jobs

Together with Stephen Wozniak, Steven Jobs invented the personal computer. Jobs was an adopted child and a loner who hated school. He attended after-school lectures at Hewlett-Packard, an electronics firm. At one lecture he asked the president of H-P to give him some parts for a school project. The president gave him both the parts and a summer job. At that job he met Stephen Wozniak, a dropout from the University of California at Berkeley who (on his own time) was perfecting a ''blue box'' which allowed individuals to make illegal, free long-distance phone calls. They first collaborated on selling these devices.

Jobs entered college in 1972, but soon dropped out. However he hung around the campus practicing meditation. In 1974 he went to India in search of spiritual enlightenment. Not finding it, he went back to Palo Alto, California, saw Wozniak again, and convinced him to work with him in perfecting and marketing a PC. Wozniak did the engineering; Jobs handled the marketing. To obtain financing, they sold Jobs's Volkswagen microbus for $1,300 and begged credit from an electronic supplier. Their product, the Apple I, was a success. It was soon followed by the Apple II and Macintosh.

By the 1980s Apple was a tremendous success. Wozniak voluntarily left the firm and Jobs was ousted in a 1985 power struggle. Everyday management of a major company was not their domain. Both left, but they left rich. Jobs used his many contacts to create the ''Next'' Computer System, designed specifically for universities. This time around, he wasn't as successful; Next has been struggling through the 1990s.

---

enormous weight to experience. So this firm may reason that in failing, the second applicant will have learned lessons that make her the better candidate. U.S. firms faced such a choice when they were invited to expand into the new market economies of Eastern Europe in the early 1990s. Should they hire the former communist managers who had failed to produce efficiently, or should they hire the reformers? (Generally they decided on the former communist managers, hoping they had learned by failing.)

Technological change offers an increase in the known range of production techniques. Technological change provides brand new ways of producing goods. For example, at one point automobile tires were made from rubber, clothing was made from cotton and wool, and buildings were made of wood. As a result of technological change, many tires are now made from petroleum distillates, much clothing is made from synthetic fibers (which in turn are made from petroleum distillates), and many buildings are constructed from steel.

Technological change can fundamentally alter the nature of production cost. Say, for instance, that physicists discovered a new method of cold fusion (combining atoms to produce energy). That discovery would greatly reduce the need for oil and other increasingly scarce and expensive sources of energy, and it would have far-reaching effects on the costs of production of almost all goods. Other possibilities for technological change with significant effects exist in the new field of genetic engineering.

Technological changes that are far less drastic in their consequences are occurring every day. A new fertilizer is developed that increases crop yield per acre; a new machine is designed that does the work of two people. These technological changes can lower costs enormously. Whenever technological change (or learning by doing) occurs, the cost curve shifts down since the same output can be produced at a lower cost.

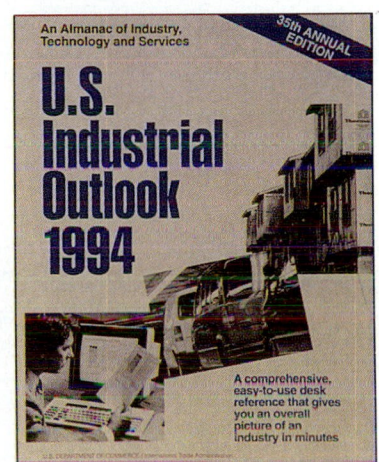

U.S. Industrial Outlook, a Commerce Department publication, provides large amounts of information about real-world industries.

Technological change An increase in the range of production techniques that provides new ways of producing goods.

Production then—The nature of production has changed considerably in the last 60 years. This picture shows a 1933 production line in which people did the work as the goods moved along the line.   *UPI/Bettmann.*

Many Dimensions

Good economic decisions take all relevant margins into account.

The only dimension in the standard model is the level of output. Many, if not most, decisions that firms make are not the one-dimensional decisions of the standard model, such as "Should we produce more or less?" They're multidimensional questions like "Should we change the quality? Should we change the wrapper? Should we improve our shipping speed? Should we increase our inventory?" Each of these questions relates to a different dimension of the production decision and each has its own marginal costs. Thus, there isn't just one marginal cost; there are 10 or 20 of them. Good economic decisions take all relevant margins into account.

The reason that the standard model is important is that each of these questions can be analyzed using the same reasoning used in the standard model. But you must remember, *in applying the analysis, it's the reasoning, not the specific model, that's important.*

Unmeasured Costs

If one were to ask, "In what area of decision making do businesses most often fail to use economic insights?" the answer most economists would give is costs. The relevant costs are generally not the costs you'll find in a firm's accounts.

Why the difference? Economists operate conceptually; they include in costs exactly what their theory says they should. Accountants who have to measure firms' costs in practice and provide the actual dollar figures take a much more pragmatic approach; their concepts of costs must reflect only those costs that are reasonably precisely measurable.

Economists Include Opportunity Cost   Let's take a few examples. First, say that a business produces 1,000 widgets that sell at $3 each for a total revenue of $3,000. To produce these widgets the business had to buy $1,000 worth of widgetgoo, which the owner has hand-shaped into widgets. An accountant would say that the total cost of producing 1,000 widgets was $1,000 and that the firm's profit was $2,000. That's because an accountant uses explicit costs that can be measured. Thus,

Accounting profit   Definition of profit used by accountants that states profit is total revenue minus explicit measurable costs.

Accounting profit = *Total revenue − Explicit measurable costs.*

Production now—The nature of production has changed considerably in the last 60 years. This picture shows a modern production line. Robots do much of the work. © *Keystone/The Image Works.*

Economic profit is different. An economist, looking at that same example, would point out that the accountant's calculation doesn't take into account the time and effort that the owner put into making the widgets. While a person's time involves no explicit cost in money, it does involve an *opportunity cost,* the forgone income that the owner could have made by spending that time working in another job. If the business takes 400 hours of the person's time and the person could have earned $6 an hour working for someone else, then the person is forgoing $2,400 in income. Economists include that implicit cost in their concept of cost. When that implicit cost is included, what looks like a $2,000 profit becomes a $400 economic loss.

Economic profit = *Implicit and explicit revenues − Implicit and explicit costs.*

Economic Depreciation versus Accounting Depreciation   Now let's take a second example. Say a firm buys a machine for $10,000 that's meant to last 10 years, but after one year, machines like that become in short supply so instead of falling, its value rises to $12,000. An accountant, looking at the firm's costs that year, would use **historical cost** (what the machine cost in terms of money actually spent) depreciated at, say, 10 percent per year, so the machine's cost for each of its 10 years of existence would be $1,000. An economist would say that since the value of the machine is rising, the machine has no cost; in fact, it provides a revenue of $2,000 to the firm. The standard model avoids such messy, real-world issues of measuring costs and instead assumes that all costs are measurable in a single time period.

I suspect that even with its simplifications, the standard model has been more than enough to learn in an introductory course. Learning the standard model, however, only provides you with the rudiments of cost analysis, in the same way that learning the rules of mechanics only provides you with the basics of mechanical engineering. In addition to a knowledge of the laws of mechanics, building a machine requires years of experience. Similarly for economics and cost analysis. Introductory economics provides you with a superb framework for starting to think about real-world cost measurement, but it can't make you an expert cost analyst.

Economic profit   Definition of profit used by economists that states profit is total implicit and explicit revenues minus total implicit and explicit costs.

Historical cost   Cost in terms of money actually spent.

The Standard Model as a Framework

NEW APPROACHES IN COST ANALYSIS

 actories run by numbers. Numbers to calculate profit and losses; to analyze the costs of new products; and to chart corporate strategy. But a lot of managers are relying on the wrong numbers.

As they adopt new manufacturing techniques like computer-aided design, just-in-time stock management, and total quality control, many firms are discovering that their existing account systems also need dragging into the 1990s. Unless the bean-counters join the manufacturing revolution, traditional cost accounting will have little place in the factory of the future.

The two previous paragraphs introduced an article in *The Economist* (March 3, 1990, p. 61) describing a conference on strategic manufacturing. This conference focused on managerial or cost accounting (the application of cost analysis to managerial decisions). Unlike *financial accounting* (which involves keeping track of income, assets, and liabilities), managerial accounting is used to help managers determine the cost of producing products and plan future investment. It's the direct application of microeconomics to production.

In the 1980s and 1990s there has been an enormous change in cost accounting. The leaders of this change—such as Robert Kaplan of the Harvard Business School—argue that cost accounting systems based on traditional concepts of fixed and variable costs lead firms consistently to make the wrong decisions. They argue that in today's manufacturing, direct labor costs have fallen substantially—in many industries to only 2 or 3 percent of the total cost—and overhead costs have risen substantially. This change in costs facing firms requires a much more careful division among types of overhead costs, and a recognition that what should and should not be assigned as a cost to a particular product differs with each decision.

These developments in managerial accounting require an even deeper understanding of costs than accountants have previously needed. As one firm's director of manufacturing was quoted in *The Economist* article, "Unless management accountants move fast [to incorporate these new concepts], they will be almost without use to the manufacturing manager of 1995."

Cost Considerations in Everyday Life: Two Examples

Let's now consider two examples of cost considerations in everyday life. Let's first consider an example of an incorrect decision often made by individuals that they would not make if they correctly specified cost; and, second, let's consider an example of a firm's pricing policy that makes sense if one understands marginal cost.

7 Marginal cost analysis can be applied to just about every decision facing you. For example, the marginal benefit of reading these marginal notes must exceed the marginal cost, or you shouldn't read them.

An Individual's Decision about Which of Two Stocks to Sell   Say you bought two stocks: one at $100, one at $10. You have a chance to sell either stock at $50. Which should you sell? Many people would answer that you should sell the stock you bought at $10 because you'll make a profit of $40, and if you sell the $100 stock, you'll sustain a loss of $50. But that reasoning is wrong. After you spent the money to buy the two stocks in the first place, that expenditure became a fixed cost and shouldn't enter into your decision about which stock to sell. You make a profit or loss when the price of the shares goes up or down, not when you sell the stock. Since you have the options of selling, the market valuation of the stock at each moment in time is used to determine your profit, not the valuation of the stock when you sell it.

Q–9:   Say you bought two stocks, one at $100 and one at $10. You have a chance to sell either stock at $50. Which should you sell? Why?

The economist's answer to the question of which of the two stocks you should sell is "It depends on what you expect to happen to the price of the stocks in the future." Decisions should not be based on the past, except to the degree that the past can be used to predict the future. Variations of this "mistake" occur all the time in business. Firms often set their prices based on invoice costs of the goods they sell, not on the current replacement or opportunity costs.

Q–10:   What is the economist's argument in favor of peak load pricing?

A Firm's Pricing Policy Based on Marginal Cost   Let's consider another example of cost and the many dimensions of output. Electric utilities often argue that they should be allowed to charge higher rates for electricity used during times of peak demand and lower rates during off-peak times. Many people argue against such a pricing policy because they believe that a firm's prices should be based on its costs. They argue that the costs of producing electricity are the same at 7 P.M. as at 4:30 A.M. and the utility should charge the same price at all times.

Understanding marginal cost and recognizing that output has multiple dimensions sheds a different light on the issue. The cost of supplying electricity consists primarily of the overhead cost that must be incurred to build facilities large enough to meet demand in the peak period. After that capacity is built, the marginal cost of supplying electricity at any point other than at the peak load is low. However the marginal cost of supplying peak load power is high. By setting different rates for peak and off-peak usage, electric companies are actually reflecting their cost structure. Economists generally support "peak load pricing" because it's based on the relevant marginal cost.

Economists generally support "peak load pricing" because it's based on the relevant marginal cost.

CONCLUSION AND A LOOK AHEAD

We've come to the end of our discussion of production, cost, and supply. The two chapters we spent on them weren't easy; there's tons of material here, and, quite frankly, it will likely require at least two or three reads and careful attention to your professor's lecture before your mind can absorb it. So if you're planning to sleep through a lecture, the ones on these chapters aren't the ones for that.

These chapters, in combination with our discussion of individual choice, will provide the framework for most of the later chapters, which really do get into interesting real-world issues. But you've got to know the basics to truly understand those issues. So, now that you've come to the end of these two chapters, unless you really feel comfortable with the analysis, it's probably time to review them from the beginning. (Sorry, but remember, there's no such thing as a free lunch.)

CHAPTER SUMMARY

- An economically efficient production process must be technically efficient, but a technically efficient process need not be economically efficient.
- Production is a social, as well as a technical, phenomenon; that's why concepts like team spirit are important.
- The long-run average total cost curve is U-shaped. Economies of scale initially cause average total cost to decrease; diseconomies eventually cause average total cost to increase.

- There is an envelope relationship between short-run average cost curves and long-run average cost curves.
- An entrepreneur is an individual who sees an opportunity to sell an item at a price higher than the average cost of producing it.
- Once one starts applying cost analysis to the real world, one must include a variety of other dimensions of costs that the standard model does not cover.

KEY TERMS

accounting profit *(542)*
diseconomies of scale *(536)*
economic profit *(543)*
economically efficient *(534)*
economies of scale *(535)*
economies of scope *(540)*

entrepreneur *(539)*
envelope relationship *(538)*
historical cost *(543)*
indivisible setup cost *(535)*
learning by doing *(540)*

minimum efficient level of
  production *(536)*
monitoring costs *(537)*
team spirit *(537)*
technical efficiency *(534)*
technological change *(541)*

QUESTIONS FOR THOUGHT AND REVIEW

The number after each question represents the estimated degree of critical thinking required. (1 = almost none; 10 = deep thought.)

1. Distinguish technical efficiency from economic efficiency. *(2)*

2. A student has just written on an exam how in the long run fixed cost will make the average total cost curve slope downward. Why will the professor mark it incorrect? *(3)*

3. What inputs do you use in studying this book? What would the long-run average total cost and marginal cost curves for studying look like? Why? *(8)*

4. Why could diseconomies of scale never occur if production relationships were only technical relationships? *(7)*

5. When economist Jacob Viner first developed the envelope relationship, he told his draftsman to make sure that (1) all the marginal cost curves went through both the minimum point of the short-run average cost curve and

(2) the point where the short-run average total cost curve was tangent to the long-run average total cost curve. The draftsman told him it couldn't be done. Viner told him to do it anyhow. Why was the draftsman right? *(8)*

6. What is the role of the entrepreneur in translating cost of production into supply? *(4)*

7. Your average total cost is 40; the price you receive for the good is 12. Should you keep on producing the good? Why? *(5)*

8. A student has just written on an exam that technological change will mean that the cost curve is downward sloping. Why did her teacher mark it wrong? *(6)*

9. Distinguish economic profit from accounting profit. *(3)*

10. If you were describing the marginal cost of an additional car driving on a road, what costs would you look at? What is the likely shape of the marginal cost curve? *(9)*

PROBLEMS AND EXERCISES

1. Visit a nearby company and ask it what would happen to its per-unit costs if sales increased by 10 percent. Try to figure out how its answer relates to the concepts in the last two chapters, remembering especially the discussion about using cost analysis in the real world.

2. Find out the total budget of your college or university. (It often takes a bit of sleuthing, but almost all college and university budgets are in the public record.) Find out the number of students. What is the total cost per student? What is the relevant marginal cost of an additional student?

   Now say you're on a planning committee charged with eliminating an expected 2 percent budget deficit next year. Using the budget figures, make some suggestions. Have a college administrator (preferably the treasurer or comptroller) come in to your class and react to those suggestions. Explain why presidents of universities and colleges don't last long.

3. A pair of shoes that wholesale for $32.50 has approximately the following costs:

Manufacturing labor	2.25
Materials	4.95
Factor overhead, operating expenses, and profit	8.50
Sales costs	4.50
Advertising	2.93
Research and development	2.00
Interest	.33
Net income	3.33
Total	32.50

   a. Which of these costs would likely be a variable cost?
   b. Which would likely be a fixed cost?

c. If output were to rise, what would likely happen to average total costs? Why?

4. Peggy-Sue's cookies are the best in the world, or so I hear. She has been offered a job by Cookie Monster, Inc. to come to work for them at $125,000 per year. Currently, she is producing her own cookies, and she has revenues of $260,000 per year. Her costs are $40,000 for labor, $10,000 for rent; $35,000 for ingredients; and $5,000 for utilities. She has $100,000 of her own money invested in the operation, which, if she leaves, can be sold for $40,000 that she can invest at 10% per year.

   a. Calculate her accounting and economic profits.
   b. Advise her as to what she should do.

5. A major issue of contention at many colleges concerns the cost of meals that is rebated when a student does not sign up for the meal plan. The administration usually says that it should rebate only the marginal cost of the food alone, which it calculates at, say, $1.25 per meal. Students say that the marginal cost should include more costs, such as the saved space from fewer students using the facilities and the reduced labor expenses on food preparation. This can raise the marginal cost to $6.00.

   a. Who is correct, the administration or the students?
   b. How might your answer differ if this argument were being conducted in the planning stage, before the dining hall is built?
   c. If one accepts the $1.25 figure of a person not eating, how could one justify using a higher figure of about $6.00 for the cost of feeding a guest at the dining hall, as many schools do?

ANSWERS TO MARGIN QUESTIONS

1. China uses more labor-intensive techniques than does the United States because the price of labor is much lower in China relative to the United States. Both countries are producing economically efficiently. *(535)*

2. Larger production runs are generally cheaper per unit than smaller production runs because of indivisible setup costs, which do not vary with the size of the run. *(535)*

3. Because the same technical process could be used over and over again at the same cost, the long-run average cost curve would never become upward sloping. *(537)*

4. The short-run average total cost curve initially slopes downward because of large average fixed costs, then begins sloping upward because of diminishing marginal productivity, giving it a U-shape. *(538)*

5. The long-run average total cost curve is generally considered to be U-shaped because initially there are

economies of scale and, for large amounts of production, there are diseconomies of scale. *(538)*

6. Economic activity does not just happen. Some dynamic, driven individual must instigate production. That dynamic individual is called an entrepreneur. *(539)*

7. Economies of scale are economies that occur because of increases in the amount one is producing of a good. Economies of scope occur when producing different types of goods lowers the cost of each of those goods. *(540)*

8. Learning by doing causes a shift in the cost curve because it is a change in the technical characteristics of production. It does not cause the cost curve to be downward sloping—it causes it to shift downward. *(540)*

9. Assuming away issues of taxation of capital gains, I would decide which stock I should sell based on what I expected to happen to the price of the stocks, not on what price I bought them for. *(544)*

10. Economists argue that peak load pricing is efficient and that most of the overhead costs should be allocated to those peak loads because it is for those peak loads that the large facilities must be built. *(544)*

25

Perfect Competition

There's no resting place for an enterprise in a competitive economy.

~Alfred P. Sloan

After reading this chapter, you should be able to:

1 List the seven conditions for perfect competition.

2 Explain why producing an output at which marginal cost equals price maximizes total profit for a perfect competitor.

3 Demonstrate why the marginal cost curve is the supply curve for a perfectly competitive firm.

4 Determine the output and profit of a perfect competitor graphically and numerically.

5 Explain why perfectly competitive firms make zero economic profit in the long run.

6 Use supply and demand curves to discuss real-world events.

7 Discuss the Pareto optimal criterion and state three criticisms of it.

In physics when you study the laws of gravity, you initially study what would happen in a vacuum. Perfect vacuums don't exist, but talking about what would happen if you dropped an object in a perfect vacuum makes the analysis easier. So too with economics. Our equivalent of a perfect vacuum is perfect competition. In perfect competition the invisible hand of the market operates unimpeded. In this chapter we'll consider how perfectly competitive markets work and see how the cost analysis developed in the previous chapter can be applied.

A **perfectly competitive** market is a market in which economic forces operate unimpeded. For a market to be called *perfectly competitive,* it must meet some stringent conditions:

1. Buyers and sellers are price takers.
2. The number of firms is large.
3. There are no barriers to entry.
4. Firms' products are homogeneous (identical).
5. Exit and entry are instantaneous and costless.
6. There is complete information.
7. Selling firms are profit-maximizing entrepreneurial firms.

These conditions are needed to ensure that economic forces operate instantaneously and are unimpeded by other invisible or visible forces. For example, say that there weren't a large number of firms. The few firms in the industry would then have an incentive to get together and limit output so they could get a higher price. They would stop the invisible hand from working. Similarly for the other conditions, although the reasoning why they're necessary can get rather complicated.

To give you a sense of these conditions, let's consider them a bit more carefully.

1. *Both buyers and sellers are price takers.* A **price taker** is a firm or individual who takes the market price as given. When you buy, say, toothpaste, you go to the store and find that the price of toothpaste is, say $1.38 for the medium-size tube; you're a price taker. The firm, however, is a price maker since it set the price at $1.38. So even though the toothpaste industry is highly competitive, it's not a perfectly competitive market. In a perfectly competitive market, supply and demand determine the price; both firms and consumers take the market price as given.

2. *The number of firms is large.* It's almost self-explanatory to say that the number of firms is large. *Large* means sufficiently large so that any one firm's output compared to the market output is imperceptible, and what one firm does has no influence on what other firms do.

3. *No barriers to entry.* **Barriers to entry** are any things that prevent other firms from entering a market. They might be legal barriers such as exist when firms acquire a patent to produce a certain product. Barriers might be technological, such as exist when the minimum efficient scale of production allows only one firm to produce at the lowest average total cost. Or barriers might be created by social forces, such as when bankers will lend only to certain types of people and not to other types. Perfect competition can have no barriers to entry.

4. *Homogeneous product.* A **homogeneous product** is a product such that each firm's output is indistinguishable from any other firm's output. Corn bought by the bushel is relatively homogeneous. One kernel is indistinguishable from every other kernel. On the other hand, you can buy 30 different brands of many goods—soft drinks, for instance: Pepsi, Coke, 7-Up, and so on. Each is slightly different from the other and thus not homogeneous.

5. *Instantaneous exit and entry.* Say all the grocery stores in your neighborhood raised their prices by 30 percent without their costs having gone up. What would happen in the next week or month? Probably nothing, other than customers

PERFECT COMPETITION

Perfectly competitive A perfectly competitive market is one in which economic forces operate unimpeded.

The Necessary Conditions for Perfect Competition

1 Seven conditions for a market to be perfectly competitive are:
1. Both buyers and sellers are price takers.
2. Large number of firms.
3. No barriers to entry.
4. Homogeneous product.
5. Instantaneous exit and entry.
6. Complete information.
7. Profit-maximizing entrepreneurial firms.

Q–1: Why is the assumption of instantaneous exit and entry necessary for the existence of perfect competition?

Commodity, currency, and stock exchanges provide the closest real world analogue to competitive markets. © *David Wells/The Image Works.*

getting mad. You'd still shop there until a new store opened in a convenient place with more reasonable prices. In a perfectly competitive market, the new store would open immediately upon hearing that the prices in the existing stores had gone up. It wouldn't wait a week, or even an hour.

6. *Complete information.* In a perfectly competitive market, not only would the store open up immediately; you'd also know about it instantaneously. So too would other firms. Similarly, if any firm experienced a technological breakthrough, all firms would know about it and would be able to use the same technology instantaneously.

7. *Profit-maximizing entrepreneurial firms.* Firms can have many goals and be organized in a variety of ways. For perfect competition to exist, firms' goals must be profit and only profit, and the people who make the decisions must receive only profits and no other form of income from the firms.

The Necessary Conditions and the Definition of Supply

These are strict, but necessary, conditions for a perfectly competitive market to exist. Combined, they create an environment in which each firm, following its own self-interest, will offer goods to the market in a predictable way. If these conditions hold, we can talk formally about the supply of a produced good. If they aren't met, then our formal definition of supply of produced goods dissolves; we can still talk *in*formally about supply of produced goods and cost conditions, but we cannot use our formal concept of supply and how it relates to costs. This follows from the definition of **supply:**

Supply   A schedule of quantities of goods that will be offered to the market at various prices.

Supply is a schedule of quantities of goods that will be offered to the market at various prices.

This definition requires the supplier to be a price taker (our first condition). In almost all other market structures (frameworks within which firms interact economically), firms are not price takers; they are price makers, and the question "How much should I supply, given a price?" will not be asked. Instead the question asked is "Given a demand curve, how much should I produce and what price should I charge?" In other market structures, the supplier sets the quantity and price, based on costs, at whatever level is best for it.[1]

---

[1] A firm's ability to set price doesn't mean that it can choose just any price it pleases. Other market structures can be highly competitive, so the range of prices a firm can charge and still stay in business is often limited. Such highly competitive firms are not perfectly competitive because they still set price, rather than supply a certain quantity and accept whatever price they get.

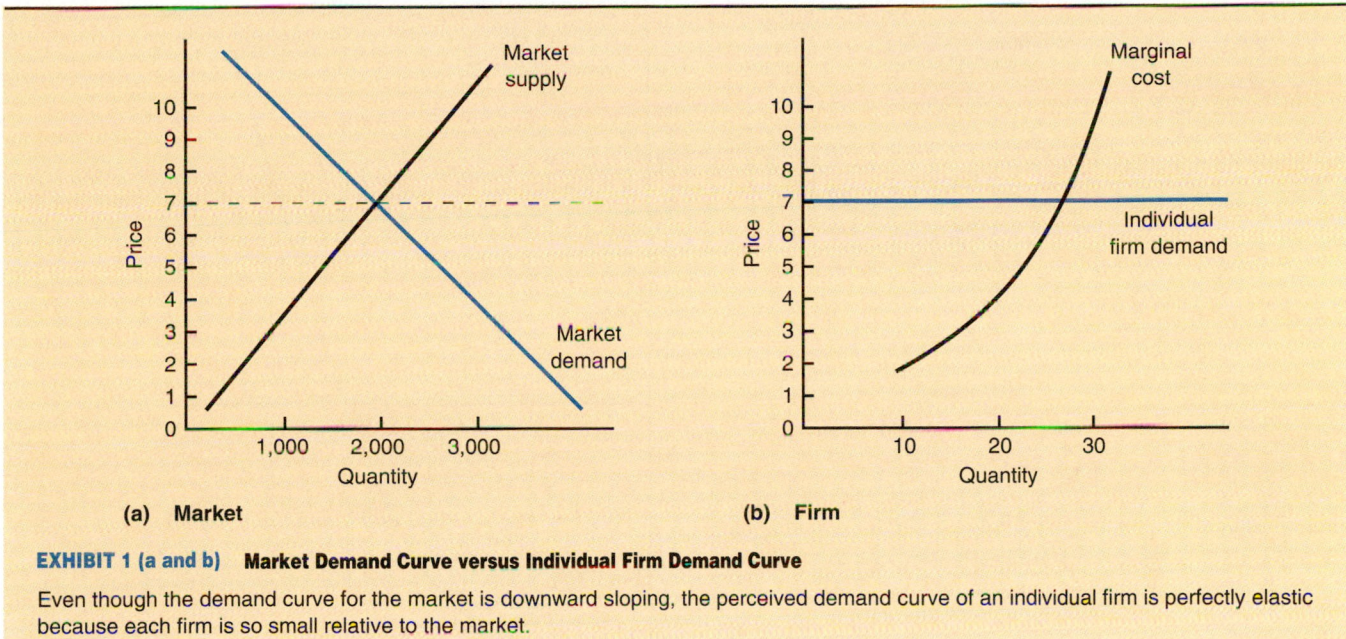

EXHIBIT 1 (a and b)   Market Demand Curve versus Individual Firm Demand Curve

Even though the demand curve for the market is downward sloping, the perceived demand curve of an individual firm is perfectly elastic because each firm is so small relative to the market.

The second condition—that the number of firms is large—is necessary so that firms have no ability to *collude* (to operate in concert so that they can get more for themselves). Conditions 3 through 6 are closely related to the first two; they make it impossible for any firm to forget that there are hundreds of other firms out there just waiting to supply a good if it doesn't. Condition 7 lets us specify a firm's goals. If we didn't know the goals, we wouldn't know how firms would react when faced with the given price.

What's nice about these conditions is that they allow us to formally relate supply to the cost concept that we developed in the last chapter: marginal cost. If the conditions hold, a firm's supply curve will be that portion of the firm's short-run marginal cost curve above the average variable cost curve, as we'll see shortly.

Of course, as later chapters will reveal, even if we can't technically specify a supply function, and even if the conditions for perfect competition don't fully exist, supply forces are still strong and many of the insights of the competitive model carry over. That's why it's important to know that competitive model well.

Even if we can't technically specify a supply function, supply forces are still strong and many of the insights of the competitive model carry over.

Demand Curves for the Firm and the Industry

Now that we've considered the competitive supply curve for the firm, let's turn our attention to the competitive demand curve for the firm. Here we must recognize that the demand curve for the industry is downward sloping as in Exhibit 1(a), but the perceived demand curve for the firm is perfectly elastic as in Exhibit 1(b). (Remember, I told you those terms would be important.)

Why the difference? It's a difference in perception. Each firm in a competitive industry is so small that it perceives its own demand curve as perfectly elastic even though the demand curve for the industry is downward sloping. Think of it as removing one piece of sand from a beach. Does that lower the level of the beach? For all practical, and even most impractical, purposes, we can assume it doesn't. Similarly for a perfectly competitive firm: Its demand curve is perfectly elastic even though the demand curve for the market is downward sloping.

This difference in perception is extremely important. It means that firms will increase their output in response to an increase in demand even though that increase in output will cause price to fall and can make all firms collectively worse off. But since, by the assumptions of perfect competition, they don't organize collectively, each firm follows its self-interest. Let's now consider that self-interest in more detail.

Q–2: How can the demand curve for the market be downward sloping but the demand curve for a competitive firm be perfectly elastic?

A perfectly competitive firm's demand schedule is perfectly elastic even though the demand curve for the market is downward sloping.

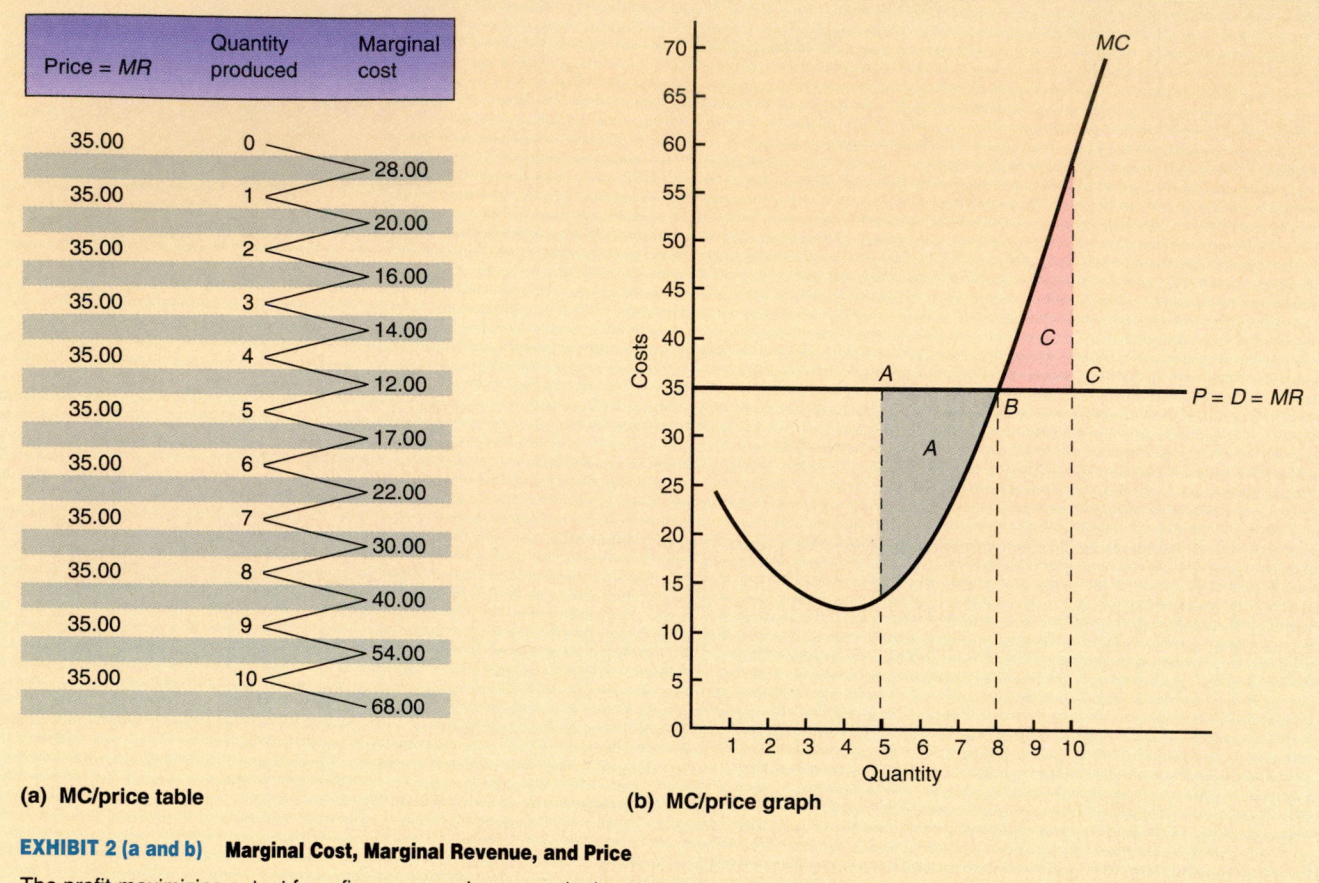

Price = MR	Quantity produced	Marginal cost
35.00	0	
		28.00
35.00	1	
		20.00
35.00	2	
		16.00
35.00	3	
		14.00
35.00	4	
		12.00
35.00	5	
		17.00
35.00	6	
		22.00
35.00	7	
		30.00
35.00	8	
		40.00
35.00	9	
		54.00
35.00	10	
		68.00

(a) MC/price table

(b) MC/price graph

EXHIBIT 2 (a and b)   Marginal Cost, Marginal Revenue, and Price

The profit-maximizing output for a firm occurs where marginal cost equals marginal revenue. Since for a competitive firm $P = MR$, its profit-maximizing output is where $MC = P$. At any other output it is forgoing profit.

PROFIT MAXIMIZATION AND EQUILIBRIUM OF A COMPETITIVE FIRM

Marginal cost   *The change in cost associated with a change in quantity.*

Marginal revenue   *The change in revenue associated with a change in quantity.*

To determine the profit-maximizing output, all you need to know is MC and MR.

The goal of a firm is to maximize profits—to get as much for itself as possible. To do so, it should produce where **marginal cost** (the change in total cost associated with a change in quantity) equals **marginal revenue** (the change in total revenue associated with a change in quantity). Any other output level will yield lower profits. Thus, the marginal cost curve is a competitive firm's supply curve because, given a price, the firm can do no better (its profits are the highest possible) than producing the quantity at which marginal cost equals price which in turn equals marginal revenue.

To see that this is the case, consider Exhibit 2(a), which lists both marginal cost and marginal revenue. The information in Exhibit 2(a) is generally presented graphically as we do in Exhibit 2(b).

A firm is interested in maximizing profit, so in its decision about what quantity to produce it will continually ask the question: What will changes in quantity do to profit? Profit is the difference between total revenue and total cost. What happens to profit in response to a change in output is determined by *marginal revenue* (*MR*) and *marginal cost* (*MC*). That's why marginal revenue and marginal cost are key concepts in determining the profit-maximizing or loss-minimizing level of output of any firm.

To emphasize the importance of *MR* and *MC*, those are the only cost and revenue figures I show in Exhibit 2. Notice that I don't list profit at all. This is because to calculate profit you must know average total cost (*ATC*). But you don't need to know what *ATC* is to determine the profit-maximizing output. All you need know is *MC* and *MR*. When marginal revenue and marginal cost are equal, the firm is maximizing profit. You only need *ATC* if you want to know what that level of profit will be.

Since *MC* and *MR* are so important, let's look at them more carefully.

Marginal Revenue

Let's first consider marginal revenue (the additional revenue the firm gets from selling another unit of output). For a competitive firm marginal revenue is simple to determine—it's the price it gets for the good. For example, if the firm increases output from 2 to 3, the price it receives for each additional unit sold is $35 so its marginal revenue is $35, the price of the good. At a price of $35 it can sell as much as it wants. So:

$$\text{For a competitive firm, } MR = P.$$

For a competitive firm, MR = P.

Marginal revenue is given in column 1 of Exhibit 2(a). As you can see, *MR* equals $35 for all levels of output. But that's what we saw in Exhibit 1 which showed that the demand curve for a perfect competitor is perfectly elastic and equal to its marginal revenue curve.

Marginal Cost

Now let's move on to marginal cost. I'll be brief since I discussed marginal cost in detail in an earlier chapter. Marginal cost is that change in cost that accompanies a change in output. Exhibit 2(a) shows marginal cost in column 3. Notice that initially in this example, marginal cost is falling, but by the fifth unit of output, it's increasing. This is consistent with our discussion in earlier chapters.

Notice also that the marginal cost figures are given for movements of one quantity to another. That's because marginal concepts tell us what happens when there's a change in something, so marginal concepts are best defined between numbers. The numbers in the shaded rows are the marginal costs. So the marginal cost of increasing output from 1 to 2 is 20, and the marginal cost of increasing output from 2 to 3 is 16. The marginal cost right at 2 (which the marginal cost graph shows) would be between 20 and 16 at approximately 18.

Profit Maximization: $MC = MR$

I just stated that, to maximize profit, a firm should produce where marginal cost equals marginal revenue. Looking at Exhibit 2(b), we see that a firm following that rule should produce at an output of 8 where $MC = MR = 35$. Now let me try to convince you that 8 is indeed the profit-maximizing output. To do so, let's consider three different possible quantities the firm might look at.

Let's say that initially it decides to produce 5, placing it at point *A* in Exhibit 2(b). At output *A*, the firm gets $35 for each widget but its marginal cost of increasing output is $17. We don't yet know the firm's profit (the difference between its total revenue and its total cost), but we do know what effect changing output will have on profit. For example, say the firm increases production from 5 to 6. Its revenue will rise by $35. (In other words, its marginal revenue is $35.) Its marginal cost of increasing output is $17. So if it increases production by one unit, profit increases by $18 (the difference between *MR*, $35, and *MC*, $17), so at an output of 5 it makes sense (meaning the firm can increase its profit) to increase output. This reasoning holds true as long as the marginal cost is below the marginal revenue. The blue shaded area (*A*) represents the entire increase in profit the firm can get by increasing output.

Now let's say that the firm decides to produce 10 widgets, placing it at point *C*. Here the firm gets $35 for each widget, but the marginal cost of producing that tenth unit is greater than that at $54. If the firm decreases production by one unit, its cost decreases by $54 and its revenue decreases by $35. Profit increases by $19 ($54 − $35 = $19), so at point *C*, it makes sense to decrease output. This reasoning holds true as long as the marginal cost is above the marginal revenue. The red shaded area (*C*) represents the increase in profits the firm can get by decreasing output.

At point *B* (output = 8) the firm gets $35 for each widget, and its marginal cost is $35, as you can see in Exhibit 2(b). If it increases output by one unit, its cost will rise by $40 and its revenue will increase by $35, so its profit falls by $5. If the firm decreases output by one unit, its cost falls by $30 and its revenue falls by $35, so its profit falls by $5. Either increasing or decreasing production will decrease profit, so point *B*, at an output of 8, where marginal cost equals marginal revenue (price), is the **profit-maximizing condition** for a perfectly competitive firm. This leads us to the following conclusion:

The profit-maximizing condition of a competitive firm is $MC = MR = P$.

Q–3: What are the two things you must know to determine the profit-maximizing output?

Profit-maximizing condition for a competitive firm: MR = P = MC.

2 If marginal revenue does not equal marginal cost, a firm obviously can increase profit by changing output. Therefore, profit is maximized when $MC = MR = P$.

You should commit this profit-maximizing condition to memory. You should also be sure that you understand the intuition behind it. If marginal revenue isn't equal to marginal cost, a firm obviously can increase profit by changing output. If that isn't obvious, the marginal benefit of an additional hour of thinking about this condition will exceed the marginal cost (whatever it is), meaning that you should . . . right, you guessed it . . . study some more.

The Marginal Cost Curve Is the Supply Curve

3 Because the marginal cost curve tells us how much of a produced good a firm will supply at a given price, the marginal cost curve *is* the firm's supply curve.

Now let's consider again the definition of the supply curve as a schedule of quantities of goods that will be offered to the market at various prices. Notice that the marginal cost curve fits that definition. It tells how much the firm will supply at a given price. If the price is $35, we showed that the firm would supply 8. If the price had been $20, the firm would have supplied 6; if the price had been $61, the firm would have supplied 10. Because the marginal cost curve tells us how much of a produced good a firm will supply at a given price, the marginal cost curve *is* the firm's supply curve. The *MC* curve tells the competitive firm how much it should produce at a given price. (As you'll see later, there's an addendum to this statement. Specifically, the marginal cost curve is the firm's supply curve only if price exceeds average variable cost.)

The Broader Importance of the $MR = MC$ Equilibrium Condition

This marginal revenue = marginal cost equilibrium condition is simple, but it's enormously powerful. As we'll see, it carries over to other market structures. If you replace revenue with benefits, it also forms the basis of economic reasoning. With whom should you go out? What's the marginal benefit? What's the marginal cost? Should you marry Pat? What's the marginal benefit? What's the marginal cost? As we discussed in Chapter 1, thinking like an economist requires thinking in these marginal terms and applying this marginal reasoning to a wide variety of activities. Understanding this condition is to economics what understanding gravity is to physics. It gives you a sense of if, how, and why prices and quantities will move.

Economic Profit, Accounting Profit, and Normal Profit

In earlier chapters I emphasized that the concept of *cost* that economists use isn't necessarily cost as measured by accountants, but is instead *opportunity cost* (the value of forgone opportunities) of using an input in its next-best alternative use. The meaning of the $MR = MC$ equilibrium condition must be interpreted in reference to this definition.

The goal of a competitive firm is to maximize profit (the residual left over after all the factors of production have been paid). *Profit* is defined:

Profit = Total Revenue − Total Costs.

$$Profit = Total\ revenue - Total\ costs$$

A profit-maximizing firm tries to hold down cost and get as much as it can for the goods it sells. A firm whose goal is profit maximization can be analyzed as an independent entity, analogous to the individual in consumer theory, but instead of maximizing utility as the individual does, the firm maximizes profit. Because profits are the difference between total revenue and total cost, the fact that there are two alternative concepts of cost means that there are two alternative concepts of profit: accounting profit and economic profit. **Accounting profit** is the profit one arrives at using the accountants' definition of cost. **Economic profit** is the profit one arrives at using the economists' definition of cost. In this discussion of the competitive firm, we're interested in *economic* profit.

Accounting profit Profit defined according to accountants' definition of cost.

Economic profit Profit defined according to economists' definition of cost.

Unfortunately, as we discussed in the last chapter, in applying the analysis to the real world often there's no measure of economic profit. Accountants do the measuring and economists are stuck with using accountants' measurements and trying to relate the unmeasured economic profit to the measured accounting profit. In doing so, economists have found that accountants consistently leave out one cost that economists believe should be included: the implicit cost of owners of business. This includes the implicit interest that owners could have received from the funds had they invested those funds in another business (the opportunity cost of capital) and the wages they could have earned if they had spent their time working as employees for

EXHIBIT 3   Accountants' versus Economists' Concepts of Profit

Accountants' concept			Economists' concept			
Total revenue		$1,000	Total revenue			$1,000
Costs			Explicit costs			
Labor	$100		Labor	$100		
Materials	600		Materials	600		
Rent	80		Rent	80		
Total costs		780	Total explicit costs		$780	
Accounting profit		$ 220	Implicit costs			
			Owner's salary	100		
			Normal profit	80		
			Total implicit costs		180	
			Total costs			960
			Economic profits			$ 40

someone else as opposed to managing their own business (the opportunity cost of their time).

Exhibit 3 gives an example that distinguishes the accountants' and the economists' concepts of cost and profit. Notice that the economists' costs include implicit costs. Thus, economists' profits are lower than accountants' profits. Because accounting profits leave out these two costs, accounting profits are often higher than economic profits, which do include these costs. To distinguish between the two, economists sometimes call implicit costs *normal profits*. **Normal profits** are the returns to the owners of business for the opportunity cost of their implicit inputs. To an economist, normal profits are actually included as a cost and are not included in *economic profit*. As we'll see later, a competitive firm earns normal profits (a normal return for the work and capital its owner puts in), but it does not earn economic profit in the long run.

Normal profits   The returns to the owners of business for the opportunity cost of their implicit inputs.

Setting *MC* = *MR* Maximizes Total Profit

I've spent great effort emphasizing that all you need to know is *MC* and *MR* to determine profit-maximizing output. Now that you know that, let's turn our attention to profit. How do we determine profit? Notice that when you talk about maximizing profit, you're talking about maximizing *total profit*, not profit per unit. Profit per unit would be maximized at a much lower output level than is total profit. Firms don't care about profit per unit; as long as an increase in output will increase total profits, a profit-maximizing firm should increase output. That's difficult to intuit, so let's consider a concrete example.

Q–4: Why do firms maximize total profit rather than profit per unit?

Say two people are selling T-shirts that cost $4 each. One sells 2 T-shirts at a price of $6 each and makes a profit per shirt of $2. His total profit is $4. The second person sells the T-shirts at $5 each, making a profit per unit of only $1 but selling 8. Her total profit is $8, twice as much as the fellow who had the $2 profit per unit. In this case, $5 (the price with the lower profit per unit), not $6, yields more total profit.

In the discussion of the firm's choice of output, given price, I carefully presented only marginal cost and price. We talked about maximizing profit, but nowhere did I mention what profit, average total cost, average variable cost, or average fixed cost is. I mentioned only marginal cost and price to emphasize that marginal cost is all that's needed to determine a competitive firm's supply curve (and a competitive firm is the only firm that has a supply curve) and the output that will maximize profit.

Determining Profit and Loss

Determining Profit from a Table of Costs   The *P* = *MR* = *MC* condition tells us how much output a competitive firm should produce to maximize profit. It does not tell us what level of profit the firm makes. The level of profit is determined by total revenue minus total cost. Exhibit 4 expands Exhibit 2(a) and presents a table of costs with all the costs relevant to the firm. Going through each of the columns and reminding yourself of the definition of each is a good review of the last chapter. If the definitions

EXHIBIT 4　Costs Relevant to a Firm

	1	2	3	4	5	6	7	8	9	10
Price = Marginal revenue	Quantity produced	Total fixed cost	Average fixed cost	Total variable cost	Average variable cost	Total cost	Average total cost	Marginal cost	Total revenue	Total profit
$35.00	0	$40.00	—	0	—	$ 40.00	—		0	$−40.00
								$28.00		
35.00	1	40.00	$40.00	$ 28.00	$28.00	68.00	$68.00		$ 35.00	−33.00
								20.00		
35.00	2	40.00	20.00	48.00	24.00	88.00	44.00		70.00	−18.00
								16.00		
35.00	3	40.00	13.33	64.00	21.33	104.00	34.67		105.00	1.00
								14.00		
35.00	4	40.00	10.00	78.00	19.50	118.00	29.50		140.00	22.00
								12.00		
35.00	5	40.00	8.00	90.00	18.00	130.00	26.00		175.00	45.00
								17.00		
35.00	6	40.00	6.67	107.00	17.83	147.00	24.50		210.00	63.00
								22.00		
35.00	7	40.00	5.71	129.00	18.43	169.00	24.14		245.00	76.00
								30.00		
35.00	8	40.00	5.00	159.00	19.88	199.00	24.88		280.00	81.00
								40.00		
35.00	9	40.00	4.44	199.00	22.11	239.00	26.56		315.00	76.00
								54.00		
35.00	10	40.00	4.00	253.00	25.30	293.00	29.30		350.00	57.00

don't come to mind immediately, you need a review. [I pause here to allow you to review; if you don't know the definitions of *MC, AVC, ATC, FC,* and *AFC,* go back and reread the previous two chapters.]

Pause

4 The profit-maximizing output can be determined in a table (as in Exhibit 4) or in a graph (as in Exhibit 5).

The firm is interested in maximizing profit. Looking at Exhibit 4, you can quickly see that the profit-maximizing position is 8, as it was before, since at an output of 8, total profit is highest.

The maximum profit the firm can earn is $81, which we calculated by subtracting total cost of $199 from total revenue of $280. Notice also that average total cost is lowest at an output of about 7, and the average variable cost is lowest at an output of about 6.[2] Thus, the profit-maximizing position (which is 8), *is not* necessarily a position that minimizes either average variable cost or average total cost. It is only the position that maximizes total profit. Notice the relationship between marginal cost and the price of $35 (which equals marginal revenue) at output level 8. Increasing output from 7 to 8 has a marginal cost of $30, which is less than $35, so it made sense to do so. Increasing output from 8 to 9 has a marginal cost of $40, which is more than $35, so it does not make sense to do so. The output 8 is the profit-maximizing output.

Determining Profit from a Graph　These relationships can be seen in a graph. In Exhibit 5(a) I add the average total cost and average variable cost curves to the graph of marginal cost and price first presented in Exhibit 2. Notice that the marginal cost curve goes through the lowest points of both average cost curves. (If you don't know why, it would be a good idea to go back again and review the previous chapter.)

Q–5: If the firm described in Exhibit 4 is producing 4 units, what would you advise it to do, and why?

The way you find profit graphically is first to find the point where *MC = MR* (point *A*). That intersection determines the quantity the firm will produce if it wants to maximize profit. Why? Because the vertical distance between a point on the marginal cost curve and a point on the marginal revenue curve represents the additional profit

---

[2] I say "about 6" and "about 7" because the table gives only whole numbers. The actual minimum point occurs at 5.55 for average variable cost and 6.55 for average total cost. The nearest whole numbers to these are 6 and 7.

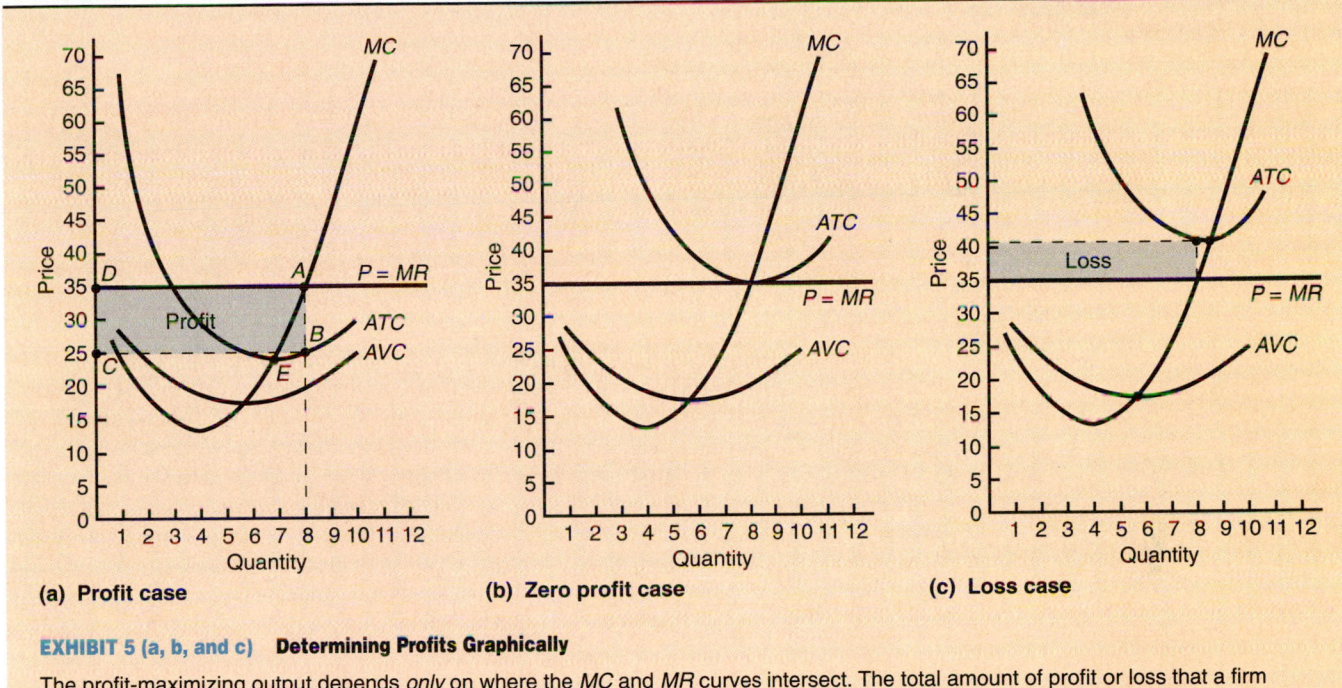

EXHIBIT 5 (a, b, and c)   Determining Profits Graphically

The profit-maximizing output depends *only* on where the *MC* and *MR* curves intersect. The total amount of profit or loss that a firm makes depends on the price it receives and its average total cost of producing the profit-maximizing output. This exhibit shows the case of (**a**) a profit, (**b**) zero profit, and (**c**) a loss.

the firm can make by changing output. For example, if it increases production from 6 to 7, its marginal cost is $22 and its marginal revenue is $35. By increasing output it can increase profit by $13 (from $63 to $76). The same reasoning holds true for any output less than 8. For outputs higher than 8, the opposite reasoning holds true. Marginal cost exceeds marginal revenue, so it pays to decrease output. So to maximize profit, the firm must see that there is no distance between the two curves—it must see where they intersect.

After having determined that quantity, drop a vertical line down to the horizontal axis and see what average total cost is at that output level (point *B*). Doing so determines the profit per unit at the profit-maximizing output because it's the distance between the price the firm receives (its average revenue) and its average cost. Since the firm will earn that profit on each unit sold, you next extend a line back to the vertical axis (point *C*). That tells us the total quantity the firm will sell. Next go up the price axis to the price that, for a competitive firm, is the marginal revenue (point *D*). That gives us the shaded rectangle, *ABCD*, which is the total profit earned by the firm (the total quantity times the profit per unit).

Notice that at the profit-maximizing position, the profit per unit isn't at its highest because average total cost is *not* at its minimum point. Profit per unit of output would be highest at point *E*. A common mistake that students make is to draw a line up from point *E* when they are finding profits. That is wrong. It is important to remember: *To determine maximum profit you must first determine what output the firm will choose to produce by seeing where MC equals MR and then determine the average total cost at that quantity by dropping a line down to the ATC curve.* Only then can you determine what maximum profit will be.

Notice also that as the curves in Exhibit 5(a) are drawn, *ATC* at the profit-maximizing position is below the price, and the firm makes a profit per unit of a little over $10. The choice of short-run average total cost curves was arbitrary and doesn't affect the firm's profit-maximizing condition: *MC = MR*. It could have been assumed that fixed cost was higher, which would have shifted the *ATC* curve up. In Exhibit 5(b) it's assumed that fixed cost is $81 higher than in Exhibit 5(a). Instead of $40, it's

To determine maximum profit, you must first determine what output the firm will choose to produce by seeing where MC equals MR, and then dropping a line down to the ATC curve.

Most real-world firms do not have profit as their only goal. The reason is that, in the real world, the decision-maker's income is part of the cost of production. For example, a paid manager has an incentive to hold down costs, but has little incentive to hold down his income which, for the firm, is a cost. Alternatively, say that a firm is a worker-managed firm. If workers receive a share of the profits, they'll push for higher profits, but they'll also see to it that in the process of maximizing profits they don't hurt their own interests—maximizing their wages.

A manager-managed firm will push for high profit, but will see to it that it doesn't achieve those profits by hurting the manager's interests. Managers' pay will be high. In short, real-world firms will hold down the costs of factors of production *except* the cost of the decision maker.

In real life, this problem of the lack of incentives to hold down costs is important. For example, firms' managerial expenses often balloon even as firms are cutting "costs." Similarly, CEOs and other high-ranking officers of the firm often have enormously high salaries. How and why the lack of incentives to hold down costs affects the economy is best seen by first considering the nature of an economy with incentives to hold down all costs. That's why we use as our standard model the profit-maximizing firm.*

_____

* *Standard model* means the model that economists use as our basis of reasoning; from it, we branch out.

Q–6: What is wrong with the following diagram?

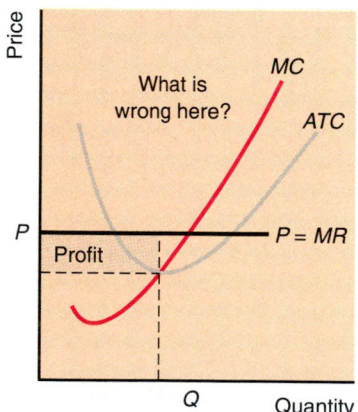

Total Revenue and Total Cost

$121. The appropriate average total cost curve for a fixed cost of $121 is drawn in Exhibit 5(b). Notice that in this case economic profit is zero and the marginal cost curve intersects the minimum point of the average total cost curve at an output of 8 and a price of $35. In this case the firm is making zero economic profit. (Remember, although economic profit is zero, all resources, including entrepreneurs, are being paid their opportunity cost, so they're getting a normal return.)

In Exhibit 5(c), fixed cost is much higher—$169. Profit-maximizing output is still 8, but now at an output of 8, the firm is making an economic loss of $6 on each unit sold, since its average total cost is $41. The loss is given by the shaded rectangle. In this case, the profit-maximizing condition is actually a loss-minimizing condition. So $MC = MR = P$ is both a profit-maximizing condition and a loss-minimization condition.

I draw these three cases to emphasize to you that determining the profit-maximizing output level doesn't depend on fixed cost or average total cost. It depends only on where marginal cost equals price.

Throughout this chapter we've emphasized the determination of profit by equating marginal cost and price. That focuses the analysis on the relevant issues since marginal changes highlight the relevant considerations in choosing the profit-maximizing output.

An alternative method to see how the firm maximizes profit, which helps distinguish between profit per unit and total profit, is to look at total revenue and total cost, as Exhibit 6 does. In it we plot the firm's total revenue and total cost curves (columns 9 and 6 of Exhibit 4). The total revenue curve is a straight line; each additional good sold increases revenue by the same amount, $35. The total cost curve is bowed upward at most quantities, reflecting the changing marginal cost at different levels of output. The firm's profit is represented by the distance between the total revenue curve and the total cost curve. For example, at output 5, the firm makes $45 in profit.

Total profit is maximized where the vertical distance between total revenue and total cost is greatest. In this example total profit is maximized at output 8, just as in the alternative approach. At that output, marginal revenue (the slope of the total revenue curve) and marginal cost (the slope of the total cost curve) are equal.

The Shutdown Point

Earlier I stated the supply curve of a competitive firm is its marginal cost curve. More specifically, the supply curve is the part of the marginal cost curve that is above the

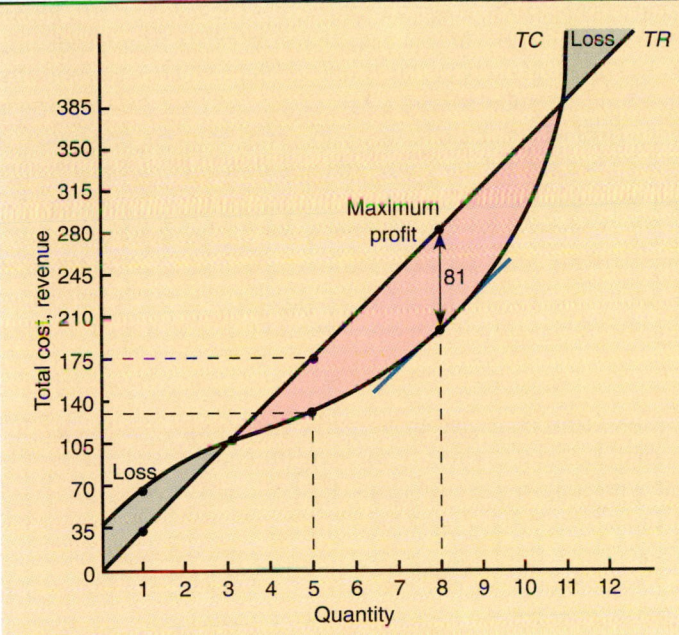

EXHIBIT 6 **Determination of Profits by Total Cost and Total Revenue Curves**

The profit-maximizing output level can also be seen by considering the total cost curve and the total revenue curve. Profit is maximized at the output where total revenue exceeds total cost by the largest amount. This occurs at an output of 8.

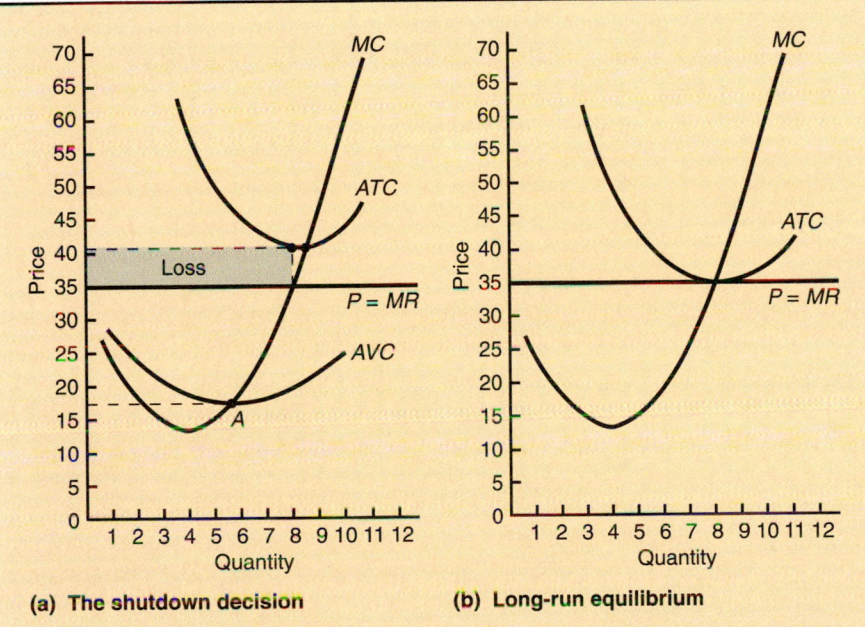

EXHIBIT 7 **The Shutdown Decision and Long-Run Equilibrium**

A firm should continue to produce as long as price exceeds average variable cost. Once price falls below that, it will do better by temporarily shutting down and saving the variable costs. This occurs at point A in (a). In (b), the long-run equilibrium position for a marginal firm in an industry is shown. In that long-run equilibrium, only normal profits are made.

(a) The shutdown decision   **(b) Long-run equilibrium**

average variable cost curve. Considering why this is the case should help the analysis stick in your mind.

Let's consider Exhibit 7 (a reproduction of Exhibit 5(c)) and the firm's decision at various prices. At a price of $35, it's incurring a loss of $6 per unit. If it's making a loss, why doesn't it shut down? The answer lies in the fixed costs. There's no use crying over spilt milk. In the short run a firm knows it must pay these fixed costs regardless of whether or not it produces. The firm only considers the costs it can save by stopping production, and those costs are its variable costs. As long as a firm is covering its variable costs, it pays to keep on producing. By producing, its loss is $48; if it stopped producing, its loss would be all the fixed costs ($169). So it makes a smaller loss by producing.

Q–7: In the 1990s, many airlines were making losses, yet they continued to operate. Why?

However, once the price falls below average variable costs (below $17.80), it will pay to shut down (point *A* in Exhibit 7(a)). In that case the firm's loss from producing would be more than $169, and it would do better to simply stop producing temporarily and save the variable cost. Thus, the point at which *MC* equals *AVC* is the **shutdown point** (that point at which the firm will gain more by temporarily shutting down than it will by staying in business). When price falls below the shutdown point, the average variable costs the firm can save by shutting down exceed the price it would get for selling the good. When price is above average variable cost, in the short run a firm should keep on producing even though it's making a loss. As long as a firm's total revenue is covering its total variable cost, temporarily producing at a loss is the firm's best strategy because it's making less of a loss than it would make if it were to shut down.

Shutdown point   Point at which the firm will gain more by shutting down than it will by staying in business.

LONG-RUN COMPETITIVE EQUILIBRIUM

5 Since profits create incentives for new firms to enter, output will increase, and the price will fall until zero profits are being made.

The analysis of the competitive firm consists of two parts: the short-run analysis just presented, and a long-run analysis. The essence of the long-run analysis is that profits and losses are inconsistent with long-run equilibrium. In the long run, only the zero-profit equilibrium shown in Exhibit 7(b) is possible. The existence of above-normal profits would cause firms to enter the industry, causing the price to fall until the marginal firm can expect zero economic profit. Similarly, the existence of losses will cause firms to exit the industry until the marginal firm can expect only the normal profit. The requirement that in the long run zero profits exist is called the **zero profit condition.**

Why is that the case, and how does it come about? Let's say that the average firm in an industry is making an economic profit. Because entry is open to anyone, the existence of profit will entice new firms to enter, putting downward pressure on the price due to the increase in output. The price will continue to fall until no new firms have an incentive to enter, which means that the average firm in the industry is not making a profit. Only at zero profit does entry stop.

Now let's say that the average firm in the industry is making a loss. It will stay in business in the short run, as long as the price it receives exceeds the *AVC*, but in the long run, as its machines wear out and as its fixed costs become variable, it will get out of the business.

As some firms get out of business, the price will rise. So when firms are making a loss there is pressure for the price in that industry to rise. Price will continue to rise until firms are no longer making a loss.

Summarizing: In the long run only one of the three total average cost curve positions is an equilibrium—the one in which there is neither an economic profit nor an economic loss (the position in which long-run average total cost equals the price, which equals marginal cost). This is known as the *zero profit condition*. It defines the long-run equilibrium of a competitive industry.

We should point out once again that *zero profit* does not mean that the entrepreneur doesn't get anything for her efforts. The entrepreneur is an input like any other input. In order to stay in the business she must receive her opportunity cost or normal profit (the amount she would have received in the next-best alternative). That normal profit is built into the costs.

Another aspect of the zero profit position deserves mention. What if one firm has superefficient workers or machinery? Won't the firm make a profit in the long run? The answer is, again, no. Other firms will see the value of those workers or machines and will bid up the price of any specialized input until all profits are eliminated. As we'll discuss later, those inputs receive what are called *rents* to their specialized ability. A **rent** is an income received by a specialized factor of production. For example, say the average worker receives $400 per week but Sarah, because she's such a good worker, receives $600. So $200 of the $600 she receives is a rent to her specialized ability.

Remember, the costs that we use in our marginal cost curve analysis are *opportunity costs* (the amount that the input would be paid in its next-best option). Thus, if the profits exist because of specialized inputs, they'll be squeezed out by rents; if the

Q–8: If a competitive firm makes zero profit, why does it stay in business?

Rent   An income received by a specialized factor of production.

The costs that we use in our marginal cost curve analysis are opportunity costs.

THE SHUTDOWN DECISION AND THE RELEVANT COSTS

he two previous chapters emphasized that it is vital to choose the relevant costs to the decision at hand. Discussing the shutdown decision gives us a chance to demonstrate the importance of those choices. Say the firm leases a large computer which it needs to operate. The rental cost of that computer is a fixed cost for most decisions, if, as long as the firm keeps the computer, the rent must be paid whether or not the computer is used. However if the firm can end the rental contract at any time, and, thereby, save the rental cost, the computer is not a fixed cost. But neither is it your normal variable cost. Since the firm can end the rental contract and save the cost only if it shuts down, that rental cost of the computer is an *indivisible set-up cost*. For the shutdown decision, the computer cost is a variable cost. For other decisions about changing quantity, it's a fixed cost.

The moral: The relevant cost can change with the decision at hand, so when you apply the analysis to real-world situations, be sure to think carefully about what is the *relevant cost.*

profits exist because of a sudden increase in demand, they'll be squeezed out by new entry. For example, say that a restaurant opens and does wonderfully because it has a super chef. The restaurant makes a large profit, but it will also discover that other restaurants will be offering to hire this super chef at double or triple her current wage. Either the first restaurant matches those offers, losing its above-normal profit, or it loses the chef, losing its above-normal profits. One way or the other, the restaurant is squeezed.

The zero profit condition is enormously powerful; it makes the analysis of competitive markets far more applicable to the real world than can a strict application of the assumption of perfect competition. If economic profit is being made, firms will enter and compete that profit away. Price will be pushed down to cost of production as long as there are no barriers to entry. As we'll see in later chapters, in their analysis of whether markets are competitive many economists focus primarily on whether barriers to entry exist.

The zero profit condition is enormously powerful; it makes the analysis of competitive markets far more applicable to the real world then would otherwise be the case.

Convergence to Equilibrium and Experimental Economics

In the last 20 years a new branch of economics—experimental economics—has developed. **Experimental economics** is that branch of economics that tests the validity of economic hypotheses by controlled experiments. Experiments are run that simulate market structures and predictions of theories. One of the results experimental economics has arrived at is that double auction markets—a certain type of competitive market in which price is established by individuals bidding without communication with one another—tend to converge relatively quickly to a competitive equilibrium (where $MC = P = MR$) when trading is repeated with the same underlying cost structure. After getting to a competitive equilibrium, price stays there even though market participants have no idea what the competitive equilibrium is (although the experimenters know precisely where it is since they set up the experiment).

These experiments have given economists some additional support for believing that certain structures of competitive markets will converge to equilibrium. But the experiments have also shown the importance of the assumptions and institutions. For example, when the experiment was changed from a double auction market to a posted price market in which sellers stated the price at which they would sell, the price converged to equilibrium much more slowly.

The Supply and Demand Curves for the Industry

Most of the preceding discussion has focused on firm supply and demand analysis. Now let's consider supply and demand in an industry. We've already discussed industry demand. Even though the firm's demand curve is perfectly elastic, the industry demand curve is downward sloping.

How about the industry supply curve? We previously demonstrated that the supply curve for a competitive firm is that firm's marginal cost curve (above the average variable cost curve). To move from individual firms' marginal cost curves or supply curves to the **market supply curve,** we must sum up all the firms' marginal cost curves horizontally and take account of any changes in input prices that might

Market supply curve   Horizontal sum of all the firms' marginal cost curves, taking account of any changes in input prices that might occur.

occur. As we sum them up, the market supply curve becomes more elastic than the individual supply curves. This means that there is a larger quantity-supplied response to an increase in price for the entire market than there is for an existing individual firm. The reason is that the supply response comes from two sources:

1. Increase in output of existing firms.
2. Entrance of new firms into the market.

To arrive at the market supply curve, we cannot simply add all the individual firms' supply curves together. When there are industry-wide changes in demand, factor prices are likely to change, which would force costs up or down for each individual firm. For example, if there were an increase in demand for the industry's output that pushed up the price of that industry's input, there would be an upward shift in each of the individual firms' marginal costs (their supply curves) and the market supply curve would be less elastic than the horizontal summation of the individual firms' supply curves. In the extreme case where all firms in an industry are competitively supplying a perfectly inelastic resource or factor input, the market supply would be perfectly inelastic. Any increase in demand would increase the price of that factor. Costs would rise in response to the increase in demand; output would not.

As a check on whether you understand the ideas behind summing up supply curves, consider the following case: There are constant returns to scale but diminishing marginal product. Input prices are fixed. What does the market supply curve look like? If you answered "perfectly elastic," you've got it! You recognized that constant returns to scale and fixed input prices mean that an infinite number of firms can enter at the market price, so output can expand without limit at the existing price. If you didn't get it, a review probably is in order.

SUPPLY AND DEMAND TOGETHER

Now that we've been through the basics of the competitive supply and demand curves, we're ready to consider the two together and to see how adjustment will likely take place in the firm and in the market.

An Increase in Demand

First, in Exhibit 8(a) and (b), let's consider a market that's in equilibrium, but that suddenly experiences an increase in demand. Exhibit 8(a) shows a representative firm's reaction. Exhibit 8(b) shows the market reaction. Originally market equilibrium occurs at a price of $7 and market supply of 700 thousand units (point A in (b)), with each firm producing 10 units (point A in (a)). Firms are making zero profit because they're in long-run equilibrium. If demand increases from D_0 to D_1, the firms will see the market price increasing and will increase their output until they're once again at a position where $MC = P$. This occurs at point B at a market output of 840 thousand units in (b) and at a firm output of 12 in (a). In the short run the existing firms make an economic profit (the shaded area in Exhibit 8(a)). Price has risen to $9 but average cost is only $7.10, so if the price remains $9 the firm is making a profit of $1.90 per unit. But price cannot remain at $9 since each firm will have an incentive to expand and new firms will have an incentive to enter the market. This will push the price down.

As existing firms expand and new firms enter, there is a movement along the long-run market supply curve. Output increases and market price falls. Eventually the new long-run market equilibrium is reached. If there are no specialized inputs at that new long-run equilibrium, the price will fall back to the original price, $7. The entry of new firms or expansion of existing firms will provide the additional output. The final equilibrium will be at a higher output but the same price. If there had been specialized inputs, or if there were diseconomies of scale, the costs to the firms would have risen and the new equilibrium price would have been higher. Then the long-run supply curve would not have been perfectly elastic; it would have been upward sloping.[3]

Q–9: If berets suddenly became the "in" thing to wear, what would you expect to happen to the price in the short run? In the long run?

---

[3] To check your understanding, ask yourself the following question: What if there had been economies of scale? If you answered, "There couldn't have been," you're really into economic thinking. (For those of you who aren't all that heavily into economic thinking, the reason is that if there had been economies of scale, the market structure would not have been perfectly competitive. One firm would have kept expanding and expanding, and as it did, its costs would have kept falling.)

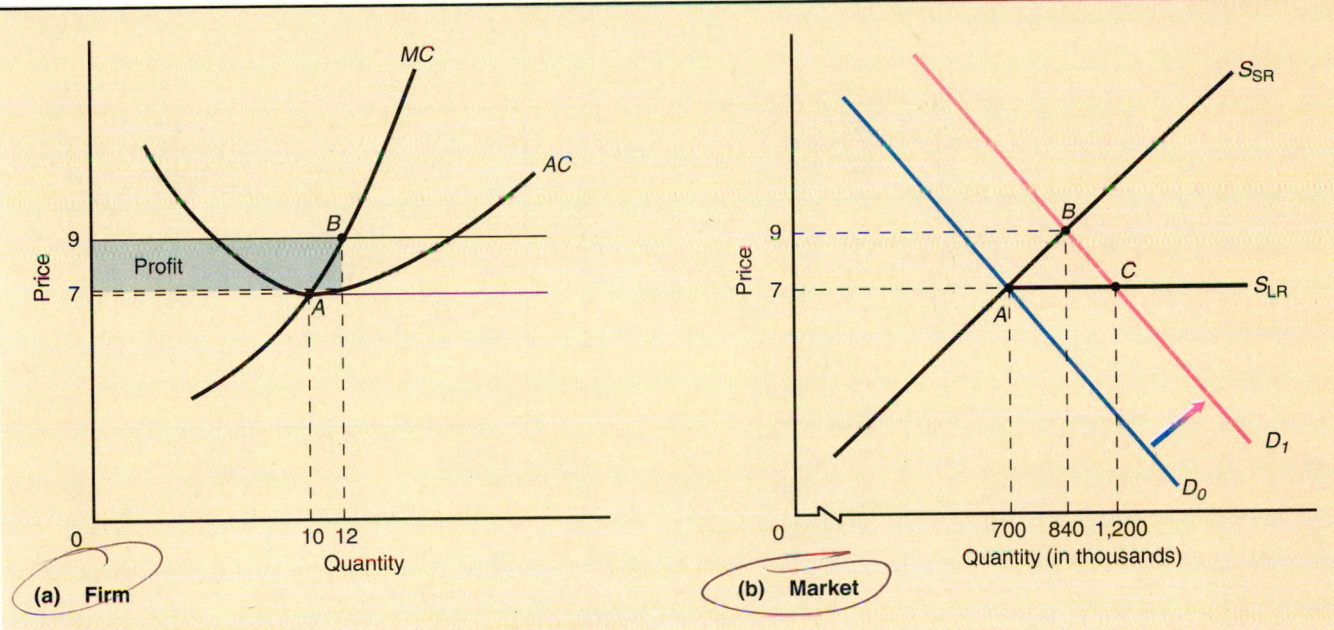

EXHIBIT 8 (a and b)   Market Response to an Increase in Demand

Faced with an increase in demand which it sees as an increase in price and hence profits, a competitive firm will respond by increasing output (from *A* to *B*) in order to maximize profit. A firm's response is shown in (**a**); the market reponse is shown in (**b**). As all firms increase output and as new firms enter, price will fall until all profit is competed away. Thus the long-run supply curve will be perfectly elastic as is S_{LR} in (**b**). The final equilibrium will be at the original price but a higher output. The original firms return to their original output (*A*) but since there are more firms in the market, the market output increases to (*C*).

Notice that in the long-run equilibrium, once again there is zero profit being made. Long-run equilibrium is defined by zero economic profit. Notice also that the long-run supply curve is much more elastic than the short-run supply curve. That's because output changes are much less costly in the short run than in the long run. *In the short run, the price does more of the adjusting. In the long run, more of the adjustment is done by quantity.*

In the short run, the price does more of the adjusting. In the long run, more of the adjustment is done by quantity.

A Technological Improvement

Next, in Exhibit 9 let's consider the effect of a technological improvement available to all firms. The initial equilibrium is at point *A*. The technological improvement lowers the marginal cost (from MC_0 to MC_1) and the average cost (from AC_0 to AC_1) for all firms. In the short run, existing firms make a profit equal to the distance between the market price and their average cost. If price would remain constant, they would increase output to point *B*. However, firms expand output and as new firms enter the market price is forced down, causing existing firms to change output to point *C* and finally to point *D*. Price falls from P_0 to P_1 to P_2 and quantity increases from Q_0 to Q_1 to Q_2, as shown in Exhibit 9(b).

As before, the increase in output eventually does not come from a movement along the short-run marginal cost curve, but instead comes from the entry of new firms or expansion by existing firms—movement along the long-run marginal cost curve.

A Decrease in Demand

Now, in Exhibit 10, let's consider a market that suddenly experiences a decrease in demand. Only this time let's also take into account the possibility of specialized inputs. Market equilibrium initially occurs at a price of $7 and market supply of 700,000 units, with each firm providing 10 units (point *A* in both (a) and (b)). Initially firms are in long-run equilibrium so there is no economic profit. Now suddenly demand decreases from D_0 to D_1. In the short run, total output falls to 560,000 units and market price falls to $5 (point *B*).

As the price falls to $5, individual firms cut output to where $MC = \$5$ at 8 units of output (Point *B*). Average total cost rises to $7.40, so individual firms will experience

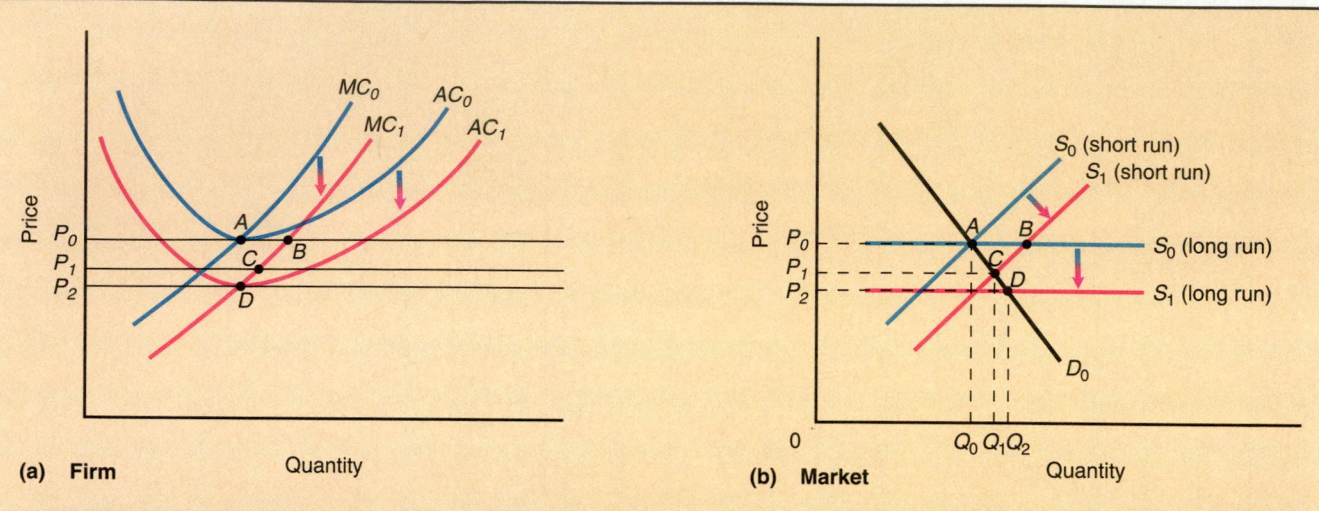

EXHIBIT 9 (a and b) **Market Response to a Technological Improvement**

A technological improvement will shift the *AC* and *MC* curves down, creating short-run profits. As existing firms expand output and as new firms enter, this profit will be competed away until the price has once again fallen to equal average total costs. The long-run equilibrium is shown by point *D* in both (**a**) and (**b**). The additional output is supplied by new firms.

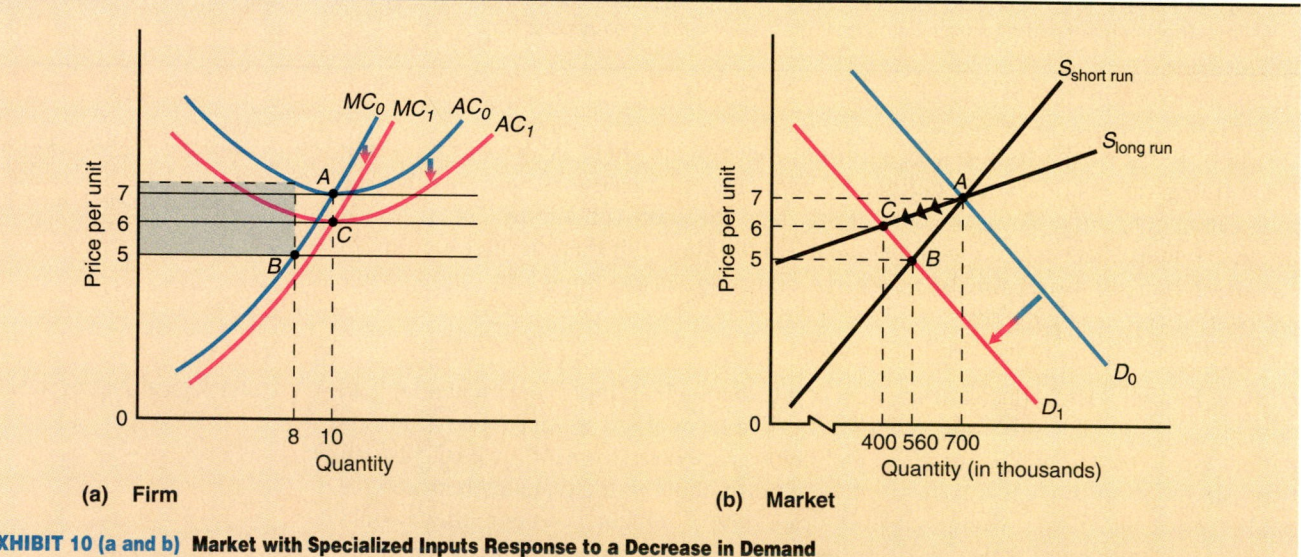

EXHIBIT 10 (a and b) **Market with Specialized Inputs Response to a Decrease in Demand**

Faced with a decrease in demand which it sees as a fall in price and hence profit, a competitive firm will respond by decreasing output in order to minimize losses. Firm output and market output will fall. In (**b**) we see the market response: as all firms decrease output, the demand for specialized inputs will fall, causing the firm's cost in (**a**) to fall from AC_0 to AC_1. The long-run equilibrium price will be lower than the original price, and the long-run supply curve S_{LR} will be upward sloping, rather than perfectly elastic.

losses, as shown in the shaded region of Exhibit 10(a). Those firms for whom price falls below average variable cost will exit the market.

As firms exit, there is a movement along the long-run market supply curve in Exhibit 10(b), which is more elastic than the short-run supply, but is not perfectly elastic. The reason is that as output decreases, the demand for, and hence the price of, specialized inputs will fall, decreasing marginal cost and average cost. Eventually a new long-run market equilibrium at a price of $6 (point *C*) will be reached at a lower quantity and lower price than the original equilibrium, but at a lower quantity and higher price than the short-run equilibrium.

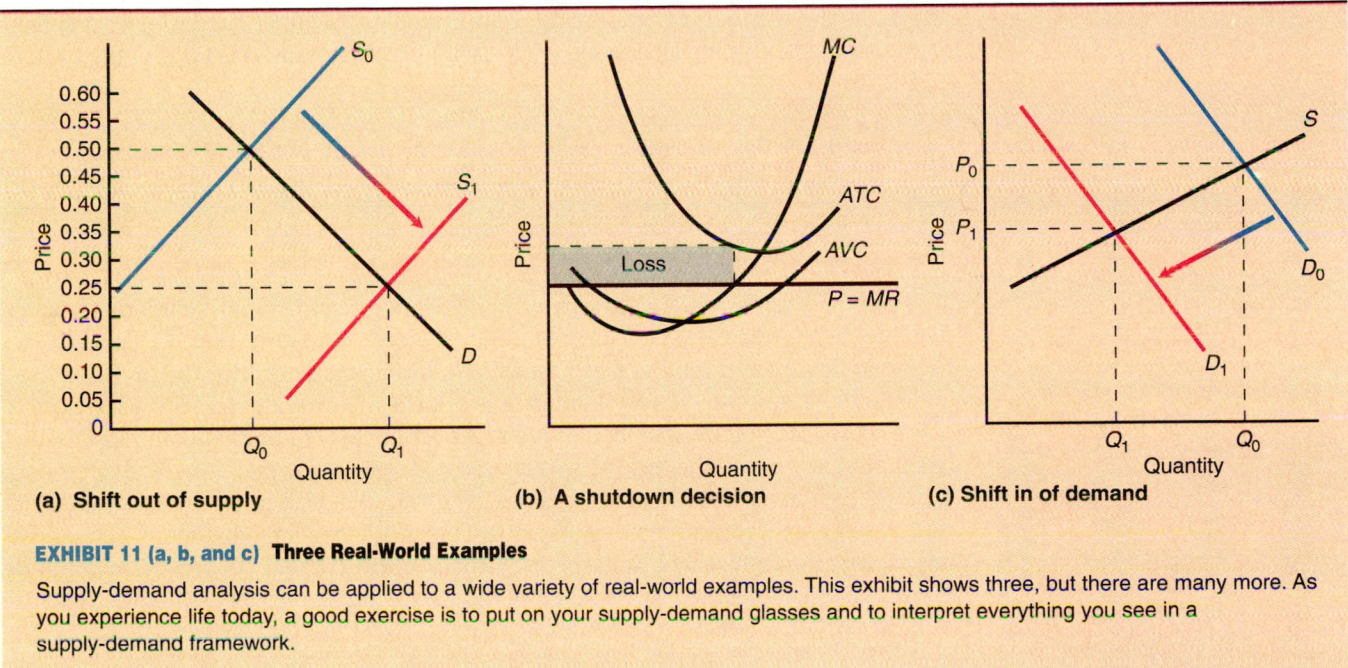

EXHIBIT 11 (a, b, and c)   **Three Real-World Examples**

Supply-demand analysis can be applied to a wide variety of real-world examples. This exhibit shows three, but there are many more. As you experience life today, a good exercise is to put on your supply-demand glasses and to interpret everything you see in a supply-demand framework.

The perfectly competitive model and the reasoning underlying it are extremely powerful. With them you have a simple model to use as a first approach to predict the effect of an event, or to explain why an event occurred. For example, consider the following events, all of which were reported in the newspapers.

Other Examples
in the Real World

1. Blueberry harvest is double what was predicted.
2. Owners of the Ames chain of department stores decide to close over 100 stores after experiencing two years of losses.
3. Tourism in Vietnam is only half of what was projected.

6 Supply and demand curves can be used to describe most real-world events.

Exhibit 11 (a, b, and c) shows these three cases. Let's briefly go through how each of them fits in with the perfectly competitive story.

In the first, the supply increases enormously so the supply curve shifts out from S_0 to S_1. In response, the price of blueberries is expected to fall. The newspaper reported that the wholesale price fell from 50¢ a pound to 25¢ a pound, as shown in Exhibit 11(a), so the event is consistent with the model.

In the second example (Exhibit 11(b)), we see a shutdown decision evolving into a long-run decision to stop producing. Initially, Ames saw the losses it was suffering as temporary. It was covering average variable cost, so it continued producing even while it was making a loss. So in the two years prior to the shutdown decision, Ames's cost curves look like those in Exhibit 11(b). Since price exceeded average variable cost, Ames continued to produce even though it was making a loss.

But after two years of losses Ames's perspective changed. The company moved from the short run to the long run. Ames began to believe that the demand wasn't temporarily low, but that it was permanently low. It began to ask: What costs are truly fixed and what costs are simply indivisible costs that we can save if we close down completely, selling our buildings and reducing our overhead? Since in the long run all costs are variable, the ATC became its relevant AVC. Ames recognized that demand had fallen below these long-run average costs. At that point, it shut down those stores for which $P < AVC$.

The third case is an example of a fall in demand. Because demand fell from D_0 to D_1, as shown in Exhibit 11(c), we would expect that the price of tourist services in Vietnam fell—which it did. Vietnamese hotels were cutting prices by 25 percent, and Vietnam was offering special tourist packages with reduced rates.

Q–10: In the early 1990s, demand for hotel rooms in Hawaii decreased substantially because the value of the Japanese yen fell. In the short run, what would you expect to happen to the prices of these hotel rooms? In the long run?

PERFECT COMPETITION, PARETO OPTIMALITY, AND JUDGING ECONOMIC SYSTEMS

7 The Pareto optimal criterion is that no person can be made better off without another being made worse off.

Don't study

The Free Market—An economics magazine that interprets current economic events from a libertarian perspective.

A Geometric Representation of the Welfare Loss of Deviations from Perfect Competition

Consumer surplus *The difference between what consumers would have been willing to pay and what they actually pay.*

Producer surplus *The difference between the price at which producers would have been willing to supply a good and the price they actually receive.*

There are hundreds of other real-world examples to which the perfectly competitive model adds insight. That's one reason why it's important to keep it in the back of your mind.

Two other related reasons why perfect competition is important are that:

1. It provides an understanding of how the invisible hand works to guide self-interest into society's interest; and
2. It provides a benchmark by which to judge economic systems.

From our earlier discussions you should have an informal sense of how the invisible hand translates self-interest into society's interest, but we haven't yet discussed that issue formally. Unfortunately, a formal sense of how the invisible hand guides self-interest into society's interest is not easy to provide, nor is it easy even to define what is meant by *society's interest*. As economists struggled with these issues, eventually they posed the following question: Can one show that a perfectly competitive equilibrium meets the **Pareto optimal criterion** that no person can be made better off without another being made worse off? This problem is one that many economists have worked on, but it was only in 1959 that Gerard Debreu succeeded in formally proving that a competitive economy met the Pareto optimal criterion under a specific set of conditions. For his work he was given a Nobel prize in 1983.

Let's briefly consider what Debreu proved. He showed that if there were a complete set of markets (a market for every possible good) now and in the future, and if all market transactions had no side effects on anyone not involved in those transactions, then if the economy were perfectly competitive, the invisible hand would guide the economy to a Pareto optimal result. In this case the supply curve (which represents the marginal cost to the individual supplier) would represent the marginal cost to society, while the demand curve would represent the marginal benefit to society. In a supply/demand equilibrium, not only would an individual be as well off as he or she possibly could be, given where he or she started from, so too would society. A perfectly competitive market equilibrium would be Pareto optimal.

Debreu's formal proof allows economists to use perfect competition as a benchmark. Since perfect competition is Pareto optimal, then any deviation from perfect competition would represent a welfare loss to society. Exhibit 12 considers an example, showing the welfare loss of a deviation from equilibrium.

As was stated earlier, the demand curve represents the marginal benefit to society; the supply curve represents the marginal cost to society. If that's the case at the competitive equilibrium, the marginal benefit equals the marginal cost and society is in a Pareto optimal position. Since the demand curve slopes downward and the supply curve slopes upward, many people are doing quite well in this competitive equilibrium. They would have been willing to pay a lot more for the good, and to supply the good at a much lower price than they actually end up doing in a competitive equilibrium. They get a surplus.

Not surprisingly, economists have developed names for the benefits consumers and producers get. Those names are *consumer surplus* and *producer surplus*. **Consumer surplus** is the difference between what consumers would have been willing to pay and what they actually pay. In Exhibit 12, at a competitive equilibrium consumer surplus is the triangle composed of areas *A, B,* and *C*. **Producer surplus** is the difference between the price at which producers would have been willing to supply a good and the price they actually receive. In Exhibit 12 it's the triangle composed of areas *D, E,* and *F*. The competitive equilibrium maximizes producer and consumer surpluses.

To fix the ideas of consumer and producer surplus in your mind, let's consider a couple of real-world examples. Think about the water you drink. What does it cost? Almost nothing. At the margin, that's how much it's worth to you, but since you'd die of thirst if you had no water, you are getting an enormous amount of consumer surplus from that water. Next, consider a ballet dancer who loves the ballet so much he'd

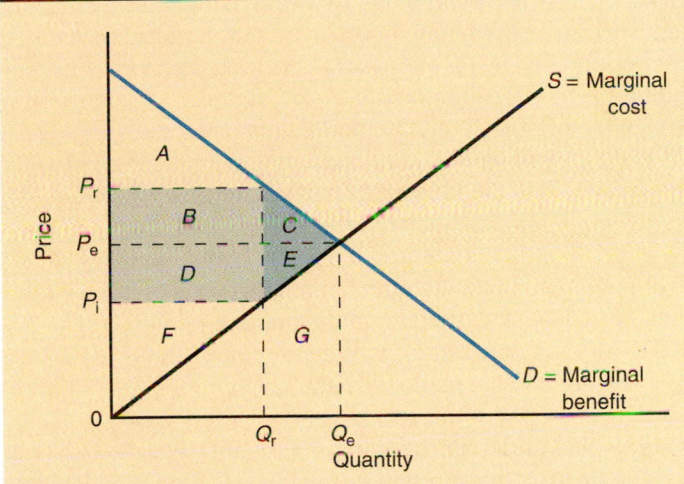

EXHIBIT 12 Welfare Loss from Deviation from Competition

The area between the equilibrium price and the demand curve (the triangle composed of areas A, B, and C) is the consumer surplus. The area between the equilibrium price and the supply curve (the triangle composed of areas D, E, and F) is the producer surplus. If producers can restrict supply to Q_r, they can charge price P_r and transfer area B from consumer surplus to producer surplus. Doing so creates a welfare loss of the areas C and E.

dance for free. But he finds that people are willing to pay to see him and that he can receive $400 a performance. He is receiving producer surplus.

Now let's say that someone places a restriction on the quantity supplied at Q_r. The price that demanders pay now rises to P_r and some consumer surplus is transferred to producer surplus. Those suppliers who are lucky enough to sell in the market receive price P_r even though they'd be willing to supply that quantity at price P_i. Producers who leave the market lose the rectangle represented by the areas E and G but gain back area G, the opportunity cost of their inputs, as they use those inputs in other pursuits, leaving E as a net loss. Producers still in the market benefit by area B. But that benefit comes at the cost of consumers who are hurt by that same area B. The restriction causes a transfer of benefits from consumers to producers. Consumers who leave the market are hurt by the triangle represented by the area C.

Notice that this transfer from consumer to producer surplus is not a total wash. The triangular area composed of areas C and E represents benefits that the excluded producers and excluded consumers won't get. That triangle is the welfare cost of a restriction on the market—the welfare cost of a deviation from perfect competition.

Because of its welfare implications, perfect competition has been used as a benchmark by which to judge the cost of deviating from competition. For example, as we'll see in later chapters, antitrust legislation is often designed to make markets more competitive, and the costs of government restrictions are often measured by their deviation from a competitive equilibrium.

Gerard Debreu won the Nobel prize in 1983 for work on competitive equilibrium theory. © *The Nobel Foundation.*

Criticism of the Pareto Optimality Benchmark

The Pareto optimality benchmark has been the subject of much controversy. Critics offer a number of criticisms of using perfect competition as a benchmark:

1. The **Nirvana criticism:** A perfectly competitive equilibrium is highly unstable. It's usually in some person's interest to restrict entry by others, and, when a market is close to a competitive equilibrium, it is in few people's interest to stop such restrictions.

    To compare reality to a situation that cannot occur (i.e., to Nirvana) is an unfair and unhelpful comparison because it leads to attempts to achieve the unachievable. A better benchmark would be a comparison with workable competition—a state of competition that one might reasonably hope could exist.

2. The **second-best criticism:** The conditions leading to the conclusion that perfect competition leads to a Pareto optimality are so restrictive that they are never even closely met in reality. If the economy deviates in hundreds of ways from perfect competition, how are we to know whether a movement toward a competitive equilibrium in one of those ways will make the economy closer to perfect competition?

Nirvana criticism   Comparing reality to a situation that cannot occur.

7 Three criticisms of the Pareto optimal criterion are:
1. The Nirvana criticism.
2. The second-best criticism.
3. The normative criticism.

Second-best criticism *If the economy is not currently at the competitive equilibrium, it is not at all clear that particular moves toward a competitive equilibrium will be in society's interest.*

Normative criticism *The desir-*
ability of a Pareto optimal position
depends on the desirability of the
starting position. If one objects to the
starting position, one will also likely
object to the Pareto optimal position.

3. The **normative criticism:** Even if the previous two criticisms didn't exist, the competitive benchmark still isn't appropriate because there is nothing necessarily wonderful about Pareto optimality. A Pareto optimal position could be a horrendous position, depending on the starting position. For example, say the starting position is the following: One person has all the world's revenues and all the other people are starving. If that rich person would be made worse off by having some money taken from him and given to the starving poor, that starting position would be Pareto optimal. By most people's normative criteria, it would also be a lousy position.

Critics of the use of the Pareto optimality goal argue that society has a variety of goals. Pareto optimality may be one of them, but it's only one. They argue that economists should take into account all of society's goals—not just Pareto optimality—when determining a benchmark for judging policies.

The Importance of the Competitive Model for All Economists

The debate between supporters and critics of the Pareto optimality benchmark is an ongoing one. Supporters argue that it's the appropriate benchmark, and that competitive equilibrium achieves Pareto optimality. Critics contend that Pareto optimality is just one of many of society's goals. But even critics agree that the forces the perfectly competitive model describes—the pressure on prices to gravitate toward costs of production and the pressure for prices to change as long as supply and demand are not in equilibrium—are strong and show themselves in a variety of real-world markets. Even critics of Pareto optimality believe there is a purpose in studying perfect competition. So, for all economists, it's absolutely necessary that everybody trained in economics understands the perfectly competitive model.

CONCLUSION

We've come to the end of the presentation of perfect competition. It was tough going, but if you went through it carefully, it will serve you well, both as a basis for later chapters and as a reference point for how real-world economies work. But like many good things, a complete understanding of the chapter doesn't come easy.

CHAPTER SUMMARY

- The necessary conditions for perfect competition are that buyers and sellers be price takers, the number of firms be large, there be no barriers to entry, firms' products be homogeneous (identical), exit and entry be instantaneous and costless, there be complete information, and sellers be profit-maximizing entrepreneurial firms.
- The supply curve of a competitive firm is its marginal cost curve. Only competitive firms have supply curves.
- The profit-maximizing position of a competitive firm is where marginal revenue equals marginal cost.

- In the short run, competitive firms can make a profit or loss. In the long run, they make zero profits.
- The shutdown price for a perfectly competitive firm is a price below the minimum point of the average variable cost curve.
- The Pareto optimal criterion is that no one can be made better off without another being made worse off.
- Three criticisms of the Pareto optimality benchmark include the Nirvana criticism, the second-best criticism, and the normative criticism.

KEY TERMS

accounting profit   *(554)*
barriers to entry   *(549)*
consumer surplus   *(566)*
economic profit   *(554)*
experimental economics   *(561)*
homogeneous product   *(549)*
marginal cost   *(552)*
marginal revenue   *(552)*

market supply curve   *(561)*
Nirvana criticism   *(567)*
normal profits   *(555)*
normative criticism   *(568)*
Pareto optimal criterion   *(566)*
perfectly competitive   *(549)*
price taker   *(549)*

producer surplus   *(566)*
profit-maximizing condition   *(553)*
rent   *(560)*
second-best criticism   *(567)*
shutdown point   *(560)*
supply   *(550)*
zero profit condition   *(560)*

QUESTIONS FOR THOUGHT AND REVIEW

The number after each question represents the estimated degree of critical thinking required. (1 = almost none; 10 = deep thought.)

1. If a firm is owned by its workers but otherwise meets all the qualifications for a perfectly competitive firm, will its price and output decisions differ from the price and output decisions of a perfectly competitive firm? Why? *(9)*

2. A profit-maximizing firm has an average total cost of $4 but gets a price of $3 for each good it sells. What would you advise it to do? *(3)*

3. How would your answer to Question 2 differ if you knew the average variable cost were $3.50? *(4)*

4. You're thinking of buying one of two firms. One has a profit margin of $8 per unit; the other has a profit margin of $4 per unit. Which should you buy? Why? *(4)*

5. Say that half of the cost of producing wheat is the rental cost of land (a fixed cost) and half is the cost of labor and machines (a variable cost). If the average total cost of producing wheat is $8 and the price of wheat is $6, what would you advise a farmer to do? ("Grow something else" is not allowed.) *(5)*

6. If marginal cost is four times the quantity produced and the price is $20, how much should the firm produce? Why? *(3)*

7. Find three events in the newspaper that can be explained or interpreted with supply/demand analysis. *(7)*

8. Show graphically the welfare loss that would occur if government established a requirement that everyone consume 10 percent more beets than he or she is currently consuming. *(9)*

9. If one can show that the welfare loss in Question 8 is small—say ½ of 1 percent of the cost of the beets—and that eating beets makes people healthy, would you support a beet-eating requirement? Why? *(9)*

10. State what is wrong with each of the graphs *(3)*.

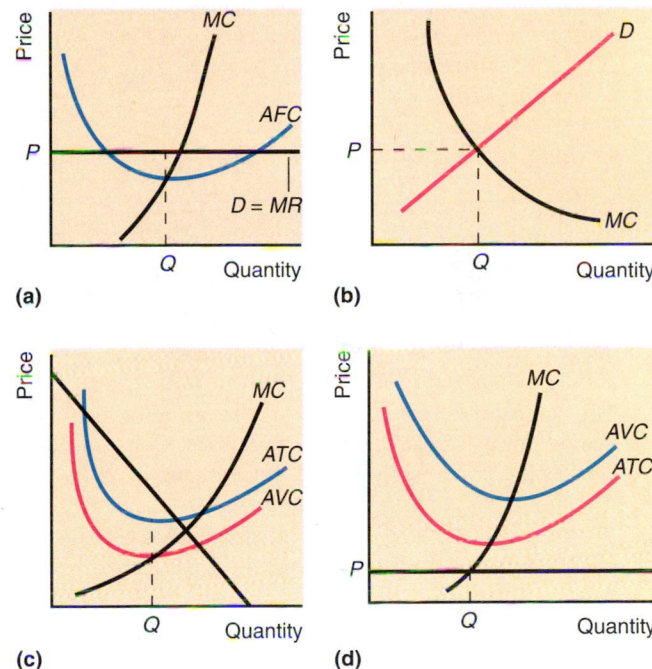

(a)   (b)

(c)   (d)

PROBLEMS AND EXERCISES

1. *a.* Based on the following table, what is the profit-maximizing output?

Output	Price	Total costs
0	$10	$ 30
1	10	40
2	10	45
3	10	48
4	10	55
5	10	65
6	10	80
7	10	100
8	10	140
9	10	220
10	10	340

   b. How would your answer change if, in response to an increase in demand, the price of the good increased to $15?

2. Economan has been infected by the free enterprise bug. He sets up a firm on extraterrestrial affairs. The rent of the building is $4,000, the cost of the two secretaries is $40,000, and the cost of electricity and gas comes to $5,000. There's a great demand for his information, and his total revenue amounts to $100,000. By working in the firm, though, Economan forfeits the $50,000 he could earn by working for the Friendly Space Agency and the $4,000 he could have earned as interest had he saved his funds instead of putting them in this business. Is he making a profit or loss by an accountant's definitions of profit and loss? How about by an economist's definition?

3. Graphically demonstrate the quantity and price of a perfectly competitive firm.
   a. Explain why a slightly larger quantity would not be preferred.
   b. Explain why a slightly lower quantity would not be preferred.
   c. Label the shutdown point in your diagram.
   d. You have just discovered that shutting down means that you would lose your land zoning permit which is required to start operating again. How does that change your answer to *c?*

4. According to an article in the *Wall Street Journal*, gener-

ally the price of a dozen live worms was $1.17 a dozen. Then there was a drought.
   a. Demonstrate graphically what will happen to the price and quantity of worms sold.
   b. If the price rose to $1.75 and the quantity sold fell from 90,000 to 60,000, what would your estimate of the elasticity of demand be?
5. A California biotechnology firm submitted a tomato to the U.S. Food and Drug Administration that will not rot for weeks. It designed such a fruit by changing the genetic structure of the tomato (it's called gene-wrecking). What effect will this technological change have
   a. On the price of tomatoes?
   b. On farmers who grow tomatoes?
   c. On the geographic areas where tomatoes are grown?

   d. On where tomatoes are generally placed on salad bars in winter?
6. Currently central banks (banks of governments) hold 35,000 tons of gold—one-third the world's supply. This is the equivalent of seventeen years' production. In the 1990s there has been discussion about the central banks selling off their gold, since it is no longer tied to money supplies. Assuming they did sell it:
   a. Demonstrate, using supply and demand analysis, the effect on the price of gold in the long run and the short run.
   b. If you were an economist advising the central banks and you believed that selling off the gold made sense, would you advise them to do it quickly or slowly? Why?

ANSWERS TO MARGIN QUESTIONS

1. Without the assumption of instantaneous exit and entry, firms could make a profit by raising price; hence their demand curve would not be perfectly elastic; and hence perfect competition would not exist. *(549)*

2. The competitive firm is such a small portion of the total market that it can have no effect on price. Consequently it takes the price as given, and hence its perceived demand curve is perfectly elastic. *(551)*

3. To determine the profit-maximizing output of a competitive firm, you must know price and marginal cost. *(553)*

4. Firms are interested in getting as much for themselves as they possibly can. Maximizing total profit does this. Maximizing profit per unit might yield very small total profits. *(555)*

5. If the firm in Exhibit 4 were producing 4 units, I would explain to it that the marginal cost of increasing output is only $12 and the marginal revenue was $35, so they should significantly expand output until 8, where the marginal cost equals the marginal revenue, or price. *(556)*

6. The diagram is drawn with the profit-maximizing wrong output and hence the wrong profit. Output is determined where marginal cost equals price and profit is the difference between the average total cost and price at that output, not at the output where marginal cost equals average total cost. The correct diagram is shown below. *(558)*

7. The marginal cost for airlines is significantly below average total cost. Since they're recovering their average variable cost, they continue to operate. In the long run, if this continues, some airlines will be forced out of business. *(559)*

8. The costs for a firm include the normal costs, which in turn include a return for all factors. Thus it is worthwhile for a competitive firm to stay in business, since it is doing better, or at least as well, as it could in any other activity. *(560)*

9. Suddenly becoming the "in" thing to wear would cause the demand for berets to shift up, pushing the price up in the short run. In the long run it would probably push the price down, as there probably are considerable economies of scale in the production of berets. *(562)*

10. A decline in demand should push the short-run price of these hotel rooms down. In the long run, however, once a number of hotels go out of business, the price of hotel rooms should eventually move back to approximately where it was before the decline, assuming constant returns to scale. *(565)*

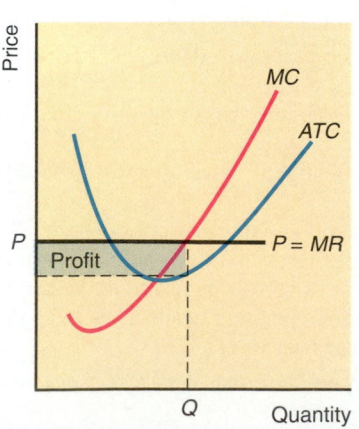

Monopoly

Monopoly is business at the end of its journey.
~Henry Demarest Lloyd

After reading this chapter, you should be able to:

1 Summarize how and why the decisions facing a monopolist differ from the collective decisions of competing firms.

2 Explain why $MC = MR$ maximizes total profit for a monopolist.

3 Determine a monopolist's price, output, and profit graphically and numerically.

4 Show why a perfectly price-discriminating monopolist will produce the same output as a perfect competitor.

5 Show graphically the welfare loss from monopoly and explain why it may underestimate people's view of the loss from monopoly.

6 Explain why, without barriers to entry, there would be no monopoly.

7 Explain why economists generally favor having government charge for monopolies.

Monopoly *A market structure in which one firm makes up the entire market.*

In the previous chapter we considered perfect competition. We now move to the other end of the spectrum: monopoly. **Monopoly** is a market structure in which one firm makes up the entire market. It is the polar opposite to competition. It is a market structure in which the firm faces no competitive pressure from other firms.

Monopolies exist because of barriers to entry into a market that prevent competition. These can be legal barriers (as in the case where a firm has a patent that prevents other firms from entering), sociological barriers where entry is prevented by the invisible handshake, or natural barriers where the firm has a unique ability to produce what other firms can't duplicate.

A key question we want to answer in this chapter is: How does a monopolist's decision differ from the collective decision of competing firms (i.e., from the competitive solution)? Answering that question brings out a key difference between a competitive firm and a monopoly. Since a competitive firm is too small to affect the price, it does not take into account the effect of its output decision on the price it receives. A competitive firm's marginal revenue (the additional revenue it receives from selling an additional unit of output) is its price. Since a monopolistic firm's output decision can affect price, it does take that effect into account; its marginal revenue is not its price. A monopolistic firm will reason: "If I increase production, the price I can get for each unit sold will fall, so I had better be careful about how much I increase production."

1 For a competitive firm, marginal revenue equals price. For a monopolist, it does not. The monopolist takes into account the fact that its decision can affect price.

Let's consider an example. Say your drawings in the margins of this book are seen by a traveling art critic who decides you're the greatest thing since Rembrandt, or at least since Andy Warhol. Carefully he tears each page out of the book, mounts them on special paper, and numbers them: Doodle Number 1 (Doodle While Contemplating Demand), Doodle Number 2 (Doodle While Contemplating Production), and so on.

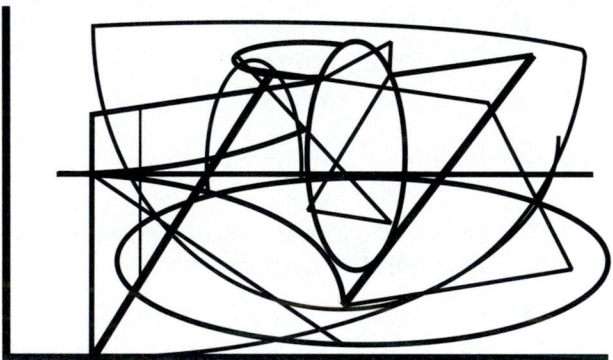

Doodle Number 27: Contemplating Costs

All told, he has 100. He figures, with the right advertising and if you're a hit on the art circuit, he'll have a monopoly in your doodles. He plans to sell them for $20,000 each: He gets 50 percent, you get 50 percent. That's $1 million for you. You tell him, "Hey, man! I can doodle my way through the entire book. I'll get you 500 doodles. Then I get $5 million and you get $5 million."

Q–1: Why should you study rather than doodle?

The art critic has a pained look on his face. He says, "You've been doodling when you should have been studying. Your doodles are worth $20,000 each only if they're rare. If there are 500, they're worth $1,000 each. And if it becomes known that you can turn them out that fast, they'll be worth nothing, I won't be able to limit quantity at all, and my monopoly will be lost. So obviously we must figure out some way that you won't doodle any more—and study instead. Oh, by the way, did you know that the price of an artist's work goes up significantly when he or she dies? Hmm." At that point you decide to forget doodling and to start studying, and to remember always that increasing production doesn't necessarily make suppliers better off.

As we saw in the last chapter, competitive firms do not take advantage of that insight. Each individual competitive firm, responding to its self-interest, is not doing what is in the interest of the firms collectively. In competitive markets, as one supplier is pitted against another, the demanders benefit. In monopolistic markets, the firm

EXHIBIT 1   Monopolistic Profit Maximization

1 Quantity	2 Price	3 Total revenue	4 Marginal revenue	5 Total cost	6 Marginal cost	7 Average total cost	8 Profit
0	$36	$ 0	—	$ 47			−$47
			$33		$1		
1	33	33		48		$48.00	−15
			27		2		
2	30	60		50		25.00	10
			21		4		
3	27	81		54		18.00	27
			15		8		
4	24	96		62		15.50	34
			9		16		
5	21	105		78		15.60	27
			3		24		
6	18	108		102		17.00	6
			−3		40		
7	15	105		142		20.29	−37
			−9		56		
8	12	96		198		24.75	−102
			−15		80		
9	9	81		278		30.89	−197

faces no competitors and does what is in its best interest. Monopolists see to it that the monopolists, not the demanders, benefit.

How much should the monopolistic firm choose to produce if it wants to maximize profit? To answer that we have to consider more carefully the effect that changing output has on the monopoly. That's what we do in this section. First, we consider a numerical example; then we consider that same example graphically. The relevant information for our example is presented in Exhibit 1.

Exhibit 1 shows the price, total revenue, marginal revenue, total cost, marginal cost, average total cost, and profit at various levels of production. It's similar to the table in Exhibit 4 of the last chapter where we determined a competitive firm's output. The big difference is that marginal revenue changes as output changes and is not equal to the price. Why?

First, let's remember the definition of marginal revenue. **Marginal revenue** is the change in total revenue that occurs as a firm changes its output. In this example, if a monopolist increases output from 4 to 5 by lowering its price from $24 to $21, its revenue increases from $96 to $105, so marginal revenue is $9. That $9 can be divided into two elements: the $21 the firm got for selling another unit minus the $3 per unit fall in the price that occurred on the other four units as the firm had to lower its price in order to sell the additional unit. That's $21 − $12 = $9.

As you can tell from the table, profits are highest ($34) at 4 units of output at a price of $24. At 3 units of output and a price of $27, the firm has total revenue of $81 and total cost of $54, yielding a profit of $27. At 5 units of output and a price of $21, the firm has a total revenue of $105 and a total cost of $78, also for a profit of $27. Thirty-four dollars is the highest profit it can make, which the firm does when it produces 4 units. This is its profit-maximizing level.

At that profit-maximizing output of 4 units, marginal revenue equals marginal cost, just as it did for the competitive firms. This cannot be seen precisely in the table since the table is for discrete jumps and does not tell us the marginal cost and marginal revenue exactly at 4; it only tells us the marginal cost and marginal revenue of moving from 3 to 4 ($8 and $15 respectively) and the marginal cost and marginal revenue of moving from 4 to 5 ($16 and $9 respectively). If small adjustments (1/100 of a unit or so) were possible, the marginal cost and marginal revenue precisely at 4 would be 12. Because drawing the curve implicitly assumes we can make very small changes, the graphs of the marginal revenue curve and marginal cost curve will intersect at an output of 4 and a marginal cost and marginal revenue of $12.

A MODEL OF MONOPOLY

Determining the Monopolist's Price and Output Numerically

Marginal revenue   *The change in total revenue that occurs as a firm changes its output.*

Q–2:   In Exhibit 1, explain why 4 is the profit-maximizing output.

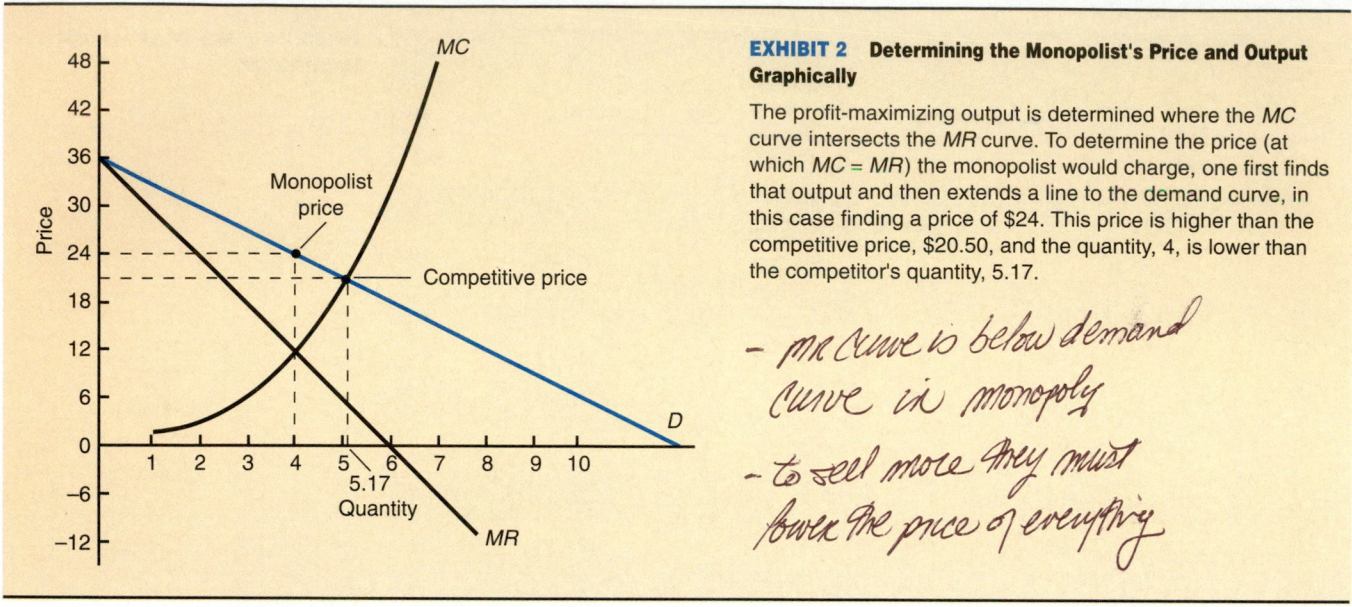

EXHIBIT 2   Determining the Monopolist's Price and Output Graphically

The profit-maximizing output is determined where the *MC* curve intersects the *MR* curve. To determine the price (at which *MC = MR*) the monopolist would charge, one first finds that output and then extends a line to the demand curve, in this case finding a price of $24. This price is higher than the competitive price, $20.50, and the quantity, 4, is lower than the competitor's quantity, 5.17.

- mc curve is below demand curve in monopoly

- to sell more they must lower the price of everything

The general rule that any firm must follow to maximize profit: Produce at an output level at which *MC = MR*.

2 If a monopolist deviates from the output level at which marginal cost equals marginal revenue, profits will decline.

Determining the Monopolist's Price and Output Graphically

Marginal revenue curve Graphical measure of the change in revenue that occurs in response to a change in price.

This is the general rule that any firm must follow to maximize profit: Produce at an output level at which *MC = MR*. What's different is that for a monopolist, marginal revenue does not equal price; marginal revenue is below price.

If you think about it, it makes sense that the point where marginal revenue equals marginal cost determines the profit-maximizing output. If the firm increases output beyond the quantity (4) where *MC > MR*, the additional revenue it gets ($9) is below the additional cost it incurs ($16). If it decreases output to 3 from 4 where *MC < MR*, the revenue it loses ($15) exceeds the additional cost it saves ($8).

The monopolist's output decision can also be seen graphically. Exhibit 2 graphs the table's information into a demand curve, a marginal revenue curve, and a marginal cost curve. The marginal cost curve is a graph of the change in the firm's cost as it changes output. It's the same curve as we saw in our discussion of perfect competition. The **marginal revenue curve** is a graph of the change in total revenue. It is graphed by plotting and connecting the points given by quantity and marginal revenue in Exhibit 1. The marginal revenue curve tells us the change in total revenue when there is a change in price.

The marginal revenue curve is new, so let's consider it a bit more carefully. It tells us the additional revenue the firm will get by expanding output. It is a downward-sloping curve that begins at the same point as the demand curve but then decreases faster. In this example marginal revenue is positive up until the firm produces six units. Then marginal revenue is negative; after six units the firm's total revenue decreases when it increases output.

Notice specifically the relationship between the demand curve (which is the average revenue curve) and the marginal revenue curve. Since the demand curve is downward sloping, the marginal revenue curve is below the average revenue curve. (Remember, if the average curve is falling, the marginal curve must be below it.)

Having plotted these curves, let's ask the same questions as we did before: What output should the monopolist produce, and what price should it charge? To answer those questions, the key curves to look at are the marginal cost curve and the marginal revenue curve.

3A The monopolist's price and output are determined as follows:

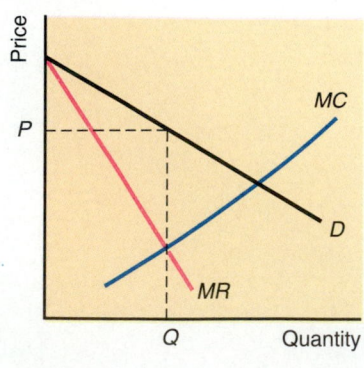

We can tell from the graph what will happen to profit by looking at the positions of the marginal revenue curve and the marginal cost curve at the output and price we're considering. At the output where the demand curve intersects the marginal cost curve, marginal cost is significantly above the marginal revenue curve. Whenever that's the case, profits will increase when output is reduced since the saving in cost

A TRICK IN GRAPHING THE MARGINAL REVENUE CURVE

Here's a trick to help you graph the marginal revenue curve. *MR* is a line that starts at the same point on the price axis as does a linear demand curve, but that intersects the quantity axis at a point half the distance from where the demand curve intersects the quantity axis. (If the demand curve isn't linear, you can use the same trick if you use lines tangent to the curved demand curve.) So you can extend the demand curve to the two axes and measure halfway on the quantity axis, and draw a line from where the demand curve intersects the price axis to that halfway mark. That line is the marginal revenue curve.

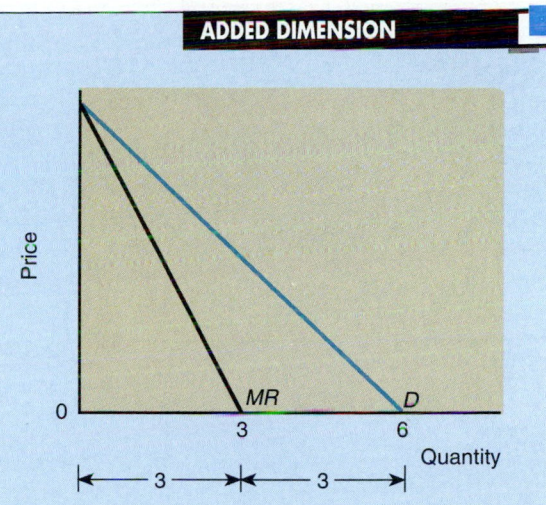

(the area under the relevant part of the marginal cost curve) is greater than the lost revenue (the area under the relevant part of the marginal revenue curve). So at an output where the demand curve intersects the marginal cost curve (5.17 in Exhibit 2) it definitely pays for the firm to restrict output.

If restricting output a little bit helps that much, how about if the monopolist restricts output some more, to 4 units? Since marginal cost exceeds marginal revenue, doing so makes sense. Well then, how about decreasing output by another unit, from 4 to 3? If you look at the graph, you'll see that doing so doesn't make sense since at all output levels below 4, marginal revenue is above marginal cost. That means that the lost revenue from reducing output will exceed the saving from reducing marginal cost.

MR = MC Determines the Profit-Maximizing Output for a Monopolist From the preceding discussion you should have a good sense of what determines whether the monopolist's profit will rise or fall with a change in output, and what output it should choose. You simply compare the marginal revenue curve to the marginal cost curve at the different output levels being considered. If the marginal revenue is below the marginal cost, it makes sense to reduce production. Doing so decreases marginal cost and increases marginal revenue. If marginal cost is below marginal revenue you should increase production. If the marginal revenue is equal to marginal cost, it does not make sense to increase or reduce production. So the monopolist should produce at the output level where *MC* = *MR*. As you can see, the output the monopolist chooses is 4 units, the same output that we determined numerically. This leads to the following insights:

> *If MR > MC, the monopolist gains profit by increasing output.*
> *If MR < MC, the monopolist gains profit by decreasing output.*
> *If MC = MR, the monopolist is maximizing profit.*

Thus **MR = MC** is the profit-maximizing rule for a monopolist.

Determining the Price a Monopolist Will Charge The *MR* = *MC* condition determines the quantity a monopolist produces; in turn, that quantity determines the price the firm will charge. Since the demand curve tells us what consumers will pay for a given quantity, to find the price a monopolist will charge you must extend the quantity line up to the demand curve. We do so in Exhibit 2 and see that the profit-maximizing output level of 4 allows a monopolist to charge a price of $24.

Comparing a Monopolist's and a Perfectly Competitive Firm's Outputs and Prices For a competitive industry, the summation of firms' marginal cost curves is the supply curve. (The above statement has some qualifications which are best left to intermedi-

Q-3: Show a monopolist's profit-maximizing price and output in the following diagram.

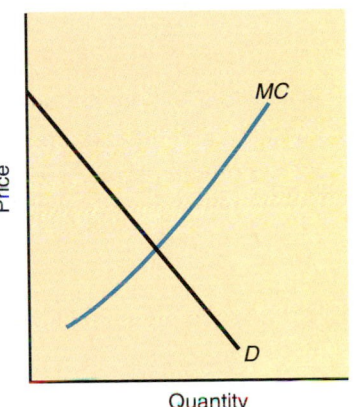

If *MR* > *MC*, the monopolist gains profit by increasing output.
If *MR* < *MC*, the monopolist gains profit by decreasing output.
If *MC* = *MR*, the monopolist is maximizing profit.

Q-4: Why does a monopolist produce less output than a perfectly-competitive firm?

A REMINDER

MONOPOLIES DON'T HAVE SUPPLY CURVES

In comparing monopoly and competition, it's important to remember the definition of a supply curve: It's the quantity that will be supplied at various prices. A supply curve shows the quantity response of *price takers*.

A monopolist is not a price taker; hence it cannot have a supply curve. A monopolist looks at its marginal cost, looks at its demand schedule, and decides what price to charge based on the intersection of its marginal revenue and marginal cost curves. It chooses output and price in a way that gives it the highest possible profit.

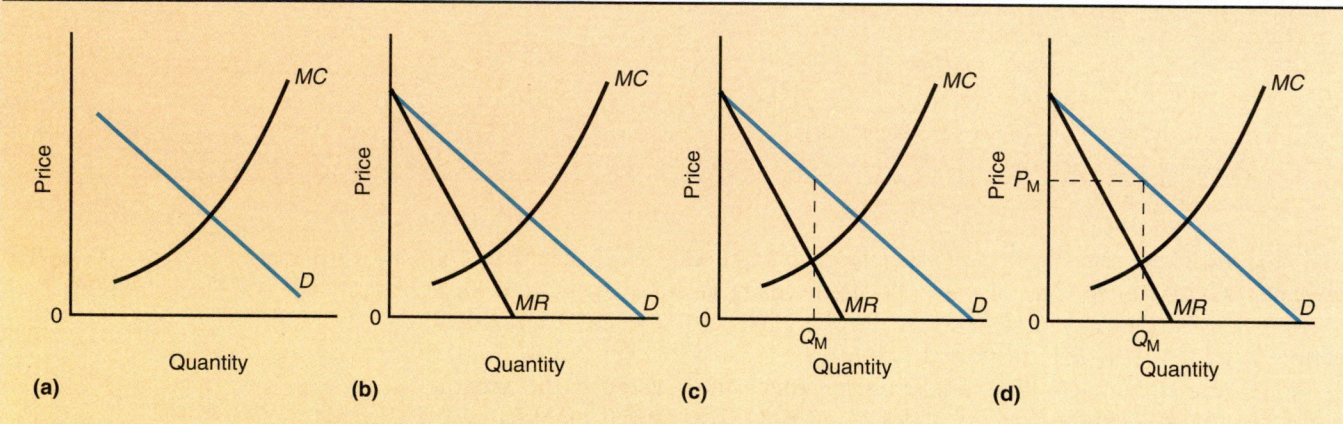

EXHIBIT 3 (a, b, c, and d)   Finding the Monopolist's Price and Output

Determining a monopolist's price and output can be tricky. In the text there is a full discussion of the steps shown in this exhibit. To make sure you understand, try to go through the steps on your own, and then check your work with the text.

ate classes.) The competitive level of output would be at 5.17 at a price of $20.50, as Exhibit 2 shows. The monopolist's output was 4 and its price was $24. So, if a monopolistic market can be made competitive, you can see that output is lower and price is higher in a monopoly than in a competitive market. The reason is that the monopolist takes into account the effect restricting output has on price.

Equilibrium output for the monopolist, like equilibrium output for the competitor, is determined by the $MC = MR$ condition, but because the monopolist's marginal revenue is below its price, its equilibrium output is different from a competitive market.

Example   We've covered a lot of material quickly, so it's probably helpful to go through an example slowly and carefully review the reasoning process. Here's the problem:

Say that a monopolist with marginal cost curve *MC* faces a demand curve *D* in Exhibit 3(a). Determine the price and output the monopolist would choose.

The first step is to draw the marginal revenue curve, since we know that a monopolist's profit-maximizing output level is determined where $MC = MR$. We do that in Exhibit 3(b), remembering the trick of extending our demand curve back to the vertical and horizontal axes and then bisecting the horizontal axis.

The second step is to determine where $MC = MR$. Having found that point, we extend a line up to the demand curve and down to the quantity axis to determine the output the monopolist chooses, Q_M. We do this in Exhibit 3(c).

Finally we see where the quantity line intersects the demand curve. Then we extend a horizontal line from that point to the price axis, as in Exhibit 3(d). This determines the price the monopolist will charge, P_M.

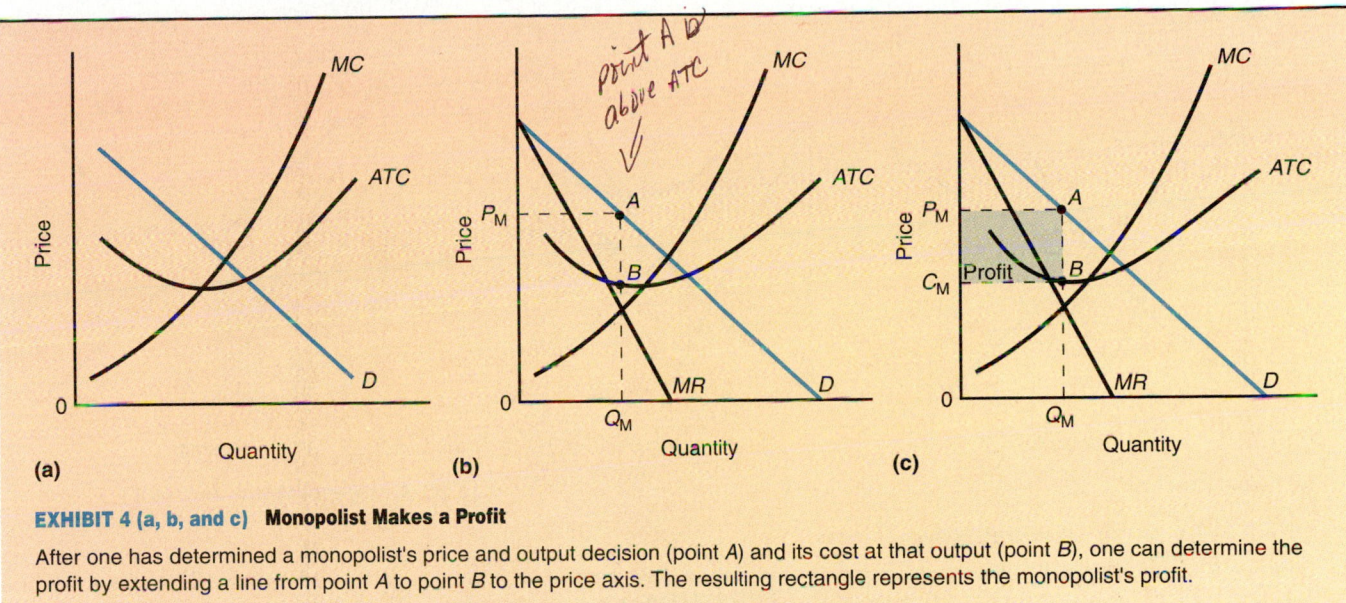

EXHIBIT 4 (a, b, and c) Monopolist Makes a Profit

After one has determined a monopolist's price and output decision (point *A*) and its cost at that output (point *B*), one can determine the profit by extending a line from point *A* to point *B* to the price axis. The resulting rectangle represents the monopolist's profit.

So far we've talked about the output and pricing decisions of a monopolist. We haven't said anything about whether the monopolist makes a profit.[1] As was the case with the perfect competitor, that can be determined only by comparing average total cost to price. So before we can determine profit, we need to add another curve: the average total cost curve. As we saw with a perfect competitor, it's important to follow the correct sequence when finding profit.

- First, determine the output the monopolist will produce by the intersection of the marginal cost and marginal revenue curves.
- Second, determine the price the monopolist will charge for that output.
- Third, determine average cost at that level of output.
- Fourth, determine the monopolist's profit (loss) by comparing $AR \ (= P)$ to average total cost.

If price exceeds average cost at the output it chooses, the monopolist will make a profit. If price equals average cost, the monopolist will make no profit (but it will make a normal return). If price is less than average cost, the monopolist will incur a loss: Total cost exceeds total revenue.

I consider the case of a profit in Exhibit 4(a), (b), and (c), going through the steps slowly. The monopolist's demand, marginal cost, and average total cost curves are presented in Exhibit 4(a). Our first step is to determine output, which we do by drawing the marginal revenue curve and finding the output level at which marginal cost equals marginal revenue. From that point draw a vertical line to the horizontal (quantity) axis. That intersection tells us the monopolist's output, Q_M in Exhibit 4(b). The second step is to find what price the monopolist will charge at that output. We do so by extending the vertical line to the demand curve (point *A*) and then extending a horizontal line over to the price axis. Doing so gives price, P_M. Our third step is to determine the average cost at that price. We do so by seeing where our vertical line at the chosen output intersects the average total cost curve (point *B*). That tells us the monopolist's average cost at its chosen output.

To determine profit, we extend lines from where the quantity line intersects the demand curve (point *A*) and the average total cost curve (point *B*) to the price axis in Exhibit 4(c). The resulting shaded rectangle represents the monopolist's profit.

PROFITS AND MONOPOLY

An Example of a Monopolist Making a Profit

3B A monopolist's profit is determined by the difference between *ATC* and price, as in the following diagram:

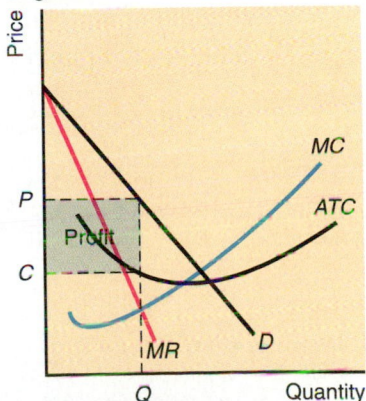

---

[1] Remember the distinction between economic profit and accounting profit. This chapter's discussion of profit considers economic profit.

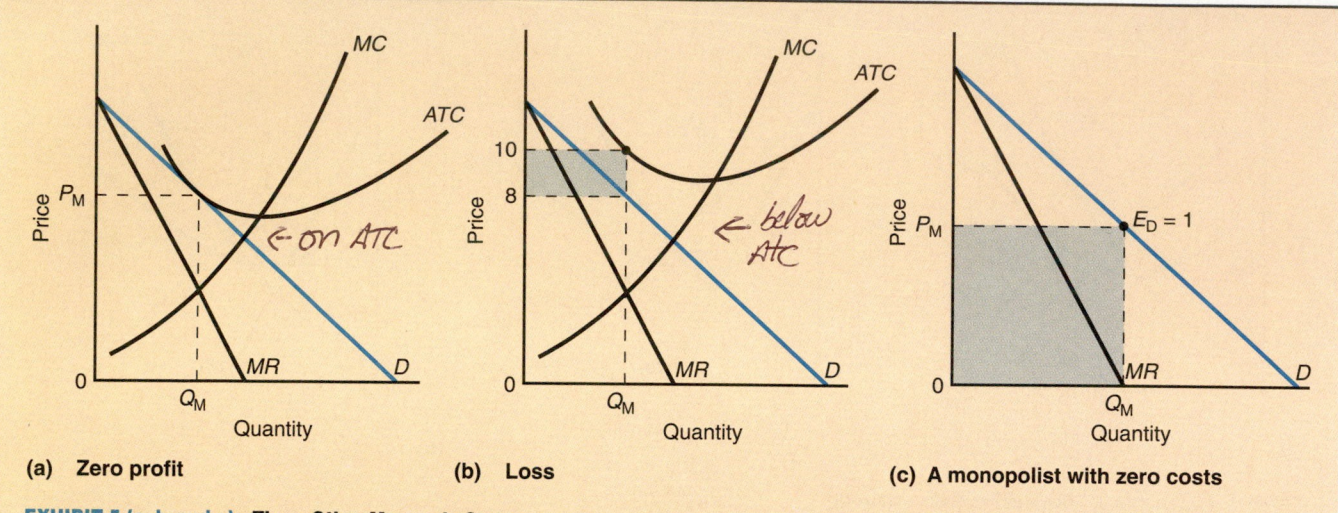

(a)   Zero profit   **(b)   Loss**   **(c) A monopolist with zero costs**

EXHIBIT 5 (a, b, and c)   Three Other Monopoly Cases

Depending on where the *ATC* curve falls, a monopolist can make a profit, break even (as in (**a**)), or make a loss (as in (**b**)) in the short run. In the long run, a monopolist who is making a loss will get out of business. (**c**) shows the equilibrium for a monopolist with zero marginal cost. When a monopolist has a zero marginal cost, the marginal cost curve is coincidental with the quantity axis. Thus, it produces an output at which the *MR* curve intersects the quantity axis and charges a price P_M. At the corresponding point on its demand curve, the elasticity is 1 because that maximizes total revenue. Assuming fixed costs are zero, *ATC* are also zero and total revenue equals total profit.

An Example of a Monopolist Breaking Even and Making a Loss

In Exhibit 5(a) and (b) we consider two other average total cost curves to show you that a monopolist may make a loss or no profit as well as an economic profit. In Exhibit 5(a) the monopolist is making zero profit; in Exhibit 5(b) it's making a loss. So clearly in the short run a monopolist can be making either a profit or a loss, or it can be breaking even.

A Monopolist with a Zero Marginal Cost

Q–5: If a monopolist receives a subsidy for each unit produced and has a zero marginal cost, show graphically its equilibrium quantity and price.

In Exhibit 5(c) let's consider what a monopolist that has no cost of production will charge and what its profit will be. Since its marginal cost is zero, it is coincidental with (lies on top of) the horizontal axis. The marginal revenue curve intersects that marginal cost at Q_M. The price the monopolist charges is P_M. Total revenue is given by the shaded area. Assuming fixed costs are also zero, and since by assumption there is no cost, total revenue is equal to profit.

As a review of the elasticity concept, ask yourself what is the elasticity at that point. If you said it's 1, you're right. If not, I'm sorry to say, you'd better review the discussion of elasticity in the chapter on demand before the next exam. I pause for you to review.

Now that you're back, I've got another question for you. Will the elasticity at the price that the normal monopolist charges be elastic (greater than 1) or inelastic (less than 1)? If you answered without hesitation that it's always elastic, you're in good shape on elasticity. If not, you've had your warnings. Remember, life is tough; no one ever said that learning difficult concepts is easy.

The Price-Discriminating Monopolist

Price discriminate   *To charge different prices to different individuals.*

Consumer surplus   *The additional amount that consumers would be willing to pay for a product above what they actually pay.*

The better to cement into your mind your understanding of the profit-maximizing condition $MC = MR$, let's consider what would happen if our monopolist suddenly gained the ability to **price discriminate**—to charge different prices to different individuals or groups of individuals (for example, students as compared to businesspeople). This means that individuals high up on the demand curve could be charged a high price; individuals low on the demand curve could be charged a lower price without affecting the price charged to other individuals.

A firm that price discriminates captures demanders' **consumer surplus** (the difference between the price demanders would have been willing to pay and the price they must actually pay). A normal monopolist, by assumption, must charge all

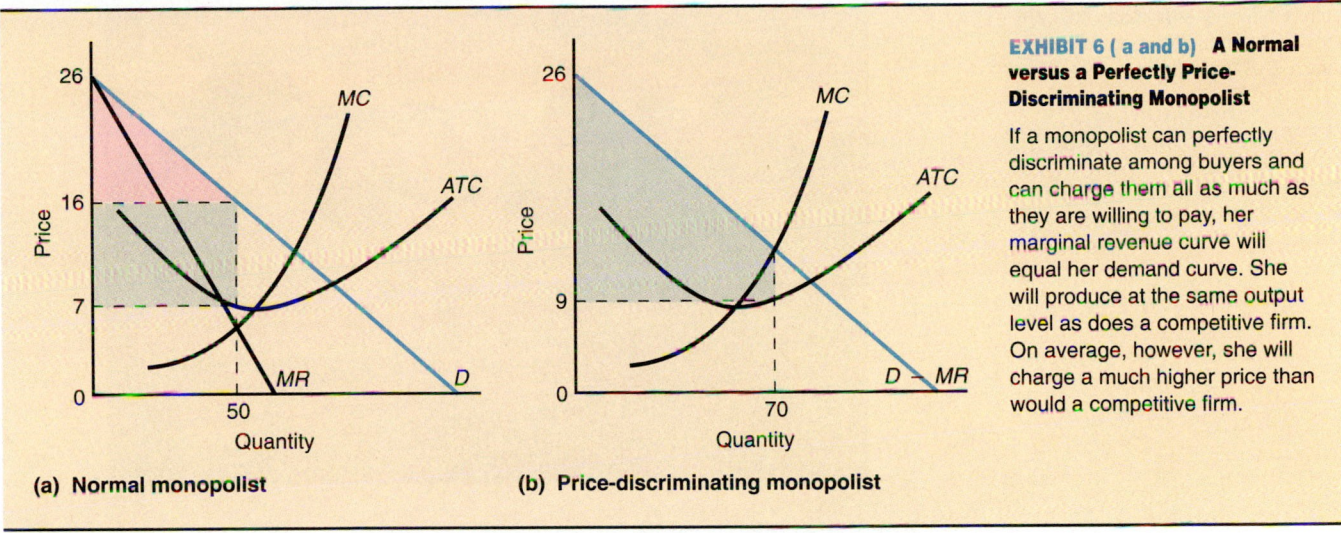

EXHIBIT 6 (a and b) **A Normal versus a Perfectly Price-Discriminating Monopolist**

If a monopolist can perfectly discriminate among buyers and can charge them all as much as they are willing to pay, her marginal revenue curve will equal her demand curve. She will produce at the same output level as does a competitive firm. On average, however, she will charge a much higher price than would a competitive firm.

individuals the same price. Thus, it's giving a good deal to some individuals who would have been willing to pay more. If a monopolist can price discriminate, it doesn't have to give any demanders a good deal. It can extract the maximum consumer surplus from each demander.

A Normal Monopolist versus a Price-Discriminating Monopolist Exhibit 6(a) graphs the decisions facing a normal monopolist. A normal monopolist will choose to produce 50 units at a price of $16 and a cost per unit of $7, making a profit of $450, the shaded rectangle. The shaded triangle is the remaining consumer surplus.

The perfectly price-discriminating monopolist is able to charge a different price to each customer. When she sells more, she doesn't have to lower her price to other customers willing to pay high prices. So she can extract the full consumer surplus. Since she doesn't have to lower her price to sell more, her marginal revenue isn't the same as the normal monopolist's. Since she doesn't need to lower the price for other customers when she sells more, her marginal revenue is the same as her average revenue (total revenue divided by quantity), which is simply her demand curve. So, for a perfectly price-discriminating monopolist: $P = AR = MR$.

In Exhibit 6(b) we consider the decision facing a price-discriminating monopolist. For a price-discriminating monopolist, we find that she will produce at an output of 70, a far higher output than the normal monopolist's, and will make a profit of $700, the shaded region, almost twice the profit of the normal monopolist. Both her profit and her output are higher than a normal monopolist's. She produces the same output that a perfectly competitive industry would have. There is no monopolistic restriction on output.

4 A price-discriminating monopolist does not lose revenue on previously-sold products, so its marginal revenue curve equals its demand curve. Thus, it will produce the same quantity as will a perfectly competitive firm.

For a perfectly price-discriminating monopolist, $P = AR = MR$.

Q–6: If a monopoly can partially price-discriminate, show graphically the range of output that it will produce.

Price Discrimination in the Real World The price discrimination just discussed is mainly of theoretical interest. It's presented to bring home the point that a price-discriminating monopolist will have an output more like a competitive firm than will a normal monopolist. In the real world it's highly unlikely that a monopolist will be able to charge everyone a different price. However, as discussed in the chapter on demand, price discrimination occurs all the time. There I pointed out the following examples:

1. *All airline Super Saver fares include Saturday night stayovers.*
    This is a method of price discrimination. Businesspeople who have highly inelastic demands generally aren't willing to stay over a Saturday night, so they're charged a high price while tourists and leisure travelers who have a far more elastic demand curve and who are willing to stay over a Saturday night are charged a low price.

Airlines typically offer many different fares in an attempt to price discriminate. © *Ray Stott/The Image Works.*

2. *Automobiles are seldom sold at list price.*

   Once again we have an example of price discrimination. Salespeople can size up the customer and determine the customer's elasticity. People who haven't done the research and don't know that selling at 10 percent off list is normal (i.e., people with inelastic demands) pay higher prices than people who search out all the alternatives (people with elastic demand).

   Now that you've analyzed price-discriminating monopolies, you should understand them better. To see whether you do, try to provide a price discrimination explanation for the following:

   1. Theaters have Monday/Tuesday night special rates.
   2. Retail tire companies run special sales about half the time.
   3. Restaurants generally make most of their profit on alcoholic drinks and just break even on food.

THE WELFARE LOSS FROM MONOPOLY

In the previous two sections, two conclusions should have started you thinking. The first is that there is no necessary reason why a monopolist must make a profit. The second is that if a monopolist is a price discriminator (which means it makes more profit than a normal monopoly), then its output is closer to the competitive output. From these two conclusions we can reason that profits aren't the primary reason that the economic model we're using sees monopoly as bad. If not because of profits, then why does the economic model see monopoly as bad?

A Partial Equilibrium Presentation of the Welfare Loss

Higher price = lower output

One reason can be seen by looking more carefully at the normal monopolist's equilibrium in Exhibit 7. A monopolist produces at Q_M at price P_M; a competitive market produces a higher quantity Q_C at a lower price P_C. Now let's consider what the benefits to society would be if the monopolist would increase output. The cost to society of increasing output from Q_M to Q_C is measured by the area under the marginal cost curve, the shaded area labeled *A*. This cost is the opportunity cost of the resources—the value of the resources in their next-best use. The benefit to society of increasing output from Q_M to Q_C is the area under the demand curve between those two quantities: areas *A, B,* and *D.* (Area *C* is neither a gain nor a loss to society. It represents a transfer of income from the monopolist to the consumer that would occur if there were a fall in price. Since both monopolist and consumer are members of society, the gain and loss net out.)

The triangular areas *B* and *D* are the net gain to society of eliminating monopoly. Thus, these triangular areas are also a measure of the welfare loss to society from the existence of monopoly. Thinking about consumer surplus (which we discussed previously) may help you to see what's going on here. As defined before, consumer surplus is the additional amount consumers would have been willing to pay for a good, but

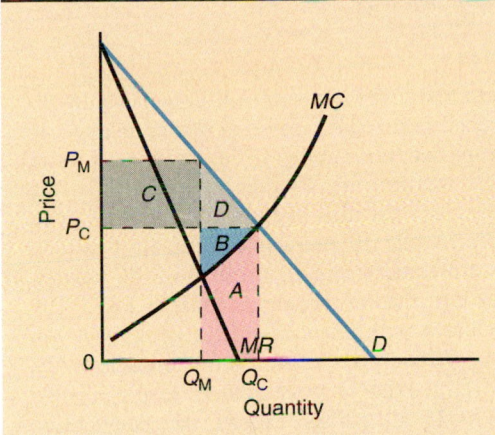

EXHIBIT 7 The Welfare Loss from Monopoly

The welfare loss of a monopolist is represented by the triangles *B* and *D*. The rectangle *C* is a transfer from consumer surplus to the monopolist. The area *A* represents the opportunity cost of diverted resources. This is not a loss to society since the resources will be used in producing other goods.

didn't have to. In a competitive market consumers would have received the areas *C* and *D* as part of their consumer surplus. But they didn't. The monopoly extracts *C* from them as its profit (that's a redistributional effect) so the consumer loses, but the monopolist gains. But the triangle *D* is lost to society; the consumer loses it but the monopolist doesn't get it. It's the cost of the monopoly restriction. The same argument can be made about the triangle *B*, only this time replace *consumer* with *producer*. *B* is the lost producer surplus.

As discussed in the previous chapter, this area designated by *B* and *D* is often called the *deadweight loss* or **welfare loss triangle;** it is a geometric representation of the welfare cost in terms of misallocated resources that are caused by monopoly. That welfare cost of monopoly is one of the reasons economists oppose monopoly. That cost can be summarized as follows: Because monopolies distort relative prices, people's decisions don't reflect the true cost to society. Price doesn't equal marginal cost. Because price doesn't equal marginal cost, people's choices are distorted; they choose to consume less of the monopolist's output and more of some other output than they would if there were competitive markets. That distinction means that the marginal cost of increasing output is lower than the marginal benefit of increasing output, so there's a welfare loss.

If the welfare loss from monopoly is large, it would seemingly make sense for the government to enter into the market and prevent monopoly. If, on the other hand, the welfare loss from monopoly is small, it would make sense for the government not to worry about monopoly. Thus, the size of the welfare loss from monopoly and other restrictions on supply is an important economic question.

To answer this question, economists have spent a fair amount of time trying to measure the welfare loss from monopoly. Almost all measurements of that welfare loss as a percentage of GDP have been rather small. One early attempt was made by Arnold Harberger (which is why welfare triangles are sometimes called *Harberger triangles*). Harberger estimated the demand elasticities for a variety of goods produced by monopolies and thereby estimated the welfare loss from monopoly. He found that the welfare loss from monopoly was only about $\frac{1}{2}$ of 1 percent of total GDP. Later estimates have differed slightly from the Harberger estimates and have shown monopoly to be more of a problem, but they too have been relatively small. Thus, at least from the welfare loss point of view, it would seem that while monopolies are a problem, they aren't an enormous problem to society when compared to issues such as unemployment or drugs.

The empirical estimates of the welfare loss due to monopoly suggest that monopolies are a relatively minor problem. But society has consistently been concerned about monopoly. Public dislike for monopolies has forced government to create laws preventing monopoly. It seems that the public opposes monopoly much more vehe-

5 The welfare loss from monopoly is a triangle as in the graph below. It is not the loss that most people consider. They are often interested in normative losses that the graph does not capture.

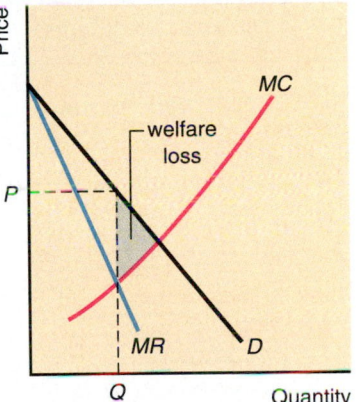

Measuring the Welfare Loss from Monopoly

Q–7: Why is area *C* in Exhibit 7 not considered a loss from monopoly?

Welfare loss triangle   Geometric representation of the welfare cost in terms of the resource misallocation caused by monopoly.

Government Policy and Monopoly

ADDED DIMENSION THE SECOND BEST AND SOME QUALIFICATIONS TO THE WELFARE LOSS

The welfare loss argument just presented requires an addendum. The loss shown in the partial equilibrium diagram is caused by relative prices being changed from competitive prices by a monopolist. But what if monopoly already exists in some other sectors and existing prices aren't competitive prices? When a monopolist changes relative prices, will that cause a similar welfare loss? The answer depends on how the demands are interrelated and whether the new complete set of relative prices is closer to the competitive set of prices than is the old set of relative prices.

Such issues were briefly introduced in the last chapter. They are called *second-best issues*. Second-best issues are issues related to determining the welfare loss due to restrictions on output if the rest of the world isn't characterized by perfect competition. In general, second-best questions can only be answered by using a complicated set of equations—such a complicated set that when I was in graduate school I could hardly work my way through them, so there's no way I'm going to foist them on you.

There's one case, however, that captures the essence of the argument and shows whether you're following the problem raised by second-best issues. Say that *all* the markets in an economy, except one, are monopolistic, and the prices in these monopolistic markets are 10 percent higher than the competitive price. Now say that the one competitive price rises by 10 percent, while all other prices remain constant. Now all markets are equally monopolized. Will the monopolization of that last market create a welfare loss? The answer is no. In fact it will create a welfare gain, since the rise in the last competitive price toward a monopolistic price must make the overall relative prices closer to the relative competitive prices. If all prices exceed the competitive prices by 10 percent, the monopolistic relative prices are identical to the competitive relative prices.

The preceding argument was worked out way back in 1926 by a brilliant mathematical economist named Frank Ramsey. Because of his work, the name *Ramsey rule* has been given to the argument that if all prices rise by an equal percentage, it's like no relative price having risen at all, and hence there's no welfare loss.

mently than one would expect it to, based on the measurement of the welfare loss from monopoly.

There are two explanations for this difference between the layperson's view of monopoly (he or she doesn't like monopoly) and the view that follows from empirical work based on the standard economic model (monopoly isn't much of a problem). One explanation is that society is wrong, that if society understood the economic model, it wouldn't be as concerned about monopoly as it is. A second explanation is that the monopolistic model isn't capturing some of people's normative arguments against monopoly. Both explanations have some validity.

Most economists would agree that the lay public often expresses a knee-jerk reaction to monopoly, not a reasoned judgment. Knee-jerk reactions are often wrong, so the argument that society is wrong to be so concerned about monopoly has a ring of truth. Knee-jerk reactions often don't hold true when subjected to careful scrutiny.

But, as discussed in the previous chapter, there are questions whether the economists' competitive equilibrium is an appropriate benchmark from which to judge welfare. The competitive benchmark doesn't take into account income distributional effects and issues of fairness. The public's judgments about real-world events do take these additional welfare considerations into account. Therefore the second explanation—that the monopolistic model isn't capturing some of people's normative arguments against monopoly—is also reasonable.

These two explanations aren't necessarily contradictory. They can complement one another. In certain instances the public might oppose monopoly because it doesn't understand the costs of monopoly, while in other instances it might dislike monopoly based on broader normative criteria that the standard model doesn't capture.

The economist's job is to help separate these two views. Doing so makes the analysis of monopoly a more complicated undertaking than simply drawing and understanding welfare triangle losses.

A BROADER VIEW OF MONOPOLY

The standard model of monopoly just presented is elegant, but, like many things elegant, it hides some issues, and these issues could help explain the difference between the standard model of monopoly (which suggests monopoly isn't much of a problem) and the public's dislike of monopoly.

One issue the standard model of monopoly hides is: What prevents other firms from entering the monopolist's market? You should be able to answer that question relatively quickly. If a monopolist exists, it must exist due to some type of **barrier to entry** (a social, political, or economic impediment that prevents firms from entering the market). Three important barriers to entry are natural ability, increasing returns to scale, and government restrictions. In the absence of barriers to entry, the monopoly would face competition from other firms, which would erode its monopoly.

This recognition is one of the main reasons why economists generally support free international trade and oppose tariffs. Tariffs are a barrier to entry to foreign firms and thus provide monopoly power to U.S. firms, allowing them to charge the consumer more than they otherwise could.

Studying how these barriers to entry are established, and what the costs of establishing them are, enriches the standard model and lets us distinguish different types of monopoly. For example, a barrier to entry might exist because a firm is better at producing a good than anyone else. It has unique qualities that make it more efficient than all other firms. The barrier to entry in this case is the firm's ability.

Such monopolies based on ability usually don't provoke the public's ire. Often in the public's mind such monopolies are "just monopolies." The standard economic model doesn't distinguish between a "just" and an "unjust" monopoly. The just/unjust distinction raises the question of whether a firm has acquired a monopoly based on its ability, or based on certain unfair positions such as initially pricing low to force competitive companies out of business but then pricing high. Many public debates over monopoly focus on such normative issues, about which the economists' standard model has nothing to say.

An alternative reason why a barrier to entry might exist is that there are significant economies of scale. If sufficiently large economies of scale exist, it would be inefficient to have two producers since if each produced half of the output, neither could take advantage of the economies of scale. Monopolies that exist because economies of scale create a barrier to entry are called **natural monopolies.** Where natural monopoly exists, the perfectly competitive solution is impossible, since average total costs are not covered where $MC = P$. Some output restriction is necessary in order for production to be feasible.

A third reason monopolies can exist is that they're created by government. The support of laissez-faire by Classical economists such as Adam Smith and their opposition to monopoly arose in large part in reaction to those government-created monopolies, not in reaction to any formal analysis of welfare loss from monopoly.

Many laypeople's views of government-created monopoly reflect the same normative judgments that Classical economists made. Classical economists considered, and much of the lay public considers, such monopolies unfair and inconsistent with liberty. Monopolies prevent people from being free to enter whatever business they want and are undesirable on normative grounds. In this view, government-created monopolies are simply wrong.

This normative argument against government-created monopoly doesn't extend to all types of government-created monopolies. The public accepts certain types of government-created monopoly that it believes have overriding social value. An example is patents. A **patent** is a legal protection of a technical innovation which gives the person holding the patent a monopoly on using that innovation. To encourage research and development of new products, government gives out patents for a wide variety of innovations, such as genetic engineering, Xerox machines, and cans that can be opened without a can opener.

A second normative argument against monopoly is that the public doesn't like the income distributional effects of monopoly. Although, as we saw in our discussion of monopoly, monopolists do not always earn an economic profit, they often do, which means that the existence of monopoly might transfer income in a way that the public (whose normative views help determine society's policy toward monopoly) doesn't

Barrier to entry   *A social, political, or economic impediment that prevents firms from entering a market.*

6 If there were no barriers to entry, profit-maximizing firms would always compete away monopoly profits.

Types of Barriers to Entry and the Public's View of Monopoly

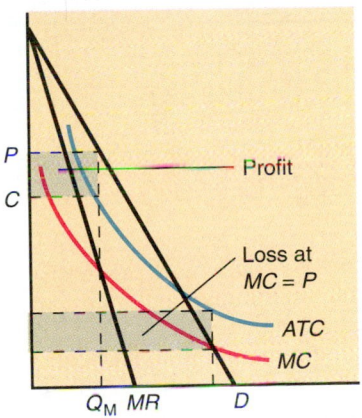

A natural monopoly would make a loss if it charged marginal cost.

Natural monopolies   *Monopolies that exist because economies of scale create a barrier to entry.*

Normative Views of Monopoly

Q–8: If a patent is a monopoly, why does the government give out patents?

Fortune—A business magazine that closely follows real-world business activities.

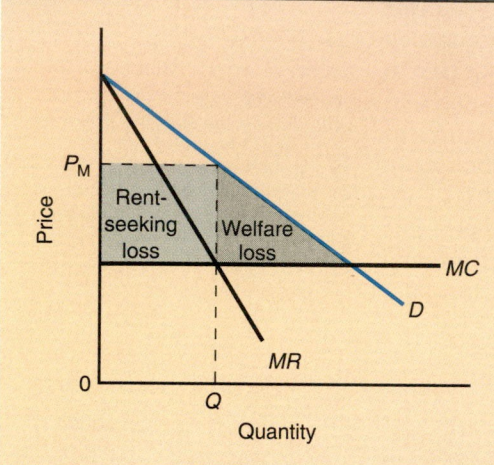

EXHIBIT 8   **The Rent-Seeking Loss from Monopoly**

If monopolies compete and spend money to achieve their monopoly profits, there will be an additional waste of resources to society, which will approximately equal the total expected profits. Thus rent-seeking analysis sees a second loss to society from monopoly.

like. This distributional effect of monopoly based on normative views of who deserves income is another reason many laypeople oppose monopoly: They believe it transfers income from ''deserving'' consumers to ''undeserving'' monopolists.

A third normative reason people oppose government-created monopoly that isn't captured by the standard model of monopoly is that the possibility of government-created monopoly encourages people to spend a lot of their time in political pursuits trying to get the government to favor them with a monopoly, and less time doing ''productive'' things.

This third normative argument against monopoly has been integrated into the standard model of monopoly by a group of political economists called **public choice economists** (economists who integrate an economic analysis of politics with their analysis of the economy). Public choice economists argue that if the government doesn't charge for a monopoly, individuals will spend large amounts of money in **rent seeking** (attempting to influence the structure of economic institutions in order to create rents for themselves). They do so by lobbying and otherwise trying to persuade government to give them the monopoly. Public choice economists further argue that the resources people spend on trying to get their monopoly is a waste of resources (that's the normative judgment) and that this waste is much larger than the traditionally incurred welfare loss from monopoly. Public choice economists argue that if there is competition for monopolies, people will spend up to the total expected amount of profit from a monopoly.

The **rent-seeking loss from monopoly** is shown in Exhibit 8. The possible profits from monopoly create a desire for monopoly and lead potential monopolists to spend resources to gain that monopoly. The resources spent are a waste (unless they serve other purposes) and hence, according to these economists who analyze rent seeking, the welfare cost of monopoly is not only the Harberger triangle, it's also the Tullock rectangle, so-named for Gordon Tullock who first made this argument back in 1967. That **Tullock rectangle** equals the entire profit of the monopolist, and its size often dwarfs the Harberger welfare triangle. According to Tullock, monopolists spend all their profits on rent seeking.

Each of these arguments probably plays a role in the public's dislike of monopoly. As you can see, these real-world arguments blend normative judgments with objective analysis, making it difficult to arrive at definite conclusions. Most real-world problems require this blending, making applied economic analysis difficult. The economist must interpret the normative judgments about what people want to achieve and explain how public policy can be designed to achieve those desired ends.

Let's now consider how economic theory might be used to analyze monopoly and to suggest some alternative policies. We first look at a debate about charging for monopolies. Then we look at a more specific example involving AIDS and AZT.

Public choice economists   *Economists who integrate an economic analysis of politics with their analysis of the economy.*

Rent-seeking   *Attempting to influence the structure of economic institutions in order to create rents for oneself.*

Rent-seeking loss from monopoly   *Waste caused by people spending money trying to get government to give them a monopoly.*

Tullock rectangle   *Graphical measure of rent-seeking loss from monopoly that results when potential monopolists spend resources to gain monopoly. The waste equals the entire profit of the monopoly.*

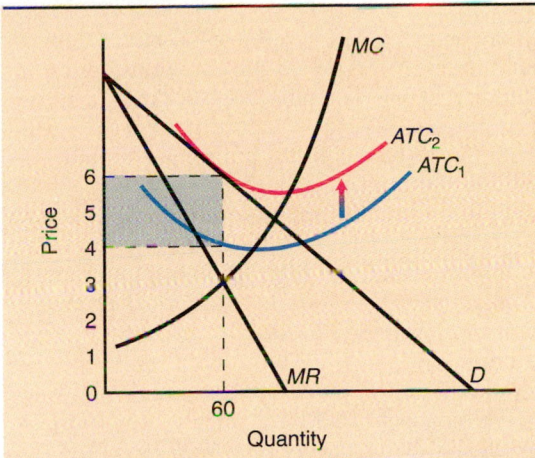

EXHIBIT 9   Selling Monopoly Rights

If the government charges a fixed fee for a monopoly, it will not affect the price, but will raise the fixed costs and hence reduce the profit (the shaded area).

Should the government charge for a monopoly that it gives out? One group argues that if the government charges, it will increase the monopolist's cost, and hence its price, so the government shouldn't charge. The other side's normative argument is that it's only fair to charge a monopolist. Let's now see where economists come out in this debate.

The first question an economist will ask is how the government will charge for the monopoly. Let's say that, if it is to charge, it will auction off the monopoly right to the highest bidder. In Exhibit 9, if the expected profits are $120, we can predict that the bidding for the monopoly right will approach that $120 economic profit. (Remember, economic profit considers the entrepreneur's effort as a cost.)

Let's say a firm buys a monopoly to sell hot dogs on the thruway, paying $119.99 for that monopoly. The $119.99 is a cost that some people say will push up the monopolist's price. Let's now consider how the economic model says this cost will affect the firm's decision on how many hot dogs to sell and what to charge for them. The economic model directs us to ask the following question: "What does the expenditure of $119.99 do to marginal cost or marginal revenue?" The answer is that it doesn't affect marginal cost or marginal revenue, so it doesn't affect the quantity or the price that the monopolist charges because both of those are determined only by where marginal cost and marginal revenue intersect.

What *does* it affect? It increases fixed cost (which is why the change has no effect on marginal cost), and in doing so it shifts up the average total cost curve to a point where the monopolist makes almost no profit. Thus, according to the economic model, the result of an auction for a monopoly is to transfer most of the monopoly profit from the monopolist to the government. It will not raise price and therefore, in regard to the two arguments posed at the beginning of this section, the economist would come out in favor of charging the full value for a monopoly. Charging for a monopoly has an additional advantage. To the degree that it eliminates profit from the monopoly, it reduces rent-seeking expenditures to get that monopoly. So in this case economic analysis supports charging for a monopoly, if you're going to have a monopoly.

As a final example of how knowledge of economics helps deal with real-world monopoly problems, let's consider the problem of AIDS and the medicinal drug AZT. AZT is believed to slow the onset of AIDS. The drug was developed by Burroughs Wellcome, which has a patent on it. That patent gives Burroughs Wellcome a monopoly. Patents are given on medicine to encourage firms to find cures for various diseases. The monopoly the patent gives them lets them charge a high price so that the firms can expect to make a profit from their research. Whether such patents are in the public interest isn't an issue since the patent has already been issued.

Should Government Charge Firms if It Gives Them a Monopoly Right?

7 Economists generally favor government charging for monopolies because those charges do not raise the price the monopolist charges, and they tend to reduce the rent-seeking expenditures spent to get that monopoly.

Q-9: Does charging for a monopoly right affect the pricing decision of a monopoly?

AIDS, AZT, and Monopoly

ADDED DIMENSION

THE WINNER'S CURSE

In the discussion about the hot dog monopoly, I was careful to specify a bid of $119.99, not $120. That still left a whole penny of economic profit. Normal profit is sufficient to keep a monopoly in a market, but, assuming a monopoly is already making a normal profit, some expected economic profit is needed to induce it to enter a new market. So some small above-normal profit has to be left to the monopolist to entice it to enter the business. Clearly a penny isn't enough, but it's enough to make the point to you: Disequilibrium adjustment from equilibrium requires the expectation of economic profit.

In real life, often there's great uncertainty about the value of a monopoly right. Individuals have differing views of what the monopoly is worth, and depending on the actual auction and the interdynamics during the bidding, the bid for a monopoly right will be higher or lower than the actual profit.

Often it's higher because of what's called the *winner's curse*. The person who wins at the auction is the person who values the monopoly right most highly, which means that the average bidder's estimate of the value of the monopoly right was lower than the amount the winner paid. If people on average are right, that means the winner paid too much and will make a loss on operating the monopoly. That's why her victory imposes the winner's curse.

A good example of the winner's curse is Donald Trump's and Merv Griffin's bidding on Resorts International and the Taj Mahal Casino. Both men figured the expected profit too high and both their businesses got into serious financial trouble, much to these tycoons' embarrassment.

Q-10: The medicinal drug tetracycline sold for animals costs about $\frac{1}{20}$ the cost of the same drug sold for human beings. What is the likely explanation?

What is an issue is what to do about AZT. Currently demand for AZT is highly inelastic, so the price Burroughs Wellcome can charge is high even though its marginal cost of producing it is low. Whether Burroughs Wellcome is making a profit on AZT depends on its cost of development. But since that cost is already spent, that's irrelevant to the current marginal cost; development cost affects Burroughs Wellcome's *ATC* curve, not its marginal cost curve. Thus, Burroughs Wellcome is charging an enormously high price for a drug that may help save people's lives and that costs Burroughs Wellcome a very small amount to produce.

What, if anything, should the government do? Some people have suggested that the government come in and regulate the price Burroughs Wellcome charges, requiring the firm to charge only its marginal cost. Doing so would make the marginal cost of producing AZT equal to the price people pay, which would make society better off. But most economists have a problem with that policy. They point out that doing so will have significant disincentive effects on drug companies. One reason drug companies spend billions of dollars for drug research is their expectation that they'll be able to make large profits if they're successful. If drug companies expect the government to come in and take away their monopoly when they're successful, they won't search for cures. So forcing Burroughs Wellcome to charge a low price for AZT would help AIDS victims, but it would hurt people suffering from diseases that are currently being researched and that might be researched in the future in the expectation of profits. So there's a strong argument not to regulate.

But the thought of people dying when a cheap cure—or at least a partially effective treatment—is available is repulsive to me and to many others. Indeed, Burroughs Wellcome has felt the pressure and has made AZT available to HIV-positive children (children infected with the AIDS virus but not yet suffering from actual AIDS) at a much lower price than it does to others (an example of price discrimination). In 1989 it lowered the price of AZT for everyone by 20 percent.

An alternative policy suggested by economic theory is for the government to buy the patent from Burroughs Wellcome and allow anyone to make AZT so the price would approach its marginal cost. Admittedly this would be expensive. It would cause negative incentive effects, as the government would have to increase taxes to cover the buyout's costs. But this approach would avoid the problem of the regulatory approach and achieve the same ends. However, it would also introduce new problems, such as determining which patents the government should buy.

Whether such a buyout policy makes sense remains to be seen, but in debating such issues the power of the simple monopoly model becomes apparent.

CONCLUSION

We've come to the end of the presentation of the formal models of perfect competition and monopoly. Working through the models takes a lot of effort, but, as my health club instructor used to say, ''No pain, no gain.'' In an earlier chapter, I quoted Einstein: ''A theory should be as simple as possible, but not more so.'' This chapter's analysis isn't simple; it takes repetition, working through models, and doing thought experiments to get it down pat. But it's as simple as possible. Even so, it's extremely easy to make a foolish mistake, as I did in my Ph.D. oral examination when I was outlining an argument on the blackboard. [''*What* did you say the output would be for this monopolist, Mr. Colander?''] As I learned then, it takes long hours of working through the models again and again to get them right.

CHAPTER SUMMARY

- The price a monopolist charges is higher than that of a competitive market due to the restriction of output; a monopolist can make a profit in the long run.
- A monopolist's profit-maximizing output is where marginal revenue equals marginal cost.
- To determine a monopolist's profit, first determine its output (where $MC = MR$). Then determine its price and average total cost at that output level.
- A perfectly price-discriminating monopolist sells more and makes a higher profit than a normal monopolist.
- The welfare loss to society from monopoly, as measured by Harberger and others, is relatively small. Normative measures of the welfare cost can increase that loss significantly.
- The public often opposes monopoly, based on normative reasons that the economic model doesn't capture.
- Three important barriers to entry are natural ability, increasing returns to scale, and government restrictions.
- Selling rights to monopoly will eliminate profit to a degree and reduce the time and money spent on rent seeking.

KEY TERMS

barrier to entry *(583)*
consumer surplus *(578)*
marginal revenue *(573)*
marginal revenue curve *(574)*
monopoly *(572)*

$MR = MC$ *(575)*
natural monopolies *(583)*
patent *(583)*
price discriminate *(578)*
public choice economists *(584)*

rent seeking *(584)*
rent-seeking loss from monopoly *(584)*
Tullock rectangle *(584)*
welfare loss triangle *(581)*

QUESTIONS FOR THOUGHT AND REVIEW

The number after each question represents the estimated degree of critical thinking required. (1 = almost none; 10 = deep thought.)

1. Demonstrate graphically the profit-maximizing positions for a perfect competitor and a monopolist. How do they differ? *(3)*
2. Monopolists differ from perfect competitors because monopolists make a profit. True or false? Why? *(4)*
3. Explain the effects on college education of the development of a teaching machine which you plug into a student's brain and which makes the student understand everything. How would your answer differ if a college could monopolize production of this machine? *(9)*
4. Say you place a lump sum tax (a tax that is treated as a fixed cost) on a monopolist. How will that affect her output and pricing decisions? *(4)*
5. A monopolist is selling fish. But if the fish don't sell, they rot. What will be the likely elasticity at the point on the demand curve at which the monopolist sets the price? *(6)*
6. Provide a price discrimination argument for the existence of the three unexplained examples of price discrimination in the text (page 580). *(6)*

7. Will the welfare loss from a monopolist with a perfectly elastic marginal cost curve be greater or less than the welfare loss from a monopolist with an upward-sloping marginal cost curve? *(5)*

8. Copyrights provide authors with a monopoly. What effect would eliminating copyrights have on the price and output of textbooks? Should copyrights be eliminated? *(8)*

9. Some authors believe that they should get a fee when-

ever someone borrows their books from the library. What effect would such a fee have on the price and quantity of books demanded? Why? Should such fees be charged? *(8)*

10. If people had to pay for monopoly, they would buy less monopoly, so the Tullock rectangle overestimates the rent-seeking loss from monopoly. True or false? Why? *(9)*

PROBLEMS AND EXERCISES

1. A monopolist with a straight line demand curve finds that it can sell two units at $12 each or 12 units at $2 each. Its fixed cost is $20 and its marginal cost is constant at $3 per unit.
   a. Draw the *MC, ATC, MR,* and demand curves for this monopolist.
   b. At what output level would the monopolist produce?
   c. At what output level would a perfectly competitive firm produce?

2. State what's wrong with the following graphs:

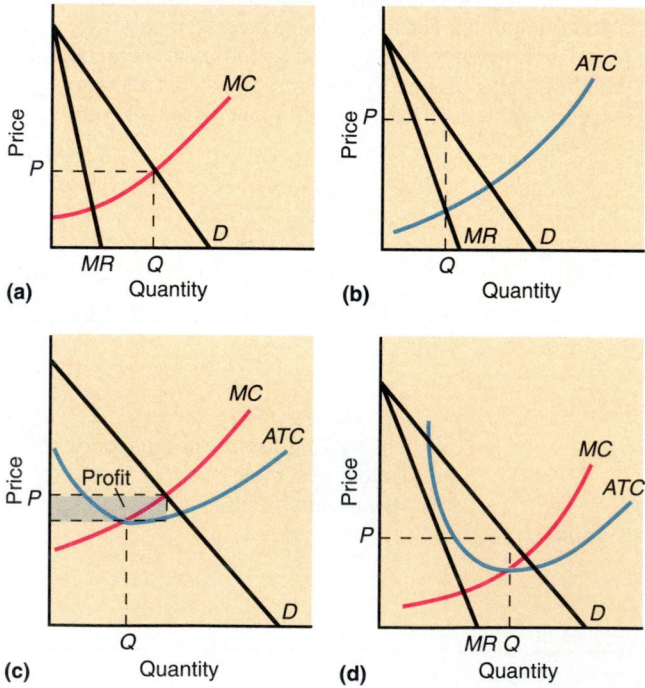

(a)

(b)

(c)

(d)

3. Wyeth-Ayerst Laboratories developed Norplant, a long-acting contraceptive, in the early 1990s. In the United States, the firm priced the contraceptive at $350, and in other countries, the firm priced it at $23.
   a. Why would the firm price it differently in different countries?
   b. Was the pricing fair?
   c. What do you think will happen to the price over time? Why?

4. Demonstrate:
   a. The welfare cost of monopoly.
   b. The rent-seeking cost of monopoly.
   c. If there were a constant marginal cost to restricting output for a monopolist, how would that cost affect your answer to *b?*
   d. How would your answer to *c* differ if there were a lump sum cost to creating monopoly?

5. New York City has issued 11,787 taxi licenses, called *medallions,* and has not changed that number since 1937.
   a. What does that limitation likely do to the price of taxi medallions?
   b. In the early 1990s, the New York City Taxi Commission promulgated a rule that required single-cab medallion owners to drive their cabs full time. What will that rule do to the price of the medallion?
   c. If New York City increased the number of medallions by 1,000, selling the additional 1,000 at the market rate, and gave half the proceeds to owners of existing medallions, what would happen to the price of medallions?
   d. What would happen to the wealth of existing medallion owners?

ANSWERS TO MARGIN QUESTIONS

1. If you doodle too much, your doodles will become worthless. Besides, if you want to pass the next test you have to study. *(572)*

2. At output 4, the marginal cost of $12 (between $8 and $16) equals the marginal revenue of $12 (between $15

and $9), making it the profit-maximizing output. It has the highest total profit, $34. *(573)*

3. To determine the profit-maximizing price and output, one must determine where the marginal revenue curve equals marginal cost. So one must first draw the margi-

nal revenue curve and see where it intersects marginal cost. That intersection determines the quantity, as in the graph below. Carrying the line up to the demand curve determines the price. *(575)*

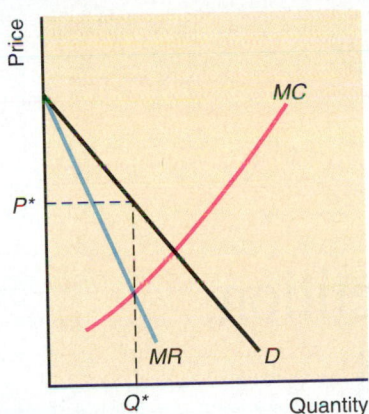

4. A monopolist produces less output than a perfectly competitive firm because it takes into account the fact that increasing output will lower the price of all previous units. *(575)*

5. The subsidy would make the monopolist's marginal cost curve below the zero axis. Price and quantity would be determined where the marginal revenue equals this marginal cost, as in the diagram below. *(578)*

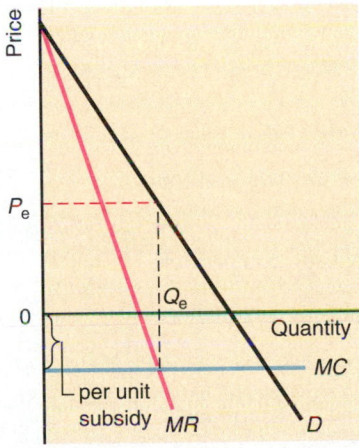

6. Since a monopolist who cannot price-discriminate would produce at Q_0 and a monopolist who could completely price-discriminate would produce at Q_1 in the diagram below, a monopolist who can partially price-discriminate would produce somewhere between Q_0 and Q_1. *(579)*

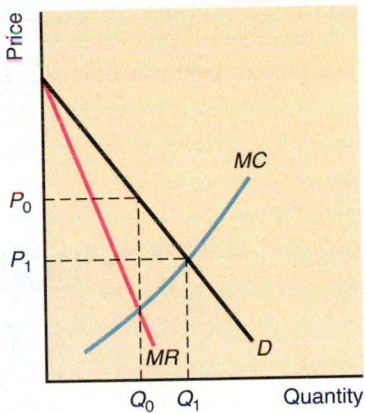

7. Area *C* represents the profit going to a monopolist. It is not considered a loss since, while consumers lose it, monopolists gain it. It is a redistribution of resources rather than an efficiency loss. *(581)*

8. The government gives out patents to encourage research and development of new products. This suggests that the public and government believe that certain monopolies have overriding social value. *(583)*

9. Charging for a monopoly right does not affect the pricing decision of the firm since it does not affect either the marginal cost curve or the price, and the output—and hence the price—of a monopolist is determined by where the marginal cost equals marginal revenue. *(585)*

10. A likely explanation for medicinal drugs being sold at a much lower cost for animals than for human beings is differing elasticities of demand. The demand for drugs for human beings is highly inelastic, whereas the demand for medicinal drugs for animals is elastic. When there is a price-discriminating monopolist for these drugs, those with more inelastic demands are charged higher prices. *(586)*

27

Monopolistic Competition, Oligopoly, and Strategic Pricing

Competition, you know, is a lot like chastity. It is widely praised, but alas, too little practiced.

~Carol Tucker

After reading this chapter, you should be able to:

1 Interpret a concentration ratio and a Herfindahl index for two- and four-digit industries.

2 List the four distinguishing characteristics of monopolistic competition.

3 Demonstrate graphically the equilibrium of a monopolistic competitor.

4 State why an oligopoly has a strong desire to form a cartel.

5 Explain why the contestable market theory would lead to determining competitiveness by performance rather than structure.

6 Summarize the important elements of various market structures.

As soon as economists start talking about real-world competition, market structure becomes a focus of the discussion. **Market structure** is the physical characteristics of the market within which firms interact. It involves the number of firms in the market, the barriers to entry, and the communication among firms. Monopoly and competition are the two polar cases of market structure that economists generally focus on. Real-world markets generally fall in between, and it is useful to introduce briefly two market structures between perfect competition and monopoly: monopolistic competition and oligopoly. They not only provide you with a sense of how the models can apply to the real world; they also help cement the concepts learned in the last chapter into your mind.

Perfect competition has an almost infinite number of firms; monopoly has one firm. Monopolistic competition and oligopoly fall between these two extremes. **Monopolistic competition** is a market structure in which there are many firms selling differentiated products. Because there are many firms, any one firm's decision is independent of other firms' decisions. Monopolistic competition falls closer to perfect competition; it has many firms, but not an uncountable number. **Oligopoly** is a market structure in which there are a few interdependent firms. Oligopoly falls closer to monopoly; it has only a few firms, but more than one firm. Exhibit 1 shows a likely distribution of the spectrum of U.S. market structures. Notice that most U.S. industry structures fall almost entirely between perfect competition and monopoly—in oligopoly and monopolistic competition. This should not be surprising to you. Using precise definitions, perfectly competitive and monopolistic industries are nearly nonexistent.

Any estimate of the distribution of market structures must be treated with care. Defining an industry is a complicated task—inevitably numerous arbitrary decisions must be made. Similarly, defining the relevant market of a given industry is complicated. For example, there are about 9,000 banks in the United States, and banking is considered reasonably competitive. However there may be only one or two banks in a particular small town, so there will be a monopoly or oligopoly with respect to banks in that town. Is the United States or the town the relevant market? The same argument exists when we think of international competition. Many firms sell in international markets and, while a group of firms may compose an oligopoly in the United States, the international market might be more accurately characterized by monopolistic competition.

Another dimension of the definitional problem concerns deciding what is to be included in an industry. If you define the industry as "the transportation industry," there are many firms. If you define it as "the automobile industry," there are fewer firms; if you define it as "the sports car industry," there are still fewer firms. Similarly with the geographic dimension of industry. There's more competition in the global market than in the local market. The narrower the definition, the fewer the firms.

To convey a sense of how specifically one is defining an industry, economists have developed a classification system of industries called a **Standard Industrial Code (SIC).** A **two-digit industry** is a broadly defined industry. For example, "furniture and fixtures" is a two-digit industry and is denoted by the number 25. All subdivisions of that broad grouping use the same first two numbers, and then add more numbers to identify the particular subdivision. For example, "metal household furniture" is a subdivision of the furniture and fixtures industry and is denoted by the number 2514.

When economists talk about industry structure, they generally talk about **four-digit industries** in the United States. This is a convention. Economists are often called upon to give expert testimony in court cases, and if an economist wants to argue that an industry is more competitive than its opponents say it is, he or she challenges this convention of using a four-digit classification of industry, asserting that the classification is arbitrary (which it is) and that the relevant market should be the two-digit

---

Market structure   *The physical characteristics of the market within which firms interact.*

Monopolistic competition   *A market structure in which many firms sell different products.*

Oligopoly   *A market structure with a few interdependent firms.*

THE PROBLEMS OF DETERMINING MARKET STRUCTURE

Classifying Industries

Standard Industrial Code (SIC)   *System for classifying industries.*

Two-digit industry   *SIC designation for broadly defined industries.*

Four-digit industry   *SIC designation for a specific type of industry within a more broadly defined two-digit industry.*

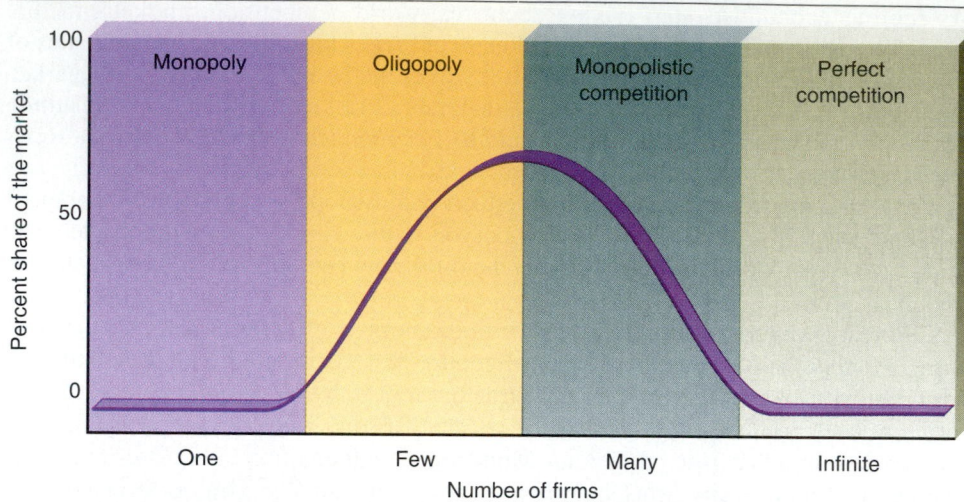

EXHIBIT 1   The Spectrum of Market Structures

There are many types of market structures, ranging from a market with one firm (monopoly) to a market with an almost infinite number of firms (perfect competition). Real-world markets generally fall between the two. Oligopoly is a market structure with a few *interdependent* firms. Monopolistic competition is a market structure in which there are more firms and their decisions are *independent*. Most industries are either oligopolistically or monopolistically competitive. Both monopoly and perfect competition are almost non-existent.

classification. Exhibit 2 presents various two- and four-digit industry groupings to give you an idea of what's included in each.

Determining Industry Structure

1A   A concentration ratio is the percentage of industry output that a specific number of the largest firms have.

Q-1:   Which would have more output: the two-digit industry 20 or the four-digit industry 2011? Explain your reasoning.

Standard Industrial Classification Manual— This Commerce Department publication provides full information about SIC codes.

To measure industry structure economists use one of two methods: the concentration ratio or a Herfindahl index (sometimes called the *Herfindahl-Hirshman index* or the *HHI*).

A **concentration ratio** is the percentage of the total industry output that the top firms of the industry have. The higher the ratio, the closer to an oligopolistic or monopolistic type of market structure. The Herfindahl index is an index of the squares of the market shares of all the firms in the industry. Generally if one index is high, so is the other. Exhibit 3 presents the four-firm concentration ratio and the Herfindahl index of selected industries. Let's consider each method in more detail.

Concentration Ratios   The most commonly used concentration ratio is the four-firm concentration ratio. For example, a four-firm concentration ratio of 60 tells you that the top four firms in the industry produce 60 percent of the industry's output. The classification of industries as monopolistically competitive or oligopolistic that you saw in Exhibit 1 was organized in large part around concentration ratios. If the four-firm concentration ratio was below 40 percent, the presumption was that the industry was monopolistically competitive. If the four-firm concentration ratio was between 40 and 60 percent, the presumption was that it was oligopolistic. If the four-firm concentration ratio was greater than 60 percent, the industry was considered monopolistic.

The Herfindahl Index   The concentration ratio measure has problems (as do all measures). For example, say an industry has a four-firm concentration ratio of 51 percent. That doesn't tell us whether one firm has 48 percent and the next three firms each have 1 percent of the market, or whether the top four firms each have 12 or 13 percent. Yet those structures are quite different from each other. Nor does the concentration ratio differentiate between industries with different numbers of firms beyond four.

To avoid these problems, an alternative definition of *market structure* has been designed—the **Herfindahl index.** It's calculated by adding the squared value of the

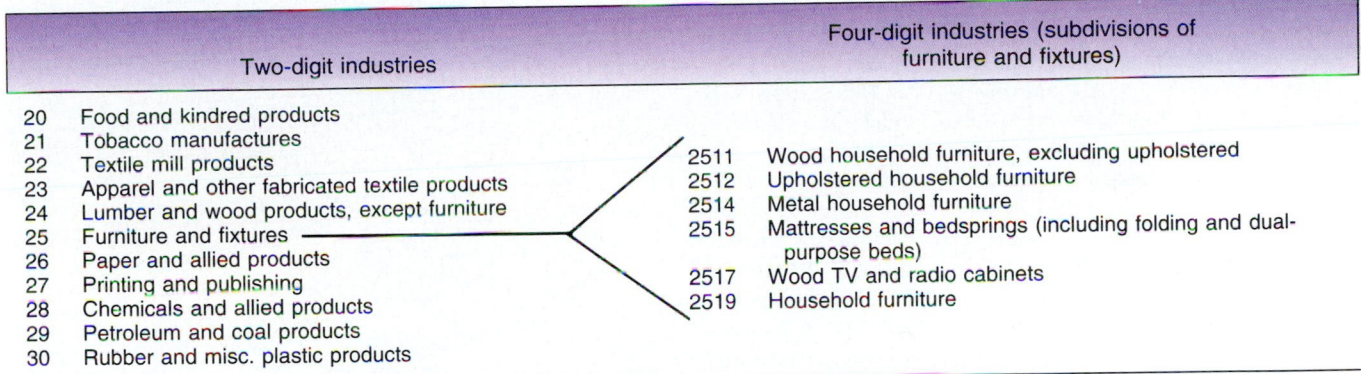

EXHIBIT 2   **Two- and Four-Digit Industry Groups**

Two-digit industries	Four-digit industries (subdivisions of furniture and fixtures)
20 Food and kindred products	
21 Tobacco manufactures	
22 Textile mill products	2511 Wood household furniture, excluding upholstered
23 Apparel and other fabricated textile products	2512 Upholstered household furniture
24 Lumber and wood products, except furniture	2514 Metal household furniture
25 Furniture and fixtures	2515 Mattresses and bedsprings (including folding and dual-purpose beds)
26 Paper and allied products	
27 Printing and publishing	2517 Wood TV and radio cabinets
28 Chemicals and allied products	2519 Household furniture
29 Petroleum and coal products	
30 Rubber and misc. plastic products	

EXHIBIT 3   **Concentration Ratios and the Herfindahl Index**

Industry	Four-firm concentration ratio	Herfindahl index
Meat packing	29	325
Canned fruit and vegetables	21	214
Cereal breakfast foods	86	NA
Women's and misses' dresses	6	24
Book publishing	17	190
Greeting card publishing	84	2840
Soap and detergent	60	1306
Men's footwear	28	378
Women's footwear	38	492
Bolts, nuts, rivets, and washers	13	102
Computing equipment	43	793
Radio and TV sets	49	751
Burial caskets	52	1247

market shares of all the firms in the industry. For example, say that 10 firms in the industry each have 10 percent of the market:

Herfindahl index $= 10^2 + 10^2 + 10^2 + 10^2 + 10^2 + 10^2 + 10^2 + 10^2 + 10^2 + 10^2 = 1,000$

1B A Herfindahl index is a method used by economists to classify how competitive an industry is.

Two advantages of the Herfindahl index are that it takes into account all firms in an industry, and it gives extra weight to a single firm that has an especially large share of the market. For example, let's consider two industries with four-firm concentration ratios of 51 percent. In the first industry the top firm has a 48 percent market share and the next three each have a 1 percent share. In the second industry the top three firms have a 13 percent share, and the fourth has a 12 percent share. Let's further assume that there are 49 other firms in the industry, each with a 1 percent share of the market.

Q-2: If the four-firm concentration ratio is 60 percent, what is the highest Herfindahl index that industry could have? What is the lowest?

The Herfindahl index of the first is:

$$(48)^2 + (1)^2 \ldots + (1)^2 = 48^2 + 52 = 2304 + 52 = 2356$$

The Herfindahl index of the second is:

$$(13)^2 + (13)^2 + (13)^2 + (12)^2 + (1)^2 + \ldots + (1)^2 = 169 + 169 + 169 + 144 + 49 = 700$$

As you can see, in certain instances the Herfindahl index gives a different view of the two industries' structures than we get from the concentration ratio method.

The Herfindahl index is important because it is used as a rule of thumb by the U.S. Department of Justice in determining whether an industry is sufficiently competitive to allow a merger between two large firms in the industry. If the Herfindahl index is less than 1,000, the Department of Justice assumes the industry is sufficiently competitive, and it doesn't look more closely at the merger. We'll discuss this in more detail in a later chapter.

FOREIGN COMPETITIVE OLIGOPOLIES

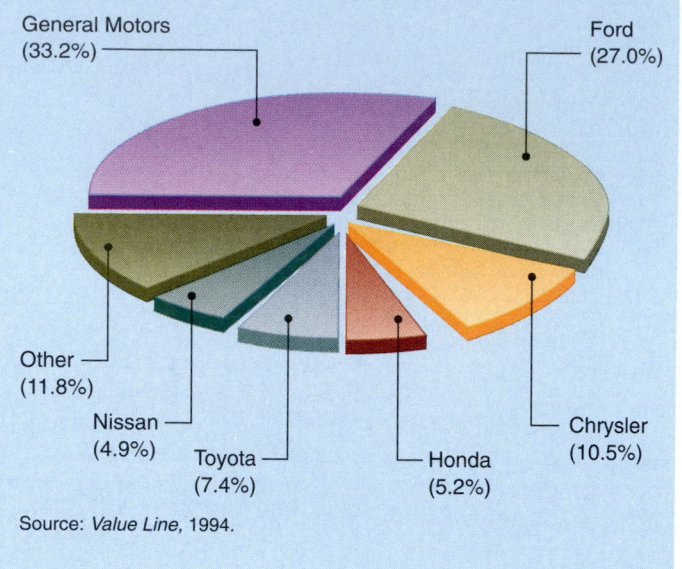

General Motors (33.2%)

Ford (27.0%)

Other (11.8%)

Nissan (4.9%)

Toyota (7.4%)

Honda (5.2%)

Chrysler (10.5%)

Source: *Value Line*, 1994.

Market structures change over time. Take, for instance, the automobile industry, which has always been used as the classic oligopoly model. Starting in the 1970s, however, foreign auto makers have made large inroads into the U.S. market and have added new competition to it. Foreign companies such as Honda, Nissan, and Toyota have entered the U.S. market as seen in the accompanying pie chart which lists major automobile companies and their market shares.

As you can see, the four-firm concentration ratio is over 75 percent, so the industry is still classified as an oligopoly. GM still considers what Ford and Chrysler's reactions will be, but with the addition of foreign competition, there are getting to be too many firms for one firm to consider the reactions of all the other firms. The auto industry is becoming more monopolistically competitive.

Such change in industry structure is to be expected. Monopoly and oligopoly allow firms to make above-normal profits. Above-normal profits invite entry, and unless there are entry barriers, the result will likely be a breakdown in that monopoly or oligopoly.

Conglomerate Firms and Bigness

Conglomerate   *A large corporation whose activities span various unrelated industries.*

Neither the four-firm concentration ratio nor the Herfindahl index gives us a picture of corporations' bigness. That's because many corporations are **conglomerates** (companies that span a variety of unrelated industries). For example, a conglomerate might produce both shoes and automobiles.

To see that concentration ratios are not an index of bigness, say there were only 11 firms in the entire United States, each with a 9 percent share of each industry. Both indices would classify the U.S. economy as reasonably competitive, but many people would seriously doubt whether that were the case. Little work has been done on classifying conglomerates or in determining whether they have any effect on an industry's competitiveness.

The Importance of Classifying Industry Structure

Now that we've talked about the classifications of industries, we need to ask why it's important to classify them in market structures such as monopolistic competition and oligopoly. The reason is that the greater the number of sellers, the greater the likelihood that an industry is competitive.

In terms of formal modeling it's important to classify industries because the number of firms in an industry plays an important role in determining whether firms explicitly take other firms' actions into account. In monopolistic competition, there are so many firms that individual firms *do not* explicitly take into account rival firms' likely responses to their decisions. In oligopoly there are fewer firms, and each firm explicitly takes into account other firms' expected reaction to its decisions. Taking explicit account of a rival's expected response to a decision you are making is called **strategic decision making.** In oligopolies all decisions, including pricing decisions, are strategic decisions. Thus, one distinguishes between monopolistic competition and oligopoly by whether or not they explicitly take into account competitors' reactions to their decisions.

Strategic decision making   *Taking explicit account of a rival's expected response to a decision you are making.*

Q–3:   Your study partner, Jean, has just said that monopolistic competitors use strategic decision making. How would you respond?

Why is the distinction important? Because it determines whether economists can model and predict the price and output of an industry. Nonstrategic decision making can be predicted relatively accurately if individuals behave rationally. Strategic decision making is much more difficult to predict, even if people behave rationally. Consistent with this distinction, economists' model of monopolistic competition has a definite prediction. A model of monopolistic competition will tell us: Here's how much will be produced and here's how much will be charged. Economists' model of oligopoly doesn't have a definite prediction. There are no unique price and output decisions at which an oligopoly will rationally arrive; there are a variety of rational oligopoly decisions.

The four distinguishing characteristics of monopolistic competition are:

1. Many sellers in a highly competitive market;
2. Differentiated products, but firms still act independently;
3. Multiple dimensions of competition; and
4. Easy entry of new firms in the long run so there are no long-run profits.

Let's consider each in turn.

MONOPOLISTIC COMPETITION

Many Sellers

When there are a few sellers, it's reasonable to explicitly take into account your competitors' reaction to the price you set. When there are many sellers, it isn't. In monopolistic competition one doesn't take into account rivals' reactions. Here's an example. There are many types of soap: Ivory, Irish Spring, Yardley's Old English, and so on. So when Ivory decides to run a sale, it won't spend a lot of time thinking of Old English's reaction. There are so many firms that one firm can't concern itself with the reaction of any specific firm. The soap industry is characterized by monopolistic competition. On the other hand, there are only a few major automobile firms, so when GM sets its price, it will explicitly consider what Ford's reaction may be. If GM raises its price, will Ford go along and also raise price? Or will it hold its price at its current level and try to sell its cars on the basis of lower prices? The automobile industry is an oligopoly.

2 Four distinguishing characteristics of monopolistic competition are:
1. Many sellers in a highly competitive market;
2. Differentiated products, but firms still act independently;
3. Multiple dimensions of competition; and
4. Easy entry of new firms in the long run so there are no long-run profits.

The fact that there are many sellers in monopolistic competition also makes collusion difficult since, when there are many firms, getting all of them to act as one is difficult. Monopolistically competitive firms act independently.

Product Differentiation

The "many sellers" characteristic gives monopolistic competition its competitive aspect. Product differentiation gives it its monopolistic aspect. In a monopolistically competitive market, the goods that are sold aren't homogeneous as in perfect competition; they are differentiated slightly. Irish Spring soap is slightly different from Ivory which in turn is slightly different from Yardley's Old English.

So in one sense each firm has a monopoly in the good it sells. But that monopoly is fleeting; it is based upon advertising to let people know, and to convince them, that one firm's good is different from the goods of competitors. The good may or may not really be different. Bleach differs little from one brand to another, yet buying Clorox makes many people feel "safe" that they're getting pure bleach. I generally don't buy it; I buy generic bleach. Ketchup, on the other hand, while made from the same basic ingredients no matter what the brand, differs among types (in my view). I buy only Heinz and would never think of getting any other type—to me, other types aren't true ketchup.

Because a monopolistic competitor has some monopoly power, advertising to increase that monopoly power (and hence increase the firm's profits) makes sense as long as the marginal benefit of advertising exceeds the marginal cost. Despite the fact that their goods are similar but differentiated, to fit the monopolistically competitive model, firms must make their decisions as if they had no effect on other firms; they must not act strategically or interdependently; that would make the industry an oligopoly.

Gasoline stations watch the competition carefully and their prices often move together. © Harriet Gan/The Image Works.

Multiple Dimensions of Competition

In perfect competition, price is the only dimension on which firms compete; in monopolistic competition, competition takes many forms. Product differentiation reflects firms' attempt to compete on perceived quality; advertising is another form competition takes. Other dimensions of competition include service and distribution outlets. These multiple dimensions of competition make it much harder to analyze a specific industry, but these alternative methods of competition follow the same general decision rules as price competition:

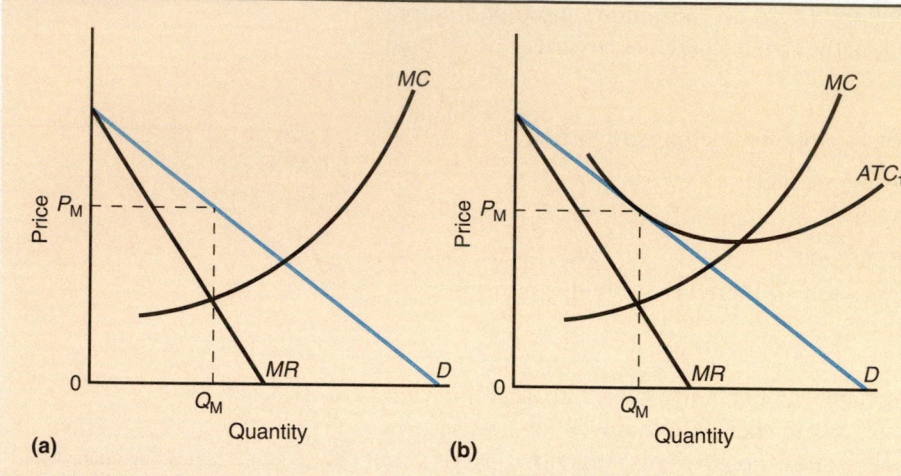

EXHIBIT 4 (a and b) Monopolistic Competition

In (a) you can see that a monopolistically competitive firm prices in the same manner as a monopolist. It sets price where marginal revenue equals marginal cost. In (b) you can see that the monopolistic competitor is not only a monopolist but also a competitor. Competition implies zero economic profit in the long run. Economic profits are determined by the average total cost (*ATC*) curve. At equilibrium, *ATC* must be equal to price. It will be equal to price only if the *ATC* curve is tangent to the demand curve at the output the firm chooses.

· Compare marginal costs and marginal benefits; and
· Change that dimension of competition until marginal costs equal marginal benefits.

Ease of Entry of New Firms in the Long Run

The last condition for a market to be considered monopolistically competitive is that entry must be relatively easy and there must be no significant barriers to entry. The absence of barriers to entry means that there can be no long-run economic profits; in monopolistic competition if there were long-run economic profits, other firms would enter. Barriers to entry create the potential for long-run economic profit and prevent competitive pressures from pushing price down to cost. When no barriers to entry exist, firms enter until no economic profit exists.

Graphical Representation of Monopolistic Competition

3 The equilibrium of a monopolistic competitor is:

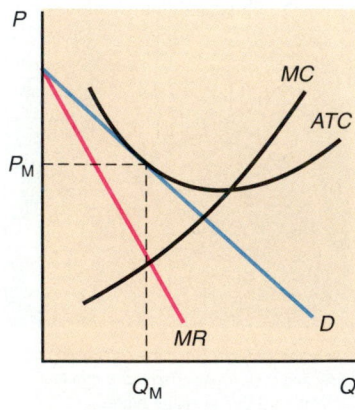

Q–4: How do the equilibrium for a monopoly and for a monopolistic competitor differ?

Although a full analysis of the multiple dimensions of monopolistic competition cannot be compressed into a two-dimensional graph, a good introduction can be gained by considering it within the standard graph.

To do so we simply consider the four propositions of monopolistic competition and see what implication they have for our curves. First, we recognize that the firm has some monopoly power; therefore a monopolistic competitor faces a downward-sloping demand curve. The downward-sloping demand curve means that in making decisions about prices, the monopolistic competitor will, as will a monopolist, use a marginal revenue curve that is below price. So at its profit-maximizing output, marginal cost will be less than price (not equal to price as it would be for a perfect competitor). We consider that case in Exhibit 4(a).

The monopolistic competitor faces the demand curve *D*, marginal revenue curve *MR*, and marginal cost curve *MC*. This demand curve is its portion of the total market demand curve. Using the $MC = MR$ rule discussed in the last chapter, you can see that the firm will choose output level Q_M (because that's the level of output at which marginal revenue intersects marginal cost). Having determined output, we extend a dotted line up to the demand curve and see that the firm will set a price equal to P_M. This price exceeds marginal cost. So far all we've done is to reproduce the monopolist's decision.

Where does the competition come in? Competition implies zero economic profit in the long run. (If there's profit, a new competitor will enter the market, decreasing the existing firms' demand [shifting it to the left].) In long-run equilibrium a perfect competitor makes only a normal profit. Economic profits are determined by *ATC*, not by *MC*, so the competition part of monopolistic competition tells us where the average total cost must be at the long-run equilibrium output. It must be equal to price, and it will be equal to price only if the *ATC* curve is tangent to the demand curve at the output the firm chooses. We add that average total cost curve to the *MC*, *MR*, and

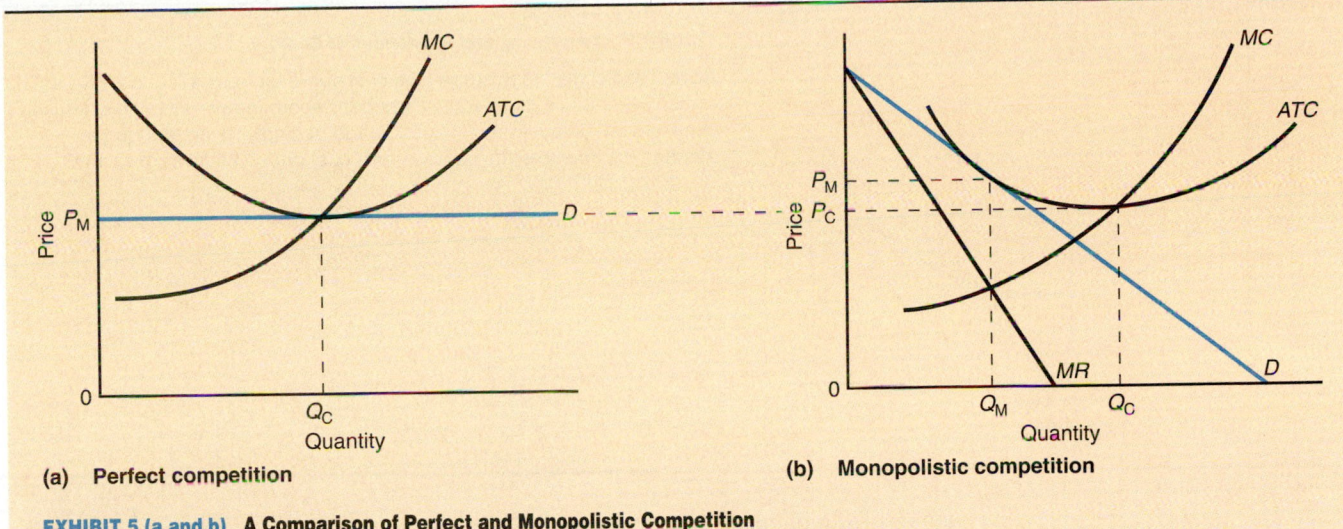

EXHIBIT 5 (a and b)   A Comparison of Perfect and Monopolistic Competition

The perfect competitor perceives its demand curve as perfectly elastic, and zero economic profit means that it produces at the minimum of the *ATC* curve, as represented in (**a**). A monopolistic competitor, on the other hand, faces a downward-sloping demand curve and produces where marginal cost equals marginal revenue, as represented in (**b**). The *ATC* curve is tangent to the demand curve at that level, which is *not* at the minimum point of the *ATC* curve. The monopolistic competitor produces Q_M at price P_M. A perfect competitor with the same marginal cost curve would produce Q_C at price P_C.

demand curves in Exhibit 4(b). Profit or loss, I hope you remember, is determined by the difference between price and average total cost at the quantity the firm chooses.

To give this condition a little more intuitive meaning, say, for instance, that the monopolistically competitive firm is making a profit. This profit would set two adjustments in motion. First, it would attract new entrants. Some of the firm's customers would defect and its portion of the market demand curve would decrease. Second, to try to protect its profits the firm would likely increase expenditures on product differentiation and advertising to offset that entry. (There would be an All New, Really New, Widget Campaign.) These expenditures would shift its average total cost curve up. These two adjustments would continue until the profits disappeared and the new demand curve was once again tangent to the average cost curve. A monopolistically competitive firm can make no long-run economic profit.

If both the monopolistic competitor and the perfect competitor make zero economic profit in the long run, it might seem that, in the long run at least, they're identical. They aren't, however. The perfect competitor perceives its demand curve as perfectly elastic, and the zero economic profit condition means that it produces at the minimum of the average total cost curve where the marginal cost curve equals price. We demonstrate that case in Exhibit 5(a).

The monopolistic competitor faces a downward-sloping demand curve. It produces where the marginal cost curve equals the marginal revenue curve, and not where *MC* equals price. In equilibrium, price exceeds marginal cost. The average total cost curve of a monopolistic competitor is tangent to the demand curve at that output level, which cannot be at the minimum point of the average total cost curve since the demand curve is sloping downward. The minimum point of the average total cost curve (where a perfect competitor produces) is at a higher output (Q_C) than that of the monopolistic competitor (Q_M). I demonstrate the monopolistically competitive equilibrium in Exhibit 5(b) to allow you to compare monopolistic competition with perfect competition.

As you can see, the difference between a monopolist and a monopolistic competitor is in the position of the average total cost curve in long-run equilibrium. For a monopolist, the average total cost curve can be, but need not be, at a position below price so that the monopolist makes a long-run economic profit. The average total cost

Comparing Monopolistic Competition with Perfect Competition

The difference between a monopolist and a monopolistic competitor is in the position of the average total cost curve in long-run equilibrium.

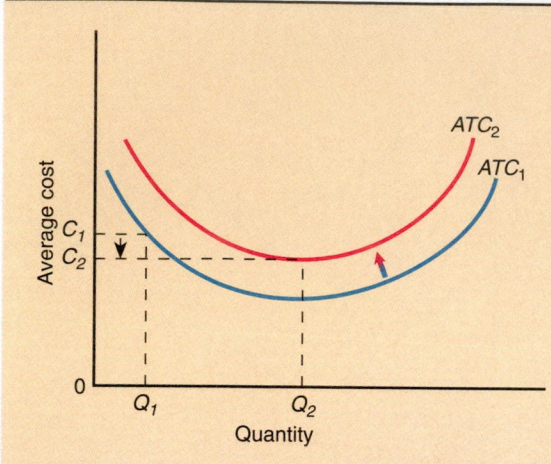

EXHIBIT 6 **Advertising and Economies of Scale**

Advertising shifts the average total cost curve up from ATC_1 to ATC_2, as shown here. Since more consumers hear about the product, the producer can increase output from Q_1 to Q_2. In the example, even though the average cost curve shifts up, the firm's cost per unit falls from C_1 to C_2.

curve of a monopolistic competitor must be tangent to the demand curve at the price and output chosen by the monopolistic competitor. No long-run economic profit is possible.

The difference between a perfect competitor and a monopolistic competitor is that the perfect competitor in long-run equilibrium produces at a point where $MC = P = ATC$. At that point, ATC is at its minimum.

For a monopolistic competitor in long-run equilibrium, $(P = ATC) \geq (MC = MR)$.

A monopolistic competitor produces at a point where $MC = MR$. Price is higher than marginal cost. For a monopolistic competitor in long-run equilibrium:

$$(P = ATC) \geq (MC = MR)$$

At that point, ATC is *not* at its minimum.

What does this distinction between a monopolistically competitive industry and a perfectly competitive industry mean in practice? It means that for a monopolistic competitor, since increasing output lowers average cost, increasing market share is a relevant concern. If only the monopolistic competitor could expand its market, it could do better. For a perfect competitor, increasing output offers no benefit in the form of lower average cost. A perfect competitor would have no concern about market share (the firm's percentage of total sales in the market).

Advertising and Monopolistic Competition

While firms in a perfectly competitive market have no incentive to advertise (since they can sell all they want at the market price), monopolistic competitors have a strong incentive. That's because their products are differentiated from the others; advertising plays an important role in providing that differentiation.

A primary goal of advertising is to shift the firm's demand curve to the right to increase demand for its product. That allows the firm to sell more, to charge a higher price, or to enjoy a combination of the two. It is advantageous to the firm if the marginal revenue of advertising exceeds the marginal cost of advertising. Advertising has two effects: It shifts the demand curve out, and it shifts the average total cost curve up.

When many firms are advertising, the advertising might be done less to shift the demand curve out than to keep the demand curve where it is—to stop demanders from shifting to a competitor's product. In either case, firms advertise to move the demand curve further out than where it would be if the firms weren't advertising. Advertising is often designed to increase the firm's market share. Market share is especially important when there are economies of scale.

Q–5: How might it be possible for advertising to lower the price of a good?

Advertising and Economies of Scale

Advertising shifts the average total cost curve up, but where there are economies of scale in production, advertising can result in lower average total costs, as Exhibit 6 shows. In it we see that advertising shifts the ATC curve upward from ATC_1 to ATC_2. (Advertising on television can cost over $1 million per minute.) However, since more consumers hear about the product, the firm can increase output, say from Q_1 to Q_2. In such a case, cost per unit declines from C_1 to

ADDED DIMENSION

THE 10 MOST POPULAR
TELEVISION ADS

The ten most popular television commercials in 1993 were:

1993 Rank	1992 Rank	Brands
1	5	McDonald's
2	2	Pepsi
3	9	Coca-Cola
4	3	Nike
5	1	Little Caesars
6	7	Budweiser
7	—	Taco Bell
8	10	Taster's Choice
9	4	DuPont Stainmaster
10	16	Lexus

Source: Video Storyboard Tests, Inc.

C_2, because of economies of scale. The lower cost from economies of scale more than offsets the cost of advertising.

Does Advertising Help or Hinder Us?   Our perception of products (the degree of trust we put in them) is significantly influenced by advertising. Think of the following pairs of goods:

Rolex	Timex
Cheerios	Oat Circles
Clorox bleach	generic bleach

Each of these names conveys a sense of what it is and how much trust we put in the product, and that determines how much we're willing to pay for it. For example, most people would pay more for Cheerios than for Oat Circles. Each year firms spend more than $125 billion on advertising. That advertising increases firms' costs but it also differentiates their products.

Are we as consumers better off or worse off with differentiated products? That's difficult to say. There's a certain waste in much of the differentiation that occurs. It shows up in the graph by the fact that monopolistic competitors don't produce at the minimum point of their average total cost curve. But there's also a sense of trust that we get from buying names we know and in having goods that are slightly different from one another. I'm a sophisticated consumer who knows that there's little difference between Clorox bleach and a no-name store brand of bleach, or between generic aspirin and Bayer aspirin. Yet sometimes I buy Clorox bleach and Bayer aspirin even though they cost more.

Edward Chamberlin, one of the originators of the description of monopolistic competition, believed that the difference between the cost of a perfect competitor and the cost of a monopolistic competitor was the cost of what he called "differentness."[1] If consumers are willing to pay that cost, then it's not a waste but, rather, it's a benefit to them.

One must be careful about drawing any implications from this analysis. Average total cost for a monopolistically competitive firm includes advertising and costs of differentiating a product. Whether we as consumers are better off with as much differentiation as we have, or whether we'd all be better off if all firms produced a generic product at a lower cost, is debatable.

Enormous amounts of product differentiation occur in the aggregate economy. Firms spend large amounts of money to convince people that their product is better. © *Mark Antman/ The Image Works.*

OLIGOPOLY

The central element of oligopoly is that there are a small number of firms in an industry so that, in any decision it makes, each firm must take into account the expected reaction of other firms. Oligopolistic firms are mutually interdependent and therefore use strategic decision making.

---

[1] About the same time as Chamberlin developed his theory of monopolistic competition, Joan Robinson, a Cambridge, England, economist, developed a theory of imperfect competition. Her theory is similar to Chamberlin's, and the two economists are generally seen as the originators of the idea.

Most industries in the United States have some oligopolistic elements. If you ask almost any businessperson whether he or she directly takes into account rivals' likely response, the answer you'll get is "In certain cases, yes; in others, no."

Most retail stores that you deal with are oligopolistic in your neighborhood or town, although by national standards they may be quite competitive. For example, how many grocery stores do you shop at? Do you think they keep track of what their competitors are doing? You bet. They keep a close eye on their competitors' prices and set their own accordingly.

Models of Oligopoly Behavior

No single general model of oligopoly behavior exists.

No single general model of oligopoly behavior exists. The reason is that there are many possible ways in which an oligopolist can decide on pricing and output strategy, and there are no compelling grounds to characterize any of them as *the* oligopoly strategy. Although there are five or six formal models, I'll focus on two informal models of oligopoly behavior that give you insight into real-world problems rather than exercise your reasoning and modeling abilities as my earlier discussion did. The two models we'll consider are the cartel model and the contestable markets model. These two models, combined with Appendix A's case study of pricing by a jewelry firm, should give you a sense of how real-world oligopolistic pricing takes place.

Why, you ask, can't economists develop a simple formal model of oligopoly? The reason lies in the interdependence of oligopolists. Since there are so few competitors, what one firm does specifically influences what other firms do, so an oligopolist's plan must always be a contingency or strategic plan. If my competitors act one way, I'll do X, but if they act another way, I'll do Y. Strategic interactions have a variety of potential outcomes rather than a single outcome such as shown in the formal models we discussed. An oligopolist spends enormous amounts of time guessing what its competitors will do, and it develops a strategy of how it will act, depending on what its competitors do.

4 If oligopolies can limit the entry of other firms and form a cartel, they increase the profits going to the combination of firms in the cartel.

Cartel   A combination of firms that acts like a single firm.

Cartel model of oligopoly   Model that assumes that oligopolies act as if they were a single monopoly.

The Cartel Model   A **cartel** (sometimes called a *trust*) is a combination of firms that acts as if it were a single firm; a cartel is a shared monopoly. If oligopolies can limit entry by other firms, they have a strong incentive to cartelize the industry and to act as a monopolist would, restricting output to a level that maximizes profit to the combination of firms. Thus, the **cartel model of oligopoly** is a model that assumes that oligopolies act as if they were monopolists that have assigned output quotas to individual member firms of the oligopoly so that total output is consistent with joint profit maximization. All firms follow a uniform pricing policy which serves their collective interest.

Since a monopolist makes the most profit that can be squeezed from a market, the cartelization strategy is the best an oligopoly can do. That strategy requires each oligopolist to hold its production below what would be in its own interest were it not to collude with the others. Such explicit formal collusion is against the law in the United States, but informal collusion is allowed and oligopolies have developed a variety of methods to collude implicitly. Thus, the cartel model has some relevance.

Q–6: Why is it difficult for firms in an industry to maintain a cartel?

There are problems with it, however. For example, various firms' interests often differ, so it isn't clear what the collective interest of the firms in the industry is. In many cases a single firm, often the largest or dominant firm, takes the lead in pricing and output decisions, and the other firms (which are often called *fringe firms*) follow suit, even though they might have preferred to adopt a different strategy.

This dominant-firm cartel model works only if there are barriers to entry to the smaller firms, or the dominant firm has significantly lower cost conditions. If that were not the case, the smaller firms would pick up an increasing share of the market, eliminating the dominant firm's monopoly. An example of such a dominant-firm market was the copier market in the 1960s and 1970s in which Xerox set the price and other firms followed. That copier market also shows the temporary nature of such a market. As the firms became more competitive on cost and quality, Xerox's market share fell, and it lost its dominant position. In the 1990s, the copier market is far more competitive than it used to be.

In other cases the various firms meet, sometimes only by happenchance, at the golf course or at a trade association gathering, and arrive at a collective decision. In the United States meetings for this purpose are illegal, but they do occur. In yet other cases the firms just happen to come to a collective decision, even though they have never met. Such collective decisions are known as **implicit collusion.**

Implicit collusion   Multiple firms making the same pricing decisions even though they have not consulted with one another.

Implicit Price Collusion   Implicit price collusion, in which firms just happen to charge the same price but didn't meet to discuss price strategy, isn't against the law. Oligopolies often operate as close to the fine edge of the law as they can. For example, many oligopolistic industries allow a price leader to set the price, and then the others follow suit. The airline and steel industries take that route. Firms just happen to charge the same price or very close to the same price.

It isn't only in major industries that you see such implicit collusion. In small towns, you'll notice that most independent carpenters charge the same price. There's no explicit collusion, but were a carpenter to offer to work for less than the others, the invisible handshake wouldn't be extended to her at morning coffee.

Or let's take another example: the Miami fish market where sport fishermen sell their catch at the dock. When I lived in Miami I often went to the docks to buy fresh fish. There were about 20 stands, all charging the same price. Price fluctuated, but it was by subtle agreement, and close to the end of the day the word would go out that the price could be reduced.

I got to know some of the sellers and asked them why they priced like that when it would be in their individual interest to set their own price. Their answer: "We like our boat and don't want it burned." They may have been talking in hyperbole, but the invisible handshake plays an important role in stabilizing prices in an oligopoly.

Cartels and Technological Change   Even if all firms in the industry cooperate, other firms, unless they are prevented from doing so, can always enter the market with a technologically superior new product at the same price or with the same good at a lower price. It is important to remember that technological changes are constantly occurring, and that a successful cartel with high profits will provide incentives for significant technological change, which can eliminate demand for its monopolized product. For example, record players gave way to cassettes and cassettes are giving way to CDs. Technologies are constantly changing, and as they do, industries, and the goods produced, must change.

Why Are Prices Sticky?   Informal collusion happens all the time in U.S. businesses. One characteristic of informal collusive behavior is that prices tend to be sticky. They don't change frequently and so the existence of informal collusion is an important reason why prices are sticky. But it's not the only reason.

Another reason is that firms don't collude, but they have certain expectations of other firms' reactions, which changes their perceived demand curves. Specifically, they perceive a kinked demand curve (not kinky, but kinked) facing them. This kinked demand curve is used especially to explain why firms often do not use lower-price strategies to increase sales.

Let's go through the reasoning behind the kinked demand curve. If a firm increases its price, and the firm believes that other firms won't go along, its perceived demand curve for increasing price will be very elastic (D_1 in Exhibit 7). It will lose lots of business to the other firms that haven't raised their price. The relevant portions of its demand curve and its marginal revenue curve are shown in blue in Exhibit 7.

The kinked demand curve assumes, however, that the firm's perception of how other firms would respond if it decreased its price is different. It assumes that all other firms would immediately match that decrease, so it would gain very few, if any, additional sales. A large fall in price would result in only a small increase in sales, so its demand is very inelastic (D_2 in Exhibit 7). This inelastic portion of the demand curve and the corresponding marginal revenue curve are shown in red in Exhibit 7.

Q–7:   If the average cost curve had a kink in it, what would the marginal cost curve look like?

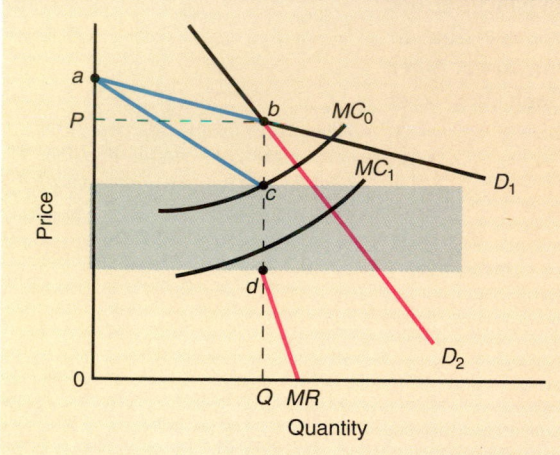

EXHIBIT 7   The Kinked Demand Curve

One explanation of why prices are sticky is that firms face a kinked demand curve. Say a firm is producing output Q at price P. If it tries to raise its price, other firms will not follow, so the demand curve is very elastic (shown by demand curve D_1). If the firm decides to decrease its price, all other firms will immediately follow suit, so demand is less elastic, as represented by demand curve D_2. To the firm, the relevant portions of D_1 and D_2 are the blue portion of D_1 and the red portion of D_2. Thus the firm's perceived demand has a kink in it. When we draw the relevant marginal revenue curve for this kinked demand we see that the corresponding MR curve is discontinuous. There is a gap in it. Shifts in marginal costs between c and d (the shaded area) will not change the price or the output that maximizes profits since they do not change the intersection of marginal cost and marginal revenue.

Notice that when you put these two curves together you get a rather strange demand curve (it's kinked) and an even stranger marginal revenue curve (one with a gap). I didn't make a mistake in drawing the curves; that's the way they come out given the assumptions. When there's a kink in the demand curve there has to be a gap in the marginal revenue curve.

When there's a kink in the demand curve, there has to be a gap in the marginal revenue curve.

If firms do indeed perceive their demand curves as kinked at the market price, we have another explanation of why prices tend to be sticky. Shifts in marginal cost in the shaded area (such as MC_0 to MC_1) will not change the firm's profit maximization position. A large shift in marginal cost is required before firms will change their price. Why should this be the case? The intuitive answer lies in the reason behind the kink. If the firm raises its price, other firms won't go along, so it will lose lots of market share. However, when the firm lowers price, other firms will go along and the firm won't gain market share. Thus, there are strong reasons for the firm not to change its price in either direction.

I should emphasize that the kinked demand curve is not a theory of oligopoly pricing. It does not say why the original price is what it is; the kinked demand curve is simply a theory of sticky prices.

The Contestable Market Model

5 In the contestable market model of oligopoly, pricing and entry decisions are based only on barriers to entry and exit, not on market structure. Thus, even if the industry contains only one firm, it could still be a competitive market if entry is open.

The Contestable Market Model   A second model of oligopoly is the *contestable market model*. The **contestable market model** is a model of oligopoly in which barriers to entry and barriers to exit, not the structure of the industry, determine a firm's price and output decisions. Thus, it places the emphasis on entry and exit conditions, and says that the price that an oligopoly will charge will exceed the cost of production and be dependent only on the entry and exit barriers to new firms. The higher the barriers, the more the price exceeds cost. If there are no barriers to entry or exit, the price an oligopolist sets will be equivalent to the competitive price. Thus, an industry that structurally looks like an oligopoly could set highly competitive prices and output levels.

Contestable market model of oligopoly   A model that bases pricing and output decisions on entry and exit conditions, not on market structure.

Comparison of the Contestable Market Model and the Cartel Model   Because of the importance of the invisible handshake in determining strategies of oligopolies, no one "oligopolistic model" exists. The stronger the ability of oligopolies to collude (i.e., the more the invisible handshake can prevent entry), the closer to a monopolist solution the oligopoly can reach. The weaker the invisible handshake and the harder it is to prevent new entry, the closer to the competitive solution the oligopoly solution is. That's as explicit as one can be.

Q–8: What are the two extremes an oligopoly model can take?

There are two extremes that an oligopoly model can take: (1) the cartel model in which an oligopoly sets a monopoly price; and (2) the contestable market model in which an oligopoly with no barriers to entry sets a competitive price. Thus, we can say that an oligopoly's price will be somewhere between the competitive price and the monopolistic price. Other models of oligopolies give results in between these two.

Much of what happens in oligopoly pricing is highly dependent on the specific legal structure within which firms interact. In Japan, where large firms are specifically allowed to collude, we see Japanese goods selling for a much higher price than those same Japanese goods sell in the United States. For example, you may well pay twice as much for a Japanese television in Japan as you would in the United States. From the behavior of Japanese firms, we get a sense of what pricing strategy U.S. oligopolists would follow in the absence of the restrictions placed on them by law.

Notice that both the cartel model and the contestable market model use **strategic pricing** decisions. They set their price based upon the expected reactions of other firms, which means that strategic pricing is a central characteristic of oligopoly.

Strategic Pricing and Oligopoly

One can see the results of strategic decision making all the time. For example, consider a firm that announces that it will not be undersold—that it will match any competitor's lower price and will even go under it. Is that a pro-competitive strategy, leading to a low price? Or is it a strategy to increase collusive information and thereby prevent other firms from breaking implicit pricing agreements? Recent work in economics suggests that it is the latter.

Let's now see how a specific consideration of strategic pricing decisions shows that the cartel model and the contestable market model are related.

New Entry as a Limit on the Cartelization Strategy   One of the things that limits oligopolies from acting as a cartel is the threat from outside competition, competition from a firm that's a potential competitor but isn't part of the social network and therefore doesn't care about the invisible handshake pressure. Often this outside competitor is much larger than the firms in the oligopoly.

For example, small-town banks have a tendency to collude (implicitly, of course), offering lower interest to savers and charging higher interest to borrowers than big banks charge, even though their average costs aren't significantly higher. When I ask small-town banks why this is, they tell me that my perceptions are faulty and that I should mind my own business. But if a big bank, which could care less about increasing the wealth of a small-town banker, enters the town and establishes a branch office, interest rates to savers seem to go up and interest rates to borrowers seem to go down. The big bank can add significant competition—competition that couldn't come from within the town.

On a national scale, the outside competition often comes from international firms. For example, implicit collusion among U.S. automobile firms led to foreign firms' entry into the U.S. automobile market. There are many such examples of this outside competition breaking down cartels with no barriers to entry. Thus, a cartel with no barriers to entry faces a long-run demand curve that's very elastic. This means that its price will be very close to its marginal cost and average cost. This is the same prediction that came from the contestable market theory.

Price Wars   Whenever there's strategic decision making there's the possibility of a war. Price wars are the result of strategic pricing decisions gone wild. Thus, in any oligopoly it's possible that firms can enter into a price war where prices fall below average total cost.

Price wars are the result of strategic pricing decisions gone wild.

The reasons for such wars are varied. Since oligopolistic firms know their competitors, they can personally dislike them; sometimes a firm's goal can be simply to drive a disliked competitor out of business, even if that process hurts the firm itself. Passion and anger play roles in oligopoly pricing because interpersonal and interfirm relations are important.

Alternatively, a firm might impersonally push the price down temporarily to drive the other firm out of business, whereupon it can charge an even higher price because potential entrants know that the existing firm will drive them out if they try to enter. It's this continual possibility that strategies can change that makes oligopoly prices so hard to predict.

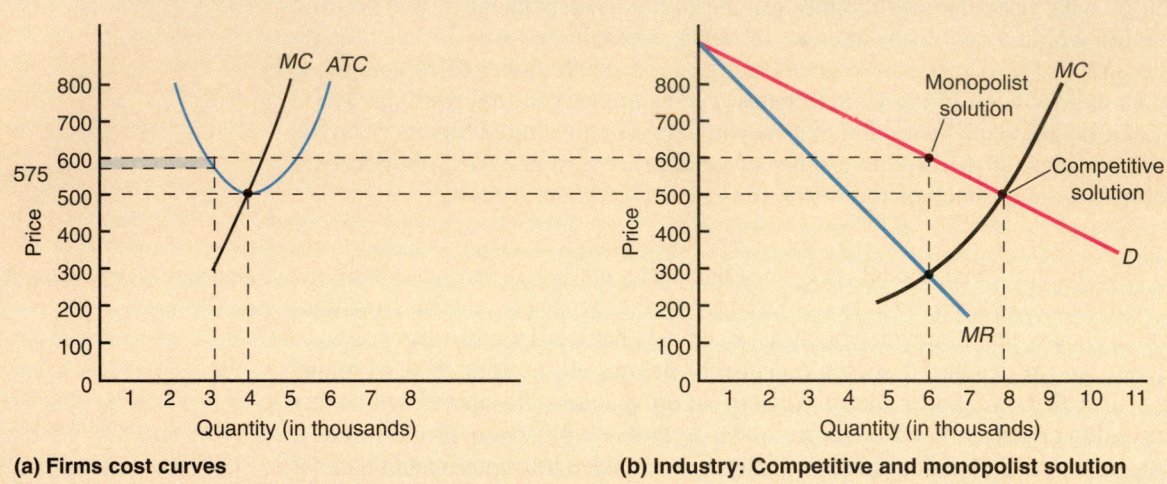

EXHIBIT 8 (a and b)   Firm and Industry Duopoly Cooperative Equilibrium

In (**a**) I show the marginal and average total cost curve for either firm in the duopoly. Thus to get the average and marginal cost for the industry, you double each. In (**b**) the industry marginal cost curve (the horizontal sum of the individual firms' marginal cost curves) is combined with the industry demand and marginal revenue curves. At the competitive solution for the industry, output is 8,000 and price is $500. As you can see in (**a**), at that price economic profits are zero. At the monopolist solution, output is 6,000 and price is $600. As you can see in (**a**), ATC are $575 at an industry output of 6,000 (firm output of 3,000), so each firm's profit is 25 x $3,000 = $75,000 (the shaded area in (**a**)).

GAME THEORY, OLIGOPOLY, AND STRATEGIC DECISION MAKING

Game theory   The application of economic principles to interdependent situations.

Prisoner's dilemma   A well-known game that nicely demonstrates the difficulty of cooperative behavior in certain circumstances.

The lack of ability to come to an explicit conclusion about what price and quantity an oligopoly will choose doesn't mean that economic reasoning and principles don't apply to oligopoly. They do. Most oligopolistic strategic decision making is carried out with the implicit or explicit use of **game theory** (the application of economic principles to interdependent situations). Game theory is economic reasoning applied to decision making.

To give you a sense of game theory, I'll present a well-known game called the **prisoner's dilemma** and show how game theory works. The standard prisoner's dilemma can be seen in the following example: Two suspects are caught and are interrogated separately. Each prisoner is offered the following options:

· If neither prisoner confesses, each will be given a 6-month sentence on a minor charge.
· If one prisoner confesses and the other does not, the one who confesses will go free and the other will be given a 10-year sentence.
· If they both confess, they'll each get a 5-year sentence.

What strategy will they choose? If the invisible handshake is weak, and neither can count on the other not to confess, the optimal strategy (the one that maximizes expected benefits) will be for each to confess, because each must assume the other will do the same. Confessing is the rational thing for each prisoner to do. That's why it's called the *prisoner's dilemma.* Trust gets one out of the prisoner's dilemma. If the prisoners can trust one another, the optimal strategy is not to confess, and they both get only a light sentence. But trust is a hard commodity to come by without an explicit enforcement mechanism.

The prisoner's dilemma has its simplest application to oligopoly when the oligopoly consists of only two firms. So let us consider the strategic decisions facing a "foam peanut" (packing material) **duopoly**—an oligopoly with only two firms. Let us assume that the average total cost and marginal cost of producing foam peanuts are the same for both firms, and are such that only two firms can exist in the industry. These costs are shown in Exhibit 8(a).

Assume that a production facility with a minimum efficient scale of 4,000 tons is the smallest that can be built. In Exhibit 8(b), the marginal costs are summed and the industry demand curve is drawn in a way that the competitive price is $500 per ton and

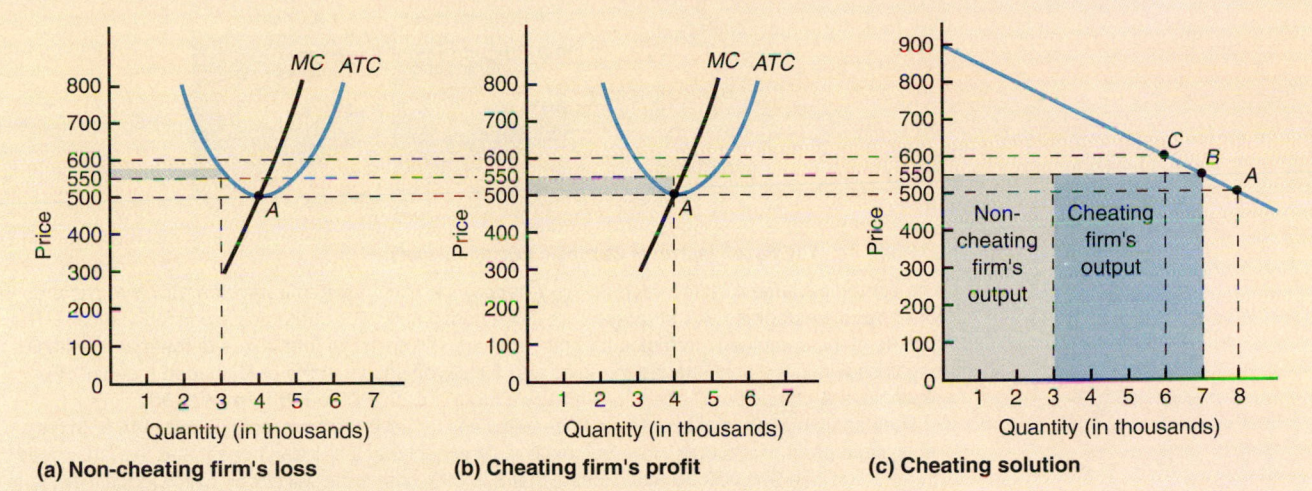

(a) Non-cheating firm's loss   (b) Cheating firm's profit   (c) Cheating solution

EXHIBIT 9 (a, b, and c)   Firm and Industry Duopoly Equilibrium when One Firm Cheats

In this Exhibit I demonstrate the three different outcomes. Exhibits (a) and (b) show the non-cheating and the cheating firm's output and profit, respectively, while (c) shows the industry output and price.

Say they both cheat. The price is $500 and output is 8,000 (4,000 per firm) (point A in (c)). Both firms make zero profit since their average total costs of $500 equal the price they receive.

If neither cheats, the industry output is 6,000, the price is $600, and their ATC is $575 as before. This outcome gives them a profit of $75,000 each and would place them at point C in (c). This outcome was considered in Exhibit 8.

If one firm cheats and the other does not, the output is 7,000 and the industry price is $550 (point B in (c)). The non-cheating firm's loss is shown by the shaded area in (a); its costs are $575, its output is 3,000, the price it receives is $550, and its loss is $75,000. The cheating firm's profit is shown by the shaded area in (b). Its average total costs are $500, the price it receives is $550, and its output is 4,000, so its profit is the shaded area in (b)—$200,000. So if one firm is cheating, it pays to be that firm; it doesn't pay to be honest when the other firm cheats.

the competitive output is 8,000 tons. The relevant industry marginal revenue curve is also drawn.

If there is full collusion, the firms will act as a joint monopolist setting total output at 6,000 tons where $MR = MC$ (3,000 tons each). This gives them a price of $600 with a cost of $575 per ton, for a joint economic profit of $150,000, or $75,000 each. The firms prefer this equilibrium to the competitive equilibrium where they earn zero economic profit.

If they can insure that they will both abide by the agreement, the monopolist output will be the joint profit maximizing output. But what if one firm cheats? What if one firm produces 4,000 tons (1,000 tons under the counter)? The additional 1,000 tons in output will cause the price to fall to $550 per ton. The cheating firm's average total costs fall to $500 as its output rises to 4,000, so its profit rises to $200,000. The non-cheating firm's profit moves in the opposite direction. Its average total costs remain $575, but the price it receives falls to $550, so it loses $75,000 instead of making $75,000. This gives it a large incentive to cheat also. The division of profits and output split is shown in Exhibit 9. If the non-cheating firm decides to become a cheating firm, it eliminates its loss and the other firm's profit, and the duopoly moves to a zero profit position.

In Exhibit 9(a), you can see that the firm that abides by the agreement and produces 3,000 units makes a loss of $75,000; its average total costs are $575 and the price it receives is $550. In Exhibit 9(b) you can see that the cheating firm makes a profit of $200,000; its average costs are $500, so it is doing much better than when it did not cheat. The combined profit of the cheating and the non-cheating firms is $200,000 − $75,000 = $125,000, which is lower than if they cooperated. By cheating, the firm has essentially transferred $125,000 from the other firm to itself and has reduced their combined profit by $25,000. Exhibit 9(c) shows the output split between the two firms. If both firms cheat, the equilibrium output moves to the competitive output, 8,000, and both the firms make zero profit.

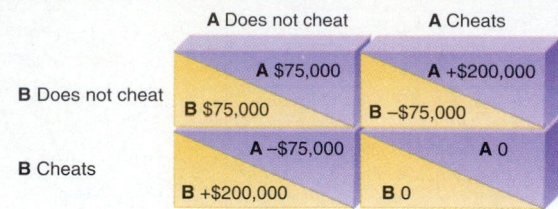

EXHIBIT 10   **The Payoff Matrix of Strategic Pricing Duopoly**

The strategic dilemma facing each firm in a duopoly can be shown in a payoff matrix that captures the four possible outcomes. **A**'s strategies are listed horizontally; **B**'s strategies are listed vertically. The payoffs of the combined strategies for both firms are shown in the four boxes of the matrix, with **B**'s payoff shown in the gold shaded triangles and **A**'s payoff shown in the blue shaded triangles. For example, if **A** cheats but **B** doesn't, **A** makes a profit of $200,000 but **B** loses $75,000.

Their combined optimal strategy is to cartelize and achieve the monopoly payoff, with both firms receiving a profit of $75,000. However, each must expect that if it doesn't cheat and the other does cheat, it will lose $75,000. To avoid losing that $75,000, both firms will cheat, which leads them to the payoff in the lower right hand corner—the competitive solution with zero profit for each firm.

Payoff matrix   *A box that contains the outcomes of a strategic game under various circumstances.*

It is precisely to provide insight into this type of strategic situation that game theory was developed. It does so by analyzing the strategies of both firms under all circumstances and placing the combinations in a **payoff matrix**—a box that contains the outcomes of a strategic game under various circumstances.

The duopoly presented above is a variation of the prisoner's dilemma game. The results can be presented in a payoff matrix that captures the essence of the prisoner's dilemma discussed above. In Exhibit 10, each square shows the payoff from a pair of decisions listed in the columns and rows. The blue triangles show A's profit; the red triangles show B's profit. For example, if neither cheats, the result for both is shown in the upper-left-hand square, and if they both cheat, the result is shown in the lower-right-hand square.

Notice the dilemma they are in if detecting cheating is impossible. If they can't detect whether the other one cheated and each believes the other is maximizing profit, each must expect the other one to cheat. But if Firm A expects Firm B to cheat, the relevant payoffs are in the second row. Given this expectation, if Firm A doesn't cheat, it loses $75,000. So Firm A's optimal strategy is to cheat. Similarly for Firm B. If it expects Firm A to cheat, its relevant payoffs are in the second column. Firm B's optimal strategy is to cheat. But if they both cheat they end up in the lower-right-hand square with zero profit.

In reality, of course, cheating is partially detectable, and even though explicit collusion and enforceable contracts are illegal in the United States, implicit collusive contracts are not. Moreover, in markets where similar conditions hold time after time, the cooperative solution is more likely since each firm will acquire a reputation based on its past actions, and firms can retaliate against other firms who cheat. But the basic dilemma remains for firms and pushes oligopolies toward a zero-profit competitive solution.

Game Theory and Experimental Economics

Experimental economics   *A branch of economics that gains insights into economic issues by conducting controlled experiments.*

Game theory has offered significant insight into the structure of economic problems but arrives at the conclusion that a number of alternative solutions are possible. A new branch of economics—**experimental economics**—has developed that offers insight into which outcome will be forthcoming. Let's consider an example.

When game theorists have done experiments, they have found that people believe that the others in the game will work toward a cooperative solution. Thus, when the gains from cheating are not too great, often people do not choose the individual profit maximizing position, but instead choose a more cooperative strategy, at least initially. Such cooperative solutions tend to break down, however, as the benefits of cheating become larger. Additionally, as the number of participants gets larger, the less likely it is that the cooperative solution will be chosen and the more likely it is that competitive solutions will be chosen.

Experimental economists have also found that the structure of the game plays an important role in deciding the solution. For example, posted price markets, in which the prices are explicitly announced, are more likely to reach a collusive result than are non-posted or uncertain price markets, where actual sale prices are not known.

Oligopoly Models, Structure, and Performance

The fourfold division of markets that I've considered so far has all been based on the structure of the markets. By *structure* I mean the number, size, and interrelationship of firms in an industry. A monopoly (one firm) is the least competitive; perfectly competitive industries (an almost infinite number of firms) are the most competitive. Classification by structure is easy for students to learn and accords nicely with intuition. The cartelization model fits best with this classification system because it assumes the structure of the market (the number of firms) is directly related to the price a firm charges. It predicts that oligopolies charge higher prices than do monopolistic competitors.

The contestable market model gives far less weight to market structure. According to it, markets that look structurally highly oligopolistic could actually be highly competitive—much more so than markets that structurally look less competitive. This contestable market model view of judging markets by performance, not structure, has had many reincarnations. Close relatives of it have previously been called the *barriers-to-entry* model, the *stay-out pricing* model, and the *limit-pricing* model. These models provide a view of competition that doesn't depend on market structure.

To see the implications of the contestable market approach, let's consider an oligopoly with a four-firm concentration ratio of 60 percent and a Herfindahl index of 1500. Using the structural approach we would say that, because of the multiplicity of oligopoly models, we're not quite sure what price firms in this industry would charge, but that it seems reasonable to assume that there would be some implicit collusion and that the price would be closer to a monopolist price than to a competitive price. If that same market had a four-firm concentration ratio of 30 percent and a Herfindahl index of 700, the industry would be more likely to have a competitive price.

A contestable market model advocate would disagree. She would argue that barriers to entry and exit are what's important. If no significant barriers to entry exist in the first case but significant barriers to entry exist in the second case, the second case would be more monopolistic than the first. An example is the Miami fish market mentioned earlier, where there were 20 sellers (none with a large percentage of the market) and significant barriers to entry (only fishermen from the pier were allowed to sell fish there and the slots at the pier were limited). Because of those entry limitations, the pricing and output decisions would be close to the monopolistic price. If you took that same structure but had free entry, you'd get much closer to competitive decisions.

As I presented the two views, I emphasized the differences in order to make the distinction clear. However, I must also point out that there's a similarity in the two views. Often barriers to entry are the reason there are only a few firms in an industry. And when there are many firms, that suggests that there are few barriers to entry. In such situations, which make up the majority of cases, the two approaches come to the same conclusion.

As you can see, the real world gets very complicated very quickly. I'll show you just how complicated in the next chapter. But don't let the complicated real world get you down on the theories presented here. It's precisely because the real world is so complicated that we need some framework, like the one presented in this chapter. That framework lets us focus on specific, hopefully the most important, issues. Because the framework is so important, as a conclusion to this chapter I summarize the primary market structures in a final exhibit, Exhibit 11.

Q-9: The Herfindahl index is 1500. Using a contestable market approach, what would you conclude about this industry?

Q-10: The Herfindahl index is 1500. Using a structural analysis of markets approach, what would you conclude about this industry?

CONCLUSION

6 Exhibit 11 gives a summary of the central differences among the four various market structures.

Characteristics \ Structure	Monopoly	Oligopoly	Monopolistic competition	Perfect competition
Number of firms	1	Few	Many	Almost infinite
Pricing decisions	$MC = MR$	Strategic pricing, between monopoly and perfect competition	$MC = MR$	$MC = MR = P$
Output decisions	Most output restriction	Output somewhat restricted	Output restricted somewhat by product differentiation	No output restriction
Interdependence	Only firm in market, not concerned about competitors	Interdependent strategic pricing and output decision	Each firm acts independently	Each firm acts independently
Profit	Possibility of long-run economic profit	Some long-run economic profit possible	No long-run economic profit possible	No long-run economic profit possible

EXHIBIT 11 **A Comparison of Various Market Structures**

This table captures the central differences among various market structures.

CHAPTER SUMMARY

- Industries are classified by SIC code, and industry structures are measured by concentration ratios and Herfindahl indexes.
- Conglomerates operate in a variety of different industries. Industry concentration measures do not assess the bigness of these conglomerates.
- In monopolistic competition firms act independently; in an oligopoly they take account of each other's actions.
- Monopolistic competitors differ from perfect competitors in that the former face a downward-sloping demand curve.

- A monopolistic competitor differs from a monopolist in that a monopolistic competitor makes zero economic profit in long-run equilibrium.
- An oligopolist's price will be somewhere between the competitive price and the monopolistic price.
- Game Theory and the Prisoner's Dilemma can shed light on strategic pricing decisions.
- A contestable market theory of oligopoly judges an industry's competitiveness more by performance and barriers to entry than by structure.

KEY TERMS

cartel (600)
cartel model of oligopoly (600)
concentration ratio (592)
conglomerate (594)
contestable market model of
  oligopoly (602)
duopoly (604)

experimental economics (606)
four-digit industry (591)
game theory (604)
Herfindahl index (592)
implicit collusion (601)
market structure (591)
monopolistic competition (591)

oligopoly (591)
payoff matrix (606)
prisoner's dilemma (604)
Standard Industrial Code (SIC) (591)
strategic decision making (594)
strategic pricing (603)
two-digit industry (591)

QUESTIONS FOR THOUGHT AND REVIEW

The number after each question represents the estimated degree of critical thinking required. (1 = almost none; 10 = deep thought.) Questions 1 and 2 require library research.

Q	20	18	16	14	12	10
P	$2	4	6	8	10	12

(5)

1. You're working for a company that buys up other companies. The company assigns you to find out whether the college textbook publishing industry is highly concentrated. Is it or isn't it? *(8)*

2. Now your company tells you to find the SIC codes for the following industries: (a) motor vehicles and car bodies, (b) robes and nightgowns, (c) chewing gum. You do what you are asked. *(6)*

3. Which industry is more highly concentrated: one with a Herfindahl index of 1200 or one with a four-firm concentration ratio of 55 percent? *(6)*

4. Does the product differentiation in monopolistic competition make us better or worse off? Why? *(8)*

5. If a monopolistic competitor has a constant marginal cost of $6 and the accompanying demand table, what output will it choose?

6. In Question 5, what will be the monopolistic competitor's average fixed cost at the output it chooses? Why? *(8)*

7. What did Adam Smith mean when he wrote, "Seldom do businessmen of the same trade get together but that it results in some detriment to the general public"? *(6)*

8. Private colleges of the same caliber generally charge roughly the same tuition. Would you characterize these colleges as a cartel type of oligopoly? *(9)*

9. What are some of the barriers to entry in the restaurant industry? In the automobile industry? *(5)*

10. Describe a situation you have faced in your lifetime that can be characterized as a prisoner's dilemma situation. *(7)*

PROBLEMS AND EXERCISES

1. A firm is convinced that if it lowers its price, no other firm in the industry will change price; however, it believes that if it raises its price, all other firms will match its increase. The current price is $8 and its marginal cost is constant at $8.
   a. Sketch the general shape of the firm's *MR, MC,* and demand curves.
   b. If the marginal cost falls to $6, what would you predict would happen to price?
   c. If the marginal cost rises to $10, what would you predict would happen to price?
   d. Do a survey of five or six firms in your area. Ask them how they believe other firms would respond to their increasing and decreasing price. Based on that survey, discuss the relevance of this kinked demand model compared to the one presented in the book.

2. You're the manager of a firm that has constant marginal cost of $6. Fixed cost is zero. The market structure is monopolistically competitive. You're faced with the following demand curve:

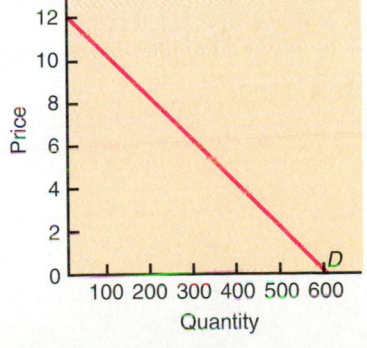

   a. Determine graphically the profit-maximizing price and output for your firm in the short run. Demonstrate what profit or loss you'll be making.
   b. Do the same for the long run.
   c. Thanks to a technological innovation, you have zero marginal cost. Demonstrate the new profit-maximizing price and output in the short run. Demonstrate graphically the short-run profit at that new profit-maximizing output.

3. The pizza market is divided as follows:

1.	Pizza Hut	20.7%
2.	Domino's	17.0%
3.	Little Caesars	6.7%
4.	Pizza Inn/Pantera's	2.2%
5.	Round Table	2.0%
6.	All others	51.4%

   b. How would you describe its market structure?
   c. What is the approximate Herfindahl index?
   d. What is the 4-firm concentration ratio?

4. In 1982 Robert Crandell, CEO of American Airlines, phoned the Braniff Airways chairman and said, "Raise your fares 20 percent and I'll raise mine the next morning."
   a. Why would he do this?
   b. If you were the Braniff Airways chairman, would you have gone along?
   c. Why should Crandell not have done this?

5. Two firms, TwiddleDee and TwiddleDum, make up the entire market for wodgets. They have identical costs. They are currently colluding and are making $2 million each. TwiddleDee has a new CEO, Mr. Notsonice, who is considering cheating. He has been informed by his able

assistant that if he cheats he can increase the firm's profit to $3 million, but that cheating will reduce TwiddleDum's profit to $1 million. You have been hired to advice Mr. Notsonice.

a. Construct a payoff matrix for him which captures the essence of the decision.

b. If the game is only played once, what strategy would you advise?

c. How would your answer to *b* change if the game were to be played many times?

d. What change in the profit made when colluding (currently $2 million) would be needed to change your advice in *b*?

6. In 1993, the infant/preschool toy market four-firm concentration ratio was 72 percent. With 8 percent of the market, Mattel was the fourth-largest firm in that market.

Mattel proposed to buy Fisher-Price, the market leader with 27 percent. At this time the new Clinton administration was trying to develop a set of rules dealing with such mergers. Your assignment is to help it decide by answering questions *a* through *d*.

a. Why would Mattel want to buy Fisher-Price?

b. What arguments can you think of in favor of allowing this acquisition?

c. What arguments can you think of against allowing this acquisition?

d. How do you think the four-firm concentration ratio for the entire toy industry would compare to this infant/preschool toy market concentration ratio?

e. What did the Clinton administration decide? (Requires library research.)

ANSWERS TO MARGIN QUESTIONS

1. The smaller the number of digits, the more inclusive the classification. Therefore, the two-digit industry would have significantly more output. *(592)*

2. The highest Herfindahl index for this industry would occur if one firm had the entire 60 percent, and all other firms had an infinitesimal amount, making the Herfindahl index slightly over 3600. The lowest Herfindahl index this industry could have would occur if each of the top four firms had 15 percent of the market, yielding a Herfindahl index of 900. *(593)*

3. I would respond that monopolistic competitors, by definition, do not take account of the expected reactions of competitors to their decisions; therefore, they cannot use strategic decision making. I would tell Jean she probably meant, "Oligopolies use strategic decision making." *(594)*

4. Both a monopoly and a monopolistic competitor produce where marginal cost equals marginal revenue. The difference is in the positioning of the average total cost curve. For a monopolistic competitor, that average total cost curve must be tangent to the demand curve because a monopolistic competitor makes no profits in the long run. A monopoly can make profits in the long run, so its average total cost can be below the price. *(596)*

5. If there are economies of scale and advertising leads to increased output, advertising, even though it costs money, could lower the price of a good. *(598)*

6. Maintaining a cartel requires firms to make decisions that are not in their individual best interest. Such decisions are hard to enforce unless there is an explicit enforcement mechanism, which is difficult in a cartel. *(600)*

7. Whenever an average cost curve has a kink in it, the related marginal cost curve has a break in it. Therefore,

in this case, the marginal cost curve would be discontinuous at the output, where the kink was, as in the diagram below. *(601)*

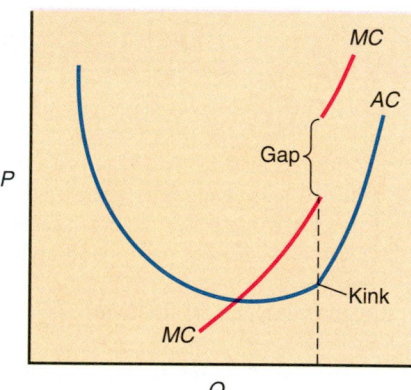

8. The two extremes an oligopoly model can take are: (1) a cartel model, which is the equivalent of a monopoly; and (2) a contestable market model, which, if there are no barriers to entry, is the equivalent of a competitive industry. *(602)*

9. The contestable markets approach looks at barriers to entry, not structure. Therefore, one could conclude nothing about the industry from the Herfindahl index. *(607)*

10. In a market with a Herfindahl index of 1500, the largest firm would have at most, slightly under 40 percent of the market. The least concentrated such an industry could be would be if seven firms each had between 14 and 15 percent of the market. In either of these two cases, the industry would probably be an oligopolistic industry and could border on monopoly. *(607)*

A Case Study

Once one gets to real-life situations, one sees that most pricing is done according to rules of thumb that exist in each industry. These rules of thumb base prices upon costs. This appendix considers the pricing strategy of a real-world retail firm and discusses how it fits into our model.

Setting Retail Prices

Most goods go through a variety of stages before they're finally sold to you, the consumer. The good is produced by a company; then it's often sold through a wholesaler to retail outlets who sell it to you. Thus, the stages are:

Manufacturer → Wholesaler → Retailer → Consumer

Manufacturers' outlet stores supposedly eliminate the wholesaler and retailer, but in fact they've become simply a new type of discount retailing.

When you talk about pricing of a retail good, you actually have to divide it up into its parts. How does the manufacturer price? How does the wholesaler price? How does the retailer price? Most of our previous discussion was mainly relevant to pricing by manufacturers. In this section we focus on pricing by wholesalers and retailers.

Neither wholesalers nor retailers have a cost of physical production. They simply buy a product and sell that same product. Their value added is their getting the product from the manufacturer to the individuals who want it.

Cost Markup Pricing

How do these firms price? Most businesses price according to rules of thumb. They add on a percentage markup over their cost to determine their selling price. These markups have evolved over time. The percentage markup is influenced by supply and demand factors so that, if entry is free, the returns to wholesaling and retailing in the long run are normal returns—enough to cover costs

and wages plus a return to the firm's inputs. Thus, the markup varies considerably among industries. In supermarkets, because of high volume relative to inventory, the markup is low—often below 10 percent. In jewelry, where inventory is high relative to volume, the markup is high—60 to 100 percent. These markups aren't fixed; they change according to supply and demand pressures. If a good isn't selling, a firm will lower its markup. If a firm wants to take an aggressive expansion stance, it will lower its markup and expand its market share.

To give you an idea of how markups work, let's consider the pricing policy of a small jewelry store. It follows what's known as a *modified Hamilton markup* as shown in the following table.

Wholesale cost	Markup
0–$25	100%
$25–$50	66
$50–$100	60
$100–$200	55
$200–$300	50
$300–$1,000	40
$1,000–special order	20

Notice that the markup falls as the price rises. That's justified because direct selling cost (salesperson's time) is as high (or higher) on a $2 item as on a $200 item. Repairs, which are sent out to a jeweler who specializes in that work, are priced at cost because they bring in customers. Thus, for repairs there is no markup. New sales cover all overhead: direct and indirect costs.

While the formula markup is set, it's not fixed in stone. When wholesale prices are rising, the owner will recalculate prices on old inventory to the latest price. He'll also walk around town, looking into competitors' windows, checking their prices, and matching his prices to theirs. Notice that in doing so he's taking supply and demand into account and serving the function of an auctioneer because he knows if his goods are priced significantly higher than competitors', he'll lose sales. If his prices are lower than theirs, he'll check his markup policy to see that he hasn't made a mistake.

When goods don't sell in a year's time, he'll lower the price on them every week until they do sell. Again the forces of supply and demand are at work.

He doesn't stock expensive items (those selling for over $1,000), but he has a supplier who'll send them to him in a day. To these items he adds only a 20 percent markup because they don't contribute to his inventory costs (and this price keeps them competitive with those at the other jewelry stores in town).

He never runs a sale. He says, "It's bad for business because people will simply wait for a sale." He's disdainful of jewelry stores that do run so-called sales when what they, in fact, do is bring in a whole new set of merchandise marked up at a 250 percent rate and sell it at "half price," bringing the actual price down close to his own normal marked-up price. Such sales aren't really sales, but are simply advertising gimmicks which he feels lower the quality of the store holding the sale and hurt total sales in the long run. (Were I to ask the other stores, I'd hear a different view.) This case isn't unique. If you went to most retail stores you'd find a similar rule-of-thumb pricing procedure.

What's relevant about the markup rules of thumb that most firms use in pricing is that they aren't inconsistent with our models. The rules develop so as to reflect the forces of supply and demand, and they change over time. To understand the economy, a blend of institutional and theoretical knowledge is required.

28

Competition in the Real World

It is ridiculous to call this an industry. This is rat eat rat; dog eat dog. I'll kill 'em, and I'm going to kill 'em before they kill me. You're talking about the American way of survival of the fittest.

~Ray Kroc (founder of McDonald's)

After reading this chapter, you should be able to:

1 Define the monitoring problem and state its implications for economics.

2 Explain how corporate takeovers can improve firms' efficiency.

3 Discuss why competition should be seen as a process, not a state.

4 Show graphically what a natural monopoly is.

5 List three ways in which firms protect their monopoly.

6 Give the advantages and disadvantages of three plans for health care reform.

7 Apply economic reasoning to real-world events.

In earlier chapters we've seen some nice, neat models, but as I discussed in the last chapter, these models don't fit reality directly. Real-world markets aren't perfectly monopolistic; they aren't perfectly competitive either. They're somewhere between the two. The monopolistic competition and oligopoly models in that last chapter come closer to reality and provide some important insights into the "in-between" markets, but, like any abstract discussion, they, too, lose dimensions of the real-world problem. In this chapter I remedy that shortcoming and give you a sense of what real-world firms, markets, and competition are like. I also apply that discussion to the health care industry and briefly discuss some proposals for health care reform.

THE GOALS OF REAL-WORLD FIRMS

Maybe the best place to start is with the assumption that firms are profit maximizers. There's a certain reasonableness to this assumption; firms definitely are concerned about profit, but are they trying to maximize profit? The answer is: It depends.

The first insight is that if firms are profit maximizers, they aren't just concerned with short-run profit; most are concerned with long-run profit. Thus, even if they can, they may not take full advantage of a potential monopolistic situation now, in order to strengthen their long-run position. For example, many stores have liberal return policies: "If you don't like it, you can return it for a full refund." Similarly, many firms spend millions of dollars improving their reputations. Most firms want to be known as "good citizens." Such expenditures on reputation and goodwill can increase long-run profit, but reduce short-run profit. These policies are inconsistent with short-run profit maximization; they aren't inconsistent with long-run profit or wealth maximization.

The Problem with Profit Maximization

Most real-world production doesn't take place in owner-operated businesses; it takes place in large corporations.

A second insight into how real-world firms differ from the model is that the decision-makers' income is often a cost of the firm. Most real-world production doesn't take place in owner-operated businesses; it takes place in large corporations with eight or nine levels of management, thousands of stockholders whose stock is often held in trust for them, and a board of directors, chosen by management, overseeing the company by meeting two or three times a year. Signing a proxy statement is as close as most stockowners get to directing "their company" to maximize profit.

Why is the structure of the firm important to the analysis? Because economic theory tells us that, unless someone is seeing to it that they do, self-interested decision makers have little incentive to hold down their pay. But their pay is a cost of the firm. And if their pay isn't held down, the firm's profit will be lower than otherwise. Most firms manage to put some pressure on managers to make at least a predesignated level of profit. (If you ask managers, they'll tell you that they face enormous pressure.) So the profit motive certainly plays a role—but to say that profit plays a role is not to say that firms maximize profit. Having dealt with many companies, I'll go out on a limb and say that there are enormous wastes and inefficiencies in many U.S. businesses.

This structure presents a problem in applying the model to the real world. The general economic model assumes individuals are utility maximizers—that they're self-seeking. Then, in the standard model of the firm, the assumption is made that firms, composed of self-seeking individuals, are profit-seeking firms, without explaining how self-seeking individuals who manage real-world corporations will find it in their interest to maximize profit for the firm. Economists recognize this problem; it's an example of the **monitoring problem** introduced in an earlier chapter.

1 The monitoring problem is that employees' incentives differ from the owner's incentives. Because monitoring these employees is expensive, some economists are studying ways to change the situation.

Incentive-compatible contract An agreement in which the incentives and goals of both parties match as closely as possible.

The general monitoring problem is that employees' incentives differ from the owner's incentives, and it's costly to see that the employee does the owner's bidding. The monitoring problem is now a central problem focused on by economists who specialize in industrial organization. They study internal structures of firms and look for an **incentive-compatible contract** which managers can be given. An incentive-compatible contract is one in which the incentives of each of the two parties to the contract correspond as closely as possible. The incentive structure is such that the firm's goals and the manager's goals match. The specific monitoring problem relevant to firm structure is that often owners find it too costly to monitor the managers to ensure that managers do what's in the owners' interest. And self-interested managers

EXHIBIT 1   Pay of Top 10 High-Level Managers, 1993

Chief executive	Company	'93 total pay in millions
1. Michael D. Eisner	Walt Disney	$203,011
2. Sanford I. Weill	Travelers	52,810
3. Joseph R. Hyde III	Autozone	32,220
4. Charles N. Mathewson	Intl. Game Technology	22,231
5. Alan C. Greenberg	Bear Stearns	15,915
6. H. Wayne Huizenga	Blockbuster Entertainment	15,557
7. Norman E. Brinker	Brinker Intl.	14,925
8. Roberto C. Goizueta	Coca-Cola	14,513
9. C. Robert Kidder	Duracell Intl.	14,172
10. Thomas M. Hahn Jr.	Georgia-Pacific	13,680

Reprinted from the April 25, 1994, issue of *Business Week* by permission.

are only interested in maximizing the firm's profit if the structure of the firm requires them to do so.

Self-interested managers are only interested in maximizing firm profit if the structure of the firm requires them to do so.

When appropriate monitoring doesn't take place, high-level managers can pay themselves very well. U.S. managers are very well paid, as can be seen in Exhibit 1; many receive multimillion-dollar salaries. But are these multimillion-dollar salaries too high? That's a difficult question. Most of the high salaries are not pure salaries, but include stock options and bonuses for performance.

Q–1: Why would most economists be concerned about third-party payment systems in which the demander and the payer are different?

One way to get an idea about an answer is to compare U.S. managers' salaries with those in Japan, where the structure of control of firms is different. Banks in Japan have significant control, and they closely monitor performance. The result is that, in Japan, high-level managers on average earn about one-fourth of what their U.S. counterparts make, while wages of low-level workers are comparable to those of low-level workers in the United States. Given Japanese companies' success in competing with U.S. companies, this suggests that high managerial pay in the United States reflects a monitoring problem inherent in the structure of corporations. There are, of course, other perspectives. When one considers what some sports, film, and music stars receive, the high salaries of U.S. managers are placed in different light.

What Do Real-World Firms Maximize?

If firms don't maximize profit, what do they maximize? What are their goals? The answer again is: It depends.

Real-world firms often have a set of complicated goals that reflect the organization structure and incentives built into the system. Clearly, profit is one of their goals. Firms spend a lot of time designing incentives to get managers to focus on profit.

But often other intermediate goals become the focus of firms. For example, many real-world firms focus on growth in sales; at other times they institute a cost-reduction program to increase long-run profit. At still other times they may simply take it easy and not push hard at all, enjoying the position they find themselves in—being what Joan Robinson (a British economist who studied intermediate market structures and who developed the reasoning behind marginal revenue curves) called **lazy monopolists**, a term descriptive of many, but not all, real-world corporations.

Lazy monopolist   Firm that does not push for efficiency, but merely enjoys the position it is already in.

The Lazy Monopolist and X-Inefficiency

Lazy monopolists see to it that they make enough profit so that the stockholders aren't squealing; they don't push as hard as they can to hold their costs down. They do their jobs as inefficiently as is consistent with keeping their jobs. The result is what economists call **X-inefficiency** (firms operating far less efficiently than they could technically). Such firms have monopoly positions, but they don't make large monopoly profits. Instead, their costs rise because of inefficiency, and they simply make a normal level of profit.

X-inefficiency   Operating less efficiently than technically possible.

The standard model avoids dealing with the monitoring problem by assuming that the owner of the firm makes all the decisions. The owners of firms who receive the profit, and only the profit, would like to see that all the firm's costs are held down.

EXHIBIT 2 **True Cost Efficiency and the Lazy Monopolist**

A monopolist producing efficiently would have costs C_M and would produce at price P_M and quantity Q_M. A lazy monopolist, on the the other hand, would let costs rise until the minimum level of profit is reached, at C_{LM}. Profit for the monopolist is represented by the entire shaded area, whereas profit for the lazy monopolist is squeezed down to area B.

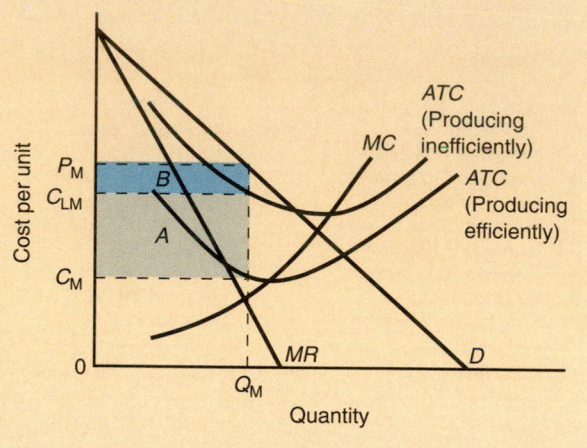

Q–2: Why doesn't a manager have the same incentive to hold costs down as an owner does?

Unfortunately, very few real-world firms operate that way. In reality owners seldom make operating decisions. They hire or appoint managers to make those decisions. The managers they hire don't have that same incentive to hold costs down. Therefore it isn't surprising to many economists that managers' pay is usually high and that high-level managers see to it that they have "perks" such as chauffeurs, jet planes, ritzy offices, and assistants to do as much of their work as possible.

The equilibrium of a lazy monopolist is presented in Exhibit 2. A monopolist would produce at price P_M and quantity Q_M. Average total cost would be C_M, so the monopolist's profit would be the entire shaded rectangle (areas A and B). The lazy monopolist would allow cost to increase until the firm reached its normal level of profit. In Exhibit 2, cost rises to C_{LM}. The profit of the lazy monopolist is area B. The remainder of the potential profit is eaten up in cost inefficiencies.

The competitive pressures a firm faces limit a firm's laziness.

What places a limit on firms' laziness is the degree of competitive pressures they face. All economic institutions must have sufficient revenue coming in to cover costs, so all economic institutions have a limit on how lazy and inefficient they can get—a limit imposed by their monopoly position. They can translate the monopoly profit into X-inefficiency, thereby benefiting the managers and workers in the firm, but once they've done so, they can't be more inefficient. They would go out of business.

How Competition Limits the Lazy Monopolist

If all individuals in the industry are lazy, then laziness becomes the norm and competitive pressures don't reduce their profits. Laziness is relative, not absolute. But if a new firm comes in all gung-ho and hard working, or if an industry is opened up to international competition, the lazy monopolists can be squeezed, and they must undertake massive restructuring to make themselves competitive. Many U.S. firms have been undergoing such restructuring in order to make themselves internationally competitive.

2 Corporate takeovers, or simply the threat of a takeover, can improve firms' efficiency.

A second way in which competitive pressure is placed on a lazy monopolist is by a **corporate takeover** in which another firm or a group of individuals issues a tender offer (that is, offers to buy up the stock of a company to gain control and to install its own managers). Usually such tender offers are financed by large amounts of debt, which means that if the takeover is successful, the firm will need to make large profits just to cover the interest payments on the debt.

Managers don't like takeovers. A takeover may mean losing their jobs and the perks that go along with the jobs, so they'll often restructure the company on their own. Such restructuring frequently means incurring large amounts of debt to finance a large payment to stockholders. These payments place more pressure on management to operate efficiently. Thus, the threat of a corporate takeover provides competitive pressure on firms to maximize profits.

Q–3: In what way does the threat of a corporate takeover provide competitive pressures on a firm?

Were profit not a motive at all, one would expect the lazy monopolist syndrome to take precedence. Thus, it's not surprising that nonprofit organizations often display these lazy monopolist tendencies. For example, some colleges, schools, libraries, jails, and nonprofit hospitals have a number of rules and ways of doing things that, upon reflection, benefit the employees of the institution rather than the customers. At most colleges, students aren't polled as to what time they would prefer classes to meet; instead, the professors and administrators decide when they want to teach. I leave it to you to figure out whether your college exhibits these tendencies and whether you'd prefer that your college, library, or hospital change to a for-profit institution. Studying these incentive-compatible problems is what management courses are all about.

Motivations for Efficiency Other than the Profit Incentive   I'm not going to discuss management theory here other than to stimulate your thinking about the problem. However I'd be remiss in presenting you this broad outline of the monitoring problem without mentioning that the drive for profit isn't the only drive that pushes for efficiency. Some individuals derive pleasure from efficiently run organizations. Such individuals don't need to be monitored. Thus, if administrators are well intentioned, they'll hold down costs even if they aren't profit maximizers. In such cases, monitoring (creating an organization and structure that gives people profit incentives) can actually reduce efficiency! It's amazing to some economists how some nonprofit organizations operate as efficiently as they do—some libraries and colleges fall into that category. Their success is built on their employees' pride in their jobs, not on their profit motive.

Most economists don't deny that such inherently efficient individuals exist, and that most people derive some pleasure from efficiency, but they believe that it's hard to maintain that push for efficiency year in, year out, when some of your colleagues are lazy monopolists enjoying the fruits of your efficiency. Most people derive some pleasure from efficiency, but, based on their observation of people's actions, economists believe that holding down costs without the profit motive takes stronger willpower than most people have.

Individuals have complicated motives; some simply have a taste for efficiency.

Even if all the assumptions for perfect competition could hold true, it's unlikely that real-world markets would be perfectly competitive. The reason is that perfect competition assumes that individuals accept a competitive institutional structure, even though there are generally significant gains to be made by changing that structure. The simple fact is that *self-seeking individuals don't like competition for themselves* (although they do like it for others), and when competitive pressures get strong and the invisible hand's push turns to shove, individuals often shove back, using either social or political means. That's why you can only understand real-world competition if you understand how the three invisible forces (the invisible hand, foot, and handshake) push against each other to create real-world economic institutions. **Real-world competition** should be seen as a process—a fight between the forces of monopolization and the forces of competition.

THE FIGHT BETWEEN COMPETITIVE AND MONOPOLISTIC FIRMS

3 When competitive pressures get strong, individuals often fight back through social and political pressures. Competition is a process—a fight between the forces of monopolization and the forces of competition.

How Monopolistic Forces Triumph over Perfect Competition

Let's consider some examples. During the Depression of the 1930s, competition was pushing down prices and wages. What was the result? Individuals socially condemned firms for unfair competition, and numerous laws were passed to prevent it. Unions were strengthened politically and given monopoly powers so they could resist the pressure to push down wages. The Robinson-Patman Act was passed, which made it illegal for many firms to lower prices! Individual states passed similar laws, and it was under one of these that Wal-Mart lost a 1993 court case in which it was challenged for charging too-low prices in its pharmacies.

As another example, consider agricultural markets which have many of the conditions for almost perfect competition. To my knowledge, not one country in the world allows a competitive agricultural market to exist! As you'll see in later chapters, the United States has a myriad of laws, regulations, and programs that prevent agricultural markets from working competitively. U.S. agricultural markets are characterized by price supports, acreage limitations, and quota systems. Thus, where perfectly competitive markets could exist, they aren't allowed to. An almost infinite number of other examples can be found. Our laws and social mores simply do not allow perfect competition to work because government emphasizes other social goals

The United States has a myriad of laws, regulations, and programs that prevent agricultural markets from working competitively.

Q-4: Explain, using supply and demand curves, why most agricultural markets are not perfectly competitive.

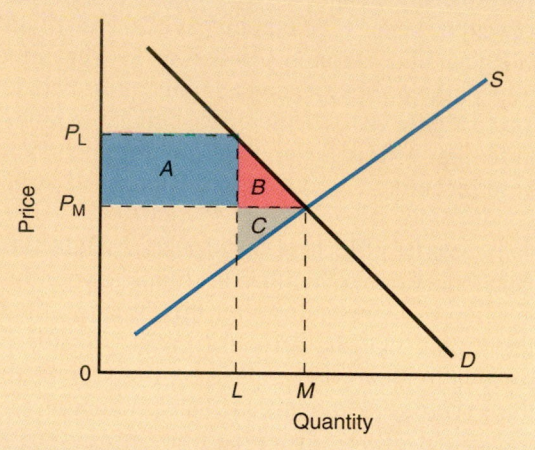

EXHIBIT 3   Movement Away from Competitive Markets

In the case where suppliers of $0L$ can restrict suppliers of LM from entering the market, they can raise the price of the good from P_M to P_L, giving the suppliers of $0L$ area A in additional income. The suppliers kept out of the market lose area C in income. The demanders, on the other hand, lose both areas A and B, giving them strong incentive to fight collusion. Often the costs of organizing for demanders are higher than the costs for the suppliers, so demanders accept the market restrictions.

besides efficiency. When competition negatively affects these other goals (which may or may not be goals that most people in society hold), government prevents competition from operating.

Economic Insights and Real-World Competition

Q–5: If demand becomes more elastic, would suppliers have a greater or a lesser desire to monopolize?

The nonexistence of perfectly competitive markets *should not* make you think that economics is irrelevant to the real world. Far from it. In fact, the movement away from perfectly competitive markets could have been predicted by economic theory!

Consider Exhibit 3. Competitive markets will exist only if suppliers or demanders don't collude. If the suppliers producing $0L$ can get together and restrict entry, preventing suppliers who would produce LM from entering the industry, the remaining suppliers can raise their price from P_M to P_L, giving them the shaded area, A, in additional income. If the cost of their colluding and preventing entry is less than that amount, economic theory predicts that these individuals will collude. The suppliers kept out of the market lose only area C so they don't have much incentive to fight the restrictions on entry. The demanders lose the areas A plus B so they have a strong incentive to fight. However, often their cost of organizing a protest is higher than the suppliers' cost of collusion, so the demanders accept the restrictions.

Suppliers introducing restrictions on entry seldom claim that the reason for the restrictions is to increase their incomes. Usually they couch the argument for restrictions in terms of the general good but, while their reasons are debatable, the net effect of restricting entry into a market is to increase suppliers' income to the detriment of demanders. In a later chapter, I'll consider the cases of licensing doctors and lawyers as examples of such restrictions. For now, all I want to point out is that economic theory predicts that there will be strong pressures away from perfectly competitive markets in the real world.

How Competitive Forces Triumph over Monopoly

Don't think that because perfect competition doesn't exist, competition doesn't exist. In the real world, competition is fierce; the invisible hand is no weakling. It holds its own against the other invisible forces.

Competition is so strong that it makes the other extreme (perfect monopolies) as rare as perfect competition. For a monopoly to exist, other firms must be prevented from entering the market. In reality it's almost impossible to prevent entry, and therefore it's almost impossible for perfect monopoly to exist. Monopoly profits send out signals to other firms. Those signals cause competition from other firms who want to get some of that profit for themselves. To get some of that profit, they break down the monopoly through political or economic means. If the monopoly is a legal monopoly, high profit will lead potential competitors to lobby to change the law underpinning that monopoly. If the law can't be changed—say the monopolist has a **patent** (a legal right to be the sole supplier of a good)—potential competitors will generally get around the obstacle by developing a slightly different product or by working on a new technology that avoids the monopoly but satisfies the relevant need.

Patent   A legal right to be the sole supplier of a good.

Say, for example, that you've just discovered the proverbial better mousetrap. You patent it and prepare to enjoy the life of a monopolist. But to patent your mousetrap, you must submit the technical drawings of how your better mousetrap works to the patent office. That gives all potential competitors (some of whom have better financing and already existing distribution systems) a chance to study your idea and see if they can think of a slightly different way (a way sufficiently different to avoid being accused of infringing on your patent) to achieve the same end. They often succeed—so often, in fact, that many firms don't apply for patents on new products because the information in the patent application spells out what's unique about the product. That information can help competitors more than the monopoly provided by the patent hurts competitors. Instead many firms try to establish an initial presence in the market and rely on inertia to protect what little monopoly profit they can extract.

Going to the patent office isn't the only way competitors gather information about competing products. Firms routinely buy other firms' products, disassemble them, figure out what's special about them, and then copy them within the limits of the law. This process is called **reverse engineering.**

Variations on reverse engineering and cloning go on in all industries. Consider the clothing industry. One firm I know of directs its secretaries to go to top department stores on their lunch hour and to buy the latest fashions that they like. The secretaries bring the clothes back and, that afternoon, the seamstresses and tailors dismantle each garment into its component parts, make a pattern of each part, and sew the original up again. The next day the secretary who chose that garment returns it to the department store, saying "I don't really like it."

Meanwhile the firm has express-mailed the patterns to its Hong Kong office, and two weeks later its shipment of garments comes in—garments that are almost, but not perfectly, identical to the ones the secretaries bought. The firm sells this shipment to other department stores at half the cost of the original.

Another example is the production of textbooks. This text (and every other text) was written only after a careful examination of all other successful—and a few of the not-so-successful—competitors. Then the publisher and I tried to determine what we liked and didn't like in the competitors' books; reviewers were asked what they liked and disliked in them too. Not until I had all that information did I sit down and write this book. There were lots of things the reviewers and I didn't like in the competitors' books, so this book significantly differs from those books. But many new books are clones of existing successful books. They have similar sections and similar discussions in slightly different words. Success breeds competition.

If you ask businesspeople, they'll tell you that competition is fierce and that profit opportunities are fleeting—which is a good sign that competition does indeed exist in the U.S. economy.

Business Week—A weekly business magazine that reports on business and economic trends.

Natural Monopolies and Competition

Certain industries enjoy strong economies of scale so average costs are continually falling. Such industries are called **natural monopolies** because it is less costly for one firm to operate than for more than one firm to operate. I demonstrate that in Exhibit 4.

If one firm produces Q_1, its cost per unit is C_1. If two firms each produce half that amount, $Q_{1/2}$, so that their total production is Q_1, the cost per unit will be C_2, which is significantly higher than C_1. In cases of natural monopoly, as the number of firms in the industry increases, the average cost of producing a fixed number of units increases. For example, if there were three firms in the industry and they each had a third of the market, each firm would have average cost C_3. It follows that, in the case of natural monopoly, even if a single firm makes some monopoly profit, the price it charges may still be lower than the price two firms making no profit would charge.

4 A natural monopoly is an industry with strong economies of scale so the average cost is continually falling. It can be demonstrated graphically that as the number of firms in a natural monopoly increases, the average cost of producing a fixed number of units also increases.

Fair Price Doesn't Necessarily Mean Low Price

If the natural monopoly has a relatively inelastic demand over the range of production, it will have an incentive to charge a high price (at which price the demand will no longer be inelastic) and will make substantial profit.

Examples of natural monopoly are local telephone service, cable TV provision, and electric utilities. But even in these cases of natural monopoly, competition works

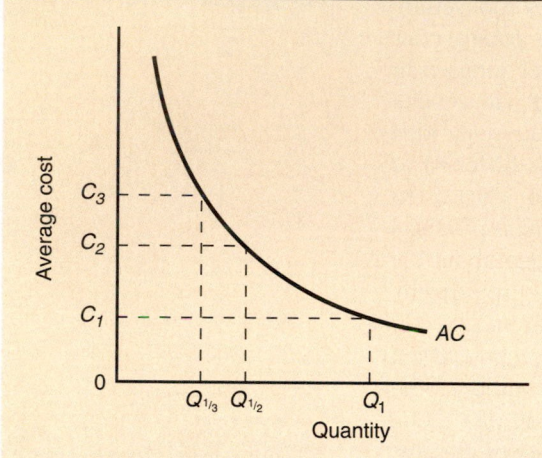

EXHIBIT 4   **Efficiency and Regulation of Natural Monopolies**

EXHIBIT 4   **Efficiency and Regulation of Natural Monopolies**

This graph shows the average cost curve for a natural monopoly. One firm producing Q_1 would have average cost of C_1. If total production remains at Q_1 and another firm enters the market, sharing quantity produced, each firm would produce $Q_{1/2}$ goods at average cost C_2. If three firms each produced $Q_{1/3}$, the average cost for each would be C_3. In a case of a natural monopoly, as the number of firms in the industry increases, the average cost of producing a fixed number of units increases.

in other ways. High monopoly profits generate research on alternative ways of supplying the product, such as sending TV signals through electrical lines or sending phone messages by satellite. When this competition doesn't work fast enough, people direct their efforts toward government, and political pressure is brought to bear either to control the monopoly through regulation or to break up the monopoly.

In the past, the pressure to regulate these natural monopolies has been stronger than competitive pressure to lower prices. Firms have been given the exclusive right to operate in the industry but, in return, they've had to agree to have the price they charge and the services they provide regulated by regulatory boards. Regulatory boards control the price that natural monopolies charge so it will be a "fair price" which they generally define as a price that includes all costs plus a normal return on capital investment (a normal profit, but no excess profit). Most states have a number of regulatory boards.

When firms are allowed to pass on all cost increases to earn a normal profit on those costs, they have little or no incentive to hold down costs.

When firms are allowed to pass on all cost increases to earn a normal profit on those costs, they have little or no incentive to hold down costs. In such cases, X-inefficiency develops with a passion, and such monopolies look for capital-intensive projects that will increase their rate bases. To fight such tendencies, regulatory boards must screen every cost and determine which costs are appropriate and which aren't—an almost impossible job. For example, nuclear power is an extremely capital-intensive method of producing electric power, and regulated electric companies favored nuclear power plants until they were told that some nuclear power plant construction costs could not be passed on.

Q–6: What is the problem with regulations that set prices relative to costs?

Once regulation gets so specific that it's scrutinizing every cost, the regulatory process becomes extremely bureaucratic, which itself increases the cost. Moreover to regulate effectively, the regulators must have independent information and must have a sophisticated understanding of economics, cost accounting, and engineering. Often regulatory boards are made up of volunteer laypeople who start with little expertise; they are exhausted or co-opted by the political infighting they have had to endure by the time they develop some of the expertise they need. As is often the case in economics, there's no easy answer to the problem.

Because of the problems with regulation, some economists argue that even in the case of natural monopoly, no regulation is desirable, and that society would be better off relying on direct competitive forces. They argue that regulated monopolies inevitably inflate their costs so much and are so inefficient and lazy that a monopoly right should never be granted.

How Firms Protect Their Monopolies   The image I've presented of competition being engendered by profits is a useful one. It shows how a market economy adjusts to ever-changing technology and demands in the real world. Competition is a dynamic, not a static, force.

Firms do not sit idly by and accept competition. They fight it. How do monopolies fight real-world competition? By spending money on maintaining their monopoly. By advertising. By lobbying. By producing products that are difficult to copy. By not taking full advantage of their monopoly position, which means charging a low price which discourages entry. Often firms could make higher short-run profits by charging a higher price, but they forgo the short-run profits in order to strengthen their long-run position in the industry.

Firms do not sit idly by and accept competition. They fight it.

5 Firms protect their monopolies by (1) advertising and lobbying, (2) producing products as nearly unique as possible, and (3) charging low prices.

Cost-Benefit Analysis of Creating and Maintaining Monopolies   Preventing real-world competition costs money. Monopolies are expensive to create and maintain. Economic theory predicts that if firms have to spend money on creating and protecting their monopoly, they're going to "buy" less monopoly than if it were free. How much will they buy? They will buy monopoly until the marginal cost of monopoly equals the marginal benefit. Thus, they'll reason:

· Does it make sense for us to hire a lobbyist to fight against this law which will reduce our monopoly power? Here is the probability that a lobbyist will be effective; here is the marginal cost; and here is the marginal benefit.

· Does it make sense for us to buy this machine? If we do, we'll be the only one to have it and are likely to get this much business. Here is the marginal cost and here is the marginal benefit.

· Does it make sense for us to advertise to further our market penetration? Here are the likely various marginal benefits; here are the likely marginal costs.

As you can see, even in those cases where the standard models of monopoly and perfect competition don't fit reality well, the reasoning process they're meant to teach (how self-seeking individuals try to structure real-world institutions based upon a decision rule relating marginal benefit and marginal cost) is a useful way to look at many real-world problems. It provides insights and often clarifies events that would otherwise be unintelligible. That doesn't mean that it will explain everything; some people aren't self-seeking. But considering how the self-seeking view of human nature explains reality is often helpful. It's how economists look at the world.

ECONOMIC REASONING AND THE REAL WORLD

To see the strength of the economist's reasoning process, let's consider a debate that will be very much in the news in the 1990s—health care reform. In considering an industry, the first thing one must do is to gather some facts and some history about the industry. The need for facts is obvious; the need for history arises because each industry follows its own path, and that path determines the present.

Competition and Health Care Reform

A Brief History of Health Care   The health care industry as we know it is a recent phenomenon. As little as 75 years ago, health care was a minor issue in people's lives. You lived your life, and when your time was up, you died. If you got sick, there were two things that could happen—you could get better on your own, or you could die. In either case, you didn't need any medical care.

Insurance was limited to catastrophic illness and accidents, and medicine was primarily focused on treating serious diseases and accident victims. The treatment could be as bad as the ailment—for example, some diseases were thought to be due to "bad blood," and therefore the treatment was blood-letting (that is, crudely, removing large volumes of blood). The germ theory of disease upon which modern medicine is based was not developed until the late 1800s. Little technology was used in medical care, other than snake oil and forceps. Barber shops doubled as hospitals, and the barber doubled as the doctor.

Beginning in the early 1900s, what is often called the medical revolution changed the nature of medical care. The germ theory of disease was gaining widespread acceptance. X-rays were discovered, and a variety of drugs were developed to combat specific germs. In 1935, sulfa drugs were discovered, and in 1945, penicillin, the first of the antibiotics. With those, and similar, discoveries, the possibility of direct

ADDED DIMENSION

- Health care in the United States is enormously expensive; as a society, we spend about 14 percent of our output on health care—that's about $1 trillion per year. In 1940, we spent about 4 percent.
- Health care is a highly regulated industry. Individuals cannot practice medicine without a license. Drugs need approval, and in every state hospitals are controlled by state boards. The economic justification for this is asymmetric information: Health care providers have access to far more information than do demanders, so it is not clear that market provision will work efficiently in providing reasonable care at a reasonable cost.
- Much of the payment for health care comes from third parties—either from government, in the form of Medicare or Medicaid, or from private insurance companies. In the early 1990s, the U.S. government paid for 27 percent and insurance companies paid for 49 percent, so total third-party payment of medical care was 76 percent. There were small, limited copayments—that is, the individual usually had to pay a small part of his or her health cost before the government or insurance kicked in—but for a large part of the market, the use of medical care involved a very low direct payment. This means the monitoring problem is relevant.
- Most private insurance is supplied by firms to groups rather than to individuals in order to avoid the **individual self-selection bias**—the skewing of risk and rates that would occur if individuals who are most likely to need insurance are left to buy it individually. This leaves large segments of U.S. society (about 37 million people) with no medical insurance. The result is a system of ''haves'' and ''have nots,'' depending on whether one has, or does not have, insurance.
- The output of health care—good health—is hard to define.
- Our moral code sees a certain level of health care as a right that individuals have. Our society will not accept that people do not receive ''adequate'' health care; our society wants everyone to receive health care that at least meets some minimal level. However, defining that ''adequate'' or ''minimal'' is extraordinarily difficult.
- A large portion of medical expenditures goes for a small number of individuals. In any given year, the majority of people use very little health care; a small number of people use enormous amounts. This small number of heavy users includes a disproportionate number of the very young—especially newborns—and the elderly.
- There are enormous technological changes occurring in health care provision. These new technologies mean that doctors can prolong and extend life. These technological advances have made our society face the question of access to these new technologies. Who should, and who should not, be eligible? For example, does a premature baby have a right to whatever care is necessary to keep him or her alive, regardless of cost or probable outcome? Does a person have a right to life-preserving medical care such as organ transplants or round-the-clock nursing care?

These, and an infinite number of similar moral questions, make health care a complicated policy question.

treatment of a variety of human afflictions became possible. Medicine expanded its horizons from treating only serious illnesses and accidents to treating less serious illnesses and overcoming physical problems that previously had been considered beyond treatment.

The ability of medicine to keep people alive and to cure previously incurable illnesses has increased at exponential rates since the 1940s. By the 1990s, premature babies weighing less than a pound, seriously injured people (such as those with a bullet lodged in the brain or a severed limb), and people with badly diseased hearts, livers, or eyes all had options available to them to correct their physical problems or at least to stay alive. These options were often expensive, but they were options nonetheless. By the end of the 1990s, these options will expand to new levels, but making these new technologies available to all will be extraordinarily expensive. Financing of health care will become a major problem.

Up until the 1940s, medical care was financed primarily by payments by individuals.

The Financing of Medical Care   Up until the 1940s, medical care was financed primarily by payments by individuals. Beginning in the early 1900s, doctors increasingly gained

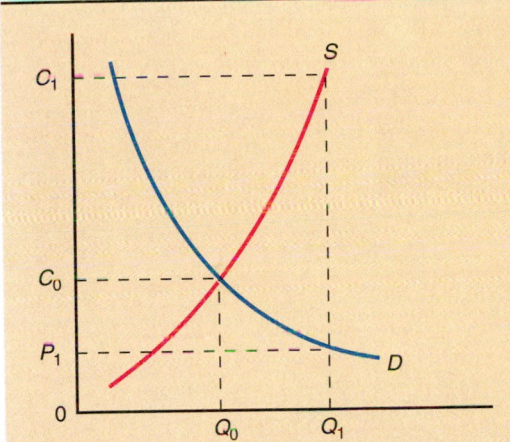

EXHIBIT 5   The Effect of Third–Party Payment

If individuals were paying for their own medical care they would choose quantity Q_0 which would have a cost of C_0. Under a third-party payee system with the individual paying P_1, the quantity demanded rises to Q_1, and the cost rises to C_1. The third party is paying both a much higher cost and is supplying a much larger quantity than under a user-pay plan.

enormous respect, due in large part to the strict standards of medical education that had been established after the Flexner Report of 1910 had condemned the then-existing quality of medical education. Doctors in this period made a good living, but for the most part they saw medicine as a calling, somewhat like that of the priesthood, to help people, not as a market job. They saw themselves as non-market professionals who stood by the Hippocratic Oath to provide medical care to all who needed it, regardless of ability to pay. Similarly, hospitals were run by charitable groups who collected money from those who could afford it but who provided service to all. Medical care was not an "economic good."

That started to change in the 1940s, and by the 1970s the regard in which the medical profession was held, the way in which it conducted its businesses, and the methods used to finance its technological development and pay its steadily increasing costs made the profession nearly unrecognizable compared to its situation in the first 40 years of the century. The reasons are varied. One important reason was the expansion of job-related health insurance. This expansion was driven by, among other things, the encouragement provided by the U.S. tax code, which allowed employers to claim the cost of health insurance as a deductible business expense and did not include medical insurance paid by employers as taxable income to employees, and by a tax code decision not to define health insurance benefits as wages.

Because there were strict wage controls during World War II, and also a significant shortage of workers, health insurance became a method of getting around the wage control laws. Almost all large companies established employee-related health benefits as a normal job benefit. With this development, the health care industry became a third-party payee industry for a growing part of the society. *The person receiving the health care differed from the person paying for the health care.* The problem presented by this separation of user and payer can be seen in a simple supply/demand framework like that in Exhibit 5.

With the advent of the third-party payments for traditional health care, the vision that doctors had of themselves as non-market professionals who somehow were indifferent to charging money for their services changed. Doctors still helped people, but health care provision became more of a business. The tradition of doctors treating problems first and thinking about payment afterwards changed to a system where payment (or the filling out of health care forms) came first and treatment came second. The family doctor who provided primary care, sometimes (but not always) with the help of a nurse, became the health care professional group, which included a nurse, a receptionist, and several administrative personnel. Providing primary health care became more and more a business, rather than a calling.

Employer-provided health care led to significantly increasing costs of medical care, both in relative and absolute terms. Since the insured faced an almost zero price, the quantity of health care demanded increased significantly. Competition could not

The U.S. Government's implicit policies played a significant role in tying together health insurance and employment.

Q–7:   What does the monitoring problem have to do with the current problems in the health care industry?

New technologies, such as radial imaging, have significantly increased the costs of health care.
© Pete Saloutos/The Stock Market.

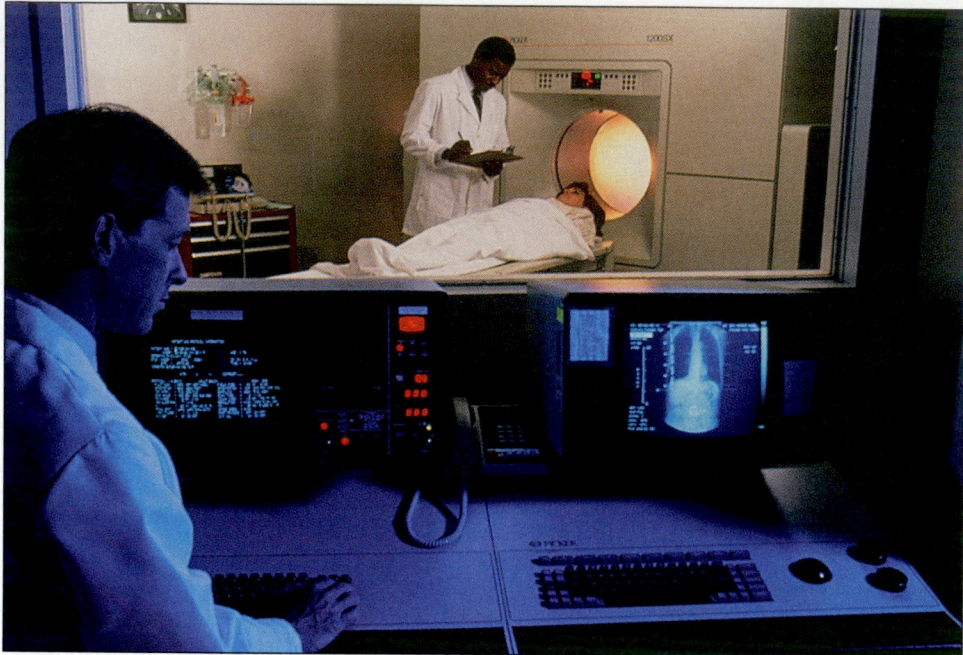

hold costs down because of the monitoring problem discussed earlier. The monitoring problem arises whenever the person paying for a service differs from the person using the service. Because the user isn't paying, he or she does not have an incentive to "monitor" or ensure that maximum value per dollar spent is received. This monitoring problem eliminated consumers' vigilance over costs. Doctors did not worry about charging people too much because the insurance company, not the individual, would be paying. This lack of monitoring of costs led to significant resources being spent on providing new drugs, diagnostic machines, and other sources of patient services. Medical workers' pay also increased absolutely and relatively.

To keep hospital health care costs lower than they would otherwise have been, and to restrict entry into the medical field, hospitals developed long residency programs that graduates of medical school had to complete. These long programs lasted from three to seven years, depending on the particular medical field the doctor wished to enter, and this residency came after four years of medical school. This long and difficult residency program worked to make medical care more like a business than it had been. Doctors felt that after expending the enormous effort to enter their field, they deserved to be handsomely compensated.

With rising health care costs not affecting the majority "insured" population, and doctors seeing health care as more of a business, health care provision became bifurcated. Those with health insurance received whatever care they needed, but the demands of those without health insurance quickly exceeded the ability of charitable groups to supply them. Better care than ever was available for those with insurance, and care of any type was being almost prohibitively costly for those without insurance. But the health care industry retained vestiges of its Hippocratic foundation—to provide care to all who needed it, regardless of cost. This commitment to open health care placed enormous strain on the health care system. The system met the need by **cost shifting**—adding the costs of providing medical care to the uninsured poor to the prices charged those who had health insurance. The result was further health care cost increases, further bifurcation of health care provision, and a strong upward trend of costs of health care as can be seen in Exhibit 6.

The commitment to open health care, regardless of cost, placed an enormous strain on the health care system.

Cost shifting   Adding the costs for one group to the prices paid by another group.

The Introduction of Medicare and Medicaid

By 1965, the situation had become so bad that the federal government felt it had no choice but to enter the field and resolve some of the problems. It established two programs, Medicare and Medicaid, to provide health care for the "have nots"—those who could not afford good insurance and

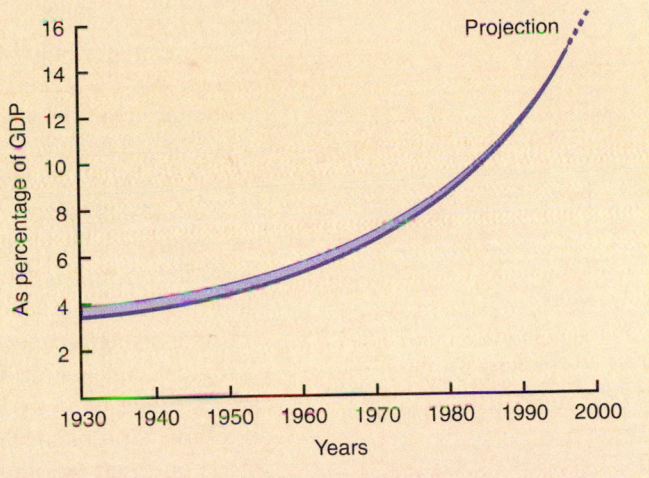

EXHIBIT 6   National Health Expenditures

U.S. health care expenses have increased dramatically since the 1930s. Their projected continued rise underlies much of the push for health care reform.

those whose physical condition or advancing age made them ineligible for most private insurance coverage.

Medicaid is a joint federal/state program providing medical care for people below a certain level of income, with the costs divided between the particular state and the federal government. Medicare is a strictly federal program, not related to income level, that covers almost all individuals who are 65 or older, as well as about 2 million severely disabled people who are under 65.

These two programs increased the quantity of health care demanded enormously, and placed a time bomb in the Medicare program that would begin to go off as baby boomers reached age 65. It also led to more cost-shifting and further bifurcation of the market. The increase in demand for medical care and increase in costs were reflected back into the price of health insurance. More and more people could not afford it, and more and more companies were trying to escape from providing it.

In the 1980s, as the government tried to limit both the quantity of medical care demanded and the cost of the care that was supplied, it set limits on what it would pay. That created a three-tier system of medical coverage in which the fully insured receive top-notch care, those under Medicare and Medicaid receive limited care, and those with no insurance at all receive poor care. All the time the quantity and quality of health care demanded by the fully insured increased and led to a continual rise in the relative price of medical care and an increase in the quality and variety of treatments.

Enormous amounts of money were spent on *new* expensive technological developments for the "haves" whose demand was not constrained by price. Equity considerations required extending some of that new technology to the have-nots, if they could somehow get into the health care system, since the health care system was still committed, in theory at least, to equal access for all. This process has continued, with expanded health care demands leading to new technology, and new technology creating new health care demands. This caused health care costs to rise from 4 percent of total output in the 1940s to 14 percent of total output in the first part of the 1990s. Left unchecked, that could increase to 20 percent by the turn of the century.

The above sketch in no way provides a full history of medical care and its finance, but it does show some highlights and gives you a sense of how the current problems have developed. The point of the history is that the problems in the health care industry did not pop up overnight; they developed over decades, and that development has been closely tied up in institutional details and government policies designed to help but which often caused additional problems of their own.

The Options   Almost all people agree that the current U.S. system of providing health care is in serious need of reform. There is little agreement about what the nature of that reform should be. Let me briefly list the broad options.

Single-Payer Plan   A single-payer system means a health care system completely financed by government, making the entire system a government-controlled business. The government, not individuals, would decide the limits of health care individuals would receive, and the government would pay the providers of that health care. To implement such a **single-payer plan** the government would set up an agency that would adjudicate all health care claims made by all people. This plan would replace the multitude of health insurance companies and health insurance plans that currently exist.

The advantages of the single-payer system are universal coverage, cost control (the single payer would have sufficient power to negotiate for low costs), and simplified administrative costs due to elimination of duplication and to the standardization of forms and benefits.

Under a single-payer arrangement, the third-party payer system would be carried to its logical conclusion. Because the government would provide all the payment for care, it would be in a position to hold costs of care down. But the single-payer option does have a problem. Since the direct costs to individuals would be zero, or close to zero, non-price rationing of government-supplied health care would be required if quantity of care is to be held down. Rationing does not mean that individuals do not have access to health care. For many aspects of health care there will be no rationing. But certain types of expensive care will necessarily be limited. And if rationing is not done by the price individuals pay, it must be done in some other manner. Non-price rationing is not necessarily bad; it may be fairer than the current rationing system that gives some individuals little health care, and others almost unlimited health care. But whether by price or other mechanisms, there must be rationing.

In the early 1990s, a proposed rationing plan along these lines was introduced by Oregon for its state health care plan. In Oregon's plan, a fixed amount of money for health care was allocated, and an independent board ranked medical conditions according to social benefit of treatment. Medical problems with the "highest social benefit of treating" would be covered down to where the allotted money ran out.

This single-payer plan changes the nature of medical care from a market good back to a right, and, ironically, is a movement back toward what the United States had in the 1950s when medical care was significantly regulated by social forces (the invisible handshake). The single-payer plan replaces that invisible handshake with political forces (the invisible foot). The government, not individuals, will ration health care and will pay for it.

The single-payer plan is a major institutional change. Any attempt to introduce it would be accompanied by enormous lobbying efforts on the part of health insurance providers, whose function would be eliminated; by many health care providers, who would face significant direct pressure from government on the fees they charge; and from some consumers who currently have extensive health care coverage provided at low cost to them by their employers.

Managed Competition   **Managed competition** is a system in which existing institutions are extended and modified, the better to take incentives into account. There are many variations on managed competition, but the basic idea is to modify our current system so that (1) all individuals are covered, (2) the power of the people is increased relative to the provider so that costs can be held down better, and (3) bureaucracy of payment is simplified, so that less money goes to administration and more goes to medical care.

Under the managed competition proposal put forward by President Clinton, all employers would be required to provide their employees with health insurance. If they did not wish to do so, they would have to contribute to a government fund set up to provide health insurance for people who do not obtain it through their employers.

The political beauty of Clinton's plan of managed health care is that it proposes to extend coverage to all individuals and pay for that extension primarily through predicted cost savings and efficiency gains. Many critics cite those features of his plan as its problems. They argue that the large cost savings predicted will not be forthcoming, since these savings can only be achieved through strict rationing of services, and/or legal caps on costs—rationing and price control that these critics doubt our political system could maintain. They ask: Is our political system really able to make the difficult decisions involved in rationing? Can our system resist responding to people's desire for the highest quality and quantity of medical care when the cost they, as individuals, face for receiving that care is close to zero?

The critics believe the answer to these questions is "No." They contend that the quantity demanded of universal medical care at an almost zero cost to the individual would eventually bankrupt the government, as cost overrun upon cost overrun developed. Supporters of managed competition argue that it is the doctor, not the patient, who controls the quantity demanded, since the doctor makes most of the health care decisions. They argue that the managed care system will force doctors to see that the cost constraint is met, and hence the managed care system will relate usefulness of treatment to cost of treatment.

Direct Competition   At the opposite end of the spectrum from the single-payer plan is a system of direct market allocation of health care in which the individual receiving the care is the person doing the paying. While a number of proposals along these lines have been suggested, they have gathered little political support.

Advocates of the **direct competition** approach argue that it was the government's decision to make health care benefits neither taxable nor subject to wage controls in the 1940s that set the United States on the path to the current problems of the system. By encouraging separation of user from payer, the decision broke down the social and economic pressures holding costs down and rationing health care through a combination of market and social mechanisms. The only way our society will be able to come to reasonable decisions about rationing health care, these critics contend, is by bringing back a system in which payer and user of health care are more, not less, closely related.

> **6C**   Direct competition involves price competition; it will avoid non-price rationing, but it will likely lead to inequities and hardships that will undermine political support for it.

To do that, the first step would be to make health benefits a taxable benefit to all employees. Such a change would increase government revenue and reduce the amount of insurance people choose because that insurance would no longer be subsidized. Second, to offset the institutional errors of the past, some direct competition advocates suggest that a certain percentage of all medical costs be required to be paid for by individuals (even those with insurance). This mandatory copayment system could be phased in over a 10-year period so that all individuals were required to pay initially 20 percent—and eventually 50 or even 75 percent—of the first $5,000 of medical bills per year. For medical expenses above some cutoff—say $5,000—the required copayment could be reduced significantly, although not completely eliminated.

Universal access to care under direct competition could be achieved with some type of a voucher system in which all individuals receive a $1,000 voucher to be used to pay uninsured medical expenses. Money not spent on medical care could be saved for another year, or translated to cash. A government-provided insurance policy covering major medical expenses could be introduced for which individuals could pay a 10-percent surcharge on their income tax or with some type of a tax credit. Making the cost of that insurance dependent on income would make the cost for low-income people much lower than the cost for high-income individuals.

Opponents of the direct competition plan argue that the voucher approach would be extremely expensive and would likely lead to significant administrative problems. They also argue that all such plans result in almost as much government involvement as do all the other plans—the voucher approach builds on the current inefficient system rather than streamlining it.

Many variations on this direct competition plan are possible, but their goal would be to reestablish consumer, rather than third-party, control over costs. The argument is that as people see, and pay for, part of the high costs of current care, they will demand reform much more quickly and more effectively than under any system in which payers and users are separate. But given the political realities, it should also be noted that, in the interim, people would likely demand an end to the "direct competition" system.

The Health Care Debate   The above discussion has been too short to provide you with details of any of the plans. But it has, I hope, stimulated your thinking about the health care system and the options. In the debate to come, political considerations will likely take precedence over economic considerations, and short-run costs will likely take precedence over long-run costs. This is the dilemma of economic policy in a democracy.

As you look further into the debate, think about the underlying economics of the various plans—of how the rationing that will be necessary under either the single-payer or the managed competition route will be accomplished, and how that rationing will affect people. Compare that rationing system to the price-rationing system that would exist under a direct competition system. Ask yourself: Which is more fair? Which is more efficient? When thinking about this problem, recognize that aspects of various plans are not necessarily mutually exclusive. For example, single-payer plans can include individual copayments of varying levels, and nondeductibility of health insurance premiums could be integrated with the managed care proposals.

Q–8: Does economic theory say that the direct competition market solution to our health care problems is the preferable solution?

Economic theory does not say which form of rationing is better, but it does say that some form of rationing is needed. Inevitably, people's ''wants'' exceed what can be provided by the economy. Somehow, ''wants'' and ''financing those wants'' must be coordinated. Any proposal that does not make clear how the needed rationing will take place should be viewed with caution.

Two Case Studies

Every market is different. The differences are in the particular problems it faces, the dimensions that competition takes, and its options in dealing with its problems. Generalizations can be made, but these generalizations necessarily give an unworldly quality to the discussion. Thus, it's helpful to consider specific case studies showing examples of particular markets and their problems. Economic knowledge comes from combining a sense of such case studies with the generalized understanding conveyed in the formal models.

Case Study 1: Competition in the Biotech Industry   The first case study, about a drug company, appeared in an article in *The Wall Street Journal*. I reprint it in its entirety to give you a sense of the type of articles you'll find in business newspapers and to show you what a business reporter, limited to 2,500 words, felt was important to include in her discussion of the firm and industry.

AMGEN, CLEARED TO SELL KIDNEY-PATIENT DRUG, STILL FACES BIG HURDLES

By Rhonda L. Rundle

Thousand Oaks, Calif.—After nine years of painstaking research, punctured dreams, and a string of recent setbacks, Amgen Inc. has approval to sell the hottest new drug in the biotechnology field.

Now comes the hard part.

First of all, Amgen must master a bagful of new tricks to transform itself from biotech boutique into a commercial drug company, selling to kidney patients a new anemia drug called EPO. Nuts-and-bolts decisions like setting prices and production schedules are

still alien to Amgen, built mainly on the brainpower and 80-hour workweeks of eager young scientists.

But Amgen can't slowly feel its way. The tiny niche it has carefully tried to carve out is under attack. A rival EPO maker is closing in on its once-comfortable lead. And, in a measure of the kinds of trouble Amgen has gotten itself into in its short life, the company is even vulnerable to competition from its marketing partner.

In bitter and distracting legal battles, Amgen is fighting both that partner and its main competitor. Amgen's falling out with the marketing partner has already had the effect of delaying the drug's approval by over two months. And Amgen's refusal to settle a dispute with the competitor over pat-

ent rights could backfire by ultimately opening the field to many others. These struggles consume precious dollars and management time—even though few people outside Amgen think the company can do better than draw.

Judgment Challenged

Thus Amgen's situation seems at least partly of its own making. ''There's a deep sense of moral righteousness at Amgen that blinds them,'' says Robert Kupor, a biotechnology analyst at Kidder, Peabody & Co. A few people are even starting to ask whether Amgen management has the mature business judgment needed to steer the company into adulthood.

Amgen's chief executive officer, Gordon Binder, dismisses such critics.

"The only thing we've lost so far is two months," he says.

Such doubts were unimaginable just a few months ago, when Amgen was being hailed as biotech's next superstar. The chief reason was EPO, or erythropoietin, a drug aimed now at the nation's 100,000 kidney-dialysis patients, but ultimately perhaps at many others, including some AIDS patients. Estimates of the anemia fighter's first-year sales are in the $100 million range, but some analysts think they could eventually top $1 billion annually, making EPO one of the most commercially successful drugs ever. Yesterday's FDA approval gives only Amgen, not its rivals, the right to sell the drug in the U.S. Among other things, the decision was a blow to Amgen's marketing partner, the Ortho Pharmaceutical unit of Johnson & Johnson.

Beyond this promise, Amgen management was until recently being praised for its entrepreneurial spirit and business sense. By cultivating relations with regulators and physicians, the company seemed to show that it had learned from the mistakes of Genentech Inc., which stumbled last year in its transition from biotech start-up to commercial drug company.

Following a Pioneer

That would be fitting. It was Genentech's initial success a decade ago that inspired two Silicon Valley venture capitalists to start a biotech company. They recruited George B. Rathmann, a Princeton-trained chemist with a knack for creating freewheeling, productive research environments. A tall, burly man with "a mind like a Cray computer," in a former employee's words, Mr. Rathmann had a charismatic style that helped Amgen hire top scientists. He also could raise money—so well that, while working earlier at Abbott Laboratories, he had been nicknamed Golden Throat. In 1981, Amgen raised $19 million in a private offering, unprecedented for a biotech company.

The early going was tough. Within two years, Amgen was on the brink of a bankruptcy filing as the funds ran out. A hot turn in the market for technology stocks saved it, as Amgen found under-writers, raced to file with regulators, and went public at $18 a share. By just a few weeks, it beat a crash in technology stocks.

The collapse was followed by Amgen's first scientific flop—a chicken growth hormone. It didn't work down on the farm. Amgen's share price plunged as low as $3.75. (Its share closed yesterday in over-the-counter trading at $41, up $.875 on FDA approval of EPO.)

Then came a big break. In 1983 an Amgen scientific team led by Fu-Kuen Lin cloned the gene for human EPO, a protein made in the kidneys that stimulates production of red blood cells. Given to people with kidney disease, it can sharply reduce or even eliminate their need for blood transfusions. And it may be broadly useful against anemia that is due to cancer therapies or to the AZT treatment of AIDS patients.

In early 1986, with EPO still unproven in human tests, Mr. Rathmann presented a bet-the-company plan to the board. He wanted to stake a huge chunk of Amgen's modest cash reserves on a $20 million plant to produce EPO. The gamble had to be taken, he argued, to stay ahead in the race to bring EPO to market.

The competitive threat turned out to be keener than Amgen knew. Early one morning in July 1987, a securities analyst tracked Mr. Rathmann down at Amgen's Boulder, Colo., office to tell him that another company had been awarded the first EPO patent.

At Amgen, there was disbelief. It had filed its application more than two years ahead of its rival, Genetics Institute Inc., based in Cambridge, Mass. But for technical reasons the two documents had been reviewed by different sections of the patent office. Genetics Institute's patent application covered the EPO molecule itself, while Amgen's covered a process for making the substance. Amgen received its own patent three months later.

The result is a legal battle. Amgen sued Genetics Institute for patent infringement in federal court in Massachusetts. Genetics Institute filed a counterclaim, then offered to cross-license, the usual remedy adopted in such disputes. Amgen refused.

Amgen executives insist a principle is at stake: Their company was first to clone the EPO gene, so it should reap the rewards. "This is what U.S. patent laws are all about; otherwise, forget rewarding innovation for small entrepreneurs," Mr. Rathmann argues.

But some analysts fear that Amgen's judgment is clouded by emotional ties to its first big product. They note that the 61-year-old Mr. Rathmann became teary-eyed during questioning about EPO at a legal hearing last year.

Other Amgen veterans feel equally possessive of EPO. It was developed when the company was still so small everyone knew everyone else, including spouses and children. Mr. and Mrs. Rathmann held picnics at their beach-front home in Ventura. EPO was truly a family affair.

When Amgen fell behind on its schedule to file an FDA license application, EPO team members leased five motel rooms to allow round-the-clock work. Ninety-three days later, their 19,578-page document was done. That morning weary workers tied yellow ribbons and a banner on the trees at corporate headquarters proclaiming: "The Simi Valley hostages are free."

Still, Genetics Institute claims that it conceived the recombinant process for making EPO ahead of Amgen. And the longer Amgen holds out for exclusive rights, the tougher terms Genetics Institute will demand, Kidder Peabody's Mr. Kupor believes. The courts could impose their own profit-sharing formula, or worse, open the door to all EPO makers by nullifying both patents. The trial is scheduled to begin in early August in federal court in Boston. Genetics Institute is backed by a cash-rich joint venture to which it has licensed the drug, Chugai-Upjohn Inc., formed by Chugai Pharmaceutical Co., Tokyo, and Upjohn Co., Kalamazoo, Mich.

The patent mess seemed like a minor blemish on Amgen's record until the marketing-partner rift surfaced in January. Johnson & Johnson's Ortho unit sued to block EPO approval until a contractual dispute was resolved. Ortho claims Amgen violated their 1985 license agreement by failing to submit to the FDA Ortho's clinical data for patients in the early stages of kidney disease. Under the agreement, Amgen sold to Ortho all rights to the drug except those for kidney patients who require regular dialysis. (J&J already sells EPO in Europe.)

Amgen management, surprised by the suit, apparently underestimated its importance. No judge would allow a commercial squabble to prevent patients from receiving EPO, Amgen believed. As the injunction hearing began in Wilmington, Del., on March 17, Amgen and the FDA were discussing dates for an imminent news conference to announce EPO approval.

But Johnson & Johnson produced scores of documents and other evidence to support its claims. Attorneys for the drug giant portrayed Amgen as capricious and sneaky. Busy making final plans for EPO's launch, Amgen executives were caught off guard by Johnson & Johnson's carefully laid offense.

The court ruled for Ortho, ordering Amgen to amend its FDA application to include Ortho's data. Amgen's stock price, which had soared more than 50% in the preceding four months, backed off a bit.

Amgen maintains that it never intended to split the kidney-disease market with Johnson & Johnson. The fledgling biotech concern tended to use "dialysis" as a synonym for "chronic renal disease" and naively agreed to inclusion of the shorter term in the agreement, officials assert.

Two years after it signed that marketing agreement, Amgen was surprised to learn that Ortho's initial EPO tests weren't for anemias associated with cancer or AIDS therapy—huge potential markets that Amgen had signed away to Ortho—but for a tiny group of "pre-dialysis" patients with kidney problems. Amgen worried that Ortho, backed by its parent's powerful marketing forces, was seeking to

invade turf Amgen thought it had reserved.

The reasoning is that nephrologists, the doctors who are the drug's real target customers, treat both pre-dialysis and dialysis patients. If Ortho should win patients in the early stages of kidney disease, their doctors might never switch brands, worries Kathleen Wiltsey, Amgen's EPO marketing director. "This is a fight for life," she says.

Whatever the merits, Amgen clearly miscalculated the strength of Ortho's case, the FDA's response, and public reaction. The FDA, criticized by the Delaware court for favorable treatment of Amgen, pulled back and began moving more cautiously. When the FDA did grant approval yesterday, it authorized EPO for chronic renal failure, not merely for dialysis patients; the effect was to perpetuate the Amgen-Ortho struggle. The next round has already begun in private arbitration talks. Amgen expects a hearing to take place this summer or early fall. The proceedings could force Amgen to allow Ortho to jointly market Epogen, Mr. Binder, Amgen's chief executive officer, said yesterday.

The approval delay eroded Amgen's prized head start over its EPO rivals. Last summer, some analysts estimated Amgen's lead at 18 months, long enough to establish trademark loyalty for its Epogen brand of EPO. Now, estimates of its lead have shrunk to six months or less.

"We've made up the lion's share of their head start," boasts a Chugai-Upjohn spokesman. While the FDA approval came with so-called orphan-drug status, which confers a seven-year marketing monopoly, the agency also said that didn't rule out the possibility of granting the same status to Chugai-Upjohn's slightly different version of EPO.

All this complicates the outlook

for EPO sales. But a more immediate question is who will pay for the drug. The annual cost for a typical kidney-dialysis patient will be between $4,000 and $8,000 a year, Amgen said yesterday. Amgen is lobbying to make sure that Medicare, which now covers roughly 90% of kidney-dialysis costs for the nation's roughly 100,000 dialysis patients, will cover most EPO costs.

Meanwhile, Amgen has been hemorrhaging financially without EPO revenue to offset the heavy launch costs. It lost nearly $9 million in its fourth quarter ended March 31. (For all of fiscal '89 it had a loss of $8.2 million on revenue of $78.1 million.) The company needs cash to continue developing its next big drug, an immune-system booster for chemotherapy patients. (The drug, granulocyte colony-stimulating factor, or G-CSF, could be ready to market late in 1990.)

Change at the Top

These problems are no longer primarily Mr. Rathmann's. He resigned as president and chief executive last October, telling astonished employees that with EPO approval near he wanted to get back to his family. Mr. Binder, now in charge, had been the chief financial officer. Harry F. Hixson, a scientist and longtime Rathmann associate, now holds the No. 2 position, with the title of president and chief operating officer.

Whether the soft-spoken Mr. Binder is the man to lead Amgen through the battles ahead remains to be seen, but some shareholders are getting impatient. Says one major holder, "I just wish these biotech companies would grow up."

The Wall Street Journal, June 2, 1989. Reprinted by permission of THE WALL STREET JOURNAL, © 1989 Dow Jones & Company, Inc. All rights reserved worldwide.

7 The economic reasoning process is a useful way to look at many real-world events.

Discussion What does this case study tell us about competition in U.S. businesses? Let's consider:

1. There's no way one would call the drug industry *perfectly competitive,* but the example shows that competition—"brutal competition"—exists. That competition isn't primarily price competition. Indeed the article doesn't even discuss pricing strategies. (They exist, but the article doesn't discuss them.) Instead, the

competition takes place in other dimensions: speed of supply; being first in the market; gaining legal rights.

2. A firm's success depends on much more than producing a better mousetrap cheaper. It depends upon handling relationships with other firms, legal knowledge, and finance. When one talks about inefficiency, one need not be referring to physical production. One might also be talking about inefficiency in public relations or financial affairs.

3. Of all the inputs for firms, skilled labor and financial capital provide the most trouble. Amgen had, and has, the skilled labor. The same story for similar firms might have focused on the problem of keeping skilled workers working for them. But Amgen had the normal finance problems. Unlike many other small companies, it overcame them, beating the crash in technology stock and coming up with the necessary financial capital when it was on the brink of bankruptcy.

4. The difference between wild success and total bankruptcy for a firm can be minute. Luck as well as skill plays a role in any business success.

5. The needs of a firm evolve over time. Often the person who organizes a company is not the best person to run it. The two stages require different skills and interests. Having the right type of person in charge at the right time is a key element in a company's success.

6. Legal monopolies from patents are of limited value. Notice that a competitor has a slightly different version of the same drug which it may be allowed to sell in direct competition.

7. The company has to do more than sell the drug to doctors. It must see to it that Medicaid will pay for it. A failure on that front could mean failure of the company.

Where does economics fit into all this? Everywhere.

- In the initial choice about what research to do, Amgen chose a research focus that had a large potential demand—$100 million to $1 billion isn't small potatoes. Most likely that decision was made on the basis of marginal cost and marginal benefit.

Q–9: What market structures does Amgen operate in?

- How the legal and financial battles come out will play a big role in Amgen's pricing strategy. If it's comfortable with its monopoly, Amgen will likely follow a high price strategy; if it's uncomfortable with it, Amgen will follow a much lower price strategy to keep other firms out on the basis of price.
- In this case economic theory doesn't say which of these two strategies will most benefit the consumer. Clearly in the short run, the low-price strategy will make consumers better off, but in the long run, expected high returns to research lead to further research and development of new drugs. If Amgen and other research-oriented companies fail to make a profit, less research will be done in the future.
- Economic analysis was used to decide what type of financing to use.
- In deciding when to negotiate with his rivals and when not to, the president might have made the economic, reasonable decision. The article suggests that he let his emotions cloud his judgment. (Interpret *emotional* as deciding at a point where marginal cost does not equal marginal benefit.) Businesspeople are judged on how economic-based their judgments are.

Were we to look more deeply into the decisions Amgen made, we'd see more instances of economics. The point is that microeconomics concerns rational, reasonable decision making, and it is that aspect of microeconomics that enters into all levels of business.

The above case was from 1989. It could be replaced by many other more recent cases, but I have left it in the text because it is of continuing interest, especially with the current debates about health care. Later, we will consider the update. In the meantime, think about what you predict the outcome of the story will be.

Case Study 2: Competition in the Casket Industry   The second case study also comes from *The Wall Street Journal*. The story it tells is not as technical as the biotech case study, but it nonetheless presents important insights into the workings of markets and competition.

INDEPENDENT COFFIN SELLERS FIGHT ESTABLISHED INDUSTRY

By John R. Emshwiller

Loma Linda, Calif.—When looking for a small business to start, Sheralee and Kyle Nyswonger thought about a florist shop or a hair salon. "But there was one of those on every corner," says the 26-year-old Mrs. Nyswonger. "We thought we should do something really different."

So they opened a store to sell coffins to the public. Their nine-month-old Hillmark Casket Gallery undersells funeral homes, the traditional retailers of coffins, by an average of 30% to 40%, says Mrs. Nyswonger, the store's manager.

On the face of it, the Nyswongers found a potential gold mine. Wholesale coffin sales exceed $800 million a year, and the nation's 22,000 funeral homes typically charge three to four times the wholesale prices. After decades of attacks by muckraking journalists and government regulators, the funeral industry hardly has a reputation as a haven of consumer bargains. What better opportunity to slash prices and clean up?

But as the Nyswongers and other would-be coffin retailers have learned, a new company bucking the longstanding practices of an established industry may have its work cut out for it. The funeral industry has come up with some potent tactics for keeping outsiders out.

Just recently, for instance, Hillmark lost a customer after a local funeral home told the family it would roughly double its funeral-service charges to more than $2,000 if the family brought in a coffin from the outside, says Mrs. Nyswonger.

More critically, the Nyswongers have had trouble simply getting coffins to sell. The world's biggest coffin maker, Batesville Casket Co. of Batesville, Ind., turned them away. Batesville will gladly sell to any licensed funeral director in the nation

and plants a tree in a national forest every time someone is buried in a Batesville coffin. But the company's policy is to reject every non-funeral director who calls. Many other major coffin manufacturers sell only to funeral homes.

"We have a system of distribution [about 16,000 funeral homes] that demands a certain loyalty or the system will fall apart," says Robert C. Smith, vice president for investor relations of Hillenbrand Industries, which owns Batesville Casket.

Inland Casket Manufacturing Co., a local coffin maker, agreed to supply Hillmark, but then changed its mind because local funeral directors were threatening to stop buying from it, says Mrs. Nyswonger. Peter Fishering, vice president of Inland Casket, declines to comment.

'Handling' Fees

But such threats aren't unusual, says Ronald Hast, a Los Angeles funeral-home owner and publisher of Mortuary Management, a national trade magazine. "If a casket company is selling to a maverick, funeral directors won't buy from it," says Mr. Hast. "I guess you call that a boycott."

In addition to threatening such boycotts, funeral homes tack on "casket-handling" fees of as much as $1,000 for customers using a coffin bought from a "third party" retailer.

Defending such practices, funeral-industry officials say they have a right to do business with whomever they choose. They contend the handling fee is to recover legitimate overhead expenses normally included in the coffin price.

But the Federal Trade Commission is investigating whether coffin-handling fees violate 1984 federal regulations aimed at increasing competition and consumer choice in the funeral business. The commission has been gathering evidence about possible anti-competitive effects of handling fees, which "seem to have put some casket

retailers out of business," says Carol Jennings, an FTC staff attorney. "This is a very controversial issue."

'Pre-Need' Buying

Spurred by the 1984 FTC rule that barred funeral homes from refusing to handle merchandise bought elsewhere, an estimated several dozen non–funeral-home vendors have started selling coffins in recent years. Most of these are cemeteries that sell coffins on a "pre-need" basis as an outgrowth of selling cemetery plots in advance.

But a small coffin maker in Chicago opened a retail outlet there, and another group, which says it got the idea from Hillmark, is considering starting a store in San Francisco.

Many of the new vendors have encountered obstacles, and the problems aren't limited to coffin makers. A local trucking company, Inland Valley Transportation Co. (no relation to the coffin maker), delivered one coffin to a local mortuary for Hillmark, but then stopped doing business with the retailer. It turned out the trucking company also did work for the mortuary. An Inland Valley official "told me the mortuary had said he could ship our caskets or their bodies," Mrs. Nyswonger recalls.

Ron Bredelis, Inland Valley's owner, confirms that he refused to handle any deliveries for Hillmark after the first one, but denies he was pressured into dropping the retailer. "It was just too controversial with funeral directors," he says.

No Identifying Marks

Resistance is so great that for fear of retaliation, Mrs. Nyswonger declines to identify her current coffin suppliers. "I've told them to leave all identifying marks off the caskets," she adds. She says one local funeral director who visited Hillmark demanded so insistently to know the identity of the firm's suppliers that she had to call the sheriff to get him to leave. (The U.S. has an estimated 400 coffin makers.)

Some local funeral directors argue that without knowing Hillmark's suppliers, it is impossible to tell whether the retailer really is selling at a discount. "Just comparing a blue casket to a blue casket is unfair," says Dennis Butler, owner of Watson-Butler Family Mortuary in Riverside, Calif.

Besides imposing coffin-handling fees, some local funeral directors are requiring customers to sign waivers absolving the funeral home of any liability if they choose a Hillmark coffin. "Suppose the bottom falls out," says Mr. Butler, the funeral-home owner.

Yet even funeral directors admit there is a certain generic quality to coffins. "How many ways can you change a box?" asks one director. As the funeral-home industry commonly uses the coffin price to cover much of the overhead, a retailer such as Hillmark can sell coffins for lower prices, adds Tom Johnson, president of Pierce Brothers Mortuaries in Los Angeles.

Casket Giveaway

Hillmark customers believe they are saving money. Mitsue Mobley of Redlands, Calif., says she paid about $600 at Hillmark for her late husband's coffin, half the price of a similar coffin at a mortuary she visited.

Thus, even with obstacles, the company survives. Mrs. Nyswonger says Hillmark's first-year revenue will be about $250,000. (Hillmark also sells cremation urns and grave markers and does floral arrangements.)

Hillmark's marketing efforts have ranged from newspaper ads to a Christmastime coffin giveaway, the latter on the theory that a death during that season would be extra tough financially on families already strapped by holiday spending. However, most of the company's customers have come from "word of mouth," says Mrs. Nyswonger.

For all the problems they have encountered, the Nyswongers were optimistic enough to open a second coffin store near here recently. Unlike the first outlet, which is in an out-of-the-way office strip next to a freeway, the new store is on a corner in downtown Santa Ana. It has two big picture windows with coffins always on display, says Mrs. Nyswonger. "You drive down Main Street and you can't miss it."

The Wall Street Journal, July 5, 1989. Reprinted by permission of THE WALL STREET JOURNAL, © 1989 Dow Jones & Company, Inc. All rights reserved worldwide.

Discussion   What does this case study tell us about real-world competition and monopoly?

1. It shows how important the invisible handshake can be. Even in a market with 400 producers of coffins and 22,000 funeral homes, the price markup on coffins can be 300 to 400 percent, and producers feel enormous pressure not to deviate from the current practices of the industry.

2. It shows how hard it is to judge competition in a particular market. Funeral homes contend that they assign much of their overhead cost to the price of coffins. If

Q–10: The fact that funeral homes make such high profits on coffins shows that the funeral market is not highly competitive. True or false? Why?

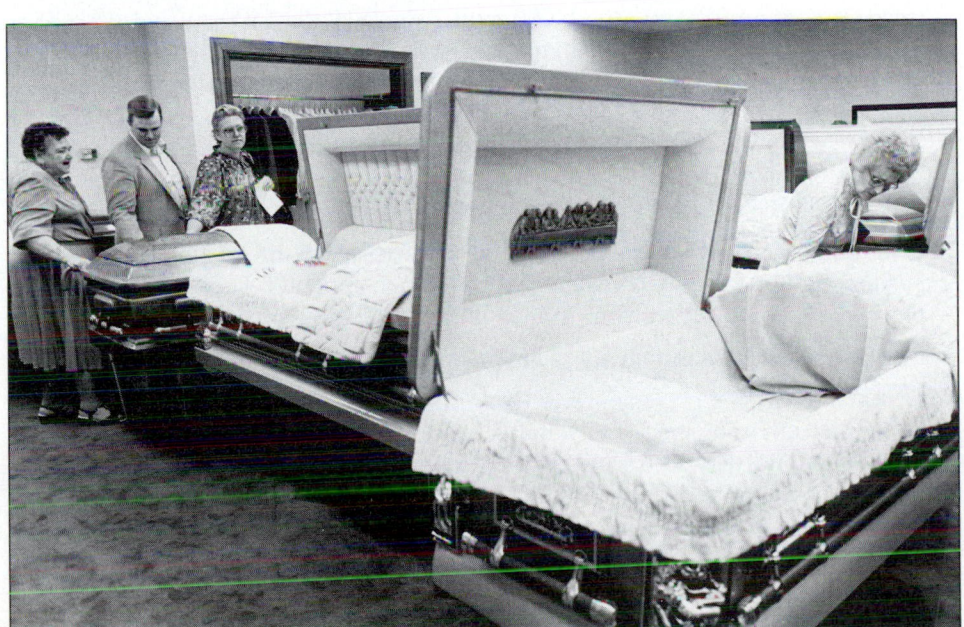

Dying is an expensive proposition, in part because the casket industry tends to be a closed monopoly maintained by funeral homes. © *Bob Daemmrich/The Image Works.*

The two case studies presented above were written in 1989. Considering the continuations of the case studies tell us a lot about the competitive process. Take the Hillmark Casket Gallery Case Study. It shows the tough side of the competitive process. Selling inexpensive caskets was a great idea—right? Well, if you look for the Hillmark Casket Gallery in Loma Linda, you won't find it anymore; the best information I could get was that it shut down sometime in 1991, even though the recession of the early 1990s should have been good for the cut-rate casket business. It seems that the funeral industry monopoly won, which isn't unexpected. Many small businesses with great ideas don't make it through the first five years.

The story does not end there, however. The problems of entrepreneurs, such as Hillmark, caught the eyes of regulators. On July 19, 1994, in response to complaints, the Federal Trade Commission established rules that make it illegal for funeral homes to charge extra when a customer buys a casket from a separate retailer. In California, bills have been introduced into the legislature that would strip the state funeral regulatory board (which the legislature believed reflected the interests of funeral homes) of many of its powers, and would redistribute them to other state regulatory boards. If these political–institutional changes are made, and it seems likely that they will be, companies like Hillmark are much more likely to succeed in the future. Of course, it will be too late for Hillmark. Such interaction between economic problems involving restraint of trade and politics is what shape the institutional structure.

The update of the Amgen story shows the other side of the competitive process. The price of their stock rose dramatically in the early 1990s as EPO came on the market and they developed a new drug, Neupogen, that stimulates white blood cell production. Sales doubled and large growth was predicted through the early 1990s.

And how about the court cases? Amgen won the case with the Genetics Institute. Part of the Johnson & Johnson case was settled in arbitration, but another part was still pending in 1994.

coffin prices were to fall, funeral homes might simply tack on the charges elsewhere, and the consumer would be no better off.

Why do they do that, you ask? Without specifically analyzing the issue, it's impossible to be definite, but a likely reason is price discrimination. Remember, a monopolist can increase its profits by price discrimination. Funeral homes aren't allowed to price discriminate in the fees they charge. However, by charging a set amount for specific types of funerals but a high markup on coffins, they can accomplish the same ends indirectly. They can sell individuals with inelastic demands ("Nothing's too good for my dear departed Joshua.") the $8,000 coffin (marked up from $2,000) at a $6,000 profit. They sell the $800 coffin (marked up from $200) for a $600 profit to individuals with elastic demands. ("Joshua always loved a bargain. Don't you have anything cheaper than a pine box? Maybe cardboard? He'd love that.")

By adding the markup to the coffin, the funeral home has charged the person with the inelastic demand $5,400 more for the funeral than it has charged the person with the elastic demand.

3. It shows how industries can protect their monopoly. By threatening to take away business from a trucking company that carried a competitor's coffins, the industry prevented the competitor firm from using that trucking company.

4. Finally it shows that despite obstacles, competition works. The competitive coffin firm is expanding.

A market environment fosters individuals who are trying to break into new markets. Where do they look? Not at the flower industry (where there's significant competition and a store on every block), but at the coffin industry (where there are high profits). Individuals looking for situations of high profits are the backbone of the competitive process.

Figuring out where economic reasoning fits into this article is much easier than with the previous article.

The article directly shows how competition works.

It shows how existing firms try to prevent competition through a variety of methods in an effort to protect their monopoly profit.

And finally it shows how potential profit leads new firms to try to figure out ways to break down those methods of protecting monopoly.

The studies presented here are but two of the millions of unfolding stories out there in the economy. Newspapers are an unending source of case studies. They report stories of monopoly and competition every day, showing how multidimensional competitive and monopolistic pressures are.

The competition and monopoly stories have no end. Both are continuous processes. Monopolies create competition. Then out of the competitive struggle monopolies emerge, only to be beaten down by competition.

Studying economics is also an unending process. The study doesn't stop with reading the textbook. By keeping your eyes and ears open, and following the economic news, you'll find that your understanding of how real-world markets work is deepened year after year.

COMPETITION AND STUDYING DYNAMIC ECONOMIC PROCESSES

CHAPTER SUMMARY

- The goals of real-world firms are many. Profit plays a role, but the actual goals depend upon the incentive structure embodied in the organizational structure of the firm.
- Competition limits the amount of X-inefficiency in a firm.
- The competitive process involves a continual fight between monopolization and competition.
- In a natural monopoly, because of economies of scale it is cheaper for one firm to produce a good than for two or more firms to produce it.

- Firms protect their monopolies by such means as advertising, lobbying, and producing products that are difficult for other firms to copy.
- Firms will spend money on monopolization until the marginal cost equals the marginal benefit.
- The current health care market is shaped by past events. Three options for health care reform are single payer, managed competition, and direct competition.
- Case studies provide insight into how economic theory relates to the real world.

KEY TERMS

corporate takeover (616)
cost shifting (624)
direct competition (627)
incentive-compatible contract (614)
individual self-selection bias (622)

lazy monopolist (615)
managed competition (626)
monitoring problem (614)
natural monopoly (619)
patent (618)

real-world competition (617)
reverse engineering (619)
single-payer plan (626)
X-inefficiency (615)

QUESTIONS FOR THOUGHT AND REVIEW

The number after each question represents the estimated degree of critical thinking required. (1 = almost none; 10 = deep thought.)

1. Are managers and high-level company officials paid high salaries because they're worth it to the firm, or because they're simply extracting profit from the company to give themselves? How would you tell whether you're correct? *(9)*

2. Some have argued that competition will eliminate X-inefficiency from firms. Will it? Why? *(7)*

3. Nonprofit colleges must be operating relatively efficiently. Otherwise for-profit colleges would develop and force existing colleges out of business. True or false? Why? *(9)*

4. If it were easier for demanders to collude than for suppliers to collude, there would often be shortages of goods. True or false? Why? *(9)*

5. If it were easier for demanders to collude than for suppliers to collude, the price of goods would be lower than the competitive price. True or false? Why? *(9)*

6. Monopolies are bad; patents give firms monopoly; therefore patents are bad. True or false? Why? *(7)*

7. In 1994, over 1,000 economists signed a petition opposing any health care plan that would require price controls. What was their likely reasoning? *(8)*

8. Natural monopolies should be broken up to improve competition. True or false? Why? *(6)*

9. Technically competent firms will succeed. True or false? Why? *(6)*

10. Would you expect the funeral home industry to be competitive? Why or why not? *(8)*

PROBLEMS AND EXERCISES

1. Econocompany is under investigation by the U.S. Department of Justice for violating antitrust laws. The government decides that Econocompany has a natural monopoly and that, if it is to keep its business, it must sell at a price equal to marginal cost. Econocompany says that it can't do that and hires you to explain to the government why it can't.
   a. You do so in reference to the following graph.
   b. What price would it charge if it were unregulated?
   c. What price would you advise that it should be allowed to change?

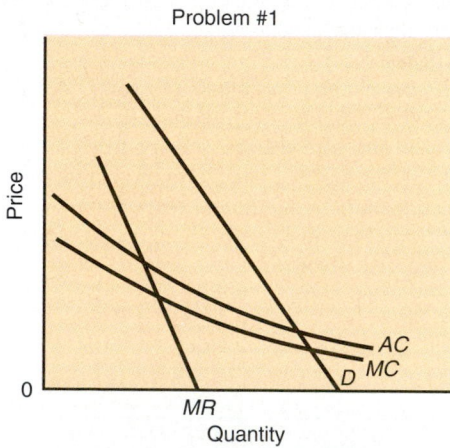

Problem #1

2. Demonstrate graphically the net gain to producers and the net loss to consumers if suppliers are able to restrict their output to Q_r in the following graph. Demonstrate the net deadweight loss to society.

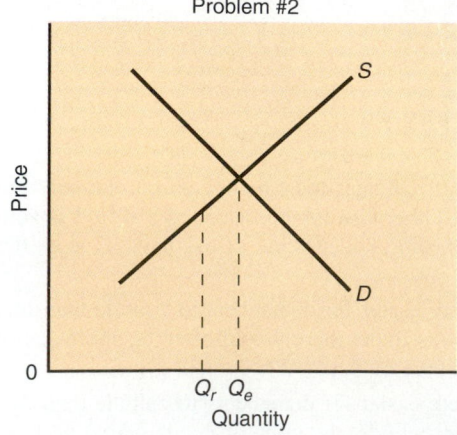

Problem #2

3. The title of an article in *The Wall Street Journal* was "Pricing of Products Is Still an Art, Often Having Little Link to Costs." In the article, the following cases were cited:
   - Vodka pricing: All vodkas are essentially indistinguishable—colorless, tasteless, and odorless—and the cost of producing vodka is independent of brand name, yet prices differ substantially.
   - Perfume: A $100 bottle of perfume may contain $4–$6 worth of ingredients.
   - Jeans and "alligator/animal" shirts: The "plain pocket" jeans and the Lacoste knockoffs often cost 40 percent less than the brand name items, yet the knockoffs are essentially identical to the brand name items.
   a. Discuss whether these differences undermine economists' analysis of pricing.
   b. What do each of these examples likely imply about fixed costs and variable costs?
   c. What do they likely imply about costs of production versus costs of selling?
   d. As what type of market would you characterize each of above examples?

4. In the Oregon health care plan for rationing Medicaid expenditures, therapy to slow the progression of AIDS and treatment for brain cancer were covered, while treatment for infectious mononucleosis and liver transplants for people with liver cancer were not covered.
   a. What criteria do you think were used to determine what was covered and what was not covered?
   b. Should an economist oppose the Oregon plan because it involves rationing?
   c. How does the rationing that occurs in the market differ from the rationing that occurs in the Oregon plan?

5. Airlines and hotels have many frequent flier and frequent visitor programs in which individuals who fly the airline or stay at the hotel receive bonuses that are the equivalent of discounts.
   a. Give two reasons why these companies have such programs rather than simply offer lower prices.
   b. Can you give other examples of such programs?
   c. What is a likely reason why firms don't monitor these programs?
   d. Should the benefits of these programs be taxable?

ANSWERS TO MARGIN QUESTIONS

1. Most economists are concerned about third-party payment systems because of the problems of monitoring. It is the demanders who have the strongest incentive to make sure that they are getting value for their money. Any third-party payment system reduces the demanders' vigilance and therefore puts less pressure on holding costs down. *(615)*

2. A manager does not have the same incentive to hold costs down as an owner does because when an owner holds costs down, the owner's profits are increased, but when a manager holds costs down, the increased profits accrue to the owner, not the manager. Thus the manager has less direct motivation to hold costs down than an owner does. This is especially true if the costs being held down are the manager's perks and pay. *(616)*

3. The threat of a corporate takeover provides competitive pressures on firms because it creates the possibility of the managers being replaced and losing all their perks and above-market-equilibrium pay. *(616)*

4. Most agricultural markets are not perfectly competitive because the gains from moving away from competitive markets are fairly large and, for small deviations from competitive markets, the costs are fairly small to those suppliers and demanders who are kept out. This can be seen in the graph below. If suppliers 0L got together, and limited supply to L, they could push the price up to P_L and could gain the rectangle A for themselves. Suppliers and demanders who are kept out of the market lose triangles B and C respectively, which, in the diagram, are not only each smaller than A, but also B and C combined are smaller than A. Of course, the area A is lost to the demanders, but the costs of organizing those demanders to fight and protect competition are often prohibitively large. *(617)*

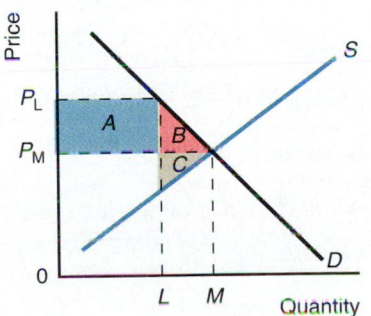

5. As demand becomes more elastic, suppliers gain less by monopolizing and therefore have a lesser desire to monopolize. (Area A, seen in the graph for the answer to question 4, becomes smaller.) *(618)*

6. The problem with cost-based regulation that sets prices relative to costs is that this removes the incentive for firms to hold down costs and can lead to X-inefficiency. While, in theory, regulators could scrutinize every cost, in practice that is impossible—it would have to create a regulatory board duplicating the work that a firm facing direct market pressure undertakes in its normal activities. *(620)*

7. Whenever the user of a service is separated from the payer for the service, there is a monitoring problem. In health care that separation is extreme, and thus the monitoring problem can go a long way toward explaining the problems in the current system. *(623)*

8. No. Economic theory simply tells us the implications of various solutions. It tells us that some rationing is necessary in whatever system we choose if costs are to be limited, and it directs us to consider the implications of the alternative methods of rationing. *(628)*

9. Amgen operates in either a monopolistic or oligopolistic market structure. It is monopolistic if the market being described is the market for EPO. It is oligopolistic if the market being described is broader and includes substitutes for EPO. In the court cases discussed in the case study, Amgen is attempting to solidify its monopolistic position. *(631)*

10. False. High profits on coffins do not necessarily show that the funeral market is not highly competitive, as the funeral homes claim. The markup they give to coffins can include large portions of their overhead costs as a way of price-discriminating among buyers. While high profits do not necessarily show that the funeral market is not highly competitive, those high profits are highly suggestive that it is not. The case study that describes actions of funeral homes to protect their monopoly and drive out the independent coffin firm suggests that the funeral market is not highly competitive, but it is the broader information, not simply the high profits on coffins, that allows one to reach that conclusion. *(633)*

29

The Regulation of Markets
Antitrust and Industrial Policies

We have always known that heedless self-interest was bad morals; we now know that it is bad economics.

~Franklin Delano Roosevelt

After reading this chapter, you should be able to:

1 Explain the difference between the structure and the performance methods of judging competition.

2 Give a brief history of U.S. antitrust policy.

3 State the resolution of the IBM and AT&T antitrust cases.

4 Differentiate among horizontal, vertical, and conglomerate mergers.

5 List five reasons why unrelated firms would want to merge.

6 Define the term *industrial policy*.

7 Give two arguments for and two against an activist industrial policy.

Antitrust policy is the government's policy toward the competitive process. It's the government's rulebook for carrying out its role as referee.[1] In volleyball, for instance, such a rulebook would answer such questions as: When should a foul be called? When has a person caught and thrown rather than hit the ball over the net? In business a referee is needed for such questions as: When can two companies merge? What competitive practices are legal? When is a company too big? To what extent is it fair for two companies to coordinate their pricing policies? When is a market sufficiently competitive or too monopolistic?

Antitrust policy   Government's policy toward the competitive process.

The United States has seen wide swings in economists' prescriptions concerning such questions, depending on which of the two views of competition has held sway. The two competing views are:

1. **Judgment by performance:** We should judge the competitiveness of markets by the *performance* (behavior) of firms in that market.
2. **Judgment by structure:** We should judge the competitiveness of markets by the *structure* of the industry.

1 Judgment by performance is the view that competitiveness of a market should be judged by the behavior of firms in that market; judgment by structure is the view that competitiveness of a market should be judged by the structure of the market.

Both views can be defended, but in refereeing the actions of businesses government can use only one of the two at any given time.

To show how the U.S. government has applied these two views of competition in refereeing the economy, this chapter considers government's application of antitrust laws to regulate business. It then considers how recent structural changes in the economy are altering the government's role as economic referee.

HISTORY OF U.S. ANTITRUST LAWS

Although U.S. ideology has always been strongly in favor of laissez-faire and government noninvolvement in business, there has simultaneously been a populist (pro-people) sensibility which fears bigness and monopoly. These fears of bigness and monopoly burst forth in the late 1800s as many firms were merging or organizing together to form trusts or cartels. As I stated two chapters ago, a trust or cartel is a combination of firms in which the firms haven't actually merged, but nonetheless act essentially as a single entity. A trust sets common prices and governs the output of individual member firms. A trust can, and often does, act like a monopolist.

In the 1870s and 1880s, trusts were forming in a number of industries, including railroads, steel, tobacco, and oil. Some of these trusts' actions are typified by John D. Rockefeller's Standard Oil. Standard Oil demanded that railroads pay it kickbacks on freight rates. These payments allowed Standard Oil to set lower prices for its products than other companies which had to pay the railroads' full price on freight. Standard Oil thus could sell at lower prices than its competitors.

2 Public outrage at the formation and activities of trusts such as Standard Oil led to the passage of the Sherman Act, the Clayton Act, and the Federal Trade Commission Act.

If prices had remained low, this would have had a positive effect on consumers and a negative effect on Standard Oil's competitors. But prices didn't remain low. By 1882, Standard Oil had driven many of its competitors out of business, and the writing was on the wall for those competitors who remained. At that time, Standard Oil created a trust and "invited" its few surviving competitors to join. Then Standard Oil Trust used the monopoly power it had gained to close down refineries, raise prices, and limit the production of oil. The price of oil rose from a competitive level to a monopolistic level, and the consumer, as well as Standard Oil's competitors, ended up suffering.

The Sherman Antitrust Act

Public outrage against trusts like Standard Oil's was high. The organizers of the trusts were widely known as *robber barons* because of their exploitation of natural resources and their other unethical behavior. The trusts were seen as making enormous profits, preventing competition, and, in general, bullying everyone in sight. In response the U.S. government passed the **Sherman Antitrust Act** of 1890.

Sherman Antitrust Act   Law passed by the U.S. Congress in 1890 to attempt to regulate the competitive process.

---

[1] As discussed earlier, the government has two roles: It's an actor, but it's also a referee.

ADDED DIMENSION

SIMPLE TOOLS AND COMPLICATED PROBLEMS

I hope the previous chapters have conveyed the complexity of real-world problems and the simplicity of the tools and concepts economists use to deal with those problems. Some of my colleagues advise me against presenting the tools and the reality in such stark contrast. They argue, "No reasonable person will ever knowingly grapple with real-world problems if he or she recognizes the disparity between the simplicity of our tools and the complexity of reality. Give the students something that will make them feel more powerful."

That's not my way. I argue that our tools, while simple, are strong if they're used conceptually and aren't pushed to answer questions they can't answer. There's nothing wrong with studying a problem and arriving at the conclusion "It depends." The world would be a better place if more people recognized that the most appropriate answer to many economic policy questions is "It depends."

My debate with my academic colleagues will continue, probably indefinitely, but I must concede one point to them: The last thing politicians want to hear from their economic advisors is "It depends." If all you have to say to politicians is "It depends," you might as well not say anything. Other far less reasonable advisors (like lawyers and members of special interest groups) present politicians with arguments based on weaker tools (in my view), but their advice tends to be specific—to tell the politicians "Do this" or "Do that." They recognize that policy decisions must be made by politicians who don't have the background or time to weigh the competing arguments and decide on their own. Politicians want their economic advisors not only to provide them with objective analysis but also to weigh the evidence and tell them what to do, given the economists' knowledge of their (the politicians') value judgments. Most politicians would agree with Harry Truman, who wanted only one-armed economists—those who cannot say, "On the one hand, . . . but on the other hand . . ."

Q–1: What are the two provisions of the Sherman Antitrust Act?

The Sherman Act is broad and sweeping, but vague.

The Sherman Act contained two main sections:

Section 1: Every contract, combination in the form of trust or otherwise, or conspiracy in restraint of trade or commerce among the several States, or with foreign nations, is hereby declared to be illegal. . . .

Section 2: Every person who shall monopolize, or attempt to monopolize, or combine or conspire with any other person or persons, to monopolize any part of the trade or commerce among the several States, or with foreign nations, shall be deemed guilty of a misdemeanor, and, on conviction thereof, shall be punished by a fine not exceeding five thousand dollars, or by imprisonment not exceeding one year, or by both said punishments, in the discretion of the court.

The Sherman Act was meant to be as sweeping and broad as its language sounds. After all, it was passed in response to a public outcry against trusts. But if you look at it carefully, in some respects it is vague and weak. For example, offenses under Section 2 were only misdemeanors, not felonies.[2] It's unclear what constitutes "restraint of trade." Moreover, although the act prohibits monopolization, it does not explicitly prohibit monopolies. In short, with the Sherman Act Congress passed the buck to the courts, letting them decide U.S. antitrust policy.[3]

The following story summarizes the courts' role in antitrust policy. Three umpires are describing their job. The youngest of the three says, "I call them as I see them." The middle-aged umpire says, "No, that's not what an umpire does. An umpire calls them the way they are." The senior umpire says, "You're both wrong. They're nothing until I call them." And that's how it is with the courts and monopoly. Whether a firm is behaving monopolistically isn't known until the court makes its decision.

As Congress was passing the Sherman Act, economists too were debating the implications of trusts and whether it was in the public interest to restrict them. Part of

---

[2] Under federal law, a misdemeanor is any misconduct punishable by only a fine or by a jail sentence of a year or less. A felony requires a sentence of more than a year.

[3] Subsequent amendments to the Sherman Act have strengthened it. For example, offenses under Section 2 are now felonies, not misdemeanors.

the debate concerned whether the mergers reflected technological changes in production and expanding transportation systems which made increased economies of scale more important (in which case restricting trusts might not be in the public interest since doing so might prevent taking advantage of economies of scale), or whether trusts simply represented attempts at monopolization to restrict output and generate monopoly profits (in which case restricting trusts would more likely be in the public interest since doing so would reduce monopoly).

A second part of the debate concerned how fast economic forces would operate and how fragile competition was. Some economists argued that competition was strong and that it would limit the profit trusts and monopolies made and force them to charge the competitive price (in which case restricting trusts might not be in the public interest). These economists were reflecting the performance viewpoint—that competition should be relied on to break down the monopolies. They argued that bigness doesn't imply the absence of market competition and that the government's role should merely be to make sure that no significant barriers to entry to new firms are created.

Other economists, reflecting the structure viewpoint, argued that competition was fragile and that it wouldn't operate unless there were a large number of small firms. They argued that trusts and monopolies (even if they don't charge monopolistic prices) are bad, that the trusts should be broken up by government, and that laws should not allow new monopolies or trusts to be formed. However the debate was for the courts, not economists, to settle.

In 1911, the U.S. Supreme Court established its interpretation of the Sherman Act by handing down its opinions in cases involving Standard Oil and the American Tobacco Company. The Court determined that both companies were structural monopolies; each company controlled 90 percent of its market. However, the Court decided that the monopolistic structure of the markets did not violate the Sherman Antitrust Act. A company's violation of the act was determined not by the structure of the industry but by the particular firm's performance—that is, by whether or not the firm engaged in "unfair business practices." This judgment by performance, not judgment by structure, is often called the *abuse theory* because a firm is legally considered a monopoly only if it commits monopolistic abuses.

In these two cases the distinction was academic. Both Standard Oil and American Tobacco were judged guilty (very guilty) of unfair business practices and were broken up. But the academic distinction played an important role in determining the industrial structure of the United States. It allowed structural monopolies to continue to exist, but it prohibited them from using certain monopolistic practices, such as demanding kickbacks.

In 1920, this structure/performance distinction was important in a case involving U.S. Steel. Here the Supreme Court ruled that, while U.S. Steel was a structural monopoly, it was not a monopoly in performance. That is, the firm had not used unfair business practices to become a monopolist and thus was not in violation of antitrust law. U.S. Steel was not required to break up into a group of smaller companies as Standard Oil had been.

In an attempt to give more guidance to the courts and to provide for more vigorous enforcement of the antitrust provisions, in 1914 Congress passed the Clayton Antitrust Act and the Federal Trade Commission Act.

The **Clayton Antitrust Act** declared that four specific monopolistic practices were illegal when their effect was to lessen competition:

1. Price discrimination, that is, selling identical goods to different customers at different prices.
2. Tie-in contracts in which the buyer must agree to deal exclusively with one seller and not to purchase goods from competing sellers.
3. Interlocking directorships in which memberships of boards of directors of two or more firms are almost identical.

The Standard Oil and American Tobacco Cases: Judging Market Competitiveness by Performance

Q-2: What was the resolution of the Standard Oil case?

The Clayton Act and the Federal Trade Commission Act

Clayton Antitrust Act   Law passed by the U.S. Congress in 1914 making four specific monopolistic practices illegal.

4. Buying stock in a competitor's company when the purpose of buying that stock is to reduce competition.

In establishing the Federal Trade Commission (FTC) in 1914, Congress gave it the power to regulate competition and police markets. The **Federal Trade Commission Act** made it illegal for firms to use "unfair methods of competition" and to engage in "unfair or deceptive acts or practices," whether or not those actions had any impact on competition. Other than that broad mandate, Congress gave the FTC little direction as to what rules it was to use to regulate trade and police markets. As a result, for more than 20 years the commission was rather ineffective. In 1938, however, it was given the job of preventing false and deceptive advertising, which remains one of its primary roles.

Federal Trade Commission Act Law passed by the U.S. Congress in 1914 making it illegal for firms to engage in certain unfair or deceptive practices.

The ALCOA Case: Judging Market Competitiveness by Structure

Q–3: What was the resolution of the ALCOA case?

Judgment by performance was the primary criterion governing U.S. antitrust policy until 1945, when the U.S. courts changed their interpretation of the law. This occurred in the ALCOA (Aluminum Company of America) case in 1945.

In the ALCOA case, the company was found guilty of violating the antitrust statutes even though the Court did not rule that ALCOA had been guilty of unfair practices. What ALCOA had done was to use its knowledge of the market to expand its capacity before any competitors had a chance to enter the market. In addition, it had kept its prices low to prevent potential entry by competitors. It showed no signs of exploiting its monopoly power to charge high prices or to force competing firms out of business. Thus, on performance standards, it was not violating the law. But in the ALCOA case, the structure of the market, not the company's performance, was used to determine whether ALCOA was in violation of antitrust law.

Judging Markets by Structure and Performance: The Reality

An important reason supporting the structure criterion is practicality.

Judgment by structure seems unfair on a gut level. After all, in economics the purpose of competition is to motivate firms to produce better goods than their competitors are producing, and to do so at lower cost. If a firm is competing so successfully that all the other firms leave the industry, the successful firm will be a monopolist, and on the basis of judgment by structure will be guilty of antitrust violations. Under the judgment-by-structure criterion, a firm is breaking the law if it does what it's supposed to be doing: producing the best product it can at the lowest possible cost.

Supporters of the judgment-by-structure criterion recognize this problem, but they nonetheless favor the structure criterion. An important reason for this is practicality.

Contextual Judgments and the Capabilities of the Courts Judgment by performance requires that each action of a firm must be analyzed on a case-by-case basis. Doing that is enormously time-consuming and expensive. In some interpretations, actions of a firm might be considered appropriate competitive behavior; in other interpretations, the same actions might be considered inappropriate. For example, say that an automobile company requires that in order for its warranty to hold, owners of its warranted vehicles must use only the company's parts and service centers. Is this requirement of the automobile company to create a monopoly position for its parts and service center divisions or to ensure proper maintenance? The answer depends on the context of the action.

But judging each case contextually is beyond the courts' capabilities. There are so many firms and so many actions that the courts can't judge all industries on their performance. They must devise a way to limit the issues they look at. In order to apply the performance criteria reasonably, the Supreme Court must set out certain guidelines to tell firms in what situations the Court will take a closer look at their performance. Because the available information concerns structure, those guidelines inevitably refer to market structure, even though it is firms' performance that will ultimately be judged. So even though judging by structure may have problems, it is necessary.

It's very much like the procedure college admissions offices use in deciding which applicants to accept. They judge applicants on their "total performance," not just on their quantitative scores on standardized tests. However, they often use a

It isn't only the federal government that has laws on competition. States have a variety of laws that govern competitive practices. One such state law is Arkansas's Unfair Practices Act, which prohibits selling, or advertising for sale, items below cost "for the purpose of injuring competitors and destroying competition." In the early 1990s, three Arkansas pharmacies sued Wal-Mart for violating this law by selling its goods at "too low" a price. The background of the case is the following.

Wal-Mart had been expanding aggressively throughout the United States in the 1980s and early 1990s, reaching a total of about 2,500 stores in 1994. It does not deny that it, like many other stores, sells some goods at below cost. But it argues that when it sells below cost it does not do so to "destroy competition" or "injure competitors," but, rather, to maintain low prices to consumers. It claims that its pricing policies promote, not destroy, competition.

In principle, most economists agree with Wal-Mart; new competition, by its very nature, hurts existing businesses—that's the way the market competitive process works. Those who don't sell for the lowest price lose, and those who sell for the lowest price gain. But most economists also recognize that Wal-Mart's brand of competition can have externalities affecting the social fabric of small town economies. A new Wal-Mart store can undermine the town centers, and replace them with commercial sprawl on the outskirts of these towns. Whether these externalities are reason to limit Wal-Mart's aggressive pricing policies is a debatable question.

Wal-Mart lost its suit in Arkansas; it is, however, appealing. But, since many states have laws similar to those of Arkansas, even if the company wins its appeal, it is likely that some time in the 1990s a suit challenging Wal-Mart's aggressive pricing policies will be successful. The very threat of these state suits therefore will likely discourage Wal-Mart from following quite as aggressive a pricing policy as it otherwise would have.

certain quantitative score as a cutoff point in order to reduce applications to a manageable number. Applicants below the cutoff point are automatically rejected; applicants above it are considered one by one.

Another argument in favor of judging competitiveness by structure is that structure can be a predictor of future performance. Advocates of the structure criterion argue that a monopolist may be pricing low now, but it is, after all, a monopolist, and it won't price low in the future. The low price will eliminate competition now, but once the competition is gone, the firm will not be able to resist the temptation to use its monopoly power.

Determining the Relevant Market and Industry   Supporters of the performance criterion admit that this standard has problems, but they point out that the structure criterion also has problems. As you saw in an earlier chapter, it's difficult to determine the relevant market (local, national, or international) and the relevant industry (two-digit or four-digit SIC code) necessary to identify the structural competitiveness of any industry.

Choosing the relevant market when evaluating competitiveness is difficult to do.

Such questions have been the center of many antitrust court cases. For example, in the ALCOA case, the company argued that metals such as copper and steel were interchangeable with aluminum, and that therefore the relevant industry to consider was the metals industry. If the Court had chosen the U.S. metals industry, and not the aluminum industry, as the relevant industry, ALCOA wouldn't have been found to have a monopoly. The Court decided, however, that aluminum had sufficiently unique properties to constitute its own market. Since it determined that ALCOA had 90 percent of the aluminum market, ALCOA was declared a monopoly and was broken up.

The arguments in the Du Pont case (1956) again centered around the definition of *industry*. There the Supreme Court found that Du Pont was innocent of monopolizing the production of cellophane even though Du Pont was the only producer of cellophane. The Court reasoned that the relevant industry was not the cellophane industry

Q-4: What was the resolution of the Du Pont case?

but, rather, the flexible wrap industry, which also included aluminum foil and wax paper. Du Pont did not have a monopoly of the flexible wrap industry and thus, the Court said, was not in violation of the antitrust laws.

Similar ambiguities exist with the decision about the relevant market. In the Pabst Brewing case (1966), the definition of the market played a key role. Pabst wanted to merge with the Blatz Brewing Company. On a national scale, both companies were relatively small, accounting together for about 4.5 percent of beer sales in the United States as a whole. Pabst argued that the United States was the relevant market. The Court, however, decided that Wisconsin, where Pabst had its headquarters, was the relevant market, and since the two firms held a 24 percent share of that market, the merger was not allowed.

What should one make of this debate? The bottom line is that both structure and performance criteria have ambiguities, and in the real world there are no definitive criteria for judging whether a firm has violated the antitrust statutes. A firm isn't at fault or in the clear until the courts make the call.

Both structure and performance criteria have ambiguities, and in the real world there are no definitive criteria for judging whether a firm has violated the antitrust statutes.

Recent Antitrust Cases

Two important cases were decided in the 1980s, and these cases have significantly influenced perceptions of antitrust in the 1990s. Thus, we'll consider them in a bit more detail than the older cases to provide a sense of how antitrust law affects companies today. One case involved IBM; the other involved AT&T.

The IBM Case   In 1969, the U.S. Department of Justice sued IBM for violating the antitrust laws. The department argued that the company had a 72-percent share of the general-purpose electronic digital computing industry, and that it had acquired that market share because of unfair business practices such as bundling of hardware, software, and maintenance services at a single price (that is, requiring customers to buy all three together). If you wanted IBM equipment (hardware), you also had to take IBM service and software whether you wanted them or not. When you bought an IBM you bought everything, so other companies had little chance to compete. Moreover, the department argued that IBM constantly redesigned its computers, making it impossible for other companies to keep up and compete fairly on the sale of any IBM mainframe–compatible item.

IBM argued that the relevant market was broader, that it included all types of computers such as military computers, programmable calculators, and other information-processing products. It further claimed that its so-called unfair practices were simply a reflection of efficient computer technology. Fast-moving technological developments required it to continually redesign its products merely to provide its customers with the latest, best equipment. And, it said, the only way to provide the best level of service to its customers was to include its maintenance services in the price of its products.

The Resolution   The case dragged on for 13 years. IBM spent over $100 million on its defense. The company constructed an entire building just to house the documents in the case. The case never went to court. In January 1982, the government withdrew its lawsuit for three reasons:

3A The IBM case was dropped by the United States, but the prosecution likely led to IBM's problems in the 1990s. It won but it also lost.

1. In the 13 years since the court case had been brought, significant competition had developed in certain parts of the computer industry—specifically, the personal computer part. Apple, DEC, and others became serious competitors. Moreover a number of Japanese companies were making major inroads into the market. This strengthened IBM's contention about which was the relevant market.

Q–5: What was the resolution of the IBM case?

2. In the 13 years since the case had been brought, the political climate had changed considerably. When the lawsuit had been started, Richard Nixon was president of the United States. By 1982, Ronald Reagan was president and he maintained a hands-off attitude toward antitrust questions. His appointees interpreted antitrust laws as less restrictive to business than their predecessors had.

3. In the 13 years since the case had been brought, the U.S. view of antitrust had changed from a U.S.-oriented view to an international view. Japanese firms were beating many U.S. firms in developing new products and in producing existing products cheaper and better.

    Some economists argued that one of the reasons for that success was the joint research and support that the Japanese government gave private firms through **MITI** (the Ministry of International Trade and Industry), a government organization which helps businesses coordinate policies. Guided by MITI, Japanese firms can form cartels and effectively coordinate their policies, thus developing international markets and increasing international market share. In contrast, these economists argued, U.S. firms have been shackled by U.S. antitrust policy. IBM is one of the few U.S. companies that was internationally successful, and here was the U.S. government prosecuting it for its success.

MITI A Japanese government organization that helps businesses coordinate policies.

IBM may have won the antitrust case against it, but in doing so, it may have lost the war. Here's why.

About the same time as the case was at its height, IBM was negotiating with a young upstart company about an operating system for a small part of its market—the PC (personal computer) market—which was just coming out. Bill Gates, the president of the young company, offered to sell its DOS (Disk Operating System) to IBM for $75,000, but IBM refused to buy it, in part because IBM was making the argument in court that it didn't control the PC portion of the market. To have bought DOS would have given IBM control over the PC market, and would have made a court-ordered breakup of IBM more likely. Instead, IBM left Bill Gates to sell DOS to IBM and everyone else, while IBM concentrated on mainframe computers.

In the early 1990s, the cost of that decision was clear. The mainframe market was dying, and IBM was hemorrhaging losses. Meanwhile, Bill Gates had become a multibillionaire, and his company—Microsoft—had become a controlling force in the PC market. Now the tables were turned and in 1994 Microsoft entered into a consent decree with the U.S. government, agreeing to make it easier for other firms, such as IBM, to compete with it.

It will never be known how important the overhang of the antitrust suit was to IBM's lack of vision about the changing market, but it is quite possible that the antitrust suit played a role in the decline of IBM in the 1990s.

The AT&T Case The other major antitrust case of the 1980s, the AT&T case, demonstrates another aspect of U.S. antitrust policy and shows how technological change plays an important role in competition and questions of industrial market structure.

Up until 1982, AT&T was what was called a *regulated monopoly*. It had the exclusive right to provide telephone service in the United States. AT&T controlled most of the telecommunications market: long-distance and local telephone service, and the production of telephones themselves as well as other communications equipment.

Why was it given that right? Because it was felt that economies of scale made supplying telephone service a **natural monopoly** (an industry in which significant economies of scale make the existence of more than one firm inefficient). Telephone service required lines to be brought into every house; those lines had to be buried underground or strung overhead on poles and connected to all other houses. It made little sense to have seven or eight companies stringing competing lines. Moreover a decision was made that universal telephone service was desired, and AT&T was required to provide universal service. Unregulated companies likely would have practiced *cream skimming* (providing service to low-cost areas and avoiding high-cost areas).

Natural monopoly An industry in which significant economies of scale make the existence of more than one firm inefficient.

In return for its monopoly, AT&T was subjected to regulatory control by the Federal Communications Commission and by state utility commissions. This government regulation was designed to limit the company's profit to a fair level and prevent it from abusing its monopoly.

Under AT&T's monopoly, phone service in the United States was the best and cheapest in the world, although some believed it could and should have been even cheaper. Some economists argued that AT&T's guarantee of a "fair" return on its investment gave it a strong incentive to act as a lazy monopolist and to invest heavily, thereby increasing costs. If a company knows it can pass on its costs to customers (and add on a profit margin as well), it has little incentive to hold down costs. But even if service was more expensive than it needed to be, on the whole most agreed that the system worked well.

In the 1970s, however, technological changes fundamentally altered the nature of the long-distance telephone industry. The development of satellite transmission and fiber optics made cable connections obsolete, so long-distance telephone service was no longer a natural monopoly. In fact, significant competition began to develop, and AT&T's new competitors claimed that they weren't being allowed reasonable access to the AT&T-controlled local telephone network. AT&T charged competing firms high fees for access to all their local lines—fees that competitors argued were unfair.

The issue was complicated by the fact that the regulatory commissions, in an attempt to see that everyone had low-cost local service, had set local charges low and long-distance rates high. As long as AT&T controlled both local and long-distance calling, AT&T didn't worry about this. But when competitors began to undercharge AT&T on long-distance service, the rate-setting system (which implicitly subsidized local service with AT&T's long-distance profits) concerned AT&T greatly. AT&T's high access charges were an attempt to see that the competitors used some of their own profits to help subsidize local rates.

As a result of these claims and counterclaims, the Department of Justice introduced an antitrust suit against AT&T in 1978, alleging that potential competitors were not being allowed reasonable access to AT&T's local telephone network. The case had merit, but so did AT&T's defense: that the problem was in the setting of rates for local and long-distance calls. As is now usual for any contested antitrust case, the case went on and on, and no conclusion was in sight.

The Resolution   Then, in January 1982 (on the same day the IBM case ended), AT&T and the Department of Justice announced that they had settled the case and that AT&T had agreed to be broken up. Specifically, AT&T agreed that by January 1, 1984, it would divest itself of 22 local operating companies (known as the *Baby Bells*) which accounted for $87 billion of AT&T's $136 billion in assets. Exhibit 1 shows the structure of AT&T before and after divestiture. You can see that AT&T ("Ma Bell") kept its long-distance telephone service, its manufacturing division (the Western Electric Company), and its research facilities (Bell Laboratories). In return, AT&T was subject to far less regulation than before. After the settlement, AT&T could enter any unregulated business it desired, such as data transmission and computers.

The result of this settlement was an enormous upheaval in the telephone industry. Local rates for phone service went up twofold or even threefold, while long-distance rates fell substantially. Two major competitors, MCI and Sprint, developed, and competition for long-distance business became frenzied. Because individual customers were now responsible for supplying their own phones, the telephone supply industry became highly competitive as cheap phones flooded the market.

AT&T may have lost the antitrust case against it, but it also may have won the war, at least temporarily. With its new-found freedom from regulation, it quickly entered into the competitive fray in a variety of industries. Its entry into the personal computer market didn't fare well, but it did much better in the broader information flow industry. It developed technology that could be used for two-way information transmittal and, ironically, became a potential competitor of cable TV monopolies, since its fiber optic networks could be used to transmit TV programs.

In 1993, AT&T expanded beyond fiber optic networks, proposing a merger with McCaw Cellular Communications. If allowed by the government, this merger will create a company that has the ability to provide a direct communications system with every household with low-cost wireless service, thereby giving it the ability to become

Q–6: What was the resolution of the AT&T case?

3B The AT&T case was settled by AT&T agreeing to be split up into regional companies handling local service, and AT&T itself competing in the long-distance market.

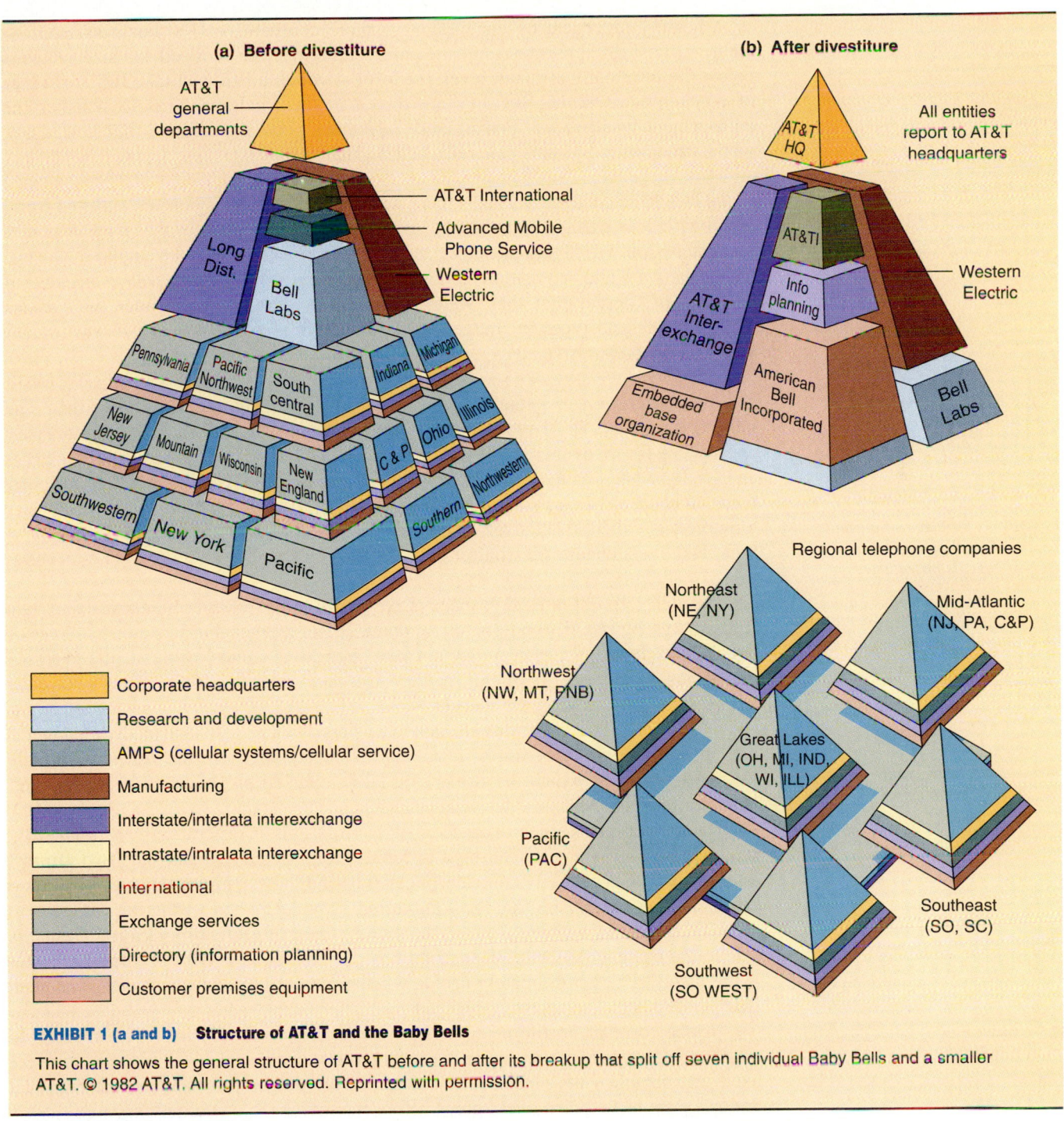

(a) Before divestiture

AT&T general departments

AT&T International

Advanced Mobile Phone Service

Western Electric

Long Dist.

Bell Labs

Pennsylvania / Pacific Northwest / South central / Indiana / Michigan

New Jersey / Mountain / Wisconsin / New England / C & P / Ohio / Illinois

Southwestern / New York / Pacific / Southern / Northwestern

(b) After divestiture

AT&T HQ

All entities report to AT&T headquarters

AT&TI

Info planning

Western Electric

AT&T Inter-exchange

American Bell Incorporated

Bell Labs

Embedded base organization

Regional telephone companies

Northeast (NE, NY)

Mid-Atlantic (NJ, PA, C&P)

Northwest (NW, MT, PNB)

Great Lakes (OH, MI, IND, WI, ILL)

Pacific (PAC)

Southeast (SO, SC)

Southwest (SO WEST)

Legend:
- Corporate headquarters
- Research and development
- AMPS (cellular systems/cellular service)
- Manufacturing
- Interstate/interlata interexchange
- Intrastate/intralata interexchange
- International
- Exchange services
- Directory (information planning)
- Customer premises equipment

EXHIBIT 1 (a and b)   Structure of AT&T and the Baby Bells

This chart shows the general structure of AT&T before and after its breakup that split off seven individual Baby Bells and a smaller AT&T. © 1982 AT&T. All rights reserved. Reprinted with permission.

direct competitors with the still-regulated Baby Bells, who had inherited the AT&T monopoly rights. Concern about that competition led the Baby Bells to complain about the merger, and to push the Justice Department to block or place restrictions on the merger. The legal maneuvering on this merger may match that of the earlier case and continue through the 1990s.

Whether AT&T will do all the things that the merger, if approved, will give it the ability to do is unclear, but it seems that in the mid-1990s AT&T may be well-positioned, perhaps because of the antitrust case which led to its breakup.

Economic scholars' overall assessment of antitrust policy is mixed. In certain cases, such as the IBM case, most agree that antitrust prosecution went too far. But most believe that other decisions (as in the 1911 Standard Oil and American Tobacco cases)

Assessment of Antitrust Policy

set a healthy precedent by encouraging a more competitive U.S. business environment. Almost all agree that antitrust enforcement has not reduced the size of firms below the minimally efficient level, the level at which a firm can take full advantage of economies of scale. But they are mixed in their judgments as to whether the enforcement was needed. Performance advocates generally believe that it was not, while structural advocates generally believe that it was.

Economists' judgment on antitrust is mixed.

In the late 1980s and early 1990s, there was not a lot of activity on the antitrust front, but nonetheless changes in industrial structure were prominent in the news. Much of that discussion was about takeovers and acquisitions of one firm by another. Most of these takeovers and acquisitions did not violate current U.S. antitrust laws because of the type of merger that they were. Thus, it's important to consider the various subcategories and types of mergers that are possible in order to put recent merger activity into perspective.

MERGERS, ACQUISITIONS, AND TAKEOVERS

Acquisitions and Takeovers

Merger   The act of combining two firms.

The term **merger** is a general term meaning the act of combining two firms. The picture it conveys is of two firms combining to form one firm. That picture isn't appropriate for many mergers. For example, often the firm buying another company is essentially what's called a *shell corporation,* which exists primarily to buy up other firms. When a shell corporation buys another firm, the combination, while technically a merger, is called a **takeover** to emphasize that little true merging is taking place. Such takeovers change the control over the firm, but do not affect market concentration.

Takeover   Purchase of a firm by another firm that then takes direct control over its operations.

Acquisition   A company buys another company; the buyer has indirect control of the resulting venture, but does not necessarily exercise direct control

Another term often used in place of *merger* is *acquisition.* In an **acquisition,** two firms merge by one firm buying out another. It is a merger, but it is not a merger of equals, and the acquiring firm may not take over direct control of the acquired firm's operations. In a merger of equals, neither firm takes over the other, and it's not clear who'll be in charge after the merger.

Hostile takeover   A merger in which one company buys another that does not want to be bought.

Takeovers and acquisitions are said to be *friendly* or *hostile.* A friendly takeover is one in which one corporation is willing to be acquired by the other. A **hostile takeover** is one in which the firm being taken over doesn't want to be taken over. How can that happen?

Remember our earlier discussion of corporations. Corporations are owned by stockholders, but are managed by a different group of individuals. The two groups' interests do not necessarily coincide. When it is said that a corporation doesn't want to be taken over, that means that the corporation's managers don't want the company to be taken over. In a hostile takeover, the management of each corporation presents its side to the shareholders of both corporations. The shareholders of the corporation that is the takeover target ultimately decide whether or not to sell their shares. If enough shareholders sell, the takeover succeeds.

In one form of hostile takeover (known as *double Pac Man*), two firms try to swallow each other, or alternatively the target of a hostile takeover bid tries to make itself unpalatable—the *poison pill* strategy. In the poison pill strategy, the firm that doesn't want to be taken over agrees before the merger to do something stupid if it's taken over so that this firm is no longer desirable to potential taking-over firms.

For example, say that Stubborn, Inc., doesn't want to be taken over. So Stubborn borrows billions of dollars and uses that money to buy some company worth about half what Stubborn pays for it. That's a stupid move. After that move, Stubborn isn't a desirable firm to be taken over. (So it wasn't so stupid, right?) Of course, after Stubborn isn't taken over, it's stuck with the company it paid too much for, and it's also stuck with the interest it has to pay on the multibillion dollar loan it took out. Stubborn has provided itself with a poison pill to keep invaders away, but it has to live with the poison pill itself. (So maybe it was a stupid move after all.)

In other cases, the takeover company doesn't really want to take over the other company. Instead, it's hoping for *greenmail* (a payment from the potential victim to halt the takeover bid).

All this financial gamesmanship has led some to believe that the government should enact laws restricting takeovers, not because of their effect on concentration

ADDED DIMENSION

WHITE KNIGHTS AND GOLDEN PARACHUTES

The specific nature of a merger is of interest to people working for the corporations involved. It determines whether employees will move up or down in the corporate pecking order, or even whether they'll keep their jobs at all. When a firm is threatened by a hostile takeover, top management is likely to hunt for another firm, a friendly one that will be a "white knight" coming to the rescue. The white knight firm, it is hoped, will keep all the management employees in their jobs. When their jobs are at stake, it is often questionable whether management searches out that firm that will pay shareholders the best price. Management's interest is likely to be in keeping their jobs, not in making money for the shareholders.

Strategies have been developed to protect shareholders from management's interest overriding shareholders' interest. One such strategy is the *golden parachute*. The board of directors of the corporation provides that if the corporation should be acquired by another corporation, people holding top management jobs are guaranteed large payments of money—as high as $40 or $50 million in some cases. This is a golden parachute. It means that management can feel comfortable when the corporation is approached by a potential buyer and will make decisions based on the shareholders' interests, not on whether management jobs will be left undisturbed.

Golden parachutes afford shareholders some assurance that if their firm receives an acquisition or takeover offer, management will consider it. Golden parachutes protect top management because either they'll keep their jobs or, if they lose their jobs, their pain will be soothed by compensation in big bucks. Golden parachutes do nothing for low-level management and ordinary workers, who may suffer demotions or layoffs after two firms have merged.

and competition, but because of their effect on managerial incentives. The disadvantage of takeovers for the economy is that managers spend too much time playing the takeover game and too little time overseeing the truly productive activities of the firm. But many economists oppose the passage of such legislation, arguing that fear of a takeover keeps managers on their toes—adding competitive pressure to the economy. To prevent takeovers would be to eliminate that competitive pressure.

Mergers

Mergers are also classified by the types of businesses that are merging. Two companies in the same industry merging is a **horizontal merger.** A firm merging with the supplier of one of its inputs is a **vertical merger.** Two firms in unrelated industries merging is a **conglomerate merger.**

Horizontal Mergers

Most U.S. antitrust policy has concerned horizontal mergers. The creation of Standard Oil, which I discussed earlier, is an example of a horizontal merger. Since the passage of the Cellar-Kefauver Act of 1950, almost all mergers of companies with substantial market shares in the same industry have been prohibited, even though enforcement was loosened in the 1980s. For example, in 1986 the FTC blocked a proposed merger between Coca-Cola and 7UP because the market share after the merger would have been 80 percent.

Exactly what is considered substantial market share has changed over time. The general guideline government used in the 1970s and early 1980s was that, in highly concentrated industries, the government would challenge all mergers involving the following combinations of market share:

4 Horizontal mergers are companies in the same industry merging together.
Vertical mergers are combinations of two companies, one of which supplied inputs to the other's production. Conglomerate mergers are combinations of unrelated businesses.

Q–7: If the long-distance phone company, AT&T, merges with McCaw, the cellular phone company, what type of merger will it be?

Acquiring firm	Acquired firm
4%	4% or more
10%	2% or more
15%	1% or more

For less-concentrated industries, the guidelines used slightly different percentages. In 1982, the Department of Justice changed the guidelines and began looking at all mergers in which the Herfindahl index, after the merger, would be above 1000. Unless one of the merging firms was on the verge of bankruptcy, such horizontal mergers among the largest firms in an industry were supposedly prohibited, but enforcement became lax in the late 1980s because President Reagan's and President Bush's appointees generally opposed antitrust enforcement.

President Bill Clinton chose appointees who were more favorable to antitrust enforcement in certain circumstances when international competitiveness was not an issue. A stricter set of guidelines was developing in the mid-1990s, which will likely result in more antitrust action. For example, in the early 1990s the FTC investigated a major computer software firm, Microsoft, for possible antitrust violations, specifically for tying buyers of its DOS computer operating system into its software. (Ironically, it was a similar antitrust investigation back in the early 1980s that played a big role in Microsoft's initial success and independence from IBM.) The FTC dropped its inquiry in 1993 without filing suit, but immediately thereafter the U.S. Justice Department started its own investigation, and in July, 1994 Microsoft agreed to limit its tying of DOS and its software.

Vertical Mergers

As I stated before, a vertical merger is a combination of two companies that are involved in different phases of producing a product, one company being a buyer of products the other company supplies. For example, if a computer company merges with an electronic chip company, a vertical merger has taken place. Similarly, if a clothes manufacturer buys a retail boutique, that's a vertical merger. If either of the merged firms is able to limit access of other buyers or sellers to the market, such a merger is in violation of the Clayton Act.

A famous vertical merger case is the Du Pont/General Motors case (1961), in which Du Pont was required to sell its 23-percent share of General Motors because Du Pont was a major supplier to the automobile industry. The Supreme Court felt Du Pont's ownership share of GM was restricting competition. Similarly in the Brown Shoe/Kinney Shoe case (1962), Brown Shoe, primarily a wholesaler, was forbidden to buy Kinney Shoe, which was a chain of shoe retailers.

In most of the 1980s, the U.S. government would challenge any vertical merger in which the supplying firm had a 10 percent or more market share and the buyer company purchased 6 percent or more of the market. This rule was loosened some as the 1980s progressed, although still, in the early 1990s, specific new guidelines have not yet replaced it.

Conglomerate Mergers

A third type of merger is a conglomerate merger. Conglomerate mergers occur when two relatively unrelated businesses merge. Conglomerate mergers are generally approved by the U.S. antitrust laws under the assumption that they do not significantly restrict competition. Thus, when GM bought Electronic Data Systems Corporation in 1984, no antitrust action was taken to prevent the merger because the two firms were unrelated.

Why would two unrelated firms want to merge? Or why would one want to be bought out by another? There are five general reasons:

1. *To achieve economies of scope.* Although the businesses are unrelated, some overlap is almost inevitable, so economies of scope are likely. For example, one firm's technical or marketing expertise may be helpful to the other firm, or the conglomerate's increased size may give it better bargaining power with its suppliers.

2. *To get a good buy.* Firms are always on the lookout for good buys. If a firm believes that another firm's stock is significantly undervalued, it can buy that stock at its low price and then sell it at a profit later when the stock is no longer undervalued.

3. *To diversify.* Many industries have a cyclical nature. In some parts of the business cycle they do poorly; in other parts of the business cycle they do just fine. Buying an unrelated company allows a firm to diversify and thereby to even out the cyclical fluctuation in its profits.

Q–8: If Ben and Jerry's, a maker of ice cream, bought a dairy farm, what type of merger would it be?

Forbes—A business magazine that closely follows major mergers and acquisitions.

5 Five reasons why unrelated firms merge include:
1. To achieve economies of scope;
2. To get a good buy;
3. To diversify;
4. To ward off a takeover bid; and
5. To strengthen their political-economic influence.

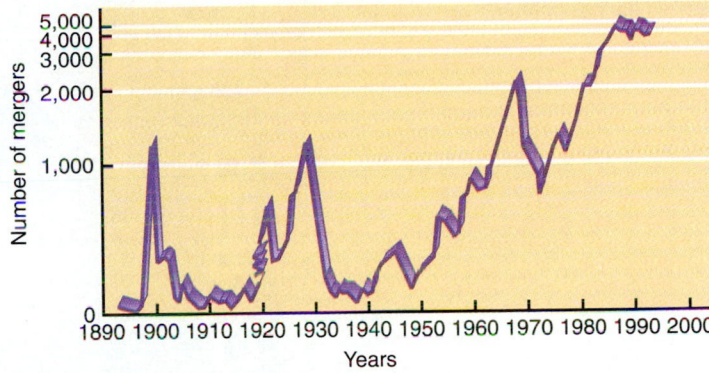

EXHIBIT 2 Mergers in the United States Since 1892

The number of mergers in the United States has fluctuated substantially in the last 100 years.
Source: Federal Trade Commission.

4. *To ward off a takeover bid.* Firms are always susceptible to being bought out by someone else. Sometimes they prevent an unwanted buyout by merging with another firm in order to become so large that they're indigestible. For example, in 1989 Time, Inc., merged with Warner Communications to reduce the likelihood that Time would be taken over by a third firm, Paramount.

5. *To strengthen their political-economic influence.* The bigger you are, the more influence you have. Individuals who run companies like to have and use influence. Merging can increase their net influence considerably.

Exhibit 2 presents the number of mergers in the United States each year since 1892. As you can see, mergers rose significantly in the last part of the 1980s. One reason is that mergers became a fad—the thing to do. Also relatively low share prices made companies a good deal. Companies' best investment was buying another company. Mergers were an especially good deal for the investment bankers who arrange the deals for a fee, and they worked hard selling the merger idea to companies. If they could persuade major companies to merge, the investment bankers stood to earn millions of dollars. It's not surprising that they pushed such deals and worked hard to find ways to finance them.

The fact that a large number of mergers took place in the late 1980s doesn't mean that the U.S. economy was seeing an overall growth in the size of companies. That's because many recent huge takeovers have been followed by **deacquisitions.** To pay off the debt it incurred to finance a takeover, a company may sell parts of the business it has bought. This is deacquisition.

For example, in 1990 Kohlberg, Kravis, Roberts, and Co. (KKR) bought RJR Nabisco. KKR raised the $24.5 billion purchase price mainly by selling high-yield, high-risk bonds (commonly called *junk bonds*). Issuing these junk bonds meant that KKR had to commit itself to pay large amounts of interest on them. But the earnings Nabisco brought KKR were less than the interest KKR needed to pay off the bondholders. The only way KKR could meet the obligation was to sell off parts of Nabisco (hoping, of course, to get more for those parts than it had paid for the whole company). Among Nabisco's well-known products were Oreos, Life Savers, Chips Ahoy, and Ritz Crackers, as well as Camel, Salem, Winston, and Vantage cigarettes. Today, many of those brands are no longer produced by RJR Nabisco. Instead they're produced and marketed by the various firms that bought the various pieces of the Nabisco company. So the net effect of this takeover is likely to be a decrease in overall concentration in the economy, although, depending on whether existing firms or new firms bought out the various Nabisco divisions, there may be an increase in concentration in particular industries.

We've introduced a lot of terms in this section and, ideally, started you thinking about the issues involved in deciding on a merger and acquisition policy. This chapter does not arrive at definite conclusions, and in this it reflects the economics profession,

Recent Merger Activity and Deacquisitions

Deacquisition   One company's sale of parts of another company it has bought.

Assessment of Mergers and Acquisitions

Among Nabisco's most valuable assets were its trademark brand names.

which has no one position on what policy the United States should follow toward mergers.

But the economics profession's failure to come to an undivided view on mergers isn't necessarily a failing of economists. Mergers have both costs and benefits, and reasonable people will assess them differently.

INTERNATIONAL COMPETITION, INDUSTRIAL POLICY, AND ANTITRUST POLICY

The nature of competition is changing in the United States. Ten or 20 years ago, when people talked about competition, they meant competition among U.S. firms. Now, however, they often mean competition between U.S. companies and foreign firms that either have started producing here in the United States or are exporting to the United States. The reason for this is the internationalization of the U.S. economy.

The large U.S. trade deficit of the 1980s was accompanied by large amounts of foreign investment in the United States. Foreign firms have strengthened their manufacturing positions here. For example, about 50 percent of the firms in the stone, clay, and glass industry in the United States are foreign-owned. Most of the large firms in the tire industry (such as Firestone, General Tire, and Armstrong) are foreign-owned. Burger King is foreign-owned. The U.S. chemical industry is 50 percent foreign-owned. There are many other examples.

Multinational corporation Firm with production facilities and a marketing force in two or more countries.

Of course the process goes the other way, too. U.S. firms more and more are becoming **multinational corporations** (sometimes called *global corporations*), with production facilities and a marketing force in one or more other countries. Just as foreign firms are investing in the United States, U.S. firms are investing in foreign countries. You can now get a McDonald's hamburger just about anywhere in the world. Walt Disney has theme parks in Japan and France. More and more firms are acquiring an international perspective in which the U.S. economy is simply becoming one market in an international economy, rather than an entire market.

The internationalization of the U.S. economy adds to competition by broadening the market and adding potential producers of a variety of goods. In the 1960s, the U.S. auto industry was dominated by the Big Three: Ford, GM, and Chrysler. Today those companies face fierce competition from foreign firms such as Toyota, Nissan, Honda, and Hyundai.

Foreign competition has played an important role in holding down U.S. prices, and thereby holding down U.S. wages.

Foreign competition has played an important role in holding down U.S. prices, and thereby holding down U.S. wages. Foreign competition has changed the relative bargaining strengths of workers and management of corporations. In the 1960s, workers were in a relatively strong position. They could threaten to strike if they didn't get the wage increases they wanted. Generally management met their demands.

The internationalization of the U.S. economy has changed that situation. If U.S. firms don't produce cheaply enough, foreign firms will replace them. Similarly in the 1990s, many U.S. firms have become multinational firms and can realistically threaten to move their production to another country. That threat gives them a much stronger bargaining position with U.S. labor. The internationalization of the U.S. economy has been furthered with the recent free trade agreement with Mexico and Canada. Since labor costs account for more than 60 percent of the value added of most products, foreign competition and the internationalization of U.S. firms have helped keep inflationary pressure in the United States lower than it would otherwise have been.

Because of this internationalization of competition, the political climate in the United States is changing. More and more, U.S. antitrust policymakers see the international market as the relevant market. The policy focus of government is shifting from "Is U.S. industry internally competitive so that it does not take advantage of the consumer?" to "Is U.S. industry internationally competitive so that it can compete effectively in the world economy?"

Other countries' approaches toward antitrust are a likely harbinger of future U.S. antitrust policy. The reason is that other countries, because almost all of them are smaller than the United States, have consistently seen the international market as the relevant market and have designed their antitrust laws accordingly. Their domestic markets were simply too small to take advantage of economies of scale.

What's interesting about other countries' antitrust laws is how weak they are compared to U.S. laws. No other country forces companies to break up for antitrust violations, although some push for price rollbacks in cases of extreme monopolization. Even when the United States has tried to export its stringent antitrust laws, as it did during its military occupation of Germany and Japan after World War II, those laws were repealed by those nations soon after the occupation ended.

One important reason other countries oppose antitrust regulation is that they recognize the importance of economies of scale. In many countries that have only small markets, the minimum efficient production level requires high concentration.

A second reason is their history. Most countries don't have the same populist worldview that exists in the United States. The ideological and cultural underpinning of strong antitrust laws (individualistic competition based on small producers) fits in nicely with the American populist worldview. In the United States, many people believe that bigness is bad. That belief is not as prevalent in other countries.

A third reason that other countries don't have strong antitrust laws is cultural. In the United States, government and business are often seen as enemies of each other. In cultures such as Japan's or Germany's, government and business are seen as allies, working together to increase exports and compete internationally.

As the U.S. economy becomes more and more internationalized, its approach to antitrust policy, in those instances where international competitiveness is at issue, will likely be less confrontational and more supportive of the idea of allowing businesses to cooperate rather than compete with each other, so that they can better compete internationally. International competition will be relied upon more heavily than domestic competition to provide competitive pressures on U.S. firms. Government will likely allow mergers and cartels that will strengthen the United States internationally, and will actively encourage cooperation among U.S. firms.

These changes have already begun. For example, in 1989 the U.S. government allowed major U.S. computer companies to organize jointly to form a chip research company so that they, as a group, could better compete with Japanese companies. Previously any such activity would have been seen as a direct violation of the antitrust laws.

Even though this consortium broke down in 1990, the fact that government allowed it to form is significant. It signals a major change in U.S. antitrust policy, and more of these exemptions can be expected in the future. Since 1991, IBM and Apple have been working together, sharing technology and information with the support of the U.S. government. Similarly, in 1993, GM, Ford, Chrysler, and the U.S. government announced that they were teaming up to develop, by the year 2003, a super-fuel-efficient automobile that will, they specify, get over 80 miles to the gallon. Whether

Antitrust Policy in Other Countries

Q-9: Does Japan have stricter or less strict antitrust laws than the United States has?

From Antitrust Policy to Industrial Policy

**ANTITRUST AGENCIES IN
SOME OTHER COUNTRIES**

Britain: British Monopoly Commission

While it has the power to recommend structural reorganization, the British Monopoly Commission generally has not done so. Instead, it has pushed for price reductions in certain industries. After World War II, a number of major industries were nationalized, putting the government in direct control of prices, but many of these industries have been privatized in the past few years.

Japan: Fair Trade Commission

The Japanese Fair Trade Commission is weak and subordinated to MITI and other government agencies. In retailing, small firms continue to dominate with the support of government. But the 1980s saw the beginnings of a retailing system with large stores, like the system in the United States. The Fair Trade Commission may take a role in suppressing that development.

Germany: Federal Cartel Office

The Federal Cartel Office is relatively small. Often it allows and even encourages cartels. It does have the authority to push for price reductions if it determines that the cartel has abused its power.

France: Commission on Competition

The Commission on Competition has been very weak and has often advocated mergers. In the 1960s, France actively promoted large-scale mergers, and during that period the government nationalized large industries without hearing objections from the Commission on Competition.

European Union

In 1992, the EU's rules officially took precedence over member nations' local rules, but it will be late in the 1990s before any practical interpretation of the rules' implications will emerge. One possibility is what happened with the European Coal and Steel Commission. Under that commission, mergers were limited in theory, but in practice none were disallowed. Another possibility is that the expansion of the market that was made possible by the integration of the EU economies in 1992 will generate significant merger activity in the mid-1990s, and since the economies of scale argument will no longer apply, a stronger antitrust policy will emerge.

---

this change in policy toward business will increase U.S. competitiveness remains to be seen.

Activist Industrial Policy

6 An industrial policy is a government's formal policy toward business.

7 Two arguments for an industrial policy are (1) that it will create gains from cooperation among firms, and (2) that it will channel funds to high-growth industries.

In the 1980s and 1990s, a rallying cry for many politicians has been that the U.S. economy needs an industrial policy. An **industrial policy** is the formal policy that government takes toward business. In actual fact, the United States has always had, and always will have, an industrial policy. What these politicians are calling for is an *activist industrial policy* under which the government would work directly with businesses, providing funds, background research, and encouragement to specific industries in order to keep the United States internationally competitive. Advocates claim that this will result in gains from cooperation and increased international competitiveness as funds are channeled to high-growth industries.

The Example of Japan's MITI   Advocates of an activist U.S. industrial policy point to Japan's Ministry of International Trade and Industry (MITI) as an example of how an activist industrial policy would work. MITI is credited by these economists with engineering Japan's economic growth over the past 40 years (although how successful MITI was is debatable). MITI worked closely with Japanese companies to improve their competitiveness. The ministry provided money and research, and saw to it that companies focused on international, rather than domestic, competition. It smoothed the flow of capital to certain industries it wanted to promote, such as the electronics industry. It did this by taking such measures as consulting with banks and encouraging

IN THE TOWERS OF THE HIGH-TECH MIRACLE

Tokyo—From inside its two office towers in Kasumigaseki, the Government center near the Imperial Palace here, the Ministry of International Trade and Industry looks more like a decrepit insurance agency than the mastermind of a high-tech miracle. Paper is piled everywhere. Employees sit elbow-to-elbow at battered gray desks that seem to date from the American occupation. Some of them do. Conferences with visitors take place on fraying couches hemmed in by filing cabinets.

There is a central computer system, but it is hardly at everyone's fingertips: Even in the information processing section, which oversees the world's second-largest computer industry, a few workers prop Toshiba laptop computers on their desks.

But appearances aside, the ministry remains the repository of much of Japan's best young talent. Ambitious throngs from the senior class of the University of Tokyo, Japan's single-school equivalent of the Ivy League, compete each year for entry-level slots at the ministry. From early on, they are given enormous respon-sibility and are rarely shy about using it. A semiconductor industry execu-tive recently fumed to a reporter that he had spent a morning at the minis-try being lectured about his business by a "condescending, arrogant little bureaucrat" young enough to be his son.

The ministry is 40 years old this year, and such complaints go back to its beginning. In its early days, it placed strict import quotas on every-thing from cars to computers and forced foreign companies to license critical technologies to Japanese part-ners if they wanted to invest directly in Japan. It used state-managed banks to funnel funds into automobiles, petrochemicals and steel. And it allo-cated scarce foreign exchange and rebuilt industrial groups into "kei-retsu," related companies with inter-locking stock ownership, usually including a trading company and a bank.

The ministry's better-known role, as the hidden hand behind Japan Inc., started in the 1960's. Wielding "administrative guidance" notices and organizing consortiums of com-panies, it navigated the oil crises, merged steel companies and began Japan's thrust into high technology.

Not everyone views its power as benign. In a controversial new book, "The Enigma of Japanese Power," Karel Van Wolferen, a Tokyo jour-nalist, argues that it is a premier blackmailer, collecting information about corporate wrongdoing and threatening companies with "expo-sure if they do not follow MITI's directions."

Not surprisingly, the ministry dis-agrees, saying that its clout in the 1960's and 1970's arose because companies were desperate to play catch-up ball and wanted the services offered by the ministry. "We had an obvious foreign competitor," said Chikao Tsukuda, a former ministry official and now a consultant to it— "I.B.M."

Source: The *New York Times*, July 9, 1989, Business Section. Copyright © 1989 by The New York Times Company. Reprinted by per-mission.

loans. MITI would say, "So-and-So is a good company," and that statement was a code to banks that they should approve So-and-So's loan application.

Questions about an Activist Industrial Policy   Japan's success did not come without problems. Its activism involved government in business decisions. This opened up significant possibilities for graft. In the late 1980s and early 1990s, a major scandal erupted in Japan when it was revealed that some Japanese corporations had given many politicians in the ruling Liberal Democratic Party options to buy stock in the companies at low prices.

Such problems are likely to arise under an activist industrial policy. Because government decisions can mean a difference of hundreds of millions of dollars to firms, companies will inevitably spend money to influence those decisions, either legally through lobbying or illegally through bribery and graft. The exposure of the scandals in Japan has already changed the composition of its elected ruling party. Whether the scandals will change Japan's industrial policy remains to be seen.

While the United States has never had an activist industrial policy like Japan's, a close connection has developed among the armed forces, the industries that manufac-ture weapons, and members of Congress from states and districts that depend heavily on the defense industry. This relationship of mutual benefit, referred to as the **military-industrial complex,** is an activist relationship in that it involves government in the decisions of privately owned defense manufacturers.

This involvement often prevents government from making tough economic choices. For example, in 1989 Congress seemed about to cut production of the B-2 Stealth bomber. Northrup, the plane's manufacturer, took out full-page newspaper

7   Two problems of an industrial policy are (1) graft and (2) the inevi-table waste inherent in bureaucracy.

Military-industrial complex   The *mutually beneficial relationship among the armed services, weapons industries, and government officials.*

ads, pointing out that parts of the B-2 were produced in 48 states and that thousands of jobs would be lost if the government canceled the contract. Congress gave in, as it has done on many other defense items that are widely regarded as nonessential to national security.

With the ending of the Cold War in the early 1990s, many felt that defense spending could be cut substantially. But whenever specific cuts were suggested, the military-industrial complex fought hard against them.

Q-10: What would a bio-educational complex likely be?

Questions about MITI's Role

Critics of an activist industrial policy also argue that Japan's success came not as a result of MITI and its activist industrial policy, but in spite of it. They point out that MITI's strategy was to develop a number of industries that, as it turned out, did not succeed in the international competitive market. These critics argue that it was only skillful decision making on the part of private firms that finessed MITI's inappropriate directives and allowed those firms to follow other paths, and that it was these firms' actions that ultimately led to MITI's success. The available information is contradictory, and the debate is likely to continue through the 1990s.

Should the United States Adopt an Activist Industrial Policy?

Any time economic decisions are made on a political basis, waste is inevitable. It's the cost of an activist industrial policy in a democratic government. But there are also benefits. Competition can be wasteful, especially in research. That's why scientific conventions (rules limiting scientists' behavior) exist that support openness and sharing of scientific knowledge. Cooperation by firms with government and universities can lead to more productive research.

Even with the problem of wasteful defense spending, the United States has maintained a technological lead in aerospace in large part because of the government's support for that industry. Some economists have argued that the United States wouldn't have remained highly competitive without the defense industry's close connection with, and subsidies by, the government. As with every decision in economics, there are both costs and benefits.

In weighing these costs and benefits, a majority of economists come out on the side of opposing an activist industrial policy for the United States. This includes most conservative economists who generally oppose activist government policies plus a number of liberal economists who are concerned about the politics of an industrial policy. They believe that a formal activist industrial policy would probably lead to more inefficiency and waste as the invisible feet of politics and law extended their influence over the invisible hand of the marketplace, yielding more costs than benefits.

To argue against an activist industrial policy is not to argue against an informal government policy of encouraging research in certain areas. This can be done by fostering connections between universities and business, by directly subsidizing private industry's basic research, or by loosening the antitrust laws. Many economists support such policies in particular cases even as they oppose a general activist industrial policy being extended to all businesses.

CHAPTER SUMMARY

- There is a debate on whether markets should be judged on the basis of structure or on the basis of performance.
- Antitrust policy is the government's policy toward the competitive process.
- Important antitrust laws include the Sherman Antitrust Act, the Clayton Act, and the Federal Trade Commission Act.
- Three types of mergers are horizontal, vertical, and con-glomerate.

- Five reasons that two unrelated firms would want to merge are economies of scope, a good buy, diversification, warding off a takeover bid, and strengthening political-economic influence.
- The increasing internationalization of the relevant U.S. market has changed U.S. policy's focus from antitrust policy to industrial policy.
- Industrial policies have advantages and disadvantages.

KEY TERMS

acquisition *(648)*
Antitrust policy *(639)*
Clayton Antitrust Act *(641)*
conglomerate merger *(649)*
deacquisition *(651)*
Federal Trade Commission Act *(642)*
horizontal merger *(649)*

hostile takeover *(648)*
industrial policy *(654)*
judgment by performance *(639)*
judgment by structure *(639)*
merger *(648)*
military-industrial complex *(655)*

MITI *(645)*
multinational corporation *(652)*
natural monopoly *(645)*
Sherman Antitrust Act *(639)*
takeover *(648)*
vertical merger *(649)*

QUESTIONS FOR THOUGHT AND REVIEW

The number after each question represents the estimated degree of critical thinking required. (1 = almost none; 10 = deep thought.)

1. How would the U.S. economy likely differ today if Standard Oil had not been broken up? *(9)*

2. Colleges require that certain courses be taken at that college in order to get a degree. Is that an example of a tie-in contract that limits consumers' choices? If so, should it be against the law? *(7)*

3. Colleges give financial aid to certain students. Is this price discrimination? If so, should it be against the law? *(7)*

4. Should interlocking directorships be against the law? Why or why not? *(6)*

5. Distinguish the basis of judgment for the Standard Oil and the ALCOA cases. *(2)*

6. If you were an economist for a firm that wanted to merge, would you argue that the two-digit or four-digit industry is the relevant market? Why? *(5)*

7. Has telephone service improved since AT&T was broken up? What does this imply about antitrust laws? *(7)*

8. Under the 1982 Department of Justice guidelines, would a merger be allowed between the number three firm in an industry and a firm with 2 percent of the market? The number four firm in the industry has 11 percent of the market. *(6)*

9. Should the United States have a policy against conglomerate mergers? Why or why not? *(7)*

10. How would you design an industrial policy to avoid the problems inherent in such a policy? *(9)*

PROBLEMS AND EXERCISES

1. You're working at the Department of Justice. Ms. Ecofame has just brought in a new index, the Ecofame index, which she argues is preferable to the Herfindahl index. The Ecofame index is calculated by cubing the market share of the top 10 firms in the industry.
   a. Calculate an Ecofame guideline that would correspond to the 1982 Department of Justice guidelines.
   b. State the advantages and disadvantages of the Ecofame index as compared to the Herfindahl index.

2. Using a monopolistic competition model, a cartel model of oligopoly, and a contestable market of oligopoly, discuss and demonstrate graphically where possible the effect of antitrust policy.

3. In 1993 Mattel proposed acquiring Fisher-Price for $1.1 billion. In the toy industry, Mattel is a major player with 11 percent of the market. Fisher-Price has 4 percent. The other two large firms are Tyco, with a 5 percent share, and Hasbro, with a 15 percent share. In the infant/preschool toy market, Mattel has an 8 percent share and Fisher-Price has a 27 percent share, the largest. The other two large firms are Hasbro, with a 25 percent share, and Rubbermaid, with a 12 percent share.
   a. What are the approximate Herfindahl and 4-firm concentration ratios for these firms in each industry?

   b. If you were Mattel's economist, which industry definition would you suggest using in court if you were challenged by the government?
   c. Give an argument why the merger might decrease competition.
   d. Give an argument why the merger might increase competition.

4. In 1992 American Airlines offered a 50-percent-off sale and cut fares. In 1993 Continental Airlines and Northwest Airlines sued American Airlines over this action.
   a. What was the likely basis of their suit?
   b. How does the knowledge that Continental and Northwest were in serious financial trouble play a role in the suit?

5. Demonstrate graphically how regulating the price of a monopolist can both increase quantity and decrease price.
   a. Why did the regulation have the effect it did?
   b. How relevant to the real world do you believe this result is in the ''contestable markets'' view of the competitive process?
   c. How relevant to the real world do you believe this result is in the ''cartel'' view of the competitive process?

ANSWERS TO MARGIN QUESTIONS

1. The Sherman Antitrust Act contained two main sections. The first stated that every contract, combination, or conspiracy in restraint of trade was illegal. The second stated that every person who shall monopolize or attempt to monopolize shall be deemed guilty of a misdemeanor. These provisions, while sounding strong, were so broad that they were almost unenforceable, and the interpretation was left to the courts. *(640)*

2. In the Standard Oil case, the Court determined that Standard Oil controlled 90 percent of the market. It said that this monopolistic structure of the market did not necessarily violate the Sherman Antitrust Act. However, the Court also decided that Standard Oil had engaged in systematic abuse and unfair business practices, and therefore was guilty of antitrust violations and must be broken up. *(641)*

3. In the ALCOA case, the Court changed the interpretation of the law. Here it found ALCOA was not guilty of any unfair practices. It agreed that ALCOA had simply used its knowledge of the market to expand capacity before any competitors had a chance to enter, and had kept its price low to prevent other entry. Thus, on performance standards, it was not violating the law. But the Court decided the structure of the market, not the company's performance, was the appropriate standard by which to judge cases and, therefore, ALCOA was in violation of the antitrust law. *(642)*

4. In the 1956 Du Pont case, the Supreme Court found that Du Pont was innocent of monopolization of the production of cellophane, even though it was the only producer. The Court's reasoning was that the relevant market was the entire flexible wrap industry, not just cellophane. Since Du Pont did not dominate the flexible wrap industry, it was not in violation of antitrust law. *(643)*

5. In the late 1960s, the Department of Justice filed suit against IBM for violating the antitrust laws. It alleged that IBM had a monopoly of the general-purpose electronic digital computing industry and that it had acquired its market share because of unfair business practices. The case dragged on for 13 years but never went to court. In 1982, the government withdrew its lawsuit. The antitrust case, however, had significant effects on IBM.

It is likely that the experience caused IBM to shy away from the then-small personal computer market. This decision by IBM very likely was the beginning of the serious problems that IBM faces in the 1990s. *(644)*

6. In 1978, the Department of Justice sued AT&T, alleging that its potential competitors were not being allowed reasonable access to AT&T's local telephone network. The case was resolved in January 1982, when AT&T agreed to let itself be broken up. Specifically, AT&T divested itself of 22 operating companies, and focused thereafter only on long-distance telephone service, manufacturing, and research and development. This settlement left AT&T free to enter into any unregulated business it desired, and in the 1990s AT&T has been expanding with fiber optic networks and has proposed merging with McCaw Cellular Communication. Ironically, these expansions placed it in direct competition with the still-regulated Baby Bells who had inherited AT&T's monopoly rights. *(646)*

7. AT&T's merger with McCaw would be a mixture of a horizontal merger and a conglomerate merger. It is a horizontal merger to the degree that one interprets the industry broadly as a "communications industry." It is a conglomerate merger if one interprets the industry narrowly and distinguishes the wireless communications industry from the wire communications industry. *(649)*

8. If Ben & Jerry's bought a dairy farm, it would be a vertical merger because Ben & Jerry's would be buying one of its suppliers. *(650)*

9. Japan has antitrust laws that are significantly less strict than those of the United States. *(653)*

10. A bio-educational complex would be a combination of biotech and education industries. With new developments in genetic engineering, it is possible that significant monopoly rights will be granted with patents to the developers of new genetic material. These patents will give the industries great power and potential income, which they will likely use to protect their turf and to influence future decisions on laws affecting these issues to favor themselves rather than the general public. *(656)*

30

Work and the Labor Market

Work banishes those three great evils: boredom, vice, and poverty.

~Voltaire

After reading this chapter, you should be able to:

1 Apply rational choice theory to the supply of labor.

2 Explain why an increase in the marginal tax rate is likely to reduce the quantity of labor supplied.

3 Determine a firm's derived demand for labor.

4 Explain why a monopolist's demand for labor will be lower than a competitive firm's demand for labor.

5 Define *monopsonist* and *bilateral monopoly.*

6 Discuss real-world characteristics of labor markets in terms of the invisible forces.

7 List three types of discrimination.

Gary Becker was awarded the 1992 Nobel prize for his work in micro-economics. He has applied economic analysis to such nontraditional areas as human capital, crime prevention, and the decision to have children. *Reuters/ Bettmann.*

Labor market *Factor market in which individuals supply labor ser-vices for wages to firms that demand labor services.*

THE INVISIBLE HAND AND THE LABOR MARKET

The Supply of Labor

Incentive effect *How much a per-son will change his or her hours worked in response to a change in the wage rate.*

1 Applying rational choice theory to the supply of labor tells us that the higher the wage, the higher the quan-tity of labor supplied.

Most of us earn our living by working. We supply labor (get a job) and get paid for doing things that other people tell us they want done. Even before we get a job, work is very much a part of our lives. We spend a large portion of our school years preparing for work. Probably many of you are taking this economics course because you've been told that it will help to prepare you for a job—or that it will get you more pay than you're getting in your present job. For you, this course is investment in "human capital." If work isn't already familiar to you, once you get out of school (unless you're sitting on a hefty trust fund or marry somebody who is), work in the marketplace will become very familiar to you.

Your job will occupy at least a third of your waking hours. To a great extent, it will define you. When someone asks, "What do you do?" you won't answer, "I clip coupons, go out on dates, visit my children . . ." Instead you'll answer, "I work for the Blank Company" or "I'm an economist" or "I'm a teacher." Defining ourselves by our work means that work is more than the way we get income. It's a part of our social and cultural makeup. If we lose our jobs, we lose part of our identity.

There's no way I can discuss all the social, political, cultural, and economic dimensions of work and labor in one chapter, but it's important to begin by at least pointing them out in order to put my discussion of labor markets in perspective. A **labor market** is a factor market in which individuals supply labor services for wages to other individuals and to firms that need (demand) labor services. The labor market is a market in which social and political pressures are particularly strong, and we can understand the nature of labor markets only by considering how the three invisible forces interact to determine our economic situation.

To do that, I first ask the question: What would labor markets be like if only economic forces—the invisible hand—operated on them? I examine how the other invisible forces interact with economic forces to produce existing labor market institutions. Finally, I consider the implications of the analysis for you and your future in the job market.

If the invisible hand were the only force that was operating, wages would be determined entirely by supply and demand. There's more to it than that, as you'll see, but it shouldn't be surprising to you that my discussion of the invisible hand and the labor market is organized around the concepts of supply and demand.

The labor supply choice facing an individual (that is, the decisions of whether, how, and how much to work) can be seen as a choice between nonmarket activities and legal market activities. Nonmarket activities include sleeping, dating, studying, play-ing, cooking, cleaning, gardening, and black market trading. Legal market activities include taking some type of paid job or working for oneself, directly supplying products or services to the consumer.

Many considerations are involved in individuals' choice of whether and how much to work and what kind of job to work at. Social background and conditioning are especially important, but the factor economists focus on is the **incentive effect** (how much a person will change his or her hours worked in response to a change in the wage rate). The incentive effect is determined by the value of supplying one's time to legal market activities relative to the value of supplying one's time to nonmarket activities. The normal relationship is:

The higher the wage, the higher the quantity of labor supplied.

This relationship between the wage rate and the quantity of labor supplied is shown in Exhibit 1. The wage rate is measured on the vertical axis; the quantity of labor supplied is measured on the horizontal axis. As you can see, its upward slope indicates that as the wage rate increases, the quantity of labor supplied increases. Why is that the normal relationship? Because work involves opportunity cost. By working one hour more, you have one hour less to devote to nonmarket activities. Alter-natively, if you devote the hour to nonmarket activities, you lose one hour's worth of income from working.

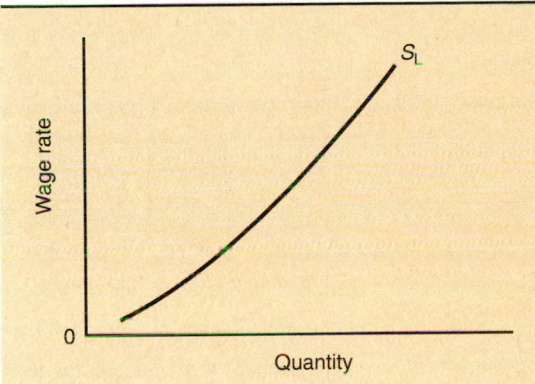

EXHIBIT 1   The Supply of Labor

The supply of labor is generally considered to be upward sloping because the opportunity cost of not working increases as wages get higher.

Say, for example, that by working you would have made $10 per hour. If you decide to work two hours less, you'll have $20 less to spend, but two hours more available for other activities (including spending the smaller amount of money). When the wage rises, say to $12 per hour, an hour of leisure has a higher opportunity cost. As the cost of leisure goes up, you buy less of it, meaning that you work more.

As I noted in my general discussions of supply and demand, the incentive effects represented by the market supply curve come from individuals' either/or decisions to enter, or leave, the labor market; and from individuals' decisions to work more, or fewer, hours. Given the institutional constraints in the labor market which require many people to work a fixed set of hours if they work at all, much of the incentive effect of higher wages works on the either/or decisions of individuals. This affects the labor force participation rate rather than adjusting the number of hours worked. For example, when wages rise, retired workers may find it worthwhile to go back to work, and many teenagers may choose to find part-time jobs.

Real Wages and the Opportunity Cost of Work   The upward-sloping supply curve of labor tells you that, other things equal, as wages go up, the quantity of labor supplied goes up. But if you look at the historical record, you see real wages in the United States increasing and the average number of hours worked per person falling. This difference is partly explained by the income effect, which is discussed below. Higher incomes make people richer, and richer people choose more leisure.

Given that people are far richer today than they were 50 or 100 years ago, it isn't surprising that they work less. What's surprising is that they work as much as they do—eight hours a day rather than the four or so hours a day that would be enough to give people the same income that they had a century ago.

The explanation of why people haven't reduced their hours of work more substantially can be found in the type of leisure taken. A century ago, conversation was an art. People could use their time for long, leisurely conversations. Letter writing was a skill all educated people had, and cooking dinner was a three-hour event. Leisure was time-intensive. If today people were satisfied with leisure consisting of long conversations, whittling, and spending quality time with their families rather than skiing, golfing, or travelling, they could get by with working perhaps only four or five hours per day instead of eight hours. But that isn't the case.

Today leisurely dinners, conversations about good books, and witty letters have been replaced by ''efficient'' leisure: a fast-food supper, a home video, and the instant analysis of current events. Microwave ovens, frozen dinners, Pop-Tarts, cellular telephones, fax machines—the list of gadgets and products designed to save time is endless. All these gadgets that increase the ''efficiency'' of leisure (increase the marginal utility per hour of leisure spent) cost money, which means people today must work more to enjoy their leisure! In the United States, one reason people work hard is so that they can play hard (and expensively).

The fast pace of modern society has led a number of people to question whether we, as a society, are better off working hard to play hard. Are we better off or simply

Q–1:   Under the usual conditions of supply, what would you expect would happen to the amount of time you study if the wage of your part-time job rises?

Modern gadgets increase the efficiency of leisure but cost money, which means people must work more to enjoy their leisure.

INCOME AND SUBSTITUTION EFFECTS

Because labor income is such an important component of most people's total income, other things often do not stay equal, and at times the effect can seem strange. For example, say that you earn $10 an hour and you decide to work eight hours per day. Suddenly demand for your services goes up and you find that you can receive $40 an hour. Will you decide to work more hours? According to the rational choice rule, you will, but you might also decide that at $40 an hour you'll work only six hours a day—$240 a day is enough; the rest of the day you want leisure time to spend your money. In such a case a higher wage means working less.

Does this violate the rational choice rule? The answer is no, because other things—specifically your income—do not remain equal. The higher wage makes you decide to work more—as the rational choice rule says; but the effect of the higher wage is overwhelmed by the effect of the higher income that allows you to decide to work less.

To distinguish between these two effects, economists have given them names. The decision, based on the rational choice rule, to work more hours when your pay goes up is called the *substitution effect*. You substitute work for leisure because the price of leisure has risen. The decision to work fewer hours when your pay goes up, based on the fact that you're richer and therefore can live a better life, is called the *income effect*.

It's possible that the income effect can exceed the substitution effect, and a wage increase can cause one to work less, but that possibility does not violate the rational choice rule, which refers to the substitution effect only. For those of you who didn't make a deal with me in the chapter on demand, a good exercise is to show the income and substitution effects with indifference curves and to demonstrate how it might be possible for an increase in the wage to lead to a decline in hours of work.

Economists do not try to answer the normative question of whether people are better off today, working hard to play hard, or simply are more harried.

more harried? Economists don't try to answer this normative question; but they do point out that people are choosing their harried lifestyle, so to argue that people are worse off, one must argue that people are choosing something they don't really want. That may be true, but it's a tough argument to prove.

The Supply of Labor and Nonmarket Activities   In addition to leisure, there are other nonmarket activities in which labor supply issues and market incentives play an important role. For example, there's a whole set of illegal activities, such as selling illegal drugs, which are alternatives to taking a legal job.

Let's say that an 18-year-old street kid figures he has only two options: Either he can work at a $4.85-an-hour job or he can deal drugs illegally. Dealing drugs involves enormous risks of getting arrested or shot, but it also means earning $50 or $75 an hour. Given that choice, many risk takers opt to sell drugs. When an emergency room doctor asked a shooting victim in New York City why he got involved in selling drugs, he responded, ''I'm not going to work for chump change. I make $2,000 a week, tax-free. What do they pay you, sucker?'' The doctor had to admit that even he wasn't making that kind of money.

For middle-class individuals who have prospects for good jobs, the cost of being arrested can be high—an arrest can destroy their future prospects. For poor street kids with little chance of getting a good job, an arrest makes little difference to their future. For them the choice is heavily weighted toward selling drugs. This is especially true for the entrepreneurial types—the risk takers—the movers and shakers who might have become the business leaders of the future. I've asked myself, had I been in their position, what decision I would have made. And I suspect I know the answer.

Prohibiting certain drugs leads to high income from selling those drugs and has significant labor market effects. The incentive effects that prohibition has on the choices facing poor teenagers in their choice of jobs is a central reason why some economists support the legalization of currently illegal drugs.

Income Taxation, Work, and Leisure   It is after-tax income, not before-tax income, that determines how much you work. Why? Because after-tax income is what you give up by not working. The government, not you, forgoes what you would have paid in taxes if you had worked. This means that when the government raises your **marginal tax rate** (the tax you pay on an additional dollar), it reduces your incentive to work. The reason is that leisure and other nonmarket activities aren't taxed, so their relative price falls. When the marginal tax rate gets really high—say 60 or 70 percent—it can significantly reduce individuals' incentive to work and earn income.

2   An increase in the marginal tax rate is likely to reduce the quantity of labor supplied because it reduces the net wage of individuals and hence, via individuals' incentive effect, causes them to work less.

One main reason why the U.S. government reduced marginal income tax rates in the 1980s was to reduce the negative incentive effects of high taxes. Whereas in the 1950s and 1960s the highest U.S. marginal income tax rate was 70 percent, in the 1990s the highest marginal income tax rate is 40 percent. European countries, which have significantly higher marginal tax rates than the United States, are currently struggling with this problem of providing incentive for people to work. The lack of incentive to work due to high marginal tax rates has even acquired a European name. It's called the **Dutch disease** because so many Dutch citizens were deciding that, given their country's high marginal tax rate and the guaranteed welfare and medical benefits they receive whether they work or not, they would not work.

Dutch disease   *Decision not to work because marginal tax rates are so high while welfare and medical benefits are guaranteed whether one works or not.*

Reducing the marginal tax rate in the United States hasn't completely eliminated the problem of negative incentive effects on individuals' work effort. The reason is that the amounts one receives from many other programs are tied to earned income. When your earned income goes up, your benefits from these other programs go down.

Say, for example, that you're getting welfare and you're deciding whether to take a $5 an hour job. Income taxes and social security taxes reduce the amount you take home from the job by 20 percent, to $4 an hour. But you also know that the Welfare Department will reduce your welfare benefits by 50¢ for every dollar you take home. This means that you lose another $2 per hour, so the marginal tax rate on your $5 an hour job isn't 20 percent; it's 60 percent. By working an hour, you've increased your net income by only $2. When you consider the transportation cost of getting to and from work, the expense of getting new clothes to wear to work, and other job-associated expenses, the net gain in income is often minimal. Your implicit marginal tax rate is almost 100 percent! At such rates, there's an enormous incentive either not to work or to work off the books (get paid in cash so you have no recorded income that the tax agent can trace).

The negative incentive effect can sometimes be even more indirect. For example, college scholarships are generally given on the basis of need. A family that earns more gets less in scholarship aid; the amount by which the scholarship is reduced as a family's income increases acts as a marginal tax on individuals' income. Why work hard to provide for yourself if there's a program to take care of you if you don't work hard? Hence, the irony in any need-based assistance program is that it reduces people's incentive to prevent themselves from being needy. These negative incentive effects on labor supply that accompany any need-based program present a public policy dilemma for which there is no easy answer.

Q–2:   What is the irony of any need-based program?

The Elasticity of the Supply of Labor

Exactly how these various incentives affect the amount of labor an individual supplies is determined by the elasticity of the individual's supply curve of labor. Exhibit 2 shows two possible supply curves of labor.[1] The supply curve of labor in Exhibit 2(a) is inelastic. (The percent change in quantity supplied divided by the percent change in wage is less than one.) The incentive effects cause little change in the number of hours an individual works. The supply curve in Exhibit 2(b) is elastic; the incentive causes a large change in the number of hours of labor supplied.

The elasticity of the market supply curve is determined by the elasticity of individuals' supply curves and by individuals entering and leaving the labor force. If a large group of people are willing to enter the labor market when wages rise, then the market labor supply will be highly elastic even if individuals' supply curves are inelastic.

The elasticity of the market supply curve is determined by the elasticity of individuals' supply curves and by individuals entering and leaving the labor market.

The elasticity of supply also depends on the type of market being discussed. For example, the elasticity of labor supply facing one firm in a small town will likely be far greater than the elasticity of the labor supply of all firms in that town. If only one firm raises its wage, it will attract workers away from other firms; if all the firms in

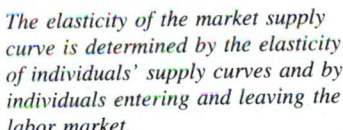

---

[1] My discussion of supply curves focuses on the incentive effect. Since wages are an important determinant of one's income, there can also be an income effect of changes in the wage: Higher wages make one richer. That income effect can also influence the elasticity of the measured supply curve. For example, higher income might lead one to work less. In certain instances, the income effect can actually make the supply curve of labor backward bending.

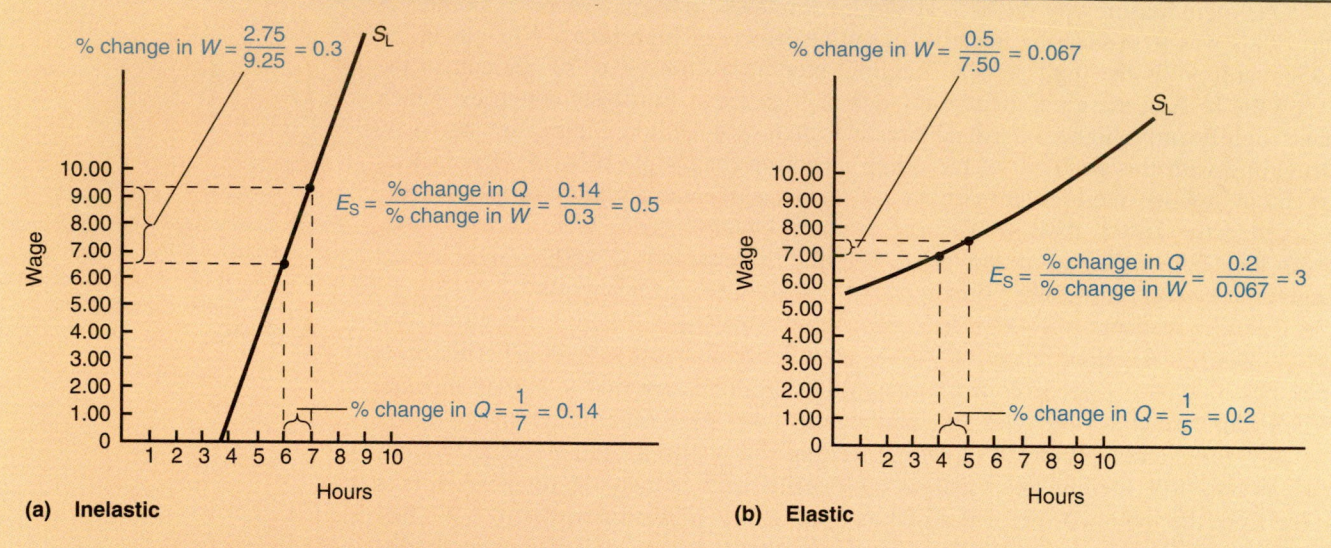

EXHIBIT 2 (a and b)   Inelastic and Elastic Supply of Labor

The elasticity of an individual's supply of labor determines to what extent various incentives affect the amount of labor an individual supplies. In (a), the individual has a highly inelastic supply of labor curve: a 30 percent drop in wages would make him work one hour less, whereas an individual with an elastic supply of labor curve, as in (b), would work one hour less if his wage were to drop only 6.7 percent.

town raise their wages, any increase in labor must come from increases in labor force participation, increases in hours worked per person, or in-migration (the movement of new workers into the town's labor market).

Existing workers prefer inelastic labor supplies because that means an increase in demand for labor will raise their wage. Employers prefer elastic supplies because that means an increase in demand for labor doesn't require large wage increases. These preferences can be seen in news reports about U.S. immigration laws, their effects, and their enforcement. Businesses such as restaurants often oppose strict immigration laws. Their reason is that jobs such as janitor, chambermaid, and busperson are frequently filled by new immigrants or illegal aliens who have comparatively low wage expectations.

Because of the importance of the elasticity of labor supply, economists have spent a great deal of time and effort estimating it. Their best estimates of labor supply elasticities to market activities are about 0.1 for heads of households and 1.1 for secondary workers in households. These elasticity figures mean that a wage increase of 10 percent will increase the supply of labor by 1 percent for heads of households (an inelastic supply) and 11 percent for secondary workers in households (an elastic supply). Why the difference? Institutional factors. Hours of work are only slightly flexible. Since most heads of households are employed, they cannot significantly change their hours worked. Many secondary workers in households are not employed, and the higher elasticity reflects new secondary workers entering the labor market.

Immigration and the International Supply of Labor   The above elasticities of labor supply are themselves based on other institutional realities, one of the most important of which is international limitation on the flow of people, and hence on labor. In many industries, wages in developing countries are one-tenth or one-twentieth the rate of wages in the United States. This large wage differential means that many people from those low-wage countries would like to move to the United States to earn the higher wages. They cannot always meet the legal immigration restrictions that limit the flow in, but in addition to about 700,000 legal immigrants per year, more than 500,000 people per year come into the United States illegally, and illegally take a variety of jobs at lower wages and worse conditions than legal residents and U.S. citizens are willing to take. The result is that the actual supply of labor is more elastic than the measured supply, especially in those jobs that cannot be easily policed.

In 1993, the European Union introduced open borders among member countries. That institutional change will likely bring about a more open flow of individuals into higher-wage EU countries from lower-wage EU countries, although other institutionalized restrictions on flows of people, such as language and culture barriers, should prevent the EU from being a unified labor market through the 1990s.

The Derived Demand for Labor

When individuals are self-employed (work for themselves), the demand for their labor is the demand for the product or service they supply—be it cutting hair, shampooing rugs, or filling teeth. You have an ability to do something; you offer to do it at a certain price; and you see who calls. You determine how many hours you work, what price you charge, and what jobs you take. The income you receive depends upon the demand for the good or service you supply and your decision about how much labor you want to supply. In analyzing self-employed individuals, one can move directly from demand for the product to demand for labor.

When a person is not self-employed, determining the demand for labor isn't as direct. It's a two-step process: Consumers demand products from firms; firms, in turn, demand labor and other factors of production to produce those products. The demand for labor by firms is a **derived demand;** it's derived from the consumer's demand for the goods that the firm sells. Thus, you can't think of demand for a factor of production such as labor separately from demand for goods. Firms translate consumers' demands into a demand for factors of production.

Derived demand   The demand for factors of production by firms, which depends upon consumers' demands.

Factors Influencing the Elasticity of Demand for Labor

The elasticity of the derived demand for labor, or for any other factor of production, depends upon a number of factors. One of the most important is (1) *the elasticity of demand for the firm's good.* The more elastic the final demand, the more elastic the derived demand. Other factors influencing the elasticity of derived demand include: (2) *the relative importance of the factor in the production process* (the more important the factor, the less elastic is the derived demand); (3) *the possibility of, and cost of, substitution in production* (the easier substitution is, the more elastic is the derived demand); and (4) *the degree to which the marginal productivity falls with an increase in the factor* (the faster productivity falls, the less elastic is the derived demand).

Q–3:   Name at least two factors that influence the elasticity of a firm's derived demand for labor.

Each of these relationships follows from the definition of *elasticity* (the percent change in quantity divided by the percent change in price) and a knowledge of production. To be sure you understand, ask yourself the following question: "If all I knew about two firms was that one was a perfect competitor and the other was a monopolist, which firm would I say is likely to have the more elastic derived demand for labor?" If your answer wasn't automatically "the competitive firm" (because its demand curve is perfectly elastic and hence more elastic than a monopolist's), I would suggest that at this point you review the discussion of factors influencing demand elasticity in the chapter on demand and relate that to this discussion. The two discussions are similar and serve as good reviews for each other.

Labor as a Factor of Production

The traditional factors of production are land, labor, capital, and entrepreneurship. When economists talk of the labor market, they're talking about two of these factors: labor and entrepreneurship. **Entrepreneurship** is a type of creative labor.

Entrepreneurship   Labor services that involve high degrees of organizational skills, concern, and creativity.

The reason for distinguishing between labor and entrepreneurship is that an hour of work is not simply an hour of work. If high degrees of organizational skill, concern, and creativity are exerted (which is what economists mean by *entrepreneurship*), one hour of such work can be the equivalent of days, weeks, or even years of simple labor. That's one reason that pay often differs between workers doing what seems to be the same job. It's also why one of the important decisions a firm makes is what type of labor to hire. Should the firm try to hire high-wage entrepreneurial labor or low-wage nonentrepreneurial labor?

We'll talk about the other two factors of production (land and capital) in the next chapter, but you should note that the formal analysis of the firm's derived demand, presented in this chapter as the derived demand for labor, is quite general and carries over to the derived demand for capital and for land. Firms translate consumers' demands for goods into derived demands for any and all of the factors of production.

The Firm's Decision to Hire   What determines a firm's decision to hire someone? The answer is simple. A profit-maximizing firm hires someone if it thinks there's money to be made by doing so. Unless there is, the firm won't hire the person. So for a firm to decide whether to hire someone, it must compare the worker's **marginal revenue product** (the marginal revenue it expects to earn from selling the additional worker's output) with the wage that it expects to pay the additional worker. For a competitive firm (for which $P = MR$), that marginal revenue product equals the worker's **value of marginal product**—the worker's **marginal physical product** (*MPP*)—which is the additional units of output that hiring an additional worker will bring about—times the price (P) at which the firm can sell the additional product.

$$\text{Marginal revenue product} = MPP \times P$$

Say, for example, that by hiring another worker a firm can produce an additional six widgets an hour, which it can sell at $2 each. That means the firm can pay up to $12 per hour and still expect to make a profit. Notice that a key question for the firm is: How much additional product will we get from hiring another worker? A competitive firm can increase its profit by hiring another worker as long as the value of the worker's marginal product (which also equals her marginal revenue product) (*MPP* × *P*) is higher than her wage.

To see whether you understand the principle, consider the example in Exhibit 3(a). Column 1 shows the number of workers, all of whom are assumed to be identical. Column 2 shows the total output of those workers. Column 3 shows the marginal physical product of an additional worker. This number is determined by looking at the change in the total product due to this person's work. For example, if the firm is currently employing 30 workers and it hires one more, the firm's total product or output will rise from 294 to 300, so the marginal product of moving from 30 to 31 workers is 6.

Notice that workers' marginal product decreases as more workers are hired. Why is this? Remember the assumption of fixed capital: More and more workers are working with the same amount of capital and there is diminishing marginal productivity.

Column 4 shows the average output per worker (**labor productivity**), a statistic commonly referred to in economic reports. It's determined by dividing the total output by the number of workers. Column 5 shows the additional worker's marginal revenue product, which, since the firm is assumed to be competitive, is determined by multiplying the price the firm receives for the product it sells ($2) by the worker's marginal physical product.

Column 5, the marginal revenue product, is of central importance to the firm. It tells the firm how much additional money it will make from hiring an additional worker. That marginal revenue product represents a competitive firm's demand for labor.

Exhibit 3(b) graphs the firm's derived demand for labor, based on the data in column 5 of Exhibit 3(a). The resulting curve is the firm's **derived demand curve for labor.** It shows the maximum amount of labor, measured in labor hours, that a firm will hire. To see this, let's assume that the wage is $9 and that the firm is hiring 30 workers. If it hires another worker so it has 31 workers, workers' marginal revenue product of $12 exceeds their wage of $9, so the firm can increase profits by doing so. It increases output and profits, since the additional revenue the firm gets from increasing workers from 30 to 31 is $12 and the additional cost the firm incurs is the wage of $9.

Now say the firm has hired 4 additional workers so it has 34 workers. As the firm hires more workers, the marginal product of workers declines. As you can see from

---

Marginal revenue product (MRP)   *The additional revenue a firm receives when it hires an additional worker.*

Value of marginal product (VMP)   *Marginal physical product times the price for which the firm can sell that product.*

Marginal physical product (MPP)   *Additional units of output that hiring an additional worker will bring about.*

Labor productivity   *Average output per worker.*

3   To determine a firm's derived demand curve for labor, you look at the marginal revenue product, because that tells you how much additional money the firm will make from hiring an additional worker.

Q–4:   In Exhibit 3, if the market wage were $7 an hour, how many workers would the firm hire?

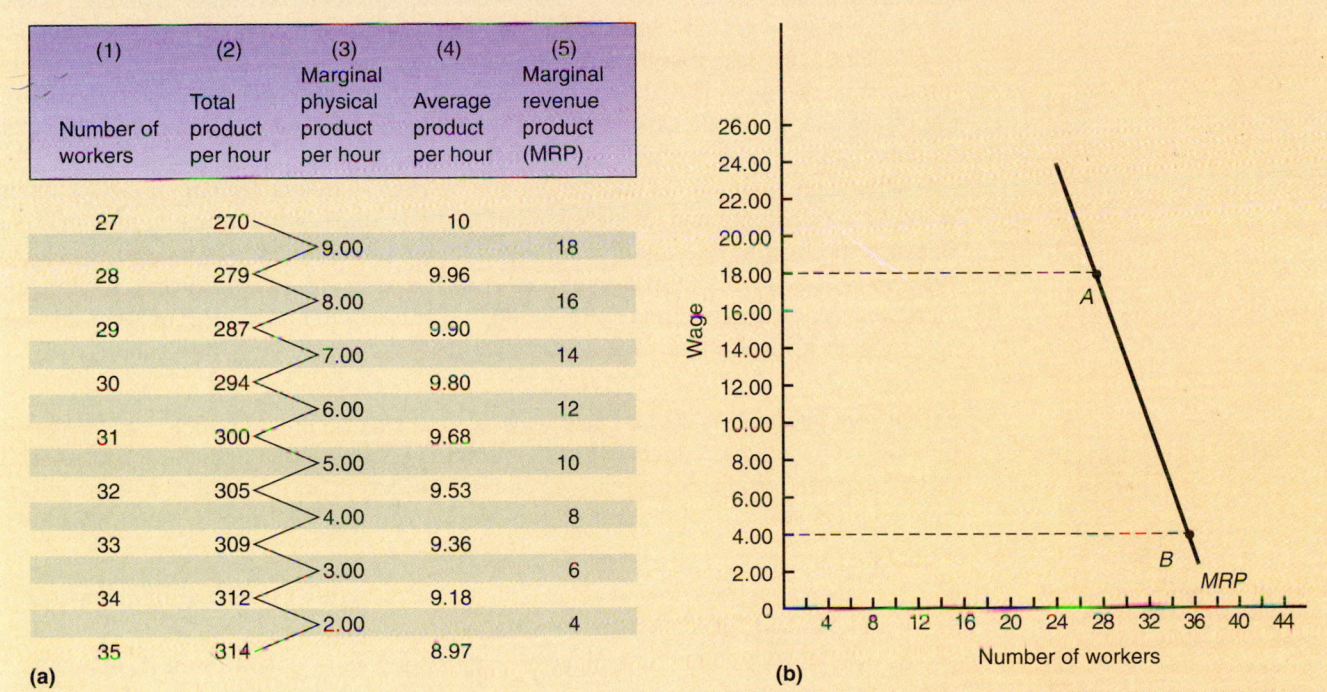

(1) Number of workers	(2) Total product per hour	(3) Marginal physical product per hour	(4) Average product per hour	(5) Marginal revenue product (MRP)
27	270		10	
		9.00		18
28	279		9.96	
		8.00		16
29	287		9.90	
		7.00		14
30	294		9.80	
		6.00		12
31	300		9.68	
		5.00		10
32	305		9.53	
		4.00		8
33	309		9.36	
		3.00		6
34	312		9.18	
		2.00		4
35	314		8.97	

(a)   (b)

EXHIBIT 3 (a and b)   Determining How Many Workers to Hire and the Firm's Derived Demand for Labor

The marginal revenue product is any firm's demand curve for labor. Since for a competitive firm $P=MR$, a competitive firm's derived demand curve is its value of the marginal product curve ($P \times MPP$). This curve tells us the additional revenue the firm gets from having an additional worker. From the chart in (a) we can see that when the firm increases from 27 to 28 workers, the marginal product per hour for each worker is 9. If the product sells for $2, then marginal revenue product is $18, which is one point on the demand curve for labor (point A in (b)). When the firm increases from 34 to 35 workers, the value of the marginal product decreases to $4. This is another point on the firm's derived demand curve (point B in (b)). By connecting the two points, as I have done in (b), you can see that the firm's derived demand curve for labor is downward sloping.

the graph in Exhibit 3(b), the marginal revenue product of decreasing from 34 to 33 workers is $6. Since the workers' marginal revenue product of $6 is less than their wage of $9, now the firm can increase profits by laying off some workers. Doing so decreases output but increases profit, because it significantly increases the average product of the remaining workers.

Only when workers' wage of $9 equals the marginal revenue product does the firm have no incentive to change the number of employees. In this example, the wage ($9) equals workers' marginal revenue product at 32 workers. When the firm is hiring 32 workers, either hiring another worker or laying off one worker will decrease profits. Decreasing from 32 to 31 workers loses $10 in revenue, but increasing from 32 to 33 workers gains $8 in revenue, but costs $9 in wages. Since the marginal revenue product curve tells the firm, given a wage, how many workers it should hire, *the marginal revenue product curve is the firm's demand curve for labor.*

The fact that the demand for labor curve is downward sloping means that as more workers are hired, workers' marginal product falls. This might tempt you to think that the last worker hired is inherently less productive than the first worker hired. But that simply can't be because, by assumption, the workers are identical. Thus, the marginal product of any worker must be identical to the marginal product of any other worker, given that a specified number of workers are working. What the falling marginal product means is that *when 30 rather than 25 workers are working,* the marginal product of any one of those 30 workers is less than the marginal product of any one of 25 of those workers when only 25 are working. When the other inputs are constant, hiring an additional worker lowers the marginal product not only of the last worker but also of any of the other workers.

To understand what's going on here you must remember that when marginal product is calculated, all other inputs are held constant—so if a firm hires another

Q–5: If the price of the firm's product fell to $1, how would your answer to Question 4 change?

Since the marginal revenue product curve tells the firm, given a wage, how many workers it should hire, the marginal revenue product curve is the firm's demand curve for labor.

worker, that worker will have to share machines or tools with other workers. When you share tools, you start running into significant bottlenecks, which cause production to fall. That's why the marginal product of workers goes down when a new worker is hired. This assumption that all other factors of production are held constant is an important one. If all other factors of production are increased, it is not at all clear that workers' productivity will fall as output increases.

Why does a firm hire another worker if doing so will lead to a fall in other workers' productivity and, possibly, a fall in the average productivity of all workers? Because the firm is interested in total profit, not productivity. As long as hiring an extra worker increases revenue by more than the worker costs, the firm's total profit increases. A profit-maximizing firm would be crazy not to hire another worker, even if by doing so it lowers the marginal product of the workers.

Factors Affecting the Demand for Labor   There are many technical issues that determine how the demand for products is translated through firms into a demand for labor (and other factors of production), but we need not go into them in detail. I will, however, state four general principles and give examples of each. The four general principles are:

Four things that affect the firm's demand for labor are: (1) the demand for the firm's product; (2) structure of the firm; (3) the price of the other factors of production; and (4) technology.

1. Changes in the demand for a firm's product will be reflected in changes in its demand for labor.

2. The structure of a firm plays an important role in determining its demand for labor.

3. A change in the other factors of production that a firm uses will change its demand for labor.

4. A change in technology will change its demand for labor.

Let's consider each of these principles in turn.

Changes in the Firm's Demand   The first principle is almost self-evident. An increase in the demand for a product leads to an increase in demand for the laborers who produce that product. The increase in demand pushes the price up, raising the marginal revenue product of labor (which, you'll remember, for a competitive firm is the price of the firm's product times the marginal physical product of labor).

The implications of this first principle, however, are not so self-evident. Often people think of firms' interests and workers' interests as being counter to one another, but this principle tells us that in many ways they are not. What benefits the firm also benefits its workers. Their interests are in conflict only when it comes to deciding how to divide up the total revenues among the owners of the firm, the workers, and the other inputs. Thus, it's not uncommon to see a firm and its workers fighting each other at the bargaining table, but also working together to prevent imports that might compete with the firm's product or to support laws that may benefit the firm.

An example of such cooperation occurred when union workers at a solar energy firm helped fight for an extension of government subsidies for solar energy. Why? Because their contract included a clause that if the solar energy subsidy bill passed, the union workers' wages would be significantly higher than if it didn't. This cooperation between workers and firms has led some economists to treat firms and workers as a single entity, out to get as much as they can as a group. These economists argue that it isn't helpful to separate out factor markets and goods markets. They argue that bargaining power models, which combine factor and goods markets, are the best way to analyze at what level wages will be set. In other words, the cost of labor to a firm should be modeled as if it is determined at the same time that its price and profitability are determined, not separately.

The Structure of the Firm and Its Demand for Labor   The way in which the demand for products is translated into a demand for labor is determined by the structure of the firm. For example, let's consider the difference between a monopolistic industry and a competitive industry. For both, the decision about whether to hire is based on whether

EXHIBIT 4   The Effect of Monopoly and Firm Structure on the Demand for Labor

1	2	3	4	5	6	7
					Marginal revenue product	
Number of workers	Wage	Price P	Marginal revenue (monopolist) MR	Marginal physical product MPP	Competitive (MPP × P)	Monopolist (MPP × MR)
5	$2.85	$1.00	$.75	5	$5.00	$3.75
6	2.85	.95	.65	3	2.85	1.95
7	2.85	.90	.55	1	.90	.55

the wage is below or above the marginal revenue product. But the firms which make up the two industries calculate their marginal revenue products differently.

The price of a competitive firm's output remains constant regardless of how many units it sells. Thus, its marginal revenue product equals the value of the marginal product. To calculate its marginal revenue product we simply multiply the price of the firm's product by the worker's marginal physical product. For a competitive firm:

Marginal revenue product of a worker = Value of the worker's marginal product = MPP × Price of product

The price of a monopolist's product decreases as more units are sold since the monopolist faces a downward-sloping demand curve. The monopolist takes that into account. That's why it focuses on marginal revenue rather than price. As it hires more labor and produces more output, the price it charges for its product will fall. Thus, for a monopolist:

Marginal revenue product of a worker = MPP × Marginal revenue

Since a monopolist's marginal revenue is always less than price, a monopolistic industry will always hire fewer workers than a comparable competitive industry, which is consistent with the result we discussed in the chapter on monopoly: that a monopolistic industry will always produce less than a competitive industry, other things equal.

To ensure that you understand the principle, let's consider the example in Exhibit 4, a table of prices, wages, marginal revenues, marginal physical products, and marginal revenue products for a firm in a competitive industry and a monopolistic industry.

A firm in a competitive industry will hire up to the point where the wage equals MPP × P (columns 5 × 3). This occurs at six workers. Hiring either fewer or more workers would mean a loss in profits for a firm in a competitive industry.

Now let's compare the competitive industry with an equivalent monopolistic industry. Whereas the firm in the competitive industry did not take into account the effect an increase in output would have on prices, the monopolist will do so. It takes into account the fact that in order to sell the additional output of an additional worker, it must lower the price of the good. The relevant marginal revenue product for the monopolist appears in column 7. At six workers, the worker's wage rate of $2.85 exceeds the worker's marginal revenue product of $1.95, which means that the monopolist would hire fewer than six workers—five full-time workers and a part-time worker.

As a second example of how the nature of firms affects the translation of demand for products into demand for labor, consider what would happen if workers controlled the firms rather than independent profit-maximizing owners. You saw before that whenever another worker is hired, other inputs constant, the marginal physical product of all similar workers falls. That can contribute to a reduction in existing workers' wages. The profit-maximizing firm doesn't take into account that effect on existing workers' wages. It wants to hold its costs down. If existing workers are making the decisions about hiring, they'll take that wage decline into account. If they believe that hiring more workers will lower their own wage, they have an incentive to see that new workers aren't hired. Thus, like the monopolist, a worker-controlled firm will hire fewer workers than a competitive profit-maximizing firm.

4 Because a monopolist's marginal revenue is below a competitive firm's price, its demand for labor will be lower, assuming all else equal.

Marginal revenue product of a worker = MPP × Marginal revenue.

ADDED DIMENSION

DIFFICULTIES IN DETERMINING MARGINAL PRODUCTIVITIES

The economic model of labor markets assumes that marginal productivities can be determined relatively easily. In reality they can't. They require guesses and estimates which are often influenced by a worker's interaction with the person doing the guessing and estimating. Thus, social interaction plays a role in determining wages. If you get along with the manager, his estimate of your marginal productivity is likely to be higher than if you don't. And for some reason, managers' estimates of their own marginal productivity tend to be high. In part because of difficulties in estimating marginal productivities, actual pay can often differ substantially from marginal productivities.

Q–6: If firms were controlled by workers, would they likely hire more, or fewer, workers? Why?

There aren't many worker-controlled firms in the United States, but a number of firms include existing workers' welfare in their decision processes. Moreover, with the growth of the team concept discussed in the chapter on production, existing workers' input into managerial decision making is increasing. In many U.S. firms workers have some say in whether additional workers will be hired and at what wage they will be hired. Other firms have an implicit understanding or a written contract with existing workers which restricts hiring and firing decisions. Some firms, such as (until recently) IBM, had never laid off a worker; if they had to reduce their workforce, they created early retirement incentives. Ultimately, however, if their business gets bad enough, the invisible hand wins out over the invisible handshake, and they lay off workers. That happened for IBM, and many large U.S. businesses, in the early 1990s.

Why do firms do such things? To be seen as a "good employer," which makes it easier for them to hire in the future. Given the strong social and legal limitations on firms' hiring and firing decisions, one cannot simply apply marginal productivity theory to the real world. One must first understand the institutional and legal structures of the labor market. However, the existence of these other forces doesn't mean that the economic forces represented by marginal productivity don't exist. Rather, it means that firms struggle to find a wage policy that accommodates both economic and social forces in their wage-setting process. For example, in the 1980s and 1990s, a number of firms (such as airline and automobile firms) negotiated two-tier wage contracts. They continued to pay their existing workers a higher wage, but paid new workers a lower wage, even though old and new workers were doing identical jobs. These two-tier wage contracts were the result of the interactions of the social and market forces.

Changes in Other Factors of Production A third principle determining the derived demand for labor is the amount of other factors of production that the firm has. Given a technology, an increase in other factors of production will increase the marginal physical product of existing workers. For example, let's say that a firm buys more machines so that each worker has more machines with which to work. The workers' marginal physical product increases, and the cost per unit of output for the firm decreases. The net effect on the demand for labor is unclear; it depends on how much the firm increases output, how much the firm's price is affected, and how easily one type of input can be substituted for another—or whether it must be used in conjunction with others.

While we can't say what the final effect on demand will be, we can determine the firm's cost minimization position. When a firm is using resources as efficiently as possible, and hence is minimizing costs, the marginal product of each factor of production divided by the price of that factor must equal that of all the other factors. Specifically, the **cost minimization condition** is:

$$MP_l/w = MP_m/P_m = MP_x/P_x$$

where

w = Wage rate
l = Labor
m = Machines
x = Any other input.

Cost minimization condition The ratio of marginal product to the price of an input is equal for all inputs. The equation is: $MP_l/w = MP_m/P_m = MP_x/P_x$.

If this cost minimizing condition is not met, the firm could hire more of the input with the higher marginal product and less of other inputs, and produce the same amount of output at a lower cost.

Let's consider a numerical example. Say the marginal product of labor is 20 and the wage is $4, while the marginal product of machines is 30 and the rental price of machines is $4. You're called in to advise the firm. You say, "Fire one worker, which will decrease output by 20 and save $4; spend that $4 on machines, which will increase output by 30." Output has increased by 10 while costs have remained constant. As long as the marginal products divided by the prices of the various inputs are unequal, you can make such recommendations to lower cost.

Changes in Technology   Our fourth and final principle governing the demand for labor concerns the effect of changes in technology. What effect will a change in technology have on the demand for an input? This question has often been debated, and it has no unambiguous answer. What economists do know is that the simple reasoning often used by laypeople when they argue that the development of new technology will decrease the demand for labor is wrong. That simple reasoning is as follows: "Technology makes it possible to replace workers with machines, so it will decrease the demand for labor." This is sometimes called *Luddite reasoning* because it's what drove the Luddites to go around smashing machines in early-nineteenth-century England.

What's wrong with Luddite reasoning? First, look at history. Technology has increased enormously, yet the demand for labor has not decreased; instead it has increased as output has increased. In other words, Luddite reasoning doesn't take into account the fact that total output can change. A second problem with Luddite reasoning is that labor is necessary for building and maintaining the machines, so increased demand for machines increases the demand for labor.

Luddite reasoning isn't *all* wrong. Technology can sometimes decrease the demand for certain types of skills. The computer has decreased demand for calligraphers; the automobile reduced demand for carriage makers. New technology changes the types of labor demanded. If you have the type of labor that will be made technologically obsolete, you can be hurt by technological change. However, technological change hasn't reduced the overall demand for labor; it has instead led to an increase in total output and a need for even more laborers to produce that output.

In the 1990s, we're likely to see an enormous increase in the use of robots to do many repetitive tasks that blue collar workers formerly did. Thus, demand for manufacturing labor will likely decrease, but it will be accompanied by an increase in demand for service industry labor—designing and repairing robots and designing activities that will fill up people's free time.

International Competitiveness and a Country's Demand for Labor   The demand for labor in a country is determined by the relative wage of labor in that country compared to the relative wage of labor in other countries. Multinational corporations are continually making decisions about where to place production facilities, and labor costs—wage rates—play an important role in those decisions. That means the country's exchange rate plays an important role in determining the demand for labor in a country. For example, in 1993 many Japanese automobile companies switched their production of cars to be sold in the United States from production facilities in Japan to facilities in the United States. Why? Because the rise in value of the yen, and fall in value of the dollar, meant that the hourly rate of labor in the United States was about $16 and the hourly rate in Japan was about $20.

But why produce in the United States when the hourly rate in Mexico was only one-fourth that in the United States? Or in Malaysia, where the hourly rate was only one-tenth that in the United States? The reasons are complicated, but include: (1) differences in workers—U.S. workers may be more productive; (2) transportation costs—producing in the country to which you're selling keeps transportation costs down; (3) potential trade restrictions—Japan was under enormous pressure from the U.S. government to reduce its trade surplus with the United States; and producing in

Q–7:   In the 1980s and 1990s, farmers have been switching from small square bales, which they hired students on summer break to store for them, to large round bales, which can be handled almost entirely by machines. What is a likely reason for the switch?

Q–8:   Should teachers be worried about the introduction of computer- and video-based teaching systems? Why or why not?

In the early 1800s, a group of British textile workers revolted against the introduction of a machine to produce cloth called a *wide frame,* which they said resulted in an inferior product. By all accounts, the wide frame produced textiles faster and reduced demand for textile workers. Angered by the introduction of these machines, a group of textile workers masked themselves and went around breaking up wide frame machines. They threatened any employee who used a wide frame. They were known as *Luddites* in memory of Ned Ludd, a worker who, 30 years earlier, had attacked stocking frames because he thought those devices were replacing workers in the manufacture of stockings.

In 1812, after a number of people had been killed, the British government stepped in and ended the movement, hanging some of the Luddite leaders and sending others to the colonies (which in those days was regarded as a severe punishment). By the 1820s, the wide frame was used throughout the British textile industry. But the term *Luddite* has remained part of the English language and is used to describe people who, in fear of losing their jobs, strongly oppose the introduction of new technology.

the U.S. helped them avoid future trade restrictions; (4) compatibility of production techniques with social institutions—production techniques must fit with a society's social institutions. If they don't, production will fall significantly. Number (5) is the focal point phenomenon—a company can't consider all places, and it costs a lot of money to explore a country's potential as a possible host country. Japanese businesses know what to expect when they open a plant in the United States; they don't know in many other countries. So the United States, and other countries that Japanese businesses have knowledge about, become focal points. They are considered as potential sites for business, while other, possibly equally good, countries are not. Combined, these reasons lead to a "follow the leader" system in which countries fall in and out of global companies' production plans. The focal-point countries expand and develop; the others don't.

The Supply of and Demand for Labor

Supply and demand forces strongly influence wages, but they do not fully determine wages.

Exhibit 5(a) puts the supply of and demand for labor on the same graph. The equilibrium wage occurs at the point where the quantity of labor supplied equals the quantity of labor demanded. The equilibrium wage is W_0 and the equilibrium quantity of labor is L_0.

Supply and demand forces strongly influence wages, but they do not fully determine wages. Real-world labor markets are filled with examples of suppliers or demanders who resist these supply and demand pressures through organizations such as labor unions, professional associations, and agreements among demanders. But, as I've emphasized throughout the book, supply and demand analysis is a useful framework for considering such resistance.

For example, say that you're advising a firm's workers on how to raise their wages. You point out that if workers want to increase their wages, they must figure out some way either to increase the demand for their services or to limit the labor supplied to the firm. One way to limit the number of workers the firm will hire (and thus keep existing workers' wages high) is to force the firm to pay an above-equilibrium wage, as in Exhibit 5(b). Say that in their contract negotiations the workers get the firm to agree to pay a wage of W_1. At wage W_1, the quantity of labor supplied is L_1 and the quantity of labor demanded is L_2. The difference, $L_1 - L_2$, represents the number of people who want jobs at wage W_1 compared to the number who have them. In such a case, jobs must be rationed. Whom you know, where you come from, or the color of your skin may play a role in whether you get a job with that firm.

As a second example, consider what would happen if U.S. immigration laws were liberalized. If you say the supply curve of labor would shift outward and the wage level would drop, you're right, as shown in Exhibit 5(c). In it the supply of labor increases from S_0 to S_1. In response, the wage falls from W_0 to W_1 and the quantity of labor demanded increases from L_0 to L_1.

In analyzing the effect of such a major change in the labor supply, however, remember that supply and demand are partial equilibrium tools, and that they're

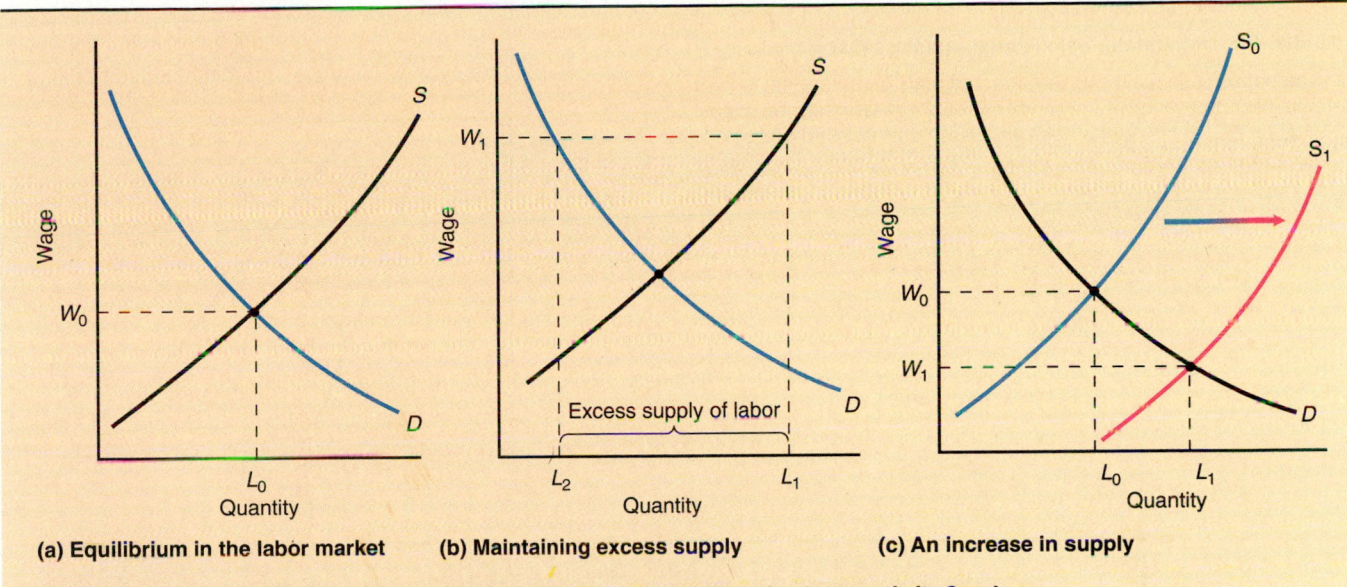

(a) Equilibrium in the labor market   **(b) Maintaining excess supply**   **(c) An increase in supply**

EXHIBIT 5 (a, b, and c)   The Supply of and Demand for Labor and the Effect of an Increase in its Supply
When the supply and the demand curves for labor are placed on the same graph, the equilibrium wage, W_0, is where the supply equals demand as in (a). At this wage, L_0 laborers are supplied. We see the effect of an above-equilibrium wage: In order for workers to increase their wages, they must increase the demand for their services or limit the quantity of workers supplied. If they force the firm to pay them a wage of W_1 instead of the equilibrium wage, there will be more workers supplied (L_1) than demanded (L_2). With an excess supply of labor, jobs must be rationed. With an increase in the supply of labor—for example, because of liberalization in the immigration laws—the supply of labor curve shifts outward from S_0 to S_1 as shown in (c). Assuming the demand for labor remains the same, the increase in the supply of labor will cause the wage level to drop from W_0 to W_1.

relevant only if the change in the supply of labor doesn't also affect the demand for labor. In reality, a change in U.S. immigration laws might increase the demand for products, thereby increasing the demand for labor and raising wages. Looking at the overall effects of a change, rather than just at the partial equilibrium effects, often makes the final result less clear-cut. That's why it's important always to remember the assumptions behind the model you're using. Those assumptions often add qualifications to the simple "right" answer.

Looking at the overall effects of a change, rather than just the partial equilibrium effects, often makes the final result less clear-cut.

I hope I've given you a sense of how supply and demand analysis can be applied to the labor market. It's applied to the labor market just as it is to any other market: It leads one to consider the incentives of the relevant decision makers, to pinpoint each decision maker's best strategy, and then to see how the various strategies interact within the framework of supply and demand.

Whenever you look at labor markets, thinking about supply, demand, incentives, and strategies is an important first step in figuring out what's going on. However, it's only a first step. As was stated in the introduction to this chapter, the invisible handshake and invisible foot play key roles in determining the wages people receive. In the remainder of this chapter, we discuss some of these issues.

Just as product markets can be imperfectly competitive, so too can labor markets. For example, there might be a **monopsony** (a market in which only a single firm hires labor). Alternatively, laborers might have organized together in a union that allows workers to operate as if there were only a single seller. In effect, the union could operate as a monopoly. Alternatively again, there might be a **bilateral monopoly** (a market with only a single seller and a single buyer). Let's briefly consider these three types of market imperfections.

Imperfect Competition and the Labor Market

5 A monopsony is a market in which only a single firm hires labor. A bilateral monopoly is a market in which a single seller faces a single buyer.

Monopsony   When there's only one buyer of labor services, it makes sense for that buyer to take into account the fact that if it hires another worker, the equilibrium wage will rise and it will have to pay more for all workers. The choice facing a monopsonist can be seen in Exhibit 6. In it, the supply curve of labor is upward sloping so that the **marginal factor cost** (the additional cost to a firm of hiring another worker) is above

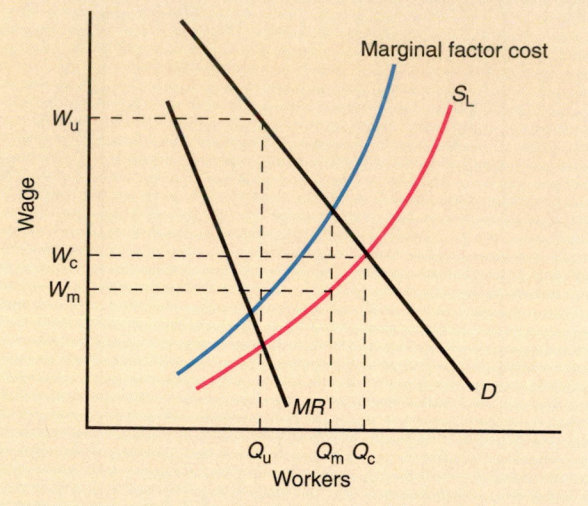

EXHIBIT 6   **Monopsony, Union Power, and the Labor Market**

A monopsonist hires fewer workers and pays them less than would a set of competitive firms. The monopsonist determines the quantity of labor, Q_m, to hire at the point where the marginal factor cost curve intersects the demand curve. The monopsonist pays a wage of W_m. A union has a tendency to push for a higher wage, W_u, and a lower quantity of workers, Q_u.

the supply curve since the monopsonist takes into account the fact that hiring another worker will increase the wage rate it must pay to all workers.

Instead of hiring Q_c workers at a wage of W_c, as would happen in a competitive labor market, the monopsonist hires Q_m workers and pays them a wage of W_m. (A good exercise to see that you understand the argument is to show that where there's a monopsonist, a minimum wage simultaneously can increase employment and raise the wage.)

Union Monopoly Power   When a union exists, it will have an incentive to act as a monopolist, restricting supply so as to increase its members' wage. To do so it must have the power to restrict both supply and union membership. The equilibrium wage and employment would depend on who is allowed to be a union member and what methods of redistributing income among union members exist. But there would be a strong tendency for the union to act like a monopolist and to move to an equilibrium somewhat similar to the monopsonist case, except for one important difference. The wage the union would set wouldn't be set below the competitive wage; instead, the wage would be above the competitive wage at W_u, as in Exhibit 6. Faced with a wage of W_u, competitive firms will hire Q_u workers. Thus, with union monopoly power, the benefits of restricting supply accrue to the union members, not to the firm as it did in the monopsonist case.

Bilateral Monopoly   As our final case, let's consider a bilateral monopoly in which a monopsonist faces a union with monopoly power. In this case, we can say that the equilibrium wage will be somewhere between the monopsonist wage, W_m, and the union monopoly power wage, W_u, and the equilibrium quantity will be somewhere between Q_u and Q_m in Exhibit 6. Where in that range the wage and equilibrium quantity will be depends on the two sides' negotiating skills and other noneconomic forces.

THE OTHER INVISIBLE FORCES AND THE LABOR MARKET

Let's now consider some real-world characteristics of labor markets. For example:

1. English teachers are paid close to what economics teachers are paid even though the quantity of English teachers supplied significantly exceeds the quantity of English teachers demanded, while the quantity of economics teachers supplied is approximately equal to the quantity demanded.

2. On average, women earn about 70 cents for every $1 earned by men.

3. The relative pay of many kinds of jobs seems to fall into a pattern in which one is always the same percentage of another. This pattern is called a *wage contour,* and it often remains constant despite shifts in supply and demand among the various jobs.

4. Certain types of jobs are undertaken primarily by members of a single ethnic group. For example, Mohawk Indians make up a large percentage of construction workers on high-rise buildings. They have an uncanny knack for keeping their balance on high, open building frames.

5. Firms often pay higher than ''market'' wages.

6. Firms often don't lay off workers even when there is a decrease in the demand for their product.

7. Wages don't fluctuate very much as unemployment rises.

8. It often seems that there are two categories of jobs: dead-end jobs and jobs with potential for career advancement. Once in a dead-end job, a person finds it almost impossible to switch to a job with potential.

9. The rate of unemployment among blacks is approximately twice as high as the rate among whites.

Supply and demand analysis alone doesn't explain these phenomena. Each of them can, however, be explained as the result of a combination of invisible forces. Thus, to understand real-world labor markets it is necessary to broaden the analysis of labor markets to include other invisible forces that limit the use of the market. These include the invisible handshake (which creates social limitations on the self-seeking activities of firms and individuals) and the invisible foot (which creates legal limitations on the self-seeking behavior of firms and individuals). Let's consider a couple of the central issues of interaction among the invisible forces and see how they affect the labor market.

> **6** Real-world labor markets are complicated and must be explained by all three invisible forces: the invisible hand, the invisible handshake, and the invisible foot.

Fairness and the Labor Market

People generally have an underlying view of what's fair. That view isn't always consistent among individuals, but it's often strongly held. The first lesson taught in a personnel or human resources course is that people aren't machines. They're human beings with feelings and emotions. If they feel good about a job, if they feel they're part of a team, then they will work hard; if they feel they're being taken advantage of, they can be highly disruptive.

On some assembly line jobs, effort is relatively easy to monitor, so individuals can be—and in the past often were—treated like machines. Their feelings and emotions were ignored. Productivity was determined by the speed of the assembly line; if workers couldn't or wouldn't keep up the pace, they were fired.

Efficiency Wages   Most modern jobs, however, require workers to make decisions and to determine how best to do a task. Today's managers are aware that workers' emotional state is important to whether they make sound decisions and do a good job. So most firms, even if they don't really care about anything but profit, will try to keep their workers happy. It's in their own interest to do so. That might mean paying workers an above-average wage, not laying them off even if layoffs would make sense economically, providing day care so the workers aren't worried about their children, or keeping wage differentials among workers small to limit internal rivalry. Such actions can often make long-run economic sense, even though they might cost the firm in the short run. They are common enough that they have acquired a name—**efficiency wages**—wages paid above marginal revenue in order to keep workers happy and productive.

> *Efficiency wages*   An above-average wage paid to a worker for bringing forth better effort.

Views of fairness also enter into wage determination through political channels. Social views of fairness influence government, which passes laws to implement those views. Minimum wage laws, comparable worth laws, and antidiscrimination laws are examples.

Comparable Worth Laws   Let's consider one of those—**comparable worth laws.** Comparable worth laws are laws mandating comparable pay for comparable work, i.e., mandatory ''fairness.'' The problem is in defining what is comparable. Do you define comparable work by the education it requires, the effort one puts out, or by other characteristics? Similarly with pay: Compensation has many dimensions and it

> *Comparable worth laws*   Laws mandating comparable pay for comparable work.

 DEMOCRACY IN THE WORKPLACE

In the United States, slavery is illegal. One cannot sell oneself to another, even if one wants to. It's an unenforceable contract. But work, which might be considered a form of partial slavery, is legal. We can sell our labor services for a specific, limited period of time.

Is there any inherent reason that such partial slavery should be seen as acceptable? The answer to that question is complicated. It deals with the rights of workers, and is based on value judgments. You must answer it for yourself. I raise it because it's a good introduction to Karl Marx's analysis of the labor market (which deals with alienation) and to some recent arguments about democracy in the workplace.

Marx saw selling one's labor as immoral, just as slavery was immoral. He believed that capitalists exploited workers by alienating them from their labor. The best equivalent I can think of is the way most people today view the selling of sex. Most people see selling sex as wrong because it alienates a person from his or her body. Marx saw all selling of labor that same way. A labor market makes one see oneself as an object, not as a human being.

The underlying philosophical issues of Marx's concern are outside of economics. Most people in the United States don't agree with Marx's philosophical underpinnings. But it's nonetheless a useful exercise to think about this issue and ask yourself whether it helps explain why we somehow treat the labor market as different than other markets and limit by law the right of employers to discriminate in the labor market.

Some of Marx's philosophical tenets are shared by the modern democracy-in-the-workplace movement. In this view, a business isn't owned by a certain group, but is an association of individuals who have come together to produce a certain product. For one group—the owners of stock—to have all the say as to how the business is run, and for another group—the regular workers—to have no say, is immoral in the same way that not having democracy in deciding on government is immoral. According to this view, work is as large a part of people's lives as is national or local politics, and a country can call itself a democracy only if it has democracy in the workplace.

As with most grandiose ideas, this one is complicated, but it's worth considering because it's reflected in certain laws. Consider, for example, the 1989 federal law that limits firms' freedom to close plants without giving notice to their workers. The view that workers have certain unalienable rights played a role in passing that law.

For those of you who say, ''Right on!'' to the idea of increasing workers' rights, let me add a word of caution. Increasing workers' rights has a cost. It makes it less likely that firms and individuals who can think up things that need doing will do so, and thus will decrease the number of jobs available. It will also enormously increase firms' desire to discriminate. If you know you must let a person play a role in decisions once you hire that person, you're going to be much more careful whom you hire.

None of these considerations mean that democracy in the workplace can't work. There are examples of somewhat democratic ''firms.'' Universities are run as partial democracies, with the faculty deciding what policies should be set. (There is, however, serious debate about how well universities are run.) But as soon as you add worker democracy to production, more questions come up: What about consumers? Shouldn't they, too, have a voice in decisions? What about the community within which the firm is located?

Economics can't answer such questions. Economics can, however, be used to predict and analyze some of the difficulties such changes might bring about.

is not at all clear which are the relevant ones, or whether the political system will focus on the relevant ones.

The problems in determining ''comparable worth'' to serve as the basis of such a law is a major deterrent to the establishment of a law on the subject. All agree about that. But it is also important not to see the issue as a simple market/nonmarket issue. Real-world markets are never simple, and labor markets, in particular, are embedded in an institutional structure in which social and intra-firm political issues are often the determining factors in setting pay.

Economists who favor comparable worth laws point out that significant portions of the current institutional structure determining pay are largely non-market structures. In fact, firms often have their own implicit or explicit comparable worth systems built into their structure. For example, seniority, not productivity, often determines pay. Bias against women and minorities and in favor of high-level management is sometimes built into those pay-setting institutions. In short, within firms, pay structure is influenced by, but is not determined by, supply and demand forces. Comparable worth laws are designed to affect those institutional biases, and thus are not necessarily any more incompatible with supply and demand forces than are current pay-setting institutions.

Discrimination is an important noneconomic factor that helps explain why labor markets don't operate as supply and demand analysis suggests they should. Managers, like many other people, have prejudices that are reflected (consciously or unconsciously) in their hiring decisions. When one group (in our society, white males) controls the hiring for most of the jobs, their prejudices can, and do, affect their hiring decisions. Whether prejudice should be allowed to affect the hiring decision is a normative question for society to settle.

In answering these normative questions, our society has passed laws making it illegal for employers to discriminate on the basis of race, religion, sex, age, disability, or national origin. The reason society has made it illegal is its ethical belief in equal opportunity for all, or at least most, individuals. (Homosexuals still aren't protected by federal legislation assuring them equal opportunities.)

Economics cannot provide answers to the normative questions of whether society should allow discrimination. Economics can, however, provide insight into how discrimination, and society's attempts to eliminate it, will affect the economy, so that if society passes laws that prevent market forces from operating, it realizes the cost of doing so.

Three Types of Direct Discrimination   In analyzing discrimination, it's important to distinguish three types of direct discrimination. One type of discrimination is based on individual characteristics that will affect job performance. For example, restaurants might discriminate against applicants with sourpuss personalities. Another example of this might be a firm trying to hire young salespeople because its clients like to buy from younger rather than older employees. A second type of discrimination is based on correctly perceived statistical characteristics of a group. A firm may correctly perceive that young people in general have a lower probability of staying on a job than do older people and therefore discriminate against younger people. A third type of discrimination is based on individual characteristics that don't affect job performance or are based on incorrectly perceived statistical characteristics of groups. A firm might not hire people over 50 because the supervisor doesn't like working with older people, even though older people may be just as productive as, or even more productive than, younger people.

Of the three types, the third will be easiest to eliminate; it doesn't have an economic motivation. In fact discrimination based on individual characteristics that don't affect job performance is costly to a firm, and market forces will work toward eliminating it. An example of the success of a firm's policy to reduce discrimination is the decision by McDonald's to create a special program to hire the learning-disabled. This group makes good employees. They have lower turnover rates and follow procedures better than do many of the other people McDonald's hires who view the job as temporary. Moreover, through advertising, McDonald's helped change people's negative view about being served by a special person into a positive view of such service. So in this case market forces and political forces are working together.

If the discrimination is of either of the first two types and is based on characteristics that do affect job performance, either directly or statistically, the discrimination will be harder to eliminate. Not discriminating can be costly to the firm, so political forces to eliminate discrimination will be working against market forces to keep discrimination.

Whenever discrimination saves the firm money, it will have an economic incentive to use subterfuges to get around an antidiscrimination law. These subterfuges will make the firm appear to be meeting the law, even when it isn't. For example, a firm will find another reason to explain why it isn't hiring an older person and will avoid using age as the reason.

Institutional Discrimination   Direct discrimination is not the only type of discrimination that can exist. There can also be institutional demand-side discrimination, in which the structure of the job makes it difficult or impossible for certain groups of individ-

Job Discrimination and the Labor Market

Q–9:   Economic theory argues that discrimination should be eliminated. True or false? Why?

7   Three types of discrimination are: (1) discrimination based on individual characteristics that will affect job performance; (2) discrimination based on correctly-perceived statistical characteristics of the group; and (3) discrimination based on individual characteristics that don't affect job performance or are incorrectly perceived.

Whenever discrimination saves the firm money, it will have an economic incentive to use subterfuges to get around an anti-discrimination law.

uals to succeed. Consider the policies of colleges and universities. To succeed as a professor, administrator, or other professional in the academic market, one must devote an enormous amount of effort during one's twenties and thirties. But these years are precisely the years when, given genetics and culture, many women have major family responsibilities that makes it difficult for them to succeed in the academic market. Were academic institutions different—say, a number of positions at universities were designed for high-level, part-time work during this time period—it would be easier for women to advance. Thus, one can argue that women face institutional demand-side discrimination in universities. Of course, one might also argue that it is the supply-side institutions where the discrimination occurs because in relationships, women get more child-rearing responsibility than men. When, for instance, parents have a sick child someone must stay home, and in the majority of relationships, the woman, not the man, stays home and jeopardizes her advancement potential.

Clearly, I have only touched on the issues; a thorough consideration is beyond the scope of the course. But it is important to note that discrimination can be deeply embedded in institutions and that the lack of direct discriminatory actions does not necessarily mean that discrimination does not exist.

Labor Markets in the Real World

Now that we've briefly considered how noneconomic forces can influence labor markets, let's turn our attention to real-world labor markets so you can have a sense of how they developed and how they might affect you.

Labor markets as we now know them developed in the 1700s and 1800s. Given the political and social rules that operated at the time, the invisible hand was free to push wage rates down to subsistence level. Work weeks were long and working conditions were poor. Laborers began to turn to other ways—besides the market—of influencing their wage. One way was to use political power to place legal restrictions on employers in their relationship with workers. A second way was to organize together—to unionize. Let's consider each in turn.

Evolving Labor Laws

Over the years, government has responded to workers' political pressure with a large number of laws that limit what can and what cannot be done in the various labor markets. For example, in many areas of production, laws limit to eight the normal number of hours a person can work on one job in a day. The laws also prescribe the amount of extra pay an employee who works more than the normal number of hours must receive. (Generally it's time-and-a-half.)

Similarly, the number and length of coffee breaks workers get are defined by law (one 15-minute coffee break every four hours). Child labor laws mandate that a person must be at least 16 in order to be hired. The safety and health conditions under which a person can work are regulated by laws. (For example, on a construction site all workers are required to wear hard hats.) Workers can be fired only for cause, and employers must show that they had cause to fire a worker. (For example, a 55-year-old employee cannot be fired simply because he or she is getting old.) Employers must not allow sexual harassment in the workplace. (Bosses can't make sexual advances to employees and firms must make a good-faith attempt to see that some employees don't sexually harass other employees.)

Combined, these laws play an enormously important role in the functioning of the labor market.

Unions and Collective Bargaining

Some of the most important labor laws concern workers' right to organize together in order to bargain collectively with employers. These laws also specify the tactics workers can use to achieve their ends. In the latter part of the 1800s, workers had few rights to organize themselves. The Knights of Labor was formed in 1869, and by 1886 it had approximately 800,000 members. But a labor riot in 1886 turned public opinion against these workers and led to the organization's breakup. In its place, the American Federation of Labor developed and began to organize strikes to achieve higher wages.

EXHIBIT 7   Change in Union Membership, 1895–1993

The graph shows union membership from 1895–1993. As can be seen, after the Depression in the 1930s, unions grew in importance. In the 1980s the importance of unions declined, even though the labor force was growing significantly.
Source: Bureau of Labor Statistics.

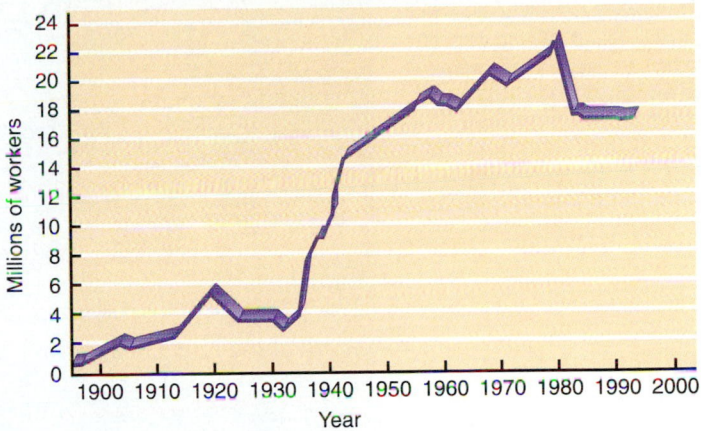

Business opposed unions' right to strike, and initially the government supported business. Police and sometimes the army were sent in to break up strikes. Under the then-existing legal structure of the economy, unions were seen as monopolistic restraints on trade and an intrusion into management rights.

In the 1920s and 1930s, society's view of unions changed, and laws such as the National Labor Relations Act and Wagner Act were passed guaranteeing workers the right to form unions, to strike, and to engage in collective bargaining. As Exhibit 7 shows, from 1935 to 1980 unions grew significantly in size and importance.

Businesses weren't happy with unions' increasing strength, and in 1947 they managed to get the Taft-Hartley Act passed. That act placed limitations on union activities. It allowed states to pass "right-to-work" laws forbidding union membership to be made a requirement for continued employment. Moreover, it made **closed shops** illegal. In a closed shop the union controls hiring; before anyone can be hired he or she must be a member of the particular union. In **union shops,** which federal law does permit, individuals are required to join a union after working for the firm for a period of time. A number of states have right-to-work laws that make union shops illegal.

Closed shop   A firm in which the union controls hiring.

Union shop   A firm in which all workers must join the union.

The Taft-Hartley Act also outlawed *secondary boycotts.* In a secondary boycott, in order to strengthen its bargaining position, a union gets other unions to refuse to buy a firm's products, even if members of the other unions aren't employed by that firm.

As we see in Exhibit 7, since the 1980s the number of workers in unions has been declining. Moreover, when the growth of the labor force is taken into account, the relative decline in labor union membership is even more significant. Unions don't have the political or economic clout they once had.

Part of the reason, ironically, is their success. By pressuring the government to pass laws that protected workers, unions made themselves less necessary. Another part of the reason is the changing nature of production in the United States. Labor unions were especially strong in manufacturing industries. As manufacturing has declined in importance in the United States and the service sector has increased in importance, the base of union membership has been reduced. Unions have somewhat compensated for this change by pushing unionization drives among public sector workers (that is, government employees), and this sector has seen the largest increase in union membership. In the 1990s, more than 40 percent of union members work in the public sector. These unions are becoming strong and will likely be exerting their influence through the 1990s.

Part of the reason labor union membership has declined in recent years is the unions' successes.

This chapter is meant to give you a sense of how the labor market works. But what does it all mean for those of you who'll soon be getting a job or are in the process of changing jobs? I'll try to answer that question in this section.

THE LABOR MARKET AND YOU

In the late 1800s, many workers worked in sweatshops; they often had quotas that required them to work 60 or more hours a week. Fines were imposed for such indiscretions as talking or smiling.   *The Bettmann Archive.*

Exhibit 8 shows a variety of potentially useful statistics about the labor market. Let's consider how some of them might affect you. For example, consider relative pay of jobs requiring a college degree compared to jobs requiring only high school degrees. Jobs requiring a college degree earn significantly more, on average, than do jobs only requiring a high school degree. In recent years the income gap between the two groups has noticeably increased. So the answer to the question of whether it's worthwhile to stick college out for another couple of years and get a degree is probably yes.

Q–10: Ph.D.s earn less than MBAs, so, therefore, one should get an MBA rather than a Ph.D. True or false? Why?

Next, consider the salaries of Ph.D.s compared to the salaries of MBAs. A *Ph.D.* is a person who has gone to graduate school after college, usually for a number of years, and earned an advanced degree called a **D**octorate of **Ph**ilosophy—even though there are many subjects besides philosophy (such as economics) in which one can earn a Ph.D. As you can see, Ph.D.s' starting salaries are lower than salaries of MBAs and professionals with other kinds of advanced degrees. Does this mean that Ph.D.s are discriminated against? Not necessarily. It's possible that Ph.D.s' lower pay suggests that Ph.D.s derive a ''psychic income'' from their work in addition to the amount of money they earn.

Since Ph.D.s are often quite smart, their willingness to accept psychic income as a substitute for higher pay suggests that there's much more to consider in a job than the salary. What's most important about a job isn't the wage, but whether you like what you're doing and the life that job is consistent with. (Of course, their lower salaries also could imply that Ph.D.s really aren't so smart.)

So my suggestion to you is definitely to finish college, especially if you enjoy it. (And with books like this, how can you help but enjoy it?) But go to graduate school only if you really enjoy learning. In picking your job, first and foremost pick a job that you enjoy (as long as it pays you enough to live on). Among jobs that you like, choose a job in a field in which the supply of labor is limited, or the demand for labor is significantly increasing. Either of those trends is likely to lead to higher wages. After all, if you're doing something you like, you might as well get paid as much as possible for it.

Jobs in which the supply will likely be limited are those in which the invisible foot has placed restrictions on entry or those requiring special abilities. If you have

The *Occupational Outlook Handbook* is an excellent Department of Labor publication for checking the outlook for various careers.

EXHIBIT 8 (a, b, c, and d)   Some Useful Labor Information

(a) Some typical starting salaries of BAs: 1994

Occupation	Private or state	U.S. government
Budget analyst	$25,000	$18,000
Management analyst	23,000	18,000
Regional planner	16,000	18,000
Physician assistant	34,000	—
Secretary	16,000	14,500
Secondary school teacher	20,000	—
Economist	20,000	18,000
Janitor	14,000	14,000
Retail sales (salary and commission)	15,000	
Insurance sales	20,000	—

Sources: Author's estimates based on *Occupational Outlook Handbook* and U.S. Dept. of Labor Statistics (pay varies significantly by region).

(b) Average weekly earnings in selected fields, 1993

Occupational category	Average weekly earnings 1993
Manufacturing	$486
Transportation and public utilities	542
Wholesale trade	447
Retail trade	210
Finance, insurance, and real estate	404
Services	351

Source: U. S. Dept. of Labor, *Employment and Earnings.*

(c) Predicted change in employment 1990–2005

Occupational group	Expected change
Total	+20%
Technicians	+37
Professional specialties	+32
Service	+29
Managerial	+27
Marketing and sales	+24
Transportation	+21
Construction	+20
Mechanics	+16
Administrative support	+13
Laborers	+8
Farming and forestry	+5
Production	−4

Source: Bureau of Labor Statistics. *Occupational Outlook Handbook.*

(d) Starting salaries for selected professional degrees, 1994*

Degree	Annual Salary
Law (3 years)	
High-ranked school	$ 80,000
Intermediate-ranked school	40,000
Low-ranked school	24,000
Engineering	
Bachelor's degree	34,000
Master's degree	47,000
Business	
Bachelor's degree	25,000
Master's (MBA) degree (2 years)	45,000
M.D. (4 years and 3 year internship)	120,000
Ph.D. (5 years)	
in economics	45,000
in humanities	40,000

* These figures are rough estimates based on data from the Dept. of Labor and informal surveys of author.

Source: U.S. Department of Labor.

some special ability, try to find a job you enjoy in which you can utilize that ability. You might also look for a job in which entry is restricted, but beware: Jobs that are restricted in supply must be rationed, so while such jobs pay higher wages, you may need personal connections to obtain one of them.

I'm sure most of you are aware that your choice of jobs is one of the most important choices you'll be making in your life. So I'm sure you feel the pressure. But you should also know that a job, unlike marriage, isn't necessarily supposed to be for life. There's enormous flexibility in the U.S. labor market. Many people change jobs six or seven times in their lifetime. So while the choice is important, a poor choice can be remedied, so don't despair if the first job you take isn't perfect. Good luck.

CHAPTER SUMMARY

- Incentive effects are important in labor supply decisions.
- The demand for labor by firms is a derived demand determined by labor's marginal revenue product.
- A firm's demand for labor is affected by the demand for a firm's product, the firm's internal structure, the price of other factors of production, and technology.

- A monopsony is a market in which only a single firm hires labor; a bilateral monopoly is a market in which there is a single seller and a single buyer.
- In the labor market, the invisible handshake and the invisible foot are very active.
- Labor laws have evolved and will continue to evolve.
- Since the 1980s, labor unions have been declining in importance.

- Discrimination is an important factor that hinders the invisible hand. It has many dimensions.
- Discrimination based on characteristics that affect job performance is hardest to eliminate.
- To be happy, finish college and choose a job you enjoy.

KEY TERMS

bilateral monopoly *(673)*
closed shop *(679)*
comparable worth laws *(675)*
cost minimization condition *(670)*
derived demand *(665)*
derived demand curve for labor *(666)*
Dutch disease *(663)*

efficiency wages *(675)*
entrepreneurship *(665)*
focal point phenomenon *(672)*
incentive effect *(660)*
labor market *(660)*
labor productivity *(666)*
marginal factor cost *(673)*

marginal physical product (MPP) *(666)*
marginal revenue product (MRP) *(666)*
marginal tax rate *(662)*
monopsony *(673)*
union shop *(679)*
value of marginal product (VMP) *(666)*

QUESTIONS FOR THOUGHT AND REVIEW

The number after each question represents the estimated degree of critical thinking required. (1 = almost none; 10 = deep thought.)

1. Why are the invisible handshake and invisible foot more active in the labor market than in most other markets? *(4)*

2. Welfare laws are bad, not for society, but for the people they are meant to help. Discuss. *(8)*

3. Which would you choose: selling illegal drugs at $75 an hour (20 percent chance per year of being arrested) or a $6-an-hour factory job? Why? *(9)*

4. If the wage goes up 20 percent and the quantity of labor supplied increases by 5 percent, what's the elasticity of labor supply? *(3)*

5. A competitive firm gets $3 per widget. A worker's average product is 4 and marginal product is 3. What is the maximum the firm should pay the worker? *(5)*

6. How would your answer to Question 5 change if the firm were a monopolist? *(6)*

7. Why might it be inappropriate to discuss the effect of immigration policy using supply and demand analysis? *(5)*

8. Comparable worth laws require employers to pay the same wage scale to workers who do comparable work or have comparable training. What likely effect would these laws have on the labor market? *(9)*

9. Why is unemployment nearly twice as high among blacks as among whites? What should be done about the situation? *(9)*

10. My brother was choosing between being a carpenter and being a plumber. I advised him to take up plumbing. Why? *(6)*

PROBLEMS AND EXERCISES

1. Fill in the following table for a competitive firm that has a $2 price of its good.

Number of workers	TP	MPP	AP	MRP
1	10		—	
2	19	—	—	—
3	—	8	—	—
4	—	—	8.5	—
5	—	—	—	12

2. Your manager comes in with three sets of proposals for a new production process. Each process uses three inputs: land, labor, and capital. Under Proposal A, the firm would be producing an output where the MPP of land is 30, labor is 42, and capital is 36. Under Proposal B, at the output produced the MPP would be 20 for land, 35 for labor, and 96 for capital. Under Proposal C, the MPP would be 40 for land, 56 for labor, and 36 for capital. Inputs' cost per hour is $5 for land, $7 for labor, and $6 for capital.

   a. Which proposal would you adopt?

   b. If the price of labor rises to $14, how will your answer change?

3. A study done by economists Daniel Hamermesh and Jeff Biddle found that people who are perceived as good looking earn an average of 10 percent more than those who are perceived as "homely" and 5 percent more than people who are perceived as "average looking." The pay differential for "homely" men was 9 percent—greater than for homely women—so the poor appearance penalty was found to be greater for men than for women.
   a. What conclusions can one draw from these findings?
   b. Do the findings necessarily mean that there is a "looks" discrimination?
   c. What might explain the larger pay penalty for males for looks?

4. In the early 1990s a teen sub-minimum training wage law was passed by which employers were allowed to pay teenagers less than the minimum wage.

   a. What effect would you predict this law would have, based on standard economic theory?
   b. In analyzing the effects of the law, Professors Card and Kreuger of Princeton University found that few businesses used it and that it had little effect. Why might that have been the case?

5. Economists Mark Blaug and Ruth Towse did a study of the market for economists in Britain. They found that the quantity demanded was about 150–200 a year, and that the supply was about 300 a year.
   a. What did they predict would happen to economists' salaries?
   b. What likely happens to the excess economists?
   c. Why doesn't the price change immediately to bring the quantity supplied and the quantity demanded into equilibrium?

ANSWERS TO MARGIN QUESTIONS

1. Under usual conditions of supply, one would expect that if the wage of my part-time job rises, the quantity of labor I supply in that part-time job also rises. Institutional constraints such as tax considerations or company rules might mean that the quantity of labor I supply doesn't change. However, under the usual conditions of supply, I will study less if the wage of my part-time job rises. *(661)*

2. The irony of any need-based program is that such a program reduces people's incentive to prevent themselves from becoming needy. *(663)*

3. Some factors that influence the elasticity of a firm's derived demand curve include (1) the elasticity of demand for a firm's good, (2) the relative importance of the factor in the production process, (3) the possibility, and cost, of substitution in production, and (4) the degree to which the marginal productivity falls with an increase in the factor. *(665)*

4. At a market wage of $7 per hour, the firm would hire 33 workers because at that number the workers' marginal revenue product is $7 per hour. *(666)*

5. If the firm's product price fell to $1, the marginal revenue product in column 5 of Exhibit 3(a) would be cut in half. If the wage remained at $7, the marginal revenue product of workers would have to equal $7. To bring this about, the firm would reduce the number of workers from 33 to 29. It would not hire 30 workers because that would reduce the marginal revenue product below the wage. The mpp of 7 is for moving from 29 to 30 workers. At 30 workers the mpp is below 7. *(667)*

6. If a firm were controlled by workers, they would take into account that hiring extra workers would reduce their marginal physical product, and hence they would hire fewer workers. *(670)*

7. A likely reason for farmers having switched from square bales handled by students on summer break to large round bales that can be handled by machinery is that there was a change in the price of students relative to the price of machinery. As students became more expensive relative to machines, the farmers substituted machinery for students, fulfilling the cost minimization condition. *(671)*

8. It depends. The introduction of computer- and video-based teaching systems could displace workers and thus cause a short-run temporary decline in the demand for teachers, lowering teacher's wages. However, that introduction will create new potential job opportunities in developing these computer- and video-based systems, into which some teachers could switch. Moreover, teachers are worried about the total learning experience of students rather than their own self-interest, and so almost all would support teaching innovations that increase learning. (Would you believe?) *(671)*

9. Economic theory does not argue that discrimination should be eliminated. Economic theory tries to stay positive. Discrimination is a normative issue. If one's normative views say that discrimination should be eliminated, economic theory might be useful to help do that most efficiently. *(677)*

10. There is more to life than income, and so it does not necessarily follow that one should take the job that pays the highest wage. (In the author's view, a Ph.D.'s life is far more fulfilling than an MBA's life, although some MBAs may disagree with that.) Each person must decide for him- or herself how to weight the various dimensions of a job. *(680)*

31

Nonwage and Asset Income:
Rents, Profits, and Interest

*The first man to fence in a piece of land, saying "This is mine,"
and who found people simple enough to believe him, was the real
founder of civil society.*

~Jean-Jacques Rousseau

After reading this chapter, you should be able to:

1 Define *rent* and explain why landowners will bear the entire burden of a tax on land.

2 Explain rent seeking and its relationship to property rights.

3 Differentiate between normal profits and economic profits.

4 Summarize the reasons an entrepreneur searches out market niches.

5 Define *interest* and demonstrate how it is used in determining present value.

6 Use the annuity rule and the rule of 72 to determine present value.

7 Explain the marginal productivity theory of income distribution.

The four traditional categories of income are wages, rent, profits, and interest. Wages, discussed in the last chapter, are determined by economic factors (the forces of supply and demand), with strong influences by political and social forces which often restrict entry or hold wages at non–market-clearing levels.

The same holds true for nonwage income: rent, profits, and interest. These forms of income are determined by the forces of supply and demand. But, as we have emphasized throughout the book, supply and demand are not necessarily the end of the story. Supply and demand determine price and income, given an institutional structure that includes **property rights** (the rights given to people to use specified property as they see fit) and the **contractual legal system** (the set of laws that govern economic behavior) of the society. If you change property rights, you change the distribution of income. Thus, in a larger sense, supply and demand don't determine the distribution of income; the distribution of property rights does.

Property rights   The rights to use specified property as one sees fit.

Contractual legal system   The set of laws that govern economic behavior.

The system of property rights and the contractual legal system that underlie the U.S. economy evolved over many years. Many people believe that property rights were unfairly distributed to begin with; if you believe that, you'll also believe that the distribution of income and the returns to those property rights are unfair. In other words, you can favor markets but object to the underlying property rights. Many political fights about income distribution concern fights over property rights, not fights over the use of markets.

Such distributional fights have been going on for a long time. In feudal times much of the land was held communally; it belonged to everyone, or at least everyone used it. It was common land—a communally held resource. As the economy evolved into a market economy, that land was appropriated by individuals, and these individuals became landholders who could determine the use of the land and could receive rent for allowing other individuals to use that land. Supply and demand can explain how much rent will accrue to a landholder; it cannot explain the initial set of property rights.

The type of issues raised by looking at the underlying property rights are in large part academic for Western societies. The property rights that exist, and the contractual legal system under which markets operate, are given. You're not going to see somebody going out and introducing a new alternative set of property rights in which the ownership of property is transferred to someone else. The government may impose shifts at the margin; for example, new **zoning laws** (laws that set limits on the use of one's property) will modify property rights and create fights about whether society has the right to impose such laws. But there will be no wholesale change in property rights. That's why most economic thinking simply takes property rights as given.

Zoning laws   Limits on the use of one's property.

But taking property rights as given isn't a reasonable assumption for the developing countries or the formerly socialist countries now in the process of establishing markets. They must decide what structure of property rights they want. Who should be given what was previously government land and property? Who should own the factories? Do those societies want land to be given to individuals in perpetuity, or do they want it given to individuals for, say, 100 years? As these questions have been raised, economists have redirected their analysis to look more closely at the underlying legal and philosophical basis of supply and demand. As they do so they are extending and modifying the economic theory of income distribution, as we'll discuss shortly.

Despite the changes that are taking place, it's helpful to consider the three traditional income categories besides wages (rent, profits, and interest) because doing so provides useful insight into forces that make our economy work and that determine who gets what.

RENT

Rent is the income from a factor of production that is in fixed supply. Traditionally rent was associated with land, which was assumed to be a totally fixed factor of production. When the supply of a factor is fixed, all we need to know to determine what the price of land (rent) will be is the amount of land there is and the demand curve. Exhibit 1 shows how the price of land is determined. In it you can see that since

1A Rent is the income from a factor of production that is in fixed supply.

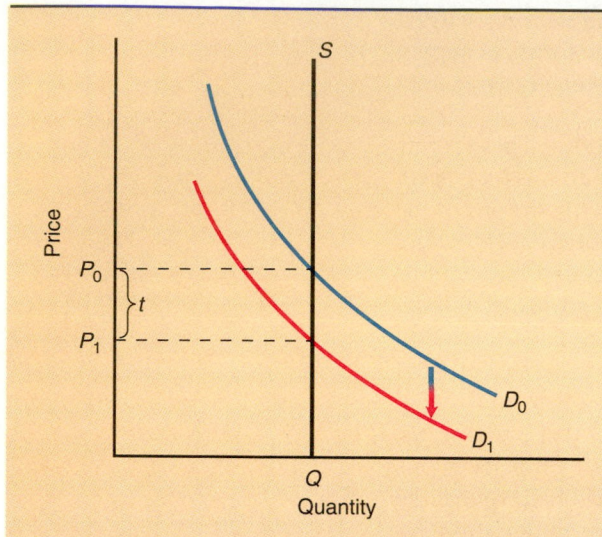

EXHIBIT 1   Rent

A tax on any factor with a perfectly inelastic supply will fall only on the supplier. A tax of t will shift the demand curve down from D_0 to D_1, leaving the after-tax price that the demander pays constant but lowering the after-tax price that the supplier receives by t—from P_0 to P_1.

the supply of land is perfectly inelastic, the level of demand determines the rent on land.

The Effect of a Tax on Land

1B As long as land is perfectly inelastic in supply, landowners will pay the entire burden of a tax on land, as in the graph below.

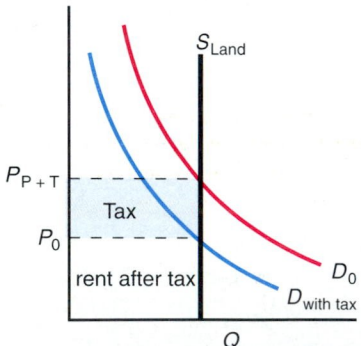

Henry George was a 19th-century economist who advocated the land tax.
Historical Pictures Service.

To check whether you understand the concept of rent, let's try a couple of questions. Say the government places a tax on the user of land. What will that tax do to the quantity of land supplied? What will that tax do to the price of the land? And who will end up bearing the burden of that tax? (Before proceeding, think, and try to answer these questions.)

The answers you should have given are that the quantity of land supplied will not change; the price of the land will not change, and the owner of the land will bear the entire burden of the tax even though the user of the land will actually pay the tax. In technical terms, the tax shifts the demand curve for land down from D_0 to D_1. Now the user simply pays part of the rental payment (t) to the government. So if the landowner were getting $100 per year in rent, after a tax of $30 per year the landowner would get only $70 per year. This follows immediately from the diagram: Given the quantity of land supplied, demanders will pay no more than the equilibrium price. By assumption, suppliers will supply the same amount of land regardless of the price they receive, so they must bear the entire burden of the tax. If they didn't, the price of land would have to rise and it cannot; demanders won't pay more for that quantity.

If you've followed the analysis, the preceding conclusion was obvious, but now let's extend it to the real world. Say the government increases the property tax. Should people who rent apartments worry that such a tax is going to raise rents? The analysis tells us no, they shouldn't; in reality, they do worry about it a lot. Part of the reason is that the assumptions don't fit reality. The supply of land isn't perfectly inelastic; new land can be created by landfills and land can be converted from useless land to useful land by a variety of methods. The supply of apartments is even more elastic since rental apartments have other uses. So the consumers are partially right.

But the model is partially right, too, because even taking these provisos into account, most economists see the supply of apartments as rather inelastic. And as long as the supply of apartments is less elastic than the demand for apartments, more of the property tax will fall on the apartment owner and most of an increase in the property tax won't be passed on to the consumer. It can look as if it's being passed on since actual rents are determined only at periodic intervals, and often the actual rent paid can deviate from the supply/demand-determined rent. Property owners often find it convenient to blame raises in rent on increased costs, even though they would have increased rent even if there had been no tax. Blaming the government is much easier than saying, "Look, apartments are in tight supply. Somebody else will pay me more, so I'm increasing your rent."

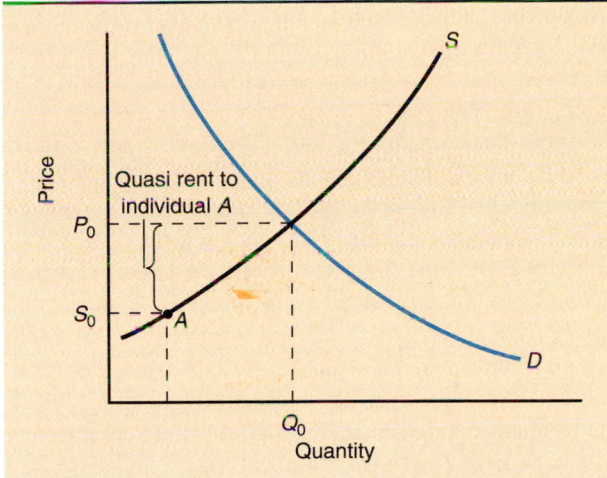

EXHIBIT 2 **Quasi Rent**

Quasi rent is the payment to a supplier above his or her opportunity cost. In this example an individual represented by point A on the supply curve would be willing to supply the good at S_0 but the market equilibrium price is P_0. The difference $P_0–S_0$ is his or her quasi rent.

The inelastic supply of land and the knowledge that ultimately most of the tax on land will be paid by the owner has led to a number of taxing proposals. One such proposal was put forward by Henry George, who argued that the government should replace all other taxes with a land tax. His proposal enjoyed significant political influence in the late 19th century; an economic institute dedicated to his ideas still exists today.

The concept of rent was extended in the 1900s to include any payment to a resource above its opportunity cost—that is, above the amount it would receive in its next-best use. This broader concept of rent is shown in Exhibit 2. In it you can see that the supply curve is upward sloping. Equilibrium is at price P_0 and quantity Q_0. Consider a person on the supply curve at point A. That person will receive price P_0, but would have been willing to supply his or her resource at S_0. The difference, $P_0 - S_0$, is the person's rent. (Sometimes this difference is called **quasi rent** or *producer surplus* to distinguish it from pure rent, in which the opportunity cost of supplying the factor is zero.)

Let's consider an example: Shaquille O'Neal. The demand for his services as a basketball player is high so he earns a multimillion dollar salary. His salary likely significantly exceeds his opportunity cost (the wage he could get at the next-best job). The difference between the two would be the quasi rent component of his salary.

This broader concept of rent applies to all types of income. For example, wage income can include a considerable rent component, as can profits and interest. As long as a supply curve is upward sloping, some suppliers are receiving some rent.[1]

The broadened definition of rent led to the insight that if individuals could somehow restrict supply, the rent they received would be higher. Restricting supply in order to increase the price suppliers receive is called **rent seeking.** The concept of rent seeking ties back into our earlier discussion of property rights. If you own something, you can get a rent for owning it. Thus, rent seeking is an attempt to create either ownership rights or institutional structures that favor you. Rent seeking is an activity in which self-interest doesn't necessarily lead to societal interest. The property rights you get might simply take away property rights from another person.

Let's consider an example: high-resolution television. For technical reasons, every country must choose a design (the number and structure of dots per inch on a television) for broadcasting. The United States made such a decision for the late 1990s

Q-1: If the demand for a good is perfectly elastic and the supply is elastic, who will bear the burden of a tax on the good, and why?

Quasi Rents

Quasi rent Any payment to a resource above the amount that the resource would receive in its next-best use. Also called producer surplus.

Q-2: How does a quasi rent differ from a rent?

Rent Seeking and Institutional Constraints

2 Rent seeking is the restricting of supply in order to increase its price. It is an attempt to change the institutional structure and hence the underlying property rights.

---

[1] One could also say that as long as the demand curve is downward sloping, some demander is receiving rent. One doesn't say that, however. The difference between what a demander would be willing to pay and what the demander actually pays is called *consumer surplus.* As was discussed in earlier chapters, consumer surplus is the demand-side equivalent of rent.

when large-screen television will probably be standard. The firms that got the law defined in a way that favored their design, rather than a competitor's, received a rent. Thus, firms expended great effort and money to lobby government to adopt their design. When they did so they were rent seeking.

Alternatively, if a group of individuals (workers and firms) can get a tariff imposed on goods that are similar to those that they produce, they'll be able to receive a higher price for their good; a component of that price will be rent, which is why the activity of getting that tariff adopted is another example of rent seeking.

Of course, it is a legitimate activity for people to try to structure property rights to benefit themselves. Sometimes it can have positive social consequences, so there's no easy answer about what is the appropriate social policy to deal with rent seeking. All rent seeking isn't bad, but there's no simple way to separate the bad from the good.

Let's consider a final hypothetical example, from the biotechnology field, which demonstrates one of the problems in making value judgments about rent seeking. Say a firm has created a new organism (a new life form) that eats nuclear waste and transforms it into humus soil. (OK, so I'm a dreamer; it could happen.) The firm will likely spend enormous amounts of money on trying to ensure that it will "own" that life form, because otherwise it won't make any income from it. In other words it will engage in rent seeking. But the rent seeking has a positive side. Unless a firm can expect to own the life form, it is unlikely to expend money on developing such a life form. Society may well be better off if property rights in such life forms exist.

There's no easy answer about what is the appropriate social policy to deal with rent seeking.

Q–3: Rent seeking causes waste. Should rent seeking be prohibited?

PROFIT

3 Normal profits are the amount that an entrepreneur can get by supplying entrepreneurship to the market. Economic profits are the entrepreneur's return above and beyond normal profits.

A second component of nonwage income is profit. **Profit** is a return on entrepreneurial activity and risk taking. As discussed in earlier chapters, profits are generally divided into normal profits and economic profits. **Normal profits** are payments to entrepreneurs as the return on their risk taking. They are an amount that an entrepreneur could get if he or she supplied entrepreneurship to the market. It is the marginal entrepreneur—the entrepreneur whose opportunity cost equals his or her expected gain—who receives a normal profit. Others receive a quasi rent in addition to profit.

Because normal profits include returns on risk taking, profits aren't normally normal. Sometimes normal profits are high; sometimes they're nonexistent; and sometimes they're negative (that is, there are losses). However, it is expected, not actual, profits that guide the entrepreneur.

Profit, Entrepreneurship, and Disequilibrium Adjustment

Economic profits *Return on entrepreneurship above and beyond normal profits.*

Economic profits are a return on entrepreneurship above and beyond normal profits. Economic profits are a sign of disequilibrium and are a signal to other entrepreneurs that it may be worthwhile to enter that market. Economic profits are the driving force of the invisible hand. The expectation of economic profit leads to innovation and creates incentives for entrepreneurs to enter into new markets. As entrepreneurs enter, they drive the price to an equilibrium price and eliminate economic profits. In this way the expectations of profits are the dynamic force in the economy, unleashing the competitive forces that will eliminate the profits.

To drive this important point home, let's relate this discussion of profit to our earlier analysis. One of the lessons you have learned (or should have learned) from the theoretical analysis of supply and demand is that competition drives the price in a market down to equal average total costs. In the long run, suppliers make normal returns on their investments—that is, zero economic profits. To remind you of that point, I show a firm in long-run equilibrium in Exhibit 3(a).

Equilibrium isn't something that just exists. It's brought about by competition—by other suppliers entering into the market. Entrepreneurs avoid highly competitive markets that are in equilibrium. Why? Because there aren't a whole lot of profits to be made in such markets. What they look for are not-so-competitive markets—markets in disequilibrium with price greater than average cost. In disequilibrium, you *can* make a lot of profits. Consider Exhibit 3(b). It represents a market in disequilibrium. Notice that the price is P_0 but the costs per unit are only C_0, which means that the supplier makes an economic profit represented by the shaded rectangle.

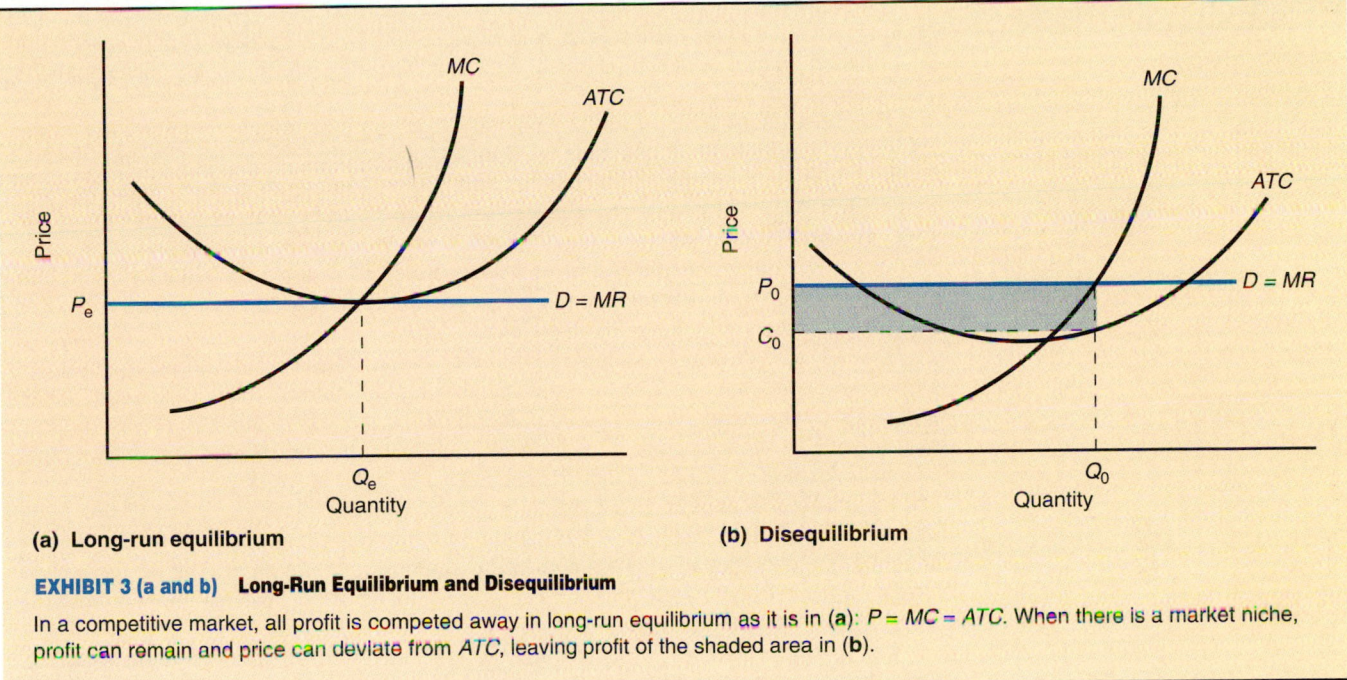

EXHIBIT 3 (a and b)   Long-Run Equilibrium and Disequilibrium

In a competitive market, all profit is competed away in long-run equilibrium as it is in (**a**): $P = MC = ATC$. When there is a market niche, profit can remain and price can deviate from *ATC*, leaving profit of the shaded area in (**b**).

What kind of markets are in disequilibrium? Ones in which competition isn't working or is working slowly. An area in which competition is not working is called a **market niche.** Entrepreneurs search for market niches. The best type of market niche to have is a monopoly, in which you're the sole supplier and you face no competition.

Such pure monopolies are rare, but temporary disequilibrium is not rare. In fact, the competitive conditions that push economic profit all the way down to zero often don't exist. For example, if no one knows you're making a profit, competitors won't enter the market to drive the price down; a disequilibrium can continue indefinitely. Bright entrepreneurs who have found a profitable market niche don't advertise the fact.

Often after an entrepreneur has made an innovation and is enjoying his above-normal economic profits, his income can look a lot like rent. This leads some people to think that society can simply tax it away with no consequence; the entrepreneur's actions won't change. That's true—if one considers those above-normal profits without historical perspective. But with historical perspective, there is a major difference. One of the driving forces behind the entrepreneur was probably the expectation of future profit. That's an important reason why she did her entrepreneurial thing.

It's true that after she's done her entrepreneurial thing, if you take what she got for doing it away from her, it won't change the past. But it will most likely change the future. Other entrepreneurs will draw the inference that their profits will be taken away from them and they won't do their entrepreneurial thing. But entrepreneurial activity is what drives the economy to equilibrium and leads to many of the innovations. If entrepreneurial incentives are removed, society may well be worse off.

The third traditional component of nonwage income is interest. **Interest is the income paid to savers—individuals who produce now but don't consume now. Instead they lend out the proceeds of their production, allowing others to invest or consume now. In return they get a promise to pay back that loan, together with whatever interest they negotiated.** Whereas profits and rents accrue to the individuals who are supplying some resource to the economy, interest is what businesses and entrepreneurs pay to those who make loans to them. High profits encourage entrepreneurial action; high interest rates discourage it.

Market Niches, Profit, and Rent

4 An entrepreneur seeks market niches because within those niches lie economic profits.

Q–4: You're at a party of suppliers. Ms. A is telling everyone how wonderful her business is; Ms. B is saying nothing. You're thinking of entering either Ms. A's or Ms. B's business. Which should you investigate first? Why?

Q–5: Why is it often difficult to distinguish rent from profit?

INTEREST

5 Interest is the income paid to savers—individuals who produce now but do not consume now.

WHERE TO FIND
A MARKET NICHE

M any kinds of market niches exist, and competition works because people search out these market niches and exploit them. In doing so, they eliminate the niches. That's what competition is.

The most likely place to find a temporary market niche may be at your current job. Say you're working for a construction firm and notice that the firm is having trouble reaching high places where it needs to work. The firm doesn't often work on high places, so it isn't worthwhile for it to buy an aerial lift truck; but when it does need to work up high, it could save enormous amounts of time and money if it had such a lift. You check out other construction firms and find they're in a similar situation. You quit your job, buy an aerial lift truck, and start your own firm, renting out your services. For a while, at least, you'll have a market niche.

That is the strategy I followed with this book. Most of the other introductory economics textbooks I read were staid and boring. I believed there was room in the market for a book with pizzazz—a book in which the author wouldn't be afraid to allow his true style to show through. This book exists in part because of market incentives that led me to exploit a market niche. It's the invisible hand at work.

But market incentives aren't the only reason I wrote this book. I wrote this book because I didn't like the way I was taught introductory economics. Given my ego, I thought I could do better—that I could make economics come alive. The desire to "do it right" was the most important reason I wrote this book. (That isn't to say that the expectation of profit didn't play a role.)

The lesson is simple: To understand the economy it's important to remember that, while the profit motive drives people, so too do other motives.

Alternative Theories of Interest

All economists agree that the interest rate is determined by the supply of and demand for something, but they don't agree on what that something is. Classical economists see the interest rate as determined by the supply of and demand for savings; that is, the interest rate depends primarily upon how much people want to save and how much they want to borrow. Keynesian economists see the interest rate as determined by the supply of and demand for money: how much money is in the economy and how much money people want to hold.

One way to partially reconcile these differences is to distinguish a short-term interest rate from a long-term interest rate. When firms or people borrow for very short periods (less than a year), the interest rate they pay is called a short-term rate. When they borrow for long periods (say, more than ten years), the interest rate they pay is called a long-term rate.

All economists agree that the supply of and demand for money significantly affects the short-term interest rate. They differ in how they see that short-term interest rate affecting long-term rates.

Keynesians see it as having a much larger effect than do Classicals. For Keynesians, a change in the short-term interest rate will lead to an equivalent long-term interest rate change. Classicals see a changing short-term interest rate often causing the long-term interest rate to move in the opposite direction. Why the difference? Because of differences in views of how quickly, if at all, changes in the money supply are reflected in changes in the price level—changes that require inflation adjustments to the interest rates.

These two theories also agree that, in macroequilibrium, the supply of and demand for both savings and investment will be equal. But they disagree about how that equilibrium is brought about. Keynesians believe that the aggregate level of income fluctuates to bring about equilibrium of savings and investment. Classical economists believe that income reflects individuals' desires, and that interest rate changes reflect those desires. For Classicals, any change in the money supply will cause an equivalent change in the price level, which will offset the initial money supply change. Thus only real changes matter.

There's no way I have time to do justice to either of these theories; all theories of interest rates are complicated. But one aspect of the interest rate is absolutely

In news magazines such as *U.S. News and World Report* one can often find information about what is happening in the stock and bond markets.

essential: its role in allowing us to determine the present value of future income flows and the future values of present income.

Present value is a method of translating a flow of future income or savings into its current worth. For example, say a smooth-talking, high-pressure salesperson is wining and dining you. "Isn't that amazing?" the salesman says. "My company will pay $10 a year not only to you, but also to your great-great-great-grandchildren, and more, for 500 years—thousands of dollars in all. And I will sell this annuity—this promise to pay money at periodic intervals in the future—to you for a payment to me now of only $800, but you must act fast. After tonight the price will rise to $2,000."

Do you buy it? My rhetoric suggests that the answer should be no—but can you explain why? And what price *would* you be willing to pay?

To decide how much an annuity is worth, you need some way of valuing that $10 per year. *You can't simply add up the $10 five hundred times.* Doing so is wrong. Instead you must *discount* all future dollars by the interest rate in the economy. Discounting is required because a dollar in the future is not worth a dollar now.

If you have $1 now, you can take that dollar, put it in the bank, and in a year you will have that dollar plus interest. If the interest rate you can get from the bank is 5 percent, that dollar will grow to $1.05 a year from now. That means also that if the interest rate in the economy is 5 percent, if you have 95¢ now, in a year it will be worth $.9975 (5% × $.95 = $.0475). Reversing the reasoning, $1 one year in the future is worth 95¢ today. So the present value of $1 one year in the future at a 5 percent interest rate is 95¢.

A dollar *two* years from now is worth even less today. Carry out that same reasoning and you'll find that if the interest rate is 5 percent, $1 two years from now is worth approximately 90¢ today. Why? Because you could take 90¢ now, put it in the bank at 5 percent interest, and in two years have $1.

The Present Value Formula   Carrying out such reasoning for every case would be a real pain. But luckily, there's a formula and a table that can be used to determine the present value (PV) of future income. The formula is:

$$PV = A_1/(1 + i) + A_2/(1 + i)^2 + A_3/(1 + i)^3 + \ldots + A_n/(1 + i)^n$$

where

A_n = the amount of money received n periods in the future
i = the interest rate in the economy (assumed constant)

Solving this formula for any time period longer than one or two years is complicated. To deal with it, people either use a business computer or a present-value table like that in Exhibit 4.

Exhibit 4(a) gives the present value of a single dollar at some time in the future at various interest rates. Notice a couple of things about the chart. The further into the future one goes and the higher the interest rate, the lower the present value. At a 12 percent interest rate, $1 fifty years from now has a present value of essentially zero.

Exhibit 4(b) is an annuity table; it tells us how much a constant stream of income for a specific number of years is worth. Notice that as the interest rate rises, the value of an annuity falls. At an 18 percent interest rate, $1 per year for 50 years has a present value of $5.55. To get the value of amounts other than $1, one simply multiplies the entry in the table by the amount. For example, $10 per year for 50 years at 18 percent interest is 10 × $5.55, or $55.50.

As you can see, the interest rate in the economy is a key to present value. *You must know the interest rate to know the value of money over time.* The higher the current (and assumed constant) interest rate, the more a given amount of money in the present will be worth in the future. Or alternatively, the higher the current interest rate, the less a given amount of money in the future will be worth in the present.

Some Rules of Thumb for Determining Present Value   Sometimes you don't have a present-value table or a business computer handy. For those times, there are a few rules of

Present value   Method of translating a flow of future income or savings into its current worth.

5   Interest plays an essential role in the present value formula.

Q–6:   A 6 percent bond will pay you $1,060 one year from now. The interest rate in the economy is 10 percent. How much is that bond worth now?

You must know the interest rate to know the value of money over time.

EXHIBIT 4 (a and b)   Sample Present Value and Annuity Tables

Year	Interest Rate						
	3%	4%	6%	9%	12%	15%	18%
1	0.97	0.96	0.94	0.92	0.89	0.87	0.85
2	0.94	0.92	0.89	0.84	0.80	0.76	0.72
3	0.92	0.89	0.84	0.77	0.71	0.66	0.61
4	0.89	0.85	0.79	0.71	0.64	0.57	0.52
5	0.86	0.82	0.75	0.65	0.57	0.50	0.44
6	0.84	0.79	0.70	0.60	0.51	0.43	0.37
7	0.81	0.76	0.67	0.55	0.45	0.38	0.31
8	0.79	0.73	0.63	0.50	0.40	0.33	0.27
9	0.77	0.70	0.59	0.46	0.36	0.28	0.23
10	0.74	0.68	0.56	0.42	0.32	0.25	0.19
15	0.64	0.56	0.42	0.27	0.18	0.12	0.08
20	0.55	0.46	0.31	0.18	0.10	0.06	0.04
30	0.41	0.31	0.17	0.08	0.03	0.02	0.01
40	0.31	0.21	0.10	0.03	0.01	0.00	0.00
50	0.23	0.14	0.05	0.01	0.00	0.00	0.00

(a) Present-Value Table (value now of $1 to be received x years in the future)

The present value table converts a future amount into a present amount.

Number of years	Interest Rate						
	3%	4%	6%	9%	12%	15%	18%
1	0.97	0.96	0.94	0.92	0.89	0.87	0.85
2	1.91	1.89	1.83	1.76	1.69	1.63	1.57
3	2.83	2.78	2.67	2.53	2.40	2.28	2.17
4	3.72	3.63	3.47	3.24	3.04	2.85	2.69
5	4.58	4.45	4.21	3.89	3.60	3.35	3.13
6	5.42	5.24	4.92	4.49	4.11	3.78	3.50
7	6.23	6.00	5.58	5.03	4.56	4.16	3.81
8	7.02	6.73	6.21	5.53	4.97	4.49	4.08
9	7.79	7.44	6.80	6.00	5.33	4.77	4.30
10	8.53	8.11	7.36	6.42	5.65	5.02	4.49
15	11.94	11.12	9.71	8.06	6.81	5.85	5.09
20	14.88	13.59	11.47	9.13	7.47	6.26	5.35
30	19.60	17.29	13.76	10.27	8.06	6.57	5.52
40	23.11	19.79	15.05	10.76	8.24	6.64	5.55
50	25.73	21.48	15.76	10.96	8.30	6.66	5.55

(b) Annuity Table (value now of $1 per year to be received for x years)

The annuity table converts a known stream of income into a present amount.

thumb and simplified formulas for which you don't need either a present-value table or a calculator. Let's consider two of them: the infinite annuity rule and the rule of 72.

The Annuity Rule   To find the present value of an annuity that will pay $1 for an infinite number of years in the future when the interest rate is 5 percent, we simply divide $1 by 5 percent (.05). Doing so gives us $20. So at 5 percent, $1 a year paid to you forever has a present value of $20. Our general **annuity rule** for any annuity is:

$$PV = X/i$$

That is, the present value of an infinite flow of income, X, is that income divided by the interest rate, i.

> **6A**   PV = X/i states the annuity rule: Present value of any annuity is the annual income it yields divided by the interest rate.

Most of the time, people don't offer to sell you annuities for the infinite future. A typical annuity runs for 30, 40, or 50 years. However, the annuity rule is still useful. As you can see from the present-value table, in 30 years at a 9 percent interest rate, the present value of $1 isn't much (it's 8¢), so we can use this infinite flow formula as an approximation of long-lasting, but less than infinite, flows of future income. We simply subtract a little bit from what we get with our formula. The longer the time period, the less we subtract. For example, say you are wondering what $200 a year for 40 years is worth when the interest rate is 8 percent. Dividing $200 by .08 gives $2,500, so we know the annuity must be worth a bit less than $2,500. (It's actually worth $2,411.)

> **Q–7:**   You are to receive $100 a year for the next 40 years. How much is it worth now if the current interest rate in the economy is 6 percent? (Use annuity table.)

The annuity rule allows us to answer the question posed at the beginning of this section: How much is $10 a year for 500 years worth right now? The answer is that it depends on the interest rate you could earn on a specified amount of money now. If the interest rate is 10 percent, the maximum you should be willing to pay for that 500-year $10 annuity is $100:

$$\$10/.10 = \$100$$

If the interest rate is 5 percent, the most you should pay is $200 ($10/.05 = $200). So now you know why you should have said no to that supersalesman who offered it to you for $800.

The Rule of 72   A second rule of thumb for determining present values of shorter time periods is the **rule of 72.** The rule of 72 states:

> **6B**   The Rule of 72 states that 72 divided by the interest rate is the number of years in which a certain amount of money will double in value.

The number of years it takes for a certain amount to double in value is equal to 72 divided by the rate of interest.

Say, for example, that the interest rate is 4 percent. How long will it take for your $100 to become worth $200? Dividing 72 by 4 gives 18. So the present value of $200 at a 4 percent interest rate 18 years in the future is about $100. (Actually it's $102.67.)

Alternatively, say that you will receive $1,000 in 10 years. Is it worth paying $500 for that amount now if the interest rate is 9 percent? Using the rule of 72, we know that at a 9 percent interest rate it will take about eight years for $500 to double:

$$72/9 = 8$$

so the future value of $500 is more than $1,000. It's probably about $1,200. (Actually it's $1,184.) So if the interest rate in the economy is 9 percent, it's not worth paying $500 now in order to get that $1,000 in 10 years. By investing that same $500 today at 9 percent, you can have $1,184 in 10 years.

The Importance of Present Value   Many business decisions require such present-value calculations. In almost any business, you'll be looking at flows of income in the future and comparing them to present costs or to other flows of money in the future. That's why understanding present value is a necessary tool.

We've completed our brief survey of rent, profit, and interest. Let's now consider how these categories of income combine with wage income to fit into a theory of income distribution.

The traditional economic theory of the distribution of income is **marginal productivity theory.** This theory states that factors are paid their marginal revenue product (what they contribute at the margin to revenue). We saw how marginal revenue product of labor was determined in the last chapter. In marginal productivity theory, that same reasoning is used to explain the income going to the other three factors. If that factor is entrepreneurship, then the income the person receives can be called *profit;* if that factor is a fixed factor, the income the person receives can be called *rent;* if the factor is current production that is not consumed, the income that person receives can be called *interest.* Marginal productivity theory essentially says that supply and demand determines who gets what.

Modern economists are in the process of extending this functional theory. One extension is to look at the theory of income distribution more abstractly than did early Classical economists. Modern-day economists focus their analysis on what "unspecified" factors of production will be paid, not on what labor or capital or entrepreneurs will be paid. Whether an unspecified factor income is interest, rent, profit, or wages doesn't matter to the analysis since the forces of supply and demand are the same in each case. Modern economists argue that what factors will be paid depends upon (1) the supply of that factor and (2) the derived demand for that factor, which in turn depends upon the marginal productivity of that factor. Thus, they still use the marginal productivity theory, but they use it more abstractly.

Modern-day economists stopped looking at the functional distribution of income among rent, profit, interest, and wages, and started to look at the issue more abstractly because the social reality had changed. The marginal productivity theory of the functional distribution of income was developed to reflect a social reality that had distinct classes of people. One class represented the workers; another represented a group of gentrified landowners who received rent; another represented a group of energetic industrialists; and the fourth represented a group who controlled much of the financial wealth of the society. The wage, rent, profit, and interest categories fit that social reality nicely.

Modern society is much more complicated and far less class-oriented, which means that the wage/rent/profit/interest components of income are often mixed. When the president of a huge corporation earns $10,000,000 a year, few economists would see that as wage income. Even the terminology describing income forms that modern economists use is different. They often don't talk about labor income as wage income. Instead they use the concept *human capital* for "labor" to emphasize the profit and rent component of wage income.

Q–8:   You are to receive $200 30 years from now. About how much is it worth now? (The interest rate is 3 percent.)

THE MARGINAL PRODUCTIVITY THEORY OF INCOME DISTRIBUTION

7 Marginal productivity theory states that factors of production are paid their marginal revenue product.

Q–9:   It is only fair that a person is paid his or her marginal product. True or false? Why?

Society's view of individuals who receive their income from investments has often been less than admiring, as seen in the 18th-century etching by Brichet of "The Financier." *Bleichroeder Print Collection, Baker Library. Harvard Business School.*

Modern economists call labor human capital to emphasize the profit and rent component of wage income.

THE PRESS AND PRESENT VALUE

The failure to understand the concept of present value often shows up in the popular press. Here are three examples.

Headline: **COURT SETTLEMENT IS $40,000,000**

Inside story: The money will be paid out over a 40-year period.

Actual value: $11,925,000 (8 percent interest rate).

Headline: **DISABLED WIDOW WINS $25 MILLION LOTTERY**

Inside story: The money will be paid over 20 years.

Actual value: $13,254,499 (8 percent interest rate).

Headline: **BOND ISSUE TO COST TAXPAYERS $68 MILLION**

Inside story: The $68 million is the total of interest and principal payments. The interest is paid yearly; the principal won't be paid back to the bond purchasers until 30 years from now.

Actual cost: $20,000,000 (8 percent interest rate).

Such stories are common. Be on the lookout for them as you read the newspaper or watch the evening news.

Marginal productivity theory explains the distribution of income, given property rights. It does not explain why property rights are what they are.

Q-10: Why have economists moved away from studying the functional distribution of income?

A second extension modern economists are making to the marginal productivity theory of the functional distribution of income is that they are looking behind it. Marginal productivity theory explains the distribution of income, *given property rights*. It does not explain why property rights are what they are. As we discussed in the beginning of this chapter, modern economists are going beyond the marginal productivity theory of income and are trying to explain why property rights are what they are. This doesn't mean that modern economists don't accept marginal productivity theory; it simply means that they are trying to get at a deeper understanding of the distribution of income.

CONCLUSION

Despite the fact that modern economists are currently expanding the theory of income distribution and are viewing the traditional categories of factors as less important, there is still much to be gained from a knowledge of the traditional theory of income distribution. For example, it tells us that factors in inelastic supply will bear the burden of a large portion of any tax on users of that factor. Similarly it highlights some key elements of the economic forces that determine who gets what—how the forces of supply and demand work. The trick is to understand that and simultaneously to understand the role that political and social forces play in determining what the underlying property rights are, and how those forces interact with economic forces. These questions are high on modern economists' research agendas. Their analysis of rent seeking will likely yield new insights in the years to come.

CHAPTER SUMMARY

- Rent is the income paid to a factor of production that is perfectly inelastic in supply.
- Rent seeking is an attempt to create ownership rights and institutional structures that favor you.
- Normal profits are payments to entrepreneurs and the return on their risk taking. Economic profits are a return on entrepreneurship above and beyond normal profits.
- Entrepreneurs search out market niches in order to earn above-normal profits. Successful search by entrepreneurs tends to eliminate those above-normal profits.

- Interest is the income paid to savers—individuals who produce now but do not consume now.
- The annuity rule and the rule of 72 are useful rules of thumb for determining present value.
- The marginal productivity theory of distribution is the theory that factors of production are paid their marginal revenue product.
- Property rights determine the distribution of income; supply and demand forces distribute income, given property rights.

KEY TERMS

annuity rule *(692)*

contractual legal system   *(685)*

economic profits *(688)*

interest *(689)*

marginal productivity theory   *(693)*

market niche   *(689)*

normal profits   *(688)*

present value   *(691)*

profit *(688)*

property rights   *(685)*

quasi rent   *(687)*

rent *(685)*

rent seeking   *(687)*

rule of 72   *(692)*

zoning laws   *(685)*

QUESTIONS FOR THOUGHT AND REVIEW

The number after each question represents the estimated degree of critical thinking required. (1 = almost none; 10 = deep thought.)

1. List the four traditional categories of income and explain why they have become less important to modern economic analysis. *(2)*

2. Some people argue that zoning laws are immoral. Based on your understanding of property rights, explain how they likely justify this position. *(8)*

3. Which would an economist normally recommend taxing: an elastic or an inelastic supply? Why? *(4)*

4. Differentiate normal profits from economic profits. *(3)*

5. Explain two reasons why the formerly socialist countries will probably have a hard time generating significant entrepreneurial activity. *(6)*

6. "In perfect competition no one would get rich quick, but the economy would stagnate." Evaluate this statement. *(8)*

7. A salesperson calls you up and offers you $200 a year for life. If the interest rate is 7 percent, how much should you be willing to pay for that annuity? *(3)*

8. The same salesperson offers you a lump sum of $20,000 in 10 years. How much should you be willing to pay? (The interest rate is still 7 percent.) *(4)*

9. Define *human capital* and explain why modern economists' use of the term makes the functional distribution of income analysis less useful. *(5)*

10. "If all people were paid their marginal product, there would be true justice in the economy." Evaluate this statement. *(9)*

PROBLEMS AND EXERCISES

1. Demonstrate graphically how the price of land is determined.
   a. Show the effect of a tax on that land.
   b. Explain why that tax won't cause the price of land to rise.
   c. Based on this analysis, would you support more extensive use of land and property taxes in the United States? Why?

2. What is the present value of a cash flow of $100 per year forever (a perpetuity), assuming:
   The interest rate is 10 percent.
   The interest rate is 5 percent.
   The interest rate is 20 percent.
   a. Working with those same three interest rates, what are the future values of $100 today in one year? How about in two years?
   b. Working with those same three interest rates, how long will it take you to double your money?

3. A team of scientific engineers has designed a new method of generating electricity and of desalinating water. It's a desert wind tower—a hollow cylinder 3,300 feet high (twice the height of the World Trade Center in New York City). Sea water is pumped into the top of the tower, where it evaporates rapidly. As the air in the tower is cooled by the evaporation, it falls faster and faster (much like the down draft of a chimney) and by the time it reaches the bottom of the tower it is going hundreds of miles per hour—fast enough to generate turbines. The cost of electricity from this process is predicted to be 2 cents per kilowatt hour—one-fourth the cost of generating electricity by oil. The evaporated water could also be condensed and used as fresh water, since the salt will have been removed.
   a. If this concept proves feasible, what would likely happen to the value of desert land near an ocean?
   b. What effect would it have on the price of oil?
   c. If you were a major oil producing country, would you encourage development of this new technology? Why or why not?

4. Taxes on goods with elastic supply have negative incentive effects, so in the late 1980s, following the advice of some economists, Margaret Thatcher, who was then Prime Minister of Great Britain, changed the property tax—in which a person's tax depended on the amount of property the person owned (a tax that had negative incentive effects)—to a poll tax—a tax at a set rate that every individual had to pay. The poll tax had no negative incentive effect.
   a. Show why the poll tax on a perfectly inelastic supply is "theoretically" preferable to a property tax in which the supply is somewhat elastic.
   b. State what you think the real-life consequences of the introduction of the poll tax were.

5. In 1986, all the land in Japan had a total market value of

$9.3 trillion, while all the land in the United States had a total value of $3.2 trillion even though there is much more usable land in the United States than there is in Japan. How could there be this difference in total land value between the two countries?

6. In divorce cases, a common debate concerns whether an

advanced degree should be considered marital property in which the academic advanced degree-holder's spouse should be given an interest.

a. What are the arguments in favor of seeing it as marital property?

b. What are the arguments against?

ANSWERS TO MARGIN QUESTIONS

1. If the demand for a product is perfectly elastic, suppliers must pay the burden of the tax, as in the diagram below. The tax shifts the after-tax demand from D_0 to $D_{\text{with tax}}$, causing quantity to decrease from Q_0 to Q_1 and the price suppliers receive to decrease from P_0 to P_1. The tax revenue is shown in the shaded part of the diagram. As you can see, the tax revenue comes entirely out of producer surplus. The reason is that with a perfectly elastic demand curve there was no demander surplus to begin with. *(687)*

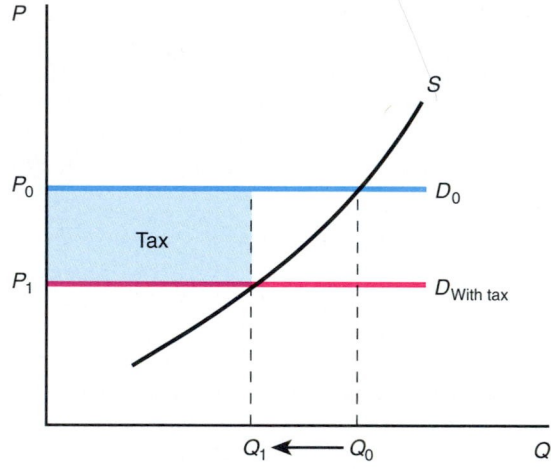

2. Pure rent is a return to a factor whose supply is perfectly inelastic. Thus the opportunity cost of supplying such a factor is zero. A quasi rent is the difference between the price a seller receives for a good and his or her opportunity cost of supplying that good in those cases when the opportunity cost is positive (i.e., when the supply curve is upward-sloping). *(687)*

3. It depends. There's no easy answer to most policy questions, including this question about whether rent seeking should be prohibited. Certain rent seeking activities cause significant waste, but others lead to positive social consequences and changes in institutions. Thus, like most questions in the art of economics, whether rent seeking should be prohibited depends on the particular instances and historical circumstances. *(688)*

4. The answer to the question of which business I should

investigate first depends upon specific psychological knowledge of the individuals. Without specific knowledge, I would probably investigate Ms. B's business first. Successful market niches depend on information not being generally available; thus, I would interpret Ms. B's silence as suggesting that she is protecting her market niche—recognizing, of course, that the reality could be that she's about to go broke and for that reason simply doesn't want to discuss business. *(689)*

5. It is often difficult to distinguish rent from profit because returns for activities are often spread out over long periods of time. For example, a textbook author may have spent an enormous amount of effort and time in developing a readable and fun text. The textbook then comes on the market and is highly successful. The author moves to the Bahamas and snorkels the rest of his or her life away, living off royalties from the textbook. Are those royalties rent, since they are received independent of the author's current effort, or profit—a return to the author's entrepreneurial effort? *(689)*

6. Substituting into the present value formula, PV = $1,060/1.1, I find that the bond is worth $964 now. *(691)*

7. Using Exhibit 4(b), the annuity table, I find that a dollar a year for 40 years with a 6 percent interest rate is worth $15.05 now. Thus $100 would be worth $1,505. *(692)*

8. Using Exhibit 4(a), the present-value table, I see that at a 3% interest rate, $1 thirty years from now is worth 41¢ now, so $200 thirty years from now would be worth $82 now. *(693)*

9. Marginal product does not necessarily have anything to do with fairness, so the answer to this question is "False." Marginal product is simply a technical relationship; whether the person deserves the attributes that led to that marginal product is a normative question upon which the assessment of "fairness" depends. *(693)*

10. Economists have moved away from studying the functional distribution of income because the institutional and social structure of society has changed and those functional classes of income are no longer the distinguishing factors. Instead, economists tend to focus on socio-economic factors determining distribution of income, such as gender and minority status. *(694)*

32

Who Gets What?
The Distribution of Income

*"God must love the poor," said Lincoln, "or he wouldn't have
made so many of them." He must love the rich, or he wouldn't
divide so much mazuma among so few of them.*

~H. L. Mencken

After reading this chapter, you should be able to:

1 State what a Lorenz curve is.

2 Explain what has happened to the U.S. Lorenz curve over time.

3 State the official definition of *poverty*.

4 Summarize the statistical findings on income and wealth distribution.

5 Explain three problems in determining whether an equal income
distribution is fair.

6 List three side effects of redistributing income.

7 Summarize U.S. expenditure programs to redistribute income.

In 1988, Michael Milken, the junk bond king who has since been convicted of insider trading, earned $550 million; that's $10,576,923 per week. Assuming he worked 70 hours per week (you have to work hard to earn that kind of money), that's $151,099 per hour.

In the mid 1990s, the average doctor earned $150,000; that's $2,885 per week. Assuming she worked 70 hours per week (she's conscientious, makes house calls, and spends time with her hospitalized patients), that's $41 per hour.

In the mid 1990s, Joe Smith, a cashier in a fast-food restaurant, earned $19,235, or $370 per week. His base wage was $4.35 per hour. But to earn enough for his family to be able to eat, he worked a lot of overtime, for which he was paid time and a half, or $6.53 per hour. So he made $370 per week by working 70 hours a week.

In the mid 1990s, Nguyen, a peasant in Vietnam, earned $260; that's $5 per week. Assuming he worked 70 hours per week (you have to work hard at that rate of pay just to keep from starving), that's 7¢ per hour.

Are such major differences typical of how income is distributed among people in general? Are such differences fair? And if they're unfair, what can be done about them? This chapter addresses such issues.

WAYS OF CONSIDERING THE DISTRIBUTION OF INCOME

There are several different ways to look at income distribution. In the 1800s, economists were concerned with how income was divided among the owners of businesses (for whom profits were the source of income), the owners of land (who received rent), and workers (who earned wages). That concern reflected the relatively sharp distinctions among social classes that existed in capitalist societies at that time. Landowners, workers, and owners of businesses were distinct groups. Few individuals moved from one group to another.

Time has changed that as the social divisions that were once important have faded. Today workers, through their pension plans and investments in financial institutions, are owners of over 25 percent of all the shares issued on the New York Stock Exchange. That percentage will likely rise to over 50 percent by the year 2000. Landowners as a group receive only a small portion of total income. Companies are run not by capitalists, but by managers who are, in a sense, workers. In short, the social lines have blurred.

But this blurring of the lines between social classes doesn't mean that we can forget the question: "Who gets what?" It simply means that our interest in who gets what has a different focus. We no longer focus on classification of income by source. Instead we look at the relative distribution of total income. How much income do the top 5 percent get? How much do the top 15 percent get? How much do the bottom 10 percent get? This relative division is called the **size distribution of income.**

A second distributional issue economists are concerned with is the **socioeconomic distribution of income** (the allocation of income among relevant socioeconomic groupings). How much do blacks get relative to whites? How much do the old get compared to the young? How much do women get compared to men?

The next three sections consider these distributional categories. Then the last three sections of the chapter ask whether the distribution of income is fair and, if it isn't, what can be done to change it?

Size distribution of income The relative division or allocation of total income among income groups.

Socioeconomic distribution of income The relative division or allocation of total income among relevant socioeconomic groups.

THE SIZE DISTRIBUTION OF INCOME

The U.S. size distribution of income measures aggregate family income, from the poorest segment of society to the richest. It ranks people by their income and tells how much the richest 20 percent (a quintile) and the poorest 20 percent receive. For example, the poorest 20 percent might get 5 percent of the income and the richest 20 percent might get 40 percent.

The Lorenz Curve

1 A Lorenz curve is a geometric representation of the size distribution of income among families in a given country at a given time.

Exhibit 1(a) presents the size distribution of income for the United States in 1992. In it you can see that the 20 percent of Americans receiving the lowest level of income got 3.8 percent of the total income. The top 20 percent of Americans received 46.8 percent of the total income. The ratio of the income of the top 20 percent compared to the income of the bottom 20 percent was about 12:1.

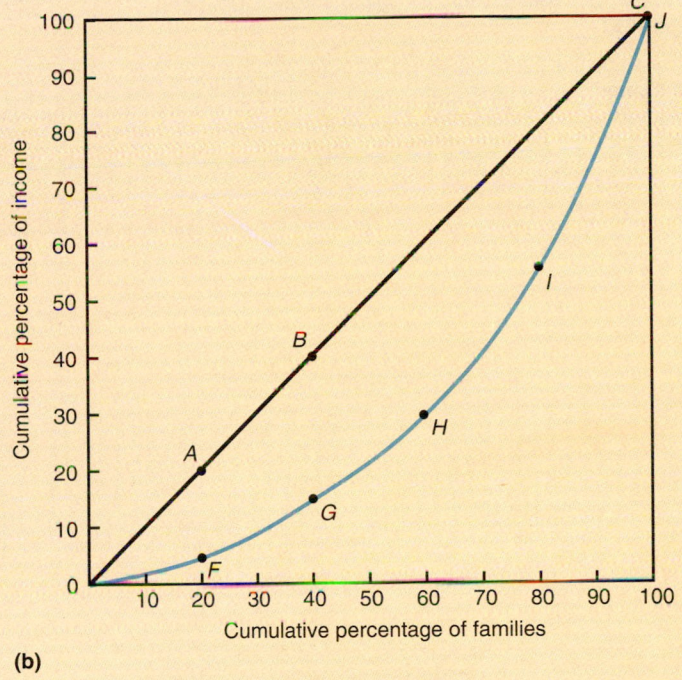

Income quintile	Percentage of total family income	Cumulative percentage of total family income
Lowest fifth	3.8	3.8
Second fifth	9.4	13.2
Third fifth	15.9	29.1
Fourth fifth	24.1	53.2
Highest fifth	46.8	100.0

(a)

(b)

EXHIBIT 1 (a and b)   A Lorenz Curve of U.S. Income (1992)

If income were perfectly equally distributed, the Lorenz curve would be a diagonal line. In (**b**) we see the U.S. Lorenz curve based on the numbers in (**a**) compared to a Lorenz curve reflecting a perfectly equal distribution of income.
Source: U.S. Bureau of the Census, *Current Population Reports, 1994.*

A **Lorenz curve** is a geometric representation of the size distribution of income among families in a given country at a given time. It measures the cumulative percentage of *families* on the horizontal axis, arranged from poorest to richest, and the cumulative percentage of *family income* on the vertical axis. Since the exhibit presents cumulative percentages (all of the families with income below a certain level), both axes start at zero and end at 100 percent.

A perfectly equal distribution of income would be represented by a diagonal line like the one in Exhibit 1(b). That is, the poorest 20 percent of the families would have 20 percent of the total income (point *A*); the poorest 40 percent of the families would have 40 percent of the income (point *B*); and 100 percent of the families would have 100 percent of the income (point *C*). An unequal distribution of income is represented by a Lorenz curve that's below the diagonal line. All real-world Lorenz curves are below the diagonal because income is always distributed unequally in the real world.

The colored line in Exhibit 1(b) represents a Lorenz curve of the U.S. income distribution presented in Exhibit 1(a)'s table. From Exhibit 1(a) you know that, in 1992, the bottom 20 percent of the families in the United States received 3.8 percent of the income. Point *F* in Exhibit 1(b) represents that combination of percentages (20 percent and 3.8 percent). To find what the bottom 40 percent received, you must add the income percentage of the bottom 20 percent and the income percentage of the next 20 percent. Doing so gives us 13.2 percent (3.8 plus 9.4 percent from column 2 of Exhibit 1(a)). Point *G* in Exhibit 1(b) represents the combination of percentages (40 percent and 13.2 percent). Continuing this process for points *H, I,* and *J,* you get a Lorenz curve that shows the size distribution of income in the United States in 1992.

Lorenz curves are most useful in visual comparisons of income distribution over time and between countries. Exhibit 2 presents Lorenz curves for the United States in 1929, 1970, and 1992. They show that from 1929 to 1970 the size distribution of income became more equal. (The curve for 1970 is closer to being diagonal than the curve for

Q–1: When drawing a Lorenz curve, what do you put on the two axes?

The *Statistical Abstract of the United States* is one of the best sources for economic and social statistics.

U.S. Income Distribution over Time

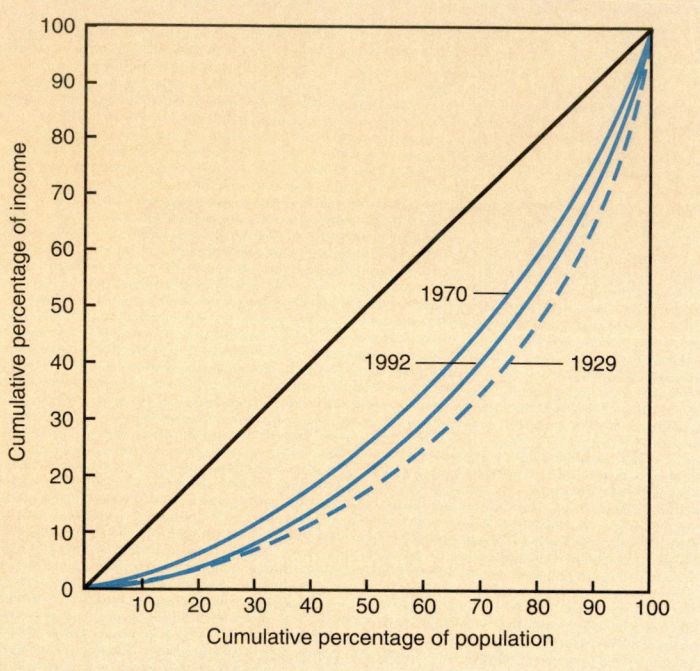

EXHIBIT 2   Lorenz Curve for United States: 1929, 1970, and 1992

The amount of inequality of income distribution has fluctuated in the United States. Until about 1970, it decreased; since then it has increased.

2 From 1929 to 1970, income equality in the United States decreased. From 1970 to 1992, it increased.

1929.) Income of the bottom fifth of families rose by a much higher proportion than did income of the top fifth. That was a continuation of a trend that had begun in the 1920s. In the 1970s that trend stopped and began to reverse. As you can see, from 1970 to 1992 income distribution became less equal. (The curve for 1992 is further from being diagonal than is the curve for 1970.) The income of the bottom fifth of families fell by over 10 percent, while the income of the top fifth rose significantly.

Important reasons for the initial increase in equality are the redistribution measures instituted by the U.S. government between the 1930s and the 1970s, including welfare programs, unemployment insurance, social security, progressive taxation (taxation of higher income at higher rates, lower income at lower rates), and improved macroeconomic performance of the economy.

The trend back toward greater inequality in the 1970s and 1980s was caused by a fall in the real income of the poor. This was due to wage increases that didn't keep up with price increases during that period, a movement away from progressive taxation, and a reduction in government funding for some social programs in the 1980s. In the early 1990s, the pendulum of social reform swung back; taxes were made more progressive, and government funding for some social programs was increased. The effects of these changes on the distribution of income won't be known for a few years.

The distribution of income over time is also affected by demographic factors. Many families have relatively low income in their early years, relatively higher income in their middle years, and then relatively low income again in their retirement years. The Lorenz curve reflects these differences, so even if lifetime income were equally distributed, income in any one year would not be. Moreover, when the percentages of these groups change the Lorenz curve will change. For example, when the baby boom generation retires and are no longer working, their income will fall from what it was when they were working. That decline in income relative to the income of the smaller number of working families will affect the Lorenz curve.

Defining Poverty

Much of the government's concern with income distribution has centered on the poorest group—those in poverty. It's tough to say exactly where poverty begins. If poverty were defined as some absolute amount of real income and that amount had been determined 50 or 60 years ago, few in the United States would be in poverty in the 1990s. Most poor families today have real incomes higher than did the middle class 50 or 60 years ago. If a relative concept of poverty were chosen, whether a

	Number of people (in millions)	Percentage of population	Poverty income of family of 4 (in dollars)
1960	39.9	22.2%	$ 3,022
1970	25.4	12.6	3,968
1975	25.9	12.3	5,500
1980	29.3	13.0	8,414
1985	33.1	14.0	10,989
1990	33.6	13.5	13,359
1991	35.7	14.2	13,924
1992	36.9	14.5	14,335
1993	NA	NA	14,764

EXHIBIT 3   Number and Percentage of Persons in Poverty, 1960–1993

Source: U.S. Bureau of the Census, *Social Security Bulletin*, 1994.

family would be classified as being in poverty would depend on what percentage of the average income it received. Poverty would then be impossible to eliminate, because some proportion of people would always be classified as poor.

The Official Definition of Poverty   The United States has adopted an official definition of **poverty** that is primarily an absolute measure but includes aspects of a relative definition. The U.S. official poverty line is drawn at three times the United States Department of Agriculture's minimum food budget, on the theory that an average family spends one-third of its income on food. If that minimum food budget is recalculated to account for rising standards of living, then the measure is a relative one. If the definition is held constant and only adjusted for changes in the prices of the foods selected in the original standard-of-living choice, then the measure is an absolute one.

The definition is currently not adjusted for rising standards of living, so it would seem to be an absolute measure of poverty. However, it is adjusted by the rate of inflation rather than by the rise in the price of the originally selected foods. But food prices have risen by less than the rise in the general price level, so the index of poverty has gone up by more than it would have had that fixed ratio of food to income remained constant, so the definition includes aspects of relativity.

The minimum food budget includes four eggs, $1\frac{1}{2}$ pounds of meat, 3 pounds of potatoes, about 4 pounds of vegetables, and other foods that cost a total of about $23.50 per person per week. If one triples that amount to about $71 (since food is said to require one-third of a family's income) and multiplies by 52 (the number of weeks in a year), one arrives at a poverty level of about $3,692 per person per year, or about $14,750 for a family of four. That's not a lot of money in today's society, even if the measure has some relativity in it.

A number of other issues regarding poverty are debated. Considering them briefly will give you a good sense of the types of statistical and data problems that economists must consider as they analyze the economy. U.S. poverty figures include the after-tax income of the poor and the cash assistance that the poor receive. However they don't include *in-kind* (noncash) *transfers,* such as food stamps and housing assistance. Nor do they take underreporting of income into account. If one makes adjustments for in-kind transfers and underreporting of income, the number of people said to be in poverty decreases to about 60 percent of the number calculated without the adjustments. Moreover, since in-kind transfers grew enormously in the 1970s, the official poverty rate underestimates the decline in poverty during that period. So, as is the case with most economic statistics, poverty statistics should be used with care.

As Exhibit 3 shows, using the official poverty measure, the number of people in poverty decreased in the 1960s and then, after remaining approximately the same for about 10 years, began increasing in the late 1970s. It remained over 30 million in the 1980s. Then in the early 1990s, with the recession, it rose even more. In 1993 and 1994 it is expected to decrease again as the U.S. economy recovers.

3   Poverty is defined by the U.S. government as being equal to or less than three times an average family's minimum food expenditures as calculated by the U.S. Department of Agriculture.

Q–2:   Is the U.S. definition of poverty an absolute or a relative definition?

U.S. poverty figures do not include in-kind transfers or underreporting of income. As usual, economic statistics should be used with care.

One of the dimensions of the poverty problem is homelessness.
AP/Wide World Photos.

The adjustments just discussed reduce the total number in poverty and some of the percent changes from year to year, but they do not modify the central conclusion that the number of people in poverty remained high in the 1980s and increased in the early 1990s. That rise has led some to question the fairness of the U.S. economy.

There are significant debates about what one should do about poverty.

Alternative Views on the Increase in Poverty   People who favor policies aimed at achieving equality of income argue that this increase in poverty is a significant cost to society. One reason is that society suffers when some of its people are in poverty, just as the entire family suffers when one member doesn't have enough to eat. Most people derive pleasure from knowing that others are not in poverty.

A second reason society as a whole benefits from a decrease in poverty is that the incentives for crime are decreased. As people's incomes increase, they have more to lose by committing crimes, and, therefore, fewer crimes are committed. In short, poverty breeds problems for society. Eliminating poverty helps to eliminate those problems. Those who favor equality of income argue that the increased poverty in the late 1970s and 1980s represents a failure of the economic policies of that period.

Others respond that the widening gap between rich and poor is not the result of government tax and spending policies. It has more to do with demographic changes. For example, the number of single-parent families increased dramatically during this period, while rapid growth of the labor force depressed wages for young, unskilled workers.

Advocates of reducing poverty respond that this argument is unconvincing. They argue that the tax cuts of the 1980s favored the rich while decreased funding for government programs hurt the poor. To compensate, they argue, free day care should be provided for children so that heads of single families can work fulltime, and the low wages of the working poor should be supplemented by government. They hold that demographic changes are not a valid excuse for ducking a question of morality.

International Dimensions of Income: The Income Distribution Question

When considering income distribution, one usually is looking at conditions within a single country. For example, the richest 5 percent of the U.S. population gets approximately 30 times what the poorest 5 percent of the American people get.

There are other ways to look at income. One might judge income inequality in the United States relative to income inequality in other countries. Is the U.S. distribution of income more or less equal than another country's? One could also look at how income is distributed among countries. Even if income is relatively equally distributed within countries, it may be unequally distributed among countries. Finally one can ask

THE WALL STREET JOURNAL ON POVERTY

Why does poverty exist? That's a tough question to answer in a whole book, let alone a box. So instead of explaining why poverty exists, I'll simply list some factors that contribute to poverty, leaving it to you to figure out how important each factor is.

Suggested causes of poverty include low ability, lack of initiative, lack of access to education, deprived childhood, lack of luck, discrimination, and statistical mistakes.

This group of causes is self-explanatory except for "statistical mistakes," but the following editorial from The Wall Street Journal should give you a good, partisan idea of what statistical mistakes mean.

Poverty Explained

In Washington, the poverty debate now centers on one crucial issue: How to blame the other guy. The Democratically controlled Ways and Means Committee recently produced a study, smilingly called "nonpartisan," that implicitly blamed the Reagan administration for recent increases in the poverty rate. To do so, it had to count 1979 and 1980 as Reagan administration years. Then it could show that poverty indeed increased between 1979 and 1987. The New York Times ran a front-page opinion piece based on this report and headlined, "Forces in Society, and Reaganism, Helped Dig Deeper Hole for Poor."

The Republican Study Committee screamed bloody murder. It used the Ways and Means data to show that between 1982 and 1987, years when Reagan budgets were actually in place, real income for those in the poorest fifth of the nation actually increased 4.1%. It was in the Carter years, it says, that the poor got poorer.

The fuss is all good politics. But it has nothing to do with poverty. Poverty trends are complex and deep; they simply can't be pegged to inauguration schedules.

Here is what really happened. Through the postwar era, the number of people living in poverty declined until about 1973. Then, remarkably, the poverty rate leveled off and began to increase. Since then, it has been fluctuating around a higher plateau. The years between 1979 and 1983 were brutal on the poor. Since 1984, the situation has been somewhat better.

The crucial question really is what happened around 1973 to cause the long decline in poverty to reverse itself. That is what honest poverty experts generally debate, some arguing that Great Society programs caused the change, some that the cultural revolution of the 1960s was responsible, others saying there had been a more fundamental change in the U.S. economy. Meanwhile it has become nothing short of hilarious to watch the political operatives in newspapers, magazines and on Capitol Hill pretend that troubling poverty trends started with Ronald Reagan.

To play their political games, the partisans rely on statistics and categories that are quaintly archaic. Back in the '60s and '70s, it was believed that poverty was a problem of scarcity. If government could divert resources to the poor, then they would be pushed out of poverty. Economists dominated the poverty debate, talking about income quintiles, and amassing data from little green books.

With the recognition of the underclass around 1982, it became obvious that behavior, not merely income level, had a lot to do with who was poor. Sociologists began to dominate discussion, and a welfare consensus emerged around the need for developing good work habits, sexual self-restraint and individual accountability. Even the liberal Ford Foundation has acknowledged that family breakdown is a major cause of social problems.

Savvy experts stopped relying on income quintiles because they tell you nothing about how poor people behave. When the Ways and Means Committee comes out and focuses on poverty rates and income distribution, it is a bit like watching a 20-year-old rerun of Dick Clark's "American Bandstand." It's hard to believe people really talked that way.

Here's a hoary old chestnut that stands as the centerpiece of the Ways and Means report: "The rich are getting richer and the poor are getting poorer." This formulation has always appealed to envy, but not much to common sense. In the first place, it's never been clear what the first observation has to do with the second. It is incoherent to pretend that the poor are getting poorer because the rich are getting richer. The economy is not finite. In fact, members of the working poor usually get richer only when the entire economy, including the rich, does better. To introduce the rich into talk of how the poor are doing is merely a lame effort to transform the problem into a pseudo-Marxian class struggle.

The more fundamental problem with the saying is that it pretends there is such a thing as "the poor." The obsolete economic perspective on poverty picks an income level and then lumps everybody under it as "the poor." In reality, 41% of this group own their own homes; many, however, are drug addicts living in the street. Some 11% have completed college, but many have virtually no marketable skills. Almost 40% of poor families have both parents in the home; the other 60% are female headed. The differences are profound, and they have to do with situation, not income.

It's time to stop defining poor people by how much they make, and to start defining them by behavior—by education, by job history, by family status. In the 1980s, we have arrived at a more realistic perception of poverty, but statistical measures haven't caught up. Until they do, we will be inundated by silly, partisan reports and nonsensical news articles.

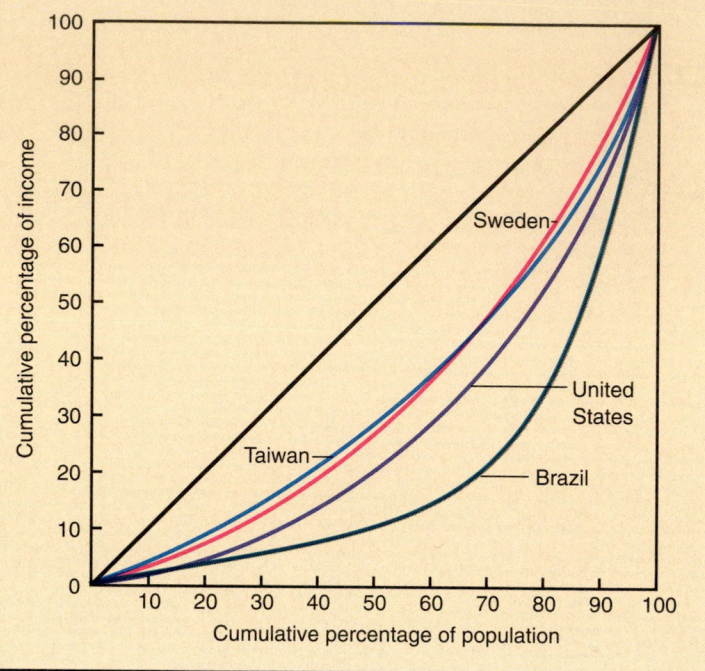

EXHIBIT 4   U.S. Income Distribution Compared to Other Countries

Among countries of the world, the United States has neither the most equal nor the most unequal distribution of income.
Source: The World Bank.

The United States has less income inequality than most developing countries but more income inequality than many developed countries.

about the total level of world income. If the poorest people in the world had incomes of $100,000 per year, would it matter that some people had incomes of $300,000 a year?

Comparing U.S. Income Distribution with That in Other Countries   Exhibit 4 gives us a sense of how the distribution of income in the United States compares to that in other countries. We see that the United States has significantly more income inequality than Sweden, but significantly less than Brazil (or most other developing and newly industrialized countries).

An important reason why the United States has more income inequality than Sweden is that Sweden's tax system is more progressive. Until recently (when Sweden's socialist party lost power), the top marginal tax rate on the highest incomes in Sweden was 80 percent, compared to about 40 percent in the United States. Given this difference, it isn't surprising that Sweden has less income inequality. In a newly industrialized country like Brazil, where a few individuals earn most of the income and, to a large degree, control the government, the government is not likely to begin redistributing income to achieve equality.

Income Distribution among Countries   When one considers the distribution of world income, the picture becomes even more unequal than the picture one sees when considering the distribution of income within countries. The reason is clear: Income is highly unequally distributed among countries. The average per capita income of the richest 5 percent of the countries of the world is more than 100 times the average income of the poorest 5 percent of the countries of the world. Thus, a Lorenz curve of world income would show much more inequality than the Lorenz curve for a particular country. Worldwide, income inequality is enormous. A minimum level in the United States would be a wealthy person's income in a poor country like Bangladesh.

The Total Amount of Income in Various Countries

To give you a better picture of income distribution problems, you need to consider not only the division of income, but also the total amounts of income in various countries. Exhibit 5 presents per capita GDP for various countries. Looking at the enormous differences of income among countries, we must ask which is more important: the distribution of income or the absolute level of income. Which would you rather be: one of four members in a family that has an income of $3,000 a year, which places you

THE GINI COEFFICIENT

A second measure economists use to talk about the degree of income inequality is the Gini coefficient of inequality. The Gini coefficient is derived from the Lorenz curve by comparing the area between the (1) Lorenz curve and the diagonal (area *A*) and (2) the total area of the triangle below the diagonal (areas *A* and *B*). That is:

Gini coefficient = Area *A*/(Areas *A* + *B*)

A Gini coefficient of zero would be perfect equality, since area *A* is zero if income is perfectly equally distributed. The highest the Gini coefficient can go is 1. So all Gini coefficients must be between zero and one. The lower the Gini coefficient, the closer income distribution is to being equal.

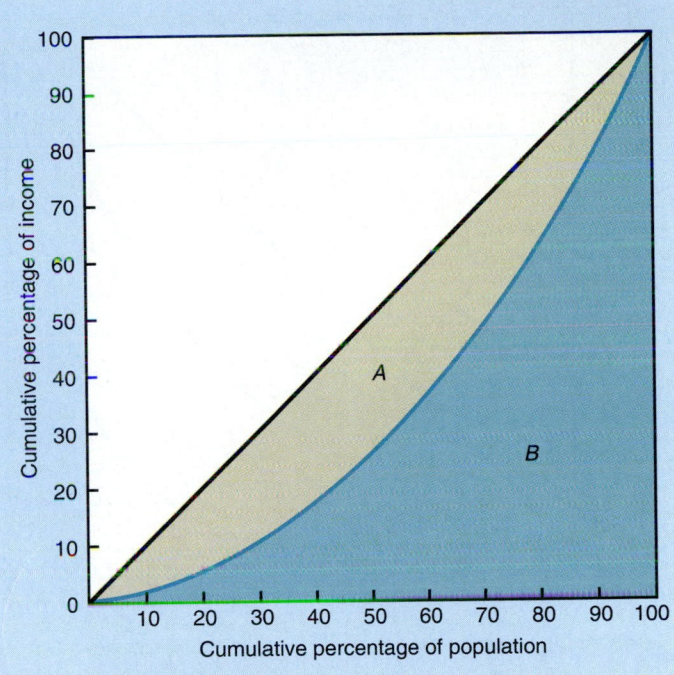

in the top 10 percent of Bangladesh's income distribution, or one of four members of a family with an income of $12,000 (four times as much), which places you in the bottom 10 percent of the income earners in the United States?

In considering equality, two measures are often used: *equality of wealth* and *equality of income*. Because of space limitations, my focus will be on income, but I want to mention wealth. **Wealth** is the value of the things individuals own. It is a *stock* concept representing the value of assets such as houses, buildings, and machines. For example, a farmer who owns a farm with a net worth of $1 million is wealthy compared to an investment banker with a net worth of $225,000.

Income, in contrast, is a *flow* concept. It's a stream through time. That farmer might have an income of $20,000 a year while the investment banker might have an income of $80,000 a year. The farmer, with $1 million worth of assets, is wealthier than the investment banker, but the investment banker has a higher income than the farmer.

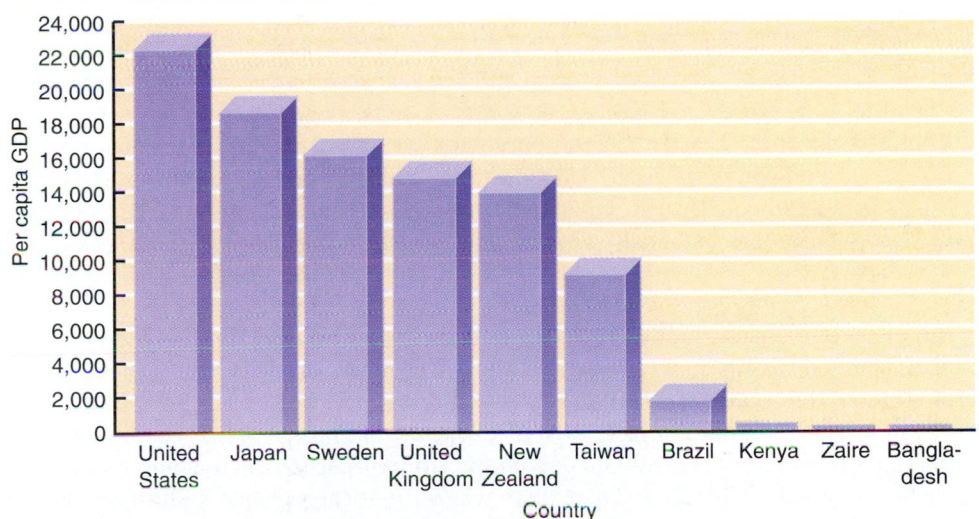

EXHIBIT 5   Per Capita GDP in Various Countries, 1992

Income is unequally distributed among the countries of the world. Source: CIA, *World Fact Book*, 1993

THE DISTRIBUTION OF WEALTH

Wealth   The value of assets an individual owns.

Income   Payments received plus or minus changes in value of one's assets in a specified time period.

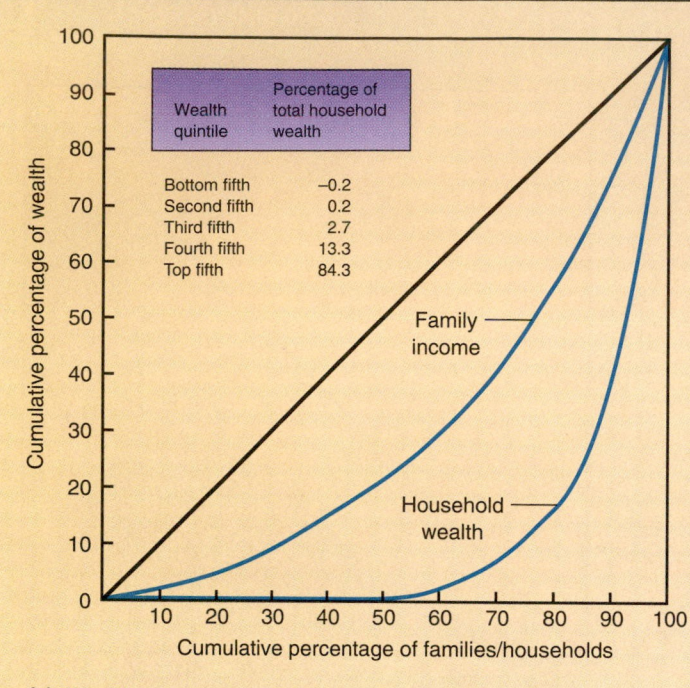

Wealth quintile	Percentage of total household wealth
Bottom fifth	-0.2
Second fifth	0.2
Third fifth	2.7
Fourth fifth	13.3
Top fifth	84.3

(a) Wealth compared to income in the United States

(b) Wealth distribution

10 Wealthiest Families in the World, 1992 (in billions of dollars)	
Walton family/USA	$25.3
Mars family/USA	9.2
Tsutsumi, Yoshaiki/Japan	9.0
du Pont family/USA	8.6
Mori, Minoru and Akira and family/Japan	7.5
Gates, William Henry III/USA	7.4
Newhouse, Samuel Irving Jr. and Donald Edward/USA	7.0
Bass, Sid, Lee, Edward and Robert/USA	6.8
Buffett, Warren Edward/USA	6.6
Haub, Erivan/Germany	6.2

EXHIBIT 6 (a and b)   Wealth Distribution in the United States and Wealth Compared to Income

Wealth is much more unequally distributed than income in the United States. In fact, the lowest 40 percent of the population have 0 percent of the wealth as shown in (**a**); they have borrowed as much as they own. Exhibit 6 (**b**) gives you a sense of how much wealth it takes to be wealthy.
Source: U.S. Bureau of the Census and Edward N. Wolff, New York University (with permission), and *FORBES* Magazine, July 5, 1993.

A Lorenz Curve of the Distribution of Wealth

4 Wealth is significantly more unequally distributed in the United States than is income.

How Much Wealth Do the Wealthy Have?

Billionaires often lose a billion here, gain a billion there; sometimes they even become multi-billionaires. Seldom do they become poor.

SOCIOECONOMIC DIMENSIONS OF INCOME INEQUALITY

Exhibit 6(a) compares the Lorenz curve for wealth in the United States with the Lorenz curve for income in the United States. You can see that wealth in the United States is more unequally distributed than income and that the bottom 40 percent of the U.S. population has essentially zero wealth, which means that they owe as much as they have.

Relative comparisons such as those depicted by Lorenz curves don't give you a sense of how much wealth it takes to be "wealthy." Exhibit 6(b) does that. It presents a list of some of the wealthiest families in the world in 1992. Most of us have little chance of joining either group; in fact, most of us have little possibility of becoming one of the top 5 percent of the wealthholders in the United States, which would require total wealth of at least $3 million. Once there was a time when people's ultimate financial goal was to be a millionaire. In the 1990s, thanks to inflation, the ultimate financial goal for the wealthiest people is to be a billionaire. The millionaire's club is no longer highly exclusive.

Of course, people on the list don't always stay there; the list is constantly changing. For example, a number of families who were on the list earlier are no longer on it. The Reichmann family had a major financial setback in 1992 and lost billions, and many of the Japanese billionaires lost billions in the fall of the Japanese stock market. Today, some of these people and families might only be multi-millionaires. (It's tough to stay a billionaire.)

The size distribution of inequality is only one of the dimensions that inequality of income and wealth can take. As I mentioned before, the distribution of income according to source of income (wages, rents, and profits) was once considered important. Today's focus is on the distribution of income based on race, ethnic background, geographic region, and other socioeconomic factors such as gender and type of job.

EXHIBIT 7   Various Socioeconomic Income Distribution Designations

Mean Income, 1992		
By Occupational Category	Male	Female
Managerial and professional specialty occupation	$46,445	$26,343
Technical, sales, and administrative support occupations	$28,036	$15,603
Service occupations	$14,735	$ 8,459
Farming, forestry, and fishing occupations	$11,956	$ 6,932
Precision production, craft, and repair occupations	$24,881	$16,475
Operators, fabricators, and laborers	$21,030	$12,063
Armed forces	$24,806	$21,576*
Average of all workers	$27,748	$16,745

* = estimated

By Region, 1992	Median Household Income
Northeast	$33,194
Midwest	$30,911
South	$27,741
West	$33,621

Mean Income				
By Sex	1970	1980	1985	1992
Male	$7,537	$15,340	$20,652	$27,748
Female	$3,138	$ 6,772	$10,584	$16,745

By Race, 1992	Median Household Income
White	$32,368
Black	$18,660
Hispanic	$22,848

Source: U.S. Bureau of the Census, *Current Population Reports, Consumer Income 1993.*

Exhibit 7 gives an idea of the distribution of income according to socioeconomic characteristics.

You can see that income differs substantially by type of job, leading some economists to argue that a new professional/nonprofessional class distinction is arising in the United States. There are also substantial differences between the incomes of women and men and between whites and blacks. Some of these variations are explained by sociological and cultural differences, but part of that variation is also the result of **discrimination** (differential treatment of individuals because of physical or social characteristics).

Discrimination exists in all walks of life: Women are paid less than men, and blacks are often directed into lower-paying jobs. Economists have done a lot of research in order to understand the facts about discrimination and what can be done about it. The first problem is to measure the amount of discrimination and get an idea of how much discrimination is caused by what. Let's consider discrimination against women.

On average, women receive somewhere around 70 percent of the pay that men receive to do the same kind of job. That has increased from about 60 percent in the 1970s. This pay gap suggests that discrimination is occurring. The economist's job is to figure out how much of this is statistically significant, and, of that portion that is caused by discrimination, what is the nature of that discrimination.

Analyzing that data, economists have found that somewhat more than half of this difference can be explained by other causes, such as length of time on the job. But that still leaves a relatively large difference that can be attributed to discrimination.

Is it direct demand-side workplace discrimination by employers? Or is it supply-side sociological discrimination which occurs in the general social interactions between men and women? It's clear what direct demand-side workplace discrimination by employers is: When an employer hires a man rather than an equally qualified woman, or pays a woman less for doing a job than the employer pays a man for that job, that's demand-side discrimination.

Supply-side sociological discrimination and demand-side institutional discrimination are more complicated. For example, sociologists have found that in personal relationships women come out on the short end. For instance, women tend to move to

Income Distribution according to Socioeconomic Characteristics

Discrimination   Differential treatment of individuals because of physical or social characteristics.

What Are the Causes of Discrimination?

Discrimination can be based on demand-side or supply-side phenomena.

be with their partners more than men move to be with their partners. In addition, women in two-parent relationships do much more work around the house and take a greater responsibility for child rearing than men do even when both the man and the woman are employed.

These observations suggest that there is sociological supply-side discrimination. Such discrimination can lead to the same pay statistics as can demand-side discrimination. The more an employer can count on an employee's total dedication to the job, the more likely the employer is to pay that employee a high wage. When a woman gives up a promotion possibility because it would require her to move away from her partner, or resigns a good job to move to be with her partner, she's lowering her average pay. Similarly when she misses a key meeting to stay with a sick child who has a 104° temperature, she may be behaving admirably, but she is lowering her advancement and pay possibilities. The fact that women, on average, take personal relationships more seriously than do men means that women, on average, will be paid less than men even if there is no demand-side discrimination.

How important are these sociological observations? In discussing discrimination I ask the members of my class to state if they expect their personal relationships with their partners to be fully equal. The usual result is the following: 80 percent of the women expect a fully equal relationship; 20 percent expect their partner to come first. Eighty percent of the men expect their careers to come first; 20 percent expect an equal relationship. I then point out that somebody's expectations aren't going to be fulfilled. Put simply, most observers believe that supply-side discrimination that occurs in interpersonal relationships is significant.

The issues become even more complicated when one allows for indirect demand-side institutional discrimination. Must careers be structured so that they require enormous time commitment at precisely the time when women's home responsibilities are greatest? Couldn't many careers be structured so that the peak time commitment occurred later, when supply-side sociological discrimination is less intensive? When one considers such issues, supply-side and demand-side factors become intertwined.

Q–3:   What is the difference between supply-side discrimination and demand-side discrimination?

Economists have made adjustments for these sociological factors, and have found that supply-side and demand-side institutional factors explain a portion of the lower pay but that direct workplace discrimination also explains a portion. How big a portion to attribute to demand-side factors and how big a portion to attribute to supply-side factors is undetermined, even though it has been subject to considerable debate. One reason for this continued debate is that the two types of discrimination interact. Say a firm doesn't have an inherent bias against women but expects that women will be less-committed employees. The firm will likely assign women to the less critical jobs. The firm is discriminating against women, but that discrimination is a reflection of its expectation of supply-side discrimination.

A final point: Even if women *in general* are less likely than men to be "fully committed employees," that does not mean that any *individual* woman will be less committed. The question of whether it is appropriate to accept discrimination against particular individuals on the basis of group characteristics is a normative issue that society, not economists, must resolve. What economists can do is to identify the nature of the discrimination and point out the consequences of policies intended to eliminate it.

International Male/Female Pay Gaps and Comparable Worth Laws

Q–4:   In what way would a comparable worth law likely reduce the pay gap between women and men?

The male/female pay gap is not consistent across countries. University of Illinois economists Francine Blau and Lawrence Kahn did a study in the early 1990s and found significant differences. In Australia, France, New Zealand, and the Scandinavian countries, women earned about 85 percent of what men earned. Why the difference between these countries and the 70 percent figure in the United States?

The answer most likely is in the institutional structure. Those countries had greater unionization or direct government involvement in the pay-setting process, or were otherwise more centralized. In Australia, for example, minimum wages are set in various occupations (as opposed to having a general minimum wage as in the United States); that pulls up the pay of some female workers.

Institutional modifications such as **comparable worth laws**—laws in which government groups will determine "fair" wages for specific jobs—have been suggested as a way of helping eliminate the pay gap, but many economists oppose such laws, feeling that they are incompatible with existing wage-setting institutions in the United States.

The supply-side/demand-side distinction is important in deciding what to do about discrimination. If the primary cause is on the supply side, it can be strongly argued that if one wants to end discrimination, the fight is best directed at the discrimination that occurs in male/female relationships. Why do women allow themselves to be "exploited" by men, and can that exploitation be reduced? If the discrimination is on the demand side because employers are reluctant to hire women, equal opportunity laws will be more successful than if the discrimination is on the supply side.

As you can see from this brief summary, discussions of discrimination quickly get complicated and intertwined with normative issues. Pointing out that seemingly simple issues are actually very complicated is something that economists often do. It's a logical conclusion of economic thinking.

Early economists focused on the distribution of income by wages, profits, and rent because that division corresponded to their class analysis of society. Landowners received rent, capitalists received profit, and workers received wages. Tensions among these classes played an important part in economists' analyses of the economy and policy.

As class divisions by income source have become blurred, they've become only a tiny part of mainstream economists' analysis of the economy. That doesn't mean that other types of socioeconomic classes no longer exist. They do. The United States has a kind of upper class. In fact, there is a company in the United States that publishes the *Social Register*, containing the names and pedigrees of about 35,000 socially prominent people who might be categorized "upper-class." Similarly, it is possible to further divide the U.S. population into a middle class and a lower class.

The difference today is that class divisions are no longer determined by income source. For example, upper-class people do not necessarily receive their income from rent and profits. Today we have "upper-class" people who derive their income from wages and "lower-class" people who derive their income from profits (usually in the form of pensions, which depend upon profits from the investment of pension funds in stocks and bonds). Nowadays in the United States, classification is based on characteristics other than source of income. For example, upper-class people don't bowl and lower-class people don't like opera—or so the classes have been stereotyped.

In acknowledging that classes exist in the United States, I want to make it clear that I in no way am condoning such stereotyping of individuals. Many people don't fit into any category; their interests, occupations, and activities fit into no class. But to pretend that classes and such stereotyping don't exist when they do, and to fail to deal with the implications of socioeconomic classes in our society, isn't going to make such stereotyping go away.

The Importance of the Middle Class What has made the most difference in today's class structure in the United States compared to its class structure in earlier periods and to the structure in today's developing countries is the tremendous growth in the relative size of the middle class. Economists used to see the class structure as a pyramid. From a base composed of a large lower class, the pyramid tapered upward through a medium-sized middle class to a peak occupied by the upper class (Exhibit 8(a)). The class structure is still pyramidal in developing countries. In the United States and other developed countries, the pyramid has bulged out into a diamond, as shown in Exhibit 8(b). The middle class has become the largest class, while the upper and lower classes are smaller in relative terms.

This enormous increase in the relative size of the middle class in developed countries has significantly blurred the distinction between capitalists and workers. In early capitalist society, the distributional fight (the fight over relative income shares)

Deciding What to Do about Economic Discrimination

Pointing out that seemingly simple issues are actually very complicated is something that economists often do. It's the logical conclusion of economic thinking.

Income Distribution according to Class

The United States has socioeconomic classes with some mobility among classes. This is not to say such classes should exist; it is only to say that they do exist.

In the United States the middle class is the largest class.

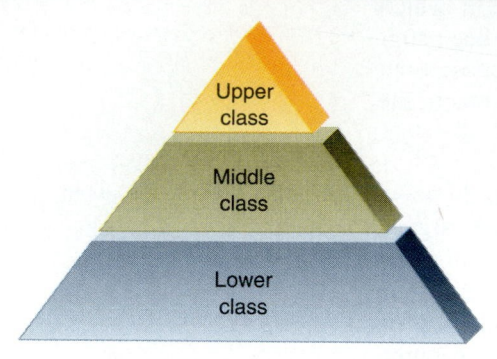 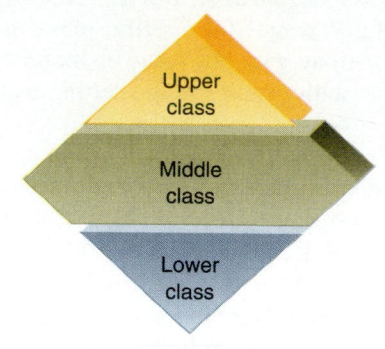

(a) Underdeveloped country's class system   **(b) U.S. class system**

EXHIBIT 8 (a and b)   The Class System as a Pyramid and as a Diamond

The class system in underdeveloped countries is a pyramid; in the United States the class system is more diamond shaped.

Q–5:   How have distributional fights about income changed over time?

was largely between workers and capitalists. In modern capitalist society, the distributional fight is among various types of individuals. Union workers are pitted against nonunion workers; salaried workers are pitted against workers paid by the hour. The old are pitted against the young; women are pitted against men; blacks are pitted against Hispanics and Asians, and all three groups are pitted against whites.

Distributional Questions and Tensions in Society   While mainstream economists tend to focus on the size distribution of income, nonmainstream economists tend to emphasize class and group structures in their analysis. Radical economists emphasize the control that the upper class has over the decision process and the political process. Conservative economists emphasize the role of special interests of all types in shaping government policy. Both radical and conservative analyses bring out the tensions among classes in society much better than does the mainstream, classless analysis.

Both radical and conservative analyses bring out the tensions in society much better than does mainstream classless analysis.

When people feel they belong to a particular class or group, they will often work to further the interests of that class or group. They also generally have stronger feelings about inequalities among classes or groups than when they lack that sense of class or group identity. Using a classless analysis means overlooking the implications of class and group solidarity in affecting the tensions in society.

Those tensions show up every day in political disputes over the tax system, in the quiet fuming of individuals as they see someone else earning more for doing the same job, and in strikes and even riots. Such tensions exist in all countries. In some transitional and developing countries they break out into the open as armed insurrections or riots over food shortages (or soap shortages or cigarette shortages, as we saw in the former USSR in the early 1990s).

Those tensions have been kept to a minimum in American society. A majority of Americans believe that income distribution is sufficiently fair for them to accept their share more or less contentedly. To remedy the unfairness that does exist, they don't demand that the entire system be replaced. Instead they work for change within the present system. They look to affirmative action laws, comparable-worth laws, minimum-wage laws, and social welfare programs for any improvement they perceive to be necessary or desirable. There's much debate about whether these government actions have achieved the desired ends, but the process itself reduces tensions and has worked toward the maintenance of the entire system.

People's acceptance of the U.S. economic system is based not only on what the distribution of income is but also on what people think it should be, what they consider fair. It is to that question that I now turn.

INCOME DISTRIBUTION AND FAIRNESS

Judgments about whether the distribution of income is fair or should be changed are normative ones, based on the values one applies to the situation. Value judgments necessarily underlie all policy prescriptions.

Philosophical Debates about Equality and Fairness

Depending on one's values, any income distribution can be justified. For example, Friedrich Nietzsche, the 19th-century German philosopher, argued that society's goal should be to support its supermen—its best and brightest. Lesser individuals' duty should be to work for the well-being of these supermen. Bertram de Juvenal, a 20th-century philosopher, has argued that a high level of income inequality is necessary to sustain the arts, beauty, education, and civilization. He and others say that a world of equally distributed income would be a world without beauty. Even if we don't personally own beautiful, expensive homes or aren't devoted opera fans, these philosophers argue, our lives are improved because some people do own such homes and because opera performances exist. Inequality creates diversity in our lives, and that diversity enriches the lives of everyone.

Other philosophers disagree strongly. They argue that equality itself is the overriding goal. That view is embodied in the U.S. Declaration of Independence: "We hold these truths to be self-evident, that all men are created equal." And for many people the inherent value of equality is not open to question—it is simply self-evident.

Believing that equality is an overriding goal does not necessarily imply that income should be equally distributed. For example, John Rawls (a Harvard University professor who believes that equality is highly desirable and that society's goal should be to maximize the welfare of the least well-off) agrees that to meet that goal some inequality is necessary. Rawls argues that if, in pursuing equality, you actually make the least well-off worse off than they otherwise would have been, then you should not pursue equality any further. For example, say under one policy there will be perfect equality and everyone receives $10,000 per year. Under another policy, the least well-off person receives $12,000 per year and all others receive $40,000. Rawls argues that the second policy is preferable to the first even though it involves more inequality.

Economists, unlike philosophers, are not concerned about justifying any particular distribution of income. In their objective role, economists limit themselves to explaining the effects that various policies will have on the distribution of income; they let the policymakers judge whether those effects are desirable.

However, in order to judge economic policies, you, in your role as a citizen who elects policymakers, must make certain judgments about income distribution because all real-world economic policies have distribution effects. Accordingly, a brief discussion of income distribution and fairness is in order.

The U.S. population has a strong general tendency to favor equality—equality is generally seen as fair. Most people, including me, share that view. However there are instances when equality of income is not directly related to people's view of fairness. For example, consider this distribution of income between John and Fred:

John gets $50,000 a year.

Fred gets $12,000 a year.

Think a minute. Is that fair? The answer I'm hoping for is that you don't yet have enough information to make the decision.

Here's some more information. Say that John gets that $50,000 for holding down three jobs at a time, while Fred gets his $12,000 for sitting around doing nothing. At this point, many of us would argue that it's possible that John should be getting even more than $50,000 and Fred should be getting less than $12,000.

But wait! What if we discover that Fred is an invalid and unless his income increases to $15,000 a year he will die? Most of us would change our minds again and argue that Fred deserves more, regardless of how much John works.

But wait! How about if, after further digging, we discover that Fred is an invalid because he squandered his health on alcohol, drugs, and fried foods? In that case some people would likely change their minds again as to whether Fred deserves more.

By now you should have gotten my point. Looking only at a person's income masks many dimensions that most people consider important in making value judgments about fairness.

When most people talk about believing in equality in income, they mean they believe in equality of opportunity for comparably endowed individuals to earn income. If equal opportunity of equals leads to inequality of income, that inequality in income is

Q–6: Is it self-evident that greater equality of income would make the society a better place to live? Why?

While economists in their objective role limit themselves to explaining the effects of various policies on the distribution of income, individuals, in order to judge economic policies, must make value judgments and concern themselves about the distributional effects of economic policy.

Fairness and Equality

Q–7: You are dividing a pie among five individuals. What would be a fair distribution of that pie?

Fairness has many dimensions and it is often difficult to say what is fair and what isn't.

5 Three problems in determining whether an equal income distribution is fair are: (1) people don't start from equivalent positions; (2) people's needs differ; and (3) people's efforts differ.

Fairness as Equality of Opportunity

The concept of fairness is crucial and complicated, and it deserves deeper consideration than just a gut reaction.

fair. Unfortunately, there's enormous latitude for debate on what constitutes equal opportunity of equals.

In the real world, needs differ, desires differ, and abilities differ. Should these differences be considered relevant differences in equality? You must supply the answers to those questions before you can judge any economic policy because to make a judgment on whether an economic policy should or should not be adopted, you must make a judgment about whether a policy's effect on income is fair. In making those judgments, most people rely on their immediate gut reaction. I hope what you have gotten out of this discussion about John and Fred and equality of opportunity is the resolve to be cautious about trusting your gut reactions. The concept of fairness is crucial and complicated, and it deserves deeper consideration than just a gut reaction.

THE PROBLEMS OF REDISTRIBUTING INCOME

Let's now say that we have considered all the issues discussed so far in this chapter and have concluded that some redistribution of income from the rich to the poor is necessary if society is to meet our ideal of fairness. How do we go about redistributing income?

To answer that question, we must consider what programs exist and what their negative side effects might be. The side effects can be substantial and they can subvert the intention of the program so that far less overall money is available for redistribution and equality is reduced less than one might think.

Three Important Side Effects of Redistributive Programs

6 Three side effects of redistribution of income include the labor/leisure incentive effect, the avoidance and evasion incentive effects, and the incentive effect to look more needy than you are.

Three important side effects that economists have found in programs to redistribute income are:

1. The incentive effects of a tax may result in a switch from labor to leisure.
2. The effects of taxes may include attempts to avoid or evade taxes, leading to a decrease in measured income.
3. The incentive effects of redistributing money may cause people to make themselves look as if they're more needy than they really are.

Appendix A provides a numerical example of each of these, showing that these effects can be substantial and make income redistribution costly in terms of reduced total income.

All economists believe that the incentive effects of taxation are important and must be taken into account in policy making. But they differ significantly in the importance they assign to incentive effects, and empirical evidence doesn't resolve the question. Some economists believe that incentive effects are so important that little taxation for redistribution should take place. They argue that when the rich do well, the total pie is increased so much that the spillover benefits to the poor are greater than the proceeds they would get from redistribution. For example, supporters of this view argue that the growth in capitalist economies was made possible by entrepreneurs. Because those entrepreneurs invested in new technology, there was more growth in society. Moreover, those entrepreneurs paid taxes. The benefits resulting from entrepreneurial action spilled over to the poor, making the poor far better off than any redistribution would. The fact that some of those entrepreneurs became rich is irrelevant because all society was better off due to their actions.

Other economists believe that there should be significant taxation for redistribution. While they agree that sometimes the incentive effects are substantial, they see the goal of equality overriding these effects.

Politics, Income Redistribution, and Fairness

Often politics, not value judgments, plays a central role in determining what taxes an individual will pay.

We began this discussion of income distribution and fairness by making the assumption that our value judgments determine the taxes we pay—that if our values led us to the conclusion that the poor deserved more income, we could institute policies that would get more to the poor. Reality doesn't necessarily work that way. Often politics, not value judgments, plays the central role in determining what taxes individuals will pay. The group that has the most votes will elect lawmakers who will enact tax policies that benefit that group at the expense of groups with fewer votes.

On the surface, the democratic system of one person/one vote would seem to suggest that the politics of redistribution would favor the poor, but it doesn't. One would expect that the poor would use their votes to make sure income was redistributed to them from the rich. Why don't they? The answer is complicated.

One reason is that many of the poor don't vote because they reason that "one vote won't make much difference." As a result, poor people's total voting strength is reduced. A second reason is that the "poor" aren't seen by most politicians as a solid voting block. There's no organization of the poor that can deliver votes to politicians. A third reason is that those poor people who do vote often cast their votes with other issues in mind. An anti–income-redistribution candidate might have a strong view on abortion as well, and for many the abortion view is the one that decides their vote.

A fourth reason is that elections require financing. Much of that financing comes from the rich. The money is used for advertising and publicity aimed at convincing the poor that voting for a person who supports the rich is actually in the best interests of the poor. Poor people are often misled by that kind of publicity, but not necessarily because they are dumb. In my view they do as well as anyone else could in processing the information they receive. The trouble is that information on the redistributive effect of a policy is often biased.

The issues are usually sufficiently complicated that a trained economist must study the information about them for a long time to determine which arguments make sense. Reasonable-sounding arguments can be made to support just about any position, and the rich have the means to see that the arguments that support their positions get the publicity. Of course, some of their arguments are also correct.

REAL-WORLD POLICIES AND PROGRAMS FOR INCOME REDISTRIBUTION

The preceding discussion provided you with a general sense of the theoretical difficulty of redistributing income. In this section I give you a sense of how income redistribution policies and programs have worked in the real world. As you've seen, there are two direct methods through which government redistributes income: taxation (policies that tax the rich more than the poor) and expenditures (programs that help the poor more than the rich).

Taxation to Redistribute Income

The U.S. federal government gets its revenue from a variety of taxes. The three largest sources of revenue are the personal income tax, the corporate income tax, and the Social Security tax. Exhibit 9 shows the 1994 rates for corporate and personal income taxes.

State and local governments get their revenue from income taxes, sales taxes, and property taxes. The rates vary among states.

Tax systems can be progressive, proportional (sometimes called *flat rate*), or regressive. A **progressive tax** is one in which the average tax rate increases with income. It redistributes income from the rich to the poor. A **proportional tax** is one in which the average rate of tax is constant regardless of income level. It is neutral in regard to income distribution. A **regressive tax** is one in which the average tax rate decreases with income. It redistributes income from poor to rich.

Progressive tax Average tax rate increases with income.

Proportional tax Average tax rate is constant with income.

Regressive tax Average tax rate decreases with income.

In the early 1940s, the federal personal income tax was made highly progressive, with a top tax rate of 90 percent on the highest incomes. The degree of progressivity went down significantly through various pieces of legislation after World War II until 1986, when the income tax system was amended to provide for an initial rate of 15 percent and a top rate of 28 percent. The changes did not reduce the actual progressivity of the personal income tax as much as they seemed to, because the 1986 reforms eliminated many of the loopholes in the U.S. Tax Code. Some loopholes had allowed rich people to legally reduce their reported incomes and to pay taxes on those lower incomes at lower rates. In 1993, as part of a deficit reduction package, the degree of progressivity was increased again and the top personal income tax rate on high-income individuals was increased to almost 40 percent.

Q–8: A progressive tax is preferable to a proportional tax. True or False? Why?

Whereas the personal income tax is progressive, the social security tax is initially proportional. All individuals pay the same tax rate on wage income (7.65 percent for employer; 7.65 percent for employee; 15.3 percent for self-employed) up to a cap of

EXHIBIT 9   Rates of Personal and Corporate Income Tax, 1993

Federal Individual Income Tax		
Joint return	Single taxpayer	Rate
$0–$38,000	$0–$22,750	15%
$38,000–$91,850	$22,751–$55,100	28
$91,851–$140,000	$55,101–$115,000	31
$140,001–$250,000	$115,001–$250,000	36
$250,001 and over	$250,001 and over	39.6

Federal Corporation Taxes	
Taxable income	Percentage rate
$0–$50,000	15%
$50,001–$75,000	25
$75,001–$100,000	34
$100,001–$335,000	39
$335,001–10,000,000	34
$10,000,001–$15,000,000	35
$15,000,001–$18,333,333	38
$18,333,334 and over	35

Source: Internal Revenue Service.

$60,600. Above that income cap, no Social Security tax is due (except for 1.45 percent for medical insurance which has no cap on the amount to which it is applied). At this income cap the social security tax becomes regressive: Higher-income individuals pay a lower percentage of their total income in Social Security taxes than do lower-income individuals. (They also receive relatively less in social security benefits, compared to what they put in. So, while the Social Security tax is regressive, taken as a whole the social security system is progressive.)

State and local governments get most of their income from the following sources:

State and local governments get most of their income from income taxes, sales taxes, and property taxes.

1. Income taxes, which are generally somewhat progressive.
2. Sales taxes, which tend to be proportional (all people pay the same tax rate on what they spend) or slightly regressive. (Since poor people often spend a higher percentage of their incomes than rich people, poor people pay a higher average tax rate as a percentage of their income than rich people.)
3. Property taxes, which are taxes paid on the value of people's property (usually real estate, but sometimes also personal property like cars). Since the value of people's property is related (although imperfectly related) to income, the property tax is considered to be roughly proportional.

When all the taxes paid by individuals to all levels of governments are combined, the conclusion that most researchers come to is that little income redistribution takes place on the tax side. The progressive taxes are offset by the regressive taxes, so the overall tax system is roughly proportional. That is, on average the tax rates individuals pay are roughly equal. Recent changes in the tax laws have increased the rate that high-income people pay and lowered the rate that lower-income people pay. These changes may make the effective tax structure slightly more progressive, but meaningful statistics won't be available for a few years.

Expenditure Programs to Redistribute Income

Since taxes don't redistribute income significantly, if the government does redistribute income, it must do so through expenditure programs. Exhibit 10 presents the federal government's expenditures on some programs that contribute to redistribution.

Program classification	Total (in billions)	Percentage* Federal	Percentage* State and local
Social insurance (including programs such as social security and unemployment insurance)	$561	81%	19%
Public aid (including programs such as Public Assistance and Supplemental Security Income)	180	37	63
Health and medical programs (excluding Medicare and Medicaid)	69	44	56
Veterans programs	33	99	1
Education	277	7	93
Housing	22	84	16
Other social welfare	20	50	50

EXHIBIT 10   Expenditures on Government Programs to Redistribute Income, 1991

Source: *Social Security Bulletin, 1994* and *Statistical Abstract, 1993*.

Social Security   The program that redistributes the most money is the **Social Security** system. It was established on a small scale during the Great Depression in 1935, but it has grown enormously since then. Almost all workers in the United States, including the self-employed, pay social security tax on their income. When you get your paycheck, this deduction is probably designated "FICA," which stands for Federal Insurance Contribution Act. This money goes into the Social Security trust fund, from which benefits are payable to eligible persons who are elderly or disabled, to certain of their dependents, and to surviving dependents of deceased workers. Social Security also has a multibillion-dollar medical insurance component called **Medicare.**

The population is aging, the death rate is going down, and the birth rate has been low. These demographic facts mean that fewer and fewer active workers are contributing to the fund while more and more people are becoming eligible for benefits. A Social Security crunch can be expected by the year 2020.

The amount of an individual's Social Security retirement, disability, or survivors' monthly cash benefits depends on a very complex formula, which is skewed in favor of lower-income workers. The program is not a pension program that pegs benefits to the amount paid in. Many people will get much more than they paid in; some who never paid anything in will get a great deal; and a few who paid in for years will get nothing. (No benefits are payable if you die before you retire and leave no survivors eligible for benefits due to your work.) On the whole, the program has been successful in keeping the elderly out of poverty. In addition, Social Security benefits have helped workers' survivors and the disabled.

In the early 1990s, there were about 40 million recipients of cash Social Security benefits, many of whom also received Medicare health insurance payments. Total benefits paid in 1990, including Medicare, came to $352.4 billion.

Public Assistance   **Public assistance** programs (more familiarly known as *welfare payments*) exist in every state of the union, although the amount paid varies greatly from state to state. The main kinds of public assistance are:

Aid to Families with Dependent Children (AFDC). Provides financial assistance to needy families with children under age 19.

Food stamps. Provides nutritional assistance in the form of coupons redeemable at most food stores.

Medicaid. Medical assistance for the poor, paid for by the individual states. It's different from, and usually more generous than, Medicare.

General assistance. State assistance to poor people when emergencies arise that aren't taken care of by any of the other programs.

By far the largest proportion of payments goes to needy families with dependent children, especially since these families are usually so poor that, in addition to

7 Expenditure programs to redistribute income include social security, public assistance, health and medical programs, veterans' programs, and education and housing programs.

Social Security   Social insurance program that provides financial benefits to the elderly and disabled and to their eligible dependents and/or survivors.

Medicare   Medical insurance component of the Social Security program.

Q–9:   The U.S. Social Security system is only a retirement system. True or false?

Public assistance ("welfare") Means-tested social programs targeted to the poor and providing financial, nutritional, medical, and housing assistance.

qualifying for AFDC, they meet the eligibility requirements for food stamps and Medicaid.

A common complaint about welfare recipients is that they should get a job. A little research reveals that this criticism is misplaced. About 70 percent of the recipients are children, and many of the adults receiving welfare are too disabled to work. Moreover, most welfare programs conduct job training and other programs designed to help recipients who are able to work get off the welfare rolls. In 1990, about $146 billion was paid in public aid (including the value of food stamps).

Supplemental Security Income (SSI)   Federal program that pays benefits, based on need, to the elderly, blind, and disabled.

Supplemental Security Income
Hundreds of thousands more people would be receiving public assistance if it weren't for **Supplemental Security Income (SSI),** a federal program administered through Social Security Administration offices. Unlike Social Security benefits, SSI pays benefits to the elderly, blind, and disabled based solely on the basis of need. Again unlike social security, the recipients pay nothing toward the cost of the program. To be eligible, though, people must have very low incomes and almost no resources except a home, if they are fortunate enough to own one, a wedding ring and engagement ring, and an automobile. In 1991, about $19 billion was paid in SSI benefits.

Unemployment compensation   Short-term financial assistance, regardless of need, to eligible individuals who are temporarily out of work.

Unemployment Compensation
Unemployment compensation is limited financial assistance to people who are out of work through no fault of their own and have worked in a covered occupation for a substantial number of weeks in the period just before they became unemployed. These programs are administered by the states, even though they are largely funded by the federal government, which in turn gets the money from a tax on employers. Employees do not have anything deducted from their paychecks for unemployment compensation. The amount and duration of benefit payments varies from state to state.

Unemployment compensation is not a long-term program, because it was designed to tide a person over who is temporarily out of work because of a lay-off or the seasonal nature of his or her occupation. A person can't just quit a job and live on unemployment benefits. While receiving unemployment benefits, people are expected to actively search for work.

Q–10:   For how long can a person normally receive unemployment benefits?

Normally a person can receive unemployment benefits for only about six months in any given year, and the amount of the benefit is always considerably less than the amount the person earned when working. Lower-income workers receive unemployment payments that are more nearly equal to their working wage than do higher-income workers, but there is no income eligibility test. In 1990, about $18 billion was paid in unemployment benefits, in 1991, $27 billion; and in 1992, $36.7 billion.

Housing Programs
Federal and state governments have many different programs to improve housing or to provide affordable housing. While many of these programs are designed to benefit "low-income" persons, there are also programs for "moderate-income" persons and "lower-income persons" (people whose incomes are lower than "moderate" but higher than "low").

The federal agency overseeing most of these programs, the Department of Housing and Urban Development (HUD), has been criticized for abuse and mismanagement. Hundreds of millions of dollars that could have benefitted the poor went instead to developers of housing and other projects, to consultants, and to others who skimmed off money before—or instead of—building or rehabilitating housing. In part because of these problems, federal funding for housing was steadily reduced during the 1980s. In 1991, about $22 billion was allocated to housing programs.

Most government redistribution works through its expenditure programs, not through taxes.

Overall Effect of Income Redistribution Programs
While the tax system has not proven to be an effective means of redistributing income, the government expenditure system has been quite effective. Exhibit 11 shows approximate Lorenz curves before and after

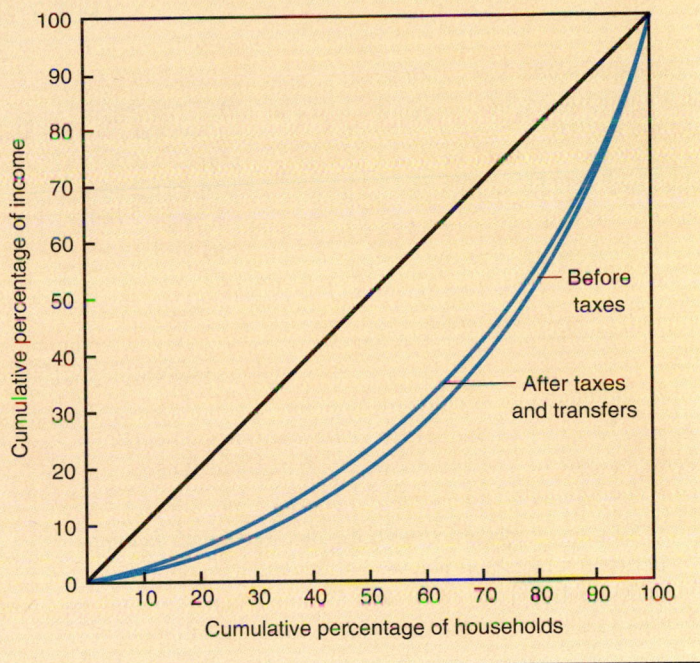

EXHIBIT 11   Distribution of Income before and after Taxes and Transfers, 1992

Although little redistribution takes place through the tax system, significant redistribution occurs through the transfer system, making the after-tax and transfer distribution of income more equal than the before-tax distribution of income.
Source: U.S. Bureau of the Census, 1993.

analyzing the effect of both taxes and government programs on the redistribution of income. As you can see, the after-transfer income is significantly closer to being equally distributed. But because of the incentive effects of collecting and distributing the money, that redistribution has come at the cost of a reduction in the total amount of income earned by the society. The debate about whether the gain in equality of income is worth the cost in reduction of total income is likely to continue indefinitely.

CONCLUSION

Much more could be said about the issues involved in income redistribution. But limitations of time and space pressure us to move on. I hope this, and the last two, chapters have convinced you that income redistribution is an important but difficult question. Specifically, I hope I have given you the sense that income distribution questions are integrally related with questions about the entire economic system. Supply and demand play a central role in the determination, of the distribution of income, but they do so in an institutional and historical context. Thus, the analysis of income distribution must include that context as well as one's ethical judgments about what is fair.

CHAPTER SUMMARY

- The Lorenz curve is a measure of the inequality of income.
- There are alternative views about government's role in reducing poverty.
- Wealth is distributed less equally than income.
- Fairness is a philosophical question. Each person must judge a program's fairness for him or herself.
- Income is difficult to redistribute because of incentive effects of taxes, avoidance and evasion effects of taxes, and incentive effects of redistribution programs.
- On the whole, the U.S. tax system is roughly proportional, so it is not very effective as a means of redistributing income.
- Government expenditure programs are more effective than tax policy in reducing income inequality in the United States.

KEY TERMS

comparable worth laws *(709)*
discrimination *(707)*
income *(705)*
Lorenz curve *(699)*
Medicare *(715)*
poverty *(701)*
progressive tax *(713)*

proportional tax *(713)*
public assistance
 (''welfare'') *(715)*
regressive tax *(713)*
size distribution of
 income *(698)*
Social Security *(715)*

socioeconomic distribution of
 income *(698)*
Supplemental Security
 Income (SSI) *(716)*
unemployment
 compensation *(716)*
wealth *(705)*

QUESTIONS FOR THOUGHT AND REVIEW

*The number after each question represents the estimated
degree of critical thinking required. (1 = almost none;
10 = deep thought.)*

1. Why are we concerned with the distribution of income
   between whites and blacks, but not between redheads
   and blonds? *(8)*

2. The Lorenz curve for Bangladesh looks like this:

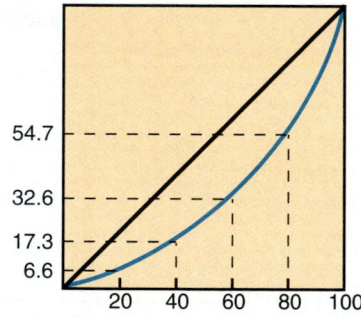

   How much income do the top 20 percent of individuals
   in Bangladesh receive? *(2)*

3. If one were to draw a Lorenz curve for lawyers, what
   would it represent? *(5)*

4. Should poverty be defined absolutely or relatively?
   Why? *(6)*

5. Some economists argue that a class distinction should be
   made between managerial decision makers and other
   workers. Do you agree? Why or why not? *(8)*

6. If a garbage collector earns more than an English
   teacher, does that mean something is wrong with the
   economy? Why or why not? *(8)*

7. Is it ever appropriate for society to:

   Let someone starve?

   Let someone be homeless?

   Forbid someone to eat chocolate? *(8)*

8. If you receive a paycheck, what percentage of it is withheld for taxes? What incentive effect does that have on
   your decision to work? *(5)*

9. Give four reasons why women earn so much less than
   men. Which reasons do you believe are most responsible
   for the difference? *(6)*

10. There are many more poor people than there are rich
    people. If the poor wanted to, they could exercise their
    power to redistribute as much money as they please to
    themselves. They don't do that, so they must see the
    income distribution system as fair. Discuss. *(6)*

PROBLEMS AND EXERCISES

1. The accompanying table shows income distribution data
   for three countries.

   | | Percentage of total income | | |
Income quintile	India	South Korea	Mexico
Lowest 20%	7.0%	5.7%	2.9%
Second quintile	9.2	11.2	7.0
Third quintile	13.5	15.1	12.0
Fourth quintile	20.5	22.4	20.4
Highest 20%	49.8	45.6	57.7

   a. Using this information, draw a Lorenz curve for each
      country.
   b. Which country has the most equal distribution of
      income?

   c. Which country has the least equal?
   d. By looking at the three Lorenz curves, can you tell
      which country has the most progressive tax system?
      Why or why not?

2. In Taxland, a tax exemption is granted for the first
   $10,000 earned per year. Between $10,000.01 and
   $30,000, the tax rate is 25 percent. Between $30,000.01
   and $50,000, it's 30 percent. Above $50,000, it's 35 percent. You're earning $75,000 a year.

   a. How much in taxes will you have to pay?
   b. What is your average tax rate? Your marginal tax rate?
   c. Taxland has just changed to a tax credit system in
      which, in lieu of any exemption, eligible individuals
      are given a check for $4,000. The two systems are
      designed to bring in the same amount of revenue.
      Would you favor or oppose the change? Why?

3. Some economists have argued against need-based scholarships because they work as an implicit tax on parents' salaries and hence discourage savings for college.

   a. If the marginal tax rate parents face is 20 percent, and 5 percent of parents' assets will be deducted from a student's financial aid each year for four years a child is in school, what is the implicit marginal tax on that portion of income that is saved? (For simplicity assume the interest rate is zero and that the parent's contribution is paid at the time the child enters college.)

   b. How would your answer differ if parents had two children with the second entering college right after the first one graduated? (How about three?) (Remember that the assets will likely decrease with each child graduating.)

   c. When parents are divorced, how should the contribution of each parent be determined? If your school has need-based scholarships, how does it determine the expected contributions of divorced parents?

   d. Given the above, would you suggest moving to an ability-based scholarship program? Why or why not?

4. Interview three female and three male professors with significant others of the opposite sex (i.e., spouses) at your college, asking them what percentage of work in the professor's household each adult household member does.

   a. Assuming your results can be extended to the population at large, what can you say about the existence of supply-side institutional discrimination?

   b. If gender-related salary data for individuals at your college are available, determine whether women or men of equal rank and experience receive higher average pay.

   c. Relate your findings in *a* and *b*.

   d. Does the existence of supply-side institutional discrimination suggest that no demand-side discrimination exists? Why or why not?

5. Some economists have proposed making the tax rate progressivity depend on the wage rate rather than the income level. Thus, an individual who works twice as long as another but who receives a lower wage would face a lower marginal tax rate.

   a. What effect would this change have on incentives to work?

   b. Would this system be fairer than our current system? Why or why not?

   c. If, simultaneously, the tax system were made regressive in hours worked so that individuals who work longer hours faced lower marginal tax rates, what effect would this change have on hours worked?

   d. What would be some of the administrative difficulties of instituting the above changes to our income tax code?

ANSWERS TO MARGIN QUESTIONS

1. When drawing a Lorenz curve, you put the cumulative percentage of income on the vertical axis and the cumulative percentage of families (or population) on the horizontal axis. *(699)*

2. The U.S. definition of poverty is an absolute measure, but the way poverty is calculated means that some relativity is included in the definition. *(701)*

3. Supply-side discrimination is structural discrimination that affects supply; it occurs in the household in interpersonal relationships within the family. Direct demand-side discrimination is discrimination that affects demand; it occurs in the firm, and represents a bias against a group independent of their qualifications. *(708)*

4. A comparable worth law would likely change the institutional structure that influences the relative pay. These changes might create inefficiency and other problems, but they would likely reduce the male/female pay gap for those women who remain working and covered by the law. *(708)*

5. In early capitalist society, the distributional fight was between workers and capitalists. In modern capitalist society, the distributional fight is more varied. For example, in the United States minorities are pitted against whites and males against females. *(710)*

6. No, it is not self-evident that greater equality of income would make society a better place to live. Unequal income distribution has its benefits. Still, most people would prefer a somewhat more equal distribution of income than currently exists. *(711)*

7. What is fair is a very difficult concept. It depends on people's needs, people's wants, to what degree people are deserving, and other factors. Still, in the absence of any more information than is given in the question, I would divide the pie equally. *(711)*

8. As a general statement, ''a progressive tax is preferable to a proportional tax'' is false. A progressive tax may well be preferable, but that is a normative judgment. Moreover, taxes have incentive effects that must be considered. *(713)*

9. False. The U.S. Social Security system includes many other aspects, such as disability benefits and survivors' benefits. *(715)*

10. Normally a person can receive unemployment benefits for only about six months in any given 12-month period. *(716)*

A Numerical Example of the Problems of Redistributing Income

To give you a better sense of the problems of redistributing income, let's consider a numerical example. In this appendix we'll once again consider our John and Fred example. This time we'll say that John and Fred are each working, one job apiece, and that they're roughly equal in ability and needs. Because they're equals, we've decided that, according to our values, it's unfair that John earns more than four times as much as Fred. We believe that Fred should get more than the $12,000 he's currently getting and John should get less than $50,000. We decide that, ideally, the income ratio between these two should be one to one. Each should get $31,000:

$$\$12,000 + \$50,000 = \$62,000/2 = \$31,000$$

One way to accomplish this end would be to institute a tax on John and give the proceeds to Fred. But in the United States, by law a tax must treat people who are equally situated equally, so our government cannot simply impose a tax on John and give the proceeds to Fred. Instead, in order to treat equals equally, the government must relate the tax to income rather than to individuals. The tax must be such that two people earning the same amount pay the same amount of tax.

Incentive Effects of Taxation

Let's say we impose a tax of 40 percent on everyone's income, hoping that the tax will bring in $20,000 from John and $4,800 from Fred for total revenue of $24,800 available for redistribution. But will our hopes be met? Probably not. Taxes have incentive effects. Both John and Fred, faced with a 40 percent tax rate, will reduce the amount of income that they earn, preferring instead to take more leisure than before. If the government is going to tax away 40 percent of your hard-earned dollars, why work so hard?

Say John reduces his income by 30 percent and Fred reduces his by 20 percent. John's after-tax income is $21,000. (He reduced his income from $50,000 to $35,000, of which the 40 percent tax takes $14,000.)

Fred's after-tax income is $5,760. (He reduced his income from $12,000 to $9,600, of which the 40 percent tax takes $3,840). Now society's total income (John's plus Fred's) falls from $62,000 to $44,600, so our total tax revenue isn't the $24,800 we hoped for, but only $17,840. As government collects tax revenue to redistribute, incentive effects shrink the total amount of income earned by the society.

Incentive Effects of Distributing Income

The next problem is how to give out the revenue we've collected for redistribution. Since our goal is to redistribute the money to Fred, we might simply give it all to Fred. But doing so would violate the law requiring equal treatment of equally situated individuals, so our redistribution system must be related to income levels and not to the characteristics of particular individuals. Let's say we decide to give the proceeds to persons who have less than $20,000 in after-tax income. We distribute this $17,840 to Fred, pulling his after-tax income up to $5,760 + $17,840 = $23,600, a level slightly higher than John's after-tax income.

But now John, seeing what we've given Fred, figures out a way to work "off the books." He works out a deal so that he's paid $5,000 of his income in cash under the table. He takes a chance by breaking the law and failing to report this $5,000 on his income tax return. That means it looks as if he's earning only $18,000 in after-tax income. He's below the $20,000 cutoff, so he can share in our income redistribution program and get back some of the tax money we collected from him. (His pretax income is still $35,000, but $5,000 of it isn't reported to the government, so he pays the 40 percent tax on only $30,000, which means that his tax is $12,000 and he's left with reported after-tax income of $18,000.) If working off the books doesn't accomplish this goal, he can simply choose to work less in order to make his after-tax income fall below the $20,000 cutoff.

Thus, there's an incentive effect of redistributing income as well as an incentive effect of collecting the money to be redistributed. As income is redistributed, individuals have an incentive to make it look as if they earn less income than they do, or to actually earn less income, in order to get a share of the redistributed income.

The negative incentive effects of redistribution further reduce the size of the income pie. In this case, if John reduces his before-tax income to $30,000, his 40 percent tax is only $12,000—and now the redistribution pot is only $15,840 ($12,000 from John and $3,840 from Fred). At the same time, the number of people eligible to share in the redistribution has doubled. Before only Fred was eligible; now both John and Fred are eligible. Now Fred receives only $7,920 from the government instead of $17,840. So his total before-tax income is $9,600 + $7,920 = $17,520. If John got his reported taxable income down to $30,000 by taking $5,000 under the table, this means that John's after-tax income is $30,920:

$30,000 total reported income
−12,000 taxes

$18,000 after-tax income
+ 5,000 under-the-table income

$23,000
+ 7,920 half share of redistribution pot

$30,920

The effect of our redistribution program on the total income in our two-person society is an aggregate reduction in income from $62,000 to $39,600 of total reported income (assuming John does take that $5,000 under the table). The initial inequality of measured income was approximately 4.2:1 (John's $50,000 to Fred's $12,000). The higher-income person earned four times as much as the lower-income person. Now the inequality of measured before-tax income is approximately 3:1 (John's reported $30,000 to Fred's $9,600), an improvement from the 4:1 it was before. The inequality of after-tax income is $18,000 (John) to $5,760 (Fred), which is also approximately a 3:1 ratio.

The absolute increase in Fred's income is $1,680 (his income is now $5,760 after-tax income plus $7,920 in redistribution proceeds), and the absolute decrease in John's income is $19,080. The net after-tax, after-redistribution positions are:

John: $30,920

Fred: $13,680

That's approximately a ratio of 2.3:1. Clearly some improvement in equality has been achieved (from 4.2:1 to 2.3:1), but it has come at a high cost in total income of the society, which has fallen from $62,000 to $44,600.

33

The Role of Government in the Economy

You've got to distinguish between a politician using economics and using economics.

~Charles Schultze

After reading this chapter, you should be able to:

1 State two insights that form the basis of most economists' support of markets.

2 Explain what an externality is.

3 State four arguments in favor of government intervention in the economy.

4 State four arguments against government intervention in the economy.

5 Define a sin tax and state why Milton Friedman would likely disapprove of it.

6 List the arguments for and against licensure.

7 Answer just about every question posed to you with, "It depends on the costs and benefits."

Should the government intervene in the private affairs of individuals? If the government does intervene, what should the nature of that intervention be? Throughout this book, these questions have been at the bottom of policy discussions. In this chapter I address these questions directly, tying together the policy discussions of the earlier chapters. I consider four justifications for government intervention in markets: to prevent restraints on trade; to offset problems of information and rationality; to correct externalities; and to prevent unfairness.

Most activities of real-world markets contain elements to which each of these reasons might apply. Thus, in most cases there's legitimate debate about whether the government should intervene, and, if it should, what form the intervention should take. Such decisions generally can be made only on the basis of specific knowledge about institutions and normative judgments, both of which are beyond the scope of an introductory economics textbook. What this book can provide you with is a framework for making such decisions. That's the purpose of this chapter.

Before you address the issues of government intervention, you must consider the question: What is government? In the United States we're all fairly clear about what we mean by **government.** It's the combination of federal, state, and local agencies whose officials are elected by the people, or are appointed by officials who are elected by the people. The federal government handles the economic matters of defense, income security, national economic regulation, and macroeconomic stability. State and local governments handle matters of education, roads, welfare, and state and local economic regulation.

Not all countries are organized like this. Many governments, especially in developing countries, are autocracies in which the leaders are not subject to elections, but hold office on the basis of power or historical precedent. The division of responsibilities among levels of authority also differs. For example, in some countries educational policy is set on the national, rather than the state and local, level.

The discussion in this chapter assumes that the government either is a functioning democracy in which the people elect their leaders or else is a beneficent autocracy in which the unelected leader tries to do what's in the people's best interests. Faced with nonbeneficent autocracies in which the leaders worry only about their own benefit, not society's benefit, and in which the leaders pursue their own self-interests, almost all economists become supporters of government nonintervention or **laissez-faire** (the philosophy that government should intervene in the economy as little as possible).

Government   The combination of federal, state, and local agencies whose officials are elected by the people or appointed by elected officials.

Q–1:   In what way does the structure of government determine economists' policy views?

Laissez-faire   The philosophy that government should intervene in the economy as little as possible.

THE ARGUMENTS FOR AND AGAINST GOVERNMENT INTERVENTION

A good way to consider the arguments for and against government intervention is to consider a debate between two imaginary economists: Paul, who favors intervention, and Milton, who opposes it. I, the author, take the role of moderator. There's one rule: Each person will be allowed to present his case without interruption.

As background for the debate, let me state two general insights that form the basis of most economists' support of markets.

1 Two insights behind economists' support of markets are: (1) if people voluntarily trade, that trade must be making them better off; and (2) excess profit generates competition and the price falls.

1. If two individuals trade in a market, one can presume that they're both better off after the trade; otherwise they wouldn't have traded.

2. If individuals are free to produce whatever goods they want, then when excess profit is being made, more people will enter into the production of that good and consumers will benefit as the price is pushed down.

Both economists in the debate accept these two insights but differ as to how many qualifications they make to them. In the imaginary debate that follows, Milton takes the position that few qualifications should be made. Paul takes the position that many qualifications should be made. The debate begins with Milton having stated the two general propositions, after which he draws the following conclusions:

Milton: *All government intervention can be seen as intervention in free trade among people. Government intervention prevents individuals from making trades that will make them both better off. Thus, government intervention can only hurt society. So let's get the government off our backs.*

ADDED DIMENSION

LAISSEZ-FAIRE IS NOT ANARCHY

Most reasons for government intervention discussed in this chapter are debatable.

There is, however, one governmental role that even the strongest laissez-faire advocates generally accept. That role is for government to set up an appropriate institutional and legal structure within which markets can operate.

The reason there's little debate about this role is that all economists recognize that markets do not operate when there is anarchy. They require institutional structures that determine the rules of ownership, what types of trade are allowable, how contracts will be enforced, and what productive institutions are most desirable.

Before anyone conducts business, he or she needs to know the rules of the game and must have a reasonable expectation that those rules will not be changed. The operation of the modern economy requires that contractual arrangements be made among individuals. These contractual arrangements must be enforced if the economy is to operate effectively.

Economists differ significantly as to what the rules for such a system should be and whether any rules that already exist should be modified. Even if the rules are currently perceived as unfair, it can be argued that they should be kept in place. Individuals have already made decisions based on those rules, and it's unfair to them to change the rules in the middle of the game.

Stability of rules is a benefit to society. When the rules are perceived as unfair and changing them is also perceived as unfair, the government must find a balance between these two degrees of unfairness. Government often finds itself in that difficult position. Thus, while there's little debate about government's role in providing some institutional framework, there's heated debate about which framework is most appropriate.

For an interesting discussion of these issues applied to antitrust law, see Walter Adams and James Brock, *Antitrust Economics on Trial: A Dialogue on the New Laissez-Faire* (Princeton, N.J.: Princeton University Press, 1991).

Paul: *Oh, come on, Milton! I'm not naive. Your argument, while it sounds nice, doesn't stand up to close scrutiny. I can list four arguments for government intervention.*

Four Arguments for Government Intervention

1. Preventing Restraints on Trade

Paul: *The first insight argues that all agreements freely entered into should be allowed. But what if two people agree to limit supply and prevent others from entering the market? That would violate the second insight since individuals would not be free to produce whatever goods they want. You'll certainly want to amend your argument against intervention to rule out certain agreements that restrain trade. Thus, one argument for government intervention is to defend competition and to prevent restraint of trade.*

2. Correcting Informational and Rationality Problems

Paul: *A second argument for intervention is an informational and rationality argument. Your free trade argument assumes that people are rational and have all the information they need to make a rational decision. What if they aren't or don't? Say two individuals make a trade: A 3-year-old says to a 17-year-old, "I'll give you my future inheritance if you'll let me play with your toy." In my view that trade is unfair because the 3-year-old isn't yet able to make rational decisions.*

Milton: *OK, I'll grant you that 3-year-olds don't fit my argument, but I'm talking about adults.*

Paul: *I am too. I only presented the argument about the 3-year-old to establish the point. Let's consider another example where the same principle applies. Let's say that your car breaks down and you have it towed to a garage where the mechanic tells you that your differential is sloppy and your clutch is chattering and that they both need to be replaced at a total cost of $1,600. Or suppose a surgeon tells you that for $32,000 you can have a quadruple coronary artery bypass which will make you feel better. Both of these cases have a potential for useful government intervention because the*

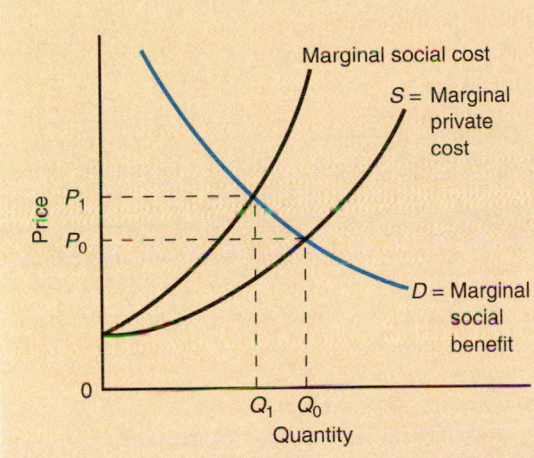

EXHIBIT 1   The Effect of an Externality

When there is a negative externality, the marginal private cost will be below the marginal social cost and the competitive price will be too low to maximize social welfare.

two sides in each transaction don't have equal access to information, meaning that the trades aren't necessarily fair. It could well be that all your car really needed was a $10 adjustment, and that you had no need for bypass surgery. How can you be sure if the mechanic and the surgeon are advising what's best for you, or if they just want the money? When both sides of a trade don't have equal access to information, the argument for nonintervention breaks down.

Similarly for rationality. People aren't always rational. Say some fast-talking salesperson convinces a 70-year-old couple to invest all their savings in a partnership to turn water into gold. They might do it voluntarily, but in my view that doesn't make it rational. Government intervention is necessary to prevent such injustices.

3. Correcting for Externalities

Paul: Let's now consider another case. Say that we agree that I'll produce steel for you. I'll build my plant on land I own, and start producing. Who can complain? It's a fair trade freely entered into by both of us, right? It's fair for the two of us—but what about my plant's neighbors? I suspect that they'll complain, and rightfully so. The resulting smoke will pollute the air they breathe; the sulphur smell will drive all the tourists away; and the factory will be an eyesore. So there's an agreement freely entered into by rational individuals that it may be better for government to prevent because the agreement affects third parties.

Such third-party effects are called **externalities** (effects of decisions not taken into account by the decision makers). Externalities provide a potential role for government intervention. I can demonstrate the effect of an externality with the simple supply/demand graph in Exhibit 1.

The supply curve, S, represents the marginal private cost to society of producing steel. It represents my opportunity cost. The demand curve, D, represents the marginal social benefit to demanders of my steel. When there are no externalities, the marginal private costs and benefits represent the marginal social costs and benefits, so the supply/demand equilibrium (P_0, Q_0) represents the point where the marginal social benefit equals the marginal social cost. At that point society is as well off as possible.

But now consider what happens when there are externalities in production, as in this example. In that case other people must bear part of the cost of our agreement. This means that the marginal social cost is different from the marginal private cost. I represent this case by adding a curve to Exhibit 1 which can be called the marginal social cost curve (to distinguish it from the marginal private cost curve). In my example, this marginal social cost curve would include all the marginal costs that my neighbors bear from my production of steel, as well as all the marginal private costs associated with that production.

When free trade is allowed, these costs aren't taken into account, and the supply/demand equilibrium is at too high a quantity, Q_0, and too low a price, P_0. The combination of price and quantity that takes into account all social costs and benefits

2 Externalities are effects of decisions not taken into account by the decision makers.

Q–2: Why would the existence of an externality prevent the market from working properly?

Q–3: Demonstrate graphically the effect of a positive externality.

An intellectual inquiry like economics is a debate of ideas. It's not a set of facts or truths. To understand arguments in economics, one must understand both sides of the arguments and the context within which a particular argument is made.

In a debate of ideas, usually a relatively simple idea is presented first. That simple idea provokes responses that can only be understood if the participants and the audience recognize that the responses are reactions to that initial idea. In order to understand ideas properly, one must know the arguments to which they are a response. These arguments require an understanding of the debate that has preceded them. For example, to understand the externality argument in favor of government intervention, one must understand the basic argument in favor of free trade to which the externality argument is a response.

There are higher and higher levels of arguments. Such higher-level arguments are the grist of academic journals and are one of the reasons many academic arguments seem unintelligible to students who don't know the history of the debate. (Another reason is that sometimes academic arguments are indeed unintelligible.)

I present this chapter as a debate to emphasize, first, that learning economics is like listening in on a conversation in which arguments build on one another, and second, that one can expect that there will always be a rebuttal to any argument. Picturing economics as such an unending clash of ideas gives one a good perspective on many economic issues.

---

occurs at P_1, Q_1, *where the marginal social benefit equals the marginal social cost. Some type of intervention to reduce production from* Q_0 *to* Q_1 *and raise price from* P_0 *to* P_1 *is needed. Government is the logical agency to make that intervention.*

Milton: *I can't let you continue. Your arguments make sense, but they're missing an essential point. And I'm not getting equal time—these boxes are extending the time allotted to Paul. I appeal to the author to let me respond.*

Author: *I'm sorry, Milton, but rules are rules; besides, good teaching requires presentation of all the arguments. So I'll let Paul state his final argument and then turn the pages over to you.*

4. Preventing Unfairness

Paul: *Thank you, Author. I'll try to be brief. My final argument is in some ways the most subtle, but in other ways is the most obvious. It goes like this: Markets operate only when there are property rights—when individuals control the items being traded. If one believes that the initial distribution of property rights is unfair, one can reasonably oppose the use of the market.*

Let's consider an example. Say a robber walks up to you and makes you an offer you can't refuse: "Your money or your life." You give him your money and in exchange he doesn't kill you. You're better off; he's better off; and no one else is worse off. But such an exchange is not one that, in my view, societies should condone. Put simply, the robber has no right to your life, so it's unfair for him to offer it in exchange for your money. Because the robber unfairly assumed property rights in your life, the result of the trade is unfair (although you're better off than if you hadn't made the trade).

Now let's change the example slightly. Instead of a robber, it's now an employer who makes you an offer you can't refuse: "You work for me on my terms or I'll fire you." The same unfairness argument can be made about this trade. One could argue that it's unfair because no one should have the right to impose arbitrary terms of employment unless those terms of employment are "fair."

Most Americans don't hold that view; they believe that employment is a fair trade, within limits, as long as other jobs exist that an individual can take. But their concept of unfairness of underlying property rights determines many of their arguments in favor of government intervention, and rightfully so. Say that a firm decides that it doesn't want to hire you because you're black or a woman. Most Americans would argue that the employer has exceeded the limitations of the "fair" employment contract at that point, because a firm shouldn't be allowed to decide whom it will hire on the basis of race or sex.

Q-4: Why can one oppose efficient markets when one does not believe the underlying property rights are fairly distributed?

EXTERNALITIES AND PUBLIC GOODS

Externalities can be positive or negative. A positive externality is the benefit conveyed to third parties by an action in which they were not actors themselves. A negative externality is the harm inflicted on third parties by an action in which they were not actors themselves. An example of a negative externality is the negative effect of pollution on society. An example of a positive externality is the effect on society of the education of its citizens.

When actions have either positive or negative third-party effects, it's not clear that society will be better off or worse off if it follows a laissez-faire policy. Unless the government intervenes, many agreements that produce negative externalities will be allowed and many agreements that produce positive externalities won't take place. Government intervention *may* be able to make individuals take third-party benefits or costs into account.

An extreme case of a positive externality is called a public good. A *public good* is a good that an individual can consume without diminishing the amount of it that other people consume. Thus, supplying a public good conveys a positive externality not only to one or two individuals but to all individuals in the society. An example of a public good is national defense. Each person in an army who defends the nation provides defense for all in the society.

Many other activities carry with them strong negative externalities. Consider fishing from a lake. Whenever you catch a fish, there's one fewer fish for all other people to catch. You're better off, but other people are worse off. But you're concerned only with your own welfare, so you won't take into account the harm done to other people. Activities like that which deplete or use up a commonly held resource involve significant negative externalities. If we allow everyone to carry on such activity unrestricted—if we follow a policy of laissez-faire—society as a whole will be worse off.

What I'm saying is that certain underlying rights—such as the right to employment—must be distributed equally for a society to be considered fair. Similarly with the right to a decent living. If the market doesn't provide that for people, then intervention is needed.

Author: *Before I turn the pages over to Milton, let me restate Paul's four arguments in favor of government intervention.*

Summary: Four Arguments for Government Intervention

1. Agreements to restrain trade should themselves be restricted.
2. When there are informational and rationality problems, government should intervene.
3. When there are externalities, intervention is necessary to see that marginal social costs and marginal social benefits are equal.
4. When property rights are unfair, government should intervene to achieve fairness.

Author: *Now go ahead, Milton.*

Milton: *It's always difficult to argue with Paul because he makes his arguments so clearly and convincingly. And in each of the cases he presents, I must agree that he captures a kernel of the truth. But all of the arguments suffer from a serious flaw. They assume that when the government comes in, it will actually correct a problem without introducing new problems that are even worse.*

Paul sees government as a group of individuals committed to doing good. That's not the way all governments work, as the author points out in the opening of this chapter. The point the author didn't make, and the point that Paul totally ignored, is that that's not the way even democratic governments operate. In my view, all government is a mechanism through which some people—people in government and people with access to government—take advantage of other people.

Once one sees government for what it truly is, then the arguments for government intervention fall apart, except for government's role in establishing a proper institutional structure within which markets can operate. But, as the author pointed out, that general role isn't in debate.

The other roles for government are in debate. The argument against government intervention rests on the difficulty of correcting economic problems through government. Yes, all the problems Paul mentions do exist, and it would be nice if they didn't exist. But it would also be nice if diamonds grew on trees. To make the four arguments

3 Four arguments for government intervention are:
1. Agreements to restrain trade should be restricted.
2. Informational and rationality problems necessitate government intervention.
3. When there are externalities, marginal social costs and marginal social benefits should be equalized.
4. When property rights are unfair, government should intervene to achieve fairness.

Four Arguments against Government Intervention

Q–5: If a positive externality exists, does that mean the market works better than if no externality existed?

Q–6: If one accepts the four explanations of market failure, how might one still oppose government intervention?

in favor of government intervention convincing, Paul would have to show that there's a better way, and that the "solution" to the problems won't make the problems worse. Paul hasn't even addressed this issue.

The reality is that government is often controlled by special interests. It's inefficient, bureaucratic, and oppressive. When you expand government, you make people worse off. So, yes, there are problems with the market, but government's attempts to correct those problems create worse problems. Laws passed in the name of the public good, in fact, generally benefit only a small group. To show you what I mean, let's consider each of the four cases that Paul presents.

1. Preventing Private Restraints on Trade Creates Even More Restraints

Milton: *There's no question that people have a desire to restrain trade, but if we look at the real world we see that the primary way they restrain trade is through governmental restrictions such as licensing requirements, antitrust legislation, and zoning regulations. Allowing government to try to stop private individuals from restricting trade opens up a Pandora's box of new possibilities for restricting trade through government. Not only will somewhat reasonable restrictions be made, but totally unreasonable restrictions also will be made. And that Pandora's box need not be opened, because without government enforcement of restrictions, competition will soon break down any private restrictions on trade. The only long-lasting restraints are those imposed by government.*

2. Correcting Informational and Rationality Problems Creates Other Problems

The central argument against using government to solve a problem is that such use creates worse problems.

Milton: *There's no doubt that informational problems like the ones Paul describes do exist. They're facts of life. But once again, using government to solve a problem creates worse problems. Say that government passes a law that all cost estimates for auto repairs must be approved as fair before the repairs can be made. Can you imagine how long you'd have to wait for the paperwork to be processed? You'd be waiting months for your car. And all that paperwork would add to your repair costs. Not only would you pay too much to have your car fixed; often you wouldn't get it back for months.*

Here's another example. The Food and Drug Administration "protects" us from unsafe drugs, but in doing so it creates enormous bureaucratic hassles for the manufacturers of all new drugs, many of which would be beneficial. For instance, the FDA prevented a number of experimental drugs from being used on AIDS patients for years, even though their use represented many people's only chance to survive, or at least to survive longer and more comfortably. By the time the FDA approved the drugs, many of the patients were dead.

3. Correcting for Externalities Creates Other Problems

Milton: *I've heard the externality argument hundreds of times, but, I swear, every time I examine a so-called externality, I discover either that it isn't a true externality that can be corrected by government or that the way in which government will correct for the externality will cause more harm than good.*

To see this, let's first consider Paul's Exhibit 1. Is it likely that government will pass a law reducing Paul's production of steel to Q_1 and raise the price to P_1? Or is it more likely that government will simply ban production of steel at Paul's house altogether? If it bans production of a good altogether, quantity will fall to zero. The good won't be available at any price, a result that would be far worse than if the market result had been left alone. Government regulatory agencies aren't designed to do the delicate balancing of benefits and costs necessary to make the marginal changes that Paul's argument calls for. Such refinements require a scalpel, and government intervention is more like a chain saw.

The same problem of government intervention causing more harm than good exists for activities with so-called positive externalities. Government intervention simply creates a possibility for special interests to come in and channel government revenue to support their own interests. In my view, positive externalities generally are the result of a poor specification of property rights. The positive externalities argument is made by some group attempting to use government for its own ends.

Government intervention for positive externalities inevitably means government subsidization, which must be paid for in higher taxes. These higher taxes are likely to offset the good the subsidized externalities might do; that is, higher taxes reduce private incentives to work and to undertake private economic activity. In my view and in the view of most noninterventionists generally, private activity done without government intervention involves as many, or more, positive externalities as do government-supported activities.

For example, in the early 1990s, as the threat from the former Soviet Union significantly diminished, it made sense to close a number of military bases around the country. But political pressure against doing so was intense. One argument used by supporters of keeping these bases open was that they had positive externalities: They created jobs for civilians in the area.

What's wrong with this argument is that in order to pay for these bases, government has to collect taxes, which discourages private activities. The net job creation is essentially zero. As was the case with negative externalities, even when government activities do have clear-cut positive externalities, it's not at all clear that the political process will choose the right level of the activity. Generally the political process won't produce a decision based on comparing marginal social costs with marginal social benefits. It will make the decision based on marginal political costs and marginal political benefits, which often have little or nothing to do with marginal social costs or benefits.

As an example of how politics guide government's decisions, consider the B-2 (Stealth) bomber, which was kept in production long after most independent observers believed it would serve no useful purpose. Why? Because the Pentagon and defense firms that wanted the bomber built understood how the system operated and saw to it that its components were built in 48 different states. Members of Congress from these states were reluctant to cancel a defense contract that provided jobs for so many of their constituents. Consideration of politics, not cost-effectiveness, almost certainly guided the government's choice.

Finally, let's now consider the argument that Paul sneaked into his presentation in the box on externalities and public goods. That's the argument about the overuse of common resources. I suggest that overfishing is not an example of market failure. It's an example of what happens when no market exists.

Paul's argument was that the lake would be overfished because of individuals' failure to take into account the full social cost of catching fish. I contend that the overfishing occurred because no one owns the lake. If someone owned the lake, that person would take into account the fact that when someone caught a fish, the catch available to others was reduced. To prevent overfishing the owner would charge people for the right to fish and would maximize his or her wealth by seeing to it that enough fish were left in the lake to reproduce for next year's fishing.

Or, alternatively, consider air pollution: If the air were owned by private individuals, those individuals would charge others for the right to pollute it and, in doing so, would decrease the amount of pollution.

Even though the air isn't privately owned, people will negotiate ways to reduce or eliminate the negative externalities of air pollution. For example, if Paul's neighbors are so worried about air pollution from the mill he proposes to build on his land, they can get together and buy his property or, at least, pay him not to build the mill. Any other solution is simply a usurping of Paul's property rights.

Q–7: Why does Milton oppose the argument that military bases have positive externalities in terms of jobs?

Overuse of a resource is the result of the lack of private ownership and markets, not the failure of markets.

4. Preventing Unfairness Creates More Unfairness

Milton: *Paul was right in saving the unfairness argument for the end because it's the argument that we market advocates find most difficult to defend against. But it too suffers from a serious flaw. It suggests that some standard of fairness other than the market standard exists by which to judge events.*

I contend that the market is a standard of fairness to which many people, including me, subscribe: People who are more productive and who work harder deserve more material rewards than people who don't work hard. By rewarding productivity and hard work, the market stimulates economic activity and provides benefits for everyone.

Let's consider Paul's example about the employer when he talked about "Preventing unfairness." Why is the employer the employer? Paul didn't answer that. He made it seem as if it was simply happenstance. But more often than not, the employer is the employer because he or she worked harder or was more productive than others. If society limits the gains of hard work and the freedom of people who work hard to do

Contemporary Economic Policy is one of the most policy-oriented of the economic journals.

ADDED DIMENSION   THE LIGHTHOUSE AND THE BEES

The debate about externalities, public goods, and differences between marginal social costs and benefits has long been conducted in economics. The examples that have been used are subject to much criticism.

For instance, an early textbook example of a public good that had to be supplied by government rather than privately was the lighthouse. If one person builds a lighthouse so coastal ships can avoid the rocks, the benefit will be there for others to enjoy. So, the textbook argument went, private business wouldn't provide lighthouses because lighthouses were a public good. However, upon searching the real world, people discovered that many private lighthouses existed and that firms had found ways to finance the lighthouses privately. The lighthouse example was dropped from the textbooks.

Another frequent textbook example of marginal social costs differing from marginal private costs has been the case of bees. The textbooks argued: Bees pollinate blossoms and therefore provide a positive externality. Because of this positive externality, there will be too few bees because the benefits they provide—pollination—are external to the beekeeper's decisions—to keep them for their honey.

But when researchers looked into beekeeping, they found a market in bee services. Orchard owners were renting bees from beekeepers in order to pollinate the flowers on their trees. The externality was being paid for and therefore wasn't an externality. The bee example was dropped from the textbooks.

Some opponents of government intervention to correct for externalities use these examples to argue that government shouldn't intervene on the basis of externalities, but that argument is too strong. The existence of private markets doesn't mean that the private market supplies enough of the good or service to make the marginal social cost equal the marginal social benefit. Nor does it mean that there aren't other, better examples in which there are no markets.

Two lessons should be drawn from these two examples:
1. One should always carefully consider the arguments that textbook writers make and compare those arguments to reality.
2. One should recognize that private sources of solutions to social problems may exist, and that before one advocates having government intervene to correct for an externality, one should carefully consider the private alternatives.

Q–8: Why does Milton oppose government intervention to prevent unfairness?

4 Four arguments against government intervention are:
1. Preventing private restraints on trade creates even more restraints.
2. Correcting informational and rationality problems creates even more problems.
3. Correcting for externalities creates other problems.
4. Preventing unfairness creates more unfairness.

Paul's Rebuttals

what they want, then society will discourage hard work. When hard work by the productive people is discouraged, society is made worse off.

That's bad, but the negative incentives created by government intervention are even worse. As soon as people see that they can get more rewards from the government than from their own hard work, productivity slows and private economic activity is discouraged. Keeping arguments about fairness out of the government decision-making process helps everyone, the poor as well as the rich. It creates more for everyone as the wealth spills over from the hard-working rich to the poor. The only workable standard of fairness is the market standard: Them that works gets; them that don't work go without—unless them that works want to help them that don't.

Author: *Paul, before you respond, I'd like to summarize Milton's four arguments against government intervention.*

Summary: Four Arguments against Government Intervention

1. Preventing private restraints on trade creates even more restraints.
2. Correcting informational and rationality problems creates even more problems.
3. Correcting for externalities creates other problems.
4. Preventing unfairness creates more unfairness.

Author: *Now, Paul, you can respond, but please be brief.*

Paul: *I must admit that there's a certain truth to each of Milton's counterarguments. But, in my view, government isn't nearly so controlled by special interests or so inefficient as Milton would have us believe. For every case of government ineffectiveness, I can point to a case of effective government intervention.*

As for property rights eliminating the need for government: Who is to establish those rights, if not government? Without government, productive activity would be impossible; people would spend all their time fighting over property rights. Governments use markets to avoid continually making judgments of who should get what. Once the initial property rights are established, the market decides. That method saves enormous political fighting and is good and necessary. But if the initial allocation of property rights leads to results that aren't to society's liking, then it's society's right to

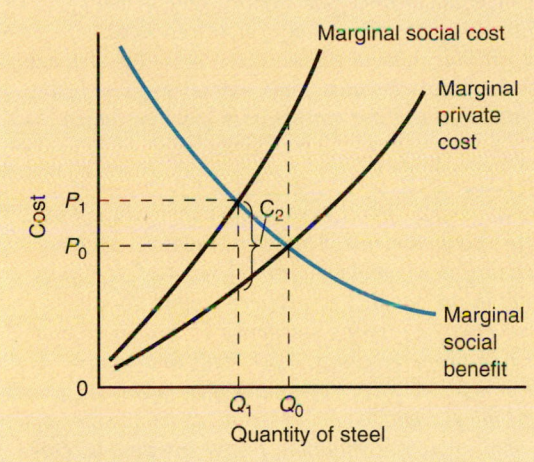

EXHIBIT 2   Regulation through Taxation

If the government sets a tax sufficient to take into account a negative externality, individuals will respond by reducing the quantity of the pollution-causing activity supplied to a level that individuals would have supplied had they included the negative externality in their decision.

modify those property rights. *Property rights aren't inalienable rights; they're conferred rights.*

What I'm saying is that the market is not above the government. Rather the government is above the market, and a democratic government will see to it that the market's allocation of property rights is within the range of fairness that society finds acceptable. If Milton doesn't agree with society's right to change property rights, then he doesn't agree with democracy. Let me give you an example of the need for government to make decisions about fairness.

Milton says, "Private individuals should own the lakes and the air." But who decides which individuals will be the owners, and who prevents unproductive fights over the allocation of property rights? If the government didn't act to prevent private individuals from usurping common resources, the social structure would break down.

Next let me deal with the argument that government intervention is a chain saw instead of the scalpel that we need. In many cases of past regulation I think Milton is right, but he's right only because economists haven't played a significant role in helping to design the government's intervention.

*All too often the type of government intervention has been administrative or regulatory. One benefit of economics is that it suggests alternatives to regulation. For example, consider pollution. If, rather than regulating the permissible amount of pollution administratively, government taxes pollution-creating activities and subsidizing the reduction of pollution—the result can be more precise and appropriate—the scalpel effect. Say that in Exhibit 2 the government determines that the additional marginal social cost of producing steel equals C_2. If government sets a firm's pollution tax on steel production at $t = C_2$, the firm will reduce its output to Q_1 on its own. It's a tribute to economists' influence that such taxes, called **effluent fees,** are now widely used in helping deal with pollution.*

An alternative way in which the government can regulate efficiently is to foster the creation of markets. As I stated, markets don't simply come into existence; they require the definition, establishment, and enforcement of property rights.

Pollution provides an example here. In dealing with pollution, governments in certain areas are establishing "pollution rights." All existing firms are required to reduce their pollution by 10 percent. New firms can pollute if they pay existing firms to reduce pollution further, by an amount that will offset the new pollution introduced by the new firms. If an existing firm is willing to reduce its pollution by 20 percent, it can sell some of its entitlements to pollute to new firms and to other existing firms which, with these permits, would be allowed to reduce pollution by less than the required 10 percent. By creating these rights and establishing a market in them, total pollution can be reduced by 10 percent, while each individual firm is still free to decide how much it will reduce pollution. Firms that have a low marginal cost of reducing pollution will reduce more than 10 percent so they can sell the right to pollute to other firms whose cost of reducing pollution is higher.

Such novel plans have problems that must be worked out before they can be widely used, but they demonstrate that government regulation can be made compatible with the market.

Effluent fees   Charges imposed by government on pollution.

Finally, let me comment on the "them that works gets" philosophy. It isn't so simple. There's nothing necessarily fair about the allocation of abilities. What's fair about Michael Jordan being endowed with his natural abilities and someone else being born a klutz? Should we let people starve simply because their market wage is below the subsistence wage? Society will continue to use the market only if it can adjust the distributional results of the market.

Milton's Rebuttals

Q–9: Do Milton's and Paul's differences result primarily from theoretical differences or from debatable judgments?

Milton: *Paul concedes many of my points and differs from me primarily in judgments. But he gives few justifications for his judgments. Those justifications aren't better than the ones I initially gave, so they don't require a direct rebuttal. It's quite clear that I have a much stronger belief in the sanctity of property rights than does Paul. Because of this belief, I find it necessary to limit government by historical and constitutional constraints, such as existing property rights. I ask Paul to compare the experience of Western market economies with socialist economies if he wants an example of the power of property rights and the market.*

As for interventionist economists improving the situation, I have my doubts. Often they have simply introduced new ways for government to intervene—ways that look as if they are compatible with markets, but actually require enormous government involvement.

The Difficult Decisions

At this point our debate must stop. General arguments are fine, but judging from historical experience, the debate is unending. Both sides of this debate about whether government should intervene in the market have valid points. No one general argument obviously wins out over the others. Decisions about government intervention will need to be made on a case-by-case basis, using a cost/benefit framework. In the remainder of this chapter, we look at two cases to give you an idea of the clash of these ideas in the real world.

THE DRUG LEGALIZATION DEBATE

Let's start by considering two letters that appeared in *The Wall Street Journal* in 1989. In the first, Milton Friedman (a well-known free market economist) advocates the legalization of marijuana. The second is a response by William Bennett, who headed the federal government's office of National Drug Control Policy. After exploring these two views, we'll consider a policy part way between the two: Legalize drugs, but tax them so heavily that their price doesn't fall.

AN OPEN LETTER TO BILL BENNETT

Dear Bill:

In Oliver Cromwell's eloquent words, "I beseech you, in the bowels of Christ, think it possible you may be mistaken" about the course you and President Bush urge us to adopt to fight drugs. The path you propose of more police, more jails, use of the military in foreign countries, harsh penalties for drug users, and a whole panoply of repressive measures can only make a bad situation worse. The drug war cannot be won by those tactics without undermining the human liberty and individual freedom that you and I cherish.

You are not mistaken in believing that drugs are a scourge that is devas-tating our society. You are not mistaken in believing that drugs are tearing asunder our social fabric, ruining the lives of many young people, and imposing heavy costs on some of the most disadvantaged among us. You are not mistaken in believing that the majority of the public share your concerns. In short, you are not mistaken in the end you seek to achieve.

Your mistake is failing to recognize that the very measures you favor are a major source of the evils you deplore. Of course the problem is demand, but it is not only demand, it is demand that must operate through repressed and illegal channels. Illegality creates obscene profits that finance the murderous tactics of the drug lords; illegality leads to the corruption of law enforcement officials; illegality monopolizes the efforts of honest law forces so that they are starved for resources to fight the simpler crimes of robbery, theft and assault.

Drugs are a tragedy for addicts. But criminalizing their use converts that tragedy into a disaster for society, for users and non-users alike. Our experience with the prohibition of drugs is a replay of our experience with the prohibition of alcoholic beverages.

In 1972 I wrote a column on "Prohibition and Drugs." The major problem then was heroin from Marseilles; today, it is cocaine from Latin America. Today, also, the problem is far more serious than it was 17 years ago: more addicts, more innocent victims; more drug pushers, more law enforcement officials; more money spent to enforce prohibition, more money spent to circumvent prohibition.

Had drugs been decriminalized 17 years ago, "crack" would never have been invented (it was invented because the high cost of illegal drugs made it profitable to provide a cheaper version) and there would today be far fewer addicts. The lives of thousands, perhaps hundreds of thousands of innocent victims would have been saved, and not only in the U.S. The ghettos of our major cities would not be drug-and-crime–infested no-man's lands. Fewer people would be in jails, and fewer jails would have been built.

Colombia, Bolivia, and Peru would not be suffering from narco-terror, and we would not be distorting our foreign policy because of narco-terror. Hell would not, in the words with which Billy Sunday welcomed Prohibition, "be forever for rent," but it would be a lot emptier.

Decriminalizing drugs is even more urgent now than in 1972, but we must recognize that the harm done in the interim cannot be wiped out, certainly not immediately. Postponing decriminalization will only make matters worse, and make the problem appear even more intractable.

Alcohol and tobacco cause many more deaths in users than do drugs. Decriminalization would not prevent us from treating drugs as we now treat alcohol and tobacco: prohibiting sales of drugs to minors, outlawing the advertising of drugs and similar measures. Such measures could be enforced, while outright prohibition cannot be. Moreover, if even a small fraction of the money we now spend on trying to enforce drug prohibition were devoted to treatment and rehabilitation, in an atmosphere of compassion not punishment, the reduction in drug usage and in the harm done to the users could be dramatic.

This plea comes from the bottom of my heart. Every friend of freedom, and I know you are one, must be as revolted as I am by the prospect of turning the United States into an armed camp, by the vision of jails filled with casual drug users and of an army of enforcers empowered to invade the liberty of citizens on slight evidence. A country in which shooting down unidentified planes "on suspicion" can be seriously considered as a drug-war tactic is not the kind of United States that either you or I want to hand on to future generations.

Milton Friedman
Senior Research Fellow
Hoover Institution
Stanford University

A RESPONSE TO MILTON FRIEDMAN

Dear Milton:

There was little, if anything, new in your open letter to me calling for the legalization of drugs. As your earlier 1972 article made clear, the legalization argument is an old and familiar one, which has recently been revived by a small number of journalists and academics who insist that the only solution to the drug problem is no solution at all. What surprises me is that you would continue to advocate so unrealistic a proposal without pausing to consider seriously its consequences.

If the argument for drug legalization has one virtue it is its sheer simplicity. Eliminate laws against drugs, and street crime will disappear. Take the profit out of the black market through decriminalization and regulation, and poor neighborhoods will no longer be victimized by drug dealers. Cut back on drug enforcement, and use the money to wage a public health campaign against drugs, as we do with tobacco and alcohol.

Counting Costs

The basic premise of all these propositions is that using our nation's laws to fight drugs is too costly. To be sure, our attempts to reduce drug use do carry with them enormous costs. But the question that must be asked—and which is totally ignored by the legalization advocates—is, what are the costs of *not* enforcing laws against drugs?

In my judgment, and in the judgment of virtually every serious scholar in this field, the potential costs of legalizing drugs would be so large as to make it a public policy disaster.

Of course, no one, including you, can say with certainty what would happen in the U.S. if drugs were suddenly to become a readily purchased product. We do know, however, that wherever drugs have been cheaper and more easily obtained, drug use—and, addiction—has skyrocketed. In opium and cocaine producing countries, addiction is rampant among the peasants involved in drug production.

Professor James Q. Wilson tells us that during the years in which heroin could be legally prescribed by doctors in Britain, the number of addicts increased forty-fold. And, after the repeal of Prohibition—an analogy favored but misunderstood by legalization advocates—consumption of alcohol soared by 350%.

Could we afford such dramatic increases in drug use? I doubt it. Already the toll of drug use on American society—measured in lost productivity, in rising health insurance costs, in hospitals flooded with drug overdose emergencies, in drug caused accidents, and in premature death—is surely more than we would like to bear.

You seem to believe that by spending just a little more money on treatment and rehabilitation, the costs of increased addiction can be avoided. That hope betrays a basic misunderstanding of the problems facing drug treatment. Most addicts don't suddenly decide to get help. They remain addicts either because treatment isn't available or because they don't seek it out. The National Drug Control Strategy announced by President Bush on Sept. 5 goes a long way in making sure that more treatment slots are available. But the simple fact remains that many drug users won't enter treatment until they are forced to—often by the very criminal justice system you think is the source of the problem.

As for the connection between drugs and crime, your unswerving commitment to a legalization solution prevents you from appreciating the complexity of the drug market. Contrary to your claim, most addicts do not turn to crime to support their habit. Research shows that many of them were involved in criminal activity before they turned to drugs. Many former addicts who have received treatment continue to commit crimes during their recovery. And even if drugs were legal, what evidence do you have that the habitual drug user wouldn't continue to rob and steal to get money for clothes, food or shelter? Drug addicts always want more drugs than they can afford, and no legalization scheme has yet come up with a way of satisfying that appetite.

The National Drug Control Strategy emphasizes the importance of reclaiming the streets and neighborhoods where drugs have wrought havoc because, I admit, the price of having drug laws is having criminals who will try to subvert them. Your proposal might conceivably reduce the amount of gang- and dealer-related crimes but it is fanciful to suggest that it would make crime vanish. Unless you are willing to distribute drugs freely and widely, there will always be a black market to undercut the regulated one. And as for the potential addicts, for the school children and for the pregnant mothers, all of whom would find drugs more accessible and legally condoned, your proposal would offer nothing at all.

So I advocate a larger criminal justice system to take drug users off the streets and deter new users from becoming more deeply involved in so hazardous an activity. You suggest that such policies would turn the country "into an armed camp." Try telling that to the public housing tenants who enthusiastically support plans to enhance security in their buildings, or to the residents who applaud police when a local crack house is razed. They recognize that drug use is a threat to the individual liberty and domestic tranquility guaranteed by the Constitution.

I remain an ardent defender of our nation's laws against illegal drug use and our attempts to enforce them because I believe drug use is wrong. A true friend of freedom understands that government has a responsibility to craft and uphold laws that help educate citizens about right and wrong. That, at any rate, was the Founders' view of our system of government.

Liberal Ridicule

Today this view is much ridiculed by liberal elites and entirely neglected by you. So while I cannot doubt the sincerity of your opinion on drug legalization, I find it difficult to respect. The moral cost of legalizing drugs is great, but it is a cost that apparently lies outside the narrow scope of libertarian policy prescriptions.

I do not have a simple solution to the drug problem. I doubt that one exists. But I am committed to fighting the problem on several fronts through imaginative policies and hard work over a long period of time. As in the past, some of these efforts will work and some won't. Your response, however, is to surrender and see what happens. To my mind that is irresponsible and reckless public policy. At a time when national intolerance for drug use is rapidly increasing, the legalization argument is a political anachronism. Its recent resurgence is, I trust, only a temporary distraction from the genuine debate on national drug policy.

William J. Bennett
Director
Office of National Drug
Control Policy

A Drug Policy Alternative

The debate laid out in the Friedman and Bennett letters leaves out a third possibility that some economists support: the legalize-but-tax alternative, a position in between Bennett's and Friedman's. It accepts a government role in controlling the use of drugs, but it uses market incentives to achieve the desired end.

5 Sin taxes are designed to discourage activities society believes are harmful to individuals. Milton Friedman would likely oppose sin taxes because they involve the government trying to direct individuals' behavior.

According to this perspective, government should legalize drug consumption but impose enormously high taxes on the sale of drugs. This possibility is sometimes called a **sin tax** approach because it discourages activities society believes are harmful (sinful) for individuals. Thus, the government is making a value judgment about what's good for individuals, but it's using market incentives rather than regulation to achieve its end. How that end could be achieved is shown in Exhibit 3.

When legalized, drugs have a price of P_e and a quantity of Q_e. A law forbidding the sale of drugs should, in principle, reduce the supply to zero. In reality, the law would only decrease the supply somewhat, depending on the degree of enforcement of the law and people's adherence to it.

Assuming that the law prohibiting drug trafficking decreases supply from S_0 to S_1, the equilibrium black market price of drugs is P_b and the black market quantity of

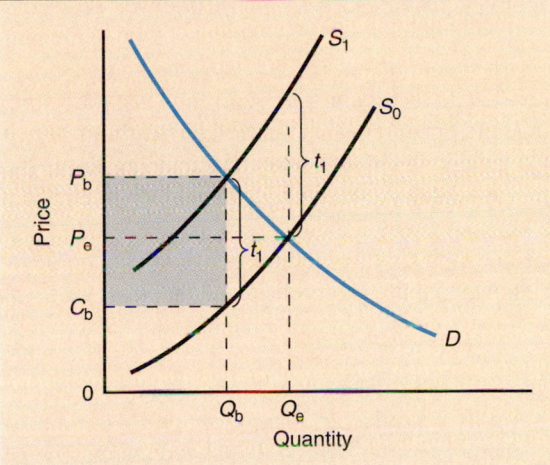

EXHIBIT 3   The Sin Tax Alternative

If drug consumption is legalized, the government can discourage drug use by imposing high taxes on the sale of drugs. If the use of the drugs is legal and no intervention takes place, along supply S_0 the price is P_e and the quantity consumed is Q_e. By instituting a high tax rate of t_1, the government can cause the supply curve to shift up from S_0 to S_1, raising the price from P_e to P_b and decreasing the quantity consumed from Q_e to Q_b. The government will receive the shaded area in taxes.

drugs sold is Q_b. Notice the large difference between the free market cost of producing Q_b, which is C_b, and the black market price, P_b. The difference (the shaded rectangle) is a cost that reflects the aversion to breaking the law, either because it represents a chance of being caught and punished or because it represents the cost to individuals who find it morally wrong to violate the law.

Those suppliers who aren't caught make enormous profits. From discussions I've had with individuals exposed to the drug trade, I understand that the pay for low-level suppliers is $50 to $100 an hour, and for high-level suppliers it's in the $1,000 to $10,000 an hour range. The profit to suppliers (the lightly shaded area in Exhibit 3) is large, as you can see. How large depends on the elasticity of the supply and demand curves, how vigorously the law is enforced, and how strongly people feel about breaking the law. The cost of producing the drugs compared to the selling price is likely to be minimal. Most of a black market drug's price is a payment for the seller's risk of getting caught.

Now let's say that instead of prohibiting drug trafficking, the government institutes an extremely high tax of t_1 on drug sales. That tax shifts the after-tax supply curve from S_0 to S_1, just as the law did, so that the price that the consumer pays to receive quantity Q_b is still P_b. Drug users are now presented with a choice: to buy illegally from a black market dealer and risk arrest, or to buy legally from a government-authorized seller at the same price but with no risk of arrest. Faced with that option, most buyers would buy from government-authorized sellers. In response, dealers would be forced to lower prices and some would be squeezed out of the market. As that happened, the government would get more of the revenue that had been going to the dealers.

The extra revenue could be substantial—perhaps as much as $50 or $60 billion if most black market sales at lower prices could be prevented. The government could greatly reduce black market sales if it used, say, one-fifth of the tax proceeds to increase the enforcement effort. Illegal dealers would be squeezed on both sides. Their costs would rise and their revenues would fall since they'd have to charge 10 or 20 percent less than the legal price to get people to buy their illegal drugs rather than the legal drugs. The remaining tax revenue could be used for drug treatment programs and for educating people about the evils of drugs. How much revenue the government would receive and how effective the tax would be in stopping drug use depends on the elasticities of supply and demand. A good exercise for you is to explain, assuming it could choose, whether the government should prefer elastic or inelastic supply and demand curves.

Many more arguments could be made for and against all three of these positions regarding government intervention in the drug trade. But the discussion should be enough to start you thinking about the myriad options available for dealing with

Summary

society's problems and about how economics provides a way to consider the costs and benefits of the various options.

THE LICENSURE DEBATE

As the drug trade example demonstrates, all government intervention is not the same. The government can respond to any specific problem or situation in any number of ways, some of which are preferable to others. As a result of political pressure, the important policy debates often concern not *whether* government should intervene, but *how*.

In the drug example we looked at taxation as the method of intervention. Now let's consider another example of government intervention—the licensing of doctors—and consider an alternative.[1]

Licensing Doctors

In the early 1800s, medical licenses were not required by law in the United States, so anyone who wanted to could set up shop as a physician. The most popular type of medical treatment at the time was heroic therapy, which consisted primarily of bloodletting, blistering, and the administration of massive doses of mineral poisons, such as mercury.[2] The practitioners of two alternative types of medicine—homeopathy (which focused on natural healing) and eclecticism (which combined a variety of approaches) together laid the foundation of modern medicine. These practitioners challenged the status quo by arguing that heroic therapy was not helping people. They pressured Congress to pass licensure laws requiring that all doctors earn a license to practice medicine by receiving training in homeopathy and eclecticism. Ever since, it has been illegal to practice medicine without a license.

To get that license, one must go through a pre-med program in college, four years of medical school, and a residency in a hospital for anywhere from one to seven years, as well as pass a series of National Medical Board examinations.

6A Licensing tends to prevent incompetents from practicing, to provide information to consumers, and to professionalize an activity.

Licensing of doctors is justified by the informational and rationality problems discussed before. Since individuals often don't have an accurate way of deciding whether a doctor is good, government intervention is necessary. The informational problem is solved because licensing requires that all doctors have at least a minimum competency. People have the *information* that a doctor must be competent because they see the license framed and hanging on the doctor's office wall.

Sometimes even when people have the information available, they don't use it *rationally*. Without licensing, businesses would be established to sell a whole set of schemes, such as using laetrile to fight cancer or using vitamin C to fight everything. According to scientific research, laetrile does not cure cancer and vitamin C does not cure everything.

A small number of economists, of whom Milton Friedman is the best known, have proposed that licensure laws be eliminated, leaving the medical field unlicensed. While such a proposal is supported by only a few economists, it's instructive to consider their proposal: Let anyone practice medicine who wishes to.

6B Licensing tends to restrict entry, restrict consumer choice, and cost money.

They argue that licensure was instituted as much, or more, to restrict supply as it was to help the consumer. Specifically, critics of medical licensure raise these questions:

Why, if licensed medical training is so great, do we even need formal restrictions to keep other types of medicine from being practiced?

Whom do these restrictions benefit: the general public or the doctors who practice mainstream medicine?

What have the long-run effects of licensure been?

---

[1] The arguments presented here about licensing doctors also apply to dentists, lawyers, college professors, cosmetologists (in some states, cosmetologists must be licensed), and other professional groups.

[2] Bloodletting involved extracting blood from the body, on the theory that the person's problem stemmed from "too much blood." Blistering involved causing blisters to form on the body, on the theory that when they burst, they would expel the poisonous matter that was making the person ill.

Even the strongest critics of licensure agree that, in the case of doctors, the informational argument for government intervention is strong. But the question is whether licensure is the right form of government intervention. Why doesn't the government simply provide the public with information about which treatments work and which don't? That would give the freest rein to **consumer sovereignty** (the right of the individual to make choices about what is consumed and produced). As for the rationality argument, critics of licensure simply reject it out of hand. They ask: Who is the government to decide for people what is, or isn't, good for them? If people have the necessary information but still choose to treat cancer with laetrile or treat influenza with massive doses of vitamin C, why should the government tell them they can't?

If the informational alternative is preferable to licensure, why didn't the government choose it? Friedman argues that government didn't follow that path because the licensing was done as much for the doctors as for the general public. Licensure has led to a monopoly position for doctors. They can restrict supply and increase price and thereby significantly increase their incomes. Friedman further argues that the group most hurt by the decision to choose the licensure alternative is the poor, who often can't afford the higher fees licensed doctors charge.

Let's now take a closer look at the informational alternative.

The informational alternative is to allow anyone to practice medicine, but to have the government certify doctors' backgrounds and qualifications. The government would require that doctors' backgrounds be made public knowledge. Each doctor would have to post the following information prominently in his or her office:

The Informational Alternative to Licensure

1. Grades in college.
2. Grades in medical school.
3. Success rate for various procedures.
4. References.
5. Medical philosophy.
6. Charges and fees.

According to supporters of the informational alternative, these data would allow individuals to make informed decisions about their medical care. Like all informed decisions, they would be complicated. For instance, doctors who take only patients with minor problems can show high "success rates," while doctors who are actually more skilled but who take on problem patients may have to provide more extensive information so people can see why their success rates shouldn't be compared to those of the doctors who take just easy patients. But despite the problems, supporters of the informational alternative argue that it's better than the current situation.

Current licensure laws don't provide any of this information to the public. All a patient knows is that a doctor has managed to get through medical school and has passed the medical board exams (which are, after all, only sets of multiple-choice questions). The doctor may have done all this 30 years ago, possibly by the skin of his or her teeth, but, once licensed, a doctor is a doctor for life. (A well-known doctor joke is the following: What do you call the person with the lowest passing grade point average in medical school? Answer: Doctor.) Thus, the informational alternative would provide much more useful data to the public than the current licensing procedure.

What do you call the person with the lowest passing grade point average in medical school? Answer: Doctor.

Let's now consider two examples of how the informational alternative would work.

Two Examples of How the Informational Alternative Would Work   Say you're wondering whether that new mole on your arm is cancerous. What do you do? Under our current system, you ask your private physician, or you go to your local hospital and ask. The physician, most likely, won't know. He or she had two or three lectures on skin cancer in medical school and may have seen some in practice, but probably isn't a specialist in cancer. So all you get is a referral to a specialist (cost: $35).

Why not go to the specialist in the first place? By agreement among doctors, specialists usually will see only those patients who have been referred to them by a general physician.[3] Now let's say that you go to the specialist, who looks at the mole and recognizes immediately that it's just a mole (cost: $50). But she orders a biopsy, just to be sure (cost: $20). She's right and you're relieved, but you're also $105 poorer. To find out from the specialist whether the mole was cancerous cost you $105 and about four hours of your time. Many people without insurance won't pay the cost. They'll just hope the mole isn't cancerous.

Consider this hypothetical informational alternative: You go to a person who hasn't been to medical school, but who's been through a special one-year training program in diagnosing malignant carcinomas (skin cancer). The success rate of detection by such persons is 99.8 percent; the fee is $10 if no biopsy is needed, $30 if one is. The process is quick, easy, and inexpensive.

Q–10:   Who would benefit and who would lose if an informational alternative to licensing doctors were introduced?

As a second example, consider surgery. This should be the strongest case for licensure. Would you want an untrained butcher to operate on you? Of course not. But opponents of licensure point out that it's not at all clear how effectively licensure prevents butchery. Ask a doctor, ''Would you send your child to any board-certified surgeon picked at random?'' The honest answer you'd get is ''No way. Some of them are butchers.'' How do they know that? Being around hospitals, they have access to information about various surgeons' success and failure rates; they've seen them operate and know whether or not they have manual dexterity.

Advocates of the informational alternative suggest that you ask yourself, ''What skill would you want in a surgeon?'' A likely answer would be ''Manual dexterity. Her fingers should be magic fingers.'' Does the existing system of licensure ensure that everyone who becomes a surgeon has magic fingers? No. To become licensed as a surgeon requires a grueling seven-year residency after four years of medical school, but manual dexterity, as such, is never explicitly tested or checked!

The informational alternative wouldn't necessarily eliminate the seven-year surgical residency. If the public believed that a seven-year residency was necessary to create skilled surgeons, many potential surgeons would choose that route. But there would be other ways to become a surgeon. For example, in high school, tests could be given for manual dexterity. Individuals with superb hand/eye coordination could go to a one-year technical college to train to be ''heart technicians,'' who would work as part of a team doing heart surgery.

Clearly open-heart surgery is the extreme case, and most people will not be convinced that it can be performed by unlicensed medical personnel. But what about minor surgery? According to informational alternative advocates, many operations could be conducted more cheaply and better (since people with better manual dexterity would be doing the work) if restrictive licensing were ended. Or, if you don't accept the argument for human medical treatments, how about for veterinarians? For cosmetologists? For plumbers? Might the informational alternatives work in these professions?

Some Words of Caution about the Informational Alternative

If you were convinced that the informational alternative was preferable to medical licensure, beware. The preceding discussion of licensure and the informational alternative presented only the arguments in favor of that alternative. It highlights the benefits of the informational alternative and the problems with the licensure alternative.

I presented the alternatives in a one-sided way to stimulate your thinking, not to convince you that doctors are monopolists concerned only with their own incomes and that eliminating the medical monopoly will solve our country's health care woes. Reality is far more complicated than that. A complete presentation would have discussed problems of the informational alternative and how, if chosen, the alternative

---

[3] Sometimes the general physician and the specialist are in the same group practice, and they each contribute a percentage of their income to a common pool, which is later divided among the members of the pool. Thus, when the doctors are in a group practice, the referring doctor gets a percentage of the specialist's fee. In such cases it's not even clear that your doctor has an incentive to send you to the most competent specialist!

could be implemented. In the real world, systems for qualifying professionals have serious problems; arguments can be made against the informational and certification alternatives that would convince you that neither is the answer.

Ultimately, one needs an intimate knowledge of the actual practice and institutions to judge whether reforms would really make things better or worse. Therein lies the problem of reform. Just about the only individuals who have detailed knowledge are those who have a vested interest in the current system. So the information you're likely to get about potential reforms may well be biased toward only those reforms that will help the vested interest.

Ultimately, one needs an intimate knowledge of the actual practice and institutions and their alternatives to judge whether reforms would really make things better or worse.

In 1994 economists and politicians were involved in major debates about health care. The next two ''letters to the editor'' give you a sense of the debate and how it relates to the principles of economics learned in this book. The first of the letters, which appeared in *The Wall Street Journal* on January 14, 1994, was signed by 562 economists and the other letter, which appeared in response in *The Wall Street Journal* on April 13, 1994, was written by a Nobel-Prize winning economist. By now, you have had enough introduction to the analysis of debates, so I leave the discussion to you. (If you are at a loss to analyze this case, you might consider problem 3 in the Problems and Exercises at the end of the chapter.)

PRICE CONTROLS IN HEALTH CARE

January 13, 1994

Dear President Clinton:

Price controls produce shortages, black markets and reduced quality. This has been the universal experience in the 4,000 years that governments have tried to artificially hold prices down using regulations.

You insist that your health care plan avoids price controls. We respectfully disagree. Your plan sets the fees charged by doctors and hospitals, caps annual spending on health care, limits insurance premiums, and imposes price limitations on new and existing drugs.

In countries that have imposed these types of regulations, patients face delays of months and years for surgery, government bureaucrats decide treatment options instead of doctors or patients, and innovations in medical techniques and pharmaceuticals are dramatically reduced. Here in America, the threat of price controls on medicines has already decreased research and development at drug companies, which will lead to reduced discoveries and the loss of life in the future.

In the 1970s, government tried to regulate the price of a simple homogenous product, gasoline. The result was a social and economic disaster. People were forced to waste hours waiting in lines to purchase gasoline. Long waits for surgery and other medical care will have far more serious consequences.

Caps, fee schedules and other government regulations may appear to reduce medical spending, but such gains are illusory. We will instead end up with lower-quality medical care, reduced medical innovation, and expensive new bureaucracies to monitor compliance. These controls will hurt people, and they will damage the economy. We urge you to remove price controls, in any form, from your health care plan.

Armen A. Alchian UCLA
Wayne Allen Delta State University
William R. Allen UCLA
Gary M. Anderson California State University at Northridge
Martin Anderson Hoover Institution, Stanford University
John Baden University of Washington
Samuel H. Baker College of William & Mary (and 552 others)
R. Robert Batemarco Manhattan College
Arleigh Bell Loyola College in Maryland

Dear *Wall Street Journal*:

Last November I received a letter from the Cato Institute inviting me to sign a statement that began with the following words: ''Price controls produce shortages, black markets and reduced quality. This has been the universal experience in the four thousand years that governments have tried to artificially hold prices down using regulations.'' It did not take me long to conclude that the statement was an economically careless one, and that a well-trained economist would not want to sign so unqualified a statement. I was, therefore, enormously surprised when, shortly thereafter, on Jan. 14, you published that statement as an open letter to President Clinton on health care reform, together with the signature of 562 economists, quite a few of them with a solid international reputation.

Nonetheless, the statement is an economically invalid one because it was not preceded, as it should have been, by some such qualification as "when markets are ideally competitive." By this we mean in particular that participants in the market do not have appreciable economic power in the sense that they can affect the price through their controls over the quantity they are prepared to sell. But once we allow for some such qualification, the relevance of the statement for the health industry becomes very questionable, for hardly anyone would argue that all participants in that market work under perfect competition conditions.

Yet without such a qualification the statement is seriously misleading; for as every economist knows or should know, in the presence of market power a price ceiling, suitably chosen, may have the effect of lowering the price below what it would be in a laissez faire market while at the same time increasing output enough to satisfy the larger demand at the lower price (thus creating no shortage). The results could well be an improvement of the general welfare, except of course that of the producers who would have to give up the extra profits they were able to reap by their artificial restriction of output. Educated economists know the classic economic text where this argument is fully developed: Abba P. Lerner's 1943 "The Economics of Control" (MacMillan, 1994), with his well-argued notion of "counter-speculation," which should be familiar to most economists.

The empirical evidence for such cogent counterexample is quite abundant. The most obvious one is provided by past experience with public utilities (electricity, gas, telephone) whose prices have typically been controlled by utility commissions, i.e. subjected to a ceiling because of the monopoly power they enjoy as the sole providers of services within their franchise. Can anyone claim that these ceilings have "universally" resulted in "shortages and black markets?" Or doubt that their elimination would result in higher prices and reduced output in many instances?

The moral of the story is, of course, not that my colleagues were wrong in opposing the Clinton program: in a free society everyone has the right and responsibility to criticize any policy he opposes. The problem is that those who signed gave the wrong impression that they were opposing the plan as professional scientific economists, relying on basic economic principle as stated in their opening paragraph.

I hope instead that this episode may serve as a lesson to economists, including me, as well as other professionals, against the temptation of cloaking our personal preferences under the mantle of science, without making certain that we are in fact relying on basic scientific principles and not on idiosyncratic value judgments.

Franco Modigliani
Institute Professor Emeritus
Alfred P. Sloan School of Management
Massachusetts Institute of Technology
Cambridge, Mass.
(Prof. Modigliani was awarded the Nobel Prize in Economics in 1985.)

CONCLUSION

As a textbook writer, I wish I could say that some conclusions can be drawn about whether the government should, or should not, enter into the economy. I certainly have views about particular instances (in case you haven't guessed, I'm a highly opinionated individual), but to lay out arguments and information that would convince a reasonable person to agree with me would take an entire book for each area in which government might intervene.

What I can do in this textbook is to stimulate your interest in discovering for yourself the information and the subtleties of the debates for and against government intervention. Just about every time you read, hear, or are asked the question "Should the government intervene in a market?" the answer is "It depends." If your first impulse is to give any answer other than that one, you may have trouble maintaining the appropriate objectivity when you start considering the costs and benefits of government intervention.

7 Should the government intervene in the market? It depends.

CHAPTER SUMMARY

- A laissez-faire policy is not anarchy.

- Possible reasons for government intervention include preventing private restraints on trade, informational and rationality problems, externalities, and unfairness.

- An externality is the result of a market transaction that is not taken into account by the transactors.

- Laissez-faire advocates argue that government intervention usually makes the situation worse, not better.

- Making something illegal creates the possibility of a

black market with large returns to breaking the law.

- Taxing an illegal activity is an alternative way of discouraging it.

- Licensure laws are often presented as helping the public, but in fact are often designed to help a particular group.

- In answer to a question "Should the government intervene?" an objective initial response is almost always "It depends."

KEY TERMS

consumer sovereignty   *(737)*
effluent fees   *(731)*

externalities   *(725)*
government   *(723)*

laissez-faire   *(723)*
sin tax   *(734)*

QUESTIONS FOR THOUGHT AND REVIEW

The number after each question represents the estimated degree of critical thinking required. (1 = almost none; 10 = deep thought.)

1. State four reasons for a potentially beneficial role of government intervention.   *(1)*

2. Would a laissez-faire advocate support or oppose anti-trust laws? Why or why not?   *(9)*

3. Should the Food and Drug Administration's role in restricting which drugs may be marketed be eliminated? Why or why not?   *(8)*

4. Pollution is often considered an externality. Should the government pass laws that prevent pollution? Why or why not?   *(8)*

5. What would be the sin tax method of controlling pollution?   *(4)*

6. Most redistribution in the United States is from one middle-class group to another middle-class group. What does that suggest about the laissez-faire/government intervention fight?   *(5)*

7. Why would Milton Friedman likely oppose the legalize-and-heavily-tax solution to the addictive drug problem?   *(5)*

8. Why would William Bennett likely oppose the legalize-and-heavily-tax solution to the addictive drug problem?   *(5)*

9. Financial analysts are currently unlicensed. Should they be licensed? Why or why not?   *(6)*

10. An advanced degree is required in order to teach at most colleges. In what sense is this a form of restricting entry through licensure?   *(5)*

PROBLEMS AND EXERCISES

1. The marginal cost, marginal social cost, and demand for a firm are given in the accompanying diagram. The social cost is higher than the private cost due to pollution emitted by the plant.

   a. What is the efficient level of output?
   b. Given the information in the accompanying diagram, if the government wanted to set a fee to force the firm to decrease emissions, what fee would you recommend?

2. Congratulations! You've been made finance minister of Happyland. The president is unhappy that so many of her subjects are taking illegal drugs. You recommend legalizing such drugs and then imposing a tax on them.

   a. Demonstrate graphically the supply/demand equilibrium for the use of illegal drugs before your program is instituted.

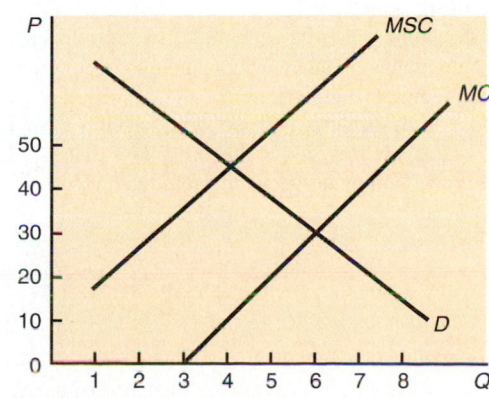

b. What should the minimum amount of tax be if the president wants to keep drug use no higher than its previous level?

c. Show graphically the government's revenue.

d. Your drug program failed miserably for political reasons. The president fires you but secretly comes to you for advice. She has heard that a cartel is taking over the drug trade and wonders what she should do about it. What advice do you give her?

3. Demonstrate graphically the effects of price controls when
   a. There is a competitive market.
   b. There is a monopoly.
   c. Relate the results of a and b to the debate about price controls presented in the chapter.

4. Economics professors Thomas Hopkins and Arthur Gosnell of the Rochester Institute of Technology have estimated that in the year 2000, regulations will cost the United States $662 billion, and that in 1992, regulations cost each U.S. family $5,700 per year.
   a. Do their findings mean that the United States has too many regulations?
   b. How would an economist decide which regulations to keep and which to do away with?

5. In 1938 Congress created a "Board of Cosmetology" in Washington, D.C., to license beauticians. In 1992 this law was used by the Board to close down a hair-braiding salon operated by Mr. Uqdah, who specialized in cornrows and braids, even though little is taught in cosmetology schools about braiding and cornrows.
   a. What possible reasons can you give for the existence of this Board?
   b. What options might you propose to change the system?
   c. What will be the political difficulties of implementing those options?

6. In the 1990s a debate about dairy products has concerned the labeling of milk produced from cows who have been injected with the hormone BST that significantly increases their milk production. Since this is a synthetically produced copy of a milk hormone that the FDA has determined is indistinguishable from the hormone produced naturally by the cow, and has also determined that milk from cows treated with BST is indistinguishable from milk that comes from cows who have not been treated with BST, some people have argued that no labeling requirement is necessary. Others argue that the consumer has a right to know.
   a. Where do you think most dairy farmers stand on this labeling issue?
   b. If consumers have a right to know, should labels inform them of other drugs, such as antibiotics, normally given to cows?
   c. Do you think dairy farmers who support BST labeling also support the broader labeling law that would be needed if other drugs were included? Why?

7. The milk industry has a number of interesting aspects. Provide economic explanations for the following:
   a. Fluid milk is 87 percent water. It can be dried and reconstituted so that it is almost indistinguishable from fresh milk. What is a likely reason that such reconstituted milk is not produced?
   b. The United States has regional milk-marketing regulations whose goals are to make each of the regions self-sufficient in milk. What is a likely reason for this?
   c. A U.S. senator from a milk-producing state has been quoted as saying, "I am absolutely convinced . . . that simply bringing down dairy price supports is not a way to cut production." Is it likely that he is correct? What is a probable reason for his statement?

8. Subtle changes in the tax laws often mean enormous amounts of money to individuals and groups. Consider the case of whiskey, as did economists Jack High and Clayton Coppin. Whiskey is distilled grain. The distilling process produces poisonous impurities, called fusel oil, that must be removed before the whiskey is drinkable. One way to remove these impurities is by aging the whiskey in wooden barrels. Whiskey produced in this manner is "straight whiskey." The second method is distillation —removing the fusel oil through additional distilling. The latter method removes more impurities and is cheaper, but it results in a whiskey with little taste. However, taste can be added back through flavorings or blending with aged whiskey. Up until 1868 distilled or blended whiskey predominated, but in that year a law was passed that allowed straight-whiskey producers who stored their whiskey in government warehouses to defer their taxes on it until it was fully aged.
   a. What advantage would this law have for straight-whiskey producers?
   b. After the tax was paid the whiskey received a tax stamp, certifying that its producers had paid the tax and that their straight whiskey had been stored in a "bonded government warehouse." If you were a straight-whiskey producer, how might you try to use that tax stamp to your advantage in advertising?
   c. How might competing producers of distilled whiskey certify the quality of their product?

9. In the third case presented in the chapter (the debate on health care) The Wall Street Journal selected 106 signatories (out of 562) whose names to print. Three of these signatories have female names.
   a. Give four alternative hypotheses about the low number of women signing the petition.
   b. How would you go about testing your hypotheses?
   c. Does the percentage of women in your economics department exceed the percentage of women signing this petition?

ANSWERS TO MARGIN QUESTIONS

1. For economists to advocate a particular government policy, they must believe that the government will do good and implement the people's desires. If the government structure precludes that, almost all economists become supporters of government nonintervention, or laissez faire. *(723)*

2. An externality is an effect of a decision not taken into account by the decision maker. When there are externalities, the private price no longer necessarily reflects the social price, and therefore the market may not work properly. *(725)*

3. When there is a positive externality, the marginal social cost is below the marginal private cost, as in the diagram below. The price for the good, P_0, is too high and the quantity Q_0, too low compared to the ideal price and quantity of P_1, Q_1. *(725)*

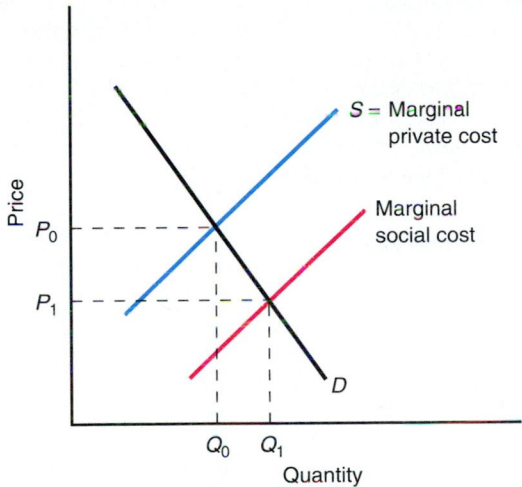

4. One can oppose efficient markets on the basis of fairness if one does not believe the underlying property rights are fairly distributed. Markets allow trades and changes in property rights, but if the underlying property rights are not fair, then the market's results can also be unfair. Market efficiency may have little meaning when there is underlying unfairness. *(726)*

5. No, the existence of a positive externality does not mean that the market works better than if no externality exis-

ted. It means that the market is not supplying a sufficient amount of the resource or activity, and insufficient supply can be as inefficient as an oversupply. *(727)*

6. One can accept all four explanations for market failure and still oppose government intervention if one believes that government intervention will cause worse problems than the market failure. *(728)*

7. Milton opposes the argument that military bases have positive externalities in terms of jobs because to pay for those bases, taxes had to be imposed, and those taxes discourage private activities that would have created jobs. The net job creation from these military bases is essentially zero, and if the bases are unnecessary, society is forgoing the positive benefit of people working at other alternative useful jobs. *(729)*

8. Milton generally opposes government intervention to prevent unfairness because that government intervention introduces new possibilities for unfairness and, based on historical views of the way the world works, government intervention has caused more unfairness than a laissez-faire policy would have created. Markets channel success to those who work hard, and that hard work creates positive externalities that bring benefits to the entire population. *(730)*

9. Milton's and Paul's differences have little to do with theoretical differences. They both use the same theory. Where they differ is in debatable judgments about how the government works and the nature of the problems. *(732)*

10. If an informational alternative to licensing were introduced, existing doctors would suffer a significant monetary loss, and students who would likely go on to medical school in existing institutions would face lower potential incomes when they entered practice. Gainers would likely be (1) those who did not want to go through an entire medical school schedule but were willing to learn a sub-specialty that required far less education and in which they had a particular proclivity to do good, and (2) demanders, who would get more for less. *(738)*

34

Politics, Economics, and Agricultural Markets

American farmers have become welfare addicts, protected and assisted at every turn by a network of programs paid for by their fellow citizens. If Americans still believe in the virtue of self-reliance, they should tell Washington to get out of the way and let farmers practice it.

~Stephen Chapman

After reading this chapter, you should be able to:

1 Explain the good/bad paradox in farming.

2 Give a brief summary of the history of U.S. farm policy.

3 State the general rule of political economy in a democracy.

4 Explain, using supply and demand curves, the distributional consequences of four alternative methods of price support.

5 Argue both sides of the question of agricultural price supports.

Agricultural markets provide good examples of the interaction of the invisible hand (the market) and the invisible foot (politics). Considering the economics of agricultural markets shows us how powerful a tool supply and demand analysis is in helping us understand not only the workings of perfectly competitive markets but also the effects of government intervention in a market. So in this chapter I consider agricultural markets and the effect of government policies on them. But bear in mind that, while the focus is on agriculture, the lessons of the analysis are applicable to a wide variety of markets in which the invisible hand and foot interact. As you read the chapter, applying the analysis to other markets will be a useful exercise.

In many ways, agricultural markets fit the classic picture of perfect competition. First, there are many independent sellers who are generally *price takers*. Second, there are many buyers. Third, the products are interchangeable: farm A's wheat can readily be substituted for farm B's wheat. And fourth, prices can, and do, vary considerably. On the basis of these inherent characteristics, it is reasonable to talk about agricultural markets as competitive markets.

In other ways, however, agricultural markets are far from perfectly competitive. The competitiveness of many agricultural markets is influenced by government programs. In fact, neither the United States nor any other country allows the market, unhindered, to control agricultural prices and output. For example, the U.S. government sets a minimum price for milk; buys up large quantities of wheat and stockpiles it; and licenses tobacco growers, allowing only those with licenses to grow tobacco.

I could have made the list of government programs much longer, because the government has a program for just about every major agricultural market. The point is clear, however: The competitive market in agriculture is not a story of the invisible hand alone. It's the story of a constant struggle between the invisible hand and the invisible foot. Whenever the invisible hand pushes prices down, farmers use their political clout (the invisible foot) to kick them back up.

Agriculture is characterized by what might be called a **good/bad paradox** (the phenomenon of doing poorly because you're doing well). This good/bad paradox shows up in a variety of ways. Looking at the long run, we see that the enormous increase in agricultural productivity over the past few centuries has reduced agriculture's importance in U.S. society and has forced many farmers off the farm. Looking at the short run, we see that when harvests are good, farmers often fare badly financially; when harvests are poor, farmers often do well financially. Let's consider these two cases in some detail.

The Long-Run Decline of Farming Most countries, the United States included, began their existence as predominantly agricultural societies. When the United States was founded a little more than 200 years ago, 97 percent of the labor force was engaged in farming, but today less than 3 percent of the U.S. labor force works in agriculture. The decline in the number of farmers isn't the result of the failure of U.S. agriculture. Rather, it's the result of its tremendous success—the enormous increase in its productivity. It used to take the majority of the population to provide food for the United States. Today it takes only a small proportion to produce more food than the U.S. population can consume.

Exhibit 1 shows how success can lead to problems. The long-run price elasticity of demand for wheat is inelastic (i.e., the percent change in quantity is small relative to the percent change in price), as it is for most agricultural products, so the exhibit shows the equilibrium in the inelastic portion of the demand curve.

In this example, initially farmers are selling quantity Q_0 for price P_0. Their total income is P_0Q_0, shown by rectangles A and B. Now say that increases in productivity shift the supply curve out from S_0 to S_1. Output increases from Q_0 to Q_1 and price falls to P_1. Income falls to P_1Q_1, shown by the B and C rectangles. Farmers have gained the C rectangle but lost the A rectangle. The net effect is the difference in size between the two rectangles. So in this example the net effect is negative.

THE NATURE OF AGRICULTURAL MARKETS

The Good/Bad Paradox in Agriculture

1 The good/bad paradox is the phenomenon of doing poorly because you're doing well.

The United States has evolved from a highly agricultural economy to one in which less than 3 percent of the labor force is engaged in farming.

THE COST OF A BOX OF WHEATIES

When people think of agricultural products, they often think of the products they buy, like Wheaties. Doing so gives them the wrong impression of the cost of agricultural products. To see why, let's consider an 18-ounce box of Wheaties which costs you, say, $3.35.

If you look at the ingredients, you'll see that you're buying sugar, salt, malt syrup, and corn syrup. So you're buying agricultural products, right? Well, a little bit. Actually, the total cost of those agricultural ingredients is probably somewhere around 25¢, less than one-tenth of the cost of the box of Wheaties. What are you spending the other nine-tenths on? Well, there's packaging, advertising, transporting the boxes, processing the ingredients, stocking the grocery store shelves, and profits. These are important components of Wheaties, but they aren't agricultural components.

The point of this example is simple. Much of our food expenditure isn't for agricultural goods; it's for the services that transform the agricultural goods into the processed foods, convince us we want to eat those foods, and get those foods to us.

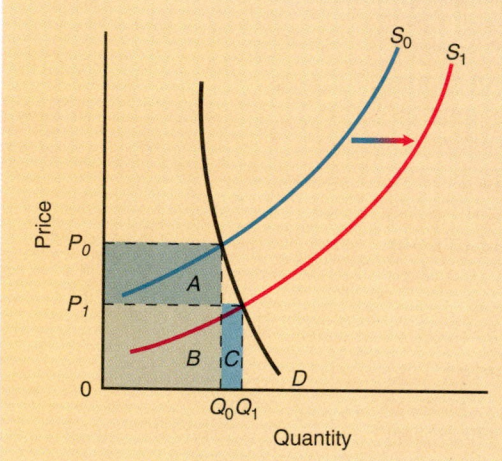

EXHIBIT 1 The Good/Bad Paradox

The good/bad paradox is demonstrated in this graph. At price P_0 the quantity of wheat produced is Q_0. Total income is $P_0 Q_0$. But if the supply of wheat increases from S_0 to S_1 due to increased productivity, the price of wheat will fall from P_0 to P_1 and quantity demanded will increase from Q_0 to Q_1. The increase in farmers' income (area C) is small. The decrease in farmers' income (area A) is large. Overall, the increased productivity has led to a decrease in farmers' incomes.

In short, productivity has increased but income has fallen, and many farmers have stopped farming altogether. They've done good by producing a lot, but the result for them is bad. This good/bad paradox will occur whenever the supply curve shifts outward in the inelastic range of the demand curve.

Due to competition among farmers, most benefits of productivity increases in agriculture have gone to consumers in the form of lower prices.

Due to competition among farmers, most benefits of productivity increases in agriculture have gone to consumers, in the form of lower prices. As an example, consider chicken. In the early 1930s, when Herbert Hoover was president of the United States and running for reelection, he promised prosperity to the country by saying there would be "two chickens in every pot." That promise meant a lot because, in today's money, chicken would have cost $8 a pound. In the mid-1990s, the price of chicken had fallen to under $2 a pound, only about one-quarter of its price in 1930.

The Short-Run Cyclical Problem Facing Farmers   The long-run good/bad paradox for farmers is mirrored by a short-run good/bad paradox: Good harvests often mean bad times and a fall in income; poor harvests often mean a rise in income.

A fact of life that farmers must deal with is that agricultural production tends to be highly unstable because it depends on weather and luck. Crops can be affected by too little rain, too much rain, insects, frost, heat, wind, hail—none of which can be easily controlled. Say you're an apple grower and you're having a beautiful spring—until the week that your trees are blossoming, when it rains continually. Bees don't fly when it rains, so they don't pollinate your trees. No pollination, no apple crop. There goes your apple crop for this year. The year 1993 provides a good example. The

Periodic flooding in the Midwest is one of the vagaries of nature with which farmers must contend. *A/P Wide World Photos.*

average rainfall for the United States that year was about normal, but, because of changing jet streams, the Midwest had floods, destroying crops as well as houses, farm machinery, farm animals, and farm land, while in the Southeast there was severe drought, making it impossible for crops to grow. (This example also shows the problems of using averages as representative of conditions.)

The short-run demand for most agricultural goods is even more inelastic than the long-run demand. Because short-run demand is so inelastic, short-run changes in supply can have a significant effect on price. The result is that good harvests for farmers in general can lower prices significantly, while poor harvests can raise prices significantly. When the short-run price effect overwhelms the short-run quantity effect (as it does when demand is inelastic), farmers face the short-run good/bad paradox.

The Difficulty of Coordinating Farm Production   This good/bad paradox caused by inelastic demand isn't lost upon farmers. They, quite naturally, aren't wild about passing on the gains to consumers instead of keeping the gains themselves. However, because agriculture is competitive, it is not in any one farmer's interest to decrease his or her supply in order to avoid encountering the paradox. Competitive farmers take the market price as given. That's the definition of a competitive industry. While it is in the industry's interest to have a ''bad year'' (to reduce total supply), it is in each individual farmer's interest to have a good year (to increase output) even if the combination of *all* farmers having a good year would cause all farmers to have a bad year.

It is, however, in farmers' joint interest to figure out ways to have continually ''bad'' years—which are, of course, actually ''good'' years for them. In other words, it's in their interest to figure out ways to limit the production of all farmers.

In a competitive industry, limiting production is easier said than done. It is difficult for farmers to limit production privately, among themselves, because although they make up only a small percentage of the total U.S. population, there are still a lot of them—2 million. That's too many to coordinate easily.

A Way around the Good/Bad Paradox   The difficulty of organizing privately to limit supply can be avoided by organizing through government. The U.S. political structure provides an alternative way for farmers (and other suppliers) to coordinate their actions and limit supply. Suppliers can organize and get government to establish programs to limit production or hold price high, thereby avoiding the good/bad paradox. And that's what farmers have done, and that's why so many government agricultural programs exist today. Before we consider how these government farm programs work, let's briefly review their history.

Q–1:   How do you think the farmers in the climatic middle, between the floods and the drought, did in 1993? Why?

Q–2:   What is the good/bad paradox?

Q–3:   What are two ways around the good/bad paradox?

ADDED DIMENSION   THE CARTEL PROBLEM

When facing an inelastic demand, it's in the interest of producers as a whole to limit production, but it's in any one producer's individual interest to produce as much as it profitably can. This difference between what's in the interest of an individual producer and what's in the interest of the group of producers is called the *cartel problem*. Agriculture is simply one example of the cartel problem; there are many other examples, such as oil production and manufacturing.

Producers have several methods to deal with the cartel problem. These methods differ among industries. For example, in the United States, *trusts* (another name for cartels) were formed in manufacturing in which each firm was allocated market share. Production was held down by agreement. These trusts were hard to enforce. Eventually, to eliminate the enforcement problem, many of the firms merged, although the amount of merger activity was limited by the U.S. antitrust laws.

Even if a group of suppliers gains a domestic cartel, it can still face competition from abroad which can undermine the domestic cartel. To be effective, a cartel often must be an international cartel. Luckily for consumers, international cartel agreements are even more difficult to enforce than domestic cartel agreements. One reason many economists support free trade is the competitive pressure it creates for domestic producers. It places a limit on domestic cartels.

Profits aren't necessarily a good measure of a cartel's effectiveness. Often its costs will rise as workers and other factors share in the gains. That's what happened in the U.S. manufacturing industries. The firms formed cartels, which led to the formation of unions and the institution of government regulations, which pushed up costs. Thus, even though we don't see U.S. manufacturing firms earning enormous profits, that doesn't necessarily mean that they haven't, to a degree, limited production to raise price.

HISTORY OF U.S. FARM PROGRAMS

2 Two reasons a persistent agricultural slump started in 1920 were (1) post-World War I demand for U.S. agricultural products declined, and (2) farm costs increased when the U.S. placed tariffs on imported manufactured goods.

I'll begin the story in the early 1900s when, because of strong growth in U.S. income, there was an increased demand for U.S. farm products, which led to high and growing income for farmers. The eruption of World War I increased demand so much that the war years, 1914–18, are known as the golden age of American farming. The depression of 1920 ended that golden age. In 1921 the U.S. economy improved, but agriculture did not; it remained in a severe slump, marked by high production, low prices, and low farm income.

The reasons for this continued severe slump were various. Two important reasons were the postwar recovery of agricultural production in Europe and the high tariffs the U.S. government placed on imported manufactured goods during the 1920s.

During the war, the number of American farms increased significantly to meet the combined demand from European countries (whose production had fallen significantly as they devoted their resources to war) and from the United States itself (which was experiencing wartime economic boom). After the war, production remained high in the United States, but demand fell as European agricultural production increased.

The impact of the low prices U.S. farmers received in the 1920s was intensified by high tariffs on imported manufactured goods. These tariffs squeezed the farmers in two ways. First, they increased the prices of goods farmers bought; and second, they further reduced demand for U.S. farm products. Unable to afford the high U.S. tariffs on their exports, the European countries, already financially weakened by the war, couldn't afford to import U.S. agricultural goods. The result of these developments was the good/bad paradox with a vengeance: low prices and high output with a tremendous fall in farm income.

The Beginnings of Government Agricultural Programs

The good/bad paradox is not a textbook concept. It has significant real-world effects. What it meant in the 1920s and 1930s was that a large number of U.S. farmers were going broke. They worked hard and got little or nothing in return. This was the time period captured in John Steinbeck's 1939 novel, *The Grapes of Wrath,* about an Oklahoma farm family forced to leave their land and migrate to California in a futile search for better conditions.

By 1929 the U.S. agricultural sector was extremely weak, but it was to become even weaker. The Great Depression that started in 1929 further devastated agricultural markets. These historical events led many to believe that competition didn't work and that the economic system used by the United States had to be changed. It was a bit like a title fight when one fighter is so bloodied and beaten that the referee steps in and

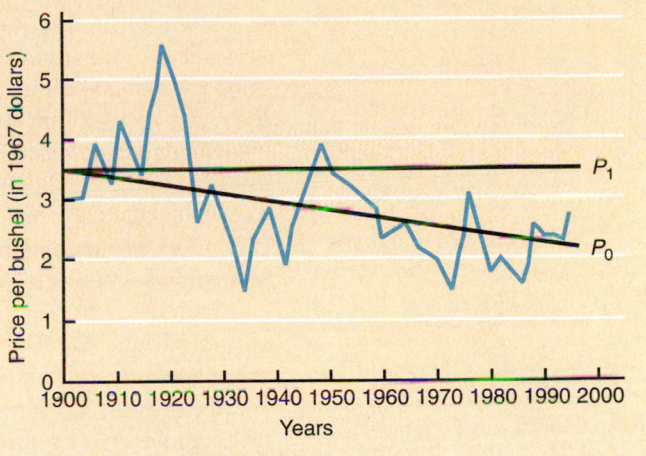

EXHIBIT 2 The Decreasing Price of Corn

If there had been no government intervention, the price of corn would have fluctuated around a downward trend as in this diagram.

stops the fight. That's what the government did; it said competition wasn't working the way society wanted it to work, and it stepped in to regulate that competition. The Great Depression marked the beginning of many of the U.S. agricultural programs that are still around today.

What would have happened without these programs is unclear. Farmers might have eventually been dominated by a few large **agrifirms** (firms that own huge farms and operate them like big corporations) which could have limited production and smoothed out price fluctuations. But as I said, achieving a private organization that limits production in agricultural markets is extraordinarily difficult. Thus, such a private "solution" to the good/bad paradox never occurred. Instead, farmers used their political clout to induce the U.S. government to step in.

In 1929, the government created the Federal Farm Board, which was given a relatively large budget to stabilize and then support agricultural prices. The difference between stabilization and support is the following: To stabilize is to smooth out short-run fluctuations, but not to affect the long-run trend. To support is to try to affect the long-run trend.

Initially the Farm Board focused on stabilizing prices by buying agricultural products directly when the price was low and selling them directly when the price was high. That was done to smooth out price fluctuations. Then direct buying and selling programs were replaced by a variety of other measures designed not only to stabilize but also to support or raise prices above their long-run trend.

Agrifirms   Large firms that own huge farms and operate them like big corporations.

Stabilization and Support for Agricultural Prices

Let's assume that you've been hired as an economist for the Federal Farm Board. Your assignment is to determine a price at which the government should buy and sell corn so as to stabilize the market by minimizing future fluctuations in its price at the lowest net cost to the government.

The jagged line in Exhibit 2 is a hypothetical line showing what the price of corn would have been from 1900 to 1995 had there been no stabilization program. It illustrates the price pattern of most agricultural goods. Two aspects of this exhibit are easily recognizable. First, the long-run trend in prices is downward. Second, there are significant short-run fluctuations around that trend.

What price would you choose? Since your object is to stabilize price at the lowest cost to the government, you should choose a price on the P_0 line that reflects the downward trend of prices. Setting the price at that trend price, you'd expect to buy corn whenever the price falls below the trend line, stopping the price from falling further and pushing the price up toward the trend line. If the price of corn rose above the trend line, you'd sell the corn you had bought. A perfect stabilization program would eliminate all price fluctuations, other than the general downward trend of prices.

If you've set the price on the trend line P_0, it's reasonable to expect that the surpluses will roughly equal the shortages. If the government chooses a stabilization price above the trend line, on average, government will accumulate surpluses; if it chooses a price below the trend line, on average, it will have shortages and will have to buy corn from abroad to meet the demand.

So if the government's goal is to minimize fluctuations in price at the lowest possible cost, it should choose a continually decreasing price that builds in the expectations of (1) increases in productivity and (2) a continually falling long-run price. That's what a **price stabilization program** is: A program designed to eliminate short-run fluctuations in prices but to allow prices to follow their long-term trend line.

Farmers aren't against such price stabilization programs. However, they're generally more interested in another type of program: a **price support program.** A price support program is one that maintains prices at a level higher than the trend of prices. If price support is your goal, you won't choose a price on trend line P_0; you'll choose a price above it on a price line such as P_1. In a price support system, surpluses and shortages don't net out. Instead, when the price trend is downward, the program generates continual surpluses which the government must figure out how to manage.

Government programs have been both stabilization and support programs. That is, they've been designed not only to minimize fluctuations in prices, but also to increase income for farmers. Farmers have come to rely on these programs to help them avoid the problems caused by the good/bad paradox.

The Choice of a Parity Price

At the center of the government's price support system has been the idea of a *parity price* that farmers should receive. A **parity price** of, say, corn, is a price of corn that keeps farmers as well off relatively as they were in a specified base year (the average of prices in the years 1910–1914). If farmers received the parity price for corn, the ratio of the prices received by farmers for that corn to prices paid by farmers would always be the same as it was in the base year. For example, say the base year price of corn was $3 a bushel and the price paid by farmers for a composite of manufactured goods was $4. If the price of manufactured goods rises to $6 (a rise of 50 percent), the parity price of corn also rises by 50 percent—to $4.50 in this hypothetical example.

Parity was justified by relatively simple arguments. Farmers argued that if they could exchange a bushel of corn for a shirt in 1912, they should also be able to exchange a bushel of corn for a shirt in 1933. If price parity is maintained, the relative prices of agricultural goods (and hence farmers' relative income) cannot fall. If price parity is maintained, the trend line of agricultural prices will be flat, not downward sloping.

The argument that farmers deserve price parity sounds logical on the surface, but it's flawed for two reasons. It doesn't allow for normal fluctuations in price, and it doesn't explain why the base should be the 1910–1914 period. Why not use 1933 as the base year?

To understand why 1910–1914 was chosen as the base year, one must recognize that U.S. government agricultural programs were designed to increase farmers' income—to support as well as stabilize prices. Choosing as the parity level the price ratio that existed during the golden age of agriculture, 1910–14, when relative agricultural prices were at their peacetime, post-1900 high, conveyed a sense that any lower price was unfair. Parity sounds good. Who would be against giving the farmers parity? Had it been called a price support system, the program would have been harder to sell politically.

Not only was a high parity price chosen, but also no downward trend was automatically built into the parity price system. The initial parity price was to be consistently maintained. If it had been maintained, increases in productivity that have occurred over time would have turned the programs more and more into support programs, with government subsidies to farmers increasing each year. However, the initial parity price has not been maintained. Instead, it has become simply a reference

Price stabilization program Program designed to eliminate short-run fluctuations in prices but allow prices to follow their long-term trend line.

Price support program Program that maintains prices at a level higher than the trend of prices.

Q-4: What is the difference between a price stabilization program and a price support program?

Parity price Price that maintains the ratio of prices received and paid by farmers at the same ratio as in a base year.

The argument that farmers deserve price parity sounds logical on the surface, but it's flawed.

Marketing Poultry a 1936 Department of Agriculture publication, is representative of the major role government has played in agriculture.

EXHIBIT 3 Parity Price Compared to Actual Price, 1910–1994

The graph shows the actual parity price farmers received from 1910 to 1994 compared to the 100 percent parity price. Parity is a ratio of the prices farmers received to the prices paid by farmers.
Source: U.S. Dept. of Agriculture.

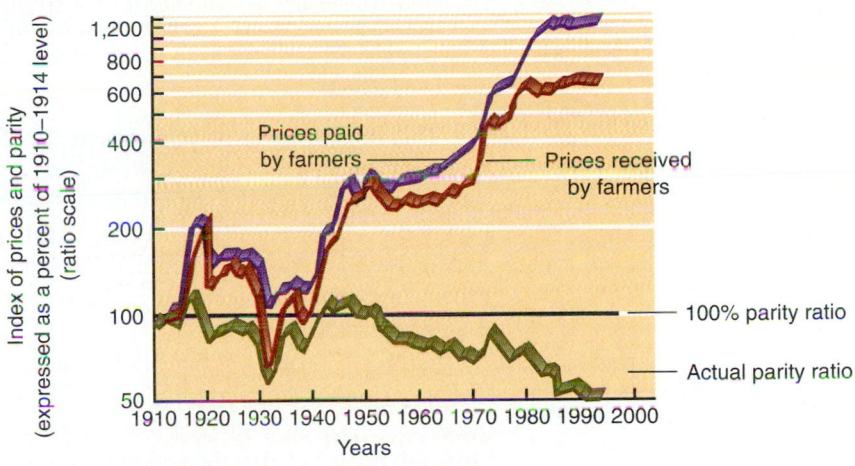

price; the actual support price is defined as a percentage or ratio of parity. The **parity ratio** is:

$$\text{Parity ratio} = \frac{\text{Index of prices received by farmers}}{\text{Index of prices paid by farmers}}$$

Parity ratio   Prices received by farmers divided by prices paid by farmers.

Exhibit 3 shows the prices farmers paid compared to the prices that farmers received from 1910 to 1994. As you can see, the prices farmers pay has increased more than the prices farmers receive. Dividing the prices received by the prices paid by farmers gives us the actual parity ratio, which can be compared to the 100-percent parity ratio that would have existed if parity had been maintained. As you can see, in the mid-1990s the actual parity ratio was about 50 percent, which means that farmers received only about 50 percent of parity price.

How high the support price has been held (which parity ratio has been guaranteed) has depended on the political power of farmers. To increase their political power they have organized a **farm lobby** (an organization of farmers whose purpose is to further political goals that will benefit farmers). Although the farm lobby has not been politically strong enough to achieve full parity with the golden age, it has been able to hold the price farmers get above what the average competitive market price would otherwise have been.

Farm lobby   Organization formed to further political goals that benefit farmers.

How do we know that this has been the case? We know because surpluses have consistently exceeded shortages. Had the government maintained prices at the average competitive price, the surpluses would be sold in time of shortage. Expressing the support price in terms of a high parity price serves a political purpose. The price support program could always be presented to the public as a limited program, going only part way to parity.

Politics and Parity   If farmers are helped by farm programs, who is hurt? The answer is taxpayers and consumers. One would expect that these broad groups would strongly oppose farm programs because farm programs cost them in two ways: (1) higher taxes that government requires in order to buy up surplus farm output, and (2) higher prices for food. It's not easy for a politician to tell her nonfarm constituents, "I'm supporting a bill that means higher prices and higher taxes for you." Nevertheless, the farm lobby has been quite successful in seeing that these programs are retained.

Economists who specialize in the relationship between economics and politics (known as *public choice economists*) have suggested that the reasons for farm groups' success involve the nature of the benefits and costs. The groups that are hurt by agricultural subsidies are large, but the negative effect on each individual in that group is relatively small. Large groups that experience small costs per individual don't provide a strong political opposition to a small group that experiences large gains. This seems to reflect a **general rule of political economy** in a democracy:

3   The general rule of political economy states that small groups that are significantly affected by a government policy will lobby more effectively than large groups that are equally affected by that same policy.

When small groups are helped by a government action and large groups are hurt by that same action, the small group tends to lobby far more effectively than the large group. Thus, policies tend to reflect the small group's interest, not the interest of the large group.

This bias in favor of farm programs is strengthened by the historical representation of farmers in Congress. Right from its beginnings in 1787, the U.S. political system has reflected the importance of agriculture. The Constitution gives representation in the Senate equally to all states. Only representation in the House of Representatives is based on a state's population. Since farm states have smaller populations than urban states, this arrangement gives farmers relatively more political power per capita than nonfarmers.

Farmers' strong political representation in Congress establishes a core of lawmakers who favor price supports.

Farmers' strong political representation in Congress establishes a core of lawmakers who favor price supports. That core, combined with the lack of political organization of large groups (consumers and taxpayers), has made it possible for the farm lobby to put together enough votes to maintain farm price support programs. When political pressure does become intense, a bit of obfuscation[1] can be used to get a bill passed. For example, what if, instead of a price support system, one introduced a loan program? Who could oppose making loans to hard-pressed farmers? That's what happened in the early 1930s, when a number of farm loan programs were enacted by Congress.

One group that could and did oppose such a loan program was the Supreme Court. In 1936, the Supreme Court overturned a set of policies that had been established to assist farmers with money raised through taxes on processors of farm commodities. In response, Congress quickly passed some slightly different legislation which got around the constitutional problems the Court had described in its 1936 decision. The revised legislation helped farmers, using general revenues rather than new tax revenues, and also established a farm credit program designed to provide low-interest mortgages and loans to farmers.

Nonrecourse loans are the equivalent of price supports.

How a Loan Program Became a Price Support Program   To implement this loan program, the government created the Commodity Credit Corporation (CCC), which had the authority to make loans to farmers using their crops as collateral at, say, $6 per bushel of corn, with $6 being the support price for corn chosen by government. The loans were nonrecourse loans, which meant that if the farmer defaulted, the CCC got the grain and nothing else. It had no recourse—no other way to collect on the loan. It couldn't seize the farm itself, for example.

Such nonrecourse loans aren't really loans at all, but are price support payments in disguise. Say, for example, that the government support price for corn was $6 and the market price of corn was $5. No farmer would sell at the market price. Instead, farmers would borrow against all of their crop. When the harvest came in, they would default on their loans and forfeit their crops. The lender (in this case the CCC) would in effect become the sole purchaser of corn.

After buying all the corn, the CCC would then sell as much as it could at the market-determined price of $5 and put the excess in storage. In that way, the CCC loan program actually worked as a pure price support system with the government holding the surpluses. During the early 1930s, the U.S. government bought substantial amounts of crops through the CCC, but when World War II began in Europe in the late 1930s, U.S. farm prices rose above the partial support level set by Congress and the surpluses disappeared.

Once the market price went above the parity support level, the CCC could sell all of its surpluses at a profit. Farmers would then sell their crops on the open market rather than deliberately defaulting on loans from the CCC. As you can see in Exhibit 3, World War II brought farmers a prosperity that continued in the years immediately

James Buchanan won the Nobel prize in 1986 for work in public choice theory. He played a major role in establishing the importance of the general rule of political economy. © The Nobel Foundation.

---

[1] *Obfuscation* is a wonderful word meaning "to make obscure, or to confuse." It comes to us from the Latin word for "to darken."

after the war. An important reason for that postwar prosperity was that, instead of instituting large tariffs on manufactured goods following the war, the United States embarked upon the Marshall Plan, a system of making large loans to European countries that allowed them, among other things, to continue to buy U.S. agricultural products. Increased exports, combined with the low interest rates of the time, were a boon to U.S. farmers, who continued to do well during the Korean War in the early 1950s.

U.S. farmers have generally done well in wars and have not done well in peacetime.

The superprosperity for farmers ended in the mid-1950s as the Korean War, which had begun in 1950, ended and the U.S. economy slowed down. Once again the parity price support levels were reached. Surpluses began building, and although the price support levels were lowered slightly in 1954, by the end of the 1950s the United States was spending almost $45 billion a year (in 1994 dollars) to purchase surplus grain.

President John F. Kennedy increased farm support prices when he took office in 1961. This would have substantially increased the amount of surplus had the government not established other programs to take land out of production through a set of *acreage control programs,* sometimes called *land bank programs.* In a land bank program, a farmer who agrees not to produce receives payments from the government.

The 1970s were good times for U.S. farmers. With land prices rising significantly and food prices high, many farmers expanded, financing that expansion by borrowing, using their land as collateral. The good times ended in the late 1970s and early 1980s as interest rates rose substantially while land and food prices fell. Once again there was a strong push on government to help the farmer. And once again the government came through, although the huge federal budget deficit kept it from being quite as generous as in the past. In the early 1990s, farm prices had recovered from the mid-1980s slump, and the cost of the government farm programs was reduced.

The combination of acreage reduction and price support systems has continued through today, although the level of support depends on what political pressures are being applied at a particular time.

Now that we've briefly reviewed the history of the U.S. government support system for agricultural prices, let's consider more carefully the theory underlying some alternative farm price support options. In doing so, we'll try to understand which options, given the political realities, would have the best chance of being implemented, and why.

HOW A PRICE SUPPORT SYSTEM WORKS IN THEORY

Four Price Support Options

In a price support system, the government maintains a higher-than-equilibrium price, as diagrammed in Exhibit 4. At support price P_1, the quantity people want to supply is Q_S, but the quantity demanded at that price is Q_D.

At price P_1 there's excess supply, which exerts a downward pressure on price (arrow *A*). To maintain price at P_1, some other force (arrow *B*) must be exerted; otherwise the invisible hand will force the price down.

The government has various options to offset that downward pressure on price:

1. Using legal and regulatory force to prevent anyone from selling or buying at a lower price.
2. Providing economic incentives to reduce the supply enough to eliminate the downward pressure on price.
3. Subsidizing the sale of the good to consumers so that while suppliers get a high price, demanders have to pay only a low price.
4. Buying up and storing, giving away, or destroying enough of the good so that the total demand (including government's demand) increases enough to eliminate downward pressure on price.

Four price support options are:
1. Regulatory force.
2. Economic incentives to reduce supply.
3. Subsidizing the sale of goods to consumers.
4. Buying up and storing, giving away, or destroying the good.

Each of these methods distributes the costs and benefits in a slightly different way. Let's consider each method in detail.

Supporting the Price by Regulatory Measures   Suppose the government simply passes a law saying that, from now on, the price of wheat will be at least $5 per bushel. No one

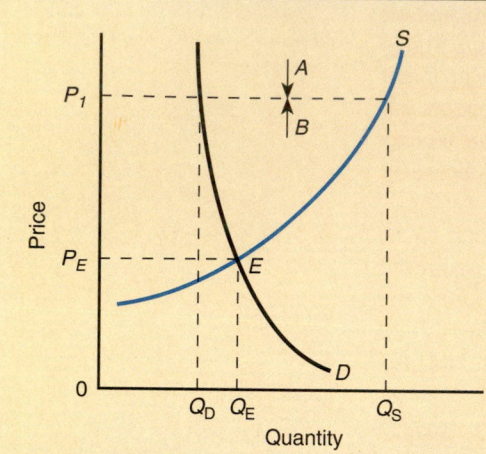

EXHIBIT 4 **A Price Support System**

In a price support system, the government maintains a higher-than-equilibrium price. At support price, P_1, the quantity of product demanded is only Q_D, while the quantity supplied is Q_S. This causes downward pressures on the price, P_1, which must be offset by various government measures.

may sell wheat at a lower price. If the competitive equilibrium price is higher than $5, the law has no effect. When the competitive equilibrium is below the price floor (say the competitive equilibrium is $3.50 per bushel), the law limits suppliers from selling their wheat at that lower price.

The price floor helps some suppliers and hurts others. Those suppliers who are lucky enough to sell their wheat benefit. Those suppliers who aren't lucky and can't find buyers for their wheat are hurt. How many suppliers will be helped and how many will be hurt depends on the elasticities of supply and demand. When supply and demand are inelastic, a large change in price brings about a small change in quantity supplied, so the hurt group is relatively small. When the supply and demand are elastic, the hurt group is larger.

In Exhibit 5(a), suppliers would like to sell quantity Q_2 but, by law, they can supply only Q_1. They end up with a surplus of wheat, $Q_2 - Q_1$. Demanders, who must pay the higher price, $5, and receive only Q_1 rather than Q_e, are hurt.

The law may or may not specify who will, and who will not, be allowed to sell, but it must establish some noneconomic method of rationing the limited demand among the suppliers. If it doesn't, buyers are likely, for example, to buy from farmers who are their friends. If individual farmers have a surplus, they'll probably try to dispose of that surplus by selling it on the black market at a price below the legal price. To maintain the support price, the government will have to arrest farmers who sell below the legal price. If the number of producers is large, such a regulatory approach is likely to break down quickly, since individual incentives to sell illegally are great and the costs of enforcing the law are accordingly high.

In understanding who benefits and who's hurt by price floors, it's important to distinguish two groups of farmers: the farmers who had been producing before the law went into effect, and the farmers who entered the market afterward. In Exhibit 5(a), the first group supplies Q_e; the second group, which would want to enter the market when the price went up, would supply $Q_2 - Q_e$. Why must the second group be clearly identified? Because one relatively easily enforceable way to limit the quantity supplied is to forbid any new farmers to enter the market. Only people who were producing at the beginning of the support program will be allowed to produce, and they will be allowed to produce only as much as they did before the program went into effect. Restricting production will reduce the quantity supplied to Q_1, leaving only $Q_e - Q_1$ to be rationed among suppliers.

This method of restriction, which is said to **grandfather in** existing suppliers, is one of the easiest to enforce and thus one of the most widely used. For example, when supply limitations were placed on tobacco, existing growers were all allowed to grow tobacco on land they were currently using for tobacco production. They could not, however, devote any new land to growing tobacco. (Later, the acreage allocations were allowed to be transferred, at a price of course, so that if old land were taken out of tobacco production, new land could be added.)

Grandfather in To pass a law affecting a specific group but providing that those in the group before the law was passed are not subject to the law.

EXHIBIT 5 (a, b, c, and d)
Alternative Methods of
Government Price Supports

Alternative methods have
different distributional
consequences. The
consequences of regulatory
measures are shown in (**a**); of
providing economic incentives to
reduce supply in (**b**); of
subsidizing the sale in (**c**); and of
buying up and storing the good in
(**d**).

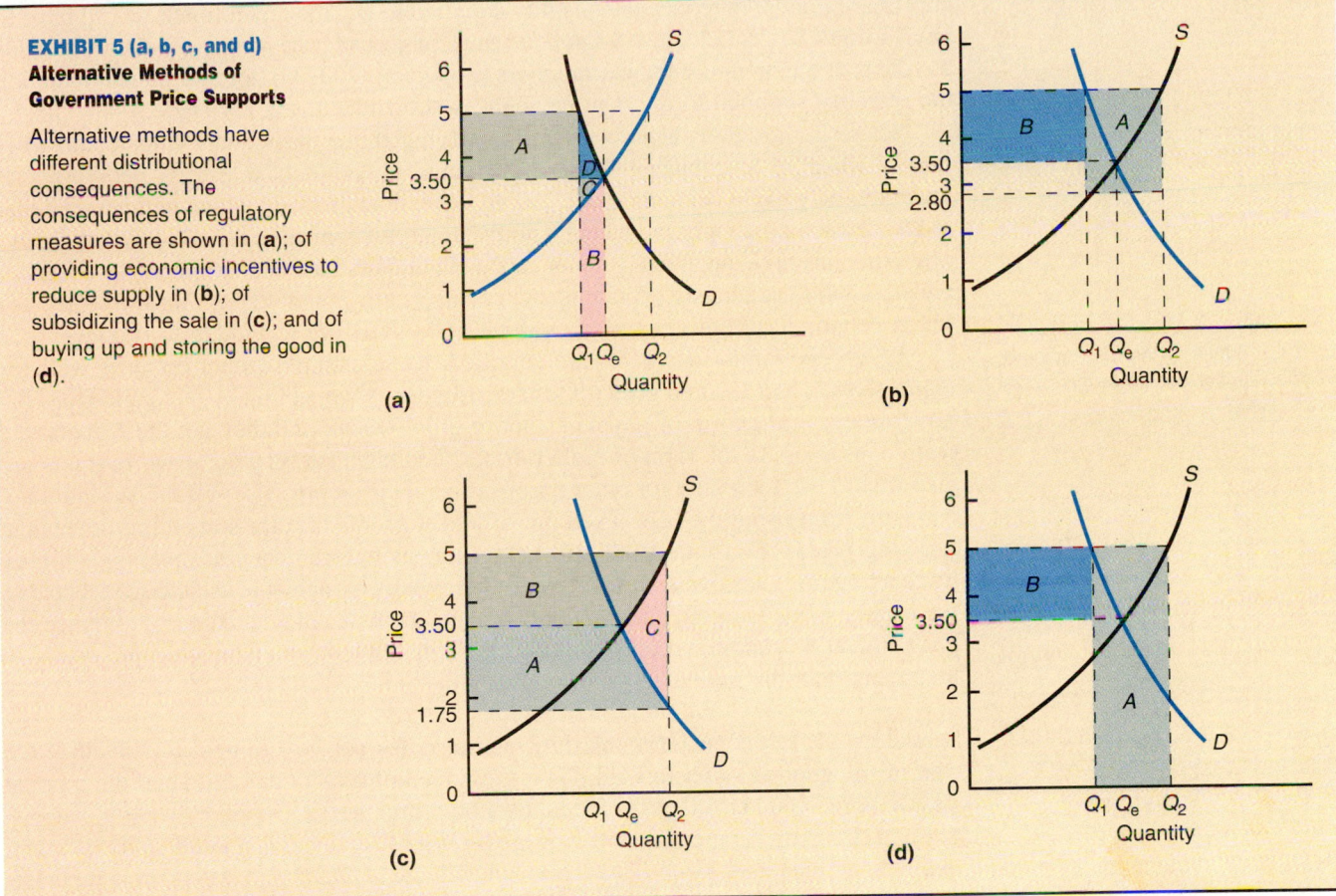

When it comes to grandfathering groups *out* of production, foreign producers are perhaps the politically easiest targets. To keep the domestic price of a good up, foreign imports must be limited as well as domestic production. U.S. taxpayers might put up with subsidizing U.S. farmers, but they're likely to balk at subsidizing foreign farmers. So most farm subsidy programs are supplemented with tariffs and quotas on foreign imports of the same commodity.

Notice that with the equilibrium in the inelastic portion of the demand curve, even though the average farmer is constrained as to how much can be sold, he or she is made better off by that constraint because the total revenue going to all farmers is higher than it would be if supply weren't constrained. The farmer's total revenue from this market increases by rectangle *A* in Exhibit 5(a) and decreases by the rectangle composed of the combined areas *B* and *C*. Of course, making the farmer better off is not cost-free. Consumers are made worse off because they must pay more for a smaller supply of wheat. There's no direct cost to taxpayers other than the cost of enforcing and administering the regulations.

Notice in the diagram the little triangle made up of areas *C* and *D*, which shows an amount of income that society loses but farmers don't get. It's simply wasted. That little triangle is a net loss to society from the restriction. It's called an **excess burden,** and it results whenever the market is prevented from operating freely. (Excess burden is also called *deadweight loss*).

4 Four methods of price support
are:
1. Regulatory methods.
2. Economic incentives to reduce supply.
3. Subsidizing the sale.
4. Buying up and storing the good.
The distributional effects are shown in Exhibit 5.

Excess burden   Loss to society caused by a policy introducing a wedge between marginal private and marginal social costs and benefits.

Providing Economic Incentives to Reduce Supply   A second way in which government can keep a price high is to provide farmers with economic incentives to reduce supply.

Looking at Exhibit 5(b), you see that at the support price, $5 per bushel, the quantity of wheat supplied is Q_2 and quantity demanded is Q_1. To avoid a surplus, the government must somehow find a way to shift the quantity supplied back from Q_2 to Q_1. For example, it could pay farmers not to grow wheat, as it did in the land bank program. How much would such an economic incentive cost? Given the way the curves are drawn, to reduce the quantity supplied to Q_1, the government would have to pay farmers $2.20 ($5.00 − $2.80) for each bushel of wheat they didn't grow. This payment of $2.20 would induce suppliers producing $Q_2 − Q_1$ not to produce, reducing the quantity supplied to Q_1. The payment is shown by the A rectangle.

There is, however, a problem in identifying those individuals who would truly supply wheat at $5 a bushel. Knowing that the government is paying people not to grow wheat, people who otherwise had no interest in growing wheat will pretend that at $5 they would supply the wheat, simply to get the subsidy. To avoid this problem, often this incentive approach is combined with our first option, regulatory restrictions. Farmers who are already producing wheat at Q_e are grandfathered in; only they are given economic incentives not to produce. All others are forbidden to produce.

Q–5: Which of the four methods of price support would farmers favor least? Why?

When economic incentives are supplied, the existing farmers do very well for themselves. Their income goes up for two reasons. They get the A rectangle from the government in the form of payments not to grow wheat, and they get the B rectangle from consumers in the form of higher prices for the wheat they do grow. Farmers are also free to use their land for other purposes, so their income rises by the amount they can earn from using the land taken out of wheat production for something other than growing wheat. Consumers are still being hurt as before: They are paying a higher price and getting less. In addition, they're being hurt in their role as taxpayers because the lightly shaded area (rectangle A) represents the taxes they must pay to finance the government's economic incentive program. Thus, this option is much more costly to taxpayers than the regulatory option.

Q–6: Which of the four methods of price support would taxpayers favor least? Why?

Subsidizing the Sale of the Good   A third option is for the government to subsidize the sale of the good in order to hold down the price consumers pay but keep the amount suppliers receive high. Exhibit 5(c) shows how this works. Suppliers supply quantity Q_2 and are paid $5 per bushel. The government then turns around and sells that quantity at whatever price it can get—in this case, $1.75. No direct transfer takes place from the consumer to the supplier. Both are made better off. Demanders get more goods at a lower price. They are benefitted by area A. Suppliers get a higher price and can supply all they want. They are benefitted by area B. What's the catch? The catch, of course, is that taxpayers foot the entire bill, paying the difference between the $5 and the $1.75 ($3.25) for each bushel sold. The cost to taxpayers is represented by areas A, B, and C. This option costs taxpayers the most of any of the four options.

Q–7: Which of the four methods of price support would consumers favor least? Why?

Buying Up and Storing, Giving Away, or Destroying the Good   The final option is for the government to buy up all the supply that demanders don't buy at the support price. This option is shown in Exhibit 5(d). Consumers buy Q_1 at price $5; the government buys $Q_2 − Q_1$ at price $5, paying the A rectangle. In this case consumers transfer the B rectangle to suppliers when they pay $5 rather than $3.50, the competitive equilibrium price. The government (i.e., the taxpayers) pays farmers rectangle A. The situation is very similar to our second option, in which the government provides suppliers with economic incentives not to produce. However, it's more expensive since the government must pay $5 per bushel rather than paying farmers $2.20 per bushel. In return for this higher payment, the government is getting something in return: $Q_2 − Q_1$ of wheat.

Of course, if the government buys the surplus wheat, it takes on the problem of what to do with this surplus. Say the government decides to give it to the poor. Since the poor were already buying food, in response to a free food program they will replace some of their purchases with the free food. This replacement brings about a drop in demand—which means that the government must buy even more surplus. Instead of giving it away, though, the government can burn the surplus or store it indefinitely in warehouses and grain elevators. Burning up the surplus or storing it, at least, doesn't increase the amount government must buy.

Why, you ask, doesn't the government give the surplus to foreign countries as a type of humanitarian aid? The reason is that just as giving the surplus to our own poor creates problems in the United States, giving the surplus to the foreign poor creates problems in the countries involved. To the degree that the foreign poor have any income, they're likely to spend most of it on food. Free food would supplant some of their demand, thus lowering the price for those who previously sold food to them. Giving anything away destroys somebody's market, and when markets are destroyed someone gets upset. So when the United States has tried to give away its surplus food, other foreign countries have put enormous pressure on the United States not to "spoil the world market."

The four price support options I've just described can, of course, be used in various combinations. It's a useful exercise at this point to think through which of the options farmers, taxpayers, and consumers would likely favor and to relate the history of the farm programs to these options.

Politics, Economics, and Price Supports

Which Group Prefers Which Option?   The first option, regulation, costs the government the least, but it benefits farmers the least. Since existing farmers are likely to be the group directly pushing for price supports, government is least likely to choose this approach. If it is chosen, most of the reduction in quantity supplied will probably be required to come from people who might enter farming at some time in the future, not from existing farmers.

The second option, economic incentives, costs the government more than the first option but less than the third and fourth options. Farmers are benefitted by economic incentive programs in two ways. They get paid not to grow a certain crop, and they can sometimes get additional income from using the land for other purposes. When farmers aren't allowed to use their land for other purposes, they usually oppose this option, preferring the third or fourth option.

The third option, subsidies on sales to keep prices down, benefits both consumers (who get low prices) and farmers (who get high prices). Taxpayers are harmed the most by this option. They must finance the subsidy payments for all subsidized farm products.

The last option, buying up and storing or destroying the goods, costs taxpayers more than the first two options but less than the third, since consumers pay part of the cost. However, it leaves the government with a surplus to deal with. If there's a group who can take that surplus without significantly reducing their current demand, then that group is likely to support this option.

As I discussed in the historical section, the two prevalent farm programs in the United States are (1) the land bank program (in which government supports prices by giving farmers economic incentives to reduce supply), and (2) the nonrecourse loan program (in which government "buys" goods in the form of collateral on defaulting loans). Programs that support prices through regulation, our first option, generally haven't been applied to existing farmers. They have often, however, been used to prevent new farmers from entering the market—which isn't surprising since the political impetus for farm programs comes from existing farmers.

The third option, to subsidize the sale of the good so the farmer gets a high price and the consumer pays a low price, hasn't been used because it would be the most costly to taxpayers. Rather than costing $10 billion or $20 billion a year, as they do now, farm programs involving direct subsidies would likely cost $60 billion to $100 billion a year. In contrast, economic incentive and government purchase programs hide the true costs of price supports better. However, direct subsidies are used in a number of developing countries where governments are under strong and conflicting political pressures from both consumers and farmers. Often the subsidies are financed by budget deficits, not taxes, so the taxpayers aren't directly confronted with the bill. (But since there's no such thing as a free lunch, they'll face the bill later when they must pay the interest on the debt.)

The two prevalent farm programs in the United States are (1) the land bank program and (2) the non-recourse loan program.

Economics, Politics, and Real-World Policies   The actual political debate is, of course, much more complicated than presented here. For example, other pressure groups are involved. Recently, farm groups and environmental groups have combined forces and

The Midwest of the North American continent has some of the best farmland in the world. © *John Eastcott/YVA Momatiuk/The Image Works.*

have become more effective in shaping and supporting farm policy. Thus, in the 1990s, restrictions on supply in farming are likely to operate in ways that environmentalists would favor, such as regulating the types of fertilizer and chemicals farmers can use.

Q–8:   Are taxpayers, farmers, and consumers separate groups that are independent of each other?

Moreover, the three interest groups discussed here—farmers, taxpayers, and consumers—aren't entirely distinct one from another. Their memberships overlap. All taxpayers are also consumers; farmers are both taxpayers and consumers; and so on. Thus, much of the political debate is simply about from whose pocket the government is going to get money to help farmers. Shall it be the consumer's pocket (through higher prices)? Or the taxpayer's (through higher taxes)? That said, the political reality is that consumer and taxpayer interests and the lobbying groups that represent them generally examine only part of the picture—the part that directly affects them. Accordingly, politicians often act as if these groups had separate memberships. Politicians weigh the options by attempting to balance their view of the general good with the power and preferences of the special interest groups that they represent or that contribute to their election campaigns.

If you think government is significantly involved in U.S. agriculture, you should see its role in other countries, such as the members of the European Union and Japan.

The final real-world complication that must be taken into account in the 1990s is the international dimension. If you think government is significantly involved in U.S. agriculture, you should see its role in other countries such as the members of the European Union and Japan. Our agricultural policy is in part determined by trade negotiations with these other countries. For example, the U.S. government could subsidize U.S. agriculture to keep U.S. agricultural products competitive with the heavily subsidized EU production. A reduction in EU subsidies could bring about a reduction in our subsidies.

AN ASSESSMENT OF FARM PRICE SUPPORT PROGRAMS

5   Price supports cause inefficiency and loss compared to a competitive solution. However, it is likely that, in the absence of price supports, private cartels would have been the outcome, and the price supports are the least inefficient practical solution.

This chapter's overview of government price support programs and their effects on farmers, consumers, and taxpayers should have given you a sense that, for society as a whole, the competitive solution would be a much better option than any of the other four approaches that we've discussed. Society would probably be better off, on average, if all the government farm programs were eliminated and replaced with a free market in agricultural goods. There would likely be much larger fluctuations in agricultural prices than there currently are, but the average price paid by consumers and the cost to taxpayers would both be lower.

But given the realities of the agricultural markets, it's unlikely that the competitive solution is a practical one. The inelastic demand for, and the fluctuating supply of, most agricultural goods create enormous pressure for cartelization of the various agricultural markets. In the absence of government programs, it's likely that the pressure would rise for the formation of private cartels—organizations of suppliers whose purpose is to limit supply—to stabilize and support agricultural prices. Had the government support programs not been established, agricultural production in the United States might today be controlled by four or five major firms which could limit supply even more than now. Agricultural prices might be higher and agricultural production lower than they currently are.

Had such private cartelization occurred, these firms would have initially made large profits, as did many of the first large manufacturing companies. The response to such profits would also likely have been similar. Agricultural workers would have organized and demanded safer working conditions and limited hours. They would have established pension systems similar to those that workers in manufacturing industries obtained. That would have significantly increased the costs of agricultural goods. The result might have been lower production and higher prices than we currently have.

To see the differences in the nature of production under our current system of private production and government support programs and under a system of private cartelization of agriculture, let's consider the question of industrial safety. To put the matter bluntly, one reason why U.S. farms are so productive is that farmers work extremely hard and skimp a lot on safety measures. Competition drives farmers to be productive, but it also kills and maims them. The accidental death rate for farmers is almost 50 per 100,000 per year. That's almost twice the death rate in mining (often considered the most dangerous occupation) and five times the national average. In a three-week period in a single year, the following accidents happened:

One reason U.S. farmers are so productive is that farmers work extremely hard and skimp a lot on safety measures.

- A man in Kempton, Indiana, was strangled when his clothes got caught in a corn picker.
- A man in Ventura, Iowa, was buried and suffocated by corn sliding into the center of the steel bin where he was working.
- A woman in Litchfield, Minnesota, was seriously injured when her clothing was caught in the machinery of a harvesting combine.
- A man in Columbus, Nebraska, was crushed by cattle in his farmyard.
- A child suffocated in a corn wagon in Boemer, Nebraska.

If those accidents had happened in any other industry, there would be demands for government intervention and new safety regulations. But not in farming. It wasn't Big Business that was responsible; it was individual farmers making their own decisions. Under a cartelized system, Big Business *would* be held responsible, and there would be a clamor for government-imposed regulations. Such requirements would significantly increase costs and decrease productivity.

Arguments like the one I am making are always tenuous because no one can say for sure what the farm industry would have been like if government programs had never existed. For example, it's possible that, even if there had been large-scale cartelization in agriculture, international competition would have forced that domestic cartel to be competitive.

Because it's unclear what the correct hypothetical comparison is, one must be extremely careful in arguing that our present system is preferable to some hypothetical alternative, just as one must be careful in arguing that perfect competition would be preferable to the present situation.

Many economists speak rather harshly about our current government agricultural programs, comparing their waste and inefficiency with the operation of a perfectly competitive market. That comparison is problematic. An alternative to current U.S. farm programs might have been, not perfect competition, but the cartelization of the entire farming industry, resulting in higher prices, lower production, and less efficiency than the existing level.

While, ideally, perfect competition might be best for our society, policy-makers must recognize the reality that competition isn't always the relevant alternative, given the nature of politics and the market.

Thus, while, ideally, perfect competition might be best for our society, policy-makers must recognize the reality that competition isn't always the relevant alternative, given the nature of politics and the market. Relevant policy choices must be made between the two most likely alternatives, not between a tidy ideal and a messy reality. Which is the better situation? As usual, there's no easy answer.

CONCLUSION

This chapter has focused on agricultural markets, but it should be clear that the discussion is about much more than just agriculture; it's about the interrelationship between economics and politics. If individuals are self-interested maximizers, it's reasonable to assume that they're maximizers in all aspects of their lives. What they can't achieve in the economic sphere, they might be able to achieve in the political sphere.

To understand the economic policies that exist, one must consider how people act in both spheres. Consideration of the economics underlying government policies often leads to useful insights. For example, a military draft can be seen as a mechanism for focusing the costs of defense away from the taxpayer and onto a specific group of individuals—young people. The government's support for the arts can be seen as a transfer from general taxpayers to a specific group of individuals who like the arts. Government support for education can be seen as a transfer from general taxpayers to a specific group of individuals: students and instructors. These groups maintain strong lobbies to achieve their political ends, and the interaction of the various lobbying groups typically strongly influences what policies government will follow.

Economics doesn't tell you whether government intervention or any particular policy is good or bad. That, you must decide for yourself. But what economics can do is pose the policy question in terms of gains and losses for particular groups. Posing the question in that framework often cuts through to the real reasons behind various groups' support for this or that policy. Farmers aren't going to tell you that they support agricultural programs because those programs transfer money from taxpayers and consumers to farmers. Similarly, academics generally aren't going to tell you that the reason they favor government support for education is that those policies transfer money to them.

The economic framework directs you to look beyond the reasons people say they support policies; it directs you to look for the self-interest. The supply/demand framework provides a neat graphical way to picture the relative gains and losses resulting from various policies, which is why the supply/demand framework is such a powerful tool, even when few industries are actually perfectly competitive.

But as usual there's an *on the other hand*. Just because some groups may support policies for self-serving reasons, it is not necessarily the case that the policies are bad, or shouldn't be adopted. Reality is complicated with many more gray answers than black-and-white ones.

Q–9: Is the military draft a cheaper way of maintaining defense than a volunteer army?

Q–10: Economic theory tells us that a volunteer army is preferable to an army maintained by a draft. True or false? Why?

CHAPTER SUMMARY

- Because most agricultural markets have an inelastic demand, they produce a good/bad paradox for farmers.

- The history of the U.S. farm program is one of government intervention to keep prices higher than they otherwise might have been.

- U.S. agriculture is enormously productive and technically efficient.

- A general rule of political economy in a democracy is that policies tend to reflect small groups' interests, not the interests of large groups.

- Farm price support options are regulations, economic incentives, subsidies, and buying up and storing or destroying.

- In judging a policy, the appropriate comparison is often the counterfactual. What would have happened if that policy had not been introduced?

- Reality is complicated, with many more gray answers than black-and-white ones.

KEY TERMS

agrifirms *(749)*

excess burden *(755)*

farm lobby *(751)*

general rule of political
  economy *(751)*

good/bad paradox *(745)*

grandfather in *(754)*

parity price *(750)*

parity ratio *(751)*

price stabilization
  program *(750)*

price support
  program *(750)*

QUESTIONS FOR THOUGHT AND REVIEW

*The number after each question represents the estimated
degree of critical thinking required. (1 = almost none;
10 = deep thought.)*

1. If the demand for farm products were elastic rather than
   inelastic, would the good/bad paradox still exist? Why
   or why not? *(5)*

2. Demonstrate, using supply and demand curves, the distributional consequences of a price support system
   achieved through acreage restriction. *(4)*

3. Which would a taxpayers' group prefer: price support
   achieved through buying up the surplus, or through providing economic incentives for not producing?
   Why? *(5)*

4. Say a city is establishing rent controls requiring rents to
   be set below market rents. What alternative methods
   could it use to ration apartments? *(8)*

5. What's the most costly method of price support to the
   taxpayer? Demonstrate graphically. *(4)*

6. What is the least costly method of price support to the
   taxpayer? Demonstrate graphically. *(4)*

7. Why do tariffs and quotas generally accompany price
   support systems? *(5)*

8. How does the elasticity of supply affect the cost of price
   supports in each of the four options? *(6)*

9. Does the comparatively high accidental death rate for
   farmers say anything about the efficiency of U.S. regulation? If so, what? *(7)*

10. All government intervention in markets makes society
    worse off. True or false? Evaluate. *(8)*

PROBLEMS AND EXERCISES

1. Show graphically how the effects of an increase in supply
   will differ according to the elasticities of supply and
   demand.
   a. Specifically, demonstrate the following combinations:
      (1) An inelastic supply and an elastic demand.
      (2) An elastic supply and an inelastic demand.
      (3) An elastic supply and an elastic demand.
      (4) An inelastic supply and an inelastic demand.
   b. Demonstrate the effect of a government guarantee of
      the price in each of the four cases.
   c. If you were a farmer, which of the four combinations
      would you prefer?

2. Congratulations. You've been appointed finance minister
   of Farmingland. The president wants to protect her political popularity by increasing farmers' incomes. She's
   considering two alternatives: (a) to bolster agricultural
   prices by adding government demand to private demand;
   and (b) to give farmers financial incentives to restrict supply and thereby increase price. She wants to use the
   measure that's least costly to the government. The conditions of supply and demand are illustrated in the
   accompanying diagram. (S_1 is what the restricted supply
   curve would look like. P_s is the price that the president
   wants to establish.) Which measure would you advise?

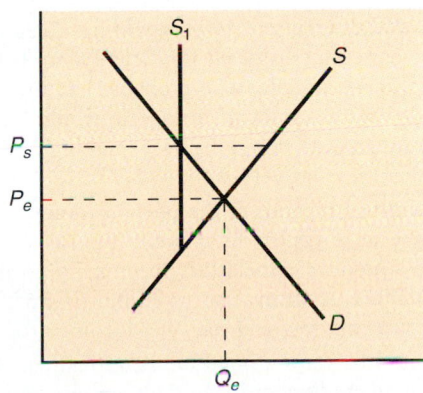

3. The Pure Food and Drug Act of 1906 is known as ''Dr.
   Wiley's Law.'' It is generally regarded by noneconomic
   historians as representing the triumph of consumer interests over producer interests.
   a. Why might an economist likely be somewhat wary of
      this interpretation?
   b. What evidence would a skeptical economist likely look
      for to determine the motives behind the passage of this
      law?
   c. What might be the significance of the fact that the

Pure Food and Drug Act was passed in 1906, right when urbanization and technological change were fostering new products that competed significantly with existing producers' interests?

4. The U.S. government makes it against the law to grow peanuts unless the grower has been granted a government quota. It also essentially forbids peanut imports and sets a minimum U.S. price of peanuts at about 50 percent higher than the price of peanuts on the world market. This program costs the government $4 million a year in administrative costs.

   a. Are there likely any other costs associated with the program?

   b. Demonstrate graphically how to come up with about $250 million of additional costs.

   c. When ''peanut land''—land with peanut quotas—is sold, what is the likely price of that land compared to equivalent land without a peanut quota?

   d. Say that, under GATT, the United States agrees to allow open imports of peanuts into the United States and guarantees that all sellers receive the current high price. What will happen to the governmental costs of the program?

   e. Say the government limits the guaranteed high price to U.S. producers. What will it have to do to make that guarantee succeed?

5. Say that a law, if passed, will reduce Mr. A's wealth by $100,000 and increase Mr. B's wealth by $100,000.

   a. How much would Mr. A be willing to spend to stop passage of the law?

   b. How much would Mr. B be willing to spend to emsure passage of the law?

   c. What implications for social policy do your answers to a and b have?

6. In 1992 the U.S. Bureau of Land Management set a fee for ranchers who graze their animals on public land equal to $1.86 per animal unit per month—the amount of forage needed to feed one cow and its calf, or five sheep, for a month. The market rate for grazing on private land is $9 per animal unit month.

   a. Why do you think there is a difference?

   b. What are the advantages of setting the lower fee?

   c. Would you expect excess demand for government grazing land? Why? Demonstrate graphically.

7. New York City has issued 11,787 taxi licenses, called ''medalions,'' and has not changed that number since 1937.

   a. What does that limitation likely do to the price of taxi medalions? Demonstrate graphically.

   b. If the New York City Taxi Commission eliminated a rule that required medalion owners who own only one cab to drive their cabs full time what would likely happen to the price of the medalion?

   c. If New York City decreased the number of medalions by 1,000 by revoking 1,000 medalions, what would happen to the price of remaining medalions?

   d. What would the political response to such a revocation be?

ANSWERS TO MARGIN QUESTIONS

1. Floods and droughts of 1993 would have had a tendency to raise agricultural prices significantly, so those farmers in the climatic middle, who probably had the agriculturally correct amount of rainfall, would likely have had large harvests. Large harvests and high prices would mean that they did very well. *(747)*

2. The good/bad paradox is the phenomenon of doing poorly because you're doing well. It exists when demand for one's product is inelastic. Specifically, as it applies to agriculture, it means that when most farmers produce a lot, prices are low and their net income drops. *(747)*

3. There are two ways around the good/bad paradox. One is for suppliers to coordinate their activity and limit supply. The second way is for suppliers to lobby and get government to establish programs to limit production, stabilizing the price and holding it high. Because of the difficulty of coordinating the large number of farmers, it is this second track that U.S. farmers have followed. *(747)*

4. A price stabilization program is designed to minimize fluctuations in prices, with the good years offsetting the bad years. A price support program is designed to *raise* the overall level of prices along with stabilizing that

level, so that the support in the bad years exceeds the amount taken away from farmers in the good years. *(750)*

5. Farmers are least likely to support the regulatory method of price support in which regulatory force is used to prevent anyone from selling or buying at a lower price. Although such a policy benefits farmers, it benefits them far less than other price support policies. *(756)*

6. Taxpayers will likely least favor the price support method of subsidizing the sale of goods to consumers, because this method costs taxpayers the most. The low price paid by consumers and the high price received by farmers necessitate large subsidies. *(756)*

7. Consumers would least favor the price support method of providing economic incentives to reduce supply and the price support method of regulatory force. Both these methods reduce the supply and push up the price. Some consumers would benefit from the buying up, giving away, or destroying method, which suggests that consumers on average would prefer this to the regulatory or the economic incentive method. *(756)*

8. While this chapter discusses taxpayers, farmers, and consumers as separate groups independent of each other, in

reality they are not. Each individual is, generally, both a taxpayer and a consumer, while farmers are generally members of all three groups. It is, nonetheless, useful to treat them as separate groups because specific interests predominate: for example, farmers' interests as farmers significantly outweigh their interests as taxpayers or as consumers. *(758)*

9. In terms of actual money payment by the government, having a military draft likely is a cheaper way of maintaining defense than is a volunteer army. However, a military draft can be seen as a type of hidden tax on a specific group of individuals—young people who are subject to the draft—to the degree that they are paid less than the going wage. If that hidden tax is also included in the cost, the military draft is not a cheaper way of maintaining defense. Because it involves inefficiencies in who can participate, it can, indeed, be seen as more expensive than an all-volunteer army. *(760)*

10. False. Economic theory tells us nothing about what is preferable. Choices about what is preferable can only be made by specifying one's value judgments. Such choices belong in normative economics and in the art of economics, where distributional effects, broader sociological issues, and value judgments are included in the analysis. *(760)*

35

Microeconomics, Social Policy, and Economic Reasoning

If an economist becomes certain of the solution of any problem, he can be equally certain that his solution is wrong.

~H. A. Innis

After reading this chapter, you should be able to:

1 List three reasons why economists sometimes differ in their views on social policy.

2 Explain why liberal and conservative economists often agree in their views on social policy.

3 Explain the typical economist's view of many regulations.

4 Define cost/benefit analysis.

5 State why economists disagree about whether the minimum wage should be raised.

6 Explain why teaching a parrot the phrase *supply and demand* will not make it an economist.

One of the important jobs that economists do is to give advice to politicians and other policymakers on a variety of questions relating to social policy: How should unemployment be dealt with? How can society distribute income fairly? Should the government redistribute income? Would a program of equal pay for jobs of comparable worth (a pay equity program) make economic sense? Should the minimum wage be increased?

Economists differ substantially in their views on these and other social policy questions. As one pundit remarked, ''If you laid all economists end to end, they still wouldn't reach a conclusion.'' Such comments have a superficial truth to them, but they also are misleading. Economists agree on many issues, and the reasons they disagree often have little to do with economics.

Understanding what economists agree and disagree about, and why, is an important part of understanding economics. Thus, this chapter considers some areas of agreement and disagreement among economists. This analysis will give you a good sense of economic reasoning as it's used in formulating social policy.

ECONOMISTS' DIFFERING VIEWS ABOUT SOCIAL POLICY

Economists have many different views on social policy because:

1. Economists' suggestions for social policy are determined by their subjective value judgments (normative views) as well as by their objective economic analyses.
2. Policy proposals must be based on imprecise empirical evidence, so there's considerable room for differences of interpretation not only about economic issues, but also about how political and social institutions work. Economic policy is an art, not a science.
3. Policy proposals are based on various models which focus on different aspects of a problem.

1 Economists' views on social policy differ widely because (1) their objective economic analyses are colored by their subjective value judgments; (2) their interpretations of economic issues and of how political and social institutions work vary widely; and (3) their proposals are often based on various models that focus on different aspects of problems.

The first and third reasons directly concern the role of ideology in economics, a controversial subject among economists. However, all economists agree that any policy proposal must embody both economic analysis *and* value judgments because the goals of policy reflect value judgments. When an economist makes a policy proposal, it's of this type: ''If A, B, and C are your goals, then you should undertake policies D, E, and F to achieve those goals most efficiently.'' In making these policy suggestions, the economist's role is much the same as an engineer's: he or she is simply telling someone else how to achieve desired ends most efficiently. Ideally the economist is, as objectively as possible, telling someone how to achieve his or her goals (which need not be the economist's goals).

How Economists' Value Judgments Creep into Policy Proposals

Even though responsible economists attempt to be as objective as possible, value judgments still creep into their analyses in three ways: interpretation of policymakers' values, interpretation of empirical evidence, and choice of economic models.

Interpretation of the Policymaker's Values
In practice, social goals are seldom so neat that they can be specified A, B, and C; they're vaguely understood and vaguely expressed. An economist will be told, for instance, ''We want to make the poor better off'' or ''We want to see that middle-income people get better housing.'' It isn't clear what *poor, better off,* and *better housing* mean. Nor is it clear how interpersonal judgments should be made when a policy will benefit some individuals at the expense of others, as real-world policies inevitably do.

In practice, social goals are seldom neat; they're generally vaguely understood and vaguely expressed.

Faced with this problem, some academic economists have argued that economists should recommend only policies that benefit some people and hurt no one. Such policies are called **Pareto optimal policies** in honor of the famous Italian economist, Wilfredo Pareto, who first suggested that kind of criterion for judging social change.[1]

Pareto optimal policies Policies that benefit some people and hurt no one.

---

[1] Pareto, in his famous book, *Mind and Society,* suggested this criterion as an analytic approach for theory, not as a criterion for real-world policy. He recognized the importance of the art of economics and that real-world policy has to be judged by much broader criteria.

It's hard to object to the notion of Pareto optimal policies because, by definition, they improve life for some people while hurting no one.

In the real world, Pareto optimal policies don't exist; all real-world policies make some people better off and some people worse off, although it is possible to design composite programs in which winners in one program compensate losers in another.

I'd give you an example of a real-world Pareto optimal policy if I could, but, unfortunately, I don't know of any. Every policy inevitably has some side effect of hurting, or at least seeming to hurt, somebody. In the real world, Pareto optimal policies don't exist. Any economist who has advised governments on real-world problems knows that all real-world policies make some people better off and some people worse off.

But that doesn't mean that economists have no policy role. In their policy proposals, economists try to spell out what a policy's income distributive effects will be, whether a policy will help a majority of people, who those people are, and whether the policy is consistent with the policymaker's value judgments. Doing so isn't easy because the policymaker's value judgments are often vague and must be interpreted by the economist. In that interpretation, the economist's value judgment often slips in.

Q–1: If someone suggests that economists should focus only on Pareto optimal policies, how would you respond?

Interpretation of Empirical Evidence Value judgments further creep into economic policy proposals through economists' interpretations of empirical evidence, which is almost always imprecise. For example, say an economist is assessing the elasticity of a product's demand. She can't run an experiment to isolate prices and quantities demanded; instead she must look at events in which hundreds of other things changed, and do her best to identify what caused what. In selecting and interpreting empirical evidence, a person's values will likely show through, try as one might to be objective. People tend to focus on evidence that supports their position. Economists are trained to be as objective as they can be, but pure objectivity is impossible.

Let's consider an example. In the 1980s, some economists proposed that a large tax be imposed on sales of disposable diapers, citing studies that suggested disposable diapers made up between 15 and 30 percent of the garbage in a landfill. Others objected, citing studies that showed disposable diapers made up only 1 or 2 percent of the refuse going into landfills. Such differences in empirical estimates are the norm, not the exception. Inevitably, if precise estimates are wanted, more studies are necessary. (In this case, the further studies showed that the lower estimates were correct.) But policy debates don't wait for further studies. Economists' value judgments influence which incomplete study they choose to believe is more accurate.

Q–2: How does a radical analysis of labor markets differ from a mainstream neoclassical analysis?

Each model captures different aspects of reality. That's why it's important to be as familiar with as many different models as possible.

Choice of Economic Models Similarly with the choice of models. A model, because it focuses on certain aspects of economic reality and not on others, necessarily reflects certain value judgments, so economists' choice of models must also reflect certain value judgments. Albert Einstein once said that theories should be as simple as possible, but not more so. To that we should add the maxim: Scientists should be as objective and as value-free as possible, but not more so.

This book presents the mainstream neoclassical model of the economy. That model directs us to certain conclusions. Two other general models that some economists follow are a Marxian (radical) model and a public choice (conservative) model. Those other models, by emphasizing different aspects of economic interrelationships, would sometimes direct us to other conclusions.

Let's consider an example. Mainstream neoclassical analysis directs us to look at how the invisible hand achieves harmony and equilibrium through the market. Thus, when neo-classical economists look at labor markets, they generally see supply and demand forces leading to equilibrium. When Marxist economists look at labor markets, their model focuses on the tensions among the social classes, and they generally see exploitation of workers by capitalists. When public choice economists look at labor markets, they see individuals using government to protect their monopolies. Their model focuses on political restrictions that provide rents to various groups. Each model captures different aspects of reality. That's why it's important to be as familiar with as many different models as possible.

Usually economists provide advice for policymakers whose values agree with their own. Economists with liberal values usually provide policy recommendations for liberal policymakers; economists with conservative values usually provide policy recommendations for conservative policymakers. Why? Because of the inevitable influence of economists' value judgments on their policy prescriptions. When economists have the same values as policymakers, they can have a better feel for a policy's harmony with the policymakers' worldview.

Let me give you a personal example. I've generally consulted for liberal policymakers even though the policies I've advocated are often classified as conservative. Why? Because my basic values are consistent with most liberals' values: I don't like people to go hungry, and I believe that we, as a society, should do what we can to help the poor. Paradoxically, much of my policy advice focuses on how existing government policies to help the poor don't achieve their desired ends, and how stronger reliance on market forces would be more effective in achieving those ends. I've found that I simply can't offer advice to politicians who, deep down, don't share my value judgments about what a just society is.

John Maynard Keynes once said that economists should be seen in the same light as dentists—as competent technicians. He was wrong, and his own experience is a contradiction of that view. In dealing with real-world economic policy, Keynes was no mere technician. He had a definite worldview, which he shared with many of the policymakers he advised. An economist who is to play a role in policy formation must be willing to combine value judgments and technical knowledge.

Why Economists Advise Policymakers Who Share Their Value Judgments

Q-3: Why do economists usually advise policymakers who have similar value judgments to the economists' own?

Despite their widely varying values, both liberal and conservative economists agree more often on policy prescriptions than most laypeople think they do. They're economists, after all, and their models focus on certain issues—specifically on incentives and individual choice. All economists believe economic incentives are important, and most economists tend to give significant weight to individuals' ability to choose reasonably. This leads economists, both liberal and conservative, to look at a problem differently than other people do.

Many people think economists of all persuasions look at the world cold-heartedly. That opinion, in my view, of course, isn't accurate, but it's understandable how people could reach it. Economists are taught to look at things in an "objective" way that takes into account a policy's long-run incentive effects as well as the short-run effects. Many of their policy proposals are based upon these long-run incentive effects, which in the short run make the policy look cold-hearted. Economists argue that they aren't being cold-hearted at all, that they're simply being reasonable, and that following their advice will lead to less suffering and more people being helped than following others' advice. They ask, "How can advice that will lead to less suffering be cold-hearted?" This is not to say that all economists' advice will lead to significant long-run benefits and less long-run suffering. Some of it may be simply misguided. You must decide your position on that, but you should decide it knowing economists' defense of their policy suggestion.

Some economists argue that comparing marginal cost and marginal benefit (making efficient decisions) will lead to the most equitable and fairest systems—interpreted as most people would interpret *equitable* and *fairest*. Economists have had problems in getting their ideas fairly expressed in public because their arguments are often long-run arguments, while the press and policymakers usually focus on short-run effects. The problem economists face is similar to the one parents face when they tell their children that they can't eat candy or must do their homework before they can play. Explaining how "being mean" is actually "being nice" to a six-year-old isn't easy.

A former colleague of mine, Abba Lerner, was well known for his strong liberal leanings. The government of Israel called on him for advice on what to do about unemployment. He went to Israel, studied the problem, and presented his advice: "Cut union wages." The government official responded, "But that's the same advice the

AGREEMENT AMONG ECONOMISTS ABOUT SOCIAL POLICY

2 Liberal and conservative economists agree on many policy prescriptions because they use the same models, which focus on incentives and individual choice.

Q-4: When can "being mean" actually be "being nice"?

Eco decisions ARE concerned w/ the long run benefits

conservative economist gave us.'' Lerner answered, ''It's good advice, too.'' The Israeli Labor government then went and did the opposite; it raised wages, thus holding onto its union support in the short run.

Another example comes from a friend who is a World Bank economist. She was lamenting that she had to advise a hospital in a developing country to turn down the offer of a free dialysis machine because the marginal cost of the filters it would have to buy to use the machine significantly exceeded the costs of other life-saving medicines. Economic reasoning involves making such hard decisions.

EXAMPLES OF ECONOMISTS' POLICY ADVICE

The best way to see the consistency and the differences in economists' policy advice is to consider some examples. Some of the following examples bring out certain common characteristics of most economists' policy advice, while others show the differences among economists in values and in empirical interpretations. Let's start with a general consideration of economists' views on regulation.

Economists' Cost/Benefit Approach to Government Regulation

Say that there has been a plane crash in which 200 people died. Newspaper headlines trumpet the disaster while news magazines are filled with stories about how the accident might have been caused, citing speculation about poor maintenance and lack of government regulation. The publicity spreads the sense that ''something must be done'' to prevent such tragedies. Politicians quickly pick up on this, feeling that the public wants action. They introduce a bill outlawing faulty maintenance, denounce poor regulatory procedures, and demand an investigation of sleepy air controllers. In short, they strike out against likely causes of the accident and suggest improved regulations to help prevent any more such crashes.

Economists differ in their views on government regulation of airlines and other businesses, but economists of all ideological persuasions find themselves opposing some of the supposedly problem-solving regulations proposed by politicians. Considering why economists react this way gives you insight into their similarity.

3 Economists believe many regulations are formulated for political expediency and do not reflect cost/benefit considerations.

''Count-from-1-to-10'' Philosophy   One reason economists unite in their opposition to many proposed government regulations is that they believe decisions should be made rationally on the basis of costs and benefits, not on the basis of political expediency.

Their position simply reflects their trained reasonableness. Reasonable people should look at the costs and the benefits of various possible courses of action, and make decisions based on those costs and benefits. After an emotional event like a plane crash, it's difficult to make rational decisions based on costs and benefits. Economists argue that laws enacted quickly in reaction to an emotional event generally will be ill thought out and will reflect the information provided by special interest groups (information that has not necessarily been processed and analyzed by independent observers). Psychologists advise patients not to make major decisions during a time of crisis; economists advise policymakers not to do so either. This advice reflects what we'll call the *count-from-1-to-10* philosophy.

In advising policymakers to stop and count to 10 before recommending new regulations, economists point out that lawmakers have an incentive to act fast—to make it look as if they're doing something when the issue is hot and they're likely to get good press. But by the same reasoning, economists have an incentive to act slowly—to advise studying the issue (by hiring economists to do so) and coming to a ''rational'' conclusion. Whether economists are offering self-serving advice or good advice is for you to decide.

Q-5: Why would a good economist advise a policymaker to be careful about economists' count-from-1-to-10 philosophy?

The Assignment of a Cost and a Benefit to Everything   A second reason economists often find themselves united with one another but at odds with the general public is that their **cost/benefit approach** to problems—assigning costs and benefits, and making one's decision on the basis of those costs and benefits—requires them to determine a quantitative cost and benefit for everything, including life. What's the value of a human life? All of us would like to answer, ''*Infinite*. Each human life is beyond price.'' But if that's true, then in a cost/benefit framework, everything of value should

4 Cost/benefit analysis is analysis in which one assigns a cost and benefit to alternatives, and draws a conclusion on the basis of those costs and benefits.

Basis for Calculation	Value of Life (in 1994 dollars)
Automobile air bag purchases	$ 453,000
Smoke detector purchases	476,000
EPA requirement for sulfur scrubbers	635,000
Wage premiums for dangerous police work	1,080,000
Auto safety features	3,175,000
EPA regulation of radium content in water	3,175,000
Wage premiums for dangerous factory jobs	4,064,000
Seat belt usage	4,070,000
OSHA rules for workplace safety	4,445,000
Premium tire usage	4,572,000
Desire for safer airline travel	15,000,000

EXHIBIT 1   The Value of a Human Life
Such figures are increasingly being used in state and federal courts to support claims for loss of enjoyment of life.

Source: Stan V. Smith, adjunct professor, DePaul College of Law, and president, Corporate Financial Group, Chicago. Used by permission. (Adjusted for inflation by author from 1987 data.)

be spent on preventing death. People should take no chances. They should drive at 30 miles per hour with airbags, triple-cushioned bumpers, double roll bars—you get the picture.

It would be possible for manufacturers to make a car in which no one would die as the result of an accident. The fact is that people don't want such cars. Many people don't buy those auto safety accessories that are already available, and many drivers ignore the present speed limit. Instead, many people want cars with style and speed.

Far from regarding human life as priceless, people make decisions every day that reflect the valuations they place on their own lives. Exhibit 1 presents one economist's estimates of some of these quantitative decisions. These values are calculated by looking at people's revealed preferences (the choices they make when they must pay the costs). To find them, economists calculate how much people will pay to reduce the possibility of their death by a certain amount. If that's what people will pay to avoid death, the cost to them of death can be calculated by multiplying the inverse of the reduced probability by the amount they pay.

For example, say someone will buy a car whose airbags add up to $500 to the vehicle's cost, but won't buy a car whose airbags add more than $500 to its cost. Also say that an airbag will reduce the chance of dying in an automobile accident by 1/720. That means that to increase the likelihood of surviving an auto accident by 1/720, the buyer will pay $500. That also means that the buyer is implicitly valuing his or her life at roughly $360,000 (720 × $500 = $360,000).

Alternatively, say that people will pay an extra $36 for a set of premium tires that reduces the risk of death by 1/100,000. As opposed to having a 3/100,000 chance per year of dying in a skid on the highway, people with premium tires all round have a 2/100,000 chance of dying. (3/100,000 − 2/100,000 = 1/100,000) Multiplying 100,000 (the inverse of the reduction in probability) by $36, the extra cost of the set of premium tires, you find that people who buy these tires are implicitly valuing their lives at $3,600,000.[2]

No one can say whether people know what they're doing in making these valuations, although the inconsistencies in the valuations people place on their lives suggest that to some degree they don't, or that other considerations are entering into their decisions. But even given the inconsistencies, it's clear that people are placing a finite value on life. Most people are aware that in order to ''live'' they must take chances on losing their lives. Economists argue that individuals' revealed choices are the best estimate that society can have of the value of life, and that in making policy society shouldn't pretend that life is beyond value.

The Economist is a British economics magazine that closely follows economic developments in the world.

Q–6: If Exhibit 1 correctly describes the valuation individuals place on life with regard to air bag purchases and safer airline travel, how would you advise them to alter their behavior in order to maximize utility?

Economists argue that individuals' revealed choices are the best estimate that society can have of the value of life, and that in making policy society shouldn't pretend that life is beyond value.

---

[2] For simplicity of exposition, I'm not considering risk preferences or other benefits of these decisions such as lowering the chance of injury.

Placing a value on human life allows economists to evaluate the cost of a crash. Say each life is worth $2 million. If 200 people die in that plane accident and a $200 million plane is destroyed, the cost of the crash is $600 million.

Right after the accident, or even long after the accident, tell a mother and father you're valuing the life of their dead daughter at $2 million and the plane at $200 million, and you'll see why economists have problems with getting their views across. Even if people can agree rationally that a value must be placed on life—that they implicitly give their own lives a value—it's not something they want to deal with emotionally, especially after an accident. Using a cost/benefit approach, an economist must be willing to say, if that's the way the analysis turns out, ''It's reasonable that my son died in this accident because the cost of preventing the accident by imposing stricter government regulations would have been greater than the benefit of preventing it.''

Economists take the emotional heat for making such valuations. Their cost/benefit approach requires them to do so.

Comparing Costs and Benefits of Different Dimensions   After the marginal cost and marginal benefit data have been gathered and processed, one is ready to make an informed decision. Will the cost of a new regulation outweigh the benefit, or vice versa? Here again, economists find themselves in a difficult position in evaluating a regulation about airplane safety. Many of the costs of regulation are small but occur in large numbers. Every time you lament some ''bureaucratic craziness'' (such as a required weekly staff meeting or a form to be signed assuring something has been done), you're experiencing a cost. But when those costs are compared to the benefits of avoiding a major accident, the dimensions of comparison are often wrong.

For example, say it were discovered that a loose bolt was the probable cause of the plane crash. A regulation requiring airline mechanics to check whether that bolt is tightened and, to ensure that they do so, requiring them to fill out a form each time the check is made, might cost $1. How can one compare $1 to the $600 million cost of the crash? Such a regulation obviously makes sense from the perspective of gaining a $600 million benefit from $1 of cost.

But wait. Each plane might have 4,000 similar bolts, each of which is equally likely to cause an accident if it isn't tightened. If it makes sense to check that one bolt, it makes sense to check all 4,000. And the bolts must be checked on each of the 4,000 flights per day. All of this increases the cost of tightening bolts to $16 million per day. But the comparison shouldn't be between $16 million and $600 million. The comparison should be between the marginal cost ($16 million) and the marginal benefit, which depends upon how much tightening bolts will contribute to preventing an accident.

Let's say that the decreased probability of having an accident because of having checked that bolt daily is .001. This means that the check will prevent one out of a thousand accidents that otherwise would have happened. The marginal benefit of checking a particular bolt isn't $600 million (which it would be if you knew a bolt was going to be loose), but is:

$$.001 \times \$600 \text{ million} = \$600,000$$

That $600,000 is the marginal benefit that must be compared to the marginal cost of $16,000,000.

Given these numbers, I leave it to you to decide: Does this hypothetical regulation make sense?

Q–7:   Why should one be very careful about any cost/benefit analysis?

Putting Cost/Benefit Analysis in Perspective   The numbers in our plane crash example are hypothetical. The numbers used in real-world decision making are not hypothetical, but they are often ambiguous. Measuring costs, benefits, and probabilities is difficult, and economists often disagree on specific costs and benefits.

Cost/benefit analyses are often used to justify what one wants to do. For example, from the 1950s to the 1980s the U.S. Army Corps of Engineers always seemed to come up with conclusions that their projects—dams, canals, and the like—made

HEARTBREAK COST/TRAFFIC
BENEFIT

■t's not only the general public that disdains economists' analyses. Sometimes economists disdain them themselves. In 1989, Herbert Stein (a well-known economist who has been, among other things, an economic advisor to a president of the United States) wrote a little piece for *The New York Times* that touched on the empirical problems of implementing cost/benefit analysis.

Stein alluded to a tendency of economists that makes ordinary people think that computer ink and not real blood runs in economists' veins; that where people anatomically locate their hearts, economists have a tidy box of microchips, electronic circuits, a few beeps, and an occasional flashing light. He invented a ''newspaper article'' announcing that a group of economists had studied the costs and benefits of traffic lights. The group concluded that the cost of installing, operating, and maintaining traffic lights, together with the costs incurred by motorists who lost time, wasted gas, and imposed wear and tear on their engines by stopping at red lights, were worth it in terms of lives saved in car accidents that didn't happen—but only just barely worth it. If the lights cost as little as 3 percent more or if lives were worth as little as 3 percent less, it would be cheaper to compensate accident victims and their families than to spend all that money on traffic lights.

Then, pointing out the human weakness for people to choose data to fit their value judgments, he invented another group of economists. The second group, he said, was very upset that any economic study would come to the conclusion that a social expense was worth the money it cost. In fact, the group was so upset that it was sure the first group must have made a mistake in analyzing its data, so the second group was going to conduct the study over again, convinced that this time it would come out the way their model said it should: Don't install traffic lights because they cost too much compared to the return on mere human life, health, and happiness.

Stein's playful story captures two aspects of economists that we've emphasized in this chapter:

1. Economists' tendency to view everything in a cost/benefit framework.
2. Economists'—and everyone else's—tendency to use empirical evidence selectively (that is, to use it to support positions they favor).

sense from a cost/benefit analysis point of view. In the 1990s, there has been a reassessment of many of the corps' projects, and in that reassessment many of the projects no longer make so much sense—the earlier analyses had not taken into account larger environmental costs.

Costs have many dimensions, some more quantifiable than others. Cost/benefit analysis is often biased toward quantifiable costs and away from nonquantifiable costs, or it involves enormous ambiguity as nonquantifiable costs are quantified.

The subjectivity and ambiguity of costs are one reason why economists differ in their views of regulation. In considering any particular regulation, some economists will favor it and some will oppose it. But their reasoning process—comparing marginal costs and marginal benefits—is the same; they differ only on the estimates they calculate.

As a case study, let's consider economists' views of the minimum wage. The basic argument in favor of the minimum wage is that it raises poor people's income. The basic economic argument against the minimum wage is that it prevents market forces from working and creates unemployment. How it does so is captured in Exhibit 2. In it you can see how the minimum wage, W_m, set above the equilibrium wage, W_e, increases the gap between the quantity of labor supplied and the quantity demanded, and thereby creates unemployment equal to $Q_s - Q_d$. The simple argument against the minimum wage is that it creates this unemployment which hurts poor people.

How does one compare the costs and benefits here? First, we must determine how many, and how much, poor people will be helped or hurt. This depends on the elasticities of supply and demand. For example, say the supply and demand curves are highly inelastic. In that case, not many people will lose their jobs because of the

Economists' Debate on Increasing the Minimum Wage

Q–8: Demonstrate graphically the effect of a maximum wage law. Does economic theory tell us such a law would be a bad idea?

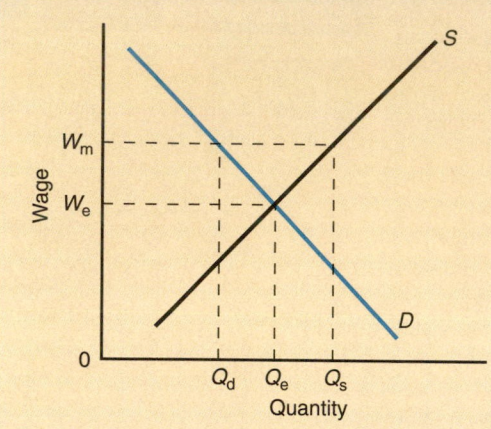

EXHIBIT 2 **The Effect of a Minimum Wage**

A minimum wage creates a gap between the quantity of labor supplied and the quantity of labor demanded, and hence creates unemployment. It helps those who manage to keep their jobs, increasing their wage from the equilibrium wage, W_e, to the minimum wage, W_m. But it hurts those who find that they can't get a job at the minimum wage, or keep a job they already had if the wage goes up (because the employer will just get along without that employee rather than pay more). This is shown by the distance $Q_s - Q_d$.

minimum wage. However if the supply and demand curves are highly elastic, a large number of people will lose their jobs when a minimum-wage law is introduced.

But estimating elasticities isn't sufficient to make a decision on whether a minimum wage is desirable. Another issue that must always be considered is the *general equilibrium* issue. Supply and demand are **partial equilibrium** concepts. They assume ''all other things remain equal.'' But all other things don't remain equal. A minimum wage will cause firms to demand labor-saving machines. This will affect the demand for machines, and the demand for machines will affect the demand for labor. To consider the things that don't remain equal is to consider the general equilibrium issue. **General equilibrium analysis** is the analysis of the simultaneous interaction of all markets. To say that something is a general equilibrium issue is to say that looking at a supply/demand model isn't sufficient. Such general equilibrium considerations make policy debates much more complicated.

You've already had far too many of my interpretations of economists' reasoning, so this time we'll look at the real thing—a debate between economists in *The Christian Science Monitor* concerning the minimum wage. As you read the following two articles, try to decide whether you agree with one or the other. Ask yourself why you agree with one and not the other, and why there's disagreement between the two sides.

Partial equilibrium analysis *Analysis that assumes all other things remain equal.*

General equilibrium analysis *The analysis of the simultaneous interaction of all markets.*

The Debate

RAISING WAGE IS NO HELP TO WORKERS

By Richard B. McKenzie and Walter Wessels

The $1.20-an-hour increase in the federal minimum wage over three years that has been passed by the House of Representatives is not as bad as the vast majority of economists say. It is much worse!

Critics of the increase have focused their analysis on the harm done to the sizable number (100,000 to 750,000, depending on the study cited) of mainly disadvantaged workers who will lose their jobs because of the increase. But the statistical work that we and other economists have done in recent years shows that the increase will even penalize those covered workers who retain their jobs at the higher $4.55 wage rate.

Both proponents and opponents of a minimum-wage increase have misguided the public debate on two counts. First, analysts have failed to recognize that legal wage constraints do not suppress competitive pressures that have kept the wages of workers with limited skills low. Wage constraints only redirect the competitive pressures and, by wiping out tens of thousands of job opportunities, worsen the competitive bind of workers covered by the wage law.

Second, the overwhelming majority of contemporary workers, even low-paid workers, are not compensated *solely* in terms of so many dollars an hour. Rather, they are paid in ''bundles of benefits''—including money, but also including relaxed work demands and a variety of fringe benefits (insurance, rest breaks, flexible schedules, discounts on personal purchases, and on-the-job training, just to name a few).

Although Congress can legislate

an increase in workers' money wage, it exerts little control over the many other nonmoney dimensions of employment. And to contain production costs in competitive markets, employers must respond to mandated money-wage increases with decreases in nonmoney benefits—for example, reductions in on-the-job training, the elimination of fringe benefits, and increases in work demands.

Unfortunately, the combination of mandated money-wage increases and reductions in nonmoney benefits makes workers relatively more costly to hire and, thereby, reduces the demand for—and worsens the competitive position of—covered workers. Though still controversial, this new perspective on the effects of minimum-wage laws is supported by a growing body of research:

- Writing in the *American Economic Review*, Nori Hashimoto found that under the 1967 minimum-wage increase, workers on average lost $1.28 worth of training for every $1 increase in the minimum wage.

- Linda Leighton and Jacob Mincer in one study and Belton Fleisher in another came to a similar conclusion: Increases in the minimum wage reduce on-the-job training—and, as a result, cause workers to lose more in future income growth than they gain from the new minimum wage.

- One of the authors of this article (Mr. Wessels) found that an increase in the minimum wage caused retail establishments in New York to increase work demands. In most stores, fewer workers were given fewer hours to do the same work.

- The research of Mr. Fleisher, William Alpert, and L. F. Dunn shows that minimum-wage increases lead to large reductions in fringe benefits and to worsening working conditions.

Given the findings of various studies, we estimate that every $1-an-hour increase in the minimum wage will cause workers to give up a minimum of $1.20 an hour in employment benefits, making them 20 cents an hour worse off in terms of the money value of their total "payment bundles." This means that the proposed $1.20-an-hour increase in the minimum wage will, on balance, make the covered workers worse off by at least 24 cents an hour. In short, increasing the minimum wage is a political recipe for making many very low-income workers, even those who retain their jobs, worse off.

Richard McKenzie is professor of economics at the University of Mississippi. Walter Wessels is an associate professor of economics at North Carolina State University.

Source: *The Christian Science Monitor*, May 8, 1989. Courtesy Richard B. McKenzie and Walter Wessels.

'BAD SIDE' OF A HIGHER WAGE ISN'T SO BAD

By George Ignatin

How can we explain the remarkable compassion that conservatives have suddenly shown toward the working poor in response to efforts to raise the minimum wage? Or some of the statements made by supposedly thoughtful economists? Like Nori Hashimoto's contention that when minimum wages are raised by $1, businesses decrease training by $1.28—as if businessmen, displaying their well-known eleemosynary tendencies, were giving their least skilled workers more training than was profitable to the business.

Which raises the point: How much and what kind of "training" do businesses provide minimum-wage workers? Picture the typical such worker: an usher at a theater, a bag boy at the supermarket, a cashier at a video-rental store. Now picture the training that is done: $1.28 worth an hour, three to eight hours a day; and for six months—as envisioned by President Bush's proposal for a sub-minimum training wage. This proposal presumes far more training than would occur and is fraught with potential abuse: Minimum-wage jobs have extremely high turnover rates. Most last less than six months. So the President's "training wage" could easily become *the* wage. All new employees would be defined as trainees; after six months, if they lasted that long, they'd be declared trained, and replaced with a new class of trainees.

Three other economists claim that an increase in the minimum wage will be offset by a reduction in benefits. Although we'd expect *some* decrease, they have the gall to count breaks from work as benefits of the job, which makes one wonder why they didn't also count the geographical knowledge obtained by employees in their trips to work.

Most economists agree that an increase in the minimum wage would cost some jobs, but the operative word is "some." The congressional bill would increase the minimum next year by about 15 percent. The best estimates are that this would lead to a decrease in employment of minimum-wage labor by one-quarter to one-fifth of that—say about 3.5 percent—or about 90,000 workers. If the minimum wage was raised to $4.55 an hour in one jump (a 36 percent increase), employment would fall by 180,000 to 240,000. Although less than 10 percent of minimum-wage workers would be laid off, more than 90 percent would keep their jobs and be paid more.

But it's not quite that simple. One of the more important concepts in economics has to do with substitution effects. When those minimum-wage workers lose their jobs, what do employers do? Sweep the floors and clean the toilets themselves? Historically, they lay off their least productive labor and hire more-productive workers, generally adult women, at slightly higher wages. Three 25-year-old women at $5 or $6 an hour to do the work of four 17-year-olds. They also pay their more highly skilled workers slightly more.

So next year, there would be a transfer of jobs, with 90,000 fewer teens and 60,000 *more* adults working—all at higher wages. And most of the unemployed teens would reenroll in school, and some of them might even improve their future job prospects.

Another thing employers do is substitute capital—machinery—for labor, and this allows workers to be more productive. Unfortunately, many minimum-wage jobs can't be performed efficiently by machines—unless we devise assembly-line hamburger shaper/cookers or motorized wash rags.

Other employers won't lay off anyone; they'll simply absorb the increase and their costs will go up. That's why businesses are opposed to the increase. Especially small businesses (with large numbers of unskilled workers) operating in highly competitive product markets that discourage price increases.

Thus, the "bad" side of a minimum wage increase isn't all that bad: For every worker or small businessman who suffers from it, there will be 15 to 30 workers who will benefit.

The US has historically paid the highest wages in the world and until the mid-1970s was highly competitive in

world markets. But in the last 15 years, it has tried the competitive method of third-world countries: low wages, small amounts of capital (relative to countries like Japan), and relatively stagnant technology. This method hasn't worked very well.

George Ignatin is associate professor of economics at the University of Alabama at Birmingham.

Source: *The Christian Science Monitor,* May 8, 1989. Courtesy George Ignatin.

Ways in which Economists Differ   Reading this debate should have brought home the point that economists differ, often substantially, about policy. On the surface, the economists who wrote these articles seem to disagree about everything. But closer examination of the articles shows that, while their conclusions differ, the assumptions underlying their analysis have much in common. For example, both use a cost/benefit framework. They also both view individuals—low-wage workers and employers—as rational. Where they differ is in their empirical estimates and in their view of the side effects of an increase in the minimum wage.

Let's consider those differences.

Differences in Empirical Estimates   Notice in both articles the wide range of empirical estimates of the effect on employment levels of an increase in the minimum wage to $4.55 an hour. McKenzie and Wessels state that anywhere from 100,000 to 750,000 workers would lose their jobs. Ignatin estimates there would be 180,000 to 240,000 additional unemployed people. Such a wide range of empirical estimates is typical of most economic debates. Even using complicated, sophisticated techniques, economists simply can't provide exact empirical estimates of a given policy's effects. Inevitably there will be disagreements and different views, depending on which estimates one believes.

Making these estimates is an important part of economists' work, and that's why one must, in order to become an economist, study statistics and have a good sense of the economic institutions to know whether one's formal empirical estimates make sense. In making and interpreting empirical estimates, it is important to recognize that much more than formal statistical training is necessary. Notice how Professor Ignatin scorns the formal empirical estimate that workers on average lose $1.28 in training for every $1 increase in the minimum wage. He asks if the reader believes that a "typical worker" receives $1.28 in training for each hour worked. He relies on the reader's institutional knowledge of how much training occurs in minimum-wage jobs and strongly suspects that the reader's answer will be no.

One must, of course, be careful in relying on the reader's institutional knowledge. The lost training is in the jobs the workers would have had if the minimum-wage increase hadn't occurred, not in the jobs they actually had. What those potential jobs would have provided in the way of training must be based on projections of future jobs, not on jobs that currently exist.

5 Economists disagree about minimum wage policy because of differences in empirical estimates of direct and of side effects.

Differences in Side Effects   A second way in which the economists differ is in the side effects they see stemming from a particular policy. McKenzie and Wessels see

How government can best contribute to quality education is much in debate. © *Bill Bachmann/The Image Works.*

employers reducing nonwage benefits of a job in response to having to pay a higher minimum wage. They argue that the minimum-wage increase will make those minimum-wage workers *who retain their jobs* worse off, as well as the ones who lose their jobs.

Ignatin focuses on a different side effect. He points out that the jobs done by the minimum-wage workers would still need to be done, and that more workers would be needed to produce the machines to do these jobs. Although there might be a decrease in the total number of minimum-wage jobs, an increase in the minimum wage would also lead to higher-paying jobs producing and using machines.

Lessons from the Debate   I presented the debate not only for you to decide who's right and who's wrong, but to show you an example of a real-world economic debate. The presentation is meant to convey to you the need for openness and caution in judging any economic debate.

Openness   Once you get into the real world, policy issues become cloudy. Any debate turns on differences in empirical estimates and on differing views of the side effects of policies, just as does this debate about the minimum wage. Reading only one side of a debate is a way to come to a conclusion about the issue, but it is not a way to come to a *correct* conclusion.

All real-world issues have many sides. To decide a question of economic policy, it's important to read and carefully consider *all* views: radical, liberal, conservative. Each has something to contribute.

Caution   Good economists can write well. Their arguments are, or at least should be, convincing. But good economists exist on all sides of most issues, and after reading all the convincing arguments, the answer you'll arrive at on many issues is "It depends." You, as an introductory student, generally don't have the background or the institutional knowledge to come to a final conclusion.

There's nothing wrong in arriving at an indefinite answer like "It depends." All too often students feel they must decide an economic issue when, in fact, they don't have sufficient economic information, experience, and training to make an informed judgment. In such cases, caution (admitting that the answer depends on a variety of factors) is well advised. That doesn't mean you don't make tentative decisions— inevitably you must decide without full information. It simply means that you keep an open mind to new evidence and arguments and always are willing to change that decision.

To decide a question of economic policy, it's important to read and carefully consider all *views: radical, liberal, conservative.*

Q–9:   A student has just answered a question by saying, "It depends." If she were in the textbook author's class, how would he likely respond?

A Political Economist Speaks about How to Make Public Schools Better

As a second case study of real-world economic policy I consider a speech that John Chubb, a senior fellow at the Brookings Institution (a Washington, DC, economic think tank), presented to a group of educators, summarizing some of his work.[3]

I present the speech for a number of reasons. First, Chubb is a good political economist, and his arguments are absorbing. Second, the topic (education) is one that most people are interested in and have some knowledge about. And third, it shows economic analysis applied to a broader issue than those to which it's usually applied in economics textbooks. Economic reasoning has had an enormous impact on the management and organizational structure of many kinds of organizations, and this selection gives you a sense of that influence.

MAKING SCHOOLS BETTER

By John Chubb

Most of you are familiar with the state of American education. Just to give you some basic statistics, for roughly 20 years from the mid-1960s until the mid-1980s, the SAT scores of American students dropped sharply. Although scores have been going up for the last few years, they've recently stalled. Our students still are well behind where they were in 1965.

In addition, the dropout rate in the United States is about 25 percent. That is to say, 25 percent of our students are not finishing high school on time. In many of our large cities only half of the students finish high school on time.

Comparing the United States to countries around the world is even more depressing. In math and science, U.S. students rank dead last in any comparison with students from the nations that are our leading competitors. . . .

There is a bit of good news. For the last five years, Americans, mostly at the state level, have been trying very hard to turn things around. . . . [W]hen reports began to come out suggesting various ways to improve our nation's school systems, a lot of skeptics said we could never find that much money. But . . . we have spent far more money than any of the skeptics thought possible.

Between 1981 and 1986 expenditures per pupil for elementary and secondary education went up 40 percent.

In real terms we now spend four times as much per child as we did in 1950. In the first half of the 1980s, teachers enjoyed larger salary increases than any other occupational group in the country. Their salaries are still arguably too low, $29,000 per year, but they have gone up very quickly. We've also spent a good deal of money to reduce the size of classes.

There has been a crackdown on teacher incompetence. Teachers are being asked to take more tests, to demonstrate that they are able. There has been a crackdown on student underachievement. Graduation and promotion requirements are being boosted around the country.

This is very heartening because it is unusual for our political system to act so forthrightly. Clearly, Americans are taking the problem seriously. Unfortunately, the prospects that these reforms will make much of a difference are not very good. That is doubly discouraging because we may be wasting a rare political opportunity to really do something.

Why am I willing to say that what has been taking place is not likely to make much of a difference? The reasons are reflected in the study I did . . . [e]ntitled "What Price Democracy?" . . .

This study included 500 randomly selected high schools nationwide, public and private. Within these high schools it included the principals, 12,000 teachers, and 12,000 students. We've never before had, in this country, a data set that puts together such detailed information on both students and the schools that they've attended. Large studies usually concentrate on either schools or students. We've combined the two.

The other thing that is virtually unique about this data set is that the students were examined not once, but twice. They were examined when they began high school as sophomores, and again when they graduated. Thus we were able to study not simply changes in the levels of student achievement over time, but how a particular group of students progressed.

We focused on one major issue . . . academic achievement. We used five tests: math, science, reading, writing, and vocabulary, and combined the results into a comprehensive measure of student achievement between sophomore year and graduation.

After determining which students were achieving and which were failing, we sought to uncover the sources of success or failure. First came a bit of bad news: The most important determinant of how students achieve is their aptitude. Bright kids learn more in high school than kids that aren't so bright. There is a certain amount of student achievement that is beyond the reach of school reformers.

But the good news is that the second most important determinant of how well students do is the school they attend. The skeptics of the 1960s and '70s, who doubted that schools could make a difference, were wrong.

---

[3] The occasion for the speech was a Manhattan Institute Seminar entitled "Making Schools Better," sponsored by a grant from the Gannett Corporation; it was published by the Manhattan Institute as Manhattan Paper #5. Reprinted with the permission of the Manhattan Institute for Policy Research.

Schools make a big difference. They are marginally more important than the influence of parents. They are far more important than the influence of peer groups.

The next question naturally is, "What makes the difference between successful and unsuccessful schools?" Let me begin by telling you what doesn't make a difference. Neither expenditures, teacher salaries, class size, graduation requirements, the amount of homework assigned, or any other individual school policy that we looked at matters. There was no correlation between student achievement and any of the variables on which school reformers have been concentrating so much time, effort, and money. That is why there is very little reason to believe that school reform, as it is proceeding, is going to work.

What will work? For any of you who are involved in management, the answer may seem pretty obvious. The thing about schools that really seems to matter is how they're organized. To begin with, good and bad schools have different goals. The schools that are succeeding, whether with poor students or the best students, consciously focus on academic achievement. If you ask personnel in these schools what their goal is, they will say, "academic achievement," or "academic excellence." People in schools that aren't doing so well say things like "the basics," "occupational training," or "citizenship." These goals may well be important. But if you want achievement the school has to focus on achievement.

I should also say that clarity and consensus about goals are as important as what you call the goal. The thing that distinguishes successful schools is that there is a real consensus within those organizations about what they are trying to achieve, whether they say, "the basics," or "academic excellence." . . . The schools in our survey that were succeeding consciously focused on one purpose.

Another important aspect of organization was leadership. The principals of successful and unsuccessful schools were as different as night and day. Successful schools were led by principals whom the teachers said had a vision,

knew where they wanted the school to go, and knew how to take the school in that direction. These are standard qualities of strong leadership. Also, the principals in the good schools were educationally oriented and thought of themselves as educational leaders, not administrators.

When we asked principals of unsuccessful schools why they became principals they would say things like: "I prefer administration to teaching." When asked what their long-term goals were, unsuccessful principals were much more likely to say, "I want to get out of the school, move up into the central office and rise in the administrative hierarchy."

In the successful schools, the principals wanted to stay in the schools. When you asked them why they became principals, they were more likely to say, "Because I wanted to take control of the school. I wanted to control personnel, I wanted to control policy." They wanted to lead, not merely manage.

The other profound organizational difference was that in successful schools [the staff's] sense of professionalism, independence, and responsibility for one's work was enormously higher. Teachers and principals in the successful schools were true professionals. Those in the unsuccessful schools weren't professionals at all. The teachers in successful schools had more independence, they participated more extensively in school decisions, and they had more influence over those decisions. Within their classrooms they were free to tailor their practices to the needs of the students. . . . In the successful schools teachers had discretion. To us, the concept that best summarized the difference between the successful and unsuccessful school organizations was that of a team. In successful schools the organization was held together by consensus and cooperation, not primarily by rules and regulations. The unsuccessful school looked like a classic bureaucracy, held together primarily by rules and regulations—a hierarchy, not a team at all.

If strong leadership, clear goals, professionalism and team spirit are what is important, how do you instill

these somewhat elusive qualities in a school? Can it be done at all?

Many state legislatures believe that it can be done by sending teachers and principals to classes. . . . But if you look around the country at successful school organizations, it doesn't appear that formal management training accounts for much.

We took a careful look at what accounts for effective organization. The key determinant, more important than anything else, turns out to be autonomy. Successful schools were relatively independent of external influence by administrators: superintendents, central office bureaucrats, and union officials. A school that was free to chart its own course was much more likely to develop effective organization and thereby breed academic achievement.

Principals who had greater influence over curriculum, instruction, discipline, and especially hiring and firing, put together effective organizations. It doesn't take much insight to figure out why. If you're a principal and you get to determine who teaches in that school and what the school's resources are, you are much more likely to trust the members of the organization, which, after all, you assembled. You are more likely to treat them as members of the team and grant them the autonomy they need to do their jobs. If you don't have control over personnel, you're less likely to treat people as if they're team members. You distrust them. You believe there is going to be conflict and you regulate. Soon you have an organization that is held together not by a common vision but by rules and regulations, that is, a bureaucracy. . . .

If you don't find autonomy in public schools except under unusual circumstances, you almost always find it in private schools, including religious schools. Private schools are more autonomous and, all things being equal, have more effective organizations and perform better than public schools. . . .

In the course of explaining about autonomy to a reporter, I told him that in New York City they have an enormous central office bureaucracy, staffed by 5,000 people, which is tremendously overbearing and leaves the principals with very little influence over their schools. I contrasted this with the Catholic school system in New York City, which despite the church's reputation for hierarchy has only 50 people in its central office, though the system has almost a quarter of the students the public schools have. [Later] I saw all these numbers and I thought, "Five thousand versus fifty! I better double-check," because [originally I had gathered them from different] sources.

I called the personnel office of the city school system and said, "I have a simple question: How many people work in the central office of the New York City School System?" The first person I reached had no idea, nor did the second or third, but they all promised to transfer me to someone who did.

Thirty-five minutes and many transfers later, I got to a person who said, "Yes, I do know the number, but if you want to know, you'll have to put your request in writing, send it through proper channels and we'll get the information back to you in a month." . . . (Finally I was told . . . it wasn't 5,000, it was 6,000.)

. . . I got someone in [the Catholic school system] central office and said, "I need some basic facts. I need to know the number of students in your school system." She told me. "I need to know the number of teachers in your school system." She told me. "I need to know the number of schools in the system." She told me. So I said, "The last thing I need to know is how many people work in the central bureaucracy of the Catholic school system in New York City."

And she said, "I'm sorry, we don't keep that kind of data."

"Well," I said, "would you have any idea? Is there any way you could get the number for me?"

And she said: "Just a minute—I'll count them." And she counted. There are 25. Twenty-five people running a school system that's a fifth to a quarter of the size of the public school system.

Public and private education are organized in an enormously different fashion. Those differences between the performance of public schools and private schools account for all of the differences between the performance of public schools and most of the differences between good public schools and bad public schools.

The message for reformers [is] . . . if you want schools to be organized more effectively and to teach more successfully, you must give them autonomy. But, as any public school administrator will tell you, you can't just turn over a school to principals and teachers without holding them accountable in some way. You've got to provide autonomy without losing accountability. And once public school administrators begin thinking about accountability, they think about tests and rules and regulations and before you know it the autonomy is done.

The only way to provide autonomy without losing accountability is to go to a different system of accountability. A top-down system will not work. You must build a system of accountability to parents and students rather than to politicians and administrators.

It works in the private sector. Private schools are held accountable to their constituency through the process of competition and choice. Similarly, the surest way to get autonomy and accountability into the public school system is not through regulation or spending, but through a mechanism of choice. There are many ways in which choice systems can be set up. Vouchers, open enrollments, magnet schools, and others.

Lessons from the Speech: Aspects of Economic Reasoning   Chubb's speech shows you economics being applied to the real world. It shows you how economists view issues that are outside the customary realm of economics. While costs and benefits aren't specifically mentioned, they lie behind Chubb's analysis. The speech also shows how economists and other social scientists use statistical data and how they apply economic reasoning in order to understand real-world problems and to propose solutions to them. Let's consider some of these aspects of economic reasoning a bit more carefully.

Economists focus on competitive pressures.

Economists Focus on Competitive Pressures   Notice that supply/demand analysis does not explicitly show up in the speech, but there's a sense of the strength of competition that supply/demand analysis is designed to convey. For example, Chubb points out that competitive pressures on private schools force them to be accountable—to meet the problems and solve them. Competitive pressures are behind the dynamic laws of supply and demand. That argument is the key to his speech.

Economists do not always favor the market solution.

Economists Do Not Always Favor the Market Solution   Although the argument concerns competitive pressures, the policies Chubb presents are not only a proposal to "create a market in educational services." At the end of the speech he presents a few ways in which accountability might be achieved: open enrollment, magnet schools, and vouchers. A voucher system, in which students are given vouchers and are allowed to spend those vouchers at whatever school they want, is a type of market solution. The others are not market solutions.

Also notice that Chubb's argument is not an argument for profit over nonprofit organizations; it's a comparison of two nonprofit school systems. Despite the fact that we focus on market incentives in introductory courses, economists don't always argue for the market and for profit-making firms over all other types of organizations. What they do argue for is the need to take competitive pressures into account in analyzing any type of organizational structure.

Economists acknowledge that spending more money doesn't necessarily solve problems. Clearly spending money on a problem is often part of the solution, but many economists believe that one should first look at the internal organization of the troubled institution. Notice that Chubb points out that in real terms spending per pupil has increased fourfold since the 1950s and yet, as a result of organizational problems, education is achieving less than it did in the 1950s.

Economists Recognize All the Invisible Forces

Economists recognize that monetary incentives (the invisible hand) aren't the only influence on behavior. In their real-world policy prescriptions, they take account of other forces as well. Chubb's argument isn't based on self-interest. He doesn't necessarily call for the privatization and profitization of schools (as some other economists have). The issues he focuses on are autonomy and accountability of teachers and administrators. Autonomy is desirable not only because it allows competitive pressures to operate, but also because it helps engender and foster a team spirit. Accountability is necessary because it makes individuals' incentives consistent with organizational goals.

In their practical work, economists take into account the strength of the invisible handshake. Much of management theory explores how the invisible hand and the invisible handshake can be integrated and made stronger.

Economists recognize all the invisible forces.

Economists Use Empirical Evidence

A fourth point to recognize is that Chubb has collected and uses empirical evidence in his argument. This is another trait of good economic reasoning. In making judgments, economists try to present quantitative data to back up their views. Notice that Chubb doesn't simply say that public education is in worse shape than it used to be. He quantifies his assertion by reporting SAT scores, dropout rates, and international comparisons.

The empirical research underlying economists' arguments helps make them persuasive. When the empirical evidence leads to a position different from the one that economic theory would have predicted, an honest economist still presents that evidence. For example, Chubb's evidence suggests that higher salaries haven't made a difference, even though the standard economic model would predict that they would. In this speech to noneconomists, Chubb didn't have any need to explore why his estimate departed from the estimate predicted by the standard model. Chubb's audience wasn't concerned with an issue like why there were deviations from the standard model. In a discussion with economists, though, that finding would have been subject to careful scrutiny.

Quantifying provides a structure for economists' research. They don't simply go and study a problem. They design a quantitative study and use information they gather from the study to structure their analysis of the problem. Of course, quantification by itself isn't sufficient. The empirical evidence must be interpreted, and general, nonquantifiable conclusions must be drawn. Chubb doesn't shy away from doing so.

Economists use empirical evidence.

Economists Tend to Dislike Bureaucracy

Chubb's speech reflects the somewhat negative attitude toward administrators and bureaucracy that many economists share. It follows from their basic view of human nature. Economists see self-interested individuals as trying to build little monopolies in order to make their lives easier. In Chubb's speech we see this view coming out in his discussion of how administrators are more interested in protecting their positions than in educating kids.

Economists tend to dislike bureaucracy.

Q-10: Why do economists tend to dislike bureaucracy?

Suppose that you are an influential member of the U.S. government and that you and a group of your powerful colleagues are worried about how expensive housing has become. Millions of low-income people are living in run-down houses or apartments or doubling up with friends and relatives. Some even sleep in their cars or spend their lives wandering the streets without any regular place to live at all.

You're in a position to write a law and get it passed. You do enact a law, a "Low-Income Housing Act." You state your purpose: "It is the policy of the United States to assist the States and their subdivisions to remedy the unsafe and unsanitary housing conditions and the acute shortage of decent, safe, and sanitary dwellings for families of low income."

You believe that when this program gets going, old housing will be rehabilitated, new housing will be built, and these units will be made available to low-income families at rents they can afford.

You institute the program and it's initially a success: All available units are rented. But its success creates an incentive problem. Once in such a unit, a family does its best to remain there. That's not what you intended; you intended that as families benefited from this assistance, they would gradually improve their circumstances and income, and move on to homes of their own or the better apartments

available on the open market. This would make room for other low-income families to move in and begin their own move up the economic ladder.

But what's the incentive for a family fortunate enough to obtain one of these units? The incentive is to remain a low-income family in order to continue to qualify for the "decent, safe, and sanitary dwelling" where it lives. Given this incentive there's little turnover in these units. When occupants die, relatives and even friends struggle to remain in the units under a provision that permits "remaining occupants" to continue to live there.

Another incentive problem is that landlords have no incentive to keep rents below the rent that similar units outside the program command, because as long as the rent doesn't exceed fair market rents in the area, the occupants need pay only 30 percent of their monthly income in rent. Rent increases don't matter to the occupants. They continue to pay only 30 percent of their income, with the government paying the difference.

How can I be so sure about the problems of such a law? Because the law I describe exists in the United States. Called *Section 8 Housing*, it's administered by the U.S. Department of Housing and Urban Development (HUD). In 1989, Congress began a series of investigations into this program's administration, and it found that the law was failing because of incentives inherent in the program.

What stops people from following their own self-interest beyond some limits is competition. Large organizations generally have little competition and, thus, economists are suspicious of them unless they are operating in a highly competitive market structure. Public school administrations generally don't face significant competition, so economists approach public administration with a certain cynicism.

At times that cynicism is unwarranted; many public administrators have a commitment to doing a good job efficiently and fairly. Economists recognize that such administrators exist, but believe that institutional incentives often undercut any commitment to efficiency even in the most committed administrator.

A Qualification   Chubb's speech is an example of good economic reasoning watered down and homogenized for presentation to the lay public. It is, however, an advocacy presentation and not a neutral presentation. For example, his argument doesn't point out some of the costs of the autonomy he recommends for principals and teachers. A critic would point out that often autonomy is used in the wrong way—to line the pockets of administrators, or to make unfair decisions and wasteful expenditures. An economist who wasn't advocating a certain position would have outlined the costs as well as the benefits.

ECONOMISTS, POLICYMAKERS, AND POLICY

Economics teaches people to be reasonable—sickeningly reasonable, some people would say. I hope that this chapter has given you some sense of what I mean by that. Economists' cost/benefit approach to problems (which pictures a world of individuals whose self-interested actions are limited only by competition) makes them look for the self-interest behind individuals' actions, and for how competition can direct that self-interest into the public interest.

In an economist's framework,

· Well-intentioned policies often are prevented by individuals' self-seeking activities.
· Policies that relieve immediate suffering often have long-run consequences that create more suffering.
· Politicians have more of an incentive to act fast—to look as if they're doing something—than to take enough time to get something done well that makes sense from a cost/benefit point of view.

I've argued that it's important for economic considerations to be taken into account in decision making, and that people are, over the long haul, rational. But in proposing policies that will work, economists must also keep in mind that, in the short run, people are often governed by emotion, swayed by mass psychology, and irrational. Politicians and other policymakers know that; the laws and regulations they propose reflect such calculations. Politicians often tell academic economists, "Yes, your arguments are reasonable, but politically I must reflect my constituents' positions. I'd be eaten alive if I followed your advice."

Politicians don't get elected and reelected by constantly saying that all choices have costs and benefits. And so, while policymakers listen to the academic economists they ask for advice, and in private frequently agree with those advisors, in practice they often choose to ignore economists' policy recommendations.

The way economic reasoning influences policy can be subtle. Sometimes one sees an elaborate charade acted out: A politician puts forward a bill that from a cost/benefit viewpoint doesn't make sense but that makes her look good. She hopes the bill won't pass, but she also hopes that presenting the bill will allow enough time to pass so that emotions can cool and a more reasonable bill can be put forward. Other times, compromise bills are proposed that incorporate as much cost/benefit policy as possible, but also appeal to voters' emotional sense. So economists and economic reasoning do influence policy.

Still, all too often (in my view), economists' advice is dumped as irrelevant, and special interest groups' policies are adopted instead. Social policy made in the real world reflects a balancing of cost/benefit analysis and special interest desires. Walking on that political tightrope is an art in which academic economists, in their role as economists, have little training.

When they propose policies, academic economists don't have to deal with such concerns. From their ivory towers they put ideas into the real world, and they help students better understand the reasoning behind those ideas. Often the ideas don't have a snowball's chance in hell of being implemented, but the ideas do make people think and influence *the way* they think. That's the payoff many economists are looking for. You'll understand policy proposals better if you bear in mind that the goal behind them isn't always to get them implemented.

As you can see, applying economics is much more than muttering "supply and demand" to explain every situation. Thomas Carlyle, who, as we saw in an earlier introductory quotation, argued that all you have to do is teach a parrot the words *supply and demand*, was wrong. Economics involves the thoughtful use of economic insights and empirical evidence. If this book is giving you a sense of the nature of that thoughtful application along with the core of economic reasoning, then it's succeeding in its purpose.

Policy for the Real World

The way economic reasoning influences policy can be subtle.

Parrots and Economic Reasoning

6 Applying economics is much more than muttering "supply and demand." Economics involves the thoughtful use of economic insights and empirical evidence.

CHAPTER SUMMARY

- Economists differ because of different underlying value judgments, because empirical evidence is subject to different interpretations, and because their underlying models differ.

- Value judgments inevitably work their way into policy advice, but good economists try to be objective.

- Economists tend to agree on certain issues because their training is similar.

- The economic approach to analyzing issues is a cost/benefit approach.

- Economists generally have reservations about regulations.

- Collecting and using empirical evidence is an important part of economics.

- Collecting and interpreting empirical evidence is difficult, which contributes to disagreements among economists.

- Economics involves the thoughtful use of economic insights and empirical evidence.

KEY TERMS

cost/benefit approach   *(768)*
general equilibrium
  analysis   *(772)*

Pareto optimal
  policies   *(765)*

partial equilibrium
  analysis   *(772)*

QUESTIONS FOR THOUGHT AND REVIEW

The number after each question represents the estimated degree of critical thinking required. (1 = almost none; 10 = deep thought.)

1. Could anyone object to a Pareto optimal policy? Why? *(8)*

2. Would it be wrong for economists to propose only Pareto optimal policies? *(9)*

3. Would all economists oppose price controls? Why or why not? *(7)*

4. Should body organs be allowed to be bought or sold? Why or why not? *(8)*

5. In cost/benefit terms, explain your decision to take an economics course. *(6)*

6. How much do you value your life in dollar terms? Are your decisions consistent in that valuation? *(9)*

7. If someone offered you $1,000,000 for one of your kidneys, would you sell it? Why or why not? *(7)*

8. Should the minimum wage be eliminated? Why? *(8)*

9. What did John Chubb find is the most important reason for the difference between a successful school and an unsuccessful school? *(5)*

10. Why might an economist propose a policy that has little chance of adoption? *(4)*

PROBLEMS AND EXERCISES

1. Demonstrate graphically, and explain why, both perfect competition and a perfectly discriminating monopoly lead to a Pareto optimal outcome.

2. Say that the cost of a car crash is $8,000. Assume further that installing a safety device in a car at a cost of $12 will reduce the probability of an accident by .05 percent. The plant makes 1,000 cars each day.
   a. If the preceding are the only relevant costs, would you favor or oppose the installation of the safety device?
   b. What other costs might be relevant?

3. In a study of hospital births, the single most important prediction factor of the percentage of vaginal births as opposed to Caesarean (C-section) births was ownership status of hospitals—whether they were for for-profit or non-profit.
   a. Which had more C-sections, and why?
   b. What implications about the health care debate can you draw from the above results?
   c. How might the results change if the for-profit hospital received a fixed per-patient payment as it would in a managed care system?

4. The technology is now developing so that road-use can be priced by computer. A computer in the surface of the road picks up a signal from your car and automatically charges you for the use of the road.

a. How could this technological change contribute to ending bottlenecks and rush hour congestion? Demonstrate how graphically.

b. How will people likely try to get around the system?

c. If people know when the prices will change, what will likely happen immediately before? How might this be avoided?

5. In the early 1990s, the 14- to 17-year-old population fell because of low birth rates in the mid-1970s. Simultaneously the echo from the past was the baby boom, and late-aging baby boomers who decided to have kids combined to increase the number of babies and hence to increase the number of parents needing baby sitters. What effect will these two events likely have on:

a. The number of times parents go out without their children?

b. The price of baby sitters?

c. The average age of baby sitters?

6. As organ transplants become more successful, scientists are working on ways to transplant animal organs to humans. Pigs are the odds-on favorites as ''donors'' since their organs are about the same size as human organs.

a. What would the development of such organ farms likely do to the price of pigs?

b. If you were an economic adviser to the government, would you say that such a development would be Pareto-optimal (for humans)?

c. Currently, there is a black market in human organs. What would this development likely do to that market?

7. If one uses a willingness-to-pay measure in which life is valued at what people are willing to pay to avoid risks that might lead to death, the value of a U.S. citizen's life is $2.6 million, a Swede's life is worth $1.2 million, and a Portuguese's life is worth $20,000 (according to an article in *The Journal of Transport Economics and Policy*).

a. What policy implications does this value schedule have?

b. Say you operate an airline. Should you spend more on safety precautions in the United States than you do in Portugal?

c. Should safety standards be lower in Portugal and Sweden than in the United States?

8. According to U.S. government statistics, the cost of averting a premature death differs among various regulations. Car seat belt standards cost $100,000 per premature death avoided while hazardous waste landfill disposal bans cost $4.2 trillion per premature death avoided.

a. If you were choosing between these two regulations, which would you choose? Why?

b. If these figures are correct, should neither, one, the other, or both of these regulations be implemented?

9. A 29-year-old politician, Anthony Zielinski, who was a member of the Milwaukee Board of Supervisors, proposed that the county government sell the organs of dead welfare recipients to help pay off the welfare recipients' welfare costs and burial expenses.

a. What was the likely effect of that proposal?

b. Why was that the effect?

10. Technology will soon exist such that individuals can choose the sex of their offspring. Assume that technology has now arrived and that 70 percent of the individuals choose male offspring.

a. What effect will that have on social institutions such as families?

b. What effect will it have on dowries—payments made by the bride's family to the groom—which are still used in a number of developing countries?

c. Why might an economist suggest that if 70 percent male were the expectation, families would be wise to have daughters rather than sons?

ANSWERS TO MARGIN QUESTIONS

1. I would respond that in the real world, Pareto optimal policies don't exist, and all real-world policies make someone better off and someone worse off. In making real-world policy judgments, one cannot avoid the difficult distributional and broader questions. It is those more difficult questions, which are value-laden, that make economic policy an art rather than a science. *(766)*

2. A radical analysis of the labor market differs from the mainstream neoclassical analysis in that it emphasizes the tensions among social classes. Thus a radical analysis will likely see exploitation built into the institutional structure. Mainstream neoclassical analysis is much more likely to take the institutional structure as given and not question it. *(766)*

3. Economists usually advise policymakers who have value judgments similar to theirs because those similar value judgments give economists a better feel for a policy's harmonies with the policymaker's worldview. Any economist who is to play a role in policy formation must be willing to combine value judgments and technical knowledge. *(767)*

4. Oftentimes being ''mean'' in the short run can actually involve being ''nice'' in the long run. The reason is that often policy effects that are beneficial in the long run have short-run costs, and people focusing on those short-run costs see the policy as ''mean.'' *(767)*

5. Economists' count-from-one-to ten philosophy emphasizes the need for rational cost/benefit analysis, which cannot be conducted in an emotionally charged environment. A good economist would advise a policymaker to be careful about economists' count-from-one-to-ten philosophy because it involves potentially self-serving advice. It can involve an increase in the demand for economists' services, and its implementation would benefit economists. Any time a policy suggested by a group favors that group, it should be carefully examined

to see whether the group's support of that policy is biased. *(768)*

6. To maximize life, one would expect that the marginal value per dollar spent should be equal in all activities. Thus, if Exhibit 1 is correct, it would suggest that you should be far less concerned about safe airline travel and far more concerned about whether your automobile has air bags or not. *(769)*

7. Costs and benefits are ambiguous; economists often disagree enormously on specific costs and benefits, or the costs and benefits are difficult or impossible to quantify. Thus, one should be extremely careful about using a cost/benefit analysis as anything more than an aid to one's analysis of the situation. *(770)*

8. A maximum wage law where the wage is set at W_{Max} in the diagram below would create a gap between the quantity of labor demanded and the quantity supplied. It

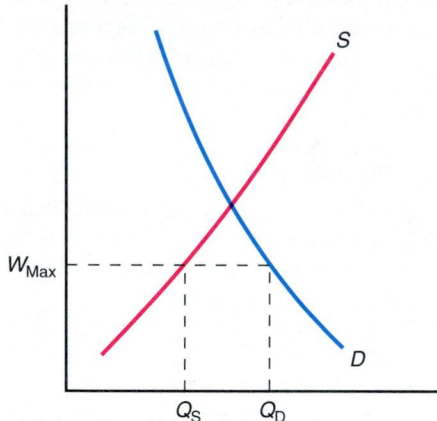

would benefit some people—specifically, the demanders of labor who can find workers and the people who buy the products—and it would hurt others—specifically, those who otherwise would get a higher wage and those demanders who can't find any workers. Economic theory does not tell us whether a law is good or bad; it involves positive analysis and simply tells us what the effect of a law would be. *(771)*

9. The textbook author would likely respond, *"Everything depends."* The student would be right, but she should have gone on to discuss the next question: What does the answer depend *on?* Inevitably, her discussion of what the answer depends on would itself depend—it would depend on her experience and institutional knowledge and judgment. This is why people generally can disagree about most economic questions. *(775)*

10. Most economists tend to dislike bureaucracy because large organizations, which engender bureaucracy, generally have little competition. They tend not to directly relate benefits and costs. *(779)*

36

Economics and the Environment

The attempt to turn a complex problem of the head into a simple moral question for the heart to answer is of course a necessary part of all political discussion.

~Frank Colby

After reading this chapter, you should be able to:

1 List four ways in which an economist's approach to environmental problems differs from a noneconomist's approach.

2 Say why correlation does not necessarily imply causation.

3 Explain why economists often oppose direct regulation.

4 Justify the notion of an optimal level of pollution.

5 Discuss economists' concerns about voluntary programs.

6 Explain why economists believe that long-term solutions to problems involve making people pay a price that reflects the cost of an externality.

7 Apply economists' reasoning to an environmental issue that has not been discussed in this chapter.

An important area of application of economic reasoning is the environment and resources. In the debate, economists who study and are concerned about these issues often have different views than do other individuals who are concerned about these areas but who aren't trained in economics. Some of the differences include:

1. Economists' understanding and statement of the environmental problem are likely to differ from those of lay conservationists.
2. Economists often oppose explicit regulation and prohibitions of certain actions (such as the use of styrofoam), preferring alternative incentive-based programs to achieve the same end.
3. Economists are often dubious about voluntary solutions.
4. Economists' methods of paying for environmental programs are likely to differ from lay conservationists' methods.

In this chapter we consider an example of each of these differences to give you some insight into how economists think and how understanding economic principles affects one's understanding of environmental problems. Then we consider a case study of a mandatory recycling program, the economic analysis of that program, and, finally, alternatives to it.

1 Four ways in which economists' approach to environmental problems differs from noneconomists' approach include (1) their understanding of the problem, (2) their opposition to explicit regulation, (3) their dubiousness about voluntary solutions, and (4) their methods for paying.

ECONOMISTS' INTERPRETATION OF THE PROBLEM

The Empirical Debate about Global Warming

Global warming theory The theory that the earth is now going through a period of warming due to the rise of carbon dioxide gases caused by the burning of fossil fuels.

One important difference between economists and laypeople is a result not so much of economists' economic training as of their statistical training. Having worked with statistics, economists know the difficulty of reaching definite conclusions about what's happening or will happen on the basis of what has happened in the past.

Let's consider this difference in relation to the **global warming theory** (the theory that the earth is now going through a period of warming due to the rise in carbon dioxide gases caused by the burning of fossil fuels). The problem of global warming and the policies we should use to deal with it have been much in the news in the 1990s. Before one can discuss what policies to use to deal with global warming, one must answer the question: Is the global warming theory correct? It's not all that easy a question to answer.

Is the Global Warming Theory Correct?   The temperature measurements in the Northern Hemisphere have been on an upward trend over the last 100 years, as we see in Exhibit 1(a). There's no debate about that. There's also no debate about the recent increase in carbon dioxide gas in the atmosphere. But to a statistician, and hence to an economist who's trained as a statistician, those facts don't necessarily mean that the global warming theory is correct.

2 Correlation does not necessarily imply causation.

Correlation Term in statistics meaning the joint movement of data points.

Causation Term in statistics meaning that a change in one data point causes another data point to change.

Correlation Does Not Imply Causation   Early on in any statistics course, all economists, like all scientists, learn that **correlation** (the joint movement of data points) does not imply **causation** (that the change in one of those data points caused the other data point to change). If the global warming theory is correct, a number of conditions are necessary. These include: (1) future temperatures must not be expected to fall unless carbon dioxide in the atmosphere falls, and (2) temperatures must be expected to continue to rise as long as carbon dioxide in the atmosphere continues to rise.

For example, if in the 1990s temperatures fall even as carbon dioxide in the atmosphere increases, the global warming theory will be shown incorrect. But even if temperatures continue to rise, the theory *won't* be *proven* correct (a theory can *never* be proven correct); it can only be corroborated. (**Corroboration** means that the data are more consistent with this theory than with any other theory, so it makes sense to use the theory.) We generally treat a corroborated theory as correct even though we're not sure it's correct.

Deciding whether the global warming theory is corroborated is a difficult statistical question with no definitive answer. It requires interpretation and integration of data from many sources. Statisticians are still debating this issue. The current state of the

Q–1: Wearing shorts and eating ice cream cones are highly correlated. Which of these would we say causes the other?

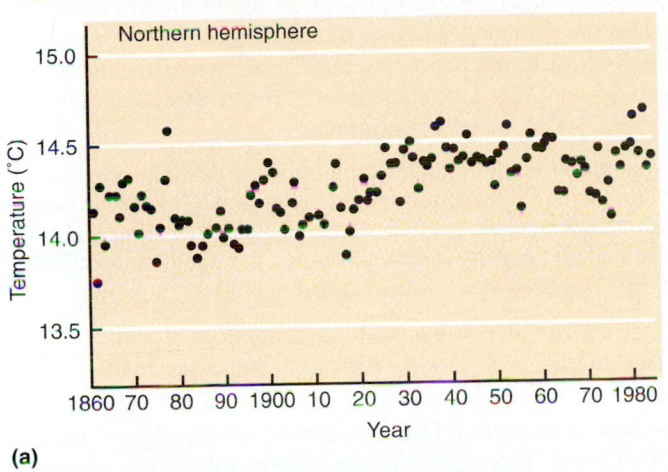

(a)

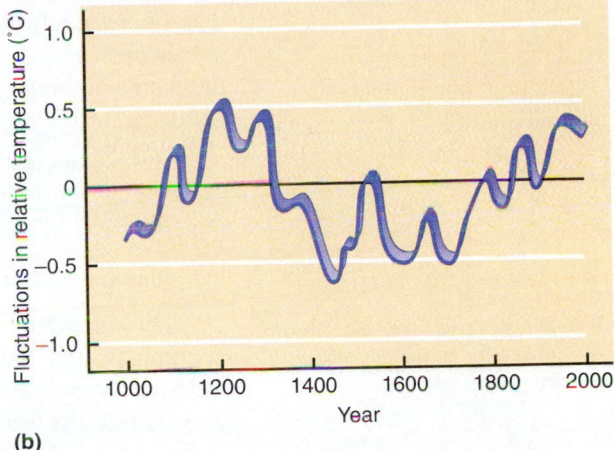

(b)

EXHIBIT 1 (a and b)   Global Warming Statistics

When we look at recent data, (**a**), the global warming theory seems reasonable. But when we look at long-run data, (**b**), we see enormous fluctuations in temperature long before the appearance of the causes identified by the global warming theory.
Source: Adapted by permission from *The Changing Atmosphere* by John Firor © Yale University Press, New Haven, CT, 1990.

debate is that interpretation of the data depends on one's prior belief.[1] If one believes that it's reasonable to assume that a qualitative change in the model has taken place, then the data are consistent with the global warming theory. Statisticians who believe that the burning of fossil fuel since the 1860s is likely to have produced a qualitative change in the nature of our weather system would take this view. If, however, one presently believes:

1. That no qualitative change in the system generating these data has taken place;
2. That the general temperature pattern is subject to significant long-run cyclical fluctuations; and
3. That potential measurement problems exist—specifically, (1) that the instruments measuring temperature aren't completely representative of global conditions but are instead representative of conditions close to inhabited areas, and (2) that the precision of the instruments in early years had problems,

then the data are inconclusive. A few statisticians believe this and the debate between the two groups of statisticians remains unresolved.

The Ambiguity of Formal Statistical Results   Like statisticians, economists who focus on this area differ in their assessments of what can be drawn from the data, but they're all far more careful about drawing inferences from the data than are the typical laypersons. Each year of new data provides more information. However, as you can see in Exhibit 1(b) (which shows estimated fluctuations in temperatures over hundreds of years), temperatures have fluctuated even before any carbon fuels were burned. We have no satisfactory explanation why. Given our lack of knowledge of the reasons for these earlier fluctuations, even another hundred years of data will be unlikely to produce conclusive evidence. Still, by the turn of the century it's possible that the

Nicholas Georgescu-Roegen was one of the earliest environmental economists. © *David Crenshaw.*

---

[1] In high-level statistical theory there's a debate between Bayesian statisticians (who believe that all statistics must be interpreted through a person's prior beliefs) and Classical statisticians (who believe that purely objective statistical estimates, not based in any way on prior beliefs, can be made). Most statisticians accept that in areas where there's much ambiguity (such as in global warming) and where precise data are so limited, it's impossible to be totally objective. This doesn't mean that the scientists are doing bad science; it only means that data limitations require interpretive assumptions that cannot be fully objective. The fact that data are limited doesn't mean the policy question shouldn't be addressed. Often policy problems must be addressed long before adequate data are available.

group believing the global warming theory is corroborated or the group believing the data are inconclusive will have strengthened its case significantly.

In an article discussing global warming, the magazine *The Economist* summarizes the data's ambiguity. It concludes that it's very possible that future effects on climate "will be unlike any seen before." The writers continue:

> This is not good news for computer modelers. Climate models are derived from weather forecasting programs that are designed to provide tomorrow's weather when told about today's. As such, they may have many assumptions built into them that have nothing to do with the underlying mechanisms governing the weather and climate. They can be inspired fudges. (*The Economist*, April 7, 1990, p. 100.)

Ambiguity of formal statistical results isn't an exception; it's the rule in economics and business.

This ambiguity of formal statistical results isn't an exception; it's the rule in economics and business. But in the real world, decisions must be made before statistically conclusive evidence is in. That's where the art of economics comes into play. One must use one's judgment, accepting that it might be wrong. Based on such judgment, not formal statistical proof, many economists believe that global warming is taking place.

Statistical Inference and Policy   Let's say that the global warming theory is correct. The next question is what to do about it. Here again, the economist's statistical training enters in. Economists recognize that averages aren't enough. Even if the average temperature has risen, the problem presented by that rise depends on how average temperature has risen. Advocates of the global warming theory's correctness claim that, based on a computer projection, a two- or three-degree increase in temperature will cause enormous problems for agriculture and create desert areas in much of the world. But that conclusion depends on when during the year, and where on the earth, the temperature rises.

Q–2: The average rainfall in the United States for 1993 was about normal. Therefore, we would expect no serious weather-related problems. True or false? Why?

Some economists point out that the data collected to date have suggested the rise in the average is occurring by winters becoming milder and summer temperatures remaining almost unchanged. Moreover, the warming is greater in polar regions than it is near the equator. Since such an asymmetrical change in temperature wouldn't create deserts, but would extend the growing season in a number of areas (reducing the cost of growing agricultural goods), it's not at all clear that such global warming will have dire negative effects on the world economy. In fact, a few economists even suggest that in certain circumstances such a global warming may benefit society. They would advocate doing nothing.

Other economists, such as William Nordhaus (a professor at Yale who did a study of policy to deal with global warming), advocate a tax on the use of carbon fuels. We'll discuss economists' policy proposals shortly.

Much real-world applied economics is slogging through data, bringing one's statistical training to bear on the data so that one can understand what the problem is.

I emphasize these interpretative statistical problems here because, before discussing policy, we must recognize how important data interpretation is. Much real-world applied economics is slogging through data, bringing one's statistical training to bear on that data so that one can understand what the problem is. If you don't understand statistical inference, you are likely to go off to solve the wrong problem.

How Limited Are Our Natural Resources?

Before moving on, let's consider another debate in which many economists have questioned the conventional wisdom based on their empirical and statistical training. That debate concerns the extent to which the world's resources are limited.

Proven reserves *Resource reserves that have been discovered, documented to date, and are recoverable with current technology.*

Proven Reserves   The layperson's conventional wisdom is that the world is running out of resources. After all, resources are fixed and, once used up, they're gone. To support this view, statistics are often cited that we have only, say, 20 years of copper left, 30 years of fossil fuel, and so on. Economists have two problems with these statistics. The first is that the available statistics don't tell us how large existing reserves of any resource are. The statistics we have concern **proven reserves** (reserves that have been discovered and are recoverable), assuming current technology and prices. The calculation of proven reserves changes over time as more resources are discovered. As reserves run low, new exploration may well find more reserves.

Q–3: Based on past experience, it is likely that in 2005 proven reserves of resources will be higher than they currently are. True or false? Why?

As an example, consider the case of copper. In 1950, proven reserves were said to be enough for 27.9 production years. Thus, in 1950 one might have predicted that copper reserves would run out by 1980. That didn't happen. In 1980, proven reserves of copper were said to be enough for 38 production years, an increase of about 10 production years. Using these data, some cynical economists facetiously argue that if the trend continues, eventually the world will be swamped with copper. That obviously won't happen, but it's not clear from the statistics we have now that we should be concerned about running out of copper in the near, or even distant, future.

The Invisible Hand at Work   A second problem economists have with these long-run projections about running out of resources is that the use of any resource depends upon its price. As the price rises, people use less of the resource (the law of demand) and spend much more time, energy, and money on finding alternatives. Rising price brings about technical change. If people expect resources to be in short supply in the future, the price of those resources will go up now, causing people to conserve. That's the market's way of conserving resources.

The fact that the price of a particular resource isn't going up now suggests that maybe the problem isn't viewed as that great by the people who produce, buy, and sell the resource. Economists point out that this group of people has the most information about future supplies and demand. Hence economists believe the current price tends to be a good signal about future shortages. If the current price isn't high or rising, then there are probably strong empirical data to support the view that we are *not* going to run out of that resource in the foreseeable future. If the price is high and rising, then one would expect that people will be undertaking more and more conservation measures without any regulatory policies to induce them to do so. The invisible hand does the work. The higher price gives them an incentive to choose to conserve. But the real price of most minerals hasn't risen. In fact, real prices of most minerals have fallen over time.

Many empirical studies suggest relative scarcity declining over time. How can scarcity decline? Remember back in the first chapter when I first discussed resources and scarcity. Available resources depend upon technology—and if technology increases faster than resources are used, relative scarcity declines.

Once again, my purpose in discussing the issue of limited resources is not to argue which view is right, but simply to point out how careful one must be in interpreting empirical evidence before discussing policy proposals.

But let's now suppose that one has come to the conclusion that there's a problem—say that we've concluded that people are using too much oil. Having come to that conclusion, let's now specifically consider the policies to which an economist and a layperson might naturally gravitate.

One difference is that a layperson is likely to favor a program of **direct regulation,** in which the amount of oil people are allowed to use is directly limited by the government. Economists are likely to oppose that solution because it does not achieve the desired end as **efficiently** (at the lowest cost possible in total resources without consideration as to who pays those costs) and fairly as possible. As we discussed in the last chapter, for an economist, coming to the conclusion that too much oil is being consumed would imply that for some reason the consumption of oil involves a negative **externality** (the result of a decision that is not taken into account by the decision maker).

As an alternative to direct regulation, economists will likely favor some type of a **market incentive program** (a program that makes the price of oil reflect the negative externality).

The reason for this difference between the layperson's and the economist's view of policy is the same reason that we discussed in the last chapter: Regulation does not get people to equate the marginal costs of reducing oil consumption with the marginal benefits.

World Watch is a strongly proenvironment magazine published by the Worldwatch Institute.

Q-4: What is the market mechanism for dealing with shortages?

Many empirical studies suggest relative scarcity is declining over time.

ALTERNATIVE POLICY APPROACHES

Economists and Direct Regulation

Direct regulation   *Program in which the amount of a resource people are allowed to use is directly limited by the government.*

Efficiently   *Achieving a desired goal at the lowest possible cost in total resources, without consideration as to who pays those costs.*

Externality   *A result of a decision that is not taken into account by the decision maker.*

Market incentive program   *Program that makes the price of a resource reflect a negative externality.*

A STORY OF TWO BETS

The prophets of doom have been around for a long time; economists generally believe they are overstating their case, not taking into account that there is a built-in market reaction to scarcity—a rise in price of the scarce good—that eliminates the scarcity. The rise in price eliminates scarcity in two ways: (1) it decreases the quantity demanded by causing demanders to substitute, and (2) it increases the quantity supplied, through such actions as investment in new technologies that replace the resource with another resource. Most economists believe that the prophets of doom significantly underestimate both these effects. One economist who has been especially outspoken on this issue is Julian Simon, author of *People: The Ultimate Resource.*

Bet 1

In 1980, Simon challenged Paul Ehrlich, an outspoken leader of the prophets of doom (and author of *The Population Bomb*), to put his money where his mouth was. He told Ehrlich to choose any five resources that he believed would become scarce. Simon was willing to put up $1,000 to back his belief that these five resources of Ehrlich's choosing would become *less scarce* in 10 years, on average—as measured by their total price in 1980 and their total price 10 years later. Put another way, he bet their prices would rise less than the inflation. So Simon wasn't even relying on the demand response to scarcity; he was relying only on the supply response—new technological developments, the breakdown of cartels, and new discoveries.

At the time, Simon's bet seemed to be a foolhardy one. Ehrlich accepted the bet, which was to cover the period October 1980 through October 1990. If, at the end of the period, the total value for specific amounts of each resource had risen above $1,000, Simon would pay Ehrlich the difference between the $1,000 and the higher value. But if the total value had fallen below $1,000, Ehrlich would pay Simon the difference between the total value and $1,000.

Ten years pass. Guess who wins? You're right: Simon. (Otherwise I wouldn't be telling this story.) The prices of the resources had fallen (some had fallen in nominal terms!). Paul Ehrlich writes a check to Simon for $576.07 and sends it to him with no note or anything. The *New York Times* hears about the bet and, in a magazine story (Sunday *New York Times,* December 2, 1990), recounts the bet, and it becomes famous—an example of the prophets of doom being mistaken again.

Bet 2

Two years pass. An economist I know is at a conference having dinner with Julian Simon. He congratulates Simon on his bet with Ehrlich and tells him that he's generally in agreement with his attack on the prophets of doom, but he argues that Simon pushes it a bit too far. Simon says that he was not strong enough in his attack on the prophets of doom; he believes not only that resources are becoming less scarce, but that the welfare of society is continually improving, not getting worse. In fact, he says he is so sure that the future is improving that he will offer my friend a bet similar to the one he offered Ehrlich. He tells my friend: "Choose any measure of human material welfare, over any time period, in any area or community. I bet you that measure will improve."

Even though my friend agrees with much of Simon's argument, he finds Simon's statement too strong, and suggests Simon modify it slightly. Simon stands firm. So my friend asks his wife, a doctor, to come up with a statistic that would qualify as a

Let's consider an example. Say we have two individuals, Mrs. Thrifty using 10 gallons of gasoline (which is made from oil) a day and Mr. Big using 20 gallons of gas a day. Say we have decided that we want to reduce these two individuals' daily gas consumption by 10 percent, or 3 gallons. The regulatory solution might require everyone to reduce consumption by some amount. Likely direct regulatory reduction strategies would be to require an equal quantity reduction (each consumer reducing consumption by 1.5 gallons) or to require an equal percentage reduction (each consumer reducing consumption by 10 percent).

Economists' problem with this direct regulatory solution is that it doesn't take into account the costs to individuals of reducing consumption. Say, for example, that

3 Economists are likely to oppose direct regulation because it does not achieve the desired end as efficiently and as fairly as possible.

"measure of human material welfare" that is highly likely—in fact, is almost guaranteed—to get worse (my friend hates to lose bets). They decide on the following measure: The number of full-blown AIDS cases in the United States as measured by Center for Disease Control (CDC) statistics in a one-year period, April 1993–April 1994." My friend bets that the statistic will increase as compared to the April 1992–April 1993 period.

Simon, having stated his position so strongly, feels he must accept the bet. (Actually, he told my friend later, he believes that the bet is a bad one for him—that the relevant measure of human welfare is life expectancy rather than a particular disease, and that a one-year period is too short for meaningful tests.) A bet is made and a contract hastily drawn up. If my friend wins, Simon will donate a specified amount of money to a charity my friend designates; if Simon wins, my friend will donate the equivalent amount of money to a charity Simon designates.

My friend, of course, thinks he has a winning bet: the number of new AIDS cases is a flow from a stock of HIV-infected people. That stock has been on an upward trend for at least 10 years and the flow from it is statistically almost guaranteed to rise in the short run.

However, about 4 o'clock the next morning he wakes up—somehow, in his sleep, he has remembered that AIDS cases had recently been redefined to include a set of women's diseases that hadn't previously been included. Depending on the decisions made by government statisticians, that redefinition could cause a one-time blip in the number of full-blown AIDS cases in the base period April 1992–April 1993. With that one-time blip, it is possible that my friend could lose the bet, since a number of AIDS cases that were actually contracted over the past 10 years could be added in the base period, artificially inflating it. With the blip, even though the number of full-blown AIDS cases has, in one sense, continually increased, the statistic measuring that increase—the number of defined AIDS cases as specified by the bet—may not have increased.

The result of the bet was still not known when this book went to press. Based on preliminary data, it will be close—the reason for the delay was that the CDC's attempts to grapple with the definitional change were taking a long time.

Lessons

Two lessons can be learned from the two bets.

1. First, don't underestimate technological change and the positive progression of history. Simon's general position is a strong one. The world will adapt to new circumstances, and most people significantly underestimate its adaptability. People have a tendency to make unfair comparisons of past and present.
2. Second, there is no sure thing. Statistics are subject to significant deviation from what one thinks they are. My friend thought he had a sure thing, but he may have lost on a definitional point. To understand statistics, you must understand how they are defined and compiled.

Why are these lessons important for economics? Because they play important roles in policy decisions; they urge caution in making "common sense" arguments, and in treating statistical facts as truth.

Mrs. Thrifty could easily (i.e., almost costlessly) reduce consumption by three gallons while Mr. Big would find it very costly to reduce consumption by even .5 gallons. In that case, either regulatory solution would be **inefficient** (more costly than necessary). It would be less costly to have Mrs. Thrifty undertake the entire reduction. Economists would prefer a policy that would automatically make the person who has the lower cost of reduction *choose* (as opposed to being *required*) to undertake the most reduction. In this case the policy should get Mrs. Thrifty to *choose* to undertake the majority of the reduction.

Two types of policies would get Mrs. Thrifty to undertake the largest share of the reduction, and economists generally favor these alternative policies if they are admin-

Inefficient More costly than necessary.

istratively feasible. One is to create a tax incentive to achieve the desired reduction; the other is to create a type of property right embodied in a permit or certificate and to allow individuals to trade these property rights freely. Let's consider each separately.

Tax Incentives to Conserve   Let's say that the government imposes a 50¢ per gallon tax on gasoline consumption. This would be an example of a **tax incentive program** (a program using a tax to create incentives for individuals to structure their activities in a way that is consistent with the desired ends). Since Mrs. Thrifty can almost costlessly reduce her gasoline consumption, she will likely respond to the tax by reducing gasoline consumption by, say, 2.75 gallons. She pays only $3.63 in tax but undertakes most of the conservation. Since Mr. Big finds it very costly to reduce his consumption of gasoline, he will likely respond by reducing gasoline consumption by very little— say by .25 gallons. He pays $9.88 in tax but does little of the conservation.

In this example, the tax has achieved the desired end in a more efficient manner than the regulatory solution would—the person for whom the reduction is least costly cuts consumption the most. Why? Because the incentive to reduce is embodied in the price, and individuals are forced to choose how much to change their consumption. The solution also has a significant element of fairness about it. The person who conserves the most pays the least tax.

Marketable Certificates and Conservation   A second method of incorporating the incentive into the individual's decision is a **marketable certificate program** (a program requiring everyone to certify that they have reduced total consumption—not necessarily their own individual consumption—by a specified amount, say 1.5 gallons). Such a program would be close to the regulatory solution but it involves a major difference. If individuals choose to reduce consumption by more than the required amount, they will be given a marketable certificate which they can sell to someone who has chosen to reduce consumption by less than that amount. By buying that certificate, the person who has not personally reduced consumption by the 1.5 gallons will have met the program's requirements. Let's see how the program would work with Mr. Big and Mrs. Thrifty.

In our example, Mr. Big finds it very costly to reduce consumption while Mrs. Thrifty finds it easy. So we can expect that Mr. Big won't reduce consumption much and will instead buy certificates from Mrs. Thrifty, who will choose to undertake significant reduction in her consumption to generate the certificates, assuming she can sell them to Mr. Big for a high enough price to make that reduction worth her while. So, as was the case in the tax incentive program, Mrs. Thrifty undertakes most of the conservation, but she reaps a financial benefit for it.

Obviously there are enormous questions about administrative feasibility of these types of proposals, but what's important to understand here is not the specifics of the proposals, but instead, the way in which the economists' policies are *more efficient* than the regulatory policy. As I stated before, *more efficient* means *less costly* in terms of resources, with no consideration paid to who is bearing those costs. Incorporating the incentive into a price and then letting individuals choose how to respond to that incentive lets those who find it least costly undertake most of the adjustment.

More and more, governments are exploring economists' policies for solving problems. Sin taxes (discussed in the preceding chapter) are an example of the tax incentive approach. Marketable pollution rights discussed in the accompanying box are an example of the marketable certificate approach. You can probably see more examples discussed in the news.

The Optimal Amount of Pollution   An **optimal policy** is one in which the marginal cost of undertaking the policy equals the marginal benefit of that policy. If a policy isn't optimal (that is, the marginal cost exceeds the marginal benefit or the marginal benefit exceeds the marginal cost), resources are being wasted because the savings from a reduction of expenditures on a program will be worth more than the gains that would be lost from reducing the program, or the benefit from spending more on a program will be worth more than the cost of expanding the program.

Tax incentive program   *Any program in which a tax is used to create incentives for individuals to structure their activities in a way that is consistent with particular desired ends.*

Q–5:   In what sense is the tax incentive approach to conservation fair?

Marketable certificate program   *A program that formalizes rights by issuing certificates and allowing trading of those rights.*

Optimal policy   *Policy whose marginal cost equals its marginal benefit.*

4 If a policy isn't optimal, resources are being wasted because the savings from reduction of expenditures on a program will be worth more than the gains that would be lost from reducing the program.

MARKETABLE PERMITS FOR POLLUTION

■arketable permits are being used more and more to deal with environmental issues. In many areas, air quality permits are required of firms before they may begin production. The only way a new firm may start production is if it buys permits from existing firms, which are allowed to sell permits only if they decrease air pollution by the amount of the permit.

Another example of the use of marketable permits is a program instituted in California to deal with a drought. The only way a construction firm is allowed to build a new house is if it reduces existing water usage by a specific amount. To do this, the firm goes around to existing home owners, offering to put in water-saving devices for free. In some areas, more than 60 percent of the existing homes have introduced these water-saving devices, which were paid for by the construction firms and hence, indirectly, by the new home buyers.

Let's consider an example of this latter case. Say the marginal benefit of a program significantly exceeds its marginal cost. That would seem good. But that would mean that we could expand the program by decreasing some other program or activity whose marginal benefit doesn't exceed its marginal cost, with a net gain in benefits to society. To spend too little on a beneficial program is as inoptimal as spending too much on a nonbeneficial program.

This concept of optimality carries over to economists' view of most problems. For example, some environmentalists would like to completely rid the economy of pollution. Most economists believe that doing so is costly and that since it's costly, one would want to take into account those costs. That means that society should reduce pollution only to the point where the marginal cost of reducing pollution equals the marginal benefit. That amount of pollution at which the marginal benefit of reducing pollution equals the marginal cost is called the **optimal level of pollution.** To reduce pollution below that level would make society as a whole worse off.

Optimal level of pollution *Amount of pollution at which the marginal benefit of reducing pollution equals the marginal cost.*

A second point upon which economists often differ from laypeople is in their view of the effectiveness of voluntary solutions. Say that one has decided that energy reduction is a desired goal. Often the first policy presented to achieve the desired end is the voluntary one: ask everyone to save energy, leaving individuals free to choose whether to save or not. Since it involves free choice, economists don't oppose this solution, but they often do question whether it will work in a large group.

Economists Are Dubious of Voluntary Solutions

To see why, let's consider Mr. Big and Mrs. Thrifty again. Say the government simply asks them to reduce their consumption voluntarily. Let's say that Mrs. Thrifty has a social conscience and undertakes most of the reduction while Mr. Big has no social conscience and does not reduce consumption significantly. Then it seems that this is a reasonably efficient solution. But what if the costs were reversed and Mr. Big had the low cost of reduction and Mrs. Thrifty had the high cost? Then the voluntary solution would not be so efficient.

The potential lack of efficiency is not the main reason economists generally are dubious about voluntary solutions. After all, when people do something voluntarily, they are choosing to do it, and, assuming they are rational, it must make them better off or they wouldn't choose to do it. So one could argue that even in the case where Mrs. Thrifty has a high cost of reduction *and* voluntarily undertakes most of the reduction, she also has a high benefit from reducing her consumption, so the person who is undertaking the reduction is getting the benefit.

Within the economists' model of rational decision makers, the preceding reasoning is correct, but most economists are quite willing to admit that this model of rational decision makers is insufficient to capture people's complex motives and psychology. Most economists fully recognize that people have a social conscience in varying degrees and do things for the good of society as well as for their own good. However, economists point out that a person's social conscience and willingness to do things for the good of society generally depend on that person's belief that others will also be helping.

5   Economists believe that a small
number of free riders will undermine
the social consciousness of many in
the society and that eventually a voluntary policy will fail.

How to Pay for Conservation

Q-6:   What will an economist
likely conclude if he or she cannot
find an externality?

6   If a program requires people to
pay a price that reflects the cost of
an externality, it will be in their
interest to change their behavior until
marginal social benefits equal marginal social costs.

A CASE STUDY:
A MANDATORY
RECYCLING PROGRAM

NIMBY   *A short way to express*
"Not In My Back Yard" when a
community objects to a proposed
development in its neighborhood.

If a socially conscious person comes to believe a large number of other people
won't contribute, he or she will often lose that social conscience: Why should I do
what's good for society if others won't? This is another example of the **free rider
problem** (individuals' unwillingness to share in the cost of a public good) which
economists believe will often limit, and eventually undermine, social actions based on
voluntary contributions. The free rider problem and its likely effect on social consciousness are the most important reasons why economists are skeptical of voluntary
solutions. They believe a small number of free riders will undermine the social
consciousness of many in the society and that eventually the voluntary policy will fail.

There are exceptions. During times of war and extreme crisis, voluntary programs
are often successful. For example, upon the advice of economists, during World War
II the war effort was in part financed through successful voluntary programs. But for
other social problems that are long run and that involve individuals accepting significant changes in their actions, generally the results of voluntary programs haven't been
positive. Economists don't oppose such voluntary programs; they simply don't have
much faith in them.

A third way in which economists' approach to environmental policy differs from
environmentalists' approach is in how to pay for any environmental program. Most
environmentalists see taxes only as a way to collect the money to pay for an
environmental program. Economists see taxes and other policies to affect prices as a
central part of the program. In fact, for an economist the incentive embodied in the
price is the single most important part of a policy.

Let's consider what this difference means. Say that the problem is too much
pollution. Immediately, an economist's training directs him or her to look at the price
of polluting and how that price can be raised. If there is too much use of carbon fuel,
an economist immediately looks at the price of carbon fuel and how it can be raised.

Moreover, as we discussed, the economist, in deciding whether there's a problem,
looks at the price and tries to reason out whether there's an externality that makes the
price too low. In many cases the externality is easy to find. For example, when people
pollute they don't pay for the cost of that pollution, so there is an argument that
pollution is an externality and the price of polluting is too low. If there is no such
externality argument, then an economist will likely conclude that there is no problem.

In most environmental issues, it is relatively easy to conclude that there is a
negative externality. Thus, economists often agree with environmentalists: There is a
social environmental problem that the current market structure doesn't solve. But the
answer to that problem for an economist is seldom direct regulation nor is it voluntary
conservation paid for by some type of tax. Rather the economist's answer is *to find a
program that makes the price people pay reflect the cost of the externality.*

Many examples presented in this book concern the federal government and national
problems. While many of the environmental issues are national and even
international—such as ozone depletion and global warming—others are local.

In the remainder of this chapter we consider a local case—one you might read
about in a small-town paper. That case is a mandatory recycling program instituted by
a small town. We'll consider the chosen policies and some alternative policies an
economically trained environmentalist might have suggested.

The case begins with trash. It seems that the people of Vermont, a state that used
to boast that it had more cows than people, were generating more trash than the
existing Vermont landfills could handle. This wasn't the result of a sudden decrease in
the amount of land. Rather, as people became more environmentally conscious, their
concerns about the potential polluting effects of landfills increased and landfills
became much more regulated. In fact, they became unacceptable to most neighborhoods. **NIMBY** (**N**ot **I**n **M**y **B**ack **Y**ard) became the political "in" word.

It was decided that something must be done to reduce the amount of trash, and
many Vermont communities instituted recycling programs. This is the story of the
path one Vermont community followed.

The first problem they had was setting up the administrative apparatus to plan and organize the recycling program. What area would it cover? The decision: A recycling coordinator was appointed, and a regional solid waste management area was established for the county. Within that regional area, the largest town was selected for an initial recycling program.

The largest town, which we'll call Big Town (population 8,293), then appointed its own part-time recycling coordinator, a recent graduate of a local college who had majored in political science and was a strong environmentalist. Working with town planners, Big Town's recycling coordinator designed the program. Her first decision was that the plan would be mandatory. It was felt that a voluntary program wouldn't achieve anywhere near the amount of desired recycling. Big Town then enacted an ordinance making the recycling of certain items mandatory for all residents.

The second decision she had to make was what would be recycled. What was there a market for? Likely candidates included certain plastics, newspapers and magazines, glass, metal containers, and corrugated boxes. Unfortunately, upon checking the second-hand market she found that the price that could be obtained for selling most of these recycled items was very low, and that no regional market existed at all for magazines and corrugated boxes. Moreover, recycling firms would take the items only if they were "uncontaminated," which meant that not only would paper have to be separated from plastic but that various types of plastic and various types of paper would have to be subdivided. For example, one could not simply recycle "paper." One would have to separate at least four different types: newspaper, glossy magazines and catalogs, colored stationery, and white stationery. For another example, only a few of the many kinds of plastic would be acceptable to recycling firms, and it would be costly to determine which types were recyclable and which were not. All this sorting would add enormously to the cost of recycling. In short, the cost of sorting trash would be so high that it would far exceed the payment the town would receive from recycling firms.

This led to a third decision: that householders would have to separate their trash themselves. This, in turn, meant that ordinary garbage trucks could not pick up the trash because the separated trash would have to be placed in individual compartments in the truck, and ordinary trucks aren't built that way. Therefore special new trucks had to be bought at a cost of about $80,000 per truck. Because no trash collection firm was willing to buy such trucks, Big Town had to find some way to pay for the trucks if there was to be any recycling.

The job of collecting recycled trash was put out to bid. Only one local trash collector was willing to take on the job. Not surprisingly, that company won the bid.

The final agreement was that this company would collect the separated trash once every two weeks and would be paid a $4 monthly pickup fee by every household, regardless of whether the household used the service. Big Town would borrow the money to buy the truck for the collector, and the collector would pay the town for its use in installments.

This $4 per month recycling fee was in addition to the fees that people were already paying private companies to pick up their trash. So at the initiation of the recycling program, people were faced with two trash fees: one for the regular trash and one for the separated trash.

Since there were about 2,600 households, this fee meant that the firm received about $10,400 per month (about $125,000 per year). From that it had to repay Big Town for the truck, pay for the labor to pick up the recycled items, and get rid of the recyclable items. (The administrative cost of the program, including the Big Town coordinator's salary, also had to be paid for. This cost was incorporated in the property tax rate payable to the town.)

The remaining problem was compliance: how to enforce the requirement that people recycle. This was done by providing a fine of up to $1,000 for each failure to recycle. Thus, households that put recyclable material in the regular trash instead of the separated trash risked a heavy fine. The final design of the program was as follows:

THE GYP CHIPPER: THE DECISION TO RECYCLE

The *Eight-Penny News*, a newspaper for light contractors, ran an article about the Gyp Chipper—a 500-pound, 4' × 4' machine that "eats wallboard at the rate of 10,000 pounds an hour and costs $8,000." Wallboard (also called *plasterboard*) is the covering on most walls in houses, and when any remodeling is done the old wallboard needs to be discarded. How much is discarded? Approximately 3 million tons a year—about 1 percent of the U.S. waste stream.

The article was written for contractors. It addressed the issue of whether it would be worthwhile to buy the machine and whether recycling wallboard would be in the interest of the construction tradespeople, called *drywallers,* who worked with wallboard. The bottom line of the article was that at "$60 a ton tippage fee (the landfill cost), it probably wasn't in their interest to recycle, but at $100 or $200 a ton it would be relatively easy to convince drywallers that recycling beats throwing away whole truckloads of wallboard."

1. Every residential building had to separate its trash according to rules published by the Big Town coordinator.

2. Each household was provided with a blue plastic box into which it would sort its recyclable trash. The householder then had to carry the recyclable trash to curbside before 7 A.M. on pickup day. Pickup was once every two weeks, with the exact day depending on the neighborhood.

3. The recycling trash collector inspected each bin and left behind any items that didn't fit the rules. For example, only plastic bottles whose bottoms bore a raised symbol including the number 2 were acceptable. If items were rejected, the collector left a notice stating the reason.

4. The recycling collector kept records of people who were not putting out the blue bins so that the town could make investigations and impose any fines that appeared justified.

5. Householders had to pay a flat $4 a month to the recycling trash collector, whether they had many, few, or no recyclable items. They could obtain any number of additional blue bins they needed, the only limitation being that they had to pay $5 for each additional one. (The first bin was free of charge because funds to pay for these had been provided by a local civic organization.)

6. It was up to the recycling collector to dispose of what was collected. If it could sell the items, it could keep the money.

The initiation of the program brought significant complaints from various groups. One group was composed of competing trash collectors whose customers were generating less trash and were therefore opting to save money by requesting fewer collections. These competing collectors were also losing business to the collector who won the bid to pick up the separated trash. This collector would give a discount to the customers who also hired this company to pick up their regular trash, giving people an incentive to switch to this company.

Another group complaining about the program were residents of households who generated almost no recyclable trash yet had to pay for its collection. There were documented instances of elderly women who put out nothing but one tin can in two weeks. A third group who complained were apartment house landlords who were responsible for paying the monthly fee and/or fines but who could not force their tenants into individual compliance. A final group who complained were civil libertarians who claimed that it was illegal to search people's regular trash to be sure no recyclable items were being put into it.

Despite the complaints, the program was considered successful by most citizens. Compliance was high (about 95 percent of households), and total trash going into the landfill was reduced by one-fifth—2,000 tons out of a total annual trash generation of about 10,000 tons. In the view of the environmentally conscious organizers of the program, at least the people of Big Town were doing something to deal with the environmental problem, and that made the program successful.

This view of the program's success wouldn't be shared by all. Specifically, many economists, even ones who strongly support environmental issues, would have a number of problems with it.

The first problem concerns whether a recycling program made sense at the time it was instituted. Recycled items sold for anywhere from $10 to $70 a ton delivered to the recycling plant. Unfortunately, there were no such plants nearby. Essentially, the delivery costs, even after the items were separated, roughly equaled the value of the recycled material! This rough equality of costs presents a major problem to an economist. The first question any economist asks about a program is whether program costs exceed the benefits. Since the delivered value of the recycled material is essentially zero, there's a significant concern about the benefit of recycling.

Deciding costs and benefits necessarily involves judgment. For example, in the publicity literature the recycling program distributed, the organizers stated that program costs were covered by the saved tipping fees (fees charged by the landfill). But for individuals, this was questionable, since the recycling program cost them $48 per year per household in direct payments but, for most people, did not reduce their trash costs significantly. Moreover, some administrative costs were part of the general town budget and not separable, so one couldn't attribute the proper amount to the recycling program. What makes it hard to come to any definite conclusion about these direct costs is that trash removal fees were rising anyhow, and the appropriate comparison is how much they would have been otherwise. So even for "direct costs" there is ambiguity.

But there is even more ambiguity in costs since for economists the comparison of direct costs and benefits is not sufficient. Because of the way the program was set up, many program costs were passed on to individuals who have to separate their trash and spend time determining what goes where. Although these costs involve no direct payment, they are included in **opportunity costs** (the costs of forgone resources). These opportunity costs of the time it takes to separate the trash do not show up when officials calculate the cost of the program, but they are still costs.

If we assume that it takes an hour per week for a household to separate its trash, then each household spends a total of 52 hours a year separating trash. How should that time be valued? The time should be valued at its opportunity cost, but that opportunity cost isn't directly measurable. Some people dislike separating trash, so they would place a high opportunity cost on their time. Others might enjoy it (they are contributing to recycling); for them, the opportunity cost is zero. In fact, for them, taking part in the program can be seen as a benefit.

How does it all net out? It would take an enormous study to figure that out, and even that study probably would not come to a conclusive result. But let us say for the sake of argument that the study concluded that the appropriate value was $2 per hour. Using this number, we arrive at a cost of $104 per year ($52 \times \$2 = \$104$). Thus, the yearly cost of the recycling program would be $152 ($48 to the collector and $104 in householder's time) per household. The administrative costs in the first year were approximately $20,000. There are about 2,600 households in the town, so, given these assumptions, the yearly cost of mandatory recycling is ($152 \times 2,600$) + $20,000 = $395,200 + $20,000 = $415,200.

For this yearly expense, approximately 2,000 tons of trash is processed through the recycling program each year. Since the landfill cost of 2,000 tons of trash is approximately $118,880 ($59.44 per ton for the town in our case study), this suggests that, if that landfill cost is the appropriate cost, the costs of this program significantly exceed the benefits. Of course, assuming the landfill cost is the appropriate cost is a big *if.* Supporters of the program see landfills as much more expensive than the actual costs, which, if true, would increase the benefits of recycling significantly.

There are also other possible benefits. For example, one could argue that separating trash is creating an environmentally aware community and is building environ-

An Economist's Cost/Benefit View of the Program

Q–7: Why would an economist have doubts about a recycling program in which the price received for recycled material was essentially zero after transportation costs were figured in?

Opportunity costs   *Costs of forgone resources.*

Until recently landfills were the primary means of waste disposal in the United States. © *Jim Sculley/The Image Works*.

Q–8: Would an economist believe that we should simply let the market deal with the pollution problem?

mentally sound habits into the population. Therefore, the argument would run, the program has significant positive external effects which should be considered.

As you can see, cost/benefit studies aren't conclusive, especially when done in a way as cursory as this one. But even a much more thorough study still wouldn't be definitive; it would reflect the assumptions put in.

Despite the ambiguity, as cost/benefit studies go, this one isn't highly favorable to the program unless one is willing to make some strong assumptions about the program's external benefits and about the value of people's time. But if these external benefits exist—if the social and landfill costs significantly exceed the actual costs paid—then for an economist the natural solution is not mandatory recycling, but is, instead, figuring out a way to get the private costs of the landfill to equal their social costs.

How would an economist handle the problem? That's unclear, but what is clear is that an economist would look much more carefully into costs and would try to build price incentives into the program. For example, if the landfill costs are only $59.44 per ton, then the entire program is called into question; but if the landfill costs were $250 per ton, the program would make sense since the savings on 2,000 tons would then be $500,000, not $118,880.

To decide whether there are significant external effects, an economist would ask whether landfill costs are for some reason not being determined by market pressures, or whether landfills create an externality that is not being taken into account in the price of the landfill. If either of those is the case, an economist would look for a program that would incorporate the externality into the price.

Perhaps a preferable program would be to push landfill prices up to a price that included the externality. Big Town's recycling program does not incorporate the price of the externality into the price the consumer pays. The Big Town program is financed with a flat $4 fee per month for every household. That flat fee is paid regardless of how much or how little recycling the household does. Thus, the fee provides no price incentive for recycling or for refraining from using the resources in the first place.

Now it's quite clear that one of the main pressures for recycling has been the decrease in the number of areas willing to accept landfills. But in that search for landfills, no one explored the possibility of allowing the price of landfills to rise by almost 300 percent and seeing how many areas might be willing to accept environmentally sound landfills at that much higher price.

It's likely that if areas were to receive large payments to accept a landfill voluntarily, as opposed to the landfill site being administratively chosen, many more

If the price is perfectly flexible, shortages can't exist. For an economist, the term *shortage* conveys a situation in which the price cannot rise to a level to equate the quantity supplied and the quantity demanded. Below, we consider how a shortage of landfills can occur.

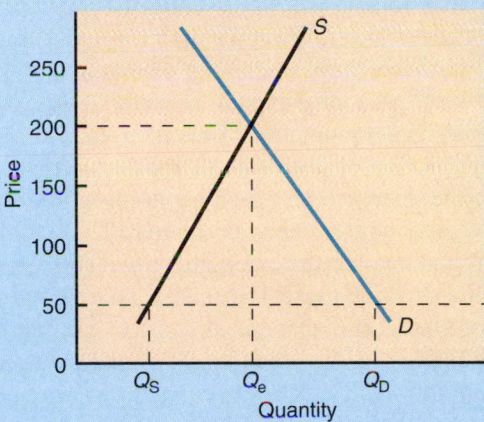

As we've drawn it, you can see that at $50 per ton of trash dumped, the quantity of landfills demanded significantly exceeds the quantity of landfills supplied, but at $200 per ton of trash dumped (with a large portion of that going to the town that allows the landfill), the supply and demand are equal. Why? Because the higher cost of getting rid of trash reduces the amount of trash and hence lowers the need for landfills and gets many more areas willing to accept landfills. Thus, supply and demand analysis suggests that NIMBY is not a necessary state of the world; it is simply a state that is characterized by too low a price of landfills and waste disposal.

In the 1980s there were dire predictions of a severe shortage of landfills. Despite that, in the 1990s, the issue, ironically, has been a shortage of waste. Many landfill owners have been trying to increase the amount of waste coming into their landfills, often by offering cut-rate prices for dumping. The reasons for this turnaround are complicated. One reason is that some of the landfills expect to be shut down and want to make money while they still can. Another reason is that some are imposing external costs on their neighbors without being concerned about these costs. A third is the success of recycling operations, and a fourth is that there never was a severe shortage. But whatever the reasons, even at existing waste-disposal prices the predicted severe shortage of landfills that played a significant role in beginning the recycling movement has not materialized.

areas would be willing to accept landfills. True, the cost of landfills would be higher, but that higher cost would create stronger incentives to recycle. Individuals would choose to recycle, not be forced to recycle by the threat of a fine. Thus, economists would look much more carefully at a policy that would raise the landfill cost to a level where the NIMBY pressure would be much weaker than it currently is.

Currently, most communities with landfills get nothing or only a minimal fee when other communities dispose of their trash in the landfill. Suppose a community with no landfill were to be charged $250 per ton of landfill accepted, with $200 of that fee going to the community that is willing to have a landfill within its borders. At $250 per ton of landfill accepted, communities that were willing to have a landfill facility could fund their services—such as schools, police, fire, streets, and street lights— even as they lowered or even eliminated their property taxes. Since a $250 landfill fee was necessary for the benefits of the mandatory recycling program to exceed the costs, if the market-determined landfill prices did not rise to that level, then an economist would seriously consider whether a mandatory recycling program made economic sense at this time.

Q–9: Say the average tipping fee paid to landfills went down in the early 1990s. How would this affect an economist's view of recycling?

The Economist's Perspective on Environmental Problems

A second way in which an economist environmentalist's solution would likely differ from a noneconomist environmentalist's solution is that the economist would look at the problem from a broader perspective. He or she would likely say that environmentally sound recycling is only part of the issue; the real issue is the total amount of trash generated.

For example, say that total trash were reduced by 20 percent through lower consumption of items that create trash rather than through recycling. Wouldn't that achieve the same end? Using such reasoning, an economist is likely to argue that the problem shouldn't be seen as a problem of recycling, but as a problem of trash generation. Why is trash generation the problem? Because when individuals buy goods, they *do not* pay the cost of disposing of those goods.

To see why this is the approach to which economists are directed, think back to our discussion of how economists view problems. They look for a reason why individual decisions might involve an externality (a result of a decision that's not taken into account by the decision maker). If there's an externality of too much trash, it is that people are not taking into account the cost of getting rid of products when they make decisions about buying the products. Thus, the externality view focuses the analysis on trash generation and not on recycling because recycling is only one of many methods to reduce the amount of trash.

Q–10: What is the advantage of including the price of disposing of the good in the price of the good itself?

What's the economist's answer to this problem? Since trash generation involves an externality, the answer is that the externality's cost must be integrated into the good's initial price. Doing so will give people incentives to create less trash by seeing to it that the price of those goods that create trash includes the cost of getting rid of that trash. Thus, rather than support a mandatory recycling program, an economist would be more likely to support (1) a "trash tax" in which the price of items sold must include the cost of disposing of the items, or (2) a "disposal requirement" on goods.

Let's consider how these economists' policies might work in regard to newspapers (a significant component of trash). We first look at the trash tax.

A Trash Tax   A trash tax of, say, 10¢ per pound of newspaper would increase the price of newspapers significantly, causing people to demand fewer newspapers and/or publishers to print fewer pages in their newspapers. Here the reduction in trash wouldn't take place through recycling; it would take place through a reduction in newspapers demanded and/or newspaper pages supplied. This approach has an added benefit. The tax money that is generated could then be used to fund environmental programs that create environmental consciousness.

A Disposal Requirement   Alternatively, the government could simply pass a law requiring publishers to cut the volume of newspapers they generate by 10 percent. In other words, newspaper publishers would be responsible for ensuring that 10 percent of their papers are either recycled or eliminated. The program would allow some newspapers to exceed a 10 percent reduction. Such newspaper firms would be given disposal certificates for the tonnage they saved in excess of 10 percent. These certificates would be marketable, which means that the firms could sell the certificates to other firms who reduced their trash generation by less than 10 percent.

Under this program, firms would have two ways to meet the law's requirements. They could either directly meet the requirement by reducing the trash they generate by 10 percent, or they could indirectly meet the requirement by buying the necessary disposal certificates from other firms that had reduced their trash generation by more than 10 percent.

This program would give newspapers a strong incentive to see that their newspapers are recycled directly. It might cause newspaper carriers to collect old newspapers when they delivered new ones. This program would also stimulate the development of a computer newspaper that would involve no paper whatsoever. People would simply wake up in the morning and flip on their computer screen or TV to get the latest headlines and the accompanying stories.

Three years after its implementation, Big Town's program was considered a success; Big Town's coordinator was promoted to supervise the entire multi-town district, and mandatory recycling was adopted in all of the District. In the meantime, the prices of recyclables fell even lower than they were when the Big Town program started, and there were reports of recycling centers sending their recycled material to landfills as stockpiles of those materials became larger and larger.

The District built a new recycling and trash transfer station, paid for by the taxpayers through the issuance of long-term bonds, the cost of which was incorporated into trash collection fees. It also began selling its trash for $47 a ton to a New Hampshire incinerator that was actively seeking trash. Trash collection fees in the area went up more than 30 percent. While this was happening, the supposed landfill crisis in the United States abated, and in the mid-1990s many landfills were competing to get trash.

Within the environment of the 1990s, it was unclear what role recycling was playing. Advocates who recognized and understood the cost/benefit analysis of recycling argued that, despite its poor current cost/benefit showing, recycling was changing people's habits, making them environmentally aware, and creating economies of scale that would eventually mean that recycling would make economic sense. Economic cynics argued that it was simply a program to make environmental yuppies feel good—to give them the sense that they were doing something about the environment—without significantly changing their lifestyles, and without having a significant impact on the environment.

Obviously there's much more to be discussed about economists' approach to recycling and various alternative programs, but this brief discussion should give you a sense of economists' approach and convince you that *to be an economist does not mean that one cannot be an environmentalist*. But it should also give you a sense that an environmentalist economist's approach to an environmental problem could differ significantly from the approach of an environmentalist untrained in economics.

Being an economist does not mean that one cannot be an environmentalist.

CONCLUSION

Environmental issues are enormously complicated and require intense study before one can come up with a viable way of dealing with the problems. There are major difficulties with the economists' solutions presented here. I did not discuss those difficulties because (1) it would have made the chapter too long, and (2) it would have taken some of the sharp edge off of the arguments—and I wanted the arguments to cut deeply and make you think.

The point of this chapter is not to convince you to believe one thing or another about environmental policy—the issues are too complicated for that. The point is simply to make sure you recognize how complicated they are. In elementary school and high school (judging from what my sons learn), environmental issues are often presented as black and white—as positions taken by (1) the mean nasty businesspeople, and (2) the good friendly environmentalists. That characterization is far too simplistic. It does not consider the trade-offs that inevitably exist, and the difficulty of making judgments on limited data and imperfect statistics.

Economists are often seen by many laypeople as opposed to environmentalism. That isn't the case. There's no fundamental difference between environmentalists and economists in terms of beliefs or concerns about the environment. What difference there is involves initial approach. An environmental economist's initial thoughts are likely to focus on market incentives, while an environmentalist untrained in economics is likely to distrust the market's effectiveness and therefore favor regulatory approaches.

To emphasize how economic training can affect one's view of environmental problems, this chapter's approach has been to contrast the two views, showing the advantages of the economist's approach and the disadvantages of the regulatory approaches. But the decision to write the chapter this way creates a problem in making some people believe that the economic answer is obviously the correct answer. It isn't.

The economist's approach, like the regulatory environmentalist's approach, has disadvantages. For example, if landfill prices rose significantly, people would likely

7 Economists' reasoning involves a general approach to all problems in which a cost/benefit analysis is taken and the program with the least cost is chosen.

burn their own trash or dump it illegally. Similarly, a trash tax would involve significant administrative problems. So you should not come away from this chapter believing that economics has all the answers, or even that economic approaches are preferable to regulatory approaches (although I believe that the economic approach is preferable). Instead I'd like you to come away from this chapter believing that economic approaches to environmental issues are worth considering, and that it is important to keep an open mind in approaching environmental problems.

CHAPTER SUMMARY

• There is no contradiction in being both an economist and an environmentalist, but an economist environmentalist's approach to solving environmental problems often differs from a lay environmentalist's approach.

• Economists often question "statistical proof" that lay-people accept without question.

• Economists generally prefer incentive-based programs to direct regulatory programs because incentive-based programs are more efficient.

• An optimal policy is one in which the marginal cost of undertaking the policy equals its marginal benefit.

• Economists are often dubious about voluntary solutions.

• NIMBY suggests that some prices are not free to fluctuate.

• All policies have problems and advantages. It is important to consider both before deciding on a policy.

KEY TERMS

causation (786)
correlation (786)
corroboration (786)
direct regulation (789)
efficiently (789)
externality (789)

free rider problem (794)
global warming theory (786)
inefficient (791)
market incentive program (789)
marketable certificate
  program (792)

NIMBY (794)
opportunity costs (797)
optimal level of pollution (793)
optimal policy (792)
proven reserves (788)
tax incentive program (792)

QUESTIONS FOR THOUGHT AND REVIEW

The number after each question represents the estimated degree of critical thinking required. (1 = almost none; 10 = deep thought.)

1. Many environmentalists agree that the data supporting the global warming theory are questionable but argue that, if the theory is correct, unless we start doing something about global warming now, it will be too late to do anything about it. Would you expect an economist to accept this argument? Why or why not? *(7)*

2. A friend tells you that by historical standards the price of gold is low, so now is a great time to buy gold. Would you agree? Why or why not? *(5)*

3. Explain why a market incentive program is more efficient than a direct regulatory program. *(6)*

4. It is sometimes said that there is a trade-off between fairness and efficiency. Explain one way in which that is true and one way in which it is not true. *(8)*

5. How would an economist likely respond to the statement "There is no such thing as acceptable pollution"? *(5)*

6. State two reasons why an economist generally opposes a solution based upon voluntary action that is not in people's self-interest. *(4)*

7. Say that the government placed a high tax on the use of oil. Would that significantly reduce the amount of pollution coming from the use of oil? Why or why not? *(4)*

8. Say that the government placed a high tax on the use of oil. Would that significantly reduce the total amount of pollution in the environment? *(8)*

9. If the price of landfills rose significantly, what problems do you see arising in the disposal of trash? *(7)*

10. How does your community deal with trash? What would an economist think of that method? *(9)*

PROBLEMS AND EXERCISES

1. There's a gas shortage in Gasland. You're presented with two proposals that will achieve the same level of reduction in the use of gas. Proposal A would force everybody to reduce their gas consumption by 5 percent. Proposal B would impose a 50¢ tax on the consumption of a gallon of gas, which would also achieve a 5 percent reduction. Demand curves for two groups are shown below.
   a. Show the effect of both proposals on each group.
   b. Which group would support a regulatory policy? Which would support a tax policy?

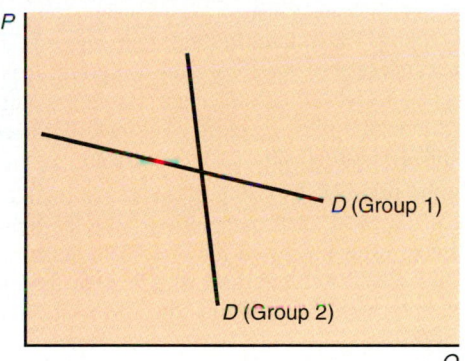

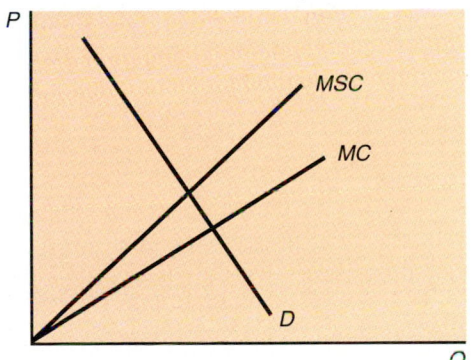

The marginal cost, marginal social cost, and demand for fish are represented by the curves at the beginning of this question. Suppose that there are no restrictions on fishing.
   a. Assuming perfect competition, what is the catch going to be, and at what price will it be sold?
   b. What are the socially efficient price and output?
   c. Some sports fishers propose a ban on commercial fishing. As the community's economic advisor, you're asked to comment on it at a public forum. What do you say?

3. You are in Seattle, watching the Seattle Stomp—a dance homeowners do in their trash cans.
   a. What can you say about trash fees in Seattle? Be as specific as possible.
   b. What change in fee structure might eliminate the Seattle Stomp?

4. In *At the Hand of Man*, Raymond Bonner argues that Africa should promote hunting, charging large fees for permits to kill animals (for example, $7,500 for a permit to shoot an elephant).
   a. What are some arguments in favor of this proposal?
   b. What are some arguments against?

5. California has passed an air quality law that requires that by 1998, 2 percent of all the cars sold in the state emit zero pollution, and that by 2003, 10 percent of all cars sold in the state meet this standard.
   a. What is the likely impact of this law?
   b. Can you think of any way in which this law might actually increase pollution rather than decrease it?
   c. How might an economist suggest modifying this law to better achieve economic efficiency?

ANSWERS TO MARGIN QUESTIONS

1. Judging from my knowledge of my decisions to wear shorts and eat ice cream, I would say that neither causes the other. Instead, they are both caused by a third phenomenon, hot weather. They are correlated with each other because they are both results of that hot weather. *(786)*

2. False. The fact that the average is normal does not necessarily mean that the components that make up that average are normal. In 1993, the Midwest had enormous floods and the Southeast had enormous drought, so even though the average rainfall was normal, there were very serious regional weather-related problems. *(788)*

3. True. Judging from past experience, proven reserves of resources have continually increased as rises in prices have led to new discoveries. Moreover, technological improvements have made us able to use a wider variety of resources, so what is considered a resource now includes elements that were not resources earlier. Sometimes that new technology is such an improvement that what was formerly considered a resource—like soft coal—ceases to be a resource. By the year 2010, oil may no longer be considered a resource. *(788)*

4. The market mechanism for dealing with shortages is twofold: (1) The rise in price causes the quantity

demanded to decrease as consumers substitute for the product; and (2) the rise in price leads existing suppliers to increase the quantity they supply, and leads others to develop new technologies and alternatives, shifting the supply curve out and the demand curve in. *(789)*

5. The tax incentive approach to conservation is fair in the following sense: Individuals who use more of the resource, pay more; and individuals who conserve more, pay less. In some broader sense, this may not be fair if one does not accept the underlying property rights that determined the initial amounts of resources that people had before the tax incentive was imposed. *(792)*

6. If an economist cannot find an externality, the economist will likely conclude that there is no problem and that we should let the market operate without interference. *(794)*

7. The price received for recycled material is the value that the market places on it, and that value is determined by the complicated interactions of many people. If the price of recycled material is zero, it means that the costs of recycling, in terms of resources as measured by current prices, are equal to the gains one gets. This does not mean that the economist will not, nonetheless, choose to support the program. Three possible reasons include: (1) current prices might not include certain social costs that the economist believed should be included; (2) the recycling program could lead to economies of scale and future recycling technological gains that would significantly raise the relative value of recycled material; and (3) individuals might get pleasure from the process of recycling—independent of the value to the environment. *(797)*

8. An economist would not necessarily believe that we should simply let the market deal with the pollution problem. Pollution clearly involves externalities. Where economists differ from many laypeople is in how they would handle the problem. An economist is likely to look much more carefully into costs, try to build price incentives into whatever program is designed, and make the marginal private cost equal the marginal social cost. *(798)*

9. If the tipping fee to landfills fell, that suggests that landfills became less scarce. Since those tipping fees are the alternative to recycling, lower tipping fees would suggest to an economist that recycling may make less sense than it would if landfills were scarce. *(799)*

10. When the price of disposing of a good is included in the price of the good itself, people will take the marginal social cost of disposing of the good into account when they buy it, and will buy less of it. Rather than recycle, they simply will not use goods that are socially harmful. *(800)*

37

International Trade

One of the purest fallacies is that trade follows the flag. Trade follows the lowest price current. If a dealer in any colony wished to buy Union Jacks, he would order them from Britain's worst foe if he could save a sixpence.

~Andrew Carnegie

After reading this chapter, you should be able to:

1 List the primary trading partners of the United States.

2 Explain the principle of absolute advantage.

3 Explain the principle of comparative advantage.

4 List three determinants of the terms of trade.

5 Explain three policies countries use to restrict trade.

6 Discuss why countries impose trade restrictions.

7 Summarize why economists generally oppose trade restrictions.

Many goods we use every day aren't made in the United States: cars, clothes, televisions—the list is endless. These goods are imported from other countries. Almost every day we hear calls from some sector of the economy to restrict foreign imports in order to save U.S. jobs and protect U.S. workers from unfair competition. Economists generally oppose these restrictions; economists favor free trade. In this chapter I consider why countries trade, why economists generally favor free trade, and why, despite what economists tell them, countries impose trade restrictions.

PATTERNS OF TRADE

Increasing but Fluctuating World Trade

Before I consider these issues, let's look at some numbers relevant to international trade to get a sense of the nature and dimensions of international trade.

In 1928, total world trade was about $430 billion (in 1993 dollars). U.S. gross domestic product was about $760 billion, so world trade as a percentage of U.S. GDP was almost 60 percent. In 1935, that ratio had fallen to less than 30 percent. In 1950 it was 20 percent. Then it started rising. In the early 1990s it was once again approximately 60 percent. As you can see, the level of world trade has fluctuated significantly.

In terms of dollar amounts, the fluctuations in international trade over the years are even greater. In constant 1980 dollars, world trade fell from $245 billion in 1928 to $110 billion in 1935. It then rose again, to well over $2 trillion in the early 1990s. The conclusion: International trade has been growing, but with significant fluctuations in that growth. Sometimes international trade has grown rapidly; at other times it has grown slowly or has even fallen.

In part, fluctuations in world trade result from fluctuations in world output. When output rises, international trade rises; when output falls, international trade falls. Fluctuations in world trade are also in part explained by trade restrictions that countries have imposed from time to time. For example, decreases in world income during the Depression caused a large decrease in trade, but that decrease was exacerbated by a worldwide increase in trade restrictions during the 1930s.

Differences in Importance of Trade

The importance of international trade to countries' economies differs widely, as we can see in Exhibit 1, which presents the importance of the shares of exports and imports for various countries. Among the countries listed, the Netherlands has the highest amount of exports compared to GDP; the United States has the lowest.

The Netherlands' imports are also the highest as a percentage of GDP. The United States has the lowest. The relationship between a country's imports and its exports is no coincidence. For most countries, imports and exports roughly correspond, though in any particular year that correspondence can be rough indeed. For the United States in recent years, imports have generally significantly exceeded exports. But that situation can't continue forever, as I'll discuss.

For most countries, imports and exports roughly correspond, though in any particular year that correspondence can be rough indeed.

Total trade figures provide us with only part of the international trade picture. We must also look at what types of goods are traded and with whom that trade is conducted. Exhibit 2 breaks U.S. international trade down into its various components. Notice that the United States both imports and exports significant amounts of manufactured goods. This isn't unusual, since much of all international trade is in manufactured goods.

1 The primary trading partners of the United States are Canada, Western Europe, Latin America, Japan, and Southeast Asia.

Exhibit 3 shows the regions with which the United States trades. Exports to Canada and Western Europe made up a large percentage of total U.S. exports in 1993. Regions from which the United States imports major quantities include Canada, Western Europe, Japan, Southeast Asia, and Latin America. Notice how the relative share of imports from Japan to total U.S. imports has increased over the years, while the percent share of U.S. exports to Japan has remained the same.

	GDP*	Exports*	% GDP	Imports*	% GDP
U.S.	$5,951	$442	7%	$544	9%
Canada	537	124	23	118	22
Netherlands	260	129	50	118	45
Germany	1,398	378	27	355	25
United Kingdom	921	187	20	211	23
Italy	1,012	169	17	170	17
France	1,080	213	20	230	21
Japan	2,468	340	14	233	9

EXHIBIT 1   Relation of Exports and Imports to GDP in Selected Countries, 1992

* Numbers in billions.

Source: *The World FactBook,* 1993.

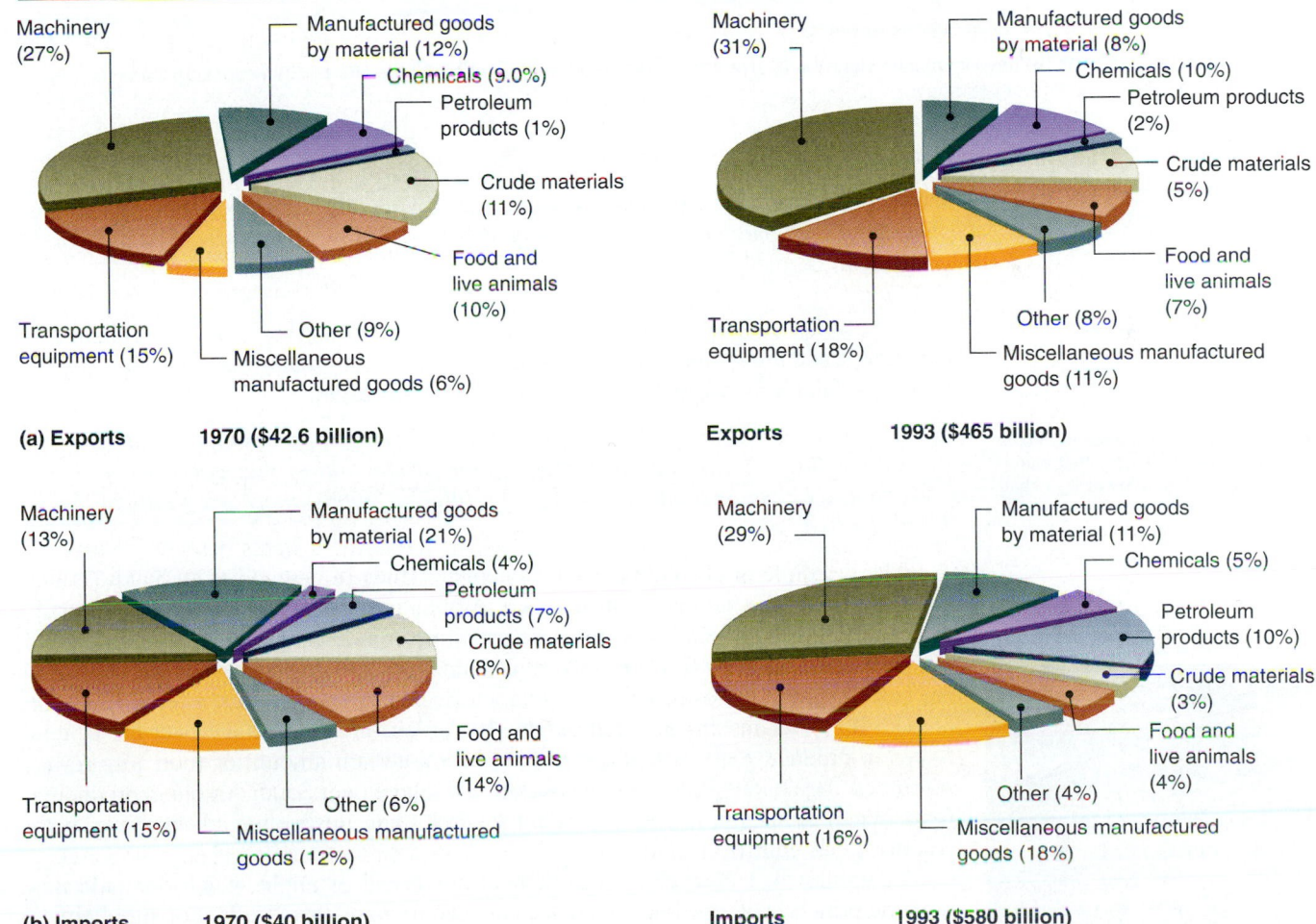

(a) Exports   1970 ($42.6 billion)

Exports   1993 ($465 billion)

(b) Imports   1970 ($40 billion)

Imports   1993 ($580 billion)

EXHIBIT 2 (a and b)   U.S. Imports and Exports by Commodity

The pie charts show the relative shares of each commodity group in exports (**a**) and imports (**b**). Notice how much of U.S. trade consists of machinery, manufactured goods, and transportation equipment. This is not unusual, because much of all international trade is in manufactured goods.

Source: U.S. Department of Commerce, *Survey of Current Business.* (Some 1993 data are estimated because of a change in classification system.)

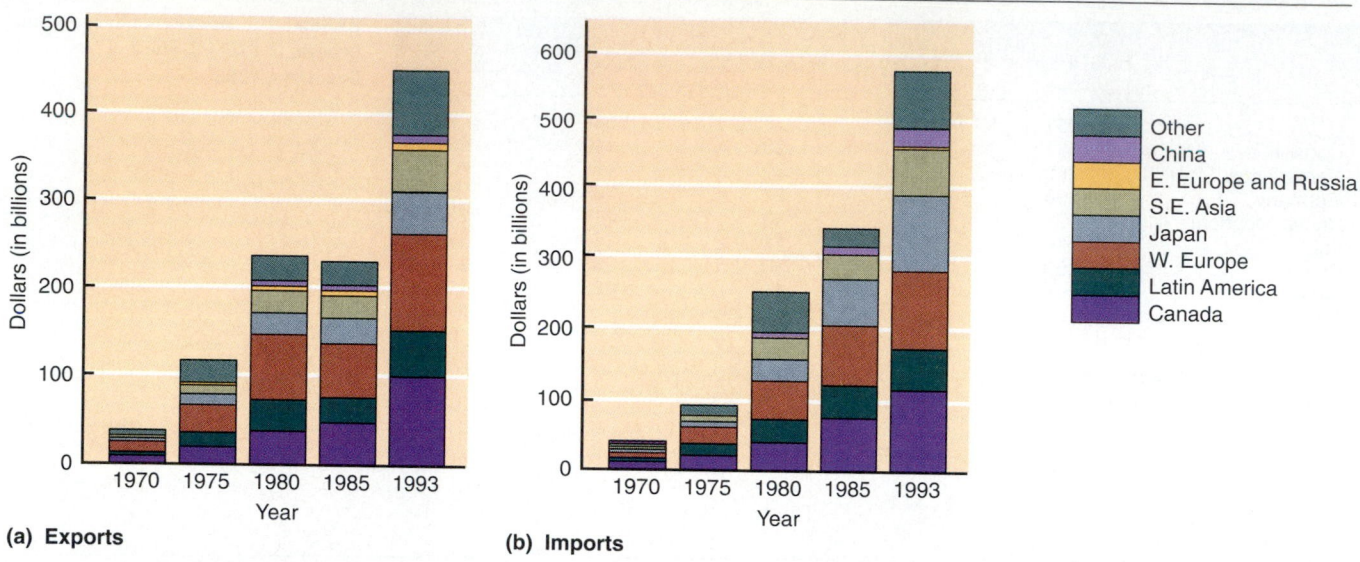

(a) Exports   **(b) Imports**

EXHIBIT 3 (a and b)   U.S. Exports and Imports by Region

U.S. exports (**a**) and imports (**b**) have increased significantly over time. Major regions that trade with the United States include Canada, Western Europe, Japan, and Southeast Asia.
Source: *Survey of Current Business.*

WHY DO NATIONS TRADE?

The Principle of Absolute Advantage

2 The principle of absolute advantage states that a country that can produce a good at a lower cost than another country has an absolute advantage in the production of that good.

International trade means that huge amounts of goods are shipped through ports. Here U.S. exports are being loaded onto a South Korean shipping line in Seattle. © *Bob Daemmrich/ The Image Works.*

International trade exists for the same reason that all trade exists: Party A has something that party B wants and party B has something that party A wants. Both parties can be made better off by trade.

Trade between countries in different types of goods is relatively easy to explain. For example, trade in raw materials and agricultural goods for manufactured goods can be easily explained by the **principle of absolute advantage:**

> *A country that can produce a good at a lower cost than another country is said to have an absolute advantage in the production of that good. When two countries have absolute advantages in different goods, there are gains of trade to be had.*

The principle of absolute advantage explains trade of, say, oil from Saudi Arabia for food from the United States. Saudi Arabia has millions of barrels of easily available oil, but growing food in its desert climate and sandy soil is expensive. The United States can grow food cheaply in its temperate climate and fertile soil, but its oil isn't as easily available or as cheap to extract. Because it can produce a certain amount of oil with fewer resources, Saudi Arabia has an absolute advantage over the United States in producing oil. Because it can produce a certain amount of food with fewer resources, the United States has an absolute advantage over Saudi Arabia in producing food. When each country specializes in the good it has an absolute advantage in, both countries can gain from trade.

In Exhibit 4, I consider a hypothetical numerical example which demonstrates how the principle of absolute advantage can lead to gains from trade. For simplicity, I assume constant opportunity costs.

Exhibits 4(b) and (d) show the choices for the United States; Exhibits 4(a) and (c) show the choices for Saudi Arabia. In Exhibits 4(a) and (b) you see that the United States and Saudi Arabia can produce various combinations of food and oil by devoting differing percentages of their resources to producing each. Comparing the two tables and assuming the resources in the two countries are comparable, we see that Saudi Arabia has an absolute advantage in the production of oil and the United States has an absolute advantage in the production of food.

Saudi Arabia

Percentage of resources devoted to oil	Oil produced (barrels)	Food produced (tons)	Row
100	1,000	0	A
80	800	20	B
60	600	40	C
40	400	60	D
20	200	80	E
0	0	100	F

(a) Saudi Arabia's Production Possibility Table

United States

Percentage of resources devoted to oil	Oil produced (barrels)	Food produced (tons)	Row
100	100	0	A
80	80	200	B
60	60	400	C
40	40	600	D
20	20	800	E
0	0	1,000	F

(b) United States's Production Possibility Table

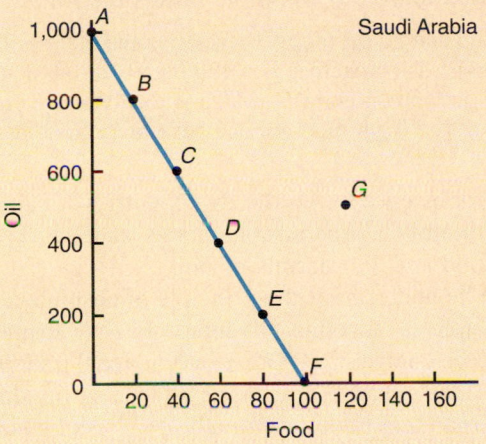

(c) Saudi Arabia's Production Possibility Curve

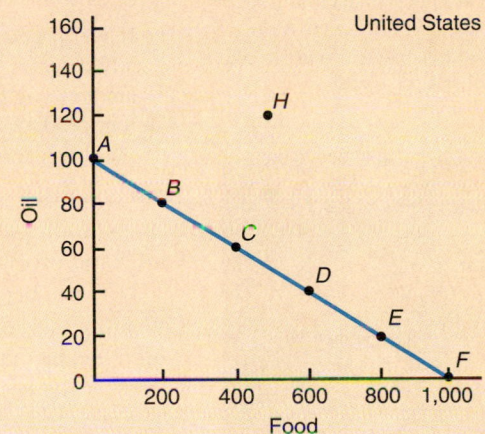

(d) United States's Production Possibility Curve

EXHIBIT 4 (a, b, c, and d)   Absolute Advantage: The United States and Saudi Arabia

Looking at tables (a) and (b), you can see that if Saudi Arabia devotes all its resources to oil, it can produce 1,000 barrels of oil, but if it devotes all of its resources to food, it can produce only 100 tons of food. For the United States, the story is the opposite: devoting all of its resources to oil, the United States can only produce 100 barrels of oil—10 times less than Saudi Arabia—but if it devotes all of its resources to food, it can produce 1,000 tons of food—10 times more than Saudi Arabia. Assuming resources are comparable, Saudi Arabia has an absolute advantage in the production of oil, and the United States has an absolute advantage in the production of food. The information in the tables is presented graphically in (c) and (d). These are the countries' production possibility curves without trade. Each point on each country's curve corresponds to a row on that country's table.

For example, when the United States and Saudi Arabia devote equal amounts of resources to oil production, Saudi Arabia can produce 10 times as much as the United States. Alternatively, when the United States devotes 60 percent of a given amount of resources to oil production, it gets 60 barrels of oil. But when Saudi Arabia devotes 60 percent of that same amount of resources to oil production, it gets 600 barrels of oil. The information in the tables is presented graphically in Exhibits 4(c) and (d). These graphs represent the two countries' production possibility curves without trade. Each combination of numbers in the table corresponds to a point on the curve. For example, point B in each graph corresponds to the entries in row B, columns 2 and 3, in the relevant table.

Let's assume that, without any international trade, the United States has chosen point C (production of 60 barrels of oil and 400 tons of food) and Saudi Arabia has chosen point D (production of 400 barrels of oil and 60 tons of food).

Now I. T. (International Trader), who understands the principle of absolute advantage, comes along and offers the following deal to Saudi Arabia:

If you produce 1,000 barrels of oil and no food (point A) and give me 500 barrels of oil while keeping 500 barrels for yourself, I guarantee you 120 tons of food, double

Q–1: Given the production possibilities in Exhibit 4, if the United States only wanted to consume food, would there be a basis for trade?

EXHIBIT 5   **Distribution of Production among the United States, Saudi Arabia, and I. T.**

	Oil (barrels)	Food (tons)
Total production	1,000	1,000
U.S. consumption	120	500
Saudi consumption	500	120
I. T.'s profit	380	380

the amount of food you're now getting. I'll put you on point *G,* which is totally above your current production possibility curve. You'll get more oil and more food. It's an offer you can't refuse.

I. T. then flies off to the United States, to whom he makes the following offer:

If you produce 1,000 tons of food and no oil (point *F*) and give me 500 tons of food while keeping 500 tons for yourself, I'll guarantee you 120 barrels of oil, double the amount you're now getting. I'll put you on point *H,* which is totally above your current production possibility curve. You'll get more oil and have more food. It's an offer you can't refuse.

Both countries accept; they'd be foolish not to. So the two countries' final consumption positions are as shown in Exhibit 5. For arranging the trade, I. T. makes a handsome profit of 380 tons of food and 380 barrels of oil.

I. T. has become rich because he understands the principle of absolute advantage. Unfortunately for I. T., the principle of absolute advantage is easy to understand, which means that he will quickly face competition. Other international traders come in and offer the countries even better deals than I. T. offered, squeezing his share. With free entry and competition in international trade, eventually I. T.'s share is squeezed down to his costs plus a normal return for his efforts.

Now obviously this hypothetical example significantly overemphasizes the gains a trader makes. Generally the person arranging the trade must compete with other traders and offer both countries a better deal than the one presented here. But the person who first recognizes a trading opportunity often makes a sizable fortune. The second and third persons who recognize the opportunity make smaller fortunes. Once the insight is generally recognized, the possibility of making a fortune is gone. Traders still make their normal returns, but the instantaneous fortunes are not to be made without new insight. In the long run, benefits of trade go to the countries, not the traders.

I. T. realizes this and spends part of his fortune on buying a Greek island, where he retires to contemplate more deeply the nature of international trade so he can triple his remaining fortune. He marries, has a daughter whom he names I. T. Too, and dies. But before he dies he teaches his daughter about international trade and how new insights can lead to fortunes. His dying words to his daughter are, "Keep searching for that new insight."

Q–2: Given the production possibilities in Exhibit 4, if Saudi Arabia only wanted to consume food, would there be a basis for trade?

Economist Edward Leamer has made significant contributions to empirically applying international trade theory. © *Philip Channing.*

Q–3: If one country had an absolute advantage in all goods, would there be a basis for trade?

The Principle of Comparative Advantage

Many years pass. I. T. Too grows up, and one day, while walking along the beach contemplates the possibilities of trade between Germany and Algeria in automobiles and food. No other traders have considered trade between these two countries because Germany is so much more productive than Algeria in *all* goods. No trade is currently taking place because Germany has an absolute advantage in production of both autos and food. Assuming the resources in the two countries are comparable, this case can be seen in Exhibit 6.

But I. T. Too is bright. She remembers what her father taught her about opportunity costs back in her first economics lesson. She reasons as follows: Germany's opportunity cost of producing an auto is 2/1. That means Germany must give up 2 tons of food to get 1 additional auto. For example, if Germany is initially producing 60 autos and 80 tons of food, if it cuts production of autos by 20, it will increase its food output by 40. For each car lost, Germany gains 2 tons of food. When Algeria cuts its

% of resources devoted to autos	Autos produced	Food produced	Row		% of rescources devoted to autos	Autos produced	Food produced	Row
100%	100	0	A		100%	20	0	A
80	80	40	B		80	16	1	B
60	60	80	C		60	12	2	C
40	40	120	D		40	8	3	D
20	20	160	E		20	4	4	E
0	0	200	F		0	0	5	F
(a) Germany					(b) Algeria			

EXHIBIT 6 (a and b)   Germany's Comparative Advantage over Algeria in the Production of Autos and Food

production of autos by 4, it gains 1 ton of food. Algeria's opportunity cost of producing another auto is 1/4. It must give up 1 ton of food to get an additional 4 autos.

I. T. Too further reasons that if Algeria needs to give up only $\frac{1}{4}$ unit of food to get an auto while Germany needs to give up 2 tons of food to produce 1 auto, there are potential gains to be made, which can be split up among the countries and herself. Then, like her father before her, she can make the countries offers they can't refuse. She walks the beach mulling the following: "*Absolute advantage* is not necessary for trade; *comparative advantage* is." A smile comes over her face; she understands.

Flying happily over the Mediterranean Sea, she formulates her insight precisely. She calls it the **principle of comparative advantage:** *As long as the relative opportunity costs of producing goods (what must be given up in one good in order to get another good) differ among countries, there are potential gains from trade, even if one country has an absolute advantage in everything.*

It is comparative advantage, not absolute advantage, that forms a basis of trade. If one country has a comparative advantage in one good, the other country must, by definition, have a comparative advantage in the other good.

Having formulated her idea, she applies it to the Germans and Algerians. She sees that, unexpectedly, Germany has a comparative advantage in producing food and Algeria has a comparative advantage in producing cars. With this insight firmly in mind, she leaves her island, flies to Germany, and makes the Germans the following offer:

> You're currently producing and consuming 60 autos and 80 tons of food (row *C* of Exhibit 6(a)). If you'll produce only 48 autos but 104 tons of food and give me 22 tons of food, I'll guarantee you 13 autos for those 22 tons of food. You'll have more autos (61) and more food (82). It's an offer you can't refuse.

She then goes to Algeria and presents the Algerians with the following offer:

> You're currently producing 4 tons of food and 4 automobiles (row *E* of Exhibit 6(b)). If you'll produce only automobiles (row *A*) and turn out 20 autos, keeping 5 for yourself and giving 15 of them to me, I'll guarantee you 5 tons of food for the 15 autos. You'll have more autos (5) and more food (5). It's an offer you can't refuse.

Absolute advantage is not necessary for trade; comparative advantage is.

3. The principle of comparative advantage states that as long as the relative opportunity costs of producing goods differ among countries, there are potential gains from trade, even if one country has an absolute advantage in everything.

Q–4:   In the Exhibit 6 example, what was the minimum amount of food I. T. Too had to offer Algeria?

	Autos	Food
Total production	68	104
German consumption	61	82
Algerian consumption	5	5
I. T. Too's profit	2	17

EXHIBIT 7   Final Consumption for Both Countries

ADDED DIMENSION

WHO FORMULATED THE PRINCIPLE OF COMPARATIVE ADVANTAGE?

In case you were wondering, I. T. Too didn't really formulate the principle of comparative advantage. It first appeared in a book called *Principles of Economics* written by an extraordinarily bright stockbroker, David Ricardo, in 1817. Thus, it's often called the *Ricardian principle of comparative advantage.*

As with many other principles of economics, the true lineage of this principle is subject to dispute. Ideas are often "in the air" long before they get into print, and the person to whom history attributes them may not be the person who formulated them. After some superb detective work, in 1976 William Thweat discovered that Ricardo's good friend, economist James Mill, and not Ricardo himself, was the first to write about comparative advantage and so deserves to be called the discoverer of the principle of comparative advantage. Not all historians agree with Thweat, but all agree that it was one of those two, not I. T. Too.

Neither Germany nor Algeria can refuse. They both agree to I. T. Too's offer. The final position appears in Exhibit 7.

I. T. Too then proceeds to visit various other countries, making similar offers. They accept the offers because it's in their interest to accept them. Countries (and people) trade because trade benefits them.

As was the case with her father, her initial returns are the greatest. Then, as other people recognize the principle of comparative advantage and offer the countries better deals than hers, her share shrinks until her return just covers her opportunity cost and the costs of transporting the goods. But because the principle of comparative advantage is more difficult to understand than the principle of absolute advantage, the competing traders enter in much more slowly. Her above-normal returns last longer than did her father's, but eventually they're competed away. When the gains decline to only normal levels, she sells out and retires.

Competitiveness, Exchange Rates, and Comparative Advantage

In microeconomics, most of our analysis is conducted in real terms, without reference to a numeraire (price level) or exchange rate.

In microeconomics, most of our analysis is conducted in real terms without reference to a numeraire (price level) or exchange rate. These financial issues are traditionally covered in macroeconomics where the study of money and financial issues is a central focus. Money and financial markets are necessary to make trade and payment imbalances possible. However, it would be inappropriate not at least to mention those issues here, since exchange rates play a central role in determining a country's absolute advantage. In fact, without implicit exchange rates, absolute advantage cannot be determined.

In turn, absolute advantage plays a big role in whether a country can have a temporary trade surplus or trade deficit—phenomena that we ruled out by assumption in this micro analysis of trade so that we keep the presentation challenging, but learnable. In micro, trade surpluses or deficits are not considered.

As discussed in Chapter 5, generally a low exchange rate encourages exports from a country and discourages imports; a high exchange rate discourages exports and encourages imports. An example of the importance of exchange rates can be seen by considering the United States and Japan: in the mid-1980s a dollar bought 200 yen, but in the mid-1990s the dollar bought only 100 yen. That change halved the absolute advantage of Japan and significantly discouraged our consumption of Japanese products. The resurgence of the U.S. auto industry is in large part due to that change in the exchange rate.

Dividing Up the Gains from Trade

The principle of comparative advantage is powerful. It determines when there are gains of trade to be made. It doesn't determine how those gains of trade will be divided up among the countries involved and among traders like I. T. Too. I can, however, offer some insights into how those gains are likely to be divided up. I've already noted the first insight:

> The more competition that exists in international trade, the less likely it is that the trader gets the gains of trade; more of the gains from trade will go to the citizens in the two countries.

INTERNATIONAL ISSUES IN PERSPECTIVE

O ver the past 20 years, international issues have become increasingly important for the U.S. economy. That statement would be correct even if the reference period went back as far as the late 1800s. The late 1800s and the first 40 years of the 1900s was an isolationist period for the United States in which the country turned inward in both economic and foreign policies.

The statement would not be correct if the reference period were earlier than the late 1800s. In the 1600s, 1700s, and most of the 1800s, international trade was vital to the American economy—even more vital than now. The American nation grew from colonial possessions of England, France, and Spain. These "new world" colonial possessions were valued for their gold, agricultural produce, and natural resources. From a European standpoint, international trade was the colonies' reason for being.*

A large portion of the U.S. government's income during much of the 1800s came from tariffs. Our technology was imported from abroad, and international issues played a central role in wars fought here. (Many historians believe that the most important cause of the U.S. Civil War was difference of views about tariffs on manufactured goods. The South opposed them because it wanted cheap manufactured goods, while the North favored them because it wanted to protect its manufacturing industries.) Up until the 1900s, no one would have studied the U.S. economy independently of international issues. Not only was there significant international trade; there was also significant immigration. The United States is a country of immigrants.

Only in the late 1800s did the United States adopt an isolationist philosophy in both politics and trade. So in reference to that isolationist period, the U.S. economy has become more integrated with the world economy. However, in a broader historical perspective, that isolationist period was an anomaly, and the 1990s is simply returning international issues to the key role they've usually played.

A second important insight is that international trade has social and cultural dimensions. While much of the chapter deals with specifically economic issues, we must also remember the cultural and social implications of trade.

Let's consider an example from history. In the Middle Ages, Greek ideas and philosophy were lost to Europe when hordes of barbarians swept over the continent. These ideas

and that philosophy were only rediscovered in the Renaissance as a by-product of trade between the Italian merchant cities and the Middle East. (The Greek ideas that had spread to the Middle East were protected there from European upheavals.) *Renaissance* means rebirth: a rebirth in Europe of Greek learning. Many of our traditions and sensibilities are based on those of the Renaissance, and that Renaissance was caused, or at least significantly influenced, by international trade. Had there been no trade, our entire philosophy of life might have been different.

Fernand Braudel, a French historian, has provided wonderful examples of the broader implications for trade. For instance, he argued that the effects of international trade, specifically Sir Walter Raleigh's introduction of the potato into England from South America in 1588, had more long-run consequences than did the celebrated 1588 battle of the English navy and Spanish Armada.

Another example, which Braudel did not live to see, is the major change in socialist countries in the 1990s. Through the 1960s China, the Soviet Union, and the Eastern European countries were relatively closed societies—behind the Iron Curtain. That changed in the 1970s and 1980s as these socialist countries opened up trade with the West as a way to speed their own economic development. That trade, and the resulting increased contact with the West, gave the people of those countries a better sense of the material goods to be had in the West. That trade also spread Western ideas of the proper organization of government and the economy to these societies. A strong argument can be made that along with trade came the seeds of discontent which changed those societies and their economies forever.

The international economics presented in this chapter does not focus on these broader cultural issues. International economics is about relatively technical issues such as the reasons for trade and the implications of tariffs. But keep in the back of your mind these broader implications as you go through the various components of international economies. They add a dimension to the story that otherwise might be forgotten.

---

* The American Indian standpoint was, I suspect, somewhat different.

This insight isn't lost upon trading companies. Numerous import/export companies exist whose business is discovering new possibilities for international trade. Individuals representing trading companies go around hawking projects or goods to countries. For example, in 1989 at the end of the Iran/Iraq war, what the business world calls the *import/export contingent* flew in to Iraq with offers of goods and services to sell. Many of these same individuals had been in Saudi Arabia when the oil price rose in the 1970s, and in the Far East when China opened its doors to international trade in the 1980s. In the early 1990s, this same group flocked to the countries of the former Soviet Union.

Selling U.S. goods is often easy for such U.S. traders. The problem generally is arranging financing. The goods must be paid for in the currency of the country doing the exporting, not in the currency of the country doing the importing. Thus, often firms

4 Three determinants of the gains of trade are:
1. The more competition, the less the trader gets.
2. Smaller countries get a larger proportion of the gain than larger countries.
3. Countries producing goods with economies of scale get a larger gain from trade.

that are doing the selling must also arrange financing for the trade. Thus, foreign exchange arrangements are important.

A second insight is:

> Once competition prevails, smaller countries tend to get a larger percentage of the gains of trade than do larger countries.

Q–5: In what circumstances would a small country not get the larger percentage of the gains from trade?

The reason, briefly, is that more opportunities are opened up for smaller countries by trade than for larger countries. The more opportunities, the larger the relative gains. Say, for instance, that the United States begins trade with Mali, a small country in Africa. Enormous new consumption possibilities are opened up for Mali—prices of all types of goods will fall. Before international trade began, cars were probably extraordinarily expensive in Mali, while fish were cheap. With international trade, the price of cars in Mali falls substantially, so Mali gets the gains. Because the U.S. economy is so large compared to Mali's, the U.S. price of fish doesn't change noticeably. Mali's fish are just a drop in the bucket. The price ratio of cars to fish doesn't change much for the United States, so it doesn't get much of the gains of trade. Mali gets almost all the gains from trade.

There's an important catch to this gains-from-trade argument. The argument holds only "once competition among traders prevails." That means that Mali residents are sold cars at the same price (plus shipping costs) as U.S. residents. International traders in small countries often have little competition from other traders and keep large shares of the gains from trade for themselves. In the preceding examples, Germany and Algeria didn't get a large share of the benefits. It was I. T. Too who got most of the benefits. Since the traders often come from the larger country, the smaller country doesn't get the benefits of the gains from trade; the larger country's international traders do.

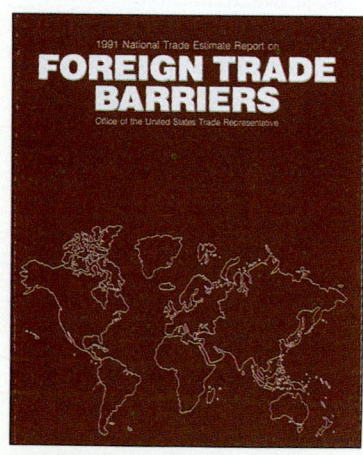

Foreign Trade Barriers is one of the many U.S. government publications that give specific information about international trade.

A third insight is:

> Gains from trade go to the countries producing goods that exhibit economies of scale.

Trade allows an increase in production. If there are economies of scale, that increase can lower the average cost of production of a good. Hence an increase in production can lower the price of the good in the producing country. The country producing the good with the largest economies of scale has its costs reduced by more, and hence gains more from trade than does its trading partner.

TRADE RESTRICTIONS

In the previous examples, I. T. Too had a relatively easy time persuading the countries to trade. All she had to do was show them that there were gains from trade to be made. Like any good trader, she didn't emphasize the potential difficulties that trade presents. In reality, international trade creates significant problems. That's why almost no country in the world allows free trade, but instead imposes a variety of trade restrictions. We briefly consider the nature of those policies to reduce trade.

Varieties of Trade Restrictions

Countries can use a variety of policies to restrict trade. These include tariffs, quotas, voluntary restraint agreements, embargoes, regulatory trade restrictions, and nationalistic appeals. I'll consider each in turn.

Industry	United States	European Union	Japan
Agriculture, forestry, and fisheries	1.8%	4.9%	18.4%
Food, beverages, and tobacco products	4.7	10.1	25.4
Textiles	9.2	7.2	3.3
Wearing apparel	22.7	13.4	13.8
Leather products	4.2	2.0	3.0
Footwear	8.8	11.6	15.7
Wood products	1.7	2.5	.3
Furniture and fixtures	4.1	5.6	5.1
Paper and products	.2	5.4	2.1
Printing and publishing	.7	2.1	.1
Chemicals	2.4	8.0	4.8
Petroleum and related products	1.4	1.2	2.2
Rubber products	2.5	3.5	1.1
Nonmetallurgical mineral products	5.3	3.7	.5
Glass and glass products	6.2	7.7	5.1
Iron and steel	3.6	4.7	2.8
Nonferrous metals	.7	2.1	1.1
Metal products	4.8	5.5	5.2
Nonelectrical machinery	3.3	4.4	4.4
Electrical machinery	4.4	7.9	4.3
Transportation equipment	2.5	8.0	1.5
Miscellaneous manufactures	4.2	4.7	4.6

EXHIBIT 8   Tariff Rates: United States, European Union, and Japan in the early 1990s. These rates will be continually changing as the changes negotiated in the latest GATT negotiations are implemented.

Source: General Agreement on Tariffs and Trade *(GATT)*.

Tariffs   Tariffs, also called *customs duties,* are taxes governments place on internationally traded goods—generally imports. Tariffs are the most-used and most familiar type of trade restriction. Tariffs operate in the same way a tax does: They make imported goods relatively more expensive than they otherwise would have been, and thereby encourage the consumption of domestically produced goods. On average, U.S. tariffs raise the price of imported goods by 5 percent. Exhibit 8 presents tariff rates on various goods imposed by the United States, the European Union, and Japan.

Probably the most infamous tariff in U.S. history is the Smoot-Hawley Tariff of 1930, which raised tariffs on imported goods an average of 60 percent. It was passed in response to the Great Depression in the United States and protect American jobs. It didn't work. Other countries responded with similar tariffs. As a result of these trade wars, international trade plummeted from $60 billion in 1928 to $25 billion in 1938, unemployment worsened, and the international depression deepened. These effects of the tariff convinced many, if not most, economists that free trade is preferable to trade restrictions. The dismal failure of the Smoot-Hawley Tariff was the main reason the **General Agreement on Tariffs and Trade (GATT)**, the regular international conference to reduce trade barriers, was established immediately following World War II. Since then, rounds of negotiations have resulted in a decline in worldwide tariffs.

Quotas   Quotas are quantity limits placed on imports. Their effect in limiting trade is similar to a tariff's effect. One big difference is in who gets the revenue. With a tariff, the government gets the revenue; with a quota, revenues accrue to producers of the protected good. For example, if the United States places quotas on foreign textiles, foreign producers of textiles will receive the proceeds of the resulting higher price. If the United States places a tariff on textile imports, the prices will also rise, but the U.S. government will receive the revenue.

A second big difference is that under a quota, any increase in domestic demand will be met by the less efficient domestic producers (who would otherwise lose in the competition) since a quota places strict numerical limitations on what can be imported. Under a tariff, part of any increase in domestic demand will be met by more efficient foreign producers since a tariff places a tax on imports but does not restrict their quantity. Needless to say, foreign producers prefer quotas to tariffs. The graphical distinction between quotas and tariffs is shown in the margin.

5 Three policies used to restrict trade are (1) tariffs (taxes on internationally traded goods), (2) quotas (quantity limits placed on imports), and (3) regulatory trade restrictions (government-imposed procedural rules that limit imports).

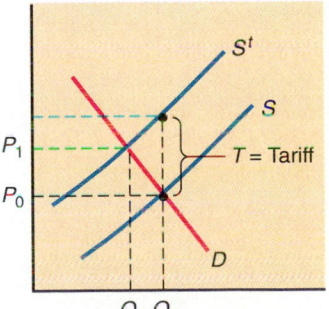

A quota of $Q_0 - Q_1$ is the equivalent of a tariff of t.

Q–6: What is the difference between a tariff and a quota?

Voluntary restraint agreements are often not all that voluntary.

Voluntary Restraint Agreements

Imposing new tariffs and quotas is specifically ruled out by GATT, but foreign countries know that GATT is voluntary and that, if a domestic industry brought sufficient political pressure on its government, GATT would be forgotten. To avoid the imposition of new tariffs on their goods, countries often voluntarily restrict their exports. That's why Japan has agreed informally to limit the number of cars it exports to the United States.

The effect of such voluntary restraint agreements is identical to the effect of quotas: They directly limit the quantity of imports, increasing the price of the good and helping domestic producers. For example, when the United States encouraged Japan to impose ''voluntary'' quotas on exports of its cars to the United States, Toyota benefitted from the quotas because it could price its limited supply of cars higher than it could if it sent in a large number of cars, so profit per car would be high. Since they faced less competition, U.S. car companies also benefitted. They could increase their prices because Toyota had done so.

Embargo   All-out restriction on import or export of a good.

Embargoes

An **embargo** is an all-out restriction on import or export of a good. Embargoes are usually established for international political reasons rather than for primarily economic reasons.

An example is the U.S. embargo of trade with Iraq. The U.S. government hoped that the embargo would so severely affect Iraq's economy that Saddam Hussein would lose political power. It did make life difficult for Iraqis, but it didn't bring about the downfall of the Hussein government.

Regulatory Trade Restrictions

Tariffs, quotas, and embargoes are the primary *direct* methods to restrict international trade. There are also indirect methods that restrict trade in not-so-obvious ways; these are called **regulatory trade restrictions** (government-imposed procedural rules that limit imports). One type of regulatory trade restriction has to do with protecting the health and safety of a country's residents. For example, a country might restrict import of all vegetables grown where certain pesticides are used, knowing full well that all other countries use those pesticides. The effect of such a regulation would be to halt the import of vegetables.

Q–7: How might a country benefit from having an inefficient customs agency?

A second type of regulatory restriction involves making import and customs procedures so intricate and time consuming that importers simply give up. For example, France requires all imported VCRs to be individually inspected in Toulouse. Since Toulouse is a provincial city, far from any port and outside the normal route for imports after they enter France, this inspection process can take months.

Some regulatory restrictions are imposed for legitimate reasons; others are designed simply to make importing more difficult.

Some regulatory restrictions are imposed for legitimate reasons; others are designed simply to make importing more difficult and hence protect domestic producers from international competition. It's often hard to tell the difference. A good example of this difficulty occurred in 1988 when the EU disallowed all imports of meat from animals that had been fed growth-inducing hormones, as the accompanying box details.

Nationalistic Appeals

Finally nationalistic appeals can help to restrict international trade. ''Buy American'' campaigns and Japanese xenophobia[1] are examples. Many Americans, given two products of equal appeal except that one is made in the United States and one is made in a foreign country, would buy the U.S. product. To get around this tendency, foreign and U.S. companies often go to great lengths to get a MADE IN U.S.A. classification on goods they sell in the United States. For example, components for many autos are made in Japan but shipped to the United States and assembled in Ohio or Tennessee so that the finished car can be called an American product.

Americans aren't the only nationalistic people on the international trade scene. Preference for Japanese goods is deeply ingrained in Japanese culture. Faced with U.S. demands that Japan reduce its trade surplus and with threats of retaliation if it

---

[1] *Xenophobia* is a Greek word meaning ''fear of foreigners.'' Pronounce the X like Z.

Trade restrictions, in practice, are often much more complicated than they seem in textbooks. Seldom does a country say, "We're limiting imports to protect our home producers." Instead the country explains the restrictions in a more politically acceptable way. Consider the fight between the European Union and the United States over U.S. meat exports. In 1988 the EU, in line with Union-wide internal requirements, banned all imports of any meat from animals treated with growth-inducing hormones, which U.S. meat producers use extensively. The result: the EU banned the meat exported from the United States.

The EU claimed that it had imposed the ban only because of public health concerns. The United States claimed that the ban was actually a trade restriction, pointing out that its own residents ate this kind of meat with confidence because a U.S. government agency had certified that the levels of hormones in the meat were far below any danger level.

The United States retaliated against the EU by imposing 100 percent tariffs on Danish and West German hams, Italian tomatoes, and certain other foods produced by EU member nations. The EU threatened to respond by placing 100 percent tariffs on $100 million worth of U.S. walnuts and dried fruits, but instead entered into bilateral meetings with the United States. Those meetings allowed untreated meats into the EU for human consumption and treated meats that would be used as dog food. In response, the United States removed its retaliatory tariff on hams and tomato sauce, but retained its tariffs on many other goods. In the 1990s, Europe's dog population seemed to be growing exponentially as Europe's imports of "dog food" increased by leaps and bounds. In 1994, talks were continuing.

Which side is right in this dispute? The answer is far from obvious. Both the U.S. and the EU have potentially justifyable positions. As I said, trade restrictions are more complicated in reality than in textbooks.

ADDED DIMENSION

HORMONES AND ECONOMICS

doesn't, the Japanese government has attempted to change its people's cultural bias and to encourage consumption of U.S. goods.

As you can see, there are many ways to restrict trade. But if trade makes sense, as it did in our example of I. T., why do countries restrict trade? Reasons for restricting trade include:

1. Unequal internal distribution of the gains from trade.
2. Haggling by companies over the gains from trade.
3. Haggling by countries over trade restrictions.
4. Specialized production: learning by doing and economies of scale.
5. Macroeconomic aspects of trade.
6. National security.
7. International politics.
8. Increased revenue brought in by tariffs.

I consider each of these obstacles to free trade in turn.

Unequal Internal Distribution of the Gains from Trade In the first example of trade discussed in this chapter, I. T. persuaded Saudi Arabia to specialize in the production of oil rather than of food, and persuaded the United States to produce more food than oil. That means, of course, that some U.S. oil workers will have to become farmers, and in Saudi Arabia some farmers will have to become oil producers.

Often people don't want to make radical changes in the kind of work they do—they want to keep on producing what they're already producing. So when these people see the same kinds of goods that they produce coming into their country from abroad, they lobby to prevent the foreign competition. Often they're successful. A good example is the "voluntary" quotas placed on Japanese cars discussed earlier. These quotas saved U.S. jobs, but forced consumers to pay higher prices for cars. Economists have estimated that it cost consumers about $100,000 for each job saved. Exhibit 9 lists economists' estimates of the cost to consumers of saving a job in some other industries.

Reasons for Trade Restrictions

6 Reasons for restricting trade include:
1. Unequal internal distribution of the gains from trade.
2. Haggling by companies over the gains from trade.
3. Haggling by countries over trade restrictions.
4. Specialized production: learning by doing and economies of scale.
5. Macroeconomic aspects of trade.
6. National security.
7. International politics.
8. Increased revenue brought in by tariffs.

EXHIBIT 9   Cost of Saving Jobs, Selected Industries

Industry	Cost of Production (per job saved)
Specialty steel	$1,000,000
Color TVs	420,000
Ceramic tiles	135,000
Clothing	36,000–82,000
Agriculture	20,000 (per farmer)
Dairy	1,800 (per cow)

Source: GATT, 1993.

The Costs of Change   Had I. T. been open about the difficulties of trading, he would have warned the countries that change is hard. It has very real costs that I. T. didn't point out when he made his offers. But these costs of change are relatively small compared to the gains from trade. Moreover, they're short-run, temporary costs, whereas gains from trade are permanent, long-run gains. Once the adjustment has been made, the costs will be gone but the benefits will still be there.

For most goods, the benefits for the large majority of the population so outweigh the small costs to some individuals that, decided on a strict cost/benefit basis, international trade is still a deal you can't refuse. With benefits so outweighing costs, it would seem that transition costs could be forgotten. But they can't.

Benefits of trade are generally widely scattered among the entire population. In contrast, costs of free trade often fall on specific small groups.

Benefits of trade are generally widely scattered among the entire population. In contrast, costs of free trade often fall on specific small groups of people who loudly oppose the particular free trade that hurts them. Though the benefits of free trade to the country at large exceed the costs of free trade to the small group of individuals, the political push from the few (who are hurt) for trade restrictions exceeds the political push from the many (who are helped) for free trade. The result is trade restrictions on a variety of products. You'll likely see TV ads supporting such restrictions under the heading SAVING U.S. JOBS. But you'll see few ads in favor of free trade to keep prices low for consumers.

It isn't only in the United States that the push for trade restrictions focuses on the small costs and not on the large benefits. For example, the European Union places large restrictions on food imports from nonmember nations. If the EU would remove those barriers, food prices in EU countries would decline significantly. For example, meat prices would probably fall by 65 percent. Consumers would benefit, but farmers would be hurt. The farmers, however, have the political clout to see that the costs are considered and the benefits aren't. The result: The EU places high duties on foreign agricultural products.

Q–8: Why does the EU place high barriers against agricultural products?

Trade Adjustment Assistance   Trade restrictions make the international trader's life more difficult but they also open up new possibilities. To see these possibilities, let's go back to I. T. Too. She has died and her son, I. T. Too II, has frittered away the entire family fortune and now must rely on his wits. Like his ancestors, he has good insights. He analyzes the problem as follows:

> Trade will make most members of society better off, but will make a particular subgroup in society worse off. Because of the country's political dynamics, this subgroup can prevent free trade. If I structure a program so that it transfers some of society's gains to individuals who are made worse off by trade, I can eliminate their opposition and thereby make society better off.

Trade adjustment assistance programs   Programs designed to compensate losers for reductions in trade restrictions.

Such programs are called **trade adjustment assistance programs.** Using this analysis, he presents the countries with the following deal:

> Given that adjustment costs of trade are small, here's what I'll do. I'll pay the adjustment costs of those people who are hurt by the trade—costs I've calculated to be only 1/20 of the gains. I'll then have eliminated the opposition to free trade. For doing this,

all I want for myself is 1/10 of the gains from trade, leaving 17/20 of the gains going to society. Now isn't this a deal you can't refuse?

Unfortunately for I. T. Too II, it's a deal most countries *can* refuse. Here's why.

Governments have tried to use trade adjustment assistance to facilitate free trade, but they've found that it's enormously difficult to limit the adjustment assistance to those who are actually hurt by international trade. As soon as people find that there's assistance for people injured by trade, they're likely to try to show that they too have been hurt and deserve assistance. Losses from free trade become exaggerated and magnified. Instead of only 1/20 of the gains from trade being needed for trade adjustment assistance, much more is demanded—often even more than the gains.

Telling people who claim to be hurt that they aren't really being hurt isn't good politics. That's why offering trade adjustment assistance as a way to relieve the pressure to restrict trade is a deal many governments can refuse. I. T. Too II must return home to go on public welfare and contemplate further the nature of international trade.

Telling people who claim to be hurt that they aren't really being hurt isn't good politics.

Haggling by Companies over the Gains from Trade

Many naturally advantageous bargains aren't consummated because each side is pushing for a larger share of the gains from trade than the other side thinks should be allotted. This is another example of the prisoner's dilemma.

To see how companies haggling over the gains of trade can cause restriction on trade, let's reconsider the original deal that I. T. proposed. I. T. got 380 tons of food and 380 barrels of oil. The United States got an additional 100 tons of food and 60 barrels of oil. Saudi Arabia got an additional 100 barrels of oil and 60 tons of food.

Suppose the Saudis had said, "Why should we be getting only 100 barrels of oil and 60 tons of food when I. T. is getting 380 barrels of oil and 380 tons of food? We want an additional 300 tons of food and another 300 barrels of oil, and we won't deal unless we get them." Similarly the United States might have said "We want an additional 300 tons of food and an additional 300 barrels of oil, and we won't go through with the deal unless we get them." If either the U.S. or the Saudi Arabian company that was involved in the trade for their country (or both) takes this position, I. T. might just walk—no deal. The potential for gains from trade is there, but tough bargaining positions can make it almost impossible to achieve them.

Such bargaining problems occur often. The side that drives the hardest bargain gets the most gain from the bargain, but it also risks making the deal fall through. Such strategic bargaining goes on all the time. **Strategic bargaining** means demanding a larger share of the gains from trade than you can reasonably expect.[2] If you're successful, you get the lion's share; if you're not successful, the deal falls apart and everyone is worse off.

Strategic bargaining   Demanding a larger share of the gains of trade than you can reasonably expect.

Haggling by Countries over Trade Restrictions

Another type of trade bargaining that often limits trade is bargaining between countries. Trade restrictions and the threat of trade restrictions play an important role in that kind of haggling. Sometimes countries must go through with trade restrictions that they really don't want to impose, just to make their threats credible.

Once one country has imposed trade restrictions, other countries attempt to get those restrictions reduced by threatening to increase their own restrictions. Again, to make the threat credible, sometimes countries must impose or increase trade restrictions simply to show they're willing to do so.

Ultimately, strategic bargaining power depends on negotiators' skills and the underlying gains from trade that a country would receive. A country that would

Q-9:   In strategic trade bargaining, it is reasonable to be unreasonable. True or false? Explain.

---

[2] Here's an example: You're buying a house. You're willing to pay $80,000, but you'd prefer to pay less. The seller is asking $85,000, but you believe the seller will accept considerably less. So what do you offer? There's no one right strategy. If you offer $75,000 and refuse to go higher, you're using strategic bargaining.

receive only a small portion of the gains from trade is in a much stronger bargaining position than a country that would receive significant gains. It's easier for the former to walk away from trade.

The United States is currently using such strategic bargaining in its attempt to get Japan to lower its restrictions on imports of U.S. goods. The U.S. Congress often threatens to restrict imports from Japan significantly if Japan doesn't ease its trade restrictions against U.S. goods. Since Japan depends heavily on exports to the United States, she takes such threats seriously. For example, in the late 1980s Japan's prime minister went on TV and asked Japanese people to buy U.S. goods. Japan also changed some of its laws governing industrial organization to make selling goods in Japan easier for U.S. companies.

Specialized Production: Learning by Doing and Economies of Scale

My discussion of absolute and comparative advantage took it as given that one country was more productive than another country in producing certain goods. But when one looks at trading patterns, it's often not at all clear why particular countries have a productive advantage in certain goods. There's no inherent reason for Switzerland to specialize in the production of watches or for South Korea to specialize in the production of cars. Much in trade cannot be explained by inherent resource endowments.

If they don't have inherent advantages, why are countries and places often so good at producing what they specialize in? Two important explanations are that they *learn by doing* and that *economies of scale* exist.

Learning by doing You become better at a task the more you perform it.

Learning by Doing

Learning by doing means that you become better at a task the more often you perform it. Take watches in Switzerland. Initially production of watches in Switzerland may have been a coincidence; the person who started the watch business happened to live there. But then people in the area became skilled in producing watches. Their skill made it attractive for other watch companies to start up. As additional companies moved in, more and more members of the labor force became skilled at watchmaking, and word went out that Swiss watches were the best in the world. That reputation attracted even more producers so Switzerland became the watchmaking capital of the world. Had the initial watch production occurred in Austria, not Switzerland, Austria might be the watch capital of the world.

When there's learning by doing, it's much harder to assign comparative advantage to a country. One must always ask: Does country A truly have a comparative advantage, or does it simply have more experience? Once country B gets the experience, will country A's comparative advantage disappear? If it will, then country B has a strong reason to limit trade with country A in order to give its own workers time to catch up as they learn by doing.

Economies of scale Costs per unit output go down as output increases.

Economies of Scale

In determining whether an inherent comparative advantage exists, a second complication is **economies of scale.** There are economies of scale when costs per unit output fall as output increases. Many manufacturing industries (such as steel and autos) exhibit economies of scale. The existence of significant economies of scale means that it makes sense (i.e., it lowers costs) for one country to specialize in one good and another country to specialize in another good. But who should specialize in what is unclear. Producers in a country can, and generally do, argue that if only the government will establish barriers, they'll be able to lower their costs per unit and eventually sell at lower costs than foreign producers.

A number of countries follow trade strategies to allow them to take advantage of economies of scale. For example, in the 1970s and 1980s Japan's government consciously directed investment into automobiles and high tech consumer products, and significantly promoted exports in these goods to take advantage of economies of scale.

Most countries recognize the importance of learning by doing and economies of scale. A variety of trade restrictions are based on these two phenomena. The most common expression of the learning-by-doing and economies-of-scale insights is the

infant industry argument, which countries use to justify many trade restrictions. They argue, ''You may now have a comparative advantage, but that's simply because you've been at it longer, or are experiencing significant economies of scale. We need trade restrictions on our _____ industry to give it a chance to catch up. Once an infant industry grows up, then we can talk about eliminating the restrictions.''

Infant industry argument   With initial protection, an industry will be able to become competitive.

Macroeconomic Aspects of Trade   The comparative advantage argument for free trade assumes full employment. When countries don't have full employment, imports can decrease domestic aggregate demand and increase unemployment. Exports can stimulate aggregate domestic demand and decrease unemployment. Similarly imports can decrease domestic economic activity. Thus, when an economy is in a recession, there is a strong macroeconomic reason to limit imports and encourage exports. These macroeconomic effects of free trade play an important role in the public's view of imports and exports. When a country is in a recession, pressure to impose trade restrictions increases substantially.

National Security   Countries often justify trade restrictions on grounds of national security. These restrictions take two forms:

1. Export restrictions on strategic materials and defense-related goods.
2. Import restrictions on defense-related goods. For example, in a war we don't want to be dependent on oil from abroad.

For a number of goods, national security considerations make sense. For example, the United States restricts the sale of certain military items to countries that are likely to be fighting the United States some day. The problem is where to draw the line about goods having a national security consideration. Should countries protect domestic agriculture? All high technology items, since they might be useful in weapons? All chemicals? Steel? The national security argument has been extended to a wide variety of goods whose importance to national security is indirect rather than direct. When a country makes a national security argument for trade, one must be careful to consider whether a domestic political reason may be lurking behind that argument.

International Politics   International politics frequently provides another reason for trade restrictions. The United States forbids trade with Cuba to punish that country for trying to extend its Marxist political and economic policies to other Latin American countries. Until 1991, the United States restricted exports to and imports from the Union of South Africa because it disapproved of South Africa's racist apartheid policies. U.S. grain exports to the Soviet Union were stopped in 1979 to protest the Soviet invasion of Afghanistan. The list can be extended, but you get the argument: Trade helps you, so we'll hurt you by stopping trade until you do what we want. So what if it hurts us too? It'll hurt you more than us.

Increased Revenue Brought in by Tariffs   A final argument made for one particular type of trade restriction—a tariff—is that tariffs bring in revenues. In the 19th century, tariffs were the U.S. government's primary source of revenue. They've receded in importance as a revenue for developed countries because those countries have instituted other forms of taxes. However, tariffs remain a primary source of revenue for many developing countries. They're relatively easy to collect and are paid by people rich enough to afford imports. These countries justify many of their tariffs with the argument that they need the revenues.

Each of the preceding arguments for trade restrictions has some validity, but most economists discount them and support free trade. The reason is that, in their considered judgment, the harm done by trade restrictions outweighs the benefits.

Economists' first argument for free trade is that, viewed from a global perspective, free trade increases total output. From a national perspective, economists agree that particular instances of trade restriction may actually help one nation, even as most

Why Economists Generally Oppose Trade Restrictions

ADDED DIMENSION

STRATEGIC TRADE POLICIES

The problem with strategic trade policies is that they can backfire. One rule of strategic bargaining is that the other side must believe that you'll go through with your threat. Thus, strategic trade policy can lead a country that actually supports free trade to impose trade restrictions, just to show how strongly it believes in free trade.

Even though most economists support free trade, they admit that in bargaining it may be necessary to adopt a strategic position. A country may threaten to impose trade restrictions if the other country does so. When such strategic trade policies are successful, they end up eliminating or reducing trade restrictions.

When should trade restrictions be used, and when should they not be used for strategic purposes? Economic theory does not tell us. That question is part of the practice of the art of economics. (It should be pointed out that economic game theorists are adding insights into the issue and that strategic trade policies is a hot area of research.)

7 Economists generally oppose trade restrictions because: (1) from a global perspective, free trade increases total output; (2) trade restrictions lead to retaliation; and (3) international trade provides competition for domestic companies.

Very few of the infant industries protected by trade restrictions have ever grown up.

Two items that the United States has been particularly successful in exporting are the know-how and ingredients for fast foods (such as hamburgers) and soda (especially Coca-Cola and Pepsi-Cola). Here we see a long line of people waiting in front of a McDonald's in Russia. *Reuters/Bettmann.*

Yes, some restrictions might benefit a country, but almost no country can limit its restrictions to the beneficial ones.

other nations are hurt. But they argue that the country imposing trade restrictions can benefit *only if the other country doesn't retaliate* with trade restrictions of its own. Retaliation is the rule, not the exception, however, and when there is retaliation, trade restrictions cause both countries to lose.

A second reason most economists support free trade is that trade restrictions reduce international competition. International competition is desirable because it forces domestic companies to stay on their toes. If trade restrictions on imports are imposed, domestic companies don't work as hard, and they become less efficient. For example, in the 1950s and 1960s the United States imposed restrictions on imported steel. U.S. steel industries responded to this protection by raising their prices and channeling profits from their steel production into other activities. By the 1970s the U.S. steel industry was a mess, internationally uncompetitive, and using outdated equipment to produce overpriced steel. Instead of making the steel industry stronger, restrictions made it a flabby, uncompetitive industry.

Economists dispose of the infant industry argument by reference to the historical record. In theory the argument makes sense. But very few of the infant industries protected by trade restrictions have ever grown up. What tends to happen instead is that infant industries become dependent on the trade restrictions and use political pressure to keep that protection. As a result, they often remain immature and internationally uncompetitive. Most economists would support the infant industry argument only if the trade restrictions included definite conditions under which the restrictions would end.

Most economists agree with the national security argument for export restrictions on goods that are directly war related. Selling bombs to Iraq, with whom the United States was at war in early 1991, doesn't make much sense (although it should be noted that the United States did exactly that throughout the 1980s when the United States supported Iraq in its war with Iran).

Economists point out that the argument is often carried far beyond goods directly related to national security. For example, in the 1980s the United States restricted exports of sugar-coated cereals to the Soviet Union for reasons of national security. Sugar-frosted flakes may be great, but they were unlikely to help the Soviet Union start a war.

Another argument that economists give against the national security rationale is that trade restrictions on military sales can often be evaded. Countries simply have another country buy the goods for them. Such third-party sales—called *transshipments*—are common in international trade and limit the effectiveness of any absolute trade restrictions for national security purposes.

Economists also argue that by fostering international cooperation, international trade makes war less likely—a significant contribution to national security.

Economists' final argument against trade restrictions is: Yes, some restrictions might benefit a country, but almost no country can limit its restrictions to the beneficial ones. Trade restrictions are addictive—the more you have, the more you want. Thus, a majority of economists take the position that the best response to such addictive policies is "just say no."

DUMPING

GATT allows countries to impose trade restrictions on imports if they can show that the goods are being dumped. *Dumping* is selling a good in a foreign country at a lower price than in the country where it's produced. On the face of it, who could complain about someone who wants to sell you a good cheaply? Why not just take advantage of the bargain price? The first objection is the learning-by-doing argument. To stay competitive, a country must keep on producing. Dumping by another country can force domestic producers out of business. Having eliminated the competition, the foreign producer has the field to itself and can raise the price. Thus, dumping can be a form of predatory pricing.

The second argument against dumping involves the short-term macroeconomic and political effects it can have on the importing country. Even if one believes that dumping is not a preliminary to predatory pricing, it can displace workers in the importing country, causing political pressure on that government to institute trade restrictions. If that country's economy is in a recession, the resulting unemployment will have substantial macroeconomic repercussions, so pressure for trade restrictions will be amplified.

Most politicians feel a strong push from constituents to impose trade barriers. Even politicians who accept free trade in principle support restrictions in practice. They have, however, found it possible to support a limited type of free trade in which a few countries agree to have free trade with each other. A **free trade association** (or *customs union*) is a group of countries that allows free trade among its members and, as a group, puts up common barriers against all other countries' goods.

Common Markets   The **European Union (EU)** is the most famous free trade association. All barriers to trade among the EU's 12 member countries were removed in 1992. During the 1990s more European countries, such as Sweden, can be expected to join the EU. In 1993, the United States and Canada agreed to enter into a similar free trade union, and they, together with Mexico, created the North American Free Trade Association (NAFTA). Under NAFTA, tariffs and other trade barriers among these countries will be reduced throughout the 1990s.

Economists have mixed reactions to free trade associations. They see free trade as beneficial, but are concerned about the possibility that these regional free trade associations will impose significant trade restrictions on nonmember countries. They also believe that bilateral negotiations between member nations will replace multilateral efforts among members and nonmembers. Whether the net effect of these bilateral negotiations is positive or negative remains to be seen.

GATT   Devastating trade wars took place during the 1930s. As a result, international trade fell by over 75 percent. This decline contributed to the worldwide Great Depression. Following that experience, countries organized to try to promote free trade among themselves. The most visible result—the General Agreement on Tariffs and Trade (GATT), established in 1947—had as its central goal the elimination of tariffs.

GATT created a mechanism for the 96 subscribing countries to establish multilateral regulations for eliminating trade barriers. Member countries meet every five years to work toward this end. Initially GATT focused on tariffs on manufactured goods, but has increasingly included services and agricultural goods as trade in these activities has expanded.

One of the goals of GATT was to equalize a country's trade barriers so that it did not discriminate against one specific country. The term **most-favored nation** refers to a country that will be charged as low a tariff on its exports as any other country. Thus, if the United States lowers tariffs on goods imported from Japan, which has most-favored nation status with the United States, it must lower tariffs on those same types of goods imported from any other country with most-favored nation status.

Trade negotiations are never easy. Here's the type of problem that continually occurs: In the 1988 Round (as GATT meetings are called), a dispute arose over agricultural policy. The United States argued that the EU's subsidies to farmers should be reduced, and that tariffs on farm exports from the United States to the EU should be

---

Free Trade Associations

Free trade association   Group of countries that allows free trade among its members and puts up common barriers against all other countries' goods.

Q–10:   What is economists' view of limited free trade associations such as the EU or NAFTA?

Most-favored nation   Country that will pay as low a tariff on its exports as will any other country.

reduced or eliminated. When the EU hesitated to go along with these proposals, there was a temporary breakdown of the talks. Eventually, in 1994 an agreement on the 1988 round of the GATT meeting was concluded. Such breakdowns demonstrate the fragility of all free trade agreements. They can quickly be replaced by trade wars which hurt all countries.

CONCLUSION

International trade will become more and more important for the United States. With international transportation and communication becoming easier and faster, and with other countries' economies growing, the U.S. economy will inevitably become more interdependent with the other economies of the world. As international trade becomes more important, the push for trade restrictions will likely increase. Various countries' strategic trade policies will likely conflict, and the world will find itself on the verge of an international trade war which would benefit no one.

Concern about that possibility leads most economists to favor free trade. As often happens, economists advise politicians to follow a policy that is politically unpopular—to take the hard course of action. Whether politicians follow economists' advice or whether they follow the politically popular policy will play a key role in determining the course of the U.S. economy in the 1990s.

CHAPTER SUMMARY

• The primary trading partners of the United States are Canada, Western Europe, and Japan, Latin America, and Southeast Asia.

• According to the principle of absolute advantage, a country that can produce a good more cheaply than another country is said to have an absolute advantage in the production of that good. When two countries have absolute advantages in different goods, there are gains from trade to be had.

• According to the principle of comparative advantage, as long as the relative opportunity costs of producing goods (what must be given up in one good in order to get another good) differ among countries, there are potential gains from trade, even if one country has an absolute advantage in everything.

• Three insights into the terms of trade include:

1. The more competition exists in international trade, the less the trader gets and the more the involved countries get.

2. Once competition prevails, smaller countries tend to get a larger percentage of the gains from trade than do larger countries.

3. Gains from trade go to countries that produce goods that exhibit economies of scale.

• Trade restrictions include: tariffs, quotas, embargoes, voluntary restraint agreements, regulatory trade restrictions, and nationalistic appeals.

• Reasons that countries impose trade restrictions include: unequal internal distribution of the gains from trade; haggling by companies over the gains from trade; haggling by countries over trade restrictions; learning by doing and economies of scale; macroeconomic aspects of trade; national security; international political reasons; and increased revenue brought in by tariffs.

• Economists generally oppose trade restrictions because of their knowledge of history and their understanding of the advantages of free trade.

KEY TERMS

economies of scale (820)
embargo (816)
European Union (EU) (823)
free trade association (823)
General Agreement on Tariffs and Trade (GATT) (815)

infant industry argument (821)
learning by doing (820)
most-favored nation (823)
principle of absolute advantage (808)
principle of comparative advantage (811)

regulatory trade restrictions (816)
quota (815)
strategic bargaining (819)
tariff (815)
trade adjustment assistance programs (818)

QUESTIONS FOR THOUGHT AND REVIEW

The number after each question represents the estimated degree of critical thinking required. (1 = almost none; 10 = deep thought.)

1. With which countries does the United States trade most? *(2)*

2. Are these countries the ones you would expect the United States to trade with, based on the law of comparative advantage? Why? *(7)*

3. Textland can produce, at most, 40 olives or 20 pickles, or some combination of olives and pickles such as the 20 olives and 10 pickles it's currently producing. Happyland can produce, at most, 120 olives or 60 pickles, or some combination of olives and pickles such as the 100 olives and 10 pickles it's currently producing. Is there a basis for trade? If so, offer the two countries a deal they can't refuse. *(6)*

4. Would your answer to Question 3 differ if you knew that there were economies of scale in the production of pickles and olives rather than the production possibilities described in the question? Why? If your answer is yes, which country would you have produce which good? *(9)*

5. Widgetland has 60 workers. Each worker can produce 4 widgets or 4 wadgets. It's considering producing only widgets. Wadgetland also has 60 workers. Each can produce 3 widgets or 12 wadgets. Its residents consume wadgets but never buy widgets. Is there a basis for trade? If so, offer the countries a deal they can't refuse. *(7)*

6. Why do smaller countries usually get most of the gains from trade? What are some reasons why a small country might not get the gains of trade? *(6)*

7. Demonstrate diagrammatically how the effects of a tariff differ from the effects of a quota. *(6)*

8. If you were economic advisor to a country that was following your advice about trade restrictions and that country fell into a recession, would you change your advice? Why, or why not? *(7)*

9. The U.S. trade balance improved significantly in early 1991. What would you say is the primary reason for that improvement? *(6)*

10. Mexico exports many vegetables to the United States. These vegetables are grown using chemicals that are not allowed in U.S. vegetable agriculture. Should the United States restrict imports of Mexican vegetables? Why, or why not? *(7)*

PROBLEMS AND EXERCISES

1. Suppose that two countries, Machineland and Farmland, have the following production possibility curves:

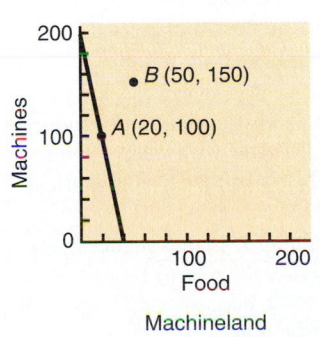

Machineland

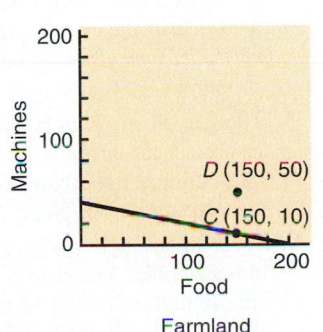

Farmland

a. Explain how these two countries can move from points A and C where they currently are to points B and D.

b. If possible, state by how much *total production* for the two countries has risen.

c. If you were a trader, how much of the gains from trade would you deserve for discovering this trade?

d. If there were economies of scale in the production of both goods, how would your analysis change?

2. The world price of textiles is P_w as in the accompanying figure of the domestic supply and demand for textiles.

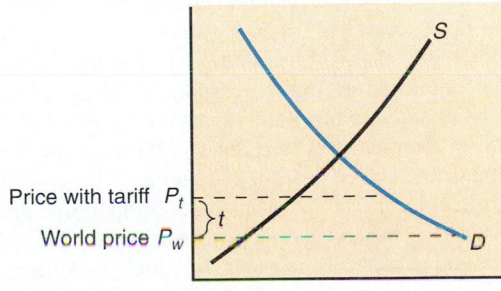

The government imposes a tariff, *t*, to protect domestic producers. For this tariff:

a. Shade in the gains to domestic producers.

b. Shade in the revenue to government.

c. Shade in the costs to domestic producers.

d. Are the gains greater than the costs? Why?

3. In 1992 the hourly cost to employers per German industrial worker was $26.90. The hourly cost to employers per U.S. industrial worker was $15.89, while the average cost per Taiwanese industrial worker was $5.19.

a. Give three reason why firms produce in Germany rather than in a lower wage country.

b. Germany has just entered into an agreement with other EU countries that allows people in any EU country, including Greece and Italy, which have lower wage rates, to travel and work in any EU country, including high-wage countries. Would you expect a significant movement of workers from Greece and Italy to Germany right away? Why or why not?

c. Workers in Thailand are paid significantly less than in Taiwan. If you were a company CEO, what other information would you want before you decided where to establish a new production facility?

4. Peter Sutherland, the director-general of GATT, published a pamphlet on the costs of trade protection. He subtitled the pamphlet ''The Sting: How Governments Buy Votes on Trade with the Consumer's Money.''

a. What does he likely mean by this subtitle?

b. If a government is out to increase votes with its trade policy, would it more likely institute tariffs or quotas? Why?

5. One of the basic economic laws is ''the law of one price.'' It says that given certain assumptions one would expect that if free trade is allowed, the price of goods in countries should converge.

a. Can you list what three of those assumptions likely are?

b. Should the law of one price hold for labor also? Why or why not?

c. Should it hold for capital more so or less so than for labor? Why or why not?

ANSWERS TO MARGIN QUESTIONS

1. In the example in Exhibit 4, if the United States only wanted to consume food, there would be no basis for trade. Since the United States is relatively more efficient at the consumption of food it would have no desire to import any oil at any price from Saudi Arabia. *(809)*

2. In the example in Exhibit 4, if Saudi Arabia only wanted to consume food when it had the absolute advantage in the production of oil, there would be an even stronger basis for trade than in the example in Exhibit 4, since Saudi Arabia would be happy to sell whatever oil it produced to get whatever food. These two examples (Questions 1 and 2) demonstrate that, while comparative advantage usually focuses on production, there is also a consumption side of comparative advantage. *(810)*

3. If a country had an absolute advantage in all goods there would be no basis for trade. However, as long as there are flexible exchange rates and, as is usually the case in microeconomics, an implicit assumption that trade flows must be equal, any absolute advantage in all goods would be eliminated by a change in the exchange rate of the countries' currencies one for another. This change would lead to one country having a comparative advantage in one good and the other country having a comparative advantage in the other, in which case there would be a basis of trade. That trade could involve one country selling produced goods and the other country selling financial and physical assets, but not produced goods. *(810)*

4. In the Exhibit 6 example, the minimum amount of food that I. T. Too had to offer Algeria for fifteen autos was slightly more than 4 units of food. Four units of food would place Algeria in a better position than it would be without trade. Whether Algeria would trade on those terms is dependent on whether or not Algeria is practicing strategic bargaining. *(811)*

5. The percentage of gains of trade that goes to a country depends upon the relative price change that occurs with respect to the goods being traded. If trade led to no change in relative prices in a small country, then that small country would get no gains from trade. Another case in which a small country gets a small percentage of the gains from trade would occur when its larger trading partner was producing a good with economies of scale and the small country was not. A third case is when the traders who extracted most of the surplus or gains from trade come from the larger country; then the small country would end up with few of the gains from trade. *(814)*

6. A tariff is a type of tax that the government places on internationally-traded goods. A quota is a quantity restriction that a country places on internationally-traded goods. *(815)*

7. An inefficient customs agency can operate with the same effect as a trade restriction, and if trade restrictions would help the country then it is possible that an inefficient customs agency could also help the country. *(816)*

8. The EU places high barriers against agricultural products to protect its farmers. As in the case with many of the international trade barriers, this is primarily for political, not economic, purposes. *(818)*

9. True. In strategic trade bargaining it is reasonable to be unreasonable. The reason it is reasonable to be unreasonable is that the belief of the other bargainer that you will be unreasonable leads you to be able to extract larger gains from trade. Of course, this leads to the logical paradox that if ''unreasonable'' is ''reasonable,'' unreasonable really is reasonable, so it is only reasonable to be reasonable. Sorting out that last statement can be left for a philosophy or logic class. *(819)*

10. Most economists have a mixed view of limited free trade associations such as NAFTA or the EU. While they see free trade as beneficial, they are concerned about the possibility that these limited trade associations will impose trade restrictions on nonmember countries. Whether the net effect of these will be positive or negative is a complicated issue. *(823)*

38

Growth and the Microeconomics of Developing Countries

It is always depressing to go back to Adam Smith, especially on economic development, as one realizes how little we have learned in nearly 200 years.

~Kenneth Boulding

After reading this chapter, you should be able to:

1 State some comparative statistics on rich and poor countries.

2 Define the dual economy and explain its relevance for developing countries.

3 List six problems facing developing countries.

4 Explain how the market can function in inappropriate ways when there is no well-developed public morality.

5 Explain why it is so difficult for developing countries to generate investment.

6 Summarize four debates about strategies for growth.

7 Defend the position that economic development is a complicated problem.

1 Seventy-five percent of the world's population lives in developing countries, with average per capita income of around $500 per year.

There are approximately 5.6 billion people in the world. Of these, 4.2 billion (about 75 percent) live in developing, rather than developed, countries. Per capita income in developing countries is around $500 per year; in the United States per capita income is about $24,000.

These averages understate the differences between the poorest country and the richest. Consider the African country of Chad—definitely one of the world's poorest. Its per capita income is about $200 per year—less than 1/100 of the per capita income in the United States. Moreover income in Chad goes primarily to the rich, so Chad's poor have per capita income of significantly less than $200.

DEVELOPMENT: PRELIMINARY CONSIDERATIONS

Before I consider the obstacles to economic development, let's consider how a person lives on that $200 per year as many people in the world do. To begin with, that person can't:

Go out for Big Macs.

Use Joy perfume (or any type of perfume).

Wear designer clothes.

And that person must:

Eat grain—usually rice or corn—for all meals, every day.

Mix fat from meat—not meat itself—with the rice on special occasions (maybe).

Live in one room with 9 or 10 other people.

Work hard from childhood to old age (if there is an old age). Those too old to work in the fields stay at home and care for those too young to work in the fields. (But children go out to work in the fields when they're about six years old.)

Go hungry, because no matter how many family members can work in the fields, probably the work and soil don't yield enough to provide the workers with an adequate number of calories per day.

In a poor person's household it's likely that a couple of the older children may have gone into the city to find work that pays money wages. If they were lucky and found jobs, they can send money home each month. That money may be the only cash income their family back in the fields has. The family uses the money to buy a few tools and cooking utensils.

A view of the difficult life of the poor in developing and middle-income countries—washing clothes and children in Rio de Janeiro, Brazil. © *McGlynn/The Image Works.*

ADDED DIMENSION

**WHAT TO CALL
DEVELOPING COUNTRIES**

In this chapter, following common usage, I call low-income countries *developing countries*. They have not always been called *developing*. In the 1950s they were called *backward*, but it was eventually realized that *backward* implied significant negative value judgments. Then these countries were called *underdeveloped*, but it was eventually realized that *underdeveloped* also implied significant negative value judgments. More recently they have been called *developing*, but eventually everyone will realize that *developing* implies significant negative value judgments. After all, in what sense are these countries "developing" any more than is the United States? All countries are evolving or developing countries. Many so-called developing countries have highly refined cultures which they don't want to lose; they may want to develop economically, but not at the cost of cultural change.

What should one call these countries? That remains to be seen, but whatever one calls them, bear in mind that language can conceal value judgments.

The preceding is, of course, only one among billions of different stories. Even Americans and Europeans who are classified as poor find it hard to contemplate what life is really like in a truly poor country.

Don't Judge Society by Its Income Alone

Poor people in developing countries survive and often find pleasure in their hard lives. There are few suicides in the poorest countries. For example, the U.S. suicide rate is approximately 13 per 100,000 people. In Costa Rica it's 4.9; in Mexico it's 1.4; and in Peru it's .5. Who has time for suicide? You're too busy surviving. There's little ambiguity and few questions about the meaning of life. Living! That's what life's all about. There's no "Mom, what am I going to do today?" You know what you're going to do: survive if you can. And survival is satisfying.

Often these economically poor societies have elaborate cultural rituals and networks of intense personal relationships that provide individuals with a deep sense of fulfillment and satisfaction.

Often economically poor societies have cultures that provide individuals with a deep sense of fulfillment and satisfaction.

Are people in these societies as happy as Americans are? If your immediate answer is no, be careful to understand the difficulty of making such a judgment. The answer isn't clear-cut. For us to say, "My God! What a failure their system is!" is wrong. It's an inappropriate value judgment about the relative worth of cultures. All too often Americans have gone into another country to try to make people better off, but have ended up making them worse off.

An economy is part and parcel of a culture. You can't judge just an economy; you must judge the entire culture. Some developing countries have cultures that, in many people's view, are preferable to ours. If one increases a country's income but takes away its culture in doing so, one may well have made its people worse off.

An economy is part and parcel of a culture.

That said, we're ready to consider whether people in developing countries would be better off if they had more income. Most people in developing countries would definitely answer yes!

Even culturally sensitive people agree that economic growth within the context of a developing country's culture would be a good thing, if only because those countries exist simultaneously with market economies. Given market societies' expansionary tendencies, without economic growth, cultures in economically poor countries would simply be overrun and destroyed by the cultures of market societies. Their land would be taken, their agricultural patterns would be changed, their traditional means of subsistence would be destroyed, and their cultures would be obliterated. So generally the choice isn't between development and preservation of the existing culture (and its accompanying ancient ways to which the poor have adjusted). Rather, the choice is between development (with its attendant wrenching cultural transitions) and continuing poverty (with exploitation by developed countries and its attendant wrenching cultural transitions).

Q-1: In what way is economic development the only choice for developing countries?

Exhibit 1 gives you a sense of the uneven distribution of production among rich and poor countries.

Some Comparative Statistics on Rich and Poor Nations

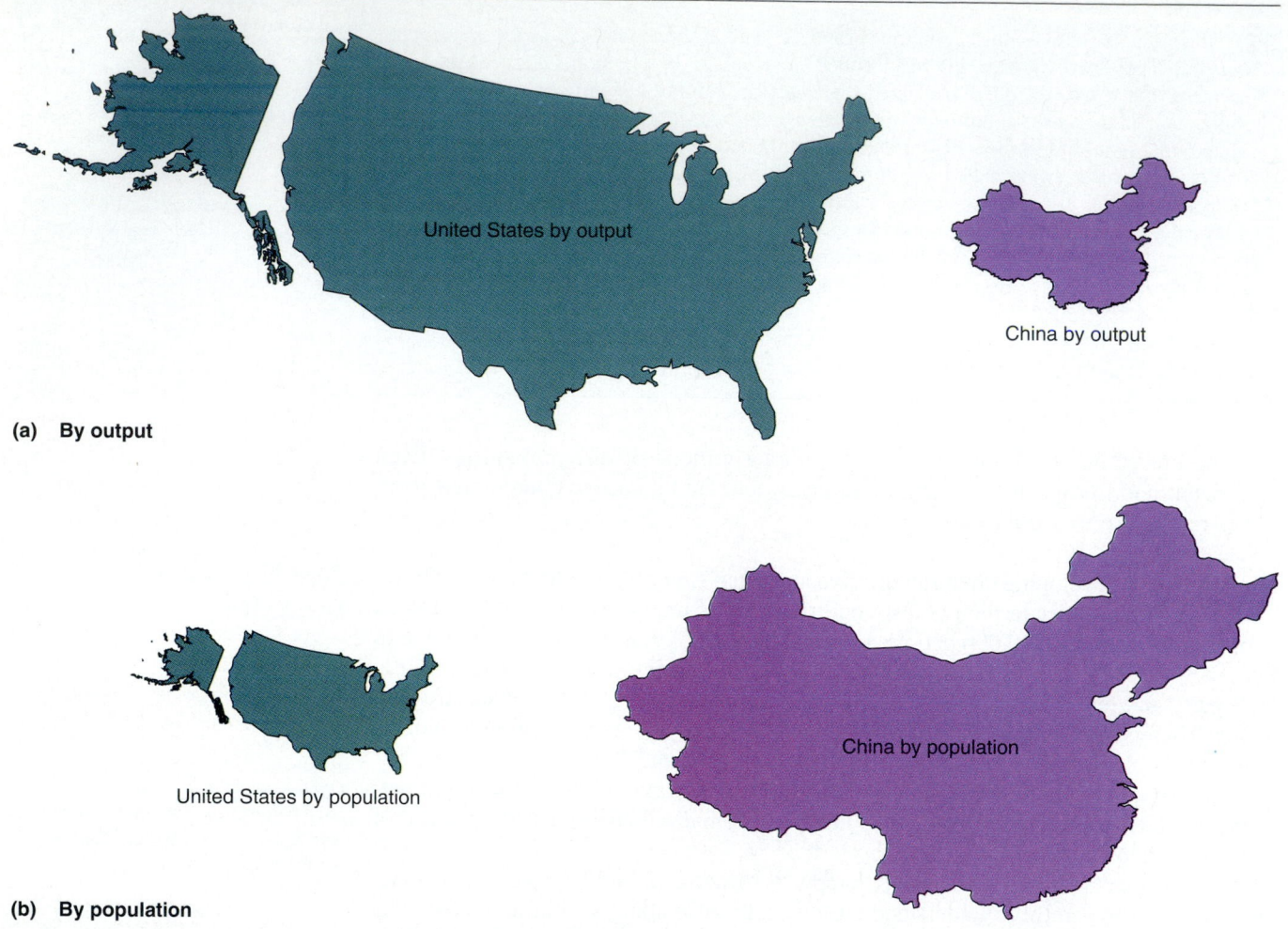

(a)   By output

(b)   By population

EXHIBIT 1   Comparing the United States and China by Output and Population

The areas of China and the United States are approximately equal. If, however, we were to scale their sizes in accordance with their relative outputs, as in (**a**), the United States would be shown double in size and China would be shown reduced to one fourth of its size. If we scaled their sizes in accordance with population, as in (**b**), it is China that would increase its size, more than doubling, while the size of the United States would be cut in half.

Purchasing power parity   Method of comparing income by looking at the domestic purchasing power of money in different countries.

The low average income in poor countries has its effects on people's lives. Life expectancy is about 50 years in most very economically poor countries (compared to about 75 years in the United States). In economically poor countries most people drink contaminated water, consume about half the number of calories the World Health Organization has determined is minimal for good health, and do physical labor (often of the kind done by machine in developed countries). Exhibit 2 compares developing countries, middle-income countries, and developed countries.

As with all statistics, care must be taken in interpreting the figures in Exhibit 2. For example, the income comparisons were all made on the basis of current exchange rates. But relative prices between rich and poor countries often differ substantially; the cost of goods relative to total income tends to be much lower for people in developing countries than for those in developed countries.

To allow for these differences, some economists have looked at the domestic purchasing power of money in various countries and have adjusted the comparisons accordingly. Rather than working with exchange rates, they compare what a specified market basket of consumer goods will cost in various countries and use these results to compare currencies' values. This is called the **purchasing power parity** method of comparing income of countries. Making these adjustments, the World Bank found that income differences among countries are cut by half. In other words, when one uses the

EXHIBIT 2   Statistics on Developing, Middle-Income, and Developed Countries: 1992

	Country	Population per physician	Daily calorie supply	Life expectancy	Infant mortality (per 1,000)	Labor force in agriculture (%)	Labor force in industry (%)	Literacy rate	People per TV receiver	GDP per capita ($)
Developing	Bangladesh	5,264	2,037	56	109	74%	11%	35	315	$ 200
	Ethiopia	36,660	1,699	52	112	80	8	62	505	130
	Haiti	6,083	2,005	53	110	66	9	53	234	340
Middle-Income	Brazil	848	2,730	63	62	31	27	81	4	2,350
	Iran	2,685	3,317	65	64	33	21	54	23	1,500
	South Korea	1,007	2,826	68	23	21	27	96	5	6,500
	Thailand	4,377	2,280	68	38	62	13	93	11	1,800
Developed	Japan	588	2,921	79	4	7	33	99	1.8	19,800
	Sweden	395	2,978	78	6	3	21	99	2.4	16,900
	United States	406	3,642	76	8	4	28	98	1.3	23,400

Sources: *U.N. Statistical Yearbook, 1993* and *The World Factbook, 1993.* Because of reporting lags, some data are for earlier years.

World Bank's purchasing power parity method of comparison, it's as if the people in developing countries had twice as much income as they had when the exchange rate method was used.

A similar adjustment can be made with the life expectancy rates. A major reason for the lower life expectancies in developing countries is their high infant mortality rates. Once children survive infancy, however, their life expectancies are much closer to those of children in developed countries. Say a country's overall life expectancy is 50 years and that 15 percent of all infants die within their first year. As a person grows older, at each birthday the person's life expectancy is higher. So if a child lives to the age of 3 years, then at that point the child has an actual life expectancy of close to 60 years, rather than 50 years.

Before the Industrial Revolution, when Western countries had low incomes compared to today's income in developing countries, Western economists focused on one question: What makes a society grow? By *growth* they meant growth of material production. It isn't surprising that the focus of the economics of developing countries is material growth: how to achieve and maintain growth in per capita income.

The Dual Economy   The fact that the average income in a country is very low does not mean that a certain group of people in a developing country may not have incomes and lifestyles equal to, or preferable to, lifestyles in developed countries. In fact, a certain group of people in virtually every country do have such lifestyles. The income level of this group of people gives them access to Western goods, which they buy on their trips to developed countries. Given the low level of wages in their own countries, their income level provides them with servants and "lifestyle employees" who care for their physical needs. Maids, cooks, and "housepeople" have disappeared almost entirely from Western countries, except for those employed by the very rich, but there are significant numbers of such employees in many developing countries, and even upper-middle-class families may have one or more household servants.

This bifurcation of the economy is often called the **dual economy,** one economy being an internationally based economy in which wage rates and lifestyles are the same as in developed countries, and the other economy being the traditional, often non-market economy. Many of the people who participate in the internationally based economic sector are what might be called "internationally mobile." They can move to some Western country if they choose. Many would not work in their own country unless its pay matched what they could earn in a developed country, and they judge themselves relative to Western standards, not the standards of the majority of citizens

Q–2: How does the exchange rate method of comparing incomes differ from the purchasing power parity method of comparing incomes?

Developing Countries Focus on Growth

2 The "dual economy" refers to the tendency of developing countries to have two somewhat unrelated economies—one an internationally-based economy, the other a traditional, often nonmarket, economy.

in their own country. It is their high income that pulls up the average income of many developing countries.

The traditional economy, on the other hand, is only tangentially related to the economies in developed countries and to the international economy. It is largely domestic, and often people in it are doing today what their ancestors did hundreds of years ago. Pay in the traditional economy is generally very low; this part of the economy pulls the average income down.

The Growth Record

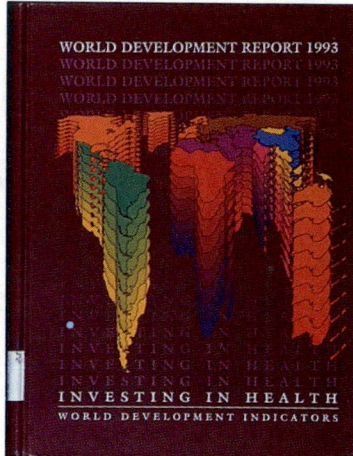

One of the best sources of information about development issues is the *World Development Report,* published by the World Bank.

In the 1990s, economists are moving away from grouping all developing countries together.

The long-term record for most countries in achieving growth isn't good. Only a small number of countries have moved out of the "developing country" ranks. One group that has moved out is the oil-producing countries. Another group of countries, called the **Asian tigers** (for example, Taiwan, South Korea, Singapore, and Hong Kong[1]) have achieved substantial economic growth and are no longer considered developing countries by some economists. They've become middle-income countries.

The Asian tigers are an exception. Considered as a group, developing countries haven't done well compared to developed countries. While from 1950 until the early 1990s, developing countries' average overall growth rates were slightly higher than growth rates of industrial market countries, their per capita growth rates were much lower. But to catch up with developed countries, the developing countries would have to grow at a much faster rate than the developed countries.

For example, if developing countries grew 4 percent a year and developed countries grew 3 percent, after 24 years the developing countries' income would have increased 156 percent while developed countries' income would have increased 103 percent. As opposed to having $\frac{1}{18}$ of a developed country's per capita income, a developing country, after 24 years of growth, would have improved to the point of having $\frac{1}{14}$ of a developed country's per capita income. But even that small gain isn't occurring for many developing countries, especially those in Africa.

Geographic Grouping of Developing Countries

In the 1990s, economists are moving away from grouping all developing countries together, and are separating out four geographic groupings—Asian, African, Latin American, and Middle Eastern. Because of cultural similarities, the problems of countries in each of these groupings often parallel those of others in that grouping.

Q–3: Which geographic group of countries has outperformed other developing countries in growth?

As you can see in Exhibit 3, the growth rates of these groupings have diverged from one another. The Asian countries have emerged as the winners in the growth sweepstakes. As mentioned earlier, a number of the Asian countries have moved into the category of "middle-income countries." Latin American and Middle Eastern developing countries have had moderate growth—often coming in spurts—and in the first half of the 1990s, Latin American countries were in another growth spurt.

Q–4: Which geographic group of countries has underperformed other developing countries in growth?

Finally come the African, especially the sub-Saharan African, countries whose growth rates have been extremely low and sometimes negative. These African growth rates are more than just statistics. They represent suffering and pain. When you hear of a famine or of starvation killing thousands of people, those events will generally be taking place in an African country.

OBSTACLES TO ECONOMIC DEVELOPMENT

What stops countries from developing economically? Economists have discovered no magic potion that will make a country develop. We can't say, "Here are steps 1, 2, 3, 4. If you follow them you'll grow, but if you don't follow them you won't grow."

What makes it so hard for developing countries to devise a successful development program is that social, political, and economic problems blend into one another and cannot be considered separately. The institutional structure that we take for granted in the United States often doesn't exist in those countries. For example,

---

[1] Hong Kong isn't an independent country. Currently it's administered by Great Britain. In 1997 it's scheduled to be returned to China. However at present, economically, it behaves very much like an independent country.

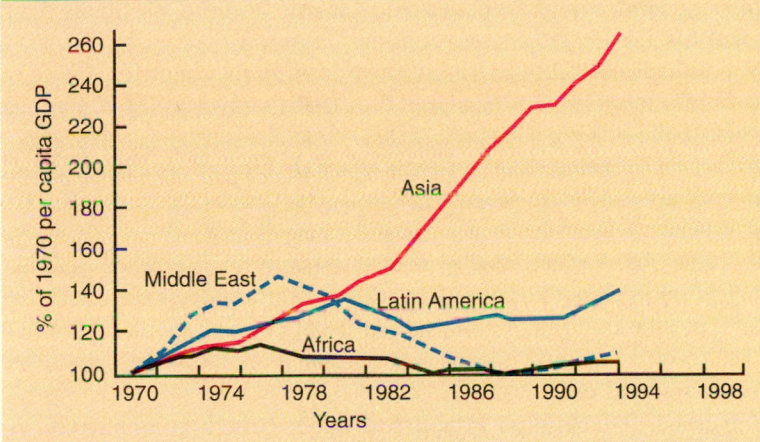

EXHIBIT 3   **Growth Rates—Groupings of Developing Countries**

Since the late 1970s, African and Middle Eastern economic growth has essentially come to a halt. Only the Asian tigers have grown faster than Europe.
Source: *World Economic Outlook* (Washington, D.C. : IMF), and author's calculations.

economists' analysis of production assumes that a stable government exists that can enforce contracts and supply basic services. In most developing countries, that assumption can't be made. Governments are often anything but stable; overnight, a coup d'état can bring a new government into power, with a whole new system of rules under which businesses have to operate. Imagine trying to figure out a reasonable study strategy if every week you had a new teacher who emphasized different things and gave totally different types of tests from last week's teacher. Firms in developing countries face similar problems.

While economists can't say, ''Here's what you have to do in order to grow,'' we have been able to identify some general obstacles that all developing countries seem to face: Such problems that fall within microeconomics include:

1. Political instability.
2. Corruption.
3. Lack of appropriate institutions.
4. Lack of investment.
5. Inappropriate education.
6. Overpopulation.

I consider each in turn.

A student's parents once asked me why their son was doing poorly in my economics class. My answer was that he could not read and he could hardly write. Until he could master those basics, there was no use talking about how he could better learn economics.

Roughly the same reasoning can be applied to the problem of political instability in developing countries. Unless a country achieves political stability (acceptance within a country of a stable system of government), it's not going to develop economically, no matter what it does.

All successful development strategies require the existence of a stable government. A mercantilist or a socialist development strategy requires an elaborate government presence. A market-based strategy requires a much smaller government role, but even with markets, a stable environment is needed for a market to function and for contracts to be made with confidence.

Many developing countries don't have that stability. Politically they haven't established a tradition of orderly governmental transition. Coups d'état or armed insurrections always remain possible.

One example is Rwanda, a small African country. In April of 1994, its president was killed and the entire country was engulfed in civil war. Another example of political instability in developing countries is to be found in Somalia. There, a civil war among competing groups led to famine and enormous hardship, which provoked the sympathy of the world. But attempts by the U.N. and the United States to establish

3 Six microeconomic problems facing developing countries are:
  1. Political instability.
  2. Corruption.
  3. Lack of appropriate institutions.
  4. Lack of investment.
  5. Inappropriate education.
  6. Overpopulation.

Political Instability

All successful development strategies require the existence of a stable government.

a stable government by sending troops there caused as many, or more, problems than they resolved, and in 1994 the United States withdrew its troops.

The problem of political instability exists in most developing countries, but it is strongest in Africa, which, in large part, accounts for Africa's low rate of economic growth relative to that of the other geographic areas.

Q–5:   Why does political insta-bility present an economic problem for developing countries?

Even countries whose governments aren't regularly toppled face threats of over-throw, and those threats are sufficient to prevent individual economic activity. To function, an economy needs some rules—any rules—that will last.

The lack of stability is often exacerbated by social and cultural differences among groups within a country. Political boundaries often reflect arbitrary decisions made by former colonial rulers, not the traditional cultural and tribal boundaries that form the real-life divisions. The result is lack of consensus among the population as a whole as well as intertribal suspicion and even warfare.

For example, Nigeria is a federation established under British colonial rule. It comprises three ethnic regions: the northern, Hausa Fulan, region; the western, Yoruba, region; and the eastern, Ibo, region. These three regions are culturally distinct and so are in continual political and military conflict. Nigeria has experienced an endless cycle of military coups, attempts at civilian rule, and threats of secession by the numerically smaller eastern region. Had each region been allowed to remain separate, economic development might have been possible; but because the British lumped the regions together and called them a country, economic development is next to impossible.

The Influence of Political Instability on Development

Do these political considerations affect economic questions? You bet. As I will discuss shortly, any development plan requires financial investment from somewhere—either external or internal. Political instability closes off both sources of investment funds.

Any serious potential investor takes political instability into account. Foreign companies considering investment in a developing country hire political specialists who analyze the degree of risk involved. Where the risk is too great, foreign companies simply don't invest.

Q–6:   Income inequality leads to higher levels of savings by the rich and therefore has significant advan-tages for developing countries. True or false? Explain your answer.

Political instability also limits internal investment. Income distribution in many developing countries is highly skewed. There are a few very rich people and an enormous number of very poor people, while the middle class is often small.

Whatever one's view of the fairness of such income inequality, it has a potential advantage for society. Members of the wealthy elite in developing countries have income to spare, and their savings are a potential source of investment funds. But when there is political instability, that potential isn't realized. Fearing that their wealth may be taken from them, the rich often channel their investment out of their own country so that, should they need to flee a revolution, they'll still be able to live comfortably. Well-off people in developing countries provide major inflows of invest-ment into the United States and other Western countries.

Ferdinand Marcos, former president of the Philippines, was reported to have $10 billion worth of assets scattered around the developed countries of the world. Had he invested those billions in the Philippines, he most likely would have lost all that money when he was deposed in 1986. Marcos, having placed his wealth abroad—often hiding its ownership—didn't lose it, or at least he didn't lose all of it, after being deposed. So the Philippines lost twice from Marcos's actions. First, he took money that didn't belong to him; and second, he deprived the Philippines of much-needed investment capital.

Political Instability and Unequal Distribution of Income

The highly skewed distribution of income in most developing countries contributes in another way to political instability. It means that the poor majority has little vested interest in maintaining the current system. A coup? Why not? What have they got to lose? The economic prospects for many people in developing countries are so bleak that they are quite willing to join or at least support a guerilla insurgency that promises to set up a new, better system. The resulting instability makes development almost impossible.

Bribery, graft, and corruption are ways of life in most developed countries. In Egypt it's called *baksheesh* (meaning "gift of money"); in Mexico it's called *la mordida* ("the bite"). If you want to park in a parking spot in Mexico City, you'd better pay the policeman, or your car will get a ticket. If you want to take a photograph of the monument to Rameses II in front of the Cairo railroad station, you'd better slip the traffic officer a few bucks, or else you may get run over.

Without a well-developed institutional setting and a public morality that condemns corruption, market forces function in a variety of areas that people in developed countries would consider inappropriate. In any country the government has the right to allow imports, to allow development, to determine where you can park your car, to say whether you can take photographs of public buildings, to decide who wins a lawsuit, and so forth. In developing countries, however, those rights can be, and often are, sold. The litigant who pays the judge the most wins. How about the right to import? Want to import a new machine? That will be 20 percent of the cost, please.

Such graft and corruption quickly become institutionalized, so that all parties involved feel that they have little choice but to take part. Government officials say that graft and bribery are built into their pay structure, so unless they take bribes, they won't have enough income to live on. Businesspeople say that if they want to stay in business they have to pay bribes. Similarly, workers must bribe business in order to get a job, and labor leaders must be bribed not to cause trouble for business.

I'm not claiming that such payments are wrong. Societies decide what is right and wrong; economists don't. The term *bribery* in English has a pejorative connotation. In many other languages the terms people use for this type of activity don't have such negative connotations.

But I *am* claiming that such payments—with the implied threat that failure to pay will have adverse consequences—make it more difficult for a society's economy to grow. Knowing that those payments must be made prevents many people from undertaking actions that might lead to growth. For example, a friend of mine wanted to build a group of apartments in the Bahamas, but when he discovered the payoffs he'd have to make to various people, he abandoned the whole idea.

Limiting an activity makes the right to undertake that limited activity valuable to the person doing the limiting. When bribery is an acceptable practice, it creates strong incentives to limit an ever-increasing number of activities—including many activities that could make a country grow.

Almost all economists agree that, to develop, a country should establish markets. Markets require the establishment of property rights—and establishing them is a difficult political process. That is the problem of a number of African countries: how to establish property rights with an undeveloped political process.

Creating markets is not enough. The markets must be meshed with the cultural and social fabric of the society. Thus, questions of economic development inevitably involve much more than supply and demand. They involve broader questions about the cultural and social institutions in a society.

Let me give an example of cultural characteristics not conducive to development. Anyone who has traveled in developing countries knows that many of these countries operate on what they call "_____ time," where the "_____" is the name of the particular country one is in. What is meant by "_____ time" is that in that country, things get done when they get done, and it is socially inappropriate to push for things to get done at specific times. Deadlines are demeaning (many students operate on "_____ time").

As a self-actualizing mentality, "_____ time" may be high-level mental development, but in an interdependent economic setting, "_____ time" doesn't fit. Economic development requires qualities such as extreme punctuality and a strong sense of individual responsibility. People who believe their being two minutes late will make the world come to an end fit far better with a high-production country than do people who are more laid back. The need to take such cultural issues into account explains why development economics tends to be far less theoretical and far more country- and region-specific than other branches of economics.

Corruption

4 When rights to conduct business are controlled and allocated by the government, economic development can be hindered.

Societies decide what is right and wrong; economists don't.

Q-7: In what way do bribes limit development?

Lack of Appropriate Institutions

Markets do not just exist; they are created, and their existence is meshed with the cultural and social fabric of the society.

As a self-actualizing mentality, "_____ time" may be a high-level mental development, but in an interdependent economic setting, "_____ time" doesn't fit.

As mentioned above, the Asian tigers have been the most successful of the developing countries. Their strategy has been a neomercantilist strategy in which the governments have played a major role in directing the economies toward establishing an export-led growth. Interest rates and exchange rates have been kept purposely low to encourage exports and promote growth. Governments have built the needed transportation and energy facilities, and domestic firms' home markets have been protected through a variety of non-tariff and tariff barriers to imports.

There is much debate about whether the cause of the Asian tigers' success is due to their neomercantilist strategy, or has occurred despite their government-oriented strategy. Many economists believe that their cultural characteristics—hard-working, high-saving, and orientation toward trading and markets—would have led to even higher growth if their governments had intervened less.

Even if the government-oriented strategy was in part responsible for their success, it is not at all clear that such a strategy can be successfully transferred to other situations since, by developing country standards, the Asian governments are relatively stable and uncorrupt.

Lack of Investment

Even if a country can overcome the political, social, and institutional constraints on development, there are also economic constraints. If a country is to grow it must somehow invest, and funds for investment must come from savings. These savings can be either brought in from abroad (as private investment or foreign government aid) or generated internally (as domestic savings). Each source of investment capital has its problems.

5 With per capita incomes of as low as $300 per year, poor people in developing countries don't have a lot left over to put into savings.

Investment Funded by Domestic Savings
In order to save, a person must first have enough to live on. With per capita incomes of $300 per year, poor people in developing countries don't have a whole lot left over to put into savings. Instead you rely on your kids, if they live, to take care of you in your old age. As for the rich, the threat of political instability often makes them put their money into savings abroad, as I discussed before. For the developing country, it's as if the rich didn't save. In fact, it's even worse because when they save abroad, the rich don't even spend the money at home as do poor people, so the rich don't generate even as much as the first-round income multiplier effects in their home country.

That leaves the middle class (small as it is) as the one hope these countries have for domestic savings. For them, the problem is: Where can they put their savings? Often these countries have an underdeveloped financial sector; there's no neighborhood bank, no venture capital fund, no government-secured savings vehicle. The only savings vehicle available may be the government savings bond. But savings bonds finance the government deficit, which supports the government bureaucracy, which is limiting activities that could lead to growth. Few middle-class people invest in those government bonds. After all, what will a government bond be worth after the next revolution? Nothing!

Some governments have taxed individuals (a type of forced savings) and channeled that money back into investment. But again, politics and corruption are likely to interfere. Instead of going into legitimate productive investment, the savings—in the form of ''consulting fees,'' outright payoffs, or ''sweetheart contracts''—go to friends of those in power. Before you get up on your high horse and say, ''How do the people allow that to happen?'' think of the United States, where it's much easier to prevent such activities but where scandals in government spending are still uncovered with depressing regularity.

Investment Funded from Abroad
The other way to generate funds for investment is from external savings, either foreign aid or foreign investment.

Foreign Aid The easiest way to finance development is with **foreign aid** (funds that developed countries loan or give to developing countries). The problem is that foreign aid generally comes with strings attached; funds are earmarked for specific purposes.

EXHIBIT 4   **Foreign Aid Given by Major Countries, 1992**

Country	Development aid 1992 (millions of U.S. dollars)	% of GDP
United States	$11,709	.20%
France	8,270	.63
United Kingdom	3,217	.31
Japan	11,151	.30
Germany	7,572	.39
Italy	4,122	.34
Austria	556	.30
Sweden	2,460	1.03
Canada	2,515	.46

Source: The World Bank, *OECD DAC Chairman's Report.*

For example, most foreign aid is military aid; helping a country prepare to fight a war isn't a good way to help it develop.

As you can see in Exhibit 4, the United States gives about $12 billion (about $45 per U.S. citizen) per year in foreign aid. For the 4.2 billion people in developing countries, total foreign aid from all countries comes to about $13 per person. That isn't going to finance a lot of economic development, especially when much of the money is earmarked for military purposes.

Total foreign aid from all countries comes to about $13.00 per person in developing countries.

Foreign Investment   If a global or multinational company believes that a country has a motivated, cheap workforce, a stable government supportive of business, and sufficient **infrastructure investment**—investment in the underlying structure of the economy, such as transportation or power facilities—it has a strong incentive to invest in the country. That's a lot of ifs, and generally the poorest countries don't measure up. What they have to offer instead are raw materials that the global corporation can develop.

Countries at the upper end of the group of developing countries (such as Mexico and Brazil) may meet all these requirements, but large amounts of foreign investment often result in political problems as citizens of these countries complain about imperialist exploitation, outside control, and significant outflows of profits. Developing countries have tried to meet such complaints by insisting that foreign investment come in the form of joint development projects under local control, but that cuts down the amount that foreign firms are willing to invest.

When the infrastructure doesn't exist, as is the case in the poorest developing countries, few firms will invest in that country, no matter how cheap the labor or how stable the government. Firms require infrastructure investment such as transportation facilities, energy availability, and housing and amenities for their employees before they will consider investing in a country. And they don't want to pay to establish this infrastructure themselves.

Q-8: The United States gives a smaller percentage of its GDP for foreign aid per U.S. citizen than any of the other major countries gives per their citizens. True or false?

Competition for Investment among Developing Countries   The world is made up of 15 to 20 highly industrial countries and about 170 other countries at various stages of development. Global companies have a choice of where to locate, and often developing countries compete to get the development located in their country. In their efforts to get the development, they may offer tax rebates, free land, guarantees of labor peace, or loose regulatory environments within which firms can operate.

This competition can be keen, and can result in many of the benefits of development being transferred from the developing country to the global company and ultimately to the Western consumer, since competition from other firms will force the global company to pass on the benefits in the form of lower price.

An example of the results of such competition can be seen in the production of chemicals. Say a company is planning to build a new plant to produce chemicals. Where does it locate? Considering the wide-ranging environmental restrictions in the United States and Western Europe, a chemical company will likely look toward a

Competition for global company investment often leads to the benefit of that investment being passed on to the Western consumer.

Q–9: Why did competition for
development projects provide a sticking point for U.S. approval of
NAFTA?

developing country that will give it loose regulation. If one country will not come
through, the chemical firm will point out that it can locate elsewhere. Concern about
Mexico's relatively loose environmental regulatory environment was one of the
sticking points of U.S. approval of NAFTA.

Focal Points and Takeoff   The scope of competition among developing countries can be
overstated. Most companies do not consider all developing countries as potential
production and investment sites. To decide to produce in a developing country
requires a knowledge of that country—its legal structure, its political structure, and its
infrastructure. Gaining this information involves a substantial initial investment, so
most companies tend to focus on a few developing countries about which they have
specific knowledge, or which they know other companies have chosen as development sites. (If company X chose it, it must meet the appropriate criteria.)

Because of this informational requirement, developing countries that have been
successful in attracting investment often get further investment. Eventually they reach
a stage called **economic takeoff**—a stage when the development process becomes
self-sustaining. Other developing countries fall by the wayside. This means that
economic development is not evenly spread over developing countries, but, rather, is
concentrated in a few.

Economic takeoff *A stage in the
development process when that process becomes self-sustaining.*

Inappropriate Education

*The right education is a necessary
component of any successful development strategy. The wrong education
is an enormous burden.*

The right education is a necessary component of any successful development strategy.
The wrong education is an enormous burden. Developing countries tend to have too
much of the wrong education and too little of the right education.

Often educational systems in developing countries resemble Western educational
systems. The reason is partly the colonial heritage of developing countries and partly
what might be described as an emulation factor. The West defines what an educated
person is, and developing countries want their citizens to be seen as educated. An
educated person should be able to discuss the ideas of Vladimir Nabokov, the poetry
of Lord Byron, the intricacies of chaos theory, the latest developments in fusion
technology, the nuances of the modern Keynesian/Classical debate, and the dissocia-
tive properties of Andy Warhol's paintings. So saith Western scholars; so be it.

But, put bluntly, that type of education is almost irrelevant to economic growth
and may be a serious detriment to growth. Basic skills—reading, writing, and
arithmetic, taught widely—are likely to be more conducive to growth than is high-
level education. When education doesn't match the needs of the society, the degrees—
the credentials—become more important than the knowledge learned. The best jobs
go to those with the highest degrees, not because the individuals holding the degrees
are better able to do the job, but simply because they hold the credentials. Such
credentialing education serves to preserve the monopoly position of these who
manage to get the degree. It has acquired the name **credentialism.**

If access to education is competitive, credentialism has its advantages. Even
irrelevant education, as long as it is difficult, serves a ''screening'' or ''selection''
role. Those individuals who work hardest at getting into, and, in, education advance
and get the good jobs. Since selecting hardworking individuals is difficult, even
irrelevant education serves this selection role.

But developing countries' current educational practices may be worse than irrelevant. Their educational systems often reflect Western culture, not their own cultures.
The best students qualify for scholarships abroad, and their education in a different
tradition makes it difficult for them to return home.

In my studies in Europe and the United States, I've come to know a large number
of the best and the brightest students from developing countries. They're superb
students and they do well in school. But as they near graduation, most of them face an
enormously difficult choice. They can return to their home country—to material
shortages, to enormous challenges for which they have little training, and to an
illiterate society whose traditional values are sometimes hostile to the values these
new graduates have learned. Or they can stay in the West, find jobs relevant to their
training, enjoy an abundance of material goods, and associate with people to whom
they've now learned to relate. Which would you choose?

Arthur Lewis won the Nobel prize in 1979 for
work on economic development. © *The
Nobel Foundation.*

The choice many of them make results in a **brain drain** (the outflow of the best and brightest students from developing countries to developed countries). Many of these good students don't return to the developing country. Those that do go home take jobs as government officials, expecting high salaries and material comforts far beyond what their society can afford. Instead of becoming the dynamic entrepreneurs of growth, they become impediments to growth.

Brain drain   The outflow of the best and brightest students from developing countries to developed countries.

There are, of course, many counterexamples to the arguments presented here. Many developing countries try to design their education system to fit their culture. And many of the dynamic, selfless leaders who make it possible for the country to develop do return home. As with most issues, there are both positive and negative attributes to the way something is done. I emphasize the problems with educational systems in developing economies because the positive attributes of education are generally accepted. Without education, development is impossible. The question is simply how that education should be structured.

Q–10:   How could too much education cause problems for development?

Two ways a country can increase per capita income are:

1. Decrease the number of people in the country (without decreasing the total income in the country).
2. Increase the income (without increasing the population).

In each case the qualifier is important, for income and population are related in complicated ways: People earn income; without people there would be no income. But often the more people there are, the less income per person there is, because the resources of the country become strained.

Overpopulation

A country's population can never be higher than the natural resources that it either has, or can import, can support. But that doesn't mean that overpopulation can't be an obstacle to development. Nature has its own ways of reducing populations that are too large: Starvation and disease are the direct opposite to development. That control system works in nature, and it would work with human societies. The problem is that we don't like it.

Thomas Carlyle gave economics its nickname, *the dismal science,* commenting on the writings of Thomas Malthus, who, in the early 1800s, said that society's prospects are dismal because population tends to outrun the means of subsistence. (Population grows geometrically—that is, at an increasing rate; the means of subsistence grow arithmetically—that is, at a constant rate.) The view was cemented into economic thinking in the law of diminishing marginal productivity: As more and more people are added to a fixed amount of land, the output per worker gets smaller and smaller.

Through technological progress, most Western economies have avoided the fate predicted by Malthus because growth in output has exceeded growth in population. In contrast, many developing economies have not avoided the Malthusian fate because diminishing marginal productivity has exceeded technological change, and limited economic growth isn't enough to offset the increase in population. The result is a constant or falling output per person.

Many developing economies have not avoided the Malthusian fate because diminishing marginal productivity has exceeded technological change.

That doesn't mean that developing countries haven't grown economically. They have. But population growth makes per capita output growth small or negative.

Population grows for a number of reasons, including:

1. As public health measures are improved, infant mortality rates and death rates for the population as a whole both decline. (Fewer people die each year.)
2. As people earn more income, they believe they can afford to have more kids.
3. In rural areas, children are useful in working the fields.

What to do? Should the government reduce the population growth rate? If it should, how can it do so? Various measures have been tried: advertising campaigns, free condoms, forced sterilization, and economic incentives. For example, in China the government has tried imposing severe economic penalties on couples who have

Even successful population control programs have their problems.

more than one child, while providing material incentives such as a free television set to couples who agreed not to have more than one child.

China's vigorous population control campaign has had a number of effects. First, it created so much anger at the government that in rural areas the campaign was dropped. Second, it led to the killing of many female babies because, if couples were to have only one baby, strong cultural and economic pressures existed to ensure that the baby was a male. Third, it led to an enormous loss of privacy. Dates of women's menstrual periods were posted in factories and officials would remind them at appropriate times that they should take precautions against getting pregnant. Only a very strong government could impose such a plan.

Even successful population control programs have their problems. In Singapore a population control campaign was so successful among educated women that the government became concerned that its "population quality" was suffering. It began a selective campaign to encourage college-educated women to have children. They issued "love tips" to men (since some college-educated women complained that their male companions were nerds and had no idea how to be romantic) and offered special monetary bonuses to college-educated women who gave birth to children. As you might imagine, the campaign provoked a backlash, and it was eventually dropped by the government.

Individuals differ substantially in their assessment of the morality of these programs, but even if one believes that population control is an appropriate government concern, it does not seem that such programs will be successful, by themselves, in limiting population growth.

It is true that birth control programs have enabled developing countries to slow their population growth, but so far their overall effect hasn't been what planners had hoped. Summarizing past attempts, Ashish Bose (head of the Population Research Center of Delhi University in India) stated, "Looking back, high tech, money, and the bureaucracy—all these have failed."

Some people, like social scientist Julian Simon, believe that all such attempts to control population are misplaced. People are the ultimate resource, he argues, and it is inconceivable that a society can have too many people. People will design technologies that will allow ever-increasing numbers to exist in a society.

STRATEGIES FOR GROWTH: AN ONGOING DEBATE

While developing countries' problems seem overwhelming, development economists have nonetheless offered a variety of strategies for growth. These strategies have been much debated, and a brief discussion of four areas of debate is appropriate at this point. All four presume that development money is available; the debate involves how best to spend it.

Balanced versus Unbalanced Growth

6 Four debates about strategies for growth are:
1. Balanced vs. unbalanced growth.
2. Agriculture vs. industry.
3. Infrastructure vs. directly productive investment.
4. Export-led growth vs. import substitution.

In deciding how to spend your development money, do you follow an **unbalanced growth plan,** focusing on one sector of the economy and hoping that that will generate development in other sectors? Or do you adopt a **balanced growth plan,** spreading the money around and trying to spur development in all sectors simultaneously? With a balanced growth plan, you risk spreading the money so thin that nothing substantial can be accomplished. With an unbalanced growth plan, you risk creating an oasis of development that the economy cannot sustain for long. The debate has sometimes been likened to a debate about how you should pull yourself up by your own bootstraps. Should you pull one side first? Or should you pull both sides together? And how can you pull yourself up at all if you are standing on the very surface you're trying to lift?

Agriculture versus Industry

Most developing countries' economies depend on agriculture. Developed countries' economies depend on industry. If you have some development money, do you spend it on agriculture, where most of your production takes place, or do you spend it on developing an industrial base for growth?

The argument for spending the money on industry is that such expenditures will allow you to decrease imports and will encourage further industrial growth so you can become like the developed countries. Advocates of this position contend that agriculture is a dead-end path.

The argument for spending the money on agriculture instead of industry is that agriculture is already built into the culture of that society, so gains in a congenial area (agriculture) are much more likely to occur than are gains in an unfamiliar area (industry).

Since agriculture is generally associated with the traditionally based economy and industry is often associated with the internationally based economy, this agriculture/industry debate might be called **"the Dueling Duals."** Should one build up the small existing industrialized economy, widening the income and cultural gap between the two economies? Or should one narrow that gap by trying to pull up the traditional economy? Notice that since the degree of inequality is tied to the strategy a country chooses, it is not clear that it will make the choice that offers the highest prospect for growth.

As I stated before, most developing countries do not have the infrastructure necessary for most kinds of production. Should you invest your development money in the infrastructure, which is indirectly productive, or in directly productive activities like building a mill or providing a fertilizer subsidy? Infrastructure investment shows no immediate monetary return. If it is to show a return, it must increase private investment which in turn generates a short-run monetary return; if private investment isn't forthcoming, the money spent on infrastructure is wasted. Thus, there is a strong incentive to use the money in directly productive investment. But directly productive investment often cannot compete internationally unless the infrastructure is in place.

Infrastructure versus Directly Productive Investment

Another of the choices developing countries face is whether to focus on *export-led growth*—trying to develop industries that will compete on the world market and that are not necessarily tied to the domestic economy—or to focus on *import substitution*—trying to develop industries that will produce for the domestic economy, replacing imports. Such an import-substitution strategy is often initiated with government-imposed tariffs on imports to provide some initial protection for an industry. It is, however, often difficult for government ever to eliminate that initial tariff protection both because (1) with the protection there is little pressure on the industry to hold costs down and become internationally competitive, and (2) the size of the market often limits the use of large-scale efficient technology.

Export-Led Growth versus Import Substitution

At this point in my course, I inevitably throw my hands up and admit that I don't know what makes it possible for a country to develop. Nor, judging from what I have read, do the development experts. The good ones (that is, the ones I agree with) admit that they don't know; others (that is, the ones I don't agree with) simply don't know that they don't know.

My gut feeling is that there are no definitive general answers that apply to all developing countries. The appropriate answer varies with each country and each situation. Each proposed solution to the development problem has a right time and a right place. Only by having a complete sense of a country, its history, and its cultural, social, and political norms can one decide whether it's the right time and place for this or that policy.

MISSION IMPOSSIBLE

7 Economic development is a complicated problem because it is entwined with cultural and social issues.

CHAPTER SUMMARY

- One must be careful in judging economies.
- The analysis of developing countries is, more and more, being divided into four geographic groupings: Asian, African, Latin American, and Middle Eastern.

- The dual structure of developing countries' economies creates political and economic tension.
- Six obstacles to economic development are political instability, corruption, lack of appropriate institutions,

lack of investment, inappropriate education, and overpopulation.

•Without an appropriate infrastructure governments can sell rights to all kinds of things and thereby limit development.

•Generating sufficient investment is a difficult problem for developing countries.

•Four debates about strategies for growth include the balanced/unbalanced growth debate, the agriculture/industry debate, the infrastructure/directly productive investment debate, and export-led growth/import substitution debate.

•Optimal strategies for growth are country-specific.

KEY TERMS

Asian tigers *(832)*
balanced growth plan   *(840)*
brain drain *(839)*
credentialism *(838)*

dual economy   *(831)*
the Dueling Duals   *(841)*
economic takeoff   *(838)*
foreign aid   *(836)*

infrastructure investment   *(837)*
purchasing power parity   *(830)*
unbalanced growth plan   *(840)*

QUESTIONS FOR THOUGHT AND REVIEW

The number after each question represents the estimated degree of critical thinking required. (1 = almost none; 10 = deep thought.)

1. If you suddenly found yourself living as a poor person in a developing country, what are some things that you now do that you would no longer be able to do? What new things would you have to do? *(2)*

2. What is wrong with saying that people in developing countries are worse off than people in the United States? *(3)*

3. Does the fact that suicide rates are lower in developing countries than in the United States imply that Americans would be better off living in a developing country? Why? *(5)*

4. Why are investment and savings so low in developing countries? *(5)*

5. If developing countries are so unstable and offer such a risky environment for investment, why do foreigners invest any money in them at all? *(5)*

6. If you were a foreign investor thinking of making an investment in a developing country, what are some things that you would be concerned about? *(4)*

7. Should developing countries send their students abroad for an education? *(5)*

8. How does corruption limit investment and economic growth? *(6)*

9. Should a country control the size and makeup of its population? Why? *(7)*

10. List four alternative strategies for growth and give an advantage and disadvantage of each strategy. *(4)*

PROBLEMS AND EXERCISES

1. Interview a foreign student in your class or school. Ask about each of the six obstacles to economic development and how her country is trying to overcome them.

2. Spend one day living like someone in a developing country. Eat almost nothing and work lifting stones for 10 hours. Then, that same evening, study this chapter and contemplate the bootstrap strategy of development.

3. In 1991 Germany passed a law requiring businesses to take back and recycle all forms of packaging. A large group of businesses formed a company to collect and recycle these packages. Its costs are 4.5 cents per pound for glass, 9.5 cents per pound for paper, and 74 cents per pound for plastic. This accounts for a recycling cost of

about $100 per ton for glass and $2,000 per ton for plastic, and the average recycling cost is $500 per ton. A developing country has offered to create a giant landfill and accept Germany's waste at a cost of $400 per ton, which includes $50 per ton sorting and transport costs and a $350-per-ton fee to be paid to the developing country.

a. Should Germany accept this proposal?

b. Will the proposal benefit the developing country?

c. What alternative or modification to the proposal might you suggest?

4. Say that you have been hired to design an education system for a developing country.

a. What skills would you want it to emphasize?

b. How might it differ from an ideal educational system here in the United States?

c. How much of the U.S. education system involves credentialism, and how much the learning of relevant skills?

5. Asian countries have grown faster than countries in other geographic areas. These countries have followed a neo-mercantalist approach in which the government takes a lead role in the development process.

a. Would you suggest other countries do the same? Why or why not?

b. What factors might have made the Asian countries successful, other than this role of government?

c. Of the six obstacles to growth, which would you say is the most important for developing countries to focus on overcoming? Why?

ANSWERS TO MARGIN QUESTIONS

1. Given market societies' expansionary tendencies, the cultures in economically poor countries that do not grow would simply be overrun and destroyed by cultures of market societies. This means that the choice is not between development and preservation of existing culture; rather, the choice is between economic development with its attendant wrenching cultural transitions, and continued poverty with exploitation by developed countries and its attendant wrenching cultural transitions. *(829)*

2. The exchange rate method of comparing incomes simply compares the income at the determined exchange rates. The purchasing power parity method of comparing incomes compares incomes adjusted by the cost of specific market baskets of consumer goods in the respective countries. *(831)*

3. The geographic grouping of countries that has grown the fastest is the grouping of Asian countries, especially the Asian tiger countries. *(832)*

4. The African countries, especially the sub-Saharan countries, have grown the least. *(832)*

5. In order for a market to operate, a set of rules—any rules—is needed. Lack of stability undermines the existence of any rules and leads to a failure of cooperation among people. *(834)*

6. It depends, but the answer is probably "false." Often the wealthy elite in a developing country fear that if they invest in their country their money will be taken away, so they often invest out of their country—meaning that the benefits of their savings go to other countries, not to the investor's own developing country. *(834)*

7. The more it costs to undertake economic activities, the fewer economic activities individuals undertake. *(835)*

8. True. While the total money amount of foreign aid given by the United States exceeds almost every other major country's grants, as a percentage of its GDP the United States gives the smallest percentage of the major developed countries. *(837)*

9. Because Mexico competes with other developing countries for investment projects, it has a tendency to give major environmental breaks to global companies seeking sites to develop. Concerns about Mexico's lack of regulatory environment led people to fear that many U.S. companies would simply locate within Mexican borders and avoid U.S. environmental rules, creating environmental havoc and costing the United States jobs. *(838)*

10. Education is absolutely necessary for development, but it is most helpful if it is the right type of education—focusing on basic skills such as reading, writing, and arithmetic. When education focuses on abstract issues, determined by different cultures and having little relevance to the country's problems, "too much" education can lead to a brain drain and a diversion of people's talent away from the central development issues. *(839)*

39

Socialist Economies in Transition

God made the world in seven days, but he didn't have an installed computer base.

~Bill Gates

After reading this chapter, you should be able to:

1 Summarize the historical roots of socialism.

2 Summarize how a centrally planned economy works.

3 Explain why most Soviet-style socialist economies suffered consistent shortages of most goods.

4 State five major problems of a centrally planned economy.

5 Summarize some transition problems former Soviet-style socialist countries are experiencing.

6 List four cautionary lessons for transitional economies in their decision to adopt Western institutions.

Most of this book has considered the operations and institutions of capitalist economies, and has discussed how economic forces work within market situations. However, as emphasized throughout this book, economic forces are at work in *all* situations. A market is simply an institution in which economic forces are allowed to predominate over political and social forces.

In this final chapter we switch gears and look at what happens when markets aren't used. We do that by considering the operation of economic forces in **Soviet-style socialist economies**—centrally planned economies in which the state owns most of the means of production—and consider some of the explanations for why these countries have moved toward an economic organization using the market rather than central planning. We'll consider how central planning has worked in practice—and how that practice differed from theory. Finally, we'll consider the ongoing transition of Soviet-style socialist economies and the problems these economies face.

The theory of modern socialist economies originated when a group of writers in the 1800s reacted to the excesses of unregulated capitalism. Looking at what the Industrial Revolution had wrought—the 10-hour work day, child labor, poor working conditions, a highly unequal distribution of income, unemployment, and starvation—they argued that there must be a better way than capitalism to organize economic society.

The doctrine of socialism itself began in the early 19th century with the work of individuals such as Louis Blanc, a French historian and government official. Blanc focused on the belief that everyone who was willing and able to work should have a job. Over time, the emphasis in socialism changed from creating an economy in which everyone had a job, to creating an economy that redistributed income from the rich to the poor, and then to creating an economy in which the government controlled production.

In the 1990s, with the downfall of Soviet-style socialist economies, the emphasis in socialist thinking was again changing. China attempted to merge markets into its socialist system, and the former Soviet bloc countries attempted to build new institutions in their formerly socialist economies. In the midst of these changes, socialists kept their belief in the existence of a better way, but they agree with mainstream economists that the Soviet-style socialist approach, with its combination of totalitarian political control and state-controlled economic planning, is not the way to go.

In a **centrally planned economy,** central planners decide the general directions the economy will take. They make the *what, how,* and *for whom* decisions. Should the economy focus on producing consumer goods? Machinery? Agriculture? Military hardware? The government's central planners decide.

In communist-dominated socialist economies like the former Soviet Union and China, or in pre-1990 Eastern Europe, the power behind the central planners was the Communist party. The Communist party nominated candidates for office. The public then ratified the choices by voting in elections in which the Communist party candidates were the only candidates. Thus, these systems were political systems as well as economic systems in which the Communist party was like an autocracy, being a government composed of a small group of people with nearly unlimited power, not of a popularly elected set of officials.

A centrally planned economy like that in the former Soviet Union differs from a market economy like that of the United States. That difference is not, however, that in one there is planning and in the other there is not. The difference lies in who does the planning, how many planners there are, and what motives guide planners' decisions.

A centrally planned economy has one central agency for economic planning, while a market economy has many planners. Since the idea of planning in a market economy may be a bit unusual to you, let's consider who does the planning in the United States.

For the 25 percent of U.S. output controlled by the various branches of government (the public sector), the government is the planner, and its decisions are peri-

Q–1: Economic forces are at work in all situations. True or false? Why?

Soviet-style socialist economies
Centrally planned economies in which the state owns most of the means of production.

THE HISTORICAL ROOTS OF SOCIALISM

1 The theory of modern socialist economies originated in the early 1800s when a group of writers reacted to the excesses of unregulated capitalism.

HOW A CENTRALLY PLANNED ECONOMY WORKS

2 In a centrally planned economy, central planners decide the general direction the economy will take. They make the *what, how,* and *for whom* decisions.

Planning in a Centrally Planned Economy and in a Market Economy

If only the world were wonderful, or at least better than it is. How many times have you thought that? Probably many, and you're not alone. Sir Thomas More in 1515 wrote a book about such a wonderful society, which he called *Utopia*. Ever since, dream worlds have gone by the name *Utopia*.

In the 18th and early 19th centuries there were many dreamers of Utopia. Democracy had been ushered in and new, better forms of government were taking hold. Why not a better economy too? Not an economy in which people starved; not an economy in which people were held under the "gun" of competition—but a society of cooperation, of concern for others, and of love.

If it sounds wonderful to you, it also sounded wonderful to numerous individuals in the early 1800s, including Robert Owen, owner of a large, successful cotton mill in Manchester, England. Owen believed sufficiently in his ideas to put his money where his mouth was. To demonstrate the superiority of his utopian ideas, he bought a mill in New Lanark, near Manchester, and instead of paying low wages and tolerating unsanitary conditions, he took a strong interest in the workers' welfare. He provided decent housing, education, and low-cost goods for his workers at the company store. The mill was a success.

Owen then expanded his mission, recommending that entire towns adopt a "cooperative," not a "competitive," structure. He suggested villages of "unity and cooperation" of about 1,200 inhabitants, with each village offering a public kitchen and dining room. Parents would care for their children until the age of three, after which children would be raised by the community so that they would be imbued with the appropriate cooperative social attitude. He believed that once society saw how wonderful these communities were, all societies would voluntarily adopt the structure and soon the whole world would embrace his ideas.

To implement his plans he moved to the United States and set up a model project—New Harmony, Indiana—in 1825. Life in New Harmony was anything but harmonious. In three years Owen was broke and the project was dead— killed by internal fights and arguments. Other similar communities suffered the same fate. The experiment in voluntary socialism was a failure.

---

odically ratified by the public through regularly scheduled elections. In the private sector the planners are business executives, and their decisions are guided by the profit motive, which in turn reflects consumer sovereignty.

In market economies there are a multitude of planners. These planners include business executives and government officials.

The multitude of planners in a market economy makes it difficult to say exactly who decides *what, how,* and *for whom* to produce. So normally economists say, "The market decides," but it's important to remember that planning does take place in a market economy. Exhibit 1 summarizes the differences in planning in market and centrally planned economies.

Planning in Practice   Planning in practice starts with a group of planners deciding what will be produced. For example, the planners might issue a general directive like the following: "Over the next five years the focus of the economy will be on producing more machinery. Production in machinery will increase 8 percent per year. We will increase agricultural goods by 4 percent per year and consumer goods by 5 percent." This directive, of course, will be made more specific—what kinds of machinery will be produced and what crops will be focused on in each of those five years.

Even when these decisions have been made, many more specifics need to be added before the plans will be meaningful enough to be carried out. For example, managers and workers need to know not only how many tractors to produce, but also their specifications: What horsepower? What size tires? What kind of steel? What inputs will be available? To give you a sense of how extensive planning was in a centrally planned economy, consider that in 1987 the former Soviet planners set quotas and prices for more than 200,000 commodities and controlled the operation of more than 37,000 enterprises. Making such decisions requires a large planning agency.

In the former Soviet planning system, an individual official in the planning agency was assigned a certain group of factories or production units, usually all in the same region of the country. This individual knew the capabilities of the factories in the region and, on the basis of that knowledge, he or she set production quotas for each factory.

For example, say the government's five-year plan emphasized plenty of bread to go around. To fulfill this plan, bread output would have to be increased by 40 percent over five years. The planners would translate that goal into an increase in the output of bread of, say, 7 percent per year, which, compounded over five years, would achieve

EXHIBIT 1   Planning in a Centrally Planned and in a Market Economy

All economies require planning. The difference between a market economy and a centrally planned economy is in who does the planning and what the planners' motivations are.

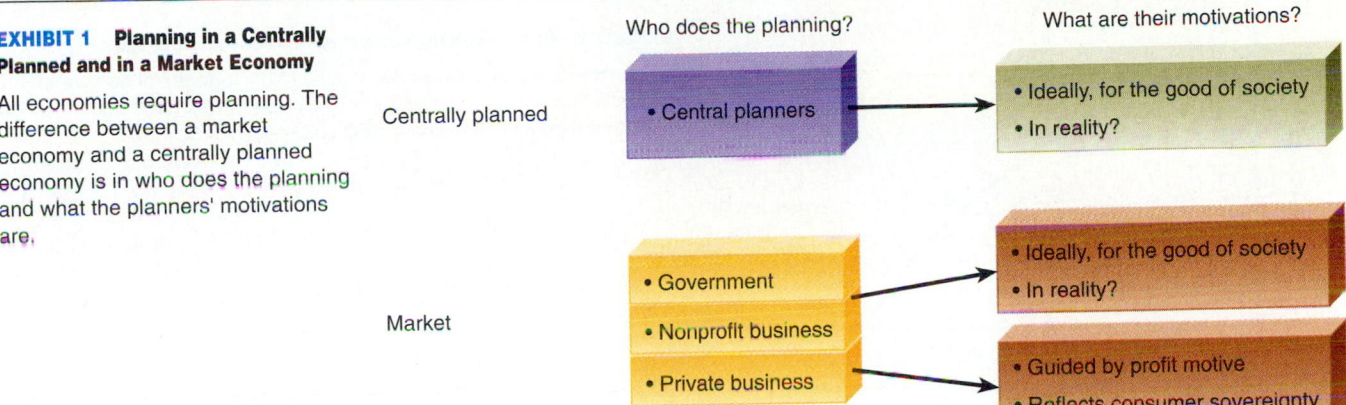

Who does the planning?

What are their motivations?

Centrally planned

- Central planners

- Ideally, for the good of society
- In reality?

Market

- Government
- Nonprofit business
- Private business

- Ideally, for the good of society
- In reality?

- Guided by profit motive
- Reflects consumer sovereignty

more than the 40 percent desired growth. The planners translated these targeted increases into specific production quotas for regions containing groups of firms—8 percent for one region, 3 percent for another, and so on.

These plans would have to be translated into directives for the managers of individual factories. Thus, a bakery manager was given a set of directives specifying what he or she would be required to produce over the next year and what inputs would be available in order to meet the goal. The directive would have read as follows: "Next year you will produce 4,000,000 loaves of white bread, 2,000,000 loaves of rye bread, 1,000,000 loaves of whole wheat bread, and 1,000,000 loaves of pumpernickel. To do so, you will be allocated 400 workers, 1 plant, and 4,000,000 pounds of grain."

This one-year directive was subdivided into monthly, weekly, and even daily input and output levels. Managers' performances were judged according to how close they came to meeting their assigned goals. Under actual conditions the plans would have been much more detailed than the hypothetical directive I've constructed, but the example gives you the general idea.

Counterplanning   The preceding description may make it seem as if, in a central planning system, the various planning agencies would continually be telling the agencies below them what to do. That was true, but the information flowed both ways. Long before a final directive was issued, the higher-level planners conferred extensively with lower-level planners. They would go over what was feasible. After talking with the lower-level planning group, the higher-level planning group would usually show the lower-level group a draft plan.

Each lower-level group had a chance to point out that it wasn't allocated the inputs necessary to achieve the output quota, or that the output quota was unrealistic. They could suggest modifications to the plan. This process of modifying the plan from below was known as **counterplanning**. Counterplanning let individuals at lower levels of the hierarchy influence decisions of those at higher levels and thereby affect the decision made by the highest level of central planners.

Counterplanning   Process that lets individuals low in the hierarchy influence the planning decisions of those higher in the hierarchy.

Coordinating the Plans: Material Balances   Directing and issuing detailed plans for an entire economy was a complicated procedure. The planners had to ensure that the output of firms whose products were used in the production of other products matched the inputs that the planners had assigned to the manufacturers of those other products. This coordination of directives was achieved through a system called *material balances*.

Using the **material balance** approach, essentially the planning board added up what was coming in, subtracted what was going out, and kept adjusting incoming and outgoing quantities of materials until they were equal—until the materials balanced. Hence the name *material balance*. The process wasn't easy. It was like trying to put a Rubik Cube back in the pattern it had when it came out of the box. One kept trying various combinations of inputs and outputs until one got everything to fit.

Material balance   Process by which central planners adjust incoming and outgoing quantities of materials until supply equals demand (at least on paper).

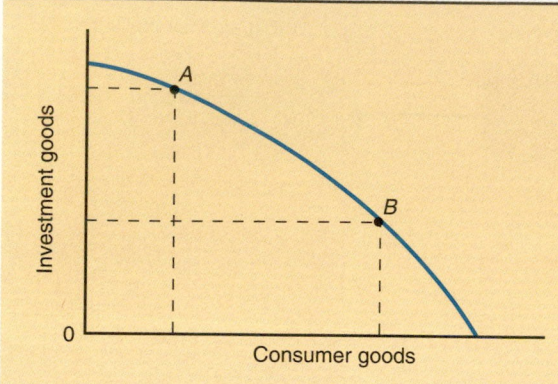

EXHIBIT 2   **Choice between Investment Goods and Consumer Goods**

One of the reasons socialist economies had shortages of consumer goods is that the planners made a conscious decision to emphasize investment goods, choosing a position like A over B.

To aid in this complex process of making inputs and outputs balance, economists designed and perfected some mathematical tools. These tools were important tools not only to planned economies; they are still important tools to Western business firms. The tools include linear programming, designed by Leonid Kantorovich (a Soviet economist), and input-output analysis, designed by Wassily Leontief (a Russian-born American economist who was interested in analyzing centrally planned economies). The two men won Nobel prizes for their work, Kantorovich in 1975 and Leontief in 1973. The material balance approach, assisted by tools such as input-output analysis and linear programming, was the most widely used system for coordinating centrally planned economic systems, and a variant is still being used in China.

Deciding What to Produce

Now that you've been introduced to the technical planning apparatus, let's consider planners' motivation in deciding what and how much of something to produce next year. There are no simple answers to these questions. The planners could, if they desired, decide how much would be wanted by consumers next year in about the same way a firm in the United States decides. Alternatively, they could look at what was produced one year, estimate how much demand for the product would increase the next year, and base their production decisions on that estimate. Or they could base their decision on other criteria.

There is a big difference between planning in socialist and capitalist economies. In capitalist economies a firm plans to make a profit. In socialist economies the central planners can follow whatever set of principles they want.

But whatever criteria they choose, there's a big difference in the motivation behind planning in a socialist economy and in a capitalist economy. In a capitalist economy a firm makes its profits by producing *what* and *how much* is wanted by consumers. To stay in business, firms must take the consumers' desires into account. Central planners in a socialist economy don't have to take consumers' desires into account. Central planners might realize that Twinkies will be wanted by consumers, but the planners might believe that Twinkies aren't good for people, so their decision might be to produce whole-wheat bread instead.

Central planners could follow any set of principles they wanted to in determining what output levels to assign the producers of various goods. Exhibit 2 presents a production possibility curve showing the range of choices that societies could make between investment goods and consumer goods. In the 1970s and 1980s, Soviet planners chose a point like *A,* focusing on investment goods (heavy equipment, large machines, space exploration, and military goods such as tanks and planes), having decided that these goods were what their society needed. Consumer goods (cars, household appliances, clothing) were given short shrift. Most market economies, in which the profit motive directs firms to produce what they think people want, choose a point like *B,* which includes more consumer goods.

The reason socialist planners chose a point like *A* was that higher production of investment goods was supposed to lead to faster growth, which would make up for the lower level of output (relative to Western developed countries) at which the former Soviet Union and other socialist countries started out. It's as if your economics instructor told you to work harder at the beginning of the term because it will pay off at the end. This strategy can be successful, but socialist economies, for reasons that I'll

Leonid Kantorovich won the Nobel prize in 1975 for work on linear programming and economic planning. © The Nobel Foundation.

EXHIBIT 3   Prices (in dollars) in East and West Germany before Unification

Item	West Germany	East Germany
Coffee (1 pound)	$3.39	$13.33
Color TV set	$600.00	$2,000.00
Electricity (1 kwh)	.17	.03
Monthly rent	$200.00	$30.00
Potatoes (10 pounds)	$1.80	.30
Refrigerator	$250.00	$570.00
Rye bread (1 kg)	.75	.10
Washing machine	$400.00	$1,000.00

Sources: Based on information collected by Deutsche Bank, World Bank, and estimates by author.

discuss later, didn't grow faster than the United States and other market economies. They grew more slowly. The payoff for choosing investment goods over consumer goods didn't come, and that missing payoff was a significant factor in the demise of centrally planned economies.

Central planners had not only to decide what goods to produce; they also had to decide what prices to charge for those goods. In a market economy, most prices are set by suppliers at a level that covers costs of production and provides them with a profit margin that they feel is appropriate. If suppliers set their prices too high, consumers will buy from other suppliers; if suppliers set their prices too low, they won't cover their costs and they'll lose money.

Pricing in a Centrally Planned Economy

In a market economy, suppliers are free to adjust their prices to make the quantity demanded equal the quantity supplied. If demand is lower than expected, firms will lower their prices to stimulate an increase in the quantity demanded. If demand is high, prices will tend to rise, encouraging consumers to economize on the good, and producers to increase their production. That's what's meant by **market-determined prices.**

In a centrally planned economy, prices are determined by the central planners, not by the market. The prices that central planners set influence the quantity demanded of various goods. When planners set a low price, the quantity demanded will be high; when they set a high price, the quantity demanded will be low. That's the same as in a capitalist economy.

In a centrally planned economy, prices are determined by the central planners, not by the market.

What are different are the criteria that central planners use to set prices. To some degree, they set prices to cover costs (not including profits, since socialist producers aren't supposed to earn profits), but they can also set prices at the level they believe is fair or at the level they believe is the social worth of a product—in short, at whatever level they want.

Q–2: Do prices play a role in a centrally planned economy?

How did central planners actually decide where to set prices? The general approach to pricing taken by socialist countries was to price necessities (like basic foods) low and luxuries (like washing machines and cars) high, independent of costs. For example, in the late 1980s Soviet rents were set at the U.S. equivalent of $80 a month for a one-bedroom apartment in Moscow. Compare this to the usual $1,000 monthly rent for a one-bedroom apartment in New York City at that time. Medical care was free. Bread and potatoes were priced far below what it cost to produce them.

Q–3: The people revolted against the formerly Soviet-style socialist governments because their economic system failed to bring them bread or electricity at a low price. True or false? Why?

Exhibit 3 shows prices of selected goods in East and West Germany in 1988, before the two nations were reunited. After unification, East Germany's prices were changed to reflect those of West Germany.

The ability to set prices at whatever level they wanted didn't free central planners from economic forces. The laws of supply and demand still operated. There were surpluses of goods whose prices were set too high relative to the quantity supplied and shortages of goods whose prices were set too low relative to the quantity supplied.

Most Soviet-style socialist economies suffered from consistent shortages of most goods. Getting an apartment required a wait of five years or even longer. Getting a car required a still longer wait. This suggests that the prices the planners chose (even the

3 Most Soviet-style socialist countries suffered from consistent shortages of goods because the planners chose too-low prices relative to demand.

This Russian photo exemplifies the shortages and queues for food that have characterized socialist economies.   *Reuters/Bettmann*

Q–4:   What rationing method did many of the formerly Soviet-style socialist countries use to determine who got what?

relatively high prices) were too low relative to demand. This was one of people's big complaints with the centrally planned economies—a consistent shortage of goods.

When there are shortages of goods, an alternative rationing system must be established to determine who gets what. In Soviet-style socialist countries, that rationing system generally involved being a member of the Communist party or being in the in-group. Officials received ''gifts,'' were put at the top of waiting lists, and were notified by distributors when scarce goods came in so that they could shop ahead of other people. In Romania, for example, before the revolution that broke out at the end of 1989, the communist leadership could get pretty much whatever consumer goods it wanted. That inequality contradicted the goals of communism, and the people's resentment of it was one cause of the uprisings against communism and Soviet-style socialism in the late 1980s and early 1990s. We'll cover this issue in more depth when we discuss reforms.

THE PROBLEMS OF CENTRAL PLANNING

Economists have identified five problems that tend to undermine central planning:

1. Nonmarket pricing and perverse incentives.
2. Inability to adjust prices quickly.
3. Lack of accurate information about demand.
4. Ambiguous production directives.
5. Inability to adjust plans quickly to changing situations.

Let's look at each of these problems in turn.

Nonmarket Pricing and Perverse Incentives

In a market economy, prices reflect costs—a central lesson of the economic analysis of production. The advantage of having prices reflect costs was a central lesson of microeconomic theory. Prices that reflect costs make people's decisions about what to consume and what to produce reflect productivity cost. The result is efficient use of resources.

Central planners can override the market and choose prices that don't reflect costs. However, as discussed in the chapter on consumer choice, when prices don't reflect costs, consumers have an incentive to use goods in a manner that reflects the cost to them and not the costs to the society. Economists call an incentive to use goods in a manner that doesn't reflect the cost to society a **perverse incentive.**

Perverse incentive   Incentive to use goods in a manner that does not reflect that use's cost to society.

Let's say that the economic planners decide that everyone in the society deserves inexpensive bread, so they lower the price of bread from 50¢ to 5¢ for a 16-ounce loaf.

Say that last year, at 50¢ a loaf, people consumed 1 million loaves, so planners figure this year, at 5¢ a loaf, 2 million loaves will be consumed. After all, how much bread can people eat? In principle, that's plenty of bread, but most likely the outcome will be a shortage of bread to eat. Why? Because at 5¢ a loaf, self-interested people will discover lots of other things one can do with bread besides eat it themselves. For example, after the fall in price, a pig farmer might buy four loaves of bread a week for his family and 7,000 loaves a week for his pigs. At 5¢ a loaf, it pays to feed bread, rather than oats or corn, to his pigs, even though the equivalent amount of oats or corn would be better for the pigs and less costly to society. Pig farming will increase enormously. If the cost to society of producing a loaf of bread is 40¢ and the cost of producing oats or corn of equal feed value is 20¢, the 5¢ price of bread not only creates a shortage of bread for people to eat, but also subsidizes pig farmers. Moreover, society will be losing 35¢ (the 40¢ it costs minus the 5¢ it gets for the bread) for each loaf of bread fed to pigs while gaining only 20¢ of value in additional output of pigs. The net loss to society will be 15¢ per loaf (the opportunity cost of the oats or corn).

If central planners have a high degree of control over which, and how, inputs are used, they can stop such "inappropriate" uses of bread simply by forbidding them. But unless people are not self-interested, policing and enforcing those additional rules require an enormous amount of central control, which requires a large, costly bureaucracy and causes other problems.

Central planners must direct individuals to do what is consistent with their plan, and must enforce their directives. The market, in contrast, uses economic incentives to guide people to do what is in society's interest.

Centrally planned pricing decisions are also not consistent with quick adjustment of prices. The reason is that the information about what is selling fast and what isn't doesn't get back to the central planners rapidly enough. Why? Sales information is often delayed by the need to flow through three or four levels of bureaucracy: A salesperson must tell his boss, who must tell the regional director, who must tell the central planning assistant director—all by memo, and memos simply don't travel very fast. It's a law of nature that administrative decisions aren't made quickly. Large firms in the United States have the same problems; they tend to adjust their prices more slowly than do small firms.

The result of central planning's inability to adjust prices quickly is a surplus of some items whose price is too high and a shortage of other goods whose price is too low. Shortages and surpluses were especially apparent in specialized consumer goods such as fashionable clothing (for example, stone-washed jeans), household appliances, and novelty items. In the United States, you can walk into stores and get almost anything you want, whenever you want. As long as some person can predict a demand and make a profit filling that demand, the demand will be filled. In the centrally planned former Soviet Union "frivolous needs" received a low priority, resulting in chronic shortages of all types of consumer goods.

China is currently changing its planning focus toward more consumer goods while simultaneously allowing more market production of consumer goods. Economic theory predicts that the market will do much better than the planners. The reason is that predicting demand for consumer items is always difficult, and central planning makes it even more difficult. In a market economy, surpluses are dealt with by running sales: "CLEARANCE SALE! TAKE 60% TO 70% OFF ALL RED-TAGGED ITEMS!" At some price, suppliers in a market economy will find demanders for those purple trousers or those dresses with last year's length.

Socialist retail firms will have trouble running sales because the need to get approval prevents them from changing prices quickly enough. So the planners' retail stores may find themselves with empty racks for jeans but overflowing racks of purple trousers.

The problems caused by the planners' inability to adjust prices are amplified by their lack of information about what products are desired. In a centrally planned economy, producers have little incentive to tell the planners that their plans will create a surplus

4 Five problems that tend to undermine central planning are:
1. Nonmarket pricing and perverse incentives.
2. Inability to adjust prices quickly.
3. Lack of accurate information about demand.
4. Ambiguous production directives.
5. Inability to adjust plans quickly to changing situations.

Q–5: What lesson does the former Soviet-style socialist countries' experience with central planning have for the health care debate in the United States in the 1990s?

Inability to Adjust Prices Quickly

It's a law of nature that administrative decisions aren't made quickly.

Lack of Accurate Information about Demand

or a shortage; nor do they have an incentive to see that their goods sell. When producers are judged by their ability to meet their production quotas, not by whether their goods sell, they don't provide planners with information about what sells. Instead they provide information that will encourage planners to set production targets that are easy to meet.

The result of such misleading feedback has been the production of lots of undesirable and unwanted goods and severe shortages of desired goods. In most centrally planned economies, consumers walked around with lots of cash and shopping bags. When they saw something they needed or liked in a store, they got in line to buy large quantities for themselves and their friends—which worsened the shortage for other consumers.

Q–6: Why would many consumers in the former socialist centrally planned economies walk around with lots of cash and shopping bags?

Ambiguous Production Directives

Another problem that centrally planned economies had is that production directives were inevitably ambiguous. To be unambiguous, a directive must give all relevant specifications of a product. One can't simply say, "Produce 4 million tons of screws." One must specify size, quality, type of material to be used, and number of threads. One perhaps apocryphal story concerns a directive for chandeliers that specified only the overall weight. To meet the directive, the plant simply built one gigantic chandelier made of lead, for which no truck large enough to move it could be found. The plant met its quota, but did not produce anything useful or desirable.

This problem is a general one of administrative control and isn't confined to centrally planned economies. At General Motors, for example, until recently managers were often given quantitative goals that left out certain qualitative specifications. In the 1970s the basic goals were to produce lots of cars quickly and cheaply. The result: low-quality cars and the decline of the U.S. auto industry.

Inability to Adjust Plans Quickly

In any economy, things never develop in quite the way they're expected to.

Another problem for centrally planned economies is that they do not adjust plans very well. In any economy, things never develop in quite the way they're expected to. Inevitably there are emergencies, breakdowns, and changes in priorities that require changes in the plan.

In market economies, decisions about adjusting plans are made by individuals and firms, using the information available to them. Firms react to market incentives. If there's a significant shortage of a good, its price rises and, as it does, some individual or firm has a monetary incentive to provide it. If an automobile manufacturer in a market economy finds that its steel supplies aren't being delivered on schedule, it calls other suppliers to round up an alternative supply. The market provides both the *information* needed to adjust the plan and *incentives* to do so.

Q–7: Why do centrally planned economies and large bureaucratic institutions generally have a difficult time implementing plans?

In a centrally planned economy, all information about the need to adjust plans must go through a central office. Say an auto plant in a centrally planned economy found that steel supplies were falling short. The managers would have to call the next level of the central planning office, which in turn would have to call the next level, which would have to call the steel producers and try to find out what was going wrong. Once a decision to adjust the plans was made, the same bureaucratic procedure was followed in reverse. The producer called the subplanner, the subplanner called the planner, and so on. By the time the information led to a change in direction, most likely everyone had said, "To hell with it." Your own experiences in dealing with some large U.S. firm or bureaucratic institution may have been merely frustrating, but centrally planned economies would have driven you crazy.

In principle, planners could have built into their plans a method of adjustment— their plans could have been contingent plans. But, in practice, merely specifying the dimensions of the product made the plans so complicated that formulating contingent plans was out of the question. There were hundreds of possible contingencies, and specifying plans for them was impossible. In short, information about what adjustment to make wasn't efficiently transmitted among producers and planners in a centrally planned economy. This was the lesson of microeconomic theory: *Market prices transmit information efficiently.*

The lesson of microeconomic theory: Market prices transmit information effectively.

THE NEED FOR PLANNING

Planned economies are often presented as the antithesis of market economies. However, while considering planned economies, remember that market economies have within them large organizations that run by plans—not by market. For example, in the United States General Motors had sales in 1993 of about $138 billion, sales larger than the GDP of all but five or six countries of the world. GM is a planned economy unto itself.

Markets could exist to coordinate activities within these firms, but they don't. Imagine, for a moment, that the United States didn't have any antitrust laws and that one of the conglomerate companies, call it Super Pac Company,

began buying more and more firms until eventually it owned all the firms in the United States. While its theoretical goals might be different (Super Pac Company would want to earn profit for its owners rather than provide a good life for its workers), its organizational problems would be exactly the same as the problems facing a socialist planner.

Thus, the economics of socialist countries is, in a sense, managerial economics. The problems managers of large U.S. firms and central planners face are similar: how to coordinate and motivate individuals without the use of the market.

Even if such information were efficiently transmitted in a centrally planned economy, the incentive to proceed with the adjustments still would not exist. It isn't easy to adjust production plans in any economy. In a market economy, competition— the threat of losing business—keeps suppliers on their toes; they have to adjust to the changing whims of consumers because if they don't, they won't make a profit. In a centrally planned economy, the profit motive doesn't exist, so it couldn't serve as an incentive to adjust plans.

Let's consider a car production manager in a centrally planned economy who discovers that delivery of steel supplies is falling behind. The question he asks is "Can I cover my backside?" The answer: "Yes, I can blame the steel company for not meeting its plan." Since the manager can't be blamed—or fired—for the steel shortages, he or she has little *incentive* to find an alternative source of steel.

The problem becomes even more difficult with consumer goods. Meeting consumer demands is tough work. Being nice to the fickle, frivolous consumer takes effort—and unless one is profiting significantly from making that effort, being nice isn't worth it. It's not from benevolence that Kmart meets your whims; it's from Kmart's self-interest. And in centrally planned economies, meeting consumer whims isn't directly in producers' self-interest.

It's not from benevolence that Kmart meets your whims; it's from Kmart's self-interest.

Again, China is currently heeding the lessons from the former Soviet Union. It is directing its retail employees to be friendly and to meet customers' whims. Chinese planners are now trying to produce what they believe the people want. Economic theory predicts that they will have trouble doing so, and will be outcompeted by firms operating in the market—if they continue to allow such firms to exist.

It's important to go over these problems with central planning, not only because they provide an understanding of why socialist countries are moving away from central planning and from socialism itself, but also because you'll see many examples of such problems in the United States.

Many larger U.S. firms face the same inefficient transmission of information and lack of incentives to adjust plans that centrally planned economies do. In fact, the difference between them, as far as these problems of unresponsiveness are concerned, is just a matter of size. The Soviet or Chinese planner would deal with a supermega company consisting of the entire economy, while U.S. managers face only the particular company they work for. Like their socialist counterparts, U.S. executives are removed from the flow of information needed for them to know what consumers want. They too often lack the incentives to meet consumer demands. The managers are often more interested in office politics and internal management promotion criteria than they are in meeting consumer demands. The reason is that in large firms the profit motive exists for the *firm* but isn't directly translated to the individual employee.

Because of this similarity, much of the training and many of the tools used in Soviet-style socialist planning are identical to those taught in business schools and

Central Planning, Bureaucracy, and Markets

Q–8: Why would U.S. business schools teach about the problems of centrally planned economies?

used in management. That training and the tools focus on how incentives within the system can be structured so that the system achieves the desired goals.

Even with training, large businesses in the United States aren't especially responsive to consumers. That's why small firms and businesses are constantly springing up, to fill in the gaps left by the large firms. These small firms keep the large firms alert to consumer demands. If the large firms don't meet those demands, they'll lose their market to small firms and go out of business.

Why do bureaucracies exist if they have such problems? The reason is simple: Markets have their problems too. Market economies have firms (which are essentially bureaucratic command and control organizations) because setting up markets and negotiating prices for every transaction would simply be too time consuming. Imagine the complexities if each day firms had to negotiate pay with workers, or students had to negotiate with every teacher how much they would pay for each lecture. Instead, institutions and contracts develop that remove some of those decisions from the market. For example, you pay tuition for a semester, not an amount per teacher and lecture; classes are then allocated by nonmarket mechanisms. Institutions, bureaucracies, and administrative controls exist because ''the market'' isn't the answer to every problem.

The difficulty, of course, is to find the middle ground between market control and coordination, and administrative control and coordination. Pinpointing that middle ground is a judgment call. Most economists are willing to make that judgment call against central planning in a large country, but similarly most economists believe that some large institutions and government coordination are necessary. The debate is about the appropriate mix.

> *Bureaucracies and the problems of bureaucracies are tolerated for the simple reason that their alternative, markets, have their problems too.*

Central Planning Is Inconsistent with Democracy

Economic efficiency is not an end in itself. It has a meaning only in relation to its contribution to the goals of society. If economic efficiency violates other goals of society, then one might say, ''To hell with economic efficiency.'' I point this out because a second argument some economists use against central planning is that it's inconsistent with democratic institutions (to which they have an ideological commitment) and that it violates the rights of individuals. If one agrees with this argument, one would oppose central planning even if it were efficient.[1]

> *The ideological argument against central planning is that it gives too much economic power to the central planners and thus is inconsistent with true democracy.*

The ideological argument against central planning is that it gives too much economic power to the central planners and thus is inconsistent with true democracy. Holders of this view argue that unless various groups in society share economic power, government will become oppressive, trample on individual rights, and destroy democracy. To give as much economic power to a small group of individuals as central planning gives can only lead to corruption. As 19th-century historian Lord Acton said, ''Power corrupts, and absolute power corrupts absolutely.''

Proponents of this view argue that this is what happened in many socialist countries. When it was first established, the Communist party in most socialist countries may have had society's goals in mind, but by the 1980s they pursued their own welfare, not society's. Thus, the system failed, even on the terms that they set out for themselves.

> Q–9: Did the formerly Soviet-style socialist economies deal more effectively with environmental externalities than have Western economies?

One example of this failure was the almost total lack of concern for the environment in these countries. Water, land, and air were far more polluted than in the United States. Environmental concerns involve externalities that the market alone cannot effectively handle. So one would have expected that a socialist government would be able to internalize the externalities and deal more effectively with environmental problems than has the United States. Yet, by all accounts, they did not.

Another example concerns the distribution of income. One of the Communist party's goals was the equal distribution of income among the people, but, as Abram Bergson (an economist at Harvard) has pointed out, the actual distribution of income

---

[1] I should point out that the argument also works in reverse: If one believes that capitalism and a market system violate individuals' rights, then one could oppose the market even though it is more efficient.

was no more equal in the former Soviet Union and most other Soviet-style socialist countries than it was in the United States.

So not only did their economies provide fewer goods than are provided in market economies, those fewer goods were not more equally divided. As we discussed, many goods in those countries were rationed, but somehow Communist party members were able to get these scarce, rationed goods that nonmembers could not. Many high-level communist leaders lived in palatial homes while ordinary citizens were crammed into tiny apartments. There were even tales of government leaders having billions of dollars stashed away in foreign bank accounts.

In the early 1990s, the perception that Communist party members were being treated ''more fairly'' than others played a major role in the overthrow of communist-dominated socialist governments. Once those governments were out of power, it quickly became apparent how badly the communist parties had failed. In free elections, large majorities in most of the formerly Soviet-style socialist countries voted to eliminate Soviet-style socialism entirely, and the countries adopted market economies.

In the 1990s, political and economic changes in Eastern Europe, the Soviet Union, and China have come so fast and so erratically that it's impossible to provide an up-to-date survey in a textbook. It is possible, however, to provide a brief background of the changes and some of the problems these countries will be experiencing.

SOCIALIST ECONOMIES IN TRANSITION

General Transition Problems

The choices these countries face aren't pleasant. They're much larger choices than the choice of an economic system. They're choices that have political and social elements as well. For example, the republics of the former Soviet Union and Eastern European countries are combinations of distinct nationalities with their own customs and allegiances. Many of these groups want political independence. The fights about the economic system will be interrelated with these political fights. As we discussed in the previous chapter on developing countries, such political and social upheavals make it impossible for any economic system to operate effectively. So one complex problem they face is political and social instability. Markets aren't going to solve this problem.

Markets are not going to solve the political and social problems that most transitional economies face. Markets require solutions to political problems before they can operate.

A second problem they face is lack of a consensus as to which direction to follow. Some groups favor maintaining a centrally planned system. Others favor moving totally to a market economy. Still others favor what they call *a third way*, an as yet undefined economic system that would supposedly provide the best of both worlds. The uncertainty accompanying these potential alternative directions will make it almost impossible for any economic system to operate. Central planning doesn't work because managers at the firm level no longer see their personal and professional futures tied to fulfillment of the centrally directed plan. But neither does the market, since a well-functioning market requires the existence of a legal structure that can see that contracts are carried out, a well-defined structure of private property, and a populace with entrepreneurial skills. And who knows what the third way requires.

5 The problems faced by transitional economies include the lack of political will to decide on an institutional structure, determining initial property rights, and developing a legal and physical infrastructure within which the economy can function.

Most of these countries decided to move to a market economy. Let's consider a couple of the specific problems one of these countries, Bulgaria, faced in implementing these decisions.

Specific Transition Problems

Deciding on Ownership   The former Bulgarian government had taken land away from landowners in the 1940s and had created collective farms. Collective farm members had lived on these farms for almost 50 years. The problem faced by the current government was how to allocate ownership of that land—should it go to the former owners, or to the current collective farm members?

The political compromise they reached was to give the land back to the former owners—or, in most cases, the heirs of the former owners—but only if these people agreed to live on the land for at least five years. Here's the problem that created: In order to establish their ownership rights, individuals who had never worked on a farm in their life were suddenly placed on a farm without equipment. It isn't difficult to guess what happened to agricultural production.

To give you a sense of the specific situation in these countries, I ask you to consider the plight of students in Bulgaria in 1991, when I was there. Before the overthrow of the socialist economy, they received free tuition and a stipend, and the universities were well funded. In the transition, education received short shrift. Stipends were eliminated, and parents' incomes had fallen by 50 percent. Faculty pay had fallen by more than that—by 75 to 80 percent—when the faculty was paid at all, which didn't happen always, because the tax system didn't allow effective collection of taxes. Schools in 1992 were starting to charge tuition, but given the economic situation, what they could charge was limited.

Fixed physical facilities were substantial, but with no operating money, they were run down; light bulbs were missing; chalk was almost nowhere to be found; and anything that broke stayed broken. Similar situations existed in all societal common areas.

Despite the physical and financial problems, the students kept coming to school and kept learning. Some professors, working with students, organized ''new schools'' that met in people's apartments, or wherever, to learn and study. And the students did learn—in many ways their technical training in mathematics and foreign languages exceeded the training of U.S. students whose education was far more costly.

The ability of individuals to cope, even in a period of institutional transition, is phenomenal, and often underestimated. The Bulgarian students' experience in the early 1990s is an example of that ability to cope.

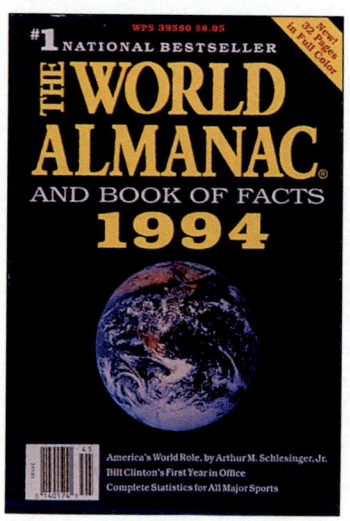

Almanacs are excellent sources of recent economic statistics.

Deciding the ownership of many buildings other than agricultural structures presented the same kind of problem, and, with the changes in the legal system that were happening simultaneously, there was no way to resolve the disputes definitively. In the meantime, the buildings sat there, deteriorating. No one was willing to fix them up because no one knew who would own them.

Where property ownership wasn't in dispute, the government tried auctioning off the properties, but here, too, they faced a catch-22. Few people had any money or access to credit. Actually, it was believed some of the former communists had a great deal of money. In the first auction the government held, one of these former communists won the auction and bought a property at a price far higher than the government had expected. But when the newspapers got hold of the story, the popular uproar was so great that the government had to investigate and tried to arrest the former communist for having so much money. Needless to say, if any former communist did have money hidden in foreign bank accounts, this example discouraged him or her from using it to develop businesses in Bulgaria.

Developing Competitive Businesses   Now let me move to the problems faced by Bulgarian businesses. Sixty percent of their trade had been with Comecon countries (former socialist Soviet-bloc countries), and that trade had broken down almost completely. Serbia, on Bulgaria's western border, was effectively closed because of the war going on there. Previously, Bulgaria had been a transshipment port for Iran and Libya, but now international pressure had closed off those markets.

In the previous system, the Soviet Union had maintained a low price for the oil and raw materials it sold to Bulgaria. Consequently Bulgaria's production facilities had been designed for very low-priced oil, which made those facilities highly energy-intensive. When the price of oil rose to $20 a barrel after the former Soviet government fell, most Bulgarian production facilities were too costly to operate, no matter what the labor costs might have been. Shortages of oil meant that electricity had to be rationed. This rationing was accomplished by having the power on for four hours, off for four hours, with alternating parts of the country being affected (that is, off for four hours in one province while it was on for those same four hours in another province). The oil shortages also meant that the dangerous Chernobyl-type nuclear reactor near Sofia, the capital of the country, had to be kept operating or else electricity would have had to be rationed much more severely.

ADDED DIMENSION   ECONOMISTS' ADVICE IN THE TRANSITION: TANSTAAFL

Like many other Western economists, the author of this book made the trip over to the formerly socialist countries. I spent two months in Bulgaria trying to understand what was going on and discussing the country's economic problems with the people there. I had an office in the former Karl Marx University (now the National Institute of International Economics), right next to the office of the university's chief administrator.

I taught classes about Western banking systems, markets, and international financial systems. Bulgarian newspaper, radio, and television reporters came to me asking what the answers were. I went over the problems and took positions on many of the controversial issues facing the Bulgarian government. But in giving my advice, I made clear to my questioners that it was contingent advice—that my knowledge of their institutions and social structure wasn't deep enough to come to conclusions. I emphasized that my training allowed me to help them understand what markets could and could not do, but it did not allow me to tell them, "This is what you should do." That, they had to decide for themselves.

But wherever I went, I told the story of King Tanstaafl. I became known as the Tanstaafl professor. If the Bulgarians learn that lesson, they will do OK, because that is the most important lesson the West has for them.

The rest of the infrastructure was similarly situated. The telephone system worked only part of the time. Bulgaria's firms had no marketing or sales departments, and no way of establishing an international marketing structure since the relative value of their currency was so low. They also faced a perception-of-quality problem: If a good came from a former socialist country, it had to be low quality; if the former socialist country tried to compete on price, the low price convinced foreigners that their perception of the quality was accurate.

I could go on, but what I have already written gives you a good sense of the dimensions of the economic problems Bulgaria, and the other transitional economies, faced.

What lessons do the principles of economics have for these countries? The answer is: Not a specific lesson, but an important general lesson.

The general lesson is that market institutions that encourage individual entrepreneurship—such as private property and moderately regulated markets—have done well for Western economies, and that, therefore, transitional countries should consider developing some variation of these institutions. In choosing these institutions these countries should recognize that a market operates given an institutional and legal structure, and an entrepreneurial mindset of the population. If these countries want to develop market economies, getting an acceptable institutional structure is the first priority.

Economics does not say that these transitional societies should adopt Western institutions. Institutions evolve, and develop to fit the situations and problems of the time. Western institutions have worked for the West, and thus they should be seriously considered. In that consideration, transitional economies should, however, remember the following:

1. The **Nirvana caution:** When you're in a situation like the one the transitional economies are in, the Western economies look like heaven, but it is important to remember that Western economies have their own problems. If they import Western institutions, they may well import these problems as well.

2. The **QWERTY caution:** The institutions that developed in Western economies, such as the QWERTY keyboard used with typewriters and computers, developed for a variety of reasons, not necessarily because they were the most efficient or most desirable. Western institutions may exist not because they are efficient, but because their inefficiency served some group's interest.

3. The **tombstone caution:** While it seems true that economies that have markets are more efficient than centrally planned economies, that doesn't necessarily mean that markets caused the higher efficiency. An efficient

Q–10: In order to sell more of their goods for export, the formerly Soviet-style socialist economies should lower their price. True or false? Why?

Cautionary Lessons for Transitional Economies from Principles of Economics

The general lesson that the principles of economics has for transitional economies is that market institutions that encourage individual entrepreneurship have done well for Western economies, and that transitional economies should consider some variation of these institutions.

6 Four cautionary lessons for transitional economies are: (1) the Nirvana caution, (2) the QWERTY caution, (3) the tombstone caution, and (4) the transplant caution.

market can exist only in a stable legal and political setting. The existence of markets may be a tombstone over those disputes about the distribution of property rights. Settling the disputes, not the creation of markets, may be the more important issue.

4. The **transplant caution:** When an organ is transplanted from one body to another, it is often rejected by the body to which it has been transplanted. Similarly, rejection can occur with transplanted institutions that don't fit the cultural or social aspects of the economy to which they are transplanted.

In the competition of economic systems, Western market economies have out-competed centrally planned economic systems.

The above four cautions are simply that—cautionary addenda to the general lesson that, in the competition of economic systems, Western market systems of the welfare capitalist variety have outcompeted centrally planned economic systems.

WHAT IS THE FUTURE?

As you can see, the issues facing transitional economies are challenging, to say the least. But the countries had no choice; they had to face those issues, and in the mid-1990s some of the countries seemed to be turning the corner and their economies seemed to be improving.

Still, uncertainty associated with the transition makes most economists pessimistic about the short-term prospects for the group of economies that were formerly centrally planned, regardless of which direction these economies follow. Whatever path they follow, the transition to a noncentrally planned economy is a rocky one.

I could list many more problems and decisions that these transitional economies are facing, but this brief discussion should give you a sense of the enormity of the transition problem. There are potential answers for each difficulty, but for each answer there are additional problems.

That does not mean that there are not better, or worse, answers. When I was in Bulgaria, I took specific positions on a variety of issues, but I carefully qualified my positions with a caveat: To understand real-world policies, one must understand economic theory, but one must also understand the culture and the institutions of the country. I didn't have the background in either the culture or the institutions of Bulgaria, so I stuck to teaching both the power and the limitations of economic theory, and encouraging my students to understand both the strengths and the weaknesses of the market. Only they can, and only they should, make the decisions that will determine their future.

CHAPTER SUMMARY

- Socialism developed as a reaction to the excesses of unregulated capitalism.

- In a centrally planned economy, central planners make the *what, how,* and *for whom* decisions.

- Centrally planned economies have been plagued by shortages of consumer goods. These shortages have been partly due to conscious decisions since central planners have generally chosen investment over consumption goods.

- Five problems of centrally planned economies are:

    1. Nonmarket pricing and perverse incentives.
    2. Inability to adjust prices quickly.
    3. Lack of information about demand.
    4. Ambiguous directives.
    5. Inability to adjust plans quickly to changing situations.

- Transforming Soviet-style socialist economies will be a difficult process. Whether the transformation will succeed is an open question.

- Two specific transition problems that the formerly socialist countries will have in switching to a market economy are (1) deciding on ownership, and (2) developing competitive businesses.

- The general lesson from principles of economics for the formerly socialist countries is that market institutions that encourage individual entrepreneurship have done well for Western economies, and that, therefore, the formerly socialist countries should consider some variation of these institutions. In that consideration, four cautions are: the Nirvana caution, the QWERTY caution, the tombstone caution, and the transplant caution.

KEY TERMS

centrally planned economy   *(845)*   Nirvana caution   *(857)*   Soviet-style socialist economies   *(845)*
counterplanning   *(847)*   perverse incentive   *(850)*   tombstone caution   *(857)*
market-determined prices   *(849)*   QWERTY caution   *(857)*   transplant caution   *(858)*
material balance   *(847)*

QUESTIONS FOR THOUGHT AND REVIEW

The number after each question represents the estimated degree of critical thinking required. (1 = almost none; 10 = deep thought.)

1. Contrast the ways a capitalist country and a Soviet-style socialist country would respond to an increase in demand for shoes. *(5)*

2. Socialist countries are fairer than capitalist countries because they price luxuries high and necessities low. True or false? Why? *(7)*

3. Perverse incentives are not only a problem of socialist economies; they are a problem of all bureaucracies organized around administrative control. Give an example of a perverse incentive you see in the United States. *(6)*

4. How would you redesign the bureaucratic structure that caused that perverse incentive? *(8)*

5. What problems would your redesign cause? *(8)*

6. If your redesigned structure would improve the efficiency of the bureaucratic structure, why hasn't the bureaucratic structure been redesigned? *(8)*

7. Market socialism is doomed to failure because prices provide information as well as coordinate action. True or false? Why? *(8)*

8. Why do many people feel that central planning is inconsistent with democracy? *(5)*

9. Explain why markets cannot resolve the ownership problem. *(7)*

10. List, and explain the relevance of, four cautions you might advise transition governments to be aware of as they attempt to develop market economies. *(6)*

PROBLEMS AND EXERCISES

1. In a centrally planned economy the government fixes the apartment rents at $50 per month, even though the equilibrium price is $100 per month.
   a. Show the likely result with supply and demand curves.
   b. Say the central planners recognize the problem and decide to eliminate the shortage by charging the equilibrium price. Show the likely result.
   c. If they do charge the equilibrium price, will the economic system be equivalent to a market system? Why?

2. Research the recent economic reforms in China, Bulgaria, and Latvia.
   a. Which country has the highest growth rate?
   b. What are the reasons for this?
   c. Would a different reform path have changed the results? Why?

3. One of the specific problems Soviet-style socialist economies had was keeping up with capitalist countries technologically.
   a. Can you think of any reason inherent to a centrally planned economy that would make innovation difficult?
   b. Can you think of any reason inherent in a capitalist country that would foster innovation?
   c. Joseph Schumpeter, a famous Harvard economist of the 1930s, predicted that as firms in capitalist societies grew in size they would innovate less. Can you suggest what his argument might have been?
   d. Schumpeter's prediction did not come true. Modern capitalist economies have had enormous innovations. Can you provide explanations why?

4. In 1993 President Clinton proposed a health care plan that would increase government involvement in the U.S. economy.
   a. What lessons from the formerly socialist countries might be relevant for this plan?
   b. Many economists supported this government-controlled health care program. What do you think their arguments were?
   c. What other major areas of the U.S. economy are government-run? Can you give reasons why they are government-run, rather than being privately run?

5. Nobel Prize winner Robert Coase has argued that firms exist in those areas where command and control are more efficient than markets. Thus, a firm replaces the market with a managerial command system.
   a. If one accepts that argument, it is legitimate to argue that the Western institutions that have developed are the most efficient? Why or why not?
   b. Can one argue that such Western institutions are the most efficient institutions for the countries in which they developed, but not necessarily for other countries?
   c. A radical economist, Steve Marglin, has argued that firms develop command and control systems to protect the monopoly position of managers, not necessarily to be more efficient. How do Marglin's and Coase's views mix?

ANSWERS TO MARGIN QUESTIONS

1. True. Economic forces operate even when no markets exist. It is market forces that operate only within market situations. The question facing the transitional economies is whether to establish the institutions that allow economic forces to operate unimpeded and hence express themselves as market forces. *(845)*

2. Yes, prices play a role in a centrally planned economy. They are, however, not market-determined prices that balance the forces of supply and demand. They are, instead, administratively imposed, which means that there can be significant shortages, surpluses, and non-price rationing. *(849)*

3. False. Most necessities such as bread and electricity were available in large quantities and at very low prices in the formerly Soviet-style socialist countries, so this was not a factor in their decision to revolt. It was the economies' failure to provide other types of quality goods, such as popular consumer goods and luxuries, together with a sense of unfairness of the system, that led to the revolts. *(849)*

4. Whenever goods are in short supply, some rationing system must be used. In many of the Soviet-style socialist countries, that rationing system involved directing goods towards members of the Communist party or members of other in-groups. This inequality went against the goals of communism and helped create people's resentment of the political system. *(850)*

5. When goods are provided at a low price to the user, some means of rationing, other than price, must be found. If health care is to have a low cost to the user, somehow the directors of the health care program must find a method to ration health care so that they eliminate inappropriate use of the health care system and encourage appropriate use. The lessons of the formerly socialist economies is that this is not an easy task to accomplish. *(851)*

6. Because of shortages of desired goods, people in the formerly socialist economies carried lots of cash and shopping bags so that, whenever they saw a desired good available, they could buy large quantities for themselves and their friends, worsening the shortage for other consumers. *(852)*

7. In any economy things never develop quite the way they were expected to, and adjustments to plans are inevitable. In a centrally planned economy and in large bureaucracies, the information generally doesn't get to the right person at the right time, and often the incentives to make the adjustments do not exist. The information often does not exist. It is difficult, costly, and time-consuming to transmit information through a large bureaucracy. The incentive doesn't exist because institutional incentives drive people, and these institutional incentives often lead to different results than anyone would want. People become more concerned with covering their backsides than with doing what needs to be done. *(852)*

8. U.S business schools teach about the problems of centrally planned economies because those problems are relevant to large corporations. These corporations have executives who are removed from the flow of information needed to know what consumers want, and they often lack the incentives to meet customer demand. *(853)*

9. No, the formerly Soviet-style socialist economies did not deal more effectively with environmental externalities than have Western economies. In many of the formerly centrally planned economies there was almost a total lack of concern for the environment. In the Western economies there may not be sufficient concern, but, compared to the formerly Soviet-style socialist economies, the governments of Western market economies have dealt more effectively with environmental problems. *(854)*

10. While general economic theory suggests that lowering price will increase quantity demanded, it is not clear that that is the case for the formerly Soviet-style socialist economies. They face a serious perception-of-quality problem, and most people to whom the goods are to be exported believe those goods are of low quality. The low price charged for the good can cement that perception of low quality into consumers' demand and cause consumers not to buy the low-priced good. *(857)*

Glossary

A

accounting profit Definition of profit used by accountants that states profit is total revenue minus explicit measurable costs. *(542, 554)*

acquisition A company buys another company; the buyer has direct control of the resulting venture, but does not necessarily exercise that direct control. *(648)*

adaptive expectations Expectations of the future based on what has been in the past. *(347)*

aggregate demand curve (AD) A schedule, graphically represented by a curve, that shows how a change in the price level will change output demanded, other things (including supply) held constant. *(187)*

aggregate demand (expenditure) management policy Policy aimed at changing the level of income in the economy by a combination of a change in autonomous expenditures and the multiplied induced expenditures resulting from that change. *(256)*

aggregate demand shock A shift in the aggregate demand curve. *(221)*

Aggregate Production/Aggregate Expenditures (AP/AE) Model Keynesian model giving *aggregate supply* the name *aggregate production* and focusing on total production changes, not on changes in output caused by price-level changes. Emphasizes the difference between the Keynesian focus and the Classical focus on quantity of aggregate supply and demand changes resulting from changes in the price level. *(229)*

aggregate expenditures The summation of all four components of expenditures: aggregate of consumption (spending by consumers), investment (spending by business), spending by government, and net foreign spending on U.S. goods (the difference between U.S. exports and U.S. imports). It is expressed by the equation $AE = C + I + G + (X - M)$. *(230, 237)*

aggregate production curve In the Keynesian model, the 45-degree line on a graph with real income measured on the horizontal axis and real production on the vertical axis. Alternatively called the *aggregate income curve*. *(230)*

aggregate supply curve (AS) A schedule graphically represented by a curve, which shows how a change in the price level will change the quantity of output supplied, other things (including expectations and aggregate demand) constant. *(189)*

agrifirms Large firms that own huge farms and operate them like big corporations. *(749)*

annuity rule Present value of any annuity is the annual income it yields divided by the interest rate. *(692)*

antitrust policy Government's policy toward the competitive process. *(639)*

approximate real-world money multiplier Measure of the amount of money ultimately created by the banking system per dollar deposited, when cash holdings of individuals and firms are treated the same as reserves of banks. The mathematical expression is $1/(r + c)$. *(314)*

arc elasticity The average elasticity of a range of points on a demand curve. *(501)*

art of economics The relating of positive economics to normative economics—the application of the knowledge learned in positive economics to the achievement of the goals determined in normative economics. *(24)*

art of macro policy An art practiced by economists who advise governments about real-world macro policy. In the practice of that art, economists recognize that economic relationships aren't certain and that conducting macroeconomic policy is not a science. *(425)*

Asian tigers Group of Asian countries that have achieved economic growth well above the level of other developing countries. *(832)*

asset management How a bank handles its loans and other assets. *(310)*

Austrian Conservative school of economists sometimes classified as libertarian. They believe in liberty of individuals first and other social goals second, and they oppose state intrusion into private property and private activities. *(468)*

automatic stabilizer Any government program or policy that will counteract the business cycle without any new government action. *(276)*

autonomous consumption Consumption that is unaffected by changes in disposable income. *(231)*

autonomous Determined by outside forces; for example, Classicals held that real output was determined by forces "autonomous" to the quantity theory of money. *(209)*

average fixed cost Fixed cost divided by quantity produced. *(525)*

average product Total output divided by the quantity of the input. *(521)*

average propensity to consume (apc) Consumption divided by disposable income. *(233)*

average propensity to save (aps) Savings divided by disposable income. *(235)*

average total cost Total cost divided by the quantity produced. Often called *average cost*. *(525)*

average variable cost Variable cost divided by quantity produced. *(525)*

B

balance of payments A country's record of all transactions between its residents and the residents of all foreign countries. *(380)*

balance of payments constraint Limitation on expansionary domestic macro policy due to a shortage of international reserves. *(459)*

balance of trade The difference between the value of goods a nation exports and the value of goods it imports. *(112, 380)*

balanced growth plan Plan that spreads money around in trying to spur development in all sectors simultaneously. *(840)*

barrier to entry A social, political, or economic impediment that prevents firms from entering a market. *(549, 583)*

basic needs Adequate food, clothing, and shelter for the people in a society. *(451)*

bilateral monopoly A market with only a single seller and a single buyer. *(673)*

bond Promissory note that a certain amount of money plus interest will be paid back in the future. *(288)*

boom In the business cycle, a very high peak representing a big jump in output. *(139)*

borrowing circle Loan system in which collateral is not required. Instead, the borrower must find friends to guarantee the repayment. It is enforced by preventing the friends from getting loans themselves unless the loan they guaranteed is paid back. *(464)*

bounded rationality Rationality based on rules of thumb rather than using the rational choice model. *(495)*

brain drain The outflow of the best and brightest students from developing countries to developed countries. *(839)*

Bretton Woods system An agreement that governed international financial relationships from the period after World War II until 1971, named for Bretton Woods, New Hampshire, where the agreement was reached at a meeting of international officials. *(394)*

Budget Enforcement Act of 1990 A federal law establishing a pay-as-you-go test for new spending and tax cuts, along with additional spending limits for government. *(404)*

business The private producing unit in our society. *(82)*

business cycle The upward or downward movement of economic activity that occurs around the growth trend. *(137)*

C

capacity utilization rate Rate at which factories and machines are operating compared to the maximum rate at which they could be used. *(140)*

capital account The part of the balance of payments account that lists all long-term flows of payments. *(380)*

capital control law A law preventing people from investing abroad. *(445)*

capital controls A government's prohibitions on its currency freely flowing into and out of the country. *(389)*

capital market Financial market in which financial assets having a maturity of more than one year are bought and sold. *(292)*

capitalism An economic system based upon private property and the market. It gives private property rights to individuals and relies on market forces to coordinate economic activity. *(63)*

capitalists Businesspeople who have acquired large amounts of money and use it to invest in businesses. *(71)*

cartel A combination of firms that acts like a single firm. *(600)*

cartel model of oligopoly Model that assumes that oligopolies act as if they were a single monopoly. *(600)*

cash flow accounting system An accounting system entering expenses and revenues only when cash is received or paid out. *(413)*

causation Term in statistics meaning that a change in one data point causes a change in another data point. *(786)*

CD (certificate of deposit) Piece of paper certifying that you have a sum of money in a savings account in the bank for a specified period of time. *(293)*

central bank A bankers' bank; it conducts monetary policy and supervises the financial system. *(328)*

centrally planned economy Economy in which central planners decide the general directions the economy will take. *(845)*

change in aggregate demand A shift of the entire demand curve. *(199)*

change in the aggregate quantity demanded A movement along the *AD* curve. *(199)*

Classical economists Economists who generally oppose government intervention. *(205)*

Classical laissez-faire economists Economists who believe that any government policies will probably make things worse, and consequently that the best policy is government disinvolvement with the economy—lowering taxes and keeping the government out of the market as much as possible. *(182)*

Classical long-run aggregate supply curve Vertical aggregate supply curve formed if price level rises but real output doesn't change. *(210)*

Classical supply-side economics Economics that focuses on incentive effects of taxes and argues that low tax rates are central to an economy's success. *(436)*

Clayton Antitrust Act Law passed by the U.S. Congress in 1914 making four specific monopolistic practices illegal. *(641)*

closed shop A firm in which the union controls hiring. *(679)*

coincidental indicators Indicators that tell us what phase of the business cycle the economy is currently in. *(140)*

commercial paper Short-term IOU of a large corporation. *(288, 293)*

comparable worth laws Laws in which government groups will determine "fair" wages for specific jobs. *(676, 709)*

comparative advantage The ability to produce a good at a lower opportunity cost (forgone production of another good) than another country can. *(13, 109)*

competition Ability of individuals to freely enter into business activities. *(97)*

competitiveness A country's ability to produce goods and services more cheaply than other countries. *(114)*

complements Goods used in conjunction with other goods. *(494)*

concentration ratio The percentage of industry output of a specific number of the largest firms. *(592)*

conditionality Making loans that are subject to specific conditions. *(459)*

conglomerate A large corporation whose activities span various unrelated industries. *(594)*

conglomerate merger Combination of unrelated businesses. *(649)*

Consumer Price Index (CPI) Index of inflation measuring prices of a fixed "basket" of consumer goods, weighted according to each component's share of an average consumer's expenditures. *(150)*

consumer sovereignty Principle that the consumer's wishes rule what's produced. *(84)*

consumer sovereignty The right of the individual to make choices about what is consumed and produced. *(737)*

consumer surplus The additional amount that consumers would be willing to pay for a product above what they actually pay. *(566, 578)*

consumption function Representation of the relationship between consumption and disposable income as a mathematical function ($C = C_o + mpcY_d$, where C = consumption expenditures, C_o = autonomous consumption, mpc = marginal propensity to consume, and Y_d = disposable income). *(231)*

contestable market model A model that bases pricing and output decisions on entry and exit conditions, not on market structure. *(602)*

contractual intermediaries Financial institution that holds and stores individuals' financial assets. *(287)*

contractual legal system The set of laws that governs economic behavior. *(685)*

convertibility on the current account System that allows people to exchange currencies freely to buy goods and services, but not to buy assets in other countries. *(459)*

corporate takeover A firm or a group of individuals issues an offer to buy up the stock of a company to gain control and to install its own managers. *(616)*

corporation Business that is treated like a person, legally owned by its stockholders. Its stockholders are not personally liable for the actions of the corporate "person." *(90)*

correlation Term in statistics meaning the joint movement of data points. *(786)*

corroboration Term meaning that the data are more consistent with a particular theory than with any other theory, so it makes sense to use that particular theory. *(786)*

cost minimization condition The ratio of marginal product to the price of an input is equal for all inputs ($MP_w = MP_c /P_c = MP_x/P_x$). *(670)*

cost shifting Adding the costs for one group to the prices paid by another group. *(624)*

cost-push inflation Inflation resulting from the pressure exerted when a significant proportion of markets (or one very important market) experiences restrictions on supply. *(153, 347)*

cost/benefit approach Approach in which one assigns a cost and benefit to alternatives, and draws a conclusion on the basis of those costs and benefits. *(768)*

countercyclical fiscal policy Fiscal policy in which the government offsets any shock that would create a business cycle. *(263)*

counterplanning Process that lets individuals low in the hierarchy influence the planning decisions of those higher in the hierarchy. *(847)*

credentialism Situation where individuals who hold the highest educational degrees get the best jobs simply because they have the credentials. *(838)*

credible systematic policies Policies that people believe will be implemented regardless of consequences. *(428)*

crowding in Positive effects of government spending on other components of spending. *(273)*

crowding out The offsetting effect on private expenditures caused by the government's sale of bonds to finance expansionary fiscal policy. *(272)*

cultural norms Standards people use when they determine whether a particular activity or behavior is acceptable. *(8)*

current account The part of the balance of payments account that lists all short-term flows of payments. *(380)*

cyclical unemployment Unemployment resulting from fluctuations in economic activity. *(141)*

D

deacquisition One company's sale of parts of another company it has bought. *(651)*

debt Accumulated deficits minus accumulated surpluses. *(95, 403)*

debt service The interest rate on debt times the total debt. *(408)*

deficit A shortfall per year of incoming revenue under outgoing payments. *(403)*

demand Schedule of quantities of a good that will be bought per unit of time at various prices. *(35)*

demand curve Curve that tells how much of a good will be bought at various prices. *(35)*

demand-pull inflation Inflation resulting from the pressure exerted when the majority of markets in the economy experience increases in demand. *(152, 347)*

demerit goods or activities   Things government believes are bad for you, although you may like them. *(99)*

depository institutions   Financial institution whose primary financial liability is deposits in checking or savings accounts. *(287)*

depreciation   Decrease in an asset's value. *(168)*

depression   A large recession. *(140)*

derived demand   The demand for factors of production by firms; the nature of this derived demand depends upon the demand for the firms' products. *(665)*

derived demand curve for labor   The curve describing the demand for labor by firms; it depends on the marginal revenue product of labor—how much additional money the firm will make from hiring additional workers. *(666)*

developing economy   An economy that has a low level of GDP per capita and a relatively undeveloped market structure, and has never had an alternative, developed economic system. *(449)*

diminishing marginal utility   At some point, as individuals increase their consumption of a good, consuming another unit of the product will simply not yield as much additional pleasure as did consuming the preceding unit. *(488)*

direct competition   Health insurance plan featuring direct allocation of health care in which the individual receiving the care is the person doing the paying. *(627)*

direct regulation   Program in which the amount of a resource people are allowed to use is directly limited by the government. *(789)*

discount rate   Rate of interest the Fed charges on loans it makes to banks. *(332)*

discouraged workers   People who do not look for a job because they feel they don't have a chance of finding one. *(146)*

discrimination   Differential treatment of individuals because of physical or social characteristics. *(707)*

diseconomies of scale   An increase in per-unit cost as a result of an increase in output. *(536)*

disequilibrium adjustment story   Story of how the economy adjusts from disequilibrium to equilibrium. *(214)*

disintermediation   Borrowing directly from an individual without going through an intermediary bank. *(293)*

disposable income   Income remaining after paying taxes. *(231)*

disposable personal income   Personal income minus personal income taxes and payroll taxes. *(172)*

diversification   Spreading of risks by holding many different types of financial assets. *(288)*

domestic income   Total income earned by residents and businesses in a country. *(170)*

downturn   Segment of the business cycle characterized by the economy starting to fall from the top of the cycle. *(139)*

dual economy   Tendency of developing countries to have two somewhat unrelated economies—one an internationally based economy, the other a traditional, often nonmarket, economy. *(453, 831)*

Dueling Duals   Debate whether a country should focus development on agriculture or on industry. *(841)*

duopoly   An oligopoly with only two firms. *(604)*

durable goods   Goods expected to last more than one year. *(167)*

Dutch disease   Decision not to work because marginal tax rates are high, while welfare and medical benefits are guaranteed whether one works or not. *(663)*

dynamic externalities   Effects of adjustment decisions that are not taken into effect by the decision maker. *(283)*

E

economic decision rule   If benefits exceed costs, do it. If costs exceed benefits, don't do it. *(9)*

economic forces   The forces of scarcity (when there isn't enough to go around, goods must be rationed). *(17)*

economic institution   Physical or mental structures that significantly influence economic decisions. *(7)*

economic policy   An action (or inaction) taken, usually by government, to influence economic events. *(8)*

economic profit   Definition of profit used by economists that states profit is total implicit and explicit revenues minus total implicit and explicit costs. *(543, 554, 688)*

economic reasoning   Making decisions on the basis of costs and benefits. *(6)*

economic system   The set of economic institutions that determine a country's important economic decisions. *(62)*

economic takeoff   A stage in the development process when that process becomes self-sustaining. *(838)*

economic theory   Generalizations about the working of an abstract economy. *(7)*

economically efficient   Using the method of production that produces a given level of output at the lowest possible cost. *(534)*

economics   The study of how human beings coordinate their wants. *(7)*

economies of scale   A decrease in per-unit cost as a result of an increase in output. *(535, 820)*

economies of scope   The costs of producing products are interdependent, so that producing one good lowers the cost of producing another. *(540)*

economy   The institutional structure through which individuals in a society coordinate their diverse wants or desires. *(7)*

effective demand   Aggregate demand that exists after suppliers cut production in response to aggregate supply exceeding aggregate demand. *(220)*

efficiency   Achieving a goal as cheaply as possible. *(16)*

efficiency wages   An above-average wage paid to a worker for bringing forth better effort. *(675)*

efficiently Achieving a desired goal at the lowest possible cost in total resources, without consideration as to who pays those costs. *(789)*

effluent fees Charges imposed by government on pollution. *(731)*

elastic Percent change in quantity is greater than percent change in price. $E_d > 1$. *(499)*

embargo All-out restriction on import or export of a good. *(816)*

entrepreneur Individual who sees an opportunity to sell an item at a price higher than the average cost of producing it. *(539)*

entrepreneurship Labor services that involve high degrees of organizational skills, concern, and creativity. *(83, 685)*

envelope relationship The relationship explaining that, at the planned output level, short-run average total cost equals long-run average total cost, but at all other levels of output, short-run average total cost is higher than long-run average total cost. *(538)*

equation of exchange $MV = PQ$ (quantity of **M**oney times **V**elocity of money equals the **P**rice level times the **Q**uantity of real goods sold). *(208)*

equilibrium A concept in which the dynamic forces cancel each other out. *(50)*

equilibrium price The price toward which the invisible hand (economic forces) drives the market. *(51)*

European Union (EU) An economic and political union of European countries that allow free trade among countries. *(119, 823)*

excess burden Loss to society caused by a policy introducing a wedge between marginal private and marginal social costs and benefits. *(755)*

excess demand Quantity demanded is greater than quantity supplied. *(48)*

excess reserves Reserves in excess of what banks are required to hold. *(318)*

excess supply Quantity supplied is greater than quantity demanded. *(48)*

exchange rate The rate at which one country's currency can be traded for another country's currency. *(366)*

exchange rate policy Deliberately affecting a country's exchange rate in order to affect its trade balance. *(266, 390, 459)*

expansion Upturn that lasts for more than two consecutive quarters of a year. *(140)*

expectations of inflation The rise in the price level that the average person expects. *(349)*

expected inflation Inflation people expect to occur. *(153)*

experimental economics A branch of economics that gains insights into economic issues by conducting controlled experiments. *(561, 606)*

export-led growth policy Any policy that increases autonomous exports or decreases autonomous imports, thereby increasing autonomous expenditures. *(266)*

exports Goods produced in the home country but sold to foreign countries. *(108)*

external government debt Government debt owed to individuals in foreign countries. *(407)*

externality A result of a decision that is not taken into account by the decision maker. *(97, 725, 789)*

F

factors of production Resources, or inputs, necessary to produce goods. *(42)*

fallacy of composition The false assumption that what is true for a part will also be true for the whole. *(184)*

farm lobby Organization formed to further political goals that benefit farmers. *(751)*

Fed Abreviation for Federal Reserve Bank.

Federal Reserve Bank (the Fed) The U.S. central bank. Its liabilities serve as cash in the United States. *(306)*

Federal Trade Commission Act Law passed by the U.S. Congress in 1914 making it illegal for firms to engage in certain unfair or deceptive practices. *(642)*

feudalism Political system divided into small communities in which a few powerful people protect those who are loyal to them. *(68)*

financial assets Assets, such as stocks or bonds, whose benefit to the owner depends on the issuer of the asset meeting certain obligations called *financial liabilities*. *(286)*

financial institution A business whose primary activity is buying, selling, or holding financial assets. *(287)*

financial liabilities Liability incurred by the issuer of a financial asset to stand behind the issued asset. *(286)*

financial market Institution that brings buyers and sellers of financial assets together. *(290)*

fine tuning Countercyclical fiscal policy designed to keep the economy always at its target or potential level of income. *(263)*

firm Economic institution that transforms factors of production into consumer goods. *(42, 520)*

first dynamic law of supply and demand When quantity demanded is greater than quantity supplied, prices tend to rise; when quantity supplied is greater than quantity demanded, prices tend to fall. *(48)*

fiscal policy Deliberate change in either government spending or taxes to stimulate or slow down the economy. *(256)*

fixed costs Costs that are spent and cannot be changed in the period of time under consideration. *(524)*

fixed exchange rate An exchange rate established by a government that chooses an exchange rate and offers to buy and sell currencies at that rate. *(366, 392)*

flexible exchange rate An exchange rate the determination of which is left totally up to the market. *(366, 392)*

focal point equilibrium Equilibrium in which goods are consumed, not because the goods are objectively preferred to all other goods, but simply because through luck or advertising they have become focal points to which people have gravitated. *(496)*

focal point phenomenon Phenomenon where a country focuses on another country as a site for business primarily because it knows the conditions in that country, while ignoring other countries that may be just as good but about which it has little knowledge. *(672)*

foreign aid Funds that developed countries loan or give to developing countries. *(836)*

foreign exchange control law A law preventing people from buying foreign currency. *(445)*

foreign exchange market Market in which one country's currency can be exchanged for another country's. *(112)*

four-digit industry SIC designation for a specific type of industry within a more broadly defined two-digit industry. *(591)*

free market in money Policy that would leave people free to use any money they want and that would significantly reduce banking regulation. *(468)*

free rider Person who participates in something for free because others have paid for it. *(98)*

free rider problem The unwillingness of individuals to share in the cost of a public good. *(794)*

free trade association Group of countries that allows free trade among its members and puts up common barriers against all other countries' goods. *(823)*

frictional unemployment Unemployment caused by new entrants to the job market and people who have left their jobs to look for and find other jobs. *(143)*

full convertibility System where there is no law preventing individuals from changing dollars into any currency they want for whatever legal purpose they want. *(458)*

full employment An economic climate in which almost everyone who wants a job has one. *(143)*

fundamental analysis Analysis of curves describing fundamental forces that will be operating in the long run. *(385)*

funded pension system Pension system in which money is collected and invested in a special fund from which payments are made. *(414)*

G

game theory The application of economic principles to interdependent situations. *(604)*

GDP deflator Index of the price level of aggregate output of the average price of the components in GDP relative to a base year. *(150)*

General Agreement on Tariffs and Trade (GATT) International agreement not to impose trade restrictions except under certain limited conditions. *(116, 815)*

General agreement on Tariffs and Trade (GATT) Periodic international conference to reduce trade barriers. *(815)*

general equilibrium analysis The analysis of the simultaneous interaction of all markets. *(772)*

general rule of political economy Small groups that are significantly affected by a government policy will lobby more effectively than large groups that are equally affected by that same policy. *(751)*

global corporations Corporations with substantial operations on both the production and sales sides in more than one country. Another name for multinational corporation. *(106, 652)*

global warming theory The theory that the earth is now going through a period of warming due to the rise of carbon dioxide gases caused by the burning of fossil fuels. *(786)*

gold specie flow mechanism Long-run adjustment mechanism under the gold standard in which flows of gold and changes in the price level bring about equilibrium. *(393)*

gold standard The system by which the value of a country's currency is fixed in relation to the price of gold and under which the country must maintain a stockpile of gold sufficiently large that it can pay in gold for as much of its currency as anyone wants to sell. *(393)*

good/bad paradox The phenomenon of doing poorly because you're doing well. *(745)*

government The combination of federal, state, and local agencies whose officials are elected by the people or appointed by elected officials. *(723)*

government budget deficit Situation when government expenditures exceed government revenues. *(96)*

government budget surplus Situation when government revenues exceed expectations. *(96)*

Gramm-Rudman-Hollings Act A federal law establishing mandatory deficit targets for the United States. *(404)*

grandfather in To pass a law affecting a specific group but providing that those in the group before the law was passed are not subject to the law. *(754)*

gross domestic product (GDP) Aggregate final output of residents and businesses in an economy in a one-year period. *(159)*

gross national product (GNP) Aggregate final output of citizens and businesses of an economy in a one-year period. *(159)*

Group of Five Group that meets to promote negotiations and coordinate economic relations among countries. The Five are Japan, Germany, Britain, France, and the United States. *(116)*

Group of Seven Group that meets to promote negotiations and coordinate economic relations among countries. The Seven are Japan, Germany, Britain, France, Canada, Italy, and the United States. *(116)*

growth-compatible institutions Institutions that foster growth. *(135)*

H

Heisenberg principle The act of looking at something changes its nature. *(473)*

Herfindahl Index A method used by economists to classify how competitive an industry is. *(592)*

heterodox economist An economist who does not accept that the mainstream economic model is the appropriate way to analyze the economy. *(468)*

historical costs Cost in terms of money actually spent. *(543)*

homogeneous product A product such that each firm's output is indistinguishable from any other firm's output. *(549)*

horizontal merger   A merger of companies in the same industry. *(649)*

hostile takeover   A merger in which one company buys another that does not want to be bought. *(648)*

households   Groups of individuals living together and making joint decisions. *(91)*

human capital   People's knowledge. *(137)*

hyperinflation   Inflation that hits triple digits (100 percent) or more. *(154)*

I

ideology   Values that are held so deeply that they are not questioned. *(93)*

implicit collusion   Multiple firms making the same pricing decisions even though they have not consulted with one another. *(601)*

import control law   A law preventing people from importing. *(445)*

imports   Goods produced in foreign countries but sold in the home country. *(108)*

incentive effect   How much a person will change his or her hours worked in response to a change in the wage rate. *(660)*

incentive-compatible contract   An agreement in which the incentives and goals of both parties match as closely as possible. *(614)*

income   Payments received plus or minus changes in value of one's assets in a specified time period. *(705)*

income adjustment mechanism   Chase between aggregate supply and aggregate demand. *(217, 229)*

incomes policy   A policy placing direct pressure on individuals to hold down their nominal wages and prices. *(361)*

indicative planning   A macroeconomic policy in which the government sets up an overall plan for various industries and selectively directs credit to certain industries. *(469)*

individual self-selection bias   The skewing of risk and rates that would occur if individuals who are most likely to need insurance are left to buy it individually. *(622)*

indivisible setup cost   The cost of an indivisible input for which a certain minimum amount of production must be undertaken before the input becomes economically feasible to use. *(535)*

induced consumption   Consumption that changes as disposable income changes. *(231)*

induced recession   A deliberate attempt by government to rid the economy of inflationary expectations. *(351)*

industrial policy   A government's formal policy toward business. *(654)*

Industrial Revolution   Period (1750–1900) during which technology and machines rapidly modernized industrial production. *(72)*

inefficiency   Getting less output from inputs which, if devoted to some other activity, would produce more output. *(15)*

inefficient   More costly than necessary. *(791)*

inelastic   Percent change in quantity is less than percent change in price. $E_d < 1$. *(499)*

infant industry argument   With initial protection, an industry will be able to become competitive. *(821)*

inferior goods   Goods whose consumption decreases when income increases. *(495)*

inflation   A continual rise in the price level. *(149, 347)*

inflation tax   An implicit tax on the holders of cash and the holders of any obligations specified in nominal terms. *(457)*

inflationary gap   The difference between equilibrium income and potential income when equilibrium income exceeds potential income. *(262)*

infrastructure investment   Investment in the underlying structure of the economy, such as transportation or power facilities. *(837)*

input   What you put in to achieve output. *(11)*

Institutionalist   An Institutionalist economist believes that the important macroeconomic policy decisions involve institutional design. *(469)*

inter-firm credit   Loans from one firm to another. *(454)*

interest   The income paid to savers—individuals who produce now but do not consume now. *(689)*

intermediate products   Products of one firm used in some other firm's production of another firm's product. *(161)*

internal government debt   Government debt owed to its own citizens. *(407)*

international effect   Given a fixed exchange rate, when the price level in a country goes down, the price of its exports decreases relative to the price of foreign goods. *(198)*

International Monetary Fund (IMF)   A multinational, international financial institution concerned primarily with monetary issues. *(116)*

interpretative Keynesian model   Keynesian model that is an aid in understanding complicated disequilibrium dynamics. *(249)*

intertemporal price-level effect   If the price level falls but is expected to rise in the future, people will decide to purchase some goods now that they would have purchased in the future. *(198)*

investment   Expenditures by business on plants and equipment. *(236)*

invisible foot   Political and legal forces that play a role in deciding whether to let market forces operate. *(18)*

invisible hand   Economic forces, that is, the price mechanism; the rise and fall of prices that guides our actions in a market. *(18)*

invisible handshake   Social and historical forces that play a role in deciding whether to let market forces operate. *(18)*

invisible hand theory   The insight that a market economy will allocate resources efficiently. *(21)*

J

J-curve   Curve describing the rise and fall in the balance of trade deficit following a fall in the exchange rate. *(391)*

judgment by performance   Judging the competitiveness of markets by the behavior of firms in that market. *(639)*

judgment by structure   Judging the competitiveness of markets by the structure of the industry. *(639)*

just-noticeable difference A threshold below which our senses don't recognize that something has changed. *(359)*

K

Keynesian activist economists Economists who believe that the government can come up with some policy proposals that will positively impact the economy. *(182)*

Keynesian economists Economists who generally favor government intervention in the aggregate economy. *(205)*

Keynesian equation Equation that tells us that income equals the multiplier times autonomous expenditures ($Y =$ *(Multiplier) (Autonomous Expenditures)*). *(239)*

Keynesian supply-side policy Policy that goes beyond the traditional Keynesian demand-side analysis and focuses on the composition of government spending and taxes, modifying that composition to expand supply and potential output, decreasing the deficit at the same time that it expands the economy. *(437)*

L

L Broad definition of "money" that includes almost all short-term assets. *(310)*

labor force The number of people in the economy willing and able to find work. *(140)*

labor market Factor market in which individuals supply labor services for wages to firms that demand labor services. *(660)*

labor productivity Average output per worker. *(666)*

laissez-faire Economic policy of leaving coordination of individuals' wants to be controlled by the market. *(72, 205, 723)*

law of aggregate demand As the price level falls the quantity of aggregate demand will increase, holding everything else constant. *(186)*

law of demand More of a good will be demanded the lower its price, other things constant. Also can be stated as: Less of a good will be demanded the higher its price, other things constant. *(35)*

law of diminishing marginal productivity As more and more of a variable input is added to an existing fixed input, after some point the additional output one gets from the additional input will fall. *(523)*

law of supply More of a good will be supplied the higher its price, other things constant. Also can be stated as: Less of a good will be supplied the lower its price, other things constant. *(42)*

lazy monopolist Firm that does not push for efficiency, but merely enjoys the position it is already in. *(615)*

leading indicators Indicators that tell us what's likely to happen 12 to 15 months from now. *(140)*

learning by doing Becoming more proficient at doing something by actually doing it; in the process, learning what works and what doesn't. *(540, 820)*

liability management How a bank attracts deposits and what it pays for them. *(310)*

libertarians Proponents of the philosophy that the liberty of

individuals comes first and other social goals come second. *(468)*

limited capital account convertibility System that allows full current account convertibility and partial capital account convertibility. *(459)*

limited liability The liability of a stockholder (owner) in a corporation; it is limited to the amount the stockholder has invested in the company. *(90)*

liquidity Ability to turn an asset into cash quickly. *(291)*

long-run decision A decision in which the firm can choose among all possible production techniques. *(520)*

long-run Phillips curve A curve showing the trade-off (or complete lack thereof) between inflation and unemployment when expectations of inflation equal actual inflation. *(349)*

long-run shift factors Shift factors that are unlikely to change substantially in the short run, but in the long run they can change significantly. *(201)*

long-run supply Level of supply consistent with an economy's potential income; it is the maximum amount of output that can be produced, given the institutional structure of the economy. *(202)*

Lorenz curve A geometric representation of the size distribution of income among families in a given country at a given time. *(699)*

M

M_1 Component of the money supply that consists of cash in the hands of the public and checking account balances. *(309)*

M_2 Component of the money supply that consists of M_1 plus savings deposits, small-denomination time deposits, and money market mutual fund shares, along with some esoteric relatively liquid assets. *(309)*

macro institutional policies Policies to change the underlying macro institutions and thereby increase output. *(460)*

macroeconomic externality Externality that affects the levels of unemployment, inflation, or growth in the economy as a whole. *(98)*

macroeconomics The study of inflation, unemployment, business cycles, and growth primarily from the whole to the parts, focusing on aggregate relationships and supplementing its analysis with microeconomic insights. *(22, 131)*

mainstream economist An economist who accepts that the mainstream economic model is the appropriate way to analyze the economy. *(468)*

managed competition Health insurance plan in which existing institutions are extended and modified, the better to take incentives into account. *(626)*

marginal benefit Additional benefit above what you've already derived. *(9)*

marginal cost The change in cost associated with a change in quantity. *(8, 525, 552)*

marginal factor cost The additional cost to a firm of hiring another worker. *(673)*

marginal physical product (MPP) Additional units of output that hiring an additional worker will bring about. *(666)*

marginal product Additional output forthcoming from an additional input, other inputs constant. *(521)*

marginal productivity theory Factors of production are paid their marginal revenue product. *(693)*

marginal propensity to consume *(mpc)* Percentage change in spending that accompanies a percentage change in income. *(220, 232)*

marginal propensity to expend *(mpe)* The additional spending that will be translated into the income stream when all induced expenditures are included. *(263)*

marginal propensity to save (mps) Percentage saved from an additional dollar of disposable income. *(235)*

marginal revenue The change in revenue associated with a change in quantity. *(552, 573)*

marginal revenue curve Graphical measure of the change in revenue that occurs in response to a change in price. *(574)*

marginal revenue product The additional revenue a firm receives when it hires an additional worker. *(666)*

marginal tax rate The tax you pay on an additional dollar. *(662)*

marginal utility The satisfaction one gets from the consumption of an incremental or additional product above and beyond what one has consumed up to that point. *(487)*

market demand curve The horizontal sum of all individual demand curves. *(39)*

market force Economic force to which society has given relatively free rein so that it has been able to work through the market. *(18)*

market incentive program Program that makes the price of a resource reflect a negative externality. *(789)*

market niche An area in which competition is not working. *(689)*

market structure The physical characteristics of the market within which firms interact. *(591)*

market supply curve Horizontal sum of all the firms' marginal cost curves, taking account of any changes in input prices that might occur. *(561)*

market-determined prices Prices are determined by supply and demand, with suppliers free to adjust their prices to make the quantity demanded equal the quantity supplied. *(849)*

marketable certificate program A program that formalizes rights by issuing certificates and allowing trading of those rights. *(792)*

material balance Process by which central planners adjust incoming and outgoing quantities of materials until supply equals demand (at least on paper). *(847)*

mechanistic Keynesian model Model picturing the economy as representable by a mechanistic, timeless model with a determinant equilibrium, with little or no discussion of the fleetingness of that equilibrium. *(248)*

mechanistic Keynesianism The belief that the simple multiplier models (or even complex variations) actually describe the aggregate adjustment process and lead to a deterministic solution that policy makers can exploit in a mechanistic way. *(426)*

Medicare Medical insurance component of the Social Security program. *(715)*

mercantilism Economic system in which government doles out the rights to undertake economic activities. *(70)*

merger The act of combining two firms. *(648)*

merit goods or activities Things government believes are good for you, although you may not think so. *(100)*

microeconomics The study of individual choice, and how that choice is influenced by economic forces. *(21)*

microfoundations of macro The decisions of individuals that underlie aggregate results. *(184)*

military-industrial complex The mutually beneficial relationship among the armed services, weapons industries, and government officials. *(94, 655)*

minimum efficient level of production The amount of the production run that spreads out setup costs sufficiently for a firm to undertake production profitably. *(536)*

MITI Japanese agency, the Ministry of International Trade and Industry, that guides the Japanese economy. *(122, 654)*

model Framework for looking at the world. *(51)*

monetary base The vault cash plus reserves that banks have at the Fed. *(340)*

monetary policy Policy of influencing the economy through changes in the money supply and credit availability. *(328)*

monetary rule A prescribed monetary policy to be followed regardless of what is happening in the economy. *(354)*

money A highly liquid financial asset that's generally accepted in exchange for other goods and is used as a reference in valuing other goods. *(208, 306)*

money market Financial market in which financial assets having a maturity of less than one year are bought and sold. *(292)*

monitoring costs Costs incurred by the organizer of production in seeing to it that employees do what they are supposed to do. *(537)*

monitoring problem Problem that employees' incentives differ from the owner's incentives and that monitoring the employees is expensive. *(614)*

monopolistic competition A market structure in which many firms sell different products. *(591)*

monopoly A market structure in which one firm makes up the entire market. *(572)*

monopoly power Ability to prevent others from entering a business field, which enables a firm to raise its price. *(97)*

monopsony A market in which only a single firm hires labor. *(673)*

mortgage A special name for a secured loan on real estate. *(300)*

most-favored nation Country that will pay as low a tariff on its exports as will any other country. *(823)*

movement along a demand curve Method of representing a change in the quantity demanded. Graphically, a change in quantity demanded will cause a movement along the demand curve. *(40)*

movement along the supply curve Method of representing a change in the quantity supplied. Graphically, a change in quantity demanded will cause a movement along the supply curve. *(46)*

MR = MC Marginal revenue curve equals marginal cost; the condition under which a monopolist is maximizing profit. *(575)*

multinational corporation Firm with production facilities and a marketing force in two or more countries. *(652)*

multiplier   Key aspect of the Keynesian model that differentiates it from the Classical model. It is a number that tells us how much income will change in response to a change in autonomous expenditures. *(239)*

N

national income (NI)   Total income earned by citizens and businesses of a country. *(170)*

national income accounting   A set of rules and definitions for measuring economic activity in the aggregate economy. *(159)*

national income accounting identity   The relationship between output and income: Whenever a good or service is produced, somebody receives an income for producing it. *(163)*

natural monopolies   Monopolies that exist because economies of scale create a barrier to entry. *(583, 619, 645)*

natural rate of unemployment   Classical term for the unemployment rate in long-run equilibrium when expectations of inflation equal the actual level of inflation. *(354)*

neomercantilism   An economic system in which the government explicitly guides the economy. *(122)*

net domestic product (NDP)   GDP adjusted to take account of depreciation. *(169)*

net exports   A country's exports minus its imports. *(236)*

net foreign factor income   Income from foreign domestic factor sources minus foreign factor incomes earned domestically. *(160)*

net national product   GDP adjusted for depreciation. *(172)*

net private investment   Gross investment minus depreciation. *(168)*

New Deal   President Franklin Roosevelt's name for the practical "do something" approach to economic policy his administration developed in the 1930s. *(439)*

Nimby   A short way to express "**N**ot **I**n **M**y **B**ack **Y**ard" when a community objects to a proposed development in its neighborhood. *(63, 794)*

Nirvana caution   Taking care not to assume that a country that looks extremely fortunate does not have any problems of its own. *(857)*

Nirvana criticism   Comparing reality to a situation that cannot occur (*i.e.*, to Nirvana). *(567)*

nominal concepts   Economic concepts specified in monetary terms (current dollars) with no adjustment for inflation. *(159)*

nominal deficit   The deficit determined by looking at the difference between expenditures and receipts. *(410)*

nominal GDP   GDP calculated at existing prices. *(175)*

nominal interest rates   Interest rates you actually see and pay. *(339)*

nominal output   Output as measured, without any adjustments. *(151)*

nonconvertible currencies   Currencies that cannot be freely exchanged with currencies of other countries. *(383)*

nondurable goods   Goods that last less than one year. *(167)*

nonprofit business   Business that does not try to make a profit. It tries only to make enough money to cover its expenses with its revenues. *(89)*

nontariff barriers   Indirect regulatory restrictions on exports and imports. *(112)*

normal goods   Goods whose consumption increases with an increase in income. *(495)*

normal profits   Payments to entrepreneurs as the return on their risk taking. *(555, 688)*

normative criticism   The desirability of a Pareto optimal position depends on the desirability of the starting position. *(568)*

normative economics   The study of what the goals of the economy should be. *(24)*

O

objective   Term applied to "analysis," meaning that the analysis keeps your subjective views—your value judgments—separate. *(23)*

off-budget expenditure   An expenditure that is not counted in the budget as an expenditure. *(414)*

official transactions account   The part of the balance of payments account that records the amount of a currency or other international reserves a nation buys. *(380)*

Okun's law   Rule of thumb economists use to translate the unemployment rate into changes in income: "A one percent fall in the unemployment rate equals a 2.5 percent increase in income." *(273)*

Okun's rule of thumb   Another name for Okun's Law: A one-percent change in the unemployment rate will cause income in the economy to change in the opposite direction by 2.5 percent. *(147)*

oligopoly   A market structure with a few independent firms. *(591)*

open market operations   The Fed's day-to-day buying and selling of government securities. *(333)*

opportunity cost   The benefit forgone, or the cost, of the best alternative to the activity you've chosen. In economic reasoning, the cost is less than the benefit of what you've chosen. *(10, 516, 797)*

optimal level of pollution   Amount of pollution at which the marginal benefit of reducing pollution equals the marginal cost. *(793)*

optimal policy   Policy whose marginal cost equals its marginal benefit. *(792)*

other things constant   An assumption that places a limitation on the implications that can be drawn from any supply/demand analysis. The elements of the particular analysis are considered under the assumption that all other elements that could affect the analysis remain constant (whether they actually remain constant or not). *(36–37, 43)*

output   The result of an activity. *(11)*

P

paradox of thrift   Individuals attempting to save more cause income to decrease; thereby, they end up saving less. *(246)*

Pareto optimal criterion   Criterion that no person can be made better off without another being made worse off. *(566)*

Pareto optimal policies   Policies that benefit some people and hurt no one. *(765)*

parity price   Price that maintains the ratio of prices received and paid by farmers at the same ratio as in a base year. *(750)*

parity ratio   Prices received by farmers divided by prices paid by farmers. *(751)*

partial equilibrium analysis   Analysis of a part of a whole; it initially assumes all other things remain equal. *(37, 185, 772)*

partially flexible exchange rate   Exchange rate where the government sometimes buys and sells currencies to influence the price directly and at other times simply accepts the exchange rate determined by supply and demand forces. *(366, 392)*

partnership   Business with two or more owners. *(90)*

passive deficit   Portion of the deficit that exists because the economy is operating below its potential level of output. *(268)*

patent   A legal protection of a technical innovation that gives the person holding the patent a monopoly on using that innovation. *(583, 618)*

path-dependent equilibrium   Equilibrium that is influenced by the adjustment process to that equilibrium. *(248)*

payoff matrix   A box that contains the outcomes of a strategic game under various circumstances. *(606)*

perfectly competitive   Market in which economic forces operate unimpeded. *(549)*

perfectly elastic   Horizontal demand curve. $E_d = $ infinity. *(502)*

perfectly inelastic   Vertical demand curve. $E_d = 0$. *(502)*

personal income (PI)   National income plus net transfer payments from government minus amounts attributed but not received. *(172)*

perverse incentive   Incentive to use goods in a manner that does not reflect that use's cost to society. *(850)*

Phillips curve   A representation of the relation between inflation and unemployment. *(348)*

planning   Deciding, before the production takes place, what will be produced, how to produce it, and for whom to produce it. *(66)*

policy change   A change in one aspect of government's actions, such as monetary policy or fiscal policy. *(454)*

policy regime   The general set of rules, whether explicit or implicit, governing the monetary and fiscal policies a country follows. *(403)*

positive economics   The study of what is, and how the economy works. *(24)*

Post-Keynesian   A Post-Keynesian macroeconomist follows Keynes's approach more so than does a mainstream macroeconomist and believes that uncertainty is a central issue in macroeconomics. *(469)*

potential income   Income level achieved at some previous point plus a normal growth factor. *(221)*

potential output   Output that would materialize at the target rate of unemployment and the target level of capacity utilization. *(140)*

poverty   As defined by the U.S. government, poverty is equal to or less than three times an average family's average annual minimum food expenditures as calculated by the U.S. Department of Agriculture. *(701)*

present value   Method of translating a flow of future income or savings into its current worth. *(298, 691)*

price ceiling   A government-imposed limit on how high a price can be charged. *(56)*

price discriminate   To charge different prices to different individuals. *(578)*

price elasticity of demand   A measure of the percent change in quantity of goods demanded divided by the percent change in the price of that good. *(498)*

price elasticity of supply   The percent change in quantity supplied divided by the percent change in price. *(517)*

price floor   A government-imposed limit on how low a price may be. *(56)*

price level   A composite price of all goods. *(187)*

price-level flexibility curve   An empirically observed curve that shows the likely price-level quantity adjustment path of any economy. *(192)*

price-level interest rate effect   A decrease in the price level will increase the real money supply. *(198)*

price stabilization program   Program designed to eliminate short-run fluctuations in prices but allow prices to follow their long-term trend line. *(750)*

price support program   Program that maintains prices at a level higher than the trend of prices. *(750)*

price taker   Firm or individual who takes the market price as given. *(549)*

primary financial market   Market in which newly issued financial assets are sold. *(290)*

principle of absolute advantage   A country that can produce a good at a lower cost than another country has an absolute advantage in the production of that good. *(808)*

principle of comparative advantage   As long as the relative opportunity costs of producing goods differ among countries, there are potential gains from trade, even if one country has an absolute advantage in everything. *(811)*

principle of increasing marginal opportunity cost   In order to get more of something, one must give up ever-increasing quantities of something else. *(14)*

principle of rational choice   Spend your money on those goods that give you the most marginal utility per dollar. *(490)*

prisoner's dilemma   A well-known game that nicely demonstrates the difficulty of cooperative behavior in certain circumstances. *(604)*

private good   A good that, when consumed by one individual, cannot be consumed by other individuals. *(98)*

private property rights   Control of an asset or a right given to an individual or a firm. *(63)*

Producer Price Index (PPI)   Composite of prices of certain raw materials. *(150)*

producer surplus   The difference between the price at which producers would have been willing to supply a good and the price they actually receive. *(566)*

production function   Equation that describes the relationships between inputs and outputs, telling the maximum amount of output that can be derived from a given number of inputs. *(521)*

production possibility curve   A curve measuring the maximum combination of outputs that can be obtained from a given number of inputs. *(12)*

production possibility table   Table that lists a choice's opportunity costs. *(11)*

production table   Table showing the output that will result from various combinations of factors of production or inputs. *(520)*

productive efficiency   Getting as much output for as few inputs as possible. *(15)*

profit   A return on entrepreneurial activity and risk taking. *(84, 688)*

profit-maximizing condition   Marginal cost equals marginal revenue (price). $MR = P = MC$. *(553)*

progressive tax   Average tax rate increases with income. *(99, 713)*

proletariat   The working class. *(74)*

property rights   The rights to use specified property as one sees fit. *(685)*

proportional tax   Average tax rate is constant with income. *(99, 713)*

proven reserves   Resource reserves that have been discovered, documented to date, and are recoverable with current technology. *(788)*

public assistance   Sometimes called *welfare*, these are means-tested social programs targeted to the poor and providing financial, nutritional, medical, and housing assistance. *(715)*

public choice economists   Economists who integrate an economic analysis of politics with their analysis of the economy. *(584)*

public goods   Goods whose consumption by one individual does not prevent their consumption by other individuals. *(98)*

purchasing power parity   Method of comparing income by looking at the domestic purchasing power of money in different countries. *(830)*

Q

quantity demanded   A specific amount that will be demanded per unit of time at a specific price. Refers to a point on a demand curve. *(35)*

quantity supplied   A specific quantity of a good offered for sale at a specific price. Refers to a point on a supply curve. *(42)*

quantity theory of money   The price level varies in response to changes in the quantity of money. *(208)*

quasi rent   Any payment to a resource above the amount that the resource would receive in its next-best use (also called *producer surplus*). *(687)*

quotas   Limitations on how much of a good can be shipped into a country. *(112, 815)*

QWERTY caution   Remembering that some economies have developed for reasons that were not necessarily the most efficient or most desirable. *(857)*

R

Radical   A radical economist focuses the analysis on major institutional changes whose purpose is to alleviate inequities in our current system. *(469)*

rational expectations   Expectations about the future based on the best current information, used in theoretical economic work that focuses on building dynamic feedback effects into macro models. *(426)*

rationing   Structural mechanism for determining who gets what. *(17)*

real concepts   Concepts adjusted for inflation. *(159)*

real deficit   The nominal deficit adjusted for inflation's effect on the debt. *(410)*

real GDP   Nominal GDP adjusted for inflation. *(175)*

real interest rate   Interest rate adjusted for expected inflation. *(200, 339)*

real output   The total amount of goods and services produced, adjusted for price level changes. *(150)*

real wage   The ratio of the wage rate to the price level. *(200, 205)*

real-world competition   A fight between the forces of monopolization and the forces of competition. *(617)*

recession   A downturn that persists for more than two consecutive quarters of a year. *(139)*

recessionary gap   The difference between equilibrium income and potential income when potential income exceeds equilibrium income. *(261)*

régime change   A change in the entire atmosphere within which the government and the company interrelate. *(454)*

regressive tax   Average tax rate decreases with income. *(99, 713)*

regulatory trade restrictions   Government-imposed procedural rules that limit imports. *(816)*

relative price   The price of a good relative to the price level. *(37, 187)*

rent   An income received by a specialized factor of production. *(560, 685)*

rent seeking   Attempting to influence the structure of economic institutions in order to create rents for oneself. *(584, 687)*

rent-seeking loss from monopoly   Waste caused by people spending money trying to get government to give them a monopoly. *(584)*

reserve currency   A currency in which countries hold reserves. *(394)*

reserve ratio   Ratio of cash or deposits a bank holds at the central bank to deposits a bank keeps as a reserve against withdrawals of cash. *(313)*

reserve requirement   The minimum percentage of deposits, as set by the Federal Reserve Bank, that a bank must keep in reserves. *(331)*

reserves   Cash and deposits at central bank that a bank keeps on hand that is sufficient to manage the normal cash inflows and outflows. *(313)*

restructuring   Changing the underlying economic institutions (of an economy). *(449)*

reverse engineering   Firm buying up other firms' products, disassembling them, figuring out what's special about them, and then copying them within the limits of the law. *(619)*

Ricardian equivalence theorem   Proposition that it makes no difference whether government spending is financed by taxes now or by a deficit (taxes later). *(430)*

Rosy Scenario policy   Government policy of making optimistic predictions and never making gloomy predictions. *(265)*

rule of 72   72 divided by the interest rate is the number of years in which a certain amount of money will double in value. *(692)*

S

Say's law   Supply creates its own demand. *(206)*

second dynamic law of supply and demand   In a market, the larger the difference between quantity supplied and quantity demanded, the greater the pressure on prices to rise (if there is excess demand) or fall (if there is excess supply). *(49)*

second-best criticism   If the economy is not currently at the competitive equilibrium, it is not at all clear that particular moves toward a competitive equilibrium will be in society's interest. *(567)*

secondary financial market   Market in which previously issued financial assets can be bought and sold. *(289)*

Sherman Antitrust Act   Law passed by the U.S. Congress in 1890 to attempt to regulate the competitive process. *(639)*

shift factors of aggregate demand   Shift factors of aggregate demand cause movements along the aggregate supply curve rather than shift the aggregate supply curve. *(201)*

shift factors of aggregate supply   Factors that shift the aggregate supply curve rather than cause movements along the aggregate supply curve. *(210)*

shift factors of demand   Something, other than the good's price, that affects how much of the good is demanded. *(37)*

shift in demand   If how much of a good is demanded is affected by a shift factor, there is said to be a shift in demand. Graphically, a shift in demand will cause the entire demand curve to shift. *(40)*

shift in supply   If how much of a good is supplied is affected by a shift factor, there is said to be a shift in supply. Graphically, a shift in supply will cause the entire supply curve to shift. *(46)*

short-run decision   Firm is constrained in regard to what production decisions it can make. *(520)*

short-run Phillips curve   A curve showing the trade-off between inflation and unemployment when expectations of inflation are constant. *(349)*

short-run shift factors   Shift factors that change significantly in the short run and that can be expected to cause short-run fluctuations in income. *(201)*

shutdown point   Point at which the firm will gain more by shutting down than it will by staying in business. *(560)*

simple money multiplier   Measure of the amount of money ultimately created by the banking system per dollar deposited, when people hold no cash. The mathematical expression is $1/r$. *(314)*

sin tax   Tax designed to discourage activities society believes are harmful to individuals. *(734)*

single-payer plan   Health insurance plan that offers universal coverage and simplified administration. *(626)*

size distribution of income   The relative division or allocation of total income among income groups. *(698)*

social capital   The habitual way of doing things that guides people in how they approach production. *(137)*

Social Security   Social insurance program that provides financial benefits to the elderly and disabled and to their eligible dependents and/or survivors. *(715)*

socialism   Economic system that tries to organize society in such a way that all people contribute what they can and get what they need, adjusting their own wants in accordance with what's available. *(64)*

socioeconomic distribution of income   The relative division or allocation of total income among relevant socioeconomic groups. *(698)*

soft budget constraint   Loose financial constraints on firms' decisions in centrally planned economies. *(454)*

sole proprietorship   Business with only one owner. *(90)*

Soviet-style socialism   Economic system that uses central planning and government ownership of the means of production to answer the questions: what, how, and for whom. *(65)*

Soviet-style socialist economies   Centrally planned economies in which the state owns most of the means of production. *(845)*

Special Drawing Rights (SDRs)   A type of international money consisting of IOUs of the IMF. *(320, 394)*

spread   The difference between the price at which traders buy and sell a currency. *(386)*

stage of production   Any of the various levels, such as manufacturing, wholesale, or retail, on which U.S. businesses are organized. *(85)*

stagflation   Combination of high inflation and high unemployment. *(355, 444)*

Standard Industrial Code (SIC)   System for classifying industries. *(591)*

state socialism   Economic system in which government sees to it that people work for the common good until they can be relied upon to do that on their own. *(75)*

stock   A partial ownership right to a company. *(90, 293)*

strategic bargaining   Demanding a larger share of the gains of trade than you can reasonably expect. *(819)*

strategic decision making   Taking explicit account of a rival's expected response to a decision you are making. *(594)*

strategic pricing   Firms set their price based upon the expected reactions of other firms. *(603)*

structural deficit   Proportion of the budget deficit that would exist even if the economy were at its potential level of income. *(268, 408)*

structural readjustment   Phenomenon of economy trying to change from what it had been doing to doing something new instead of repeating what it had done in the past. *(143, 222)*

structural unemployment   Unemployment resulting from changes in the economy itself. *(141)*

subjective   Term applied to ''analysis,'' meaning that the analysis reflects the analyst's views of how things should be. *(24)*

substitutes   Goods that can be used in place of one another. *(494)*

Supplemental Security Income (SSI)   Federal program that pays benefits, based on need, to the elderly, blind, and disabled. *(716)*

supply   A schedule of quantities of goods that will be offered to the market at various prices. *(42, 550)*

supply price shocks   Shocks that cause a rise in nominal wages and prices. *(441)*

supply-side policies   Policies that focus on incentive effects of taxes and advocate lower tax rates or modifying the composition of government spending and taxes to stimulate supply, expand potential output, and allow the economy to grow, with the result that the growth decreases the budget deficit and creates jobs—that is, creates growth, prosperity, and low unemployment. *(435)*

T

takeover   Purchase of a firm by another firm that then takes direct control over its operations. *(648)*

target rate of unemployment   Lowest sustainable rate of unemployment economists believe is possible under existing conditions. *(140)*

tariff   A tax governments place on internationally traded goods—generally imports. Tariffs are also called *customs duties. (112, 815)*

tax incentive program   Any program in which a tax is used to create incentives for individuals to structure their activities in a way that is consistent with particular desired ends. *(792)*

tax-based income policies   Policies in which the government tries to directly affect the nominal wage- and price-setting institutions. *(469)*

team spirit   The feelings of friendship and being part of a team that bring out people's best effort. *(537)*

technical efficiency   A situation in which as few inputs as possible are used to produce a given output. *(534)*

technological change   An increase in the range of production techniques that provides new ways of producing goods. *(541)*

third dynamic law of supply and demand   When quantity supplied equals quantity demanded, prices have no tendency to change. *(49)*

tombstone caution   Remembering that markets may not be the cause of high efficiency but instead may be merely covering over disputes about the distribution of property rights. *(857)*

total cost   Sum of the fixed and variable costs. *(524)*

total utility   The satisfaction one gets from one's entire consumption of a product. *(487)*

trade adjustment assistance programs   Programs designed to compensate losers for reductions in trade restrictions. *(818)*

trade balance   The difference between a country's exports and its imports. *(367)*

trade credits   Short-term loans to facilitate inter-firm trade. *(455)*

trade deficit   The result of a country's imports exceeding its exports. *(112)*

trade surplus   The result of a country's exports exceeding its imports. *(112)*

transactions costs   Costs of undertaking trades through the market. *(520)*

transfer payments   Payments by government to individuals that are not in payment for goods or services. *(168, 259)*

transitional economy   An economy that has had an alternative, developed, socialist economic system, but is in the process of changing from that system to a market system. *(449)*

transplant caution   Remembering that when an institution is transplanted from one economy to another, the institution can be rejected if it doesn't fit the cultural or social aspects of the economy to which it is transplanted. *(858)*

Treasury Accord   An agreement between the Fed and the U.S. Treasury Department in which the Fed was freed from holding the interest rate on government bonds constant. *(439)*

Tullock rectangle   Graphical measure of rent-seeking loss from monopoly that results when potential monopolists spend resources to gain monopoly. The waste equals the entire profit of the monopoly. *(584)*

two-digit industry   SIC designation for broadly defined industries. *(591)*

U

unbalanced growth plans   Plan that focuses on one sector of the economy in the hope that that will generate development in other sectors. *(840)*

unemployment compensation   Short-term financial assistance, regardless of need, to eligible individuals who are temporarily out of work. *(716)*

unemployment rate   The percentage of people in the labor force who can't find a job. *(140)*

unexpected inflation   Inflation that surprises people. *(153)*

unfunded pension system   Pension system in which pensions are paid from current revenues. *(414)*

union shop   A firm in which all workers must join the union. *(679)*

unitary elasticity   Percent change in quantity equals percent change in price. $E_d = 1$. *(499)*

upturn   Period characterized by the economy starting to come out of the trough, or lowest point on the business cycle. *(140)*

utility   A measure of the pleasure or satisfaction one gets from consuming a good or service. *(487)*

V

value added   The contribution that each stage of production makes to the final value of a good. *(162, 519)*

value of marginal product   Marginal physical product times the price for which the firm can sell that product. *(666)*

variable costs   The costs of variable inputs; they change as output changes. *(524)*

veil-of-money assumption   Real output is not influenced by changes in the money supply. *(209)*

velocity of money   Number of times per year, on average, a dollar goes around to generate a dollar's worth of income; or amount of income per year generated by a dollar of money. *(209)*

vertical merger   Combination of two companies, one of which supplied inputs to the other's production. *(649)*

W

wage and price controls   Legal limits on prices and wages. *(441)*

Wealth Accounts   A balance sheet of an economy's stock of assets and liabilities. *(161)*

wealth   The value of assets an individual owns. *(705)*

wealth effect   If the price level falls, people feel wealthier because each of their dollars will buy more than they did before, so people will increase their spending until aggregate goods demanded equals aggregate supply. *(197)*

welfare capitalism   Economic system in which the market operates but government regulates markets significantly. *(74)*

welfare loss triangle   Geometric representation of the welfare cost in terms of the resource misallocation caused by monopoly. *(579)*

World Bank   A multinational, international financial institution that works with developing countries to secure low-interest loans. *(116)*

X

X-inefficiency   Operating less efficiently than technically possible. *(615)*

Z

zero profit condition   In the long run, zero profits exist. *(560)*

zoning laws   Limits on the use of one's property. *(685)*

Index